TABLE OF CONTENTS

Canadian Dividend Achievers

American Depositary Receipts Dividend Achievers

Notes From The Editor

Since 1979, Mergent, Inc. has been identifying companies that have increased their regular annual dividend payments for ten or more consecutive years. These dividend paying companies or "Dividend Achievers," which have historically been blue chip companies with a strong cash reserve, have a proven track record of solid, steady earnings growth. More importantly, they outlasted the technology bubble, declining market returns, and corporate malfeasance. For a quarter of a century, this elite group of companies has been profiled in Mergent's Dividend Achievers handbook.

On December 19, 2003, Mergent introduced its Dividend Achievers Index. The value of the Index, which is comprised of the constituents of Mergent's Dividend Achievers handbook, is calculated in real time by the American Stock Exchange using a market capitalization weighted scheme under the ticker symbol "DAA".

On June 30, 2004, Mergent launched its Dividend Achievers50 Index (DA 50). The Index, a subset of the broader Dividend Achievers Index, is comprised of the top 50 Dividend Achievers by highest yield. The DA 50 Index, which is yield weighted and excludes real estate investment trusts and limited partnerships, is calculated in real time by the American Stock Exchange under the ticker symbol "DAY."

Mergent's Dividend Achievers Index is currently comprised of 314 companies. The list includes three companies that boast 51 years of consecutive dividend increases: American States Water Company, Diebold, Inc., and Procter and Gamble Co. The Index includes 72 companies with at least 30 years of consecutive dividend increases.

For the trailing ten years ended April 30, 2005, the total return for Mergent's Dividend Achievers Index outperformed the S&P 500 (S&P 500) and the Dow Jones Industrial Average (DJIA) indexes. The Dividend Achievers posted a total return of 13.54% compared with 10.26% for the S&P 500 and 11.10% for the DJIA. Moreover, for the trailing five years ended April, 30, 2005, Mergent's total return amounted to 3.66%, while the S&P 500 reported a loss of 2.94% and DJIA grew less than 1.0%.

Meanwhile, for the trailing ten years ended April 30, 2005, Mergent's DA 50 Index reported total return of 15.73%, while the Dow Jones Select Dividend Achievers (DVY) Index was 15.94%. However, DVY encountered significantly more volatility as the standard deviation was 15.82% versus only 12.15% for the DA 50. For the trailing five years ended April 30, 2005, total return for the DA 50 amounted to 17.78% compared with 16.38% for DVY. Once again, the standard deviation for the DA 50 was considerably less at 12.86% versus 15.24% for DVY.

It is important to note that standard deviation is used to measure the volatility of an asset class relative to its historical returns. As many investors are risk averse, they tend to favor assets that have lower volatility with respect to their expected returns. According to "Beating the S&P with Dividends: How to Build a Superior Portfolio of Dividend Yielding Stocks", which was written by Mergent's Chief Executive Officer, Jonathan Worrall and Peter O'Shea, "The Mergent dividend investment strategy mitigates the risk involved in dividend investing by minimizing one of the biggest uncertainties: an irregular dividend payment. It creates a higher level of certainty around the issuance of dividends by relying on history."

Furthermore, the Book mentions that "A consistent payment history suggests a company has built shareholder returns into its financial plan and has a commitment to making distributions to shareholders from its profits."

The Book delves into and reveals the strategies and techniques that Mergent professionals use to continually uncover these high-return/low risk stocks, and explain how it can be implemented in virtually any portfolio. Explaining how to invest in high-quality stocks that not only provide outstanding dividend performance, but also benefit from lower tax rates on dividends, this comprehensive resource is ideal for any independent investor looking to make positive cash flow an important part of their investment strategy.

The newly-released publication, available on www.wiley.com or www.amazon.com, is the perfect companion to the Dividend Achievers handbook

With this "dividend-investment strategy" in mind and due to the compelling results of the DA 50, PowerShares Capital Management, LLC, a portfolio management company, licensed the stock selection methodology from Mergent in December of 2004 to create an exchange traded fund called the High Yield Equity Dividend Achievers Portfolio. The ETF trades on the American Stock Exchange under the ticker symbol "PEY." As of June 1, 2005, the market capitalization of PEY exceeded $375 million.

Options on the PowerShares High Yield Equity Dividend Achievers Portfolio are listed on the American Stock Exchange.

Over the past two years, Mergent has entered into three licensing agreements with BlackRock, one of the largest publicly traded investment management firms in the United States with $391 billion in assets under management as of March 31, 2005. The agreements became the basis for two actively managed closed end funds and one actively managed open end fund.

The first closed end fund, which was listed on the NYSE under the ticker symbol "BDV" on December 19, 2003, is based on the top 100 Dividend Achievers by yield. As of March 31, 2005, the Fund had total net assets of $790.5 million.

The second closed end fund, listed on the NYSE under the ticker symbol "BDT," reflects the small and mid cap Dividend Achievers. The Fund was launched on March 26, 2004 and as of March 31, 2005, had total net assets of $398.4 million

The open end fund, launched October 18, 2004 and called BlackRock Dividend Achievers Portfolio, is based the large cap Dividend Achievers. The Fund, which trades under five different share classes, had total net assets of $26.3 million.

Mergent, in its quest to become the premier provider of dividend-related investment products, currently offers 13 indexes. Many more indexes are in the product pipeline. The following table represents a breakdown of the indexes along with their total returns through April 30, 2005.

Dividend Achievers Indexes	Weighting	Annualized 1 Yr	3 Yrs	5 Yrs	10 Yrs
Broad	Market Cap	4.67%	3.81%	3.66%	13.54%
Over The Counter	Market Cap	4.75%	1.58%	8.03%	13.75%
Compound Avg Growth Rate	Market Cap	-0.29%	1.79%	1.04%	12.18%
Compound Avg Growth Rate	Modified Market Cap	-0.22%	2.62%	3.47%	12.96%
Canadian	Market Cap	19.51%	10.76%	12.81%	14.07%
Canadian	Equal Weighted	15.09%	7.67%	13.26%	16.01%
Canadian	Dividend Yield Weighted	10.76%	8.03%	14.98%	16.68%
North American (70%US/30%CAN)	Market Cap	9.03%	5.94%	6.43%	13.85%
Global High Yield 50	Equal Weighted	14.08%	9.81%	13.80%	13.91%
Dividend Achiever 50	Dividend Yield Weighted	11.77%	8.20%	17.78%	15.73%
ADR	Market Cap	18.08%	11.34%	0.20%	5.25%
ADR	Equal Weighted	18.62%	14.74%	11.14%	9.79%
ADR	Dividend Yield Weighted	21.71%	14.16%	11.25%	12.81%

Mergent's Dividend Achievers continue to reward their shareholders with increasing dividend payments. These increasing dividend payments protect the purchasing power of investors at rates that are typically higher than inflation. Investors who agree with Mergent's proprietary stock selection methodology realize that a portfolio of these companies will likely outperform, on an absolute and risk adjusted basis, their comparative benchmark over the long term. This methodology works whether one invests in United States, Canadian or international equities. Investors also continue to benefit from the new dividend tax laws.

Moreover, the products that are based on Mergent's methodology continue to gain market acceptance as many investors are opting for a policy that endorses dividend growth rather than a policy of dividend stability, which is promoted by the Dow Jones Select Dividend Index. A dividend growth strategy hinges on a company's ability to increase its earnings stream in order to pay the increasing dividends. However, a strategy of dividend stability highlights the fact that a company does not necessarily have to grow its top line as dividends can remain stagnant for many years.

Mergent will continue to explore and introduce new dividend-related investment methodologies in the coming months. Be sure to visit www.dividendachievers.com for all the latest information.

Kevin Heckert
Manager, Equity Research

Dividend Achievers Index 10 Year Performance

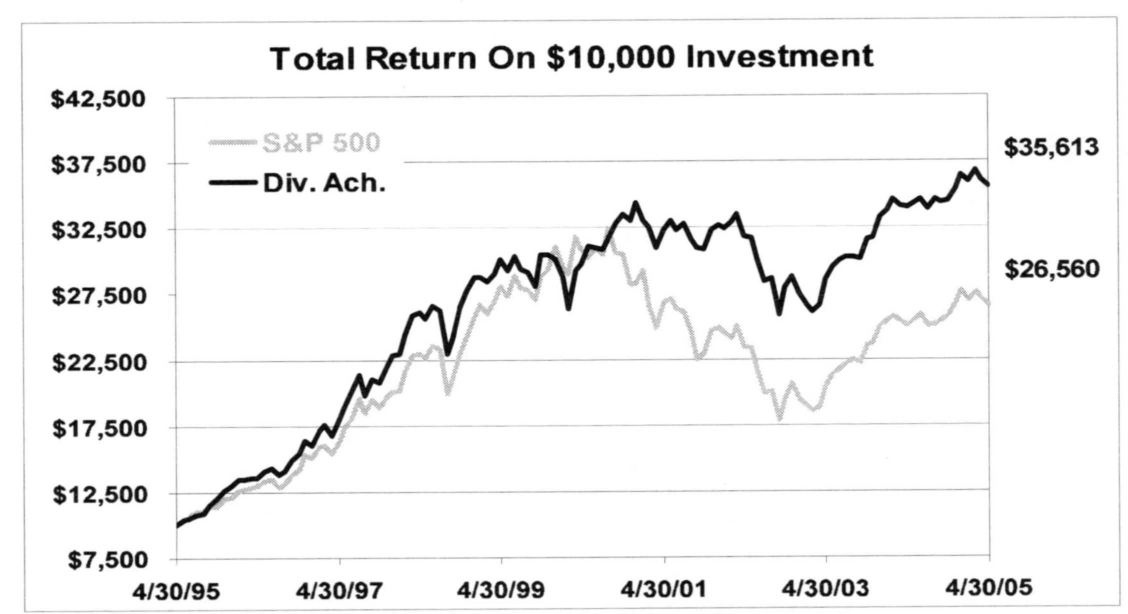

Ranking The 2005 Dividend Achievers

Companies are listed by the 10-year average annual compound growth of their dividends. Also shown are total numbers of consecutive years of dividend growth.

Rank	Name	10-Year CAGR	Years
1	City National Corp.	38.30	10
2	MAF Bancorp, Inc.	38.01	10
3	Sky Financial Group, Inc.	36.44	10
4	Paychex Inc.	35.37	16
5	Expeditors Int'l of Washington, Inc.	33.21	10
6	Citigroup Inc.	32.51	18
7	North Fork Bancorporation, Inc.	30.89	10
8	Raven Industries, Inc.	29.59	17
9	Harley-Davidson, Inc.	27.74	11
10	First State Bancorporation	27.12	10
11	Matthews International Corp.	27.10	10
12	Doral Financial Corp.	26.37	15
13	Linear Technology Corp.	26.19	12
14	Home Depot, Inc.	25.57	17
15	Home Properties Inc.	25.35	10
16	Texas Regional Bancshares, Inc.	24.36	10
17	Commerce Group, Inc.	24.20	10
18	MBT Financial Corp.	24.17	11
19	Anchor BanCorp Wisconsin, Inc.	24.16	11
20	Forest City Enterprises, Inc.	23.94	10
20	Pier 1 Imports Inc.	23.94	13
22	DENTSPLY International, Inc.	23.72	10
23	Ross Stores, Inc.	23.62	10
24	Corus Bankshares, Inc.	23.40	18
25	SEI Investments Co.	23.33	13
26	CVB Financial Corp.	23.32	14
27	Stryker Corp.	23.11	12
28	Sterling Bancorp	22.49	10
29	Fidelity National Financial, Inc.	22.42	17
30	Eaton Vance Corp.	22.05	23
31	M & T Bank Corp.	21.95	24
32	Caterpillar Inc.	21.37	11
33	First Oak Brook Bancshares, Inc.	21.06	13
34	Granite Construction Inc.	21.04	10
35	Medtronic, Inc.	20.89	27
36	TD Banknorth Group Inc.	20.74	10
37	Essex Property Trust, Inc.	20.27	10
38	Cullen/Frost Bankers, Inc.	19.98	11
39	Arrow International,Inc.	19.62	12
39	TCF Financial Corp.	19.62	13
39	Wal-Mart Stores, Inc.	19.62	29
42	LSI Industries Inc.	19.60	11
43	T Rowe Price Group Inc.	19.31	18
44	Archer Daniels Midland Co.	19.24	30
45	Sysco Corp.	19.17	28
46	Wolverine World Wide, Inc.	19.12	11
47	Liberty Property Trust	18.88	10
48	Washington Mutual Inc.	18.79	15
49	Realty Income Corp.	18.62	10
50	Roper Industries, Inc.	18.59	12
51	SLM Corp.	18.53	24
52	Fifth Third Bancorp	18.49	32
53	People's Bank	18.39	11
54	Synovus Financial Corp.	18.29	28
55	WestAmerica Bancorporation	18.20	15
56	Meridian Bioscience Inc.	17.81	12
57	AFLAC Inc.	17.75	22
58	Cintas Corporation	17.74	22
59	Nucor Corp.	17.53	32
60	MBNA Corp.	17.44	13
61	Leggett & Platt, Inc.	17.36	33
62	Jack Henry & Associates, Inc.	17.28	13
63	Courier Corp.	17.21	11
64	Wells Fargo & Co.	17.14	17
65	Pacific Capital Bancorp	17.09	35
66	WPS Resources Corp.	17.07	46
67	Talbots, Inc.	16.93	10
68	Independent Bank Corporation	16.87	16
69	Popular Inc.	16.79	12
70	McDonald's Corp.	16.75	28
71	F.N.B. Corp.	16.69	20
72	First Bancorp	16.53	17
73	Freddie Mac	16.53	14
74	Chittenden Corp.	16.46	12
75	Gallagher (Arthur J.) & Co.	16.04	20
76	Southwest Bancorp, Inc.	15.98	10
77	Legg Mason, Inc.	15.94	21
78	Pfizer Inc.	15.81	37
79	BancFirst Corp.	15.68	11
80	Alberto-Culver Co.	15.67	20
80	Praxair, Inc.	15.67	12
82	Franklin Electric Co., Inc.	15.64	11
82	State Street Corp.	15.64	24
84	Mercury General Corp.	15.51	18
85	Golden West Financial Corp.	15.43	21
86	Brown & Brown, Inc.	15.27	11
87	Sigma-Aldrich Corp.	15.21	23
88	Commerce Bancorp, Inc.	15.21	13
89	American International Group Inc	15.21	19
90	Hudson United Bancorp	15.17	14
91	Automatic Data Processing Inc.	14.87	29
91	Hibernia Corp.	14.87	11
91	McGrath RentCorp	14.87	14
94	Applebee's International, Inc.	14.69	13
95	Harleysville National Corp.	14.67	18
96	Glacier Bancorp, Inc.	14.61	13
97	Superior Industries Intl. Inc.	14.58	19
98	Republic Bancorp, Inc.	14.52	12
99	Johnson & Johnson	14.51	42
100	South Financial Group Inc	14.50	10
101	Albemarle Corp.	14.48	10
102	Wiley (John) & Sons Inc.	14.37	11

Ranking The 2005 Dividend Achievers

Companies are listed by the 10-year average annual compound growth of their dividends. Also shown are total numbers of consecutive years of dividend growth.

Rank	Name	10-Year CAGR	Years	Rank	Name	10-Year CAGR	Years
103	AptarGroup Inc.	14.36	11	161	Abbott Laboratories	10.73	32
104	Sterling Bancshares, Inc.	14.27	11	162	Valspar Corp.	10.72	26
105	Trustmark Corp.	14.22	31	163	Community Banks, Inc.	10.69	13
106	S & T Bancorp, Inc.	14.04	15	164	Marshall & Ilsley Corp.	10.63	32
107	Illinois Tool Works, Inc.	13.99	42	165	State Auto Financial Corp.	10.38	13
108	Tootsie Roll Industries Inc.	13.88	41	166	PennRock Financial Services	10.34	18
109	Danaher Corp.	13.87	11	167	Fulton Financial Corp.	10.34	31
110	First Community Bancshares, Inc.	13.78	14	168	Hershey Corp.	10.33	30
111	BB&T Corp.	13.73	33	169	BancorpSouth Inc.	10.31	18
112	Bank of America Corp.	13.72	27	169	Meredith Corp.	10.31	11
113	Old Republic International Corp.	13.70	23	171	RLI Corp.	10.16	28
114	Brady Corp.	13.64	20	172	Merck & Co., Inc.	10.09	21
115	First Financial Holdings, Inc.	13.54	12	173	Comerica, Inc.	9.92	21
116	Irwin Financial Corp.	13.52	15	174	Kimco Realty Corp.	9.88	12
117	Mine Safety Appliances Co.	13.48	34	175	Coca-Cola Co.	9.87	42
118	Peoples Bancorp, Inc.	13.43	12	176	HNI Corp.	9.79	16
119	Fannie Mae	13.24	19	177	MBIA Inc.	9.74	17
120	Webster Financial Corp.	13.22	12	178	Dover Corp.	9.73	49
121	Martin Marietta Materials, Inc.	13.20	10	179	Johnson Controls Inc.	9.60	29
121	Northern Trust Corp.	13.20	19	180	Colgate-Palmolive Co.	9.57	42
123	Commerce Bancshares, Inc.	13.04	36	181	Protective Life Corp.	9.56	15
124	General Electric Co.	12.79	29	182	First Charter Corp.	9.52	12
125	Washington Trust Bancorp, Inc.	12.77	12	183	NACCO Industries Inc.	9.51	21
126	Teleflex Incorporated	12.71	27	184	General Growth Properties, Inc.	9.39	11
127	Lowe's Cos., Inc.	12.70	43	185	Anheuser-Busch Cos., Inc.	9.36	30
128	Whitney Holding Corp.	12.62	11	186	Sherwin-Williams Co.	9.28	25
129	Park National Corp.	12.58	17	187	Beckman Coulter, Inc.	9.15	13
130	Capital City Bank Group, Inc.	12.54	11	188	Pentair, Inc.	9.10	28
131	Becton, Dickinson and Co.	12.49	32	189	Community Bank System, Inc.	9.05	13
132	Nuveen Investments Inc.	12.46	12	190	Bemis, Inc.	9.01	21
133	Franklin Resources, Inc.	12.29	15	191	Carlisle Companies Inc.	9.00	28
134	Associated Banc-Corp.	12.11	34	192	Bank of Hawaii Corp.	8.99	27
135	First Midwest Bancorp, Inc.	12.07	12	193	Vulcan Materials Co.	8.98	12
136	Regions Financial Corp.	12.05	33	194	Avon Products, Inc.	8.96	14
137	First Indiana Corp.	12.03	13	195	Pitney Bowes, Inc.	8.90	21
138	Compass Bancshares Inc.	12.03	23	196	Sara Lee Corp.	8.89	28
139	ABM Industries, Inc.	12.00	40	197	McCormick & Co., Inc.	8.84	18
140	SunTrust Banks, Inc.	11.72	19	198	Clorox Co.	8.79	28
141	Chemical Financial Corp.	11.69	29	199	AmSouth Bancorporation	8.75	34
142	Avery Dennison Corp.	11.65	29	200	First Commonwealth Financial	8.72	17
143	National Penn Bancshares, Inc.	11.63	26	201	PepsiCo Inc.	8.66	33
144	Allstate Corp.	11.61	11	202	Prologis	8.64	10
144	Family Dollar Stores, Inc.	11.61	28	203	Sterling Financial Corp.	8.60	17
146	Procter & Gamble Co.	11.47	51	204	Lilly (Eli) & Co.	8.55	37
147	Jefferson-Pilot Corp.	11.44	37	205	National City Corp.	8.55	12
148	United Technologies Corp.	11.41	11	206	First Merchants Corp.	8.50	20
149	Cincinnati Financial Corp.	11.39	44	207	Nordson Corp.	8.36	24
150	Transatlantic Holdings, Inc.	11.38	14	208	TEPPCO Partners, L.P.	8.33	12
151	Altria Group Inc.	11.28	39	209	Pinnacle West Capital Corp.	8.26	11
152	Ecolab, Inc.	11.27	12	210	Air Products & Chemicals, Inc.	8.15	22
153	Lancaster Colony Corp.	11.09	35	211	Valley National Bancorp	8.14	13
154	Macerich Co.	11.04	10	212	Walgreen Co.	8.06	29
155	Ambac Financial Group, Inc.	11.04	13	213	FirstMerit Corp	7.97	22
156	Holly Corp.	10.95	11	214	Shurgard Storage Centers, Inc.	7.94	10
157	ConAgra Foods, Inc.	10.91	27	215	Washington Federal Inc.	7.92	21
158	Mercantile Bankshares Corp.	10.83	28	216	Target Corp.	7.92	33
159	Myers Industries Inc.	10.80	28	217	Wilmington Trust Corp.	7.82	23
160	Marsh & McLennan Cos., Inc.	10.79	43	218	CBL & Associates Properties	7.81	10

Ranking The 2005 Dividend Achievers

Companies are listed by the 10-year average annual compound growth of their dividends. Also shown are total numbers of consecutive years of dividend growth.

Rank	Name	10-Year CAGR	Years	Rank	Name	10-Year CAGR	Years
219	Midland Co.	7.80	18	267	Hilb Rogal & Hobbs Co.	5.01	18
220	General Dynamics Corp.	7.57	13	268	Universal Corp.	4.97	34
221	McGraw-Hill Cos., Inc.	7.54	31	269	Bard (C.R.), Inc.	4.95	33
222	Harleysville Group, Inc.	7.50	18	270	CenturyTel, Inc.	4.92	31
223	Wrigley (William) Jr. Co.	7.47	24	271	VF Corp.	4.91	32
224	Rohm & Haas Co.	7.29	27	272	SBC Communications, Inc.	4.81	20
225	Emerson Electric Co.	7.28	48	273	PPG Industries, Inc.	4.80	33
226	Old National Bancorp	7.28	21	274	Fuller (H.B.) Company	4.76	37
227	Grainger (W.W.) Inc.	7.25	33	275	Genuine Parts Co.	4.75	48
228	Duke Realty Corp.	7.24	11	276	ServiceMaster Co.	4.69	34
229	Universal Forest Products Inc.	7.18	11	277	Harsco Corp.	4.62	10
229	Alfa Corp.	7.18	19	278	Progressive Corp.	4.62	35
231	The St Paul Travelers Companies	6.99	18	279	Stanley Works	4.58	37
232	Susquehanna Bancshares, Inc.	6.98	34	280	Colonial Properties Trust	4.47	10
233	Banta Corporation	6.97	26	281	Regency Centers Corp.	4.42	10
234	United Bankshares, Inc.	6.86	23	282	Gannett Co., Inc.	4.37	33
235	KeyCorp	6.84	25	283	United Dominion Realty Trust	4.34	23
236	Masco Corp.	6.70	46	284	Questar Corp..	4.17	25
237	Hillenbrand Industries, Inc.	6.70	34	285	NICOR Inc.	4.05	17
238	La-Z-Boy Inc.	6.61	23	286	MDU Resources Group Inc.	4.02	14
239	Diebold, Inc.	6.58	51	287	Vectren Corp.	3.96	29
240	West Pharmaceutical Services	6.57	12	288	Briggs & Stratton Corp.	3.87	13
241	Smith (A.O.) Corp	6.40	12	289	Healthcare Realty Trust, Inc.	3.84	11
242	Bandag, Inc.	6.39	28	290	Exxon Mobil Corp.	3.84	22
243	Telephone and Data Systems	6.25	30	291	May Department Stores Co.	3.72	29
244	Media General, Inc.	6.16	10	292	National Fuel Gas Co.	3.50	33
244	Haverty Furniture Cos., Inc.	6.16	34	293	Black Hills Corporation	3.49	33
246	Sonoco Products Co.	6.12	21	294	Wesco Financial Corp.	3.48	33
247	Hormel Foods Corp.	6.05	37	295	Tanger Factory Outlet Centers	3.30	11
248	Brown-Forman Corp.	6.03	20	296	Atmos Energy Corp.	3.25	17
249	Wesbanco, Inc.	5.86	19	297	Energen Corp.	3.22	22
250	Kimberly-Clark Corp.	5.82	30	298	Progress Energy, Inc.	3.07	16
251	Aqua America Inc.	5.70	13	299	Lexington Corporate Prop Trust	2.92	10
252	Cedar Fair, L.P.	5.67	17	300	Helmerich & Payne, Inc.	2.87	28
253	Sun Communities, Inc.	5.66	10	301	Tennant Co.	2.84	32
254	Donnelley (R.R.) & Sons Co.	5.65	35	302	UGI Corp.	2.80	17
255	Parker-Hannifin Corp.	5.51	48	303	Supervalu Inc.	2.72	32
256	Lincoln National Corp.	5.49	21	304	Otter Tail Corp.	2.49	29
257	Chubb Corp.	5.39	40	305	Federal Realty Investment Trust	2.35	37
258	Health Care Property Investors	5.37	19	306	Clarcor Inc.	1.93	24
259	Washington REIT	5.35	35	307	Universal Health Realty Inc	1.85	17
260	ALLTEL Corp.	5.34	44	308	Peoples Energy Corp.	1.82	21
261	RPM International Inc.	5.33	31	309	WGL Holdings, Inc.	1.60	28
262	Piedmont Natural Gas Co., Inc.	5.22	25	310	California Water Service Group	1.33	37
263	EastGroup Properties, Inc.	5.17	12	311	Commercial Net Lease Realty	1.24	15
264	Chevron Corp.	5.16	17	312	Consolidated Edison, Inc.	1.23	30
265	Weingarten Realty Investors	5.06	16	313	American States Water Co.	1.05	51
266	3M Co.	5.05	46	314	MGE Energy Inc.	0.87	29

Longest Records Of Dividend Achievement

These Dividend Achievers boast more than a quarter of a century of consecutive annual dividend increases.

Rank	Years	Name	Ticker
1	51	American States Water Co.	AWR
	51	Diebold, Inc.	DBD
	51	Procter & Gamble Co.	PG
4	49	Dover Corp.	DOV
5	48	Emerson Electric Co.	EMR
	48	Genuine Parts Co.	GPC
	48	Parker-Hannifin Corp.	PH
8	46	3M Co.	MMM
	46	Masco Corp.	MAS
	46	WPS Resources Corp.	WPS
11	44	ALLTEL Corp.	AT
	44	Cincinnati Financial Corp.	CINF
13	43	Lowe's Cos., Inc.	LOW
	43	Marsh & McLennan Cos., Inc.	MMC
15	42	Coca-Cola Co.	KO
	42	Colgate-Palmolive Co.	CL
	42	Illinois Tool Works, Inc.	ITW
	42	Johnson & Johnson	JNJ
19	41	Tootsie Roll Industries Inc.	TR
20	40	ABM Industries, Inc.	ABM
	40	Chubb Corp.	CB
22	39	Altria Group Inc.	MO
23	37	California Water Service Group	CWT
	37	Federal Realty Investment Trust	FRT
	37	Fuller (H.B.) Company	FUL
	37	Hormel Foods Corp.	HRL
	37	Jefferson-Pilot Corp.	JP
	37	Lilly (Eli) & Co.	LLY
	37	Pfizer Inc.	PFE
	37	Stanley Works	SWK
31	36	Commerce Bancshares, Inc.	CBSH
	35	Donnelley (R.R.) & Sons Co.	RRD
33	35	Lancaster Colony Corp.	LANC
	35	Pacific Capital Bancorp	PCBC
	35	Progressive Corp.	PGR
	35	Washington Real Estate Inv. Trust	WRE
37	34	AmSouth Bancorporation	ASO
	34	Associated Banc-Corp.	ASBC
	34	Haverty Furniture Cos., Inc.	HVT
	34	Hillenbrand Industries, Inc.	HB
	34	Mine Safety Appliances Co.	MSA
	34	ServiceMaster Co.	SVM
	34	Susquehanna Bancshares, Inc.	SUSQ
	34	Universal Corp.	UVV
45	33	Bard (C.R.), Inc.	BCR
	33	BB&T Corp.	BBT
	33	Black Hills Corporation	BKH
	33	Gannett Co., Inc.	GCI
	33	Grainger (W.W.) Inc.	GWW
	33	Leggett & Platt, Inc.	LEG
	33	National Fuel Gas Co.	NFG
	33	PepsiCo Inc.	PEP
	33	PPG Industries, Inc.	PPG
	33	Regions Financial Corp.	RF
	33	Target Corp.	TGT
	33	Wesco Financial Corp.	WSC

Rank	Years	Name	Ticker
57	32	Abbott Laboratories	ABT
	32	Becton, Dickinson and Co.	BDX
	32	Fifth Third Bancorp	FITB
	32	Marshall & Ilsley Corp.	MI
	32	Nucor Corp.	NUE
	32	Supervalu Inc.	SVU
	32	Tennant Co.	TNC
	32	VF Corp.	VFC
65	31	CenturyTel, Inc.	CTL
	31	Fulton Financial Corp.	FULT
	31	McGraw-Hill Cos., Inc.	MHP
	31	RPM International Inc.	RPM
	31	Trustmark Corp.	TRMK
70	30	Anheuser-Busch Cos., Inc.	BUD
	30	Archer Daniels Midland Co.	ADM
	30	Consolidated Edison, Inc.	ED
	30	Hershey Corp.	HSY
	30	Kimberly-Clark Corp.	KMB
	30	Telephone and Data Systems, Inc.	TDS
76	29	Automatic Data Processing Inc.	ADP
	29	Avery Dennison Corp.	AVY
	29	Chemical Financial Corp.	CHFC
	29	General Electric Co.	GE
	29	Johnson Controls Inc.	JCI
	29	May Department Stores Co.	MAY
	29	MGE Energy Inc.	MGEE
	29	Otter Tail Corp.	OTTR
	29	Vectren Corp.	VVC
	29	Walgreen Co.	WAG
	29	Wal-Mart Stores, Inc.	WMT
87	28	Bandag, Inc.	BDG
	28	Carlisle Companies Inc.	CSL
	28	Clorox Co.	CLX
	28	Family Dollar Stores, Inc.	FDO
	28	Helmerich & Payne, Inc.	HP
	28	McDonald's Corp.	MCD
	28	Mercantile Bankshares Corp.	MRBK
	28	Myers Industries Inc.	MYE
	28	Pentair, Inc.	PNR
	28	RLI Corp.	RLI
	28	Sara Lee Corp.	SLE
	28	Synovus Financial Corp.	SNV
	28	Sysco Corp.	SYY
	28	WGL Holdings, Inc.	WGL
101	27	Bank of America Corp.	BAC
	27	Bank of Hawaii Corp.	BOH
	27	ConAgra Foods, Inc.	CAG
	27	Medtronic, Inc.	MDT
	27	Rohm & Haas Co.	ROH
	27	Teleflex Incorporated	TFX
107	26	Banta Corporation	BN
	26	National Penn Bancshares, Inc.	NPBC
	26	Valspar Corp.	VAL
110	25	KeyCorp	KEY
	25	Piedmont Natural Gas Co., Inc.	PNY
	25	Questar Corp..	STR
	25	Sherwin-Williams Co.	SHW

Dividend Achievers Arrivals

The following companies, which recorded at least ten consecutive years of dividend increases in 2005 mark their debut as Dividend Achievers.

Albemarle Corp.
Capital City Bank Group, Inc.
CBL & Associates Properties, Inc.
City National Corp.
Colonial Properties Trust
Commerce Group, Inc.
Community Banks, Inc.
DENTSPLY International, Inc.
Essex Property Trust, Inc.
Expeditors International of Washington, Inc.
First Bancorp
First Oak Brook Bancshares, Inc.
First State Bancorporation
Forest City Enterprises, Inc.
Granite Construction Inc.
Harsco Corp.
Home Properties Inc
Lexington Corporate Properties Trust
Liberty Property Trust
LSI Industries Inc.
Macerich Co.
MAF Bancorp, Inc.
Martin Marietta Materials, Inc.
Matthews International Corp
MBT Financial Corp.
Media General, Inc.
North Fork Bancorporation, Inc.
PennRock Financial Services Corp.
Peoples Bancorp, Inc.
Prologis
Realty Income Corp.
Regency Centers Corp.
Ross Stores, Inc.
Shurgard Storage Centers, Inc.
Sky Financial Group, Inc.
South Financial Group Inc
Southwest Bancorp, Inc.
Sterling Bancorp
Sun Communities, Inc.
Talbots, Inc.
Texas Regional Bancshares, Inc
TD Banknorth Group Inc
Universal Forest Products Inc.
Washington Trust Bancorp, Inc.

Dividend Achievers Departures

The following former Dividend Achievers have not increased their regular cash dividends in 2004.

Camden Property Trust
Citizens Banking Corp
Cleco Corp.
Federal Signal Corp.
Heinz (H.J.) Co.
SWS Group, Inc.
Unizan Financial Corp

The following former Dividend Achievers did not meet volume/liquidity requirements.

1st Source Corp.
Artesian Resources Corp.
Badger Meter, Inc.
Bowl America Inc.
Community Trust Bancorp, Inc.
Connecticut Water Service, Inc.
EnergySouth, Inc.
Farmer Bros. Co.
First Financial Corp.
Florida Public Utilities Co.
Frisch's Restaurants, Inc.
Gorman-Rupp Co.
Middlesex Water Co.
National Security Group, Inc
Pennichuck Corp.
Quaker Chemical Corp.
Quixote Corp.
Simmons First National Corp.
SJW Corp.
Stepan Co.
United Mobile Homes, Inc.
Weyco Group, Inc

Dividend Achievers Name Changes

Old Name	*New Name*
Banknorth Group Inc	TD Banknorth Group Inc
Hershey Foods Corp.	Hershey Corp.
ChevronTexaco Corp.	Chevron Corp.

Top 20 by Return on Equity

Based on latest available year-end information. Ratios determined using net income.

Rank	Company	R.O.E.	Rank	Company	R.O.E.
1	Colgate-Palmolive Co.	99.9	11	Procter & Gamble Co.	32.5
2	Clorox Co.	99.9	12	Cincinnati Financial Corp.	32.3
3	Avon Products, Inc.	75.1	13	Sara Lee Corp.	31.4
4	Anheuser-Busch Cos., Inc.	69.4	14	Altria Group Inc.	30.9
5	SLM Corp.	55.5	15	Merck & Co., Inc.	30.6
6	Hershey Corp.	51.2	16	Sysco Corp.	30.1
7	Nucor Corp.	38.2	17	PepsiCo Inc.	28.7
8	SEI Investments Co.	36.8	18	Doral Financial Corp.	28.4
9	Pitney Bowes, Inc.	36.3	19	Coca-Cola Co.	28.4
10	ServiceMaster Co.	34.0	20	Chevron Corp.	28.1

Top 20 by Return on Assets

Based on latest available year-end information. Ratios determined using net income.

Rank	Company	R.O.A	Rank	Company	R.O.A
1	SEI Investments Co.	26.7	11	Coca-Cola Co.	15.4
2	Avon Products, Inc.	20.2	12	Linear Technology Corp.	15.2
3	Raven Industries, Inc.	20.2	13	Hershey Corp.	15.0
4	Colgate-Palmolive Co.	19.7	14	Bard (C.R.), Inc.	14.7
5	Nucor Corp.	18.2	15	Applebee's International, Inc.	14.5
6	Eaton Vance Corp.	17.8	16	PepsiCo Inc.	14.5
7	T Rowe Price Group Inc.	16.9	17	Nuveen Investments Inc.	14.2
8	Harley-Davidson, Inc.	16.0	18	Clorox Co.	14.1
9	Johnson & Johnson	15.8	19	3M Co.	14.0
10	Wrigley (William) Jr. Co.	15.5	20	Chevron Corp.	13.8

Top 20 by Current Yield

Based on closing prices at April 30, 2005

Rank	Company	Yield	Rank	Company	Yield
1	Sun Communities, Inc.	7.2	11	Home Properties Inc.	6.0
2	Colonial Properties Trust	7.0	12	TEPPCO Partners, L.P.	6.0
3	Commercial Net Lease Realty, Inc.	6.8	13	Progress Energy, Inc.	5.6
4	Healthcare Realty Trust, Inc.	6.7	14	Tanger Factory Outlet Centers	5.6
5	Health Care Property Investors, Inc.	6.5	15	Realty Income Corp.	5.5
6	Lexington Corporate Properties Trust	6.3	16	Peoples Energy Corp.	5.5
7	Universal Health Realty Income Trust	6.2	17	SBC Communications, Inc.	5.4
8	Duke Realty Corp.	6.1	18	United Dominion Realty Trus	5.4
9	Cedar Fair, L.P.	6.1	19	Consolidated Edison, Inc.	5.3
10	Liberty Property Trust	6.1	20	Shurgard Storage Centers, Inc	5.3

Highest Price/Earnings Ratios

Based on latest available year-end information. Ratios determined using net income.
Based on closing prices at April 30, 2005

Rank	Company	P/E Ratio	Rank	Company	P/E Ratio
1	United Dominion Realty Trust, Inc.	276.9	11	People's Bank	38.1
2	Telephone and Data Systems, Inc.	105.7	12	EastGroup Properties, Inc.	37.5
3	Shurgard Storage Centers, Inc.	102.0	13	Helmerich & Payne, Inc.	35.9
4	Marsh & McLennan Cos., Inc.	87.6	14	Gallagher (Arthur J.) & Co.	35.7
5	Home Properties Inc.	62.5	15	Paychex Inc.	35.6
6	Wesco Financial Corp.	56.8	16	Teleflex Incorporated	35.4
7	Forest City Enterprises, Inc.	49.7	17	Tanger Factory Outlet Centers, Inc.	35.1
8	Federal Realty Investment Trust	47.8	18	Expeditors Int'l of Washington, Inc.	34.8
9	Macerich Co.	43.4	19	General Growth Properties, Inc.	32.6
10	Stryker Corp.	39.5	20	Prologis	32.2

Lowest Price/Earnings Ratios

Based on latest available year-end information. Ratios determined using net income.
Based on closing prices at April 30, 2005

Rank	Company	P/E Ratio	Rank	Company	P/E Ratio
1	Cincinnati Financial Corp.	3.4	11	MBIA Inc.	9.5
2	Doral Financial Corp.	3.5	12	Old Republic International Corp.	9.8
3	Fidelity National Financial, Inc.	5.5	13	Chubb Corp.	9.9
4	Nucor Corp.	6.0	14	Ambac Financial Group, Inc.	10.1
5	Fannie Mae	6.8	15	Mercury General Corp.	10.1
6	Chevron Corp.	8.4	16	Midland Co.	10.4
7	National City Corp.	8.7	17	Protective Life Corp.	10.9
8	Commerce Group, Inc.	8.9	18	Colonial Properties Trust	11.2
9	Freddie Mac	9.1	19	Irwin Financial Corp.	11.3
10	State Auto Financial Corp.	9.4	20	Supervalu Inc.	11.3

Highest Price/Book Ratios

Based on latest available year-end information. Ratios determined using net income.
Based on closing prices at April 30, 2005

Rank	Company	P/B Ratio	Rank	Company	P/B Ratio
1	Colgate-Palmolive Co.	28.45	11	Procter & Gamble Co.	6.78
2	Avon Products, Inc.	16.91	12	Stryker Corp.	6.69
3	Hershey Corp.	13.80	13	SLM Corp.	6.53
4	Anheuser-Busch Cos., Inc.	11.84	14	PepsiCo Inc.	6.43
5	Paychex Inc.	8.60	15	Coca-Cola Co.	6.29
6	Pitney Bowes, Inc.	7.54	16	Eaton Vance Corp.	6.28
7	SEI Investments Co.	7.32	17	Expeditors Int'l of Washington, Inc.	6.12
8	Sysco Corp.	7.24	18	Johnson & Johnson	6.07
9	Meridian Bioscience Inc.	6.93	19	Lilly (Eli) & Co.	5.98
10	Wrigley (William) Jr. Co.	6.82	20	Medtronic, Inc.	5.95

Lowest Price/Book Ratios

Based on latest available year-end information. Ratios determined using net income.
Based on closing prices at April 30, 2005

Rank	Company	P/B Ratio	Rank	Company	P/B Ratio
1	Superior Industries Intl., Inc.	0.89	11	Haverty Furniture Cos., Inc.	1.16
2	Myers Industries Inc.	0.94	12	La-Z-Boy Inc.	1.17
3	Doral Financial Corp.	1.00	13	Fidelity National Finl., Inc.	1.19
4	Harleysville Group, Inc.	1.05	14	Protective Life Corp.	1.19
5	MBIA Inc.	1.08	15	Media General, Inc.	1.21
6	Old Republic International Corp.	1.10	16	NACCO Industries Inc.	1.22
7	Cincinnati Financial Corp.	1.11	17	Lincoln National Corp.	1.24
8	Irwin Financial Corp.	1.11	18	Wesco Financial Corp.	1.26
9	The St Paul Travelers Com., Inc.	1.14	19	Pinnacle West Capital Corp.	1.28
10	CenturyTel, Inc.	1.16	20	Susquehanna Banc., Inc.	1.29

Top 20 By Revenues

Based on latest available year-end information (in million's US$)

Rank	Name	Revenues	Rank	Name	Revenues
1	Exxon Mobil Corp.	298,035	11	Procter & Gamble Co.	51,407
2	Wal-Mart Stores, Inc.	287,989	12	Bank of America Corp.	48,065
3	Chevron Corp.	155,300	13	Johnson & Johnson	47,348
4	General Electric Co.	152,363	14	Target Corp.	46,839
5	Citigroup Inc.	94,713	15	SBC Communications, Inc.	40,787
6	Altria Group Inc.	89,610	16	Walgreen Co.	37,508
7	American International Group Inc.	81,303	17	United Technologies Corp.	37,445
8	Home Depot, Inc.	73,094	18	Lowe's Cos., Inc.	36,464
9	Fannie Mae	53,768	19	Archer Daniels Midland Co.	36,151
10	Pfizer Inc.	52,516	20	Freddie Mac	34,288

Top 20 By Net Income

Based on latest available year-end information (in million's US$)

Rank	Name		Net Income	Rank	Name		Net Income
1	Exxon Mobil Corp.	$	25,330	11	Fannie Mae	$	7,905
2	Citigroup Inc.	$	17,853	12	Procter & Gamble Co.	$	6,481
3	General Electric Co.	$	16,593	13	Wells Fargo & Co.	$	6,202
4	Chevron Corp.	$	13,328	14	SBC Communications, Inc.	$	5,887
5	Pfizer Inc.	$	11,361	15	Merck & Co., Inc.	$	5,813
6	Bank of America Corp.	$	10,810	16	Home Depot, Inc.	$	5,001
7	Wal-Mart Stores, Inc.	$	10,267	17	Coca-Cola Co.	$	4,847
8	Altria Group Inc.	$	9,416	18	Freddie Mac	$	4,147
9	American Intl. Group Inc.	$	9,274	19	Washington Mutual Inc.	$	3,880
10	Johnson & Johnson	$	8,509	20	PepsiCo Inc.	$	3,568

Top 20 by Market Capitalization

Based on latest available year-end information (in million's US$)
Based on closing prices at April 30, 2005

Rank	Name	Current Value	Rank	Name	Current Value
1	General Electric Co.	383,716	11	Chevron Corp.	109,439
2	Exxon Mobil Corp.	364,387	12	Coca-Cola Co.	104,695
3	Citigroup Inc.	244,976	13	Wells Fargo & Co.	101,610
4	Johnson & Johnson	204,085	14	PepsiCo Inc.	93,364
5	Pfizer Inc.	202,658	15	SBC Communications, Inc.	78,621
6	Wal-Mart Stores, Inc.	199,148	16	Abbott Laboratories	76,636
7	Bank of America Corp.	182,574	17	Home Depot, Inc.	76,353
8	Procter & Gamble Co.	136,599	18	Merck & Co., Inc.	74,855
9	Altria Group Inc.	134,438	19	Lilly (Eli) & Co.	66,229
10	American Int'l Group Inc.	132,444	20	Medtronic, Inc.	63,741

Bottom 20 by Market Capitalization

Based on latest available year-end information (in million's US$)
Based on closing prices at April 30, 2005

Rank	Name	Current Value	Rank	Name	Current Value
1	Southwest Bancorp, Inc.	230	11	Tennant Co.	320
2	LSI Industries Inc.	239	12	Washington Trust Bancorp, Inc	323
3	PennRock Financial Services Corp.	256	13	MBT Financial Corp.	325
4	Meridian Bioscience Inc.	265	14	Haverty Furniture Cos., Inc.	326
5	First State Bancorporation	270	15	First Financial Holdings, Inc.	327
6	Peoples Bancorp, Inc.	270	16	Myers Industries Inc.	333
7	First Oak Brook Bancshares	279	17	Raven Industries, Inc.	343
8	First Bancorp	286	18	First Indiana Corp.	347
9	Community Banks, Inc.	298	19	Universal Health Realty Inc Tr	386
10	First Community Bancshares	313	20	Courier Corp.	395

Top 20 by Total Assets

Based on latest available year-end information (in million's US$)

Rank	Name	Total Assets	Rank	Name	Total Assets
1	Citigroup Inc.	1,264,032	11	National City Corp.	139,280
2	Fannie Mae	1,009,569	12	SunTrust Banks, Inc.	125,393
3	General Electric Co.	750,330	13	Pfizer Inc.	123,684
4	Bank of America Corp.	736,445	14	Wal-Mart Stores, Inc.	120,223
5	American International Group Inc.	678,346	15	Lincoln National Corp.	116,219
6	Freddie Mac	617,340	16	SBC Communications, Inc.	108,844
7	Wells Fargo & Co.	387,798	17	Golden West Financial Corp.	106,889
8	Washington Mutual Inc.	275,178	18	Altria Group Inc.	101,648
9	Exxon Mobil Corp.	195,256	19	BB&T Corp.	100,509
10	Allstate Corp.	149,725	20	Fifth Third Bancorp	94,456

About Total Return

Total return represents one of the best measures of how well an investor of a given stock has fared as it reflects both dividend income and price appreciation. Mergent calculates total return for each Dividend Achievers company on the basis that cash dividends were reinvested on the ex-dividend date of each dividend payment. The following table demonstrates the effect of compounding as well as each stock's performance and the level of dividends paid. Total returns have been adjusted for splits, stock dividends and spin-offs. In the case of a spin-off, shares in the spun-off company were assumed to be converted to cash and reinvested in the original company's stock.

How to read the rankings: On the following pages, the Dividend Achievers companies are listed alphabetically with their respective total returns and rankings over trailing one, three and five year periods ending January 31, 2005. For example, an investor who purchased shares of 3M Co. on January 31, 2004, and sold them on January 31, 2005, would have realized a total return of 8.41% on their original investment. Following each company's one-year total return are its three-year and five-year annualized total returns and their respective rankings for each period. The three-year annualized total return is based on an investment made on January 31, 2002, and the five-year annualized total return represents an investment made on January 31, 2000. Thus an investment made in 3M Co. at January 31, 2002, would have generated an annualized total return of 17.03% during the three year period ended January 31, 2005. If an investor had bought shares in 3M Co. on January 31, 2000, and sold them on January 31, 2005, their annualized total return would have been 14.72%.

Ranking The Dividend Achievers By Total Return

Based on the 1,3 and 5 year periods ending April 30, 2005

Name	1-Year Tot. Ret.	1-Year Rank	3-Year Tot. Ret.	3-Year Rank	5-Year Tot. Ret.	5-Year Rank
3M Co.	(10.08)	278	8.63	144	14.23	161
Abbott Laboratories	22.03	68	1.51	240	8.74	231
ABM Industries, Inc.	0.35	229	0.42	254	9.91	220
AFLAC Inc.	(2.78)	249	11.78	103	11.63	193
Air Products & Chemicals, Inc.	20.20	79	8.93	141	15.74	144
Albemarle Corp.	27.14	46	9.20	140	14.01	165
Alberto-Culver Co.	(5.05)	263	7.78	159	24.10	40
Alfa Corp.	4.03	203	(2.78)	278	11.53	195
Allstate Corp.	25.00	53	14.76	75	21.41	68
ALLTEL Corp.	15.96	109	7.64	162	(0.63)	291
Altria Group Inc.	22.38	66	11.22	109	30.55	15
Ambac Financial Group, Inc.	(2.49)	246	2.73	232	16.63	126
American International Group Inc.	(28.68)	309	(9.37)	306	(6.72)	306
American States Water Co.	13.27	131	2.49	235	8.51	232
AmSouth Bancorporation	23.50	61	8.86	142	17.08	120
Anchor BanCorp Wisconsin, Inc.	10.78	156	8.11	155	12.89	175
Anheuser-Busch Cos., Inc.	(6.90)	272	(2.47)	275	7.54	243
Applebee's International, Inc.	(4.00)	257	12.86	92	18.37	99
AptarGroup Inc.	24.25	57	10.10	127	12.09	189
Aqua America Inc.	33.31	30	14.03	85	19.64	84
Archer Daniels Midland Co.	4.00	204	12.53	98	16.73	124
Arrow International,Inc.	12.23	141	12.96	90	15.22	150
Associated Banc-Corp.	16.33	105	10.70	118	20.79	75
Atmos Energy Corp.	11.01	153	7.68	161	15.85	140
Automatic Data Processing Inc.	0.45	227	(3.90)	283	(3.19)	298
Avery Dennison Corp.	(16.63)	294	(4.37)	285	(2.31)	295
Avon Products, Inc.	(3.34)	252	14.36	78	15.80	141
BancFirst Corp.	29.88	40	19.85	38	23.34	51
BancorpSouth Inc.	7.70	174	1.72	237	9.90	221
Bandag, Inc.	2.19	215	7.11	173	16.45	131
Bank of America Corp.	15.71	111	11.16	111	17.05	121
Bank of Hawaii Corp.	10.96	154	21.26	31	21.52	67
Banta Corporation	(4.97)	262	5.19	195	18.56	95
Bard (C.R.), Inc.	34.93	28	38.87	4	28.43	22
BB&T Corp.	17.33	94	4.25	211	11.41	197
Beckman Coulter, Inc.	20.46	74	12.80	94	16.57	128
Becton, Dickinson and Co.	17.11	96	17.69	53	19.33	89
Bemis, Inc.	4.29	199	3.39	224	10.94	206
Black Hills Corporation	16.18	106	3.25	226	12.37	182
Brady Corp.	54.90	7	19.91	36	17.47	111
Briggs & Stratton Corp.	(6.06)	268	17.93	52	13.82	166
Brown & Brown, Inc.	12.93	133	10.42	121	35.27	6
Brown-Forman Corp.	20.45	75	14.21	80	17.48	110
California Water Service Group	20.28	77	14.17	82	11.38	198
Capital City Bank Group, Inc.	(1.19)	239	21.29	30	22.02	61
Carlisle Companies Inc.	22.87	64	23.05	24	13.80	168
Caterpillar Inc.	15.27	114	19.77	40	20.40	78
CBL & Associates Properties, Inc.	59.68	5	34.06	9	34.09	11
Cedar Fair, L.P.	1.34	221	14.76	76	16.16	136
CenturyTel, Inc.	7.01	181	4.20	212	5.32	264
Chemical Financial Corp.	(5.79)	267	3.75	220	6.89	251
Chevron Corp.	16.76	102	9.74	133	7.38	244
Chittenden Corp.	5.63	190	0.94	248	11.26	201
Chubb Corp.	20.90	72	4.39	209	7.33	245
Cincinnati Financial Corp.	5.70	189	0.42	253	4.19	274
Cintas Corporation	(13.86)	287	(8.74)	303	0.06	288
Citigroup Inc.	0.96	224	8.26	150	4.87	269
City National Corp.	16.52	103	10.42	122	15.92	138

Ranking The Dividend Achievers By Total Return

Based on the 1,3 and 5 year periods ending April 30, 2005

Name	1-Year Tot. Ret.	1-Year Rank	3-Year Tot. Ret.	3-Year Rank	5-Year Tot. Ret.	5-Year Rank
Clarcor Inc.	16.11	108	17.52	54	24.82	35
Clorox Co.	24.45	56	14.94	71	13.82	167
Coca-Cola Co.	(12.20)	283	(6.06)	292	0.03	289
Colgate-Palmolive Co.	(12.33)	284	(0.43)	262	(1.27)	292
Colonial Properties Trust	13.95	125	8.24	151	16.40	132
Comerica, Inc.	14.44	121	0.37	255	9.75	222
Commerce Bancorp, Inc.	(0.52)	235	5.69	192	24.87	34
Commerce Bancshares, Inc.	14.73	119	9.76	132	16.70	125
Commerce Group, Inc.	30.80	36	16.64	58	18.50	98
Commercial Net Lease Realty, Inc.	20.33	76	14.03	84	19.81	81
Community Bank System, Inc.	11.55	149	12.55	96	18.02	101
Community Banks, Inc.	(19.26)	301	7.94	157	17.24	115
Compass Bancshares Inc.	14.97	118	9.29	139	22.17	60
ConAgra Foods, Inc.	(4.23)	259	7.03	174	11.27	200
Consolidated Edison, Inc.	9.64	162	4.39	210	9.52	224
Corus Bankshares, Inc.	32.78	32	27.91	15	34.16	10
Courier Corp.	20.66	73	23.10	23	35.02	8
Cullen/Frost Bankers, Inc.	2.15	216	7.13	171	14.58	157
CVB Financial Corp.	6.73	183	13.59	86	23.28	54
Danaher Corp.	9.57	163	12.40	100	12.28	184
DENTSPLY International, Inc.	13.21	132	11.76	105	23.70	44
Diebold, Inc.	6.43	186	10.18	126	12.73	178
Donnelley (R.R.) & Sons Co.	15.05	117	4.45	207	12.93	174
Doral Financial Corp.	(56.48)	313	(1.82)	269	23.59	45
Dover Corp.	(7.78)	274	0.80	249	(5.11)	303
Duke Realty Corp.	9.75	160	10.76	117	13.58	169
EastGroup Properties, Inc.	35.09	26	20.61	33	19.43	86
Eaton Vance Corp.	30.12	38	10.02	129	18.51	97
Ecolab, Inc.	10.85	155	15.46	66	12.17	186
Emerson Electric Co.	6.49	184	8.27	148	5.31	265
Energen Corp.	51.90	8	32.55	11	30.41	16
Essex Property Trust, Inc.	29.09	43	18.48	48	19.94	80
Expeditors International of Washington,	22.67	65	19.78	39	18.55	96
Exxon Mobil Corp.	36.80	24	15.04	70	10.44	215
F.N.B. Corp.	0.23	230	13.56	87	21.60	64
Family Dollar Stores, Inc.	(15.12)	289	(7.08)	295	8.22	235
Fannie Mae	(19.77)	303	(9.91)	307	(0.24)	290
Federal Realty Investment Trust	49.04	12	31.28	12	27.60	24
Fidelity National Financial, Inc.	11.92	145	26.06	19	32.68	13
Fifth Third Bancorp	(16.88)	296	(12.28)	309	2.49	281
First Bancorp	1.62	217	10.19	125	18.80	90
First Charter Corp.	7.36	177	5.87	190	13.34	172
First Commonwealth Financial Corp.	(3.07)	251	3.41	222	7.17	246
First Community Bancshares, Inc.	0.23	231	1.11	243	15.88	139
First Financial Holdings, Inc.	(3.99)	256	(1.09)	266	17.58	109
First Indiana Corp.	39.74	20	10.90	114	14.02	164
First Merchants Corp.	12.38	139	4.47	206	11.01	204
First Midwest Bancorp, Inc.	(0.97)	238	4.92	200	13.21	173
First Oak Brook Bancshares, Inc.	(0.02)	233	9.97	130	25.42	31
First State Bancorporation	12.65	134	15.56	65	23.97	42
FirstMerit Corp	7.92	173	(1.23)	267	12.48	179
Forest City Enterprises, Inc.	21.66	70	18.94	46	27.51	25
Franklin Electric Co., Inc.	18.99	86	13.06	89	16.09	137
Franklin Resources, Inc.	26.01	49	18.73	47	17.13	117
Freddie Mac	7.24	178	(0.28)	260	7.67	239
Fuller (H.B.) Company	12.39	138	0.74	251	11.44	196
Fulton Financial Corp.	9.20	166	8.23	153	12.22	185
Gallagher (Arthur J.) & Co.	(10.99)	281	(5.93)	291	10.80	209
Gannett Co., Inc.	(10.09)	279	2.89	228	5.15	267
General Dynamics Corp.	13.73	126	4.19	213	14.11	163

Ranking The Dividend Achievers By Total Return

Based on the 1,3 and 5 year periods ending April 30, 2005

Name	1-Year Tot. Ret.	1-Year Rank	3-Year Tot. Ret.	3-Year Rank	5-Year Tot. Ret.	5-Year Rank
General Electric Co.	23.56	60	7.28	168	(5.23)	304
General Growth Properties, Inc.	49.26	11	42.45	3	35.21	7
Genuine Parts Co.	22.92	63	10.81	115	14.17	162
Glacier Bancorp, Inc.	11.24	151	22.30	26	26.89	27
Golden West Financial Corp.	19.05	85	22.66	25	30.14	17
Grainger (W.W.) Inc.	6.93	182	0.95	247	6.59	255
Granite Construction Inc.	15.60	112	0.99	246	9.12	229
Harley-Davidson, Inc.	(15.90)	291	(3.41)	280	3.80	276
Harleysville Group, Inc.	12.64	136	(9.24)	305	8.08	236
Harleysville National Corp.	(17.69)	298	5.63	194	17.74	105
Harsco Corp.	25.76	50	10.78	116	15.79	142
Haverty Furniture Cos., Inc.	(19.49)	302	(7.45)	296	6.55	256
Health Care Property Investors, Inc.	12.50	137	14.18	81	21.00	73
Healthcare Realty Trust, Inc.	13.31	130	14.83	74	25.14	33
Helmerich & Payne, Inc.	43.99	17	9.62	136	12.16	187
Hershey Foods Corp.	46.02	14	25.59	20	25.19	32
Hibernia Corp.	46.94	13	19.33	44	27.81	23
Hilb Rogal & Hobbs Co.	(1.25)	241	(0.61)	263	21.36	69
Hillenbrand Industries, Inc.	(16.70)	295	(3.42)	281	14.80	153
HNI Corp.	38.70	22	21.00	32	17.11	119
Holly Corp.	106.32	1	60.52	1	71.40	1
Home Depot, Inc.	1.42	219	(7.88)	299	(8.36)	310
Home Properties Inc.	17.52	93	10.91	113	15.21	151
Hormel Foods Corp.	3.73	207	9.80	131	17.30	113
Hudson United Bancorp	(0.93)	237	5.88	189	14.79	154
Illinois Tool Works, Inc.	(1.69)	244	6.47	183	6.89	250
Independent Bank Corporation	11.64	148	17.47	55	34.39	9
Irwin Financial Corp.	(14.04)	288	2.70	233	4.83	270
Jack Henry & Associates, Inc.	(5.29)	265	(8.88)	304	(2.05)	294
Jefferson-Pilot Corp.	4.08	202	2.85	229	5.14	268
Johnson & Johnson	29.34	42	4.12	214	12.40	181
Johnson Controls Inc.	1.56	218	10.06	128	13.51	171
KeyCorp	15.30	113	9.64	135	17.12	118
Kimberly-Clark Corp.	(0.68)	236	1.50	241	4.02	275
Kimco Realty Corp.	34.35	29	25.44	21	21.92	62
Lancaster Colony Corp.	2.74	212	4.61	205	11.94	191
La-Z-Boy Inc.	(41.71)	312	(25.21)	312	(3.59)	299
Legg Mason, Inc.	16.40	104	29.41	14	23.92	43
Leggett & Platt, Inc.	21.63	71	3.02	227	7.03	248
Lexington Corporate Properties Trust	30.44	37	19.77	41	23.58	47
Liberty Property Trust	14.10	124	13.47	88	16.94	122
Lilly (Eli) & Co.	(19.03)	299	(1.99)	271	(3.69)	300
Lincoln National Corp.	2.96	210	1.08	244	8.41	233
Linear Technology Corp.	1.26	222	(1.98)	270	(8.40)	311
Lowe's Cos., Inc.	0.39	228	7.47	166	16.34	134
LSI Industries Inc.	7.03	180	(6.70)	293	6.92	249
M & T Bank Corp.	23.61	58	8.12	154	20.34	79
Macerich Co.	49.37	10	33.34	10	28.90	20
MAF Bancorp, Inc.	0.60	226	4.74	202	18.64	94
Marsh & McLennan Cos., Inc.	(36.36)	310	(15.87)	311	(8.70)	312
Marshall & Ilsley Corp.	18.16	91	12.46	99	15.24	149
Martin Marietta Materials, Inc.	29.08	44	14.04	83	2.26	283
Masco Corp.	14.62	120	6.21	187	9.46	226
Matthews International Corp.	16.90	99	9.66	134	25.92	29
May Department Stores Co.	17.28	95	3.64	221	8.25	234
MBIA Inc.	(9.62)	277	0.56	252	11.28	199
MBNA Corp.	(17.51)	297	(4.23)	284	3.66	277
MBT Financial Corp.	12.18	142	12.88	91	3.00	278
McCormick & Co., Inc.	2.86	211	12.32	101	19.38	87
McDonald's Corp.	9.53	164	2.60	234	(3.94)	302

Ranking The Dividend Achievers By Total Return

Based on the 1,3 and 5 year periods ending April 30, 2005

Name	1-Year Tot. Ret.	1-Year Rank	3-Year Tot. Ret.	3-Year Rank	5-Year Tot. Ret.	5-Year Rank
McGrath RentCorp	45.44	15	21.77	29	25.78	30
McGraw-Hill Cos., Inc.	11.97	144	12.55	97	12.41	180
MDU Resources Group Inc.	23.61	59	14.85	73	16.58	127
Media General, Inc.	(13.72)	285	(2.52)	276	5.84	263
Medtronic, Inc.	5.12	191	6.29	185	0.84	286
Mercantile Bankshares Corp.	21.70	69	10.32	123	15.42	148
Merck & Co., Inc.	(25.11)	306	(10.25)	308	(10.08)	313
Mercury General Corp.	6.33	187	4.62	204	17.26	114
Meredith Corp.	(6.85)	271	4.07	215	12.10	188
Meridian Bioscience Inc.	57.69	6	35.38	8	23.98	41
MGE Energy Inc.	10.73	157	9.60	137	18.11	100
Midland Co.	19.78	80	11.12	112	21.58	66
Mine Safety Appliances Co.	32.95	31	38.41	5	41.60	3
Myers Industries Inc.	(23.93)	305	(8.50)	301	4.44	272
NACCO Industries Inc.	24.51	55	14.31	79	20.45	77
National City Corp.	1.22	223	6.54	182	19.34	88
National Fuel Gas Co.	15.13	115	8.74	143	6.82	252
National Penn Bancshares, Inc.	(4.19)	258	7.40	167	13.58	170
NICOR Inc.	13.48	128	(3.21)	279	6.42	259
Nordson Corp.	(5.32)	266	3.32	225	9.74	223
North Fork Bancorporation, Inc.	16.89	100	5.87	191	24.66	38
Northern Trust Corp.	8.43	169	(3.79)	282	(5.56)	305
Nucor Corp.	73.78	2	22.14	28	20.65	76
Nuveen Investments Inc.	35.36	25	7.59	164	23.28	55
Old National Bancorp	(13.74)	286	(0.74)	264	(3.02)	297
Old Republic International Corp.	3.64	208	4.94	199	23.01	58
Otter Tail Corp.	(3.40)	254	(7.01)	294	2.61	280
Pacific Capital Bancorp	7.38	176	15.90	61	16.17	135
Park National Corp.	(6.25)	269	4.41	208	5.98	261
Parker-Hannifin Corp.	9.69	161	7.78	160	6.80	253
Paychex Inc.	(16.38)	292	(5.03)	290	(1.46)	293
PennRock Financial Services Corp.	18.37	90	15.17	69	27.03	26
Pentair, Inc.	35.08	27	19.86	37	17.95	104
Peoples Bancorp, Inc.	11.77	147	5.99	188	16.52	129
People's Bank	51.53	9	38.01	7	31.16	14
Peoples Energy Corp.	(1.35)	242	5.05	196	10.01	219
PepsiCo Inc.	3.83	206	3.84	217	10.18	218
Pfizer Inc.	(22.31)	304	(7.54)	297	(7.01)	307
Piedmont Natural Gas Co., Inc.	17.08	97	11.17	110	14.63	156
Pier 1 Imports Inc.	(28.27)	308	(14.06)	310	6.52	258
Pinnacle West Capital Corp.	11.40	150	2.81	230	7.78	238
Pitney Bowes, Inc.	4.75	193	4.89	201	5.31	266
Popular Inc.	12.64	135	19.04	45	21.03	72
PPG Industries, Inc.	16.79	101	12.01	102	7.58	242
Praxair, Inc.	29.92	39	19.59	42	17.71	106
Procter & Gamble Co.	4.21	200	8.45	145	14.96	152
Progress Energy, Inc.	2.65	213	(2.56)	277	7.64	240
Progressive Corp.	4.42	197	16.82	57	33.40	12
Prologis	39.14	21	25.26	22	20.82	74
Protective Life Corp.	8.12	171	8.26	149	11.99	190
Questar Corp..	67.55	3	30.73	13	28.52	21
Raven Industries, Inc.	18.50	89	51.30	2	57.82	2
Realty Income Corp.	31.61	34	18.24	51	24.43	39
Regency Centers Corp.	44.19	16	27.17	17	26.20	28
Regions Financial Corp.	0.92	225	2.10	236	14.56	158
Republic Bancorp, Inc.	10.04	158	7.15	170	18.79	91
RLI Corp.	25.06	52	15.62	64	23.33	53

Ranking The Dividend Achievers By Total Return

Based on the 1,3 and 5 year periods ending April 30, 2005

Name	1-Year Tot. Ret.	1-Year Rank	3-Year Tot. Ret.	3-Year Rank	5-Year Tot. Ret.	5-Year Rank
Rohm & Haas Co.	15.08	116	7.93	158	6.54	257
Roper Industries, Inc.	40.30	19	14.65	77	17.46	112
Ross Stores, Inc.	(11.65)	282	10.20	124	21.60	65
RPM International Inc.	17.84	92	3.84	218	15.43	147
S & T Bancorp, Inc.	22.10	67	11.37	106	17.95	103
Sara Lee Corp.	(4.53)	261	3.40	223	10.49	214
SBC Communications, Inc.	(0.15)	234	(4.51)	286	(8.35)	309
SEI Investments Co.	11.78	146	(0.38)	261	10.96	205
ServiceMaster Co.	8.20	170	0.19	257	2.02	284
Sherwin-Williams Co.	18.98	87	15.27	68	14.67	155
Shurgard Storage Centers, Inc.	31.32	35	11.29	108	16.49	130
Sigma-Aldrich Corp.	3.96	205	8.27	147	15.79	143
Sky Financial Group, Inc.	12.25	140	7.11	172	15.72	145
SLM Corp.	26.42	47	15.84	62	37.26	4
Smith (A.O.) Corp	(2.69)	247	(0.98)	265	9.21	228
Sonoco Products Co.	12.14	143	1.00	245	8.85	230
South Financial Group Inc	(3.05)	250	6.78	179	16.38	133
Southwest Bancorp, Inc.	15.80	110	16.61	59	29.09	19
Stanley Works	3.43	209	0.11	258	10.77	210
State Auto Financial Corp.	(2.12)	245	19.46	43	23.12	57
State Street Corp.	(3.95)	255	(2.03)	273	0.14	287
Sterling Bancorp	2.55	214	10.64	120	29.98	18
Sterling Bancshares, Inc.	7.21	179	0.78	250	14.39	160
Sterling Financial Corp.	1.37	220	18.42	49	21.09	71
Stryker Corp.	(1.67)	243	22.19	27	22.18	59
Sun Communities, Inc.	4.92	192	0.20	256	6.78	254
SunTrust Banks, Inc.	9.89	159	5.04	197	10.32	217
Superior Industries International, Inc.	(39.12)	311	(25.56)	313	(7.51)	308
Supervalu Inc.	4.35	198	4.02	216	11.60	194
Susquehanna Bancshares, Inc.	(7.18)	273	(1.99)	272	12.78	177
Synovus Financial Corp.	20.27	78	3.81	219	11.12	202
Sysco Corp.	(8.15)	275	7.56	165	14.43	159
T Rowe Price Group Inc.	9.11	168	18.31	50	9.47	225
Talbots, Inc.	(25.90)	307	(8.31)	300	1.29	285
Tanger Factory Outlet Centers, Inc.	26.31	48	27.34	16	24.77	36
Target Corp.	7.70	175	2.76	231	7.58	241
TCF Financial Corp.	4.57	196	1.56	239	19.65	83
TD Banknorth Group Inc.	N.A.	N.A.	N.A.	N.A.	N.A.	N.A.
Teleflex Incorporated	19.20	84	(0.20)	259	10.87	208
Telephone and Data Systems, Inc.	18.89	88	(1.64)	268	(3.90)	301
Tennant Co.	(8.66)	276	(4.92)	289	2.49	282
TEPPCO Partners, L.P.	23.34	62	17.19	56	23.58	46
Texas Regional Bancshares, Inc.	0.19	232	12.73	95	23.34	52
The St Paul Travelers Companies Inc.	(10.12)	280	(7.84)	298	2.82	279
Tootsie Roll Industries Inc.	(5.14)	264	(8.71)	302	4.49	271
Transatlantic Holdings, Inc.	(19.26)	300	(4.68)	287	5.95	262
Trustmark Corp.	5.83	188	4.70	203	11.10	203
UGI Corp.	63.95	4	38.17	6	35.51	5
United Bankshares, Inc.	4.75	194	1.42	242	10.50	213
United Dominion Realty Trust, Inc.	28.80	45	15.64	63	24.76	37
United Technologies Corp.	19.70	81	14.86	72	11.89	192
Universal Corp.	(6.38)	270	5.65	193	23.43	50
Universal Forest Products Inc.	40.83	18	15.45	67	23.56	48
Universal Health Realty Income Trust	32.03	33	16.41	60	23.50	49

Ranking The Dividend Achievers By Total Return

Based on the 1,3 and 5 year periods ending April 30, 2005

Name	1-Year Tot. Ret.	1-Year Rank	3-Year Tot. Ret.	3-Year Rank	5-Year Tot. Ret.	5-Year Rank
Valley National Bancorp	(1.21)	240	1.63	238	10.92	207
Valspar Corp.	(15.52)	290	(2.19)	274	4.34	273
Vectren Corp.	16.15	107	6.94	176	10.64	211
VF Corp.	24.84	54	11.33	107	17.67	107
Vulcan Materials Co.	16.98	98	7.18	169	6.07	260
Walgreen Co.	25.53	51	4.97	198	9.38	227
Wal-Mart Stores, Inc.	(16.48)	293	(4.78)	288	(2.53)	296
Washington Federal Inc.	7.99	172	7.63	163	19.53	85
Washington Mutual Inc.	9.16	167	6.75	180	23.25	56
Washington Real Estate Investment Trus	14.34	123	6.61	181	18.77	92
Washington Trust Bancorp, Inc.	(3.36)	253	8.23	152	12.85	176
Webster Financial Corp.	6.44	185	6.88	177	18.66	93
Weingarten Realty Investors	29.35	41	20.12	35	21.13	70
Wells Fargo & Co.	9.28	165	8.28	146	10.53	212
Wesbanco, Inc.	(2.74)	248	6.82	178	7.14	247
Wesco Financial Corp.	(4.30)	260	6.35	184	10.43	216
West Pharmaceutical Services, Inc.	38.13	23	26.61	18	19.76	82
WestAmerica Bancorporation	4.14	201	6.21	186	17.23	116
WGL Holdings, Inc.	11.19	152	8.11	156	7.87	237
Whitney Holding Corp.	13.41	129	10.67	119	17.99	102
Wiley (John) & Sons Inc.	19.20	83	11.77	104	16.93	123
Wilmington Trust Corp.	4.67	195	7.03	175	12.34	183
Wolverine World Wide, Inc.	14.44	122	20.39	34	21.79	63
WPS Resources Corp.	19.40	82	12.84	93	17.61	108
Wrigley (William) Jr. Co.	13.65	127	9.51	138	15.56	146

Ranking the Dividend Achievers by Total Return

Based on the trailing 1-year period ending April 30, 2005

Rank	Company	Ticker	1-Year Tot. Ret	Rank	Company	Ticker	1-Year Tot. Ret
1	Holly Corp.	HOC	106.32	11	General Growth Properties, Inc.	GGP	49.26
2	Nucor Corp.	NUE	73.78	12	Federal Realty Investment Trust	FRT	49.04
3	Questar Corp..	STR	67.55	13	Hibernia Corp.	HIB	46.94
4	UGI Corp.	UGI	63.95	14	Hershey Foods Corp.	HSY	46.02
5	CBL & Associates Prop.	CBL	59.68	15	McGrath RentCorp	MGRC	45.44
6	Meridian Bioscience Inc.	VIVO	57.69	16	Regency Centers Corp.	REG	44.19
7	Brady Corp.	BRC	54.90	17	Helmerich & Payne, Inc.	HP	43.99
8	Energen Corp.	EGN	51.90	18	Universal Forest Products Inc.	UFPI	40.83
9	People's Bank	PBCT	51.53	19	Roper Industries, Inc.	ROP	40.30
10	Macerich Co.	MAC	49.37	20	First Indiana Corp.	FINB	39.74

Based on the trailing 3-year period ending April 30, 2005

Rank	Company	Ticker	3-Year Tot. Ret	Rank	Company	Ticker	3-Year Tot. Ret
1	Holly Corp.	HOC	60.52	11	Energen Corp.	EGN	32.55
2	Raven Industries, Inc.	RAVN	51.30	12	Federal Realty Investment Trust	FRT	31.28
3	General Growth Properties	GGP	42.45	13	Questar Corp..	STR	30.73
4	Bard (C.R.), Inc.	BCR	38.87	14	Legg Mason, Inc.	LM	29.41
5	Mine Safety Appliances Co.	MSA	38.41	15	Corus Bankshares, Inc.	CORS	27.91
6	UGI Corp.	UGI	38.17	16	Tanger Factory Outlet Centers, Inc.	SKT	27.34
7	People's Bank	PBCT	38.01	17	Regency Centers Corp.	REG	27.17
8	Meridian Bioscience Inc.	VIVO	35.38	18	West Pharmaceutical Services, Inc.	WST	26.61
9	CBL & Associates Prop., Inc	CBL	34.06	19	Fidelity National Financial, Inc.	FNF	26.06
10	Macerich Co.	MAC	33.34	20	Hershey Foods Corp.	HSY	25.59

Based on the trailing 5-year period ending April 30, 2005

Rank	Company	Ticker	5-Year Tot. Ret	Rank	Company	Ticker	5-Year Tot. Ret
1	Holly Corp.	HOC	71.40	11	CBL & Associates Properties, Inc.	34.09	34.99
2	Raven Industries, Inc.	RAVN	57.82	12	Progressive Corp.	33.40	34.07
3	Mine Safety Appliances Co.	MSA	41.60	13	Fidelity National Financial, Inc.	32.68	33.60
4	SLM Corp.	SLM	37.26	14	People's Bank	31.16	32.81
5	UGI Corp.	UGI	35.51	15	Altria Group Inc.	30.55	32.72
6	Brown & Brown, Inc.	BRO	35.27	16	Energen Corp.	30.41	32.43
7	General Growth Prop.	GGP	35.21	17	Golden West Financial Corp.	30.14	31.56
8	Courier Corp.	CRRC	35.02	18	Sterling Bancorp	29.98	30.71
9	Independent Bank Corp.	IBCP	34.39	19	Southwest Bancorp, Inc.	29.09	30.70
10	Corus Bankshares, Inc.	CORS	34.16	20	Macerich Co.	28.90	30.59

Web Site And Dividend Reinvestment Plan Information

Company	Ticker	Web Site	DRIP
3M Co.	MMM	www.3m.com	Yes
Abbott Laboratories	ABT	www.abbott.com	Yes
ABM Industries, Inc.	ABM	www.abm.com	No
AFLAC Inc.	AFL	www.aflac.com	Yes
Air Products & Chemicals, Inc.	APD	www.airproducts.com	Yes
Albemarle Corp.	ALB	www.albemarle.com	Yes
Alberto-Culver Co.	ACV	www.alberto.com	No
Alfa Corp.	ALFA	www.alfains.com	Yes
Allstate Corp.	ALL	www.allstate.com	Yes
ALLTEL Corp.	AT	www.alltel.com	Yes
Altria Group Inc.	MO	www.philipmorris.com	Yes
Ambac Financial Group, Inc.	ABK	www.ambac.com	No
American International Group Inc.	AIG	www.aig.com	No
American States Water Co.	AWR	www.aswater.com	Yes
AmSouth Bancorporation	ASO	www.amsouth.com	Yes
Anchor BanCorp Wisconsin, Inc.	ABCW	www.anchorbank.com	No
Anheuser-Busch Cos., Inc.	BUD	www.anheuser-busch.com	Yes
Applebee's International, Inc.	APPB	www.applebees.com	No
AptarGroup Inc.	ATR	www.aptargroup.com	No
Aqua America Inc.	WTR	www.suburbanwater.com	Yes
Archer Daniels Midland Co.	ADM	www.admworld.com	Yes
Arrow International,Inc.	ARRO	www.arrowintl.com	No
Associated Banc-Corp.	ASBC	www.associatedbank.com	Yes
Atmos Energy Corp.	ATO	www.atmosenergy.com	Yes
Automatic Data Processing Inc.	ADP	www.adp.com	No
Avery Dennison Corp.	AVY	www.averydennison.com	Yes
Avon Products, Inc.	AVP	www.avon.com	Yes
BancFirst Corp.	BANF	www.bancfirst.com	No
BancorpSouth Inc.	BXS	www.bancorpsouth.com	Yes
Bandag, Inc.	BDG	www.bandag.com	Yes
Bank of America Corp.	BAC	www.bankofamerica.com	Yes
Bank of Hawaii Corp.	BOH	www.boh.com	Yes
Banta Corporation	BN	www.banta.com	Yes
Bard (C.R.), Inc.	BCR	www.crbard.com	Yes
BB&T Corp.	BBT	www.bbandt.com	Yes
Beckman Coulter, Inc.	BEC	www.beckmancoulter.com	Yes
Becton, Dickinson and Co.	BDX	www.bd.com	Yes
Bemis, Inc.	BMS	www.bemis.com	Yes
Black Hills Corporation	BKH	www.blackhillscorp.com	Yes
Brady Corp.	BRC	www.bradycorp.com	Yes
Briggs & Stratton Corp.	BGG	www.briggsandstratton.com	Yes
Brown & Brown, Inc.	BRO	www.bbinsurance.com	No
Brown-Forman Corp.	BF B	www.brown-forman.com	No
California Water Service Group	CWT	www.calwater.com	Yes
Capital City Bank Group, Inc.	CCBG	www.mycapitalcitybank.com	No
Carlisle Companies Inc.	CSL	www.carlisle.com	Yes
Caterpillar Inc.	CAT	www.CAT.com	Yes
CBL & Associates Properties, Inc.	CBL	www.cblproperties.com	Yes
Cedar Fair, L.P.	FUN	www.cedarfair.com	Yes
CenturyTel, Inc.	CTL	www.centurytel.com	Yes
Chemical Financial Corp.	CHFC	www.chemicalbankmi.com	Yes
Chevron Corp.	CVX	www.chevrontexaco.com	Yes
Chittenden Corp.	CHZ	www.chittendencorp.com	Yes
Chubb Corp.	CB	www.chubb.com	Yes
Cincinnati Financial Corp.	CINF	www.cinfin.com	Yes
Cintas Corporation	CTAS	www.cintas.com	No
Citigroup Inc.	C	www.citigroup.com	Yes
City National Corp.	CYN	www.cnb.com	No
Clarcor Inc.	CLC	www.clarcor.com	Yes
Clorox Co.	CLX	www.clorox.com	Yes
Coca-Cola Co.	KO	www.coca-cola.com	Yes
Colgate-Palmolive Co.	CL	www.colgate.com	Yes
Colonial Properties Trust	CLP	www.colonialprop.com	Yes

Web Site And Dividend Reinvestment Plan Information

Company	Ticker	Web Site	DRIP
Comerica, Inc.	CMA	www.comerica.com	Yes
Commerce Bancorp, Inc.	CBH	www.commerceonline.com	Yes
Commerce Bancshares, Inc.	CBSH	www.commercebank.com	Yes
Commerce Group, Inc.	CGI	www.commerceinsurance.com	No
Commercial Net Lease Realty, Inc.	NNN	www.cnlreit.com	Yes
Community Bank System, Inc.	CBU	www.communitybankna.com	Yes
Community Banks, Inc.	CMTY	www.communitybanks.com	Yes
Compass Bancshares Inc.	CBSS	www.compassweb.com	Yes
ConAgra Foods, Inc.	CAG	www.conagrafoods.com	Yes
Consolidated Edison, Inc.	ED	www.conedison.com	Yes
Corus Bankshares, Inc.	CORS	www.corusbank.com	No
Courier Corp.	CRRC	www.courier.com	No
Cullen/Frost Bankers, Inc.	CFR	www.frostbank.com	No
CVB Financial Corp.	CVBF	www.cbbank.com	No
Danaher Corp.	DHR	www.danaher.com	No
DENTSPLY International, Inc.	XRAY	www.dentsply.com	No
Diebold, Inc.	DBD	www.diebold.com	Yes
Donnelley (R.R.) & Sons Co.	RRD	www.rrdonnelley.com	Yes
Doral Financial Corp.	DRL	www.doralfinancial.com	No
Dover Corp.	DOV	www.dovercorporation.com	Yes
Duke Realty Corp.	DRE	www.dukerealty.com	Yes
EastGroup Properties, Inc.	EGP	www.eastgroup.net	Yes
Eaton Vance Corp.	EV	www.eatonvance.com	No
Ecolab, Inc.	ECL	www.ecolab.com	Yes
Emerson Electric Co.	EMR	www.gotoemerson.com	Yes
Energen Corp.	EGN	www.energen.com	Yes
Essex Property Trust, Inc.	ESS	www.expresspropertytrust.com	Yes
Expeditors International of Washington, Inc.	EXPD	www.expditors.com	No
Exxon Mobil Corp.	XOM	www.exxonmobil.com	Yes
F.N.B. Corp.	FNB	www.fnbcorporation.com	Yes
Family Dollar Stores, Inc.	FDO	www.familydollar.com	No
Fannie Mae	FNM	www.fanniemae.com	Yes
Federal Realty Investment Trust	FRT	www.federalrealty.com	Yes
Fidelity National Financial, Inc.	FNF	www.fnf.com	No
Fifth Third Bancorp	FITB	www.53.com	Yes
First Bancorp	FBNC	wwwfirstbancorp.com	Yes
First Charter Corp.	FCTR	www.firstcharter.com	Yes
First Commonwealth Financial Corp.	FCF	www.fcbanking.com	Yes
First Community Bancshares, Inc.	FCBC	www.fcbinc.com	No
First Financial Holdings, Inc.	FFCH	www.firstfinancialholdings.com	Yes
First Indiana Corp.	FINB	www.firstindiana.com	Yes
First Merchants Corp.	FRME	www.firstmerchants.com	Yes
First Midwest Bancorp, Inc.	FMBI	www.firstmidwest.com	Yes
First Oak Brook Bancshares, Inc.	FOBB	www.firstoakbrook.com	No
First State Bancorporation	FSNM	www.fsbnm.com	Yes
FirstMerit Corp	FMER	www.firstmerit.com	Yes
Forest City Enterprises, Inc.	FCE A	www.fceinc.com	Yes
Franklin Electric Co., Inc.	FELE	www.franklin-electric.com	No
Franklin Resources, Inc.	BEN	www.frk.com	Yes
Freddie Mac	FRE	www.freddiemac.com	Yes
Fuller (H.B.) Company	FUL	www.hbfuller.com	Yes
Fulton Financial Corp.	FULT	www.fult.com	Yes
Gallagher (Arthur J.) & Co.	AJG	www.ajg.com	No
Gannett Co., Inc.	GCI	www.gannett.com	Yes
General Dynamics Corp.	GD	www.generaldynamics.com	No
General Electric Co.	GE	www.ge.com	Yes
General Growth Properties, Inc.	GGP	www.generalgrowth.com	Yes
Genuine Parts Co.	GPC	www.genpt.com	Yes
Glacier Bancorp, Inc.	GBCI	www.glacierbancorp.com	Yes
Golden West Financial Corp.	GDW	www.gdw.com	No
Grainger (W.W.) Inc.	GWW	www.grainger.com	No
Granite Construction Inc.	GVA	www.graniteconstruction.com	Yes
Harley-Davidson, Inc.	HDI	www.harley-davidson.com	Yes

Web Site And Dividend Reinvestment Plan Information

Company	Ticker	Web Site	DRIP
Harleysville Group, Inc.	HGIC	www.harleysvillegroup.com	Yes
Harleysville National Corp.	HNBC	www.hncbank.com	Yes
Harsco Corp.	HSC	www.harsco.com	Yes
Haverty Furniture Cos., Inc.	HVT	www.havertys.com	No
Health Care Property Investors, Inc.	HCP	www.hcpi.com	Yes
Healthcare Realty Trust, Inc.	HR	www.healthcarerealty.com	Yes
Helmerich & Payne, Inc.	HP	www.hpinc.com	No
Hershey Corp.	HSY	www.hersheys.com	Yes
Hibernia Corp.	HIB	www.hibernia.com	Yes
Hilb Rogal & Hobbs Co.	HRH	www.hrh.com	No
Hillenbrand Industries, Inc.	HB	www.hillenbrand.com	Yes
HNI Corp.	HNI	www.honi.com	No
Holly Corp.	HOC	www.hollycorp.com	No
Home Depot, Inc.	HD	www.homedepot.com	Yes
Home Properties Inc.	HME	www.homeproperties.com	Yes
Hormel Foods Corp.	HRL	www.hormel.com	Yes
Hudson United Bancorp	HU	www.hudsonunitedbank.com	Yes
Illinois Tool Works, Inc.	ITW	www.itw.com	Yes
Independent Bank Corporation	IBCP	www.ibcp.com	Yes
Irwin Financial Corp.	IFC	www.irwinfinancial.com	Yes
Jack Henry & Associates, Inc.	JKHY	www.jackhenry.com	Yes
Jefferson-Pilot Corp.	JP	www.jpfinancial.com	Yes
Johnson & Johnson	JNJ	www.jnj.com	Yes
Johnson Controls Inc.	JCI	www.johnsoncontrols.com	Yes
KeyCorp	KEY	www.key.com	Yes
Kimberly-Clark Corp.	KMB	www.kimberly-clark.com	Yes
Kimco Realty Corp.	KIM	www.kimcorealty.com	Yes
Lancaster Colony Corp.	LANC	www.lancastercolony.com	Yes
La-Z-Boy Inc.	LZB	www.la-z-boy.com	Yes
Legg Mason, Inc.	LM	www.leggmason.com	No
Leggett & Platt, Inc.	LEG	www.leggett.com	No
Lexington Corporate Properties Trust	LXP	www.lxp.com	No
Liberty Property Trust	LRY	www.libertyproperty.com	Yes
Lilly (Eli) & Co.	LLY	www.lilly.com	Yes
Lincoln National Corp.	LNC	www.lfg.com	Yes
Linear Technology Corp.	LLTC	www.linear.com	No
Lowe's Cos., Inc.	LOW	www.lowes.com	Yes
LSI Industries Inc.	LYTS	www.lsi-industries.com	Yes
M & T Bank Corp.	MTB	www.mandtbank.com	Yes
Macerich Co.	MAC	www.macerich.com	Yes
MAF Bancorp, Inc.	MAFB	www.mafbancorp.com	No
Marsh & McLennan Cos., Inc.	MMC	www.mmc.com	Yes
Marshall & Ilsley Corp.	MI	www.micorp.com	Yes
Martin Marietta Materials, Inc.	MLM	www.martinmarietta.com	No
Masco Corp.	MAS	www.masco.com	Yes
Matthews International Corp.	MATW	www.matw.com	No
May Department Stores Co.	MAY	www.maycompany.com	Yes
MBIA Inc.	MBI	www.mbia.com	No
MBNA Corp.	KRB	www.mbna.com	No
MBT Financial Corp.	MBTF	www.MBandT.com	No
McCormick & Co., Inc.	MKC	www.mccormick.com	No
McDonald's Corp.	MCD	www.mcdonalds.com	Yes
McGrath RentCorp	MGRC	www.mgrc.com	No
McGraw-Hill Cos., Inc.	MHP	www.mcgraw-hill.com	Yes
MDU Resources Group Inc.	MDU	www.mdu.com	Yes
Media General, Inc.	MEG	www.mediageneral.com	Yes
Medtronic, Inc.	MDT	www.medtronic.com	Yes
Mercantile Bankshares Corp.	MRBK	www.mercantile.com	Yes
Merck & Co., Inc.	MRK	www.merck.com	Yes
Mercury General Corp.	MCY	www.mercuryinsurance.com	No
Meredith Corp.	MDP	www.meredith.com	No
Meridian Bioscience Inc.	VIVO	www.meridianbioscience.com	Yes
MGE Energy Inc.	MGEE	www.mge.com	Yes

Web Site And Dividend Reinvestment Plan Information

Company	Ticker	Web Site	DRIP
Midland Co.	MLAN	www.midlandcompany.com	Yes
Mine Safety Appliances Co.	MSA	www.msanet.com	No
Myers Industries Inc.	MYE	www.myersind.com	Yes
NACCO Industries Inc.	NC	www.naccoind.com	No
National City Corp.	NCC	www.nationalcity.com	Yes
National Fuel Gas Co.	NFG	www.nationalfuelgas.com	Yes
National Penn Bancshares, Inc.	NPBC	www.nationalpennbancshares.com	Yes
NICOR Inc.	GAS	www.nicor.com	Yes
Nordson Corp.	NDSN	www.nordson.com	Yes
North Fork Bancorporation, Inc.	NFB	www.northforkbank.com	Yes
Northern Trust Corp.	NTRS	www.northerntrust.com	No
Nucor Corp.	NUE	www.nucor.com	Yes
Nuveen Investments Inc.	JNC	www.nuveen.com	No
Old National Bancorp	ONB	www.oldnational.com	Yes
Old Republic International Corp.	ORI	www.oldrepublic.com	Yes
Otter Tail Corp.	OTTR	www.ottertail.com	Yes
Pacific Capital Bancorp	PCBC	www.pcbancorp.com	No
Park National Corp.	PRK	www.parknationalcorp.com	Yes
Parker-Hannifin Corp.	PH	www.phstock.com	Yes
Paychex Inc.	PAYX	www.paychex.com	Yes
PennRock Financial Services Corp.	PRFS	www.pennrock.com	Yes
Pentair, Inc.	PNR	www.pentair.com	Yes
Peoples Bancorp, Inc.	PEBO	www.peoplesbancorp.com	No
People's Bank	PBCT	www.peoples.com	Yes
Peoples Energy Corp.	PGL	www.peoplesenergy.com	Yes
PepsiCo Inc.	PEP	www.pepsico.com	Yes
Pfizer Inc.	PFE	www.pfizer.com	Yes
Piedmont Natural Gas Co., Inc.	PNY	www.piedmontng.com	Yes
Pier 1 Imports Inc.	PIR	www.pier1.com	Yes
Pinnacle West Capital Corp.	PNW	www.pinnaclewest.com	Yes
Pitney Bowes, Inc.	PBI	www.pb.com	Yes
Popular Inc.	BPOP	www.popularinc.com	Yes
PPG Industries, Inc.	PPG	www.ppg.com	Yes
Praxair, Inc.	PX	www.praxair.com	Yes
Procter & Gamble Co.	PG	www.pg.com	Yes
Progress Energy, Inc.	PGN	www.progress-energy.com	Yes
Progressive Corp.	PGR	www.progressive.com	No
Prologis	PLD	www.prologis.com	Yes
Protective Life Corp.	PL	www.protective.com	Yes
Questar Corp..	STR	www.questar.com	Yes
Raven Industries, Inc.	RAVN	www.ravenind.com	Yes
Realty Income Corp.	O	www.realtyincome.com	No
Regency Centers Corp.	REG	www.regencyrealty.com	Yes
Regions Financial Corp.	RF	www.regions.com	Yes
Republic Bancorp, Inc.	RBNC	www.republicbancorp.com	Yes
RLI Corp.	RLI	www.rlicorp.com	Yes
Rohm & Haas Co.	ROH	www.rohmhaas.com	Yes
Roper Industries, Inc.	ROP	www.roperind.com	No
Ross Stores, Inc.	ROST	www.rossstores.com	No
RPM International Inc.	RPM	www.rpminc.com	Yes
S & T Bancorp, Inc.	STBA	www.stbank.com	Yes
Sara Lee Corp.	SLE	www.saralee.com	Yes
SBC Communications, Inc.	SBC	www.sbc.com	Yes
SEI Investments Co.	SEIC	www.seic.com	No
ServiceMaster Co.	SVM	www.servicemaster.com	Yes
Sherwin-Williams Co.	SHW	www.sherwin.com	Yes
Shurgard Storage Centers, Inc.	SHU	www.shurgard.com	No
Sigma-Aldrich Corp.	SIAL	www.sigma-aldrich.com	No
Sky Financial Group, Inc.	SKYF	www.skyfi.com	Yes
SLM Corp.	SLM	www.salliemae.com	No
Smith (A.O.) Corp	AOS	www.aosmith.com	Yes
Sonoco Products Co.	SON	www.sonoco.com	Yes
South Financial Group Inc	TSFG	www.thesouthgroup.com	Yes

Web Site And Dividend Reinvestment Plan Information

Company	Ticker	Web Site	DRIP
Southwest Bancorp, Inc.	OKSB	www.oksb.com	No
Stanley Works	SWK	www.stanleyworks.com	Yes
State Auto Financial Corp.	STFC	www.stauto.com	Yes
State Street Corp.	STT	www.statestreet.com	Yes
Sterling Bancorp	STL	www.sterlingbancorp.com	Yes
Sterling Bancshares, Inc.	SBIB	www.sterlingfi.com	No
Sterling Financial Corp.	SLFI	www.sterlingfi.com	Yes
Stryker Corp.	SYK	www.stryker.com	No
Sun Communities, Inc.	SUI	www.suncommunities.com	No
SunTrust Banks, Inc.	STI	www.suntrust.com	Yes
Superior Industries International, Inc.	SUP	www.supind.com	Yes
Supervalu Inc.	SVU	www.supervalu.com	Yes
Susquehanna Bancshares, Inc.	SUSQ	www.susqbanc.com	Yes
Synovus Financial Corp.	SNV	www.synovus.com	Yes
Sysco Corp.	SYY	www.sysco.com	Yes
T Rowe Price Group Inc.	TROW	www.troweprice.com	No
Talbots, Inc.	TLB	www.talbots.com	No
Tanger Factory Outlet Centers, Inc.	SKT	www.tangeroutlet.com	Yes
Target Corp.	TGT	www.targetcorp.com	Yes
TCF Financial Corp.	TCB	www.tcfexpress.com	Yes
TD Banknorth Group Inc.	BNK	www.banknorth.com	No
Teleflex Incorporated	TFX	www.teleflex.com	Yes
Telephone and Data Systems, Inc.	TDS	www.teldta.com	Yes
Tennant Co.	TNC	www.tennantco.com	Yes
TEPPCO Partners, L.P.	TPP	www.teppco.com	No
Texas Regional Bancshares, Inc.	TRBS	www.trbsinc.com	No
The St Paul Travelers Companies Inc.	STA	www.stpaul.com	Yes
Tootsie Roll Industries Inc.	TR	www.tootsie.com	No
Transatlantic Holdings, Inc.	TRH	www.transre.com	No
Trustmark Corp.	TRMK	www.trustmark.com	Yes
UGI Corp.	UGI	www.ugicorp.com	Yes
United Bankshares, Inc.	UBSI	www.ubsi-wv.com	Yes
United Dominion Realty Trust, Inc.	UDR	www.udrt.com	Yes
United Technologies Corp.	UTX	www.utc.com	Yes
Universal Corp.	UVV	www.universalcorp.com	Yes
Universal Forest Products Inc.	UFPI	www.ufpi.com	No
Universal Health Realty Income Trust	UHT	www.uhrit.com	Yes
Valley National Bancorp	VLY	www.valleynationalbank.com	Yes
Valspar Corp.	VAL	www.valspar.com	Yes
Vectren Corp.	VVC	www.vectren.com	Yes
VF Corp.	VFC	www.vfc.com	Yes
Vulcan Materials Co.	VMC	www.vulcanmaterials.com	Yes
Walgreen Co.	WAG	www.walgreens.com	Yes
Wal-Mart Stores, Inc.	WMT	www.wal-mart.com	Yes
Washington Federal Inc.	WFSL	www.washingtonfederal.com	No
Washington Mutual Inc.	WM	www.wamu.com	Yes
Washington Real Estate Investment Trust	WRE	www.writ.com	Yes
Washington Trust Bancorp, Inc.	WASH	www.washtrust.com	Yes
Webster Financial Corp.	WBS	www.websteronline.com	Yes
Weingarten Realty Investors	WRI	www.weingarten.com	Yes
Wells Fargo & Co.	WFC	www.wellsfargo.com	Yes
Wesbanco, Inc.	WSBC	www.wesbanco.com	Yes
Wesco Financial Corp.	WSC	www.wescofinancial.com	No
West Pharmaceutical Services, Inc.	WST	www.westpharma.com	Yes
WestAmerica Bancorporation	WABC	www.westamerica.com	Yes
WGL Holdings, Inc.	WGL	www.wglholdings.com	Yes
Whitney Holding Corp.	WTNY	www.whitneybank.com	Yes
Wiley (John) & Sons Inc.	JW A	www.wiley.com	No
Wilmington Trust Corp.	WL	www.wilmingtontrust.com	Yes
Wolverine World Wide, Inc.	WWW	www.wolverineworldwide.com	No
WPS Resources Corp.	WPS	www.wpsr.com	Yes
Wrigley (William) Jr. Co.	WWY	www.wrigley.com	Yes

NAICS Classification of Companies By Industry Sector

Accommodation and Food Services
Applebee's International, Inc.
McDonald's Corporation

Admin & Support & Waste Mgmt & Remed Svcs
ServiceMaster Co.
Johnson Controls Inc.

Arts, Entertainment, and Recreation
Cedar Fair, L.P.

Construction
ABM Industries, Inc.
Forest City Enterprises, Inc.
Granite Construction Inc.
Martin Marietta Materials, Inc.
MDU Resources Group Inc.

Finance and Insurance
AFLAC Inc.
Alfa Corp.
Allstate Corp.
Ambac Financial Group, Inc.
American International Group Inc.
AmSouth Bancorporation
Anchor BanCorp Wisconsin, Inc.
Associated Banc-Corp.
BancFirst Corp.
BancorpSouth Inc.
Bank of America Corp.
Bank of Hawaii Corp.
BB&T Corp.
Brown & Brown, Inc.
Capital City Bank Group, Inc.
Chemical Financial Corp.
Chittenden Corp.
Chubb Corp.
Cincinnati Financial Corp.
Citigroup Inc.
City National Corp.
Comerica, Inc.
Commerce Bancorp, Inc.
Commerce Bancshares, Inc.
Commerce Group, Inc.
Community Bank System, Inc.
Community Banks, Inc.
Compass Bancshares Inc.
Corus Bankshares, Inc.
Cullen/Frost Bankers, Inc.
CVB Financial Corp.
Doral Financial Corp.
Eaton Vance Corp.
F.N.B. Corp.
Fannie Mae
Fidelity National Financial, Inc.
Fifth Third Bancorp
First Bancorp
First Charter Corp.
First Commonwealth Financial Corp.
First Community Bancshares, Inc.

Finance and Insurance
First Financial Holdings, Inc.
First Indiana Corp.
First Merchants Corp.
First Midwest Bancorp, Inc.
First Oak Brook Bancshares, Inc.
First State Bancorporation
FirstMerit Corp
Franklin Resources, Inc.
Freddie Mac
Fulton Financial Corp.
Gallagher (Arthur J.) & Co.
Glacier Bancorp, Inc.
Golden West Financial Corp.
Harleysville Group, Inc.
Harleysville National Corp.
Hibernia Corp.
Hilb Rogal & Hobbs Co.
Hudson United Bancorp
Independent Bank Corporation
Irwin Financial Corp.
Jefferson-Pilot Corp.
KeyCorp
Legg Mason, Inc.
Lincoln National Corp.
M & T Bank Corp.
MAF Bancorp, Inc.
Marsh & McLennan Cos., Inc.
Marshall & Ilsley Corp.
MBIA Inc.
MBNA Corp.
MBT Financial Corp.
Mercantile Bankshares Corp.
Mercury General Corp.
Midland Co.
National City Corp.
National Penn Bancshares, Inc.
North Fork Bancorporation, Inc.
Northern Trust Corp.
Nuveen Investments Inc.
Old National Bancorp
Old Republic International Corp.
Pacific Capital Bancorp
Park National Corp.
PennRock Financial Services Corp.
Peoples Bancorp, Inc.
People's Bank
Popular Inc.
Progressive Corp.
Protective Life Corp.
Regions Financial Corp.
Republic Bancorp, Inc.
RLI Corp.
S & T Bancorp, Inc.
SEI Investments Co.
Sky Financial Group, Inc.
SLM Corp.
South Financial Group Inc
Southwest Bancorp, Inc.
State Auto Financial Corp.
State Street Corp.

NAICS Classification of Companies By Industry Sector

Finance and Insurance
Sterling Bancorp
Sterling Bancshares, Inc.
Sterling Financial Corp.
SunTrust Banks, Inc.
Susquehanna Bancshares, Inc.
Synovus Financial Corp.
T Rowe Price Group Inc.
TCF Financial Corp.
TD Banknorth Group Inc.
Texas Regional Bancshares, Inc.
The St Paul Travelers Companies Inc.
Transatlantic Holdings, Inc.
Trustmark Corp.
United Bankshares, Inc.
Valley National Bancorp
Washington Federal Inc.
Washington Mutual Inc.
Washington Trust Bancorp, Inc.
Webster Financial Corp.
Wells Fargo & Co.
Wesbanco, Inc.
WestAmerica Bancorporation
Whitney Holding Corp.
Wilmington Trust Corp.

Information
ALLTEL Corp.
Automatic Data Processing Inc.
CenturyTel, Inc.
Gannett Co., Inc.
McGraw-Hill Cos., Inc.
Media General, Inc.
Meredith Corp.
Telephone and Data Systems, Inc.
Wiley (John) & Sons Inc.

Management of Companies and Enterprises
SBC Communications, Inc.
Universal Corp.

Manufacturing
3M Co.
Abbott Laboratories
Air Products & Chemicals, Inc.
Albemarle Corp.
Alberto-Culver Co.
Altria Group Inc.
Anheuser-Busch Cos., Inc.
AptarGroup Inc.
Archer Daniels Midland Co.
Arrow International,Inc.
Avery Dennison Corp.
Avon Products, Inc.
Bandag, Inc.
Banta Corporation
Bard (C.R.), Inc.
Beckman Coulter, Inc.
Becton, Dickinson and Co.

Manufacturing
Brady Corp.
Briggs & Stratton Corp.
Brown-Forman Corp.
Carlisle Companies Inc.
Caterpillar Inc.
Chevron Corp.
Cintas Corporation
Clarcor Inc.
Clorox Co.
Coca-Cola Co.
Colgate-Palmolive Co.
ConAgra Foods, Inc.
Courier Corp.
Danaher Corp.
DENTSPLY International, Inc.
Diebold, Inc.
Donnelley (R.R.) & Sons Co.
Dover Corp.
Ecolab, Inc.
Emerson Electric Co.
Exxon Mobil Corp.
Franklin Electric Co., Inc.
Fuller (H.B.) Company
General Dynamics Corp.
General Electric Co.
Harley-Davidson, Inc.
Harsco Corp.
Hershey Corp.
Hillenbrand Industries, Inc.
HNI Corp.
Holly Corp.
Hormel Foods Corp.
Illinois Tool Works, Inc.
Johnson & Johnson
Kimberly-Clark Corp.
Lancaster Colony Corp.
La-Z-Boy Inc.
Leggett & Platt, Inc.
Lilly (Eli) & Co.
Linear Technology Corp.
LSI Industries Inc.
Masco Corp.
Matthews International Corp.
McCormick & Co., Inc.
Medtronic, Inc.
Merck & Co., Inc.
Meridian Bioscience Inc.
Myers Industries Inc.
NACCO Industries Inc.
Nordson Corp.
Nucor Corp.
Parker-Hannifin Corp.
Pentair, Inc.
PepsiCo Inc.
Pfizer Inc.
PPG Industries, Inc.
Praxair, Inc.
Procter & Gamble Co.

NAICS Classification of Companies By Industry Sector

Manufacturing
Raven Industries, Inc.
Rohm & Haas Co.
Roper Industries, Inc.
RPM International Inc.
Sara Lee Corp.
Sherwin-Williams Co.
Smith (A.O.) Corp
Sonoco Products Co.
Stanley Works
Stryker Corp.
Superior Industries International, Inc.
Teleflex Incorporated
Tennant Co.
Tootsie Roll Industries Inc.
United Technologies Corp.
Universal Forest Products Inc.
Valspar Corp.
VF Corp.
West Pharmaceutical Services, Inc.
Wolverine World Wide, Inc.
Wrigley (William) Jr. Co.

Mining
Helmerich & Payne, Inc.
Vulcan Materials Co.

Professional, Scientific, and Technical Services
Expeditors International of Washington, Inc.
Jack Henry & Associates, Inc.
Paychex Inc.

Real Estate Investment Trusts
CBL & Associates Properties, Inc.
Colonial Properties Trust
Commercial Net Lease Realty, Inc.
Duke Realty Corp.
EastGroup Properties, Inc.
Essex Property Trust, Inc.
Federal Realty Investment Trust
General Growth Properties, Inc.
Health Care Property Investors, Inc.
Healthcare Realty Trust, Inc.
Home Properties Inc.
Kimco Realty Corp.
Lexington Corporate Properties Trust
Liberty Property Trust
Macerich Co.
McGrath RentCorp
Prologis
Realty Income Corp.
Regency Centers Corp.
Shurgard Storage Centers, Inc.
Sun Communities, Inc.
Tanger Factory Outlet Centers, Inc.
United Dominion Realty Trust, Inc.
Universal Health Realty Income Trust
Washington Real Estate Investment Trust
Weingarten Realty Investors

Retail Trade
Family Dollar Stores, Inc.
Haverty Furniture Cos., Inc.
Home Depot, Inc.
Lowe's Cos., Inc.
May Department Stores Co.
Pier 1 Imports Inc.
Ross Stores, Inc.
Talbots, Inc.
Target Corp.
Walgreen Co.
Wal-Mart Stores, Inc.

Transportation and Warehousing
Atmos Energy Corp.
TEPPCO Partners, L.P.

Utilities
American States Water Co.
Aqua America Inc.
Black Hills Corporation
California Water Service Group
Consolidated Edison, Inc.
Energen Corp.
MGE Energy Inc.
National Fuel Gas Co.
NICOR Inc.
Otter Tail Corp.
Peoples Energy Corp.
Piedmont Natural Gas Co., Inc.
Pinnacle West Capital Corp.
Progress Energy, Inc.
Questar Corp..
UGI Corp.
Vectren Corp.
WGL Holdings, Inc.
WPS Resources Corp.

Wholesale Trade
Genuine Parts Co.
Grainger (W.W.) Inc.
Mine Safety Appliances Co.
Pitney Bowes, Inc.
Sigma-Aldrich Corp.
Supervalu Inc.
Sysco Corp.
Wesco Financial Corp.

Canadian Company Rankings

Canadian Dividend Achievers Index
10 Year Performance

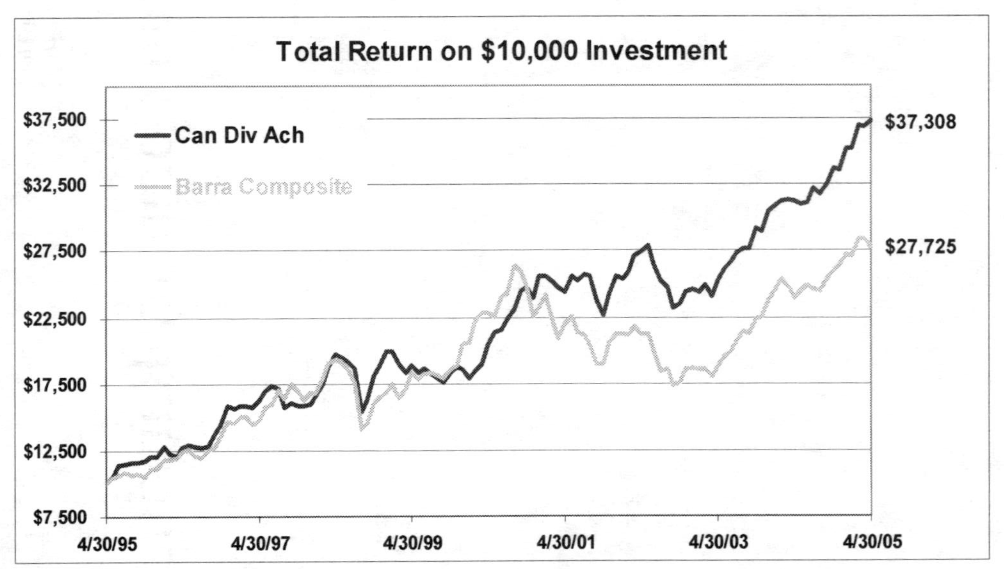

Ranking The 2005 Canadian Dividend Achievers

Canadian companies are listed by the five-year average annual compound growth rate of their dividends.

Rank	Company	5-Year CAGR	Rank	Company	5-Year CAGR
1	C.I. Fund Management	61.54	19	Rothmans Inc.	14.14
2	Home Capital Group Inc	39.77	20	Toronto Dominion Bank	13.56
3	Saputo Inc.	35.10	21	Canadian Imperial Bank of Comm	12.89
4	BMTC Group Inc.	29.46	22	Toromont Industries Ltd.	12.70
5	Loblaw Cos. Ltd.	28.14	23	Atco Ltd.	11.84
5	Weston (George) Limited	26.86	24	Melcor Developments Ltd.	11.38
7	Empire Co Ltd	25.74	25	Bank of Montreal	11.08
8	AGF Management Ltd	22.28	26	Buhler Industries, Inc.	10.20
9	Metro Inc	21.20	27	Enbridge Inc	8.90
10	Great-West Lifeco Inc.	20.92	28	Sico, Inc.	8.45
11	Bank of Nova Scotia	20.39	29	Terasen Inc	7.21
12	Ensign Resource Service Group	20.01	30	West Fraser Timber Co., Ltd.	4.64
13	Power Financial Corp	19.14	31	Canadian Utilities Ltd.	4.27
14	IGM Financial Inc	18.90	32	Fortis Inc.	3.71
15	Power Corp. of Canada	17.81	33	Imperial Oil Ltd.	3.53
16	Royal Bank of Canada	16.53	34	Thomson Corp.	2.80
17	National Bank of Canada	15.20	35	Emera Inc.	1.18
18	Canadian National Railway Co.	14.29	36	Leon's Furniture Ltd.	-3.44

Longest Record Of Dividend Achievement

Companies are listed by the number of consecutive annual dividend increases.

Rank	Company	Years of Growth	Rank	Company	Years of Growth
1	Canadian Utilities Ltd.	22	19	Melcor Developments Ltd.	9
2	Toromont Industries Ltd.	15	20	Metro Inc	9
3	Bank of Nova Scotia	13	21	National Bank of Canada	9
4	BMTC Group Inc.	13	22	Power Corp. of Canada	9
5	IGM Financial Inc	13	23	Weston (George) Limited	9
5	Bank of Montreal	12	24	AGF Management Ltd	8
7	Emera Inc.	12	25	Buhler Industries, Inc.	8
8	Great-West Lifeco Inc.	12	26	Canadian National Railway Co.	8
9	Power Financial Corp	12	27	Leon's Furniture Ltd.	8
10	West Fraser Timber Co., Ltd.	12	28	Terasen Inc	8
11	Atco Ltd.	11	29	C.I. Fund Management	7
12	Loblaw Cos. Ltd.	11	30	Saputo Inc	6
13	Thomson Corp.	11	31	Canadian Imperial Bank of Comm	5
14	Toronto Dominion Bank	11	32	Ensign Resource Service Group	5
15	Empire Co Ltd	10	33	Fortis Inc.	5
16	Imperial Oil Ltd.	10	34	Home Capital Group Inc	5
17	Royal Bank of Canada	10	35	Rothmans Inc.	5
18	Enbridge Inc	9	36	Sico, Inc.	5

Ranking By Market Capitalization

Based on latest available year-end information (C$ in million's) Based on closing prices at April 30, 2005

Rank	Company	Current Value	Rank	Company	Current Value
1	Royal Bank of Canada	47,953	19	Saputo Inc	3,650
2	Bank of Nova Scotia	40,330	20	Terasen Inc	2,862
3	Toronto Dominion Bank	33,018	21	Metro Inc	2,801
4	Imperial Oil Ltd.	31,140	22	Empire Co Ltd	2,431
5	Bank of Montreal	28,376	23	Emera Inc.	1,941
6	Thomson Corp.	27,246	24	Ensign Resource Service Group	1,938
7	Canadian Imperial Bank of Comm	25,968	25	West Fraser Timber Co., Ltd.	1,922
8	Great-West Lifeco Inc.	24,578	26	Atco Ltd.	1,866
9	Power Financial Corp	23,294	27	Fortis Inc.	1,715
10	Loblaw Cos. Ltd.	20,932	28	Rothmans Inc.	1,683
11	Canadian National Railway Co.	20,454	29	AGF Management Ltd	1,535
12	Weston (George) Limited	14,822	30	Toromont Industries Ltd.	1,402
13	Power Corp. of Canada	14,201	31	Home Capital Group Inc	1,178
14	Enbridge Inc	10,983	32	Leon's Furniture Ltd.	692
15	IGM Financial Inc	9,949	33	BMTC Group Inc.	464
16	National Bank of Canada	8,773	34	Melcor Developments Ltd.	205
17	C.I. Fund Management	4,974	35	Sico, Inc.	187
18	Canadian Utilities Ltd.	3,906	36	Buhler Industries, Inc.	181

Ranking By Return on Equity

Based on latest available year-end information. Ratios determined using net income.

Rank	Company	R.O.E.	Rank	Company	R.O.E.
1	Rothmans Inc.	44.9	19	Toromont Industries Ltd.	16.2
2	BMTC Group Inc.	31.2	20	Saputo Inc	15.9
3	Imperial Oil Ltd.	29.6	21	C.I. Fund Management	15.8
4	Home Capital Group Inc	26.0	22	Royal Bank of Canada	15.2
5	Great-West Lifeco Inc.	19.2	23	Power Corp. of Canada	14.8
6	Metro Inc	18.8	24	Canadian Utilities Ltd.	14.2
7	Bank of Nova Scotia	18.7	25	Buhler Industries, Inc.	13.7
8	Power Financial Corp	18.7	26	West Fraser Timber Co., Ltd.	13.4
9	Ensign Resource Service Group	18.4	27	Sico, Inc.	12.7
10	IGM Financial Inc	18.4	28	Atco Ltd.	12.5
11	Bank of Montreal	17.9	29	Melcor Developments Ltd.	12.1
12	Canadian Imperial Bank of Comm	17.7	30	Terasen Inc	10.8
13	Leon's Furniture Ltd	17.4	31	Empire Co Ltd	10.1
14	Toronto Dominion Bank	17.3	32	Fortis Inc. (Canada)	10.1
15	Loblaw Cos. Ltd.	17.1	33	Weston (George) Limited	10.1
16	Canadian National Railway Co.	16.9	34	Emera Inc. (Canada)	9.6
17	National Bank of Canada	16.9	35	Thomson Corp.	9.2
18	Enbridge Inc	16.8	36	AGF Management Ltd	8.3

Ranking by Return on Assets

Based on latest available year-end information. Ratios determined using net income.

Rank	Company	R.O.A	Rank	Company	R.O.A
1	Rothmans Inc.	18.6	19	Enbridge Inc	4.5
2	BMTC Group Inc.	17.5	20	Empire Co Ltd	3.7
3	Imperial Oil Ltd.	14.3	21	AGF Management Ltd	3.6
4	Leon's Furniture Ltd.	12.5	22	Emera Inc.	3.4
5	Metro Inc	10.7	23	Terasen Inc	3.0
6	Ensign Resource Service Group	10.5	24	Fortis Inc.	2.7
7	Saputo Inc	10.3	25	Atco Ltd.	2.3
8	C.I. Fund Management	9.7	26	Weston (George) Limited	2.3
9	IGM Financial Inc	9.2	27	Great-West Lifeco Inc.	1.7
10	Sico, Inc.	9.1	28	Home Capital Group Inc	1.7
11	Loblaw Cos. Ltd.	7.4	29	Power Financial Corp	1.4
12	Toromont Industries Ltd.	7.4	30	Bank of Nova Scotia	1.0
13	Buhler Industries, Inc.	7.1	31	Bank of Montreal	0.9
14	Canadian National Railway Co.	6.7	32	Power Corp. of Canada	0.9
15	Melcor Developments Ltd.	6.7	33	National Bank of Canada	0.8
16	West Fraser Timber Co., Ltd.	6.3	34	Canadian Imperial Bank of Comm	0.7
17	Canadian Utilities Ltd.	4.8	35	Toronto Dominion Bank	0.7
18	Thomson Corp.	4.7	36	Royal Bank of Canada	0.6

Ranking by Current Yield

Based on closing prices at April 30, 2005

Rank	Company	Yield	Rank	Company	Yield
1	Emera Inc.	4.9	19	Thomson Corp.	2.4
2	Great-West Lifeco Inc.	4.3	20	Atco Ltd.	2.2
3	Rothmans Inc.	3.5	21	Buhler Industries, Inc.	1.9
4	Bank of Nova Scotia	3.4	22	Melcor Developments Ltd.	1.8
5	Canadian Utilities Ltd.	3.4	23	Sico, Inc.	1.7
6	Power Financial Corp	3.3	24	Leon's Furniture Ltd.	1.3
7	IGM Financial Inc	3.1	25	Saputo Inc	1.3
8	Terasen Inc	3.1	26	Weston (George) Limited	1.3
9	Fortis Inc.	3.0	27	Metro Inc	1.2
10	Power Corp. of Canada	3.0	28	Toromont Industries Ltd.	1.2
11	Canadian Imperial Bank of Comm	2.9	29	West Fraser Timber Co., Ltd.	1.2
12	Enbridge Inc	2.9	30	Canadian National Railway Co.	1.1
13	Bank of Montreal	2.8	31	Empire Co Ltd	1.1
14	National Bank of Canada	2.7	32	Ensign Resource Service Group	1.1
15	Royal Bank of Canada	2.7	33	Imperial Oil Ltd.	1.0
16	Toronto Dominion Bank	2.7	34	Loblaw Cos. Ltd.	1.0
17	C.I. Fund Management	2.6	35	BMTC Group Inc.	0.8
18	AGF Management Ltd	2.4	36	Home Capital Group Inc	0.4

Ranking By Price/Earnings Ratios

Based on latest available year-end information. Ratios determined using net income.
Based on closing prices at April 30, 2005

Rank	Company	P/E Ratio	Rank	Company	P/E Ratio
1	Weston (George) Limited	37.0	19	Imperial Oil Ltd.	15.5
2	Home Capital Group Inc	26.3	20	Great-West Lifeco Inc.	15.4
3	Thomson Corp.	24.6	21	Power Corp. of Canada	15.4
4	Loblaw Cos. Ltd.	21.6	22	Leon's Furniture Ltd.	15.3
5	C.I. Fund Management	20.5	23	Emera Inc.	14.9
6	Toromont Industries Ltd.	20.0	24	Toronto Dominion Bank	14.8
7	AGF Management Ltd	19.9	25	Buhler Industries, Inc.	14.5
8	Terasen Inc	19.0	26	Empire Co Ltd	14.1
9	Rothmans Inc.	18.5	27	Bank of Nova Scotia	13.9
10	Royal Bank of Canada	17.5	28	Canadian Imperial Bank of Comm	13.3
11	Saputo Inc	17.2	29	National Bank of Canada	12.8
12	Fortis Inc.	16.8	30	Canadian Utilities Ltd.	12.6
13	Metro Inc	16.8	31	Bank of Montreal	12.5
14	IGM Financial Inc	16.6	32	Sico, Inc.	12.1
15	Enbridge Inc	16.4	33	Atco Ltd.	11.7
16	Ensign Resource Service Group	16.3	34	Melcor Developments Ltd.	10.8
17	Canadian National Railway Co.	15.9	35	BMTC Group Inc.	10.7
18	Power Financial Corp	15.6	36	West Fraser Timber Co., Ltd.	7.8

Ranking By Price/Book Ratios

Based on latest available year-end information. Ratios determined using net income.
Based on closing prices at April 30, 2005

Rank	Company	P/B Ratio	Rank	Company	P/B Ratio
1	Rothmans Inc.	8.31	19	Bank of Nova Scotia	2.61
2	Home Capital Group Inc	6.83	20	Toronto Dominion Bank	2.55
3	Imperial Oil Ltd.	4.59	21	Canadian Imperial Bank of Comm	2.36
4	Weston (George) Limited	3.74	22	Power Corp. of Canada	2.28
5	Loblaw Cos. Ltd.	3.70	23	Thomson Corp.	2.28
6	BMTC Group Inc.	3.35	24	Bank of Montreal	2.24
7	C.I. Fund Management	3.24	25	National Bank of Canada	2.16
8	Toromont Industries Ltd.	3.24	26	Terasen Inc	2.06
9	Metro Inc	3.15	27	Buhler Industries, Inc.	1.99
10	IGM Financial Inc	3.06	28	Canadian Utilities Ltd.	1.80
11	Ensign Resource Service Group	2.98	29	Fortis Inc.	1.70
12	Great-West Lifeco Inc.	2.96	30	AGF Management Ltd	1.65
13	Power Financial Corp	2.92	31	Sico, Inc.	1.54
14	Enbridge Inc	2.77	32	Atco Ltd.	1.45
15	Saputo Inc	2.74	33	Emera Inc.	1.42
16	Canadian National Railway Co.	2.69	34	Empire Co Ltd	1.42
17	Leon's Furniture Ltd.	2.65	35	Melcor Developments Ltd.	1.31
18	Royal Bank of Canada	2.65	36	West Fraser Timber Co., Ltd.	1.05

Ranking by Total Revenues

Based on latest available year-end information (in million's C$)

Rank	Name	Total Revenues	Rank	Name	Total Revenues
1	Weston (George) Limited	29,798	19	Atco Ltd.	3,349
2	Loblaw Cos. Ltd.	26,209	20	Canadian Utilities Ltd.	3,090
3	Royal Bank of Canada	25,204	21	West Fraser Timber Co., Ltd.	2,400
4	Power Corp. of Canada	24,323	22	IGM Financial Inc	2,119
5	Power Financial Corp	23,922	23	Terasen Inc	1,957
6	Imperial Oil Ltd.	22,408	24	Toromont Industries Ltd.	1,487
7	Great-West Lifeco Inc.	21,871	25	Emera Inc.	1,222
8	Canadian Imperial Bank of Comm	16,723	26	Fortis Inc.	1,145
9	Bank of Nova Scotia	16,497	27	Ensign Resource Service Group Inc.	1,059
10	Toronto Dominion Bank	16,015	28	C.I. Fund Management	845
11	Bank of Montreal	13,246	29	BMTC Group Inc.	802
12	Empire Co Ltd	11,269	30	AGF Management Ltd	640
13	Thomson Corp.	10,469	31	Rothmans Inc.	620
14	Canadian National Railway Co.	6,548	32	Leon's Furniture Ltd.	505
15	Enbridge Inc	6,541	33	Sico, Inc.	303
16	Metro Inc	5,999	34	Buhler Industries, Inc.	206
17	National Bank of Canada	4,771	35	Home Capital Group Inc	176
18	Saputo Inc	3,570	36	Melcor Developments Ltd.	88

Ranking by Net Income

Based on latest available year-end information (in million's C$)

Rank	Name	Net Income	Rank	Name	Net Income
1	Bank of Nova Scotia	2,894	19	C.I. Fund Management	242
2	Royal Bank of Canada	2,745	20	Saputo Inc	213
3	Bank of Montreal	2,269	21	Empire Co Ltd	173
4	Toronto Dominion Bank	2,237	22	Metro Inc	167
5	Imperial Oil Ltd.	2,009	23	Atco Ltd.	160
6	Canadian Imperial Bank of Comm	1,945	24	Terasen Inc	150
7	Great-West Lifeco Inc.	1,594	25	Emera Inc.	130
8	Power Financial Corp	1,494	26	Ensign Resource Service Group Inc	119
9	Canadian National Railway Co.	1,288	27	Fortis Inc.	102
10	Thomson Corp.	1,107	28	Rothmans Inc.	91
11	Loblaw Cos. Ltd.	968	29	AGF Management Ltd	77
12	Power Corp. of Canada	921	30	Toromont Industries Ltd.	70
13	National Bank of Canada	686	31	Leon's Furniture Ltd.	45
14	Enbridge Inc	668	32	Home Capital Group Inc	45
15	IGM Financial Inc	598	33	BMTC Group Inc.	43
16	Weston (George) Limited	401	34	Melcor Developments Ltd.	19
17	Canadian Utilities Ltd.	309	35	Sico, Inc.	15
18	West Fraser Timber Co., Ltd.	246	36	Buhler Industries, Inc.	13

Ranking By Total Assets

Based on latest available year-end information (in million's C$)

Rank	Name	Total Assets	Rank	Name	Total Assets
1	Royal Bank of Canada	428,415	19	Terasen Inc	4,970
2	Toronto Dominion Bank	310,769	20	Empire Co Ltd	4,686
3	Bank of Nova Scotia	278,157	21	West Fraser Timber Co., Ltd.	3,928
4	Canadian Imperial Bank of Comm	277,525	22	Fortis Inc.	3,838
5	Bank of Montreal	265,194	23	Emera Inc.	3,813
6	Power Corp. of Canada	105,367	24	Home Capital Group Inc	2,568
7	Power Financial Corp	103,626	25	C.I. Fund Management	2,493
8	Great-West Lifeco Inc.	93,802	26	AGF Management Ltd	2,167
9	National Bank of Canada	88,483	27	Saputo Inc	2,066
10	Thomson Corp.	23,571	28	Metro Inc	1,560
11	Canadian National Railway Co.	19,271	29	Ensign Resource Service Group Inc.	1,139
12	Weston (George) Limited	17,797	30	Toromont Industries Ltd.	944
13	Enbridge Inc	14,760	31	Rothmans Inc.	488
14	Imperial Oil Ltd.	14,027	32	Leon's Furniture Ltd.	361
15	Loblaw Cos. Ltd.	13,046	33	Melcor Developments Ltd.	282
16	Atco Ltd.	7,039	34	BMTC Group Inc.	247
17	IGM Financial Inc	6,473	35	Buhler Industries, Inc.	175
18	Canadian Utilities Ltd.	6,463	36	Sico, Inc.	169

Ranking the Dividend Achievers by Total Return

Based on the trailing 1-year period ending April 30, 2005

Rank	Name	Tot. Ret	Rank	Name	Tot. Ret
1	Metro Inc	53.56%	19	BMTC Group Inc.	17.12%
2	Rothmans Inc.	51.52%	20	Bank of Nova Scotia	13.77%
3	Home Capital Group Inc	49.40%	21	Terasen Inc	13.46%
4	Imperial Oil Ltd.	48.21%	22	Ensign Resource Service Group Inc.	13.37%
5	Melcor Developments Ltd.	43.68%	23	Toronto Dominion Bank	13.17%
6	Canadian National Railway Co.	39.75%	24	Fortis Inc.	12.59%
7	Empire Co Ltd	38.84%	25	Canadian Imperial Bank of Commerce	11.25%
8	Loblaw Cos. Ltd.	29.94%	26	Buhler Industries, Inc.	10.69%
9	Atco Ltd.	28.27%	27	Saputo Inc	10.00%
10	Enbridge Inc	26.52%	28	Great-West Lifeco Inc.	9.61%
11	Leon's Furniture Ltd.	25.75%	29	Bank of Montreal	9.15%
12	Weston (George) Limited	25.44%	30	IGM Financial Inc	8.70%
13	Sico, Inc.	25.00%	31	Canadian Utilities Ltd.	5.63%
14	Royal Bank of Canada	22.97%	32	C.I. Fund Management	3.69%
15	Toromont Industries Ltd.	20.92%	33	West Fraser Timber Co., Ltd.	3.45%
16	Power Financial Corp	18.46%	34	Thomson Corp.	-4.72%
17	National Bank of Canada	17.83%	35	Emera Inc.	-7.46%
18	Power Corp. of Canada	17.68%	36	AGF Management Ltd	-8.65%

Based on the trailing 3-year period ending April 30, 2005

Rank	Name	Tot. Ret	Rank	Name	Tot. Ret
1	Home Capital Group Inc	66.68%	19	Terasen Inc	11.58%
2	BMTC Group Inc.	34.55%	20	Enbridge Inc	11.32%
3	Toromont Industries Ltd.	24.79%	21	Sico, Inc.	11.20%
4	Imperial Oil Ltd.	23.90%	22	Canadian Imperial Bank of Commerce	10.97%
5	Melcor Developments Ltd.	23.88%	23	Royal Bank of Canada	10.89%
6	Power Financial Corp	18.52%	24	Empire Co Ltd	8.62%
7	Ensign Resource Service Group Inc.	16.27%	25	Loblaw Cos. Ltd.	8.51%
8	National Bank of Canada	16.20%	26	Leon's Furniture Ltd.	7.06%
9	Power Corp. of Canada	16.10%	27	Atco Ltd.	7.00%
10	Rothmans Inc.	15.21%	28	IGM Financial Inc	6.69%
11	Buhler Industries, Inc.	14.74%	29	West Fraser Timber Co., Ltd.	6.48%
12	Bank of Montreal	14.56%	30	Toronto Dominion Bank	6.33%
13	Fortis Inc.	14.31%	31	Canadian Utilities Ltd.	3.28%
14	Bank of Nova Scotia	14.02%	32	Emera Inc.	2.76%
15	Metro Inc	13.49%	33	Saputo Inc	1.92%
16	Great-West Lifeco Inc.	13.45%	34	Weston (George) Limited	-1.07%
17	Canadian National Railway Co.	13.36%	35	Thomson Corp.	-7.98%
18	C.I. Fund Management	11.98%	36	AGF Management Ltd	-9.43%

Based on the trailing 5-year period ending April 30, 2005

Rank	Name	Tot. Ret	Rank	Name	Tot. Ret
1	Home Capital Group Inc	76.35%	19	Bank of Montreal	16.08%
2	BMTC Group Inc.	42.82%	20	Weston (George) Limited	15.48%
3	Melcor Developments Ltd.	30.91%	21	Terasen Inc	15.18%
4	Rothmans Inc.	27.23%	22	Enbridge Inc	14.67%
5	Metro Inc	26.65%	23	Canadian Imperial Bank of Commerce	14.01%
6	Canadian National Railway Co.	21.25%	24	Loblaw Cos. Ltd.	13.97%
7	Toromont Industries Ltd.	21.22%	25	Atco Ltd.	13.75%
8	Imperial Oil Ltd.	20.77%	26	IGM Financial Inc	13.57%
9	Power Financial Corp	20.66%	27	Ensign Resource Service Group Inc.	13.27%
10	Buhler Industries, Inc.	20.53%	28	Leon's Furniture Ltd.	11.57%
11	National Bank of Canada	20.30%	29	Canadian Utilities Ltd.	10.13%
12	Saputo Inc	19.74%	30	Sico, Inc.	9.46%
13	Great-West Lifeco Inc.	19.66%	31	West Fraser Timber Co., Ltd.	8.93%
14	Power Corp. of Canada	19.27%	32	Toronto Dominion Bank	8.01%
15	Bank of Nova Scotia	18.83%	33	C.I. Fund Management	7.48%
16	Fortis Inc.	18.30%	34	Emera Inc.	5.84%
17	Empire Co Ltd	18.18%	35	AGF Management Ltd	-1.47%
18	Royal Bank of Canada	16.48%	36	Thomson Corp.	-3.19%

NAICS Classification of Canadian Companies By Industry Sector

Agriculture, Forestry, Fishing and Hunting
West Fraser Timber Co., Ltd.

Mining
Ensign Resource Service Group Inc.
Imperial Oil Ltd.

Utilities
Atco Ltd.
Canadian Utilities Ltd.
Emera Inc.
Fortis Inc.

Construction
Melcor Developments Ltd.

Manufacturing
Leon's Furniture Ltd.
Sico, Inc.
Toromont Industries Ltd.
Weston (George) Limited

Retail Trade
BMTC Group Inc.
Loblaw Cos. Ltd.

Management of Companies and Enterprises
Power Corp. of Canada

Wholesale Trade
Buhler Industries, Inc.
Empire Co Ltd.
Metro Inc.
Rothmans Inc.
Saputo Inc.

Transportation and Warehousing
Canadian National Railway Co.
Enbridge Inc.
Terasen Inc.

Information
Thomson Corp.

Finance and Insurance
AGF Management Ltd.
Bank of Montreal
Bank of Nova Scotia
Canadian Imperial Bank of Commerce
C.I. Fund Management
Great-West Lifeco Inc.
Home Capital Group Inc.
IGM Financial Inc.
National Bank of Canada
Power Financial Corp.
Royal Bank of Canada
Toronto Dominion Bank

Web Site And Dividend Reinvestment Plan Information

Company	Ticker	Web Site	DRIP
AGF Management Ltd.	AGF NV	www.agf.com	No
Atco Ltd.	ACO Y	www.atco.com	No
Bank of Montreal	BMO	www.bmo.com	Yes
Bank of Nova Scotia	BNS	www.scotiabank.com	Yes
BMTC Group Inc.	GBT SVA	www.braultetmartineau.com	No
Buhler Industries, Inc.	BUI	www.buhler.com	No
Canadian Imperial Bank of Commerce	CM	www.cibc.com	No
Canadian National Railway Co.	CNR	www.cn.ca	No
Canadian Utilities Ltd.	CU X	www.canadian-utilities.com	No
C.I. Fund Management	CIX	www.cix.com	No
Emera Inc.	EMA	www.emera.com	No
Empire Co Ltd.	EMP NVA	www.empireco.ca	No
Enbridge Inc.	ENB	www.enbridge.com	Yes
Ensign Resource Service Group Inc.	ESI	www.ensigngroup.com	No
Fortis Inc.	FTS	www.fortisinc.com	No
Great-West Lifeco Inc.	GWO	www.greatwestlifeco.com	No
Home Capital Group Inc.	HCG	www.homecapital.com	No
IGM Financial Inc.	IGI	www.investorsgroup.com	No
Imperial Oil Ltd.	IMO	www.imperialoil.ca	Yes
Leon's Furniture Ltd.	LNF	www.leons.ca	No
Loblaw Cos. Ltd.	L	www.loblaw.com	No
Melcor Developments Ltd.	MRD	www.melcor.ca	No
Metro Inc.	MRU SVA	www.metro.ca	No
National Bank of Canada	NA	www.nbc.ca	No
Power Corp. of Canada	POW SV	www.powercorporation.com	No
Power Financial Corp.	PWF	www.powerfinancial.com	No
Rothmans Inc.	ROC	www.rothmansinc.ca	No
Royal Bank of Canada	RY	www.rbc.com	Yes
Saputo Inc.	SAP	www.saputo.com	No
Sico, Inc.	SIC	www.sico.com	No
Terasen Inc.	TER	www.terasen.com	Yes
Thomson Corp.	TOC	www.thomson.com	No
Toromont Industries Ltd.	TIH	www.toromont.com	No
Toronto Dominion Bank	TD	www.td.com	Yes
West Fraser Timber Co., Ltd.	WFT	www.westfraser.com	No
Weston (George) Limited	WN	www.weston.ca	No

Mergent's 2005 International Dividend Achievers

Company	Country	Exchange	Ticker
ABN AMRO Holding N.V.	Netherlands	NYS	ABN
ACE Ltd.	Bermuda	NYS	ACE
Allied Irish Banks Plc	Ireland	NYS	AIB
Aracruz Celulose S.A.	Brazil	NYS	ARA
Canadian Imperial Bank of Commerce	Canada	NYS	BCM
Barclays PLC	United Kingdom	NYS	BCS
Bank of Montreal	Canada	NYS	BMO
Bunzl Plc	United Kingdom	NYS	BNL
Bank of Nova Scotia	Canada	NYS	BNS
Compania de Minas Buenaventura S.A.	Peru	NYS	BVN
Canon, Inc.	Japan	NYS	CAJ
Canadian National Railway Co.	Canada	NYS	CNI
Ciba Specialty Chemicals Holdings, Inc.	Switzerland	NYS	CSB
Consolidated Water Co., Inc.	Cayman Islands	NMS	CWCO
Dassault Systemes S.A.	France	NMS	DAST Y
ENI S.p.A.	Italy	NYS	E
Grupo Elektra S.A. de C.V.	Mexico	NYS	EKT
Endesa S.A.	Spain	NYS	ELE
Enbridge Inc	Canada	NYS	ENB
E.ON AG	Germany	NYS	EON
Fresenius Medical Care AG	Germany	NYS	FMS
HSBC Holdings Plc	United Kingdom	NYS	HBC
Huaneng Power International, Inc.	China	NYS	HNP
Imperial Oil Ltd.	Canada	ASE	IMO
Infosys Technologies Ltd.	India	NMS	INFY
Governor & Co. of the Bank of Ireland	Ireland	NYS	IRE
Imperial Tobacco Group Plc	United Kingdom	NYS	ITY
Luxottica Group S.P.A.	Italy	NYS	LUX
Nam Tai Electronics, Inc.	Hong Kong	NYS	NTE
Novo-Nordisk A/S	Denmark	NYS	NVO
Novartis AG Basel	Switzerland	NYS	NVS
Pioneer Corp	Japan	NYS	PIO
PartnerRe Ltd.	Bermuda	NYS	PRE
Pfeiffer Vacuum Technology AG	Germany	NYS	PV
RenaissanceRe Holdings Ltd.	Bermuda	NYS	RNR
Royal Bank of Canada	Canada	NYS	RY
Signet Group Plc	United Kingdom	NYS	SIG
Sappi Ltd.	South Africa	NYS	SPP
Sasol Ltd.	South Africa	NYS	SSL
Banco Santander Central Hispano SA	Spain	NYS	STD
Toronto Dominion Bank	Canada	NYS	TD
Teva Pharmaceutical Industries Ltd.	Israel	NMS	TEVA
Thomson Corp.	Canada	NYS	TOC
Total S.A.	France	NYS	TOT
Unilever Plc	United Kingdom	NYS	UL
Volvo AB	Sweden	NMS	VOLV Y
WPP Group Plc	United Kingdom	NMS	WPPG Y
XL Capital Ltd.	Bermuda	NYS	XL

Dividend Achievers ADR Index 10 Year Performance

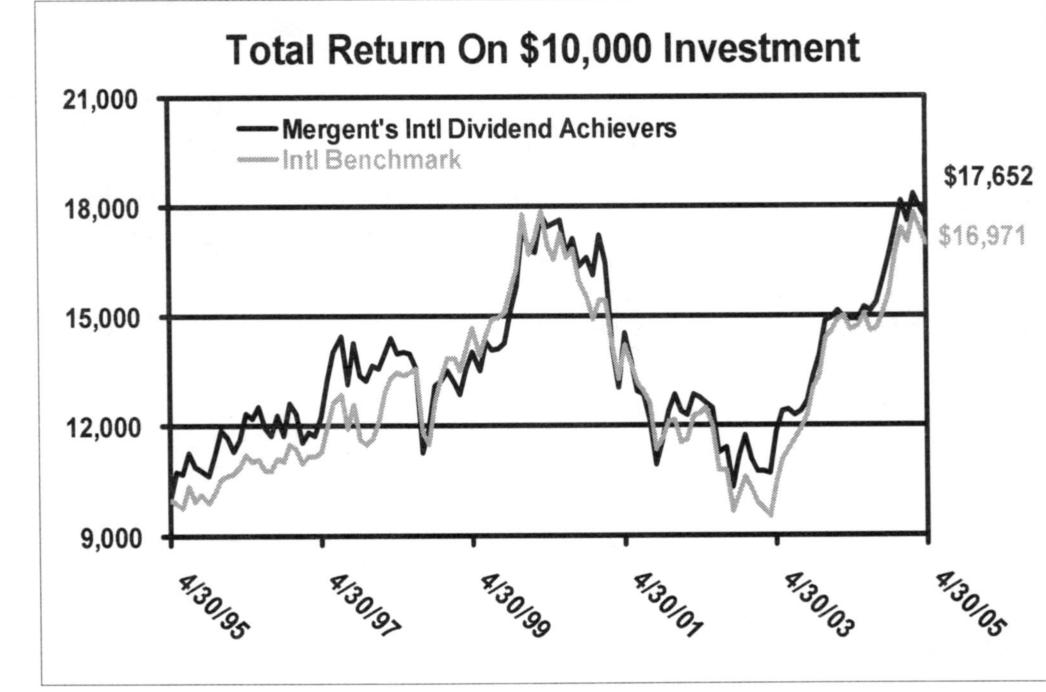

Ranking The 2005 International Dividend Achievers

International companies are listed by the five-year average annual compound growth rate of their dividends.

Rank	Company	CAGR	Rank	Company	CAGR
1	Infosys Technologies Ltd.	145.22	19	Consolidated Water Co., Inc.	22.98
2	Aracruz Celulose S.A.	67.45	20	AB Electrolux	22.55
3	Huaneng Power International, Inc.	65.76	21	Governor & Co. of Bk of Ireland	21.06
4	Novo-Nordisk A/S	44.17	22	Bank of Nova Scotia	20.39
5	Teva Pharmaceutical Industries Ltd.	42.74	23	Signet Group Plc	18.49
5	Canon, Inc.	40.73	24	E.ON AG	17.99
7	Volvo AB	37.70	25	Fresenius Medical Care AG	17.16
8	HSBC Holdings Plc	36.05	26	Royal Bank of Canada	16.53
9	Nam Tai Electronics, Inc.	34.27	27	Barclays PLC	16.27
10	Total S.A.	33.93	28	Imperial Tobacco Group Plc	15.89
11	Compania de Minas Buenaventura S.A.	32.51	29	Banco Santander Cntrl Hispano	15.53
12	Grupo Elektra S.A. de C.V.	31.24	30	Allied Irish Banks Plc	15.44
13	Luxottica Group S.P.A.	27.62	31	Ciba Spec Chemicals Hldgs, Inc	15.24
14	Pfeiffer Vacuum Technology AG	25.10	32	ACE Ltd.	14.87
15	Sasol Ltd.	24.93	33	Canadian National Railway Co.	14.29
16	Pioneer Corp	24.36	34	Novartis AG Basel	14.05
17	WPP Group Plc	24.26	35	ABN AMRO Holding N.V.	13.95
18	ENI S.p.A.	23.06	36	Toronto Dominion Bank	13.56

Longest Record Of Dividend Achievement

Companies are listed by the number of consecutive annual dividend increases.

Rank	Company	Years of Growth	Rank	Company	Years of Growth
1	Bank of Nova Scotia	13	17	Canadian National Railway Co.	8
2	Bank of Montreal	12	18	Consolidated Water Co., Inc.	8
3	Novartis AG Basel	12	19	ENI S.p.A.	8
4	ACE Ltd.	11	20	Novo-Nordisk A/S	8
5	Allied Irish Banks Plc	11	21	Pioneer Corp	8
5	Barclays PLC	11	22	WPP Group Plc	8
7	Luxottica Group S.P.A.	11	23	Dassault Systemes S.A.	7
8	Toronto Dominion Bank	11	24	Governor & Co. of Bk of Ireland	7
9	Thomson Corp.	11	25	Imperial Tobacco Group Plc	7
10	Imperial Oil Ltd.	10	26	Volvo AB	7
11	Nam Tai Electronics, Inc.	10	27	Ciba Spec Chemicals Hldgs, Inc.	6
12	PartnerRe Ltd.	10	28	Endesa S.A.	6
13	Royal Bank of Canada	10	29	AB Electrolux	6
14	Enbridge Inc (Canada)	9	30	Fresenius Medical Care AG	6
15	RenaissanceRe Holdings Ltd.	9	31	XL Capital Ltd.	6
16	Unilever Plc	9			

Ranking By Market Capitalization

Based on latest available year-end information (in US$000's) Based on closing prices at April 29, 2005

Rank	Company	Current Value	Rank	Company	Current Value
1	HSBC Holdings Plc (United Kingdom)	178,864,930	19	Canadian Imperial Bank of Commerce	20,244,171
2	Novartis AG Basel (Switzerland)	118,258,456	20	Teva Pharmaceutical Ind. Ltd. (Israel)	19,581,232
3	ENI S.p.A.	100,479,017	21	Allied Irish Banks Plc	18,768,231
4	Banco Santander Central Hispano SA	72,549,840	22	Novo-Nordisk A/S (Denmark)	16,887,743
5	Total S.A. (New)	67,220,567	23	Canadian National Railway Co. (Canada)	16,196,151
6	Barclays PLC (United Kingdom)	66,955,697	24	Gov. & Co. of the Bank of Ireland (Ireland)	14,456,601
7	E.ON AG (Germany)	55,962,124	25	Sasol Ltd.	14,209,469
8	Canon, Inc. (Japan)	46,151,986	26	WPP Group Plc (United Kingdom)	12,850,393
9	ABN AMRO Holding N.V. (Netherlands)	40,613,899	27	ACE Ltd. (Cayman Islands)	12,221,197
10	Royal Bank of Canada (Montreal, Quebec)	38,412,178	28	Volvo AB (Sweden)	11,274,948
11	Bank of Nova Scotia (Toronto, Canada)	31,736,400	29	XL Capital Ltd. (Cayman Islands)	9,766,953
12	Unilever Plc (United Kingdom)	27,920,888	30	Luxottica Group S.P.A. (Italy)	8,925,002
13	Toronto Dominion Bank	26,327,377	31	Enbridge Inc (Canada)	8,734,626
14	Imperial Oil Ltd. (Canada)	24,675,965	32	Infosys Technologies Ltd. (India)	7,890,301
15	Endesa S.A. (Spain)	23,133,733	33	Dassault Systemes S.A. (France)	5,263,064
16	Bank of Montreal (Canada)	22,544,161	34	Bunzl Plc (United Kingdom)	4,436,571
17	Thomson Corp.	21,665,209	35	Ciba Specialty Chemicals Holdings, Inc.	4,166,839
18	Imperial Tobacco Group Plc (UK)	21,150,472	36	PartnerRe Ltd.	3,196,914

Ranking By Return on Equity

Based on latest available year-end information. Ratios determined using net income.

Rank	Company	R.O.E.	Rank	Company	R.O.E.
1	Imperial Tobacco Group Plc (United Kingdom)	99.9	19	Luxottica Group S.P.A. (Italy)	18.0
2	Unilever Plc (United Kingdom)	45.5	20	E.ON AG (Germany)	17.9
3	Infosys Technologies Ltd. (India)	33.9	21	Signet Group Plc (United Kingdom)	17.8
4	Imperial Oil Ltd. (Canada)	32.3	22	Novo-Nordisk A/S (Denmark)	17.4
5	Compania de Minas Buenaventura S.A. (Peru)	31.5	23	Toronto Dominion Bank	16.9
6	Aracruz Celulose S.A. (Brazil)	31.1	24	Novartis AG Basel (Switzerland)	16.8
7	Bunzl Plc (United Kingdom)	28.4	25	Enbridge Inc (Canada)	16.7
8	Grupo Elektra S.A. de C.V. (Mexico)	28.3	26	Teva Pharmaceutical Industries Ltd. (Israel)	16.6
9	ENI S.p.A.	28.2	27	Bank of Montreal (Canada)	16.3
10	Total S.A. (New)	27.8	28	Canon, Inc. (Japan)	15.8
11	ABN AMRO Holding N.V. (Netherlands)	27.6	29	Sasol Ltd.	15.7
12	Nam Tai Electronics, Inc.	24.3	30	Royal Bank of Canada (Montreal, Quebec)	15.6
13	Governor & Co. of the Bank of Ireland (Ireland)	22.3	31	Canadian Imperial Bank of Commerce	14.9
14	Dassault Systemes S.A. (France)	20.4	32	PartnerRe Ltd.	14.8
15	Banco Santander Central Hispano SA	19.2	33	XL Capital Ltd. (Cayman Islands)	14.8
16	Bank of Nova Scotia (Toronto, Canada)	18.7	34	Endesa S.A. (Spain)	14.2
17	Allied Irish Banks Plc	18.4	35	Huaneng Power International, Inc. (China)	14.2
18	Barclays PLC (United Kingdom)	18.1	36	Canadian National Railway Co. (Canada)	13.8

Ranking by Return on Assets

Based on latest available year-end information. Ratios determined using net income.

Rank	Company	R.O.A	Rank	Company	R.O.A
1	Infosys Technologies Ltd. (India)	35.6	19	Unilever Plc (United Kingdom)	5.5
2	Compania de Minas Buenaventura S.A. (Peru)	20.6	20	Thomson Corp.	5.1
3	Dassault Systemes S.A. (France)	17.3	21	E.ON AG (Germany)	4.8
4	Imperial Oil Ltd. (Canada)	17.2	22	Grupo Elektra S.A. de C.V. (Mexico)	4.7
5	Nam Tai Electronics, Inc.	14.3	23	Enbridge Inc (Canada)	4.5
6	ENI S.p.A.	14.0	24	PartnerRe Ltd.	3.8
7	Novo-Nordisk A/S (Denmark)	13.9	25	Fresenius Medical Care AG (Germany)	3.6
8	Aracruz Celulose S.A. (Brazil)	12.0	26	Endesa S.A. (Spain)	3.1
9	Signet Group Plc (United Kingdom)	10.7	27	Ciba Specialty Chemicals Holdings, Inc.	2.9
10	Pfeiffer Vacuum Technology AG	9.4	28	Pioneer Corp (Japan)	2.7
11	Canon, Inc. (Japan)	8.2	29	Teva Pharmaceutical Industries Ltd. (Israel)	2.6
12	Bunzl Plc (United Kingdom)	8.1	30	XL Capital Ltd. (Cayman Islands)	2.3
13	Sasol Ltd.	8.1	31	RenaissanceRe Holdings Ltd.	2.0
14	Huaneng Power International, Inc. (China)	7.3	32	ACE Ltd. (Cayman Islands)	1.9
15	Consolidated Water Co., Inc. (Cayman Islands)	7.1	33	Volvo AB (Sweden)	1.8
16	Imperial Tobacco Group Plc (United Kingdom)	6.9	34	WPP Group Plc (United Kingdom)	1.8
17	Luxottica Group S.P.A. (Italy)	6.3	35	Banco Santander Central Hispano SA	1.6
18	Canadian National Railway Co. (Canada)	5.5	36	Sappi Ltd. (South Africa)	1.6

Ranking by Current Yield

Based on closing prices at April 29, 2005

Rank	Company	Yield	Rank	Company	Yield
1	Huaneng Power International, Inc. (China)	7.9	19	Banco Santander Central Hispano SA	2.9
2	Aracruz Celulose S.A. (Brazil)	5.7	20	Toronto Dominion Bank	2.9
3	Ciba Specialty Chemicals Holdings, Inc.	5.0	21	XL Capital Ltd. (Cayman Islands)	2.8
4	ABN AMRO Holding N.V. (Netherlands)	5.0	22	Royal Bank of Canada (Montreal, Quebec)	2.8
5	Barclays PLC (United Kingdom)	4.3	23	ENI S.p.A.	2.6
6	HSBC Holdings Plc (United Kingdom)	3.9	24	Volvo AB (Sweden)	2.6
7	Allied Irish Banks Plc	3.7	25	PartnerRe Ltd.	2.4
8	Governor & Co. of the Bank of Ireland (Ireland	3.6	26	Signet Group Plc (United Kingdom)	2.4
9	Endesa S.A. (Spain)	3.5	27	Bunzl Plc (United Kingdom)	2.3
10	Unilever Plc (United Kingdom)	3.4	28	Thomson Corp.	2.3
11	Total S.A. (New)	3.4	29	E.ON AG (Germany)	2.2
12	Canadian Imperial Bank of Commerce	3.3	30	ACE Ltd. (Cayman Islands)	2.0
13	Bank of Nova Scotia (Toronto, Canada)	3.3	31	Novartis AG Basel (Switzerland)	1.8
14	Imperial Tobacco Group Plc (United Kingdom)	3.2	32	RenaissanceRe Holdings Ltd.	1.7
15	Sasol Ltd.	3.1	33	Enbridge Inc (Canada)	1.4
16	Sappi Ltd. (South Africa)	3.0	34	Pfeiffer Vacuum Technology AG	1.4
17	Nam Tai Electronics, Inc.	3.0	35	Grupo Elektra S.A. de C.V. (Mexico)	1.4
18	Bank of Montreal (Canada)	2.9	36	Consolidated Water Co., Inc. (Cayman Islands)	1.4

Ranking By Price/Earnings Ratios

Based on latest available year-end information. Ratios determined using net income.

Rank	Company	P/E Ratio	Rank	Company	P/E Ratio
1	Consolidated Water Co., Inc. (Cayman Islands)	38.5	19	Royal Bank of Canada (Montreal, Quebec)	16.0
2	Pioneer Corp (Japan)	33.1	20	Ciba Specialty Chemicals Holdings, Inc.	15.9
3	Infosys Technologies Ltd. (India)	29.5	21	Canadian National Railway Co. (Canada)	15.6
4	Pfeiffer Vacuum Technology AG	29.1	22	Sasol Ltd.	15.6
5	Unilever Plc (United Kingdom)	27.3	23	Imperial Oil Ltd. (Canada)	15.3
6	Dassault Systemes S.A. (France)	27.0	24	HSBC Holdings Plc (United Kingdom)	14.9
7	Imperial Tobacco Group Plc (United Kingdom)	25.3	25	Toronto Dominion Bank	14.7
8	Luxottica Group S.P.A. (Italy)	24.9	26	Canon, Inc. (Japan)	13.7
9	Thomson Corp.	24.4	27	Huaneng Power International, Inc. (China)	13.6
10	WPP Group Plc (United Kingdom)	21.8	28	Bank of Nova Scotia (Toronto, Canada)	13.5
11	Teva Pharmaceutical Industries Ltd. (Israel)	21.4	29	Endesa S.A. (Spain)	13.4
12	Sappi Ltd. (South Africa)	20.6	30	Allied Irish Banks Plc	13.1
13	Novartis AG Basel (Switzerland)	19.8	31	Nam Tai Electronics, Inc.	12.9
14	Novo-Nordisk A/S (Denmark)	19.8	32	Bank of Montreal (Canada)	12.6
15	Fresenius Medical Care AG (Germany)	19.1	33	Volvo AB (Sweden)	12.6
16	Bunzl Plc (United Kingdom)	18.1	34	Canadian Imperial Bank of Commerce	12.5
17	Enbridge Inc (Canada)	16.8	35	Signet Group Plc (United Kingdom)	12.5
18	Banco Santander Central Hispano SA	16.4	36	ACE Ltd. (Cayman Islands)	11.0

Ranking By Price/Book Ratios

Based on latest available year-end information. Ratios determined using net income.
Based on closing prices at April 29, 2005

Rank	Company	P/E Ratio	Rank	Company	P/E Ratio
1	Imperial Tobacco Group Plc (UK)	89.1	19	Grupo Elektra S.A. de C.V. (Mexico)	2.7
2	Unilever Plc (United Kingdom)	12.4	20	Bank of Nova Scotia (Canada)	2.5
3	Infosys Technologies Ltd. (India)	10.0	21	Royal Bank of Canada (Quebec)	2.5
4	Dassault Systemes S.A. (France)	5.5	22	Toronto Dominion Bank	2.5
5	Bunzl Plc (United Kingdom)	5.1	23	Sasol Ltd.	2.4
6	Imperial Oil Ltd. (Canada)	5.0	24	Allied Irish Banks Plc	2.4
7	Luxottica Group S.P.A. (Italy)	4.5	25	Gover. & Co. of the Bank of Ireland	2.4
8	Cons. Water Co., Inc. (Cay. Islands)	4.3	26	Aracruz Celulose S.A. (Brazil)	2.2
9	Teva Pharmaceutical Industries Ltd. (Israel)	3.6	27	Signet Group Plc (UK)	2.2
10	Novo-Nordisk A/S (Denmark)	3.4	28	Canon, Inc. (Japan)	2.2
11	Pfeiffer Vacuum Technology AG	3.4	29	Canadian National Railway Co. (Can)	2.2
12	Novartis AG Basel (Switzerland)	3.3	30	Thomson Corp.	2.2
13	Banco Santander Central Hisp.SA	3.2	31	Bank of Montreal (Canada)	2.1
14	Nam Tai Electronics, Inc.	3.1	32	HSBC Holdings Plc (UK)	2.0
15	Total S.A. (New)	3.0	33	ABN AMRO Holding N.V. (Neth)	1.9
16	Compania de Minas Buena. (Peru)	3.0	34	Huaneng Power Intl., Inc. (China)	1.9
17	ENI S.p.A.	2.9	35	Barclays PLC (United Kingdom)	1.9
18	Enbridge Inc (Canada)	2.8	36	Endesa S.A. (Spain)	1.9

Ranking by Total Revenues

Based on latest available year-end information (in 000's US$)

Rank	Name	Total Revenues	Rank	Name	Total Revenues
1	Total S.A. (New)	166,209,000	19	Bank of Montreal (Canada)	10,833,000
2	ENI S.p.A.	79,084,000	20	XL Capital Ltd. (Cayman Islands)	10,175,800
3	HSBC Holdings Plc (United Kingdom)	70,860,000	21	Sasol Ltd.	9,456,000
4	E.ON AG (Germany)	66,515,000	22	WPP Group Plc (United Kingdom)	8,243,000
5	Unilever Plc (United Kingdom)	55,075,370	23	Thomson Corp.	8,098,000
6	ABN AMRO Holding N.V. (Netherlands)	45,139,000	24	Allied Irish Banks Plc	7,090,000
7	Barclays PLC (United Kingdom)	40,016,000	25	Pioneer Corp (Japan)	6,845,000
8	Canon, Inc. (Japan)	33,344,700	26	Fresenius Medical Care AG (Germany)	6,228,000
9	Volvo AB (Sweden)	31,813,000	27	Ciba Specialty Chemicals Holdings, Inc.	6,158,000
10	Banco Santander Central Hispano SA	31,796,600	28	Governor & Co. of the Bank of Ireland (Irelar	6,022,000
11	Novartis AG Basel (Switzerland)	28,247,000	29	Imperial Tobacco Group Plc (United Kingdon	5,495,000
12	Endesa S.A. (Spain)	24,471,000	30	Canadian National Railway Co. (Canada)	5,457,000
13	Royal Bank of Canada (Montreal, Quebec)	20,672,000	31	Enbridge Inc (Canada)	5,450,900
14	Imperial Oil Ltd. (Canada)	18,675,000	32	Novo-Nordisk A/S (Denmark)	5,327,000
15	Canadian Imperial Bank of Commerce	13,701,000	33	Bunzl Plc (United Kingdom)	5,168,000
16	Bank of Nova Scotia (Toronto, Canada)	13,521,000	34	Teva Pharmaceutical Industries Ltd. (Israel)	4,798,900
17	Toronto Dominion Bank	13,136,000	35	Sappi Ltd. (South Africa)	4,728,000
18	ACE Ltd. (Cayman Islands)	12,329,800	36	Luxottica Group S.P.A. (Italy)	4,367,100

Ranking by Net Income

Based on latest available year-end information (in 000's US$)

Rank	Name	Net Income	Rank	Name	Net Income
1	Total S.A. (New)	13,020,000	19	Volvo AB (Sweden)	1,414,000
2	HSBC Holdings Plc (UK)	11,840,000	20	XL Capital Ltd. (Cayman Islands)	1,166,600
3	ENI S.p.A.	9,854,000	21	Gov. & Co. of the Bank of Ireland (Ireland)	1,160,000
4	Barclays PLC (United Kingdom)	6,265,000	22	ACE Ltd. (Cayman Islands)	1,139,100
5	E.ON AG (Germany)	5,878,000	23	Canadian National Railway Co. (Canada)	1,081,000
6	Novartis AG Basel (Switzerland)	5,767,000	24	Thomson Corp.	1,011,000
7	ABN AMRO Hold. N.V. (Netherlands)	5,566,000	25	Novo-Nordisk A/S (Denmark)	920,000
8	Unilever Plc (United Kingdom)	3,664,778	26	Sasol Ltd.	862,000
9	Canon, Inc. (Japan)	3,301,400	27	Imperial Tobacco Group Plc (UK)	806,000
10	Banco Santander Central His. SA	3,282,300	28	Huaneng Power International, Inc. (China)	643,100
11	Bank of Nova Scotia (Canada)	2,404,000	29	WPP Group Plc (United Kingdom)	560,400
12	Royal Bank of Canada (Quebec)	2,311,000	30	Enbridge Inc (Canada)	543,500
13	Bank of Montreal (Canada)	1,928,000	31	PartnerRe Ltd.	492,400
14	Toronto Dominion Bank	1,895,000	32	Infosys Technologies Ltd. (India)	419,000
15	Allied Irish Banks Plc	1,886,061	33	Fresenius Medical Care AG (Germany)	402,000
16	Endesa S.A. (Spain)	1,868,000	34	Luxottica Group S.P.A. (Italy)	388,600
17	Canadian Imperial Bank of Commerce	1,804,000	35	Teva Pharmaceutical Ind. Ltd. (Israel)	331,800
18	Imperial Oil Ltd. (Canada)	1,710,000	36	Ciba Specialty Chemicals Holdings, Inc.	328,000

Ranking By Total Assets

Based on latest available year-end information (in 000's US$)

Rank	Name	Total Assets	Rank	Name	Total Assets
1	HSBC Holdings Plc (United Kingdom)	1,276,778,000	19	XL Capital Ltd. (Cayman Islands)	49,014,600
2	Barclays PLC (United Kingdom)	1,000,949,000	20	Canon, Inc. (Japan)	34,490,600
3	ABN AMRO Holding N.V. (Netherlands)	824,441,000	21	Volvo AB (Sweden)	33,702,000
4	Banco Santander Central Hispano SA	442,271,100	22	Thomson Corp.	19,643,000
5	Royal Bank of Canada (Montreal, Quebec)	352,027,000	23	WPP Group Plc (United Kingdom)	19,626,900
6	Toronto Dominion Bank	255,104,000	24	Canadian National Railway Co. (Canada)	16,060,000
7	Bank of Nova Scotia (Toronto, Canada)	229,010,000	25	PartnerRe Ltd.	12,511,200
8	Canadian Imperial Bank of Commerce	228,642,000	26	Enbridge Inc (Canada)	12,421,900
9	Bank of Montreal (Canada)	217,512,000	27	Imperial Oil Ltd. (Canada)	11,690,000
10	E.ON AG (Germany)	154,508,000	28	Imperial Tobacco Group Plc (United Kingdon	11,651,000
11	Allied Irish Banks Plc	138,494,000	29	Sasol Ltd.	11,057,000
12	Governor & Co. of the Bank of Ireland (Irelan	130,963,000	30	Ciba Specialty Chemicals Holdings, Inc.	9,645,000
13	Total S.A. (New)	114,004,000	31	Teva Pharmaceutical Industries Ltd. (Israel)	9,632,000
14	ENI S.p.A.	84,655,000	32	Huaneng Power International, Inc. (China)	8,791,800
15	Endesa S.A. (Spain)	65,063,000	33	Fresenius Medical Care AG (Germany)	7,961,500
16	Unilever Plc (United Kingdom)	56,417,940	34	Novo-Nordisk A/S (Denmark)	6,869,000
17	ACE Ltd. (Cayman Islands)	56,342,400	35	Pioneer Corp (Japan)	6,816,400
18	Novartis AG Basel (Switzerland)	54,469,000	36	Sappi Ltd. (South Africa)	6,106,000

Ranking the Dividend Achievers by Total Return

Total Return
Based on the 1-year period ending April 29, 2005

Rank	Name	1-Year Tot. Ret	Rank	Name	1-Year Tot. Ret
1	Consolidated Water Co., Inc. (Cay Islands)	68.92	16	ENI S.p.A.	26.63
2	Imperial Oil Ltd. (Canada)	62.83	17	Canadian Imperial Bank of Commerce	26.30
3	Sasol Ltd.	57.22	18	Total S.A. (New)	24.75
4	Canadian National Railway Co. (Canada)	53.27	19	Grupo Elektra S.A. de C.V. (Mexico)	24.56
5	Infosys Technologies Ltd. (India)	49.04	20	ABN AMRO Holding N.V. (Nether)	23.67
6	Allied Irish Banks Plc	44.53	21	Endesa S.A. (Spain)	23.07
7	Enbridge Inc (Canada)	42.59	22	Pfeiffer Vacuum Technology AG	22.90
8	Royal Bank of Canada (Montreal, Quebec)	38.12	23	Luxottica Group S.P.A. (Italy)	22.79
9	Imperial Tobacco Group Plc (UK)	33.42	24	Bank of Montreal (Canada)	22.61
10	Nam Tai Electronics, Inc.	32.57	25	Bunzl Plc (United Kingdom)	18.34
11	E.ON AG (Germany)	31.04	26	Fresenius Medical Care AG (Germany)	17.64
12	Volvo AB (Sweden)	30.37	27	Barclays PLC (United Kingdom)	17.58
13	Governor & Co. of the Bank of Ireland	29.65	28	Dassault Systemes S.A. (France)	16.82
14	Bank of Nova Scotia (Toronto, Canada)	28.92	29	HSBC Holdings Plc (United Kingdom)	14.99
15	Toronto Dominion Bank	27.33	30	Banco Santander Central Hispano SA	12.45

Annualized Total Return
Based on the 3-year period ending April 29, 2005

Rank	Name	3-Year Tot. Ret	Rank	Name	3-Year Tot. Ret
1	Nam Tai Electronics, Inc.	62.70	16	ENI S.p.A.	21.93
2	Consol. Water Co., Inc. (Cayman Islands)	36.48	17	Novo-Nordisk A/S (Denmark)	21.62
3	Imperial Oil Ltd. (Canada)	35.66	18	E.ON AG (Germany)	21.48
4	Volvo AB (Sweden)	34.23	19	Allied Irish Banks Plc	20.07
5	Sasol Ltd.	33.44	20	Compania de Minas Buena. S.A. (Peru)	18.72
6	Huaneng Power International, Inc. (China)	32.67	21	Toronto Dominion Bank	17.88
7	Teva Pharmaceutical Industries Ltd. (Israel)	31.34	22	Aracruz Celulose S.A. (Brazil)	17.39
8	Imperial Tobacco Group Plc (UK)	30.33	23	Total S.A. (New)	16.68
9	Bank of Nova Scotia (Toronto, Canada)	27.15	24	Grupo Elektra S.A. de C.V. (Mexico)	16.44
10	Bank of Montreal (Canada)	26.98	25	Endesa S.A. (Spain)	16.40
11	Infosys Technologies Ltd. (India)	25.05	26	HSBC Holdings Plc (United Kingdom)	14.36
12	Enbridge Inc (Canada)	23.79	27	ABN AMRO Holding N.V. (Nether)	13.90
13	Canadian Imperial Bank of Commerce	23.59	28	Governor & Co. of the Bank of Ireland	13.29
14	Canadian National Railway Co. (Canada)	23.03	29	Fresenius Medical Care AG (Germany)	11.86
15	Royal Bank of Canada (Montreal, Quebec)	22.77	30	Pfeiffer Vacuum Technology AG	11.18

Annualized Total Return
Based on the 5-year period ending April 29, 2005

Rank	Name	5-Year Tot. Ret	Rank	Name	5-Year Tot. Ret
1	Huaneng Power International, Inc. (China)	54.62	16	Luxottica Group S.P.A. (Italy)	20.90
2	Consol.Water Co., Inc. (Cayman Islands)	44.56	17	Governor & Co. of the Bank of Ireland	20.70
3	Imperial Tobacco Group Plc (UK)	42.44	18	Signet Group Plc (United Kingdom)	20.08
4	Nam Tai Electronics, Inc.	41.78	19	Allied Irish Banks Plc	19.28
5	Sasol Ltd.	37.06	20	Volvo AB (Sweden)	16.27
6	RenaissanceRe Holdings Ltd.	31.85	21	Bunzl Plc (United Kingdom)	15.41
7	Imperial Oil Ltd. (Canada)	26.85	22	Toronto Dominion Bank	14.80
8	Canadian National Railway Co. (Canada)	26.75	23	Aracruz Celulose S.A. (Brazil)	14.51
9	Royal Bank of Canada (Montreal, Quebec)	23.83	24	ACE Ltd. (Cayman Islands)	14.46
10	Teva Pharmaceutical Industries Ltd. (Israel)	23.76	25	Novo-Nordisk A/S (Denmark)	14.30
11	Bank of Montreal (Canada)	23.13	26	Grupo Elektra S.A. de C.V. (Mexico)	14.02
12	ENI S.p.A.	22.66	27	E.ON AG (Germany)	13.15
13	Enbridge Inc (Canada)	22.08	28	Barclays PLC (United Kingdom)	12.34
14	Compania de Minas Buenaven. S.A. (Peru)	21.48	29	PartnerRe Ltd.	12.09
15	Canadian Imperial Bank of Commerce	21.27	30	Novartis AG Basel (Switzerland)	12.01

NAICS Classification of International Companies By Industry Sector

Manufacturing

Aracruz Celulose S.A. (Brazil)
Canon, Inc. (Japan)
Ciba Specialty Chemicals Holdings, Inc.
ENI S.p.A.
Fresenius Medical Care AG (Germany)
Luxottica Group S.P.A. (Italy)
Nam Tai Electronics, Inc.
Novartis AG Basel (Switzerland)
Novo-Nordisk A/S (Denmark)
Pfeiffer Vacuum Technology AG
Pioneer Corp (Japan)
Sappi Ltd. (South Africa)
Teva Pharmaceutical Industries Ltd. (Israel)
Unilever Plc (United Kingdom)
Volvo AB (Sweden)

Mining

Compania de Minas Buenaventura S.A. (Peru)
Imperial Oil Ltd. (Canada)
Sasol Ltd.
Total S.A. (New)

Transportation and Warehousing

Canadian National Railway Co. (Canada)
Enbridge Inc (Canada)

Utilities

Consolidated Water Co., Inc. (Cayman Islands)
E.ON AG (Germany)
Endesa S.A. (Spain)
Huaneng Power International, Inc. (China)

Finance and Insurance

ACE Ltd. (Cayman Islands)
Allied Irish Banks Plc
Banco Santander Central Hispano SA
Bank of Montreal (Canada)
Bank of Nova Scotia (Toronto, Canada)
Barclays PLC (United Kingdom)
Canadian Imperial Bank of Commerce
Governor & Co. of the Bank of Ireland (Ireland)
HSBC Holdings Plc (United Kingdom)
PartnerRe Ltd.
RenaissanceRe Holdings Ltd.
Royal Bank of Canada (Montreal, Quebec)
Toronto Dominion Bank
XL Capital Ltd. (Cayman Islands)

Information

Thomson Corp.
WPP Group Plc (United Kingdom)

Professional, Scientific, and Technical Services

Dassault Systemes S.A. (France)
Infosys Technologies Ltd. (India)

Wholesale Trade

Bunzl Plc (United Kingdom)
Imperial Tobacco Group Plc (United Kingdom)

Retail Trade

Grupo Elektra S.A. de C.V. (Mexico)
Signet Group Plc (United Kingdom)

Web Site And Dividend Reinvestment Plan Information

Company	Ticker	Web Site	DRIP
ABN AMRO Holding N.V. (Netherlands)	ABN	www.abnamro.com	No
ACE Ltd. (Cayman Islands)	ACE	www.acelimited.com	No
Allied Irish Banks Plc	AIB	www.aibgroup.com	No
Aracruz Celulose S.A. (Brazil)	ARA	www.aracruz.com.br	No
Banco Santander Central Hispano SA	STD	www.gruposantander.com	No
Bank of Montreal (Canada)	BMO	www.bmo.com	Yes
Bank of Nova Scotia (Toronto, Canada)	BNS	www.scotiabank.com	Yes
Barclays PLC (United Kingdom)	BCS	www.barclays.com	No
Bunzl Plc (United Kingdom)	BNL	www.bunzl.com	No
Canadian Imperial Bank of Commerce	BCM	www.cibc.com	No
Canadian National Railway Co. (Canada)	CNI	www.cn.ca	No
Canon, Inc. (Japan)	CAJ	www.canon.co.jp	No
Ciba Specialty Chemicals Holdings, Inc.	CSB	www.cibasc.com	No
Compania de Minas Buenaventura S.A. (Peru)	BVN	www.buenaventura.com.pe	Yes
Consolidated Water Co., Inc. (Cayman Islands)	CWCO	www.cwco.com	No
Dassault Systemes S.A. (France)	DAST Y	www.3ds.com	No
E.ON AG (Germany)	EON	www.eon.com	No
Enbridge Inc (Canada)	ENB	www.enbridge.com	Yes
Endesa S.A. (Spain)	ELE	www.endesa.es	Yes
ENI S.p.A.	E	www.eni.it	No
Fresenius Medical Care AG (Germany)	FMS	www.fmc-ag.com	Yes
Governor & Co. of the Bank of Ireland (Ireland)	IRE	www.bankofireland.ie	No
Grupo Elektra S.A. de C.V. (Mexico)	EKT	www.grupoelektra.com.mx	Yes
HSBC Holdings Plc (United Kingdom)	HBC	www.hsbc.com	Yes
Huaneng Power International, Inc. (China)	HNP	www.hpi.com.cn	No
Imperial Oil Ltd. (Canada)	IMO	www.imperialoil.ca	Yes
Imperial Tobacco Group Plc (United Kingdom)	ITY	www.imperial-tobacco.com	No
Infosys Technologies Ltd. (India)	INFY	www.infosys.com	No
Luxottica Group S.P.A. (Italy)	LUX	www.luxottica.com	Yes
Nam Tai Electronics, Inc.	NTE	www.namtai.com	No
Novartis AG Basel (Switzerland)	NVS	www.novartis.com	No
Novo-Nordisk A/S (Denmark)	NVO	www.novonordisk.com	No
PartnerRe Ltd.	PRE	www.partnerre.com	No
Pfeiffer Vacuum Technology AG	PV	www.pfeiffer-vacuum.de	No
Pioneer Corp (Japan)	PIO	www.pioneer.co.jp	No
RenaissanceRe Holdings Ltd.	RNR	www.renre.com	No
Royal Bank of Canada (Montreal, Quebec)	RY	www.rbc.com	Yes
Sappi Ltd. (South Africa)	SPP	www.sappi.com	No
Sasol Ltd.	SSL	www.sasol.com	No
Signet Group Plc (United Kingdom)	SIG	www.signetgroupplc.com	No
Teva Pharmaceutical Industries Ltd. (Israel)	TEVA	www.tevapharm.com	No
Thomson Corp.	TOC	www.thomson.com	No
Toronto Dominion Bank	TD	www.td.com	Yes
Total S.A. (New)	TOT	www.total.com	No
Unilever Plc (United Kingdom)	UL	www.unilever.com	Yes
Volvo AB (Sweden)	VOLV Y	www.volvo.com	Yes
WPP Group Plc (United Kingdom)	WPPG Y	www.wpp.com	No
XL Capital Ltd. (Cayman Islands)	XL	www.xlcapital.com	Yes

Frequently Asked Questions

Topics Questions:

- How does a dividend-paying company become a Dividend Achiever?
- What percentage of dividend-paying companies classified as Dividend Achievers?
- How many economic sectors and industries are represented by Dividend Achievers?
- What distinguishes Dividend Achievers from other U.S. listed companies?
- How often is the Dividend Achievers Index reconstituted?
- How are corporate actions handled?
- What type of information is available on the Dividend Achievers constituents?

Q: How does a dividend-paying company become a Dividend Achiever?

A: A publicly-traded company that has increased its dividends for the last ten or more consecutive years will be classified as a Dividend Achiever. Depending on the industry, companies must also meet certain capitalization requirements in order to be considered a Dividend Achiever.

Q: What percentage of dividend-paying companies classified as Dividend Achievers?

A: Just 3.0% of 10,000-plus North American-listed, dividend-paying common stocks are classified as Dividend Achievers.

Q: How many economic sectors and industries are represented by Dividend Achievers?

A: Dividend Achievers represent five economic sectors and more than 50 industries.

Q: What distinguishes Dividend Achievers from other U.S. listed companies?

A: Dividend Achievers have demonstrated the ability to consistently increase dividend payments over a substantial period of time, through volatile markets and challenging political climates.

Q: Does Mergent Inc. offer a Dividend Achiever Index?

A: Mergent currently offers an Index that tracks the daily performance of Dividend Achiever constituents. The inception date was January 17, 2003. The real time price appreciation values are published by the American Stock Exchange under the Symbol ^DAA.

Q: How often is the Index reconstituted?

A: The Dividend Achievers Index is reconstituted annually.

Q: How are corporate actions handled?

A: If an Index constituent is acquired and is no longer actively traded, the company will cease classification as a Dividend Achiever. If an Index constituent spins off a portion of its business or merges with another company, it will be handled on a case by case basis.

HOW TO USE THIS BOOK

MERGENT'S Dividend Achievers is a compact, easy-to-use reference that provides basic financial and business information on companies that have increased their cash dividend payments for at least ten consecutive years, adjusting for splits. The presentation of background information plus current and historical data provides the answers to four basic questions for each company:

1. What does the company do? (See G.)
2. How has it done in the past? (See B, J.)
3. How is it doing now? (See C, D, H.)
4. How will it fare in the future? (See I.)

A. CAPSULE STOCK INFORMATION shows where the stock is traded and its symbol, a recent price and price/earnings ratio, plus the yield afforded by the indicated dividend based on a recent price. The indicated dividend is the current annualized dividend based on the most recent regular cash payment. Also shown is the 52-week range of the Company's stock price.

B. LONG-TERM PRICE CHART illustrates the pattern of monthly stock price movements, fully adjusted for stock dividends and splits. The chart points out the degree of volatility in the price movement of the company's stock and what its long-term trend has been. It also shows how it has performed long-term relative to an initial investment in the S&P 500 Index equal to the price of the company's stock at the beginning of the period shown in the price chart. It indicates areas of price support and resistance, plus other technical points to be considered by the investor. The bars at the base of the long-term price chart indicate the monthly trading volume. Monthly trading volume offers the individual an opportunity to recognize at what periods stock accumulation occurs and what percent of a company's outstanding shares are traded.

PRICE SCORES – Above each company's price/volume chart are its ***Mergent's Price Scores***. These are basic measures of the stock's performance. Each stock is measured against the New York Stock Exchange Composite Index.

A score of 100 indicates that the stock did as well as the New York Stock Exchange Composite Index during the time period. A score of less than 100 means that the stock did not do as well; a score of more than 100 means that the stock outperformed the NYSE Composite Index. All stock prices are adjusted for splits and stock dividends. The time periods measured for each company conclude with the date of the recent price shown in the top line of each company's profile.

The ***7 YEAR PRICE SCORE*** mirrors the common stock's price growth over the previous seven years. The higher the price score, the better the relative performance. It is based on the ratio of the latest 12-month average price to the current seven-year average. This ratio is then indexed against the same ratio for the market as a whole (the New York Stock Exchange Composite Index), which is taken as 100.

The ***12 MONTH PRICE SCORE*** is a similar measurement but for a shorter period of time. It is based on the ratio of the latest two-month average price to the current 12-month average. As was done for the Long-Term Price Score, this ratio is also indexed to the same ratio for the market as a whole.

C. INTERIM EARNINGS (Per Share) – Figures are reported before effect of extraordinary items, discontinued operations and cumulative effects of accounting changes. Each figure is for the quarterly period indicated. These figures are essentially as reported by the company, although all figures are adjusted for all stock dividends and splits.

D. INTERIM DIVIDENDS (Per Share) – The cash dividends are the actual dollar amounts declared by the company. No adjustments have been made for stock dividends and splits. **Ex-Dividend Date**: a stockholder must purchase the stock prior to this date in order to be entitled to the dividend. The **Record Date** indicates the date on which the shareholder had to have been a holder of record in order to qualify for the dividend. The **Payable Date** indicates the date the company paid or intends to pay the dividend. The cash amount shown in the first column is followed by a letter (example "Q" for quarterly) to indicate the frequency of the dividend. A notation of "Dividend payment suspended" indicates that dividend payments have been suspended within the most recent ten years.

ILLUSTRATIVE INC.

Exchange		Symbol	Price	52Wk Range	Yield	P/E
NYS	A	III	$46.28 (5/31/2005)	50.72-42.63	2.85	13.30

*7 Year Price Score 114.48 *NYSE Composite Index=100 *12 Month Price Score 95.35

Interim Earnings (Per Share)

Qtr.	Mar	Jun	Sep	Dec
2002	(2.21)	0.57	1.02	0.87
2003	0.12	0.45	1.03	1.50
2004	0.20	0.60	1.02	1.56
2005	0.30	...	...	...

C

Interim Dividends (Per Share)

Amt	Decl	Ex	Rec	Pay
0.325Q	8/17/2004	9/15/2004	9/17/2004	10/18/2004
0.33Q	11/9/2004	12/16/2004	12/20/2004	1/20/2005
0.33Q	3/15/2005	3/23/2005	3/28/2005	4/20/2005
0.33Q	5/3/2005	6/16/2005	6/20/2005	7/20/2005

D

Indicated Div: $1.32 (Div. Reinv. Plan)

Valuation Analysis E

Forecast P/E	15.29 (5/28/2005)		
Market Cap	$905.8 Million	Book Value	535.8 Million
Price/Book	1.69	Price/Sales	1.03

Dividend Achiever Status F

Rank	242	10 Year Growth Rate	6.39%
Total Years of Dividend Growth			28

Business Summary: Rubber Products (MIC: 11.6 SIC: 011 NAIC: 26211) G

Illustrative manufactures precured tread rubber, equipment and supplies for retreading tires. At Dec 31 2004, Co. and its licensees have 900 franchisees worldwide. The majority of Co.'s franchisees are independent operators of full service tire distributorships. Co. sells and maintains new and retread tires to principally commercial and industrial customers through its wholly-owned subsidiary, Tires-R-Always Systems. Also, Co. provides quick-service truck lubrication and tire service through its subsidiary, Stupendous Jacks Lube, through 30 on-highway locations.

Recent Developments: H For the quarter ended Mar 31 2005, net income increased 48.3% to $5,962,000 from net income of $4,019 thousand in the year-earlier quarter. Revenues were $189,041 thousand, up 7.8% from $175,291 thousand the year before. Operating income was $8,675 thousand versus an income of $5,932 thousand in the prior-year quarter, an increase of 46.2%. Total direct expense was $123,294 thousand versus $112,803 thousand in the prior-year quarter, an increase of 9.3%. Total indirect expense was $57,072 thousand versus $56,556 thousand in the prior-year quarter, an increase of 0.9%.

Prospects: I Results reflect strength in the North American trucking industry, offset in part by global high raw material and transportation costs, which are pressuring margins in its traditional business. On the positive side, Co. believes continued strength in the trucking industry in its major markets will work to its benefit as it continues delivering an expanded array of valued-added vehicle services, which complement its traditional business. At the same time, Co. recognizes that continued increases in raw material and transportation costs will be a concern throughout 2005.

Financial Data

(US$ in Thousands) J	3 Mos	12/31/2004	12/31/2003	12/31/2002	12/31/2001	12/31/2000	12/31/1999	12/31/1998
Earnings Per Share	3.48	3.39	3.11	0.14	2.12	2.90	2.40	2.63
Cash Flow Per Share	4.20	4.92	4.08	6.65	5.66	4.78	5.18	3.85
Tang Book Value Per Share	25.74	25.55	24.61	21.97	21.22	20.03	18.62	17.84
Dividends Per Share	1.310	1.305	1.285	1.265	1.230	1.190	1.150	1.110
Dividend Payout %	37.64	38.50	41.32	903.57	58.02	41.03	47.92	42.21
Income Statement								
Total Revenue	189,041	867,953	828,186	911,953	982,209	1,013,426	1,027,878	1,079,498
EBITDA	15,157	109,191	113,482	110,708	120,036	158,572	155,581	161,695
Depn & Amortn	6,482	27,182	27,179	32,333	46,155	50,465	53,764	51,410
Income Before Taxes	10,032	84,902	83,900	71,518	66,505	99,375	92,090	99,513
Income Taxes	4,193	17,648	23,700	21,465	22,673	39,042	39,760	40,194
Net Income	5,962	66,880	60,200	2,793	43,832	60,333	52,330	59,319
Average Shares	19,707	19,707	19,369	19,888	20,686	20,778	21,764	22,559
Balance Sheet								
Current Assets	476,100	486,255	466,286	416,082	450,174	427,179	428,118	439,124
Total Assets	722,731	730,727	660,529	617,827	718,572	714,549	722,421	755,729
Current Liabilities	146,412	158,558	148,193	147,861	186,075	132,735	154,053	174,909
Long-Term Obligations	31,025	17,143	22,857	28,571	94,286	100,000	100,000	100,000
Total Liabilities	186,889	198,440	183,452	193,234	229,576	240,392	268,346	288,432
Stockholders' Equity	535,842	532,287	477,077	424,593	488,996	474,157	454,075	467,297
Shares Outstanding	19,572	19,451	19,268	19,151	20,641	20,561	20,770	21,955
Statistical Record								
Return on Assets %	9.90	9.59	9.42	0.42	6.12	8.37	7.08	7.17
Return on Equity %	13.53	13.22	13.35	0.61	9.10	12.96	11.36	12.75
EBITDA Margin %	8.02	12.58	13.70	12.14	12.22	15.65	15.14	14.98
Net Margin %	3.15	7.71	7.27	0.31	4.46	5.95	5.09	5.50
Asset Turnover	1.27	1.24	1.30	1.36	1.37	1.41	1.39	1.30
Current Ratio	3.25	3.07	3.15	2.81	2.42	3.22	2.78	2.51
Debt to Equity	0.06	0.03	0.05	0.07	0.19	0.21	0.22	0.21
Price Range	51.05-38.98	51.05-38.98	42.30-28.67	41.16-26.47	46.19-25.34	42.63-22.38	41.25-23.63	59.50-28.38
P/E Ratio	14.67-11.20	15.06-11.50	13.60-9.22	294.00-189.07	21.79-11.95	14.70-7.72	17.19-9.84	22.62-10.79
Average Yield %	2.84	2.86	3.58	3.63	3.99	4.10	3.62	2.52

Address: Owen Lars Highway, Muscatine, IA R2D2 - C3PO	**Officers:** Leia Organa - Chmn., Pres., C.E.O. Wicket W. Warrick - V.P., C.F.O., Sec.	**Investor Contact:** 563-260-0001
Telephone: 520-260-0000	**Transfer Agents:** EquiServe Trust Company, N.A. Providence, RI	**No of Institutions:** 106
Web Site: www.illustrative.com K		**Shares:** 5,793,709 **% Held:** 63.55 L

HOW TO USE THIS BOOK

Indicated Dividend This is the annualized amount (fully adjusted for splits) of the latest regular cash dividend. Companies with Dividend Reinvestment Plans are indicated here.

E. VALUATION ANALYSIS is a tool for evaluating a company's stock. Included are: Forecast Price/Earnings, Market Capitalization, Book Value, Price/Book and Price/Sales.

F. DIVIDEND ACHIEVER STATUS – The company's rank among the Dividend Achievers for dividend growth is indicated. Each company is ranked by its ten-year compound annual average cash dividend growth rate, which is also shown here, along with the total consecutive years of increases.

G. BUSINESS SUMMARY explains what a company does in terms of the products or services it sells, its markets, and the position the company occupies in its industry. For a quick reference, included are the Company's Standard Industrial Classification (SIC), North American Industry Classification (NAIC) and Mergent's Industry Classification (MIC).

H. RECENT DEVELOPMENTS – This section captures what has happened in the most recent quarter for which results are available. It provides analysis of recently released sales and earnings figures, including special charges and credits, and may also include results by sector, expense trends and ratios, and other current information.

I. PROSPECTS – This section focuses on what is anticipated for the immediate future, as well as the outlook for the next few years, based on analysis by Mergent.

J. FINANCIAL DATA (fully adjusted for stock dividends and splits) is provided for at least the past seven fiscal years preceded by the most recent three-, six- and nine-month results if available.

Fiscal Years are the annual financial reporting periods as determined by each company. Annual prices and dividends are displayed based on the Company's fiscal year.

Per Share Data:

The Earnings Per Share figure is based on a trailing 12-month period. Earnings per share, and all per share figures, are adjusted for subsequent stock dividends and splits. Earnings per share reported after 12/15/97 are presented on a diluted basis, as described by Financial Accounting Standards Board Statement 128. Prior to that date, earnings per share are presented on a primary basis.

Cash Flow Per Share represents the annualized cash flow from operating activities (or for quarters, TTM cash flow from operating activities) divided by the average shares outstanding.

Tangible Book Value Per Share is calculated as stockholders equity (the value of common shares, paid-in capital and retained earnings) minus preferred stock and intangibles such as goodwill, patents and excess acquisition costs, divided by shares outstanding. It demonstrates the underlying cash value of each common share if the company were to be liquidated as of that date.

Dividends Per Share is the total of cash payments made per share to shareholders for the trailing 12-month period.

Dividend Payout % is the proportion of earnings available for common stock that is paid to common shareholders in the form of cash dividends. It is significant because it indicates what percentage of earnings is being reinvested in the business for internal growth.

EDITOR'S NOTE: TTM net income is net income for the last 365 days (normally four reported quarters) ended on the quarterly balance sheet date. Where that last 365 days does not exactly equate to the last four reported quarters the net income for any included partial quarter is adjusted on a pro-rata basis.

INCOME STATEMENT, BALANCE SHEET AND STATISTICAL RECORD

Includes pertinent earnings and balance sheet information essential to analyzing a corporation's performance. The comparisons provide the necessary historical perspective to intelligently review the various operating and financial trends. Generic definitions follow.

Income Statement:

Total Revenues consists of all revenues from operations.

EBITDA represents earnings before, interest, taxes, depreciation and amortization, and special items.

Depreciation and Amortization includes all non-cash charges such as depletion and amortization as well as depreciation.

HOW TO USE THIS BOOK

Income Before Taxes is the remaining income *after* deducting all costs, expenses, property charges, interest etc. but *before* deducting income taxes.

Income Taxes includes the amount charged against earnings to provide for current and deferred income taxes.

Net Income consists of all revenues less all expenses (operating and non-operating), and is presented before preference and common dividends.

Average Shares Outstanding is the weighted average number of shares including common equivalent shares outstanding during the year, as reported by the corporation and fully adjusted for all stock dividends and splits. The use of *average shares* minimizes the distortion in *earnings per share* which could result from issuance of a large amount of stock or the company's purchase of a large amount of its own stock during the year.

Balance Sheet:

Current Assets includes the short-term assets expected to be realized or consumed within one year. Normally includes cash and cash equivalents, short term investments, receivables, prepayments and inventories.

Total Assets represents all of the assets of the company, including tangible and intangible, and current and non-current.

Current Liabilities are all of the obligations of the company normally expected to be paid within one year. Includes bank overdrafts, short-term debt, payables and accruals.

Long-Term Obligations are the total long-term debts (due beyond one year) reported by the company, including bonds, capital lease obligations, notes, mortgages, debentures, etc.

Total Liabilities represents all liabilities of the company, whether current or non-current.

Stockholders' Equity is the sum of all capital stock accounts – paid in capital (including additional premium), retained earnings, and all other capital balances.

Shares Outstanding is the number of shares outstanding as of the date of the company's quarterly/annual report, exclusive of treasury stock and adjusted for subsequent stock dividends and splits.

Statistical Record:

Return on Assets % represents the ratio of annualized net income (or for Mos, TTM net income) to average total assets. This ratio represents how effectively assets are being used to produce a profit.

Return on Equity % is the ratio of annualized net income (or for Mos, TTM net income) to average stockholders' equity, expressed as a percentage. This ratio illustrates how effectively the investment of the stockholders is being utilized to earn a profit.

EBITDA Margin % represents earnings before interest, taxes, depreciation and amortization as a percentage of total revenue.

Net Margin % is net income expressed as a percentage of total revenues.

Asset Turnover is annualized total revenue (or for Mos, TTM net income) divided by average total assets. A measure of efficiency of the use of assets.

Current Ratio represents current assets divided by current liabilities. The higher the figure the better the company is able to meet its current liabilities out of its current assets. A key measure of liquidity for industrial companies.

Debt to Equity is the ratio of long-term obligations to stockholders' equity.

Price Ranges are based on each Company's fiscal year. Where actual stock sales did not take place, a range of lowest bid and highest asked prices is shown.

Price/Earnings Ratio is shown as a range. The figures are calculated by dividing the stock's highest price for the year and its lowest price by the year's earnings per share. Growth stocks tend to command higher P/Es than cyclical stocks.

Average Yield % is the ratio of annual dividends to the real average of the prices over the fiscal year.

EDITOR'S NOTE: In order to preserve the historical relationships between prices, earnings and dividends, figures are not restated to reflect subsequent events. Figures are presented in U.S. dollars unless otherwise indicated.

K. ADDITIONAL INFORMATION on each stock includes the officers of the company, investor relations contact, address, telephone number, web site and transfer agents.

L. INSTITUTIONAL HOLDINGS indicates the number of investment companies, insurance companies, mutual funds, bank trust and college endowment funds holding the stock and the total number of shares held as last reported.

OTHER DEFINITIONS

Factors Pertaining Especially to Banks

Interest Income is all interest income, including income from loans and leases, securities and deposits.

Interest Expense is all interest expense, including from loans and leases, securities and deposits.

Net Interest Income is interest income less interest expense. This figure is presented before provision for losses.

Provision for Losses represents the amount charged against earnings to increase the provision made for losses on loans and leases.

Non-Interest Income is any income that is not interest-related. Such income could include trading revenue and gains on the sale of assets.

Non-Interest Expense is all expenses that are not interest-related, including employment costs, office costs, marketing costs, etc.

Net Loans & Leases includes all loans and leases net of provisions for losses. May include commercial, agricultural, real estate, consumer and foreign loans.

Total Deposits are all time and demand deposits entrusted to a bank.

Factors Pertaining Especially to Utilities

Net Property, Plant & Equip is the cost of property, plant and equipment, less its accumulated depreciation.

PPE Turnover represents annualized total revenue (or for Mos, TTM net income) divided by average net property, plant and equipment.

Net Interest Margin % is net interest income before provisions expressed as a percentage of total interest income. A key measure of bank profitability.

Efficiency Ratio % is non-interest expense expressed as a percentage of total revenue.

Loans to Deposits are net loans and leases divided by total deposits. A key measure of bank liquidity.

Factors Pertaining Especially to Insurance Companies

Premium Income is the amount of insurance premiums received from policyholders. This is the primary revenue source for insurance companies.

Benefits and Claims represents the payments made to policyholders under the terms of insurance contracts.

Loss Ratio % is benefits and claims expressed as a percentage of premium income. A key ratio of insurance company profitability.

Factors Pertaining Especially to Real Estate Investment Trusts

Property Income is income from property rental and other associated activities.

Non-Property Income includes interest income and other income not from property activities.

HOW TO USE THIS BOOK

ABBREVIATIONS AND SYMBOLS

A……………………………………………………….Annual
ASE……………………………… American Stock Exchange
()………………………………………………………… Deficit
(Div. Reinv. Plan)….Dividend Reinvestment Plan offered
E………………………………………………………….Extra
M………………………………………………..Monthly
N/A………………………………………….....Not Applicable
N.M…………………………………………..Not Meaningful
NYS……………………………...New York Stock Exchange
OTC……………………………….Over-The-Counter Market
Q………………………………………………………..Quarterly
Sp…………………………………………….Special Dividend
U………………………………………..... Frequency Unknown

ABBOTT LABORATORIES

Exchange	Symbol	Price	52Wk Range	Yield	P/E
NYS	ABT	$48.24 (5/31/2005)	49.87-38.36	2.28	23.42

*7 Year Price Score 92.88 *NYSE Composite Index=100 *12 Month Price Score 106.45

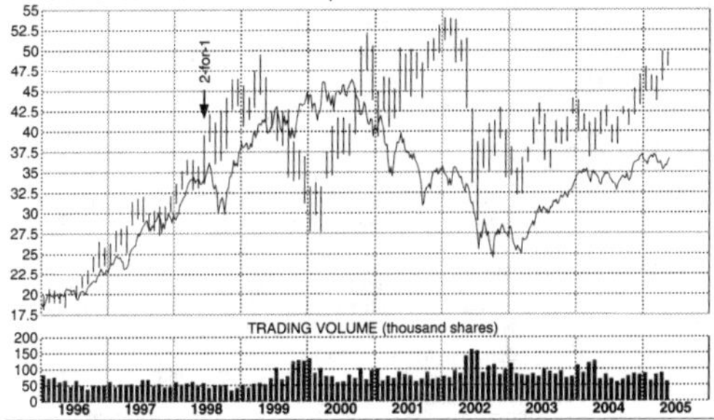

Interim Earnings (Per Share)

Qtr.	Mar	Jun	Sep	Dec
2002	0.54	0.38	0.46	0.40
2003	0.51	0.16	0.48	0.60
2004	0.52	0.40	0.51	0.62
2005	0.53	...	...	...

Interim Dividends (Per Share)

Amt	Decl	Ex	Rec	Pay
0.26Q	6/11/2004	7/13/2004	7/15/2004	8/15/2004
0.26Q	9/10/2004	10/13/2004	10/15/2004	11/15/2004
0.26Q	12/10/2004	1/12/2005	1/14/2005	2/15/2005
0.275Q	2/18/2005	4/13/2005	4/15/2005	5/15/2005

Indicated Div: $1.10 (Div. Reinv. Plan)

Valuation Analysis

Forecast P/E 19.29 (5/28/2005)
Market Cap $74.8 Billion Book Value 14.2 Billion
Price/Book 5.28 Price/Sales 3.66

Dividend Achiever Status

Rank 161 **10 Year Growth Rate** 10.73%
Total Years of Dividend Growth 32

Business Summary: Pharmaceuticals (MIC: 9.1 SIC: 834 NAIC: 25412)

Abbott Laboratories' principal business is the discovery, development, manufacture, and sale of health care products. The Pharmaceutical Products segment includes a line of adult and pediatric pharmaceuticals sold primarily on prescription, or recommendation of physicians. Principal products include: Depakote®, TriCor®, HUMIRA®, Synthroid®, Mavik® and Meridia®. The Diagnostic Products segment includes diagnostic systems and tests. The Hospital Products segment includes acute care injectable drugs and systems. The Ross Products segment includes a line of pediatric and adult nutritionals. The International segment includes products marketed and manufactured primarily outside of the U.S.

Recent Developments: For the quarter ended Mar 31 2005, net income increased 1.8% to $837,888 thousand from net income of $822,909 thousand in the year-earlier quarter. Revenues were $5,382,679 thousand, up 16.0% from $4,640,855 thousand the year before. Operating income was $1,135,871 thousand versus an income of $950,140 thousand in the prior-year quarter, an increase of 19.5%. Total direct expense was $2,522,531 thousand versus $2,073,422 thousand in the prior-year quarter, an increase of 21.7%. Total indirect expense was $1,724,277 thousand versus $1,617,293 thousand in the prior-year quarter, an increase of 6.6%.

Prospects: Co.'s results are benefiting from strong sales growth in both medical products and pharmaceuticals. Co. is also encouraged by the performance of its global diabetes care business, which is exceeding expectations, as well as the strong demand for its global pharmaceutical brands. In the Medical Products group, Abbott Diabetes Care blood glucose monitoring products have been moved to preferred status on the United Healthcare formulary, effective May 1 2005, allowing greater access for diabetics to Co.'s MediSense and TheraSense products. Looking ahead to full-year 2005, Co. expects earnings to range from $2.47 to $2.53 per share, before one-time items and accounting changes.

Financial Data

(US$ in Thousands)	3 Mos	12/31/2004	12/31/2003	12/31/2002	12/31/2001	12/31/2000	12/31/1999	12/31/1998
Earnings Per Share	2.06	2.06	1.75	1.78	0.99	1.78	1.57	1.51
Cash Flow Per Share	2.23	2.75	2.40	2.68	2.30	2.00	1.91	1.79
Tang Book Value Per Share	2.25	2.22	2.90	1.93	1.14	4.54	3.78	2.88
Dividends Per Share	1.040	1.025	0.970	0.915	0.820	0.740	0.660	0.585
Dividend Payout %	50.49	49.76	55.43	51.40	82.83	41.57	42.04	38.74
Income Statement								
Total Revenue	5,382,679	19,680,016	19,680,561	17,684,663	16,285,246	13,745,916	13,177,625	12,477,845
EBITDA	1,565,006	5,563,387	5,154,531	5,055,978	3,285,925	4,667,059	4,306,659	4,128,960
Depn & Amortn	344,880	1,288,700	1,273,991	1,177,345	1,168,018	827,431	828,006	784,243
Income Before Taxes	1,177,856	4,125,600	3,734,417	3,673,413	1,883,148	3,816,407	3,396,888	3,240,599
Income Taxes	339,968	949,764	981,184	879,710	332,758	1,030,430	951,129	907,368
Net Income	837,888	3,235,851	2,753,233	2,793,703	1,550,390	2,785,977	2,445,759	2,333,231
Average Shares	1,569,505	1,570,611	1,571,869	1,573,293	1,565,963	1,565,579	1,557,655	1,545,658
Balance Sheet								
Current Assets	10,351,123	10,734,485	10,290,415	9,121,772	8,419,189	7,376,241	6,419,754	5,553,136
Total Assets	28,857,214	28,767,494	26,715,342	24,259,102	23,296,423	15,283,254	14,471,044	13,216,213
Current Liabilities	7,367,978	6,825,644	7,639,535	7,002,202	7,926,817	4,297,540	4,516,711	4,962,126
Long-Term Obligations	4,697,835	4,787,934	3,452,329	4,273,973	4,335,493	1,076,368	1,336,789	1,339,694
Total Liabilities	14,679,666	14,441,711	13,643,084	13,594,549	14,236,991	6,712,348	7,043,449	7,502,552
Stockholders' Equity	14,177,548	14,325,783	13,072,258	10,664,553	9,059,432	8,570,906	7,427,595	5,713,661
Shares Outstanding	1,550,677	1,560,023	1,564,517	1,563,068	1,554,530	1,545,934	1,547,019	1,516,063
Statistical Record								
Return on Assets %	11.42	11.63	10.80	11.75	8.04	18.68	17.67	18.46
Return on Equity %	23.48	23.56	23.20	28.33	17.59	34.73	37.22	43.56
EBITDA Margin %	29.07	28.27	26.19	28.59	20.18	33.95	32.68	33.09
Net Margin %	15.57	16.44	13.99	15.80	9.52	20.27	18.56	18.70
Asset Turnover	0.72	0.71	0.77	0.74	0.84	0.92	0.95	0.99
Current Ratio	1.40	1.57	1.35	1.30	1.06	1.72	1.42	1.12
Debt to Equity	0.33	0.33	0.26	0.40	0.48	0.13	0.18	0.23
Price Range	47.96-37.65	46.99-36.81	44.10-32.16	53.97-29.00	53.10-39.34	52.15-27.71	49.51-31.16	46.53-30.63
P/E Ratio	23.28-18.28	22.81-17.87	25.20-18.38	30.32-16.29	53.64-39.74	29.30-15.57	31.54-19.85	30.82-20.29
Average Yield %	2.43	2.47	2.51	2.13	1.75	1.90	1.62	1.53

Address: 100 Abbott Park Road, Abbott Park, IL 60064-6400
Telephone: 847-937-6100
Web Site: www.abbott.com

Officers: Miles D. White - Chmn., C.E.O. Richard A. Gonzalez - Pres., C.O.O., Medical Products **Transfer Agents:** EquiServe, Providence, RI

Investor Contact: 847-937-3923
No of Institutions: 958
Shares: 931,653,824 **% Held:** 59.76

ABM INDUSTRIES, INC.

Exchange	Symbol	Price	52Wk Range	Yield	P/E
NYS	ABM	$19.07 (5/31/2005)	22.39-16.92	2.20	30.27

***7 Year Price Score 109.08** *NYSE Composite Index=100 ***12 Month Price Score 94.88**

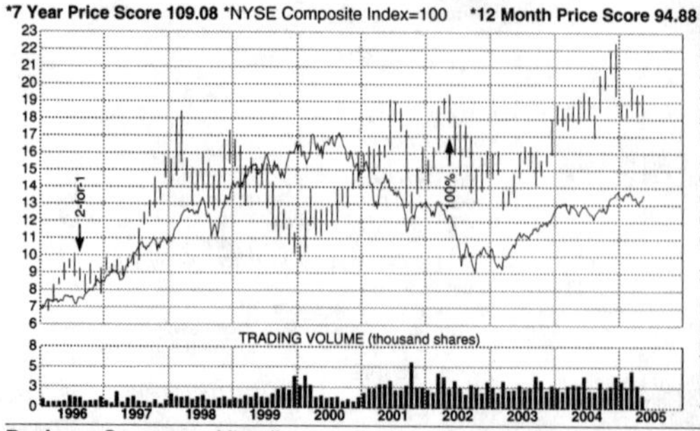

TRADING VOLUME (thousand shares)

Interim Earnings (Per Share)

Qtr.	Jan	Apr	Jul	Oct
2001-02	0.16	0.27	0.25	0.24
2002-03	0.09	0.20	0.23	1.29
2003-04	0.14	0.14	0.27	0.06
2004-05	0.16	...	...	...

Interim Dividends (Per Share)

Amt	Decl	Ex	Rec	Pay
0.10Q	6/8/2004	7/8/2004	7/12/2004	8/2/2004
0.10Q	9/8/2004	10/6/2004	10/11/2004	11/1/2004
0.105Q	12/13/2004	1/12/2005	1/14/2005	2/7/2005
0.105Q	3/7/2005	4/6/2005	4/8/2005	5/2/2005

Indicated Div: $0.42

Valuation Analysis

Forecast P/E	18.97 (5/28/2005)		
Market Cap	$946.3 Million	Book Value	457.5 Million
Price/Book	2.07	Price/Sales	0.38

Dividend Achiever Status

Rank	139	**10 Year Growth Rate**	12.00%
Total Years of Dividend Growth			40

Business Summary: Miscellaneous Business Services (MIC: 12.8 SIC: 349 NAIC: 38210)

ABM Industries and its subsidiaries provide janitorial, parking, security, engineering, lighting and mechanical services for commercial, industrial, institutional and retail facilities throughout the United States and in British Columbia, Canada. At Oct 31 2004, Co.'s seven business segments were Janitorial, Parking, Security, Engineering, Lighting, Mechanical, and Facility Services. Co.'s customer base, includes, but is not limited to, commercial office buildings, industrial plants, financial institutions, retail stores, shopping centers, warehouses, airports, health and educational facilities, stadiums and arenas, government buildings, apartment complexes, and theme parks.

Recent Developments: For the quarter ended Jan 31 2005, net income increased 25.1% to $7,924 thousand from net income of $6,335 thousand in the year-earlier quarter. Revenues were $647,363 thousand, up 13.4% from $570,823 thousand the year before. Total indirect expense was $634,347 thousand versus $560,720 thousand in the prior-year quarter, an increase of 13.1%. Comparisons were made with restated prior-year figures.

Prospects: Co.'s prospects appear favorable, reflecting recent top-line growth and improved operating profit from across its business segments. Accordingly, Co. increased its fiscal 2005 guidance to $0.98 to $1.03 per diluted share. Co. noted that its guidance is exclusive of future acquisitions, and does not include the expensing of stock options. Separately, on Mar 4 2005, Co. announced that its subsidiary, Security Services of America, completed the acquisition of Amguard Security and Patrol Services for $1.1 million in cash. Amguard, with annual revenues in excess of $4.5 million, is a provider of security officer services, primarily to high-rise, commercial and residential structures.

Financial Data

(US$ in Thousands)	3 Mos	10/31/2004	10/31/2003	10/31/2002	10/31/2001	10/31/2000	10/31/1999	10/31/1998
Earnings Per Share	0.63	0.61	1.81	0.92	0.65	0.93	0.82	0.72
Cash Flow Per Share	1.32	0.69	1.23	2.26	1.38	0.42	0.80	0.76
Tang Book Value Per Share	3.94	3.95	5.01	4.46	5.08	4.48	3.82	3.12
Dividends Per Share	0.405	0.400	0.380	0.360	0.330	0.310	0.280	0.240
Dividend Payout %	64.44	65.57	20.99	39.13	50.77	33.51	33.94	33.33
Income Statement								
Total Revenue	647,363	2,416,223	2,262,476	2,191,957	1,950,038	1,807,557	1,629,716	1,501,827
EBITDA	17,570	64,029	69,681	84,510	79,273	96,217	87,930	77,101
Depn & Amortn	4,806	17,667	14,829	15,182	26,328	23,524	20,698	19,593
Income Before Taxes	12,764	46,362	54,852	69,328	52,945	72,693	67,232	57,508
Income Taxes	4,840	15,889	18,454	22,600	20,119	28,350	27,565	23,578
Net Income	7,924	30,473	90,458	46,728	32,826	44,343	39,667	33,930
Average Shares	50,402	50,064	50,004	51,015	50,020	47,418	47,496	46,322
Balance Sheet								
Current Assets	504,568	486,088	500,648	437,785	465,541	436,819	367,589	324,308
Total Assets	874,904	842,524	795,983	704,939	683,100	641,985	563,384	501,363
Current Liabilities	269,432	254,428	256,691	227,090	235,999	212,620	183,310	157,824
Long-Term Obligations	...	...	...	...	942	36,811	28,903	33,720
Total Liabilities	417,390	400,363	351,947	318,269	321,923	319,276	280,033	257,429
Stockholders' Equity	457,514	442,161	444,036	386,670	361,177	316,309	276,951	237,534
Shares Outstanding	49,624	48,707	48,367	48,997	48,778	45,998	44,814	43,202
Statistical Record								
Return on Assets %	3.75	3.71	12.05	6.73	4.95	7.34	7.45	7.01
Return on Equity %	6.88	6.86	21.78	12.50	9.69	14.91	15.42	15.59
EBITDA Margin %	2.71	2.65	3.08	3.86	4.07	5.32	5.40	5.13
Net Margin %	1.22	1.26	4.00	2.13	1.68	2.45	2.43	2.26
Asset Turnover	2.99	2.94	3.01	3.16	2.94	2.99	3.06	3.10
Current Ratio	1.87	1.91	1.95	1.93	1.97	2.05	2.01	2.05
Debt to Equity	...	...	...	...	N.M.	0.12	0.10	0.14
Price Range	22.39-16.92	20.87-15.25	16.44-12.72	19.43-13.05	19.10-12.50	13.97-9.69	17.31-11.00	18.41-12.63
P/E Ratio	35.54-26.86	34.21-25.00	9.08-7.03	21.12-14.18	29.38-19.23	15.02-10.42	21.11-13.41	25.56-17.53
Average Yield %	2.13	2.20	2.56	2.23	2.08	2.57	1.94	1.62

Address: 160 Pacific Avenue, Suite 222, San Francisco, CA 94111
Telephone: 415-733-4000
Web Site: www.abm.com

Officers: Martin H. Mandles - Chmn., Chief Admin. Officer Henrik C. Slipsager - Pres., C.E.O. **Transfer Agents:** Mellon Investor Services LLC, San Francisco, CA

No of Institutions: 128
Shares: 29,804,928 **% Held:** 59.93

AFLAC INC.

Exchange	Symbol	Price	52Wk Range	Yield	P/E
NYS	AFL	$41.55 (5/31/2005)	41.81-35.70	1.06	16.29

***7 Year Price Score 116.96** *NYSE Composite Index=100 ***12 Month Price Score 97.57**

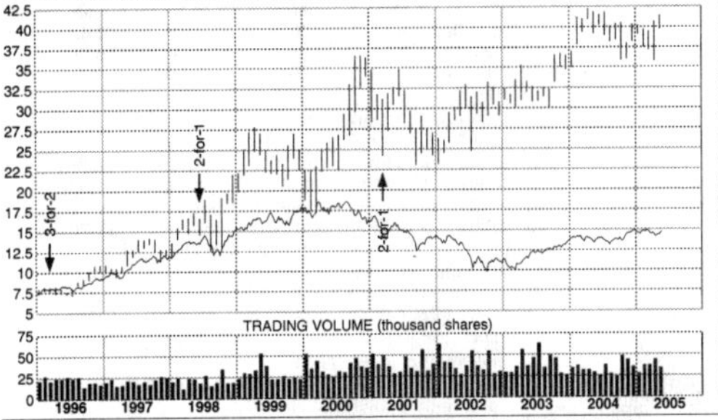

TRADING VOLUME (thousand shares)

Interim Earnings (Per Share)

Qtr.	Mar	Jun	Sep	Dec
2002	0.34	0.40	0.45	0.35
2003	0.45	0.48	0.45	0.14
2004	0.61	0.51	0.58	0.82
2005	0.64	...	...	...

Interim Dividends (Per Share)

Amt	Decl	Ex	Rec	Pay
0.095Q	7/27/2004	8/11/2004	8/13/2004	9/1/2004
0.095Q	10/26/2004	11/9/2004	11/12/2004	12/1/2004
0.11Q	1/31/2005	2/16/2005	2/18/2005	3/1/2005
0.11Q	4/26/2005	5/18/2005	5/20/2005	6/1/2005

Indicated Div: $0.44 (Div. Reinv. Plan)

Valuation Analysis

Forecast P/E 15.77 (5/28/2005)
Market Cap $20.9 Billion Book Value 7.8 Billion
Price/Book 2.68 Price/Sales 1.54

Dividend Achiever Status

Rank 57 **10 Year Growth Rate** 17.75%
Total Years of Dividend Growth 22

Business Summary: Insurance (MIC: 8.2 SIC: 321 NAIC: 24114)

AFLAC primarily sells supplemental health and life insurance in the United States and Japan. Co.'s insurance operations are conducted through American Family Life Assurance Company of Columbus, which operates in the U.S. and as a branch in Japan. Aflac Japan sells cancer plans, care plans, general medical expense plans, medical/sickness riders to its cancer plan, a living benefit life plan, ordinary life insurance plans and annuities. Aflac U.S. sells cancer plans and various types of health insurance, including accident and disability, fixed-benefit dental, personal sickness and hospital indemnity, hospital intensive care, long-term care, ordinary life, and short-term disability plans.

Recent Developments: For the quarter ended Mar 31 2005, net income increased 7.9% to $328,000 thousand from net income of $304,000 thousand in the year-earlier quarter. Revenues were $3,559,000 thousand, up 8.5% from $3,280,000 thousand the year before. Net premiums earned were $3,041,000 thousand versus $2,773,000 thousand in the prior-year quarter, an increase of 9.7%.

Prospects: Co.'s outlook appears promising. In Aflac Japan, which has benefited from the introduction of new medical products, Co.'s objective for 2005 is a 5.0% to 10.0% increase in total new annualized premium sales in yen. Meanwhile, during the first quarter of 2005, Aflac U.S. recruited more than 6,400 new sales associates. At Mar 31 2005, Aflac U.S. was represented by 60,300 licensed sales associates, or 4.6% higher than last year, which could aid top line growth going forward. Co. is also optimistic that the introduction of a new vision product will benefit sales in the second half of 2005. Co.'s objective for Aflac U.S. for 2005 is a 3.0% to 8.0% increase in total new annualized premium.

Financial Data (US$ in Thousands)	3 Mos	12/31/2004	12/31/2003	12/31/2002	12/31/2001	12/31/2000	12/31/1999	12/31/1998
Earnings Per Share	2.55	2.52	1.52	1.55	1.28	1.26	1.03	0.88
Cash Flow Per Share	8.83	8.82	6.60	5.87	5.43	6.17	5.28	4.68
Tang Book Value Per Share	15.49	15.04	13.03	12.43	10.40	8.87	7.28	7.09
Dividends Per Share	0.395	0.380	0.300	0.230	0.193	0.165	0.145	0.126
Dividend Payout %	15.49	15.08	19.74	14.84	15.04	13.10	14.01	14.35
Income Statement								
Premium Income	3,041,000	11,302,000	9,921,000	8,595,000	8,061,000	8,239,000	7,264,000	5,943,000
Total Revenue	3,559,000	13,281,000	11,447,000	10,257,000	9,598,000	9,720,000	8,640,000	7,104,000
Benefits & Claims	2,266,000	8,482,000	7,529,000	6,589,000	6,303,000	6,618,000	5,885,000	4,877,000
Income Before Taxes	506,000	1,807,000	1,225,000	1,259,000	1,081,000	1,012,000	778,000	551,000
Income Taxes	178,000	508,000	430,000	438,000	394,000	325,000	207,000	64,000
Net Income	328,000	1,299,000	795,000	821,000	687,000	687,000	571,000	487,000
Average Shares	509,449	516,421	522,138	528,326	537,380	544,906	550,846	551,744
Balance Sheet								
Total Assets	57,041,000	59,326,000	50,964,000	45,058,000	37,860,000	37,232,000	37,041,000	31,183,000
Total Liabilities	49,265,000	51,753,000	44,318,000	38,664,000	32,435,000	32,538,000	33,173,000	27,413,000
Stockholders' Equity	7,776,000	7,573,000	6,646,000	6,394,000	5,425,000	4,694,000	3,868,000	3,770,000
Shares Outstanding	501,987	503,608	509,892	514,439	521,615	529,209	531,482	531,368
Statistical Record								
Return on Assets %	2.38	2.35	1.66	1.98	1.83	1.84	1.67	1.61
Return on Equity %	17.77	18.22	12.19	13.89	13.58	16.00	14.95	13.53
Loss Ratio %	74.51	75.05	75.89	76.66	78.19	80.33	81.02	82.06
Net Margin %	9.22	9.78	6.95	8.00	7.16	7.07	6.61	6.86
Price Range	42.23-35.79	42.23-34.95	36.67-30.08	33.17-23.12	34.83-23.01	36.53-17.19	27.81-19.88	22.00-11.73
P/E Ratio	16.56-14.04	16.76-13.87	24.13-19.79	21.40-14.92	27.21-17.98	28.99-13.64	27.00-19.30	25.00-13.33
Average Yield %	1.00	0.96	0.92	0.78	0.67	0.62	0.61	0.77

Address: 1932 Wynnton Road, Columbus, GA 31999
Telephone: 706-323-3431
Web Site: www.aflac.com

Officers: Daniel P. Amos - Chmn., C.E.O. Kriss Cloninger III - Pres., C.F.O., Treas. **Transfer Agents:** AFLAC Incorporated, Columbus, GA

Investor Contact: 706-596-3264
No of Institutions: 488
Shares: 279,546,528 **% Held:** 55.70

AIR PRODUCTS & CHEMICALS, INC.

Exchange	Symbol	Price	52Wk Range	Yield	P/E
NYS	APD	$60.23 (5/31/2005)	65.14-48.42	2.13	20.70

Interim Earnings (Per Share)

Qtr.	Dec	Mar	Jun	Sep
2001-02	0.52	0.57	0.63	0.65
2002-03	0.56	0.51	0.12	0.59
2003-04	0.58	0.62	0.71	0.73
2004-05	0.72	0.75	...	...

Interim Dividends (Per Share)

Amt	Decl	Ex	Rec	Pay
0.29Q	9/16/2004	9/29/2004	10/1/2004	11/8/2004
0.29Q	11/18/2004	12/30/2004	1/3/2005	2/14/2005
0.32Q	3/18/2005	3/30/2005	4/1/2005	5/9/2005
0.32Q	5/19/2005	6/29/2005	7/1/2005	8/8/2005

Indicated Div: $1.28 (Div. Reinv. Plan)

Valuation Analysis

Forecast P/E	19.30 (6/2/2005)		
Market Cap	$13.8 Billion	Book Value	4.9 Billion
Price/Book	2.81	Price/Sales	1.76

Dividend Achiever Status

Rank	210	10 Year Growth Rate	8.15%
Total Years of Dividend Growth			22

Business Summary: Chemicals (MIC: 11.1 SIC: 813 NAIC: 25120)

Air Products & Chemicals is engaged in the business of industrial gas and related industrial process equipment and is a producer of certain chemicals. The gases business segment recovers and distributes industrial gases such as oxygen, nitrogen, helium, argon, and hydrogen, and a variety of medical and specialty gases, and also includes Co.'s healthcare business. The chemicals business segment produces and markets performance materials and chemical intermediates. The equipment business segment designs and manufactures equipment for cryogenic air separation, gas processing, natural gas liquefaction, and hydrogen purification.

Recent Developments: For the first quarter ended Mar 31 2005, net income advanced 24.2% to $175.3 million compared with $141.2 million in the corresponding prior-year quarter. Sales increased 7.9% to $2.00 billion from $1.86 billion a year earlier. Cost of sales climbed 7.3% to $1.47 billion from $1.37 billion the year before. Operating income was $252.2 million versus $210.1 million in the previous year, an increase of 20.0%.

Prospects: Despite concerns about slowing growth in the manufacturing sector, Co. expects continued volume gains during the second half of 2005, primarily in its refinery hydrogen, equipment and homecare businesses. Meanwhile, Co. will continue to focus on offsetting increases in raw materials and energy costs with productivity and pricing improvements. Co. is targeting third-quarter 2005 earnings per share in the range of $0.77 to $0.82, and earnings of between $3.00 and $3.15 for the full year. On Apr 21 2005, Co. announced plans to construct a new hydrogen production plant in Port Arthur, TX to supply 110 million standard cubic feet per day of hydrogen to The Premcor Refining Group Inc.'s refinery.

Financial Data

(US$ in Thousands)	6 Mos	3 Mos	09/30/2004	09/30/2003	09/30/2002	09/30/2001	09/30/2000	09/30/1999
Earnings Per Share	2.91	2.77	2.64	1.78	2.36	2.12	0.57	2.09
Cash Flow Per Share	6.07	5.45	4.84	4.72	4.90	5.05	5.49	5.13
Tang Book Value Per Share	16.98	16.36	15.45	12.99	13.33	13.67	12.30	11.39
Dividends Per Share	1.190	1.100	1.040	0.880	0.820	0.780	0.740	0.700
Dividend Payout %	40.89	39.67	39.39	49.44	34.75	36.79	129.82	33.49
Income Statement								
Total Revenue	3,994,300	1,991,000	7,411,400	6,297,300	5,401,200	5,722,700	5,495,500	5,039,800
EBITDA	897,700	443,200	1,687,300	1,343,700	1,491,600	1,520,600	908,700	1,373,700
Depn & Amortn	356,500	179,400	714,900	654,800	584,800	592,400	593,900	545,600
Income Before Taxes	483,600	236,000	851,400	565,400	784,500	737,000	118,100	669,000
Income Taxes	132,700	64,900	226,600	147,200	240,800	219,000	(13,700)	203,400
Net Income	342,100	166,800	604,100	397,300	525,400	465,600	124,200	450,500
Average Shares	234,300	232,300	228,900	223,600	222,700	219,300	216,200	216,000
Balance Sheet								
Current Assets	2,771,200	2,611,000	2,416,900	2,067,900	1,909,300	1,684,800	1,805,000	1,782,400
Total Assets	10,707,300	10,653,400	10,040,400	9,431,900	8,495,000	8,084,100	8,270,500	8,235,500
Current Liabilities	1,845,400	1,804,900	1,705,600	1,581,200	1,256,200	1,352,400	1,374,800	1,857,800
Long-Term Obligations	2,115,000	2,241,400	2,113,600	2,168,600	2,041,000	2,027,500	2,615,800	1,961,600
Total Liabilities	5,611,100	5,728,800	5,427,500	5,461,300	4,850,200	4,860,300	5,333,700	5,146,600
Stockholders' Equity	4,910,100	4,740,800	4,444,000	3,782,500	3,460,400	3,105,800	2,821,300	2,961,600
Shares Outstanding	229,187	227,311	227,301	227,265	227,219	227,186	229,305	229,304
Statistical Record								
Return on Assets %	6.51	6.24	6.19	4.43	6.34	5.69	1.50	5.73
Return on Equity %	14.88	14.62	14.65	10.97	16.00	15.71	4.28	16.01
EBITDA Margin %	22.47	22.26	22.77	21.34	27.62	26.57	16.54	27.26
Net Margin %	8.56	8.38	8.15	6.31	9.73	8.14	2.26	8.94
Asset Turnover	0.76	0.75	0.76	0.70	0.65	0.70	0.66	0.64
Current Ratio	1.50	1.45	1.42	1.31	1.52	1.25	1.31	0.96
Debt to Equity	0.43	0.47	0.48	0.57	0.59	0.65	0.93	0.66
Price Range	65.14-48.02	58.87-47.02	55.00-44.50	48.64-37.49	53.05-36.82	48.00-32.94	39.00-24.19	49.13-27.94
P/E Ratio	22.38-16.50	21.25-16.97	20.83-16.86	27.33-21.06	22.48-15.60	22.64-15.54	68.42-42.43	23.50-13.37
Average Yield %	2.18	2.11	2.07	2.04	1.77	1.93	2.35	1.88

Address: 7201 Hamilton Boulevard, Allentown, PA 18195-1501 **Telephone:** 610-481-4911 **Web Site:** www.airproducts.com	**Officers:** John P. Jones III - Chmn., Pres., C.E.O. W. Douglas Brown - V.P., Gen. Couns., Sec. **Transfer Agents:** American Stock Transfer & Trust Company, New York, NY	**Investor Contact:** 610-481-5775 **No of Institutions:** 451 **Shares:** 189,671,056 **% Held:** 83.34

ALBEMARLE CORP.

Exchange	Symbol	Price	52Wk Range	Yield	P/E
NYS	ALB	$38.04 (5/31/2005)	40.32-28.75	1.58	25.53

Interim Earnings (Per Share)

Qtr.	Mar	Jun	Sep	Dec
2002	0.38	0.48	0.48	0.39
2003	0.50	0.54	0.23	0.44
2004	0.32	0.49	0.02	0.46
2005	0.52	...	...	...

Interim Dividends (Per Share)

Amt	Decl	Ex	Rec	Pay
0.145Q	6/30/2004	9/13/2004	9/15/2004	10/1/2004
0.15Q	11/17/2004	12/13/2004	12/15/2004	1/1/2005
0.15Q	2/2/2005	3/11/2005	3/15/2005	4/1/2005
0.15Q	4/19/2005	6/13/2005	6/15/2005	7/1/2005

Indicated Div: $0.60

Valuation Analysis

Forecast P/E 16.82 (5/28/2005)
Market Cap $1.8 Billion Book Value 871.6 Million
Price/Book 2.03 Price/Sales 1.04

Dividend Achiever Status

Rank 101 **10 Year Growth Rate** 14.48%
Total Years of Dividend Growth 10

Business Summary: Chemicals (MIC: 11.1 SIC: 821 NAIC: 25211)

Albemarle is a worldwide producer of specialty chemicals. Co.'s operations are managed and reported in two operating segments: Polymer Chemicals and Fine Chemicals. The Polymer Chemicals segment consists of a broad range of chemicals, including flame retardants, catalysts and polymer additives. The Fine Chemicals segment includes a broad range of chemicals, including pharmachemicals, agrichemicals, fine chemistry services and intermediates and performance chemicals. Most of Co.'s products are additives to plastics, polymers and elastomers, cleaning products, personal care products, agricultural compounds, pharmaceuticals, drilling compounds, paper processing chemicals, and biocides.

Recent Developments: For the quarter ended Mar 31 2005, net income increased 78.7% to $24,319 thousand from net income of $13,607 thousand in the year-earlier quarter. Revenues were $509,965 thousand, up 58.4% from $322,009 thousand the year before. Operating income was $39,316 thousand versus an income of $21,344 thousand in the prior-year quarter, an increase of 84.2%. Total direct expense was $402,643 thousand versus $261,225 thousand in the prior-year quarter, an increase of 54.1%. Total indirect expense was $68,006 thousand versus $39,440 thousand in the prior-year quarter, an increase of 72.4%.

Prospects: Operating results are being driven by stronger demand for hydroprocessing catalysts, excellent pricing momentum and cost synergies. Also contributing to the results is the Fine Chemicals segment, which is showing dramatic improvement with the introduction of higher value products. Moreover, Co.'s Polymer Additives segment is continuing to see strong growth in net sales. Going forward, Co. will continue to implement its aggressive cost-cutting initiatives, coupled with its exceptional pricing execution across its business segments, to remain competitive and further support margin improvement in fiscal 2005.

Financial Data

(US$ in Thousands)	3 Mos	12/31/2004	12/31/2003	12/31/2002	12/31/2001	12/31/2000	12/31/1999	12/31/1998
Earnings Per Share	1.49	1.29	1.71	1.73	1.47	2.18	1.87	1.63
Cash Flow Per Share	3.17	4.60	3.64	3.44	3.15	3.37	3.50	2.66
Tang Book Value Per Share	9.96	7.33	12.58	12.82	12.34	11.71	10.23	9.16
Dividends Per Share	0.590	0.585	0.565	0.540	0.520	0.460	0.400	0.370
Dividend Payout %	39.60	45.35	33.04	31.21	35.37	21.10	21.39	22.70
Income Statement								
Total Revenue	509,965	1,513,737	1,110,237	980,215	916,899	917,549	845,925	820,862
EBITDA	74,757	186,462	177,445	189,486	180,342	227,249	212,867	202,297
Depn & Amortn	29,045	97,268	84,014	80,603	77,610	73,750	75,750	75,012
Income Before Taxes	35,459	71,844	88,055	103,813	97,196	147,501	128,738	122,798
Income Taxes	11,140	17,005	13,890	29,068	29,029	45,725	39,909	38,066
Net Income	24,319	54,839	71,945	74,745	68,167	101,776	88,829	84,732
Average Shares	46,885	42,527	42,146	43,137	46,524	46,606	47,513	52,136
Balance Sheet								
Current Assets	841,911	747,410	481,369	413,064	383,661	315,154	332,599	311,530
Total Assets	2,503,374	2,442,745	1,387,291	1,192,956	1,129,475	981,803	954,094	937,797
Current Liabilities	391,116	373,746	210,071	165,007	303,837	142,116	131,353	107,936
Long-Term Obligations	820,456	899,584	228,389	180,137	12,353	97,681	158,981	192,530
Total Liabilities	1,631,806	1,731,370	751,070	623,216	536,173	422,896	463,530	486,130
Stockholders' Equity	871,568	711,375	636,221	569,740	593,302	558,907	490,564	451,667
Shares Outstanding	46,572	41,898	41,153	41,692	45,498	45,823	46,199	47,008
Statistical Record								
Return on Assets %	3.37	2.86	5.58	6.44	6.46	10.49	9.39	9.28
Return on Equity %	8.67	8.12	11.93	12.85	11.83	19.34	18.86	17.49
EBITDA Margin %	14.66	12.32	15.98	19.33	19.67	24.77	25.16	24.64
Net Margin %	4.77	3.62	6.48	7.63	7.43	11.09	10.50	10.32
Asset Turnover	0.88	0.79	0.86	0.84	0.87	0.95	0.89	0.90
Current Ratio	2.15	2.00	2.29	2.50	1.26	2.22	2.53	2.89
Debt to Equity	0.94	1.26	0.36	0.32	0.02	0.17	0.32	0.43
Price Range	40.32-27.35	40.32-27.35	30.44-22.28	32.89-22.40	25.05-17.35	25.69-14.56	25.19-16.81	26.00-16.63
P/E Ratio	27.06-18.36	31.26-21.20	17.80-13.03	19.01-12.95	17.04-11.80	11.78-6.68	13.47-8.99	15.95-10.20
Average Yield %	1.75	1.83	2.09	1.92	2.36	2.20	1.96	1.70

Address: 330 South Fourth Street, P.O. Box 1335, Richmond, VA 23219
Telephone: 804-788-6000
Web Site: www.albemarle.com

Officers: William M. Gottwald - Chmn. Floyd D. Gottwald Jr. - Vice-Chmn. **Transfer Agents:**

Investor Contact: 225-388-7320
No of Institutions: 144
Shares: 22,105,396 **% Held:** 47.47

ALBERTO-CULVER CO.

Exchange	Symbol	Price	52Wk Range	Yield	P/E
NYS	ACV	$44.33 (5/31/2005)	55.40-42.05	1.04	20.71

*7 Year Price Score 140.58 *NYSE Composite Index=100 *12 Month Price Score 91.33

Interim Earnings (Per Share)

Qtr.	Dec	Mar	Jun	Sep
2001-02	0.33	0.37	0.41	0.44
2002-03	0.40	0.42	0.47	0.51
2003-04	0.02	0.44	0.56	0.52
2004-05	0.53	0.53	...	...

Interim Dividends (Per Share)

Amt	Decl	Ex	Rec	Pay
0.10Q	4/22/2004	4/29/2004	5/3/2004	5/20/2004
0.10Q	10/28/2004	11/3/2004	11/5/2004	11/19/2004
0.115Q	1/27/2005	2/3/2005	2/7/2005	2/18/2005
0.115Q	4/28/2005	5/5/2005	5/9/2005	5/20/2005

Indicated Div: $0.46

Valuation Analysis

Forecast P/E	18.80 (5/28/2005)		
Market Cap	$4.1 Billion	Book Value	1.4 Billion
Price/Book	2.82	Price/Sales	1.20

Dividend Achiever Status

Rank	80	10 Year Growth Rate	15.67%
Total Years of Dividend Growth			20

Business Summary: Chemicals (MIC: 11.1 SIC: 844 NAIC: 25620)

Alberto-Culver operates two businesses: Global Consumer Products and Beauty Supply Distribution. The Global Consumer Products segment develops, manufactures, and markets beauty, health care, food and household products to the U.S., Canada and internationally. Products include Alberto V05, St. Ives, TRESemme, Motions, Just for Me, Mrs. Dash and Molly McButter. Beauty Supply Distribution, is comprised of two operations: Sally Beauty Supply, a chain of cash-and-carry outlets offering professional beauty supplies to both salon professionals and retail consumers, and Beauty Systems Group, a beauty products distributor offering professional brands to salons and through professional-only stores.

Recent Developments: For the quarter ended Mar 31 2005, net income increased 20.9% to $49,078 thousand from net income of $40,585 thousand in the year-earlier quarter. Revenues were $884,075 thousand, up 7.9% from $819,321 thousand the year before. Operating income was $77,743 thousand versus an income of $68,267 thousand in the prior-year quarter, an increase of 13.9%. Total direct expense was $438,192 thousand versus $401,810 thousand in the prior-year quarter, an increase of 9.1%. Total indirect expense was $368,140 thousand versus $349,244 thousand in the prior-year quarter, an increase of 5.4%.

Prospects: On May 9 2005, Co. announced that it has signed an agreement in principle to purchase substantially all of the assets of Nexxus Products Company related to its Nexxus brand of hair care products including trademarks, inventory, accounts receivable and other items. Terms of the cash purchase, which is expected to be completed by the end of May 2005, were not disclosed. Meanwhile, results are benefiting from increased sales of TRESemme shampoos, conditioners and styling products, as well as the introduction of new Alberto VO5 and St. Ives products both domestically and internationally.

Financial Data

(US$ in Thousands)	6 Mos	3 Mos	09/30/2004	09/30/2003	09/30/2002	09/30/2001	09/30/2000	09/30/1999
Earnings Per Share	2.14	2.05	1.54	1.80	1.55	1.27	1.22	1.01
Cash Flow Per Share	2.06	2.70	2.87	2.50	2.69	1.96	1.51	1.06
Tang Book Value Per Share	8.60	8.17	8.24	7.04	5.03	4.60	3.44	3.87
Dividends Per Share	0.415	0.399	0.105	0.405	0.352	0.323	0.290	0.255
Dividend Payout %	19.39	19.50	6.82	22.50	22.79	25.33	23.77	25.33
Income Statement								
Total Revenue	1,731,609	847,534	3,257,996	2,891,417	2,650,976	2,494,180	2,247,163	1,975,928
EBITDA	184,093	91,419	285,212	322,618	281,642	284,181	256,965	216,738
Depn & Amortn	28,588	13,657	51,142	48,827	47,214	95,115	83,475	70,236
Income Before Taxes	151,533	76,028	212,644	251,400	211,792	167,236	154,281	133,783
Income Taxes	53,037	26,610	70,874	89,247	74,127	56,860	51,097	47,493
Net Income	98,496	49,418	141,770	162,153	137,665	110,376	103,184	86,290
Average Shares	93,163	92,450	91,832	89,956	88,821	86,757	84,615	85,743
Balance Sheet								
Current Assets	1,121,973	1,103,655	1,118,433	1,165,489	984,217	876,949	740,537	645,554
Total Assets	2,185,426	2,147,667	2,058,780	1,945,609	1,729,491	1,516,501	1,389,819	1,184,534
Current Liabilities	513,850	518,230	532,434	465,509	460,447	390,303	340,789	336,401
Long-Term Obligations	124,665	141,368	121,246	320,587	320,181	321,183	340,948	225,173
Total Liabilities	742,550	756,390	745,074	883,480	867,032	780,492	753,338	615,714
Stockholders' Equity	1,442,876	1,391,277	1,313,706	1,062,129	862,459	736,009	636,481	568,820
Shares Outstanding	91,892	91,165	90,764	88,460	87,268	85,242	83,909	83,588
Statistical Record								
Return on Assets %	9.21	9.06	7.06	8.82	8.48	7.60	7.99	7.66
Return on Equity %	14.95	14.82	11.90	16.85	17.22	16.08	17.07	15.65
EBITDA Margin %	10.63	10.79	8.75	11.16	10.62	11.39	11.44	10.97
Net Margin %	5.69	5.83	4.35	5.61	5.19	4.43	4.59	4.37
Asset Turnover	1.58	1.60	1.62	1.57	1.63	1.72	1.74	1.75
Current Ratio	2.18	2.13	2.10	2.50	2.14	2.25	2.17	1.92
Debt to Equity	0.09	0.10	0.09	0.30	0.37	0.44	0.54	0.40
Price Range	55.40-42.05	50.49-39.81	50.49-39.21	39.39-31.45	38.19-25.61	30.28-19.13	21.08-13.04	18.46-14.71
P/E Ratio	25.89-19.65	24.63-19.42	32.79-25.46	21.88-17.47	24.64-16.52	23.84-15.06	17.28-10.69	18.28-14.56
Average Yield %	0.24	0.22	0.24	1.18	1.09	1.23	1.68	1.51

Address: 2525 Armitage Avenue, Melrose Park, IL 60160 **Telephone:** 708-450-3000 **Web Site:** www.alberto.com	**Officers:** Carol L. Bernick - Chmn. Bernice E. Lavin - Vice-Chmn., Treas., Sec. **Transfer Agents:** The Corporation Trust Company, Wilmington, DE	**No of Institutions:** 268 **Shares:** 60,880,248 **% Held:** 66.78

ALFA CORP

Exchange	Symbol	Price	52Wk Range	Yield	P/E
NMS	ALFA	$14.32 (5/31/2005)	15.60-12.82	2.79	13.38

*7 Year Price Score 109.55 *NYSE Composite Index=100 *12 Month Price Score 94.64

TRADING VOLUME (thousand shares)

Interim Earnings (Per Share)

Qtr.	Mar	Jun	Sep	Dec
2002	0.23	0.20	0.22	0.25
2003	0.23	0.24	0.23	0.27
2004	0.32	0.26	0.26	0.28
2005	0.27	...	...	...

Interim Dividends (Per Share)

Amt	Decl	Ex	Rec	Pay
0.087Q	7/26/2004	8/11/2004	8/13/2004	9/1/2004
0.087Q	10/27/2004	11/10/2004	11/15/2004	12/1/2004
0.087Q	1/24/2005	2/11/2005	2/15/2005	3/1/2005
0.10Q	4/28/2005	5/11/2005	5/13/2005	6/1/2005

Indicated Div: $0.40 (Div. Reinv. Plan)

Valuation Analysis

Forecast P/E	12.67 (5/28/2005)		
Market Cap	$1.1 Billion	Book Value	699.6 Million
Price/Book	1.64	Price/Sales	1.70

Dividend Achiever Status

Rank	229	10 Year Growth Rate	7.18%
Total Years of Dividend Growth			19

Business Summary: Insurance (MIC: 8.2 SIC: 331 NAIC: 24126)

Alfa is a financial services holding company that operates predominantly in the insurance industry through its wholly owned subsidiaries Alfa Life Insurance Corporation, Alfa Insurance Corporation, Alfa General Insurance Corporation, Alfa Vision Insurance Corporation, Alfa Agency Mississippi, Inc. and Alfa Agency Georgia, Inc. Co.'s insurance subsidiaries write life insurance in Alabama, Georgia and Mississippi, and property and casualty insurance in Georgia and Mississippi. Co.'s wholly owned non-insurance subsidiaries include Alfa Financial Corporation and Alfa Benefits Corporation, which are engaged in consumer financing, commercial leasing, and benefit services for the Alfa Group.

Recent Developments: For the quarter ended Mar 31 2005, net income decreased 15.3% to $21,570,344 from net income of $25,476,887 in the year-earlier quarter. Revenues were $179,747,866 , up 10.0% from $163,456,080 the year before. Net premiums earned were $154,778,156 versus $139,180,803 in the prior-year quarter, an increase of 11.2%. Net investment income rose 4.9% to $22,975,156 from $21,901,161 a year ago.

Prospects: Earnings are being negatively affected by losses stemming from a series of thunderstorms that struck Alabama and Mississippi in the first quarter of 2005. These storms caused damage to both automobiles and homes, generating claims of more than $20.0 million. Meanwhile, top-line growth is being driven by the recent acquisition of Alfa Vision Insurance Group. Separately, during the fourth quarter of 2004, Co. committed a plan to sell the OFC Capital commercial leasing division of its wholly owned subsidiary, Alfa Financial Corporation. Co. expects to complete the sale of this operation during the second quarter of 2005.

Financial Data

(US$ in Thousands)	3 Mos	12/31/2004	12/31/2003	12/31/2002	12/31/2001	12/31/2000	12/31/1999	12/31/1998
Earnings Per Share	1.07	1.11	0.98	0.90	0.88	0.85	0.80	0.69
Cash Flow Per Share	1.73	1.84	1.27	1.36	1.31	1.52	1.39	1.17
Tang Book Value Per Share	8.44	8.66	7.96	7.09	6.50	6.05	5.17	5.31
Dividends Per Share	0.350	0.343	0.315	0.297	0.282	0.255	0.236	0.219
Dividend Payout %	32.71	30.86	32.14	33.06	32.10	30.00	29.53	31.70
Income Statement								
Premium Income	154,778	561,356	525,229	491,105	452,869	429,197	405,330	391,838
Total Revenue	179,748	660,368	618,047	587,548	546,296	510,313	482,261	460,986
Benefits & Claims	111,019	389,969	364,533	346,456	312,944	295,881	281,716	277,901
Income Before Taxes	28,449	120,629	106,597	99,345	98,094	94,746	92,077	83,265
Income Taxes	6,879	31,184	28,128	27,637	28,133	27,925	27,520	26,549
Net Income	21,570	89,445	78,469	71,708	69,506	66,821	64,557	56,716
Average Shares	80,680	80,489	80,390	79,546	78,963	78,814	80,471	82,296
Balance Sheet								
Total Assets	2,284,373	2,222,698	2,045,075	1,884,055	1,697,604	1,546,303	1,335,347	1,246,659
Total Liabilities	1,584,791	1,531,245	1,406,562	1,317,957	1,188,493	1,072,742	926,679	823,037
Stockholders' Equity	699,585	691,452	638,512	566,098	509,112	473,561	408,667	423,622
Shares Outstanding	80,212	79,833	80,217	79,278	78,359	78,297	79,084	79,736
Statistical Record								
Return on Assets %	3.89	4.18	3.99	4.00	4.29	4.63	5.00	4.69
Return on Equity %	12.53	13.41	13.03	13.34	14.15	15.11	15.51	14.06
Loss Ratio %	71.73	69.47	69.40	70.55	69.10	68.94	69.50	70.92
Net Margin %	12.00	13.54	12.70	12.20	12.72	13.09	13.39	12.30
Price Range	15.60-12.98	15.60-12.86	13.50-10.92	16.05-10.75	12.35-9.06	9.69-7.31	12.13-7.50	12.13-8.13
P/E Ratio	14.58-12.13	14.05-11.59	13.78-11.14	17.83-11.94	14.03-10.30	11.40-8.60	15.16-9.38	17.57-11.78
Average Yield %	2.48	2.47	2.50	2.31	2.69	2.93	2.63	2.24

Address: 2108 East South Boulevard, Montgomery, AL 36116-2015
Telephone: 334-288-3900
Web Site: www.alfains.com

Officers: Jerry A. Newby - Chmn., Pres. C. Lee Ellis - Exec. V.P., Oper., Treas. **Transfer Agents:** American Stock Transfer and Trust Co., New York, NY

Investor Contact: 334-288-3900
No of Institutions: 58
Shares: 6,640,623 **% Held:** 8.28

ALLSTATE CORP. (THE)

Exchange	Symbol	Price	52Wk Range	Yield	P/E
NYS	ALL	$58.20 (5/31/2005)	58.43-43.46	2.20	12.02

*7 Year Price Score 115.69 *NYSE Composite Index=100 *12 Month Price Score 107.59

Interim Earnings (Per Share)

Qtr.	Mar	Jun	Sep	Dec
2002	0.60	0.48	0.35	0.63
2003	0.94	0.84	0.97	1.08
2004	1.34	1.47	0.09	1.64
2005	1.64	...	...	...

Interim Dividends (Per Share)

Amt	Decl	Ex	Rec	Pay
0.28Q	7/13/2004	8/27/2004	8/31/2004	10/1/2004
0.28Q	11/10/2004	11/26/2004	11/30/2004	1/3/2005
0.32Q	2/22/2005	3/9/2005	3/11/2005	4/1/2005
0.32Q	5/17/2005	5/26/2005	5/31/2005	7/1/2005

Indicated Div: $1.28 (Div. Reinv. Plan)

Valuation Analysis

Forecast P/E 9.95 (5/28/2005)

Market Cap $39.1 Billion Book Value 21.3 Billion

Price/Book 1.83 Price/Sales 1.14

Dividend Achiever Status

Rank 144 **10 Year Growth Rate** 11.61%

Total Years of Dividend Growth 11

Business Summary: Insurance (MIC: 8.2 SIC: 331 NAIC: 24126)

Allstate is a holding company for Allstate Insurance. Co.'s business is conducted principally through Allstate Insurance, Allstate Life Insurance and their subsidiaries. Co. is engaged, principally in the U.S. and Canada, in the personal property and casualty insurance business and the life insurance and savings business. As of Dec 31 2004, Co. provided insurance products to more than 16.0 million households through about 13,600 exclusive agents and financial specialists. Co. operates in four business segments: Allstate Protection, Allstate Financial, discontinued lines and coverages, and corporate and other business.

Recent Developments: For the quarter ended Mar 31 2005, net income increased 18.3% to $1,123 million from net income of $949 million in the year-earlier quarter. Revenues were $8,705 million, up 4.7% from $8,311 million the year before. Net premiums earned were $7,205 million versus $6,867 million in the prior-year quarter, an increase of 4.9%. Net investment income rose 8.6% to $1,384 million from $1,274 million a year ago.

Prospects: Co. is off to a solid start for 2005, lead by solid growth in policies in force (PIF). For instance, Allstate brand standard auto and homeowners PIF increased 4.9% and 6.0%, respectively, from the first quarter of 2004, with both standard auto and homeowners experiencing growth in most states. Also, Allstate brand standard auto and homeowners new business premiums written grew 5.3% and 8.4%, respectively, compared with quarter ended Mar 31 2004. Accordingly, Co. confirmed its annual operating income per diluted share guidance for 2005, assuming the level of average expected catastrophe losses used in pricing for the year, in the range of $5.40 to $5.80.

Financial Data
(US$ in Thousands)

	3 Mos	12/31/2004	12/31/2003	12/31/2002	12/31/2001	12/31/2000	12/31/1999	12/31/1998
Earnings Per Share	4.84	4.54	3.83	1.60	1.60	2.95	3.38	3.94
Cash Flow Per Share	8.12	7.84	8.09	6.26	3.18	2.32	2.83	3.47
Tang Book Value Per Share	30.51	30.74	27.89	23.52	22.35	22.26	19.51	21.08
Dividends Per Share	1.160	1.120	0.930	0.840	0.760	0.680	0.600	0.540
Dividend Payout %	23.97	24.67	24.28	52.50	47.50	23.05	17.75	13.71
Income Statement								
Premium Income	7,205,000	28,061,000	26,981,000	25,654,000	24,427,000	24,076,000	21,735,000	20,826,000
Total Revenue	8,705,000	33,936,000	32,149,000	29,579,000	28,865,000	29,134,000	26,959,000	25,879,000
Benefits & Claims	4,474,000	19,461,000	19,283,000	19,427,000	19,203,000	19,585,000	17,257,000	16,016,000
Income Before Taxes	1,538,000	4,586,000	3,571,000	1,540,000	1,285,000	3,047,000	3,907,000	4,745,000
Income Taxes	415,000	1,230,000	846,000	65,000	73,000	795,000	1,148,000	1,422,000
Net Income	1,123,000	3,181,000	2,705,000	1,134,000	1,158,000	2,211,000	2,720,000	3,294,000
Average Shares	683,100	700,300	706,200	709,900	723,300	748,700	803,800	836,600
Balance Sheet								
Total Assets	151,466,000	149,725,000	134,142,000	117,426,000	109,175,000	104,808,000	98,119,000	87,691,000
Total Liabilities	130,141,000	127,902,000	113,577,000	99,788,000	91,779,000	86,607,000	80,554,000	69,701,000
Stockholders' Equity	21,325,000	21,823,000	20,565,000	17,438,000	17,196,000	17,451,000	16,601,000	17,240,000
Shares Outstanding	672,000	683,000	704,000	702,000	712,000	728,000	787,000	818,000
Statistical Record								
Return on Assets %	2.32	2.24	2.15	1.00	1.08	2.17	2.93	3.91
Return on Equity %	15.64	14.97	14.24	6.55	6.68	12.95	16.08	20.05
Loss Ratio %	62.10	69.35	71.47	75.73	78.61	81.35	79.40	76.90
Net Margin %	12.90	9.37	8.41	3.83	4.01	7.59	10.09	12.73
Price Range	54.75-43.22	51.76-42.71	43.03-30.68	41.32-31.56	45.21-31.02	44.00-17.75	40.50-23.50	51.50-37.31
P/E Ratio	11.31-8.93	11.40-9.41	11.23-8.01	25.82-19.72	28.26-19.39	14.92-6.02	11.98-6.95	13.07-9.47
Average Yield %	2.39	2.39	2.52	2.27	2.01	2.41	1.77	1.22

Address: 2775 Sanders Road, Northbrook, IL 60062-6127
Telephone: 847-402-5000
Web Site: www.allstate.com

Officers: Edward M. Liddy - Chmn., Pres., C.E.O. Danny L. Hale - V.P., C.F.O. **Transfer Agents:** Wells Fargo Bank, N.A., St. Paul, MN

Investor Contact: 800-416-8803
No of Institutions: 638
Shares: 447,002,816 **% Held:** 65.81

ALLTEL CORP.

Exchange	Symbol	Price	52Wk Range	Yield	P/E
NYS	AT	$58.17 (5/31/2005)	60.56-49.23	2.61	15.23

*7 Year Price Score 86.93 *NYSE Composite Index=100 *12 Month Price Score 99.55

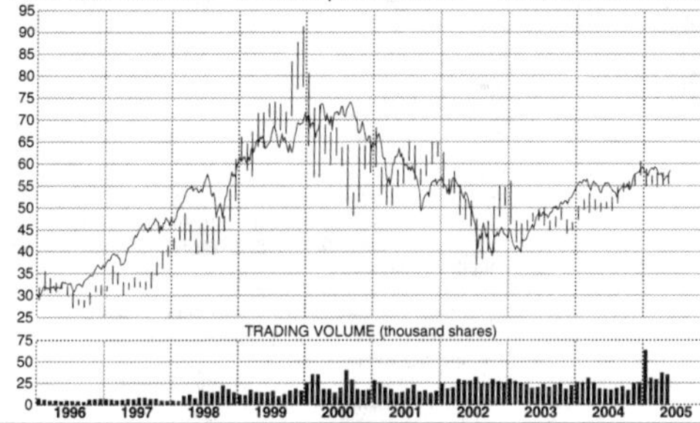

Interim Earnings (Per Share)

Qtr.	Mar	Jun	Sep	Dec
2002	0.68	0.69	0.76	0.82
2003	0.90	1.75	0.78	0.82
2004	0.61	0.85	1.05	0.89
2005	1.03	...	...	...

Interim Dividends (Per Share)

Amt	Decl	Ex	Rec	Pay
0.37Q	7/22/2004	9/8/2004	9/10/2004	10/3/2004
0.38Q	10/21/2004	12/8/2004	12/10/2004	1/3/2005
0.38Q	1/20/2005	2/22/2005	2/24/2005	4/3/2005
0.38Q	4/21/2005	6/8/2005	6/10/2005	7/3/2005

Indicated Div: $1.52 (Div. Reinv. Plan)

Valuation Analysis

Forecast P/E 16.76 (5/28/2005)
Market Cap $17.6 Billion Book Value 7.2 Billion
Price/Book 2.43 Price/Sales 2.09

Dividend Achiever Status

Rank 260 10 Year Growth Rate 5.34%
Total Years of Dividend Growth 44

Business Summary: Communications (MIC: 10.1 SIC: 813 NAIC: 17310)

ALLTEL provides wireless and wireline local, long-distance, network access and Internet services. Telecommunications products are warehoused and sold by Co.'s distribution subsidiary. A subsidiary also publishes telephone directories for affiliates and other independent telephone companies. Another subsidiary provides billing, customer care and other data processing and outsourcing services to telecommunications companies. As of Dec 31 2004, including customers of its wireless, wireline and long-distance services, Co. served over 13 million communications customers in 26 states. Co. also provides Internet, high-speed data services, paging and cable television services in select markets.

Recent Developments: For the quarter ended Mar 31 2005, net income increased 64.9% to $313,000 thousand from net income of $189,800 thousand in the year-earlier quarter. Revenues were $2,126,000 thousand, up 8.4% from $1,961,200 thousand the year before. Operating income was $469,300 thousand versus an income of $394,800 thousand in the prior-year quarter, an increase of 18.9%. Total direct expense was $908,100 thousand versus $818,100 thousand in the prior-year quarter, an increase of 11.0%. Total indirect expense was $748,600 thousand versus $748,300 thousand in the prior-year quarter, an increase of 0.0%.

Prospects: On Apr 15 2005, Co. announced that it has completed the purchase of certain assets from Cingular Wireless LLC. Under the terms of the agreement, Co. acquired former AT&T Wireless properties, including licenses and network assets and subscribers, in Oklahoma City and Grant, OK; Sherman, Denison and Jack, TX; Owensboro and Fulton, KY; Litchfield, CT and Yalobusha, MS. Co. also acquired 20 MHz of spectrum and the network assets formerly held by AT&T Wireless in Wichita, KS, along with spectrum in various counties in Georgia and Texas. The companies also swapped certain partnership interests. Co.'s total consideration included $165.0 million in cash paid to Cingular.

Financial Data

(US$ in Thousands)	3 Mos	12/31/2004	12/31/2003	12/31/2002	12/31/2001	12/31/2000	12/31/1999	12/31/1998
Earnings Per Share	3.82	3.39	4.25	2.96	3.40	6.08	2.47	1.89
Cash Flow Per Share	8.91	8.01	7.94	8.34	6.65	4.75	4.79	4.55
Tang Book Value Per Share	3.41	3.13	2.66	N.M.	6.87	5.92	7.03	5.82
Dividends Per Share	1.500	1.490	1.420	1.370	1.330	1.290	1.235	1.175
Dividend Payout %	39.27	43.95	33.41	46.28	39.12	21.22	50.00	62.17
Income Statement								
Total Revenue	2,126,000	8,246,100	7,979,900	7,983,400	7,598,900	7,067,000	6,302,271	5,194,008
EBITDA	923,600	3,244,200	3,160,400	2,993,500	3,208,400	4,649,900	2,473,199	1,943,137
Depn & Amortn	341,200	1,299,700	1,247,700	1,178,600	1,167,700	988,400	862,172	707,129
Income Before Taxes	495,700	1,592,000	1,534,100	1,465,500	1,751,800	3,350,700	1,330,852	972,339
Income Taxes	182,700	565,300	580,600	541,200	704,300	1,385,300	547,218	446,864
Net Income	313,000	1,046,200	1,330,100	924,300	1,067,000	1,928,800	783,634	525,475
Average Shares	303,500	308,400	312,800	312,300	313,500	317,200	316,814	277,276
Balance Sheet								
Net PPE	7,500,400	7,548,100	7,620,800	7,708,700	6,781,300	6,549,000	5,734,545	4,828,068
Total Assets	16,773,200	16,603,700	16,661,100	16,389,100	12,609,000	12,182,000	10,774,203	9,374,226
Long-Term Obligations	4,924,600	5,352,400	5,581,200	6,145,500	3,861,500	4,611,700	3,750,413	3,491,755
Total Liabilities	9,533,100	9,475,000	9,638,900	10,391,000	7,043,200	7,086,600	6,568,466	6,103,354
Stockholders' Equity	7,240,100	7,128,700	7,022,200	5,998,100	5,565,800	5,095,400	4,205,737	3,270,872
Shares Outstanding	302,562	302,267	312,643	311,182	310,529	312,983	314,257	281,198
Statistical Record								
Return on Assets %	7.02	6.27	8.05	6.37	8.61	16.76	7.78	7.00
Return on Equity %	16.54	14.75	20.43	15.99	20.02	41.36	20.96	19.18
EBITDA Margin %	43.44	39.34	39.60	37.50	42.22	65.80	39.24	37.41
Net Margin %	14.72	12.69	16.67	11.58	14.04	27.29	12.43	10.12
PPE Turnover	1.12	1.08	1.04	1.10	1.14	1.15	1.19	1.30
Asset Turnover	0.50	0.49	0.48	0.55	0.61	0.61	0.63	0.69
Debt to Equity	0.68	0.75	0.79	1.02	0.69	0.91	0.89	1.07
Price Range	60.56-49.00	60.56-46.58	56.05-41.15	62.58-36.93	68.25-50.49	82.69-48.13	91.38-57.06	61.13-39.25
P/E Ratio	15.85-12.83	17.86-13.74	13.19-9.68	21.14-12.48	20.07-14.85	13.60-7.92	36.99-23.10	32.34-20.77
Average Yield %	2.78	2.84	3.03	2.76	2.27	2.07	1.74	2.61

Address: One Allied Drive, Little Rock, AR 72202
Telephone: 501-905-8000
Web Site: www.alltel.com

Officers: Joe T. Ford - Chmn. Scott T. Ford - Pres., C.E.O. **Transfer Agents:** Wachovia Bank, Charlotte, NC

Investor Contact: 501-905-8991
No of Institutions: 499
Shares: 200,967,632 **% Held:** 66.44

ALTRIA GROUP INC

Exchange	Symbol	Price	52Wk Range	Yield	P/E
NYS	MO	$67.14 (5/31/2005)	68.00-45.15	4.35	14.13

*7 Year Price Score 113.62 *NYSE Composite Index=100 *12 Month Price Score 112.46

Interim Earnings (Per Share)

Qtr.	Mar	Jun	Sep	Dec
2002	1.09	1.21	2.06	0.87
2003	1.07	1.20	1.22	1.02
2004	1.07	1.27	1.29	0.94
2005	1.25	...	...	...

Interim Dividends (Per Share)

Amt	Decl	Ex	Rec	Pay
0.73Q	8/25/2004	9/13/2004	9/15/2004	10/12/2004
0.73Q	12/15/2004	12/22/2004	12/27/2004	1/10/2005
0.73Q	2/23/2005	3/11/2005	3/15/2005	4/11/2005
0.73Q	5/25/2005	6/13/2005	6/15/2005	7/11/2005

Indicated Div: $2.92 (Div. Reinv. Plan)

Valuation Analysis

Forecast P/E	13.17 (5/28/2005)		
Market Cap	$138.9 Billion	Book Value	32.4 Billion
Price/Book	4.29	Price/Sales	1.52

Dividend Achiever Status

Rank	151	10 Year Growth Rate	11.28%
Total Years of Dividend Growth			39

Business Summary: Tobacco Products (MIC: 4.2 SIC: 111 NAIC: 12221)

Altria Group, through its wholly-owned subsidiaries, Philip Morris USA Inc., Philip Morris International Inc. and its 85.4% majority-owned subsidiary, Kraft Foods Inc., is engaged in the manufacture and sale of various consumer products, including cigarettes, packaged grocery products, snacks, beverages, cheese and convenient meals. Philip Morris USA's major premium brands are Marlboro, Virginia Slims and Parliament. Its principal discount brand is Basic. Philip Morris Capital Corporation, another wholly-owned subsidiary, is primarily engaged in leasing activities.

Recent Developments: For the quarter ended Mar 31 2005, income from continuing operations increased 18.3% to $2,584,000 thousand from income of $2,185,000 thousand in the year-earlier quarter. Net income increased 18.3% to $2,596,000 thousand from net income of $2,194,000 thousand in the year-earlier quarter. Revenues were $23,618,000 thousand, up 8.7% from $21,721,000 thousand the year before. Operating income rose 12.5% to $4,176,000 thousand. Total direct expense was $15,827,000 thousand versus $14,329,000 thousand in the prior-year quarter, an increase of 10.5%. Total indirect expense was $3,847,000 thousand versus $3,680,000 thousand in the prior-year quarter, an increase of 4.5%.

Prospects: Co. is pleased with overall results in the first quarter that are in line with its expectations. For example, Co.'s Philip Morris USA is generating increases in retail share, driven by Marlboro, and strong income growth. Despite difficult conditions for the entire cigarette industry in Western Europe, Philip Morris International is posting share gains and an increase in income, which was fueled by favorable currency and a one-time inventory sale to its new distributor in Italy. Meanwhile, Co.'s Food business, Kraft continues to make solid progress on its growth plan. For 2005, Co. expects diluted earnings from continuing operations to range from $4.95 to $5.05 per share.

Financial Data

(US$ in Thousands)	3 Mos	12/31/2004	12/31/2003	12/31/2002	12/31/2001	12/31/2000	12/31/1999	12/31/1998
Earnings Per Share	4.75	4.56	4.52	5.21	3.87	3.75	3.19	2.20
Cash Flow Per Share	4.91	5.31	5.33	5.03	4.08	4.87	4.75	3.34
Dividends Per Share	2.870	2.820	2.640	2.440	2.220	2.020	1.840	1.680
Dividend Payout %	60.42	61.84	58.41	46.83	57.36	53.87	57.68	76.36
Income Statement								
Total Revenue	23,618,000	89,610,000	81,832,000	80,408,000	89,924,000	80,356,000	78,596,000	74,391,000
EBITDA	4,302,000	16,787,000	17,350,000	20,563,000	18,039,000	16,396,000	15,192,000	11,667,000
Depn & Amortn	407,000	1,607,000	1,440,000	1,331,000	2,337,000	1,717,000	1,702,000	1,690,000
Income Before Taxes	3,895,000	14,004,000	14,760,000	18,098,000	14,284,000	13,960,000	12,695,000	9,087,000
Income Taxes	1,291,000	4,540,000	5,151,000	6,424,000	5,407,000	5,450,000	5,020,000	3,715,000
Net Income	2,596,000	9,416,000	9,204,000	11,102,000	8,560,000	8,510,000	7,675,000	5,372,000
Average Shares	2,081,000	2,063,000	2,038,000	2,129,000	2,210,000	2,272,000	2,403,000	2,446,000
Balance Sheet								
Current Assets	31,732,000	25,901,000	21,382,000	17,441,000	17,275,000	17,238,000	20,895,000	20,230,000
Total Assets	102,280,000	101,648,000	96,175,000	87,540,000	84,968,000	79,067,000	61,381,000	59,920,000
Current Liabilities	22,945,000	23,574,000	21,393,000	19,082,000	20,141,000	25,949,000	18,017,000	16,379,000
Long-Term Obligations	18,224,000	18,683,000	21,163,000	21,355,000	19,163,000	20,181,000	12,226,000	12,615,000
Total Liabilities	69,871,000	70,934,000	71,098,000	68,062,000	65,348,000	64,062,000	46,076,000	43,723,000
Stockholders' Equity	32,409,000	30,714,000	25,077,000	19,478,000	19,620,000	15,005,000	15,305,000	16,197,000
Shares Outstanding	2,069,121	2,059,527	2,037,263	2,039,259	2,152,503	2,208,897	2,338,520	2,430,535
Statistical Record								
Return on Assets %	9.92	9.49	10.02	12.87	10.44	12.09	12.65	9.27
Return on Equity %	33.14	33.66	41.32	56.79	49.44	56.00	48.73	34.53
EBITDA Margin %	18.21	18.73	21.20	25.57	20.06	20.40	19.33	15.68
Net Margin %	10.99	10.51	11.25	13.81	9.52	10.59	9.77	7.22
Asset Turnover	0.92	0.90	0.89	0.93	1.10	1.14	1.30	1.28
Current Ratio	1.38	1.10	1.00	0.91	0.86	0.66	1.16	1.24
Debt to Equity	0.56	0.61	0.84	1.10	0.98	1.34	0.80	0.78
Price Range	67.00-44.95	61.60-44.95	54.92-28.10	57.72-36.17	53.00-40.13	45.25-18.94	55.25-21.50	58.25-35.19
P/E Ratio	14.11-9.46	13.51-9.86	12.15-6.22	11.08-6.94	13.70-10.37	12.07-5.05	17.32-6.74	26.48-15.99
Average Yield %	5.27	5.40	6.39	5.11	4.70	7.32	5.05	3.79

Address: 120 Park Avenue, New York, NY 10017 **Telephone:** 917-663-5000 **Web Site:** www.altria.com	**Officers:** Louis C. Camilleri - Chmn., C.E.O. André Calantzopoulos - Pres., C.E.O. **Transfer Agents:** First Chicago Trust Company, Jersey City, NJ	**Investor Contact:** 917-663-3460 **No of Institutions:** 836 **Shares:** 1,416,123,264 **% Held:** 68.47

AMBAC FINANCIAL GROUP, INC.

Exchange	Symbol	Price	52Wk Range	Yield	P/E
NYS	ABK	$72.15 (5/31/2005)	84.42-62.20	0.69	10.88

***7 Year Price Score 121.98** *NYSE Composite Index=100 ***12 Month Price Score 89.87**

Interim Earnings (Per Share)

Qtr.	Mar	Jun	Sep	Dec
2002	1.07	1.09	1.21	0.59
2003	1.27	1.48	1.45	1.45
2004	1.55	1.63	1.65	1.69
2005	1.66	...	...	...

Interim Dividends (Per Share)

Amt	Decl	Ex	Rec	Pay
0.11Q	5/5/2004	5/13/2004	5/17/2004	6/2/2004
0.125Q	10/20/2004	11/8/2004	11/10/2004	12/1/2004
0.125Q	1/26/2005	2/8/2005	2/10/2005	3/2/2005
0.125Q	5/3/2005	5/12/2005	5/16/2005	6/1/2005

Indicated Div: $0.50

Valuation Analysis

Forecast P/E	10.99 (5/28/2005)		
Market Cap	$7.8 Billion	Book Value	5.1 Billion
Price/Book	1.53	Price/Sales	5.35

Dividend Achiever Status

Rank	155	10 Year Growth Rate	11.04%
Total Years of Dividend Growth			13

Business Summary: Insurance (MIC: 8.2 SIC: 351 NAIC: 24130)

Ambac Financial Group is a holding company whose subsidiaries provide financial guarantee products and other financial services to clients in the public and private sectors. Co. provides financial guarantees for public finance and structured finance obligations through its principal operating subsidiary, Ambac Assurance. Through its financial services subsidiaries, Co. provides financial and investment products including investment agreements, interest rate and total return swaps and funding conduits, primarily to its clients of the financial guarantee business, which include municipalities and other public entities, health care organizations and asset-backed and structured finance issuers.

Recent Developments: For the quarter ended Mar 31 2005, net income increased 8.1% to $185,543 thousand from net income of $171,611 thousand in the year-earlier quarter. Net premiums earned were $255,753 thousand versus $192,548 thousand in the prior-year quarter, an increase of 32.8%. Net investment income rose 10.2% to $58,090 thousand from $52,720 thousand a year ago.

Prospects: Co. sees weakness in its U.S. structured finance as increased activity in collateralized debt obligations, structured insurance and investor owned utilities is offset by slower consumer asset-backed securities writings. In addition, Co. is experiencing a substantial decline in international writings as very few deals have closed in 2005 demonstrating the unpredictable nature of this sector. However, Co. is experiencing increased deal activity, particularly internationally, and expects backlog and deal flow to drive improvement in future quarters. Looking ahead to full-year 2005, Co. expects earnings growth in the range of 4.0% to 8.0%.

Financial Data (US$ in Thousands)	3 Mos	12/31/2004	12/31/2003	12/31/2002	12/31/2001	12/31/2000	12/31/1999	12/31/1998
Earnings Per Share	6.63	6.53	5.66	3.97	3.97	3.41	2.87	2.37
Cash Flow Per Share	9.24	8.64	9.42	7.60	6.36	4.57	4.33	3.22
Tang Book Value Per Share	47.22	46.13	39.71	34.20	28.26	24.60	19.23	19.98
Dividends Per Share	0.485	0.470	0.420	0.380	0.340	0.307	0.280	0.253
Dividend Payout %	7.32	7.20	7.42	9.57	8.56	8.99	9.74	10.67
Income Statement								
Premium Income	199,634	716,659	620,317	471,534	378,734	311,276	264,426	113,920
Total Revenue	390,820	1,406,708	1,272,208	971,818	724,920	621,310	533,317	457,036
Benefits & Claims	23,472	69,600	53,400	26,700	20,000	15,000	11,000	6,000
Income Before Taxes	251,972	976,782	849,589	564,190	568,727	482,124	404,658	328,912
Income Taxes	66,429	250,942	221,490	131,596	135,821	115,952	96,741	74,918
Net Income	185,543	724,551	618,915	432,594	432,906	366,172	307,917	253,994
Average Shares	111,772	110,898	109,409	109,066	108,948	107,415	107,049	106,995
Balance Sheet								
Total Assets	18,625,776	18,585,258	16,747,314	15,355,538	12,267,695	10,120,300	11,345,096	11,212,311
Total Liabilities	13,512,548	13,560,801	12,492,756	11,730,359	9,284,007	7,524,186	9,326,646	9,116,221
Stockholders' Equity	5,113,228	5,024,457	4,254,558	3,625,179	2,983,688	2,596,114	2,018,450	2,096,090
Shares Outstanding	108,290	108,915	107,144	105,990	105,584	105,550	104,936	104,913
Statistical Record								
Return on Assets %	4.09	4.09	3.86	3.13	3.87	3.40	2.73	2.61
Return on Equity %	15.32	15.57	15.71	13.09	15.52	15.83	14.97	12.80
Loss Ratio %	11.76	9.71	8.61	5.66	5.28	4.82	4.16	5.27
Net Margin %	47.48	51.51	48.65	44.51	59.72	58.94	57.74	55.57
Price Range	84.42-64.04	84.42-64.04	72.19-44.51	69.69-49.90	63.43-45.50	58.31-26.13	40.92-30.08	43.79-27.54
P/E Ratio	12.73-9.66	12.93-9.81	12.75-7.86	17.55-12.57	15.98-11.46	17.10-7.66	14.26-10.48	18.48-11.62
Average Yield %	0.64	0.63	0.68	0.63	0.61	0.77	0.76	0.69

Address: One State Street Plaza, New York, NY 10004 **Telephone:** 212-668-0340 **Web Site:** www.ambac.com	**Officers:** Phillip B. Lassiter - Chmn. Howard C. Pfeffer - Vice-Chmn., Sr. Managing Dir., Public Fin., Investment & Fin. Serv. **Transfer Agents:** Citibank, N.A., New York, NY	**Investor Contact:** 800-221-1854 **No of Institutions:** 363 **Shares:** 101,171,808 **% Held:** 92.87

AMERICAN INTERNATIONAL GROUP INC

Exchange	Symbol	Price	52Wk Range	Yield	P/E
NYS	AIG	$55.55 (5/31/2005)	74.80-50.35	0.90	48.73

Interim Earnings (Per Share)

Qtr.	Mar	Jun	Sep	Dec
2001	0.65	0.69	0.12	0.70
2002	0.75	0.68	0.70	(0.03)
2003	0.74	0.87	0.89	1.03
2004	1.01	1.09	0.95	1.14

Interim Dividends (Per Share)

Amt	Decl	Ex	Rec	Pay
0.075Q	9/15/2004	12/1/2004	12/3/2004	12/17/2004
0.125Q	1/5/2005	3/2/2005	3/4/2005	3/18/2005
0.125Q	3/16/2005	6/1/2005	6/3/2005	6/17/2005
0.125Q	5/18/2005	8/31/2005	9/2/2005	9/16/2005

Indicated Div: $0.50

Valuation Analysis

Forecast P/E	12.75 (5/28/2005)		
Market Cap	$144.7 Billion	Book Value	78.9 Billion
Price/Book	1.83	Price/Sales	1.53

Dividend Achiever Status

Rank	89	**10 Year Growth Rate**	15.21%
Total Years of Dividend Growth			19

Business Summary: Insurance (MIC: 8.2 SIC: 331 NAIC: 24126)

American International Group is a financial services organization, with operations in more than 130 countries and jurisdictions. Co.'s subsidiaries serve commercial, institutional and individual customers. In the U.S., Co.'s subsidiaries underwrite commercial, industrial and life insurance. Co.'s global businesses also include financial services, retirement services and asset management. Co.'s financial services businesses include aircraft leasing, financial products, trading and market making. Co. is engaged in consumer finance through American General Finance, retirement services through AIG SunAmerica and AIG VALIC, and life insurance through AIG American General.

Recent Developments: For the year ended Dec 31 2004, net income advanced 19.1% to $11.05 billion compared with $9.27 billion in the previous year. Results for 2004 included a settlement charge of $53.0 million related to final settlement with the Securities and Exchange Commission with respect to issues arising from certain transactions with Brightpoint, Inc. and The PNC Financial Services Group. Total revenues increased 21.3% to $98.61 billion from $81.30 billion a year earlier. Notably, General Insurance Operations net premiums earned rose 24.3% to $39.46 billion, and Life Insurance & Retirement Services Operations premiums grew 20.9% to $28.40 billion.

Prospects: On May 1 2005, Co. announced that it has decided to restate its financial statements for the years ended Dec 31 2003, 2002, 2001 and 2000, the quarters ended Mar 31, June 30 and Sep 30, 2004 and 2003 and the quarter ended Dec 31 2003. Also, based on its internal review to date, Co. has determined that consolidated shareholders' equity at Dec 31 2004 would be reduced by about $2.70 billion as a result of the adjustments for items classified as corrections of accounting errors totaling approximately $2.00 billion, or as fourth quarter changes in estimates, including estimates for tax accruals, deferred acquisition costs, and other contingencies and allowances, totaling about $700.0 million.

Financial Data

(US$ in Thousands)	9 Mos	6 Mos	3 Mos	12/31/2003	12/31/2002	12/31/2001	12/31/2000	12/31/1999
Earnings Per Share	4.07	4.01	3.79	3.53	2.10	2.02	2.41	2.15
Cash Flow Per Share	13.75	14.28	13.96	13.85	7.15	2.94	2.55	4.44
Tang Book Value Per Share	27.07	25.12	26.49	24.39	20.32	19.94	16.98	14.33
Dividends Per Share	0.270	0.260	0.242	0.224	0.178	0.158	0.141	0.126
Dividend Payout %	6.64	6.48	6.38	6.35	8.48	7.82	5.84	5.87
Income Statement								
Premium Income	50,150,000	32,460,000	16,139,000	54,613,000	44,589,000	38,608,000	31,017,000	27,486,000
Total Revenue	72,857,000	47,446,000	23,637,000	81,303,000	67,482,000	55,459,000	42,440,000	37,751,000
Benefits & Claims	42,709,000	27,275,000	13,734,000	46,886,000	41,927,000	27,222,000	18,565,000	16,738,000
Income Before Taxes	12,638,000	8,680,000	4,291,000	13,908,000	8,142,000	8,139,000	8,349,000	7,512,000
Income Taxes	4,037,000	2,757,000	1,356,000	4,264,000	2,328,000	2,339,000	2,458,000	2,219,000
Net Income	8,030,000	5,518,000	2,656,000	9,274,000	5,519,000	5,363,000	5,636,000	5,055,000
Average Shares	2,628,000	2,631,000	2,633,000	2,628,000	2,634,000	2,650,000	2,343,000	2,350,500
Balance Sheet								
Total Assets	776,420,000	735,982,000	724,154,000	678,346,000	561,229,000	492,982,000	306,577,000	268,238,000
Total Liabilities	697,324,000	662,213,000	647,182,000	606,901,000	499,973,000	438,630,000	265,611,000	234,037,000
Stockholders' Equity	78,903,000	73,577,000	76,779,000	71,253,000	59,103,000	52,150,000	39,619,000	33,306,000
Shares Outstanding	2,604,571	2,605,398	2,608,226	2,608,447	2,609,600	2,615,432	2,332,713	2,323,692
Statistical Record								
Return on Assets %	1.50	1.55	1.51	1.50	1.05	1.34	1.96	2.19
Return on Equity %	14.56	14.85	14.31	14.23	9.92	11.69	15.41	16.73
Loss Ratio %	85.16	84.03	85.10	85.85	94.03	70.51	59.85	60.90
Net Margin %	11.02	11.63	11.24	11.41	8.18	9.67	13.28	13.39
Price Range	76.77-56.59	76.77-55.18	75.12-49.45	66.28-44.47	79.61-51.10	96.88-67.05	103.69-54.29	74.46-51.53
P/E Ratio	18.86-13.90	19.14-13.76	19.82-13.05	18.78-12.60	37.91-24.33	47.96-33.19	43.02-22.53	34.63-23.97
Average Yield %	0.39	0.39	0.39	0.39	0.27	0.19	0.17	0.20

Address: 70 Pine Street, New York, NY 10270 **Telephone:** 212-770-7000 **Web Site:** www.aig.com	**Officers:** Maurice R. Greenberg - Chmn. Thomas R. Tizzio - Sr. Vice-Chmn., Gen. Insurance **Transfer Agents:** EquiServe Trust Company, N.A. Providence, RI	**Investor Contact:** 212-770-6293 **No of Institutions:** 1065 **Shares:** 1,553,557,248 **% Held:** 59.65

AMERICAN STATES WATER CO.

Exchange	Symbol	Price	52Wk Range	Yield	P/E
NYS	AWR	$27.98 (5/31/2005)	28.26-21.90	3.22	21.20

Interim Earnings (Per Share)

Qtr.	Mar	Jun	Sep	Dec
2002	0.25	0.36	0.50	0.23
2003	0.20	0.19	0.51	(0.12)
2004	0.08	0.44	0.52	0.14
2005	0.22	...	...	...

Interim Dividends (Per Share)

Amt	Decl	Ex	Rec	Pay
0.221Q	7/27/2004	8/5/2004	8/9/2004	9/1/2004
0.225Q	11/2/2004	11/9/2004	11/12/2004	12/1/2004
0.225Q	1/31/2005	2/8/2005	2/10/2005	3/1/2005
0.225Q	4/28/2005	5/6/2005	5/10/2005	6/1/2005

Indicated Div: $0.90 (Div. Reinv. Plan)

Valuation Analysis

Forecast P/E 20.81 (5/28/2005)
Market Cap $469.3 Million Book Value 251.8 Million
Price/Book 1.86 Price/Sales 2.03

Dividend Achiever Status

Rank 313 **10 Year Growth Rate** 1.05%
Total Years of Dividend Growth 51

Business Summary: Water Utilities (MIC: 7.2 SIC: 941 NAIC: 21310)

American States Water is a public utility that purchases, produces, distributes, and sells water, and distributes electricity through its primary subsidiary Southern California Water Company (SCW). SCW is organized into one electric customer service area and three water service regions operating within 75 communities in 10 counties in California and provides water service in 21 customer service areas. Through its American States Utility Services subsidiary, Co. performs non-regulated, water related services and operations on a contract basis. Co.'s subsidiary, Chaparral City Water Company, is an Arizona public utility company serving Fountain Hills, AZ and a portion of Scottsdale, AZ.

Recent Developments: For the quarter ended Mar 31 2005, net income increased 228.4% to $3,764 thousand from net income of $1,146 thousand in the year-earlier quarter. Revenues were $49,794 thousand, up 6.7% from $46,651 thousand the year before. Operating income was $8,473 thousand versus an income of $5,550 thousand in the prior-year quarter, an increase of 52.7%. Total direct expense was $23,844 thousand versus $24,234 thousand in the prior-year quarter, a decrease of 1.6%. Total indirect expense was $17,477 thousand versus $16,867 thousand in the prior-year quarter, an increase of 3.6%.

Prospects: Co. is benefiting from strong revenues, largely due to rate increases for nearly all of its Southern California Water Company's water customers in 2004. Also, Co. is benefiting from an increase in water consumption from changes in weather conditions, as well as higher electric revenues due to increased customer usage. Meanwhile, Co. is experiencing higher operating expenses, reflecting increased supply costs due to higher purchased water expenses, partially offset by decreased power purchased for pumping, caused by the need to replace groundwater supply due to wells being removed from service for water quality and mechanical reasons.

Financial Data (US$ in Thousands)	3 Mos	12/31/2004	12/31/2003	12/31/2002	12/31/2001	12/31/2000	12/31/1999	12/31/1998
Earnings Per Share	1.32	1.18	0.78	1.34	1.33	1.27	1.19	1.08
Cash Flow Per Share	2.93	3.21	3.08	1.70	2.62	2.18	2.90	2.34
Tang Book Value Per Share	14.30	14.30	13.97	14.05	13.23	12.75	11.82	11.48
Dividends Per Share	0.892	0.888	0.884	0.871	0.867	0.857	0.853	0.840
Dividend Payout %	67.58	75.25	113.33	65.02	65.00	67.28	71.51	77.78
Income Statement								
Total Revenue	49,794	228,005	212,669	209,205	197,514	183,960	173,421	148,060
Depn & Amortn	5,635	20,824	19,792	18,302	17,951	15,339	14,364	12,929
Income Taxes	...	7,594	6,070	12,949	15,379	15,127	13,345	10,130
Net Income	3,764	18,541	11,892	20,339	20,447	18,086	16,101	14,623
Average Shares	16,805	15,663	15,227	15,157	15,256	14,116	13,437	13,437
Balance Sheet								
Net PPE	676,739	664,165	602,298	563,311	539,842	509,096	449,595	414,753
Total Assets	816,252	810,277	757,475	701,650	683,764	616,646	533,181	484,671
Long-Term Obligations	228,902	228,902	229,799	231,089	245,692	176,452	167,363	120,809
Total Liabilities	564,468	558,812	544,988	488,371	482,182	422,323	372,735	328,772
Stockholders' Equity	251,784	251,465	212,487	213,279	201,582	194,323	160,446	155,899
Shares Outstanding	16,771	16,752	15,212	15,180	15,119	15,113	13,436	13,437
Statistical Record								
Return on Assets %	2.71	2.36	1.63	2.94	3.14	3.14	3.16	3.11
Return on Equity %	9.15	7.97	5.59	9.81	10.33	10.17	10.18	9.48
Net Margin %	7.56	8.13	5.59	9.72	10.35	9.83	9.28	9.88
PPE Turnover	0.36	0.36	0.36	0.38	0.38	0.38	0.40	0.37
Asset Turnover	0.30	0.29	0.29	0.30	0.30	0.32	0.34	0.31
Debt to Equity	0.91	0.91	1.08	1.08	1.22	0.91	1.04	0.77
Price Range	27.55-21.37	26.78-21.37	28.71-21.80	28.85-21.01	25.32-19.35	24.75-17.00	26.50-14.88	19.42-14.50
P/E Ratio	20.87-16.19	22.69-18.11	36.81-27.95	21.53-15.68	19.04-14.55	19.49-13.39	22.27-12.50	17.98-13.43
Average Yield %	3.64	3.65	3.56	3.54	3.86	4.21	4.20	5.03

Address: 630 East Foothill Blvd., San Dimas, CA 91773-1212 **Telephone:** 909-394-3600 **Web Site:** www.aswater.com	**Officers:** Lloyd E. Ross - Chmn. Floyd E. Wicks - Pres., C.E.O. **Transfer Agents:** ChaseMellon Shareholder Services, L.L.C., Ridgefield Park, NJ.	**Investor Contact:** 909-394-3633 **No of Institutions:** 106 **Shares:** 5,533,284 **% Held:** 33.00

AMSOUTH BANCORPORATION

Exchange	Symbol	Price	52Wk Range	Yield	P/E
NYS	ASO	$26.66 (5/31/2005)	26.90-23.84	3.75	14.89

*7 Year Price Score 102.65 *NYSE Composite Index=100 *12 Month Price Score 98.99

Interim Earnings (Per Share)

Qtr.	Mar	Jun	Sep	Dec
2002	0.40	0.42	0.43	0.43
2003	0.44	0.44	0.45	0.45
2004	0.45	0.47	0.33	0.49
2005	0.50	...	...	...

Interim Dividends (Per Share)

Amt	Decl	Ex	Rec	Pay
0.24Q	7/15/2004	9/15/2004	9/17/2004	10/1/2004
0.25Q	10/21/2004	12/16/2004	12/20/2004	1/3/2005
0.25Q	1/20/2005	3/16/2005	3/18/2005	4/1/2005
0.25Q	4/21/2005	6/15/2005	6/17/2005	7/1/2005

Indicated Div: $1.00 (Div. Reinv. Plan)

Valuation Analysis

Forecast P/E 13.18 (6/2/2005)
Market Cap $9.4 Billion Book Value 3.5 Billion
Price/Book 2.70 Price/Sales 2.90

Dividend Achiever Status

Rank 199 **10 Year Growth Rate** 8.75%
Total Years of Dividend Growth 34

TRADING VOLUME (thousand shares)

Business Summary: Commercial Banking (MIC: 8.1 SIC: 022 NAIC: 22110)

AmSouth Bancorporation is a regional bank holding company headquartered in Birmingham, AL. As of Dec 31 2004, Co. had assets of $49.70 billion and operated more than 685 branch banking offices and over 1,250 automated teller machines in the following southeastern states: Alabama, Florida, Tennessee, Mississippi, Georgia, and Louisiana. Co., through its affiliates, provides a full line of traditional and nontraditional financial services including consumer and commercial banking, small business banking, mortgage lending, equipment leasing, annuity and mutual fund sales, and trust and investment management services.

Recent Developments: For the quarter ended Mar 31 2005, net income increased 11.6% to $178,645 thousand from net income of $160,099 thousand in the year-earlier quarter. Net interest income was $379,748 thousand, up 5.6% from $359,497 thousand the year before. Provision for loan losses was $20,600 thousand versus $28,100 thousand in the prior-year quarter, a decrease of 26.7%. Non-interest income fell 2.3% to $215,436 thousand, while non-interest expense declined 0.9% to $319,517 thousand.

Prospects: Co. is pleased with its operating performance, supported by strong, broad-based growth in loans and stronger growth in deposits. The growth in loans has also led to considerable improvement in Co.'s net interest income, which increased 5.6% during the first quarter of fiscal 2005 versus the year before. Also, Co. is enjoying an increase in return on average equity, a higher return on average assets and an improved efficiency ratio. Co. attributes its improved performance to its efforts to capitalize on disruption caused by other banks' merger in many of its largest markets, which it expects to continue to take advantage of in the coming months.

Financial Data

(US$ in Thousands)	3 Mos	12/31/2004	12/31/2003	12/31/2002	12/31/2001	12/31/2000	12/31/1999	12/31/1998
Earnings Per Share	1.79	1.74	1.77	1.68	1.45	0.86	0.86	1.45
Cash Flow Per Share	3.46	2.72	3.06	3.92	2.40	2.23	0.88	1.13
Tang Book Value Per Share	9.89	10.02	9.18	8.82	8.14	7.53	7.56	8.05
Dividends Per Share	0.980	0.970	0.930	0.890	0.850	0.810	0.707	0.567
Dividend Payout %	54.75	55.75	52.54	52.98	58.62	94.19	82.17	39.17
Income Statement								
Interest Income	581,174	2,165,661	2,086,451	2,254,116	2,634,540	3,070,426	2,932,750	1,462,541
Interest Expense	201,426	689,636	671,816	781,476	1,239,656	1,691,323	1,424,804	763,571
Net Interest Income	379,748	1,476,025	1,414,635	1,472,640	1,394,884	1,379,103	1,507,946	698,970
Provision for Losses	20,600	127,750	173,700	213,550	187,100	227,600	165,626	58,134
Non-Interest Income	215,436	1,032,142	855,778	739,361	748,222	669,494	847,557	346,626
Non-Interest Expense	319,517	1,456,938	1,205,577	1,126,622	1,185,394	1,366,435	1,648,506	582,117
Income Before Taxes	255,067	923,479	891,136	871,829	770,612	454,562	541,371	405,345
Income Taxes	76,422	299,981	265,015	262,682	234,266	125,435	200,903	142,633
Net Income	178,645	623,498	626,121	609,147	536,346	329,127	340,468	262,712
Average Shares	358,812	357,952	354,308	362,329	370,948	384,677	396,515	181,921
Balance Sheet								
Net Loans & Leases	32,658,601	32,434,563	28,955,240	26,969,339	24,760,886	24,236,001	25,903,283	12,693,788
Total Assets	50,011,458	49,548,371	45,615,516	40,571,272	38,600,414	38,935,978	43,406,554	19,901,679
Total Deposits	34,828,520	34,232,779	30,440,353	27,315,624	26,167,017	26,623,304	27,912,443	13,283,804
Total Liabilities	46,519,736	45,979,530	42,385,847	37,455,275	35,645,315	36,122,571	40,447,349	18,474,050
Stockholders' Equity	3,491,722	3,568,841	3,229,669	3,115,997	2,955,099	2,813,407	2,959,205	1,427,629
Shares Outstanding	353,051	356,310	351,891	353,424	363,035	373,806	391,374	177,376
Statistical Record								
Return on Assets %	1.32	1.31	1.45	1.54	1.38	0.80	1.08	1.36
Return on Equity %	18.71	18.29	19.73	20.07	18.60	11.37	15.52	18.68
Net Interest Margin %	65.34	68.16	67.80	65.33	52.95	44.92	51.42	47.79
Efficiency Ratio %	40.11	45.56	40.97	37.64	35.04	36.54	43.61	32.18
Loans to Deposits	0.94	0.95	0.95	0.99	0.95	0.91	0.93	0.96
Price Range	26.90-21.95	26.90-21.95	24.58-19.09	22.88-18.28	20.15-15.13	19.88-11.88	33.92-18.94	30.42-21.42
P/E Ratio	15.03-12.26	15.46-12.61	13.89-10.79	13.62-10.88	13.90-10.43	23.11-13.81	39.44-22.02	20.98-14.77
Average Yield %	3.93	3.92	4.28	4.24	4.75	5.08	2.72	2.19

Address: AMSOUTH CENTER, 1900 Fifth Avenue North, Birmingham, AL 35203
Telephone: 205-320-7151
Web Site: www.amsouth.com

Officers: C. Dowd Ritter - Chmn., Pres., C.E.O. Candice W. Bagby - Sr. Exec. V.P., Consumer Banking, Mktg. **Transfer Agents:** The Bank of New York, New York, NY

Investor Contact: 205-801-0265
No of Institutions: 327
Shares: 145,126,928 **% Held:** 41.10

ANCHOR BANCORP WISCONSIN, INC

Exchange	Symbol	Price	52Wk Range	Yield	P/E
NMS	ABCW	$27.62 (5/31/2005)	29.61-24.65	1.96	12.79

*7 Year Price Score 116.31 *NYSE Composite Index=100 *12 Month Price Score 97.82

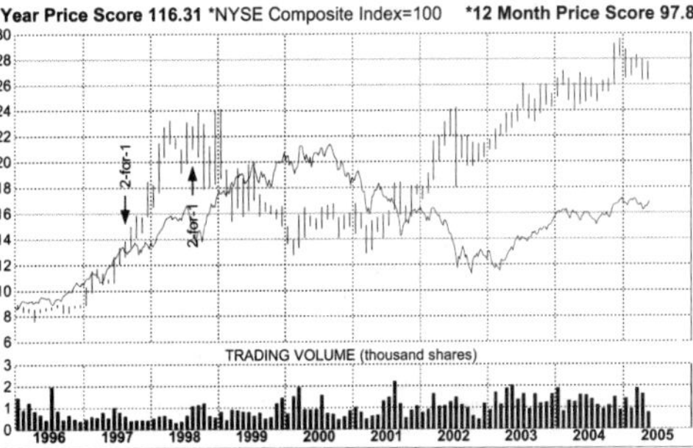

Interim Earnings (Per Share)

Qtr.	Jun	Sep	Dec	Mar
2001-02	0.35	0.37	0.37	0.46
2002-03	0.42	0.49	0.55	0.55
2003-04	0.59	0.48	0.43	0.52
2004-05	0.46	0.46	0.47	0.77

Interim Dividends (Per Share)

Amt	Decl	Ex	Rec	Pay
0.125Q	7/20/2004	7/28/2004	7/30/2004	8/13/2004
0.125Q	10/22/2004	10/28/2004	11/1/2004	11/15/2004
0.125Q	1/21/2005	1/27/2005	1/31/2005	2/15/2005
0.135Q	4/18/2005	4/26/2005	4/28/2005	5/13/2005

Indicated Div: $0.54

Valuation Analysis

Forecast P/E 13.95 (6/2/2005)
Market Cap $634.1 Million Book Value 320.7 Million
Price/Book 1.98 Price/Sales 2.15

Dividend Achiever Status

Rank 19 **10 Year Growth Rate** 24.16%
Total Years of Dividend Growth 11

Business Summary: Other Depository Banking (MIC: 8.5 SIC: 036 NAIC: 22120)

Anchor BanCorp Wisconsin is engaged in the savings and loan business through its wholly-owned banking subsidiary, AnchorBank, fsb. Co. also has a non-banking subsidiary, Investment Directions, Inc., which invests in real estate partnerships. Through AnchorBank, Co. offers checking, savings, money market accounts, mortgages, home equity and other consumer loans, student loans, credit cards, annuities and related consumer financial services. AnchorBank also offers banking services to businesses, including checking accounts, lines of credit, secured loans and commercial real estate loans. As of Mar 31 2004, total assets were $3.81 billion and total deposits amounted to $2.60 billion.

Recent Developments: For the twelve months ended Mar 31 2005, net income increased 4.9% to $49.7 million compared with $47.4 million a year earlier. Net interest income advanced 9.4% to $120.7 million from $110.4 million the previous year. Provision for loan losses amounted to $1.6 million versus $2.0 million in 2004. Total non-interest income climbed 67.1% to $137.2 million compared with $82.1 million the year before. Total non-interest income for 2005 and 2004 included real estate investment partnership revenue of $106.3 million and $49.7 million, respectively. Total non-interest expense rose 48.4% to $162.6 million.

Prospects: Co. is looking to continue its momentum in earnings growth in fiscal 2006, following a year in which experienced considerable gains in its bottom line. Co. attributes its growth to increases in its overall loan portfolio and deposit base. Also, Co. saw considerable gains in its net interest margin, which climbed to 3.29% in the fourth quarter of fiscal 2005 from 3.03% in the previous-year period. Looking ahead to the coming fiscal year, Co. anticipates continuing growth as a result of its upcoming branch expansions in Wisconsin, primarily in Green Bay and the greater Milwaukee area.

Financial Data

(US$ in Thousands)	9 Mos	6 Mos	3 Mos	03/31/2004	03/31/2003	03/31/2002	03/31/2001	03/31/2000
Earnings Per Share	1.90	1.87	1.88	2.02	2.02	1.55	1.16	0.78
Cash Flow Per Share	2.68	5.71	4.90	3.84	2.41	(1.43)	2.41	0.97
Tang Book Value Per Share	13.10	12.87	12.51	12.27	11.40	11.12	9.63	9.02
Dividends Per Share	0.470	0.455	0.440	0.430	0.362	0.323	0.295	0.250
Dividend Payout %	24.68	24.39	23.34	21.29	17.95	20.81	25.43	32.05
Income Statement								
Interest Income	147,183	95,826	47,036	190,262	209,605	225,701	228,647	202,065
Interest Expense	57,711	38,005	18,830	79,907	92,856	128,454	148,096	119,393
Net Interest Income	89,472	57,821	28,206	110,355	116,749	97,247	80,551	82,672
Provision for Losses	1,414	750	450	1,950	1,800	2,485	945	1,306
Non-Interest Income	76,259	53,046	30,263	82,076	32,753	21,615	13,503	13,717
Non-Interest Expense	106,926	73,427	40,428	113,641	68,004	59,531	51,450	59,985
Income Before Taxes	52,426	33,748	16,009	76,840	79,698	56,846	41,659	35,098
Income Taxes	20,227	12,469	5,412	29,471	30,135	20,479	14,682	15,596
Net Income	32,199	21,279	10,597	47,369	49,563	36,367	26,977	19,502
Average Shares	23,059	23,123	23,077	23,399	24,592	23,462	23,207	25,159
Balance Sheet								
Net Loans & Leases	3,304,155	3,238,883	3,173,168	3,066,812	2,770,988	2,627,248	2,414,976	2,302,721
Total Assets	3,934,387	3,914,257	3,839,653	3,810,386	3,538,621	3,507,076	3,127,474	2,911,152
Total Deposits	2,705,495	2,681,757	2,663,376	2,602,954	2,574,188	2,553,987	2,119,320	1,897,369
Total Liabilities	3,606,671	3,591,384	3,525,648	3,502,147	3,245,617	3,229,564	2,907,862	2,693,937
Stockholders' Equity	320,749	316,359	307,715	301,548	293,004	277,512	219,612	217,215
Shares Outstanding	22,958	23,028	22,997	22,954	23,942	24,950	22,814	24,088
Statistical Record								
Return on Assets %	1.16	1.14	1.17	1.29	1.41	1.10	0.89	0.77
Return on Equity %	14.27	14.19	14.41	15.89	17.37	14.63	12.35	10.82
Net Interest Margin %	61.63	60.70	59.97	58.00	55.70	43.09	35.23	40.91
Efficiency Ratio %	44.92	46.11	52.30	41.73	28.06	24.07	21.25	27.80
Loans to Deposits	1.22	1.21	1.19	1.18	1.08	1.03	1.14	1.21
Price Range	29.61-24.00	27.10-23.48	27.10-23.08	27.10-21.95	24.25-17.99	21.64-13.13	16.75-12.88	20.00-12.75
P/E Ratio	15.58-12.63	14.49-12.56	14.41-12.28	13.42-10.87	12.00-8.91	13.96-8.47	14.44-11.10	25.64-16.35
Average Yield %	1.80	1.78	1.74	1.74	1.69	1.94	1.92	1.54

Address: 25 West Main Street, Madison, WI 53703
Telephone: 608-252-8700
Web Site: www.anchorbank.com

Officers: Douglas J. Timmerman - Chmn., Pres., C.E.O. Michael W. Helser - C.F.O., Treas. **Transfer Agents:** American Stock Transfer & Trust Company, New York, NY

Investor Contact: 608-252-1810
No of Institutions: 96
Shares: 8,772,373 **% Held:** 38.58

ANHEUSER-BUSCH COS., INC.

Exchange	Symbol	Price	52Wk Range	Yield	P/E
NYS	BUD	$46.85 (5/31/2005)	54.29-45.10	2.09	17.04

Interim Earnings (Per Share)

Qtr.	Mar	Jun	Sep	Dec
2002	0.51	0.66	0.71	0.32
2003	0.57	0.75	0.80	0.36
2004	0.67	0.83	0.85	0.42
2005	0.65	...	...	...

Interim Dividends (Per Share)

Amt	Decl	Ex	Rec	Pay
0.245Q	7/28/2004	8/5/2004	8/9/2004	9/9/2004
0.245Q	10/27/2004	11/5/2004	11/9/2004	12/9/2004
0.245Q	1/12/2005	2/7/2005	2/9/2005	3/9/2005
0.245Q	4/27/2005	5/5/2005	5/9/2005	6/9/2005

Indicated Div: $0.98 (Div. Reinv. Plan)

Valuation Analysis

Forecast P/E	17.27 (5/28/2005)		
Market Cap	$36.4 Billion	Book Value	2.6 Billion
Price/Book	13.99	Price/Sales	2.42

Dividend Achiever Status

Rank	185	**10 Year Growth Rate**	9.36%
Total Years of Dividend Growth			30

Business Summary: Food (MIC: 4.1 SIC: 082 NAIC: 12120)

Anheuser-Busch Companies is the parent holding company of Anheuser-Busch, Inc., the world's largest brewer of beer. Co.'s beer is sold under brand names including Budweiser, Michelob, Busch, and Natural Light. Worldwide sales of Co.'s beer brands aggregated 116.8 million barrels in 2004. Additionally, theme park operations are conducted through Co.'s subsidiary, Busch Entertainment Corporation, which owned nine theme parks as of Dec 31 2004. Co. also engages in packaging, malt and rice production, international beer, non-beer beverages, real estate development, marketing communications, and transportation services.

Recent Developments: For the quarter ended Mar 31 2005, net income decreased 6.7% to $512,800 thousand from net income of $549,900 thousand in the year-earlier quarter. Revenues were $7,127,400 thousand, up 2.5% from $6,954,000 thousand the year before. Operating income was $732,400 thousand versus an income of $821,400 thousand in the prior-year quarter, a decrease of 10.8%. Total direct expense was $2,227,200 thousand versus $2,073,300 thousand in the prior-year quarter, an increase of 7.4%. Total indirect expense was $604,100 thousand versus $582,300 thousand in the prior-year quarter, an increase of 3.7%.

Prospects: Earnings are being negatively affected by volume declines in the U.S. and increased commodity cost pressures, partially offset by sharply higher international volume. In an effort to enhance beer volume growth, Co. is implementing a number of initiatives, including increased investments in domestic marketing, the continued roll out of new products, led by Budweiser Select, stepped up on premise sales initiatives, new packaging, and strategic price promotions. As a result, Co. anticipates full-year 2005 earnings per share growth in the range of 1.0% to 4.0%, or about $2.76 to $2.84 per share, excluding one-time items.

Financial Data

(US$ in Thousands)	3 Mos	12/31/2004	12/31/2003	12/31/2002	12/31/2001	12/31/2000	12/31/1999	12/31/1998
Earnings Per Share	2.75	2.77	2.48	2.20	1.89	1.69	1.47	1.26
Cash Flow Per Share	3.70	3.67	3.60	3.19	2.65	2.48	2.22	2.26
Tang Book Value Per Share	1.83	1.88	2.74	3.19	4.15	4.11	3.79	3.96
Dividends Per Share	0.955	0.930	0.830	0.750	0.690	0.630	0.580	0.540
Dividend Payout %	34.73	33.57	33.47	34.09	36.51	37.28	39.46	42.69
Income Statement								
Total Revenue	3,563,700	14,934,200	14,146,700	13,566,400	12,911,500	12,261,800	11,703,700	11,245,800
EBITDA	988,700	4,332,400	4,076,900	3,820,600	3,545,300	3,297,200	3,069,900	2,850,700
Depn & Amortn	236,800	932,700	877,200	847,300	834,500	803,500	777,000	738,400
Income Before Taxes	644,300	2,999,400	2,824,300	2,623,600	2,377,600	2,179,900	2,007,600	1,852,600
Income Taxes	237,400	1,163,200	1,093,300	1,041,500	913,200	828,300	762,900	704,300
Net Income	512,800	2,240,300	2,075,900	1,933,800	1,704,500	1,551,600	1,402,200	1,233,300
Average Shares	785,900	808,500	837,000	878,900	901,600	919,700	953,600	975,000
Balance Sheet								
Current Assets	2,044,700	1,818,400	1,630,300	1,504,700	1,550,400	1,547,900	1,600,600	1,640,400
Total Assets	16,537,200	16,173,400	14,689,500	14,119,500	13,862,000	13,084,500	12,640,400	12,484,300
Current Liabilities	2,143,500	1,969,000	1,857,200	1,787,700	1,732,300	1,675,700	1,987,200	1,730,300
Long-Term Obligations	8,585,600	8,278,600	7,285,400	6,603,200	5,983,900	5,374,500	4,880,600	4,718,600
Total Liabilities	13,938,000	13,505,300	11,977,800	11,067,200	9,800,500	8,955,600	8,718,900	8,268,300
Stockholders' Equity	2,599,200	2,668,100	2,711,700	3,052,300	4,061,500	4,128,900	3,921,500	4,216,000
Shares Outstanding	776,367	785,000	813,100	846,600	879,100	903,600	922,200	953,200
Statistical Record								
Return on Assets %	13.92	14.48	14.41	13.82	12.65	12.03	11.16	10.19
Return on Equity %	82.84	83.06	72.03	54.37	41.62	38.44	34.46	29.87
EBITDA Margin %	27.74	29.01	28.82	28.16	27.46	26.89	26.23	25.35
Net Margin %	14.39	15.00	14.67	14.25	13.20	12.65	11.98	10.97
Asset Turnover	0.95	0.97	0.98	0.97	0.96	0.95	0.93	0.93
Current Ratio	0.95	0.92	0.88	0.84	0.89	0.92	0.81	0.95
Debt to Equity	3.30	3.10	2.69	2.16	1.47	1.30	1.24	1.12
Price Range	54.29-47.26	54.29-49.45	53.69-45.92	54.97-44.00	46.51-38.50	49.81-27.47	40.81-32.59	34.13-21.72
P/E Ratio	19.74-17.19	19.60-17.85	21.65-18.52	24.99-20.00	24.61-20.37	29.47-16.25	27.76-22.17	27.08-17.24
Average Yield %	1.88	1.80	1.65	1.49	1.62	1.62	1.59	2.11

Address: One Busch Place, St. Louis, MO 63118 **Telephone:** 314-577-2000 **Web Site:** www.anheuser-busch.com	**Officers:** August A. Busch III - Chmn. Keith M. Kasen - Chmn. **Transfer Agents:** Mellon Investor Services, LLC, Ridgefield Park, NJ	**Investor Contact:** 314-577-9629 **No of Institutions:** 705 **Shares:** 447,269,248 **% Held:** 57.57

APPLEBEE'S INTERNATIONAL, INC.

Exchange	Symbol	Price	52Wk Range	Yield	P/E
NMS	APPB	$27.27 (5/31/2005)	28.91-22.79	0.22	19.91

*7 Year Price Score 150.46 *NYSE Composite Index=100 *12 Month Price Score 98.95

Interim Earnings (Per Share)

Qtr.	Mar	Jun	Sep	Dec
2002	0.24	0.25	0.25	0.24
2003	0.29	0.24	0.30	0.27
2004	0.35	0.34	0.34	0.31
2005	0.38	...	...	...

Interim Dividends (Per Share)

Amt	Decl	Ex	Rec	Pay
0.04A	12/12/2002	12/24/2002	12/27/2002	1/30/2003
0.047A	12/12/2003	12/23/2003	12/26/2003	1/23/2004
50%	5/13/2004	6/16/2004	5/28/2004	6/15/2004
0.06A	12/10/2004	12/21/2004	12/24/2004	1/21/2005

Indicated Div: $0.06

Valuation Analysis

Forecast P/E	18.15 (6/3/2005)		
Market Cap	$2.2 Billion	Book Value	520.8 Million
Price/Book	4.25	Price/Sales	1.94

Dividend Achiever Status

Rank	94	10 Year Growth Rate	14.69%
Total Years of Dividend Growth			13

Business Summary: Hospitality & Tourism (MIC: 5.1 SIC: 812 NAIC: 22110)

Applebee's International develops, franchises and operates a national chain of casual dining restaurants under the trademark of "Applebee's Neighborhood Grill & Bar." Each of the restaurants is designed as a neighborhood establishment, featuring a selection of moderately-priced food and beverage items with full-service luncheon and evening dining. The restaurants feature a selection of entrees, including beef, chicken, seafood and pasta items prepared in a variety of cuisines, as well as appetizers, salads, sandwiches, specialty drinks and desserts. As of Dec 26 2004, there were 1,671 Applebee's restaurants in 49 states and 12 countries.

Recent Developments: For the first quarter ended Mar 27 2005, net earnings increased 6.5% to $31.7 million compared with $29.7 million in the corresponding prior-year quarter. Results for 2005 and 2004 included losses on dispositions of restaurants and equipment of $297,000 and $495,000, respectively. Total revenues rose 9.8% to $304.5 million from $277.4 million a year earlier. Company restaurant sales advanced 11.0% to $270.5 million, while franchise royalties and fees grew 7.5% to $33.0 million. Other franchise income dropped 65.8% to $1.1 million. Operating earnings increased 6.6% to $48.3 million from $45.4 million the year before.

Prospects: Co. is aware of sales trends and remains intent on maintaining its proposition with continued food initiatives, including its spring menu launched in April 2005. Co.'s brand awareness is being enhanced by the more than 30.0% increase in its national advertising budget that is designed to convey multiple messages to its guests. In addition to accelerating its development pace, Co. plans to optimize its initiatives and will continue to focus on improving operations throughout the system, as well as leveraging key strategies including Carside To Go™ and its alliance with Weight Watchers.

Financial Data

(US$ in Thousands)	3 Mos	12/26/2004	12/28/2003	12/29/2002	12/30/2001	12/31/2000	12/26/1999	12/27/1998
Earnings Per Share	1.37	1.33	1.09	0.97	0.76	0.71	0.56	0.49
Cash Flow Per Share	2.58	2.34	2.13	1.63	1.27	1.23	1.05	0.91
Tang Book Value Per Share	4.88	4.58	4.27	3.64	2.92	2.30	1.80	1.93
Dividends Per Share	0.060	0.060	0.047	0.040	0.036	0.033	0.030	0.027
Dividend Payout %	4.37	4.51	4.27	4.11	4.71	4.58	5.29	5.45
Income Statement								
Total Revenue	304,531	1,111,634	990,138	826,796	744,344	690,152	669,584	647,562
EBITDA	62,060	216,835	188,706	167,990	149,612	146,118	132,154	125,481
Depn & Amortn	13,318	46,714	40,788	35,686	38,279	36,876	35,605	35,150
Income Before Taxes	48,405	168,495	146,185	130,136	103,877	99,938	85,735	80,409
Income Taxes	16,748	57,630	52,627	47,109	38,227	36,777	31,537	29,753
Net Income	31,657	110,865	93,558	83,027	64,401	63,161	54,198	50,015
Average Shares	82,375	83,600	85,408	85,383	85,315	88,755	96,528	102,549
Balance Sheet								
Current Assets	98,767	100,657	86,622	69,579	67,999	53,181	34,211	34,909
Total Assets	775,750	754,431	644,001	566,114	500,411	471,707	442,216	510,904
Current Liabilities	153,536	151,698	149,332	115,186	97,746	93,835	77,662	65,951
Long-Term Obligations	25,412	35,472	20,670	52,186	74,525	90,461	106,293	145,522
Total Liabilities	254,935	257,704	184,269	173,533	175,228	189,989	188,343	214,851
Stockholders' Equity	520,815	496,727	459,732	392,581	325,183	281,718	253,873	296,053
Shares Outstanding	81,074	81,128	82,789	83,082	83,722	85,116	89,765	99,697
Statistical Record								
Return on Assets %	15.74	15.90	15.51	15.61	13.29	13.60	11.40	11.29
Return on Equity %	22.91	23.25	22.01	23.20	21.28	23.20	19.77	17.10
EBITDA Margin %	20.38	19.51	19.06	20.32	20.10	21.17	19.74	19.38
Net Margin %	10.40	9.97	9.45	10.04	8.65	9.15	8.09	7.72
Asset Turnover	1.59	1.59	1.64	1.55	1.54	1.49	1.41	1.46
Current Ratio	0.64	0.66	0.58	0.60	0.70	0.57	0.44	0.53
Debt to Equity	0.05	0.07	0.04	0.13	0.23	0.32	0.42	0.49
Price Range	28.91-22.79	28.39-22.79	26.59-15.39	18.18-13.09	16.24-8.50	11.07-6.56	10.22-6.00	7.65-4.81
P/E Ratio	21.10-16.64	21.35-17.14	24.40-14.12	18.74-13.49	21.37-11.18	15.60-9.23	18.25-10.71	15.61-9.83
Average Yield %	0.23	0.24	0.23	0.25	0.29	0.39	0.35	0.42

Address: 4551 W. 107th Street, Overland Park, KS 66207
Telephone: 913-967-4000
Web Site: www.applebees.com

Officers: Lloyd L. Hill - Chmn., Pres., C.E.O. Steven K. Lumpkin - Exec. V.P., C.F.O., Treas. **Transfer Agents:** American Stock Transfer & Trust Co, New York, NY

Investor Contact: 913-967-4109
No of Institutions: 198
Shares: 63,501,784 **% Held:** 78.32

APTARGROUP INC.

Exchange	Symbol	Price	52Wk Range	Yield	P/E
NYS	ATR	$50.00 (5/31/2005)	54.43-40.12	1.20	19.69

***7 Year Price Score 127.72** *NYSE Composite Index=100 ***12 Month Price Score 102.16**

TRADING VOLUME (thousand shares)

Interim Earnings (Per Share)

Qtr.	Mar	Jun	Sep	Dec
2002	0.36	0.48	0.49	0.50
2003	0.53	0.58	0.51	0.54
2004	0.57	0.61	0.68	0.65
2005	0.60	...	...	...

Interim Dividends (Per Share)

Amt	Decl	Ex	Rec	Pay
0.15Q	7/16/2004	7/23/2004	7/27/2004	8/17/2004
0.15Q	10/13/2004	10/26/2004	10/28/2004	11/18/2004
0.15Q	1/20/2005	1/31/2005	2/2/2005	2/24/2005
0.15Q	4/14/2005	4/27/2005	4/29/2005	5/20/2005

Indicated Div: $0.60

Valuation Analysis

Forecast P/E	18.33 (5/28/2005)		
Market Cap	$1.8 Billion	Book Value	848.0 Million
Price/Book	2.09	Price/Sales	1.34

Dividend Achiever Status

Rank	103	**10 Year Growth Rate**	14.36%
Total Years of Dividend Growth			11

Business Summary: Plastics (MIC: 11.7 SIC: 089 NAIC: 26199)

AptarGroup designs, manufactures and sells consumer product dispensing systems for the personal care, fragrance/cosmetic, pharmaceutical, household and food/beverage markets. Operations are divided into two segments, Dispensing Systems and SeaquistPerfect. The Dispensing Systems segment sells primarily non-aerosol spray and lotion pumps, plastic dispensing and non-dispensing closures, and metered dose aerosol valves to the fragrance/cosmetic, pharmaceutical, personal care, household and food/beverage markets. SeaquistPerfect sells primarily aerosol valves and accessories and certain non-aerosol spray and lotion pumps mainly for the personal care, household and food/beverage markets.

Recent Developments: For the quarter ended Mar 31 2005, net income increased 3.9% to $22,068 thousand from net income of $21,235 thousand in the year-earlier quarter. Revenues were $343,999 thousand, up 9.0% from $315,603 thousand the year before. Operating income was $34,349 thousand versus an income of $31,703 thousand in the prior-year quarter, an increase of 8.3%. Total direct expense was $232,478 thousand versus $211,581 thousand in the prior-year quarter, an increase of 9.9%. Total indirect expense was $77,172 thousand versus $72,319 thousand in the prior-year quarter, an increase of 6.7%.

Prospects: Co. is seeing increased demand for its products across all of the markets it serves, which, along with price increases, is leading to strong sales performance. Demand for Co.'s dispensing systems is particularly strong from the food/beverage, personal care and household markets. Higher sales levels are allowing Co. to overcome the negative effects of the weaker dollar on imports to the U.S., higher costs of materials and continuing price competition. Looking ahead, Co. expects this momentum to continue into the second quarter of 2005 with particularly strong demand anticipated from the personal care, pharmaceutical and food/beverage markets.

Financial Data

(US$ in Thousands)	3 Mos	12/31/2004	12/31/2003	12/31/2002	12/31/2001	12/31/2000	12/31/1999	12/31/1998
Earnings Per Share	2.54	2.51	2.16	1.82	1.61	1.78	1.59	1.65
Cash Flow Per Share	5.03	5.05	3.87	4.30	3.60	3.63	3.26	2.36
Tang Book Value Per Share	19.31	18.81	16.76	12.11	9.01	8.55	8.03	10.13
Dividends Per Share	0.520	0.440	0.260	0.240	0.220	0.200	0.180	0.160
Dividend Payout %	20.47	17.53	12.04	13.19	13.66	11.24	11.32	9.70
Income Statement								
Total Revenue	343,999	1,296,608	1,114,689	926,691	891,986	883,481	834,317	713,506
EBITDA	59,908	237,427	210,023	179,111	175,689	186,109	173,524	158,940
Depn & Amortn	25,532	94,493	85,852	72,141	73,584	70,949	68,670	54,446
Income Before Taxes	32,453	137,177	117,270	98,358	88,355	97,922	91,778	99,189
Income Taxes	10,385	43,890	37,591	31,711	29,447	33,256	33,066	38,368
Net Income	22,068	93,287	79,679	66,647	58,844	64,666	58,712	60,821
Average Shares	36,773	37,157	36,901	36,623	36,529	36,369	36,913	36,799
Balance Sheet								
Current Assets	645,372	661,229	602,454	447,196	374,915	407,549	351,234	316,649
Total Assets	1,363,676	1,374,026	1,264,343	1,047,671	915,327	952,239	863,298	714,673
Current Liabilities	292,145	276,861	283,220	162,688	154,151	203,102	159,905	167,433
Long-Term Obligations	142,228	142,581	125,196	219,182	239,387	252,752	235,649	80,875
Total Liabilities	515,651	500,829	481,292	453,204	446,123	511,699	443,029	299,165
Stockholders' Equity	848,025	873,197	783,051	594,467	469,204	440,540	420,269	415,508
Shares Outstanding	35,492	38,200	37,700	37,200	37,000	36,600	36,500	36,100
Statistical Record								
Return on Assets %	7.12	7.05	6.89	6.79	6.30	7.10	7.44	9.36
Return on Equity %	11.48	11.23	11.57	12.53	12.94	14.98	14.05	16.06
EBITDA Margin %	17.42	18.31	18.84	19.33	19.70	21.07	20.80	22.28
Net Margin %	6.42	7.19	7.15	7.19	6.60	7.32	7.04	8.52
Asset Turnover	1.00	0.98	0.96	0.94	0.96	0.97	1.06	1.10
Current Ratio	2.21	2.39	2.13	2.75	2.43	2.01	2.20	1.89
Debt to Equity	0.17	0.16	0.16	0.37	0.51	0.57	0.56	0.19
Price Range	54.43-37.83	54.43-37.38	39.48-26.51	38.70-25.12	36.90-27.38	30.00-19.88	30.81-22.75	32.94-20.25
P/E Ratio	21.43-14.89	21.69-14.89	18.28-12.27	21.26-13.80	22.92-17.00	16.85-11.17	19.38-14.31	19.96-12.27
Average Yield %	1.13	1.01	0.75	0.75	0.69	0.80	0.66	0.56

Address: 475 West Terra Cotta Avenue, Suite E, Crystal Lake, IL 60014
Telephone: 815-477-0424
Web Site: www.aptargroup.com

Officers: King Harris - Chmn. Peter Pfeiffer - Vice-Chmn. **Transfer Agents:** Mellon Investor Services, LLC, South Hackensack, NJ

No of Institutions: 175
Shares: 30,079,144 **% Held:** 84.13

AQUA AMERICA INC

Exchange	Symbol	Price	52Wk Range	Yield	P/E
NYS	WTR	$27.22 (5/31/2005)	27.92-18.91	1.91	30.58

*7 Year Price Score 124.65 *NYSE Composite Index=100 *12 Month Price Score 111.09

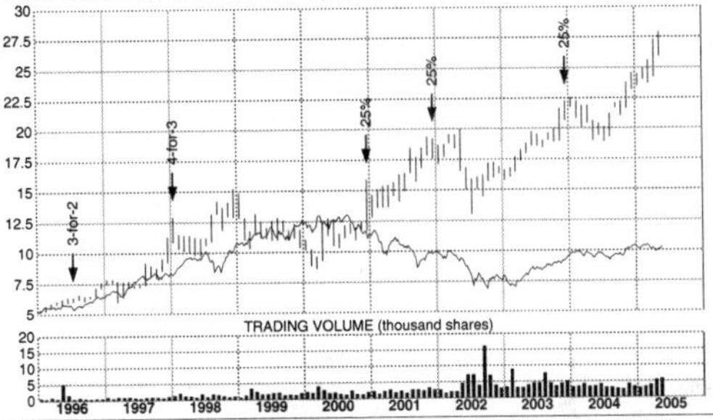

TRADING VOLUME (thousand shares)

Interim Earnings (Per Share)

Qtr.	Mar	Jun	Sep	Dec
2002	0.14	0.17	0.25	0.22
2003	0.15	0.18	0.26	0.20
2004	0.17	0.19	0.26	0.24
2005	0.20	...	...	...

Interim Dividends (Per Share)

Amt	Decl	Ex	Rec	Pay
0.12Q	8/3/2004	8/12/2004	8/16/2004	9/1/2004
0.13Q	8/3/2004	11/10/2004	11/15/2004	12/1/2004
0.13Q	1/28/2005	2/10/2005	2/14/2005	3/1/2005
0.13Q	5/4/2005	5/16/2005	5/18/2005	6/1/2005

Indicated Div: $0.52 (Div. Reinv. Plan)

Valuation Analysis

Forecast P/E	28.57 (5/28/2005)		
Market Cap	$2.6 Billion	Book Value	760.2 Million
Price/Book	3.43	Price/Sales	5.71

Dividend Achiever Status

Rank	251	10 Year Growth Rate	5.70%
Total Years of Dividend Growth			13

Business Summary: Water Utilities (MIC: 7.2 SIC: 941 NAIC: 21310)

Aqua America is a holding company. Through its subsidiaries, Co. is engaged in operating regulated utilities that provide water or wastewater services to approximately 2.5 million people in 14 states. Co.'s largest subsidiary, Aqua Pennsylvania, Inc. provides water or wastewater services to about 1.3 million residents in the suburban areas north and west of the city of Philadelphia and 19 other counties in PA. Co. also provides water and wastewater services through operating and maintenance contracts with municipal authorities and other parties close to its operating companies' service territories. Co. is the largest U.S.-based publicly-traded water utility based on number of people served.

Recent Developments: For the quarter ended Mar 31 2005, net income increased 21.2% to $18,871 thousand from net income of $15,575 thousand in the year-earlier quarter. Revenues were $113,988 thousand, up 14.3% from $99,768 thousand the year before. Operating income was $42,771 thousand versus an income of $36,444 thousand in the prior-year quarter, an increase of 17.4%. Total direct expense was $47,309 thousand versus $41,831 thousand in the prior-year quarter, an increase of 13.1%. Total indirect expense was $23,908 thousand versus $21,493 thousand in the prior-year quarter, an increase of 11.2%.

Prospects: Co. is benefiting from its continuing growth-through-acquisition strategy, as Co. has completed eleven acquisitions and growth ventures throughout several states in recent months. Co. believes that these acquisitions are forming the building blocks for its future growth. They should provide Co. with new platforms for future expansions and consolidation as well as new opportunities to invest needed capital, which in turns helps to support Co.'s earnings growth. Meanwhile, Co. prepares to enter the higher customer demand period of May to September and is pleased to report that all reservoirs are filled to capacity. Co. expects weather to affect earnings during this period from 5.0% to 10.0%.

Financial Data (US$ in Thousands)	3 Mos	12/31/2004	12/31/2003	12/31/2002	12/31/2001	12/31/2000	12/31/1999	12/31/1998
Earnings Per Share	0.89	0.85	0.79	0.78	0.70	0.65	0.45	0.53
Cash Flow Per Share	1.88	1.86	1.62	1.42	1.20	1.07	0.93	1.03
Tang Book Value Per Share	7.94	7.64	7.12	5.81	5.53	5.13	4.58	4.28
Dividends Per Share	0.500	0.490	0.486	0.430	0.404	0.376	0.358	0.340
Dividend Payout %	56.18	57.65	61.52	55.41	57.99	58.12	79.55	64.56
Income Statement								
Total Revenue	113,988	442,039	367,233	322,028	307,280	275,538	257,326	150,977
EBITDA	59,527	239,674	212,843	193,970	179,114	161,455	128,516	85,030
Depn & Amortn	15,911	58,864	51,463	44,322	40,168	34,100	31,903	17,630
Income Before Taxes	30,821	132,131	116,718	109,252	99,087	86,995	62,915	48,424
Income Taxes	11,950	52,124	45,923	42,046	38,976	34,105	26,531	19,605
Net Income	18,871	80,007	70,795	67,206	60,111	52,890	36,384	28,819
Average Shares	96,665	94,282	89,244	86,538	85,943	81,767	80,673	54,445
Balance Sheet								
Net PPE	2,088,799	2,069,812	1,824,291	1,486,703	1,368,115	1,251,427	1,135,364	609,808
Total Assets	2,348,552	2,340,248	2,069,736	1,717,069	1,560,339	1,414,010	1,280,805	701,450
Long-Term Obligations	811,000	784,461	696,666	582,910	516,520	468,769	413,752	261,826
Total Liabilities	1,588,315	1,591,780	1,410,706	1,223,972	1,086,506	981,663	911,904	466,691
Stockholders' Equity	760,237	748,468	659,030	493,097	473,833	432,347	368,901	234,759
Shares Outstanding	95,749	95,384	92,589	84,895	85,483	83,868	80,102	54,154
Statistical Record								
Return on Assets %	3.76	3.62	3.74	4.10	4.04	3.91	3.67	4.37
Return on Equity %	11.67	11.34	12.29	13.90	13.27	13.17	12.05	13.42
EBITDA Margin %	52.22	54.22	57.96	60.23	58.29	58.60	49.94	56.32
Net Margin %	16.56	18.10	19.28	20.87	19.56	19.20	14.14	19.09
PPE Turnover	0.23	0.23	0.22	0.23	0.23	0.23	0.29	0.26
Asset Turnover	0.21	0.20	0.19	0.20	0.21	0.20	0.26	0.23
Debt to Equity	1.07	1.05	1.06	1.18	1.09	1.08	1.12	1.12
Price Range	25.63-18.91	24.59-18.91	22.25-15.77	19.98-13.02	19.39-12.80	15.88-8.64	15.14-10.30	15.23-9.76
P/E Ratio	28.80-21.25	28.93-22.25	28.16-19.96	25.62-16.70	27.69-18.29	24.43-13.29	33.64-22.90	28.74-18.42
Average Yield %	2.27	2.30	2.61	2.54	2.51	3.33	3.02	2.88

Address: 762 W. Lancaster Avenue, Bryn Mawr, PA 19010-3489
Telephone: 610-524-8000
Web Site: www.suburbanwater.com

Officers: Nicholas DeBenedictis - Chmn., Pres. Roy H. Stahl - Exec. V.P., Sec., Gen. Couns. **Transfer Agents:** BankBoston, N.A., Boston, MA

Investor Contact: 610-525-1400
No of Institutions: 172
Shares: 26,244,578 **% Held:** 27.49

ARCHER DANIELS MIDLAND CO.

Exchange	Symbol	Price	52Wk Range	Yield	P/E
NYS	ADM	$19.85 (5/31/2005)	25.32-15.43	1.71	17.41

***7 Year Price Score 125.87** *NYSE Composite Index=100 ***12 Month Price Score 100.08**

Interim Earnings (Per Share)

Qtr.	Sep	Dec	Mar	Jun
2001-02	0.20	0.23	0.18	0.17
2002-03	0.17	0.20	0.18	0.15
2003-04	0.23	0.34	0.35	(0.16)
2004-05	0.41	0.48	0.41	...

Interim Dividends (Per Share)

Amt	Decl	Ex	Rec	Pay
0.075Q	8/5/2004	8/18/2004	8/20/2004	9/10/2004
0.075Q	11/4/2004	11/17/2004	11/19/2004	12/10/2004
0.085Q	2/3/2005	2/15/2005	2/17/2005	3/10/2005
0.085Q	5/5/2005	5/17/2005	5/19/2005	6/9/2005

Indicated Div: $0.34 (Div. Reinv. Plan)

Valuation Analysis

Forecast P/E	N/A		
Market Cap	$13.0 Billion	Book Value	8.6 Billion
Price/Book	1.52	Price/Sales	0.36

Dividend Achiever Status

Rank	44	10 Year Growth Rate	19.24%
Total Years of Dividend Growth			30

Business Summary: Food (MIC: 4.1 SIC: 075 NAIC: 11225)

Archer-Daniels-Midland is engaged in procuring, transporting, storing, processing and merchandising agricultural commodities and products. Co.'s operations are classified into three business segments. The Oilseeds Processing segment includes processing oilseeds, such as soybeans, cottonseed, sunflower seeds, canola, peanuts, and flaxseed into vegetable oils and meals. The Corn Processing segment includes the production of syrups, starches, dextros and sweeteners used in the food and beverage industry. The Agricultural Services segment buys, stores, cleans and transports agricultural commodities. The Other segment consists of food and feed ingredient businesses and financial activities.

Recent Developments: For the quarter ended Mar 31 2005, net income increased 18.7% to $269,095 thousand from net income of $226,769 thousand in the year-earlier quarter. Revenues were $8,484,171 thousand, down 8.9% from $9,309,019 thousand the year before. Total direct expense was $7,909,315 thousand versus $8,722,000 thousand in the prior-year quarter, a decrease of 9.3%. Total indirect expense was $280,395 thousand versus $251,701 thousand in the prior-year quarter, an increase of 11.4%.

Prospects: Co.'s outlook is tempered by recent lackluster operating results exhibited across its business segments. For instance, Co.'s Oilseeds Processing operating profit for the quarter ended Mar 31 2005 was hurt by lower oilseed crush margins in North and South America. Also, Corn Processing operating profits were negatively affected by higher net corn and energy costs and lower lysine average selling prices. Finally, Co.'s Agricultural Services operating profits were pressured by lower global grain merchandising results, principally due to improved crop conditions in Europe, which resulted in decreased demand in Europe for imported agricultural commodities and agricultural commodity products.

Financial Data

(US$ in Thousands)	9 Mos	6 Mos	3 Mos	06/30/2004	06/30/2003	06/30/2002	06/30/2001	06/30/2000
Earnings Per Share	1.14	1.08	0.94	0.76	0.70	0.78	0.58	0.45
Cash Flow Per Share	4.54	2.84	1.33	0.05	1.67	2.31	1.30	1.21
Tang Book Value Per Share	12.53	12.48	11.56	11.31	10.43	10.39	9.56	9.39
Dividends Per Share	0.310	0.300	0.285	0.270	0.240	0.198	0.188	0.179
Dividend Payout %	27.19	27.88	30.44	35.53	34.29	25.34	32.45	40.05
Income Statement								
Total Revenue	26,520,108	18,035,937	8,972,411	36,151,394	30,708,033	23,453,561	20,051,421	12,876,817
EBITDA	1,998,837	1,338,995	632,433	1,749,860	1,639,670	1,688,963	1,542,004	1,378,280
Depn & Amortn	507,599	337,086	167,447	689,858	648,726	614,070	621,974	647,639
Income Before Taxes	1,249,335	840,299	385,937	718,011	630,973	718,937	521,899	353,237
Income Taxes	400,434	260,493	119,640	223,301	179,828	207,844	138,615	52,334
Net Income	848,901	579,806	266,297	494,710	451,145	511,093	383,284	300,903
Average Shares	658,904	654,985	652,325	647,698	646,086	656,955	664,507	669,279
Balance Sheet								
Current Assets	10,044,596	10,083,993	9,854,313	10,338,996	8,421,857	7,363,231	6,150,301	6,162,367
Total Assets	18,981,797	19,375,223	18,893,383	19,368,821	17,182,879	15,416,273	14,339,931	14,423,100
Current Liabilities	5,460,878	5,793,611	6,138,694	6,750,237	5,147,472	4,719,297	3,866,981	4,332,945
Long-Term Obligations	3,575,477	3,695,432	3,690,147	3,739,875	3,872,287	3,111,294	3,351,067	3,277,218
Total Liabilities	10,408,691	10,844,527	10,989,927	11,670,605	10,113,682	8,661,452	8,008,248	8,312,857
Stockholders' Equity	8,573,106	8,530,696	7,903,456	7,698,216	7,069,197	6,754,821	6,331,683	6,110,243
Shares Outstanding	656,488	655,953	654,512	650,935	644,855	649,993	662,378	650,682
Statistical Record								
Return on Assets %	3.72	3.57	3.33	2.70	2.77	3.44	2.67	2.11
Return on Equity %	9.06	8.69	8.05	6.68	6.53	7.81	6.16	4.86
EBITDA Margin %	7.54	7.42	7.05	4.84	5.34	7.20	7.69	10.70
Net Margin %	3.20	3.21	2.97	1.37	1.47	2.18	1.91	2.34
Asset Turnover	1.81	1.88	2.03	1.97	1.88	1.58	1.39	0.90
Current Ratio	1.84	1.74	1.61	1.53	1.64	1.56	1.59	1.42
Debt to Equity	0.42	0.43	0.47	0.49	0.55	0.46	0.53	0.54
Price Range	25.32-15.43	22.36-14.95	17.59-13.11	17.59-12.08	14.28-10.54	15.60-12.00	15.20-7.92	13.34-8.22
P/E Ratio	22.21-13.54	20.70-13.84	18.71-13.95	23.14-15.89	20.40-15.06	20.00-15.38	26.21-13.65	29.63-18.27
Average Yield %	1.62	1.73	1.79	1.78	1.98	1.44	1.65	1.66

Address: 4666 Faries Parkway, Box 1470, Decatur, IL 62525
Telephone: 217-424-5200
Web Site: www.admworld.com

Officers: G. Allen Andreas - Chmn., C.E.O. Paul B. Mulhollem - Pres., C.O.O. **Transfer Agents:** Hickory Point Bank & Trust, fsb, Decatur, IL

Investor Contact: 217-424-4647
No of Institutions: 392
Shares: 408,760,352 **% Held:** 62.32

ARROW INTERNATIONAL,INC.

Exchange	Symbol	Price	52Wk Range	Yield	P/E
NMS	ARRO	$33.80 (5/31/2005)	36.02-26.61	1.78	33.80

***7 Year Price Score 133.54** *NYSE Composite Index=100 ***12 Month Price Score 102.69**

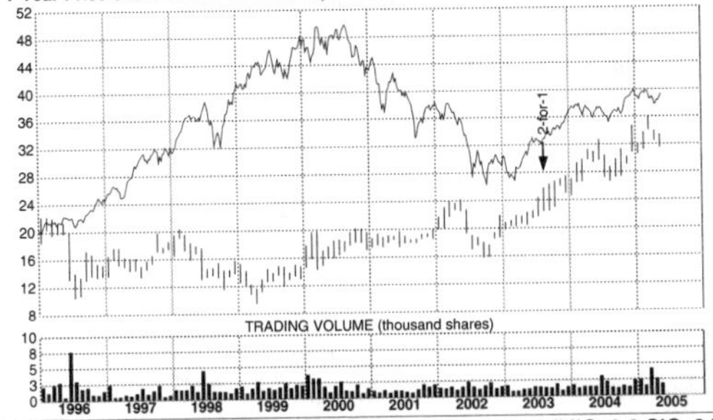

TRADING VOLUME (thousand shares)

Interim Earnings (Per Share)

Qtr.	Nov	Feb	May	Aug
2001-02	0.27	0.29	0.26	0.07
2002-03	0.26	0.27	0.33	0.18
2003-04	0.33	0.35	0.26	0.32
2004-05	0.30	0.12	...	...

Interim Dividends (Per Share)

Amt	Decl	Ex	Rec	Pay
0.09Q	8/16/2004	8/26/2004	8/30/2004	9/13/2004
0.09Q	11/9/2004	11/24/2004	11/29/2004	12/13/2004
0.15Q	2/14/2005	2/24/2005	2/28/2005	3/14/2005
0.15Q	5/16/2005	5/26/2005	5/31/2005	6/13/2005

Indicated Div: $0.60

Valuation Analysis

Forecast P/E	23.80 (6/2/2005)		
Market Cap	$1.5 Billion	Book Value	478.0 Million
Price/Book	3.15	Price/Sales	3.39

Dividend Achiever Status

Rank	39	**10 Year Growth Rate**	19.62%
Total Years of Dividend Growth			12

Business Summary: Medical Instruments & Equipment (MIC: 9.6 SIC: 841 NAIC: 39112)

Arrow International develops, manufactures and markets a range of disposable catheters, heart assist devices and related products for critical and cardiac care. Co.'s critical care products are used principally for central vascular access in the administration of fluids, drugs and blood products, patient monitoring and diagnostic purposes. Co.'s cardiac care products are used by interventional cardiologists, cardiac surgeons, interventional radiologists and electrophysiologists for such purposes as the diagnosis and treatment of heart and vascular disease and to provide short-term cardiac assist following cardiac surgery, serious heart attack or balloon angioplasty.

Recent Developments: For the three months ended Feb 28 2005, net income was $5.4 million compared with $15.5 million in the corresponding year-earlier period. Results for 2005 included a restructuring charge of $930,000. Net sales rose to $109.2 million from $108.3 million the previous year. On a product basis, Central Venous Catheters sales rose 2.2% to $ 57.0 million; Specialty Catheters sales grew 3.3% to $34.3; and Stepic Distributed Products sales fell 36.7% to $1.9 million. Cardiac Care sales slipped 1.8% to $16.0 million. Operating income declined 69.1% to $7.1 million versus $23.0 million the year before.

Prospects: On Apr 7 2005, Co. announced that it has discontinued the development, sales and marketing programs related to its LionHeart Left Ventricular Assist System (LVAS). There were no sales of Co.'s LionHeart devices during either of the first two quarters of fiscal year 2005. As a result, Co. made a provision in its second fiscal quarter of $2.1 million for LionHeart inventory in excess of anticipated requirements. Also, Co. wrote off in the second fiscal quarter of 2005 its remaining investment in the LionHeart program, which included $2.8 million in equipment and components. Co. stated that it will continue the clinical trial of its CorAide continuous flow ventricular assist device in Europe.

Financial Data (US$ in Thousands)	6 Mos	3 Mos	08/31/2004	08/31/2003	08/31/2002	08/31/2001	08/31/2000	08/31/1999
Earnings Per Share	1.00	1.23	1.26	1.04	0.89	1.05	1.02	0.77
Cash Flow Per Share	1.77	1.87	2.11	1.82	1.78	0.97	1.26	1.22
Tang Book Value Per Share	8.81	8.59	8.30	8.04	7.32	6.43	5.60	5.26
Dividends Per Share	0.420	0.360	0.350	0.195	0.138	0.128	0.117	0.108
Dividend Payout %	42.00	29.36	27.78	18.75	15.45	12.14	11.46	13.96
Income Statement								
Total Revenue	221,934	112,725	433,134	380,376	340,759	334,042	320,340	295,946
EBITDA	39,457	26,013	106,916	88,941	79,862	94,063	92,326	74,922
Depn & Amortn	12,693	6,459	23,778	23,226	21,693	22,696	20,931	18,606
Income Before Taxes	26,961	19,679	82,877	66,918	57,777	69,470	69,450	55,341
Income Taxes	8,324	6,396	26,935	21,248	18,777	22,925	23,266	19,646
Net Income	18,637	13,283	55,942	45,670	39,000	46,545	46,184	35,695
Average Shares	45,009	44,526	44,301	43,773	44,211	44,240	45,037	46,390
Balance Sheet								
Current Assets	322,130	304,396	290,076	241,880	224,873	203,985	179,651	166,627
Total Assets	595,539	576,576	549,208	493,897	425,680	417,710	385,814	357,484
Current Liabilities	88,583	89,182	80,474	77,966	50,425	78,429	89,601	58,726
Long-Term Obligations	...	...	...	3,735	300	600	900	11,105
Total Liabilities	117,489	111,706	102,877	103,251	65,324	91,621	100,610	79,317
Stockholders' Equity	478,050	464,870	446,331	390,646	360,356	326,089	285,204	278,167
Shares Outstanding	44,485	43,944	43,774	43,285	43,941	44,002	44,001	46,115
Statistical Record								
Return on Assets %	7.92	9.97	10.70	9.93	9.25	11.59	12.39	10.49
Return on Equity %	9.91	12.51	13.33	12.16	11.36	15.23	16.35	13.57
EBITDA Margin %	17.78	23.08	24.68	23.38	23.44	28.16	28.82	25.32
Net Margin %	8.40	11.78	12.92	12.01	11.45	13.93	14.42	12.06
Asset Turnover	0.79	0.81	0.83	0.83	0.81	0.83	0.86	0.87
Current Ratio	3.64	3.41	3.60	3.10	4.46	2.60	2.01	2.84
Debt to Equity	...	...	...	0.01	N.M.	N.M.	N.M.	0.04
Price Range	34.68-26.61	32.72-24.61	32.72-22.43	25.80-15.75	24.20-16.93	20.16-17.06	19.81-11.88	15.69-9.44
P/E Ratio	34.68-26.61	26.60-20.01	25.97-17.80	24.81-15.14	27.19-19.02	19.20-16.25	19.42-11.64	20.37-12.26
Average Yield %	1.41	1.27	1.27	0.95	0.68	0.68	0.74	0.81

Address: 2400 Bernville Road, Reading, PA 19605
Telephone: 610-378-0131
Web Site: www.arrowintl.com

Officers: Carl G. Anderson Jr. - Chmn, C.E.O. Philip B. Fleck - Pres., C.O.O. **Transfer Agents:** Registrar and Transfer Company, Cranford, NJ

Investor Contact: 610-478-3116
No of Institutions: 103
Shares: 18,991,708 **% Held:** 43.12

ASSOCIATED BANC-CORP.

Exchange	Symbol	Price	52Wk Range	Yield	P/E
NMS	ASBC	$33.42 (5/31/2005)	34.85-28.76	3.23	14.47

*7 Year Price Score 124.23 *NYSE Composite Index=100 *12 Month Price Score 96.45

Interim Earnings (Per Share)

Qtr.	Mar	Jun	Sep	Dec
2002	0.46	0.45	0.47	0.47
2003	0.51	0.51	0.53	0.50
2004	0.53	0.58	0.57	0.57
2005	0.59	...	...	...

Interim Dividends (Per Share)

Amt	Decl	Ex	Rec	Pay
0.25Q	7/28/2004	8/4/2004	8/6/2004	8/16/2004
0.25Q	10/28/2004	11/4/2004	11/8/2004	11/15/2004
0.25Q	1/26/2005	2/3/2005	2/7/2005	2/15/2005
0.27Q	4/27/2005	5/5/2005	5/9/2005	5/16/2005

Indicated Div: $1.08 (Div. Reinv. Plan)

Valuation Analysis

Forecast P/E	13.41 (5/28/2005)		
Market Cap	$4.3 Billion	Book Value	2.0 Billion
Price/Book	2.14	Price/Sales	4.05

Dividend Achiever Status

Rank	134	10 Year Growth Rate	12.11%
Total Years of Dividend Growth			34

Business Summary: Commercial Banking (MIC: 8.1 SIC: 022 NAIC: 22110)

Associated Banc-Corp. is a bank holding company. Through its banking subsidiaries and various nonbanking subsidiaries, Co. provides a range of banking and nonbanking products and services to individuals and businesses in the communities it serves. Co.'s banking and wealth management activities are conducted primarily in Wisconsin, Minnesota, and Illinois, and are primarily delivered through branch facilities in this tri-state area, as well as supplemented through loan production offices, supermarket branches, a customer service call center and 24-hour phone-banking services, an interstate ATM network, and internet banking services. As of Dec 31 2004, Co. had total assets of $20.52 billion.

Recent Developments: For the quarter ended Mar 31 2005, net income increased 30.1% to $77,470 thousand from net income of $59,560 thousand in the year-earlier quarter. Net interest income was $165,908 thousand, up 28.5% from $129,075 thousand the year before. Provision for loan losses was $2,327 thousand versus $5,176 thousand in the prior-year quarter, a decrease of 55.0%. Non-interest income rose 54.5% to $71,373 thousand, while non-interest expense advanced 39.5% to $121,242 thousand.

Prospects: Following its integration of First Federal Capital Corp., which was acquired on Oct 29 2004, Co. believes it is well positioned to capitalize on selling its expanded product line to First Federal customers. Meanwhile, Co.'s near-term outlook is tempered by the rate environment and competitive loan and deposit environment. For the quarter ended Mar 31 2005, Co.'s net interest margin was 3.68%, versus 3.74% and 3.80% for fourth and first quarters of 2004, respectively. Co. noted that the flattening of the yield curve and competitive pricing pressures have substantially offset the benefits to the margin from interest rate increases that began in the second half of 2004 and continue into 2005.

Financial Data
(US$ in Thousands)

	3 Mos	12/31/2004	12/31/2003	12/31/2002	12/31/2001	12/31/2000	12/31/1999	12/31/1998
Earnings Per Share	2.31	2.25	2.05	1.86	1.64	1.49	1.42	1.36
Cash Flow Per Share	3.05	3.37	4.49	2.67	(0.00)	1.68	2.34	1.21
Tang Book Value Per Share	9.45	9.39	9.64	9.14	10.92	8.88	7.93	7.70
Dividends Per Share	1.000	0.977	0.887	0.808	0.739	0.671	0.639	0.575
Dividend Payout %	43.29	43.41	43.32	43.43	45.19	45.01	45.14	42.44
Income Statement								
Interest Income	251,148	767,122	727,364	792,106	880,622	931,157	814,520	785,765
Interest Expense	85,240	214,495	216,602	290,840	458,637	547,590	418,775	411,028
Net Interest Income	165,908	552,627	510,762	501,266	421,985	383,567	395,745	374,737
Provision for Losses	2,327	14,668	46,813	50,699	28,210	20,206	19,243	14,740
Non-Interest Income	71,373	210,247	246,435	220,308	195,603	184,196	165,906	167,951
Non-Interest Expense	121,242	377,869	388,668	374,549	338,369	317,736	305,092	294,985
Income Before Taxes	113,712	370,337	321,716	296,326	251,009	229,821	237,316	232,963
Income Taxes	36,242	112,051	93,059	85,607	71,487	61,838	72,373	75,943
Net Income	77,470	258,286	228,657	210,719	179,522	167,983	164,943	157,020
Average Shares	131,358	115,025	111,760	113,239	109,751	112,876	116,270	115,777
Balance Sheet								
Net Loans & Leases	13,733,279	13,692,125	10,114,188	10,140,684	8,891,660	8,793,147	8,244,752	7,173,020
Total Assets	20,502,442	20,520,136	15,247,894	15,043,275	13,604,374	13,128,394	12,519,902	11,250,667
Total Deposits	12,193,904	12,786,239	9,792,843	9,124,852	8,612,611	9,291,646	8,691,829	8,557,819
Total Liabilities	18,477,371	18,502,717	13,899,467	13,771,092	12,533,958	12,159,698	11,610,113	10,371,946
Stockholders' Equity	2,025,071	2,017,419	1,348,427	1,272,183	1,070,416	968,696	909,789	878,721
Shares Outstanding	129,748	129,770	110,040	111,420	98,003	109,091	114,708	114,139
Statistical Record								
Return on Assets %	1.53	1.44	1.51	1.47	1.34	1.31	1.39	1.43
Return on Equity %	16.15	15.31	17.45	17.99	17.61	17.84	18.44	18.56
Net Interest Margin %	66.06	72.04	70.22	63.28	47.92	41.19	48.59	47.69
Efficiency Ratio %	37.59	38.66	39.91	37.00	31.44	28.49	31.12	30.93
Loans to Deposits	1.13	1.07	1.03	1.11	1.03	0.95	0.95	0.84
Price Range	34.85-27.09	34.85-27.09	28.75-21.43	25.50-18.13	22.37-18.03	18.87-12.29	23.73-16.70	24.30-14.74
P/E Ratio	15.09-11.73	15.49-12.04	14.03-10.46	13.71-9.75	13.64-10.99	12.66-8.25	16.71-11.76	17.87-10.84
Average Yield %	3.21	3.22	3.57	3.57	3.57	4.44	3.25	2.73

Address: 1200 Hansen Road, Green Bay, WI 54304
Telephone: 920-491-7000
Web Site: www.associatedbank.com

Officers: Robert C. Gallagher - Chmn. John C. Seramur - Vice-Chmn. **Transfer Agents:** National City Bank, Cleveland, OH

Investor Contact: 920-491-7120
No of Institutions: 209
Shares: 53,406,600 **% Held:** 41.20

ATMOS ENERGY CORP.

Exchange	Symbol	Price	52Wk Range	Yield	P/E
NYS	ATO	$28.29 (5/31/2005)	29.09-24.38	4.38	15.80

*7 Year Price Score 97.51 *NYSE Composite Index=100 *12 Month Price Score 99.54

TRADING VOLUME (thousand shares)

Interim Earnings (Per Share)

Qtr.	Dec	Mar	Jun	Sep
2001-02	0.50	1.01	0.08	(0.14)
2002-03	0.60	1.07	0.00	(0.11)
2003-04	0.57	1.12	0.09	(0.20)
2004-05	0.79	1.11	...	...

Interim Dividends (Per Share)

Amt	Decl	Ex	Rec	Pay
0.305Q	8/10/2004	8/23/2004	8/25/2004	9/10/2004
0.31Q	11/9/2004	11/22/2004	11/24/2004	12/10/2004
0.31Q	2/8/2005	2/23/2005	2/25/2005	3/10/2005
0.31Q	5/9/2005	5/23/2005	5/25/2005	6/10/2005

Indicated Div: $1.24 (Div. Reinv. Plan)

Valuation Analysis

Forecast P/E	16.73 (5/28/2005)		
Market Cap	$2.3 Billion	Book Value	1.6 Billion
Price/Book	1.38	Price/Sales	0.55

Dividend Achiever Status

Rank	296	**10 Year Growth Rate**	3.25%
Total Years of Dividend Growth			17

Business Summary: Gas Utilities (MIC: 7.4 SIC: 922 NAIC: 86210)

Atmos Energy is engaged in the natural gas utility business as well as certain non-regulated natural gas businesses. As of Sept. 30, 2004, Co. distributes natural gas through sales and transportation arrangements to about 1,700,000 residential, commercial public authority and industrial customers through its regulated utility operations in 12 states. Co. also transports natural gas through its distribution system. Co. provides natural gas management and marketing services to industrial customers, municipalities and other local gas distribution companies in 18 states. Co. also supplements natural gas used by its customers through natural gas storage fields located in Kentucky and Louisiana.

Recent Developments: For the quarter ended Mar 31 2005, net income increased 51.8% to $88,502 thousand from net income of $58,305 thousand in the year-earlier quarter. Revenues were $1,685,085 thousand, up 50.8% from $1,117,485 thousand the year before. Operating income was $172,181 thousand versus an income of $105,414 thousand in the prior-year quarter, an increase of 63.3%. Total direct expense was $1,306,502 thousand versus $911,359 thousand in the prior-year quarter, an increase of 43.4%. Total indirect expense was $206,402 thousand versus $100,712 thousand in the prior-year quarter, an increase of 104.9%.

Prospects: Results are being positively affected by Co.'s acquisition of the gas distribution and pipeline operations of TXU Gas Company in October 2004. Meanwhile, results are being hampered by unseasonably warm weather in parts of Co.'s 12-state service area where customer gas rates are not adjusted by regulators for the effects of the weather. Co. remains focused on seeking rate design to mitigate the effects of weather, conservation and regulatory lag on its utility margins. Looking ahead, Co. is targeting full-year 2005 earnings per diluted share at the lower end of the $1.65 to $1.75 range.

Financial Data (US$ in Thousands)	6 Mos	3 Mos	09/30/2004	09/30/2003	09/30/2002	09/30/2001	09/30/2000	09/30/1999
Earnings Per Share	1.79	1.79	1.58	1.54	1.45	1.47	1.14	0.58
Cash Flow Per Share	4.80	4.30	5.00	1.07	7.20	2.18	1.72	2.77
Tang Book Value Per Share	11.40	10.55	14.25	11.35	9.19	12.43	12.28	12.09
Dividends Per Share	1.230	1.225	1.220	1.200	1.180	1.160	1.140	1.100
Dividend Payout %	68.72	68.52	77.22	77.92	81.38	78.91	100.00	189.66
Income Statement								
Total Revenue	3,053,709	1,368,624	2,920,037	2,799,916	950,849	1,442,275	850,152	690,196
EBITDA	391,521	173,056	301,314	279,225	237,931	206,939	166,980	125,271
Depn & Amortn	89,323	43,997	98,112	89,194	83,921	70,470	66,920	61,674
Income Before Taxes	236,583	96,517	137,765	126,371	94,836	89,458	56,237	27,299
Income Taxes	88,482	36,918	51,538	46,910	35,180	33,368	20,319	9,555
Net Income	148,101	59,599	86,227	71,688	59,656	56,090	35,918	17,744
Average Shares	79,760	75,725	54,416	46,496	41,250	38,247	31,594	30,819
Balance Sheet								
Net PPE	3,251,595	3,223,143	1,722,521	1,515,989	1,300,320	1,335,398	982,346	965,782
Total Assets	5,412,444	5,406,096	2,869,883	2,518,508	1,980,221	2,036,180	1,348,758	1,230,537
Long-Term Obligations	2,254,817	2,255,173	861,311	863,918	670,463	692,399	363,198	377,483
Total Liabilities	3,780,174	3,867,018	1,736,424	1,660,991	1,406,986	1,452,316	956,292	852,874
Stockholders' Equity	1,632,270	1,539,078	1,133,459	857,517	573,235	583,864	392,466	377,663
Shares Outstanding	79,877	79,257	62,799	51,475	41,675	40,791	31,952	31,247
Statistical Record								
Return on Assets %	3.56	2.81	3.19	3.19	2.97	3.31	2.78	1.50
Return on Equity %	11.42	9.56	8.64	10.02	10.31	11.49	9.30	4.74
EBITDA Margin %	12.82	12.64	10.32	9.97	25.02	14.35	19.64	18.15
Net Margin %	4.85	4.35	2.95	2.56	6.27	3.89	4.22	2.57
PPE Turnover	1.67	1.48	1.80	1.99	0.72	1.24	0.87	0.73
Asset Turnover	0.99	0.85	1.08	1.24	0.47	0.85	0.66	0.58
Debt to Equity	1.38	1.47	0.76	1.01	1.17	1.19	0.93	1.00
Price Range	29.09-23.68	27.43-23.68	26.86-23.68	25.45-20.70	24.46-18.37	26.25-19.31	25.00-14.75	32.69-23.06
P/E Ratio	16.25-13.23	15.32-13.23	17.00-14.99	16.53-13.44	16.87-12.67	17.86-13.14	21.93-12.94	56.36-39.76
Average Yield %	4.75	4.81	4.87	5.21	5.37	5.08	5.85	4.11

Address: Three Lincoln Centre, Suite 1800, 5430 LBJ Freeway, Dallas, TX 75240
Telephone: 972-934-9227
Web Site: www.atmosenergy.com

Officers: Robert W. Best - Chmn., Pres., C.E.O. John P. Reddy - Sr. V.P., C.F.O. **Transfer Agents:** EquiServe Trust Company, Providence, RI.

No of Institutions: 173
Shares: 42,210,588 **% Held:** 53.20

AUTOMATIC DATA PROCESSING INC.

Exchange	Symbol	Price	52Wk Range	Yield	P/E
NYS	ADP	$43.80 (5/31/2005)	46.23-38.88	1.42	25.92

***7 Year Price Score 83.77** *NYSE Composite Index=100 ***12 Month Price Score 99.39**

Interim Earnings (Per Share)

Qtr.	Sep	Dec	Mar	Jun
2001-02	0.31	0.42	0.56	0.46
2002-03	0.34	0.43	0.54	0.36
2003-04	0.32	0.38	0.50	0.35
2004-05	0.35	0.42	0.57	...

Interim Dividends (Per Share)

Amt	Decl	Ex	Rec	Pay
0.14Q	8/11/2004	9/8/2004	9/10/2004	10/1/2004
0.155Q	11/9/2004	12/8/2004	12/10/2004	1/1/2005
0.155Q	1/27/2005	3/10/2005	3/14/2005	4/1/2005
0.155Q	4/28/2005	6/8/2005	6/10/2005	7/1/2005

Indicated Div: $0.62

Valuation Analysis

Forecast P/E	22.18 (5/28/2005)		
Market Cap	$25.6 Billion	Book Value	5.8 Billion
Price/Book	4.43	Price/Sales	3.09

Dividend Achiever Status

Rank	91	**10 Year Growth Rate**	14.87%
Total Years of Dividend Growth			29

Business Summary: IT & Technology (MIC: 10.2 SIC: 374 NAIC: 18210)

Automatic Data Processing provides computerized transaction processing, data communication, and information services. Co.'s Employer Services group offers payroll processing, human resource and benefits administration products and services. Co.'s Brokerage Services group provides transaction processing systems, desktop productivity applications and investor communications services to the financial services industry. Co.'s Dealer Services group provides dealer management computer systems to automotive retailers and their manufacturers. Co.'s Claims Services group offers business services to clients in the property and casualty insurance, auto collision repair and auto recycling industries.

Recent Developments: For the quarter ended Mar 31 2005, net income increased 12.7% to $338,371 thousand from net income of $300,250 thousand in the year-earlier quarter. Revenues were $2,348,963 thousand, up 10.7% from $2,121,435 thousand the year before. Total indirect expense was $1,813,078 thousand versus $1,653,792 thousand in the prior-year quarter, an increase of 9.6%.

Prospects: The Employer Services segment is benefiting from investments in sales and new products, which are now more evident across all of its market segments. Also, Co.'s Brokerage Services segment is seeing revenue growth primarily driven by expansion in investor communications, which is leading to a slightly lower overall margin. Meanwhile, the Dealer Services segment recently was awarded new sales contracts to be the sole dealer management systems provider for two of the largest dealership groups in the U.S. This will result in about 240 additional dealer sites over the next 18 to 30 months. Separately, the Securities Clearing and Outsourcing Services segment continues its positive momentum.

Financial Data

(US$ in Thousands)	9 Mos	6 Mos	3 Mos	06/30/2004	06/30/2003	06/30/2002	06/30/2001	06/30/2000
Earnings Per Share	1.69	1.61	1.58	1.56	1.68	1.75	1.44	1.31
Cash Flow Per Share	2.24	2.61	2.55	2.35	2.61	2.48	2.37	1.70
Tang Book Value Per Share	4.47	4.30	4.25	4.23	4.57	5.25	4.97	4.71
Dividends Per Share	0.590	0.575	0.560	0.540	0.475	0.448	0.395	0.339
Dividend Payout %	34.91	35.61	35.54	34.62	28.27	25.57	27.43	25.86
Income Statement								
Total Revenue	6,197,229	3,848,266	1,854,682	7,754,942	7,147,017	7,004,263	7,017,570	6,287,512
EBITDA	1,542,786	911,159	421,120	1,867,276	1,822,307	1,968,539	1,860,126	1,587,022
Depn & Amortn	321,760	215,676	107,942	436,694	274,682	279,077	320,856	284,282
Income Before Taxes	1,266,510	728,560	330,940	1,494,530	1,645,200	1,786,970	1,525,010	1,289,600
Income Taxes	469,875	270,296	122,779	558,960	627,050	686,200	600,290	448,800
Net Income	796,635	458,264	208,161	935,570	1,018,150	1,100,770	924,720	840,800
Average Shares	590,512	591,086	589,952	598,749	605,917	630,579	645,989	646,098
Balance Sheet								
Current Assets	4,489,340	4,193,873	3,028,533	2,761,589	3,675,501	2,817,257	3,083,460	3,064,452
Total Assets	32,772,727	28,189,379	23,787,478	21,120,559	19,833,671	18,276,522	17,889,090	16,850,816
Current Liabilities	2,754,277	2,600,640	1,659,933	1,768,424	1,998,783	1,411,102	1,336,273	1,296,668
Long-Term Obligations	75,937	75,926	76,508	76,200	84,674	90,648	110,227	132,017
Total Liabilities	27,003,085	22,532,856	18,373,944	15,702,889	14,462,198	13,162,317	13,188,093	12,267,998
Stockholders' Equity	5,769,642	5,656,523	5,413,534	5,417,670	5,371,473	5,114,205	4,700,997	4,582,818
Shares Outstanding	583,451	583,096	582,537	587,115	594,839	616,317	623,936	628,746
Statistical Record								
Return on Assets %	3.47	3.66	4.45	4.56	5.34	6.09	5.32	7.40
Return on Equity %	17.70	17.53	17.59	17.30	19.42	22.43	19.92	19.52
EBITDA Margin %	24.89	23.68	22.71	24.08	25.50	28.10	26.51	25.24
Net Margin %	12.85	11.91	11.22	12.06	14.25	15.72	13.18	13.37
Asset Turnover	0.28	0.30	0.37	0.38	0.38	0.39	0.40	0.55
Current Ratio	1.63	1.61	1.82	1.56	1.84	2.00	2.31	2.36
Debt to Equity	0.01	0.01	0.01	0.01	0.02	0.02	0.02	0.03
Price Range	46.84-38.88	46.84-38.88	46.84-35.85	46.84-33.86	44.70-27.25	60.27-43.10	68.88-49.56	57.69-38.00
P/E Ratio	27.72-23.01	29.09-24.15	29.65-22.69	30.03-21.71	26.61-16.22	34.44-24.63	47.83-34.42	44.04-29.01
Average Yield %	1.37	1.34	1.36	1.33	1.30	0.85	0.68	0.71

Address: One ADP Boulevard, Roseland, NJ 07068-1728
Telephone: 973-974-5000
Web Site: www.adp.com

Officers: Arthur F. Weinbach - Chmn., C.E.O. Gary C. Butler - Pres., C.O.O. **Transfer Agents:** Mellon Investor Services, Ridgefield Park, NJ

Investor Contact: 973-974-5858
No of Institutions: 718
Shares: 415,017,536 **% Held:** 71.17

AVERY DENNISON CORP.

Exchange	Symbol	Price	52Wk Range	Yield	P/E
NYS	AVY	$52.45 (5/31/2005)	65.78-51.35	2.90	18.80

*7 Year Price Score 92.31 *NYSE Composite Index=100 *12 Month Price Score 88.78

Interim Earnings (Per Share)

Qtr.	Mar	Jun	Sep	Dec
2002	0.66	0.74	0.64	0.56
2003	0.71	0.71	0.67	0.60
2004	0.52	0.68	0.75	0.83
2005	0.57	...	...	...

Interim Dividends (Per Share)

Amt	Decl	Ex	Rec	Pay
0.37Q	7/22/2004	8/30/2004	9/1/2004	9/15/2004
0.38Q	10/28/2004	11/29/2004	12/1/2004	12/15/2004
0.38Q	1/27/2005	2/28/2005	3/2/2005	3/16/2005
0.38Q	4/28/2005	5/27/2005	6/1/2005	6/15/2005

Indicated Div: $1.52 (Div. Reinv. Plan)

Valuation Analysis

Forecast P/E	18.14 (5/28/2005)		
Market Cap	$5.3 Billion	Book Value	1.5 Billion
Price/Book	3.42	Price/Sales	0.98

Dividend Achiever Status

Rank	142	**10 Year Growth Rate**	11.65%
Total Years of Dividend Growth			29

Business Summary: Paper Products (MIC: 11.11 SIC: 672 NAIC: 22222)

Avery Dennison is divided into three primary business segments. Pressure-sensitive Materials manufactures and sells pressure-sensitive roll label materials, films for graphic applications, reflective highway safety products, performance polymers (largely adhesives used to manufacture pressure-sensitive materials), and extruded films. Office and Consumer Products manufactures and sells a variety of products, including labels, binders, dividers, sheet protectors, and writing instruments. Retail Information Services designs, manufactures and sells a wide variety of price marking and brand identification products, including tickets, tags and labels, and related supplies and equipment.

Recent Developments: For the quarter ended Apr 2 2005, net income increased 9.7% to $57,700 thousand from net income of $52,600 thousand in the year-earlier quarter. Revenues were $1,346,300 thousand, up 8.0% from $1,246,700 thousand the year before. Total direct expense was $958,500 thousand versus $880,200 thousand in the prior-year quarter, an increase of 8.9%. Total indirect expense was $292,000 thousand versus $257,700 thousand in the prior-year quarter, an increase of 13.3%.

Prospects: Based on first quarter results and preliminary trends in the second quarter, Co. is updating its reported revenue growth target for the full year to 5.0% to 6.0%, down from its previous guidance of 6.0% to 10.0%. Co. adjusted its earnings per share guidance down for the full year to a range of $2.85 to $3.15 per share. Also, Co. anticipates earnings for the second and third quarters combined to be in the range of $1.45 to $1.65 per share. Co. indicated that its revised guidance assumes lower unit volume growth than originally anticipated for the year, along with continued raw material inflation through the second quarter, offset by the benefit of targeted cost reductions.

Financial Data (US$ in Thousands)	3 Mos	01/01/2005	12/27/2003	12/28/2002	12/29/2001	12/30/2000	01/01/2000	01/02/1999
Earnings Per Share	2.79	2.78	2.68	2.59	2.47	2.84	2.13	2.15
Cash Flow Per Share	4.41	5.09	3.38	5.32	3.85	4.18	4.40	4.10
Tang Book Value Per Share	6.56	6.45	4.53	2.53	4.70	3.93	4.18	6.88
Dividends Per Share	1.500	1.490	1.450	1.350	1.230	1.110	0.990	0.870
Dividend Payout %	53.86	53.60	54.10	52.12	49.80	39.08	46.48	40.47
Income Statement								
Total Revenue	1,346,300	5,340,900	4,762,600	4,206,900	3,803,300	3,893,500	3,768,200	3,459,900
EBITDA	134,300	534,400	492,100	501,600	515,800	583,200	480,800	463,900
Depn & Amortn	41,800	161,000	157,200	136,800	156,000	156,900	150,400	127,200
Income Before Taxes	78,000	373,400	334,900	364,800	359,800	426,300	330,400	336,700
Income Taxes	20,300	93,700	92,100	107,600	116,400	142,800	115,000	113,400
Net Income	57,700	279,700	267,900	257,200	243,200	283,500	215,400	223,300
Average Shares	100,700	100,500	100,000	99,400	98,600	99,800	101,300	104,100
Balance Sheet								
Current Assets	1,502,400	1,542,400	1,440,900	1,215,500	982,500	982,400	956,000	802,000
Total Assets	4,296,200	4,399,300	4,105,300	3,652,400	2,819,200	2,699,100	2,592,500	2,142,600
Current Liabilities	1,303,000	1,387,300	1,496,000	1,296,100	951,300	800,700	850,400	664,300
Long-Term Obligations	995,000	1,007,200	887,700	837,200	626,700	772,900	617,500	465,900
Total Liabilities	2,758,700	2,850,600	2,786,600	2,596,000	1,889,800	1,871,000	1,782,600	1,309,300
Stockholders' Equity	1,537,500	1,548,700	1,318,700	1,056,400	929,400	828,100	809,900	833,300
Shares Outstanding	100,177	100,113	99,569	110,467	109,890	110,245	98,800	100,000
Statistical Record								
Return on Assets %	6.69	6.47	6.93	7.97	8.84	10.74	9.12	10.49
Return on Equity %	19.41	19.19	22.62	25.98	27.75	34.71	26.29	26.30
EBITDA Margin %	9.98	10.01	10.33	11.92	13.56	14.98	12.76	13.41
Net Margin %	4.29	5.24	5.63	6.11	6.39	7.28	5.72	6.45
Asset Turnover	1.28	1.24	1.23	1.30	1.38	1.48	1.60	1.63
Current Ratio	1.15	1.11	0.96	0.94	1.03	1.23	1.12	1.21
Debt to Equity	0.65	0.65	0.67	0.79	0.67	0.93	0.76	0.56
Price Range	65.78-54.90	65.78-54.90	63.51-47.75	69.49-52.86	60.24-44.39	78.00-43.31	72.88-39.75	60.75-40.88
P/E Ratio	23.58-19.68	23.66-19.75	23.70-17.82	26.83-20.41	24.39-17.97	27.46-15.25	34.21-18.66	28.26-19.01
Average Yield %	2.47	2.44	2.64	2.19	2.34	1.88	1.71	1.74

Address: 150 North Orange Grove Boulevard, Pasadena, CA 91103
Telephone: 626-304-2000
Web Site: www.averydennison.com

Officers: Philip M. Neal - Chmn. Dean A. Scarborough - Pres., C.E.O. **Transfer Agents:** EquiServe Trust Company, N.A., Providence, RI

Investor Contact: 626-304-2204
No of Institutions: 367
Shares: 79,791,520 **% Held:** 72.24

AVON PRODUCTS, INC.

Exchange	Symbol	Price	52Wk Range	Yield	P/E
NYS	AVP	$39.74 (5/31/2005)	46.14-37.45	1.66	21.84

***7 Year Price Score 138.98** *NYSE Composite Index=100 ***12 Month Price Score 94.49**

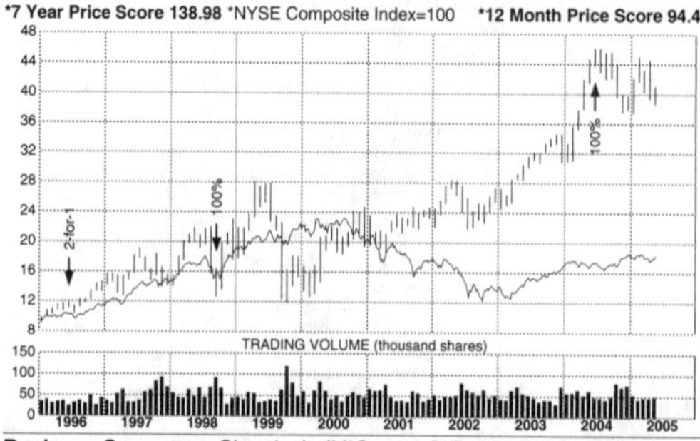

Interim Earnings (Per Share)

Qtr.	Mar	Jun	Sep	Dec
2002	0.20	0.32	0.19	0.40
2003	0.21	0.35	0.28	0.55
2004	0.31	0.49	0.37	0.60
2005	0.36	...	...	...

Interim Dividends (Per Share)

Amt	Decl	Ex	Rec	Pay
0.14Q	8/5/2004	8/16/2004	8/18/2004	9/1/2004
0.14Q	11/4/2004	11/12/2004	11/16/2004	12/1/2004
0.165Q	2/1/2005	2/10/2005	2/14/2005	3/1/2005
0.165Q	5/5/2005	5/17/2005	5/19/2005	6/1/2005

Indicated Div: $0.66 (Div. Reinv. Plan)

Valuation Analysis

Forecast P/E	18.71 (5/28/2005)		
Market Cap	$18.8 Billion	Book Value	993.0 Million
Price/Book	18.89	Price/Sales	2.39

Dividend Achiever Status

Rank	194	10 Year Growth Rate	8.96%
Total Years of Dividend Growth			14

Business Summary: Chemicals (MIC: 11.1 SIC: 844 NAIC: 25620)

Avon Products is a global manufacturer and marketer of beauty and related products. Co.'s business is conducted worldwide primarily in one channel, direct selling. Co.'s reportable segments are based on geographic operations in North America, Europe, Latin America and Asia Pacific. Sales are made to the customers principally by independent Avon Representatives. Product categories include Beauty, which consists of cosmetics, fragrance, skin care and toiletries; Beauty Plus, which consists of fashion jewelry, watches, apparel and accessories; and Beyond Beauty, which consists of home products, gift and decorative products, candles and toys.

Recent Developments: For the quarter ended Mar 31 2005, net income increased 16.1% to $172,000 thousand from net income of $148,100 thousand in the year-earlier quarter. Revenues were $1,881,100 thousand, up 6.6% from $1,764,800 thousand the year before. Operating income was $260,500 thousand versus an income of $229,400 thousand in the prior-year quarter, an increase of 13.6%. Total direct expense was $698,200 thousand versus $666,200 thousand in the prior-year quarter, an increase of 4.8%. Total indirect expense was $922,400 thousand versus $869,200 thousand in the prior-year quarter, an increase of 6.1%.

Prospects: Co. expects revenue growth in the second-quarter of 2005 to accelerate ahead of the first quarter, with dollar-denominated and local-currency growth expected to be in the ranges of 10.0% and 6.0%, respectively. Operating profit is forecast to increase approximately in line with revenue growth, including an acceleration of consumer investments in emerging markets as well as funding for the China direct-selling test. For full-year 2005, Co. is expecting continuing strong results in its international regions, partially offset by U.S. performance during this period of repositioning, with its emerging markets once again expected to deliver another full year of stand-out revenue growth.

Financial Data

(US$ in Thousands)	3 Mos	12/31/2004	12/31/2003	12/31/2002	12/31/2001	12/31/2000	12/31/1999	12/31/1998
Earnings Per Share	1.82	1.77	1.39	1.11	0.90	1.00	0.58	0.51
Cash Flow Per Share	1.88	1.86	1.58	1.20	1.59	0.68	0.90	0.62
Tang Book Value Per Share	2.10	2.02	0.79	...	...	...	...	0.54
Dividends Per Share	0.585	0.560	0.420	0.400	0.380	0.370	0.360	0.340
Dividend Payout %	32.14	31.64	30.22	36.04	42.46	37.19	61.54	66.67
Income Statement								
Total Revenue	1,881,100	7,747,800	6,876,000	6,228,300	5,994,500	5,714,600	5,289,100	5,212,700
EBITDA	287,500	1,343,000	1,161,500	1,022,000	846,400	864,300	621,700	546,700
Depn & Amortn	31,500	135,300	133,200	142,900	124,000	97,100	83,000	72,000
Income Before Taxes	253,700	1,187,500	993,500	835,600	665,700	691,000	506,600	455,900
Income Taxes	79,800	330,600	318,900	292,300	230,900	201,700	204,200	190,800
Net Income	172,000	846,100	664,800	534,600	430,000	478,400	302,400	270,000
Average Shares	477,000	477,960	483,140	490,940	492,100	485,900	518,740	531,900
Balance Sheet								
Current Assets	2,602,900	2,506,400	2,226,100	2,048,200	1,889,100	1,545,700	1,337,800	1,341,400
Total Assets	4,211,800	4,148,100	3,562,300	3,327,500	3,193,100	2,826,400	2,528,600	2,433,500
Current Liabilities	1,637,800	1,525,500	1,587,700	1,975,500	1,461,000	1,359,300	1,712,800	1,329,500
Long-Term Obligations	850,700	866,300	877,700	767,000	1,236,300	1,108,200	701,400	201,000
Total Liabilities	3,218,800	3,197,900	3,191,000	3,455,200	3,267,700	3,042,200	2,934,700	2,148,400
Stockholders' Equity	993,000	950,200	371,300	(127,700)	(74,600)	(215,800)	(406,100)	285,100
Shares Outstanding	472,015	471,530	470,596	470,515	473,362	476,324	475,790	525,040
Statistical Record								
Return on Assets %	22.55	21.89	19.30	16.40	14.29	17.82	12.19	11.47
Return on Equity %	123.19	127.70	545.81	...	...	...	...	94.72
EBITDA Margin %	15.28	17.33	16.89	16.41	14.12	15.12	11.75	10.49
Net Margin %	9.14	10.92	9.67	8.58	7.17	8.37	5.72	5.18
Asset Turnover	2.04	2.00	2.00	1.91	1.99	2.13	2.13	2.22
Current Ratio	1.59	1.64	1.40	1.04	1.29	1.14	0.78	1.01
Debt to Equity	0.86	0.91	2.36	...	...	...	...	0.71
Price Range	46.14-37.45	46.14-30.86	34.67-24.58	28.48-21.86	24.80-18.39	24.78-12.69	28.09-11.91	23.09-12.69
P/E Ratio	25.35-20.58	26.07-17.44	24.95-17.68	25.66-19.69	27.55-20.43	24.78-12.69	48.44-20.53	45.28-24.88
Average Yield %	1.39	1.40	1.38	1.58	1.71	1.94	1.69	1.82

Address: 1345 Avenue of the Americas, New York, NY 10105-0196
Telephone: 212-282-5000
Web Site: www.avon.com

Officers: Andrea Jung - Chmn., C.E.O. Susan J. Kropf - Pres., C.O.O. **Transfer Agents:** EquiServe Trust Company, N.A. Providence, RI

Investor Contact: 212-282-5320
No of Institutions: 446
Shares: 395,068,864 **% Held:** 83.79

BANCFIRST CORP.

Exchange	Symbol	Price	52Wk Range	Yield	P/E
NMS	BANF	$78.74 (5/31/2005)	79.58-56.80	1.42	15.78

*7 Year Price Score 132.87 *NYSE Composite Index=100 *12 Month Price Score 101.90

Interim Earnings (Per Share)

Qtr.	Mar	Jun	Sep	Dec
2002	0.96	1.02	1.07	1.01
2003	1.07	1.02	0.93	0.98
2004	1.03	1.08	1.17	1.38
2005	1.36	...	...	...

Interim Dividends (Per Share)

Amt	Decl	Ex	Rec	Pay
0.25Q	5/27/2004	6/28/2004	6/30/2004	7/15/2004
0.28Q	8/26/2004	9/28/2004	9/30/2004	10/15/2004
0.28Q	11/18/2004	12/29/2004	12/31/2004	1/14/2005
0.28Q	2/24/2005	3/29/2005	3/31/2005	4/15/2005

Indicated Div: $1.12

Valuation Analysis

Forecast P/E	14.57 (6/2/2005)		
Market Cap	$613.2 Million	Book Value	277.6 Million
Price/Book	2.21	Price/Sales	3.03

Dividend Achiever Status

Rank	79	**10 Year Growth Rate**	15.68%
Total Years of Dividend Growth			11

Business Summary: Commercial Banking (MIC: 8.1 SIC: 021 NAIC: 22110)

BancFirst is a bank holding company that provides a range of commercial banking services to retail customers and small to medium-sized businesses both in the non-metropolitan trade centers of Oklahoma and the metropolitan markets of Oklahoma City, Tulsa, Lawton, Muskogee, Norman and Shawnee. Retail and commercial banking services include commercial, real estate, agricultural and consumer lending; depository and funds transfer services; collections; safe deposit boxes; cash management services; retail brokerage services; and other services tailored for both individual and corporate customers. As of Dec 31 2004, total assets were $3.05 billion and deposits amounted to $2.66 billion.

Recent Developments: For the quarter ended Mar 31 2005, net income increased 32.9% to $10,887 thousand from net income of $8,191 thousand in the year-earlier quarter. Net interest income was $31,706 thousand, up 13.6% from $27,920 thousand the year before. Provision for loan losses was $792 thousand versus $720 thousand in the prior-year quarter, an increase of 10.0%. Non-interest income rose 5.5% to $12,348 thousand, while non-interest expense advanced 3.0% to $26,978 thousand.

Prospects: Co.'s outlook for the balance of 2005 appears promising, supported by continued momentum in loan growth and the underlying strength of the Oklahoma economy. Co. noted that its net interest income was up nearly 14% year over year to $31.7 million for the first quarter of 2005. Co. attributes the increase to loan growth, combined with a rising interest rate environment. Moreover, Co.'s net interest margin was 4.67% for the first quarter of 2005 versus 4.20% in the same period the year before. At Mar 31 2005, Co.'s total assets were $3.10 billion, with total loans of $2.10 billion, up 10.6% from $1.90 billion a year earlier. Deposits totaled $2.70 billion, unchanged from Mar 31 2004.

Financial Data (US$ in Thousands)	3 Mos	12/31/2004	12/31/2003	12/31/2002	12/31/2001	12/31/2000	12/31/1999	12/31/1998
Earnings Per Share	4.99	4.65	4.00	4.06	3.34	3.19	2.75	2.27
Cash Flow Per Share	20.11	17.14	4.05	5.17	4.27	3.82	3.41	2.80
Tang Book Value Per Share	31.02	30.77	28.51	28.25	24.34	21.18	17.34	19.14
Dividends Per Share	1.090	1.060	0.940	0.800	0.720	0.660	0.580	0.500
Dividend Payout %	21.84	22.80	23.50	19.70	21.56	20.69	21.09	22.03
Income Statement								
Interest Income	39,693	144,765	141,032	157,139	182,643	182,389	159,384	161,042
Interest Expense	7,987	27,519	31,915	47,809	77,711	80,054	66,149	68,290
Net Interest Income	31,706	117,246	109,117	109,330	104,932	102,335	93,235	92,752
Provision for Losses	792	2,699	3,722	5,276	1,780	4,045	2,521	2,211
Non-Interest Income	12,348	51,855	48,820	45,212	36,908	29,902	28,707	24,019
Non-Interest Expense	26,978	108,744	105,382	98,380	96,620	87,724	81,453	80,482
Income Before Taxes	16,284	57,658	48,833	50,886	43,440	40,468	37,968	34,078
Income Taxes	5,397	20,482	16,951	17,324	15,479	14,251	14,019	12,528
Net Income	10,887	37,176	31,882	33,562	27,961	26,217	23,949	21,550
Average Shares	8,009	7,995	7,972	8,260	8,371	8,224	8,699	9,510
Balance Sheet								
Net Loans & Leases	2,121,287	2,067,769	1,921,075	1,790,495	1,692,902	1,640,958	1,432,933	1,319,220
Total Assets	3,068,215	3,046,977	2,921,369	2,796,862	2,757,045	2,570,255	2,335,807	2,335,883
Total Deposits	2,674,914	2,657,434	2,585,690	2,428,648	2,401,328	2,267,397	2,082,696	2,024,800
Total Liabilities	2,790,586	2,769,480	2,665,997	2,545,354	2,533,877	2,373,297	2,171,093	2,133,966
Stockholders' Equity	277,629	277,497	255,372	251,508	223,168	196,958	164,714	201,917
Shares Outstanding	7,788	7,840	7,822	8,136	8,260	8,112	8,112	9,291
Statistical Record								
Return on Assets %	1.30	1.24	1.12	1.21	1.05	1.07	1.03	1.17
Return on Equity %	14.74	13.92	12.58	14.14	13.31	14.46	13.06	13.27
Net Interest Margin %	79.88	80.99	77.37	69.58	57.45	56.11	58.50	57.59
Efficiency Ratio %	51.84	55.31	55.51	48.62	44.01	41.32	43.31	43.49
Loans to Deposits	0.79	0.78	0.74	0.74	0.70	0.72	0.69	0.65
Price Range	79.58-55.00	79.58-55.00	59.80-42.85	51.74-34.45	43.25-33.75	40.25-24.88	37.13-30.50	48.25-32.88
P/E Ratio	15.95-11.02	17.11-11.83	14.95-10.71	12.74-8.49	12.95-10.10	12.62-7.80	13.50-11.09	21.26-14.48
Average Yield %	1.68	1.74	1.83	1.83	1.86	2.11	1.69	1.24

Address: 101 North Broadway, Oklahoma City, OK 73102-8401
Telephone: 405-270-1086
Web Site: www.bancfirst.com

Officers: H. E. Rainbolt - Chmn. James R. Daniel - Vice-Chmn. **Transfer Agents:** BancFirst Trust and Investment Management, Oklahoma City, OK

Investor Contact: 405-270-1044
No of Institutions: 54
Shares: 1,422,713 **% Held:** 18.15

BANCORPSOUTH INC.

Exchange	Symbol	Price	52Wk Range	Yield	P/E
NYS	BXS	$22.35 (5/31/2005)	25.22-20.01	3.40	15.10

Interim Earnings (Per Share)

Qtr.	Mar	Jun	Sep	Dec
2002	0.36	0.38	0.33	0.32
2003	0.50	0.37	0.43	0.37
2004	0.35	0.40	0.36	0.32
2005	0.40	...	...	...

Interim Dividends (Per Share)

Amt	Decl	Ex	Rec	Pay
0.18Q	7/21/2004	9/13/2004	9/15/2004	10/1/2004
0.19Q	10/27/2004	12/13/2004	12/15/2004	1/3/2005
0.19Q	1/26/2005	3/11/2005	3/15/2005	4/1/2005
0.19Q	4/27/2005	6/13/2005	6/15/2005	7/1/2005

Indicated Div: $0.76 (Div. Reinv. Plan)

Valuation Analysis

Forecast P/E	15.11 (5/28/2005)		
Market Cap	$1.7 Billion	Book Value	921.5 Million
Price/Book	1.90	Price/Sales	2.51

Dividend Achiever Status

Rank	169	10 Year Growth Rate	10.31%
Total Years of Dividend Growth			18

Business Summary: Commercial Banking (MIC: 8.1 SIC: 022 NAIC: 22110)

BancorpSouth is a bank holding company headquartered in Tupelo, MS with assets of $10.85 billion and total deposits of $9.06 billion as of Dec 31 2004. Co. operates 256 commercial banking, insurance, trust, broker/dealer and consumer finance locations in Mississippi, Tennessee, Alabama, Arkansas, Texas and Louisiana. Co. and its subsidiaries provide a range of financial services to individuals and small-to-medium size businesses. Co. operates investment services, consumer finance, credit insurance and insurance agency subsidiaries. Co.'s trust department offers a variety of services including personal trust and estate services, and certain employee benefit accounts and plans.

Recent Developments: For the quarter ended Mar 31 2005, net income increased 16.9% to $31,744 thousand from net income of $27,165 thousand in the year-earlier quarter. Net interest income was $87,129 thousand, up 4.4% from $83,482 thousand the year before. Provision for loan losses was $4,787 thousand versus $4,015 thousand in the prior-year quarter, an increase of 19.2%. Non-interest income rose 17.1% to $53,919 thousand, while non-interest expense advanced 4.3% to $89,688 thousand.

Prospects: Operating results reflect improvements in the economic, interest rate and operating environment in Co.'s market. Co. believes it is well-positioned to leverage these trends to strengthen its position in its existing markets and enter new, fast-growing markets, either within or contiguous to its six-state franchise. In pursuing these growth opportunities, Co. remains committed to customer service, high credit quality and a strong capitalization, which is integral to its long-term growth strategies. Separately, on Apr 1 2005, Co. announced the acquisition of Kyzar and Company, P.A., of Hattiesburg, MS and incorporation of the employees benefits firm into its Stewart Sneed Hewes division.

Financial Data

(US$ in Thousands)	3 Mos	12/31/2004	12/31/2003	12/31/2002	12/31/2001	12/31/2000	12/31/1999	12/31/1998
Earnings Per Share	1.48	1.43	1.68	1.39	1.19	0.88	1.20	1.01
Cash Flow Per Share	1.32	1.39	3.12	2.10	1.15	1.65	2.12	0.95
Tang Book Value Per Share	10.44	10.34	10.38	10.40	9.92	9.39	8.68	8.48
Dividends Per Share	0.740	0.730	0.660	0.610	0.570	0.530	0.490	0.450
Dividend Payout %	50.00	51.05	39.29	43.88	47.90	60.23	40.83	44.55
Income Statement								
Interest Income	132,111	497,629	526,911	590,418	665,835	674,035	414,187	383,519
Interest Expense	44,982	163,837	175,805	218,892	331,093	346,883	196,686	187,412
Net Interest Income	87,129	333,792	351,106	371,526	334,742	327,152	217,501	196,107
Provision for Losses	4,787	17,485	25,130	29,411	22,259	26,166	14,689	15,014
Non-Interest Income	53,919	183,519	190,086	132,239	128,633	85,578	79,331	53,018
Non-Interest Expense	89,688	342,945	322,594	312,398	295,313	274,227	183,000	152,084
Income Before Taxes	46,573	156,881	193,468	161,956	145,803	112,337	99,143	82,027
Income Taxes	14,829	46,261	62,334	49,938	47,340	37,941	30,190	27,550
Net Income	31,744	110,620	131,134	112,018	98,463	74,396	68,953	54,477
Average Shares	78,518	77,378	78,164	80,481	82,979	84,811	57,524	53,871
Balance Sheet								
Net Loans & Leases	6,814,681	6,745,025	6,140,955	6,301,510	5,990,050	6,013,585	3,997,975	3,419,083
Total Assets	10,829,104	10,848,193	10,305,035	10,189,247	9,395,429	9,044,034	5,776,926	5,203,741
Total Deposits	9,079,407	9,059,091	8,599,128	8,548,918	7,856,840	7,480,920	4,815,415	4,441,923
Total Liabilities	9,907,588	9,931,765	9,436,129	9,381,424	8,590,026	8,254,458	5,279,526	4,747,384
Stockholders' Equity	921,516	916,428	868,906	807,823	805,403	789,576	497,400	456,357
Shares Outstanding	78,256	78,037	77,926	77,680	81,225	84,043	57,304	53,833
Statistical Record								
Return on Assets %	1.08	1.04	1.28	1.14	1.07	1.00	1.26	1.16
Return on Equity %	12.77	12.36	15.64	13.89	12.35	11.53	14.46	13.34
Net Interest Margin %	65.95	67.08	66.63	62.93	50.27	48.54	52.51	51.13
Efficiency Ratio %	48.21	50.35	44.99	43.23	37.17	36.10	37.08	34.84
Loans to Deposits	0.75	0.74	0.71	0.74	0.76	0.80	0.83	0.77
Price Range	25.22-19.82	25.22-19.82	24.45-17.72	22.00-16.30	17.00-12.88	17.13-11.88	19.13-15.50	23.75-17.00
P/E Ratio	17.04-13.39	17.64-13.86	14.55-10.55	15.83-11.73	14.29-10.82	19.46-13.49	15.94-12.92	23.51-16.83
Average Yield %	3.32	3.25	3.12	3.11	3.76	3.61	2.91	2.19

Address: One Mississippi Plaza, 201 South Spring Street, Tupelo, MS 38804 **Telephone:** 662-680-2000 **Web Site:** www.bancorpsouth.com	**Officers:** Aubrey B. Patterson - Chmn., C.E.O. James V. Kelley - Pres., C.O.O. **Transfer Agents:** SunTrust Bank, Atlanta, GA	**No of Institutions:** 103 **Shares:** 15,228,640 % **Held:** 19.45

BANDAG, INC.

Exchange	Symbol	Price	52Wk Range	Yield	P/E
NYS	BDG	$46.28 (5/31/2005)	50.72-42.63	2.85	13.30

*7 Year Price Score 114.48 *NYSE Composite Index=100 *12 Month Price Score 95.35

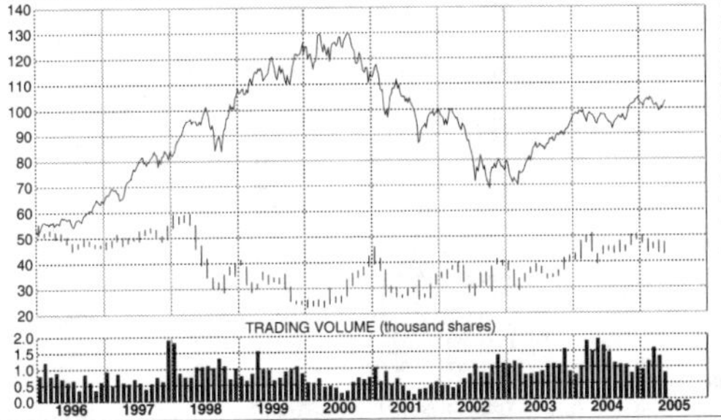

TRADING VOLUME (thousand shares)

Interim Earnings (Per Share)

Qtr.	Mar	Jun	Sep	Dec
2002	(2.21)	0.57	1.02	0.87
2003	0.12	0.45	1.03	1.50
2004	0.20	0.60	1.02	1.56
2005	0.30	...	...	...

Interim Dividends (Per Share)

Amt	Decl	Ex	Rec	Pay
0.325Q	8/17/2004	9/15/2004	9/17/2004	10/18/2004
0.33Q	11/9/2004	12/16/2004	12/20/2004	1/20/2005
0.33Q	3/15/2005	3/23/2005	3/28/2005	4/20/2005
0.33Q	5/3/2005	6/16/2005	6/20/2005	7/20/2005

Indicated Div: $1.32 (Div. Reinv. Plan)

Valuation Analysis

Forecast P/E	15.29 (5/28/2005)		
Market Cap	$905.8 Million	Book Value	535.8 Million
Price/Book	1.69	Price/Sales	1.03

Dividend Achiever Status

Rank	242	10 Year Growth Rate	6.39%
Total Years of Dividend Growth			28

Business Summary: Rubber Products (MIC: 11.6 SIC: 011 NAIC: 26211)

Bandag manufactures and sells precured tread rubber, equipment and supplies for retreading tires. At Dec 31 2004, Co. and its licensees have 985 franchisees worldwide. The majority of Co.'s franchisees are independent operators of full service tire distributorships. Co. sells and maintains new and retread tires to principally commercial and industrial customers through its wholly-owned subsidiary, Tire Distribution Systems. Also, Co. provides quick-service truck lubrication and tire service through its 87.5%-owned subsidiary, Speedco through 33 on-highway locations.

Recent Developments: For the quarter ended Mar 31 2005, net income increased 48.3% to $5,962 thousand from net income of $4,019 thousand in the year-earlier quarter. Revenues were $189,041 thousand, up 7.8% from $175,291 thousand the year before. Operating income was $8,675 thousand versus an income of $5,932 thousand in the prior-year quarter, an increase of 46.2%. Total direct expense was $123,294 thousand versus $112,803 thousand in the prior-year quarter, an increase of 9.3%. Total indirect expense was $57,072 thousand versus $56,556 thousand in the prior-year quarter, an increase of 0.9%.

Prospects: Results reflect growing strength in the North American trucking industry, offset in part by global high raw material and transportation costs, which are pressuring margins in its traditional business. On the positive side, Co. believes continued strength in the trucking industry in its major markets will work to its benefit as it continues delivering an expanded array of valued-added vehicle services, which complement its traditional business. At the same time, Co. recognizes that continued increases in raw material and transportation costs will be a concern throughout 2005.

Financial Data

(US$ in Thousands)	3 Mos	12/31/2004	12/31/2003	12/31/2002	12/31/2001	12/31/2000	12/31/1999	12/31/1998
Earnings Per Share	3.48	3.39	3.11	0.14	2.12	2.90	2.40	2.63
Cash Flow Per Share	4.20	4.92	4.08	6.65	5.66	4.78	5.18	3.85
Tang Book Value Per Share	25.74	25.55	24.61	21.97	21.22	20.03	18.62	17.84
Dividends Per Share	1.310	1.305	1.285	1.265	1.230	1.190	1.150	1.110
Dividend Payout %	37.64	38.50	41.32	903.57	58.02	41.03	47.92	42.21
Income Statement								
Total Revenue	189,041	867,953	828,186	911,953	982,209	1,013,426	1,027,878	1,079,498
EBITDA	15,157	109,191	113,482	110,708	120,036	158,572	155,581	161,695
Depn & Amortn	6,482	27,182	27,179	32,333	46,155	50,465	53,764	51,410
Income Before Taxes	10,032	84,902	83,900	71,518	66,505	99,375	92,090	99,513
Income Taxes	4,193	17,648	23,700	21,465	22,673	39,042	39,760	40,194
Net Income	5,962	66,880	60,200	2,793	43,832	60,333	52,330	59,319
Average Shares	19,707	19,707	19,369	19,888	20,686	20,778	21,764	22,559
Balance Sheet								
Current Assets	476,100	486,255	466,286	416,082	450,174	427,179	428,118	439,124
Total Assets	722,731	730,727	660,529	617,827	718,572	714,549	722,421	755,729
Current Liabilities	146,412	158,558	148,193	147,861	186,075	132,735	154,053	174,909
Long-Term Obligations	31,025	17,143	22,857	28,571	94,286	100,000	100,000	100,000
Total Liabilities	186,889	198,440	183,452	193,234	229,576	240,392	268,346	288,432
Stockholders' Equity	535,842	532,287	477,077	424,593	488,996	474,157	454,075	467,297
Shares Outstanding	19,572	19,451	19,268	19,151	20,641	20,561	20,770	21,955
Statistical Record								
Return on Assets %	9.90	9.59	9.42	0.42	6.12	8.37	7.08	7.17
Return on Equity %	13.53	13.22	13.35	0.61	9.10	12.96	11.36	12.75
EBITDA Margin %	8.02	12.58	13.70	12.14	12.22	15.65	15.14	14.98
Net Margin %	3.15	7.71	7.27	0.31	4.46	5.95	5.09	5.50
Asset Turnover	1.27	1.24	1.30	1.36	1.37	1.41	1.39	1.30
Current Ratio	3.25	3.07	3.15	2.81	2.42	3.22	2.78	2.51
Debt to Equity	0.06	0.03	0.05	0.07	0.19	0.21	0.22	0.21
Price Range	51.05-38.98	51.05-38.98	42.30-28.67	41.16-26.47	46.19-25.34	42.63-22.38	41.25-23.63	59.50-28.38
P/E Ratio	14.67-11.20	15.06-11.50	13.60-9.22	294.00-189.07	21.79-11.95	14.70-7.72	17.19-9.84	22.62-10.79
Average Yield %	2.84	2.86	3.58	3.63	3.99	4.10	3.62	2.52

Address: 2905 North Highway 61, Muscatine, IA 52761-5886
Telephone: 563-262-1400
Web Site: www.bandag.com

Officers: Martin G. Carver - Chmn., Pres., C.E.O. Warren W. Heidbreder - V.P., C.F.O., Sec. **Transfer Agents:** EquiServe Trust Company, N.A. Providence, RI

Investor Contact: 319-262-1260
No of Institutions: 106
Shares: 5,793,709 **% Held:** 63.55

BANK OF AMERICA CORP.

Exchange	Symbol	Price	52Wk Range	Yield	P/E
NYS	BAC	$46.32 (5/31/2005)	47.44-41.27	3.89	11.85

Interim Earnings (Per Share)

Qtr.	Mar	Jun	Sep	Dec
2002	0.69	0.70	0.72	0.84
2003	0.80	0.90	0.96	0.91
2004	0.92	0.93	0.91	0.93
2005	1.14	...	...	...

Interim Dividends (Per Share)

Amt	Decl	Ex	Rec	Pay
100%	6/23/2004	8/30/2004	8/6/2004	8/27/2004
0.45Q	10/27/2004	12/1/2004	12/3/2004	12/22/2004
0.45Q	1/26/2005	3/2/2005	3/4/2005	3/25/2005
0.45Q	4/27/2005	6/1/2005	6/3/2005	6/24/2005

Indicated Div: $1.80 (Div. Reinv. Plan)

Valuation Analysis

Forecast P/E 10.98 (6/2/2005)

Market Cap $186.9 Billion Book Value 98.5 Billion

Price/Book 1.90 Price/Sales 2.65

Dividend Achiever Status

Rank 112 **10 Year Growth Rate** 13.72%

Total Years of Dividend Growth 27

Business Summary: Commercial Banking (MIC: 8.1 SIC: 021 NAIC: 22110)

Bank of America, with $1.110 trillion in total assets as of Dec 31 2004, is a bank holding and financial holding company. Co.'s Global Consumer and Small Business Banking segment provides range of products and services to individuals and small businesses. Global Business and Financial Services primarily provides commercial lending and treasury management services to middle-market companies. Global Capital Markets and Investment Banking provides capital-raising services, advisory services, derivatives capabilities, equity and debt sales and trading. Global Wealth and Investment Management offers an array of services to institutional clients, high-net-worth individuals and retail customers.

Recent Developments: For the quarter ended Mar 31 2005, net income increased 75.1% to $4,695,000 thousand from net income of $2,681,000 thousand in the year-earlier quarter. Net interest income was $7,873,000 thousand, up 35.7% from $5,801,000 thousand the year before. Provision for loan losses was $580,000 thousand versus $624,000 thousand in the prior-year quarter, a decrease of 7.1%. Non-interest income rose 64.9% to $6,149,000 thousand, while non-interest expense advanced 30.0% to $7,057,000 thousand.

Prospects: Co.'s prospects appear satisfactory, reflecting in part the continuing integration of the Fleet franchise that should enhance its ability to achieve future growth. During 2004, Co. rebranded all banking centers in the former FleetBoston franchise, as well as a majority of outstanding credit cards. In addition, Co. began to rollout customer service platforms, including Premier Banking, to the Northeast. Co. also completed several key systems conversions necessary for full integration. Meanwhile, Co. indicated that during the quarter ended Mar 31 2005 it experienced improving commercial loan growth across its franchise and strong deposit growth, further strengthening its near-term outlook.

Financial Data

(US$ in Thousands)	3 Mos	12/31/2004	12/31/2003	12/31/2002	12/31/2001	12/31/2000	12/31/1999	12/31/1998
Earnings Per Share	3.91	3.69	3.56	2.96	2.09	2.26	2.24	1.45
Cash Flow Per Share	0.03	(1.05)	8.18	(3.95)	(4.02)	1.59	3.50	3.90
Tang Book Value Per Share	11.53	11.80	11.38	11.88	10.40	9.50	7.83	8.34
Dividends Per Share	1.750	1.700	1.440	1.220	1.140	1.030	0.925	0.795
Dividend Payout %	44.76	46.07	40.39	41.29	54.55	45.58	41.29	54.83
Income Statement								
Interest Income	13,153,000	43,227,000	31,643,000	32,161,000	38,293,000	43,258,000	37,323,000	38,588,000
Interest Expense	5,280,000	14,430,000	10,179,000	11,238,000	18,003,000	24,816,000	19,086,000	20,290,000
Net Interest Income	7,873,000	28,797,000	21,464,000	20,923,000	20,290,000	18,442,000	18,237,000	18,298,000
Provision for Losses	580,000	2,769,000	2,839,000	3,697,000	4,287,000	2,535,000	1,820,000	2,920,000
Non-Interest Income	6,808,000	20,097,000	16,422,000	13,571,000	14,348,000	14,514,000	14,309,000	13,206,000
Non-Interest Expense	7,057,000	27,027,000	20,127,000	18,436,000	20,709,000	18,633,000	18,511,000	20,536,000
Income Before Taxes	7,044,000	21,221,000	15,861,000	12,991,000	10,117,000	11,788,000	12,215,000	8,048,000
Income Taxes	2,349,000	7,078,000	5,051,000	3,742,000	3,325,000	4,271,000	4,333,000	2,883,000
Net Income	4,695,000	14,143,000	10,810,000	9,249,000	6,792,000	7,517,000	7,882,000	5,165,000
Average Shares	4,099,062	3,823,943	3,030,356	3,130,934	3,251,308	3,329,858	3,520,116	3,551,520
Balance Sheet								
Net Loans & Leases	521,153,000	513,211,000	365,300,000	335,904,000	322,278,000	385,355,000	363,834,000	350,206,000
Total Assets	1,212,239,000	1,110,457,000	736,445,000	660,458,000	621,764,000	642,191,000	632,574,000	617,679,000
Total Deposits	629,987,000	618,570,000	414,113,000	386,458,000	373,495,000	364,244,000	347,273,000	357,260,000
Total Liabilities	1,113,720,000	1,010,812,000	688,465,000	610,139,000	573,244,000	594,563,000	588,142,000	571,741,000
Stockholders' Equity	98,519,000	99,645,000	47,980,000	50,319,000	48,520,000	47,628,000	44,432,000	45,938,000
Shares Outstanding	4,035,319	4,046,546	2,882,286	3,001,382	3,118,594	3,227,264	3,354,546	3,448,968
Statistical Record								
Return on Assets %	1.59	1.53	1.55	1.44	1.07	1.18	1.26	1.17
Return on Equity %	21.94	19.11	21.99	18.72	14.13	16.29	17.44	15.35
Net Interest Margin %	59.86	66.62	67.83	65.06	52.99	42.63	48.86	47.42
Efficiency Ratio %	35.35	42.68	41.87	40.31	39.34	32.25	35.85	39.65
Loans to Deposits	0.83	0.83	0.88	0.87	0.86	1.06	1.05	0.98
Price Range	47.44-38.96	47.44-38.96	41.77-32.81	38.45-27.07	32.50-23.38	30.50-19.00	37.75-24.00	43.97-24.03
P/E Ratio	12.13-9.96	12.86-10.56	11.73-9.22	12.99-9.15	15.55-11.18	13.50-8.41	16.85-10.71	30.32-16.57
Average Yield %	3.99	3.99	3.82	3.61	3.98	4.23	2.87	2.35

Address: Bank of America Corporate Center, 100 N. Tryon Street, Charlotte, NC 28255
Telephone: 704-386-8486
Web Site: www.bankofamerica.com

Officers: Kenneth D. Lewis - Chmn., C.E.O. Marc D. Oken - Exec. V.P., C.F.O. **Transfer Agents:** Mellon Investor Services LLC, South Hackensack, NJ

Investor Contact: 704-386-5681
No of Institutions: 1106
Shares: 2,373,363,456 **% Held:** 58.55

BANK OF HAWAII CORP

Exchange	Symbol	Price	52Wk Range	Yield	P/E
NYS	BOH	$48.73 (5/31/2005)	50.95-43.24	2.71	15.13

*7 Year Price Score 145.47 *NYSE Composite Index=100 *12 Month Price Score 96.96

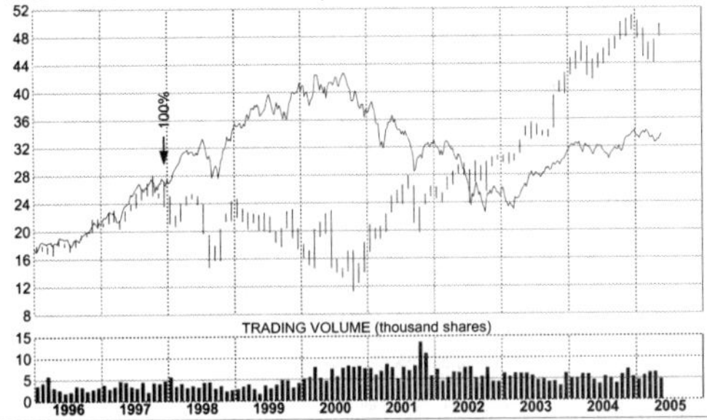

Interim Earnings (Per Share)

Qtr.	Mar	Jun	Sep	Dec
2002	0.41	0.42	0.43	0.44
2003	0.47	0.48	0.61	0.65
2004	0.69	0.79	0.78	0.82
2005	0.83	...	...	...

Interim Dividends (Per Share)

Amt	Decl	Ex	Rec	Pay
0.30Q	7/23/2004	8/26/2004	8/30/2004	9/15/2004
0.33Q	10/22/2004	11/24/2004	11/29/2004	12/14/2004
0.33Q	1/24/2005	2/24/2005	2/28/2005	3/14/2005
0.33Q	4/25/2005	5/26/2005	5/31/2005	6/14/2005

Indicated Div: $1.32 (Div. Reinv. Plan)

Valuation Analysis

Forecast P/E	N/A		
Market Cap	$2.6 Billion	Book Value	716.7 Million
Price/Book	3.59	Price/Sales	3.83

Dividend Achiever Status

Rank	192	10 Year Growth Rate	8.99%
Total Years of Dividend Growth			27

Business Summary: Commercial Banking (MIC: 8.1 SIC: 022 NAIC: 22110)

Bank of Hawaii, with assets of $9.77 billion as of Dec 31 2004, is a bank holding company. Co. operates in Hawaii, Guam and nearby islands, and American Samoa. The Retail banking segment offers loan, lease and deposit products to consumers and small businesses. The Commercial banking segment provides corporate banking and commercial real estate loans, lease financing, auto dealer financing, deposit and cash management products to mid-to-large sized companies. The Investment Services group includes private banking, trust services, asset management, institutional investment advice and retail brokerage. The Treasury and Other Corporate segment provides corporate asset and liability management.

Recent Developments: For the first quarter ended Mar 31 2005, net income advanced 14.4% to $45.5 million compared with $39.8 million in the corresponding prior-year quarter. Net interest income increased 4.8% to $100.7 million from $96.0 million a year earlier. Total non-interest income climbed 7.1% to $52.3 million from $48.8 million the year before, reflecting increased fee income due to increases in average assets under management and higher investment advisory fees on money market assets. Total non-interest expense declined 2.6% to $80.9 million from $83.0 million in the previous year.

Prospects: Co.'s strong performance continues to be supported by overall credit and asset quality and the strong Hawaiian economy. At the end of the first quarter of 2005, Co.'s non-performing assets were $13.4 million, a decrease of 52.0% compared with $27.9 million at the end of the corresponding prior-year quarter. Meanwhile, Co.'s net interest margin continues to improve, primarily the result of higher volume in its investment portfolio. Separately, Hawaii's economy is benefiting from renewed tourism growth in early 2005 which is augmenting the strength in residential investment. As a result, Co. now expects full-year 2005 net income to range from $176.0 million to $179.0 million.

Financial Data (US$ in Thousands)	3 Mos	12/31/2004	12/31/2003	12/31/2002	12/31/2001	12/31/2000	12/31/1999	12/31/1998
Earnings Per Share	3.22	3.08	2.21	1.70	1.46	1.42	1.64	1.32
Cash Flow Per Share	7.63	4.87	5.46	9.13	(3.28)	3.50	1.95	2.48
Tang Book Value Per Share	12.55	13.83	13.38	15.09	16.16	13.93	12.57	12.07
Dividends Per Share	1.260	1.230	0.870	0.730	0.720	0.710	0.680	0.657
Dividend Payout %	39.13	39.94	39.37	42.94	49.32	50.00	41.46	49.81
Income Statement								
Interest Income	120,158	455,014	442,521	516,538	828,262	1,057,493	1,026,519	1,099,786
Interest Expense	19,500	64,424	76,579	146,307	368,584	501,262	451,776	523,185
Net Interest Income	100,658	390,590	365,942	370,231	459,678	556,231	574,743	576,601
Provision for Losses	...	(10,000)	...	11,616	74,339	142,853	60,915	84,014
Non-Interest Income	52,315	205,094	198,720	199,921	452,619	263,429	265,581	211,751
Non-Interest Expense	80,863	334,440	357,875	370,835	597,616	496,430	553,238	540,279
Income Before Taxes	72,110	271,244	206,787	187,701	239,959	179,990	225,686	163,613
Income Taxes	26,588	97,905	71,592	66,521	122,164	66,329	92,729	56,649
Net Income	45,522	173,339	135,195	121,180	117,795	113,661	132,957	106,964
Average Shares	55,020	56,241	61,085	71,447	80,577	79,813	80,044	81,142
Balance Sheet								
Net Loans & Leases	5,910,784	5,880,134	5,628,095	5,216,151	5,493,539	9,168,140	9,280,848	9,416,809
Total Assets	9,908,030	9,766,191	9,461,647	9,516,418	10,627,797	14,013,816	14,440,315	15,016,563
Total Deposits	7,760,662	7,564,667	7,332,779	6,920,161	6,673,596	9,080,581	9,394,218	9,576,342
Total Liabilities	9,191,374	8,951,357	8,668,515	8,500,659	9,380,785	12,712,460	13,227,985	13,830,969
Stockholders' Equity	716,656	814,834	793,132	1,015,759	1,247,012	1,301,356	1,212,330	1,185,594
Shares Outstanding	52,826	54,960	54,928	63,015	73,218	79,612	80,036	80,326
Statistical Record								
Return on Assets %	1.80	1.80	1.42	1.20	0.96	0.80	0.90	0.71
Return on Equity %	23.84	21.50	14.95	10.71	9.24	9.02	11.09	9.29
Net Interest Margin %	83.77	85.84	82.69	71.68	55.50	52.60	55.99	52.43
Efficiency Ratio %	46.88	50.66	55.81	51.76	46.66	37.58	42.82	41.19
Loans to Deposits	0.76	0.78	0.77	0.75	0.82	1.01	0.99	0.98
Price Range	50.95-41.70	50.95-41.70	42.72-29.43	30.75-23.88	27.88-16.94	22.94-11.25	24.69-17.38	25.44-14.75
P/E Ratio	15.82-12.95	16.54-13.54	19.33-13.32	18.09-14.05	19.10-11.60	16.15-7.92	15.05-10.59	19.27-11.17
Average Yield %	2.70	2.68	2.54	2.62	3.13	4.26	3.25	3.03

Address: 130 Merchant Street, Honolulu, HI 96813
Telephone: 808-538-4727
Web Site: www.boh.com

Officers: Allan R. Landon - Chmn., Pres., C.E.O. Alton T. Kuioka - Vice-Chair, Commercial Banking
ransfer Agents:

Investor Contact: 808-537-8037
No of Institutions: 181
Shares: 35,634,364 **% Held:** 66.65

BANTA CORPORATION

Exchange	Symbol	Price	52Wk Range	Yield	P/E
NYS	BN	$43.92 (5/31/2005)	46.34-36.84	1.64	15.80

*7 Year Price Score 120.89 *NYSE Composite Index=100 *12 Month Price Score 96.50

Interim Earnings (Per Share)

Qtr.	Mar	Jun	Sep	Dec
2002	0.41	0.52	0.76	0.01
2003	0.44	0.28	0.62	0.47
2004	0.54	0.60	0.76	0.78
2005	0.63	...	...	...

Interim Dividends (Per Share)

Amt	Decl	Ex	Rec	Pay
0.17Q	7/27/2004	10/13/2004	10/15/2004	11/1/2004
0.17Q	12/7/2004	1/19/2005	1/21/2005	2/1/2005
0.17Q	1/25/2005	4/13/2005	4/15/2005	5/2/2005
0.18Q	4/26/2005	7/13/2005	7/15/2005	8/1/2005

Indicated Div: $0.72 (Div. Reinv. Plan)

Valuation Analysis

Forecast P/E	15.31 (5/28/2005)		
Market Cap	$1.1 Billion	Book Value	531.5 Million
Price/Book	2.05	Price/Sales	0.71

Dividend Achiever Status

Rank	233	**10 Year Growth Rate**	6.97%
Total Years of Dividend Growth			26

Business Summary: Printing (MIC: 13.4 SIC: 759 NAIC: 23119)

Banta operates in three business segments. Co.'s printing services segment provides printing and digital imaging applications to publishers and direct marketers. Products and services include books, catalogs, publications, product brochures, literature management services, educational materials and e-business services. The global supply-chain management services unit provides outsourcing capabilities to technology companies. Services range from materials sourcing, product configuration and customized kitting, to order fulfillment and global distribution. Co.'s healthcare segment produces and sources disposable products used in outpatient clinics, dental offices and hospitals.

Recent Developments: For the quarter ended Apr 2 2005, income from continuing operations increased 7.3% to $13,747 thousand from income of $12,817 thousand in the year-earlier quarter. Net income increased 13.7% to $16,007 thousand from net income of $14,074 thousand in the year-earlier quarter. Revenues were $386,277 thousand, up 10.5% from $349,528 thousand the year before. Operating income was $20,622 thousand versus an income of $21,160 thousand in the prior-year quarter, a decrease of 2.5%. Total direct expense was $302,358 thousand versus $277,302 thousand in the prior-year quarter, an increase of 9.0%. Total indirect expense was $63,297 thousand versus $51,066 thousand in the prior-year quarter, an increase of 24.0%.

Prospects: Co.'s outlook for full-year 2005 remains positive, although Co. expects its operating earnings growth to be back-end loaded into the second half of the year. Co.'s second quarter plans include productivity-enhancing projects that will generate one-time costs in the second quarter, but create long-term benefits beginning mid-year. During the second quarter, three presses will be out of service and undergoing rebuilds. Two are being relocated to operations needing additional capacity, and one is undergoing the most-extensive rebuild in Co.'s history. Co. anticipates additional expenses related to its Literature Management Group formation and the rollout of its corporate productivity programs.

Financial Data

(US$ in Thousands)	3 Mos	01/01/2005	01/03/2004	12/28/2002	12/29/2001	12/30/2000	01/01/2000	01/02/1999
Earnings Per Share	2.78	2.67	1.81	1.71	2.01	2.35	0.59	1.80
Cash Flow Per Share	3.38	3.38	4.26	5.89	7.26	5.05	4.64	4.64
Tang Book Value Per Share	18.75	18.83	17.35	15.46	13.89	12.41	12.31	11.83
Dividends Per Share	0.680	0.680	0.660	0.640	0.610	0.600	0.560	0.510
Dividend Payout %	24.50	25.47	36.46	37.43	30.35	25.53	94.92	28.33
Income Statement								
Total Revenue	386,277	1,523,252	1,418,497	1,366,457	1,457,935	1,537,729	1,278,278	1,335,796
EBITDA	35,496	169,462	146,682	161,574	171,295	189,141	115,184	163,777
Depn & Amortn	14,460	59,943	63,848	78,430	75,378	75,744	68,212	66,862
Income Before Taxes	20,217	105,430	74,414	71,801	82,197	96,643	34,610	86,090
Income Taxes	6,470	37,425	27,800	28,002	32,200	37,900	18,600	33,150
Net Income	16,007	68,005	46,614	43,799	49,997	58,743	16,010	52,940
Average Shares	25,400	25,508	25,742	25,565	24,857	24,980	27,177	29,474
Balance Sheet								
Current Assets	523,193	524,241	523,166	460,150	373,616	406,675	355,861	354,620
Total Assets	895,852	905,573	886,023	805,264	788,046	854,524	773,344	769,966
Current Liabilities	219,474	223,606	223,851	185,782	184,750	240,319	245,353	196,491
Long-Term Obligations	61,073	62,333	87,712	111,489	130,981	179,202	113,520	120,628
Total Liabilities	364,331	367,607	372,594	352,151	380,768	483,612	419,569	360,035
Stockholders' Equity	531,521	537,966	513,429	453,113	407,278	370,912	353,775	409,931
Shares Outstanding	24,828	25,046	25,791	25,247	24,729	24,566	23,942	28,260
Statistical Record								
Return on Assets %	8.05	7.61	5.42	5.51	6.10	7.24	2.08	6.84
Return on Equity %	13.84	12.97	9.49	10.21	12.88	16.26	4.20	12.88
EBITDA Margin %	9.19	11.13	10.34	11.82	11.75	12.30	9.01	12.26
Net Margin %	4.14	4.46	3.29	3.21	3.43	3.82	1.25	3.96
Asset Turnover	1.77	1.71	1.65	1.72	1.78	1.89	1.66	1.73
Current Ratio	2.38	2.34	2.34	2.48	2.02	1.69	1.45	1.80
Debt to Equity	0.11	0.12	0.17	0.25	0.32	0.48	0.32	0.29
Price Range	47.00-36.84	47.00-36.84	40.93-27.34	38.91-29.30	30.92-22.93	25.42-17.56	27.00-17.25	34.88-21.88
P/E Ratio	16.91-13.25	17.60-13.80	22.61-15.10	22.75-17.13	15.38-11.41	10.82-7.47	45.76-29.24	19.38-12.15
Average Yield %	1.60	1.60	1.95	1.90	2.23	2.92	2.46	1.78

Address: 225 Main Street, Menasha, WI 54952-8003 **Telephone:** 920-751-7777 **Web Site:** www.banta.com	**Officers:** Stephanie A. Streeter - Chmn., Pres., C.E.O. Michael B. Allen - Pres., Print Sector **Transfer Agents:** American Stock Transfer & Trust Company, New York, NY	**Investor Contact:** 920-751-7777 **No of Institutions:** 172 **Shares:** 21,092,238 **% Held:** 83.91

BARD (C.R.), INC.

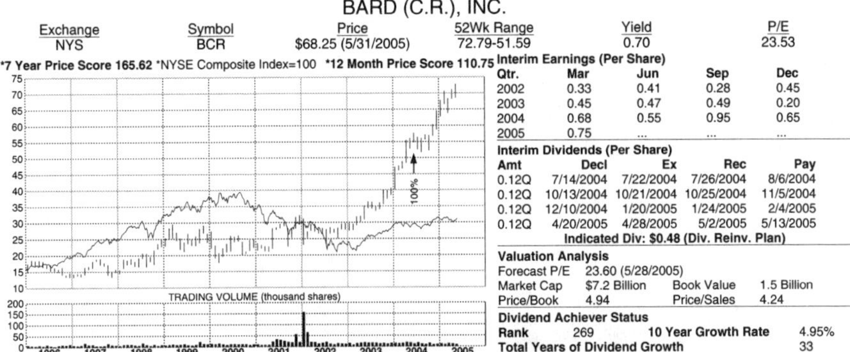

Exchange	Symbol	Price	52Wk Range	Yield	P/E
NYS	BCR	$68.25 (5/31/2005)	72.79-51.59	0.70	23.53

Interim Earnings (Per Share)

Qtr.	Mar	Jun	Sep	Dec
2002	0.33	0.41	0.28	0.45
2003	0.45	0.47	0.49	0.20
2004	0.68	0.55	0.95	0.65
2005	0.75	...	...	...

Interim Dividends (Per Share)

Amt	Decl	Ex	Rec	Pay
0.12Q	7/14/2004	7/22/2004	7/26/2004	8/6/2004
0.12Q	10/13/2004	10/21/2004	10/25/2004	11/5/2004
0.12Q	12/10/2004	1/20/2005	1/24/2005	2/4/2005
0.12Q	4/20/2005	4/28/2005	5/2/2005	5/13/2005

Indicated Div: $0.48 (Div. Reinv. Plan)

Valuation Analysis

Forecast P/E	23.60 (5/28/2005)		
Market Cap	$7.2 Billion	Book Value	1.5 Billion
Price/Book	4.94	Price/Sales	4.24

Dividend Achiever Status

Rank	269	10 Year Growth Rate	4.95%
Total Years of Dividend Growth			33

Business Summary: Medical Instruments & Equipment (MIC: 9.6 SIC: 841 NAIC: 39112)

C.R. Bard is engaged in the design, manufacture, packaging, distribution and sale of medical, surgical, diagnostic and patient-care devices. Co.'s product for the peripheral vascular market include minimally invasive vascular products, electrophysiology products, and fabrics, meshes and implantable vascular grafts. Co.'s urology products include Foley catheters, as well as surgical sling and injectable tissue bulking products and urine monitoring and collection systems. Co. also provides a range of oncology devices for the treatment and management of cancer as well as several surgical specialty products, such as meshes for soft tissue repair, irrigation devices and hemostasis products.

Recent Developments: For the quarter ended Mar 31 2005, net income increased 13.1% to $81,300 thousand from net income of $71,900 thousand in the year-earlier quarter. Revenues were $428,600 thousand, up 8.8% from $393,800 thousand the year before. Total direct expense was $164,900 thousand versus $161,600 thousand in the prior-year quarter, an increase of 2.0%. Total indirect expense was $155,800 thousand versus $143,900 thousand in the prior-year quarter, an increase of 8.3%.

Prospects: Co. is experiencing strong revenue growth across all of its major product groups, reflecting the strength of its product portfolio and the importance of new technologies. Co.'s earnings are benefiting from gross margin expansion and lower operating expenses. Meanwhile, Co. expects improving operating efficiencies to provide it the necessary capital to invest in its key franchises. Going forward, Co.'s key growth initiatives include additional focus on research and development, the expansion of its sales organization, business development activities and improved manufacturing efficiencies. Co. also plans to increase sales through selective business, product and technology acquisitions.

Financial Data

(US$ in Thousands)	3 Mos	12/31/2004	12/31/2003	12/31/2002	12/31/2001	12/31/2000	12/31/1999	12/31/1998
Earnings Per Share	2.90	2.82	1.60	1.47	1.38	1.04	1.14	2.25
Cash Flow Per Share	2.93	2.65	2.54	2.62	2.42	2.03	0.88	1.87
Tang Book Value Per Share	7.90	7.26	5.35	4.84	3.97	2.53	2.34	2.03
Dividends Per Share	0.475	0.470	0.450	0.430	0.420	0.410	0.390	0.370
Dividend Payout %	16.38	16.67	28.13	29.25	30.55	39.23	34.21	16.41
Income Statement								
Total Revenue	428,600	1,656,100	1,433,100	1,273,800	1,181,300	1,098,800	1,036,500	1,164,700
EBITDA	124,400	460,500	261,300	245,500	238,700	199,900	220,300	517,100
Depn & Amortn	16,700	54,700	44,700	41,000	40,000	49,600	49,100	58,700
Income Before Taxes	111,200	414,200	223,200	211,000	204,900	154,000	173,300	464,400
Income Taxes	29,900	111,400	54,700	56,000	61,700	47,100	55,200	212,100
Net Income	81,300	302,800	168,500	155,000	143,200	106,900	118,100	252,300
Average Shares	108,200	107,200	105,200	105,600	104,001	102,443	103,763	111,940
Balance Sheet								
Current Assets	1,078,900	1,054,000	875,100	758,000	647,400	526,600	529,100	488,500
Total Assets	2,067,800	2,009,100	1,692,000	1,416,700	1,231,100	1,089,200	1,126,400	1,079,800
Current Liabilities	380,600	390,300	421,900	316,900	234,500	224,500	352,500	302,800
Long-Term Obligations	151,400	151,400	151,500	152,200	156,400	204,300	158,400	160,000
Total Liabilities	614,600	649,000	646,300	536,300	442,400	475,300	552,100	512,200
Stockholders' Equity	1,453,200	1,360,100	1,045,700	880,400	788,700	613,900	574,300	567,600
Shares Outstanding	105,113	104,672	103,509	103,205	104,767	101,817	101,563	102,995
Statistical Record								
Return on Assets %	16.20	16.32	10.84	11.71	12.34	9.62	10.71	21.39
Return on Equity %	24.02	25.10	17.50	18.57	20.42	17.94	20.68	44.24
EBITDA Margin %	29.02	27.81	18.23	19.27	20.21	18.19	21.25	44.40
Net Margin %	18.97	18.28	11.76	12.17	12.12	9.73	11.39	21.66
Asset Turnover	0.88	0.89	0.92	0.96	1.02	0.99	0.94	0.99
Current Ratio	2.83	2.70	2.07	2.39	2.76	2.35	1.50	1.61
Debt to Equity	0.10	0.11	0.14	0.17	0.20	0.33	0.28	0.28
Price Range	70.65-48.33	64.58-40.20	40.63-27.41	32.25-23.13	32.26-21.00	27.34-17.63	29.56-21.13	24.75-14.34
P/E Ratio	24.36-16.66	22.90-14.26	25.39-17.13	21.94-15.73	23.37-15.21	26.29-16.95	25.93-18.53	11.00-6.38
Average Yield %	0.81	0.88	1.33	1.57	1.62	1.82	1.55	1.95

Address: 730 Central Avenue, Murray Hill, NJ 07974 **Telephone:** 908-277-8000 **Web Site:** www.crbard.com	**Officers:** Timothy M. Ring - Chmn., C.E.O. John H. Weiland - Pres., C.O.O. **Transfer Agents:** EquiServe Trust Company, N.A., Providence, RI	**Investor Contact:** 908-277-8139 **No of Institutions:** 359 **Shares:** 86,930,896 **% Held:** 83.00

BB&T CORP.

Exchange	Symbol	Price	52Wk Range	Yield	P/E
NYS	BBT	$39.94 (5/31/2005)	43.25-36.54	3.51	13.68

***7 Year Price Score 99.60** *NYSE Composite Index=100 ***12 Month Price Score 95.72**

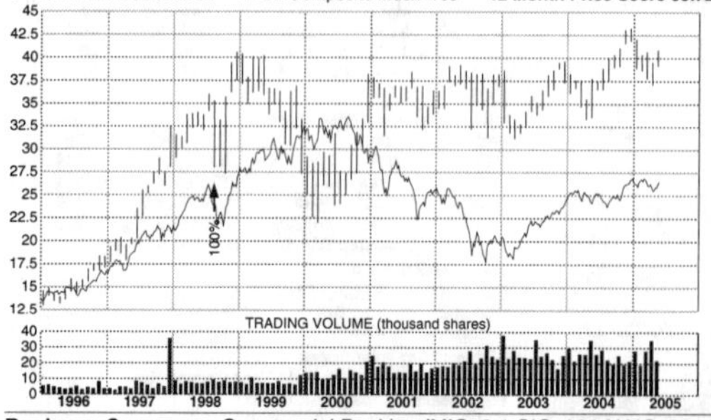

TRADING VOLUME (thousand shares)

Interim Earnings (Per Share)

Qtr.	Mar	Jun	Sep	Dec
2002	0.66	0.68	0.68	0.70
2003	0.69	0.67	0.21	0.56
2004	0.60	0.72	0.74	0.75
2005	0.71	...	...	...

Interim Dividends (Per Share)

Amt	Decl	Ex	Rec	Pay
0.35Q	6/22/2004	7/14/2004	7/16/2004	8/2/2004
0.35Q	8/24/2004	10/13/2004	10/15/2004	11/1/2004
0.35Q	12/14/2004	1/12/2005	1/14/2005	2/1/2005
0.35Q	2/22/2005	4/13/2005	4/15/2005	5/2/2005

Indicated Div: $1.40 (Div. Reinv. Plan)

Valuation Analysis

Forecast P/E 13.10 (6/2/2005)

Market Cap $21.9 Billion Book Value 10.8 Billion

Price/Book 2.02 Price/Sales 3.19

Dividend Achiever Status

Rank 111 **10 Year Growth Rate** 13.73%

Total Years of Dividend Growth 33

Business Summary: Commercial Banking (MIC: 8.1 SIC: 021 NAIC: 22110)

BB&T, a multi-bank holding company with assets of $100.51 billion as of Dec 31 2004, operates more than 1,400 banking offices in the Carolinas, Virginia, West Virginia, Tennessee, Kentucky, Georgia, Maryland, Florida, Alabama, Indiana and Washington, D.C. Co.'s largest subsidiary is Branch Banking and Trust Company (BB&T-NC). BB&T-NC's subsidiaries include BB&T Leasing Corp., BB&T Investment Services, and BB&T Insurance Services. Co.'s other subsidiaries include Branch Banking and Trust Co. of South Carolina, Branch Banking and Trust Co. of Virginia, and Fidelity Service Corporation.

Recent Developments: For the quarter ended Mar 31 2005, net income increased 20.4% to $395,384 thousand from net income of $328,500 thousand in the year-earlier quarter. Net interest income was $849,183 thousand, up 5.3% from $806,823 thousand the year before. Provision for loan losses was $41,045 thousand versus $63,418 thousand in the prior-year quarter, a decrease of 35.3%. Non-interest income rose 8.7% to $516,621 thousand, while non-interest expense declined 0.5% to $730,706 thousand.

Prospects: On Apr 1 2005, Co. completed its acquisition of a 70.0% ownership interest in Sterling Capital Management LLC of Charlotte, NC. Privately-held Sterling Capital Management, with more than $8.00 billion in assets under management, provides investment management services to institutional clients and high net worth individuals. Meanwhile, earnings growth is being driven by Co.'s disciplined expense control, continued excellent credit quality, and strong loan growth. In addition, results are benefiting from noninterest income growth, which is being fueled by higher revenues from mortgage banking and Co.'s insurance operations, as well as an increase in other nondeposit fees and commissions.

Financial Data (US$ in Thousands)	3 Mos	12/31/2004	12/31/2003	12/31/2002	12/31/2001	12/31/2000	12/31/1999	12/31/1998
Earnings Per Share	2.92	2.80	2.07	2.72	2.12	1.55	1.83	1.71
Cash Flow Per Share	6.10	5.49	7.47	1.73	0.21	0.62	5.06	0.61
Tang Book Value Per Share	11.22	11.33	10.92	12.04	13.50	11.91	9.66	9.51
Dividends Per Share	1.370	1.340	1.220	1.100	0.980	0.860	0.750	0.660
Dividend Payout %	46.92	47.86	58.94	40.44	46.23	55.48	40.98	38.60
Income Statement								
Interest Income	1,243,492	4,546,695	4,354,792	4,434,044	4,849,538	4,339,674	3,115,780	2,481,182
Interest Expense	394,309	1,198,472	1,272,787	1,686,584	2,415,053	2,322,046	1,534,065	1,233,778
Net Interest Income	849,183	3,348,223	3,082,005	2,747,460	2,434,485	2,017,628	1,581,715	1,247,404
Provision for Losses	41,045	249,269	248,000	263,700	224,318	127,431	92,097	80,310
Non-Interest Income	516,621	2,119,271	1,889,135	1,692,475	1,378,691	777,022	761,356	528,002
Non-Interest Expense	730,706	2,895,863	2,721,212	2,385,538	2,228,430	1,761,539	1,346,904	961,374
Income Before Taxes	594,053	2,322,362	1,617,030	1,790,697	1,360,428	905,680	904,070	733,722
Income Taxes	198,669	763,987	552,127	497,468	386,790	279,238	291,223	231,897
Net Income	395,384	1,558,375	1,064,903	1,303,009	973,638	626,442	612,847	501,825
Average Shares	553,654	556,041	514,082	478,792	459,269	398,915	335,298	293,571
Balance Sheet								
Net Loans & Leases	67,955,367	66,744,193	60,794,990	50,416,621	44,891,339	38,932,351	28,524,467	22,350,692
Total Assets	102,015,086	100,508,641	90,466,613	80,216,816	70,869,945	59,340,228	43,480,996	34,427,227
Total Deposits	66,836,339	67,699,337	59,349,785	51,280,016	44,733,275	38,014,501	27,251,142	23,046,907
Total Liabilities	91,189,802	89,634,167	80,531,882	72,828,902	64,719,736	54,554,303	40,281,837	31,668,679
Stockholders' Equity	10,825,284	10,874,474	9,934,731	7,387,914	6,150,209	4,785,925	3,199,159	2,758,548
Shares Outstanding	548,638	550,406	541,942	470,452	455,682	401,678	331,170	290,211
Statistical Record								
Return on Assets %	1.66	1.63	1.25	1.72	1.50	1.22	1.57	1.58
Return on Equity %	15.30	14.94	12.29	19.25	17.81	15.65	20.57	20.09
Net Interest Margin %	68.29	73.64	70.77	61.96	50.20	46.49	50.76	50.27
Efficiency Ratio %	41.51	43.44	43.58	38.94	35.78	34.43	34.74	31.95
Loans to Deposits	1.02	0.99	1.02	0.98	1.00	1.02	1.05	0.97
Price Range	43.25-33.33	43.25-33.33	39.66-31.15	39.23-31.26	38.48-31.42	38.25-22.00	40.44-27.31	40.63-27.31
P/E Ratio	14.81-11.41	15.45-11.90	19.16-15.05	14.42-11.49	18.15-14.82	24.68-14.19	22.10-14.92	23.76-15.97
Average Yield %	3.52	3.50	3.46	2.99	2.75	3.06	2.11	1.98

Address: 200 West Second Street, Winston-Salem, NC 27102
Telephone: 336-733-2000
Web Site: www.bbandt.com

Officers: John A. Allison IV - Chmn., C.E.O. Scott E. Reed - Sr. Exec. V.P., C.F.O. **Transfer Agents:** Branch Banking & Trust Company, Wilson, NC

Investor Contact: 336-733-3058
No of Institutions: 377
Shares: 155,554,048 **% Held:** 28.36

BECKMAN COULTER, INC.

Exchange	Symbol	Price	52Wk Range	Yield	P/E
NYS	BEC	$70.06 (5/31/2005)	72.02-52.21	0.80	21.36

Interim Earnings (Per Share)

Qtr.	Mar	Jun	Sep	Dec
2002	0.43	0.64	0.49	0.52
2003	0.70	0.82	0.62	1.07
2004	0.54	0.88	0.87	0.91
2005	0.62	...	...	...

Interim Dividends (Per Share)

Amt	Decl	Ex	Rec	Pay
0.13Q	7/26/2004	8/11/2004	8/13/2004	9/2/2004
0.13Q	10/11/2004	10/14/2004	10/18/2004	11/5/2004
0.14Q	1/28/2005	2/16/2005	2/18/2005	3/10/2005
0.14Q	4/13/2005	5/11/2005	5/13/2005	6/2/2005

Indicated Div: $0.56 (Div. Reinv. Plan)

Valuation Analysis

Forecast P/E	19.33 (5/28/2005)		
Market Cap	$4.3 Billion	Book Value	1.1 Billion
Price/Book	3.87	Price/Sales	1.77

Dividend Achiever Status

Rank	187	**10 Year Growth Rate**	9.15%
Total Years of Dividend Growth			13

Business Summary: Instruments and Related Products (MIC: 11.15 SIC: 826 NAIC: 34516)

Beckman Coulter designs, manufactures, and markets systems, which consist of instruments, chemistries, software and supplies that are designed to meet a variety of biomedical laboratory needs. Co.'s products are used in a range of applications from instruments used for medical research, clinical research and drug discovery to diagnostic systems. Co. operates in two segments: The clinical diagnostics segment encompasses diagnostic applications, principally in hospital laboratories. The biomedical research segment includes life sciences and drug discovery applications in universities, medical schools, medical centers, reference laboratories and pharmaceutical and biotechnology companies.

Recent Developments: For the quarter ended Mar 31 2005, net income increased 16.3% to $41,400 thousand from net income of $35,600 thousand in the year-earlier quarter. Revenues were $576,100 thousand, up 7.3% from $536,800 thousand the year before. Operating income was $75,800 thousand versus an income of $67,700 thousand in the prior-year quarter, an increase of 12.0%. Total direct expense was $303,100 thousand versus $282,500 thousand in the prior-year quarter, an increase of 7.3%. Total indirect expense was $197,200 thousand versus $186,600 thousand in the prior-year quarter, an increase of 5.7%.

Prospects: On Apr 27 2005, Co. announced plans to acquire Agencourt Bioscience Corporation, a provider of genomic services and nucleic acid purification products in the biomedical research market. Agencourt's 2004 sales were about $27.0 million. Terms of the agreement include a payment at closing of $100.0 million and up to $40.0 million of contingent payments through 2007. Meanwhile, Co.'s prospects appear decent, bolstered by new products from both its Clinical Diagnostics and Biomedical Research segments. So, including the effect of its pending acquisition of Agencourt, Co.'s full year sales outlook calls for growth in the 7.0% to 9.0% range. Earnings per diluted share should be from $3.51 to $3.61.

Financial Data

(US$ in Thousands)	3 Mos	12/31/2004	12/31/2003	12/31/2002	12/31/2001	12/31/2000	12/31/1999	12/31/1998
Earnings Per Share	3.28	3.21	3.21	2.08	2.16	2.03	1.78	0.57
Cash Flow Per Share	5.12	4.32	3.68	5.12	4.57	3.55	3.70	(0.03)
Tang Book Value Per Share	6.74	6.19	2.99	N.M.	N.M.	N.M.	N.M.	N.M.
Dividends Per Share	0.510	0.480	0.400	0.350	0.340	0.325	0.320	0.305
Dividend Payout %	15.55	14.95	12.46	16.83	15.74	16.01	17.93	53.51
Income Statement								
Total Revenue	576,100	2,408,300	2,192,500	2,059,400	1,984,000	1,886,900	1,808,700	1,718,200
EBITDA	63,700	416,400	409,900	326,600	378,300	383,600	364,400	273,400
Depn & Amortn	...	115,200	106,800	109,800	126,400	136,100	143,700	152,400
Income Before Taxes	57,600	278,200	272,800	178,900	205,000	181,900	154,700	46,600
Income Taxes	16,200	67,300	65,600	43,400	63,500	56,400	48,700	13,100
Net Income	41,400	210,900	207,200	135,500	138,400	125,500	106,000	33,500
Average Shares	66,501	65,773	64,493	65,060	64,011	61,800	59,400	58,600
Balance Sheet								
Current Assets	1,281,200	1,279,600	1,161,200	1,056,200	1,035,600	927,800	966,400	956,600
Total Assets	2,788,500	2,795,000	2,558,200	2,263,600	2,178,000	2,018,200	2,110,800	2,133,300
Current Liabilities	591,300	613,300	578,200	611,600	509,900	501,100	575,900	719,300
Long-Term Obligations	605,800	611,700	625,600	626,600	760,300	862,800	980,700	982,200
Total Liabilities	1,667,700	1,700,700	1,660,500	1,671,500	1,659,800	1,674,300	1,882,900	2,006,400
Stockholders' Equity	1,120,800	1,094,300	897,700	592,100	518,200	343,900	227,900	126,900
Shares Outstanding	61,900	61,600	62,000	61,000	61,200	59,700	58,000	56,800
Statistical Record								
Return on Assets %	8.14	7.86	8.59	6.10	6.60	6.06	5.00	1.50
Return on Equity %	21.21	21.12	27.82	24.41	32.11	43.78	59.75	32.10
EBITDA Margin %	11.06	17.29	18.70	15.86	19.07	20.33	20.15	15.91
Net Margin %	7.19	8.76	9.45	6.58	6.98	6.65	5.86	1.95
Asset Turnover	0.92	0.90	0.91	0.93	0.95	0.91	0.85	0.77
Current Ratio	2.17	2.09	2.01	1.73	2.03	1.85	1.68	1.33
Debt to Equity	0.54	0.56	0.70	1.06	1.47	2.51	4.30	7.74
Price Range	72.02-52.21	67.70-49.99	51.31-28.50	52.47-25.78	47.01-34.50	41.94-23.66	27.56-20.00	31.81-20.00
P/E Ratio	21.96-15.92	21.09-15.57	15.98-8.88	25.23-12.39	21.76-15.97	20.66-11.65	15.48-11.24	55.81-35.09
Average Yield %	0.83	0.84	0.98	0.84	0.83	1.00	1.34	1.15

Address: 4300 N. Harbor Boulevard, Fullerton, CA 92835
Telephone: 714-871-4848
Web Site: www.beckmancoulter.com

Officers: Scott Garrett - Pres., C.E.O. James T. Glover - V.P., C.F.O. **Transfer Agents:** EquiServe Trust Company, N.A., Providence, RI

Investor Contact: 714-773-7620
No of Institutions: 285
Shares: 48,294,544 **% Held:** 77.86

BECTON, DICKINSON AND CO.

Exchange	Symbol	Price	52Wk Range	Yield	P/E
NYS	BDX	$57.45 (5/31/2005)	59.98-46.41	1.25	26.85

*7 Year Price Score 126.97 *NYSE Composite Index=100 *12 Month Price Score 104.25

TRADING VOLUME (thousand shares)

Interim Earnings (Per Share)

Qtr.	Dec	Mar	Jun	Sep
2001-02	0.37	0.48	0.44	0.50
2002-03	0.43	0.54	0.49	0.61
2003-04	0.48	0.62	0.41	0.26
2004-05	0.75	0.72	...	...

Interim Dividends (Per Share)

Amt	Decl	Ex	Rec	Pay
0.15Q	7/27/2004	9/7/2004	9/9/2004	9/30/2004
0.18Q	11/23/2004	12/9/2004	12/13/2004	1/3/2005
0.18Q	2/1/2005	3/8/2005	3/10/2005	3/31/2005
0.18Q	5/24/2005	6/7/2005	6/9/2005	6/30/2005

Indicated Div: $0.72 (Div. Reinv. Plan)

Valuation Analysis

Forecast P/E	19.88 (5/28/2005)		
Market Cap	$14.5 Billion	Book Value	3.4 Billion
Price/Book	4.25	Price/Sales	2.83

Dividend Achiever Status

Rank	131	10 Year Growth Rate	12.49%
Total Years of Dividend Growth			32

Business Summary: Medical Instruments & Equipment (MIC: 9.6 SIC: 841 NAIC: 39112)

Becton, Dickinson and Co. is engaged principally in the manufacture and sale of a range of medical supplies, devices, laboratory equipment and diagnostic products used by healthcare institutions, life science researchers, clinical laboratories, industry and the general public. Co.'s operations consist of three worldwide business segments: BD Medical, BD Diagnostics and BD Biosciences. BD Medical includes products such as hypodermic syringes and needles for injection. BD Diagnostics includes products such as clinical and industrial microbiology, and sample collection products. BD Biosciences includes products and services for a variety of applications in life sciences.

Recent Developments: For the quarter ended Mar 31 2005, net income increased 13.9% to $188,150 thousand from net income of $165,160 thousand in the year-earlier quarter. Revenues were $1,365,530 thousand, up 8.9% from $1,253,633 thousand the year before. Operating income was $255,185 thousand versus an income of $229,599 thousand in the prior-year quarter, an increase of 11.1%. Total direct expense was $678,018 thousand versus $629,516 thousand in the prior-year quarter, an increase of 7.7%. Total indirect expense was $432,327 thousand versus $394,518 thousand in the prior-year quarter, an increase of 9.6%.

Prospects: Co.'s earnings are continuing to benefit from revenue growth across all three segments and in every global business unit. Co.'s Biosciences segment's revenue growth is being driven primarily by improvement in sales of its instruments, including its FACSCanto™ and BD™ LSR II flow cytometers. Also contributing to this segment's growth were higher sales of its Discovery Labware unit. Co.'s results also continue to reflect its disciplined cost control and supply chain productivity. Looking ahead, Co. expects earnings from continuing operations to range from $0.66 to $0.68 per diluted share for the fiscal third quarter and $2.80 to $2.84 per diluted share for fiscal year 2005.

Financial Data

(US$ in Thousands)	6 Mos	3 Mos	09/30/2004	09/30/2003	09/30/2002	09/30/2001	09/30/2000	09/30/1999
Earnings Per Share	2.14	2.03	1.77	2.07	1.79	1.49	1.49	1.04
Cash Flow Per Share	4.04	4.54	4.35	3.56	3.24	3.03	2.43	1.73
Tang Book Value Per Share	9.47	9.06	8.01	7.60	6.48	7.16	5.70	4.76
Dividends Per Share	0.660	0.630	0.600	0.400	0.390	0.380	0.370	0.340
Dividend Payout %	30.84	30.99	33.90	19.32	21.79	25.50	24.83	32.69
Income Statement								
Total Revenue	2,653,899	1,288,369	4,934,745	4,527,940	4,033,069	3,754,302	3,618,334	3,418,412
EBITDA	693,821	342,522	1,035,487	1,003,889	901,204	937,864	882,386	703,570
Depn & Amortn	193,042	94,686	253,012	257,623	239,311	305,700	288,255	258,863
Income Before Taxes	487,101	238,714	752,868	709,706	628,589	576,750	519,934	372,655
Income Taxes	106,194	44,316	170,364	162,650	148,607	138,348	127,037	96,936
Net Income	383,501	195,351	467,402	547,056	479,982	401,652	392,897	275,719
Average Shares	262,016	261,970	263,337	263,635	268,183	268,833	263,239	264,580
Balance Sheet								
Current Assets	2,893,173	2,815,625	2,641,334	2,338,569	1,928,707	1,762,942	1,660,677	1,683,725
Total Assets	6,003,464	5,973,425	5,752,579	5,572,253	5,040,460	4,802,287	4,505,096	4,436,958
Current Liabilities	1,138,963	1,165,472	1,050,082	1,043,374	1,252,453	1,264,676	1,353,538	1,329,322
Long-Term Obligations	1,051,369	1,061,341	1,171,506	1,184,031	802,967	782,996	779,569	954,169
Total Liabilities	2,586,133	2,631,213	2,684,716	2,675,299	2,552,486	2,473,520	2,549,098	2,668,270
Stockholders' Equity	3,417,331	3,342,212	3,067,863	2,896,954	2,487,974	2,328,767	1,955,998	1,768,688
Shares Outstanding	252,518	252,915	249,334	251,133	255,529	259,236	253,496	250,797
Statistical Record								
Return on Assets %	9.56	9.25	8.23	10.31	9.75	8.63	8.76	6.66
Return on Equity %	17.04	16.77	15.63	20.32	19.93	18.75	21.04	16.30
EBITDA Margin %	26.14	26.59	20.98	22.17	22.35	24.98	24.39	20.58
Net Margin %	14.45	15.16	9.47	12.08	11.90	10.70	10.86	8.07
Asset Turnover	0.87	0.87	0.87	0.85	0.82	0.81	0.81	0.83
Current Ratio	2.54	2.42	2.52	2.24	1.54	1.39	1.23	1.27
Debt to Equity	0.31	0.32	0.38	0.41	0.32	0.34	0.40	0.54
Price Range	59.98-46.41	57.83-41.03	53.25-35.71	40.43-28.40	38.47-25.01	39.00-26.56	34,13-22.38	46.88-25.63
P/E Ratio	28.03-21.69	28.49-20.21	30.08-20.18	19.53-13.72	21.49-13.97	26.17-17.83	22.90-15.02	45.07-24.64
Average Yield %	1.25	1.26	1.31	1.17	1.14	1.12	1.35	0.95

Address: 1 Becton Drive, Franklin Lakes, NJ 07417-1880
Telephone: 201-847-6800
Web Site: www.bd.com

Officers: Edward J. Ludwig - Chmn., Pres., C.E.O. Gary M. Cohen - Pres. **Transfer Agents:** EquiServe Trust Company, N.A., Jersey City, NJ

Investor Contact: 800-284-6845
No of Institutions: 477
Shares: 214,850,560 **% Held:** 84.95

BEMIS, INC.

Exchange	Symbol	Price	52Wk Range	Yield	P/E
NYS	BMS	$27.16 (5/31/2005)	31.36-24.98	2.65	17.30

*7 Year Price Score 113.06 *NYSE Composite Index=100 *12 Month Price Score 97.78

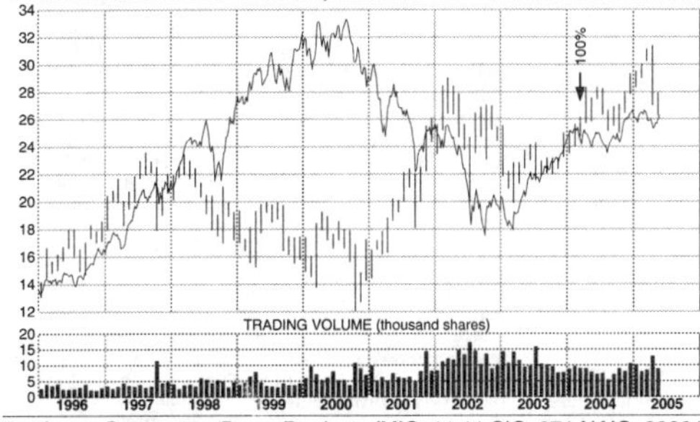

TRADING VOLUME (thousand shares)

Interim Earnings (Per Share)

Qtr.	Mar	Jun	Sep	Dec
2002	0.33	0.41	0.41	0.40
2003	0.33	0.36	0.32	0.36
2004	0.40	0.42	0.41	0.44
2005	0.30	...	...	...

Interim Dividends (Per Share)

Amt	Decl	Ex	Rec	Pay
0.16Q	7/29/2004	8/16/2004	8/18/2004	9/1/2004
0.16Q	10/28/2004	11/15/2004	11/17/2004	12/1/2004
0.18Q	2/3/2005	2/14/2005	2/16/2005	3/1/2005
0.18Q	5/5/2005	5/18/2005	5/20/2005	6/1/2005

Indicated Div: $0.72 (Div. Reinv. Plan)

Valuation Analysis

Forecast P/E 16.08 (5/28/2005)

Market Cap $3.1 Billion Book Value 1.3 Billion

Price/Book 2.38 Price/Sales 1.06

Dividend Achiever Status

Rank 190 **10 Year Growth Rate** 9.01%

Total Years of Dividend Growth 21

Business Summary: Paper Products (MIC: 11.11 SIC: 671 NAIC: 22221)

Bemis manufactures flexible packaging products and pressure-sensitive materials. The flexible packing segment produces consumer and industrial packaging, including multilayer flexible polymer film structures and barrier laminates sold for food, medical, and personal care products as well as non-food applications. Additional products include stretchfilm products, carton sealing tapes and application equipment, thermoformed plastic packaging, paper bags, printed paper roll stock, and bag closing materials. Co.'s pressure-sensitive materials products include pressure sensitive paper, films, digital screen printers and micro-thin film adhesives for the label, graphic and technical markets.

Recent Developments: For the quarter ended Mar 31 2005, net income decreased 25.1% to $32,224 thousand from net income of $43,027 thousand in the year-earlier quarter. Revenues were $831,869 thousand, up 21.6% from $684,037 thousand the year before. Total direct expense was $676,599 thousand versus $540,079 thousand in the prior-year quarter, an increase of 25.3%. Total indirect expense was $92,053 thousand versus $75,041 thousand in the prior-year quarter, an increase of 22.7%.

Prospects: Rapid raw material cost increases have, in the short term, outpaced Co.'s ability to increase selling prices in its flexible packaging business segment and substantially increased the cost of normal production waste. Co. remains cautious about how higher selling prices may affect customer order trends. As a result, Co. is reducing its expectations of earnings per share growth for 2005. Co. expects 2005 earnings to be slightly ahead of 2004 earnings of $1.67 per share, including $0.08 to $0.10 per share expected accretion from the recent acquisition of Dixie Toga, a large Brazilian packaging company. Co. expects 2005 capital expenditures to range from $160.0 million to $175.0 million.

Financial Data (US$ in Thousands)	3 Mos	12/31/2004	12/31/2003	12/31/2002	12/31/2001	12/31/2000	12/31/1999	12/31/1998
Earnings Per Share	1.57	1.67	1.37	1.54	1.32	1.22	1.09	1.04
Cash Flow Per Share	2.24	2.53	2.93	2.71	3.01	1.97	1.77	2.08
Tang Book Value Per Share	5.43	7.48	5.81	4.11	4.39	4.76	5.51	4.88
Dividends Per Share	0.660	0.640	0.560	0.520	0.500	0.480	0.460	0.440
Dividend Payout %	42.04	38.32	40.88	33.77	37.88	39.34	42.20	42.11
Income Statement								
Total Revenue	831,869	2,834,394	2,635,018	2,369,038	2,293,104	2,164,583	1,918,025	1,848,004
EBITDA	93,027	425,549	367,440	386,246	351,572	319,632	283,592	270,842
Depn & Amortn	40,103	131,882	128,195	119,231	124,147	108,130	97,717	88,910
Income Before Taxes	52,924	293,667	239,245	267,015	227,425	211,502	185,875	181,932
Income Taxes	20,700	113,700	92,100	101,500	87,100	80,900	71,100	70,500
Net Income	32,224	179,967	147,145	165,515	140,325	130,602	114,775	111,432
Average Shares	108,411	107,942	107,733	107,492	106,243	107,106	105,314	106,648
Balance Sheet								
Current Assets	1,069,682	873,767	751,906	721,655	586,897	639,959	583,581	517,939
Total Assets	2,966,078	2,486,743	2,292,932	2,256,650	1,922,974	1,888,643	1,532,143	1,453,054
Current Liabilities	453,366	375,143	315,586	325,853	238,182	495,097	253,268	242,788
Long-Term Obligations	841,879	533,886	583,399	718,277	595,249	437,952	372,267	371,363
Total Liabilities	1,616,851	1,175,904	1,148,802	1,293,236	1,034,698	1,088,316	766,750	745,010
Stockholders' Equity	1,322,847	1,307,866	1,138,733	958,974	886,148	798,757	725,895	670,807
Shares Outstanding	115,962	106,947	106,242	105,887	105,739	105,204	104,378	104,538
Statistical Record								
Return on Assets %	6.40	7.51	6.47	7.92	7.36	7.61	7.69	7.92
Return on Equity %	13.49	14.67	14.03	17.94	16.66	17.09	16.44	17.00
EBITDA Margin %	11.18	15.01	13.94	16.30	15.33	14.77	14.79	14.66
Net Margin %	3.87	6.35	5.58	6.99	6.12	6.03	5.98	6.03
Asset Turnover	1.13	1.18	1.16	1.13	1.20	1.26	1.29	1.31
Current Ratio	2.36	2.33	2.38	2.21	2.46	1.29	2.30	2.13
Debt to Equity	0.64	0.41	0.51	0.75	0.67	0.55	0.51	0.55
Price Range	31.15-24.98	29.31-23.48	25.53-19.89	29.04-19.94	26.08-14.41	19.25-12.03	19.97-15.22	23.47-16.97
P/E Ratio	19.84-15.91	17.55-14.06	18.64-14.52	18.85-12.95	19.76-10.91	15.78-9.86	18.32-13.96	22.57-16.32
Average Yield %	2.38	2.42	2.47	2.03	2.50	2.93	2.57	2.16

Address: 222 South 9th Street, Suite 2300, Minneapolis, MN 55402-4099
Telephone: 612-376-3000
Web Site: www.bemis.com

Officers: John H. Roe - Chmn. Jeffrey H. Curler - Pres., C.E.O. **Transfer Agents:** Wells Fargo Bank Minnesota, South St. Paul, MN

Investor Contact: 612-376-3000
No of Institutions: 250
Shares: 58,833,544 **% Held:** 54.96

BLACK HILLS CORPORATION

Exchange	Symbol	Price	52Wk Range	Yield	P/E
NYS	BKH	$36.62 (5/31/2005)	36.62-26.72	3.50	18.88

***7 Year Price Score 92.48** *NYSE Composite Index=100 ***12 Month Price Score 110.59**

Interim Earnings (Per Share)

Qtr.	Mar	Jun	Sep	Dec
2002	0.52	0.51	0.64	0.58
2003	0.52	0.54	0.69	0.22
2004	0.30	0.35	0.52	0.59
2005	0.48	...	...	...

Interim Dividends (Per Share)

Amt	Decl	Ex	Rec	Pay
0.31Q	7/28/2004	8/12/2004	8/16/2004	9/1/2004
0.31Q	11/5/2004	11/15/2004	11/17/2004	12/1/2004
0.32Q	2/4/2005	2/11/2005	2/15/2005	3/1/2005
0.32Q	4/28/2005	5/16/2005	5/18/2005	6/1/2005

Indicated Div: $1.28 (Div. Reinv. Plan)

Valuation Analysis

Forecast P/E	18.52 (5/28/2005)		
Market Cap	$1.2 Billion	Book Value	737.7 Million
Price/Book	1.62	Price/Sales	1.03

Dividend Achiever Status

Rank	293	**10 Year Growth Rate**	3.49%
Total Years of Dividend Growth			33

Business Summary: Electricity (MIC: 7.1 SIC: 911 NAIC: 21121)

Black Hills is an energy and communications company with three segments. Co.'s Wholesale Energy group generates and sells electricity, produces coal, natural gas and crude oil primarily in the Rocky Mountain region, and markets and transports fuel products. Co.'s Electric Utility group engages in the generation, transmission and distribution of electricity to about 62,000 customers in South Dakota, Wyoming and Montana. Co.'s Communications group offers broadband telecommunications services, including local and long distance telephone, expanded cable television, cable modem Internet access and high-speed data and video services to residential and business customers in part of South Dakota.

Recent Developments: For the quarter ended Mar 31 2005, income from continuing operations increased 58.7% to $15,865 thousand from income of $9,994 thousand in the year-earlier quarter. Net income increased 60.8% to $15,740 thousand from net income of $9,786 thousand in the year-earlier quarter. Revenues were $305,685 thousand, up 11.4% from $274,328 thousand the year before. Operating income was $35,042 thousand versus an income of $28,306 thousand in the prior-year quarter, an increase of 23.8%. Total direct expense was $215,502 thousand versus $197,360 thousand in the prior-year quarter, an increase of 9.2%. Total indirect expense was $55,141 thousand versus $48,662 thousand in the prior-year quarter, an increase of 13.3%.

Prospects: Co. is seeing considerable improvement in its power generation results, reflecting the contracted status of the Las Vegas Cogeneration II power plant, which ran merchant in difficult market conditions during the first quarter of 2004. Meanwhile, Co. will continue to pursue other strategic goals, including sustaining the production growth of its oil and gas operation, integrating Cheyenne Light into its business operations, and pursuing balanced, risk-managed energy projects in the West. Separately, in April 2005, Co. announced a definitive agreement to sell its Communications business. Cash proceeds from the sale are to be used for debt repayment or for investments in energy projects.

Financial Data

(US$ in Thousands)	3 Mos	12/31/2004	12/31/2003	12/31/2002	12/31/2001	12/31/2000	12/31/1999	12/31/1998
Earnings Per Share	1.94	1.76	1.97	2.26	3.42	2.37	1.73	1.19
Cash Flow Per Share	4.96	4.21	5.59	8.16	6.99	3.36	3.53	2.53
Tang Book Value Per Share	20.42	20.37	19.55	15.42	14.67	10.45	10.14	9.52
Dividends Per Share	1.250	1.240	1.200	1.160	1.120	1.080	1.040	1.000
Dividend Payout %	64.43	70.45	60.91	51.33	32.75	45.57	60.12	84.03
Income Statement								
Total Revenue	305,685	1,121,701	1,250,052	423,919	1,558,558	1,623,836	791,875	679,254
EBITDA	58,862	222,442	219,209	206,360	234,106	150,610	89,769	73,399
Depn & Amortn	23,519	87,833	80,791	69,738	54,051	32,864	25,067	24,037
Income Before Taxes	22,964	84,525	86,915	96,017	142,807	94,479	52,856	37,516
Income Taxes	8,514	26,704	29,920	29,662	50,544	30,358	15,789	11,708
Net Income	15,740	57,973	61,222	61,452	88,077	52,848	37,067	25,808
Average Shares	33,009	32,912	31,015	27,167	25,771	22,281	21,482	21,665
Balance Sheet								
Net PPE	1,554,802	1,445,732	1,442,422	1,677,877	1,238,224	794,281	464,189	389,607
Total Assets	2,152,703	2,056,163	2,063,225	2,035,169	1,658,767	1,320,320	674,806	559,417
Long-Term Obligations	756,544	733,581	868,459	618,862	415,798	307,092	160,700	162,030
Total Liabilities	1,410,127	1,320,398	1,353,478	1,500,006	1,143,603	1,037,974	458,200	352,751
Stockholders' Equity	737,682	735,765	709,747	535,163	515,164	282,346	216,606	206,666
Shares Outstanding	32,536	32,477	32,297	27,102	26,890	22,921	21,371	21,719
Statistical Record								
Return on Assets %	3.04	2.81	2.99	3.33	5.91	5.28	6.01	4.83
Return on Equity %	8.83	8.00	9.84	11.70	22.09	21.13	17.51	12.53
EBITDA Margin %	19.26	19.83	17.54	48.68	15.02	9.27	11.34	10.81
Net Margin %	5.15	5.17	4.90	14.50	5.65	3.25	4.68	3.80
PPE Turnover	0.77	0.77	0.80	0.29	1.53	2.57	1.85	1.72
Asset Turnover	0.55	0.54	0.61	0.23	1.05	1.62	1.28	1.27
Debt to Equity	1.03	1.00	1.22	1.16	0.81	1.09	0.74	0.78
Price Range	33.22-26.72	32.25-26.72	33.35-22.26	36.84-19.15	58.05-26.35	45.13-20.56	26.38-20.50	27.38-20.75
P/E Ratio	17.12-13.77	18.32-15.18	16.93-11.30	16.30-8.47	16.97-7.70	19.04-8.68	15.25-11.85	23.00-17.44
Average Yield %	4.18	4.17	4.08	3.99	2.86	4.17	4.51	4.21

Address: 625 Ninth Street, Rapid City, SD 57701	**Officers:** David R. Emery - Chmn., Pres., C.E.O. Mark T. Thies - Exec. V.P., C.F.O., Chief Acctg. Officer	**Investor Contact:** 605-721-1700
Telephone: 605-721-1700	**Transfer Agents:**	**No of Institutions:** 141
Web Site: www.blackhillscorp.com	Wells Fargo Shareowner Services	**Shares:** 17,403,696 **% Held:** 53.51

BRADY CORP.

Exchange	Symbol	Price	52Wk Range	Yield	P/E
NYS	BRC	$30.57 (5/31/2005)	35.40-20.45	1.44	11.99

Interim Earnings (Per Share)

Qtr.	Oct	Jan	Apr	Jul
2001-02	0.17	0.13	0.18	0.70
2002-03	0.17	0.06	0.19	0.48
2003-04	0.22	0.17	0.34	1.39
2004-05	0.41	0.41	...	...

Interim Dividends (Per Share)

Amt	Decl	Ex	Rec	Pay
100%	11/18/2004	1/3/2005	12/10/2004	12/31/2004
0.11Q	11/18/2004	1/6/2005	1/10/2005	1/31/2005
0.11Q	2/15/2005	4/6/2005	4/8/2005	5/2/2005
0.11Q	5/17/2005	7/6/2005	7/8/2005	7/29/2005

Indicated Div: $0.44 (Div. Reinv. Plan)

Valuation Analysis

Forecast P/E	18.32 (5/28/2005)		
Market Cap	$1.5 Billion	Book Value	459.4 Million
Price/Book	3.27	Price/Sales	1.97

Dividend Achiever Status

Rank	114	10 Year Growth Rate	13.64%
Total Years of Dividend Growth			20

Business Summary: Consumer Accessories (MIC: 4.6 SIC: 993 NAIC: 39950)

Brady is an international manufacturer and marketer of identification products and specialty materials. Co.'s products include labels and signs, printing systems and software, label-application and data-collection systems, safety devices and precision die-cut materials. Co.'s major products include identification applications and specialty tape products, including wire and cable markers, high-performance labels, laboratory identification products, stand-alone printing systems, bar-code and other software, graphics and workplace applications. Co. serves customers in electronics, telecommunications, manufacturing, electrical, construction, education and other industries.

Recent Developments: For the quarter ended Jan 31 2005, net income increased 156.2% to $20,579 thousand from net income of $8,033 thousand in the year-earlier quarter. Revenues were $196,216 thousand, up 28.3% from $152,948 thousand the year before. Operating income was $30,934 thousand versus an income of $11,643 thousand in the prior-year quarter, an increase of 165.7%. Total direct expense was $91,260 thousand versus $75,138 thousand in the prior-year quarter, an increase of 21.5%. Total indirect expense was $74,022 thousand versus $66,167 thousand in the prior-year quarter, an increase of 11.9%.

Prospects: Looking ahead, Co. intends to continue its growth strategies of developing proprietary products, making acquisitions that expand its product range, technical expertise or market penetration, and further improving processes to best serve customers. As a result of Co.'s improving profitability, it is increasing its guidance for fiscal 2005. Co. anticipates sales of $790.0 million to $810.0 million, with net income between $78.0 million and $80.0 million and earnings per share of $1.55 to $1.60, up from previous guidance of sales of $780.0 million to $800.0 million, net income of $66.0 million to $69.0 million and earnings per share of $1.35 to $1.41.

Financial Data

(US$ in Thousands)	6 Mos	3 Mos	07/31/2004	07/31/2003	07/31/2002	07/31/2001	07/31/2000	07/31/1999
Earnings Per Share	2.55	2.31	2.12	0.90	1.19	1.17	2.04	1.72
Cash Flow Per Share	2.20	1.92	0.89	0.60	0.59	0.58	0.53	0.68
Tang Book Value Per Share	1.92	1.37	1.69	4.47	4.61	4.44	4.13	4.09
Dividends Per Share	0.430	0.425	0.420	0.400	0.380	0.360	0.340	0.320
Dividend Payout %	16.89	18.41	19.86	44.69	32.07	30.90	16.71	18.66
Income Statement								
Total Revenue	396,635	200,419	671,219	554,866	516,962	545,944	541,077	470,862
EBITDA	76,756	38,851	91,748	50,347	59,847	67,854	94,542	80,376
Depn & Amortn	13,253	6,775	20,190	17,771	16,630	22,646	17,833	15,149
Income Before Taxes	59,327	29,937	70,327	32,455	43,135	44,790	76,131	64,782
Income Taxes	18,391	9,580	19,456	11,035	14,882	17,244	28,930	25,198
Net Income	40,936	20,357	50,871	21,420	28,253	27,546	47,201	39,584
Average Shares	49,988	49,230	95,624	93,508	93,358	92,428	91,732	90,731
Balance Sheet								
Current Assets	273,549	248,902	251,923	215,157	210,026	194,993	203,183	203,169
Total Assets	761,440	735,149	694,330	449,519	420,525	392,476	398,134	351,120
Current Liabilities	117,514	120,241	120,217	91,279	74,262	71,163	87,099	73,285
Long-Term Obligations	150,000	150,000	150,019	568	3,751	4,144	4,157	1,402
Total Liabilities	302,083	303,547	291,015	110,558	96,283	89,897	106,910	90,556
Stockholders' Equity	459,357	431,602	403,315	338,961	324,242	302,579	291,224	260,564
Shares Outstanding	49,129	48,651	48,160	46,618	46,242	45,828	45,462	45,209
Statistical Record								
Return on Assets %	11.74	10.10	8.87	4.92	6.95	6.97	12.57	11.94
Return on Equity %	17.75	15.49	13.67	6.46	9.01	9.28	17.06	16.03
EBITDA Margin %	19.35	19.38	13.67	9.07	11.58	12.43	17.47	17.07
Net Margin %	10.32	10.16	7.58	3.86	5.47	5.05	8.72	8.41
Asset Turnover	1.22	1.19	1.17	1.28	1.27	1.38	1.44	1.42
Current Ratio	2.33	2.07	2.10	2.36	2.83	2.74	2.33	2.77
Debt to Equity	0.33	0.35	0.37	N.M.	0.01	0.01	0.01	0.01
Price Range	32.13-17.45	27.49-17.30	23.10-15.90	17.70-12.89	20.30-13.65	19.47-13.88	17.91-12.38	17.50-8.19
P/E Ratio	12.60-6.84	11.90-7.49	10.90-7.50	19.67-14.32	17.06-11.47	16.64-11.86	8.78-6.07	10.17-4.76
Average Yield %	1.84	2.04	2.18	2.53	2.23	2.23	2.24	2.62

Address: 6555 West Good Hope Road, Milwaukee, WI 53223 **Telephone:** 414-358-6600 **Web Site:** www.bradycorp.com	**Officers:** Frank M. Jaehnert - Pres., C.E.O. David R. Hawke - Exec. V.P. **Transfer Agents:** Wells Fargo Bank Minnesota, N.A., St. Paul, MN	**Investor Contact:** 414-438-6940 **No of Institutions:** 125 **Shares:** 52,036,752 **% Held:** N/A

BRIGGS & STRATTON CORP.

Exchange	Symbol	Price	52Wk Range	Yield	P/E
NYS	BGG	$33.86 (5/31/2005)	44.20-31.69	2.01	13.65

*7 Year Price Score 133.22 *NYSE Composite Index=100 *12 Month Price Score 85.34

2-for-1

TRADING VOLUME (thousand shares)

Interim Earnings (Per Share)

Qtr.	Sep	Dec	Mar	Jun
2001-02	(0.41)	0.06	0.79	0.66
2002-03	(0.16)	0.27	0.91	0.69
2003-04	0.09	0.44	1.44	0.79
2004-05	(0.03)	0.14	1.56	...

Interim Dividends (Per Share)

Amt	Decl	Ex	Rec	Pay
0.17Q	8/4/2004	8/23/2004	8/25/2004	10/1/2004
0.17Q	10/20/2004	11/29/2004	12/1/2004	1/3/2005
0.17Q	1/19/2005	2/25/2005	3/1/2005	4/1/2005
0.17Q	4/20/2005	5/27/2005	6/1/2005	6/30/2005

Indicated Div: $0.68 (Div. Reinv. Plan)

Valuation Analysis

Forecast P/E 10.67 (5/28/2005)

Market Cap	$1.8 Billion	Book Value	901.2 Million
Price/Book	1.94	Price/Sales	0.75

Dividend Achiever Status

Rank 288 **10 Year Growth Rate** 3.87%

Total Years of Dividend Growth 13

Business Summary: Industrial Machinery and Equipment (MIC: 11.5 SIC: 519 NAIC: 33618)

Briggs & Stratton is a producer of air cooled gasoline engines for outdoor power equipment. Co. designs, manufactures, markets and services these products for original equipment manufacturers (OEMs) worldwide. These engines are primarily aluminum alloy gasoline engines ranging from 3 to 31 horsepower. Co.'s engines are marketed under various brand names including Classic™, Sprint™, Quattro™, Quantum®, INTEK™, I/C®, Industrial Plus™ and Vanguard™. Additionally, through its wholly owned subsidiary, Briggs & Stratton Power Products Group, LLC, Co. designs, manufactures and markets portable generators, pressure washers and related accessories.

Recent Developments: For the quarter ended Mar 27 2005, net income increased 13.1% to $80,624 thousand from net income of $71,268 thousand in the year-earlier quarter. Revenues were $840,463 thousand, up 28.4% from $654,681 thousand the year before. Operating income was $97,484 thousand versus an income of $114,504 thousand in the prior-year quarter, a decrease of 14.9%. Total direct expense was $674,735 thousand versus $486,914 thousand in the prior-year quarter, an increase of 38.6%. Total indirect expense was $68,244 thousand versus $53,263 thousand in the prior-year quarter, an increase of 28.1%.

Prospects: Co. is experiencing strong growth in net sales primarily as a result of the acquisition of Simplicity Manufacturing in July 2004 and contributions from lawn and garden equipment due to acquisition of selected assets of the bankrupt Murray, Inc. in February 2005. Co.'s Power Products segment is also benefiting from strong generator demand due to replenishment of inventory. Co.'s net income is being pressured by increased spending on raw materials and other manufacturing costs and lower production volume in the Engines segment. For fiscal year 2005, Co. expects revenues of about $2.60 billion, including $200.0 million from Murray, and earnings in the range of $2.76 to $2.85 per diluted share.

Financial Data

(US$ in Thousands)	9 Mos	6 Mos	3 Mos	06/27/2004	06/29/2003	06/30/2002	07/01/2001	07/02/2000
Earnings Per Share	2.48	2.34	2.64	2.77	1.75	1.18	1.11	2.98
Cash Flow Per Share	2.52	0.18	0.77	1.01	3.88	4.63	1.58	1.67
Tang Book Value Per Share	10.70	9.30	9.29	13.03	8.15	6.67	5.77	9.26
Dividends Per Share	0.675	0.670	0.665	0.660	0.640	0.630	0.620	0.600
Dividend Payout %	27.26	28.57	25.23	23.87	36.68	53.39	56.11	20.10
Income Statement								
Total Revenue	1,783,158	942,695	438,995	1,947,364	1,657,633	1,529,372	1,312,446	1,590,557
EBITDA	181,952	61,193	23,677	306,597	219,993	188,722	160,180	287,671
Depn & Amortn	54,182	35,837	17,886	66,898	63,526	65,968	59,711	51,370
Income Before Taxes	100,616	8,442	(2,328)	205,004	118,578	80,510	71,873	216,623
Income Taxes	34,220	2,870	(840)	68,890	37,940	27,390	23,860	80,150
Net Income	86,196	5,572	(1,488)	136,114	80,638	53,120	48,013	136,473
Average Shares	51,710	51,751	51,191	50,680	48,960	48,904	43,932	45,684
Balance Sheet								
Current Assets	1,124,710	1,018,395	838,394	981,993	807,147	669,944	613,430	471,997
Total Assets	2,050,732	1,933,897	1,748,350	1,637,153	1,475,193	1,349,033	1,296,195	930,245
Current Liabilities	426,239	510,367	328,961	300,561	301,395	266,023	242,182	312,778
Long-Term Obligations	486,131	360,941	360,752	360,562	503,397	499,022	508,134	98,512
Total Liabilities	1,149,520	1,107,431	922,660	819,558	960,206	899,387	873,443	520,780
Stockholders' Equity	901,212	826,466	825,690	817,595	514,987	449,646	422,752	409,465
Shares Outstanding	51,684	51,618	51,615	51,090	43,570	43,278	43,198	43,492
Statistical Record								
Return on Assets %	6.86	6.78	8.16	8.77	5.73	4.03	4.32	14.87
Return on Equity %	16.66	17.05	19.27	20.48	16.76	12.21	11.57	34.63
EBITDA Margin %	10.20	6.49	5.39	15.74	13.27	12.34	12.20	18.09
Net Margin %	4.83	0.59	N.M.	6.99	4.86	3.47	3.66	8.58
Asset Turnover	1.26	1.24	1.29	1.25	1.18	1.16	1.18	1.73
Current Ratio	2.64	2.00	2.55	3.27	2.68	2.52	2.53	1.51
Debt to Equity	0.54	0.44	0.44	0.44	0.98	1.11	1.20	0.24
Price Range	44.20-33.59	44.20-31.68	44.20-29.36	43.70-25.25	25.40-15.59	24.06-15.12	24.00-15.44	31.50-15.66
P/E Ratio	17.82-13.54	18.89-13.54	16.74-11.12	15.78-9.12	14.51-8.91	20.39-12.81	21.62-13.91	10.57-5.25
Average Yield %	1.74	1.79	1.85	2.01	3.16	3.12	3.10	2.45

Address: 12301 West Wirth Street, Wauwatosa, WI 53222 **Telephone:** 414-259-5333 **Web Site:** www.briggsandstratton.com	**Officers:** John S. Shiely - Chmn., Pres., C.E.O. Todd J. Teske - Sr. V.P. **Transfer Agents:** National City Bank, Cleveland, OH	**Investor Contact:** 414-259-5333 **No of Institutions:** 219 **Shares:** 43,585,580 **% Held:** 84.58

BROWN & BROWN, INC.

Exchange	Symbol	Price	52Wk Range	Yield	P/E
NYS	BRO	$44.56 (5/31/2005)	48.25-39.50	0.72	22.85

*7 Year Price Score 157.35 *NYSE Composite Index=100 *12 Month Price Score 98.05

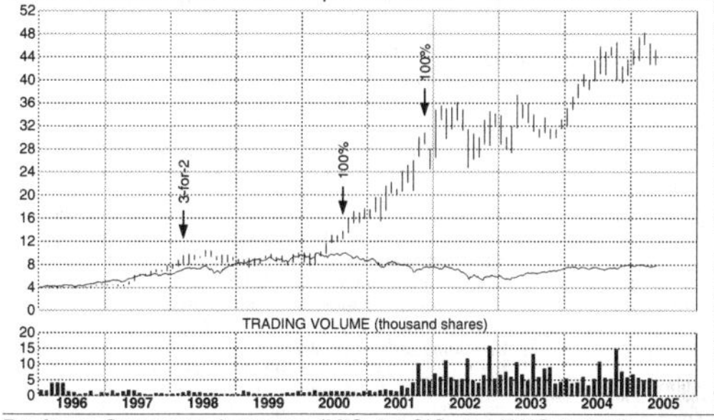

Interim Earnings (Per Share)

Qtr.	Mar	Jun	Sep	Dec
2002	0.31	0.31	0.29	0.31
2003	0.44	0.41	0.38	0.37
2004	0.53	0.46	0.43	0.44
2005	0.62	...	...	...

Interim Dividends (Per Share)

Amt	Decl	Ex	Rec	Pay
0.07Q	7/21/2004	8/2/2004	8/4/2004	8/18/2004
0.08Q	10/20/2004	11/1/2004	11/3/2004	11/17/2004
0.08Q	1/19/2005	1/31/2005	2/2/2005	2/16/2005
0.08Q	4/21/2005	5/3/2005	5/5/2005	5/19/2005

Indicated Div: $0.32

Valuation Analysis

Forecast P/E 20.58 (6/2/2005)

Market Cap $3.1 Billion Book Value 662.5 Million

Price/Book 4.65 Price/Sales 4.51

Dividend Achiever Status

Rank 86 **10 Year Growth Rate** 15.27%

Total Years of Dividend Growth 11

Business Summary: Insurance (MIC: 8.2 SIC: 411 NAIC: 24210)

Brown & Brown is engaged in the property and casualty business. Co.'s business is divided into four divisions. The Retail Division sells insurance products to commercial, professional and individual clients. The National Programs Division is comprised of two units: Professional Programs, which provides professional liability and related package products; and Special Programs, which markets targeted applications for specific industries, trade groups, governmental entities and market niches. The Brokerage Division sells commercial insurance via independent agents and brokers. The Service Division provides third-party administration for workers' compensation and employee benefit markets.

Recent Developments: For the quarter ended Mar 31 2005, net income increased 18.4% to $43,018 thousand from net income of $36,348 thousand in the year-earlier quarter. Total revenues were $202,374 thousand, up 22.2% from $165,565 thousand the year before. Commisions and fees climbed 21.9% to $200,315 thousand, while investment income jumped 40.3% to $965 thousand. Other income rose 94.3% to 1,094 thousand. Total expenses increased 24.2% to $131,861 thousand versus $106,205 thousand in the prior-year quarter.

Prospects: Co. is pleased with its results, considering the current softening of commercial insurance premium rates. Co.'s goal is to maintain its intense focus on the execution of its stated plan and to continue providing solid service to its growing list of clients across the nation. In the mergers and acquisitions arena, 2005 has started even better than Co. imagined. Co. has completed several acquisitions during the first quarter, with estimated annualized revenues of $91.6 million. Most of these entities already operate within Co.'s desired operating profit percent range. Co. will continue to exercise its selective discipline to choose the best acquisitions.

Financial Data

(US$ in Thousands)	3 Mos	12/31/2004	12/31/2003	12/31/2002	12/31/2001	12/31/2000	12/31/1999	12/31/1998
Earnings Per Share	1.95	1.86	1.60	1.22	0.85	0.58	0.50	0.43
Cash Flow Per Share	2.37	2.46	2.09	1.39	1.12	0.77	0.72	0.68
Tang Book Value Per Share	N.M.	N.M.	0.40	0.17	N.M.	0.35	0.20	0.09
Dividends Per Share	0.300	0.290	0.242	0.200	0.160	0.135	0.115	0.102
Dividend Payout %	15.38	15.59	15.16	16.39	18.82	23.28	23.23	23.84
Income Statement								
Total Revenue	202,374	646,934	551,040	455,742	365,029	209,706	176,413	153,791
Income Before Taxes	70,513	206,949	176,482	134,664	90,478	53,978	44,208	37,485
Income Taxes	27,495	78,106	66,160	49,271	34,834	20,792	17,036	14,432
Net Income	43,018	128,843	110,322	83,122	53,913	33,186	27,172	23,053
Average Shares	69,711	69,444	68,897	68,043	63,222	57,326	54,944	53,724
Balance Sheet								
Total Assets	1,461,525	1,249,517	865,854	754,349	488,737	276,719	235,163	230,513
Total Liabilities	799,026	625,192	367,819	362,759	313,452	154,808	132,137	146,305
Stockholders' Equity	662,499	624,325	498,035	391,590	175,285	121,911	103,026	84,208
Shares Outstanding	69,158	69,159	68,561	68,178	63,194	57,398	54,880	53,992
Statistical Record								
Return on Assets %	11.38	12.15	13.62	13.37	14.09	12.93	11.67	10.86
Return on Equity %	22.61	22.90	24.80	29.33	36.28	29.43	29.02	28.58
Price Range	48.25-38.32	46.60-32.08	37.44-27.29	36.13-24.74	30.81-15.45	17.72-7.81	10.03-7.42	10.42-7.24
P/E Ratio	24.74-19.65	25.05-17.25	23.40-17.06	29.61-20.28	36.25-18.18	30.55-13.47	20.06-14.84	24.24-16.84
Average Yield %	0.70	0.72	0.76	0.63	0.71	1.09	1.31	1.15

Address: 220 South Ridgewood Ave., Daytona Beach, FL 32114
Telephone: 368-252-9601
Web Site: www.bbinsurance.com

Officers: J. Hyatt Brown - Chmn., C.E.O. Jim W. Henderson - Pres., C.O.O., Asst. Treas. **Transfer Agents:** Wachovia Bank N.A., Charlotte, NC

Investor Contact: 904-239-7250
No of Institutions: 179
Shares: 42,458,032 **% Held:** 61.39

BROWN-FORMAN CORP.

Exchange	Symbol	Price	52Wk Range	Yield	P/E
NYS	BF A	$61.29 (5/31/2005)	61.29-44.62	1.60	24.52

***7 Year Price Score 123.42** *NYSE Composite Index=100 ***12 Month Price Score 109.41**

Interim Earnings (Per Share)

Qtr.	Jul	Oct	Jan	Apr
2001-02	0.28	0.58	0.42	0.38
2002-03	0.27	0.59	0.51	0.45
2003-04	0.26	0.72	0.66	0.47
2004-05	0.42	0.84	0.78	...

Interim Dividends (Per Share)

Amt	Decl	Ex	Rec	Pay
0.212Q	7/22/2004	9/2/2004	9/7/2004	10/1/2004
0.245Q	11/18/2004	12/2/2004	12/6/2004	1/1/2005
0.245Q	1/27/2005	3/8/2005	3/10/2005	4/1/2005
0.245Q	5/26/2005	6/2/2005	6/6/2005	7/1/2005

Indicated Div: $0.98

Valuation Analysis

Forecast P/E 21.05 (5/28/2005)

Market Cap	$7.5 Billion	Book Value	1.2 Billion
Price/Book	6.01	Price/Sales	3.21

Dividend Achiever Status

Rank	248	10 Year Growth Rate	6.03%
Total Years of Dividend Growth			20

Business Summary: Food (MIC: 4.1 SIC: 084 NAIC: 12130)

Brown-Forman operates in two business segments: beverages and consumer durables. The beverages segment manufactures, bottles, imports, exports and markets a wide variety of alcoholic beverage brands. Co. also manufactures and markets new and used oak barrels. Co.'s principal beverage brands include: Jack Daniel's, Southern Comfort, Finlandia Vodka, Canadian Mist, Korbel champagnes, and Fetzer Vineyards, Bolla and Bel Arbor wines. The consumer durables segment sells fine china dinnerware, crystal stemware and giftware, stainless steel flatware, and silver-plated and metal giftware under the Lenox, Gorham and Dansk brand names, as well as Hartmann luggage.

Recent Developments: For the quarter ended Jan 31 2005, net income increased 19.4% to $96,100 thousand from net income of $80,500 thousand in the year-earlier quarter. Revenues were $630,500 thousand, up 6.4% from $592,600 thousand the year before. Operating income was $94,700 thousand versus an income of $126,900 thousand in the prior-year quarter, a decrease of 25.4%. Total direct expense was $255,200 thousand versus $249,000 thousand in the prior-year quarter, an increase of 2.5%. Total indirect expense was $280,600 thousand versus $216,700 thousand in the prior-year quarter, an increase of 29.5%.

Prospects: Following strong growth in earnings through the third quarter of fiscal 2005, only moderate growth is expected for the remainder of the fiscal year. Continued solid consumer demand for several of Co.'s beverage brands is forecasted to be partially offset by increases in advertising investments and reductions in global trade inventory levels related to both supply chain efficiency initiatives and potential distribution changes in continental Europe. Meanwhile, Co. expects fiscal 2005 earnings to range from $2.47 to $2.51 per share. Separately, on Apr 27 2005, Co. announced that it joined a consortium led by Constellation Brands to consider a potential bid to acquire Allied Domecq.

Financial Data

(US$ in Thousands)	9 Mos	6 Mos	3 Mos	04/30/2004	04/30/2003	04/30/2002	04/30/2001	04/30/2000
Earnings Per Share	2.50	2.38	2.27	2.11	1.81	1.67	1.70	1.59
Cash Flow Per Share	3.29	2.96	2.85	2.51	1.80	1.83	1.69	1.75
Tang Book Value Per Share	5.12	5.22	4.36	4.99	2.43	7.79	6.75	5.68
Dividends Per Share	0.882	0.850	0.825	0.800	0.725	0.680	0.640	0.605
Dividend Payout %	35.23	35.67	36.39	37.91	39.94	40.84	37.65	38.05
Income Statement								
Total Revenue	1,796,600	1,166,100	496,000	2,213,000	2,060,000	1,958,000	1,924,000	1,877,000
EBITDA	453,900	270,700	97,000	463,000	433,000	408,000	438,000	410,000
Depn & Amortn	43,800	28,900	14,100	56,000	55,000	55,000	64,000	62,000
Income Before Taxes	398,500	232,300	78,000	388,000	373,000	348,000	366,000	343,000
Income Taxes	147,900	77,800	26,100	130,000	128,000	120,000	133,000	125,000
Net Income	250,600	154,500	51,900	258,000	245,000	228,000	233,000	218,000
Average Shares	122,482	122,417	122,414	121,986	135,126	137,000	137,200	137,200
Balance Sheet								
Current Assets	1,310,900	1,276,000	1,086,000	1,083,000	1,068,000	1,029,000	994,000	1,020,000
Total Assets	2,622,200	2,563,700	2,372,700	2,376,000	2,264,000	2,016,000	1,939,000	1,802,000
Current Liabilities	489,200	483,700	368,200	369,000	548,000	495,000	538,000	522,000
Long-Term Obligations	600,800	601,100	630,200	630,000	629,000	40,000	40,000	41,000
Total Liabilities	1,381,000	1,360,900	1,279,400	1,291,000	1,424,000	705,000	752,000	754,000
Stockholders' Equity	1,241,200	1,202,800	1,093,300	1,085,000	840,000	1,311,000	1,187,000	1,048,000
Shares Outstanding	121,763	121,784	121,796	104,731	121,134	136,696	136,918	137,024
Statistical Record								
Return on Assets %	12.44	11.70	11.94	11.09	11.45	11.53	12.46	12.29
Return on Equity %	27.82	27.42	28.82	26.73	22.78	18.25	20.85	22.13
EBITDA Margin %	25.26	23.21	19.56	20.92	21.02	20.84	22.77	21.84
Net Margin %	13.95	13.25	10.46	11.66	11.89	11.64	12.11	11.61
Asset Turnover	0.94	0.92	0.96	0.95	0.96	0.99	1.03	1.06
Current Ratio	2.68	2.64	2.95	2.93	1.95	2.08	1.85	1.95
Debt to Equity	0.48	0.50	0.58	0.58	0.75	0.03	0.03	0.04
Price Range	51.90-44.62	51.90-43.01	51.90-39.50	51.90-38.51	40.25-30.16	39.20-30.32	34.75-24.56	34.50-21.00
P/E Ratio	20.76-17.85	21.81-18.07	22.86-17.40	24.60-18.25	22.24-16.66	23.47-18.16	20.44-14.45	21.70-13.21
Average Yield %	1.81	1.77	1.77	1.79	2.02	2.05	2.19	2.17

Address: 850 Dixie Highway, Louisville, KY 40210 **Telephone:** 502-585-1100 **Web Site:** www.brown-forman.com	**Officers:** Owsley Brown II - Chmn., C.E.O. Michael B. Crutcher - Vice-Chmn., Sec., Gen. Couns. **Transfer Agents:** National City Bank, Cleveland, OH	**No of Institutions:** 54 **Shares:** 30,971,086 **% Held:** 54.49

CALIFORNIA WATER SERVICE GROUP

Exchange	Symbol	Price	52Wk Range	Yield	P/E
NYS	CWT	$36.08 (5/31/2005)	37.70-26.19	3.16	N/A

*7 Year Price Score 104.17 *NYSE Composite Index=100 *12 Month Price Score 105.53

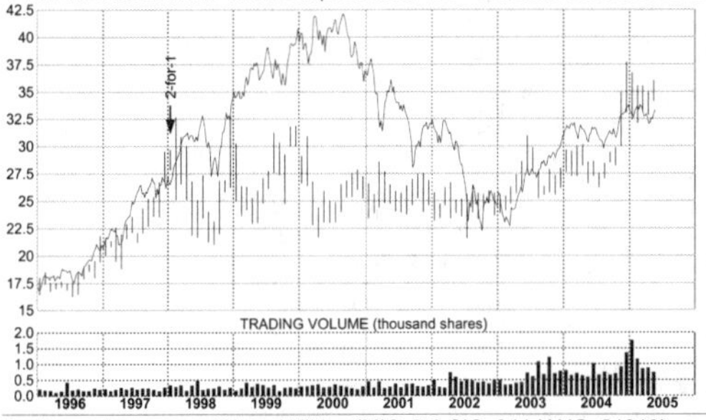

Interim Earnings (Per Share)

Qtr.	Mar	Jun	Sep	Dec
2002	0.12	0.43	0.50	0.19
2003	(0.05)	0.30	0.53	0.42
2004	0.08	0.59	0.59	0.19
2005	0.03	...	...	...

Interim Dividends (Per Share)

Amt	Decl	Ex	Rec	Pay
0.282Q	7/28/2004	8/5/2004	8/9/2004	8/20/2004
0.282Q	10/28/2004	11/4/2004	11/8/2004	11/19/2004
0.285Q	1/26/2005	2/3/2005	2/7/2005	2/18/2005
0.285Q	4/27/2005	5/5/2005	5/9/2005	5/20/2005

Indicated Div: $1.14 (Div. Reinv. Plan)

Valuation Analysis

Forecast P/E	N/A		
Market Cap	$662.9 Million	Book Value	286.6 Million
Price/Book	2.31	Price/Sales	2.10

Dividend Achiever Status

Rank	310	**10 Year Growth Rate**	1.33%
Total Years of Dividend Growth			37

Business Summary: Water Utilities (MIC: 7.2 SIC: 941 NAIC: 21310)

California Water Service Group is a utility water company that provides regulated and non-regulated water utility services to over 2.0 million customers in 100 communities in California, Washington, New Mexico and Hawaii as of Dec 31 2004. Co. is the parent company of California Water Service Company, Washington Water Service Company, New Mexico Water Service Company, Hawaii Water Service Company, Inc. and CWS Utility Services. The sole business of Co. consists of the production, purchase, storage, purification, distribution and sale of water for domestic, industrial, public, and irrigation uses, and for fire protection.

Recent Developments: For the quarter ended Mar 31 2005, net income decreased 53.0% to $680 thousand from net income of $1,446 thousand in the year-earlier quarter. Revenues were $60,303 thousand, up 0.1% from $60,240 thousand the year before. Operating income was $4,465 thousand versus an income of $5,391 thousand in the prior-year quarter, a decrease of 17.2%. Total direct expense was $45,422 thousand versus $44,679 thousand in the prior-year quarter, an increase of 1.7%. Total indirect expense was $10,416 thousand versus $10,170 thousand in the prior-year quarter, an increase of 2.4%.

Prospects: Results are being hampered by reduced water usage in Southern California stemming from heavy rainfall during the first quarter of 2005. Going forward, Co. will continue to pursue rate relief in an effort to offset the higher costs of providing services. In addition, results should benefit from Co.'s efforts to expand its customer base and improve operating efficiencies. Separately, on Apr 27 2005, Co. announced that it has completed its purchase of the assets of the Los Trancos County Water District, which serves 270 homes in the areas of Portola Valley and unincorporated San Mateo County in California.

Financial Data

(US$ in Thousands)	3 Mos	12/31/2004	12/31/2003	12/31/2002	12/31/2001	12/31/2000	12/31/1999	12/31/1998
Earnings Per Share	1.40	1.46	1.21	1.25	0.97	1.31	1.53	1.45
Cash Flow Per Share	4.05	3.13	2.80	2.20	2.54	2.28	3.30	2.97
Tang Book Value Per Share	15.41	15.66	14.44	13.12	12.95	13.13	13.70	13.38
Dividends Per Share	1.133	1.130	1.125	1.120	1.115	1.100	1.085	1.070
Dividend Payout %	80.93	77.40	92.98	89.60	114.95	83.97	70.92	73.79
Income Statement								
Total Revenue	60,303	315,567	277,128	263,151	246,820	244,806	206,440	186,273
Depn & Amortn	6,996	26,114	23,256	21,238	19,226	18,368	15,802	14,563
Income Taxes	...	17,084	12,898	12,568	...	...	...	...
Net Income	680	26,026	19,417	19,073	14,965	19,963	19,919	18,395
Average Shares	18,403	17,674	15,893	15,185	15,285	15,173	12,936	12,619
Balance Sheet								
Net PPE	809,515	800,305	759,498	696,988	624,342	582,008	515,354	478,305
Total Assets	950,390	942,853	873,035	800,582	710,214	666,605	587,618	548,499
Long-Term Obligations	274,414	274,821	272,226	250,365	202,600	187,098	156,572	136,345
Total Liabilities	663,757	651,773	625,036	597,890	510,120	464,296	406,961	376,220
Stockholders' Equity	286,633	291,080	247,999	202,692	200,094	202,309	180,657	172,279
Shares Outstanding	18,372	18,367	16,932	15,182	15,182	15,146	12,936	12,619
Statistical Record								
Return on Assets %	2.77	2.86	2.32	2.52	2.17	3.17	3.51	3.41
Return on Equity %	9.51	9.63	8.62	9.47	7.44	10.40	11.29	10.83
Net Margin %	1.13	8.25	7.01	7.25	6.06	8.15	9.65	9.88
PPE Turnover	0.40	0.40	0.38	0.40	0.41	0.44	0.42	0.40
Asset Turnover	0.35	0.35	0.33	0.35	0.36	0.39	0.36	0.35
Debt to Equity	0.96	0.94	1.10	1.24	1.01	0.92	0.87	0.79
Price Range	37.70-26.19	37.70-26.19	30.97-23.65	26.69-21.60	28.60-23.38	30.94-21.69	31.88-22.94	32.75-21.00
P/E Ratio	26.93-18.71	25.82-17.94	25.60-19.55	21.35-17.28	29.48-24.10	23.62-16.56	20.83-14.99	22.59-14.48
Average Yield %	3.69	3.86	4.22	4.53	4.37	4.28	3.99	4.16

Address: 1720 North First Street, San Jose, CA 95112
Telephone: 408-367-8200
Web Site: www.calwater.com

Officers: Robert W. Foy - Chmn. Peter C. Nelson - Pres., C.E.O. **Transfer Agents:**
State Street Bank and Trust Company, Boston, MA

Investor Contact: 408-367-8200
No of Institutions: 84
Shares: 4,165,628 **% Held:** 22.67

CAPITAL CITY BANK GROUP, INC.

Exchange	Symbol	Price	52Wk Range	Yield	P/E
NMS	CCBG	$40.20 (5/31/2005)	45.41-34.49	1.89	17.79

*7 Year Price Score 132.56 *NYSE Composite Index=100 *12 Month Price Score 93.90

Interim Earnings (Per Share)

Qtr.	Mar	Jun	Sep	Dec
2002	0.38	0.41	0.44	0.50
2003	0.48	0.49	0.47	0.46
2004	0.37	0.48	0.82	0.51
2005	0.45	...	...	...

Interim Dividends (Per Share)

Amt	Decl	Ex	Rec	Pay
0.19Q	11/23/2004	12/2/2004	12/6/2004	12/20/2004
0.19Q	2/24/2005	3/3/2005	3/7/2005	3/21/2005
25%	4/26/2005	7/5/2005	6/17/2005	7/1/2005
0.19Q	5/26/2005	6/2/2005	6/6/2005	6/20/2005

Indicated Div: $0.76

Valuation Analysis

Forecast P/E	19.80 (6/2/2005)		
Market Cap	$569.3 Million	Book Value	260.1 Million
Price/Book	2.19	Price/Sales	3.53

Dividend Achiever Status

Rank	130	10 Year Growth Rate	12.54%
Total Years of Dividend Growth			11

Business Summary: Commercial Banking (MIC: 8.1 SIC: 022 NAIC: 22110)

Capital City Bank Group, with $2.36 billion in total assets as of Dec 31 2004, is a financial holding company. Co.'s principal asset is the capital stock of Capital City Bank (CCB). In addition to its banking subsidiary, Co. has seven other indirect subsidiaries, Capital City Trust, Capital City Mortgage (inactive), Capital City Securities, Capital City Services, First Insurance Agency of Grady County, Southern Oaks, and FNB Financial Services, all of which are wholly-owned subsidiaries of CCB, and one additional direct subsidiary, CCBG Capital Trust I, a wholly-owned subsidiary of Co. CCB is a Florida chartered full-service bank engaged in the commercial and retail banking business.

Recent Developments: For the quarter ended Mar 31 2005, net income increased 31.6% to $6,377 thousand from net income of $4,847 thousand in the year-earlier quarter. Net interest income was $24,554 thousand, up 26.0% from $19,492 thousand the year before. Provision for loan losses was $410 thousand versus $961 thousand in the prior-year quarter, a decrease of 57.3%. Non-interest income rose 11.9% to $11,060 thousand, while non-interest expense advanced 19.9% to $25,267 thousand.

Prospects: Co. turned in a solid performance for the first quarter and is gaining momentum as it heads into the second quarter. Co.'s margin is responding well to rising rates, evidenced by a 17 basis point improvement over the fourth quarter of 2004. Loan growth picked up during the latter half of the first quarter and credit quality remains at historically strong levels. Expansion into the Alachua/Gainesville market adds tremendous growth potential to Co.'s franchise, and expansion continues with the pending acquisition of First Alachua Banking, with $230.0 million in assets, which is expected to close in May 2005.

Financial Data

(US$ in Thousands)	3 Mos	12/31/2004	12/31/2003	12/31/2002	12/31/2001	12/31/2000	12/31/1999	12/31/1998
Earnings Per Share	2.26	2.18	1.90	1.74	1.27	1.42	1.20	1.19
Cash Flow Per Share	3.17	3.28	2.86	2.88	2.52	2.10	1.92	1.24
Tang Book Value Per Share	12.78	12.47	13.37	11.94	10.49	9.92	8.41	7.49
Dividends Per Share	0.740	0.730	0.656	0.502	0.476	0.436	0.394	0.360
Dividend Payout %	32.74	33.49	34.53	28.92	37.42	30.62	32.83	30.20
Income Statement								
Interest Income	30,474	101,525	99,487	106,095	118,983	109,334	99,685	79,253
Interest Expense	5,920	15,441	14,839	22,503	48,249	46,234	41,247	31,342
Net Interest Income	24,554	86,084	84,648	83,592	70,734	63,100	58,438	47,911
Provision for Losses	410	2,141	3,436	3,297	3,983	3,120	2,440	2,160
Non-Interest Income	11,060	50,553	41,939	37,176	32,037	26,769	24,761	21,751
Non-Interest Expense	25,267	89,226	84,378	81,698	72,804	59,147	58,028	47,309
Income Before Taxes	9,937	45,270	38,773	35,773	25,984	27,602	22,731	20,193
Income Taxes	3,560	15,899	13,580	12,691	9,118	9,449	7,479	7,005
Net Income	6,377	29,371	25,193	23,082	16,866	18,153	15,252	13,188
Average Shares	14,165	13,448	13,251	13,273	13,292	12,768	12,745	11,072
Balance Sheet								
Net Loans & Leases	1,827,763	1,812,788	1,329,203	1,272,726	1,231,255	1,041,268	918,557	755,208
Total Assets	2,349,092	2,364,013	1,846,502	1,824,771	1,821,423	1,527,460	1,430,520	1,329,405
Total Deposits	1,889,358	1,894,886	1,474,205	1,434,200	1,550,101	1,268,367	1,202,658	1,160,284
Total Liabilities	2,088,994	2,107,213	1,643,693	1,638,240	1,649,640	1,379,853	1,298,304	1,217,705
Stockholders' Equity	260,098	256,800	202,809	186,531	171,783	147,607	132,216	111,700
Shares Outstanding	14,162	14,155	13,236	13,196	13,303	12,635	12,737	11,067
Statistical Record								
Return on Assets %	1.44	1.39	1.37	1.27	1.01	1.22	1.11	1.13
Return on Equity %	13.23	12.75	12.94	12.88	10.56	12.94	12.51	12.43
Net Interest Margin %	80.57	84.79	85.08	78.79	59.45	57.71	58.62	60.45
Efficiency Ratio %	60.83	58.67	59.66	57.02	48.21	43.46	46.63	46.84
Loans to Deposits	0.97	0.96	0.90	0.89	0.79	0.82	0.76	0.65
Price Range	45.41-34.49	45.99-34.49	46.55-27.25	31.59-18.40	20.80-15.95	20.35-13.80	22.10-16.15	26.00-19.10
P/E Ratio	20.09-15.26	21.10-15.82	24.50-14.34	18.16-10.57	16.38-12.56	14.33-9.72	18.42-13.46	21.85-16.05
Average Yield %	1.87	1.81	1.84	2.09	2.55	2.71	2.10	1.53

Address: 217 North Monroe Street, Tallahassee, FL 32301 **Telephone:** 850-671-0300 **Web Site:** www.mycapitalcitybank.com	**Officers:** William G. Smith Jr. - Chmn., Pres., C.E.O. J. Kimbrough Davis - Exec. V.P., C.F.O. **Transfer Agents:**	**Investor Contact:** 850-671-0316 **No of Institutions:** 45 **Shares:** 2,233,531 **% Held:** 15.77

CARLISLE COMPANIES INC.

Exchange	Symbol	Price	52Wk Range	Yield	P/E
NYS	CSL	$69.32 (5/31/2005)	74.62-57.33	1.33	25.77

*7 Year Price Score 125.16 *NYSE Composite Index=100 *12 Month Price Score 107.10

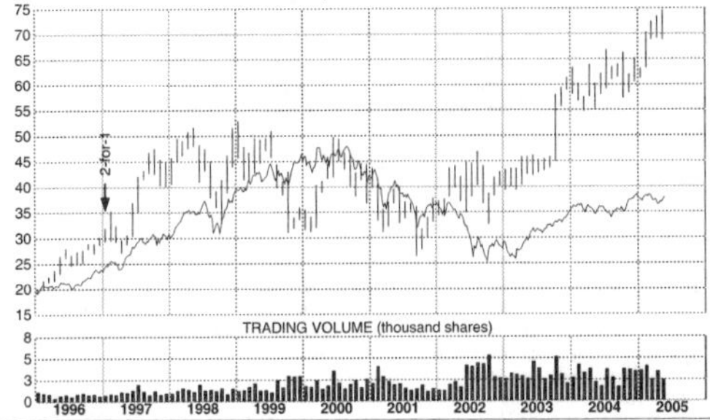

Interim Earnings (Per Share)

Qtr.	Mar	Jun	Sep	Dec
2002	0.42	0.81	0.65	(0.94)
2003	0.56	0.93	0.80	0.60
2004	0.76	1.19	0.92	(0.32)
2005	0.90	...	...	...

Interim Dividends (Per Share)

Amt	Decl	Ex	Rec	Pay
0.23Q	8/2/2004	8/17/2004	8/19/2004	9/1/2004
0.23Q	11/3/2004	11/16/2004	11/18/2004	12/1/2004
0.23Q	2/2/2005	2/16/2005	2/18/2005	3/1/2005
0.23Q	5/4/2005	5/13/2005	5/17/2005	6/1/2005

Indicated Div: $0.92 (Div. Reinv. Plan)

Valuation Analysis

Forecast P/E 16.53 (5/28/2005)

Market Cap $2.1 Billion Book Value 716.9 Million

Price/Book 3.00 Price/Sales 0.95

Dividend Achiever Status

Rank 191 **10 Year Growth Rate** 9.00%

Total Years of Dividend Growth 28

TRADING VOLUME (thousand shares)

Business Summary: Rubber Products (MIC: 11.6 SIC: 011 NAIC: 26211)

Carlisle Companies manufactures and distributes a wide variety of products across a broad range of industries, including roofing, construction, trucking, foodservice, industrial equipment, lawn and garden and aircraft manufacturing. Co. markets its products both as a component supplier to original equipment manufacturers, as well as directly to end-users. Co.'s businesses are divided into four reportable segments: Industrial Components, Construction Materials, Specialty Products and Transportation Products, as well as an all other category labeled General Industry.

Recent Developments: For the quarter ended Mar 31 2005, income from continuing operations increased 28.9% to $30,072 thousand from income of $23,326 thousand in the year-earlier quarter. Net income increased 19.1% to $28,255 thousand from net income of $23,727 thousand in the year-earlier quarter. Revenues were $592,328 thousand, up 17.7% from $503,206 thousand the year before. Total direct expense was $474,605 thousand versus $402,739 thousand in the prior-year quarter, an increase of 17.8%. Total indirect expense was $64,025 thousand versus $58,773 thousand in the prior-year quarter, an increase of 8.9%.

Prospects: Though Co.'s key markets remain strong and its outlook for improved pricing and margins is positive, it must temper its optimism as uncertainties surrounding future costs of oil-based commodities and certain chemicals as well as the impact of rising interest rates require that Co. maintain its 2005 guidance of $4.10 to $4.25 per diluted share for income from continuing operations. The Mar 31 2005 backlog from continuing operations of $373.9 million was 8.8% below $410.1 million at Dec 31 2004, reflecting decreased backlog for the Construction Materials, Industrial Components and General Industry segments. Also, Co. expects to dispose of the automotive components operations in 2005.

Financial Data (US$ in Thousands)	3 Mos	12/31/2004	12/31/2003	12/31/2002	12/31/2001	12/31/2000	12/31/1999	12/31/1998
Earnings Per Share	2.69	2.54	2.88	0.94	0.82	3.14	3.13	2.77
Cash Flow Per Share	2.07	3.59	3.81	7.43	7.37	4.13	4.51	3.21
Tang Book Value Per Share	13.51	12.94	10.37	8.09	6.72	9.79	10.63	8.85
Dividends Per Share	0.910	0.900	0.870	0.850	0.820	0.760	0.680	0.600
Dividend Payout %	33.83	35.43	30.21	90.43	100.00	24.20	21.73	21.66
Income Statement								
Total Revenue	592,328	2,227,614	2,108,164	1,971,280	1,849,477	1,771,067	1,611,256	1,517,494
EBITDA	58,227	238,329	206,560	184,645	131,005	238,432	222,051	208,205
Depn & Amortn	13,839	52,639	60,366	56,994	63,960	59,549	47,414	45,221
Income Before Taxes	44,388	170,340	131,733	110,500	37,925	150,865	155,483	140,269
Income Taxes	14,316	52,026	42,813	38,122	13,084	54,685	59,689	55,403
Net Income	28,255	79,612	88,920	28,625	24,841	96,180	95,794	84,866
Average Shares	31,331	31,409	30,863	30,583	30,450	30,599	30,635	30,674
Balance Sheet								
Current Assets	750,062	652,269	584,381	481,508	553,272	576,477	541,038	478,525
Total Assets	1,598,097	1,501,241	1,436,909	1,315,900	1,397,987	1,305,679	1,080,662	1,022,852
Current Liabilities	461,810	384,022	339,343	324,262	273,779	399,948	240,378	255,337
Long-Term Obligations	257,886	259,554	294,581	293,124	461,744	281,864	281,744	273,521
Total Liabilities	881,188	802,754	804,979	762,823	857,703	757,800	602,529	615,947
Stockholders' Equity	716,909	698,487	631,930	553,077	540,284	547,879	478,133	406,905
Shares Outstanding	31,014	30,896	30,991	30,597	30,263	30,251	30,127	30,178
Statistical Record								
Return on Assets %	5.47	5.40	6.46	2.11	1.84	8.04	9.11	9.01
Return on Equity %	12.30	11.94	15.01	5.24	4.57	18.70	21.65	22.46
EBITDA Margin %	9.83	10.70	9.80	9.37	7.08	13.46	13.78	13.72
Net Margin %	4.77	3.57	4.22	1.45	1.34	5.43	5.95	5.59
Asset Turnover	1.47	1.51	1.53	1.45	1.37	1.48	1.53	1.61
Current Ratio	1.62	1.70	1.72	1.48	2.02	1.44	2.25	1.87
Debt to Equity	0.36	0.37	0.47	0.53	0.85	0.51	0.59	0.67
Price Range	72.43-55.25	66.90-54.71	61.49-39.24	46.91-32.65	43.69-26.40	49.75-31.19	52.94-31.06	51.75-32.88
P/E Ratio	26.93-20.54	26.34-21.54	21.35-13.63	49.90-34.73	53.28-32.20	15.84-9.93	16.91-9.92	18.68-11.87
Average Yield %	1.46	1.49	1.87	2.12	2.33	1.86	1.60	1.34

Address: 13925 Ballantyne Corporate Place, Suite 400, Charlotte, NC 28277
Telephone: 704-501-1100
Web Site: www.carlisle.com

Officers: Stephen P. Munn - Chmn. Richmond D. McKinnish - Pres., C.E.O. **Transfer Agents:** Computershare Investor Services, LLC., Chicago, IL

Investor Contact: 704-501-1100
No of Institutions: 144
Shares: 19,927,836 **% Held:** 64.18

CATERPILLAR INC.

Exchange	Symbol	Price	52Wk Range	Yield	P/E
NYS	CAT	$94.11 (5/31/2005)	99.96-69.62	1.74	15.30

Interim Earnings (Per Share)

Qtr.	Mar	Jun	Sep	Dec
2002	0.23	0.58	0.61	0.88
2003	0.37	1.15	0.62	0.98
2004	1.16	1.55	1.41	1.56
2005	1.63	...	...	...

Interim Dividends (Per Share)

Amt	Decl	Ex	Rec	Pay
0.41Q	6/9/2004	7/16/2004	7/20/2004	8/20/2004
0.41Q	10/13/2004	10/21/2004	10/25/2004	11/20/2004
0.41Q	12/8/2004	1/18/2005	1/20/2005	2/19/2005
0.41Q	4/13/2005	4/21/2005	4/25/2005	5/20/2005

Indicated Div: $1.64 (Div. Reinv. Plan)

Valuation Analysis

Forecast P/E	11.88 (5/28/2005)		
Market Cap	$32.2 Billion	Book Value	7.7 Billion
Price/Book	4.15	Price/Sales	1.00

Dividend Achiever Status

Rank	32	**10 Year Growth Rate**	21.37%
Total Years of Dividend Growth			11

Business Summary: Industrial Machinery and Equipment (MIC: 11.5 SIC: 531 NAIC: 33120)

Caterpillar operates in three principal lines of business. The machinery division designs, manufactures and markets construction, mining, agricultural and forestry machinery. The engines division designs, manufactures and markets engines for Caterpillar machinery; electric power generation systems; on-highway trucks and locomotives; marine, petroleum, construction, industrial, agricultural, and other applications; and related parts. Engines range from 5 to over 22,000 horsepower, and turbines range from 1,200 to 20,500 horsepower. The financial products division consists primarily of Caterpillar Financial Services Corporation, Caterpillar Insurance Holdings, Inc. and their subsidiaries.

Recent Developments: For the quarter ended Mar 31 2005, net income increased 38.3% to $581 million from net income of $420 million in the year-earlier quarter. Revenues were $8,339 million, up 28.7% from $6,480 million the year before. Operating income was $756 million versus an income of $568 million in the prior-year quarter, an increase of 33.1%. Total direct expense was $6,215 million versus $4,701 million in the prior-year quarter, an increase of 32.2%. Total indirect expense was $1,198 million versus $1,092 million in the prior-year quarter, an increase of 9.7%.

Prospects: Prospects appear favorable, reflecting continued economic growth in key global markets. Results are expected to benefit as mining companies continue to add capacity to meet anticipated growth in demand for the next several years. In addition, results will likely be positively affected by increased global demand for energy, including coal as well as gas, along with higher levels of commercial construction and housing in most countries. Accordingly, Co. expects 2005 sales and revenues to advance between 16.0% and 18.0% and profit per share to increase between 35.0% and 40.0% from 2004.

Financial Data

(US$ in Thousands)	3 Mos	12/31/2004	12/31/2003	12/31/2002	12/31/2001	12/31/2000	12/31/1999	12/31/1998
Earnings Per Share	6.15	5.75	3.13	2.30	2.32	3.02	2.63	4.11
Cash Flow Per Share	(11.43)	(11.63)	5.98	6.88	5.79	5.92	7.23	4.90
Tang Book Value Per Share	17.04	16.63	12.92	11.01	11.47	11.92	11.09	10.89
Dividends Per Share	1.600	1.560	1.420	1.400	1.380	1.330	1.250	1.100
Dividend Payout %	26.02	27.13	45.37	60.87	59.48	44.04	47.53	26.76
Income Statement								
Total Revenue	8,339,000	30,251,000	22,763,000	20,152,000	20,450,000	20,175,000	19,702,000	20,977,000
EBITDA	1,236,000	4,334,000	3,070,000	2,613,000	2,623,000	2,842,000	2,635,000	3,303,000
Depn & Amortn	372,000	1,397,000	1,347,000	1,220,000	1,169,000	1,022,000	945,000	865,000
Income Before Taxes	799,000	2,707,000	1,477,000	1,114,000	1,169,000	1,528,000	1,421,000	2,174,000
Income Taxes	232,000	731,000	398,000	312,000	367,000	447,000	455,000	665,000
Net Income	581,000	2,035,000	1,099,000	798,000	805,000	1,053,000	946,000	1,513,000
Average Shares	356,600	353,700	351,400	346,900	347,100	348,897	359,367	368,130
Balance Sheet								
Current Assets	20,224,000	20,856,000	16,791,000	14,628,000	13,400,000	12,521,000	11,734,000	11,459,000
Total Assets	44,347,000	43,091,000	36,465,000	32,851,000	30,657,000	28,464,000	26,635,000	25,128,000
Current Liabilities	14,787,000	16,210,000	12,621,000	11,344,000	10,276,000	8,568,000	8,178,000	7,565,000
Long-Term Obligations	17,909,000	15,837,000	14,078,000	11,596,000	11,291,000	11,334,000	9,928,000	9,404,000
Total Liabilities	36,600,000	35,624,000	30,387,000	27,379,000	25,046,000	22,864,000	21,170,000	19,997,000
Stockholders' Equity	7,747,000	7,467,000	6,078,000	5,472,000	5,611,000	5,600,000	5,465,000	5,131,000
Shares Outstanding	341,694	342,936	343,762	344,255	343,376	343,396	353,748	357,198
Statistical Record								
Return on Assets %	5.31	5.10	3.17	2.51	2.72	3.81	3.66	6.59
Return on Equity %	30.99	29.97	19.03	14.40	14.36	18.98	17.86	30.85
EBITDA Margin %	14.82	14.33	13.49	12.97	12.83	14.09	13.37	15.75
Net Margin %	6.97	6.73	4.83	3.96	3.94	5.22	4.80	7.21
Asset Turnover	0.78	0.76	0.66	0.63	0.69	0.73	0.76	0.91
Current Ratio	1.37	1.29	1.33	1.29	1.30	1.46	1.43	1.51
Debt to Equity	2.31	2.12	2.32	2.12	2.01	2.02	1.82	1.83
Price Range	99.96-69.62	98.47-69.62	84.75-42.04	59.79-33.86	56.20-40.09	53.31-29.81	65.50-43.13	60.69-40.25
P/E Ratio	16.25-11.32	17.13-12.11	27.08-13.43	26.00-14.72	24.22-17.28	17.65-9.87	24.90-16.40	14.77-9.79
Average Yield %	1.92	1.96	2.34	2.91	2.84	3.44	2.31	2.18

Address: 100 NE Adams Street, Peoria, IL 61629-7310
Telephone: 309-675-1000
Web Site: www.CAT.com

Officers: James W. Owens - Chmn., C.E.O. David B. Burritt - V.P., C.F.O. **Transfer Agents:** Mellon Investor Services of South Hackensack, NJ

Investor Contact: 309-675-4549
No of Institutions: 608
Shares: 250,007,264 **% Held:** 73.27

CBL & ASSOCIATES PROPERTIES, INC.

Exchange	Symbol	Price	52Wk Range	Yield	P/E
NYS	CBL	$81.47 (5/31/2005)	82.58-52.26	1.99	26.89

*7 Year Price Score 157.37 *NYSE Composite Index=100 *12 Month Price Score 110.27

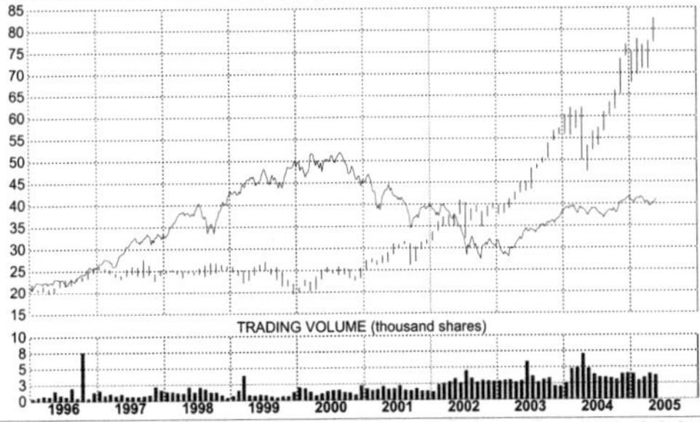

TRADING VOLUME (thousand shares)

Interim Earnings (Per Share)

Qtr.	Mar	Jun	Sep	Dec
2002	0.64	0.63	0.57	0.65
2003	0.74	0.68	0.65	1.93
2004	0.96	0.68	0.62	0.95
2005	0.78	...	...	...

Interim Dividends (Per Share)

Amt	Decl	Ex	Rec	Pay
0.362Q	9/9/2004	9/28/2004	9/30/2004	10/15/2004
0.406Q	11/4/2004	12/29/2004	12/31/2004	1/14/2005
0.406Q	3/3/2005	3/29/2005	3/31/2005	4/15/2005
100%	3/21/2005	6/16/2005	6/1/2005	6/15/2005

Indicated Div: $1.625

Valuation Analysis

Forecast P/E	13.70 (5/28/2005)		
Market Cap	$2.6 Billion	Book Value	1.1 Billion
Price/Book	2.42	Price/Sales	3.21

Dividend Achiever Status

Rank	218	10 Year Growth Rate	7.81%
Total Years of Dividend Growth			10

Business Summary: Property, Real Estate & Development (MIC: 8.3 SIC: 798 NAIC: 25930)

CBL & Associates Properties is a self-managed, self-administered, fully-integrated real estate investment trust that is engaged in the ownership, development, acquisition, leasing, management and operation of regional shopping malls and community centers. Co.'s shopping center properties are located mostly in the southeast and midwest, as well as in select markets in other regions of the U.S. As of Dec 31 2004, Co. owned controlling interests in 64 regional malls; 25 associated centers, each adjacent to a regional shopping mall; 12 community centers and its corporate office building. Co. owned non-controlling interests in five regional malls, one associated centers and 48 community centers.

Recent Developments: For the quarter ended Mar 31 2005, net income decreased 4.6% to $33,013 thousand from net income of $34,605 thousand in the year-earlier quarter. Revenues were $210,905 thousand, up 22.5% from $172,159 thousand the year before. Operating income was $97,280 thousand versus an income of $77,418 thousand in the prior-year quarter, an increase of 25.7%.

Prospects: Co. is now benefiting from a more favorable environment with more productive tenants, retailers pursuing expansion plans and a stronger economy overall. Based on its outlook and Co.'s first quarter results, it is offering guidance for 2005 funds from operations in the range of $5.88 to $5.96 per share. Separately, on May 3 2005, Co. announced that it has entered into an agreement to acquire a 70.0% joint venture interest in Laurel Park Place in Livonia, MI, from Schostak Brothers & Company. Co. acquired the interest for a total consideration of $82.2 million, $50.9 million represents debt held by the joint venture to which the property is subject, including closing costs.

Financial Data (US$ in Thousands)	3 Mos	12/31/2004	12/31/2003	12/31/2002	12/31/2001	12/31/2000	12/31/1999	12/31/1998
Earnings Per Share	3.03	3.21	3.99	2.49	2.11	2.37	1.94	1.53
Cash Flow Per Share	10.79	10.98	9.16	9.55	6.67	4.72	4.63	3.70
Tang Book Value Per Share	33.62	33.64	27.61	24.87	20.38	17.35	16.96	16.91
Dividends Per Share	1.538	1.494	1.345	1.160	1.065	1.020	0.975	0.930
Dividend Payout %	50.76	46.53	33.71	46.59	50.47	43.04	50.26	60.78
Income Statement								
Property Income	205,486	739,066	653,355	583,236	539,569	351,400	313,412	251,936
Non-Property Income	5,419	20,098	14,176	15,858	4,806	5,088	4,191	2,704
Total Revenue	210,905	759,164	667,531	599,094	544,375	356,488	317,603	254,640
Depn & Amortn	40,098	141,707	119,176	101,937	89,444	61,910	55,240	45,357
Interest Expense	48,921	177,219	153,373	143,164	154,477	94,597	82,505	67,329
Net Income	33,013	121,111	144,139	84,906	60,908	65,722	54,595	40,499
Average Shares	32,397	32,002	31,193	29,668	25,833	25,021	24,834	24,340
Balance Sheet								
Total Assets	5,178,780	5,204,500	4,264,310	3,795,114	3,372,851	2,115,565	2,018,838	1,855,347
Long-Term Obligations	3,369,302	3,371,679	2,738,102	2,402,079	2,315,955	1,424,337	1,360,753	1,208,204
Total Liabilities	3,555,667	3,583,743	2,899,579	2,553,411	2,419,662	1,502,565	1,424,989	1,270,670
Stockholders' Equity	1,056,003	1,054,151	837,300	741,190	522,088	434,825	419,887	415,782
Shares Outstanding	31,404	31,333	30,323	29,797	25,616	25,067	24,755	24,591
Statistical Record								
Return on Assets %	2.50	2.55	3.58	2.37	2.22	3.17	2.82	2.61
Return on Equity %	12.53	12.77	18.26	13.44	12.73	15.34	13.07	10.85
Net Margin %	15.65	15.95	21.59	14.17	11.19	18.44	17.19	15.90
Price Range	77.84-47.42	76.63-47.42	57.38-37.56	40.89-31.50	31.85-25.13	25.88-20.13	27.00-19.44	26.88-23.38
P/E Ratio	25.69-15.65	23.87-14.77	14.38-9.41	16.42-12.65	15.09-11.91	10.92-8.49	13.92-10.02	17.57-15.28
Average Yield %	2.43	2.51	2.90	3.16	3.69	4.34	4.05	3.72

Address: 2030 Hamilton Place Blvd., Suite 500, Chattanooga, TN 37421-6000
Telephone: 423-855-0001
Web Site: www.cblproperties.com

Officers: Charles B. Lebovitz - Chmn., C.E.O. John N. Foy - Vice-Chmn., C.F.O., Treas. **Transfer Agents:** SunTrust Bank, Atlanta, GA

Investor Contact: 423-855-0001
No of Institutions: 158
Shares: 23,526,804 **% Held:** 74.93

CEDAR FAIR, L.P.

Exchange	Symbol	Price	52Wk Range	Yield	P/E
NYS	FUN	$31.05 (5/31/2005)	33.95-28.86	5.93	20.70

***7 Year Price Score 111.21** *NYSE Composite Index=100 ***12 Month Price Score 95.62**

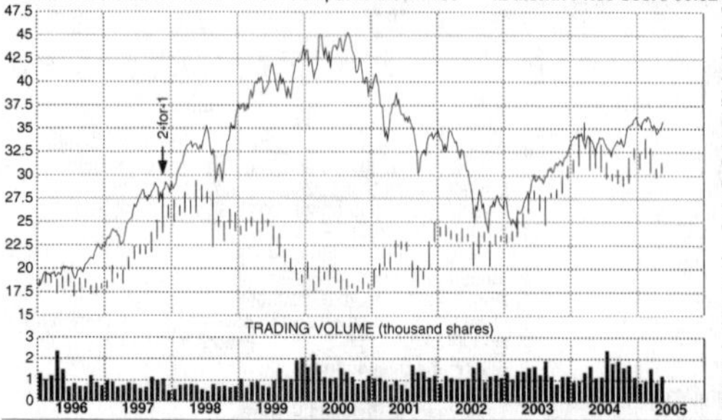

Interim Earnings (Per Share)

Qtr.	Mar	Jun	Sep	Dec
2002	(0.63)	0.40	2.01	(0.39)
2003	(0.62)	0.33	2.16	(0.21)
2004	(0.59)	0.25	2.02	(0.30)
2005	(0.46)	...	...	...

Interim Dividends (Per Share)

Amt	Decl	Ex	Rec	Pay
0.45Q	6/24/2004	7/1/2004	7/6/2004	8/16/2004
0.45Q	9/23/2004	10/1/2004	10/5/2004	11/15/2004
0.45Q	12/16/2004	1/3/2005	1/5/2005	2/15/2005
0.46Q	3/7/2005	4/1/2005	4/5/2005	5/16/2005

Indicated Div: $1.84 (Div. Reinv. Plan)

Valuation Analysis

Forecast P/E N/A
Market Cap $1.7 Billion Book Value N/A
Price/Book N/A Price/Sales 3.06

Dividend Achiever Status

Rank 252 **10 Year Growth Rate** 5.67%
Total Years of Dividend Growth 17

Business Summary: Sporting & Recreational (MIC: 13.5 SIC: 996 NAIC: 13110)

Cedar Fair is a limited partnership managed by Cedar Fair Mgmt. As of Dec 31 2004, Co. owned and operated seven amusement parks: Cedar Point on Lake Erie in Sandusky, OH; Knott's Berry Farm, located in Buena Park, CA; Dorney Park & Wildwater Kingdom, near Allentown, PA; Geauga Lake in Aurora, OH; Valleyfair, near Minneapolis, MN; Worlds of Fun in Kansas City, MO; and Michigan's Adventure, near Muskegon, MI. Co.'s five water parks are located near San Diego and Palm Springs, CA, and adjacent to Cedar Point, Knott's Berry Farm and Worlds of Fun. Co. owns and operates four hotel facilities. Co. operates Knott's Camp Snoopy at the Mall of America in Bloomington, MN under a management contract.

Recent Developments: For the quarter ended Mar 27 2005, net loss increased 19.6% to $24,564 thousand from net loss of $20,535 thousand in the year-earlier quarter. Revenues were $24,801 thousand, up 6.9% from $23,210 thousand the year before. Operating loss was $27,445 thousand versus a loss of $24,085 thousand in the prior-year quarter, an increase of 14.0%. Total direct expense was $3,516 thousand versus $3,480 thousand in the prior-year quarter, an increase of 1.0%. Total indirect expense was $48,730 thousand versus $43,815 thousand in the prior-year quarter, an increase of 11.2%.

Prospects: Co. is confident that the $80.0 million in capital it has invested in its parks, along with the continued momentum of Castaway Bay, will position it to have a successful year. Although Knott's Berry Farm got off to a slow start due to poor weather, Co. remains optimistic that it can generate revenue growth of 6.0% to 8.0% over the year before, as well as full-year adjusted earnings before interest, taxes, depreciation and amortization in the $185.0 million to $195.0 million range. At that level, Co. should be positioned to achieve its goal of continued growth in cash distributions to its unitholders in 2005.

Financial Data

(US$ in Thousands)	3 Mos	12/31/2004	12/31/2003	12/31/2002	12/31/2001	12/31/2000	12/31/1999	12/31/1998
Earnings Per Share	1.50	1.47	1.67	1.39	1.13	1.50	1.63	1.58
Cash Flow Per Share	2.58	2.84	2.67	2.90	2.46	2.22	2.39	2.52
Dividends Per Share	1.800	1.790	1.740	1.650	1.580	1.502	1.388	0.965
Dividend Payout %	119.74	121.77	104.19	118.71	139.82	100.17	85.12	61.08
Income Statement								
Total Revenue	24,801	541,972	509,976	502,851	477,256	472,920	438,001	419,500
EBITDA	(23,532)	172,983	172,569	155,225	141,043	155,088	151,837	144,673
Depn & Amortn	3,454	50,690	44,693	41,682	42,486	39,572	35,082	32,065
Income Before Taxes	(33,487)	97,030	103,806	88,576	74,414	94,159	101,384	97,948
Income Taxes	(8,923)	18,715	17,918	17,159	16,520	16,353	15,580	14,507
Net Income	(24,564)	78,315	85,888	71,417	57,894	77,806	85,804	83,441
Average Shares	53,487	53,315	51,334	51,263	51,113	51,679	52,390	52,414
Balance Sheet								
Current Assets	38,698	32,960	29,777	29,237	26,868	25,378	24,184	20,967
Total Assets	1,020,757	993,208	819,341	822,257	810,231	764,143	708,961	631,325
Current Liabilities	114,626	121,517	111,694	106,338	96,700	114,024	86,559	77,231
Long-Term Obligations	516,261	442,084	348,647	365,150	373,000	300,000	261,200	200,350
Total Liabilities	697,722	622,725	510,450	516,937	501,981	433,554	358,975	289,334
Shares Outstanding	53,542	53,480	50,673	50,549	50,514	50,813	51,798	51,980
Statistical Record								
Return on Assets %	8.95	8.62	10.46	8.75	7.35	10.53	12.80	13.56
EBITDA Margin %	N.M.	31.92	33.84	30.87	29.55	32.79	34.67	34.49
Net Margin %	N.M.	14.45	16.84	14.20	12.13	16.45	19.59	19.89
Asset Turnover	0.58	0.60	0.62	0.62	0.61	0.64	0.65	0.68
Current Ratio	0.34	0.27	0.27	0.27	0.28	0.22	0.28	0.27
Price Range	34.97-28.86	35.71-28.86	31.03-22.74	24.79-20.30	24.98-18.03	20.75-17.56	26.00-18.50	29.44-22.31
P/E Ratio	23.31-19.24	24.29-19.63	18.58-13.62	17.83-14.60	22.11-15.96	13.83-11.71	15.95-11.35	18.63-14.12
Average Yield %	5.76	5.69	6.51	7.10	7.50	8.05	6.07	3.66

Address: One Cedar Point Drive, Sandusky, OH 44870-5259
Telephone: 419-626-0830
Web Site: www.cedarfair.com

Officers: Richard L. Kinzel - Chmn., Pres., C.E.O. Bruce A. Jackson - V.P., Fin., C.F.O. **Transfer Agents:** American Stock Transfer & Trust Company, New York, NY

Investor Contact: 419-627-2233
No of Institutions: 112
Shares: 11,115,618 **% Held:** 20.78

CENTURYTEL, INC.

Exchange	Symbol	Price	52Wk Range	Yield	P/E
NYS	CTL	$32.79 (5/31/2005)	35.49-29.25	0.73	13.55

*7 Year Price Score 86.45 *NYSE Composite Index=100 *12 Month Price Score 94.27

TRADING VOLUME (thousand shares)

Interim Earnings (Per Share)

Qtr.	Mar	Jun	Sep	Dec
2002	0.50	0.55	4.26	0.30
2003	0.58	0.60	0.63	0.56
2004	0.58	0.60	0.63	0.60
2005	0.59	...	...	...

Interim Dividends (Per Share)

Amt	Decl	Ex	Rec	Pay
0.058Q	8/24/2004	9/2/2004	9/7/2004	9/17/2004
0.058Q	11/18/2004	12/1/2004	12/3/2004	12/17/2004
0.06Q	2/22/2005	3/2/2005	3/4/2005	3/18/2005
0.06Q	5/24/2005	6/1/2005	6/3/2005	6/17/2005

Indicated Div: $0.24 (Div. Reinv. Plan)

Valuation Analysis

Forecast P/E 13.93 (5/28/2005)
Market Cap $4.3 Billion Book Value 3.4 Billion
Price/Book 1.26 Price/Sales 1.79

Dividend Achiever Status

Rank 270 **10 Year Growth Rate** 4.92%
Total Years of Dividend Growth 31

Business Summary: Communications (MIC: 10.1 SIC: 813 NAIC: 17110)

CenturyTel is an integrated communications company engaged primarily in providing local exchange, long distance, Internet access and broadband services. Co. bundles its service offerings to provide its customers with a complete offering of integrated communications services. As of Dec 31 2004, Co.'s local exchange telephone subsidiaries operated approximately 2.3 million telephone access lines, primarily in rural, suburban and small urban areas in 22 states, with over 70.0% of these lines located in Wisconsin, Missouri, Alabama, Arkansas and Washington.

Recent Developments: For the quarter ended Mar 31 2005, net income decreased 4.4% to $79,616 thousand from net income of $83,279 thousand in the year-earlier quarter. Revenues were $595,282 thousand, up 0.3% from $593,704 thousand the year before. Operating income was $176,860 thousand versus an income of $183,557 thousand in the prior-year quarter, a decrease of 3.6%. Total direct expense was $191,993 thousand versus $181,549 thousand in the prior-year quarter, an increase of 5.8%. Total indirect expense was $226,429 thousand versus $228,598 thousand in the prior-year quarter, a decrease of 0.9%.

Prospects: For second quarter of 2005, Co. expects total revenues of $590.0 million to $605.0 million and diluted earnings per share of $0.53 to $0.57. The decline in diluted earnings per share from first quarter to second quarter 2005 is primarily due to increased operating costs related to expected growth in Co.'s DSL, long distance and fiber operations, annual wage adjustments effective in the second quarter and the seasonal impact of maintenance activities for its outside plant. For full-year 2005, diluted earnings per share is expected to be in the range of $2.25 to $2.35 versus the previous guidance of $2.20 to $2.35.

Financial Data (US$ in Thousands)	3 Mos	12/31/2004	12/31/2003	12/31/2002	12/31/2001	12/31/2000	12/31/1999	12/31/1998
Earnings Per Share	2.42	2.41	2.38	5.61	2.41	1.63	1.70	1.64
Cash Flow Per Share	7.03	6.95	7.44	5.62	4.73	4.00	2.94	3.41
Tang Book Value Per Share	N.M.	N.M.	N.M.	N.M.	N.M.	N.M.	1.39	N.M.
Dividends Per Share	0.233	0.230	0.220	0.210	0.200	0.190	0.180	0.173
Dividend Payout %	9.61	9.54	9.24	3.74	8.30	11.66	10.59	10.57
Income Statement								
Total Revenue	595,282	2,407,372	2,380,745	1,971,996	2,117,469	1,845,926	1,676,669	1,577,085
EBITDA	311,883	1,259,327	1,229,351	926,927	1,251,963	957,543	928,645	883,564
Depn & Amortn	132,175	500,904	470,641	411,626	473,384	388,056	348,816	328,554
Income Before Taxes	127,083	547,372	531,959	293,456	553,056	386,185	429,272	387,458
Income Taxes	47,467	210,128	187,252	103,537	210,025	154,711	189,503	158,701
Net Income	79,616	337,244	344,707	801,624	343,031	231,474	239,769	228,757
Average Shares	137,169	142,144	144,700	142,879	142,307	141,864	141,432	140,105
Balance Sheet								
Net PPE	3,287,849	3,341,401	3,455,481	3,531,645	2,999,563	2,959,293	2,256,458	2,351,453
Total Assets	7,702,524	7,796,953	7,895,852	7,770,408	6,318,684	6,393,290	4,705,407	4,935,455
Long-Term Obligations	2,694,203	2,762,019	3,109,302	3,578,132	2,087,500	3,050,292	2,078,311	2,558,000
Total Liabilities	4,273,340	4,387,188	4,417,336	4,682,404	3,981,304	4,361,211	2,857,415	3,403,973
Stockholders' Equity	3,429,184	3,409,765	3,478,516	3,088,004	2,337,380	2,032,079	1,847,992	1,531,482
Shares Outstanding	131,272	132,373	144,364	142,955	141,232	140,667	139,945	138,083
Statistical Record								
Return on Assets %	4.28	4.29	4.40	11.38	5.40	4.16	4.97	4.74
Return on Equity %	9.75	9.77	10.50	29.55	15.70	11.90	14.19	16.16
EBITDA Margin %	52.39	52.31	51.64	47.00	59.13	51.87	55.39	56.03
Net Margin %	13.37	14.01	14.48	40.65	16.20	12.54	14.30	14.51
PPE Turnover	0.72	0.71	0.68	0.60	0.71	0.71	0.73	0.68
Asset Turnover	0.31	0.31	0.30	0.28	0.33	0.33	0.35	0.33
Debt to Equity	0.79	0.81	0.89	1.16	0.89	1.50	1.12	1.67
Price Range	35.49-26.51	35.49-26.33	36.63-25.51	35.20-22.18	39.00-26.18	47.38-24.50	48.88-36.44	45.00-21.75
P/E Ratio	14.67-10.95	14.73-10.93	15.39-10.72	6.27-3.95	16.18-10.86	29.06-15.03	28.75-21.43	27.44-13.26
Average Yield %	0.73	0.74	0.69	0.71	0.64	0.57	0.43	0.56

Address: 100 CenturyTel Drive, Monroe, LA 71203
Telephone: 318-388-9000
Web Site: www.centurytel.com

Officers: Glen F. Post III - Chmn., C.E.O. Karen A. Puckett - Pres., C.O.O. **Transfer Agents:** Computershare Investor Services, LLC, Chicago, IL

Investor Contact: 800-833-1188
No of Institutions: 287
Shares: 108,921,296 % **Held:** 82.11

CHEMICAL FINANCIAL CORP.

Exchange	Symbol	Price	52Wk Range	Yield	P/E
NMS	CHFC	$31.98 (5/31/2005)	41.11-28.97	3.31	14.41

*7 Year Price Score 108.93 *NYSE Composite Index=100 *12 Month Price Score 86.76

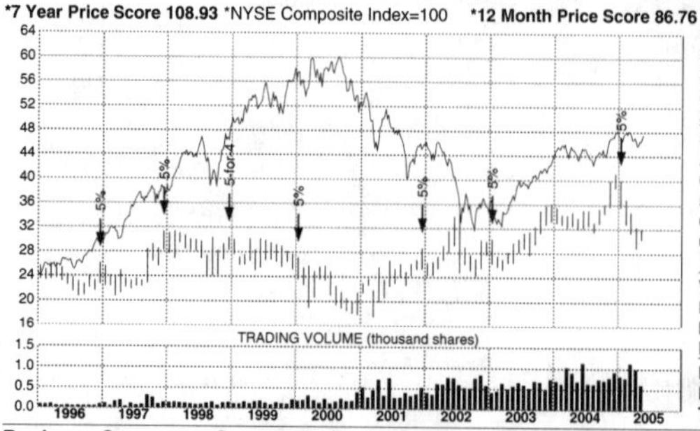

Interim Earnings (Per Share)

Qtr.	Mar	Jun	Sep	Dec
2002	0.53	0.52	0.54	0.62
2003	0.56	0.55	0.58	0.54
2004	0.56	0.55	0.56	0.57
2005	0.53	...	...	...

Interim Dividends (Per Share)

Amt	Decl	Ex	Rec	Pay
0.252Q	10/19/2004	12/1/2004	12/3/2004	12/17/2004
5%	12/13/2004	1/6/2005	1/10/2005	1/28/2005
0.265Q	1/17/2005	3/2/2005	3/4/2005	3/18/2005
0.265Q	4/18/2005	6/1/2005	6/3/2005	6/17/2005

Indicated Div: $1.06 (Div. Reinv. Plan)

Valuation Analysis

Forecast P/E 14.97 (6/2/2005)

Market Cap $805.4 Million Book Value 486.7 Million

Price/Book 1.65 Price/Sales 3.51

Dividend Achiever Status

Rank 141 10 Year Growth Rate 11.69%

Total Years of Dividend Growth 29

TRADING VOLUME (thousand shares)

Business Summary: Commercial Banking (MIC: 8.1 SIC: 022 NAIC: 22110)

Chemical Financial is a multibank holding company with total assets of $3.76 billion as of Dec 31 2004. Through its subsidiaries, Co. offers a full range of commercial banking and fiduciary products and services. These include business and personal checking accounts, savings and individual retirement accounts, time deposit instruments, electronically accessed banking products, residential and commercial real estate financing, commercial lending, consumer financing, debit cards, safe deposit services, automated teller machines, access to insurance and investment products, money transfer services, corporate and personal trust services and other banking services.

Recent Developments: For the quarter ended Mar 31 2005, net income decreased 4.4% to $13,504 thousand from net income of $14,119 thousand in the year-earlier quarter. Net interest income was $35,947 thousand, down 2.4% from $36,822 thousand the year before. Provision for loan losses was $730 thousand versus $746 thousand in the prior-year quarter, a decrease of 2.1%. Non-interest income rose 2.2% to $10,180 thousand, while non-interest expense declined 0.7% to $49,966 thousand.

Prospects: Earnings are being adversely affected by lower net interest income and a slightly higher effective federal income tax rate. Also, average interest-earning assets are down primarily due to a decline in deposits. In addition, Co. is seeing a decline in total loans. For instance, total loans were $2.58 billion at Mar 31 2005, down 0.3% from $2.59 billion at Dec 31 2004. Although Co. achieved an increase in commercial loans and real estate construction loans, these increases are being offset by decreases in the remaining three loan categories, with the largest decrease occurring in consumer loans. Consumer loans saw a sequential 3.0% decline to $520.8 million at Mar 31 2005.

Financial Data

(US$ in Thousands)	3 Mos	12/31/2004	12/31/2003	12/31/2002	12/31/2001	12/31/2000	12/31/1999	12/31/1998
Earnings Per Share	2.22	2.25	2.24	2.20	1.71	1.78	1.68	1.57
Cash Flow Per Share	3.08	3.22	4.21	3.86	0.10	2.08	1.93	1.85
Tang Book Value Per Share	16.40	16.31	15.25	15.68	13.97	17.41	16.06	15.48
Dividends Per Share	1.022	1.010	0.952	0.871	0.829	0.760	0.691	0.632
Dividend Payout %	46.08	44.87	42.55	39.58	48.37	42.72	41.24	40.19
Income Statement								
Interest Income	47,960	189,250	185,037	211,044	219,250	131,085	121,917	121,633
Interest Expense	12,013	41,616	45,265	65,352	89,182	54,035	47,071	49,146
Net Interest Income	35,947	147,634	139,772	145,692	130,068	77,050	74,846	72,487
Provision for Losses	730	3,819	2,834	3,765	2,004	487	483	964
Non-Interest Income	10,180	39,329	39,094	34,534	31,873	17,364	16,003	15,610
Non-Interest Expense	24,983	98,469	91,923	93,526	94,597	50,860	48,986	48,307
Income Before Taxes	20,414	84,675	84,109	82,935	65,340	43,067	41,380	38,826
Income Taxes	6,910	27,993	28,393	27,990	22,617	14,061	13,671	12,780
Net Income	13,504	56,682	55,716	54,945	42,723	29,006	27,709	26,046
Average Shares	25,247	25,217	24,943	24,929	24,876	16,303	16,509	16,575
Balance Sheet								
Net Loans & Leases	2,542,619	2,551,419	2,448,096	2,044,514	2,151,547	1,067,636	990,827	880,222
Total Assets	3,796,890	3,764,125	3,708,888	3,568,893	3,488,306	1,973,424	1,890,376	1,872,626
Total Deposits	2,927,947	2,863,473	2,967,236	2,847,272	2,789,524	1,606,217	1,561,702	1,554,271
Total Liabilities	3,310,199	3,279,289	3,250,839	3,138,554	3,098,850	1,704,695	1,640,795	1,630,787
Stockholders' Equity	486,691	484,836	458,049	430,339	389,456	268,729	249,581	241,839
Shares Outstanding	25,185	25,169	24,991	24,868	24,821	15,439	15,539	15,623
Statistical Record								
Return on Assets %	1.45	1.51	1.53	1.56	1.56	1.50	1.47	1.43
Return on Equity %	11.72	11.99	12.54	13.40	12.98	11.16	11.28	11.18
Net Interest Margin %	74.95	78.01	75.54	69.03	59.32	58.78	61.39	59.59
Efficiency Ratio %	42.97	43.08	41.01	38.08	37.67	34.26	35.52	35.20
Loans to Deposits	0.87	0.89	0.83	0.72	0.77	0.66	0.63	0.57
Price Range	41.11-31.38	41.11-31.51	36.10-25.27	34.43-24.22	28.79-17.52	27.53-17.80	30.23-25.05	31.44-24.01
P/E Ratio	18.52-14.14	18.27-14.01	16.12-11.28	15.65-11.01	16.84-10.24	15.47-10.00	18.00-14.91	20.03-15.30
Average Yield %	2.93	2.92	3.19	3.15	3.48	3.41	2.51	2.22

Address: 333 East Main Street, Midland, MI 48640-0569
Telephone: 989-839-5350
Web Site: www.chemicalbankmi.com

Officers: Frank P. Popoff - Chmn. David B. Ramaker - Pres., C.E.O. **Transfer Agents:** Computershare Investor Services, LLC, Chicago, IL

Investor Contact: 989-839-5350
No of Institutions: 83
Shares: 7,147,107 **% Held:** 28.38

CHEVRON CORPORATION

Exchange	Symbol	Price	52Wk Range	Yield	P/E
NYS	CVX	$53.78 (5/31/2005)	62.08-45.00	3.35	8.46

*7 Year Price Score 107.93 *NYSE Composite Index=100 *12 Month Price Score 99.14

Interim Earnings (Per Share)

Qtr.	Mar	Jun	Sep	Dec
2002	0.34	0.20	(0.42)	0.42
2003	0.91	0.75	1.01	0.81
2004	1.20	1.94	1.51	1.63
2005	1.28	...	...	...

Interim Dividends (Per Share)

Amt	Decl	Ex	Rec	Pay
0.40Q	7/28/2004	8/17/2004	8/19/2004	9/10/2004
0.40Q	10/27/2004	11/16/2004	11/18/2004	12/10/2004
0.40Q	1/26/2005	2/14/2005	2/16/2005	3/10/2005
0.45Q	4/27/2005	5/17/2005	5/19/2005	6/10/2005

Indicated Div: $1.80

Valuation Analysis

Forecast P/E	9.94 (6/7/2005)		
Market Cap	$112.8 Billion	Book Value	46.6 Billion
Price/Book	2.42	Price/Sales	0.69

Dividend Achiever Status

Rank	264	**10 Year Growth Rate**	5.16%
Total Years of Dividend Growth			17

Business Summary: Oil and Gas (MIC: 14.2 SIC: 911 NAIC: 24110)

Chevron is a global energy company engaged in fully integrated petroleum operations, chemicals operations and coal mining activities. Co. also holds investments in power generation and gasification businesses. Petroleum operations consist of exploring for, developing and producing crude oil and natural gas; refining crude oil into finished petroleum products; marketing crude oil, natural gas and the many products derived from petroleum; and transporting crude oil, natural gas and petroleum products. As of Dec 31 2004, net proved reserves of natural gas were 16,128 billion cubic feet and net proved reserves of crude oil, condensate and natural gas liquids totaled 8,199 million barrels.

Recent Developments: For the quarter ended Mar 31 2005, net income increased 4.5% to $2,677,000 thousand from net income of $2,562,000 thousand in the year-earlier quarter. Revenues were $41,607,000 thousand, up 23.7% from $33,645,000 thousand the year before. Total direct expense was $26,491,000 thousand versus $20,027,000 thousand in the prior-year quarter, an increase of 32.3%. Total indirect expense was $10,081,000 thousand versus $9,228,000 thousand in the prior-year quarter, an increase of 9.2%.

Prospects: On Apr 4 2005, Co. announced that it has entered into an agreement to acquire Unocal Corporation for approximately $18.00 billion, including the assumption of about $1.60 billion of debt. The acquisition would expand Co.'s presence in several of its core areas of operation, including the Asia Pacific region, the Gulf of Mexico, and the Caspian region. In addition, Co. anticipates the transaction will generate annual savings of more than $325.0 million before tax stemming from operational synergies and reduced corporate expenses. Also, Co. expects proceeds of more that $2.00 billion from asset sales after the acquisition is completed.

Financial Data (US$ in Thousands)	3 Mos	12/31/2004	12/31/2003	12/31/2002	12/31/2001	12/31/2000	12/31/1999	12/31/1998
Earnings Per Share	6.36	6.28	3.48	0.54	1.54	3.98	1.57	1.02
Cash Flow Per Share	7.16	6.92	5.80	4.68	5.40	6.65	3.41	2.85
Tang Book Value Per Share	22.21	21.47	16.97	14.79	15.91	15.54	13.52	12.90
Dividends Per Share	1.565	1.530	1.430	1.400	1.325	1.300	1.240	1.220
Dividend Payout %	24.61	24.36	41.09	261.68	85.76	32.62	78.98	119.61
Income Statement								
Total Revenue	41,607,000	155,300,000	121,761,000	99,049,000	106,245,000	52,129,000	36,586,000	30,557,000
EBITDA	6,348,000	25,892,000	18,628,000	9,952,000	16,183,000	12,578,000	6,986,000	4,559,000
Depn & Amortn	1,334,000	4,935,000	5,384,000	5,231,000	7,059,000	2,848,000	2,866,000	2,320,000
Income Before Taxes	4,907,000	20,551,000	12,770,000	4,156,000	8,291,000	9,270,000	3,648,000	1,834,000
Income Taxes	2,230,000	7,517,000	5,344,000	3,024,000	4,360,000	4,085,000	1,578,000	495,000
Net Income	2,677,000	13,328,000	7,230,000	1,132,000	3,288,000	5,185,000	2,070,000	1,339,000
Average Shares	2,099,899	2,122,000	2,128,000	2,126,800	2,125,800	1,302,200	1,319,000	1,314,200
Balance Sheet								
Current Assets	31,159,000	28,503,000	19,426,000	17,776,000	18,327,000	8,213,000	8,297,000	6,297,000
Total Assets	95,803,000	93,208,000	81,470,000	77,359,000	77,572,000	41,264,000	40,668,000	36,540,000
Current Liabilities	19,674,000	18,795,000	16,111,000	19,876,000	20,654,000	7,674,000	8,889,000	7,166,000
Long-Term Obligations	10,422,000	10,456,000	10,894,000	10,911,000	8,989,000	5,153,000	5,485,000	4,393,000
Total Liabilities	49,211,000	47,978,000	45,175,000	45,755,000	43,614,000	21,339,000	22,919,000	19,506,000
Stockholders' Equity	46,592,000	45,230,000	36,295,000	31,604,000	33,958,000	19,925,000	17,749,000	17,034,000
Shares Outstanding	2,098,220	2,107,120	2,138,295	2,136,273	2,134,441	1,282,120	1,312,692	1,320,000
Statistical Record								
Return on Assets %	14.86	15.22	9.10	1.46	5.53	12.62	5.36	3.72
Return on Equity %	31.72	32.61	21.30	3.45	12.20	27.45	11.90	7.76
EBITDA Margin %	15.26	16.67	15.30	10.05	15.23	24.13	19.09	14.92
Net Margin %	6.43	8.58	5.94	1.14	3.09	9.95	5.66	4.38
Asset Turnover	1.81	1.77	1.53	1.28	1.79	1.27	0.95	0.85
Current Ratio	1.58	1.52	1.21	0.89	0.89	1.07	0.93	0.88
Debt to Equity	0.22	0.23	0.30	0.35	0.26	0.26	0.31	0.26
Price Range	62.08-43.89	55.41-42.22	43.20-30.93	45.43-32.95	49.02-39.38	47.14-35.53	51.78-36.84	44.47-35.56
P/E Ratio	9.76-6.90	8.82-6.72	12.41-8.89	84.13-61.02	31.83-25.57	11.84-8.93	32.98-23.47	43.60-34.87
Average Yield %	3.06	3.20	4.04	3.51	2.98	3.07	2.76	3.00

Address: 6001 Bollinger Canyon Road, San Ramon, CA 94583-2324
Telephone: 925-842-1000
Web Site: www.chevrontexaco.com

Officers: David J. O'Reilly - Chmn., C.E.O. Peter J. Robertson - Vice-Chmn. **Transfer Agents:** Mellon Investor Services LLC, Ridgefield Park, NJ

Investor Contact: 415-894-5690
No of Institutions: 1033
Shares: 1,246,345,088 **% Held:** 59.22

CHITTENDEN CORP. (BURLINGTON, VT.)

Exchange	Symbol	Price	52Wk Range	Yield	P/E
NYS	CHZ	$26.25 (5/31/2005)	30.06-24.50	2.74	15.91

*7 Year Price Score 111.57 *NYSE Composite Index=100 *12 Month Price Score 91.21

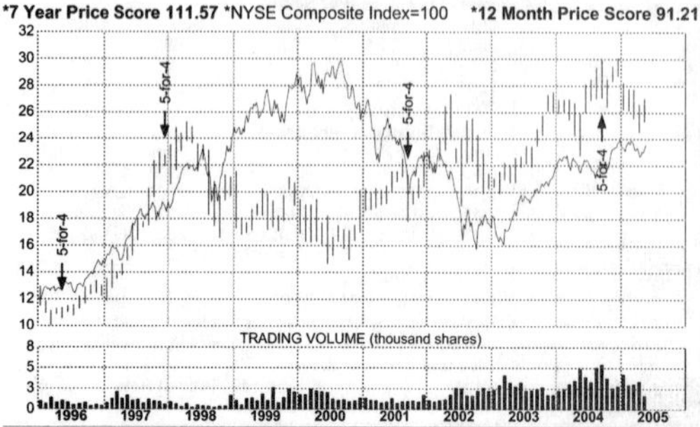

Interim Earnings (Per Share)

Qtr.	Mar	Jun	Sep	Dec
2002	0.37	0.38	0.38	0.44
2003	0.39	0.41	0.43	0.42
2004	0.38	0.39	0.42	0.43
2005	0.41	...	...	...

Interim Dividends (Per Share)

Amt	Decl	Ex	Rec	Pay
0.176Q	7/22/2004	7/28/2004	7/30/2004	8/13/2004
0.18Q	10/21/2004	10/27/2004	10/29/2004	11/12/2004
0.18Q	1/20/2005	1/26/2005	1/28/2005	2/11/2005
0.18Q	4/20/2005	4/27/2005	4/29/2005	5/13/2005

Indicated Div: $0.72 (Div. Reinv. Plan)

Valuation Analysis

Forecast P/E	15.17 (6/2/2005)		
Market Cap	$1.2 Billion	Book Value	617.5 Million
Price/Book	1.97	Price/Sales	3.47

Dividend Achiever Status

Rank	74	10 Year Growth Rate	16.46%
Total Years of Dividend Growth			12

TRADING VOLUME (thousand shares)

Business Summary: Commercial Banking (MIC: 8.1 SIC: 022 NAIC: 22110)

Chittenden is a bank holding company with assets totaling $6.07 billion as of Dec 31 2004. Through its subsidiaries, Co. is engaged in providing financial services. Co. offers a variety of lending services, including commercial loans and residential real estate loans. In addition, Co. offers acceptance of demand, savings, NOW, money market, cash management and time deposits. Also, Co. provides personal trust services, including services as executor, trustee, administrator, custodian and guardian. Corporate trust services are also provided, including services as trustee for pension and profit sharing plans. Asset management services are provided for personal and corporate trust clients.

Recent Developments: For the three months ended Mar 31 2005, net income increased 9.2% to $19,082 thousand from net income of $17,467 thousand a year earlier. Net interest income was $58,985 thousand, up 7.8% from $54,711 thousand the year before. Provision for loan losses was $1,075 thousand versus $427 thousand in the prior year, an increase of 151.8%. Non-interest income fell 2.5% to $17,559 thousand, while non-interest expense rose 1.9% to $45,440 thousand.

Prospects: Co. is pleased with its recent operating performance, which saw notable gains in earnings per share and deposits on a year over year for the three months ended Mar 31 2005. Also, Co. enjoying solid growth in total loans, lead by increases in its commercial loan portfolio, the commercial real estate loan portfolio and in the 1-4 family residential loan portfolio. Additionally, higher yields on loans as well as continued improvement in Co.'s earning asset mix is benefiting Co.'s net interest margin. Based on these factors, Co. believes it is well-positioned to continue its solid operating performance for 2005.

Financial Data

(US$ in Thousands)	3 Mos	12/31/2004	12/31/2003	12/31/2002	12/31/2001	12/31/2000	12/31/1999	12/31/1998
Earnings Per Share	1.65	1.61	1.66	1.57	1.44	1.38	(0.06)	1.34
Cash Flow Per Share	2.60	2.33	3.53	1.02	2.31	1.67	2.50	1.57
Tang Book Value Per Share	7.97	8.02	7.17	8.66	7.55	7.31	7.76	7.34
Dividends Per Share	0.712	0.692	0.640	0.632	0.613	0.602	0.550	0.499
Dividend Payout %	43.10	42.98	38.65	40.31	42.56	43.72	N.M.	37.32
Income Statement								
Interest Income	73,212	269,767	271,442	259,019	266,497	288,102	288,216	151,511
Interest Expense	14,227	44,269	53,379	66,404	96,192	121,030	113,235	60,508
Net Interest Income	58,985	225,498	218,063	192,615	170,305	167,072	174,981	91,003
Provision for Losses	1,075	4,377	7,175	8,331	8,041	8,700	8,700	5,100
Non-Interest Income	17,559	73,405	97,031	65,060	63,733	54,810	64,226	32,402
Non-Interest Expense	45,440	176,372	191,371	151,544	135,760	126,462	203,929	71,767
Income Before Taxes	30,029	118,154	116,548	97,800	90,237	86,720	26,578	46,538
Income Taxes	10,947	43,027	41,749	34,155	31,736	28,033	29,074	15,873
Net Income	19,082	75,127	74,799	63,645	58,501	58,687	(2,496)	30,665
Average Shares	46,918	46,731	45,150	40,618	40,683	42,625	44,743	22,942
Balance Sheet								
Net Loans & Leases	4,068,066	4,018,162	3,667,220	2,925,666	2,792,909	2,815,843	2,854,651	1,375,593
Total Assets	6,081,227	6,070,210	5,900,644	4,920,544	4,153,714	3,769,861	3,827,297	2,122,019
Total Deposits	5,063,163	5,038,730	4,969,891	4,126,092	3,669,846	3,292,407	3,204,098	1,890,754
Total Liabilities	5,463,745	5,449,953	5,320,693	4,501,752	3,783,060	3,427,795	3,464,837	1,946,872
Stockholders' Equity	617,482	620,257	579,951	418,792	370,654	342,066	362,460	175,147
Shares Outstanding	46,401	46,341	45,795	39,924	44,679	44,670	44,340	22,159
Statistical Record								
Return on Assets %	1.29	1.25	1.38	1.40	1.48	1.54	N.M.	1.50
Return on Equity %	12.61	12.48	14.98	16.12	16.42	16.61	N.M.	18.18
Net Interest Margin %	80.57	83.59	80.34	74.36	63.91	57.99	60.71	60.06
Efficiency Ratio %	50.06	51.39	51.94	46.76	41.11	36.88	57.86	39.02
Loans to Deposits	0.80	0.80	0.74	0.71	0.76	0.86	0.89	0.73
Price Range	30.06-22.71	30.06-22.71	27.52-19.89	27.34-18.97	23.00-17.80	20.16-14.64	21.52-16.80	25.28-16.56
P/E Ratio	18.22-13.76	18.67-14.11	16.58-11.98	17.42-12.08	15.97-12.36	14.61-10.61	...	18.87-12.36
Average Yield %	2.61	2.55	2.78	2.76	3.03	3.50	2.96	2.29

Address: Two Burlington Square, Burlington, VT 05401
Telephone: 802-658-4000
Web Site: www.chittendencorp.com

Officers: Paul A. Perrault - Chmn., Pres., C.E.O. Kirk W. Walters - Exec. V.P., C.F.O., Treas. **Transfer Agents:** Computershare Investor Services, LLC, Chicago, IL

Investor Contact: 802-660-1412
No of Institutions: 131
Shares: 26,956,454 **% Held:** 58.10

CHUBB CORP.

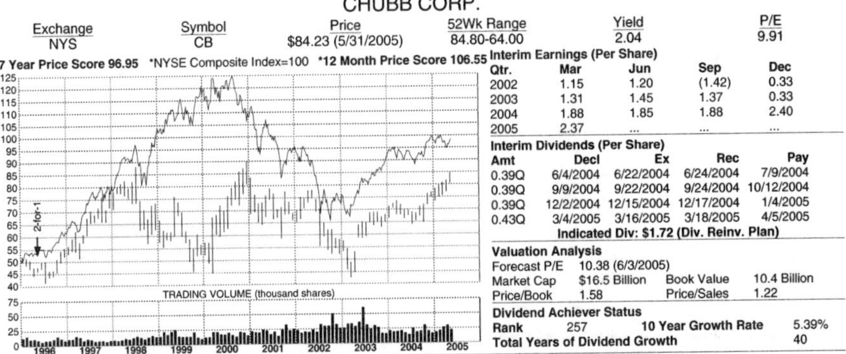

Exchange	Symbol	Price	52Wk Range	Yield	P/E
NYS	CB	$84.23 (5/31/2005)	84.80-64.00	2.04	9.91

*7 Year Price Score 96.95 *NYSE Composite Index=100 *12 Month Price Score 106.55

Interim Earnings (Per Share)

Qtr.	Mar	Jun	Sep	Dec
2002	1.15	1.20	(1.42)	0.33
2003	1.31	1.45	1.37	0.33
2004	1.88	1.85	1.88	2.40
2005	2.37	...	...	...

Interim Dividends (Per Share)

Amt	Decl	Ex	Rec	Pay
0.39Q	6/4/2004	6/22/2004	6/24/2004	7/9/2004
0.39Q	9/9/2004	9/22/2004	9/24/2004	10/12/2004
0.39Q	12/2/2004	12/15/2004	12/17/2004	1/4/2005
0.43Q	3/4/2005	3/16/2005	3/18/2005	4/5/2005

Indicated Div: $1.72 (Div. Reinv. Plan)

Valuation Analysis

Forecast P/E	10.38 (6/3/2005)		
Market Cap	$16.5 Billion	Book Value	10.4 Billion
Price/Book	1.58	Price/Sales	1.22

Dividend Achiever Status

Rank	257	10 Year Growth Rate	5.39%
Total Years of Dividend Growth			40

Business Summary: Insurance (MIC: 8.2 SIC: 331 NAIC: 24126)
Chubb is engaged in the property and casualty insurance business. Operations are divided into three strategic business units. Chubb Commercial Insurance specializes in commercial customer insurance products, including coverage for multiple peril, casualty, workers' compensation and property and marine. Chubb Specialty Insurance provides executive protection and professional liability products for privately and publicly-owned companies. Chubb Specialty Insurance also includes Co.'s surety and accident businesses, as well as its reinsurance business. Chubb Personal Insurance offers products for individuals who require more coverage choices and higher limits than standard insurance policies.

Recent Developments: For the quarter ended Mar 31 2005, net income increased 30.2% to $469,600 thousand from net income of $360,700 thousand in the year-earlier quarter. Revenues were $3,448,700 thousand, up 8.5% from $3,178,300 thousand the year before. Net premiums earned were $3,035,100 thousand versus $2,794,000 thousand in the prior-year quarter, an increase of 8.6%.

Prospects: Results are benefiting from the continued solid performance of Co.'s commercial insurance lines and ongoing significant improvement in homeowners insurance. Co. is on track to achieve or exceed its operating earnings guidance of $7.60 to $8.00 per share for 2005. Operating earnings guidance continues to assume 3 points of catastrophe losses for the year and to exclude results from the non-insurance business of Chubb Financial Solutions. In a more competitive market environment, Co. has maintained underwriting discipline and strict expense vigilance in order to protect and enhance its profitability. This core strategy will continue to guide the Co. forward.

Financial Data (US$ in Thousands)	3 Mos	12/31/2004	12/31/2003	12/31/2002	12/31/2001	12/31/2000	12/31/1999	12/31/1998
Earnings Per Share	8.50	8.01	4.46	1.29	0.63	4.01	3.66	4.19
Cash Flow Per Share	21.80	21.47	18.77	13.97	5.87	5.52	7.98	7.33
Tang Book Value Per Share	50.85	50.13	42.85	37.33	35.62	37.13	32.85	34.78
Dividends Per Share	1.600	1.560	1.440	1.400	1.360	1.320	1.283	1.240
Dividend Payout %	18.82	19.48	32.29	108.53	215.87	32.92	35.04	29.59
Income Statement								
Premium Income	3,035,100	11,635,700	10,182,500	8,085,300	6,656,400	6,145,900	5,652,000	5,303,800
Total Revenue	3,448,700	13,177,200	11,394,000	9,140,300	7,754,000	7,251,500	6,729,600	6,349,800
Benefits & Claims	1,835,000	7,320,900	6,867,200	6,064,600	5,357,400	4,127,700	3,942,000	3,493,700
Income Before Taxes	611,800	2,068,200	933,600	168,400	(66,000)	851,000	710,100	849,700
Income Taxes	142,200	519,800	124,800	(54,500)	(177,500)	136,400	89,000	142,700
Net Income	469,600	1,548,400	808,800	222,900	111,500	714,600	621,100	707,000
Average Shares	198,400	193,200	181,300	172,900	175,800	178,300	169,800	168,600
Balance Sheet								
Total Assets	45,547,800	44,260,300	38,360,600	34,114,400	29,449,000	25,026,700	23,537,000	20,746,000
Total Liabilities	35,146,500	34,133,900	29,838,600	27,255,200	22,923,700	18,045,000	17,265,200	15,101,900
Stockholders' Equity	10,401,300	10,126,400	8,522,000	6,859,200	6,525,300	6,981,700	6,271,800	5,644,100
Shares Outstanding	195,341	192,676	187,963	171,201	170,071	174,919	175,489	162,267
Statistical Record								
Return on Assets %	3.85	3.74	2.23	0.70	0.41	2.93	2.81	3.50
Return on Equity %	17.04	16.56	10.52	3.33	1.65	10.75	10.42	12.51
Loss Ratio %	60.46	62.92	67.44	75.01	80.48	67.16	69.75	65.87
Net Margin %	13.62	11.75	7.10	2.44	1.44	9.85	9.23	11.13
Price Range	80.95-64.00	77.00-64.00	69.24-42.45	78.20-52.20	83.44-58.59	90.00-44.75	75.94-45.50	88.25-57.00
P/E Ratio	9.52-7.53	9.61-7.99	15.52-9.52	60.62-40.47	132.44-93.00	22.44-11.16	20.75-12.43	21.06-13.60
Average Yield %	2.23	2.23	2.42	2.13	1.91	1.93	2.13	1.68

Address: 15 Mountain View Road, P.O. Box 1615, Warren, NJ 07061-1615
Telephone: 908-903-2000
Web Site: www.chubb.com

Officers: John D. Finnegan - Chmn., Pres., C.E.O. Michael O'Reilly - Vice-Chmn., C.F.O., Chief Invest. Officer **Transfer Agents:**
EquiServe Trust Company, N.A., Jersey City, NJ

Investor Contact: 908-903-3579
No of Institutions: 450
Shares: 163,842,816 **% Held:** 84.38

CINCINNATI FINANCIAL CORP.

Exchange	Symbol	Price	52Wk Range	Yield	P/E
NMS	CINF	$39.48 (5/31/2005)	43.73-36.95	3.09	12.07

*7 Year Price Score 100.75 *NYSE Composite Index=100 *12 Month Price Score 96.30

Interim Earnings (Per Share)

Qtr.	Mar	Jun	Sep	Dec
2002	0.42	0.19	0.40	0.32
2003	0.32	0.47	0.58	0.73
2004	0.86	0.87	0.50	1.09
2005	0.81	...	...	...

Interim Dividends (Per Share)

Amt	Decl	Ex	Rec	Pay
0.262Q	11/12/2004	12/20/2004	12/22/2004	1/14/2005
0.29Q	2/7/2005	3/22/2005	3/25/2005	4/15/2005
5%	2/7/2005	4/4/2005	4/6/2005	4/26/2005
0.305Q	5/27/2005	6/22/2005	6/24/2005	7/15/2005

Indicated Div: $1.22 (Div. Reinv. Plan)

Valuation Analysis

Forecast P/E	13.90 (6/3/2005)		
Market Cap	$6.9 Billion	Book Value	6.0 Billion
Price/Book	1.15	Price/Sales	1.89

Dividend Achiever Status

Rank	149	10 Year Growth Rate	11.39%
Total Years of Dividend Growth			44

Business Summary: Insurance (MIC: 8.2 SIC: 331 NAIC: 24126)

Cincinnati Financial offers property and casualty insurance, its main business, through The Cincinnati Insurance Company, The Cincinnati Indemnity Company and The Cincinnati Casualty Company. The Cincinnati Life Insurance Company markets life and disability income insurance and annuities. CFC Investment Company supports the insurance subsidiaries and their independent agent representatives through commercial leasing and financing activities. CinFin Capital Management Company provides asset management services to institutions, corporations and high net worth individuals.

Recent Developments: For the quarter ended Mar 31 2005, net income decreased 1.4% to $144.0 million from net income of $146.0 million in the year-earlier quarter. Total revenues were $916.0 million, up 5.3% from $870.0 million the year before. Net premiums earned climbed 4.9% to $776.0 million from $740.0 million the previous year. Net investment income rose 5.8% to $127.0 million from $120.0 million the prior year.

Prospects: Co. is targeting full-year 2005 written premium growth in the range of 3.0% to 5.0% for its commercial lines business, along with a combined ratio, or claims and expenses expressed as a percentage of premiums, of approximately 90.0%. Meanwhile, Co. anticipates a mid-single digit decline in personal lines written premiums in 2005, reflecting increased competition and a slowdown in new business. Separately, Co. plans to open 100 new agencies by the end of 2006. In the second quarter of 2005, Co. plans to open agencies in three of the eight new territories expected for the year, including Chicago, IL, Birmingham, AL, and a second Maryland territory that encompasses Delaware.

Financial Data

(US$ in Thousands)	3 Mos	12/31/2004	12/31/2003	12/31/2002	12/31/2001	12/31/2000	12/31/1999	12/31/1998
Earnings Per Share	3.27	3.28	2.10	1.32	1.08	0.66	1.38	1.28
Cash Flow Per Share	3.85	4.65	4.61	3.74	3.04	2.01	3.79	1.49
Tang Book Value Per Share	34.33	35.64	35.17	31.34	33.58	33.80	30.35	30.59
Dividends Per Share	1.076	1.035	0.907	0.807	0.762	0.689	0.617	0.556
Dividend Payout %	32.94	31.60	43.29	60.96	70.59	104.11	44.74	43.49
Income Statement								
Premium Income	776,000	3,020,000	2,748,000	2,478,000	2,152,000	1,906,922	1,731,950	1,612,735
Total Revenue	916,000	3,614,000	3,181,000	2,843,000	2,561,000	2,330,994	2,128,223	2,054,289
Benefits & Claims	481,000	1,846,000	1,887,000	1,826,000	1,663,000	1,581,123	1,254,363	1,221,118
Income Before Taxes	195,000	800,000	480,000	279,000	221,000	108,664	321,573	307,107
Income Taxes	51,000	216,000	106,000	41,000	28,000	(9,701)	66,851	65,540
Net Income	144,000	584,000	374,000	238,000	193,000	118,365	254,722	241,567
Average Shares	177,000	178,376	178,292	179,920	178,605	180,722	185,898	189,715
Balance Sheet								
Total Assets	15,798,000	16,107,000	15,509,000	14,059,000	13,959,000	13,287,091	11,380,214	11,086,503
Total Liabilities	9,791,000	9,858,000	9,305,000	8,461,000	7,961,000	7,292,096	5,958,930	5,465,567
Stockholders' Equity	6,007,000	6,249,000	6,204,000	5,598,000	5,998,000	5,994,995	5,421,284	5,620,936
Shares Outstanding	175,000	175,350	176,400	178,605	178,605	177,382	178,628	183,765
Statistical Record								
Return on Assets %	3.68	3.68	2.53	1.70	1.42	0.96	2.27	2.35
Return on Equity %	9.52	9.35	6.34	4.10	3.22	2.07	4.61	4.67
Loss Ratio %	61.98	61.13	68.67	73.69	77.28	82.91	72.42	75.72
Net Margin %	15.72	16.16	11.76	8.37	7.54	5.08	11.97	11.76
Price Range	43.73-36.95	43.34-36.95	37.91-30.52	42.67-29.65	38.73-32.03	38.89-24.21	38.32-27.32	42.55-27.89
P/E Ratio	13.37-11.30	13.21-11.27	18.05-14.53	32.32-22.46	35.86-29.66	58.92-36.68	27.77-19.80	33.25-21.79
Average Yield %	2.66	2.60	2.60	2.21	2.16	2.13	1.85	1.55

Address: 6200 S. Gilmore Road, Fairfield, OH 45014-5141
Telephone: 513-870-2000
Web Site: www.cinfin.com

Officers: John J. Schiff Jr. - Chmn., Pres., C.E.O. James E. Benoski - Vice-Chmn., Chief Insurance Officer **Transfer Agents:** Cincinnati Financial Corporation, Fairfield, OH

Investor Contact: 513-870-2639
No of Institutions: 278
Shares: 89,625,512 **% Held:** 53.59

CINTAS CORPORATION

Exchange	Symbol	Price	52Wk Range	Yield	P/E
NMS	CTAS	$40.37 (5/31/2005)	47.86-38.21	0.79	24.03

*7 Year Price Score 90.03 *NYSE Composite Index=100 *12 Month Price Score 89.77

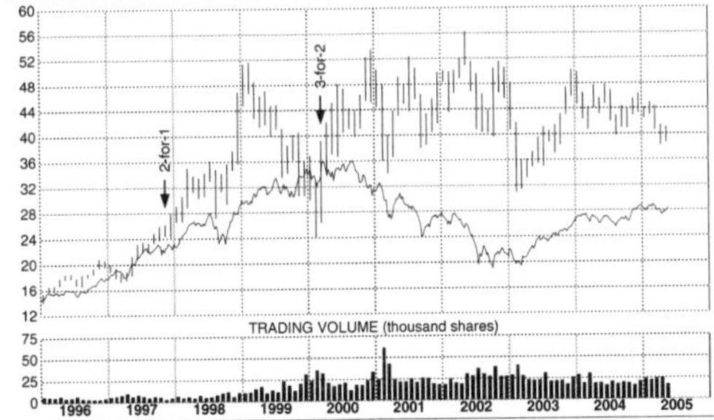

TRADING VOLUME (thousand shares)

Interim Earnings (Per Share)

Qtr.	Aug	Nov	Feb	May
2001-02	0.33	0.34	0.32	0.37
2002-03	0.36	0.37	0.34	0.38
2003-04	0.37	0.40	0.39	0.42
2004-05	0.42	0.43	0.41	...

Interim Dividends (Per Share)

Amt	Decl	Ex	Rec	Pay
0.25A	1/31/2002	2/13/2002	2/15/2002	4/8/2002
0.27A	1/24/2003	2/5/2003	2/7/2003	3/14/2003
0.29A	1/27/2004	2/6/2004	2/10/2004	3/16/2004
0.32A	1/28/2005	2/4/2005	2/8/2005	3/15/2005

Indicated Div: $0.32

Valuation Analysis

Forecast P/E	20.34 (6/2/2005)		
Market Cap	$6.9 Billion	Book Value	2.1 Billion
Price/Book	3.34	Price/Sales	2.32

Dividend Achiever Status

Rank	58	**10 Year Growth Rate**	17.74%
Total Years of Dividend Growth			22

Business Summary: Apparel (MIC: 4.4 SIC: 326 NAIC: 15225)

Cintas designs, manufactures, and implements corporate identity uniform programs, provides entrance mats, restroom supplies, promotional products, first aid and safety products and services and document management services for over 500,000 businesses. Co.'s Rentals segment designs and manufactures corporate identity uniforms which it rents to customers along with other items, including mats, fender covers, towels, mops, linen. Co.'s Other Services segment involves the design, manufacture and direct sale of uniforms to customers along with ancillary services including restroom supplies, first aid and safety products and services, document management services and cleanroom supplies.

Recent Developments: For the quarter ended Feb 28 2005, net income increased 7.3% to $71,332 thousand from net income of $66,493 thousand in the year-earlier quarter. Revenues were $755,241 thousand, up 8.4% from $696,940 thousand the year before. Rentals revenue climbed 6.4% to $582,619 thousand from $547,474 thousand the previous year, while other services revenue rose 15.5% to $172,622 thousand from $149,466 thousand the prior year. Income before taxes was $113,192 thousand, up 7.3% versus $105,540 thousand a year earlier.

Prospects: Co.'s revenue growth continues to accelerate as it adds more new customers across all of its business divisions. Recently, Co. expanded its product and service offerings with the addition of fire protection services, such as fire extinguishers, and further expanded its new Document Management division to include document storage. Meanwhile, Co. is continuing to generate solid gross margins despite higher energy prices. As a result, Co.'s balance sheet is strengthening with its debt to total capitalization continuing to decline. For fiscal year 2005, Co. expects revenues to be in a rang of $3.05 billion to $3.07 billion, and earning to range from $1.71 to $1.75 per share.

Financial Data (US$ in Thousands)	9 Mos	6 Mos	3 Mos	05/31/2004	05/31/2003	05/31/2002	05/31/2001	05/31/2000
Earnings Per Share	1.68	1.66	1.63	1.58	1.45	1.36	1.30	1.14
Cash Flow Per Share	2.55	2.65	2.85	2.97	1.94	2.22	1.46	1.54
Tang Book Value Per Share	6.18	6.32	5.88	6.25	5.33	4.39	7.27	6.20
Dividends Per Share	0.320	0.290	0.290	0.290	0.270	0.250	0.220	0.187
Dividend Payout %	19.05	17.52	17.84	18.35	18.62	18.38	16.92	16.37
Income Statement								
Total Revenue	2,258,037	1,502,796	745,956	2,814,059	2,686,585	2,271,052	2,160,700	1,901,991
EBITDA	455,515	305,202	151,746	575,339	538,820	491,610	468,543	411,272
Depn & Amortn	110,185	73,064	36,428	143,259	143,061	120,025	112,089	99,513
Income Before Taxes	345,330	232,138	115,318	432,080	395,759	371,585	356,454	311,759
Income Taxes	127,772	85,912	42,652	159,875	146,506	137,334	134,003	118,372
Net Income	217,558	146,226	72,666	272,205	249,253	234,251	222,451	193,387
Average Shares	172,790	172,664	172,660	172,372	172,037	172,244	171,629	169,987
Balance Sheet								
Current Assets	1,192,253	1,185,510	1,059,451	1,034,243	877,544	853,250	819,670	721,470
Total Assets	3,055,523	2,994,095	2,847,014	2,810,297	2,582,946	2,519,234	1,752,224	1,581,342
Current Liabilities	385,358	344,083	279,964	325,686	304,839	312,634	250,903	235,392
Long-Term Obligations	462,202	465,178	474,266	473,685	534,763	703,250	220,940	254,378
Total Liabilities	974,619	938,974	880,649	922,328	936,614	1,095,475	520,909	538,466
Stockholders' Equity	2,080,904	2,055,121	1,966,365	1,887,969	1,646,332	1,423,759	1,231,315	1,042,876
Shares Outstanding	172,068	171,689	171,516	171,377	170,599	169,930	169,370	168,281
Statistical Record								
Return on Assets %	9.99	10.01	10.32	10.07	9.77	10.97	13.35	12.90
Return on Equity %	14.92	14.82	15.27	15.36	16.24	17.65	19.56	20.15
EBITDA Margin %	20.17	20.31	20.34	20.45	20.06	21.65	21.68	21.62
Net Margin %	9.63	9.73	9.74	9.67	9.28	10.31	10.30	10.17
Asset Turnover	1.03	1.03	1.06	1.04	1.05	1.06	1.30	1.27
Current Ratio	3.09	3.45	3.78	3.18	2.88	2.73	3.27	3.06
Debt to Equity	0.22	0.23	0.24	0.25	0.32	0.49	0.18	0.24
Price Range	47.86-39.75	50.21-39.75	50.21-37.01	50.21-34.93	52.21-30.90	56.28-37.92	53.56-34.00	45.19-24.25
P/E Ratio	28.49-23.66	30.25-23.95	30.80-22.71	31.78-22.11	36.01-21.31	41.38-27.88	41.20-26.15	39.64-21.27
Average Yield %	0.73	0.65	0.66	0.68	0.64	0.53	0.50	0.51

Address: 6800 Cintas Boulevard, Cincinnati, OH 45262-5737
Telephone: 513-459-1200
Web Site: www.cintas.com

Officers: Richard T. Farmer - Chmn. Robert J. Kohlhepp - Vice-Chmn. **Transfer Agents:** Computershare Investor Services LLC, Chicago, IL

Investor Contact: 513-459-1200
No of Institutions: 366
Shares: 108,408,032 **% Held:** 63.13

CITIGROUP INC

Exchange	Symbol	Price	52Wk Range	Yield	P/E
NYS	C	$47.11 (5/31/2005)	49.78-42.56	3.74	14.28

***7 Year Price Score 101.25** *NYSE Composite Index=100 ***12 Month Price Score 97.09**

Interim Earnings (Per Share)

Qtr.	Mar	Jun	Sep	Dec
2002	0.93	0.78	0.76	0.47
2003	0.79	0.83	0.90	0.91
2004	1.01	0.22	1.02	1.02
2005	1.04	...	...	...

Interim Dividends (Per Share)

Amt	Decl	Ex	Rec	Pay
0.40Q	7/20/2004	7/29/2004	8/2/2004	8/27/2004
0.40Q	10/19/2004	10/28/2004	11/1/2004	11/24/2004
0.44Q	1/20/2005	2/3/2005	2/7/2005	2/25/2005
0.44Q	4/19/2005	4/28/2005	5/2/2005	5/27/2005

Indicated Div: $1.76 (Div. Reinv. Plan)

Valuation Analysis

Forecast P/E	11.20 (6/2/2005)		
Market Cap	$245.1 Billion	Book Value	110.5 Billion
Price/Book	2.22	Price/Sales	2.20

Dividend Achiever Status

Rank	6	**10 Year Growth Rate**	32.51%
Total Years of Dividend Growth			18

Business Summary: Commercial Banking (MIC: 8.1 SIC: 021 NAIC: 23930)

Citigroup is a bank holding company that provides financial services to consumers and corporations. Co.'s Global Consumer segment delivers banking, lending, insurance and investment services. Co.'s Global Corporate and Investment Bank segment provides corporations, governments, institutions and investors with financial products and services. Co.'s Global Wealth Management provides wealth management services to high-net-worth and affluent clients through the Smith Barney Private Client and Global Equity Research businesses and the Citigroup Private Bank. Co.'s Global Investment Management segment offers life insurance, annuity, asset management products and services.

Recent Developments: For the quarter ended Mar 31 2005, income from continuing operations increased 2.9% to $5,168 million from income of $5,024 million in the year-earlier quarter. Net income increased 3.2% to $5,441 million from net income of $5,273 million in the year-earlier quarter. Total revenues were $28,961 million, up 17.1% from $24,742 million the year before. Interest expense jumped 66.5% to $7,428 million from $4,460 million the previous year. Total operating expenses rose 11.9% to $11,655 million from $10,420 million the prior year.

Prospects: On Mar 31 2005, Co. announced that it has completed its acquisition of First American Bank in Texas. Immediately prior to the acquisition, the privately held bank was converted to a National Association banking charter and renamed Citibank Texas, N.A. Terms of the deal were not disclosed. The acquisition provides a presence in the attractive Texas retail banking market. Meanwhile, Co. is experiencing strong earnings growth, primarily due to growth in customer balances, which is helping to offset net interest margin compression from rising short-term interest rates. Separately, Co. is continuing to expand its growth franchises through branch expansion, advertising, and technology.

Financial Data

(US$ in Thousands)	3 Mos	12/31/2004	12/31/2003	12/31/2002	12/31/2001	12/31/2000	12/31/1999	12/31/1998
Earnings Per Share	3.30	3.26	3.42	2.94	2.72	2.62	2.12	1.22
Cash Flow Per Share	1.77	(0.47)	(2.92)	5.13	5.28	0.54	2.06	1.08
Tang Book Value Per Share	11.87	11.72	10.75	9.70	15.57	12.84	10.64	8.94
Dividends Per Share	1.640	1.600	1.100	0.700	0.600	0.520	0.405	0.278
Dividend Payout %	49.70	49.08	32.16	23.81	22.06	19.85	19.08	22.84
Income Statement								
Interest Income	17,535,000	66,709,000	57,047,000	58,939,000	66,565,000	64,939,000	44,900,000	46,239,000
Premium Income	735,000	3,993,000	3,749,000	3,410,000	13,460,000	12,429,000	10,441,000	9,850,000
Interest Expense	7,428,000	22,086,000	17,271,000	21,248,000	31,965,000	36,638,000	24,768,000	27,495,000
Benefits & Claims	217,000	3,801,000	3,895,000	3,478,000	11,759,000	10,147,000	8,671,000	8,365,000
Income Before Taxes	7,848,000	24,182,000	26,333,000	20,537,000	21,897,000	21,143,000	15,948,000	9,269,000
Income Taxes	2,516,000	6,909,000	8,195,000	6,998,000	7,526,000	7,525,000	5,703,000	3,234,000
Net Income	5,441,000	17,046,000	17,853,000	15,276,000	14,126,000	13,519,000	9,867,000	5,807,000
Average Shares	5,225,999	5,207,399	5,193,599	5,166,199	5,146,999	5,122,199	4,591,331	4,630,398
Balance Sheet								
Total Assets	1,489,891,000	1,484,101,000	1,264,032,000	1,097,190,000	1,051,450,000	902,210,000	716,937,000	668,641,000
Total Liabilities	1,379,355,000	1,374,810,000	1,166,018,000	1,010,472,000	970,203,000	831,084,000	662,331,000	621,473,000
Stockholders' Equity	110,536,000	109,291,000	98,014,000	86,718,000	81,247,000	66,206,000	49,686,000	42,708,000
Shares Outstanding	5,202,176	5,194,642	5,156,949	5,140,681	5,118,688	5,022,221	4,490,031	4,515,998
Statistical Record								
Return on Assets %	1.23	1.24	1.51	1.42	1.45	1.67	1.42	1.10
Return on Equity %	16.21	16.40	19.33	18.19	19.16	23.27	21.36	18.26
Net Interest Margin %	57.64	66.89	69.72	63.95	51.98	43.58	44.84	40.54
Loss Ratio %	29.52	95.19	103.89	101.99	87.36	81.64	83.05	84.92
Price Range	52.29-42.56	52.29-42.56	49.00-31.42	48.55-25.21	52.57-33.95	54.97-33.61	40.61-23.20	33.78-14.90
P/E Ratio	15.85-12.90	16.04-13.06	14.33-9.19	16.51-8.57	19.33-12.48	20.98-12.83	19.16-10.94	27.68-12.22
Average Yield %	3.52	3.40	2.63	1.84	1.31	1.16	1.27	1.12

Address: 399 Park Avenue, New York, NY 10043
Telephone: 212-559-1000
Web Site: www.citigroup.com

Officers: Sanford I. Weill - Chmn. William R. Rhodes - Sr. Vice-Chmn. **Transfer Agents:** Mellon Investor Services, LLC, Ridgefield Park, NJ

Investor Contact: 212-559-9446
No of Institutions: 1209
Shares: 3,320,400,640 **% Held:** 63.54

CITY NATIONAL CORP. (BEVERLY HILLS, CA)

Exchange	Symbol	Price	52Wk Range	Yield	P/E
NYS	CYN	$71.03 (5/31/2005)	71.25-62.12	2.03	17.20

*7 Year Price Score 128.83 *NYSE Composite Index=100 *12 Month Price Score 99.78

Interim Earnings (Per Share)

Qtr.	Mar	Jun	Sep	Dec
2002	0.87	0.88	0.94	0.87
2003	0.87	0.93	1.05	0.87
2004	1.00	1.03	1.04	0.97
2005	1.09	...	...	...

Interim Dividends (Per Share)

Amt	Decl	Ex	Rec	Pay
0.32Q	7/28/2004	8/9/2004	8/11/2004	8/23/2004
0.32Q	10/27/2004	11/8/2004	11/10/2004	11/22/2004
0.36Q	1/20/2005	1/31/2005	2/2/2005	2/15/2005
0.36Q	5/4/2005	5/16/2005	5/18/2005	5/31/2005

Indicated Div: $1.44

Valuation Analysis

Forecast P/E	15.37 (6/2/2005)		
Market Cap	$3.5 Billion	Book Value	1.3 Billion
Price/Book	2.66	Price/Sales	4.30

Dividend Achiever Status

Rank	1	**10 Year Growth Rate**	38.30%
Total Years of Dividend Growth			10

Business Summary: Commercial Banking (MIC: 8.1 SIC: 021 NAIC: 22110)

City National, with assets of $14.20 billion as of Dec 31 2004, conducts its business through City National Bank (the Bank). The Bank provides banking, investment and trust services through 52 offices, including 12 full-service regional centers, in Southern California, the San Francisco Bay Area, and New York City. Co. offers a range of lending, deposit, cash management, international banking, and other products and services. Co. also offers investment management and advisory services and brokerage services, including portfolio management, securities trading and asset management; personal and business trust and investment services; and estate and financial planning and custodial services.

Recent Developments: For the quarter ended Mar 31 2005, net income increased 9.0% to $55,461 thousand from net income of $50,898 thousand in the year-earlier quarter. Net interest income was $146,426 thousand, up 11.8% from $130,972 thousand the year before. Non-interest income rose 8.1% to $50,358 thousand from $46,570 thousand the previous year, while non-interest expense advanced 12.7% to $106,504 thousand from $94,531 thousand the prior year.

Prospects: Co. continues to expect net income per diluted common share for full-year 2005 to be approximately 11.0% to 14.0% higher than net income per diluted common share for 2004, based on economic conditions, business indicators and an expectation that the federal funds rate will rise by 75 basis points in 2005. Co. also expects that average loans will grow at a faster rate than in 2004, while average deposits are expected to grow at a slower rate than in 2004. Additionally, Co. is projecting that net interest income will grow at a much higher rate in 2005, as a result of interest rate changes that occurred in 2004, expected rate increases in 2005 and higher loan balances.

Financial Data (US$ in Thousands)	3 Mos	12/31/2004	12/31/2003	12/31/2002	12/31/2001	12/31/2000	12/31/1999	12/31/1998
Earnings Per Share	4.13	4.04	3.72	3.56	2.96	2.72	2.30	2.00
Cash Flow Per Share	3.87	4.23	5.71	3.72	3.06	3.98	2.45	2.90
Tang Book Value Per Share	20.84	21.27	18.65	17.42	14.81	11.50	9.78	10.61
Dividends Per Share	1.320	1.280	0.970	0.780	0.740	0.700	0.660	0.560
Dividend Payout %	31.96	31.68	26.08	21.91	25.00	25.74	28.70	28.00
Income Statement								
Interest Income	167,650	604,325	575,725	609,700	625,248	646,288	470,446	423,949
Interest Expense	21,224	58,437	61,110	94,444	191,094	239,772	148,441	130,278
Net Interest Income	146,426	545,888	514,615	515,256	434,154	406,516	322,005	293,671
Provision for Losses	...	...	29,000	67,000	35,000	21,500	...	...
Non-Interest Income	50,358	184,265	177,225	146,293	132,384	109,484	87,212	67,684
Non-Interest Expense	106,504	395,410	364,178	332,591	313,395	294,770	241,803	211,331
Income Before Taxes	88,469	329,751	294,623	261,958	218,143	199,730	167,414	150,024
Income Taxes	33,008	123,429	107,946	78,858	71,973	68,070	59,307	53,796
Net Income	55,461	206,322	186,677	183,100	146,170	131,660	108,107	96,228
Average Shares	51,030	51,074	50,198	51,389	49,376	48,393	46,938	48,141
Balance Sheet								
Net Loans & Leases	8,437,856	8,345,619	7,716,756	7,834,968	7,016,344	6,391,710	5,356,592	4,395,088
Total Assets	13,918,038	14,231,513	13,018,242	11,870,392	10,176,316	9,096,669	7,213,619	6,427,781
Total Deposits	11,762,624	11,986,915	10,937,063	9,839,698	8,131,202	7,408,670	5,669,409	4,887,402
Total Liabilities	12,572,330	12,856,616	11,772,942	10,760,433	9,285,739	8,353,021	6,641,973	5,865,978
Stockholders' Equity	1,320,183	1,348,535	1,219,256	1,109,959	890,577	743,648	571,646	561,803
Shares Outstanding	49,377	49,546	49,204	48,983	48,149	47,629	45,456	46,007
Statistical Record								
Return on Assets %	1.55	1.51	1.50	1.66	1.52	1.61	1.58	1.65
Return on Equity %	16.47	16.03	16.03	18.31	17.89	19.97	19.08	17.98
Net Interest Margin %	87.34	90.33	89.39	84.51	69.44	62.90	68.45	69.27
Efficiency Ratio %	48.85	50.14	48.37	43.99	41.37	39.00	43.36	42.99
Loans to Deposits	0.72	0.70	0.71	0.80	0.86	0.86	0.94	0.90
Price Range	70.91-58.09	70.75-57.93	64.00-39.25	56.14-40.40	49.38-33.91	40.75-25.88	41.63-30.38	41.63-26.56
P/E Ratio	17.17-14.07	17.51-14.34	17.20-10.55	15.77-11.35	16.68-11.46	14.98-9.51	18.10-13.21	20.81-13.28
Average Yield %	1.99	2.00	1.96	1.57	1.80	1.99	1.87	1.56

Address: City National Center, 400 North Roxbury Drive, Beverly Hills, CA 90210
Telephone: 310-888-6000
Web Site: www.cnb.com

Officers: Bram Goldsmith - Chmn. Russell D. Goldsmith - Vice-Chmn., C.E.O. **Transfer Agents:** Continental Stock Transfer & Trust Co.

Investor Contact: 310-888-6700
No of Institutions: 204
Shares: 29,421,412 **% Held:** 59.33

CLARCOR INC.

Exchange	Symbol	Price	52Wk Range	Yield	P/E
NYS	CLC	$28.09 (5/31/2005)	28.42-21.28	0.91	22.29

***7 Year Price Score 146.70** *NYSE Composite Index=100 ***12 Month Price Score 104.09**

Interim Earnings (Per Share)

Qtr.	Feb	May	Aug	Nov
2001-02	0.16	0.21	0.24	0.32
2002-03	0.19	0.26	0.28	0.34
2003-04	0.23	0.29	0.30	0.41
2004-05	0.25	...	...	...

Interim Dividends (Per Share)

Amt	Decl	Ex	Rec	Pay
0.064Q	9/20/2004	10/13/2004	10/15/2004	10/29/2004
0.064Q	12/13/2004	1/12/2005	1/14/2005	1/28/2005
0.064Q	3/21/2005	4/13/2005	4/15/2005	4/29/2005
2-for-1	3/21/2005	5/2/2005	4/15/2005	4/29/2005

Indicated Div: $0.26 (Div. Reinv. Plan)

Valuation Analysis

Forecast P/E	20.85 (5/28/2005)		
Market Cap	$1.4 Billion	Book Value	443.1 Million
Price/Book	3.27	Price/Sales	1.79

Dividend Achiever Status

Rank	306	10 Year Growth Rate	1.93%
Total Years of Dividend Growth			24

Business Summary: Automotive (MIC: 15.1 SIC: 714 NAIC: 36399)

Clarcor conducts its business through three industry segments. Co.'s Engine/Mobile Filtration segment includes filters for oil, air, fuel, coolants and hydraulic fluids. Industrial/Environmental Filtration products include air and antimicrobial treated filters, high efficiency electronic air cleaners, specialty filters, industrial process liquid filters, filters for pharmaceutical processes and beverages, filtration systems for aircraft refueling, anti-pollution, sewage treatment and water recycling, bilge separators, sand control filters for oil and gas drilling and woven wire and metallic products. Packaging products include a variety of custom-styled containers and packaging items.

Recent Developments: For the quarter ended Feb 26 2005, net income increased 12.8% to $13,154 thousand from net income of $11,661 thousand in the year-earlier period. Revenues were $196,261 thousand, up 11.9% from $175,275 thousand the year before. Operating income was $21,080 thousand versus an income of $17,813 thousand in the prior-year quarter, an increase of 18.3%. Total direct expense was $139,242 thousand versus $123,788 thousand the year before, an increase of 12.4%. Total indirect expense was $35,939 thousand versus $33,671 thousand in the prior-year period, an increase of 6.7%.

Prospects: Recent top line growth, coupled with improving operating margins, strengthens Co.'s outlook. Accordingly, Co. expects full-year 2005 earnings per share will be in the $2.63 to $2.71 range, which includes the effect of expensing stock options. Co. noted that it has been able to pass through most of the steel price increases it incurred last year and so far in 2005; however, in addition to steel, prices for many other commodities and manufactured materials continue to rise. Separately, on Mar 1 2005, Co. announced that it has acquired Niagara Screen Products Limited, a manufacturer of woven wire and metallic screening and filtration products, located in St. Catharines, Ontario, Canada.

Financial Data

(US$ in Thousands)	3 Mos	11/30/2004	11/30/2003	11/30/2002	11/30/2001	11/30/2000	11/27/1999	11/28/1998
Earnings Per Share	1.26	1.24	1.08	0.93	0.84	0.82	0.73	0.65
Cash Flow Per Share	1.38	1.46	1.75	1.71	1.29	1.10	0.81	0.87
Tang Book Value Per Share	5.73	5.48	4.90	3.87	3.20	2.88	2.49	3.45
Dividends Per Share	0.253	0.251	0.246	0.241	0.236	0.231	0.226	0.221
Dividend Payout %	20.00	20.26	22.91	26.08	28.13	28.20	30.99	34.04
Income Statement								
Total Revenue	196,261	787,686	741,358	715,563	666,964	652,148	477,869	426,773
EBITDA	26,326	118,272	106,576	96,822	97,200	95,402	73,269	64,780
Depn & Amortn	5,529	19,151	18,985	19,760	21,850	21,079	15,372	12,380
Income Before Taxes	20,768	99,060	86,059	71,450	65,734	63,487	55,615	51,347
Income Taxes	7,536	34,717	31,371	24,773	23,804	23,201	20,137	19,262
Net Income	13,154	63,997	54,552	46,601	41,893	40,237	35,412	32,079
Average Shares	52,321	51,506	50,745	50,343	49,784	49,012	48,627	49,297
Balance Sheet								
Current Assets	298,859	303,990	257,402	259,746	244,350	230,479	227,670	168,173
Total Assets	621,000	627,797	538,237	546,119	530,617	501,930	472,991	305,766
Current Liabilities	111,078	126,272	111,373	174,255	94,931	97,826	97,475	61,183
Long-Term Obligations	16,042	24,130	16,913	22,648	135,203	141,486	145,981	36,419
Total Liabilities	177,936	199,335	167,845	230,658	256,356	259,837	262,273	118,959
Stockholders' Equity	443,064	428,462	370,392	315,461	274,261	242,093	210,718	186,807
Shares Outstanding	51,519	51,223	50,618	49,837	49,252	48,762	48,039	47,898
Statistical Record								
Return on Assets %	11.22	10.95	10.06	8.66	8.11	8.16	9.12	10.94
Return on Equity %	15.91	15.98	15.91	15.80	16.23	17.58	17.87	17.97
EBITDA Margin %	13.41	15.02	14.38	13.53	14.57	14.63	15.33	15.18
Net Margin %	6.70	8.12	7.36	6.51	6.28	6.17	7.41	7.52
Asset Turnover	1.39	1.35	1.37	1.33	1.29	1.32	1.23	1.45
Current Ratio	2.69	2.41	2.31	1.49	2.57	2.36	2.34	2.75
Debt to Equity	0.04	0.06	0.05	0.07	0.49	0.58	0.69	0.19
Price Range	28.00-20.43	26.26-20.43	22.95-15.53	17.00-12.82	13.80-8.56	10.69-8.34	10.63-7.66	12.17-7.25
P/E Ratio	22.22-16.21	21.18-16.47	21.25-14.37	18.28-13.78	16.43-10.19	13.03-10.18	14.55-10.49	18.72-11.15
Average Yield %	1.07	1.12	1.31	1.61	1.94	2.47	2.45	2.29

Address: 840 Crescent Centre Drive, Suite 600, Franklin, TN 37067 **Telephone:** 615-771-3100 **Web Site:** www.clarcor.com	**Officers:** Norman E. Johnson - Chmn., Pres., C.E.O. William B. Walker - Vice-Chmn. **Transfer Agents:** First Chicago Trust Company of New York, Jersey City, NJ	**No of Institutions:** 167 **Shares:** 20,142,756 **% Held:** 78.19

CLOROX CO.

Exchange	Symbol	Price	52Wk Range	Yield	P/E
NYS	CLX	$58.41 (5/31/2005)	65.27-49.56	1.92	9.95

Interim Earnings (Per Share)

Qtr.	Sep	Dec	Mar	Jun
2001-02	0.33	0.22	0.20	0.62
2002-03	0.65	0.40	0.50	0.67
2003-04	0.60	0.51	0.59	0.86
2004-05	0.57	3.68	0.76	...

Interim Dividends (Per Share)

Amt	Decl	Ex	Rec	Pay
0.27Q	9/15/2004	10/27/2004	10/29/2004	11/15/2004
0.28Q	11/17/2004	1/27/2005	1/31/2005	2/15/2005
0.28Q	3/16/2005	4/26/2005	4/28/2005	5/13/2005
0.28Q	5/13/2005	7/27/2005	7/29/2005	8/15/2005

Indicated Div: $1.12 (Div. Reinv. Plan)

Valuation Analysis

Forecast P/E	19.20 (5/28/2005)		
Market Cap	$9.0 Billion	Book Value	N/A
Price/Book	N/A	Price/Sales	2.04

Dividend Achiever Status

Rank	198	10 Year Growth Rate	8.79%
Total Years of Dividend Growth			28

Business Summary: Chemicals (MIC: 11.1 SIC: 842 NAIC: 25612)

Clorox is engaged in the production and marketing of consumer products sold primarily through grocery, mass merchandise, club and other retail stores. Co. has three business segments: Household Products-North America, Specialty Products, and Household Products-Latin America/Other. Co.'s principal products include plastic bags, wraps and containers, home care cleaning products such as disinfecting sprays and wipes, toilet bowl cleaners, dilutable, spray and gel household cleaners, glass and surface cleaners, carpet cleaners, reusable cleaning cloths, drain openers and septic-system treatments, steel-wool soap pads and scrubber sponges, mildew removers, and soap scum and bathroom cleaners.

Recent Developments: For the quarter ended Mar 31 2005, income from continuing operations increased 0.9% to $116,000 thousand from income of $115,000 thousand in the year-earlier quarter. Net income decreased 6.3% to $118,000 thousand from net income of $126,000 thousand in the year-earlier quarter. Revenues were $1,086,000 thousand, up 3.3% from $1,051,000 thousand the year before. Total direct expense was $632,000 thousand versus $584,000 thousand in the prior-year quarter, an increase of 8.2%. Total indirect expense was $272,000 thousand versus $289,000 thousand in the prior-year quarter, a decrease of 5.9%.

Prospects: Results are benefiting from strong sales across nearly all of Co.'s business segments, most notably home care, Glad® trash bags, and the Latin America division. Meanwhile, top-line growth is being positively affected by strong shipments of new products, including Co.'s new Clorox ToiletWand disposable toilet cleaning system, and recent price increases on Glad trash bags and GladWare containers. Co. is considering raising prices on more products to help offset higher commodity costs. Looking ahead, Co. is targeting full fiscal-2005 sales growth in the range of 4.0% to 6.0%, along with earnings from continuing operations of between $2.80 and $2.86 per diluted share.

Financial Data

(US$ in Thousands)	9 Mos	6 Mos	3 Mos	06/30/2004	06/30/2003	06/30/2002	06/30/2001	06/30/2000
Earnings Per Share	5.87	5.69	2.52	2.56	2.23	1.37	1.35	1.64
Cash Flow Per Share	5.41	5.20	4.57	4.24	3.68	3.78	3.16	2.78
Tang Book Value Per Share	...	...	1.43	0.77	N.M.	0.24	1.38	1.10
Dividends Per Share	1.090	1.080	1.080	1.080	0.880	0.840	0.840	0.800
Dividend Payout %	18.57	18.97	42.78	42.19	39.46	61.31	62.22	48.78
Income Statement								
Total Revenue	3,134,000	2,048,000	1,090,000	4,324,000	4,144,000	4,061,000	3,903,000	4,083,000
EBITDA	640,000	455,000	236,000	1,028,000	965,000	668,000	639,000	776,000
Depn & Amortn	142,000	94,000	47,000	162,000	138,000	135,000	74,000	66,000
Income Before Taxes	498,000	361,000	189,000	840,000	802,000	498,000	487,000	622,000
Income Taxes	139,000	116,000	66,000	294,000	288,000	176,000	162,000	228,000
Net Income	940,000	822,000	123,000	549,000	493,000	322,000	323,000	394,000
Average Shares	156,104	189,806	215,117	214,371	220,692	234,704	239,483	239,614
Balance Sheet								
Current Assets	1,128,000	1,047,000	1,130,000	1,043,000	951,000	1,002,000	1,103,000	1,454,000
Total Assets	3,756,000	3,710,000	3,772,000	3,834,000	3,652,000	3,630,000	3,995,000	4,353,000
Current Liabilities	1,286,000	1,469,000	1,095,000	1,268,000	1,451,000	1,225,000	1,069,000	1,541,000
Long-Term Obligations	2,123,000	2,124,000	474,000	475,000	495,000	678,000	685,000	590,000
Total Liabilities	4,102,000	4,167,000	2,128,000	2,294,000	2,437,000	2,276,000	2,095,000	2,559,000
Stockholders' Equity	(346,000)	(457,000)	1,644,000	1,540,000	1,215,000	1,354,000	1,900,000	1,794,000
Shares Outstanding	154,151	153,385	213,376	212,988	213,676	223,009	236,691	235,361
Statistical Record								
Return on Assets %	30.14	30.97	14.78	14.63	13.54	8.45	7.74	9.26
Return on Equity %	227.96	310.88	38.69	39.75	38.38	19.79	17.49	23.36
EBITDA Margin %	20.42	22.22	21.65	23.77	23.29	16.45	16.37	19.01
Net Margin %	29.99	40.14	11.28	12.70	11.90	7.93	8.28	9.65
Asset Turnover	1.18	1.21	1.19	1.15	1.14	1.07	0.94	0.96
Current Ratio	0.88	0.71	1.03	0.82	0.66	0.82	1.03	0.94
Debt to Equity	...	...	0.29	0.31	0.41	0.50	0.36	0.33
Price Range	63.00-48.91	59.16-46.83	54.68-45.20	53.95-42.00	48.24-32.18	47.62-34.64	47.94-30.06	56.97-29.88
P/E Ratio	10.73-8.33	10.40-8.23	21.70-17.94	21.07-16.41	21.63-14.43	34.76-25.28	35.51-22.27	34.74-18.22
Average Yield %	1.98	2.07	2.16	2.26	2.07	2.07	2.28	1.83

Address: 1221 Broadway, Oakland, CA 94612-1888
Telephone: 510-271-7000
Web Site: www.clorox.com

Officers: R. W. Matschullat - Chmn. G. E. Johnston - Pres., C.E.O. **Transfer Agents:** EquiServe Trust Company N.A., Providence, RI

No of Institutions: 387
Shares: 109,220,960 **% Held:** 71.21

COCA-COLA CO (THE)

Exchange	Symbol	Price	52Wk Range	Yield	P/E
NYS	KO	$44.63 (5/31/2005)	52.71-38.65	2.51	22.77

***7 Year Price Score 72.91** *NYSE Composite Index=100 ***12 Month Price Score 97.06**

Interim Earnings (Per Share)

Qtr.	Mar	Jun	Sep	Dec
2002	(0.05)	0.52	0.47	0.29
2003	0.34	0.55	0.50	0.38
2004	0.46	0.65	0.39	0.50
2005	0.42	...	...	...

Interim Dividends (Per Share)

Amt	Decl	Ex	Rec	Pay
0.25Q	7/22/2004	9/13/2004	9/15/2004	10/1/2004
0.25Q	10/21/2004	11/29/2004	12/1/2004	12/15/2004
0.28Q	2/17/2005	3/11/2005	3/15/2005	4/1/2005
0.28Q	4/20/2005	6/13/2005	6/15/2005	7/1/2005

Indicated Div: $1.12 (Div. Reinv. Plan)

Valuation Analysis

Forecast P/E	21.35 (6/2/2005)		
Market Cap	$107.5 Billion	Book Value	16.5 Billion
Price/Book	6.51	Price/Sales	4.85

Dividend Achiever Status

Rank	175	**10 Year Growth Rate**	9.87%
Total Years of Dividend Growth			42

Business Summary: Food (MIC: 4.1 SIC: 086 NAIC: 12111)

The Coca-Cola Company is engaged in the manufacturing, distributing and marketing of nonalcoholic beverage concentrates and syrups. Co.'s beverage products include, but are not limited to: Coca-Cola, Coca-Cola Classic, Diet Coke, Vanilla Coke, Sprite, Mr. Pibb, Mello Yellow, Barq's, Powerade, Dasani plus other assorted diet and caffeine-free versions. Co. also produces, distributes and markets juice and juice-drink products including Minute Maid juices and juice drinks, Simply Orange orange juice, Odwalla super premium juices and drinks, Five Alive, Bacardi tropical fruit mixers (manufactured and marketed under a license from Bacardi & Company Limited) and Hi-C ready to serve fruit drinks.

Recent Developments: For the three months ended Mar 31 2005, net income slipped 11.1% to $1,002 million from net income of $1,127 million a year earlier. Revenues were $5,266 million, up 3.7% from $5,078 million the year before. Gross profit totaled $3,457 million, or 65.6% of revenues, up 4.0% compared with $3,325 million, or 65.5% of revenues, the previous year. Operating income declined 6.3% to $1,359 million from $1,451 million in the prior year.

Prospects: In Mar 2005, Co. and Coca-Cola Hellenic Bottling Company S.A., a Coca-Cola bottler, announced an agreement to jointly acquire Multon, a Russian juice company, for a total purchase price of approximately $501.0 million. The transaction closed on Apr 20 2005. The total purchase price has been split equally between Co. and Coca-Cola HBC. Multon has production facilities in Moscow and St. Petersburg and produces and distributes juice products under the brands Rich, Nico and Dobry. Looking ahead, Co. intends to increase its investments in marketing, as well as new product innovation. In North America during the quarter ended Mar 31 2005, Co. launched Coca-Cola with Lime and Dasani Flavors.

Financial Data (US$ in Thousands)	3 Mos	12/31/2004	12/31/2003	12/31/2002	12/31/2001	12/31/2000	12/31/1999	12/31/1998
Earnings Per Share	1.96	2.00	1.77	1.23	1.60	0.88	0.98	1.42
Cash Flow Per Share	2.57	2.45	2.22	1.91	1.65	1.44	1.57	1.39
Tang Book Value Per Share	5.26	5.02	4.14	3.34	3.53	2.98	3.06	3.19
Dividends Per Share	1.030	1.000	0.880	0.800	0.720	0.680	0.640	0.600
Dividend Payout %	52.55	50.00	49.72	65.04	45.00	77.27	65.31	42.25
Income Statement								
Total Revenue	5,266,000	21,962,000	21,044,000	19,564,000	20,092,000	20,458,000	19,805,000	18,813,000
EBITDA	1,682,000	7,016,000	6,187,000	6,114,000	6,437,000	4,274,000	4,688,000	5,901,000
Depn & Amortn	226,000	755,000	690,000	625,000	803,000	773,000	792,000	645,000
Income Before Taxes	1,448,000	6,222,000	5,495,000	5,499,000	5,670,000	3,399,000	3,819,000	5,198,000
Income Taxes	446,000	1,375,000	1,148,000	1,523,000	1,691,000	1,222,000	1,388,000	1,665,000
Net Income	1,002,000	4,847,000	4,347,000	3,050,000	3,969,000	2,177,000	2,431,000	3,533,000
Average Shares	2,410,000	2,429,000	2,462,000	2,483,000	2,487,000	2,487,000	2,487,000	2,496,000
Balance Sheet								
Current Assets	12,286,000	12,094,000	8,396,000	7,352,000	7,171,000	6,620,000	6,480,000	6,380,000
Total Assets	31,614,000	31,327,000	27,342,000	24,501,000	22,417,000	20,834,000	21,623,000	19,145,000
Current Liabilities	10,636,000	10,971,000	7,886,000	7,341,000	8,429,000	9,321,000	9,856,000	8,640,000
Long-Term Obligations	1,141,000	1,157,000	2,517,000	2,701,000	1,219,000	835,000	854,000	687,000
Total Liabilities	15,103,000	15,392,000	13,252,000	12,701,000	11,051,000	11,518,000	12,110,000	10,742,000
Stockholders' Equity	16,511,000	15,935,000	14,090,000	11,800,000	11,366,000	9,316,000	9,513,000	8,403,000
Shares Outstanding	2,408,973	2,409,339	2,441,531	2,470,979	2,486,228	2,484,762	2,471,575	2,466,000
Statistical Record								
Return on Assets %	15.54	16.48	16.77	13.00	18.35	10.23	11.93	19.58
Return on Equity %	30.30	32.20	33.58	26.33	38.38	23.06	27.14	44.97
EBITDA Margin %	31.94	31.95	29.40	31.25	32.04	20.89	23.67	31.37
Net Margin %	19.03	22.07	20.66	15.59	19.75	10.64	12.27	18.78
Asset Turnover	0.73	0.75	0.81	0.83	0.93	0.96	0.97	1.04
Current Ratio	1.16	1.10	1.06	1.00	0.85	0.71	0.66	0.74
Debt to Equity	0.07	0.07	0.18	0.23	0.11	0.09	0.09	0.08
Price Range	53.00-38.65	53.00-38.65	50.75-37.07	57.64-43.47	60.82-42.85	66.88-43.31	70.50-47.56	87.94-56.19
P/E Ratio	27.04-19.72	26.50-19.32	28.67-20.94	46.86-35.34	38.01-26.78	75.99-49.22	71.94-48.53	61.93-39.57
Average Yield %	2.31	2.15	2.00	1.61	1.48	1.23	1.03	0.83

Address: One Coca-Cola Plaza, Atlanta, GA 30313 **Telephone:** 404-676-2121 **Web Site:** www.coca-cola.com	**Officers:** E. Neville Isdell - Chmn., C.E.O. Gary P. Fayard - Exec. V.P., C.F.O. **Transfer Agents:** EquiServe Trust Company, N.A., Providence, RI	**Investor Contact:** 404-676-5766 **No of Institutions:** 911 **Shares:** 1,398,016,384 **% Held:** 58.01

COLGATE-PALMOLIVE CO.

Exchange	Symbol	Price	52Wk Range	Yield	P/E
NYS	CL	$49.97 (5/31/2005)	58.73-43.06	2.32	22.01

Interim Earnings (Per Share)

Qtr.	Mar	Jun	Sep	Dec
2002	0.49	0.55	0.57	0.59
2003	0.56	0.62	0.63	0.65
2004	0.59	0.66	0.58	0.50
2005	0.53	...	...	...

Interim Dividends (Per Share)

Amt	Decl	Ex	Rec	Pay
0.24Q	7/8/2004	7/22/2004	7/26/2004	8/16/2004
0.24Q	10/7/2004	10/21/2004	10/25/2004	11/15/2004
0.24Q	1/13/2005	1/24/2005	1/26/2005	2/15/2005
0.29Q	2/10/2005	4/22/2005	4/26/2005	5/13/2005

Indicated Div: $1.16 (Div. Reinv. Plan)

Valuation Analysis

Forecast P/E	19.12 (5/28/2005)		
Market Cap	$26.1 Billion	Book Value	1.0 Billion
Price/Book	25.76	Price/Sales	2.42

Dividend Achiever Status

Rank	180	**10 Year Growth Rate**	9.57%
Total Years of Dividend Growth			42

Business Summary: Chemicals (MIC: 11.1 SIC: 844 NAIC: 25620)

Colgate-Palmolive is a global consumer products company. Co.'s Oral, Personal and Home Care products include toothpaste, oral rinses and toothbrushes, bar and liquid hand soaps, shower gels, shampoos, conditioners, deodorants and antiperspirants, shave products, laundry and dishwashing detergents, fabric conditioners, cleansers and cleaners, bleaches and other similar items. Co.'s Pet Nutrition products include pet food products manufactured and marketed by Hill's Pet Nutrition. Principal global and regional trademarks include Colgate, Palmolive, Kolynos, Sorriso, Elmex, Mennen, Protex, Softsoap, Irish Spring, Ajax, Soupline, Suavitel, Hill's Science Diet and Hill's Prescription Diet.

Recent Developments: For the quarter ended Mar 31 2005, net income decreased 11.3% to $300,100 thousand from net income of $338,500 thousand in the year-earlier quarter. Revenues were $2,743,000 thousand, up 9.1% from $2,513,500 thousand the year before. Operating income was $492,600 thousand versus an income of $531,300 thousand in the prior-year quarter, a decrease of 7.3%. Total direct expense was $1,239,400 thousand versus $1,113,900 thousand in the prior-year quarter, an increase of 11.3%. Total indirect expense was $944,400 thousand versus $844,300 thousand in the prior-year quarter, an increase of 11.9%.

Prospects: Co.'s 2004 restructuring program appears on track. Co. projects the program will result in cumulative aftertax charges of between $550.0 and $650.0 million by 2008, with annual aftertax savings expected to be in the range of $250.0 to $300.0 million also by 2008. Co. also expects savings to begin ramping up late in second quarter 2005. Meanwhile, Co. sees top-line growth continuing throughout 2005, and gross profit margin, before the effect of the 2004 restructuring charges, improving. Thus, Co. expects to achieve its expectations, excluding restructuring charges, of high single-digit earnings per share growth for 2005 and is hopeful for double-digit earnings per share growth in 2006.

Financial Data

(US$ in Thousands)	3 Mos	12/31/2004	12/31/2003	12/31/2002	12/31/2001	12/31/2000	12/31/1999	12/31/1998
Earnings Per Share	2.27	2.33	2.46	2.19	1.89	1.70	1.47	1.30
Cash Flow Per Share	3.45	3.30	3.29	2.97	2.87	2.66	2.22	2.00
Dividends Per Share	0.960	0.960	0.900	0.720	0.675	0.630	0.590	0.550
Dividend Payout %	42.29	41.20	36.59	32.88	35.71	37.06	40.14	42.15
Income Statement								
Total Revenue	2,743,000	10,584,200	9,903,400	9,294,300	9,427,800	9,357,900	9,118,200	8,971,600
EBITDA	575,800	2,449,900	2,481,500	2,309,600	2,171,000	2,078,300	1,906,400	1,753,300
Depn & Amortn	83,200	327,800	315,500	296,500	336,200	337,800	340,200	330,300
Income Before Taxes	461,000	2,002,400	2,041,900	1,870,300	1,668,700	1,567,200	1,394,600	1,250,100
Income Taxes	160,900	675,300	620,600	582,000	522,100	503,400	457,300	401,500
Net Income	300,100	1,327,100	1,421,300	1,288,300	1,146,600	1,063,800	937,300	848,600
Average Shares	561,700	569,300	578,800	589,100	607,700	627,300	638,800	648,400
Balance Sheet								
Current Assets	2,944,200	2,739,900	2,496,500	2,228,100	2,203,400	2,347,200	2,354,800	2,244,900
Total Assets	8,691,500	8,672,900	7,478,800	7,087,200	6,984,800	7,252,300	7,423,100	7,685,200
Current Liabilities	3,090,800	2,730,700	2,445,400	2,148,700	2,123,500	2,244,100	2,273,500	2,114,400
Long-Term Obligations	2,969,900	3,089,500	2,684,900	3,210,800	2,812,000	2,536,900	2,243,300	2,300,600
Total Liabilities	7,676,500	7,427,500	6,591,700	6,736,900	6,138,400	5,784,200	5,589,400	5,599,600
Stockholders' Equity	1,015,000	1,245,400	887,100	350,300	846,400	1,468,100	1,833,700	2,085,600
Shares Outstanding	523,178	526,625	533,697	536,001	550,722	566,655	578,863	585,420
Statistical Record								
Return on Assets %	15.92	16.39	19.52	18.31	16.11	14.46	12.41	11.15
Return on Equity %	141.43	124.12	229.72	215.31	99.08	64.26	47.83	39.80
EBITDA Margin %	20.99	23.15	25.06	24.85	23.03	22.21	20.91	19.54
Net Margin %	10.94	12.54	14.35	13.86	12.16	11.37	10.28	9.46
Asset Turnover	1.34	1.31	1.36	1.32	1.32	1.27	1.21	1.18
Current Ratio	0.95	1.00	1.02	1.04	1.04	1.05	1.04	1.06
Debt to Equity	2.93	2.48	3.03	9.17	3.32	1.73	1.22	1.10
Price Range	58.92-43.06	58.92-43.06	60.88-49.10	58.73-44.36	62.50-51.00	65.00-42.75	65.00-37.53	48.47-32.78
P/E Ratio	25.96-18.97	25.29-18.48	24.75-19.96	26.82-20.26	33.07-26.98	38.24-25.15	44.22-25.53	37.28-25.22
Average Yield %	1.84	1.82	1.64	1.33	1.19	1.13	1.18	1.31

Address: 300 Park Avenue, New York, NY 10022-7499 **Telephone:** 212-310-2000 **Web Site:** www.colgate.com	**Officers:** Reuben Mark - Chmn., C.E.O. Javier G. Teruel - Vice-Chmn. **Transfer Agents:** EquiServe Trust Company, N.A., Providence, RI	**Investor Contact:** 212-310-3072 **No of Institutions:** 675 **Shares:** 330,828,896 **% Held:** 62.99

COLONIAL PROPERTIES TRUST (AL)

Exchange	Symbol	Price	52Wk Range	Yield	P/E
NYS	CLP	$40.80 (5/31/2005)	42.44-35.55	6.62	11.76

*7 Year Price Score 108.28 *NYSE Composite Index=100 *12 Month Price Score 96.32

Interim Earnings (Per Share)

Qtr.	Mar	Jun	Sep	Dec
2002	0.60	0.97	0.53	0.48
2003	0.52	0.15	0.26	0.37
2004	0.50	0.24	0.18	0.54
2005	2.51	...	...	...

Interim Dividends (Per Share)

Amt	Decl	Ex	Rec	Pay
0.67Q	7/20/2004	7/28/2004	7/30/2004	8/6/2004
0.67Q	10/19/2004	10/27/2004	10/29/2004	11/5/2004
0.675Q	1/21/2005	1/27/2005	1/31/2005	2/7/2005
0.675Q	4/27/2005	5/5/2005	5/9/2005	5/16/2005

Indicated Div: $2.70

Valuation Analysis

Forecast P/E	10.66 (5/28/2005)		
Market Cap	$1.1 Billion	Book Value	675.1 Million
Price/Book	1.69	Price/Sales	3.13

Dividend Achiever Status

Rank	280	10 Year Growth Rate	4.47%
Total Years of Dividend Growth			10

Business Summary: Property, Real Estate & Development (MIC: 8.3 SIC: 798 NAIC: 25930)

Colonial Properties is a self-administered equity real estate investment trust. Co. owns, develops and operates multifamily, office and retail properties in the Sunbelt region of the U.S. Co. is a fully-integrated real estate company, whose activities include ownership of a diversified portfolio of 153 wholly and partially-owned properties as of Dec 31 2004, located in Alabama, Arizona, Florida, Georgia, Mississippi, Nevada, New Mexico, North Carolina, South Carolina, Tennessee, Texas, and Virginia. Co. is the direct general partner of, and holds approx. 72.7% of the interests in, Colonial Realty Limited Partnership, a Delaware limited partnership.

Recent Developments: For the quarter ended Mar 31 2005, income from continuing operations decreased 71.3% to $1,815 thousand from income of $6,333 thousand in the year-earlier quarter. Net income increased 330.8% to $73,600 thousand from net income of $17,084 thousand in the year-earlier quarter. Revenues were $91,770 thousand, up 29.2% from $71,028 thousand the year before. Operating income was $25,559 thousand versus an income of $23,880 thousand in the prior-year quarter, an increase of 7.0%.

Prospects: On Apr 1 2005, Co. announced that it has completed its acquisition of Cornerstone Realty Income Trust, Inc., which has assets primarily consisting of 87 apartment communities with 22,981 apartment homes, a third party property management business, apartment land under development and ownership in four real estate joint ventures. As part of the transaction, Co. assumed approximately $830.4 million of debt, of which $338.5 million was paid off subsequent to the closing of the acquisition. Looking ahead, Co. expects full-year 2005 earnings per share to range from $3.20 to $4.73 per diluted share, and funds from operations to range between $3.68 and $3.76 per diluted share.

Financial Data
(US$ in Thousands)

	3 Mos	12/31/2004	12/31/2003	12/31/2002	12/31/2001	12/31/2000	12/31/1999	12/31/1998
Earnings Per Share	3.47	1.45	1.29	2.58	2.02	1.82	1.83	1.59
Cash Flow Per Share	4.87	4.98	5.52	6.41	6.57	4.96	5.39	4.69
Tang Book Value Per Share	24.14	21.92	22.80	23.53	24.19	21.88	22.56	23.34
Dividends Per Share	2.685	2.680	2.660	2.640	2.520	2.400	2.320	2.200
Dividend Payout %	77.38	184.83	206.20	102.33	124.75	131.87	126.78	138.36
Income Statement								
Property Income	88,464	309,151	308,001	303,764	293,837	283,587	264,837	242,836
Non-Property Income	3,306	28,259	26,241	26,102	22,488	18,723	17,727	14,531
Total Revenue	91,770	337,410	334,242	329,866	316,325	302,310	282,564	257,367
Depn & Amortn	29,590	88,875	88,814	82,835	72,357	63,884	55,185	48,647
Interest Expense	23,696	78,933	66,666	65,265	71,397	71,855	57,211	52,063
Income Taxes	...	...	...	...	15	...	...	...
Net Income	73,600	54,618	52,265	73,377	55,609	49,590	55,776	50,222
Average Shares	27,824	27,462	25,232	22,408	20,792	21,249	24,478	24,641
Balance Sheet								
Total Assets	2,971,297	2,801,343	2,194,927	2,129,856	2,014,623	1,944,099	1,863,518	1,755,449
Long-Term Obligations	1,930,958	1,855,787	1,267,865	1,262,193	1,191,791	1,179,095	1,039,863	909,322
Total Liabilities	2,008,041	1,930,335	1,323,140	1,317,759	1,245,537	1,209,859	1,082,254	946,055
Stockholders' Equity	675,121	605,026	601,733	537,803	507,435	453,826	493,575	610,447
Shares Outstanding	27,962	27,599	26,394	22,850	20,976	20,742	21,872	26,147
Statistical Record								
Return on Assets %	4.29	2.18	2.42	3.54	2.81	2.60	3.08	3.19
Return on Equity %	17.29	9.03	9.17	14.04	11.57	10.44	10.10	9.12
Net Margin %	80.20	16.19	15.64	22.24	17.58	16.40	19.74	19.51
Price Range	42.44-33.93	42.44-33.93	40.31-30.77	38.95-31.15	31.60-25.20	28.63-22.69	28.63-22.00	32.13-24.38
P/E Ratio	12.23-9.78	29.27-23.40	31.25-23.85	15.10-12.07	15.64-12.48	15.73-12.47	15.64-12.02	20.20-15.33
Average Yield %	6.98	6.85	7.59	7.64	8.68	9.36	8.78	7.61

Address: 2101 Sixth Avenue North, Suite 750, Birmingham, AL 35203
Telephone: 205-250-8700
Web Site: www.colonialprop.com

Officers: Thomas H. Lowder - Chmn., Pres., C.E.O. John P. Rigrish - Exec. V.P., Chief Admin. Officer
ransfer Agents:

Investor Contact: 205-250-8880
No of Institutions: 133
Shares: 18,301,496 **% Held:** 65.38

COMERICA, INC.

Exchange	Symbol	Price	52Wk Range	Yield	P/E
NYS	CMA	$55.88 (5/31/2005)	63.46-53.17	3.94	12.15

*7 Year Price Score 93.77 *NYSE Composite Index=100 *12 Month Price Score 93.44

TRADING VOLUME (thousand shares)

Interim Earnings (Per Share)

Qtr.	Mar	Jun	Sep	Dec
2002	1.20	1.03	0.14	1.18
2003	1.00	0.97	0.89	0.89
2004	0.92	1.10	1.13	1.21
2005	1.16	...	...	...

Interim Dividends (Per Share)

Amt	Decl	Ex	Rec	Pay
0.52Q	7/27/2004	9/13/2004	9/15/2004	10/1/2004
0.52Q	11/23/2004	12/13/2004	12/15/2004	1/1/2005
0.55Q	1/25/2005	3/11/2005	3/15/2005	4/1/2005
0.55Q	5/17/2005	6/13/2005	6/15/2005	7/1/2005

Indicated Div: $2.20 (Div. Reinv. Plan)

Valuation Analysis

Forecast P/E	12.45 (5/28/2005)		
Market Cap	$9.4 Billion	Book Value	5.0 Billion
Price/Book	1.87	Price/Sales	3.00

Dividend Achiever Status

Rank	173	10 Year Growth Rate	9.92%
Total Years of Dividend Growth			21

Business Summary: Commercial Banking (MIC: 8.1 SIC: 021 NAIC: 22110)

Comerica is a bank holding company with assets of $51.77 billion and total deposits of $40.90 billion as of Dec 31 2004. Co. operates banking subsidiaries in Michigan, Texas and California, banking operations in Florida, and businesses in several other states. Co. is a diversified financial services provider, offering a broad range of financial products and services for businesses and individuals. Through its subsidiaries, the Company has aligned its operations into three major lines of business: the Business Bank, the Individual Bank and the Investment Bank. Co. also has an investment services affiliate, Munder Capital Management, and operates banking subsidiaries in Canada and Mexico.

Recent Developments: For the quarter ended Mar 31 2005, net income increased 22.8% to $199,000 thousand from net income of $162,000 thousand in the year-earlier quarter. Net interest income was $46,000,0thousand, up 3.4% from $44,500,0thousand the year before. Provision for loan losses was $100,0thousand versus $6,500,0thousand in the prior-year quarter, a decrease of 98.5%. Non-interest income fell 4.5% to $420,000 thousand, while non-interest expense advanced 1.4% to $374,000 thousand.

Prospects: Results are being positively affected by improving credit trends and Co.'s efforts to reduce expenses. In addition, Co. is enjoying solid loan growth across all businesses and geographies. Co. noted that average loans increased approximately $1.00 billion, or nearly 10.0% on an annualized basis, in the first quarter of 2005. Meanwhile, net interest margin improvement is being driven by an increased mix of noninterest-bearing deposits and the effects of the change in earning asset mix from short-term investments to loans. Going forward, Co. will continue to focus on its strategy of relationship-based middle market lending to small businesses and individuals.

Financial Data

(US$ in Thousands)	3 Mos	12/31/2004	12/31/2003	12/31/2002	12/31/2001	12/31/2000	12/31/1999	12/31/1998
Earnings Per Share	4.60	4.36	3.75	3.40	3.88	4.63	4.14	3.72
Cash Flow Per Share	6.15	5.96	7.55	7.02	5.63	5.07	6.64	4.43
Tang Book Value Per Share	29.81	29.95	29.20	28.30	27.15	23.94	20.60	17.94
Dividends Per Share	2.110	2.080	2.000	1.920	1.760	1.600	1.440	1.280
Dividend Payout %	45.87	47.71	53.33	56.47	45.36	34.56	34.78	34.41
Income Statement								
Interest Income	607,000	2,237,000	2,412,000	2,797,000	3,393,547	3,261,636	2,672,710	2,616,774
Interest Expense	147,000	427,000	486,000	665,000	1,291,209	1,602,785	1,125,569	1,155,503
Net Interest Income	460,000	1,810,000	1,926,000	2,132,000	2,102,338	1,658,851	1,547,141	1,461,271
Provision for Losses	1,000	64,000	377,000	635,000	236,000	145,000	114,000	113,000
Non-Interest Income	210,000	857,000	887,000	900,000	803,332	825,890	716,888	603,148
Non-Interest Expense	374,000	1,493,000	1,483,000	1,515,000	1,559,033	1,188,370	1,116,957	1,020,044
Income Before Taxes	295,000	1,110,000	953,000	882,000	1,110,637	1,151,371	1,033,072	931,375
Income Taxes	96,000	353,000	292,000	281,000	401,059	402,045	360,483	324,299
Net Income	199,000	757,000	661,000	601,000	709,578	749,326	672,589	607,076
Average Shares	171,000	174,000	176,000	177,000	177,665	156,398	158,397	158,757
Balance Sheet								
Net Loans & Leases	41,100,000	40,170,000	39,499,000	41,490,000	40,541,248	35,522,235	32,216,808	30,152,454
Total Assets	53,510,000	51,766,000	52,592,000	53,301,000	50,731,973	41,985,185	38,653,332	36,600,831
Total Deposits	42,706,000	40,936,000	41,463,000	41,775,000	37,570,379	27,168,012	23,291,403	24,313,133
Total Liabilities	48,480,000	46,661,000	47,482,000	48,354,000	45,924,509	37,977,919	35,178,688	33,554,218
Stockholders' Equity	5,030,000	5,105,000	5,110,000	4,947,000	4,807,464	4,007,266	3,474,644	3,046,613
Shares Outstanding	168,746	170,475	175,000	174,775	177,074	156,943	156,517	155,881
Statistical Record								
Return on Assets %	1.47	1.45	1.25	1.16	1.53	1.85	1.79	1.67
Return on Equity %	15.69	14.78	13.15	12.32	16.10	19.98	20.63	20.90
Net Interest Margin %	75.78	80.91	79.85	76.22	61.95	50.86	57.89	55.84
Efficiency Ratio %	45.78	48.25	44.95	40.98	37.15	29.07	32.95	31.68
Loans to Deposits	0.96	0.98	0.95	0.99	1.08	1.31	1.38	1.24
Price Range	63.46-51.02	63.46-51.02	56.31-37.61	65.30-35.53	64.95-44.66	60.31-33.81	69.75-44.94	71.58-50.13
P/E Ratio	13.80-11.09	14.56-11.70	15.02-10.03	19.21-10.45	16.74-11.51	13.03-7.30	16.85-10.85	19.24-13.47
Average Yield %	3.65	3.62	4.33	3.47	3.11	3.29	2.45	1.99

Address: Comerica Tower at Detroit Center, 500 Woodward Avenue, MC 3391, Detroit, MI 48226-3509
Telephone: 313-222-9743
Web Site: www.comerica.com

Officers: Ralph W. Babb Jr. - Chmn., Pres., C.E.O. Elizabeth S. Acton - Exec. V.P., C.F.O. **Transfer Agents:** Wells Fargo Shareowner Services, South St. Paul, MN

Investor Contact: 313-222-2840
No of Institutions: 360
Shares: 106,810,592 **% Held:** 62.76

COMMERCE BANCORP, INC. (NJ)

Exchange	Symbol	Price	52Wk Range	Yield	P/E
NYS	CBH	$27.75 (5/31/2005)	32.85-24.12	1.59	16.23

*7 Year Price Score 137.94 *NYSE Composite Index=100 *12 Month Price Score 96.90

Interim Earnings (Per Share)

Qtr.	Mar	Jun	Sep	Dec
2002	0.23	0.25	0.27	0.28
2003	0.30	0.32	0.34	0.35
2004	0.38	0.40	0.42	0.44
2005	0.45	...	...	...

Interim Dividends (Per Share)

Amt	Decl	Ex	Rec	Pay
0.095Q	9/21/2004	9/30/2004	10/4/2004	10/20/2004
0.11Q	12/21/2004	1/4/2005	1/6/2005	1/20/2005
2-for-1	2/15/2005	3/8/2005	2/25/2005	3/7/2005
0.11Q	3/15/2005	3/30/2005	4/1/2005	4/15/2005

Indicated Div: $0.44 (Div. Reinv. Plan)

Valuation Analysis

Forecast P/E	N/A		
Market Cap	$4.5 Billion	Book Value	1.7 Billion
Price/Book	2.63	Price/Sales	2.59

Dividend Achiever Status

Rank	88	10 Year Growth Rate	15.21%
Total Years of Dividend Growth			13

Business Summary: Commercial Banking (MIC: 8.1 SIC: 021 NAIC: 22110)

Commerce Bancorp, with assets of $30.50 billion and deposits of $27.66 billion as of Dec 31 2004, is a bank holding company primarily serving the Metropolitan Philadelphia, New Jersey, Delaware and New York markets. Co. operates four bank subsidiaries: Commerce Bank, Commerce Bank/Pennsylvania, Commerce Bank/Delaware, and Commerce Bank/North. As of Dec 31 2004, these banks provided a full range of retail and commercial banking services through 319 retail branch offices. Lending services are focused on commercial real estate and commercial and consumer loans to local borrowers. Co. also has securities, investment banking and brokerage activities, and an insurance brokerage agency.

Recent Developments: For the quarter ended Mar 31 2005, net income increased 24.5% to $77,137 thousand from net income of $61,975 thousand in the year-earlier quarter. Net interest income was $278,901 thousand, up 1.5% from $230,212 thousand the year before. Provision for loan losses was $6,250 thousand versus $9,500 thousand in the prior-year quarter, a decrease of 34.2%. Non-interest income rose 20.2% to $103,689 thousand, while non-interest expense advanced 22.8% to $258,406 thousand.

Prospects: On May 5 2005, Co. announced that it has launched a Spanish language version of its Commerce Online Banking Web site. Separately, Co. is continuing to experience strong net income growth and higher net interest income despite margin compression caused by the flattening yield curve. Co.'s primary strength is in building customer relationships and growing market share in deposits, loans and related services. Consumer and small business loan growth is primarily due to Co.'s significant increase in branch locations, market expansion and additions in lending personnel. Co. expects to open between 55 and 60 new locations in 2005 in Metro New York, Metro Washington, D.C. and Metro Philadelphia.

Financial Data

(US$ in Thousands)	3 Mos	12/31/2004	12/31/2003	12/31/2002	12/31/2001	12/31/2000	12/31/1999	12/31/1998
Earnings Per Share	1.71	1.63	1.30	1.02	0.76	0.62	0.54	0.47
Cash Flow Per Share	3.25	3.08	3.67	1.46	0.05	0.79	(0.03)	0.04
Tang Book Value Per Share	10.56	10.42	8.35	6.77	4.83	3.87	2.99	2.98
Dividends Per Share	0.410	0.380	0.330	0.300	0.275	0.242	0.207	0.218
Dividend Payout %	24.05	23.31	25.29	29.41	36.42	38.89	38.16	46.26
Income Statement								
Interest Income	370,480	1,238,291	915,631	755,371	604,367	505,300	386,448	289,280
Interest Expense	91,579	220,506	159,765	182,616	203,041	208,370	142,081	115,553
Net Interest Income	278,901	1,017,785	755,866	572,755	401,326	296,930	244,367	173,727
Provision for Losses	6,250	39,238	31,850	33,150	26,384	13,931	9,175	5,867
Non-Interest Income	103,689	375,071	332,478	257,466	196,805	150,760	114,596	88,947
Non-Interest Expense	258,406	938,778	763,392	579,168	420,036	315,357	252,523	181,967
Income Before Taxes	117,934	414,840	293,102	217,903	151,711	118,402	97,265	74,840
Income Taxes	40,797	141,422	98,815	73,088	48,689	38,355	31,305	25,522
Net Income	77,137	273,418	194,287	144,815	103,022	80,047	65,960	49,318
Average Shares	176,323	172,603	148,924	141,806	136,204	128,444	121,860	104,794
Balance Sheet								
Net Loans & Leases	9,836,604	9,318,991	7,328,519	5,731,856	4,516,431	3,638,580	2,922,706	1,904,954
Total Assets	31,869,976	30,501,645	22,712,180	16,403,981	11,363,703	8,296,516	6,635,793	4,894,065
Total Deposits	29,487,958	27,658,885	20,701,400	14,548,841	10,185,594	7,387,594	5,608,920	4,435,115
Total Liabilities	30,164,017	28,835,940	21,434,892	15,485,971	10,727,133	7,804,292	6,279,037	4,593,349
Stockholders' Equity	1,705,959	1,665,705	1,277,288	918,010	636,570	492,224	356,756	300,716
Shares Outstanding	161,591	159,840	153,012	135,666	131,665	127,045	119,377	100,821
Statistical Record								
Return on Assets %	1.02	1.02	0.99	1.04	1.05	1.07	1.14	1.12
Return on Equity %	18.27	18.53	17.70	18.63	18.25	18.81	20.06	17.89
Net Interest Margin %	75.28	82.19	82.55	75.82	66.40	58.76	63.23	60.05
Efficiency Ratio %	54.50	58.19	61.16	57.18	52.43	48.07	50.40	48.11
Loans to Deposits	0.33	0.34	0.35	0.39	0.44	0.49	0.52	0.43
Price Range	33.38-24.12	33.38-24.12	26.65-18.18	25.12-18.21	19.67-13.45	17.50-7.83	11.90-9.45	11.99-7.81
P/E Ratio	19.52-14.11	20.48-14.80	20.50-13.99	24.63-17.85	25.88-17.70	28.23-12.63	22.05-17.50	25.51-16.62
Average Yield %	1.40	1.30	1.53	1.35	1.60	2.06	2.01	2.26

Address: Commerce Atrium, 1701 Route 70 East, Cherry Hill, NJ 08034-5400
Telephone: 856-751-9000
Web Site: www.commerceonline.com

Officers: Vernon W. Hill II - Chmn., Pres., C.E.O. Peter M. Musumeci Jr. - Exec. V.P., Sr. Credit Officer, Treas., Asst. Sec. **Transfer Agents:** Mellon Investor Services, LLP, New York, NY

Investor Contact: 888-751-9000
No of Institutions: 252
Shares: 129,463,144 **% Held:** 81.59

COMMERCE BANCSHARES, INC.

Exchange	Symbol	Price	52Wk Range	Yield	P/E
NMS	CBSH	$48.75 (5/31/2005)	50.20-42.29	1.97	15.63

Interim Earnings (Per Share)

Qtr.	Mar	Jun	Sep	Dec
2002	0.61	0.66	0.67	0.69
2003	0.63	0.68	0.75	0.74
2004	0.71	0.75	0.89	0.75
2005	0.73	...	...	...

Interim Dividends (Per Share)

Amt	Decl	Ex	Rec	Pay
0.219Q	10/22/2004	11/24/2004	11/29/2004	12/13/2004
5%	10/22/2004	11/24/2004	11/29/2004	12/13/2004
0.24Q	1/28/2005	3/7/2005	3/9/2005	3/28/2005
0.24Q	4/20/2005	6/3/2005	6/7/2005	6/27/2005

Indicated Div: $0.96 (Div. Reinv. Plan)

Valuation Analysis

Forecast P/E	14.61 (6/2/2005)		
Market Cap	$3.3 Billion	Book Value	1.4 Billion
Price/Book	2.39	Price/Sales	3.47

Dividend Achiever Status

Rank	123	**10 Year Growth Rate**	13.04%
Total Years of Dividend Growth			36

Business Summary: Commercial Banking (MIC: 8.1 SIC: 022 NAIC: 22110)

Commerce Bancshares is a bank holding company. Co. conducts its principal activities through its banking and non-banking subsidiaries from approximately 330 locations throughout Missouri, Illinois and Kansas. Co. owns three national banking associations, which are headquartered in Missouri, Kansas and Nebraska. The Nebraska bank is limited to the issuance of credit cards. Principal activities include retail and commercial banking, investment management, securities brokerage, mortgage banking, credit related insurance, venture capital and real estate activities. As of Dec 31 2004, Co. had total assets of $14.25 billion and total deposits of $10.43 billion.

Recent Developments: For the quarter ended Mar 31 2005, net income decreased 2.9% to $49,846 thousand from net income of $51,324 thousand in the year-earlier quarter. Net interest income was $121,477 thousand, down 1.2% from $122,984 thousand the year before. Provision for loan losses was $2,368 thousand versus $10,250 thousand in the prior-year quarter, a decrease of 76.9%. Non-interest income fell 6.1% to $80,691 thousand, while non-interest expense advanced 4.2% to $123,922 thousand.

Prospects: Co.'s net income is being adversely affected by the declines in both net interest income and non-interest income. Co. is seeing significantly reduced provisions for loan losses due to favorable credit experience, however, its investment securities gains have fallen substantially versus the prior year. Meanwhile, Co. is continues to grow its average loan balances and a planned reduction in its securities portfolio is driving slightly lower net interest income. Separately, on Apr 11 2005, Co. announced the purchase of property at the corner of South National and Lakewood St. where it will build a new south Springfield, MO Banking Center, which is expected to open in early 2007.

Financial Data

(US$ in Thousands)	3 Mos	12/31/2004	12/31/2003	12/31/2002	12/31/2001	12/31/2000	12/31/1999	12/31/1998
Earnings Per Share	3.12	3.10	2.81	2.62	2.36	2.27	2.03	1.81
Cash Flow Per Share	3.87	3.77	3.71	3.49	3.59	3.03	2.65	2.65
Tang Book Value Per Share	19.67	20.16	19.62	18.51	16.13	14.27	12.71	12.25
Dividends Per Share	0.897	0.876	0.707	0.561	0.527	0.486	0.448	0.412
Dividend Payout %	28.79	28.26	25.18	21.42	22.33	21.39	22.06	22.83
Income Statement								
Interest Income	160,853	610,090	617,410	652,553	750,962	812,168	750,626	728,471
Interest Expense	39,376	112,759	115,018	152,588	283,052	331,515	284,625	300,726
Net Interest Income	121,477	497,331	502,392	499,965	467,910	480,653	466,001	427,745
Provision for Losses	2,368	30,351	40,676	34,108	36,423	35,159	35,335	36,874
Non-Interest Income	80,691	326,931	301,667	280,572	277,512	252,808	236,209	214,037
Non-Interest Expense	123,922	482,769	472,144	452,927	439,638	430,381	419,015	379,344
Income Before Taxes	75,878	311,142	291,239	293,502	269,361	267,921	247,860	225,564
Income Taxes	26,032	90,801	84,715	94,004	87,387	89,347	81,647	75,473
Net Income	49,846	220,341	206,524	199,498	181,974	178,574	166,213	150,091
Average Shares	68,582	71,066	73,617	76,114	77,239	78,588	80,976	83,225
Balance Sheet								
Net Loans & Leases	8,275,150	8,172,965	8,007,458	7,745,326	7,508,509	7,778,220	7,453,850	6,929,760
Total Assets	14,103,272	14,250,368	14,287,164	13,308,415	12,902,806	11,115,117	11,400,936	11,402,023
Total Deposits	10,685,423	10,434,309	10,206,208	9,913,311	10,031,966	9,081,738	9,164,123	9,530,197
Total Liabilities	12,731,703	12,823,488	12,836,210	11,892,078	11,630,323	9,971,362	10,321,104	10,321,238
Stockholders' Equity	1,371,569	1,426,880	1,450,954	1,416,337	1,272,483	1,143,755	1,079,832	1,080,785
Shares Outstanding	67,256	68,337	71,366	73,980	75,751	76,063	79,607	81,959
Statistical Record								
Return on Assets %	1.53	1.54	1.50	1.52	1.52	1.58	1.46	1.38
Return on Equity %	15.33	15.27	14.41	14.84	15.06	16.02	15.39	14.56
Net Interest Margin %	75.52	81.52	81.37	76.62	62.31	59.18	62.08	58.72
Efficiency Ratio %	51.30	51.52	51.37	48.54	42.75	40.41	42.46	40.25
Loans to Deposits	0.77	0.78	0.78	0.78	0.75	0.86	0.81	0.73
Price Range	50.20-41.96	50.20-41.96	46.93-32.14	40.16-30.02	35.53-27.35	34.96-21.06	32.18-25.56	35.71-25.32
P/E Ratio	16.09-13.45	16.19-13.54	16.70-11.44	15.33-11.46	15.06-11.59	15.40-9.28	15.85-12.59	19.73-13.99
Average Yield %	1.95	1.92	1.85	1.55	1.69	1.83	1.53	1.26

Address: 1000 Walnut, Kansas City, MO 64106 **Telephone:** 816-234-2000 **Web Site:** www.commercebank.com	**Officers:** David W. Kemper - Chmn., Pres., C.E.O. Johnathan M. Kemper - Vice-Chmn. **Transfer Agents:** EquiServe Trust Company, N.A, Jersey City, NJ	**Investor Contact:** 800-892-7100 **No of Institutions:** 157 **Shares:** 26,284,484 **% Held:** 38.95

COMMERCE GROUP, INC. (MA)

Exchange	Symbol	Price	52Wk Range	Yield	P/E
NYS	CGI	$59.60 (5/31/2005)	69.70-45.66	2.55	8.95

*7 Year Price Score 136.07 *NYSE Composite Index=100 *12 Month Price Score 104.25

TRADING VOLUME (thousand shares)

Interim Earnings (Per Share)

Qtr.	Mar	Jun	Sep	Dec
2002	1.06	(0.01)	0.27	0.09
2003	0.40	2.22	0.71	1.66
2004	1.56	1.14	1.64	2.16
2005	1.72	...	...	...

Interim Dividends (Per Share)

Amt	Decl	Ex	Rec	Pay
0.33Q	8/20/2004	8/26/2004	8/30/2004	9/10/2004
0.33Q	11/19/2004	11/24/2004	11/29/2004	12/10/2004
0.33Q	2/18/2005	2/24/2005	2/28/2005	3/11/2005
0.38Q	5/20/2005	5/26/2005	5/31/2005	6/10/2005

Indicated Div: $1.52

Valuation Analysis

Forecast P/E	9.79 (5/28/2005)		
Market Cap	$2.0 Billion	Book Value	1.2 Billion
Price/Book	1.74	Price/Sales	1.10

Dividend Achiever Status

Rank	17	10 Year Growth Rate	24.20%
Total Years of Dividend Growth			10

Business Summary: Insurance (MIC: 8.2 SIC: 331 NAIC: 24126)

Commerce Group provides personal and commercial property and casualty insurance primarily in Massachusetts and in other states. Co.'s core product lines are personal automobile, homeowners, and commercial automobile. Co. markets its products exclusively through its network of independent agents in all states, except California, where it uses agents and brokers. Co. manages its business in four reportable segments: property and casualty insurance - Massachusetts, property and casualty insurance - other than Massachusetts, real estate and commercial lending, and corporate and other.

Recent Developments: For the quarter ended Mar 31 2005, net income increased 13.7% to $58,038 thousand from net income of $51,040 thousand in the year-earlier quarter. Revenues were $467,809 thousand, up 3.8% from $450,886 thousand the year before. Net premiums earned were $423,202 thousand versus $395,568 thousand in the prior-year quarter, an increase of 7.0%. Net investment income rose 4.6% to $29,087 thousand from $27,815 thousand a year ago.

Prospects: Co.'s results continue to benefit from its consolidated combined ratio, which improved to 89.1% from 93.7% for 2004. Co. attributed the decrease in the combined ratio to a decline in the loss ratio, partially offset by an increase in the underwriting ratio. Co.'s consolidated loss ratio for the first quarter ended Mar 31 2005 decreased to 66.0% from 71.3% during the same period last year. Co. attributed the improvement to several factors, including higher average earned premium revenue per automobile; more favorable loss reserve development; improved results from Commonwealth Automobile Reinsurers; and, and a decrease in the current year personal automobile bodily injury claim frequency.

Financial Data

(US$ in Thousands)	3 Mos	12/31/2004	12/31/2003	12/31/2002	12/31/2001	12/31/2000	12/31/1999	12/31/1998
Earnings Per Share	6.66	6.51	4.99	1.42	2.75	3.87	2.94	2.68
Cash Flow Per Share	10.61	9.87	8.13	6.94	3.16	4.32	3.57	1.81
Tang Book Value Per Share	34.31	33.45	28.40	24.53	24.44	23.08	18.73	18.57
Dividends Per Share	1.320	1.310	1.270	1.230	1.190	1.150	1.110	1.070
Dividend Payout %	19.82	20.12	25.45	86.62	43.27	29.72	37.76	39.93
Income Statement								
Premium Income	423,202	1,638,833	1,445,628	1,210,040	1,043,652	954,483	871,830	745,620
Total Revenue	467,809	1,806,571	1,640,822	1,257,119	1,153,838	1,099,480	987,540	852,330
Benefits & Claims	279,158	1,044,840	1,070,147	909,769	777,543	686,157	625,090	531,429
Income Before Taxes	83,760	304,186	219,305	52,026	115,425	170,066	128,790	124,467
Income Taxes	25,488	89,003	58,068	17,063	23,194	38,306	27,154	27,975
Net Income	58,038	214,431	160,943	46,755	93,094	132,080	102,588	96,492
Average Shares	33,823	32,952	32,254	33,028	33,794	34,121	34,940	36,042
Balance Sheet								
Total Assets	3,741,614	3,610,396	3,164,231	2,382,688	2,140,082	2,075,614	1,871,472	1,755,983
Total Liabilities	2,583,961	2,489,114	2,247,630	1,588,530	1,327,808	1,292,665	1,223,650	1,050,198
Stockholders' Equity	1,152,413	1,116,156	912,211	790,052	812,274	781,881	646,634	705,785
Shares Outstanding	33,588	33,322	32,060	32,116	33,130	33,753	34,359	38,000
Statistical Record								
Return on Assets %	6.19	6.31	5.80	2.07	4.42	6.67	5.66	5.50
Return on Equity %	20.77	21.09	18.91	5.84	11.68	18.44	15.17	14.24
Loss Ratio %	65.96	63.76	74.03	75.19	74.50	71.89	71.70	71.27
Net Margin %	12.41	11.87	9.81	3.72	8.07	12.01	10.39	11.32
Price Range	69.70-42.98	62.12-39.40	40.94-32.30	42.05-29.48	40.05-24.63	30.81-23.25	35.44-20.75	39.25-23.00
P/E Ratio	10.47-6.45	9.54-6.05	8.20-6.47	29.61-20.76	14.56-8.96	7.96-6.01	12.05-7.06	14.65-8.58
Average Yield %	2.47	2.69	3.40	3.31	3.46	4.24	4.41	3.20

Address: 211 Main Street, Webster, MA 01570
Telephone: 508-943-9000
Web Site: www.commerceinsurance.com

Officers: Arthur J. Remillard Jr. - Chmn., Pres., C.E.O. Gerald Fels - Exec. V.P., C.F.O. **Transfer Agents:** EquiServe Trust Company N.A., Kansas City, MO

No of Institutions: 97
Shares: 10,660,336 **% Held:** 31.76

COMMERCIAL NET LEASE REALTY, INC.

Exchange	Symbol	Price	52Wk Range	Yield	P/E
NYS	NNN	$19.40 (5/31/2005)	21.20-16.50	6.70	14.59

***7 Year Price Score 114.33** *NYSE Composite Index=100 ***12 Month Price Score 98.88**

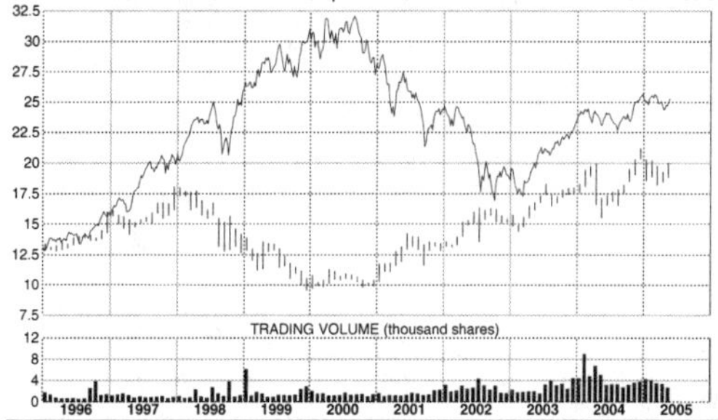

TRADING VOLUME (thousand shares)

Interim Earnings (Per Share)

Qtr.	Mar	Jun	Sep	Dec
2002	0.29	0.31	0.19	0.31
2003	0.23	0.28	0.32	0.30
2004	0.29	0.22	0.30	0.34
2005	0.47	...	...	...

Interim Dividends (Per Share)

Amt	Decl	Ex	Rec	Pay
0.325Q	7/14/2004	7/28/2004	7/30/2004	8/13/2004
0.325Q	10/15/2004	10/27/2004	10/29/2004	11/15/2004
0.325Q	1/14/2005	1/27/2005	1/31/2005	2/15/2005
0.325Q	4/15/2005	4/27/2005	4/29/2005	5/13/2005

Indicated Div: $1.30 (Div. Reinv. Plan)

Valuation Analysis

Forecast P/E	12.91 (5/28/2005)		
Market Cap	$1.0 Billion	Book Value	765.4 Million
Price/Book	1.32	Price/Sales	7.66

Dividend Achiever Status

Rank	311	**10 Year Growth Rate**	1.24%
Total Years of Dividend Growth			15

Business Summary: Property, Real Estate & Development (MIC: 8.3 SIC: 798 NAIC: 25930)

Commercial Net Lease Realty is a fully integrated, self-administered real estate investment trust. Co. and its wholly-owned subsidiaries acquire, own, manage and indirectly, through investment interests, develop primarily single-tenant retail, office and industrial properties that are generally leased under long-term commercial net leases. As of Dec 31 2004, Co. owned 362 properties in 38 states that are generally leased to major retail businesses under long-term commercial net leases. These businesses include Academy, Barnes & Noble, Best Buy, Borders, CVS, Eckerd, OfficeMax, The Sports Authority, United Rentals, and the United States of America.

Recent Developments: For the quarter ended Mar 31 2005, income from continuing operations increased 15.7% to $14,578 thousand from income of $12,602 thousand in the year-earlier quarter. Net income increased 59.8% to $26,004 thousand from net income of $16,268 thousand in the year-earlier quarter. Revenues were $33,081 thousand, up 11.7% from $29,610 thousand the year before. Operating income was $20,311 thousand versus an income of $16,735 thousand in the prior-year quarter, an increase of 21.4%.

Prospects: Co. is benefiting from increased revenue, driven largely from the efficient execution of streamlining its retail property sector activities. Meanwhile, Co. continues to be able to increase its stable rental revenue stream, and its acquisitions and development teams continue building relationships that should position Co. to take advantage of profitable opportunities and generate repeat business. For example, during the first quarter, Co. invested $47.0 million in its investment portfolio, including acquiring 21 properties. Co.'s investment portfolio occupancy was 97.5% at Mar 31 2005 compared with 96.7% at Mar 31 2004.

Financial Data

(US$ in Thousands)	3 Mos	12/31/2004	12/31/2003	12/31/2002	12/31/2001	12/31/2000	12/31/1999	12/31/1998
Earnings Per Share	1.33	1.15	1.13	1.09	0.91	1.26	1.16	1.10
Cash Flow Per Share	1.49	1.45	1.26	1.45	1.21	1.65	1.58	1.41
Tang Book Value Per Share	13.33	13.20	13.22	12.49	12.68	12.93	12.94	13.00
Dividends Per Share	1.295	1.290	1.280	1.270	1.260	1.245	1.240	1.230
Dividend Payout %	97.37	112.17	113.27	116.51	138.46	98.81	106.90	111.82
Income Statement								
Property Income	31,304	121,591	95,790	85,316	69,851	73,776	72,275	61,750
Non-Property Income	1,777	7,718	6,868	8,511	10,675	7,115	4,268	3,023
Total Revenue	33,081	129,309	102,658	93,827	80,526	80,891	76,543	64,773
Depn & Amortn	4,531	17,064	13,119	11,315	8,803	8,702	8,445	6,774
Interest Expense	(7,866)	32,463	27,731	26,720	24,952	26,528	21,920	13,460
Income Before Taxes	12,912	44,589	...	...	...	...	...	...
Income Taxes	(570)	(2,542)	...	...	...	...	...	...
Net Income	26,004	64,934	53,473	48,058	28,963	38,251	35,311	32,441
Average Shares	53,539	51,742	43,896	40,588	31,717	30,407	30,408	29,397
Balance Sheet								
Total Assets	1,321,406	1,300,048	1,208,310	954,108	1,006,628	761,611	749,789	685,595
Long-Term Obligations	503,935	506,341	437,338	345,689	327,933	258,681	242,271	154,807
Total Liabilities	554,459	541,022	477,556	404,967	441,988	367,710	358,427	301,705
Stockholders' Equity	765,380	756,998	730,754	549,141	564,640	393,901	391,362	383,890
Shares Outstanding	52,189	52,077	50,001	40,403	40,599	30,456	30,255	29,521
Statistical Record								
Return on Assets %	5.77	5.16	4.95	4.90	3.28	5.05	4.92	5.31
Return on Equity %	9.85	8.71	8.36	8.63	6.04	9.72	9.11	8.70
Net Margin %	78.61	50.22	52.09	51.22	35.97	47.29	46.13	50.08
Price Range	21.20-15.49	21.20-15.49	18.30-14.37	16.34-13.00	14.25-10.25	11.31-9.69	13.88-9.50	18.00-12.63
P/E Ratio	15.94-11.65	18.43-13.47	16.19-12.72	14.99-11.93	15.66-11.26	8.98-7.69	11.96-8.19	16.36-11.48
Average Yield %	7.04	7.06	7.70	8.50	9.97	11.94	10.38	7.92

Address: 450 South Orange Avenue, Suite 900, Orlando, FL 32801
Telephone: 407-265-7348
Web Site: www.cnlreit.com

Officers: James M. Seneff Jr. - Chmn. Robert A. Bourne - Vice-Chmn. **Transfer Agents:** Wachovia Bank, N.A., Charlotte, NC

Investor Contact: 407-265-7348
No of Institutions: 120
Shares: 22,051,716 **% Held:** 42.33

COMMUNITY BANK SYSTEM, INC.

Exchange	Symbol	Price	52Wk Range	Yield	P/E
NYS	CBU	$23.30 (5/31/2005)	28.35-21.26	3.09	13.79

Interim Earnings (Per Share)

Qtr.	Mar	Jun	Sep	Dec
2002	0.28	0.31	0.42	0.37
2003	0.38	0.38	0.44	0.30
2004	0.38	0.40	0.45	0.41
2005	0.43	...	...	...

Interim Dividends (Per Share)

Amt	Decl	Ex	Rec	Pay
0.18Q	8/19/2004	9/13/2004	9/15/2004	10/11/2004
0.18Q	11/19/2004	12/13/2004	12/15/2004	1/10/2005
0.18Q	2/18/2005	3/11/2005	3/15/2005	4/11/2005
0.18Q	5/12/2005	6/13/2005	6/15/2005	7/11/2005

Indicated Div: $0.72 (Div. Reinv. Plan)

Valuation Analysis

Forecast P/E	14.12 (6/2/2005)		
Market Cap	$706.5 Million	Book Value	460.4 Million
Price/Book	1.53	Price/Sales	2.67

Dividend Achiever Status

Rank	189	10 Year Growth Rate	9.05%
Total Years of Dividend Growth			13

Business Summary: Commercial Banking (MIC: 8.1 SIC: 021 NAIC: 22110)

Community Bank System is a bank holding company with $4.39 billion in assets and total deposits of $2.93 billion as of Dec 31 2004. As of Dec 31 2004, Co.'s wholly-owned community banking subsidiary, Community Bank, N.A., operated 125 customer facilities throughout 22 counties of Upstate New York and five counties of Northeastern Pennsylvania offering a range of commercial and retail banking services. Another Co. subsidiary, Benefit Plans Administrative Services, Inc., provides administration, consulting and actuarial services to sponsors of employee benefit plans.

Recent Developments: For the quarter ended Mar 31 2005, net income increased 19.5% to $13,334,000 from net income of $11,155,000 in the year-earlier quarter. Net interest income was $37,702,000, up 4.9% from $35,954,000 the year before. Provision for loan losses was $1,875,000 versus $2,050,000 in the prior-year quarter, a decrease of 8.5%. Non-interest income rose 23.1% to $12,959,000, while non-interest expense advanced 4.3% to $31,031,000 .

Prospects: Co.'s results are benefiting from decent growth from several non-interest income sources. For the first quarter ended Mar 31 2005, non-interest income, excluding securities gains, grew 6.8% to $11.2 million versus $10.5 million last year, aided by improvement from Co.'s employee benefits plan administration and consulting business. Deposit service fees and trust, investment and asset management fees also rose. Additionally, Co. noted that it took advantage of market conditions in the first quarter of 2005 by selling certain securities in order to maximize their expected total return attributes and shorten the average life of the portfolio, generating an after-tax $0.03 per share gain.

Financial Data (US$ in Thousands)	3 Mos	12/31/2004	12/31/2003	12/31/2002	12/31/2001	12/31/2000	12/31/1999	12/31/1998
Earnings Per Share	1.69	1.64	1.50	1.47	0.81	1.43	1.21	1.02
Cash Flow Per Share	2.76	2.85	2.78	2.24	1.92	1.94	2.16	2.41
Tang Book Value Per Share	7.58	7.90	7.37	7.33	4.87	6.32	4.04	4.50
Dividends Per Share	0.700	0.680	0.610	0.560	0.540	0.520	0.480	0.430
Dividend Payout %	41.42	41.46	40.80	38.23	66.67	36.49	39.67	41.95
Income Statement								
Interest Income	55,223	212,795	191,129	204,870	197,850	145,221	123,888	122,938
Interest Expense	17,521	61,752	59,301	77,020	101,195	74,012	55,947	58,543
Net Interest Income	37,702	151,043	131,828	127,850	96,655	71,208	67,941	64,395
Provision for Losses	1,875	8,750	11,195	12,222	7,097	7,182	5,136	5,123
Non-Interest Income	12,959	44,445	34,981	32,600	29,083	20,989	15,487	17,040
Non-Interest Expense	31,031	119,899	102,461	95,824	89,039	55,989	52,733	51,876
Income Before Taxes	17,755	66,839	53,153	52,404	29,602	29,027	25,559	24,436
Income Taxes	4,421	16,643	12,773	13,887	8,891	8,708	7,923	8,902
Net Income	13,334	50,196	40,380	38,517	19,129	20,319	17,635	15,728
Average Shares	31,192	30,670	27,034	26,334	23,650	14,271	14,590	15,341
Balance Sheet								
Net Loans & Leases	2,302,497	2,326,715	2,099,414	1,780,574	1,708,969	1,084,112	995,802	904,779
Total Assets	4,354,652	4,393,831	3,855,397	3,434,204	3,210,833	2,022,635	1,840,702	1,680,689
Total Deposits	2,976,953	2,928,978	2,725,488	2,505,356	2,545,970	1,457,730	1,360,306	1,378,066
Total Liabilities	3,894,226	3,919,203	3,450,569	3,109,166	2,942,853	1,883,260	1,732,214	1,560,523
Stockholders' Equity	460,426	474,628	404,828	325,038	267,980	139,376	108,487	120,165
Shares Outstanding	30,322	30,641	28,330	25,957	25,805	13,986	14,592	14,592
Statistical Record								
Return on Assets %	1.28	1.21	1.11	1.16	0.73	1.05	1.00	0.95
Return on Equity %	11.86	11.38	11.07	12.99	9.39	16.35	15.43	13.21
Net Interest Margin %	68.27	70.98	68.97	62.41	48.85	49.03	54.84	52.38
Efficiency Ratio %	45.51	46.61	45.31	40.35	39.24	33.69	37.84	37.06
Loans to Deposits	0.77	0.79	0.77	0.71	0.67	0.74	0.73	0.66
Price Range	28.35-19.25	28.35-19.25	25.13-15.55	17.01-13.07	14.82-12.45	13.02-10.13	16.31-11.31	19.09-12.50
P/E Ratio	16.78-11.39	17.29-11.74	16.75-10.37	11.57-8.89	18.30-15.37	9.10-7.08	13.48-9.35	18.72-12.25
Average Yield %	2.91	2.84	3.07	3.67	3.95	4.55	3.73	2.73

Address: 5790 Widewaters Parkway, DeWitt, NY 13214-1883 **Telephone:** 315-445-2282 **Web Site:** www.communitybankna.com	**Officers:** James A. Gabriel - Chmn. Sanford A. Belden - Pres., C.E.O. **Transfer Agents:** ChaseMellon Shareholder Services, L.L.C., Ridgefield Park, NJ	**Investor Contact:** 315-445-2282 **No of Institutions:** 100 **Shares:** 11,534,923 **% Held:** 38.05

COMMUNITY BANKS, INC. (PA)

Exchange	Symbol	Price	52Wk Range	Yield	P/E
NMS	CMTY	$24.76 (5/31/2005)	31.47-23.04	3.07	14.07

Interim Earnings (Per Share)

Qtr.	Mar	Jun	Sep	Dec
2002	0.36	0.37	0.38	0.37
2003	0.41	0.40	0.41	0.41
2004	0.41	0.43	0.45	0.44
2005	0.44	...	...	...

Interim Dividends (Per Share)

Amt	Decl	Ex	Rec	Pay
0.17Q	8/3/2004	9/14/2004	9/16/2004	10/1/2004
0.17Q	11/2/2004	12/15/2004	12/17/2004	1/3/2005
0.17Q	2/8/2005	3/15/2005	3/17/2005	4/1/2005
0.19Q	5/13/2005	6/14/2005	6/16/2005	7/1/2005

Indicated Div: $0.76

Valuation Analysis

Forecast P/E	13.60 (6/2/2005)		
Market Cap	$304.8 Million	Book Value	151.8 Million
Price/Book	2.01	Price/Sales	2.44

Dividend Achiever Status

Rank	163	**10 Year Growth Rate**	10.69%
Total Years of Dividend Growth			13

Business Summary: Commercial Banking (MIC: 8.1 SIC: 021 NAIC: 22110)

Community Banks is a financial holding company. Through its banking subsidiary, Co. conducts a full service commercial and retail banking business and provides limited trust services through 48 banking offices, which are located in Adams, Cumberland, Dauphin, Luzerne, Northumberland, Schuylkill, Snyder, and York Counties in Pennsylvania and Carroll County in Maryland. Lending services include secured and unsecured commercial loans, residential and commercial mortgages and various forms of consumer lending. Deposit services include a variety of checking, savings, time and money market deposits. At Dec 31 2004, Co. had total assets of $1.95 billion and total deposits of $1.31 billion.

Recent Developments: For the quarter ended Mar 31 2005, net income increased 6.0% to $5,487 thousand from net income of $5,175 thousand in the year-earlier quarter. Net interest income was $14,690 thousand, up 9.3% from $13,439 thousand the year before. Provision for loan losses was $550 thousand versus $850 thousand in the prior-year quarter, a decrease of 35.3%. Non-interest income fell 7.3% to $5,210 thousand, while non-interest expense advanced 6.5% to $12,659 thousand.

Prospects: Co.'s earnings are benefiting from improvement in net interest income, which is up in part to and expansion of net interest margin, a signal that pricing compression may be subsiding, after being a major obstacle to earnings improvement in the last several years as interest rates declined. At the same time, revenue growth from service and fee income sources continues to be a critical component of Co.'s revenue diversification initiatives. Co.'s non-interest income continues to grow as it continues to integrate financial service capabilities from non-bank acquisitions. Separately, Co. expects to complete its previously announced acquisition of PennRock Financial Services Corp. by mid-2005.

Financial Data

(US$ in Thousands)	3 Mos	12/31/2004	12/31/2003	12/31/2002	12/31/2001	12/31/2000	12/31/1999	12/31/1998
Earnings Per Share	1.76	1.73	1.63	1.47	1.15	1.29	1.17	1.03
Cash Flow Per Share	2.40	2.44	2.93	1.26	1.41	0.73	1.30	0.91
Tang Book Value Per Share	12.33	12.45	11.34	10.52	9.42	8.89	7.48	8.22
Dividends Per Share	0.680	0.672	0.627	0.546	0.484	0.440	0.413	0.386
Dividend Payout %	38.64	38.84	38.52	37.02	42.10	34.18	35.41	37.49
Income Statement								
Interest Income	26,183	99,799	94,865	96,700	98,075	79,578	66,264	57,000
Interest Expense	11,493	43,242	42,329	46,212	52,140	41,720	32,213	26,887
Net Interest Income	14,690	56,557	52,536	50,488	45,935	37,858	34,051	30,113
Provision for Losses	550	3,100	2,500	3,350	5,080	2,308	1,298	1,464
Non-Interest Income	5,210	23,213	20,441	13,975	12,141	7,363	5,668	4,960
Non-Interest Expense	12,659	49,993	45,718	39,300	36,521	25,774	22,937	20,025
Income Before Taxes	6,691	26,677	24,759	21,813	16,475	17,139	15,484	13,584
Income Taxes	1,204	4,879	4,359	3,367	2,879	4,288	3,681	3,534
Net Income	5,487	21,798	20,400	18,446	13,596	12,851	11,803	10,050
Average Shares	12,564	12,575	12,497	12,491	11,868	11,650	10,147	9,761
Balance Sheet								
Net Loans & Leases	1,231,150	1,201,530	1,065,433	892,225	845,146	684,044	581,859	495,308
Total Assets	2,012,653	1,954,799	1,860,130	1,679,898	1,509,734	1,121,372	971,824	851,674
Total Deposits	1,348,250	1,305,537	1,230,685	1,132,913	1,003,225	779,246	693,436	595,905
Total Liabilities	1,860,895	1,802,458	1,716,724	1,550,736	1,398,485	1,034,229	900,743	772,798
Stockholders' Equity	151,758	152,341	143,406	129,162	111,249	87,143	71,081	78,876
Shares Outstanding	12,312	12,236	12,230	12,108	11,707	9,779	9,447	9,518
Statistical Record								
Return on Assets %	1.12	1.14	1.15	1.16	1.03	1.22	1.29	1.53
Return on Equity %	14.63	14.70	14.97	15.35	13.71	16.20	15.74	15.20
Net Interest Margin %	56.11	56.67	55.38	52.21	46.84	47.57	51.39	52.83
Efficiency Ratio %	40.32	40.64	39.65	35.51	33.14	29.65	31.89	32.32
Loans to Deposits	0.91	0.92	0.87	0.79	0.84	0.88	0.84	0.83
Price Range	31.58-23.70	34.52-25.35	32.14-20.83	22.45-17.71	21.49-14.05	15.94-10.97	16.65-13.10	17.67-13.68
P/E Ratio	17.94-13.47	19.96-14.65	19.72-12.78	15.27-12.05	18.69-12.22	12.36-8.50	14.23-11.20	17.16-13.28
Average Yield %	2.42	2.30	2.54	2.71	2.78	3.19	2.80	2.46

Address: 750 East Park Dr., Harrisburg, PA 17111 **Telephone:** 717-920-1698 **Web Site:** www.communitybanks.com	**Officers:** Eddie L. Dunklebarger - Chmn., Pres., C.E.O. Donald F. Holt - Exec. V.P., Fin., C.F.O. **Transfer Agents:** Community Banks, Inc., Millersburg, PA	**No of Institutions:** 37 **Shares:** 1,655,146 **% Held:** 13.46

COMPASS BANCSHARES INC.

Exchange	Symbol	Price	52Wk Range	Yield	P/E
NMS	CBSS	$44.60 (5/31/2005)	48.67-40.78	3.14	14.67

***7 Year Price Score 131.34** *NYSE Composite Index=100 ***12 Month Price Score 95.71**

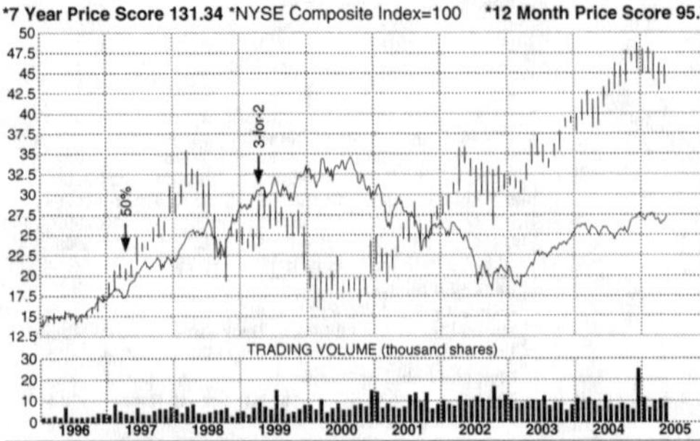

TRADING VOLUME (thousand shares)

Interim Earnings (Per Share)

Qtr.	Mar	Jun	Sep	Dec
2002	0.59	0.60	0.61	0.62
2003	0.64	0.68	0.68	0.69
2004	0.69	0.73	0.75	0.78
2005	0.78	...	...	...

Interim Dividends (Per Share)

Amt	Decl	Ex	Rec	Pay
0.313Q	8/17/2004	9/13/2004	9/15/2004	10/1/2004
0.313Q	11/18/2004	12/13/2004	12/15/2004	1/4/2005
0.35Q	2/21/2005	3/11/2005	3/15/2005	4/1/2005
0.35Q	5/17/2005	6/13/2005	6/15/2005	7/1/2005

Indicated Div: $1.40 (Div. Reinv. Plan)

Valuation Analysis

Forecast P/E	13.94 (6/2/2005)		
Market Cap	$5.5 Billion	Book Value	2.1 Billion
Price/Book	2.65	Price/Sales	2.85

Dividend Achiever Status

Rank	138	**10 Year Growth Rate**	12.03%
Total Years of Dividend Growth			23

Business Summary: Commercial Banking (MIC: 8.1 SIC: 021 NAIC: 22110)

Compass Bancshares is a bank holding company headquartered in Birmingham, AL, with total assets of $28.18 billion as of Dec 31 2004. Co.'s principal subsidiary is Compass Bank, which operates 382 banking centers, including 139 in Texas, 89 in Alabama, 73 in Arizona, 41 in Florida, 30 in Colorado, and 10 in New Mexico. In addition, Compass Bank operates loan production offices in Georgia and Maryland. Compass Bank provides general commercial banking and trust services such as receiving demand and time deposits, making personal and commercial loans and furnishing personal and commercial checking accounts.

Recent Developments: For the quarter ended Mar 31 2005, net income increased 14.5% to $98,756 thousand from net income of $86,247 thousand in the year-earlier quarter. Net interest income was $236,276 thousand, up 6.0% from $222,861 thousand the year before. Provision for loan losses was $20,273 thousand versus $24,345 thousand in the prior-year quarter, a decrease of 16.7%. Non-interest income rose 8.9% to $154,561 thousand, while non-interest expense advanced 5.6% to $221,872 thousand.

Prospects: Results are benefiting from strong deposit generation, particularly low-cost deposits, and solid loan production. Given the strength of Co.'s revenue growth, its sales and service culture and the momentum of its core businesses, Co. is cautiously optimistic about the remainder of 2005 in spite of the challenges of an uncertain economic environment. While the expectations of a rising interest rate environment and the flattening of the yield curve will likely continue to put pressure on percent net interest margins, Co.'s focus remains on generating sufficient volumes of high-quality loans and continued growth of low-cost deposits.

Financial Data

(US$ in Thousands)	3 Mos	12/31/2004	12/31/2003	12/31/2002	12/31/2001	12/31/2000	12/31/1999	12/31/1998
Earnings Per Share	3.04	2.95	2.69	2.42	2.11	2.00	1.88	1.57
Cash Flow Per Share	4.46	4.19	3.28	4.21	3.24	1.76	3.46	1.63
Tang Book Value Per Share	14.27	14.14	12.93	13.06	13.53	12.24	10.52	10.30
Dividends Per Share	1.288	1.250	1.120	1.000	0.920	0.880	0.800	0.700
Dividend Payout %	42.35	42.37	41.64	41.32	43.60	44.00	42.55	44.68
Income Statement								
Interest Income	347,952	1,273,526	1,277,287	1,386,923	1,517,721	1,432,844	1,247,571	1,134,544
Interest Expense	111,676	361,698	367,757	462,068	691,862	752,044	608,403	555,157
Net Interest Income	236,276	911,828	909,530	924,855	825,859	680,800	639,168	579,387
Provision for Losses	20,273	105,658	119,681	136,331	106,241	53,539	31,122	38,445
Non-Interest Income	154,561	617,590	526,184	441,063	376,378	298,904	241,109	222,500
Non-Interest Expense	221,872	868,478	797,883	752,429	685,770	569,589	517,916	491,017
Income Before Taxes	148,692	555,282	518,150	477,158	410,226	356,576	331,239	272,425
Income Taxes	49,936	185,498	176,282	162,759	139,829	115,985	114,194	91,545
Net Income	98,756	369,784	341,868	314,399	270,397	240,591	217,045	180,880
Average Shares	126,388	125,416	127,186	129,850	129,138	120,454	114,441	113,745
Balance Sheet								
Net Loans & Leases	18,920,462	18,598,583	17,120,920	16,248,490	13,515,893	11,340,877	10,645,849	9,964,608
Total Assets	28,795,231	28,184,628	26,963,113	23,884,709	23,015,000	19,992,242	18,150,752	17,288,908
Total Deposits	17,637,774	17,039,151	15,687,823	15,135,387	13,735,245	14,033,244	12,808,918	12,013,446
Total Liabilities	26,712,688	26,139,375	25,091,230	21,953,207	21,299,359	18,511,780	16,954,548	16,092,767
Stockholders' Equity	2,082,543	2,045,253	1,871,883	1,931,502	1,715,641	1,480,462	1,196,204	1,196,141
Shares Outstanding	123,826	123,264	122,086	126,116	126,800	120,972	113,708	113,350
Statistical Record								
Return on Assets %	1.36	1.34	1.34	1.34	1.26	1.26	1.22	1.18
Return on Equity %	19.07	18.83	17.98	17.24	16.92	17.93	18.14	16.78
Net Interest Margin %	67.90	71.60	71.21	66.68	54.41	47.51	51.23	51.07
Efficiency Ratio %	44.15	45.92	44.24	41.16	36.21	32.89	34.79	36.18
Loans to Deposits	1.07	1.09	1.09	1.07	0.98	0.81	0.83	0.83
Price Range	48.67-38.20	48.67-37.77	39.59-29.99	35.87-26.18	29.08-19.13	24.28-15.75	30.50-20.69	35.46-19.25
P/E Ratio	16.01-12.57	16.50-12.80	14.72-11.15	14.82-10.82	13.78-9.06	12.14-7.88	16.22-11.00	22.58-12.26
Average Yield %	2.90	2.91	3.23	3.16	3.74	4.64	3.06	2.48

Address: 15 South 20th Street, Birmingham, AL 35233
Telephone: 205-297-3000
Web Site: www.compassweb.com

Officers: D. Paul Jones Jr. - Chmn., C.E.O. George M. Boltwood - Sr. Exec. V.P., Corp. Banking **Transfer Agents:** Continental Stock Transfer & Trust Company, New York, NY

Investor Contact: 205-297-3331
No of Institutions: 242
Shares: 47,652,300 **% Held:** 38.56

CONAGRA FOODS, INC.

Exchange	Symbol	Price	52Wk Range	Yield	P/E
NYS	CAG	$26.15 (5/31/2005)	30.00-25.59	4.17	18.29

Interim Earnings (Per Share)

Qtr.	Aug	Nov	Feb	May
2001-02	0.36	0.44	0.31	0.36
2002-03	0.43	0.45	0.30	0.28
2003-04	0.37	0.51	0.38	0.40
2004-05	0.26	0.47	0.32	...

Interim Dividends (Per Share)

Amt	Decl	Ex	Rec	Pay
0.26Q	7/9/2004	7/29/2004	8/2/2004	9/1/2004
0.273Q	9/23/2004	10/28/2004	11/1/2004	12/1/2004
0.273Q	12/2/2004	1/28/2005	2/1/2005	3/1/2005
0.273Q	4/8/2005	4/28/2005	5/2/2005	6/1/2005

Indicated Div: $1.09 (Div. Reinv. Plan)

Valuation Analysis

Forecast P/E	16.76 (6/2/2005)		
Market Cap	$13.5 Billion	Book Value	4.9 Billion
Price/Book	2.77	Price/Sales	0.92

Dividend Achiever Status

Rank	157	**10 Year Growth Rate**	10.91%
Total Years of Dividend Growth			27

Business Summary: Food (MIC: 4.1 SIC: 011 NAIC: 11611)

ConAgra Foods is a food company that operates in different areas of the food industry, with a focus on the sale of branded and value-added consumer products. Co.'s operations are classified into three segments. The Retail Products segment includes branded foods in the shelf-stable, frozen and refrigerated temperature classes. The Foodservice Products segment includes branded and customized food products, including meals, entrees, prepared potatoes, meats, seafood, sauces, and custom-manufactured culinary products. The Food Ingredients segment includes branded and commodity food ingredients, including milled grain ingredients, seasonings, blends and flavorings.

Recent Developments: For the thirteen weeks ended Feb 27 2005, income from continuing operations was $164.5 million compared with income of $203.8 million a year earlier. Results for 2005 included a gain of $185.7 million on the sale of Pilgrim's Pride Corporation common stock. Net sales increased 1.3% to $3.57 billion from $3.53 billion the previous year. Retail Products sales eased to $2.08 billion from $2.09 billion last year. Foodservice Products sales rose 1.1% to $885.6 million. Food Ingredients sales increased 8.9% to $607.5 million versus $558.0 million the year before. Comparisons were made with restated prior-year results.

Prospects: Co.'s results are being adversely affected by increased input costs in its retail packaged meats business, as well as short-term manufacturing challenges resulting from installing new equipment and consolidating and transferring production across plant locations, which have produced lower sales realizations as orders for certain high-margin products go unfilled. Looking ahead, Co. is focused on improving margins and returns on capital over the long term with its multi-year marketing, operations and information systems initiatives. Co. expects operating improvements going forward as it increases prices to cover higher input and packaging costs and focuses on high-margin, high-volume products.

Financial Data

(US$ in Thousands)	9 Mos	6 Mos	3 Mos	05/30/2004	05/25/2003	05/26/2002	05/27/2001	05/28/2000
Earnings Per Share	1.43	1.48	1.52	1.66	1.46	1.47	1.24	0.86
Cash Flow Per Share	1.37	1.54	1.30	1.40	1.35	4.48	0.24	1.46
Tang Book Value Per Share	0.52	0.43	0.06	0.41	N.M.	N.M.	N.M.	1.22
Dividends Per Share	1.065	1.053	1.040	1.028	0.978	0.930	0.878	0.789
Dividend Payout %	74.71	70.88	68.58	61.90	66.95	63.27	70.85	91.74
Income Statement								
Total Revenue	11,181,700	7,611,800	3,495,600	14,522,100	19,839,200	27,629,600	27,194,200	25,385,800
EBITDA	1,228,200	778,500	303,300	1,778,500	1,949,100	2,292,900	2,120,300	1,506,000
Depn & Amortn	264,700	174,000	88,900	352,300	396,700	623,200	592,900	536,500
Income Before Taxes	963,500	604,500	214,400	1,151,300	1,276,100	1,268,200	1,104,100	666,100
Income Taxes	386,400	227,900	81,100	355,300	436,000	483,200	421,600	253,100
Net Income	539,700	377,300	135,000	879,800	774,800	783,000	638,600	413,000
Average Shares	520,300	517,500	521,400	530,700	530,700	528,000	514,300	478,600
Balance Sheet								
Current Assets	4,944,600	5,487,100	4,903,400	5,144,900	6,059,600	6,433,900	7,362,600	5,966,500
Total Assets	13,321,300	14,202,100	14,021,800	14,230,100	15,071,400	15,496,200	16,480,800	12,295,800
Current Liabilities	2,924,100	3,651,100	2,954,000	3,001,600	3,803,400	4,313,400	6,935,600	5,489,200
Long-Term Obligations	4,353,400	4,589,300	5,287,400	5,280,700	5,395,200	5,743,700	4,109,500	2,566,800
Total Liabilities	8,429,800	9,341,400	9,361,400	9,390,600	10,449,700	11,188,000	12,497,600	9,331,700
Stockholders' Equity	4,891,500	4,860,700	4,660,400	4,839,500	4,621,700	4,308,200	3,983,200	2,964,100
Shares Outstanding	517,751	514,998	514,286	521,194	536,765	537,040	537,067	492,212
Statistical Record								
Return on Assets %	5.33	5.42	5.43	5.91	5.08	4.91	4.45	3.39
Return on Equity %	15.18	15.96	17.06	18.30	17.40	18.94	18.43	14.10
EBITDA Margin %	10.98	10.23	8.68	12.25	9.82	8.30	7.80	5.93
Net Margin %	4.83	4.96	3.86	6.06	3.91	2.83	2.35	1.63
Asset Turnover	1.06	1.03	0.98	0.98	1.30	1.73	1.90	2.08
Current Ratio	1.69	1.50	1.66	1.71	1.59	1.49	1.06	1.09
Debt to Equity	0.89	0.94	1.13	1.09	1.17	1.33	1.03	0.87
Price Range	30.00-25.59	29.34-24.50	29.34-21.15	29.34-21.15	27.65-19.65	25.64-19.02	26.13-17.99	28.06-15.50
P/E Ratio	20.98-17.90	19.82-16.55	19.30-13.91	17.67-12.74	18.94-13.46	17.44-12.94	21.07-14.51	32.63-18.02
Average Yield %	3.88	3.92	4.00	4.10	4.06	4.06	4.12	3.49

Address: One ConAgra Drive, Omaha, NE 68102-5001 **Telephone:** 402-595-4000 **Web Site:** www.conagrafoods.com	**Officers:** Bruce C. Rohde - Chmn., Pres., C.E.O. Frank S. Sklarsky - Exec. V.P., C.F.O. **Transfer Agents:** Wells Fargo Shareowner Services, St. Paul, MN	**Investor Contact:** 800-214-0349 **No of Institutions:** 443 **Shares:** 289,613,824 **% Held:** 56.18

CONSOLIDATED EDISON, INC.

Exchange	Symbol	Price	52Wk Range	Yield	P/E
NYS	ED	$45.51 (5/31/2005)	45.78-38.61	5.01	19.62

*7 Year Price Score 91.95 *NYSE Composite Index=100 *12 Month Price Score 99.31

TRADING VOLUME (thousand shares)

Interim Earnings (Per Share)

Qtr.	Mar	Jun	Sep	Dec
2002	0.78	0.46	1.33	0.55
2003	0.72	0.29	1.16	0.21
2004	0.68	0.37	1.01	0.19
2005	0.75	...	...	...

Interim Dividends (Per Share)

Amt	Decl	Ex	Rec	Pay
0.565Q	7/22/2004	8/9/2004	8/11/2004	9/15/2004
0.565Q	10/21/2004	11/8/2004	11/10/2004	12/15/2004
0.57Q	1/27/2005	2/14/2005	2/16/2005	3/15/2005
0.57Q	4/21/2005	5/16/2005	5/18/2005	6/15/2005

Indicated Div: $2.28 (Div. Reinv. Plan)

Valuation Analysis

Forecast P/E	15.97 (6/2/2005)		
Market Cap	$10.0 Billion	Book Value	7.4 Billion
Price/Book	1.36	Price/Sales	1.01

Dividend Achiever Status

Rank	312	**10 Year Growth Rate**	1.23%
Total Years of Dividend Growth			30

Business Summary: Electricity (MIC: 7.1 SIC: 931 NAIC: 21121)

Consolidated Edison provides a range of energy-related products and services through six subsidiaries. Consolidated Edison Company of New York is a regulated utility providing electric, gas and steam service to New York City and Westchester County, New York. Orange and Rockland Utilities is a regulated utility serving customers in southeastern New York state and adjacent sections of northern New Jersey and northeastern Pennsylvania. Con Edison Solutions is a retail energy supply and services company and Con Edison Energy is a wholesale energy supply company. Con Edison Development owns and operates generating plants and energy and other infrastructure projects.

Recent Developments: For the quarter ended Mar 31 2005, net income increased 16.8% to $181,000 thousand from net income of $155,000 thousand in the year-earlier quarter. Revenues were $5,602,000 thousand, up 4.6% from $5,358,000 thousand the year before. Operating income was $283,000 thousand versus an income of $259,000 thousand in the prior-year quarter, an increase of 9.3%. Total direct expense was $1,997,000 thousand versus $1,894,000 thousand in the prior-year quarter, an increase of 5.4%. Total indirect expense was $521,000 thousand versus $526,000 thousand in the prior-year quarter, a decrease of 1.0%.

Prospects: Co.'s improved results reflect the continuing strengthening of the local economy and Con Edison of New York's (CENY) new gas and steam rate plans that took effect October 2004 and have their greatest effect in the winter months. Meanwhile, in March 2005, the New York Public Service Commission approved a three-year electric rate plan for CENY's electric delivery service. Under the plan, rates were increased $104.6 million, effective Apr 1 2005, and will be increased $220.4 million effective Apr 1 2007. Looking ahead to full-year 2005, Co. expects its earnings to be in the range of $2.75 to $2.90 a share.

Financial Data

(US$ in Thousands)	3 Mos	12/31/2004	12/31/2003	12/31/2002	12/31/2001	12/31/2000	12/31/1999	12/31/1998
Earnings Per Share	2.32	2.27	2.38	3.02	3.21	2.74	3.13	3.04
Cash Flow Per Share	6.41	5.58	5.97	7.07	6.36	4.51	5.39	5.83
Tang Book Value Per Share	30.19	27.00	29.15	25.40	24.21	26.39	25.90	25.88
Dividends Per Share	2.265	2.260	2.240	2.220	2.200	2.180	2.140	2.120
Dividend Payout %	97.63	99.56	94.12	73.51	68.54	79.56	68.37	69.74
Income Statement								
Total Revenue	2,801,000	9,758,000	9,827,000	8,481,860	9,633,962	9,431,391	7,491,323	7,093,048
Depn & Amortn	141,000	551,000	529,000	494,553	526,235	586,407	526,182	518,514
Income Taxes	(4,000)	284,000	327,000	388,881	(21,922)	(10,622)	(26,891)	(2,229)
Net Income	181,000	537,000	528,000	646,036	682,242	582,835	700,615	712,742
Average Shares	243,400	236,400	221,800	214,049	212,919	212,186	223,442	234,308
Balance Sheet								
Net PPE	15,400,000	16,106,000	15,225,000	13,329,175	12,248,375	11,893,419	11,353,845	11,406,543
Total Assets	23,430,000	22,560,000	20,966,000	18,820,310	16,996,111	16,767,245	15,531,476	14,381,403
Long-Term Obligations	6,979,000	6,594,000	6,769,000	6,206,917	5,542,305	5,446,913	4,559,148	4,087,403
Total Liabilities	16,078,000	15,265,000	14,288,000	12,677,761	11,070,708	11,045,243	9,869,856	8,106,185
Stockholders' Equity	7,352,000	7,054,000	6,423,000	5,921,079	5,666,268	5,472,389	5,412,007	6,025,605
Shares Outstanding	219,779	242,514	202,629	213,932	212,146	188,816	192,452	232,833
Statistical Record								
Return on Assets %	2.51	2.46	2.65	3.61	4.04	3.60	4.68	4.90
Return on Equity %	8.01	7.95	8.55	11.15	12.25	10.68	12.25	11.92
Net Margin %	6.46	5.50	5.37	7.62	7.08	6.18	9.35	10.05
PPE Turnover	0.66	0.62	0.69	0.66	0.80	0.81	0.66	0.63
Asset Turnover	0.44	0.45	0.49	0.47	0.57	0.58	0.50	0.49
Debt to Equity	0.95	0.93	1.05	1.05	0.98	1.00	0.84	0.68
Price Range	45.59-37.26	45.59-37.26	45.99-37.00	45.10-33.58	42.18-32.38	39.25-26.19	52.88-33.75	55.94-39.56
P/E Ratio	19.65-16.06	20.08-16.41	19.32-15.55	14.93-11.12	13.14-10.09	14.32-9.56	16.89-10.78	18.40-13.01
Average Yield %	5.38	5.35	5.53	5.35	5.72	6.65	4.89	4.57

Address: 4 Irving Place, New York, NY 10003
Telephone: 212-460-4600
Web Site: www.conedison.com

Officers: Eugene R. McGrath - Chmn., Pres., C.E.O. Joan S. Freilich - Exec. V.P., C.F.O. **Transfer Agents:** The Bank of New York, New York, NY

Investor Contact: 212-460-6611
No of Institutions: 345
Shares: 100,384,048 **% Held:** 41.38

CORUS BANKSHARES, INC.

Exchange	Symbol	Price	52Wk Range	Yield	P/E
NMS	CORS	$51.32 (5/31/2005)	53.12-38.70	2.73	13.69

*7 Year Price Score 161.76 *NYSE Composite Index=100 *12 Month Price Score 104.42

Interim Earnings (Per Share)

Qtr.	Mar	Jun	Sep	Dec
2002	0.36	0.48	0.51	0.37
2003	0.44	0.46	0.56	0.60
2004	0.62	0.85	0.98	0.95
2005	0.97	...	...	...

Interim Dividends (Per Share)

Amt	Decl	Ex	Rec	Pay
0.313Q	8/4/2004	9/23/2004	9/27/2004	10/8/2004
0.313Q	11/17/2004	12/22/2004	12/27/2004	1/10/2005
0.35Q	2/15/2005	3/22/2005	3/25/2005	4/8/2005
0.35Q	4/21/2005	6/22/2005	6/24/2005	7/8/2005

Indicated Div: $1.40

Valuation Analysis

Forecast P/E	13.69 (6/2/2005)		
Market Cap	$1.4 Billion	Book Value	604.7 Million
Price/Book	2.36	Price/Sales	5.30

Dividend Achiever Status

Rank	24	10 Year Growth Rate	23.40%
Total Years of Dividend Growth			18

Business Summary: Commercial Banking (MIC: 8.1 SIC: 022 NAIC: 22110)

Corus Bankshares is a bank holding company with total assets of $5.02 billion and total deposits of $4.10 billion as of Dec 31 2004. Co. provides consumer and corporate banking products and services through its wholly-owned banking subsidiary, Corus Bank, N.A. The two main business activities for Co. are commercial real estate lending and deposit gathering. The third, and smaller, business is servicing the check cashing industry. The bank has eleven retail branches in the Chicago metropolitan area and offers general banking services such as checking, savings, money market and time deposit accounts, as well as safe deposit boxes and a variety of additional services.

Recent Developments: For the quarter ended Mar 31 2005, net income increased 56.8% to $28,120 thousand from net income of $17,935 thousand in the year-earlier quarter. Total interest, loan fees, and dividend income soared 62.6% to $82,526 thousand from $50,732 thousand in 2004. Net interest income was $51,549 thousand, up 40.2% from $36,781 thousand the year before. Non-interest income rose 31.2% to $6,215 thousand, while non-interest expense advanced 1.4% to $14,428 thousand.

Prospects: Co. continues to see solid prospects for its commercial real estate portfolio. For instance, Co.'s total loans outstanding crossed $3.00 billion for the first time in the first quarter of 2005 and its pipeline of loans pending remains strong. Co.'s assets are continuing to grow as a result of strong deposit growth. Meanwhile, Co.'s net interest income is growing as a result of the continuing strong loan growth and increasing yields on loans. The higher loan yields are resulting from an increased focus on condominium loans, faster payoffs of all types of commercial loans causing loan fees to be amortized over a shorter time period and increases in short-term interest rates.

Financial Data

(US$ in Thousands)	3 Mos	12/31/2004	12/31/2003	12/31/2002	12/31/2001	12/31/2000	12/31/1999	12/31/1998
Earnings Per Share	3.75	3.40	2.04	1.73	1.90	2.62	1.41	1.38
Cash Flow Per Share	3.24	2.78	2.01	1.97	1.51	1.28	0.95	1.30
Tang Book Value Per Share	21.58	21.41	19.32	16.91	15.76	14.03	11.09	10.58
Dividends Per Share	1.288	1.250	0.830	0.318	0.308	0.297	0.287	0.278
Dividend Payout %	34.33	36.76	40.69	18.41	16.23	11.38	20.39	20.18
Income Statement								
Interest Income	82,526	222,059	170,239	152,878	188,630	223,676	196,580	187,525
Interest Expense	30,977	70,595	46,812	54,591	80,921	102,625	90,449	89,305
Net Interest Income	51,549	151,464	123,427	98,287	107,709	121,051	106,131	98,220
Provision for Losses	...	...	...	...	...	...	...	10,000
Non-Interest Income	6,215	14,066	14,554	15,821	17,881	36,416	20,241	20,539
Non-Interest Expense	14,428	56,273	52,533	47,472	51,100	52,908	63,096	51,889
Income Before Taxes	43,336	146,606	87,814	73,894	82,325	113,657	61,983	61,997
Income Taxes	15,216	48,667	29,404	24,580	28,142	38,903	21,257	21,369
Net Income	28,120	97,939	58,410	49,314	54,183	74,754	40,726	40,628
Average Shares	28,861	28,818	28,703	28,590	28,618	28,604	28,928	29,546
Balance Sheet								
Net Loans & Leases	2,973,269	2,760,946	2,397,323	1,705,340	1,434,788	1,512,279	1,695,267	1,515,814
Total Assets	5,597,947	5,017,787	3,643,830	2,617,050	2,659,322	2,598,467	2,388,198	2,589,415
Total Deposits	4,632,893	4,100,152	2,846,402	2,059,773	2,121,456	2,107,630	1,964,420	2,154,676
Total Liabilities	4,993,238	4,418,196	3,097,650	2,135,009	2,208,436	2,196,114	2,060,373	2,271,285
Stockholders' Equity	604,709	599,591	546,180	482,041	450,886	402,353	327,825	318,130
Shares Outstanding	27,808	27,795	28,036	28,238	28,319	28,286	28,738	29,102
Statistical Record								
Return on Assets %	2.33	2.26	1.87	1.87	2.06	2.99	1.64	1.68
Return on Equity %	18.68	17.05	11.36	10.57	12.70	20.42	12.61	13.33
Net Interest Margin %	62.46	68.21	72.50	64.29	57.10	54.12	53.99	52.38
Efficiency Ratio %	16.26	23.83	28.43	28.14	24.74	20.34	29.10	24.94
Loans to Deposits	0.64	0.67	0.84	0.83	0.68	0.72	0.86	0.70
Price Range	52.24-36.50	50.19-31.02	32.09-19.73	26.69-19.48	30.57-20.26	24.94-10.22	17.94-11.50	23.44-14.31
P/E Ratio	13.93-9.73	14.76-9.12	15.73-9.67	15.43-11.26	16.09-10.66	9.52-3.90	12.72-8.16	16.98-10.37
Average Yield %	2.92	3.02	3.32	1.37	1.25	1.97	1.89	1.42

Address: 3959 N. Lincoln Avenue, Chicago, IL 60613-2431 **Telephone:** 773-832-3088 **Web Site:** www.corusbank.com	**Officers:** Joseph C. Glickman - Chmn. Robert J. Glickman - Pres., C.E.O. **Transfer Agents:** Mellon Investor Services, LLC, Ridgefield Park, NJ	**Investor Contact:** 773-832-3088 **No of Institutions:** 106 **Shares:** 9,414,345 **% Held:** 33.80

COURIER CORP.

Exchange	Symbol	Price	52Wk Range	Yield	P/E
NMS	CRRC	$35.04 (5/31/2005)	37.05-25.67	1.14	13.69

*7 Year Price Score 170.34 *NYSE Composite Index=100 *12 Month Price Score 104.59

Interim Earnings (Per Share)

Qtr.	Dec	Mar	Jun	Sep
2001-02	0.33	0.36	0.51	0.99
2002-03	0.56	0.47	0.59	0.86
2003-04	0.48	0.47	0.63	0.92
2004-05	0.50	0.50	...	...

Interim Dividends (Per Share)

Amt	Decl	Ex	Rec	Pay
0.10Q	11/4/2004	11/10/2004	11/15/2004	11/26/2004
0.10Q	1/20/2005	2/9/2005	2/11/2005	2/25/2005
50%	3/10/2005	5/31/2005	5/6/2005	5/27/2005
0.10Q	3/10/2005	5/4/2005	5/6/2005	5/27/2005

Indicated Div: $0.40

Valuation Analysis

Forecast P/E 18.86 (5/28/2005)
Market Cap $284.6 Million Book Value 141.9 Million
Price/Book 2.01 Price/Sales 1.29

Dividend Achiever Status

Rank 63 **10 Year Growth Rate** 17.21%
Total Years of Dividend Growth 11

Business Summary: Printing (MIC: 13.4 SIC: 732 NAIC: 23117)

Courier and its subsidiaries are engaged in book manufacturing and specialty publishing. Co. has two business segments. Co.'s book manufacturing segment produces hard and softcover books, as well as related services involved in managing the process of creating and distributing these products. Co.'s specialty publishing segment publishes books in over 30 specialty categories, including fine and commercial arts, children's books, crafts, musical scores, graphic design, mathematics, physics and other areas of science, puzzles, games, social science, stationery items, and classics of literature for both juvenile and adult markets, including the Dover Thrift Editions.

Recent Developments: For the quarter ended Mar 26 2005, net income increased 7.9% to $4,154,000 from net income of $3,851,000 in the year-earlier quarter. Revenues were $53,495,000 , up 7.7% from $49,663,000 the year before. Total direct expense was $37,141,000 versus $34,136,000 in the prior-year quarter, an increase of 8.8%. Total indirect expense was $9,915,000 versus $9,636,000 in the prior-year quarter, an increase of 2.9%.

Prospects: Results are benefiting from strong sales to the education market, reflecting gains in its book manufacturing segment due to growing demand for Co.'s expanded capabilities in four-color textbook production. Repeated investment in service, technology and capacity is enabling the textbook business to outpace the overall market, as customers are relying on Co. to produce a larger share of their books. Meanwhile, within the specialty publishing segment, Co. has initiated changes in Dover Publications' sales and marketing organization to improve long-term sales. For fiscal 2005, Co. expects sales between $223.0 million and $228.0 million and earnings ranging from $2.60 to $2.75 per diluted share.

Financial Data

(US$ in Thousands)	6 Mos	3 Mos	09/25/2004	09/27/2003	09/28/2002	09/29/2001	09/30/2000	09/25/1999
Earnings Per Share	2.56	2.53	2.50	2.48	2.03	1.69	1.40	1.12
Cash Flow Per Share	4.07	3.70	3.57	3.98	3.76	3.71	3.00	2.00
Tang Book Value Per Share	13.38	13.15	12.67	11.42	9.00	7.15	5.55	6.43
Dividends Per Share	0.375	0.362	0.350	0.300	0.267	0.240	0.213	0.187
Dividend Payout %	14.68	14.35	14.00	12.10	13.16	14.17	15.24	16.67
Income Statement								
Total Revenue	104,764	51,269	211,179	202,002	202,184	211,943	188,320	163,991
EBITDA	18,791	9,383	42,457	39,376	35,278	33,729	24,273	21,363
Depn & Amortn	5,935	2,966	10,929	9,798	10,687	11,796	8,062	8,282
Income Before Taxes	12,925	6,444	31,551	29,526	24,111	20,034	15,886	12,557
Income Taxes	4,640	2,313	11,011	10,254	7,936	6,817	5,249	4,181
Net Income	8,285	4,131	20,540	20,120	16,175	13,217	10,637	8,376
Average Shares	8,326	8,290	8,221	8,120	7,992	7,797	7,589	7,467
Balance Sheet								
Current Assets	83,944	81,147	86,837	77,673	61,722	59,709	71,353	49,266
Total Assets	175,782	173,463	175,199	151,101	131,658	133,615	142,241	91,512
Current Liabilities	23,046	23,381	29,363	26,813	27,755	31,029	38,006	27,351
Long-Term Obligations	469	490	510	593	674	16,501	31,327	1,193
Total Liabilities	33,859	34,314	40,209	35,681	35,739	53,290	74,470	33,953
Stockholders' Equity	141,923	139,149	134,990	115,420	95,919	80,325	67,771	57,559
Shares Outstanding	8,123	8,052	8,031	7,931	7,822	7,668	7,524	7,274
Statistical Record								
Return on Assets %	12.81	12.78	12.62	14.27	12.23	9.61	8.95	9.38
Return on Equity %	15.95	16.11	16.45	19.09	18.41	17.90	16.70	15.65
EBITDA Margin %	17.94	18.30	20.10	19.49	17.45	15.91	12.89	13.03
Net Margin %	7.91	8.06	9.73	9.96	8.00	6.24	5.65	5.11
Asset Turnover	1.34	1.33	1.30	1.43	1.53	1.54	1.59	1.84
Current Ratio	3.64	3.47	2.96	2.90	2.22	1.92	1.88	1.80
Debt to Equity	N.M.	N.M.	N.M.	0.01	0.01	0.21	0.46	0.02
Price Range	37.05-25.46	35.29-25.40	30.41-22.63	24.89-15.74	19.78-9.33	12.73-8.00	9.11-6.33	9.19-5.33
P/E Ratio	14.47-9.95	13.95-10.04	12.16-9.05	10.04-6.35	9.74-4.60	7.54-4.73	6.51-4.52	8.20-4.76
Average Yield %	1.24	1.27	1.29	1.42	1.66	2.43	2.85	2.75

Address: 15 Wellman Avenue, North Chelmsford, MA 01863
Telephone: 978-251-6000
Web Site: www.courier.com

Officers: James F. Conway III - Chmn., Pres., C.E.O. George Q. Nichols - Corp. Sr. V.P. **Transfer Agents:** EquiServe Trust Company, N.A.

Investor Contact: 978-251-6000
No of Institutions: 55
Shares: 3,451,055 **% Held:** 42.85

CULLEN/FROST BANKERS, INC.

Exchange	Symbol	Price	52Wk Range	Yield	P/E
NYS	CFR	$44.61 (5/31/2005)	49.00-41.87	2.69	16.22

Interim Earnings (Per Share)

Qtr.	Mar	Jun	Sep	Dec
2002	0.52	0.61	0.51	0.58
2003	0.59	0.67	0.62	0.57
2004	0.62	0.65	0.68	0.72
2005	0.70	...	...	...

Interim Dividends (Per Share)

Amt	Decl	Ex	Rec	Pay
0.265Q	7/29/2004	8/30/2004	9/1/2004	9/15/2004
0.265Q	10/28/2004	11/29/2004	12/1/2004	12/15/2004
0.265Q	1/27/2005	2/25/2005	3/1/2005	3/15/2005
0.30Q	4/28/2005	5/27/2005	6/1/2005	6/15/2005

Indicated Div: $1.20

Valuation Analysis

Forecast P/E	14.72 (6/2/2005)		
Market Cap	$2.3 Billion	Book Value	808.0 Million
Price/Book	2.86	Price/Sales	3.61

Dividend Achiever Status

Rank	38	10 Year Growth Rate	19.98%
Total Years of Dividend Growth			11

Business Summary: Commercial Banking (MIC: 8.1 SIC: 029 NAIC: 22110)

Cullen/Frost Bankers is a financial holding company offering a broad range of banking and financial services to retail and commercial customers throughout Texas. As of Dec 31 2004, Co. operated 78 financial centers in Texas through its wholly-owned subsidiary, The Frost National Bank. In addition to general commercial banking, Co.'s other product and services include trust and investment management, investment banking, insurance brokerage, leasing, asset-based lending, treasury management and item processing. As of Dec 31 2004, Co. had consolidated total assets of $9.95 billion and total deposits of $8.11 billion.

Recent Developments: For the quarter ended Mar 31 2005, net income increased 13.6% to $37.4 million compared with $32.9 million in the equivalent 2004 quarter. Net interest income grew 15.0% to $90.1 million versus $78.3 million. Provision for possible loan losses totaled $2.4 million compared with $500,000 a year earlier. The provision for possible loan losses increased in part due to an increase in the level of criticized loans combined with an increase in the historical loss ratios applied to these pools of criticized loans. Also, the increase partly reflects the overall growth in the loan portfolio. Non-interest income rose 1.1% to $58.0 million, while non-interest expense advanced 4.5% to $90.5 million.

Prospects: Co. is seeing solid growth in net interest income. Co. attributes this momentum to the asset-sensitive nature of its balance sheet, which in a rising rate environment, will allow its margin to move up at a faster pace. Meanwhile, in Co.'s fee income, trust fees continue to grow steadily, up 9.0% for the first quarter of 2005 versus the year before. Also, Co. is seeing solid growth in loans, which is being driven by a positive economic climate in Texas and continued sales discipline, as well as a steady level of deposits. Separately, Co. announced a merger agreement with Horizon Capital Bank of Houston, which is expected to increase it presence and reach in the Houston area.

Financial Data

(US$ in Thousands)	3 Mos	12/31/2004	12/31/2003	12/31/2002	12/31/2001	12/31/2000	12/31/1999	12/31/1998
Earnings Per Share	2.75	2.66	2.48	2.23	1.52	2.03	1.78	1.39
Cash Flow Per Share	2.63	2.49	3.93	5.34	1.91	2.48	2.56	2.17
Tang Book Value Per Share	13.37	13.59	12.65	11.40	11.58	11.14	9.64	9.60
Dividends Per Share	1.060	1.035	0.940	0.875	0.840	0.760	0.675	0.575
Dividend Payout %	38.55	38.91	37.90	39.24	55.26	37.44	37.92	41.52
Income Statement								
Interest Income	112,923	393,544	368,946	389,898	460,976	512,331	447,580	428,091
Interest Expense	22,820	62,106	55,188	75,865	144,759	189,568	150,602	160,118
Net Interest Income	90,103	331,438	313,758	314,033	316,217	322,763	296,978	267,973
Provision for Losses	2,400	2,500	10,544	22,546	40,031	14,103	12,427	10,393
Non-Interest Income	58,039	225,110	215,361	200,709	192,891	170,865	157,085	138,666
Non-Interest Expense	90,487	345,030	326,035	312,142	352,606	313,280	293,015	278,506
Income Before Taxes	55,255	209,018	192,540	180,054	116,471	166,245	148,621	117,740
Income Taxes	17,888	67,693	62,039	57,821	38,565	57,428	50,979	42,095
Net Income	37,367	141,325	130,501	116,986	80,916	108,817	97,642	75,645
Average Shares	53,069	53,140	52,658	52,423	53,348	53,657	54,746	54,678
Balance Sheet								
Net Loans & Leases	5,326,442	5,089,181	4,507,245	4,436,329	4,445,727	4,471,380	4,108,383	3,592,987
Total Assets	9,849,192	9,952,787	9,672,114	9,552,318	8,369,584	7,660,372	6,996,680	6,869,605
Total Deposits	8,003,268	8,105,678	8,068,857	7,628,143	7,098,007	6,499,690	5,953,832	5,845,487
Total Liabilities	9,041,212	9,130,392	8,902,110	8,848,528	7,774,665	7,087,346	6,487,369	6,356,686
Stockholders' Equity	807,980	822,395	770,004	703,790	594,919	573,026	509,311	512,919
Shares Outstanding	51,817	51,923	51,776	51,295	51,355	51,430	52,823	53,426
Statistical Record								
Return on Assets %	1.47	1.44	1.36	1.31	1.01	1.48	1.41	1.25
Return on Equity %	18.37	17.70	17.71	18.02	13.86	20.05	19.10	16.42
Net Interest Margin %	79.79	84.22	85.04	80.54	68.60	63.00	66.35	62.60
Efficiency Ratio %	52.93	55.77	55.80	52.85	53.93	45.86	48.46	49.14
Loans to Deposits	0.67	0.63	0.56	0.58	0.63	0.69	0.69	0.61
Price Range	49.00-41.17	49.00-38.90	41.00-29.40	40.04-29.40	41.19-23.84	43.19-19.63	29.94-23.00	30.41-20.78
P/E Ratio	17.82-14.97	18.42-14.62	16.53-11.85	17.96-13.18	27.10-15.68	21.27-9.67	16.82-12.92	21.88-14.95
Average Yield %	2.33	2.35	2.69	2.53	2.54	2.69	2.58	2.14

Address: 100 W. Houston Street, San Antonio, TX 78205 **Telephone:** 210-220-4011 **Web Site:** www.frostbank.com	**Officers:** Tom C. Frost - Sr. Chmn. Richard W. Evans Jr. - Chmn., C.E.O. **Transfer Agents:** Bank of New York, New York, NY	**Investor Contact:** 210-220-5632 **No of Institutions:** 171 **Shares:** 33,814,452 **% Held:** 65.15

CVB FINANCIAL CORP.

Exchange	Symbol	Price	52Wk Range	Yield	P/E
NMS	CVBF	$18.44 (5/31/2005)	22.34-16.16	2.39	16.32

*7 Year Price Score 143.65 *NYSE Composite Index=100 *12 Month Price Score 93.62

Interim Earnings (Per Share)

Qtr.	Mar	Jun	Sep	Dec
2002	0.20	0.19	0.21	0.20
2003	0.21	0.20	0.22	0.23
2004	0.16	0.29	0.28	0.27
2005	0.29	...	...	...

Interim Dividends (Per Share)

Amt	Decl	Ex	Rec	Pay
0.104Q	9/15/2004	9/27/2004	9/29/2004	10/14/2004
5-for-4	12/15/2004	1/14/2005	12/29/2004	1/13/2005
0.11Q	12/15/2004	12/28/2004	12/30/2004	1/13/2005
0.11Q	3/18/2005	3/31/2005	4/4/2005	4/18/2005

Indicated Div: $0.44

Valuation Analysis

Forecast P/E	15.95 (5/28/2005)		
Market Cap	$1.1 Billion	Book Value	324.2 Million
Price/Book	3.51	Price/Sales	4.70

Dividend Achiever Status

Rank	26	10 Year Growth Rate	23.32%
Total Years of Dividend Growth			14

Business Summary: Commercial Banking (MIC: 8.1 SIC: 022 NAIC: 22110)

CVB Financial is a bank holding company, with assets of $4.51 billion and deposits of $2.88 billion as of Dec 31 2004. Co.'s Citizens Business Bank, operates 37 business financial centers located in the Inland Empire, San Gabriel Valley, Orange County, Los Angeles County, Fresno County, Tulare County and Kern County. Co. provides a full complement of banking products and services to businesses and consumers, including asset management services. Golden West Enterprises, Inc. provides automobile and equipment leasing, and brokers mortgage loans. Community Trust Deed Services prepares and files notices of default and reconveyances and acts as a trustee under deeds of trust.

Recent Developments: For the quarter ended Mar 31 2005, net income increased 75.7% to $17,701,000 from net income of $10,072,000 in the year-earlier quarter. Net interest income was $58,667,000, up 14.8% from $51,090,000 the year before. Non-interest income rose 806.4% to $7,079,000 , while non-interest expense declined 3.8% to $20,697,000 .

Prospects: On Mar 1 2005, Co. and its principal subsidiary, Citizens Business Bank, announced that they have completed the acquisition of Granite State Bank for an aggregate purchase price of $19 per share, or approximately $27.0 million, including the costs associated with the cancellation of stock options. Co. paid half of the total purchase price in its common stock and the other half in cash in a cash/stock election merger. The acquisition should expand Co.'s presence in the San Gabriel Valley market and compliment its business and banking strategy going forward.

Financial Data

(US$ in Thousands)	3 Mos	12/31/2004	12/31/2003	12/31/2002	12/31/2001	12/31/2000	12/31/1999	12/31/1998
Earnings Per Share	1.13	1.00	0.86	0.81	0.66	0.57	0.43	0.41
Cash Flow Per Share	1.24	1.25	1.19	1.02	0.67	0.72	0.70	0.59
Tang Book Value Per Share	4.55	4.81	4.30	4.08	3.58	3.05	2.27	2.17
Dividends Per Share	0.420	0.406	0.445	0.320	0.256	0.203	0.162	0.123
Dividend Payout %	37.17	40.60	51.75	39.64	38.94	35.48	37.65	30.05
Income Statement								
Interest Income	55,996	197,702	166,346	154,323	155,877	150,867	128,478	96,840
Interest Expense	15,059	46,517	37,053	40,439	52,806	56,760	38,466	31,248
Net Interest Income	40,937	151,185	129,293	113,884	103,071	94,107	90,012	65,592
Provision for Losses	...	...	...	...	1,750	2,800	2,700	2,500
Non-Interest Income	7,079	27,907	29,989	29,018	22,192	19,023	18,630	14,976
Non-Interest Expense	20,697	89,722	77,794	66,056	60,155	56,345	64,737	45,024
Income Before Taxes	27,319	89,370	81,488	76,846	63,358	53,985	41,205	33,043
Income Taxes	9,618	27,884	28,656	27,101	23,300	19,302	15,245	12,256
Net Income	17,701	61,486	52,832	49,745	40,058	34,683	25,960	20,787
Average Shares	61,730	61,279	61,387	61,294	60,869	60,512	60,183	50,871
Balance Sheet								
Net Loans & Leases	2,184,021	2,117,580	1,738,659	1,424,343	1,167,071	1,032,341	935,791	675,668
Total Assets	4,831,993	4,511,011	3,854,349	3,123,411	2,514,102	2,307,996	2,010,757	1,555,207
Total Deposits	3,017,194	2,875,039	2,660,510	2,309,964	1,876,959	1,595,030	1,501,073	1,215,305
Total Liabilities	4,507,762	4,193,528	3,567,628	2,863,590	2,293,354	2,119,366	1,869,987	1,439,500
Stockholders' Equity	324,231	317,483	286,721	259,821	220,748	188,630	140,770	115,707
Shares Outstanding	61,666	60,666	60,361	59,858	59,781	59,424	58,412	48,838
Statistical Record								
Return on Assets %	1.56	1.47	1.51	1.76	1.66	1.60	1.46	1.48
Return on Equity %	22.27	20.30	19.33	20.70	19.57	21.00	20.24	19.09
Net Interest Margin %	73.11	76.47	77.73	73.80	66.12	62.38	70.06	67.73
Efficiency Ratio %	32.81	39.77	39.62	36.03	33.78	33.17	44.01	40.27
Loans to Deposits	0.72	0.74	0.65	0.62	0.62	0.65	0.62	0.56
Price Range	22.34-15.72	22.34-15.13	16.10-13.35	15.55-10.01	11.43-6.75	8.42-5.71	10.03-6.37	8.87-5.77
P/E Ratio	19.77-13.91	22.34-15.13	18.72-15.53	19.19-12.35	17.31-10.23	14.77-10.02	23.32-14.81	21.63-14.07
Average Yield %	2.29	2.30	3.02	2.57	2.97	2.99	2.03	1.69

Address: 701 North Haven Avenue, Suite 350, Ontario, CA 91764 **Telephone:** 909-980-4030 **Web Site:** www.cbbank.com	**Officers:** George A. Borba - Chmn. D. Linn Wiley - Pres., C.E.O. **Transfer Agents:** U.S. Stock Transfer Corporation, Glendale, CA	**Investor Contact:** 909-980-4030 **No of Institutions:** 66 **Shares:** 8,873,948 **% Held:** 14.43

DANAHER CORP.

Exchange	Symbol	Price	52Wk Range	Yield	P/E
NYS	DHR	$55.13 (5/31/2005)	58.64-46.80	0.11	22.69

***7 Year Price Score 139.61** *NYSE Composite Index=100 ***12 Month Price Score 94.76**

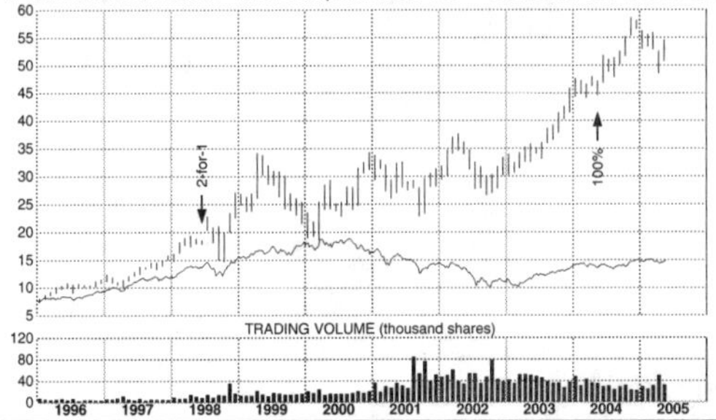

TRADING VOLUME (thousand shares)

Interim Earnings (Per Share)

Qtr.	Mar	Jun	Sep	Dec
2002	(0.29)	0.33	0.37	0.52
2003	0.33	0.40	0.44	0.53
2004	0.45	0.56	0.62	0.67
2005	0.58	...	...	...

Interim Dividends (Per Share)

Amt	Decl	Ex	Rec	Pay
0.015Q	9/17/2004	9/22/2004	9/24/2004	10/29/2004
0.015Q	12/20/2004	12/29/2004	12/31/2004	1/28/2005
0.015Q	3/21/2005	3/22/2005	3/25/2005	4/29/2005
0.015Q	5/6/2005	6/22/2005	6/24/2005	7/29/2005

Indicated Div: $0.06

Valuation Analysis

Forecast P/E	20.05 (6/2/2005)		
Market Cap	$17.0 Billion	Book Value	4.7 Billion
Price/Book	3.60	Price/Sales	2.37

Dividend Achiever Status

Rank	109	**10 Year Growth Rate**	13.87%
Total Years of Dividend Growth			11

Business Summary: Metal Products (MIC: 11.4 SIC: 429 NAIC: 32510)

Danaher designs, manufactures and markets industrial and consumer products in three business segments: Professional Instrumentation, Industrial Technologies, and Tools & Components. The Professional Instrumentation segment offers professional and technical customers various products and services that are used in connection with the performance of their work. The Industrial Technologies segment manufactures products and sub-systems that are typically incorporated by original equipment manufacturers into various end-products and systems. The Tools & Components segment is primarily engaged in the production of general purpose mechanics' hand tools.

Recent Developments: For the quarter ended Apr 1 2005, net income increased 29.6% to $188.3 million compared with $145.2 million in the equivalent 2004 quarter. Revenues advanced 18.3% to $1.83 billion from $1.54 billion the year before. Gross profit increased 22.8% to $775.2 million, or 42.5% as a percentage of sales, versus $631.3 million, or 40.9%, a year earlier. The improvement in gross profit was primarily due to leverage on increased sales volume, ongoing cost improvements in existing business units and low-cost region initiatives, generally higher gross profit margins in businesses recently acquired, and cost reductions in recently acquired business units. Operating income grew 20.8% to $271.8 million.

Prospects: Results are benefiting from added sales from recent acquisitions and favorable foreign currency exchange rates. On Jan 5 2005, Co. announced that it has completed its acquisition of approximately 97.0% of the outstanding common shares of Linx Printing Technologies PLC, a U.K.-based supplier of industrial non-contact coding and marking equipment based on inkjet and laser technologies with fiscal 2004 revenues of approximately $93.0 million. Separately, Co. is targeting second-quarter earnings in the range of $0.62 to $0.67 per share. Looking ahead, Co. is projecting full-year 2005 earnings of between $2.67 and $2.77 per share.

Financial Data

(US$ in Thousands)	3 Mos	12/31/2004	12/31/2003	12/31/2002	12/31/2001	12/31/2000	12/31/1999	12/31/1998
Earnings Per Share	2.43	2.30	1.69	0.94	1.00	1.12	0.90	0.66
Cash Flow Per Share	3.54	3.33	2.81	2.36	2.12	1.79	1.48	1.23
Tang Book Value Per Share	N.M.	N.M.	0.99	0.01	N.M.	0.28	1.46	0.25
Dividends Per Share	0.060	0.058	0.050	0.045	0.040	0.035	0.030	0.028
Dividend Payout %	2.46	2.50	2.97	4.79	3.98	3.14	3.35	4.17
Income Statement								
Total Revenue	1,825,948	6,889,301	5,293,876	4,577,232	3,782,444	3,777,777	3,197,238	2,910,038
EBITDA	271,837	1,261,261	979,431	830,687	680,401	701,870	572,648	434,693
Depn & Amortn	...	156,128	133,436	129,565	178,390	149,721	126,419	108,651
Income Before Taxes	259,664	1,057,717	797,035	657,468	476,264	522,924	429,562	301,111
Income Taxes	71,408	311,717	260,201	223,327	178,599	198,711	167,938	118,165
Net Income	188,256	746,000	536,834	290,391	297,665	324,213	261,624	182,946
Average Shares	329,390	327,701	323,140	316,964	303,696	290,998	292,178	277,770
Balance Sheet								
Current Assets	2,916,956	2,918,690	2,942,151	2,387,266	1,874,615	1,474,306	1,202,117	886,904
Total Assets	8,622,702	8,493,893	6,890,050	6,029,145	4,820,483	4,031,679	3,047,071	2,738,715
Current Liabilities	2,206,931	2,202,286	1,380,003	1,265,312	1,017,294	1,018,540	708,786	688,705
Long-Term Obligations	927,536	925,535	1,284,498	1,197,422	1,119,333	713,557	341,037	412,918
Total Liabilities	3,883,774	3,874,211	3,243,341	3,019,546	2,591,897	2,089,346	1,338,317	1,386,884
Stockholders' Equity	4,738,928	4,619,682	3,646,709	3,009,599	2,228,586	1,942,333	1,708,754	1,351,831
Shares Outstanding	309,200	308,920	307,362	305,064	286,628	284,026	284,880	270,214
Statistical Record								
Return on Assets %	9.94	9.67	8.31	5.35	6.73	9.14	9.04	7.92
Return on Equity %	18.56	18.00	16.13	11.09	14.27	17.71	17.10	16.13
EBITDA Margin %	14.89	18.31	18.50	18.15	17.99	18.58	17.91	14.94
Net Margin %	10.31	10.83	10.14	6.34	7.87	8.58	8.18	6.29
Asset Turnover	0.90	0.89	0.82	0.84	0.85	1.06	1.11	1.26
Current Ratio	1.32	1.33	2.13	1.89	1.84	1.45	1.70	1.29
Debt to Equity	0.20	0.20	0.35	0.40	0.50	0.37	0.20	0.31
Price Range	58.64-44.48	58.64-43.99	45.98-30.23	37.66-26.62	33.84-22.77	34.34-18.56	34.28-21.56	27.16-14.69
P/E Ratio	24.13-18.30	25.50-19.13	27.20-17.88	40.07-28.32	33.84-22.77	30.66-16.57	38.09-23.96	41.15-22.25
Average Yield %	0.12	0.12	0.14	0.14	0.14	0.14	0.11	0.14

Address: 2099 Pennsylvania Ave. NW, 12th Floor, Washington, DC 20006-1813
Telephone: 202-828-0850
Web Site: www.danaher.com

Officers: Steven M. Rales - Chmn. Mitchell P. Rales - Exec. Chmn. **Transfer Agents:** SunTrust Bank

Investor Contact: 202-828-0850
No of Institutions: 464
Shares: 209,166,384 **% Held:** 67.65

DENTSPLY INTERNATIONAL, INC. (NEW)

Exchange	Symbol	Price	52Wk Range	Yield	P/E
NMS	XRAY	$57.05 (5/31/2005)	57.97-46.74	0.42	21.94

*7 Year Price Score 146.47 *NYSE Composite Index=100 *12 Month Price Score 100.62

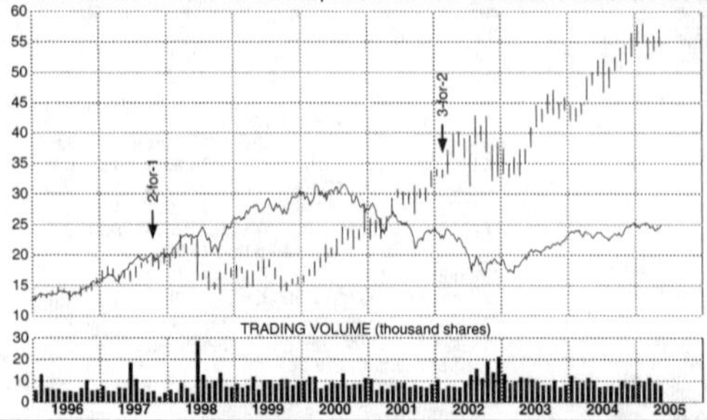

Interim Earnings (Per Share)

Qtr.	Mar	Jun	Sep	Dec
2002	0.42	0.46	0.45	0.53
2003	0.48	0.55	0.51	0.62
2004	1.09	0.60	0.57	0.83
2005	0.60	...	...	...

Interim Dividends (Per Share)

Amt	Decl	Ex	Rec	Pay
0.052Q	7/21/2004	9/23/2004	9/27/2004	10/7/2004
0.06Q	9/22/2004	12/23/2004	12/28/2004	1/7/2005
0.06Q	2/15/2005	3/22/2005	3/24/2005	4/5/2005
0.06Q	5/11/2005	6/22/2005	6/24/2005	7/7/2005

Indicated Div: $0.24

Valuation Analysis

Forecast P/E	21.41 (5/28/2005)		
Market Cap	$4.6 Billion	Book Value	1.4 Billion
Price/Book	3.21	Price/Sales	2.73

Dividend Achiever Status

Rank	22	10 Year Growth Rate	23.72%
Total Years of Dividend Growth			10

Business Summary: Medical Instruments & Equipment (MIC: 9.6 SIC: 843 NAIC: 39114)

Dentsply International designs, develops, manufactures and markets a broad range of products including dental prosthetics, precious metal dental alloys, dental ceramics, endodontic instruments and materials, prophylaxis paste, dental sealants, ultrasonic scalers, dental injectible anesthetics and crown and bridge materials, dental x-ray equipment, dental handpieces, intraoral cameras, dental x-ray film holders, film mounts and bone substitute/grafting materials, impression materials, orthodontic appliances, dental cutting instruments and dental implants to the dental market.

Recent Developments: For the quarter ended Mar 31 2005, net income decreased 44.8% to $49,049 thousand from net income of $88,832 thousand in the year-earlier quarter. Revenues were $406,975 thousand, down 1.8% from $414,359 thousand the year before. Operating income was $70,125 thousand versus an income of $70,106 thousand in the prior-year quarter, an increase of 0.0%. Total direct expense was $198,034 thousand versus $210,467 thousand in the prior-year quarter, a decrease of 5.9%. Total indirect expense was $138,816 thousand versus $133,786 thousand in the prior-year quarter, an increase of 3.8%.

Prospects: Co.'s stable of product offerings and its balanced geographic footprint should help to provide a solid foundation for future growth. Co. is continuing to make investments in product developments and technology to enhance its position in dental product innovations. Co.'s recent product launches include the introduction of ORAQIX, a new dental needle-less anesthetic, and BIOPURE MTAD, an antibacterial root canal cleanser. Meanwhile, Co. has acquired the rights to the compound SATIF from SANOFI-AVENTIS Group. SATIF is a Titanium-Fluoride derivative demonstrating the ability to protect tooth surfaces. Additionally, Co. announced its earnings guidance of $2.59 to $2.63 for 2005.

Financial Data

(US$ in Thousands)	3 Mos	12/31/2004	12/31/2003	12/31/2002	12/31/2001	12/31/2000	12/31/1999	12/31/1998
Earnings Per Share	2.60	3.09	2.16	1.85	1.54	1.29	1.13	0.43
Cash Flow Per Share	3.52	3.80	3.27	2.21	2.72	1.87	1.53	1.20
Tang Book Value Per Share	2.61	2.35	N.M.	N.M.	N.M.	2.26	1.51	0.86
Dividends Per Share	0.225	0.218	0.197	0.184	0.183	0.171	0.154	0.140
Dividend Payout %	8.65	7.04	9.12	9.95	11.90	13.28	13.60	32.31
Income Statement								
Total Revenue	406,975	1,694,232	1,570,925	1,513,742	1,129,094	889,796	830,864	800,456
EBITDA	87,799	343,080	321,062	292,229	260,035	202,446	192,283	106,743
Depn & Amortn	13,432	49,296	45,661	43,859	54,334	41,359	39,624	37,474
Income Before Taxes	70,350	274,155	251,196	220,985	185,127	151,796	138,019	55,101
Income Taxes	21,301	63,869	81,343	73,033	63,631	50,780	48,156	20,276
Net Income	49,049	253,165	174,183	147,952	121,496	101,016	89,863	34,825
Average Shares	82,289	82,014	80,647	79,994	78,975	78,559	79,366	80,395
Balance Sheet								
Current Assets	1,025,692	1,056,409	727,452	541,001	484,243	325,454	314,668	322,452
Total Assets	2,696,417	2,798,145	2,445,587	2,087,033	1,798,151	866,615	859,588	895,322
Current Liabilities	393,418	404,607	337,684	365,745	358,517	168,138	176,220	194,376
Long-Term Obligations	700,900	779,940	790,202	769,823	723,524	109,500	145,312	217,491
Total Liabilities	1,262,012	1,353,572	1,323,100	1,249,846	1,188,195	341,684	388,217	478,783
Stockholders' Equity	1,433,818	1,443,973	1,122,069	835,928	609,519	520,370	468,872	413,801
Shares Outstanding	80,600	80,600	79,300	78,400	77,900	77,550	79,200	78,900
Statistical Record								
Return on Assets %	8.19	9.63	7.69	7.62	9.12	11.67	10.24	4.17
Return on Equity %	16.12	19.68	17.79	20.47	21.51	20.37	20.36	8.31
EBITDA Margin %	21.57	20.25	20.44	19.31	23.03	22.75	23.14	13.34
Net Margin %	12.05	14.94	11.09	9.77	10.76	11.35	10.82	4.35
Asset Turnover	0.65	0.64	0.69	0.78	0.85	1.03	0.95	0.96
Current Ratio	2.61	2.61	2.15	1.48	1.35	1.94	1.79	1.66
Debt to Equity	0.49	0.54	0.70	0.92	1.19	0.21	0.31	0.53
Price Range	57.97-44.33	56.48-41.97	47.19-32.70	42.89-31.27	33.83-22.54	28.42-15.54	19.33-14.13	23.33-13.67
P/E Ratio	22.30-17.05	18.28-13.58	21.85-15.14	23.18-16.90	21.97-14.64	22.03-12.05	17.11-12.50	54.26-31.78
Average Yield %	0.43	0.44	0.49	0.50	0.65	0.82	0.93	0.77

Address: 221 West Philadelphia Street, York, PA 17405-0872
Telephone: 717-845-7511
Web Site: www.dentsply.com

Officers: Gary K. Kunkle Jr. - Chmn., C.E.O. Thomas L. Whiting - Pres., C.O.O. **Transfer Agents:** Computershare Investor Services, LLC

Investor Contact: 717-849-4269
No of Institutions: 299
Shares: 58,308,516 **% Held:** 72.22

DIEBOLD, INC.

Exchange	Symbol	Price	52Wk Range	Yield	P/E
NYS	DBD	$50.06 (5/31/2005)	57.58-45.00	1.64	19.94

*7 Year Price Score 122.47 *NYSE Composite Index=100 *12 Month Price Score 96.93

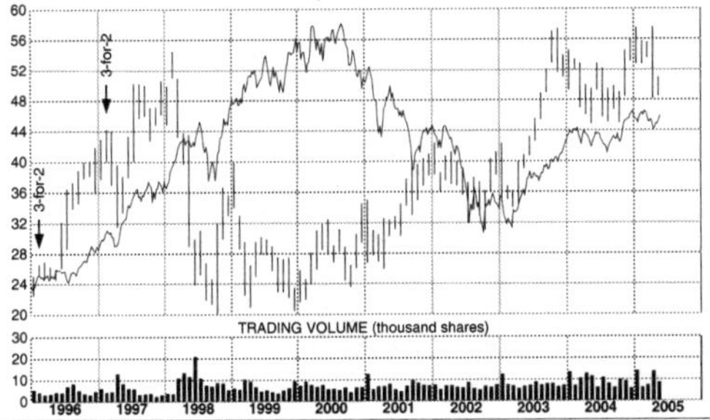

Interim Earnings (Per Share)

Qtr.	Mar	Jun	Sep	Dec
2002	0.37	0.55	0.61	0.30
2003	0.36	0.57	0.66	0.81
2004	0.40	0.60	0.67	0.87
2005	0.37	...	...	...

Interim Dividends (Per Share)

Amt	Decl	Ex	Rec	Pay
0.185Q	8/5/2004	8/11/2004	8/13/2004	9/3/2004
0.185Q	10/7/2004	11/9/2004	11/12/2004	12/3/2004
0.205Q	2/10/2005	2/16/2005	2/18/2005	3/11/2005
0.205Q	4/28/2005	5/11/2005	5/13/2005	6/3/2005

Indicated Div: $0.82 (Div. Reinv. Plan)

Valuation Analysis

Forecast P/E	17.05 (5/28/2005)		
Market Cap	$3.6 Billion	Book Value	1.3 Billion
Price/Book	2.85	Price/Sales	1.48

Dividend Achiever Status

Rank	239	10 Year Growth Rate	6.58%
Total Years of Dividend Growth			51

TRADING VOLUME (thousand shares)

Business Summary: Office Equipment Supplies (MIC: 11.12 SIC: 578 NAIC: 33313)

Diebold develops, manufactures, sells and services self-service transaction systems, electronic and physical security systems, software and various products used to equip bank facilities to global financial and commercial markets and electronic voting terminals and solutions to the government. Co.'s primary customers include banks and financial institutions, as well as hospitals, colleges and universities, public libraries, government agencies, utilities and various retail outlets. Sales of systems and equipment are made directly to customers by Co.' sales personnel and by manufacturer's representatives and distributors.

Recent Developments: For the quarter ended Mar 31 2005, net income decreased 8.6% to $26,675 thousand from net income of $29,169 thousand in the year-earlier quarter. Revenues were $1,080,468 thousand, up 8.4% from $996,510 thousand the year before. Operating income was $40,947 thousand versus an income of $43,830 thousand in the prior-year quarter, a decrease of 6.6%. Total direct expense was $399,833 thousand versus $358,228 thousand in the prior-year quarter, an increase of 11.6%. Total indirect expense was $99,454 thousand versus $96,197 thousand in the prior-year quarter, an increase of 3.4%.

Prospects: On May 2 2005, Co. announced that it has completed its acquisition of TASC Security, a London-based security systems integration company. TASC is a provider of customizable electronic security solutions that include alarms, access control, closed-circuit television and video surveillance systems. Meanwhile, Co. is encouraged by its continued strong order growth in financial self-service, particularly in the Europe, Middle East and Africa region. Looking ahead, Co. is targeting full-year 2005 revenue growth in the 10.0% to 13.0% range, along with earnings per share of between $2.80 and $2.93, including restructuring charges of $0.09 to $0.12 per share.

Financial Data

(US$ in Thousands)	3 Mos	12/31/2004	12/31/2003	12/31/2002	12/31/2001	12/31/2000	12/31/1999	12/31/1998
Earnings Per Share	2.51	2.54	2.40	1.37	0.93	1.92	1.85	1.10
Cash Flow Per Share	4.21	3.22	2.90	2.27	2.16	2.04	2.72	2.57
Tang Book Value Per Share	11.92	11.84	11.24	9.32	8.79	8.94	9.63	9.87
Dividends Per Share	0.760	0.740	0.680	0.660	0.640	0.620	0.600	0.560
Dividend Payout %	30.28	29.13	28.33	48.18	68.82	32.29	32.43	50.91
Income Statement								
Total Revenue	540,234	2,380,910	2,109,673	1,940,163	1,760,297	1,743,608	1,259,177	1,185,707
EBITDA	62,344	354,583	330,609	306,526	157,960	257,939	236,047	145,456
Depn & Amortn	19,897	74,983	64,301	61,296	45,453	35,901	34,709	25,649
Income Before Taxes	39,695	268,943	257,023	218,551	99,839	204,357	201,338	119,807
Income Taxes	13,020	84,986	82,247	86,250	32,946	67,438	72,482	43,659
Net Income	26,675	183,957	174,776	99,154	66,893	136,919	128,856	76,148
Average Shares	72,246	72,534	72,924	72,297	71,783	71,479	69,562	69,310
Balance Sheet								
Current Assets	1,177,111	1,234,632	1,105,159	924,888	952,426	804,363	647,936	543,548
Total Assets	2,081,900	2,135,552	1,900,502	1,625,081	1,651,913	1,585,427	1,298,831	1,004,188
Current Liabilities	672,939	728,623	618,653	564,962	658,018	566,792	382,407	235,533
Long-Term Obligations	...	...	...	...	20,800	20,800	20,800	20,800
Total Liabilities	821,485	875,077	752,264	684,258	748,803	649,361	454,436	305,065
Stockholders' Equity	1,260,415	1,260,475	1,148,238	940,823	903,110	936,066	844,395	699,123
Shares Outstanding	71,725	71,592	72,649	72,111	71,356	71,547	71,096	68,880
Statistical Record								
Return on Assets %	9.06	9.09	9.91	6.05	4.13	9.47	11.19	7.63
Return on Equity %	15.04	15.23	16.73	10.75	7.27	15.34	16.70	11.14
EBITDA Margin %	11.54	14.89	15.67	15.80	8.97	14.79	18.75	12.27
Net Margin %	4.94	7.73	8.28	5.11	3.80	7.85	10.23	6.42
Asset Turnover	1.21	1.18	1.20	1.18	1.09	1.21	1.09	1.19
Current Ratio	1.75	1.69	1.79	1.64	1.45	1.42	1.69	2.31
Debt to Equity	...	...	...	...	0.02	0.02	0.02	0.03
Price Range	57.51-44.85	56.06-44.85	57.43-33.94	42.41-31.00	41.00-25.96	34.56-21.63	39.88-20.50	54.50-20.13
P/E Ratio	22.91-17.87	22.07-17.66	23.93-14.14	30.96-22.63	44.09-27.91	18.00-11.26	21.55-11.08	49.55-18.30
Average Yield %	1.50	1.48	1.52	1.76	1.93	2.24	2.22	1.59

Address: 5995 Mayfair Road, North Canton, OH 44720-8077
Telephone: 330-490-4000
Web Site: www.diebold.com

Officers: Walden W. O'Dell - Chmn., C.E.O. Eric C. Evans - Pres., C.O.O. **Transfer Agents:** The Bank of New York, New York, NY

Investor Contact: 330-490-5900
No of Institutions: 299
Shares: 51,740,780 **% Held:** 72.16

DONNELLEY (R.R.) & SONS CO.

Exchange	Symbol	Price	52Wk Range	Yield	P/E
NYS	RRD	$33.25 (5/31/2005)	35.29-29.42	3.13	20.65

*7 Year Price Score 98.52 *NYSE Composite Index=100 *12 Month Price Score 97.75

TRADING VOLUME (thousand shares)

Interim Earnings (Per Share)

Qtr.	Mar	Jun	Sep	Dec
2002	0.20	0.22	0.42	0.42
2003	0.05	0.17	0.47	0.85
2004	(0.39)	(0.06)	0.51	0.67
2005	0.49	...	...	...

Interim Dividends (Per Share)

Amt	Decl	Ex	Rec	Pay
0.26Q	7/22/2004	8/5/2004	8/9/2004	9/1/2004
0.26Q	9/30/2004	11/4/2004	11/8/2004	12/1/2004
0.26Q	1/27/2005	2/8/2005	2/10/2005	3/1/2005
0.26Q	3/24/2005	5/6/2005	5/10/2005	6/1/2005

Indicated Div: $1.04 (Div. Reinv. Plan)

Valuation Analysis

Forecast P/E	N/A		
Market Cap	$7.1 Billion	Book Value	3.7 Billion
Price/Book	1.92	Price/Sales	0.90

Dividend Achiever Status

Rank	254	10 Year Growth Rate	5.65%
Total Years of Dividend Growth			35

Business Summary: Printing (MIC: 13.4 SIC: 752 NAIC: 23110)

R. R. Donnelley & Sons is engaged in preparing, producing and delivering integrated communications services designed to produce, manage and deliver its customers' content, regardless of the communications medium. Co.'s services include content creation, digital content management, production and distribution. Co. operates primarily in three business segments: print, logistics and financial. Co. serves the following end-markets: magazines, catalogs and retail, telecommunications, book publishing premedia, financial services, direct mail, international, and logistics.

Recent Developments: For the quarter ended Mar 31 2005, net income was $106,900 thousand versus net loss of $58,900 thousand in the year-earlier quarter. Revenues were $1,926,500 thousand, up 49.5% from $1,288,700 thousand the year before. Operating income was $197,100 thousand versus a loss of $48,600 thousand in the prior-year quarter, an increase of 505.6%. Total direct expense was $1,367,000 thousand versus $1,025,100 thousand in the prior-year quarter, an increase of 33.4%. Total indirect expense was $362,400 thousand versus $312,200 thousand in the prior-year quarter, an increase of 16.1%.

Prospects: On Apr 18 2005, Co. announced that it has signed a definitive agreement to acquire The Astron Group for approximately $990.0 million in cash. The Astron Group is a provider of transactional print and mail services, data and print management, document production and marketing support services with projected revenues of about $550.0 million in 2005. The acquisition is expected to close during the summer of 2005, subject to regulatory approval. Looking ahead, Co. is targeting full-year 2005 earnings from continuing operations of $1.97 per diluted share.

Financial Data

(US$ in Thousands)	3 Mos	12/31/2004	12/31/2003	12/31/2002	12/31/2001	12/31/2000	12/31/1999	12/31/1998
Earnings Per Share	1.61	0.88	1.54	1.24	0.21	2.17	2.38	2.08
Cash Flow Per Share	3.87	4.05	3.13	3.62	4.70	6.04	4.93	5.25
Tang Book Value Per Share	2.79	3.81	5.14	4.51	3.92	5.06	6.01	6.85
Dividends Per Share	1.040	1.040	1.020	0.980	0.940	0.900	0.860	0.820
Dividend Payout %	64.60	118.18	66.23	79.03	447.62	41.47	36.13	39.42
Income Statement								
Total Revenue	1,926,500	7,156,400	4,787,162	4,754,937	5,297,760	5,764,335	5,183,408	5,018,436
EBITDA	295,200	828,200	564,641	562,050	524,800	914,025	969,075	955,274
Depn & Amortn	98,700	385,500	306,005	323,499	378,723	390,402	374,382	367,803
Income Before Taxes	175,400	356,800	208,277	175,733	74,894	433,984	506,529	509,305
Income Taxes	66,500	92,600	31,768	33,496	49,906	167,084	195,014	214,725
Net Income	106,900	178,300	176,509	142,237	24,988	266,900	308,314	294,580
Average Shares	217,000	204,200	114,302	114,372	118,498	123,093	129,566	141,865
Balance Sheet								
Current Assets	2,364,600	2,600,600	999,510	866,439	940,194	1,206,449	1,229,850	1,144,993
Total Assets	8,284,800	8,553,700	3,188,950	3,151,772	3,400,017	3,914,202	3,853,464	3,787,819
Current Liabilities	1,546,700	1,487,300	883,582	954,730	984,290	1,190,561	1,203,463	898,300
Long-Term Obligations	1,577,500	1,581,200	752,497	752,870	881,318	739,190	748,498	998,978
Total Liabilities	4,559,900	4,567,100	2,205,798	2,237,178	2,511,610	2,681,654	2,715,206	2,486,941
Stockholders' Equity	3,724,900	3,986,600	983,152	914,594	888,407	1,232,548	1,138,258	1,300,878
Shares Outstanding	214,900	222,400	113,674	113,124	113,121	140,889	123,237	134,322
Statistical Record								
Return on Assets %	4.17	3.03	5.57	4.34	0.68	6.85	8.07	7.44
Return on Equity %	9.28	7.16	18.60	15.78	2.36	22.45	25.28	20.37
EBITDA Margin %	15.32	11.57	11.79	11.82	9.91	15.86	18.70	19.04
Net Margin %	5.55	2.49	3.69	2.99	0.47	4.63	5.95	5.87
Asset Turnover	0.96	1.22	1.51	1.45	1.45	1.48	1.36	1.27
Current Ratio	1.53	1.75	1.13	0.91	0.96	1.01	1.02	1.27
Debt to Equity	0.42	0.40	0.77	0.82	0.99	0.60	0.66	0.77
Price Range	35.29-28.50	35.29-27.95	30.15-17.05	31.96-19.06	31.62-24.83	27.00-19.00	43.81-22.81	47.75-34.00
P/E Ratio	21.92-17.70	40.10-31.76	19.58-11.07	25.77-15.37	150.57-118.24	12.44-8.76	18.41-9.59	22.96-16.35
Average Yield %	3.26	3.32	4.29	3.70	3.33	3.88	2.65	1.98

Address: 77 West Wacker Drive, Chicago, IL 60601 **Telephone:** 312-326-8000 **Web Site:** www.rrdonnelley.com	**Officers:** Stephen M. Wolf - Chmn. Mark A. Angelson - C.E.O. **Transfer Agents:** EquiServe Trust Company, N.A., Jersey City, NJ	**Investor Contact:** 312-326-8313 **No of Institutions:** 361 **Shares:** 184,027,184 **% Held:** 85.44

DORAL FINANCIAL CORP.

Exchange	Symbol	Price	52Wk Range	Yield	P/E
NYS	DRL	$11.59 (5/31/2005)	49.45-11.52	6.21	2.93

*7 Year Price Score 177.60 *NYSE Composite Index=100 *12 Month Price Score 41.74

Interim Earnings (Per Share)

Qtr.	Mar	Jun	Sep	Dec
2000	0.20	0.20	0.20	0.21
2001	0.32	0.29	0.33	0.37
2002	0.40	0.45	0.49	0.55
2003	0.60	0.64	0.70	0.78
2004	0.86	0.96	1.01	1.12

Interim Dividends (Per Share)

Amt	Decl	Ex	Rec	Pay
0.15Q	7/14/2004	8/25/2004	8/27/2004	9/10/2004
0.18Q	10/13/2004	11/9/2004	11/12/2004	12/3/2004
0.18Q	1/24/2005	2/9/2005	2/11/2005	3/4/2005
0.18Q	4/20/2005	5/12/2005	5/16/2005	6/3/2005

Indicated Div: $0.72

Valuation Analysis

Forecast P/E	N/A		
Market Cap	$1.3 Billion	Book Value	2.0 Billion
Price/Book	0.63	Price/Sales	1.22

Dividend Achiever Status

Rank	12	**10 Year Growth Rate**	26.37%
Total Years of Dividend Growth			15

Business Summary: Finance Intermediaries & Services (MIC: 8.7 SIC: 162 NAIC: 22292)

Doral Financial, with $15.10 billion in total assets as of Dec 31 2004, is a diversified financial services company engaged in mortgage banking, banking (including thrift operations), institutional securities operations and insurance agency activities. As of Dec 31 2004, Doral Bank PR operated 40 branches in Puerto Rico, concentrated in the greater San Juan metropolitan area and the Island's northeast region. Co. operates primarily in Puerto Rico, but it also has one mortgage banking office and six branches of Doral Bank-NY, a federally chartered savings bank in New York City.

Recent Developments: On Apr 19 2005, Co. announced that it had determined that the previously filed interim and audited financial statements for the periods from Jan 1 2000 through Dec 31 2004 should no longer be relied on and that the financial statements for some or all of the periods included therein should be restated. Co. is working on the restatement, but it does not yet have sufficient information to announce an expected date for filing the Form 10-Q for the quarter ended Mar 31 2005. For the quarter ended Dec 31 2004, net income increased 52.3% to $489.6 million compared with $321.3 million in the year-earlier quarter. Net interest income advanced 46.5% to $265.9 million from $181.5 million in 2003.

Prospects: The matters that Co. has identified to date as requiring restatement of financial statements for periods ended on or prior to Dec 31 2004 are as follows: Co. is reviewing the accounting for its portfolio of floating rate interest only strips (IOs) originated from 2000 through 2004, and noted that an expected change in its valuation model will result in a substantial reduction in the recorded fair value of its floating rate IOs. Also, Co. has been developing new procedures to improve its control over the valuation process for its IOs. Lastly, Co. is reviewing all the assumptions and processes used to value its IOs and mortgage servicing rights and to calculate gains on sale of mortgage loans.

Financial Data (US$ in Thousands)	12/31/2004	12/31/2003	12/31/2002	12/31/2001	12/31/2000	12/31/1999	12/31/1998	12/31/1997
Earnings Per Share	3.95	2.72	1.89	1.31	0.82	0.67	0.56	0.24
Cash Flow Per Share	(4.20)	2.98	(11.62)	(4.99)	(4.50)	(4.46)	(10.01)	(5.25)
Tang Book Value Per Share	12.97	9.45	7.58	5.92	3.89	4.11	2.90	2.18
Dividends Per Share	0.600	0.400	0.280	0.211	0.169	0.133	0.102	0.086
Dividend Payout %	15.19	14.71	14.79	16.10	20.54	20.00	18.25	36.32
Income Statement								
Interest Income	570,847	452,570	415,600	356,095	325,545	211,679	148,051	90,131
Interest Expense	304,949	271,090	263,178	271,668	283,241	161,795	114,786	61,438
Net Interest Income	265,898	181,480	152,422	84,427	42,304	49,884	33,265	28,693
Provision for Losses	5,507	14,085	7,429	4,445	4,078	2,626	883	600
Non-Interest Income	450,384	411,772	255,393	191,132	164,585	126,911	88,340	45,286
Non-Interest Expense	209,052	185,802	139,410	112,854	106,659	97,556	60,883	35,582
Income Before Taxes	501,723	393,365	260,976	158,260	96,152	76,613	59,839	37,797
Income Taxes	12,098	72,066	40,008	20,338	11,496	8,687	7,007	5,249
Net Income	489,625	321,299	220,968	143,851	84,656	67,926	52,832	20,231
Average Shares	119,744	110,434	109,438	102,381	94,710	95,448	94,338	87,139
Balance Sheet								
Net Loans & Leases	1,752,490	1,410,849	1,022,342	644,113	398,191	231,184	166,987	133,055
Total Assets	15,102,401	10,393,996	8,421,689	6,694,283	5,463,386	4,537,343	2,918,113	1,857,789
Total Deposits	3,643,080	2,971,272	2,217,211	1,669,909	1,303,525	1,010,424	533,113	300,494
Total Liabilities	13,129,632	8,801,556	7,376,718	5,932,163	4,957,676	4,152,361	2,648,554	1,670,834
Stockholders' Equity	1,972,769	1,592,440	1,044,971	762,120	505,710	384,982	269,559	186,955
Shares Outstanding	107,908	107,903	107,761	107,573	95,384	90,965	90,965	82,788
Statistical Record								
Return on Assets %	3.83	3.42	2.92	2.37	1.69	1.82	2.21	1.37
Return on Equity %	27.39	24.36	24.46	22.69	18.96	20.76	23.15	11.99
Net Interest Margin %	46.58	40.10	36.68	23.71	12.99	23.57	22.47	31.83
Efficiency Ratio %	20.47	21.50	20.78	20.62	21.76	28.81	25.76	26.28
Loans to Deposits	0.48	0.47	0.46	0.39	0.31	0.23	0.31	0.44
Price Range	49.25-29.87	34.67-18.73	19.94-13.68	17.50-9.97	11.36-3.89	9.83-4.72	10.08-4.67	5.67-2.72
P/E Ratio	12.47-7.56	12.75-6.89	10.55-7.24	13.36-7.61	13.86-4.74	14.68-7.05	18.01-8.33	23.61-11.34
Average Yield %	1.60	1.45	1.69	1.53	2.80	1.87	1.43	2.28

Address: 1451 Franklin D. Roosevelt Avenue, San Juan, PR 00920-2717
Telephone: 787-474-6700
Web Site: www.doralfinancial.com

Officers: Salomon Levis - Chmn., C.E.O. Zoila Levis - Pres., C.O.O. **Transfer Agents:** Mellon Investor Services, LLC, Ridgefield Park, NJ

Investor Contact: 212-329-3729
No of Institutions: 201
Shares: 64,458,412 **% Held:** 59.73

DOVER CORP.

Exchange	Symbol	Price	52Wk Range	Yield	P/E
NYS	DOV	$37.87 (5/31/2005)	42.61-34.70	1.69	18.12

*7 Year Price Score 92.56 *NYSE Composite Index=100 *12 Month Price Score 91.80

Interim Earnings (Per Share)

Qtr.	Mar	Jun	Sep	Dec
2002	(1.22)	0.27	0.28	0.07
2003	0.29	0.36	0.41	0.37
2004	0.41	0.54	0.59	0.48
2005	0.48	...	...	...

Interim Dividends (Per Share)

Amt	Decl	Ex	Rec	Pay
0.16Q	8/5/2004	8/27/2004	8/31/2004	9/15/2004
0.16Q	11/4/2004	11/26/2004	11/30/2004	12/15/2004
0.16Q	2/10/2005	2/24/2005	2/28/2005	3/15/2005
0.16Q	5/5/2005	5/26/2005	5/31/2005	6/15/2005

Indicated Div: $0.64 (Div. Reinv. Plan)

Valuation Analysis

Forecast P/E	16.12 (5/28/2005)		
Market Cap	$7.7 Billion	Book Value	3.1 Billion
Price/Book	2.46	Price/Sales	1.35

Dividend Achiever Status

Rank	178	10 Year Growth Rate	9.73%
Total Years of Dividend Growth			49

Business Summary: Industrial Machinery and Equipment (MIC: 11.5 SIC: 531 NAIC: 33120)

Dover is a diversified industrial manufacturing corporation made up of 49 operating companies. Dover Diversified's products include packaging and printing machinery, heat transfer equipment, food refrigeration and display cases as well as products for use in the defense, aerospace and automotive industries. Dover Industries makes products for use in the waste handling, bulk transport, automotive service, commercial food service and packaging, welding, cash dispenser and construction industries. Dover Technologies' products include automated assembly and testing equipment, specialized electronic components and industrial printers. Dover Resources manufactures products for various industries.

Recent Developments: For the quarter ended Mar 31 2005, income from continuing operations increased 19.6% to $100,265 thousand from income of $83,809 thousand in the year-earlier quarter. Net income increased 18.1% to $98,134 thousand from net income of $83,112 thousand in the year-earlier quarter. Revenues were $1,449,034 thousand, up 16.6% from $1,242,380 thousand in 2004. Operating income was $146,054 thousand versus income of $132,688 thousand in the prior-year quarter. Total direct expense was $951,543 thousand versus $806,515 thousand in the prior-year quarter, an increase of 18.0%. Total indirect expense was $351,437 thousand versus $303,177 thousand in the prior-year quarter, an increase of 15.9%.

Prospects: All of Co.'s companies continue to see improvement in their operations, including lowering costs through sourcing and process improvements, while bringing new products to market at the same time. Co. noted that it is seeing considerable gains in its industrial companies, especially in its North American markets. Also, Co. believes that its new operating structure, which consists of six segments and 13 operating groups, is helping it to improve its focus on markets served and enhance its management capacity to react to growth opportunities. Co.'s balance sheet remains strong and continues to actively search for acquisition candidates to meet its criteria.

Financial Data

(US$ in Thousands)	3 Mos	12/31/2004	12/31/2003	12/31/2002	12/31/2001	12/31/2000	12/31/1999	12/31/1998
Earnings Per Share	2.09	2.02	1.44	(0.60)	1.22	2.54	4.41	1.69
Cash Flow Per Share	2.49	2.93	2.93	1.95	3.35	2.73	2.21	2.19
Tang Book Value Per Share	1.99	2.16	2.70	2.65	1.97	1.82	1.10	2.14
Dividends Per Share	0.630	0.620	0.570	0.540	0.520	0.480	0.440	0.400
Dividend Payout %	30.14	30.69	39.58	...	42.62	18.90	9.98	23.67
Income Statement								
Total Revenue	1,449,034	5,488,112	4,413,296	4,183,664	4,459,695	5,400,717	4,446,420	3,977,666
EBITDA	193,029	774,281	585,367	495,523	533,677	1,064,194	833,121	702,771
Depn & Amortn	42,496	160,845	151,309	161,003	219,963	203,384	183,244	167,687
Income Before Taxes	134,386	552,146	371,892	269,691	238,434	772,315	615,004	488,646
Income Taxes	34,121	143,006	86,676	58,542	71,595	239,108	209,950	162,249
Net Income	98,134	412,755	292,927	(121,261)	248,537	519,612	928,992	378,845
Average Shares	204,904	204,786	203,614	203,346	204,013	204,677	210,679	224,386
Balance Sheet								
Current Assets	2,306,932	2,149,947	1,849,640	1,658,001	1,654,928	1,974,849	1,611,562	1,304,524
Total Assets	6,006,176	5,792,179	5,133,752	4,437,385	4,602,202	4,892,116	4,131,940	3,627,276
Current Liabilities	1,530,964	1,355,976	910,801	696,938	819,171	1,604,640	1,334,865	989,747
Long-Term Obligations	755,443	753,063	1,003,915	1,030,299	1,033,243	631,846	608,025	610,090
Total Liabilities	2,867,163	2,673,497	2,391,081	2,042,762	2,082,663	2,450,541	2,093,184	1,716,392
Stockholders' Equity	3,139,013	3,118,682	2,742,671	2,394,623	2,519,539	2,441,575	2,038,756	1,910,884
Shares Outstanding	203,727	203,496	202,912	202,402	202,579	203,183	204,628	220,407
Statistical Record								
Return on Assets %	7.60	7.53	6.12	N.M.	5.24	11.48	23.95	10.97
Return on Equity %	14.45	14.05	11.40	N.M.	10.02	23.13	47.04	20.96
EBITDA Margin %	13.32	14.11	13.26	11.84	11.97	19.70	18.74	17.67
Net Margin %	6.77	7.52	6.64	N.M.	5.57	9.62	20.89	9.52
Asset Turnover	1.01	1.00	0.92	0.93	0.94	1.19	1.15	1.15
Current Ratio	1.51	1.59	2.03	2.38	2.02	1.23	1.21	1.32
Debt to Equity	0.24	0.24	0.37	0.43	0.41	0.26	0.30	0.32
Price Range	42.61-36.03	44.02-36.03	40.08-23.35	43.31-23.91	43.32-28.77	53.81-36.00	47.50-29.50	39.81-25.94
P/E Ratio	20.39-17.24	21.79-17.84	27.83-16.22	...	35.51-23.58	21.19-14.17	10.77-6.69	23.56-15.35
Average Yield %	1.60	1.56	1.76	1.63	1.39	1.07	1.14	1.17

Address: 280 Park Avenue, New York, NY 10017 **Telephone:** 212-922-1640 **Web Site:** www.dovercorporation.com	**Officers:** Thomas L. Reece - Chmn. Ronald L. Hoffman - Pres., C.E.O. **Transfer Agents:** Mellon Investor Services, Ridgefield Park, NJ	**Investor Contact:** 212-922-1640 **No of Institutions:** 375 **Shares:** 156,596,640 **% Held:** 76.88

DUKE REALTY CORP.

Exchange	Symbol	Price	52Wk Range	Yield	P/E
NYS	DRE	$30.87 (5/31/2005)	35.77-29.40	6.03	30.56

***7 Year Price Score 111.65** *NYSE Composite Index=100 ***12 Month Price Score 91.35**

Interim Earnings (Per Share)

Qtr.	Mar	Jun	Sep	Dec
2002	0.34	0.36	0.29	0.21
2003	0.28	0.25	0.30	0.37
2004	0.23	0.24	0.30	0.29
2005	0.18	...	...	...

Interim Dividends (Per Share)

Amt	Decl	Ex	Rec	Pay
0.465Q	7/28/2004	8/11/2004	8/13/2004	8/31/2004
0.465Q	10/27/2004	11/9/2004	11/12/2004	11/30/2004
0.465Q	1/26/2005	2/10/2005	2/14/2005	2/28/2005
0.465Q	4/27/2005	5/10/2005	5/12/2005	5/31/2005

Indicated Div: $1.86 (Div. Reinv. Plan)

Valuation Analysis

Forecast P/E	N/A		
Market Cap	$4.4 Billion	Book Value	2.8 Billion
Price/Book	1.58	Price/Sales	3.73

Dividend Achiever Status

Rank	228	**10 Year Growth Rate**	7.24%
Total Years of Dividend Growth			11

Business Summary: Property, Real Estate & Development (MIC: 8.3 SIC: 798 NAIC: 25930)

Duke Realty is a self-administered and self-managed real estate investment trust company that focuses on major cities in the Midwest and the Southeast. As of Dec 31 2004, Co.'s 893 rental properties encompass over 114.2 million rentable square feet and are leased by approximately 4,200 tenants whose businesses include manufacturing, retailing, wholesale trade, distribution and professional services. Also, Co. owns or controls nearly 4,600 acres of unencumbered land ready for development. Through its service operations, Co. provides, on a fee basis, leasing, property and asset management, development, construction, build-to-suit, and other tenant-related services.

Recent Developments: For the quarter ended Mar 31 2005, income from continuing operations decreased 15.6% to $33,361 thousand from income of $39,548 thousand in the year-earlier quarter. Net income decreased 15.9% to $37,101 thousand from net income of $44,100 thousand in the year-earlier quarter. Revenues were $106,460 thousand, up 15.7% from $91,996 thousand the year before. Operating income was $34,330 thousand versus an income of $36,596 thousand in the prior-year quarter, a decrease of 6.2%.

Prospects: On Apr 28 2005, Co. announced $102.0 million of new developments through its National Development Group. The most significant project is a 350,000 square foot office headquarters for HealthNow in Buffalo, NY. This project is 100.0% pre-leased for 15 years. The other development consists of two projects that will be developed in Co.'s medical office joint venture with Bremner Healthcare. The first is a 71,000 square foot development for Adena Healthcare System in Chillicothe, OH. The project is 64.0% pre-leased by Adena for 11 years. The second project is a 72,000 square foot development in Summit, NJ that is 43.0% pre-leased to Atlantic Health System for 10 years.

Financial Data (US$ in Thousands)	3 Mos	12/31/2004	12/31/2003	12/31/2002	12/31/2001	12/31/2000	12/31/1999	12/31/1998
Earnings Per Share	1.01	1.06	1.19	1.19	1.75	1.66	1.32	1.12
Cash Flow Per Share	2.62	2.67	2.72	4.25	3.34	3.53	3.27	2.74
Tang Book Value Per Share	14.94	15.18	15.57	16.11	16.56	16.45	16.36	14.20
Dividends Per Share	1.855	1.850	1.830	1.810	1.760	1.640	1.460	1.280
Dividend Payout %	183.66	174.53	153.78	152.10	100.57	98.80	110.61	114.29
Income Statement								
Property Income	191,030	744,065	706,722	684,311	691,958	697,270	523,950	337,768
Non-Property Income	106,460	421,934	343,074	268,319	341,695	97,355	65,644	35,573
Total Revenue	297,490	1,165,999	1,049,796	952,630	1,033,653	794,625	589,594	373,341
Depn & Amortn	64,770	233,486	199,860	179,346	164,303	163,415	112,643	70,128
Interest Expense	35,226	135,130	129,160	117,073	113,830	133,948	86,757	60,217
Net Income	37,101	188,701	199,232	206,325	282,409	261,939	182,240	110,704
Average Shares	157,720	157,062	151,141	150,839	151,710	147,441	120,511	92,468
Balance Sheet								
Total Assets	5,945,877	5,896,643	5,561,249	5,348,823	5,330,033	5,460,036	5,486,238	2,853,653
Long-Term Obligations	2,351,753	2,518,704	2,335,536	2,106,285	1,814,856	1,973,215	2,113,476	1,007,317
Total Liabilities	2,954,648	2,875,661	2,681,706	2,424,002	2,149,834	2,311,829	2,383,897	1,176,812
Stockholders' Equity	2,800,374	2,825,869	2,666,749	2,616,180	2,785,009	2,712,890	2,668,596	1,570,112
Shares Outstanding	143,442	142,894	136,594	135,007	131,416	127,932	125,823	86,053
Statistical Record								
Return on Assets %	3.14	3.28	3.65	3.86	5.23	4.77	4.37	4.40
Return on Equity %	6.62	6.85	7.54	7.64	10.27	9.71	8.60	7.89
Net Margin %	12.47	16.18	18.98	21.66	27.32	32.96	30.91	29.65
Price Range	35.77-28.76	35.77-28.76	31.75-24.50	28.95-22.42	25.97-22.00	25.75-17.88	23.94-16.81	24.94-19.81
P/E Ratio	35.42-28.48	33.75-27.13	26.68-20.59	24.33-18.84	14.84-12.57	15.51-10.77	18.13-12.74	22.27-17.69
Average Yield %	5.72	5.68	6.53	7.15	7.36	7.45	6.85	5.56

Address: 600 East 96th Street, Suite 100, Indianapolis, IN 46240 **Telephone:** 317-808-6000 **Web Site:** www.dukerealty.com	**Officers:** Thomas L. Hefner - Chmn., C.E.O. Dennis D. Oklak - Pres., C.O.O. **Transfer Agents:** American Stock Transfer & Trust Company, New York, NY	**Investor Contact:** 317-808-6005 **No of Institutions:** 263 **Shares:** 85,906,496 **% Held:** 60.11

EASTGROUP PROPERTIES, INC.

Exchange	Symbol	Price	52Wk Range	Yield	P/E
NYS	EGP	$40.72 (5/31/2005)	41.25-31.20	4.76	40.32

***7 Year Price Score 127.21** *NYSE Composite Index=100 ***12 Month Price Score 102.98**

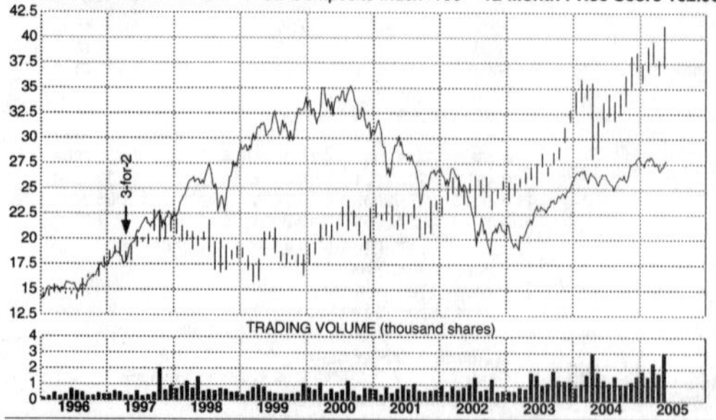

Interim Earnings (Per Share)

Qtr.	Mar	Jun	Sep	Dec
2002	0.22	0.27	0.16	0.18
2003	0.17	0.21	0.13	0.20
2004	0.21	0.22	0.32	0.24
2005	0.23	...	...	...

Interim Dividends (Per Share)

Amt	Decl	Ex	Rec	Pay
0.48Q	5/27/2004	6/16/2004	6/18/2004	6/30/2004
0.48Q	9/2/2004	9/15/2004	9/17/2004	9/30/2004
0.48Q	12/3/2004	12/15/2004	12/17/2004	12/30/2004
0.485Q	3/15/2005	3/22/2005	3/25/2005	3/31/2005

Indicated Div: $1.94 (Div. Reinv. Plan)

Valuation Analysis

Forecast P/E	15.40 (5/28/2005)		
Market Cap	$892.6 Million	Book Value	377.3 Million
Price/Book	2.37	Price/Sales	7.58

Dividend Achiever Status

Rank	263	**10 Year Growth Rate**	5.17%
Total Years of Dividend Growth			12

Business Summary: Property, Real Estate & Development (MIC: 8.3 SIC: 798 NAIC: 25930)

Eastgroup Properties is a self-administered, equity real estate investment trust focused on the acquisition, operation and development of industrial properties in the major Sunbelt markets throughout the U.S. with an emphasis in the states of Arizona, California, Florida and Texas. Co.'s strategy for growth is based on ownership of premier distribution facilities generally clustered near major transportation features in supply constrained submarkets. As of Dec 31 2004, Co.'s portfolio included 21.1 million square feet with an additional 439,000 square feet under development.

Recent Developments: For the quarter ended Mar 31 2005, income from continuing operations increased 4.2% to $5,126 thousand from income of $4,918 thousand in the year-earlier quarter. Net income increased 10.5% to $5,536 thousand from net income of $5,012 thousand in the year-earlier quarter. Revenues were $30,654 thousand, up 11.7% from $27,448 thousand the year before.

Prospects: Co. is targeting full-year 2005 funds from operations (FFO) per share in the range of $2.59 to $2.69. Also, Co. anticipates earnings of between $0.95 and $1.00 per share during the year. Co. noted that its projections were based on assumptions that include 2005 average occupancy of between 90.0% and 92.5%; same store property net operating income (PNOI) increases of 1.2% to 4.4%; existing development contributions of $0.14 per share in PNOI; acquisitions, net of dispositions, of $25.0 million to $30.0 million during 2005; lease termination fees of $168,000; floating rate bank debt at an average rate of 4.0%; and new fixed rate debt of $25.0 million on Jul 1 2005 at 6.0%.

Financial Data

(US$ in Thousands)	3 Mos	12/31/2004	12/31/2003	12/31/2002	12/31/2001	12/31/2000	12/31/1999	12/31/1998
Earnings Per Share	1.01	0.98	0.70	0.84	1.51	1.68	1.99	1.66
Cash Flow Per Share	2.73	2.76	2.84	3.39	3.23	3.38	2.91	1.81
Tang Book Value Per Share	15.39	14.98	16.05	15.40	16.48	16.84	16.76	16.25
Dividends Per Share	1.925	1.920	1.900	1.880	1.800	1.580	1.480	1.400
Dividend Payout %	190.59	195.92	271.43	223.81	119.21	94.05	74.37	84.34
Income Statement								
Property Income	30,579	114,051	107,771	103,048	100,560	93,906	83,320	74,312
Non-Property Income	75	633	670	2,762	4,735	4,197	2,916	2,416
Total Revenue	30,654	114,684	108,441	105,810	105,295	98,103	86,236	76,728
Depn & Amortn	9,036	30,059	32,397	30,818	27,413	23,821	20,178	16,574
Interest Expense	5,970	20,481	19,015	17,387	17,823	18,570	17,688	16,948
Net Income	5,536	23,327	20,445	23,626	34,182	36,512	38,355	29,336
Average Shares	21,196	21,088	18,194	16,237	16,046	15,798	17,362	16,432
Balance Sheet								
Total Assets	825,895	768,664	729,267	702,341	683,782	666,205	632,151	567,548
Long-Term Obligations	325,342	303,674	285,722	248,343	205,014	168,709	148,665	122,494
Total Liabilities	446,806	414,974	360,518	344,097	311,333	289,116	260,499	248,821
Stockholders' Equity	377,255	351,806	366,945	356,485	370,710	375,392	369,312	316,024
Shares Outstanding	21,920	21,059	20,853	16,104	15,912	15,849	15,555	16,307
Statistical Record								
Return on Assets %	3.05	3.11	2.86	3.41	5.06	5.61	6.39	5.98
Return on Equity %	6.45	6.47	5.65	6.50	9.16	9.78	11.19	10.23
Net Margin %	18.06	20.34	18.85	22.33	32.46	37.22	44.48	38.23
Price Range	39.67-28.01	38.59-28.01	32.90-23.88	26.35-22.40	23.90-20.19	23.88-17.56	21.13-15.75	22.06-16.69
P/E Ratio	39.28-27.73	39.38-28.58	47.00-34.11	31.37-26.67	15.83-13.37	14.21-10.45	10.62-7.91	13.29-10.05
Average Yield %	5.58	5.70	6.93	7.61	8.10	7.55	8.09	7.14

Address: 300 One Jackson Place, 188 East Capitol Street, Jackson, MS 39201-2195
Telephone: 601-354-3555
Web Site: www.eastgroup.net

Officers: Leland R. Speed - Chmn. David H. Hoster II - Pres., C.E.O. **Transfer Agents:** First Chicago Trust Company of New York, Jersey City, NJ

No of Institutions: 106
Shares: 13,998,148 **% Held:** 66.39

EATON VANCE CORP

Exchange	Symbol	Price	52Wk Range	Yield	P/E
NYS	EV	$24.36 (5/31/2005)	27.30-17.79	1.31	22.77

*7 Year Price Score 138.07 *NYSE Composite Index=100 *12 Month Price Score 100.67

Interim Earnings (Per Share)

Qtr.	Jan	Apr	Jul	Oct
2001-02	0.23	0.23	0.22	0.17
2002-03	0.19	0.18	0.19	0.20
2003-04	0.22	0.25	0.25	0.28
2004-05	0.27	0.27	...	...

Interim Dividends (Per Share)

Amt	Decl	Ex	Rec	Pay
0.08Q	10/20/2004	10/27/2004	10/29/2004	11/8/2004
2-for-1	12/15/2004	1/18/2005	12/31/2004	1/14/2005
0.08Q	1/12/2005	1/27/2005	1/31/2005	2/14/2005
0.08Q	4/14/2005	4/27/2005	4/29/2005	5/9/2005

Indicated Div: $0.32

Valuation Analysis

Forecast P/E 21.66 (6/3/2005)
Market Cap $3.2 Billion Book Value 459.5 Million
Price/Book 7.06 Price/Sales 4.74

Dividend Achiever Status

Rank 30 **10 Year Growth Rate** 22.05%
Total Years of Dividend Growth 23

Business Summary: Wealth Management (MIC: 8.8 SIC: 282 NAIC: 23930)

Eaton Vance is engaged in the provision of investment advisory and distribution services to mutual funds and other investment funds, and investment management and counseling services to individual high-net-worth investors, family offices and institutional clients. Co. operates in one business segment, namely as an investment adviser managing fund and separate account assets. Co. provides investment advisory or administration services to over 150 funds, 1,300 separately managed individual and institutional accounts, and participates in more than 40 retail managed account broker/dealer programs.

Recent Developments: For the quarter ended Apr 30 2005, Co. reported net income of $37,627,000 compared with net income of $35,169,000 in the equivalent period a year earlier. Results for 2005 included a $77,000 gain on investments and a $1,840,000 impairment loss on investments. Results for 2004 included an $83,000 loss on investments and a $29,000 foreign currency loss. Total revenue rose 10.4% to $182,504,000 from $165,291,000 in the corresponding quarter the year before. Operating income was $61,450,000, up 9.4% versus $56,175,000 in the comparable 2004 period.

Prospects: Results are being positively affected by higher average assets under management, which amounted to $98.00 billion at the end of the first quarter of 2005, up 17.2% from the year before. The improvement in assets under managements reflects the positive effects of long-term fund and separate account net inflows, market price appreciation and $1.90 billion of separate accounts acquired from Deutsche Bank in July 2004. Meanwhile, results are benefiting from Co.'s successful closed-end fund offerings as net fund and separate account inflows were $1.30 billion in the first quarter of fiscal 2005.

Financial Data (US$ in Thousands)	3 Mos	10/31/2004	10/31/2003	10/31/2002	10/31/2001	10/31/2000	10/31/1999	10/31/1998
Earnings Per Share	1.04	1.00	0.76	0.85	0.80	0.79	0.11	0.20
Cash Flow Per Share	1.37	0.87	0.32	0.97	1.02	0.52	0.15	0.07
Tang Book Value Per Share	2.46	2.37	2.06	1.92	1.40	1.82	1.37	1.47
Dividends Per Share	0.295	0.275	0.200	0.149	0.126	0.101	0.080	0.064
Dividend Payout %	28.30	27.64	26.49	17.50	15.78	12.82	74.42	31.48
Income Statement								
Total Revenue	181,781	661,813	523,133	522,985	486,372	429,566	429,566	249,987
Income Before Taxes	63,239	221,658	164,858	186,241	178,666	187,179	85,910	50,038
Income Taxes	23,368	79,797	57,700	65,184	62,469	71,128	33,505	19,515
Net Income	38,409	138,943	106,123	121,057	116,020	116,051	15,798	30,523
Average Shares	143,711	139,578	140,750	142,824	144,600	146,444	148,988	151,028
Balance Sheet								
Total Assets	709,574	743,566	658,702	616,619	675,301	432,989	358,229	380,260
Total Liabilities	211,571	226,190	234,734	242,919	373,210	178,039	163,961	168,451
Stockholders' Equity	459,497	449,506	416,277	372,302	301,126	254,950	194,268	211,809
Shares Outstanding	133,182	133,581	136,810	138,514	137,233	139,087	141,039	142,663
Statistical Record								
Return on Assets %	20.81	19.76	16.64	18.74	20.94	29.25	4.28	7.95
Return on Equity %	33.10	32.01	26.91	35.95	41.73	51.53	7.78	13.93
Price Range	26.07-16.46	21.81-16.46	17.80-11.70	20.36-11.98	19.10-11.16	13.69-8.47	9.72-4.75	6.19-4.05
P/E Ratio	25.07-15.83	21.81-16.46	23.42-15.39	23.95-14.09	23.88-13.95	17.33-10.72	88.35-43.18	30.94-20.23
Average Yield %	1.44	1.45	1.30	0.90	0.81	0.94	1.20	1.21

Address: 255 State Street, Boston, MA 02109
Telephone: 617-482-8260
Web Site: www.eatonvance.com

Officers: James B. Hawkes - Chmn., Pres., C.E.O. Thomas E. Faust Jr. - Exec. V.P., Chief Investment Officer **Transfer Agents:**
EquiServe Trust Company, N.A., Kansas City, MO

Investor Contact: 617-482-8260
No of Institutions: 201
Shares: 77,278,352 **% Held:** 57.99

ECOLAB, INC.

Exchange	Symbol	Price	52Wk Range	Yield	P/E
NYS	ECL	$32.33 (5/31/2005)	35.26-29.37	1.08	26.50

***7 Year Price Score 125.84** *NYSE Composite Index=100 ***12 Month Price Score 97.49**

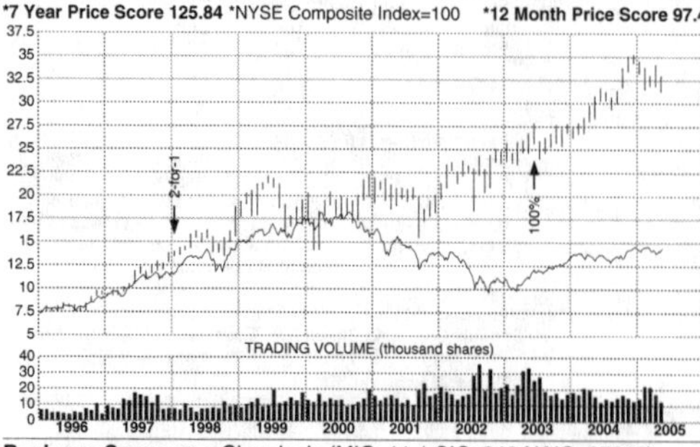

Interim Earnings (Per Share)

Qtr.	Mar	Jun	Sep	Dec
2002	0.15	0.20	0.28	0.19
2003	0.21	0.25	0.33	0.26
2004	0.25	0.30	0.36	0.27
2005	0.29	...	...	...

Interim Dividends (Per Share)

Amt	Decl	Ex	Rec	Pay
0.08Q	8/13/2004	9/17/2004	9/21/2004	10/15/2004
0.087Q	12/9/2004	12/17/2004	12/21/2004	1/18/2005
0.087Q	2/28/2005	3/11/2005	3/15/2005	4/15/2005
0.087Q	5/6/2005	6/17/2005	6/21/2005	7/15/2005

Indicated Div: $0.35 (Div. Reinv. Plan)

Valuation Analysis

Forecast P/E	24.50 (5/28/2005)		
Market Cap	$8.3 Billion	Book Value	1.5 Billion
Price/Book	5.39	Price/Sales	1.93

Dividend Achiever Status

Rank	152	**10 Year Growth Rate**	11.27%
Total Years of Dividend Growth			12

Business Summary: Chemicals (MIC: 11.1 SIC: 842 NAIC: 25612)

Ecolab develops and markets products and services for the hospitality, foodservice, institutional and industrial markets. Co. operates in three business segments. The Cleaning and Sanitizing segment consists of seven business units and offers cleaners, sanitizers, detergents, lubricants, chemical cleaning, animal health, water treatment, infection control and janitorial products. Other U.S. Services consists of two business units focused on the elimination and prevention of pests, and the manufacturing of dishwashing and customized machines for the foodservice industry. The International segment serves customers in Europe, Asia Pacific, Canada, Latin America, the Middle East and Africa.

Recent Developments: For the quarter ended Mar 31 2005, net income increased 13.1% to $74,648 thousand from net income of $66,006 thousand in the year-earlier quarter. Revenues were $1,069,880 thousand, up 9.2% from $979,371 thousand the year before. Operating income was $126,369 thousand versus an income of $116,139 thousand in the prior-year quarter, an increase of 8.8%. Total direct expense was $526,556 thousand versus $474,094 thousand in the prior-year quarter, an increase of 11.1%. Total indirect expense was $416,955 thousand versus $389,138 thousand in the prior-year quarter, an increase of 7.1%.

Prospects: Co. continues to enjoy strong sales growth across the U.S. and Latin America, along with improved sales growth in Canada and the Asia Pacific region. For the second quarter of 2005, Co. expects sales for both domestic and international operations to increase over 2004 levels. Gross margins are expected to be approximately 51.0% of sales, while selling, general and administrative expenses are expected to be in the 39.0% range. In addition, earnings are projected to be in the range of $0.32 to $0.33. Looking ahead, Co. expects full-year 2005 earnings per share of between $1.30 and $1.34.

Financial Data

(US$ in Thousands)	3 Mos	12/31/2004	12/31/2003	12/31/2002	12/31/2001	12/31/2000	12/31/1999	12/31/1998
Earnings Per Share	1.22	1.19	1.06	0.80	0.72	0.78	0.66	0.72
Cash Flow Per Share	2.18	2.26	2.04	1.64	1.43	1.23	1.13	0.91
Tang Book Value Per Share	1.17	1.33	1.14	0.83	0.41	1.77	1.98	1.75
Dividends Per Share	0.335	0.328	0.297	0.275	0.263	0.245	0.218	0.195
Dividend Payout %	27.46	27.52	28.07	34.38	36.21	31.41	33.21	27.08
Income Statement								
Total Revenue	1,069,880	4,184,933	3,761,819	3,403,585	2,354,723	2,264,313	2,080,012	1,888,226
EBITDA	188,322	769,345	716,475	607,606	481,169	491,575	424,481	383,951
Depn & Amortn	61,953	235,223	222,712	211,740	162,990	148,436	134,530	121,971
Income Before Taxes	115,179	488,778	448,418	351,971	289,745	318,534	267,238	240,238
Income Taxes	40,531	178,290	171,070	140,081	117,408	129,495	109,769	101,782
Net Income	74,648	310,488	277,348	209,770	188,170	206,127	175,786	192,506
Average Shares	260,044	261,776	262,737	261,574	259,856	263,892	268,838	268,094
Balance Sheet								
Current Assets	1,347,008	1,279,066	1,150,340	1,015,937	929,583	600,568	577,321	503,514
Total Assets	3,798,334	3,716,174	3,228,918	2,878,429	2,525,000	1,714,011	1,585,946	1,470,995
Current Liabilities	1,114,902	939,547	851,942	866,350	827,952	532,034	470,674	399,791
Long-Term Obligations	566,636	645,445	604,441	539,743	512,280	234,377	169,014	227,041
Total Liabilities	2,266,753	2,153,655	1,933,492	1,778,678	1,644,648	957,004	823,930	780,454
Stockholders' Equity	1,531,581	1,562,519	1,295,426	1,099,751	880,352	757,007	762,016	690,541
Shares Outstanding	255,313	257,541	257,416	259,880	255,800	254,322	258,832	258,958
Statistical Record								
Return on Assets %	8.80	8.92	9.08	7.76	8.88	12.46	11.50	13.33
Return on Equity %	22.18	21.67	23.16	21.19	22.98	27.07	24.20	30.99
EBITDA Margin %	17.60	18.38	19.05	17.85	20.43	21.71	20.41	20.33
Net Margin %	6.98	7.42	7.37	6.16	7.99	9.10	8.45	10.20
Asset Turnover	1.18	1.20	1.23	1.26	1.11	1.37	1.36	1.31
Current Ratio	1.21	1.36	1.35	1.17	1.12	1.13	1.23	1.26
Debt to Equity	0.37	0.41	0.47	0.49	0.58	0.31	0.22	0.33
Price Range	35.26-28.05	35.26-26.22	27.91-23.36	25.07-18.36	21.97-15.48	22.34-14.13	22.09-16.06	18.84-13.42
P/E Ratio	28.90-22.99	29.63-22.03	26.33-22.04	31.34-22.96	30.51-21.51	28.65-18.11	33.48-24.34	26.17-18.64
Average Yield %	1.05	1.08	1.16	1.22	1.33	1.31	1.13	1.30

Address: 370 Wabasha Street North, St. Paul, MN 55102-1390
Telephone: 651-293-2233
Web Site: www.ecolab.com

Officers: Douglas M. Baker Jr. - Pres., C.E.O. Steven L. Fritze - Exec. V.P., C.F.O. **Transfer Agents:** EquiServe Trust Company, N.A., Providence, RI

Investor Contact: 612-293-2809
No of Institutions: 327
Shares: 131,004,440 **% Held:** 51.02

EMERSON ELECTRIC CO.

Exchange	Symbol	Price	52Wk Range	Yield	P/E
NYS	EMR	$66.47 (5/31/2005)	70.44-58.77	2.50	20.90

Interim Earnings (Per Share)

Qtr.	Dec	Mar	Jun	Sep
2001-02	0.61	0.65	0.68	0.59
2002-03	0.52	0.56	0.85	0.66
2003-04	0.58	0.75	0.81	0.84
2004-05	0.70	0.83	...	...

Interim Dividends (Per Share)

Amt	Decl	Ex	Rec	Pay
0.40Q	8/3/2004	8/11/2004	8/13/2004	9/10/2004
0.415Q	11/2/2004	11/9/2004	11/12/2004	12/10/2004
0.415Q	2/1/2005	2/9/2005	2/11/2005	3/10/2005
0.415Q	5/3/2005	5/11/2005	5/13/2005	6/10/2005

Indicated Div: $1.66 (Div. Reinv. Plan)

Valuation Analysis

Forecast P/E	19.42 (5/28/2005)		
Market Cap	$27.7 Billion	Book Value	7.6 Billion
Price/Book	3.64	Price/Sales	1.69

Dividend Achiever Status

Rank	225	10 Year Growth Rate	7.28%
Total Years of Dividend Growth			48

Business Summary: Electrical (MIC: 11.14 SIC: 621 NAIC: 35312)

Emerson designs and supplies product technology and delivers engineering services in a range of industrial, commercial and consumer markets around the world. Co. is organized into five business segments, based on the nature of the products and services rendered. These segments are Process Management, Industrial Automation, Network Power, Climate Technologies, and Appliance and Tools. Through these segments Co. provides goods and services to allow customer to improve plant efficiency, quality control, power optimization, and storage capabilities. Co. operates under various trade and brand names in each of its segments.

Recent Developments: For the quarter ended Mar 31 2005, net income increased 9.4% to $348,000 thousand from net income of $318,000 thousand in the year-earlier quarter. Revenues were $4,227,000 thousand, up 9.5% from $3,859,000 thousand the year before. Total direct expense was $2,725,000 thousand versus $2,503,000 thousand in the prior-year quarter, an increase of 8.9%. Total indirect expense was $893,000 thousand versus $807,000 thousand in the prior-year quarter, an increase of 10.7%.

Prospects: Co. is benefiting from sales volume leverage and its previous restructuring actions, which are offsetting higher material costs and the dilution from the Marconi acquisition. Going forward, Co. expects that its shift to best-cost manufacturing, together with its aggressive sourcing initiatives, productivity improvements, and price increases will allow it to deliver improvement in operating margins in the coming quarters. Meanwhile, the acceleration of underlying orders in Asia and Latin America, combined with solid demand in the U.S., should help drive sales growth between 9.0% and 11.0% for fiscal 2005 and allow Co. to deliver 12.0% to 16.0% earnings per share growth.

Financial Data

(US$ in Thousands)	6 Mos	3 Mos	09/30/2004	09/30/2003	09/30/2002	09/30/2001	09/30/2000	09/30/1999
Earnings Per Share	3.18	3.09	2.98	2.59	0.29	2.40	3.30	3.00
Cash Flow Per Share	5.24	5.23	5.27	4.13	4.34	4.01	4.29	4.17
Tang Book Value Per Share	4.45	4.58	4.72	3.60	1.98	2.22	2.53	4.43
Dividends Per Share	1.630	1.615	1.600	1.570	1.550	1.530	1.430	1.300
Dividend Payout %	51.26	52.24	53.69	60.62	534.48	63.75	43.33	43.33
Income Statement								
Total Revenue	8,197,000	3,970,000	15,615,000	13,958,000	13,824,000	15,479,600	15,544,800	14,269,500
EBITDA	1,314,000	625,000	2,619,000	2,179,000	2,339,000	2,601,400	3,144,400	2,848,100
Depn & Amortn	276,000	137,000	557,000	534,000	541,000	708,500	678,500	637,500
Income Before Taxes	932,000	434,000	1,852,000	1,414,000	1,565,000	1,588,600	2,178,300	2,020,900
Income Taxes	287,000	137,000	595,000	401,000	505,000	556,800	755,900	707,300
Net Income	645,000	297,000	1,257,000	1,089,000	122,000	1,031,800	1,422,400	1,313,600
Average Shares	420,900	421,900	422,200	420,900	420,900	429,500	431,400	438,400
Balance Sheet								
Current Assets	7,146,000	6,841,000	6,416,000	5,500,000	4,961,000	5,320,100	5,482,700	5,124,400
Total Assets	17,263,000	16,956,000	16,361,000	15,194,000	14,545,000	15,046,400	15,164,300	13,623,500
Current Liabilities	5,107,000	4,749,000	4,339,000	3,417,000	4,400,000	5,379,100	5,218,800	4,590,400
Long-Term Obligations	2,881,000	2,886,000	3,136,000	3,733,000	2,990,000	2,255,600	2,247,700	1,317,100
Total Liabilities	9,652,000	9,301,000	9,123,000	8,734,000	8,804,000	8,932,400	8,761,500	7,443,000
Stockholders' Equity	7,611,000	7,655,000	7,238,000	6,460,000	5,741,000	6,114,000	6,402,800	6,180,500
Shares Outstanding	416,698	419,585	419,428	421,154	420,709	419,625	427,476	433,044
Statistical Record								
Return on Assets %	8.05	8.00	7.95	7.32	0.82	6.83	9.85	10.00
Return on Equity %	18.34	18.17	18.30	17.85	2.06	16.49	22.55	21.92
EBITDA Margin %	16.03	15.74	16.77	15.61	16.92	16.81	20.23	19.96
Net Margin %	7.87	7.48	8.05	7.80	0.88	6.67	9.15	9.21
Asset Turnover	0.98	0.98	0.99	0.94	0.93	1.02	1.08	1.09
Current Ratio	1.40	1.44	1.48	1.61	1.13	0.99	1.05	1.12
Debt to Equity	0.38	0.38	0.43	0.58	0.52	0.37	0.35	0.21
Price Range	70.44-56.56	70.44-56.56	68.46-52.65	56.79-42.42	65.51-43.20	78.81-45.80	70.19-41.13	70.94-51.81
P/E Ratio	22.15-17.79	22.80-18.30	22.97-17.67	21.93-16.38	225.90-148.97	32.84-19.08	21.27-12.46	23.65-17.27
Average Yield %	2.55	2.56	2.62	3.11	2.88	2.34	2.47	2.09

Address: 8000 W. Florissant Avenue, St. Louis, MO 63136
Telephone: 314-553-2000
Web Site: www.gotoemerson.com

Officers: David N. Farr - Chmn., C.E.O. James G. Berges - Pres. **Transfer Agents:** EquiServe Trust Company, N.A., Providence, RI

Investor Contact: 314-553-2197
No of Institutions: 742
Shares: 293,541,856 **% Held:** 70.00

ENERGEN CORP.

Exchange	Symbol	Price	52Wk Range	Yield	P/E
NYS	EGN	$65.18 (5/31/2005)	67.95-43.57	1.23	18.95

*7 Year Price Score 161.39 *NYSE Composite Index=100 *12 Month Price Score 109.94

TRADING VOLUME (thousand shares)

Interim Earnings (Per Share)

Qtr.	Mar	Jun	Sep	Dec
2002	1.24	0.37	0.01	0.47
2003	1.56	0.66	0.33	0.57
2004	1.65	0.61	0.37	0.86
2005	1.60	...	...	...

Interim Dividends (Per Share)

Amt	Decl	Ex	Rec	Pay
0.193Q	10/27/2004	11/10/2004	11/15/2004	12/1/2004
0.20Q	1/26/2005	2/11/2005	2/15/2005	3/1/2005
0.20Q	4/27/2005	5/11/2005	5/13/2005	6/1/2005
100%	4/27/2005	6/2/2005	5/13/2005	6/1/2005

Indicated Div: $0.80 (Div. Reinv. Plan)

Valuation Analysis

Forecast P/E	14.00 (5/28/2005)		
Market Cap	$2.4 Billion	Book Value	798.8 Million
Price/Book	2.99	Price/Sales	2.52

Dividend Achiever Status

Rank	297	**10 Year Growth Rate**	3.22%
Total Years of Dividend Growth			22

Business Summary: Gas Utilities (MIC: 7.4 SIC: 924 NAIC: 21210)

Energen is a diversified energy holding company engaged primarily in the acquisition, development, exploration and production of oil, natural gas and natural gas liquids in the continental United States and in the purchase, distribution, and sale of natural gas, principally in central and north Alabama. Co.'s two subsidiaries are Energen Resources Corporation, which operates Co.'s oil and gas operations and Alabama Gas Corporation (Alagasco). As of Dec 31 2004, Energen Resources' proved oil and gas reserves totaled 1,554 billion cubic feet equivalent. Alagasco's service territory is located in central and parts of north Alabama and includes 191 cities and communities in 28 counties.

Recent Developments: For the quarter ended Mar 31 2005, income from continuing operations decreased 2.0% to $58,941 thousand from income of $60,161 thousand in the year-earlier quarter. Net income decreased 1.9% to $59,046 thousand from net income of $60,185 thousand in the year-earlier quarter. Revenues were $361,008 thousand, up 2.8% from $351,282 thousand the year before. Operating income was $105,128 thousand versus an income of $105,982 thousand in the prior-year quarter, a decrease of 0.8%. Total direct expense was $197,262 thousand versus $191,860 thousand in the prior-year quarter, an increase of 2.8%. Total indirect expense was $58,618 thousand versus $53,440 thousand in the prior-year quarter, an increase of 9.7%.

Prospects: Citing its recent operating results, on Apr 27 2005 Co. reaffirmed its full-year 2005 earnings guidance range of $4.45 to $4.65 per diluted share. Co. noted that this guidance includes an estimated $0.03 per diluted share from an unidentified acquisition of $200.0 million budgeted to occur in the fourth quarter of 2005. Co.'s 2005 guidance also assumes that prices applicable to Energen Resources' unhedged production will average: $6.50 per thousand cubic feet for gas (May through December); $45 per barrel for oil (April through December); and $0.70 per gallon for natural gas liquids (April through December). Co. also reaffirmed its 2006 earnings guidance of $5.00 to $5.20 per diluted share.

Financial Data

(US$ in Thousands)	3 Mos	12/31/2004	12/31/2003	12/31/2002	12/31/2001	09/30/2001	09/30/2000	09/30/1999
Earnings Per Share	3.44	3.49	3.10	2.03	0.12	2.18	1.75	1.38
Cash Flow Per Share	8.50	8.00	6.86	6.35	0.54	5.09	3.48	4.41
Tang Book Value Per Share	21.80	21.97	19.30	16.77	15.18	15.61	13.21	12.09
Dividends Per Share	0.770	0.755	0.730	0.710	0.690	0.685	0.665	0.645
Dividend Payout %	22.38	21.63	23.55	34.98	575.00	31.42	38.00	46.74
Income Statement								
Total Revenue	361,008	937,384	842,221	677,175	146,164	784,973	555,595	497,517
EBITDA	136,666	366,766	334,440	245,575	36,013	212,917	184,649	167,333
Depn & Amortn	31,453	120,960	117,785	110,767	25,184	86,975	87,073	88,615
Income Before Taxes	93,543	203,063	174,393	91,095	195	83,872	59,807	41,545
Income Taxes	34,602	75,613	64,128	20,509	(3,384)	15,976	6,789	135
Net Income	59,046	127,463	110,654	68,639	3,658	67,896	53,018	41,410
Average Shares	36,828	36,558	35,716	33,838	31,277	31,083	30,359	29,920
Balance Sheet								
Net PPE	1,800,548	1,783,059	1,433,451	1,256,803	1,005,679	998,334	907,829	861,107
Total Assets	2,233,949	2,181,739	1,781,432	1,530,891	1,240,356	1,223,879	1,203,041	1,184,895
Long-Term Obligations	692,895	612,891	552,842	512,954	544,133	544,110	353,932	371,824
Total Liabilities	1,435,156	1,378,073	1,082,400	948,081	766,151	743,112	802,181	823,391
Stockholders' Equity	798,793	803,666	699,032	582,810	474,205	480,767	400,860	361,504
Shares Outstanding	36,640	36,582	36,223	34,745	31,248	30,799	30,350	29,903
Statistical Record								
Return on Assets %	6.20	6.41	6.68	4.95	0.24	5.60	4.43	3.80
Return on Equity %	16.39	16.92	17.26	12.99	0.67	15.40	13.87	11.99
EBITDA Margin %	37.86	39.13	39.71	36.26	24.64	27.12	33.23	33.63
Net Margin %	16.36	13.60	13.14	10.14	2.50	8.65	9.54	8.32
PPE Turnover	0.58	0.58	0.63	0.60	0.12	0.82	0.63	0.62
Asset Turnover	0.46	0.47	0.51	0.49	0.10	0.65	0.46	0.46
Debt to Equity	0.87	0.76	0.79	0.88	1.15	1.13	0.88	1.03
Price Range	67.95-40.30	59.80-39.99	41.96-28.23	29.80-21.86	25.20-22.00	39.71-22.21	30.05-14.75	20.25-13.63
P/E Ratio	19.75-11.72	17.13-11.46	13.54-9.11	14.68-10.77	210.00-183.33	18.22-10.19	17.17-8.43	14.67-9.87
Average Yield %	1.48	1.60	2.14	2.76	2.91	2.27	3.36	3.62

Address: 605 Richard Arrington Jr. Blvd. N., Birmingham, AL 35203-2707
Telephone: 205-326-2700
Web Site: www.energen.com

Officers: William Michael Warren Jr. - Chmn., Pres., C.E.O. Geoffrey C. Ketcham - Exec. V.P., C.F.O., Treas. **Transfer Agents:** EquiServe Trust Company, N.A., Providence, RI

Investor Contact: 800-654-3206
No of Institutions: 198
Shares: 24,190,678 **% Held:** 66.04

ESSEX PROPERTY TRUST, INC.

Exchange	Symbol	Price	52Wk Range	Yield	P/E
NYS	ESS	$80.00 (5/31/2005)	85.11-65.20	4.05	18.87

Interim Earnings (Per Share)

Qtr.	Mar	Jun	Sep	Dec
2002	0.61	1.14	0.57	0.50
2003	0.48	0.50	0.43	0.28
2004	0.26	0.23	1.49	1.39
2005	1.13	...	...	...

Interim Dividends (Per Share)

Amt	Decl	Ex	Rec	Pay
0.79Q	9/17/2004	9/28/2004	9/30/2004	10/15/2004
0.79Q	12/14/2004	12/29/2004	12/31/2004	1/15/2005
0.81Q	2/24/2005	3/29/2005	3/31/2005	4/15/2005
0.81Q	5/17/2005	6/28/2005	6/30/2005	7/15/2005

Indicated Div: $3.24

Valuation Analysis

Forecast P/E	17.67 (5/28/2005)		
Market Cap	$1.8 Billion	Book Value	606.4 Million
Price/Book	3.04	Price/Sales	6.21

Dividend Achiever Status

Rank	37	**10 Year Growth Rate**	20.27%
Total Years of Dividend Growth			10

Business Summary: Property, Real Estate & Development (MIC: 8.3 SIC: 798 NAIC: 25930)

Essex Property Trust is a self-administered equity real estate investment trust engaged in the ownership, acquisition, development and management of multifamily apartment communities. Co.'s multifamily portfolio as of Dec 31 2004 consisted of ownership interests in 120 properties (25,518 apartment units), of which 13,755 units are located in Southern California (Los Angeles, Ventura, Orange, San Diego and Riverside counties), 5,810 units are located in Northern California (the San Francisco Bay Area), 5,651 are located in the Pacific Northwest (4,776 units in the Seattle metropolitan area and 875 units in the Portland, OR metropolitan area), and 302 units are located in Houston, TX.

Recent Developments: For the quarter ended Mar 31 2005, income from continuing operations increased 316.6% to $25,176 thousand from income of $6,043 thousand in the year-earlier quarter. Net income increased 316.7% to $26,877 thousand from net income of $6,450 thousand in the year-earlier quarter. Revenues were $82,330 thousand, up 17.2% from $70,264 thousand the year before.

Prospects: In the first quarter of 2005, Co.'s earnings benefited from stronger-than-expected performance of its properties and one-time revenues which contributed to solid growth in funds from operations. Co.'s apartment fundamentals continue to improve with same-store property revenues in each region, except the San Francisco Bay Area, increasing substantially in the last four quarters. Co. anticipates that these positive trends, coupled with the benefits of its supply constrained markets, will continue to support the overall improvement in its operating results. As a result, Co. is increasing its guidance for full-year 2005 funds from operations to a range of $4.47 to $4.53 per diluted share.

Financial Data (US$ in Thousands)	3 Mos	12/31/2004	12/31/2003	12/31/2002	12/31/2001	12/31/2000	12/31/1999	12/31/1998
Earnings Per Share	4.24	3.36	1.70	2.82	2.59	2.37	2.36	1.36
Cash Flow Per Share	5.39	5.30	4.81	4.63	5.36	5.04	4.77	3.55
Tang Book Value Per Share	25.21	24.58	24.74	23.41	20.98	21.27	21.48	23.42
Dividends Per Share	3.180	3.160	3.120	3.080	2.800	2.380	2.150	1.950
Dividend Payout %	75.00	94.05	183.53	109.22	108.11	100.42	91.10	143.38
Income Statement								
Property Income	77,321	283,483	222,868	177,265	183,482	167,771	140,427	122,042
Non-Property Income	...	...	11,582	22,857	22,152	10,969	5,618	3,217
Total Revenue	77,321	283,483	234,450	200,122	205,634	178,740	146,045	125,259
Depn & Amortn	20,203	74,510	50,417	37,841	36,952	31,404	26,716	22,666
Interest Expense	18,147	63,023	42,751	35,012	39,105	30,384	21,268	19,374
Net Income	26,877	79,693	37,947	52,874	48,545	44,353	43,564	26,328
Average Shares	23,330	23,156	21,678	18,725	18,768	18,657	18,491	16,808
Balance Sheet								
Total Assets	2,230,988	2,217,217	1,728,564	1,619,734	1,329,458	1,281,849	1,062,313	931,796
Long-Term Obligations	1,317,955	1,316,984	832,229	804,063	638,660	595,535	384,108	361,515
Total Liabilities	1,392,415	1,385,810	895,064	865,890	691,379	652,044	436,331	411,564
Stockholders' Equity	606,435	591,277	589,701	491,314	386,599	391,675	387,693	389,800
Shares Outstanding	23,059	23,033	22,825	20,983	18,428	18,417	18,049	16,640
Statistical Record								
Return on Assets %	4.63	4.03	2.27	3.59	3.72	3.77	4.37	3.15
Return on Equity %	17.02	13.46	7.02	12.05	12.48	11.35	11.21	6.68
Net Margin %	34.76	28.11	16.19	26.42	23.61	24.81	29.83	21.02
Price Range	85.11-60.05	85.11-60.05	66.08-49.50	55.75-45.23	55.94-43.20	57.75-32.81	35.38-26.13	35.00-27.25
P/E Ratio	20.07-14.16	25.33-17.87	38.87-29.12	19.77-16.04	21.60-16.68	24.37-13.84	14.99-11.07	25.74-20.04
Average Yield %	4.41	4.55	5.36	6.11	5.67	5.36	6.77	6.12

Address: 925 East Meadow Drive, Palo Alto, CA 94303 **Telephone:** 650-494-3700 **Web Site:** www.expresspropertytrust.com	**Officers:** George M. Marcus - Chmn. Keith R. Guericke - Vice-Chmn., Pres., C.E.O. **Transfer Agents:**	**Investor Contact:** 650-849-1600 **No of Institutions:** 125 **Shares:** 19,347,530 **% Held:** 84.31

EXPEDITORS INTERNATIONAL OF WASHINGTON, INC.

Exchange	Symbol	Price	52Wk Range	Yield	P/E
NMS	EXPD	$50.98 (5/31/2005)	57.71-45.80	0.59	34.92

*7 Year Price Score 157.99 *NYSE Composite Index=100 *12 Month Price Score 94.11

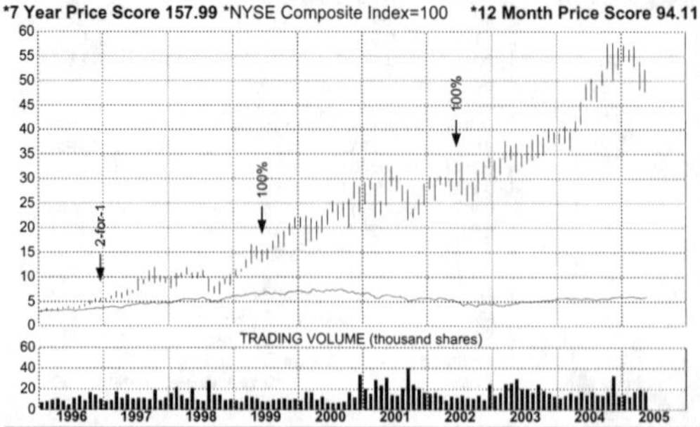

Interim Earnings (Per Share)

Qtr.	Mar	Jun	Sep	Dec
2002	0.20	0.22	0.28	0.33
2003	0.23	0.26	0.30	0.33
2004	0.29	0.34	0.39	0.39
2005	0.34	...	...	...

Interim Dividends (Per Share)

Amt	Decl	Ex	Rec	Pay
0.08S	11/10/2003	11/26/2003	12/1/2003	12/15/2003
0.11S	5/6/2004	5/27/2004	6/1/2004	6/15/2004
0.11S	11/8/2004	11/29/2004	12/1/2004	12/15/2004
0.15S	5/9/2005	5/27/2005	6/1/2005	6/15/2005

Indicated Div: $0.30

Valuation Analysis

Forecast P/E	31.13 (5/28/2005)		
Market Cap	$5.4 Billion	Book Value	831.9 Million
Price/Book	6.53	Price/Sales	1.57

Dividend Achiever Status

Rank	5	10 Year Growth Rate	33.21%
Total Years of Dividend Growth			10

Business Summary: Misc. Transportation Services (MIC: 15.4 SIC: 731 NAIC: 41614)

Expeditors International of Washington is engaged in the business of providing global logistics services. Co. offers its customers an international network supporting the movement and strategic positioning of goods. Co.'s services include the consolidation or forwarding of air and ocean freight. Co. also provides additional services including distribution management, vendor consolidation, cargo insurance, purchase order management and customized logistics information. As of May 4 2005, Co. had 159 full-service offices, 53 satellite locations and seven international service centers located on six continents.

Recent Developments: For the quarter ended Mar 31 2005, net income increased 18.5% to $37,744 thousand from net income of $31,844 thousand in the year-earlier quarter. Revenues were $825,164 thousand, up 20.1% from $686,850 thousand the year before. Operating income was $57,557 thousand versus an income of $48,808 thousand in the prior-year quarter, an increase of 17.9%. Total direct expense was $528,408 thousand versus $433,471 thousand in the prior-year quarter, an increase of 21.9%. Total indirect expense was $239,199 thousand versus $204,571 thousand in the prior-year quarter, an increase of 16.9%.

Prospects: During the first quarter of 2005, Co. opened several new offices and is continuing to strengthen its presence in China. Separately, earnings could benefit from a lower tax rate in 2005 stemming from the adoption of a plan under Internal Revenue Code (IRC) 965, which was added by the Jobs Act. Although, this lower tax rate will only affect 2005 results if the plan is adopted. Meanwhile, Co. expects to spend approximately $30.0 million for normal capital expenditures in 2005; however, total capital expenditures in 2005 will likely exceed $100.0 million if Co. adopts a plan calling for capital expenditures to meet the investment requirements of IRC 965.

Financial Data

(US$ in Thousands)	3 Mos	12/31/2004	12/31/2003	12/31/2002	12/31/2001	12/31/2000	12/31/1999	12/31/1998
Earnings Per Share	1.46	1.41	1.12	1.03	0.89	0.76	0.55	0.45
Cash Flow Per Share	1.99	1.81	1.09	1.12	1.61	1.51	0.53	0.54
Tang Book Value Per Share	7.63	7.40	5.96	4.98	4.02	3.52	2.79	2.20
Dividends Per Share	0.220	0.220	0.160	0.120	0.100	0.070	0.050	0.035
Dividend Payout %	15.07	15.60	14.29	11.65	11.30	9.21	9.09	7.87
Income Statement								
Total Revenue	825,164	3,317,499	2,624,941	2,296,903	1,652,633	1,695,181	1,444,575	1,063,707
EBITDA	66,092	271,933	217,122	195,544	170,232	150,854	115,029	89,941
Depn & Amortn	7,339	27,978	25,816	23,675	24,618	23,401	21,567	16,083
Income Before Taxes	60,871	249,580	195,642	177,990	154,294	133,348	94,645	75,577
Income Taxes	22,074	88,415	71,142	65,461	57,051	50,313	35,470	28,303
Net Income	37,744	156,126	121,952	112,529	97,243	83,035	59,175	47,274
Average Shares	112,151	110,817	109,001	108,881	109,741	109,358	107,655	106,116
Balance Sheet								
Total Assets	1,385,388	1,364,053	1,040,847	879,948	688,437	661,740	511,780	406,596
Total Liabilities	553,445	549,177	392,122	356,136	273,814	299,956	229,395	189,398
Stockholders' Equity	831,943	807,404	645,501	523,812	414,623	361,784	282,385	217,198
Shares Outstanding	106,618	106,643	105,056	104,220	103,223	102,902	101,288	98,728
Statistical Record								
Return on Assets %	12.92	12.95	12.70	14.35	14.40	14.11	12.89	12.63
Return on Equity %	21.41	21.43	20.86	23.98	25.05	25.71	23.69	24.42
EBITDA Margin %	8.01	8.20	8.27	8.51	10.30	8.90	7.96	8.46
Net Margin %	4.57	4.71	4.65	4.90	5.88	4.90	4.10	4.44
Asset Turnover	2.76	2.75	2.73	2.93	2.45	2.88	3.15	2.84
Price Range	57.71-39.36	57.71-35.75	40.28-29.90	34.27-25.40	32.64-21.63	29.44-16.31	22.16-10.19	12.03-6.50
P/E Ratio	39.53-26.96	40.93-25.35	35.96-26.70	33.27-24.66	36.67-24.30	38.73-21.46	40.28-18.52	26.74-14.44
Average Yield %	0.44	0.48	0.45	0.41	0.37	0.31	0.32	0.37

Address: 1015 Third Avenue, 12th Floor, Seattle, WA 98104 **Telephone:** 206-674-3400 **Web Site:** www.expd.com	**Officers:** Peter J. Rose - Chmn., C.E.O. Glenn M. Alger - Pres., C.O.O. **Transfer Agents:** EquiServe Trust Company, N.A., New Jersey, NJ	**Investor Contact:** 206-674-3427 **No of Institutions:** 271 **Shares:** 90,695,232 **% Held:** 84.92

EXXON MOBIL CORP.

Exchange	Symbol	Price	52Wk Range	Yield	P/E
NYS	XOM	$56.20 (5/31/2005)	63.57-43.37	2.06	13.13

*7 Year Price Score 111.84 *NYSE Composite Index=100 *12 Month Price Score 107.44

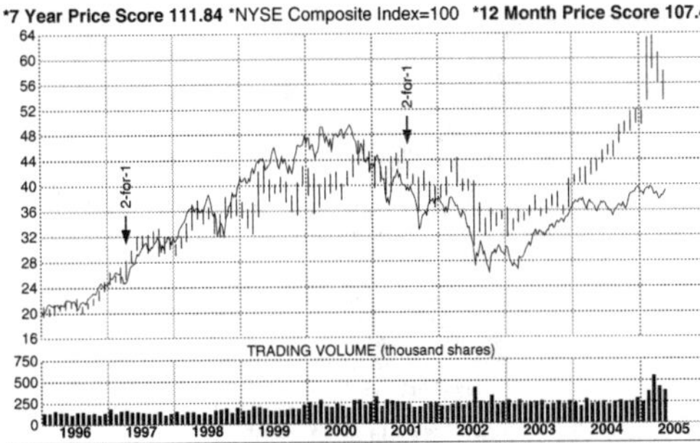

Interim Earnings (Per Share)

Qtr.	Mar	Jun	Sep	Dec
2002	0.30	0.38	0.39	0.60
2003	1.05	0.62	0.55	1.01
2004	0.83	0.88	0.88	1.30
2005	1.22	...	...	...

Interim Dividends (Per Share)

Amt	Decl	Ex	Rec	Pay
0.27Q	7/28/2004	8/11/2004	8/13/2004	9/10/2004
0.27Q	10/27/2004	11/9/2004	11/12/2004	12/10/2004
0.27Q	1/26/2005	2/8/2005	2/10/2005	3/10/2005
0.29Q	4/27/2005	5/11/2005	5/13/2005	6/10/2005

Indicated Div: $1.16 (Div. Reinv. Plan)

Valuation Analysis

Forecast P/E	12.70 (6/2/2005)		
Market Cap	$357.8 Billion	Book Value	103.7 Billion
Price/Book	3.45	Price/Sales	1.14

Dividend Achiever Status

Rank	290	**10 Year Growth Rate**	3.84%
Total Years of Dividend Growth			22

Business Summary: Oil and Gas (MIC: 14.2 SIC: 911 NAIC: 24110)

Exxon Mobil's principal business is energy, involving exploration for, and production of, crude oil and natural gas, manufacturing of petroleum products and transportation and sale of crude oil, natural gas and petroleum products. Co. is a major manufacturer and marketer of basic petrochemicals, including olefins, aromatics, polyethylene and polypropylene plastics and a wide variety of specialty products. Co. also has interests in electric power generation facilities. As of Dec 31 2004, worldwide proved developed and undeveloped reserves were: crude oil and natural gas liquids, 8,395 million barrels; and natural gas, 31,843 billion cubic feet.

Recent Developments: For the quarter ended Mar 31 2005, net income increased 44.5% to $7,860 million from net income of $5,440 million in the year-earlier quarter. Revenues were $82,051 million, up 21.4% from $67,602 million the year before. Total direct expense was $45,397 million versus $36,068 million in the prior-year quarter, an increase of 25.9%. Total indirect expense was $23,600 million versus $22,370 million in the prior-year quarter, an increase of 5.5%.

Prospects: Results are being positively affected by continued strong earnings growth from Co.'s exploration and production operations due to sharply higher crude oil and natural gas prices, partially offset by declining output in mature oil fields and production stoppages. Meanwhile, Co.'s refining and marketing operations are benefiting from improved refining margins in the U.S., while earnings growth at Co.'s chemical business is being driven by strong market conditions. Separately, Co. is continuing to actively invest in capital spending and exploration projects. Co. is projecting capital expenditures of between $15.00 billion and $16.00 billion in 2005.

Financial Data

(US$ in Thousands)	3 Mos	12/31/2004	12/31/2003	12/31/2002	12/31/2001	12/31/2000	12/31/1999	12/31/1998
Earnings Per Share	4.28	3.89	3.23	1.68	2.21	2.52	1.13	1.29
Cash Flow Per Share	6.82	6.24	4.30	3.15	3.33	3.29	2.17	2.28
Tang Book Value Per Share	16.29	15.90	13.69	11.13	10.74	10.21	9.12	8.99
Dividends Per Share	1.080	1.060	0.980	0.920	0.910	0.880	0.835	0.820
Dividend Payout %	25.23	27.25	30.34	54.76	41.18	34.92	74.22	63.57
Income Statement								
Total Revenue	82,051,000	298,035,000	246,738,000	204,506,000	213,488,000	232,748,000	185,527,000	117,772,000
EBITDA	15,456,000	51,646,000	41,220,000	26,218,000	32,356,000	35,800,000	20,149,000	14,496,000
Depn & Amortn	2,553,000	9,767,000	9,047,000	8,310,000	7,944,000	8,130,000	8,304,000	5,340,000
Income Before Taxes	12,903,000	41,241,000	31,966,000	17,510,000	24,119,000	27,081,000	11,150,000	9,056,000
Income Taxes	5,043,000	15,911,000	11,006,000	6,499,000	9,014,000	11,091,000	3,240,000	2,616,000
Net Income	7,860,000	25,330,000	21,510,000	11,460,000	15,320,000	17,720,000	7,910,000	6,370,000
Average Shares	6,420,999	6,519,001	6,662,001	6,803,001	6,941,001	7,034,001	6,906,001	4,855,999
Balance Sheet								
Current Assets	68,590,000	60,377,000	45,960,000	38,291,000	35,681,000	40,399,000	31,141,000	17,593,000
Total Assets	201,252,000	195,256,000	174,278,000	152,644,000	143,174,000	149,000,000	144,521,000	92,630,000
Current Liabilities	47,757,000	42,981,000	38,386,000	33,175,000	30,114,000	38,191,000	38,733,000	19,412,000
Long-Term Obligations	5,015,000	5,013,000	4,756,000	6,655,000	7,099,000	7,280,000	8,402,000	4,530,000
Total Liabilities	97,554,000	93,500,000	84,363,000	78,047,000	70,013,000	78,243,000	81,055,000	48,880,000
Stockholders' Equity	103,698,000	101,756,000	89,915,000	74,597,000	73,161,000	70,757,000	63,466,000	43,750,000
Shares Outstanding	6,365,734	6,400,999	6,568,001	6,700,001	6,809,001	6,930,001	6,959,785	4,855,999
Statistical Record								
Return on Assets %	14.55	13.67	13.16	7.75	10.49	12.04	6.67	6.75
Return on Equity %	28.41	26.36	26.15	15.51	21.29	26.33	14.76	14.57
EBITDA Margin %	18.84	17.33	16.71	12.82	15.16	15.38	10.86	12.31
Net Margin %	9.58	8.50	8.72	5.60	7.18	7.61	4.26	5.41
Asset Turnover	1.64	1.61	1.51	1.38	1.46	1.58	1.56	1.25
Current Ratio	1.44	1.40	1.20	1.15	1.18	1.06	0.80	0.91
Debt to Equity	0.05	0.05	0.05	0.09	0.10	0.10	0.13	0.10
Price Range	63.57-41.52	51.97-40.10	41.00-31.82	44.38-30.27	45.77-35.83	47.22-35.53	43.22-32.41	38.28-29.06
P/E Ratio	14.85-9.70	13.36-10.31	12.69-9.85	26.42-18.02	20.71-16.21	18.74-14.10	38.25-28.68	29.68-22.53
Average Yield %	2.21	2.34	2.71	2.44	2.20	2.12	2.18	2.37

Address: 5959 Las Colinas Boulevard, Irving, TX 75039-2298
Telephone: 972-444-1000
Web Site: www.exxonmobil.com

Officers: Lee R. Raymond - Chmn., C.E.O. R. W. Tillerson - Pres. **Transfer Agents:** EquiServe Trust Company, N.A., Providence, RI

No of Institutions: 1195
Shares: 3,256,652,800 **% Held:** 51.00

F.N.B. CORP

Exchange	Symbol	Price	52Wk Range	Yield	P/E
NYS	FNB	$18.58 (5/31/2005)	22.72-17.77	4.95	15.23

***7 Year Price Score 126.20** *NYSE Composite Index=100 ***12 Month Price Score 89.35**

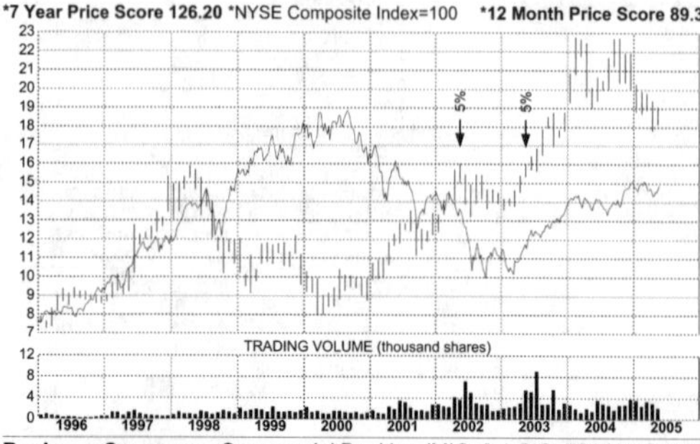

Interim Earnings (Per Share)

Qtr.	Mar	Jun	Sep	Dec
2002	(0.19)	0.50	0.51	0.51
2003	0.50	0.53	0.01	0.22
2004	0.34	0.32	0.31	0.31
2005	0.28	...	...	...

Interim Dividends (Per Share)

Amt	Decl	Ex	Rec	Pay
0.23Q	8/18/2004	8/30/2004	9/1/2004	9/15/2004
0.23Q	11/10/2004	11/29/2004	12/1/2004	12/15/2004
0.23Q	2/16/2005	2/25/2005	3/1/2005	3/15/2005
0.23Q	5/18/2005	5/27/2005	6/1/2005	6/15/2005

Indicated Div: $0.92 (Div. Reinv. Plan)

Valuation Analysis

Forecast P/E	N/A		
Market Cap	$1.0 Billion	Book Value	452.7 Million
Price/Book	2.31	Price/Sales	3.10

Dividend Achiever Status

Rank	71	**10 Year Growth Rate**	16.69%
Total Years of Dividend Growth			20

Business Summary: Commercial Banking (MIC: 8.1 SIC: 021 NAIC: 22110)

F.N.B., with assets of $5.03 billion as of Dec 31 2004, is a financial holding company that provides a range of financial services to consumers and small- to medium-size businesses in its market areas. Co. operates in Pennsylvania and northeastern Ohio. As of Dec 31 2004, Co.'s Community Banking segment consisted of a regional community bank. The Wealth Management segment consisted of a trust company, a registered investment advisor and a broker dealer subsidiary. The Insurance segment consisted of an insurance agency and a reinsurer. The Consumer Finance segment consisted of a multi-state consumer finance company.

Recent Developments: For the quarter ended Mar 31 2005, net income decreased 8.1% to $14,910 thousand from net income of $16,222 thousand in the year-earlier quarter. Net interest income was $45,910 thousand, up 8.8% from $42,205 thousand the year before. Provision for loan losses was $2,331 thousand versus $4,622 thousand in the prior-year quarter, a decrease of 49.6%. Non-interest income fell 11.3% to $18,416 thousand, while non-interest expense advanced 16.5% to $40,338 thousand.

Prospects: Co.'s results continue to be influenced by its recent expansion initiatives. For instance, on Oct 8 2004 Co. completed its acquisition of Slippery Rock Financial Corporation, parent company of First National Bank of Slippery Rock, with $335.0 million in assets. Further, on Feb 18 2005 Co. completed its acquisition of NSD, the parent company of NorthSide Bank, with $503.0 million in assets. Separately, on Apr 25 2005, Co. announced the signing of a definitive agreement to acquire North East Bancshares, Inc. of North East, PA in Erie County. The stock transaction is valued at $15.5 million. Co. anticipates that the transaction will be completed during the fourth quarter of 2005.

Financial Data

(US$ in Thousands)	3 Mos	12/31/2004	12/31/2003	12/31/2002	12/31/2001	12/31/2000	12/31/1999	12/31/1998
Earnings Per Share	1.22	1.29	1.25	1.34	1.52	1.62	1.48	1.32
Cash Flow Per Share	1.60	2.23	2.17	1.05	1.36	2.17	2.78	(1.02)
Tang Book Value Per Share	4.67	4.79	8.73	11.08	13.02	12.51	11.35	11.77
Dividends Per Share	0.920	0.920	0.930	0.810	0.698	0.678	0.645	0.615
Dividend Payout %	75.41	71.32	74.36	60.32	45.92	41.85	43.58	46.59
Income Statement								
Interest Income	69,400	254,448	423,313	426,784	296,693	290,936	254,916	235,985
Interest Expense	23,490	84,390	129,836	145,671	125,667	135,308	106,467	103,385
Net Interest Income	45,910	170,058	293,477	281,113	171,026	155,628	148,449	132,600
Provision for Losses	2,331	16,280	24,339	19,094	12,915	10,877	9,240	7,255
Non-Interest Income	18,416	78,141	130,571	120,873	82,799	55,645	46,928	31,745
Non-Interest Expense	40,338	142,587	315,323	289,444	174,830	137,501	129,679	109,174
Income Before Taxes	21,657	89,332	84,386	93,448	66,080	62,895	56,458	47,916
Income Taxes	6,747	27,537	25,597	30,113	21,508	20,119	17,163	16,044
Net Income	14,910	61,795	58,789	63,335	44,572	42,776	39,295	31,872
Average Shares	53,808	48,012	46,972	47,073	29,311	25,484	26,468	24,265
Balance Sheet								
Net Loans & Leases	3,633,235	3,338,994	5,634,336	5,152,098	3,161,659	2,923,336	2,767,463	2,298,834
Total Assets	5,609,386	5,027,009	8,308,310	7,090,232	4,129,087	3,886,548	3,706,184	3,250,695
Total Deposits	3,915,323	3,598,087	6,159,499	5,426,157	3,292,392	3,102,937	2,909,434	2,708,572
Total Liabilities	5,156,710	4,702,907	7,701,401	6,491,636	3,759,890	3,565,304	3,415,869	2,978,537
Stockholders' Equity	452,676	324,102	606,909	598,596	369,197	321,244	290,315	272,158
Shares Outstanding	56,274	50,058	46,313	46,055	28,346	25,541	25,385	22,928
Statistical Record								
Return on Assets %	1.18	0.92	0.76	1.13	1.11	1.12	1.13	1.08
Return on Equity %	17.21	13.24	9.75	13.09	12.91	13.95	13.97	12.68
Net Interest Margin %	66.15	66.83	69.33	65.87	57.64	53.49	58.23	56.19
Efficiency Ratio %	45.93	42.87	56.93	52.85	46.07	39.67	42.96	40.78
Loans to Deposits	0.93	0.93	0.91	0.95	0.96	0.94	0.95	0.85
Price Range	22.72-18.72	22.77-18.80	18.80-13.58	16.03-12.39	13.52-9.85	10.42-7.96	12.22-9.14	15.89-10.18
P/E Ratio	18.62-15.34	17.65-14.57	15.04-10.87	11.96-9.24	8.89-6.48	6.43-4.92	8.25-6.18	12.04-7.71
Average Yield %	4.50	4.40	5.75	5.62	5.97	7.38	6.04	4.72

Address: 2150 Goodlette Road North, Naples, FL 34102
Telephone: 239-262-7600
Web Site: www.fnbcorporation.com

Officers: Peter Mortensen - Chmn. Stephen J. Gurgovits - Pres., C.E.O. **Transfer Agents:** F.N.B. Shareholder Services, Naples, FL

Investor Contact: 239-659-9894
No of Institutions: 92
Shares: 15,947,890 **% Held:** 28.41

FAMILY DOLLAR STORES, INC.

Exchange	Symbol	Price	52Wk Range	Yield	P/E
NYS	FDO	$25.67 (5/31/2005)	34.98-24.00	1.48	17.00

*7 Year Price Score 97.01 *NYSE Composite Index=100 *12 Month Price Score 88.68

TRADING VOLUME (thousand shares)

Interim Earnings (Per Share)

Qtr.	Nov	Feb	May	Aug
2001-02	0.29	0.37	0.35	0.24
2002-03	0.33	0.42	0.40	0.28
2003-04	0.37	0.47	0.43	0.26
2004-05	0.33	0.48	...	...

Interim Dividends (Per Share)

Amt	Decl	Ex	Rec	Pay
0.085Q	8/17/2004	9/13/2004	9/15/2004	10/15/2004
0.085Q	11/2/2004	12/13/2004	12/15/2004	1/14/2005
0.095Q	1/20/2005	3/11/2005	3/15/2005	4/15/2005
0.095Q	5/16/2005	6/13/2005	6/15/2005	7/15/2005

Indicated Div: $0.38

Valuation Analysis

Forecast P/E 18.27 (6/2/2005)

Market Cap $4.3 Billion Book Value 1.4 Billion

Price/Book 2.99 Price/Sales 0.77

Dividend Achiever Status

Rank 144 **10 Year Growth Rate** 11.61%

Total Years of Dividend Growth 28

Business Summary: Retail - General (MIC: 5.2 SIC: 331 NAIC: 52990)

Family Dollar Stores is engaged in the operation of a chain of self-service retail discount stores. The stores offer a variety of hardlines and softlines merchandise. Hardlines merchandise includes primarily household chemicals and paper products, candy, snacks and other foods, health and beauty aids, electronics, housewares and giftware, pet food and supplies, toys, stationery and school supplies, seasonal goods, hardware and automotive supplies. Softlines merchandise includes men's, women's, boys', girls' and infants' clothing, shoes, and domestic items such as blankets, sheets and towels. As of Oct 1 2004, Co. operated 5,481 stores in 44 states and the District of Columbia.

Recent Developments: For the quarter ended Feb 26 2005, net income decreased 0.4% to $80.1 million from net income of $80.4 million in the year-earlier quarter. Revenues were $1.59 billion, up 13.1% from $1.40 billion in the equivalent 2004 quarter. The improvement in sales was primarily attributed to an increase in sales in comparable stores with the balance of the increases primarily relating to sales from new stores opened as part of Co.'s new store expansion program. Selling, general and administrative expenses increased 13.6% to $394.4 million, primarily reflecting additional costs arising from the growth in the number of stores in operation.

Prospects: Co.'s outlook is mixed. On the positive side, sales in comparable stores for the second quarter ended Feb 26 2005 rose approximately 4.5% above the second quarter last fiscal year, including an increase of about 5.8% in sales of hardlines and no change in sales of softlines. However, gross profit margin as a percent to sales decreased to 32.8% from 33.8% in the year-ago period, due to stronger sales of lower margin basic consumables and higher freight costs. Meanwhile, Co. has begun the planned installation in selected stores of coolers for the sale of perishable food. By the end of the second quarter of 2005, coolers had been installed and stocked with perishable food in about 200 stores.

Financial Data

(US$ in Thousands)	6 Mos	3 Mos	08/28/2004	08/30/2003	08/31/2002	09/01/2001	08/26/2000	08/28/1999
Earnings Per Share	1.51	1.49	1.53	1.43	1.25	1.10	1.00	0.81
Cash Flow Per Share	1.76	2.00	2.21	1.72	2.34	0.95	1.07	0.64
Tang Book Value Per Share	8.58	8.40	8.13	7.61	6.66	5.57	4.66	4.00
Dividends Per Share	0.340	0.330	0.320	0.280	0.250	0.230	0.210	0.190
Dividend Payout %	22.59	22.09	20.92	19.58	20.00	20.91	21.00	23.46
Income Statement								
Total Revenue	2,966,999	1,380,245	5,281,888	4,750,171	4,162,652	3,665,362	3,132,639	2,751,181
EBITDA	264,728	111,844	512,098	478,040	418,636	366,107	325,421	266,468
Depn & Amortn	53,066	25,216	97,883	88,315	77,015	67,685	54,509	43,788
Income Before Taxes	211,662	86,628	414,215	389,725	341,621	298,422	270,911	222,679
Income Taxes	77,160	31,273	151,530	142,250	124,692	108,917	98,894	82,600
Net Income	134,502	55,355	262,685	247,475	216,929	189,505	172,017	140,079
Average Shares	168,361	168,008	171,624	173,354	174,049	172,774	172,648	172,511
Balance Sheet								
Current Assets	1,376,378	1,268,289	1,225,308	1,156,492	1,055,859	807,265	750,673	719,955
Total Assets	2,350,927	2,227,417	2,167,422	1,985,695	1,754,619	1,399,745	1,243,714	1,095,252
Current Liabilities	824,143	724,455	713,551	595,331	530,780	390,294	412,017	378,546
Total Liabilities	914,246	819,510	807,022	674,726	599,671	440,730	445,750	404,601
Stockholders' Equity	1,436,681	1,407,907	1,360,400	1,310,969	1,154,948	959,015	797,964	690,651
Shares Outstanding	167,429	167,687	167,396	172,208	173,329	172,035	171,131	172,750
Statistical Record								
Return on Assets %	11.30	11.93	12.72	13.27	13.79	14.11	14.75	13.79
Return on Equity %	17.78	18.31	19.78	20.13	20.58	21.22	23.17	22.14
EBITDA Margin %	8.92	8.10	9.70	10.06	10.06	9.99	10.39	9.69
Net Margin %	4.53	4.01	4.97	5.21	5.21	5.17	5.49	5.09
Asset Turnover	2.51	2.55	2.56	2.55	2.65	2.73	2.69	2.71
Current Ratio	1.67	1.75	1.72	1.94	1.99	2.07	1.82	1.90
Price Range	38.55-25.60	39.39-25.60	43.61-25.60	40.25-24.16	36.86-24.56	30.09-16.88	23.25-14.38	25.56-12.69
P/E Ratio	25.53-16.95	26.44-17.18	28.50-16.73	28.15-16.90	29.49-19.65	27.35-15.34	23.25-14.38	31.56-15.66
Average Yield %	1.11	1.05	0.92	0.87	0.80	0.96	1.13	0.92

Address: 10401 Old Monroe Road, Matthews, NC 28105
Telephone: 704-847-6961
Web Site: www.familydollar.com

Officers: Howard R. Levine - Chmn., C.E.O. R. James Kelly - Vice-Chmn., C.F.O., Admin. Officer **Transfer Agents:** Mellon Investor Services LLC, Ridgefield Park, NJ

Investor Contact: 704-847-6961
No of Institutions: 246
Shares: 143,756,896 **% Held:** 85.72

FANNIE MAE

Exchange	Symbol	Price	52Wk Range	Yield	P/E
NYS	FNM	$59.24 (5/31/2005)	77.54-51.46	1.76	N/A

*7 Year Price Score 83.35 *NYSE Composite Index=100 *12 Month Price Score 82.01

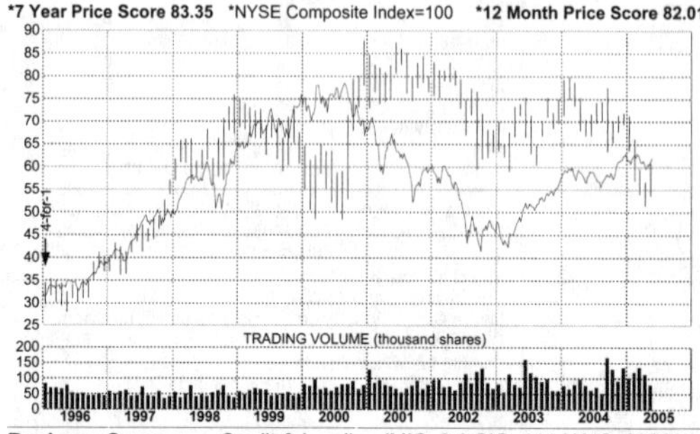

Interim Earnings (Per Share)

Qtr.	Mar	Jun	Sep	Dec
2001	1.25	1.36	1.33	0.00
2002	1.17	1.44	0.98	0.92
2003	1.93	1.09	2.69	2.21
2004	1.90	1.10	...	...

Interim Dividends (Per Share)

Amt	Decl	Ex	Rec	Pay
0.52Q	7/20/2004	7/28/2004	7/30/2004	8/25/2004
0.52Q	10/19/2004	10/27/2004	10/31/2004	11/25/2004
0.26Q	1/18/2005	1/27/2005	1/31/2005	2/25/2005
0.26Q	4/19/2005	4/27/2005	4/30/2005	5/25/2005

Indicated Div: $1.04 (Div. Reinv. Plan)

Valuation Analysis

Forecast P/E	16.97 (12/30/2003)		
Market Cap	$57.3 Billion	Book Value	26.1 Billion
Price/Book	2.20	Price/Sales	N/A

Dividend Achiever Status

Rank	119	10 Year Growth Rate	13.24%
Total Years of Dividend Growth			19

TRADING VOLUME (thousand shares)

Business Summary: Credit & Lending (MIC: 8.6 SIC: 111 NAIC: 22292)

Fannie Mae is a federally chartered, private, shareholder-owned co., and an investor in home mortgage loans in the U.S. Co. operates in the secondary mortgage market by purchasing mortgages and mortgage-related securities, including mortgage-related securities guaranteed by Co., from primary market institutions, such as commercial banks, savings and loan associations, mortgage cos., and other investors. Co. provides additional liquidity in the secondary mortgage market by issuing and guaranteeing mortgage-related securities. Co. provides liquidity in the secondary mortgage market through Co.'s two primary business segments: the Portfolio Investment business and the Credit Guaranty business.

Recent Developments: For the quarter ended June 30 2004, net income totaled $1.11 billion, up 0.9% compared with $1.10 billion in the corresponding prior-year quarter. Results for 2004 and 2003 included a $23.5 million gain and a $739.8 million loss, respectively, from the retirement of debt, and purchased options expenses of $1.98 billion and $1.88 billion. Net interest income fell 11.1% to $3.11 billion, while net interest margin dropped 26 basis points to 1.04%. Guaranty fee income climbed 3.9% to $656.7 million, driven by a 13.6% rise in average outstanding mortgage-backed security growth, partially offset by a 1.8 basis point decline in the effective guaranty fee rate on that business.

Prospects: On Mar 17 2005, filed a Form 12b-25 with the Securities and Exchange Commission (SEC) to report that it has determined that it will not be able to file its Form 10-K for the year ended Dec 31 2004 by the Mar 16 2005 due date or by Mar 31 2005 and, thus, Co. is not requesting the fifteen-day extension permitted by the rules of the SEC. Co. stated that it is not able to file a timely Form 10-K because Co. has not completed its financial statements for 2004. Also, as previously announced, Co. has determined that its previously filed interim and audited financial statements for the periods from Jan 2001 through the second quarter of 2004 must be restated and should no longer be relied upon.

Financial Data (US$ in Thousands)	6 Mos	3 Mos	12/31/2003	12/31/2002	12/31/2001	12/31/2000	12/31/1999	12/31/1998
Earnings Per Share	7.89	70.88	7.91	4.53	5.72	4.29	3.72	3.23
Cash Flow Per Share	26.98	21.45	19.98	12.24	14.70	12.44	11.58	7.48
Tang Book Value Per Share	22.74	17.21	18.83	13.76	15.86	18.58	16.02	13.95
Dividends Per Share	1.940	1.810	1.680	1.320	1.200	1.120	1.080	0.960
Dividend Payout %	24.59	22.97	21.24	29.14	20.98	26.11	29.03	29.72
Income Statement								
Interest Income	24,399,000	12,344,000	50,920,000	50,853,000	49,170,000	42,781,000	35,495,000	29,995,000
Interest Expense	18,090,000	9,148,000	37,351,000	40,287,000	41,080,000	37,107,000	30,601,000	25,885,000
Net Interest Income	6,309,000	3,196,000	13,569,000	10,566,000	8,090,000	5,674,000	4,894,000	4,110,000
Provision for Losses	20,000	32,000	100,000	128,000	(115,000)	(120,000)	(120,000)	(50,000)
Non-Interest Income	1,226,000	739,000	2,848,000	2,048,000	1,633,000	1,307,000	1,473,000	1,504,000
Non-Interest Expense	770,000	410,000	3,631,000	5,764,000	1,354,000	905,000	800,000	708,000
Income Before Taxes	3,839,000	2,558,000	10,413,000	6,048,000	8,291,000	5,982,000	5,440,000	4,645,000
Income Taxes	827,000	659,000	2,693,000	1,429,000	2,224,000	1,566,000	1,519,000	1,201,000
Net Income	3,012,000	1,899,000	7,905,000	4,619,000	5,894,000	4,448,000	3,912,000	3,418,000
Average Shares	970,000	975,000	981,000	997,000	1,006,000	1,009,000	1,031,000	1,037,000
Balance Sheet								
Net Loans & Leases	239,673,000	237,788,000	240,582,000	186,055,000	705,167,000	607,399,000	522,780,000	415,223,000
Total Assets	989,341,000	995,268,000	1,009,569,000	887,515,000	799,791,000	675,072,000	575,167,000	485,014,000
Total Liabilities	963,220,000	974,463,000	987,196,000	871,227,000	781,673,000	654,234,000	557,538,000	469,561,000
Stockholders' Equity	26,121,000	20,805,000	22,373,000	16,288,000	18,118,000	20,838,000	17,629,000	15,453,000
Shares Outstanding	968,000	970,000	970,000	989,000	997,000	999,000	1,019,000	1,025,000
Statistical Record								
Return on Assets %	0.45	0.76	0.83	0.55	0.80	0.71	0.74	0.78
Return on Equity %	42.61	36.51	40.89	26.85	30.26	23.06	23.65	23.37
Net Interest Margin %	25.82	25.89	26.65	20.78	16.45	13.26	13.79	13.70
Efficiency Ratio %	2.87	3.13	6.75	10.90	2.67	2.05	2.16	2.25
Price Range	79.88-60.40	79.88-60.40	75.37-58.93	83.15-59.54	87.49-72.95	87.81-48.38	75.00-59.00	75.94-56.31
P/E Ratio	...	...	9.53-7.45	18.36-13.14	15.30-12.75	20.47-11.28	20.16-15.86	23.51-17.43
Average Yield %	2.73	2.54	2.45	1.78	1.50	1.78	1.60	1.51

Address: 3900 Wisconsin Avenue, NW, Washington, DC 20016-2892
Telephone: 202-752-7000
Web Site: www.fanniemae.com

Officers: Stephen B. Ashley - Non-Exec. Chmn. Daniel H. Mudd - Vice-Chmn., Interim C.E.O., C.O.O.
ransfer Agents: Equiserve Trust Company NA., Providence RI

Investor Contact: 202-752-7115
No of Institutions: 698
Shares: 874,985,344 **% Held:** 90.40

FEDERAL REALTY INVESTMENT TRUST (MD)

Exchange	Symbol	Price	52Wk Range	Yield	P/E
NYS	FRT	$55.20 (5/31/2005)	56.65-39.21	3.66	36.32

*7 Year Price Score 146.75 *NYSE Composite Index=100 *12 Month Price Score 107.23

Interim Earnings (Per Share)

Qtr.	Mar	Jun	Sep	Dec
2002	(0.15)	0.74	0.31	(0.07)
2003	0.26	0.29	0.44	0.67
2004	0.28	0.45	0.30	0.37
2005	0.40	...	...	...

Interim Dividends (Per Share)

Amt	Decl	Ex	Rec	Pay
0.49Q	6/10/2004	6/22/2004	6/24/2004	7/15/2004
0.505Q	9/7/2004	9/22/2004	9/24/2004	10/15/2004
0.505Q	12/14/2004	12/30/2004	1/3/2005	1/17/2005
0.505Q	3/3/2005	3/14/2005	3/16/2005	4/15/2005

Indicated Div: $2.02 (Div. Reinv. Plan)

Valuation Analysis

Forecast P/E	18.17 (5/28/2005)		
Market Cap	$2.9 Billion	Book Value	800.8 Million
Price/Book	3.62	Price/Sales	7.18

Dividend Achiever Status

Rank	305	**10 Year Growth Rate**	2.35%
Total Years of Dividend Growth			37

Business Summary: Property, Real Estate & Development (MIC: 8.3 SIC: 798 NAIC: 25930)

Federal Realty Investment Trust specializes in the ownership, management, development and redevelopment of retail and mixed-use properties. As of Dec 31 2004, Co. owned or had a majority ownership interest in 106 community and neighborhood shopping centers and retail mixed-use properties comprising approximately 16.9 million square feet, located primarily in densely populated and affluent communities throughout the Northeast and Mid-Atlantic United States, as well as California and one apartment complex in Maryland. Also, a joint venture in which Co. owns a 30.0% interest owned four neighborhood shopping centers totaling approximately 500,000 square feet as of Dec 31 2004.

Recent Developments: For the quarter ended Mar 31 2005, income from continuing operations increased 20.7% to $20,059 thousand from income of $16,622 thousand in the year-earlier quarter. Net income increased 39.1% to $23,997 thousand from net income of $17,246 thousand in the year-earlier quarter. Revenues were $103,507 thousand, up 9.8% from $94,232 thousand the year before. Operating income was $43,176 thousand versus an income of $38,769 thousand in the prior-year quarter, an increase of 11.4%.

Prospects: Co. expects its results for full-year 2005 to benefit from a combination of a number of factors, including increased earnings in its same center portfolio, higher earnings from its real estate partnership established in July 2004, increased earnings as it expands its portfolio through property acquisitions, and improved occupancy and rental rates on retail and/or residential space at its Santana Row development. Co. is also exploring the possibility of selling as many as 219 residential units at Santana as condominiums. In the event Co. determines that it is financially feasible to sell residential units and is able to obtain all necessary approvals, sales of units could begin in mid-2005.

Financial Data

(US$ in Thousands)	3 Mos	12/31/2004	12/31/2003	12/31/2002	12/31/2001	12/31/2000	12/31/1999	12/31/1998
Earnings Per Share	1.52	1.41	1.59	0.85	1.52	1.35	1.02	0.94
Cash Flow Per Share	3.01	3.15	2.58	2.86	2.77	2.73	2.58	2.31
Tang Book Value Per Share	12.68	12.57	11.31	9.40	8.92	9.31	10.00	10.73
Dividends Per Share	2.005	1.990	1.950	1.930	1.900	2.290	0.900	...
Dividend Payout %	131.91	141.13	122.64	227.06	125.00	169.63	88.24	...
Income Statement								
Property Income	100,220	389,359	352,497	313,678	293,912	271,749	257,064	232,533
Non-Property Income	3,287	4,915	5,379	5,156	6,590	7,532	7,649	5,945
Total Revenue	103,507	394,274	357,876	318,834	300,502	279,281	264,713	238,478
Depn & Amortn	22,595	90,438	74,616	64,529	59,914	53,259	50,011	46,047
Interest Expense	22,063	85,058	75,232	65,054	69,313	66,418	61,492	55,125
Net Income	23,997	84,156	94,497	55,287	68,756	60,523	48,443	44,960
Average Shares	53,179	51,547	48,619	42,882	40,266	39,910	40,638	40,080
Balance Sheet								
Total Assets	2,327,325	2,266,896	2,143,435	1,999,378	1,837,978	1,621,079	1,534,048	1,484,317
Long-Term Obligations	978,103	979,006	949,357	1,003,212	935,625	809,200	757,862	583,769
Total Liabilities	1,506,983	1,457,408	1,422,479	1,325,725	1,212,572	1,105,504	986,891	908,828
Stockholders' Equity	800,831	790,534	691,374	644,287	592,388	467,654	501,827	529,947
Shares Outstanding	52,492	52,136	49,200	43,535	40,071	39,469	40,201	40,080
Statistical Record								
Return on Assets %	3.97	3.81	4.56	2.88	3.98	3.83	3.21	3.21
Return on Equity %	12.25	11.33	14.15	8.94	12.97	12.45	9.39	8.30
Net Margin %	23.18	21.34	26.40	17.34	22.88	21.67	18.30	18.85
Price Range	52.55-34.73	52.55-34.73	39.80-26.75	28.75-22.93	23.71-18.98	22.31-17.88	24.50-16.63	25.88-19.56
P/E Ratio	34.57-22.85	37.27-24.63	25.03-16.82	33.82-26.98	15.60-12.49	16.53-13.24	24.02-16.30	27.53-20.81
Average Yield %	4.43	4.57	5.81	7.32	9.03	11.37	4.20	...

Address: 1626 East Jefferson Street, Rockville, MD 20852-4041
Telephone: 301-998-8100
Web Site: www.federalrealty.com

Officers: Mark Ordan - Chmn. Donald C. Wood - Pres., C.E.O., C.O.O. **Transfer Agents:** American Stock Transfer & Trust Company, New York, NY

No of Institutions: 157
Shares: 38,052,564 **% Held:** 72.56

FIDELITY NATIONAL FINANCIAL, INC.

Exchange	Symbol	Price	52Wk Range	Yield	P/E
NYS	FNF	$35.99 (5/31/2005)	46.77-30.45	2.78	6.16

***7 Year Price Score 158.25** *NYSE Composite Index=100 ***12 Month Price Score 82.86**

TRADING VOLUME (thousand shares)

Interim Earnings (Per Share)

Qtr.	Mar	Jun	Sep	Dec
2002	0.75	0.82	1.05	1.29
2003	1.05	1.62	1.81	1.13
2004	0.88	1.26	1.09	0.98
2005	2.51	...	...	...

Interim Dividends (Per Share)

Amt	Decl	Ex	Rec	Pay
0.25Q	9/7/2004	11/15/2004	11/17/2004	12/1/2004
0.25Q	1/26/2005	3/8/2005	3/10/2005	3/24/2005
10.00Sp	3/9/2005	3/29/2005	3/21/2005	3/28/2005
0.25Q	4/26/2005	6/3/2005	6/7/2005	6/21/2005

Indicated Div: $1.00

Valuation Analysis

Forecast P/E	10.77 (6/3/2005)		
Market Cap	$6.3 Billion	Book Value	3.4 Billion
Price/Book	1.87	Price/Sales	0.72

Dividend Achiever Status

Rank	29	**10 Year Growth Rate**	22.42%
Total Years of Dividend Growth			17

Business Summary: Insurance (MIC: 8.2 SIC: 361 NAIC: 24127)

Fidelity National Financial, through its principal subsidiaries, is a major U.S. title insurance and diversified real estate-related services company. As of Dec 31 2004, Co. provided title insurance in 49 states, the District of Columbia, Guam, Puerto Rico, the U.S. Virgin Islands and in Canada and Mexico. Also, Co. provides information-based technology applications and processing services to financial institutions and the mortgage and financial services industries. Co.'s reporting segments include title insurance, specialty insurance, financial institution software and services, lender outsourcing solutions, information services, and corporate and other.

Recent Developments: For the quarter ended Mar 31 2005, net income increased 195.9% to $444,497 thousand from net income of $150,241 thousand in the year-earlier quarter. Revenues were $2,271,638 thousand, up 23.7% from $1,836,818 thousand the year before. Net premiums earned were $1,064,108 thousand versus $1,119,951 thousand in the prior-year quarter, a decrease of 5.0%.

Prospects: The first quarter is off to a solid start as Co. successfully completed the recapitalization of FIS, the minority equity interest sale in FIS. Co. continues to make progress on its diversification efforts. Further, Co. was able to generate more than 6.0% organic growth and improve pre-tax margins in its information services businesses, despite the slowing mortgage market. Co.'s default management business continued to grow, despite operating in a historically low mortgage delinquency market. Co. achieved 2.5% organic growth in its FISS segment and is optimistic that the existing pipeline will allow it to meet its goal of 5.0% organic growth in the second half of the year.

Financial Data

(US$ in Thousands)	3 Mos	12/31/2004	12/31/2003	12/31/2002	12/31/2001	12/31/2000	12/31/1999	12/31/1998
Earnings Per Share	5.84	4.21	5.63	3.91	2.29	1.07	1.36	1.94
Cash Flow Per Share	6.75	6.83	8.65	6.21	3.31	1.64	1.01	1.54
Tang Book Value Per Share	N.M.	4.57	6.84	9.55	12.65	10.53	9.56	8.25
Dividends Per Share	10.860	0.790	0.633	0.292	0.246	0.240	0.228	0.153
Dividend Payout %	185.96	18.76	11.24	7.47	10.74	22.45	16.74	7.88
Income Statement								
Premium Income	1,064,108	4,978,584	4,873,482	3,547,729	2,694,479	1,946,159	939,452	910,278
Total Revenue	2,271,638	8,296,002	7,715,215	5,082,640	3,874,107	2,741,994	1,352,204	1,288,465
Benefits & Claims	79,627	282,124	255,694	177,391	134,724	97,322	52,713	59,294
Income Before Taxes	530,280	1,184,091	1,420,639	851,300	518,641	194,140	...	...
Income Taxes	80,335	438,114	539,843	306,468	207,456	85,825	46,975	69,442
Net Income	444,497	740,962	861,820	531,717	305,476	108,315	70,853	105,692
Average Shares	177,327	176,000	153,171	135,870	133,189	101,382	52,135	55,692
Balance Sheet								
Total Assets	10,058,665	9,270,535	7,295,339	5,245,744	4,415,998	3,833,985	1,029,173	969,470
Total Liabilities	6,525,349	4,551,570	3,407,145	2,860,011	2,729,962	2,721,656	592,066	571,198
Stockholders' Equity	3,374,016	4,700,091	3,873,359	2,253,936	1,638,870	1,106,737	432,494	396,740
Shares Outstanding	174,990	172,555	164,840	131,594	129,592	105,117	45,234	48,074
Statistical Record								
Return on Assets %	11.49	8.92	13.74	11.01	7.41	4.44	7.09	13.46
Return on Equity %	27.54	17.24	28.13	27.32	22.25	14.04	17.09	35.64
Loss Ratio %	7.48	5.67	5.25	5.00	5.00	5.00	5.61	6.51
Net Margin %	19.57	8.93	11.17	10.46	7.89	3.95	5.24	8.20
Price Range	46.77-32.00	45.67-33.34	35.25-22.36	24.44-15.78	22.20-12.08	23.67-7.14	18.33-8.26	23.53-13.28
P/E Ratio	8.01-5.48	10.85-7.92	6.26-3.97	6.25-4.04	9.69-5.28	22.12-6.67	13.48-6.08	12.13-6.85
Average Yield %	27.49	2.08	2.34	1.44	1.50	2.12	2.12	0.83

Address: 601 Riverside Avenue, Jacksonville, FL 32204 **Telephone:** 904-854-8100 **Web Site:** www.fnf.com	**Officers:** William P. Foley II - Chmn., C.E.O. Frank P. Willey - Vice-Chmn. **Transfer Agents:** EquiServe Trust Company, N.A., Providence, RI	**Investor Contact:** 904-854-8120 **No of Institutions:** 295 **Shares:** 99,275,232 **% Held:** 56.90

FIFTH THIRD BANCORP

Exchange	Symbol	Price	52Wk Range	Yield	P/E
NMS	FITB	$42.67 (5/31/2005)	55.52-40.50	3.28	16.10

*7 Year Price Score 81.56 *NYSE Composite Index=100 *12 Month Price Score 86.52

Interim Earnings (Per Share)

Qtr.	Mar	Jun	Sep	Dec
2002	0.66	0.68	0.70	0.72
2003	0.72	0.75	0.76	0.80
2004	0.75	0.79	0.83	0.31
2005	0.72	...	...	...

Interim Dividends (Per Share)

Amt	Decl	Ex	Rec	Pay
0.32Q	6/15/2004	6/28/2004	6/30/2004	7/15/2004
0.32Q	9/21/2004	9/28/2004	9/30/2004	10/14/2004
0.35Q	12/21/2004	12/30/2004	12/31/2004	1/18/2005
0.35Q	3/22/2005	3/29/2005	3/31/2005	4/14/2005

Indicated Div: $1.40 (Div. Reinv. Plan)

Valuation Analysis

Forecast P/E	13.76 (6/2/2005)		
Market Cap	$23.6 Billion	Book Value	8.9 Billion
Price/Book	2.66	Price/Sales	3.52

Dividend Achiever Status

Rank	52	10 Year Growth Rate	18.49%
Total Years of Dividend Growth			32

TRADING VOLUME (thousand shares)

Business Summary: Commercial Banking (MIC: 8.1 SIC: 022 NAIC: 22110)

Fifth Third Bancorp is a bank holding company. Co.'s subsidiaries engage primarily in commercial and retail banking, electronic payment processing services and investment advisory services. Co. provides financial products and services to the retail, commercial, financial, governmental, educational and medical sectors, including a variety of checking, savings and money market accounts, and credit products such as credit cards, installment loans, mortgage loans and leasing. As of Dec 31 2004, Co. had $94.46 billion in assets and operated 17 affiliates with 1,011 banking centers located throughout Ohio, Kentucky, Indiana, Michigan, Illinois, Florida, Tennessee, West Virginia and Pennsylvania.

Recent Developments: For the quarter ended Mar 31 2005, net income decreased 5.8% to $405,000 thousand from net income of $430,000 thousand in the year-earlier quarter. Net interest income was $751,000 thousand, up 0.1% from $750,000 thousand the year before. Provision for loan losses was $67,000 thousand versus $87,000 thousand in the prior-year quarter, a decrease of 23.0%. Non-interest income fell 3.0% to $607,000 thousand, while non-interest expense advanced 8.8% to $705,000 thousand.

Prospects: Co. is encouraged by deposit trends, the solid addition of new customers and excellent overall results from Fifth Third Processing Solutions. Co. also sees considerable strength in its lending businesses highlighted by growth in both commercial and consumer loans. Ultimately, Co. expects higher interest rates combined with loan and deposit growth to result in stronger spread-based revenues. Credit quality in its loan and lease portfolios is steady and Co. continues to see solid returns from its new banking center additions. Meanwhile, Co. is working to achieve revenue growth in some of its service businesses and increase efficiency to help drive improved results over the remainder of 2005.

Financial Data

(US$ in Thousands)	3 Mos	12/31/2004	12/31/2003	12/31/2002	12/31/2001	12/31/2000	12/31/1999	12/31/1998
Earnings Per Share	2.65	2.68	3.03	2.76	1.86	1.83	1.43	1.17
Cash Flow Per Share	6.35	6.23	14.19	3.84	1.66	1.70	2.26	1.02
Tang Book Value Per Share	10.99	13.33	12.92	12.65	13.09	10.50	8.80	7.94
Dividends Per Share	1.340	1.310	1.130	0.980	0.830	0.700	0.587	0.473
Dividend Payout %	50.57	48.88	37.29	35.51	44.62	38.25	40.93	40.34
Income Statement								
Interest Income	1,145,000	4,114,000	3,991,000	4,129,000	4,709,000	3,263,000	2,738,000	2,018,677
Interest Expense	394,000	1,102,000	1,086,000	1,429,000	2,276,000	1,793,000	1,333,000	1,015,853
Net Interest Income	751,000	3,012,000	2,905,000	2,700,000	2,433,000	1,470,000	1,405,000	1,002,824
Provision for Losses	67,000	268,000	399,000	246,000	236,000	89,000	134,000	109,171
Non-Interest Income	607,000	2,465,000	2,483,000	2,194,000	1,797,000	1,013,000	877,000	636,194
Non-Interest Expense	705,000	2,972,000	2,442,000	2,216,000	2,341,000	1,119,000	1,122,000	803,577
Income Before Taxes	586,000	2,237,000	2,547,000	2,432,000	1,653,000	1,275,000	1,026,000	726,270
Income Taxes	181,000	712,000	805,000	759,000	550,000	412,000	358,000	250,142
Net Income	405,000	1,525,000	1,755,000	1,635,000	1,094,000	863,000	668,000	476,128
Average Shares	562,000	568,000	580,000	592,020	591,316	475,978	471,855	398,007
Balance Sheet								
Net Loans & Leases	64,185,000	59,095,000	51,538,000	45,245,000	40,924,000	25,569,000	24,597,000	17,512,163
Total Assets	102,713,000	94,456,000	91,143,000	80,894,000	71,026,000	45,857,000	41,589,000	28,921,782
Total Deposits	65,311,000	58,226,000	57,095,000	52,208,000	45,854,000	30,948,000	26,083,000	18,780,355
Total Liabilities	93,825,000	85,532,000	82,618,000	71,958,000	62,966,000	40,966,000	37,512,000	25,743,260
Stockholders' Equity	8,888,000	8,924,000	8,525,000	8,475,000	7,639,000	4,891,000	4,077,000	3,178,522
Shares Outstanding	554,054	557,648	566,685	574,355	582,674	465,651	463,329	400,377
Statistical Record								
Return on Assets %	1.53	1.64	2.04	2.15	1.87	1.97	1.89	1.89
Return on Equity %	16.90	17.43	20.65	20.29	17.46	19.19	18.41	17.45
Net Interest Margin %	65.59	73.21	72.79	65.39	51.67	45.05	51.31	49.68
Efficiency Ratio %	40.24	45.17	37.72	35.05	35.98	26.17	31.04	30.27
Loans to Deposits	0.98	1.01	0.90	0.87	0.89	0.83	0.94	0.93
Price Range	56.91-42.05	59.90-45.78	61.81-47.73	69.40-55.86	64.43-47.19	60.50-30.00	50.29-39.42	48.92-32.33
P/E Ratio	21.48-15.87	22.35-17.08	20.40-15.75	25.14-20.24	34.64-25.37	33.06-16.39	35.17-27.56	41.81-27.64
Average Yield %	2.70	2.49	2.03	1.54	1.44	1.54	1.30	1.21

Address: 38 Fountain Square Plaza, Cincinnati, OH 45263
Telephone: 513-534-5300
Web Site: www.53.com

Officers: George A. Schaefer Jr. - Pres., C.E.O. Paul L. Reynolds - Exec. V.P., Gen. Couns., Sec. **Transfer Agents:** Fifth Third Bank, Cincinnati, OH

Investor Contact: 513-579-4356
No of Institutions: 512
Shares: 358,917,472 **% Held:** 64.87

FIRST BANCORP

Exchange	Symbol	Price	52Wk Range	Yield	P/E
NMS	FBNC	$20.90 (5/31/2005)	29.30-19.08	3.25	14.93

***7 Year Price Score 130.22** *NYSE Composite Index=100 ***12 Month Price Score 89.52**

Interim Earnings (Per Share)

Qtr.	Mar	Jun	Sep	Dec
2002	0.27	0.28	0.32	0.37
2003	0.33	0.33	0.35	0.34
2004	0.33	0.34	0.36	0.37
2005	0.33	...	...	...

Interim Dividends (Per Share)

Amt	Decl	Ex	Rec	Pay
3-for-2	9/29/2004	11/16/2004	10/29/2004	11/15/2004
0.17Q	11/23/2004	12/29/2004	12/31/2004	1/25/2005
0.17Q	2/22/2005	3/29/2005	3/31/2005	4/25/2005
0.17Q	5/24/2005	6/28/2005	6/30/2005	7/25/2005

Indicated Div: $0.68

Valuation Analysis

Forecast P/E	N/A		
Market Cap	$295.5 Million	Book Value	150.8 Million
Price/Book	1.96	Price/Sales	2.92

Dividend Achiever Status

Rank	72	**10 Year Growth Rate**	16.53%
Total Years of Dividend Growth			17

Business Summary: Commercial Banking (MIC: 8.1 SIC: 022 NAIC: 22110)

First Bancorp is a bank holding company. The principal activity of Co. is the ownership and operation of First Bank (the "Bank"), a state chartered bank with its main office in Troy, NC. The Bank engages in a range of banking activities, providing such services as checking, savings, NOW and money market accounts; loans for business, agriculture, real estate, personal uses, home improvement and automobiles; credit cards; debit cards; letters of credit; IRAs; safe deposit box rentals; bank money orders; electronic funds transfer services, including wire transfers, automated teller machines, and bank-by-phone capabilities and Internet banking. As of Dec 31 2004, the Bank operated 59 branches.

Recent Developments: For the quarter ended Mar 31 2005, net income decreased 0.1% to $4,716 thousand from net income of $4,720 thousand in the year-earlier quarter. Net interest income was $16,285 thousand, up 10.2% from $14,773 thousand the year before. Provision for loan losses was $580 thousand versus $570 thousand in the prior-year quarter, an increase of 1.8%. Non-interest income fell 2.2% to $3,710 thousand, while non-interest expense advanced 9.4% to $11,715 thousand.

Prospects: Results were negatively impacted by incremental expenses associated with complying with Section 404 of the Sarbanes-Oxley Act of 2002 and a higher effective tax rate, which negated the positive earnings generated from increases in Co.'s loan and deposit bases. Separately, Co. has begun construction of new buildings in north Asheboro, Anderson Creek and Salisbury that will replace existing facilities. Also, Co. has begun construction of a new branch in Thomasville, which will complement the existing branch in Thomasville. Meanwhile, Apr 4 2005, Co. opened its newest bank branch in Rose Hill, NC, which is located in close proximity to its existing branches in Wallace and Kenansville.

Financial Data

(US$ in Thousands)	3 Mos	12/31/2004	12/31/2003	12/31/2002	12/31/2001	12/31/2000	12/31/1999	12/31/1998
Earnings Per Share	1.40	1.40	1.35	1.23	0.98	0.69	0.95	0.81
Cash Flow Per Share	2.01	1.97	2.95	0.81	0.89	1.06	2.06	2.09
Tang Book Value Per Share	7.17	7.04	6.44	7.22	6.75	8.01	5.67	5.10
Dividends Per Share	0.667	0.657	0.627	0.600	0.587	0.467	0.302	0.267
Dividend Payout %	47.51	46.90	46.31	48.65	59.86	67.96	31.70	32.79
Income Statement								
Interest Income	22,915	81,593	74,667	73,261	76,773	72,915	39,294	35,344
Interest Expense	6,630	20,303	18,907	23,871	35,720	34,220	15,810	14,356
Net Interest Income	16,285	61,290	55,760	49,390	41,053	38,695	23,484	20,988
Provision for Losses	580	2,905	2,680	2,545	1,151	1,605	910	990
Non-Interest Income	4,005	15,864	14,918	11,968	9,655	4,729	5,121	4,656
Non-Interest Expense	11,715	43,717	37,964	32,301	28,634	26,741	17,816	15,912
Income Before Taxes	7,700	30,532	30,034	26,512	20,923	15,078	9,879	8,742
Income Taxes	2,984	10,418	10,617	9,282	7,307	5,736	3,260	3,059
Net Income	4,716	20,114	19,417	17,230	13,616	9,342	6,619	5,683
Average Shares	14,363	14,395	14,351	13,981	13,910	13,605	6,948	6,986
Balance Sheet								
Net Loans & Leases	1,380,258	1,352,336	1,205,326	987,640	880,922	738,196	413,085	352,830
Total Assets	1,687,160	1,638,913	1,475,769	1,218,146	1,144,691	915,167	559,447	491,838
Total Deposits	1,448,692	1,388,768	1,249,364	1,055,957	1,000,281	770,379	480,023	440,266
Total Liabilities	1,536,381	1,490,435	1,333,913	1,094,161	1,027,965	804,483	515,505	451,344
Stockholders' Equity	150,779	148,478	141,856	123,985	116,726	110,684	43,942	40,494
Shares Outstanding	14,138	14,083	14,152	13,682	13,668	13,241	6,827	6,797
Statistical Record								
Return on Assets %	1.26	1.29	1.44	1.46	1.32	1.26	1.26	1.27
Return on Equity %	13.65	13.82	14.61	14.32	11.97	12.05	15.68	14.71
Net Interest Margin %	71.07	75.12	74.68	67.42	53.47	53.07	59.76	59.38
Efficiency Ratio %	43.52	44.86	42.38	37.90	33.13	34.44	40.11	39.78
Loans to Deposits	0.95	0.97	0.96	0.94	0.88	0.96	0.86	0.80
Price Range	29.30-18.61	29.30-18.61	21.37-15.49	18.34-13.72	17.63-10.58	11.50-8.04	13.33-9.78	18.67-10.67
P/E Ratio	20.93-13.30	20.93-13.30	15.83-11.48	14.91-11.15	17.99-10.80	16.67-11.65	14.04-10.29	23.05-13.17
Average Yield %	2.90	2.93	3.48	3.78	4.05	4.66	2.56	1.87

Address: 341 North Main Street, Troy, NC 27371
Telephone: 910-576-6171
Web Site: wwwfirstbancorp.com

Officers: William E. Samuels - Vice-Chmn. James H. Garner - Pres., C.E.O., Treas. **Transfer Agents:** Registrar & Transfer Co., Inc, Cranford, NJ

Investor Contact: 800-548-9377
No of Institutions: 42
Shares: 1,519,382 **% Held:** 10.76

FIRST CHARTER CORP.

Exchange	Symbol	Price	52Wk Range	Yield	P/E
NMS	FCTR	$22.05 (5/31/2005)	28.11-20.27	3.45	15.53

*7 Year Price Score 111.17 *NYSE Composite Index=100 *12 Month Price Score 91.27

Interim Earnings (Per Share)

Qtr.	Mar	Jun	Sep	Dec
2002	0.28	0.32	0.33	0.37
2003	0.33	(0.14)	0.30	(0.02)
2004	0.31	0.34	0.38	0.36
2005	0.34	...	...	...

Interim Dividends (Per Share)

Amt	Decl	Ex	Rec	Pay
0.19Q	7/29/2004	9/22/2004	9/24/2004	10/18/2004
0.19Q	10/20/2004	12/15/2004	12/17/2004	1/18/2005
0.19Q	1/26/2005	3/16/2005	3/18/2005	4/18/2005
0.19Q	4/27/2005	6/15/2005	6/17/2005	7/18/2005

Indicated Div: $0.76 (Div. Reinv. Plan)

Valuation Analysis

Forecast P/E	14.69 (6/2/2005)		
Market Cap	$667.6 Million	Book Value	312.3 Million
Price/Book	2.14	Price/Sales	2.61

Dividend Achiever Status

Rank	182	10 Year Growth Rate	9.52%
Total Years of Dividend Growth			12

Business Summary: Commercial Banking (MIC: 8.1 SIC: 021 NAIC: 22110)

First Charter is a regional financial services company with assets of $4.43 billion as of Dec 31 2004. Co. is the holding company for First Charter Bank, which operates 53 financial centers, one mortgage origination office, and seven insurance offices and 110 ATMs located in 18 counties throughout the piedmont and western half of North Carolina. Co. also operates one mortgage origination office in Virginia. Co. provides businesses and individuals with a broad range of financial services, including banking, financial planning, funds management, investments, insurance, mortgages and employee benefit programs.

Recent Developments: For the quarter ended Mar 31 2005, net income increased 11.6% to $10,309 thousand from net income of $9,240 thousand in the year-earlier quarter. Net interest income was $30,574 thousand, up 0.7% from $30,373 thousand the year before. Provision for loan losses was $1,900 thousand versus $3,000 thousand in the prior-year quarter, a decrease of 36.7%. Non-interest income rose 7.8% to $15,814 thousand, while non-interest expense advanced 2.0% to $28,869 thousand.

Prospects: Co. is pleased with its operating performance, which is being driven by fee revenue growth, a continued focus on expense management and solid credit quality. This solid performance in early 2005 is a continuation of the earnings momentum experienced in 2004. Meanwhile, Co. is leveraging its Community Banking Model, which is based on acquiring new customers and deepening relationships with existing customers through solid service. Furthermore, Co. is encouraged about the continued growth in checking account balances as well as the initial progress of its Raleigh market entry.

Financial Data

(US$ in Thousands)	3 Mos	12/31/2004	12/31/2003	12/31/2002	12/31/2001	12/31/2000	12/31/1999	12/31/1998
Earnings Per Share	1.42	1.40	0.47	1.30	1.12	0.79	1.45	0.50
Cash Flow Per Share	1.13	1.07	(3.61)	1.20	1.43	2.65	2.46	1.17
Tang Book Value Per Share	9.60	9.70	10.08	10.80	10.06	9.79	12.96	13.34
Dividends Per Share	0.755	0.750	0.740	0.730	0.720	0.700	0.680	0.610
Dividend Payout %	53.17	53.57	157.45	56.15	64.29	88.61	46.90	122.00
Income Statement								
Interest Income	51,282	187,303	178,292	196,388	215,276	216,244	136,717	136,509
Interest Expense	20,708	64,293	70,490	83,227	109,912	108,314	67,269	70,623
Net Interest Income	30,574	123,010	107,802	113,161	105,364	107,930	69,448	65,886
Provision for Losses	1,900	8,425	27,518	8,270	4,465	7,615	3,350	2,376
Non-Interest Income	15,814	60,896	64,180	47,631	38,773	30,565	18,213	13,650
Non-Interest Expense	28,869	111,017	127,032	97,772	87,579	92,727	45,869	59,166
Income Before Taxes	15,619	64,464	17,432	54,750	52,093	38,153	38,442	17,994
Income Taxes	5,310	22,022	3,286	14,947	16,768	13,312	12,350	8,758
Net Income	10,309	42,442	14,146	39,803	35,325	24,841	26,092	9,236
Average Shares	30,630	30,277	30,007	30,702	31,660	31,580	18,053	18,572
Balance Sheet								
Net Loans & Leases	2,676,707	2,412,529	2,227,030	2,045,266	1,929,052	2,128,960	1,408,953	1,406,967
Total Assets	4,513,053	4,431,605	4,206,693	3,745,949	3,332,737	2,932,199	1,894,317	1,864,357
Total Deposits	2,702,708	2,609,846	2,427,897	2,322,647	2,162,945	1,998,234	1,149,512	1,123,035
Total Liabilities	4,200,799	4,116,918	3,907,254	3,421,263	3,023,396	2,622,912	1,666,605	1,618,385
Stockholders' Equity	312,254	314,687	299,439	324,686	309,341	309,287	227,712	245,972
Shares Outstanding	30,275	30,054	29,720	30,069	30,742	31,601	17,571	18,442
Statistical Record								
Return on Assets %	0.99	0.98	0.36	1.12	1.13	1.03	1.39	0.70
Return on Equity %	14.01	13.78	4.53	12.56	11.42	9.23	11.02	5.71
Net Interest Margin %	59.62	65.67	60.46	57.62	48.94	49.91	50.80	48.26
Efficiency Ratio %	43.03	44.73	52.39	40.07	34.47	37.57	29.61	39.40
Loans to Deposits	0.99	0.92	0.92	0.88	0.89	1.07	1.23	1.25
Price Range	28.11-20.05	28.11-19.52	21.20-16.69	20.57-15.33	18.75-13.44	17.50-12.50	24.88-14.00	27.00-14.00
P/E Ratio	19.80-14.12	20.08-13.94	45.11-35.51	15.82-11.79	16.74-12.00	22.15-15.82	17.16-9.66	54.00-28.00
Average Yield %	3.24	3.32	3.92	4.11	4.37	4.78	3.46	2.78

Address: 10200 David Taylor Drive, Charlotte, NC 28262
Telephone: 704-688-4300
Web Site: www.firstcharter.com

Officers: J. Roy Davis Jr. - Chmn. Michael R. Coltrane - Vice-Chmn. **Transfer Agents:** Registrar & Transfer Company, Cranford, NJ

Investor Contact: 800-422-4650
No of Institutions: 63
Shares: 6,331,990 **% Held:** 20.97

FIRST COMMONWEALTH FINANCIAL CORP.

Exchange	Symbol	Price	52Wk Range	Yield	P/E
NYS	FCF	$13.36 (5/31/2005)	15.76-12.50	4.94	22.27

*7 Year Price Score 99.67 *NYSE Composite Index=100 *12 Month Price Score 92.99

TRADING VOLUME (thousand shares)

Interim Earnings (Per Share)

Qtr.	Mar	Jun	Sep	Dec
2002	0.13	0.19	0.21	0.22
2003	0.23	0.23	0.23	0.21
2004	0.22	0.18	(0.04)	0.24
2005	0.22	...	...	...

Interim Dividends (Per Share)

Amt	Decl	Ex	Rec	Pay
0.16Q	6/15/2004	6/28/2004	6/30/2004	7/15/2004
0.16Q	9/21/2004	9/28/2004	9/30/2004	10/15/2004
0.165Q	12/21/2004	12/29/2004	12/31/2004	1/14/2005
0.165Q	3/15/2005	3/29/2005	3/31/2005	4/15/2005

Indicated Div: $0.66 (Div. Reinv. Plan)

Valuation Analysis

Forecast P/E N/A
Market Cap $934.0 Million Book Value 513.1 Million
Price/Book 1.82 Price/Sales 2.77

Dividend Achiever Status

Rank 200 **10 Year Growth Rate** 8.72%
Total Years of Dividend Growth 17

Business Summary: Commercial Banking (MIC: 8.1 SIC: 021 NAIC: 22110)

First Commonwealth Financial is a financial services holding company with $6.20 billion in assets, as of Dec 31 2004. Co. operates 103 community banking offices in Pennsylvania through First Commonwealth Bank, a Pennsylvania chartered bank. Financial services and insurance products are also provided by First Commonwealth Trust, First Commonwealth Financial Advisors, and First Commonwealth Insurance Agency. Co. also operates First Commonwealth Systems, a data processing subsidiary, First Commonwealth Professional Resources, a support services subsidiary, and jointly owns Commonwealth Trust Credit Life Insurance, a credit life reinsurance company.

Recent Developments: For the quarter ended Mar 31 2005, net income increased 14.2% to $15,219 thousand from net income of $13,323 thousand in the year-earlier quarter. Net interest income was $44,932 thousand, up 22.1% from $36,807 thousand the year before. Provision for loan losses was $1,744 thousand versus $2,100 thousand in the prior-year quarter, a decrease of 17.0%. Non-interest income fell 15.8% to $11,440 thousand, while non-interest expense advanced 11.6% to $35,393 thousand.

Prospects: Results are being positively affected by increases in average earning assets and improvement in net interest margin, reflecting continued strong loan and deposit growth during the first quarter of 2005. Meanwhile, on Mar 16 2005, Co. announced plans to open two new branches in Washington County, PA. Separately, on Mar 8 2005, Co. announced that it has entered into an agreement to sell one of its branches located in State College, PA to Clearfield Bank and Trust Company, which will assume approximately $16.5 million of deposit liabilities that are associated with the office. The transaction is expected to be completed during the second quarter of 2005, subject to regulatory approvals.

Financial Data

(US$ in Thousands)	3 Mos	12/31/2004	12/31/2003	12/31/2002	12/31/2001	12/31/2000	12/31/1999	12/31/1998
Earnings Per Share	0.60	0.58	0.90	0.74	0.86	0.82	0.88	0.54
Cash Flow Per Share	0.62	0.59	0.97	0.99	0.80	1.15	0.87	0.86
Tang Book Value Per Share	5.33	5.59	6.55	6.67	6.33	5.74	4.93	5.74
Dividends Per Share	0.650	0.645	0.625	0.605	0.585	0.565	0.515	0.445
Dividend Payout %	108.33	111.21	69.44	81.76	68.02	68.90	58.52	82.41
Income Statement								
Interest Income	75,637	278,025	243,773	275,568	308,891	311,882	297,507	283,421
Interest Expense	30,705	110,690	100,241	122,673	167,170	174,539	152,653	148,282
Net Interest Income	44,932	167,335	143,532	152,895	141,721	137,343	144,854	135,139
Provision for Losses	1,744	8,070	12,770	12,223	11,495	10,030	9,450	15,049
Non-Interest Income	11,440	47,649	48,444	37,206	40,224	33,683	30,853	26,338
Non-Interest Expense	35,393	164,555	112,655	125,441	105,007	99,461	93,615	100,201
Income Before Taxes	19,235	42,359	66,551	52,437	65,443	61,535	72,642	46,227
Income Taxes	4,016	3,707	13,251	8,911	15,254	14,289	19,612	12,229
Net Income	15,219	38,652	53,300	43,526	50,189	47,246	53,030	33,374
Average Shares	70,024	66,487	59,387	58,742	58,118	57,618	60,569	61,666
Balance Sheet								
Net Loans & Leases	3,513,647	3,473,770	2,787,497	2,574,138	2,533,777	2,457,226	2,466,520	2,342,546
Total Assets	6,200,590	6,198,478	5,189,195	4,524,743	4,583,530	4,372,312	4,340,846	4,096,789
Total Deposits	3,891,682	3,844,475	3,288,275	3,044,124	3,093,150	3,064,146	2,948,829	2,931,131
Total Liabilities	5,687,453	5,666,500	4,758,249	4,123,353	4,213,464	4,038,156	4,054,163	3,741,384
Stockholders' Equity	513,137	531,978	430,946	401,390	370,066	334,156	286,683	355,405
Shares Outstanding	69,912	69,868	60,712	58,962	58,451	58,195	58,142	61,876
Statistical Record								
Return on Assets %	0.71	0.68	1.10	0.96	1.12	1.08	1.26	0.95
Return on Equity %	8.47	8.01	12.81	11.28	14.25	15.18	16.52	10.64
Net Interest Margin %	59.40	60.19	58.88	55.48	45.88	44.04	48.69	47.68
Efficiency Ratio %	40.65	50.53	38.55	40.11	30.08	28.78	28.51	32.35
Loans to Deposits	0.90	0.90	0.85	0.85	0.82	0.80	0.84	0.80
Price Range	15.76-12.01	15.76-12.01	14.98-11.50	14.12-10.84	15.00-9.50	12.00-8.63	14.31-10.16	17.53-11.50
P/E Ratio	26.27-20.02	27.17-20.71	16.64-12.78	19.08-14.65	17.44-11.05	14.63-10.52	16.26-11.54	32.47-21.30
Average Yield %	4.66	4.60	4.82	4.87	5.03	5.72	4.34	3.30

Address: Old Courthouse Square, 22 North Sixth Street, Indiana, PA 15701-0400
Telephone: 724-349-7220
Web Site: www.fcbanking.com

Officers: E. James Trimarchi - Chmn. Johnston A. Glass - Vice-Chmn. **Transfer Agents:** The Bank of New York, New York, NY

Investor Contact: 800-331-4107
No of Institutions: 86
Shares: 14,438,987 **% Held:** 20.66

FIRST COMMUNITY BANCSHARES, INC.

Exchange	Symbol	Price	52Wk Range	Yield	P/E
NMS	FCBC	$30.08 (5/31/2005)	37.67-26.31	3.39	14.12

Interim Earnings (Per Share)

Qtr.	Mar	Jun	Sep	Dec
2002	0.56	0.54	0.59	0.56
2003	0.62	0.63	0.55	0.46
2004	0.37	0.50	0.57	0.53
2005	0.53	...	...	...

Interim Dividends (Per Share)

Amt	Decl	Ex	Rec	Pay
0.25Q	8/18/2004	9/13/2004	9/15/2004	9/30/2004
0.25Q	11/3/2004	11/29/2004	12/1/2004	12/15/2004
0.255Q	2/18/2005	3/11/2005	3/15/2005	3/29/2005
0.255Q	5/24/2005	6/13/2005	6/15/2005	6/30/2005

Indicated Div: $1.02

Valuation Analysis

Forecast P/E	13.38 (6/2/2005)		
Market Cap	$339.1 Million	Book Value	184.3 Million
Price/Book	1.84	Price/Sales	2.90

Dividend Achiever Status

Rank	110	**10 Year Growth Rate**	13.78%
Total Years of Dividend Growth			14

Business Summary: Commercial Banking (MIC: 8.1 SIC: 022 NAIC: 22110)

First Community Bancshares is a one-bank holding company. Co. serves as the holding company for First Community Bank, N.A. (the Bank), a national association that conducts commercial banking operations within the states of Virginia, West Virginia, North Carolina and Tennessee. The Bank also owns Stone Capital Management, an investment advisory firm. As of Dec 31 2004, the Bank had total consolidated assets of approximately $1.83 billion and conducted commercial and mortgage banking business through 53 full-service banking locations, six loan production offices, and two trust and investment management offices.

Recent Developments: For the quarter ended Mar 31 2005, income from continuing operations increased 8.0% to $6,051 thousand from income of $5,602 thousand in the year-earlier quarter. Net income increased 43.5% to $5,971 thousand from net income of $4,161 thousand in the year-earlier quarter. Net interest income was $17,753 thousand, up 11.1% from $15,984 thousand the year before. Provision for loan losses was $691 thousand versus $532 thousand in the prior-year quarter, an increase of 29.9%. Non-interest income rose 14.8% to $3,722 thousand, while non-interest expense advanced 14.5% to $12,496 thousand.

Prospects: Co. is focusing on its core community banking business following its strategic decision in 2004 to exit the wholesale mortgage banking business. This should reduce Co.'s exposure to risk associated with the large fluctuations previously experienced in the volume-driven, wholesale business and the related interest rate volatility associated with the mortgage banking business. During the first quarter of 2005, Co. completed another phase of its strategic branch expansion plan, by consummating the planned sale of a tract of land to a charitable foundation. The sale allowed Co. to acquire a prime branch location in a southern West Virginia market.

Financial Data

(US$ in Thousands)	3 Mos	12/31/2004	12/31/2003	12/31/2002	12/31/2001	12/31/2000	12/31/1999	12/31/1998
Earnings Per Share	2.13	1.97	2.25	2.25	1.75	1.61	1.58	1.54
Cash Flow Per Share	4.30	3.05	7.28	2.95	(2.02)	2.23	1.64	2.83
Tang Book Value Per Share	10.89	10.84	11.95	11.53	9.75	8.82	7.58	9.12
Dividends Per Share	1.005	1.000	0.973	0.909	0.810	0.785	0.727	0.694
Dividend Payout %	47.18	50.76	43.23	40.32	46.40	48.72	46.07	45.16
Income Statement								
Interest Income	25,188	96,136	93,040	96,204	92,829	85,958	76,492	81,213
Interest Expense	7,435	26,953	28,374	35,008	42,409	39,379	32,250	38,128
Net Interest Income	17,753	69,183	64,666	61,196	50,420	46,579	44,242	43,085
Provision for Losses	691	2,671	3,419	4,208	5,134	3,986	2,893	6,250
Non-Interest Income	3,700	17,329	21,707	20,049	20,275	12,492	10,732	11,182
Non-Interest Expense	12,496	48,035	47,351	42,269	38,025	30,968	27,457	28,752
Income Before Taxes	8,288	35,806	35,603	34,768	27,536	24,117	24,624	19,265
Income Taxes	2,237	9,786	10,365	10,049	8,402	7,054	7,772	6,164
Net Income	5,971	22,364	25,238	24,719	19,134	17,063	16,852	13,101
Average Shares	11,339	11,337	11,198	10,970	10,979	10,567	10,607	8,518
Balance Sheet								
Net Loans & Leases	1,266,003	1,222,417	1,011,567	913,211	890,544	810,523	692,196	600,089
Total Assets	1,886,836	1,830,822	1,672,727	1,524,363	1,478,235	1,218,017	1,088,162	1,054,006
Total Deposits	1,401,872	1,359,064	1,225,617	1,139,727	1,078,260	899,903	833,258	875,996
Total Liabilities	1,702,563	1,647,589	1,497,692	1,371,901	1,345,194	1,097,335	984,674	952,269
Stockholders' Equity	184,273	183,233	175,035	152,462	133,041	120,682	103,488	101,737
Shares Outstanding	11,271	11,250	11,242	10,877	10,930	10,938	10,559	8,486
Statistical Record								
Return on Assets %	1.35	1.27	1.58	1.65	1.42	1.48	1.57	1.25
Return on Equity %	13.34	12.45	15.41	17.32	15.08	15.18	16.42	13.13
Net Interest Margin %	70.48	71.96	69.50	63.61	54.31	54.19	57.84	53.05
Efficiency Ratio %	43.26	42.33	41.27	36.36	33.62	31.46	31.48	31.12
Loans to Deposits	0.90	0.90	0.83	0.80	0.83	0.90	0.83	0.69
Price Range	37.67-25.00	37.67-25.00	37.60-25.73	30.60-23.11	28.10-14.26	15.91-11.57	20.56-14.88	28.26-17.52
P/E Ratio	17.69-11.74	19.12-12.69	16.71-11.44	13.60-10.27	16.06-8.15	9.88-7.19	13.01-9.42	18.35-11.38
Average Yield %	3.16	3.13	3.00	3.32	3.77	5.63	4.15	2.99

Address: One Community Place, Bluefield, VA 24605
Telephone: 276-326-9000
Web Site: www.fcbinc.com

Officers: Harold V. Groome Jr. - Chmn. John M. Mendez - Pres., C.E.O. **Transfer Agents:**

Investor Contact: 276-326-9000
No of Institutions: 41
Shares: 2,409,581 **% Held:** 21.40

FIRST FINANCIAL HOLDINGS, INC.

Exchange	Symbol	Price	52Wk Range	Yield	P/E
NMS	FFCH	$28.44 (5/31/2005)	33.70-25.55	3.23	13.87

***7 Year Price Score 110.87** *NYSE Composite Index=100 ***12 Month Price Score 89.79**

Interim Earnings (Per Share)

Qtr.	Dec	Mar	Jun	Sep
2001-02	0.49	0.54	0.51	0.50
2002-03	0.50	0.54	0.50	0.53
2003-04	0.41	0.50	0.52	0.50
2004-05	0.47	0.56	...	...

Interim Dividends (Per Share)

Amt	Decl	Ex	Rec	Pay
0.22Q	7/23/2004	8/4/2004	8/6/2004	8/20/2004
0.23Q	10/29/2004	11/9/2004	11/12/2004	11/26/2004
0.23Q	1/28/2005	2/9/2005	2/11/2005	2/25/2005
0.23Q	4/29/2005	5/11/2005	5/13/2005	5/27/2005

Indicated Div: $0.92 (Div. Reinv. Plan)

Valuation Analysis

Forecast P/E	14.58 (6/2/2005)		
Market Cap	$351.3 Million	Book Value	170.9 Million
Price/Book	2.06	Price/Sales	N/A

Dividend Achiever Status

Rank	115	**10 Year Growth Rate**	13.54%
Total Years of Dividend Growth			12

Business Summary: Other Depository Banking (MIC: 8.5 SIC: 035 NAIC: 22120)

First Financial Holdings is a savings and loan holding company. Through its subsidiaries, Co. is engaged in making construction, consumer, non-residential mortgage and commercial business loans and invests in mortgage-backed securities, federal government and agency obligations, money market obligations and certain corporate obligations. Co. also engages in full-service brokerage activities, property, casualty, life and health insurance, third party administrative services, trust and fiduciary services, reinsurance of private mortgage insurance, premium finance activities and certain investment activities. At Sep 30 2004, Co. had total assets of $2.44 billion and deposits of $1.52 billion.

Recent Developments: For the quarter ended Mar 31 2005, net income increased 10.3% to $7,047 thousand from net income of $6,390 thousand in the year-earlier quarter. Net interest income was $18,932 thousand, down 3.5% from $19,609 thousand the year before. Provision for loan losses was $1,300 thousand versus $1,825 thousand in the prior-year quarter, a decrease of 28.8%. Non-interest income rose 20.0% to $12,508 thousand, while non-interest expense advanced 4.3% to $19,083 thousand.

Prospects: Co. is pleased with its results for its fiscal second quarter ended Mar 31 2005. Non-interest income was $12.5 million for the second quarter of fiscal 2005, an increase of 20.0% over the comparable quarter last year. Commissions on insurance comprised 46.4% of total other income for the second quarter of 2005, and advanced 15.5% to $1.8 million compared with $5.0 million in the comparable quarter ended Mar 31 2004. Looking ahead, Co.'s results could benefit from the recent addition of strategic lending resources in some of its markets. Co. also stated that it believes that general market conditions are favorable in the major markets in which it operates.

Financial Data

(US$ in Thousands)	6 Mos	3 Mos	09/30/2004	09/30/2003	09/30/2002	09/30/2001	09/30/2000	09/30/1999
Earnings Per Share	2.05	1.98	1.92	2.07	2.04	1.64	1.47	1.40
Cash Flow Per Share	2.48	1.59	1.26	4.37	0.04	2.40	1.61	2.92
Tang Book Value Per Share	11.99	11.80	11.60	13.02	12.55	11.71	10.35	9.43
Dividends Per Share	0.900	0.890	0.880	0.760	0.680	0.620	0.560	0.480
Dividend Payout %	43.90	44.85	45.83	36.71	33.33	37.80	38.10	34.29
Income Statement								
Interest Income	63,893	31,981	126,593	134,381	154,026	173,277	161,642	140,832
Interest Expense	25,815	12,835	49,991	55,921	71,342	102,908	98,888	80,394
Net Interest Income	38,078	19,146	76,602	78,460	82,684	70,369	62,754	60,438
Provision for Losses	2,600	1,300	5,675	6,235	5,888	4,975	2,745	2,765
Non-Interest Income	24,713	12,205	42,175	40,965	30,959	24,918	18,310	15,314
Non-Interest Expense	39,888	20,805	74,764	70,781	63,944	55,143	47,884	43,280
Income Before Taxes	20,303	9,246	38,338	42,409	43,811	35,169	30,435	29,707
Income Taxes	7,343	3,333	13,784	15,198	15,659	12,610	10,507	10,400
Net Income	12,960	5,913	24,554	27,211	28,152	22,559	19,928	19,307
Average Shares	12,569	12,605	12,818	13,173	13,832	13,733	13,559	13,786
Balance Sheet								
Net Loans & Leases	1,857,223	1,837,779	1,813,531	1,781,881	1,924,828	1,905,333	1,838,497	1,742,150
Total Assets	2,473,065	2,456,593	2,442,313	2,322,882	2,264,674	2,325,664	2,256,511	2,070,752
Total Deposits	1,547,696	1,505,251	1,520,817	1,481,651	1,440,271	1,395,785	1,241,295	1,219,848
Total Liabilities	2,302,161	2,289,066	2,277,126	2,159,876	2,099,026	2,168,771	2,118,660	1,944,871
Stockholders' Equity	170,904	167,527	165,187	163,006	165,648	156,893	137,851	125,881
Shares Outstanding	12,351	12,306	12,303	12,522	13,195	13,395	13,317	13,353
Statistical Record								
Return on Assets %	1.05	1.03	1.03	1.19	1.23	0.98	0.92	0.99
Return on Equity %	15.18	15.13	14.92	16.56	17.46	15.31	15.07	15.38
Net Interest Margin %	59.33	59.87	60.51	58.39	53.68	40.61	38.82	42.91
Efficiency Ratio %	42.96	47.09	44.30	40.37	34.57	27.82	26.61	27.72
Loans to Deposits	1.20	1.22	1.19	1.20	1.34	1.37	1.48	1.43
Price Range	33.70-27.05	33.70-27.05	33.10-27.05	30.96-23.70	32.74-22.04	26.00-15.13	19.06-12.75	20.88-14.50
P/E Ratio	16.44-13.20	17.02-13.66	17.24-14.09	14.96-11.45	16.05-10.80	15.85-9.22	12.97-8.67	14.91-10.36
Average Yield %	3.02	2.98	2.95	2.84	2.51	3.07	3.75	2.58

Address: 34 Broad Street, Charleston, SC 29401 **Telephone:** 843-529-5933 **Web Site:** www.firstfinancialholdings.com	**Officers:** A. Thomas Hood - Pres., C.E.O. Susan E. Baham - Exec. V.P., C.F.O. **Transfer Agents:** Register & Transfer Company, Cranford, NJ	**Investor Contact:** 843-529-5933 **No of Institutions:** 66 **Shares:** 3,575,488 **% Held:** 29.04

FIRST INDIANA CORP.

Exchange	Symbol	Price	52Wk Range	Yield	P/E
NMS	FINB	$26.95 (5/31/2005)	26.95-18.11	2.67	27.22

***7 Year Price Score 105.22** *NYSE Composite Index=100 ***12 Month Price Score 110.36**

Interim Earnings (Per Share)

Qtr.	Mar	Jun	Sep	Dec
2002	0.41	0.43	0.43	0.07
2003	0.30	(0.11)	(0.16)	0.12
2004	0.34	0.32	(0.08)	0.35
2005	0.40	...	...	...

Interim Dividends (Per Share)

Amt	Decl	Ex	Rec	Pay
0.165Q	7/21/2004	9/2/2004	9/7/2004	9/16/2004
0.18Q	10/27/2004	12/3/2004	12/7/2004	12/16/2004
0.18Q	1/21/2005	3/2/2005	3/4/2005	3/16/2005
0.18Q	4/20/2005	6/3/2005	6/7/2005	6/16/2005

Indicated Div: $0.72 (Div. Reinv. Plan)

Valuation Analysis

Forecast P/E 16.15 (6/2/2005)

Market Cap $375.7 Million Book Value 173.1 Million

Price/Book 2.17 Price/Sales 2.71

Dividend Achiever Status

Rank 137 **10 Year Growth Rate** 12.03%

Total Years of Dividend Growth 13

Business Summary: Other Depository Banking (MIC: 8.5 SIC: 035 NAIC: 22120)

First Indiana is the holding company for First Indiana Bank, N.A. (the "Bank"). The Bank is a community bank offering a full range of banking services in central Indiana. The Bank attracts deposits and originates commercial and consumer loans and offers cash management and trust/investment advisory services through 31 banking centers. Additionally, the Bank originates home equity loans on a national basis through a network of agents and brokers. These loans are primarily sold to investors. As of Dec 31 2004, Co. had total assets of $1.90 billion.

Recent Developments: For the quarter ended Mar 31 2005, net income increased 32.2% to $5,622 thousand from income from continuing operations of $4,254 thousand in the year-earlier quarter. Net interest income was $16,340 thousand, down 7.3% from $17,626 thousand the year before. Provision for loan losses was $2,550 thousand versus $3,000 thousand in the prior-year quarter, a decrease of 185.0%. Non-interest income fell 39.6% to $5,959 thousand, while non-interest expense declined 10.2% to $16,010 thousand.

Prospects: Loans outstanding were $1.48 billion at Mar 31 2005, compared with $1.50 billion at Dec 31 2004, and $1.76 billion at Mar 31 2004. Business loans decreased 5.0% to $474.9 million at Mar 31 2005, compared with $499.7 million at Mar 31 2004. Co. attributed the decrease in business loans primarily to the deliberate and continuing shift in the mix of loans in the Bank's portfolios to emphasize credits that match Co.'s targeted risk profile and the reduction of non-performing and under-performing loans. Accordingly, for the first quarter ended Mar 31 2005 non- performing assets decreased to $15.8 million from $21.4 million at Dec 31 2004, and $38.5 million at Mar 31 2004.

Financial Data

(US$ in Thousands)	3 Mos	12/31/2004	12/31/2003	12/31/2002	12/31/2001	12/31/2000	12/31/1999	12/31/1998
Earnings Per Share	0.99	0.93	0.16	1.34	1.25	1.55	1.42	1.15
Cash Flow Per Share	14.97	13.24	1.24	1.63	2.25	0.66	6.26	(1.66)
Tang Book Value Per Share	9.95	9.51	10.37	13.40	12.69	11.87	11.31	10.45
Dividends Per Share	0.690	0.675	0.660	0.640	0.512	0.448	0.416	0.384
Dividend Payout %	69.70	72.58	412.50	47.76	40.96	28.87	29.38	33.33
Income Statement								
Interest Income	24,097	101,644	114,330	125,923	157,128	172,810	146,426	135,834
Interest Expense	7,757	32,203	37,430	52,143	83,079	95,042	75,575	73,080
Net Interest Income	16,340	69,441	76,900	73,780	74,049	77,768	70,851	62,754
Provision for Losses	(2,550)	11,550	38,974	20,756	15,228	9,756	9,410	9,780
Non-Interest Income	5,959	40,435	49,563	46,765	43,963	25,638	26,958	23,773
Non-Interest Expense	16,010	71,478	83,637	66,502	70,501	53,728	52,346	45,756
Income Before Taxes	8,839	26,848	3,852	33,287	32,283	39,922	36,053	30,991
Income Taxes	3,217	9,665	1,323	12,107	12,274	15,105	13,320	11,844
Net Income	5,622	14,678	2,529	21,180	20,009	24,817	22,733	19,147
Average Shares	14,116	15,788	15,720	15,809	15,998	15,997	16,049	16,571
Balance Sheet								
Net Loans & Leases	1,426,802	1,447,018	1,761,794	1,793,164	1,719,351	1,750,848	1,673,422	1,518,543
Total Assets	1,832,033	1,898,263	2,193,137	2,125,214	2,046,657	2,085,948	1,979,774	1,795,990
Total Deposits	1,383,294	1,370,697	1,489,972	1,339,204	1,379,478	1,399,983	1,312,115	1,227,918
Total Liabilities	1,658,938	1,726,120	1,984,243	1,904,003	1,837,626	1,887,136	1,802,671	1,626,230
Stockholders' Equity	173,095	172,143	208,894	221,211	209,031	198,812	177,103	165,970
Shares Outstanding	13,939	14,022	15,546	15,540	15,443	15,574	15,653	15,878
Statistical Record								
Return on Assets %	0.75	0.72	0.12	1.02	0.97	1.22	1.20	1.12
Return on Equity %	7.72	7.68	1.18	9.85	9.81	13.17	13.25	12.00
Net Interest Margin %	67.81	68.32	67.26	58.59	47.13	45.00	48.39	46.20
Efficiency Ratio %	53.27	50.31	51.03	38.51	35.06	27.07	30.19	28.67
Loans to Deposits	1.03	1.06	1.18	1.34	1.25	1.25	1.28	1.24
Price Range	25.49-17.76	23.75-17.76	20.39-15.30	22.46-16.25	21.48-16.12	20.85-13.45	20.90-14.40	24.00-13.90
P/E Ratio	25.75-17.94	25.54-19.10	127.44-95.63	16.76-12.13	17.18-12.90	13.45-8.68	14.72-10.14	20.87-12.09
Average Yield %	3.28	3.34	3.67	3.39	2.64	2.78	2.47	2.02

Address: 135 North Pennsylvania Street, Indianapolis, IN 46204
Telephone: 317-269-1200
Web Site: www.firstindiana.com

Officers: Marni M. McKinney - Chmn., C.E.O. Robert H. Warrington - Pres. **Transfer Agents:** National City, Corporate Trust Operations, Cleveland, OH

Investor Contact: 317-472-2184
No of Institutions: 48
Shares: 2,546,027 **% Held:** 18.14

FIRST MERCHANTS CORP.

Exchange	Symbol	Price	52Wk Range	Yield	P/E
NMS	FRME	$24.87 (5/31/2005)	28.99-23.21	3.70	15.94

Interim Earnings (Per Share)

Qtr.	Mar	Jun	Sep	Dec
2002	0.39	0.46	0.46	0.38
2003	0.32	0.48	0.39	0.31
2004	0.37	0.40	0.41	0.40
2005	0.35	...	...	...

Interim Dividends (Per Share)

Amt	Decl	Ex	Rec	Pay
0.23Q	8/10/2004	9/1/2004	9/6/2004	9/20/2004
0.23Q	10/12/2004	12/2/2004	12/6/2004	12/20/2004
0.23Q	2/8/2005	3/3/2005	3/7/2005	3/21/2005
0.23Q	4/14/2005	6/2/2005	6/6/2005	6/20/2005

Indicated Div: $0.92 (Div. Reinv. Plan)

Valuation Analysis

Forecast P/E	14.53 (6/2/2005)		
Market Cap	$460.0 Million	Book Value	310.6 Million
Price/Book	1.48	Price/Sales	2.37

Dividend Achiever Status

Rank	206	10 Year Growth Rate	8.50%
Total Years of Dividend Growth			20

Business Summary: Commercial Banking (MIC: 8.1 SIC: 021 NAIC: 22110)

First Merchants is a bank holding company. Through its bank subsidiaries, Co. offers a range of financial services, including accepting time, savings and demand deposits; making consumer, commercial, agri-business and real estate mortgage loans; renting safe deposit facilities; providing personal and corporate trust services; providing full service brokerage; and providing other corporate services. Through various nonbank subsidiaries, Co. also offers personal and commercial lines of insurance and engages in the title agency business and the reinsurance of credit life, accident, and health insurance. As of Dec 31 2004, Co. had total assets of $3.19 billion and deposits of $2.41 billion.

Recent Developments: For the quarter ended Mar 31 2005, net income decreased 5.3% to $6,567 thousand from net income of $6,935 thousand in the year-earlier quarter. Net interest income was $26,942 thousand, up 5.1% from $25,632 thousand the year before. Provision for loan losses was $2,667 thousand versus $1,372 thousand in the prior-year quarter, an increase of 94.4%. Non-interest income rose 10.1% to $9,046 thousand, while non-interest expense grew 7.4% to $24,231 thousand.

Prospects: Co. noted that it is pleased with its recent earnings performance before the adverse impact of increased provision expense and curtailment expense. With the burden of a volatile defined benefit pension plan behind it and its allowance for loan losses equal to 1.01% of loans positions, Co.'s earnings outlook for the remainder appears promising. Separately, on Jan 1 2005, Co. combined Randolph County Bank and Union County National Bank and renamed the combined entity United Communities National Bank. The data conversions are complete and the related expenses are reflected in first quarter results.

Financial Data

(US$ in Thousands)	3 Mos	12/31/2004	12/31/2003	12/31/2002	12/31/2001	12/31/2000	12/31/1999	12/31/1998
Earnings Per Share	1.56	1.58	1.50	1.69	1.61	1.51	1.36	1.30
Cash Flow Per Share	2.44	2.15	3.60	1.08	2.28	2.26	1.85	1.40
Tang Book Value Per Share	9.19	9.33	8.71	8.98	10.52	10.53	9.75	11.00
Dividends Per Share	0.920	0.920	0.898	0.855	0.815	0.777	0.726	0.668
Dividend Payout %	58.97	58.23	59.87	50.74	50.45	51.43	53.16	51.21
Income Statement								
Interest Income	41,315	156,974	155,530	146,682	120,435	116,528	100,463	79,728
Interest Expense	14,373	51,585	52,388	53,759	56,074	60,546	46,898	38,050
Net Interest Income	26,942	105,389	103,142	92,923	64,361	55,982	53,565	41,678
Provision for Losses	2,667	5,705	9,477	7,174	3,576	2,625	2,241	1,984
Non-Interest Income	9,046	34,554	35,902	27,077	18,543	16,634	14,573	11,725
Non-Interest Expense	...	91,642	91,279	71,009	45,195	40,083	35,906	27,895
Income Before Taxes	9,090	42,596	38,288	41,817	34,133	29,908	29,187	23,524
Income Taxes	2,523	13,185	10,717	13,981	11,924	9,968	10,099	8,125
Net Income	6,567	29,411	27,571	27,836	22,209	19,940	19,088	15,399
Average Shares	18,696	18,667	18,371	16,502	13,769	13,442	14,026	11,808
Balance Sheet								
Net Loans & Leases	2,389,611	2,405,503	2,328,010	1,981,960	1,344,445	1,163,132	988,767	735,560
Total Assets	3,187,586	3,191,668	3,076,812	2,678,687	1,787,035	1,621,063	1,474,048	1,177,172
Total Deposits	2,452,219	2,408,150	2,362,101	2,036,688	1,421,251	1,288,299	1,147,203	926,844
Total Liabilities	2,876,988	2,877,065	2,772,847	2,417,558	1,607,907	1,465,000	1,347,752	1,045,675
Stockholders' Equity	310,598	314,603	303,965	261,129	179,128	156,063	126,296	131,497
Shares Outstanding	18,497	18,573	18,512	17,138	13,969	12,823	12,660	11,675
Statistical Record								
Return on Assets %	0.93	0.94	0.96	1.25	1.30	1.28	1.44	1.40
Return on Equity %	9.37	9.48	9.76	12.65	13.25	14.09	14.81	12.15
Net Interest Margin %	65.21	67.14	66.32	63.35	53.44	48.04	53.32	52.28
Efficiency Ratio %	...	47.85	47.68	40.87	32.52	30.10	31.21	30.50
Loans to Deposits	0.97	1.00	0.99	0.97	0.95	0.90	0.86	0.79
Price Range	28.99-22.51	28.99-22.51	27.25-21.29	27.21-19.95	22.66-18.09	23.00-16.20	25.05-18.57	26.92-18.72
P/E Ratio	18.58-14.43	18.35-14.25	18.17-14.19	16.10-11.81	14.07-11.23	15.23-10.73	18.42-13.66	20.71-14.40
Average Yield %	3.65	3.68	3.72	3.70	4.01	4.04	3.55	2.91

Address: 200 East Jackson Street, Muncie, IN 47305-2814 **Telephone:** 765-747-1500 **Web Site:** www.firstmerchants.com	**Officers:** Michael L. Cox - Pres., C.E.O. Roger M. Arwood - Exec. V.P., C.O.O. **Transfer Agents:** First Merchants Bank, N.A., Muncie, IN	**Investor Contact:** 800-262-4261Ext7282 **No of Institutions:** 60 **Shares:** 2,813,508 **% Held:** 15.17

FIRST MIDWEST BANCORP, INC.

Exchange	Symbol	Price	52Wk Range	Yield	P/E
NMS	FMBI	$34.69 (5/31/2005)	38.19-31.30	2.88	16.06

***7 Year Price Score 116.21** *NYSE Composite Index=100 ***12 Month Price Score 93.29**

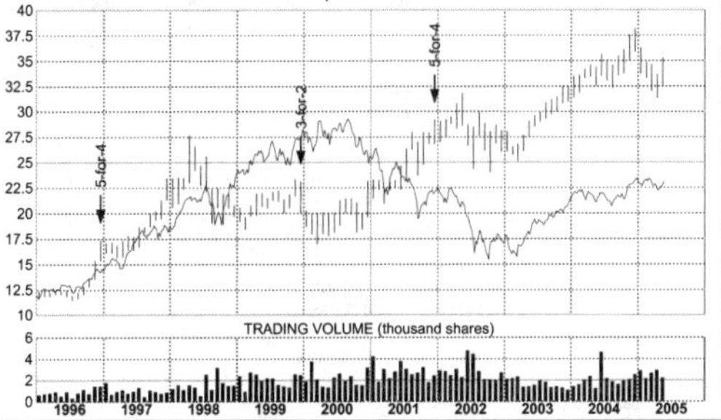

TRADING VOLUME (thousand shares)

Interim Earnings (Per Share)

Qtr.	Mar	Jun	Sep	Dec
2002	0.45	0.47	0.47	0.47
2003	0.48	0.53	0.45	0.51
2004	0.51	0.53	0.54	0.54
2005	0.55	...	...	...

Interim Dividends (Per Share)

Amt	Decl	Ex	Rec	Pay
0.22Q	8/19/2004	9/22/2004	9/24/2004	10/19/2004
0.24Q	11/17/2004	12/21/2004	12/23/2004	1/18/2005
0.24Q	2/23/2005	3/22/2005	3/24/2005	4/19/2005
0.25Q	5/18/2005	6/22/2005	6/24/2005	7/19/2005

Indicated Div: $1.00 (Div. Reinv. Plan)

Valuation Analysis

Forecast P/E	15.08 (6/2/2005)		
Market Cap	$1.6 Billion	Book Value	519.2 Million
Price/Book	3.06	Price/Sales	3.93

Dividend Achiever Status

Rank	135	**10 Year Growth Rate**	12.07%
Total Years of Dividend Growth			12

Business Summary: Commercial Banking (MIC: 8.1 SIC: 021 NAIC: 22110)

First Midwest Bancorp is a bank holding company with assets of $6.86 billion and deposits of $4.91 billion as of Dec 31 2004. Co. operates two wholly-owned subsidiaries, First Midwest Bank and First Midwest Insurance Company. First Midwest Bank is engaged in commercial and retail banking and offers a range of lending, depository, and related financial services. As of Dec 31 2004, First Midwest Bank operated 67 banking offices that are located in various communities throughout Northern Illinois. First Midwest Insurance Company operates as a reinsurer of credit life, accident, and health insurance sold through First Midwest Bank, primarily in conjunction with the consumer lending operations.

Recent Developments: For the quarter ended Mar 31 2005, net income increased 4.9% to $25,207 thousand from net income of $24,032 thousand in the year-earlier quarter. Net interest income was $57,109 thousand, up 0.4% from $56,889 thousand the year before. Provision for loan losses was $3,150 thousand versus $1,928 thousand in the prior-year quarter, an increase of 63.4%. Non-interest income rose 15.9% to $20,146 thousand, while non-interest expense declined 1.1% to $39,772 thousand.

Prospects: Looking ahead to the remainder of 2005, Co. expects to see net interest margin expansion to a range of 3.85% to 3.95% as a result of higher yield on the securities portfolio, improving returns on floating rate assets and a lag in repricing transactional and time deposits. Meanwhile, improvement in fee revenues stemming from new initiatives, coupled with Co.'s ongoing expense controls should also contribute to earnings growth. As a result, Co. expects 2005 earnings to range from $2.26 to $2.36 per diluted share. In addition, based on robust deal flow and strong pipelines, Co. expects strong commercial, commercial real estate and real estate construction loan growth for the balance of 2005.

Financial Data

(US$ in Thousands)	3 Mos	12/31/2004	12/31/2003	12/31/2002	12/31/2001	12/31/2000	12/31/1999	12/31/1998
Earnings Per Share	2.16	2.12	1.97	1.86	1.63	1.46	1.34	0.98
Cash Flow Per Share	3.56	3.19	2.67	2.74	1.74	1.49	2.87	(1.54)
Tang Book Value Per Share	9.25	9.45	9.09	10.07	9.18	8.75	7.19	8.32
Dividends Per Share	0.920	0.900	0.790	0.700	0.650	0.592	0.528	0.488
Dividend Payout %	42.59	42.45	40.10	37.63	39.88	40.44	39.52	49.72
Income Statement								
Interest Income	83,155	315,342	291,067	329,664	385,218	421,517	361,279	364,597
Interest Expense	26,046	86,478	81,313	110,910	180,838	231,906	168,615	177,016
Net Interest Income	57,109	228,864	209,754	218,754	204,380	189,611	192,664	187,581
Provision for Losses	3,150	12,923	10,805	15,410	19,084	9,094	5,760	5,542
Non-Interest Income	20,146	79,381	74,170	66,991	68,866	63,198	58,334	55,462
Non-Interest Expense	39,772	163,338	149,452	148,052	145,356	144,416	149,809	158,802
Income Before Taxes	34,333	131,984	123,667	122,283	108,806	99,299	95,429	78,699
Income Taxes	9,126	32,848	30,889	32,133	26,668	23,759	24,520	23,995
Net Income	25,207	99,136	92,778	90,150	82,138	75,540	70,909	54,704
Average Shares	46,164	46,860	46,982	48,415	50,401	51,603	53,071	55,880
Balance Sheet								
Net Loans & Leases	4,097,484	4,078,560	4,003,378	3,358,917	3,324,561	3,188,103	2,919,842	2,621,127
Total Assets	6,910,482	6,863,381	6,906,658	5,980,533	5,667,919	5,906,484	5,511,588	5,192,887
Total Deposits	4,962,859	4,905,378	4,815,108	4,172,954	4,193,921	4,252,205	4,001,183	4,050,451
Total Liabilities	6,391,319	6,331,343	6,384,118	5,488,580	5,220,652	5,459,761	5,142,327	4,739,989
Stockholders' Equity	519,163	532,038	522,540	491,953	447,267	446,723	369,261	452,898
Shares Outstanding	45,732	46,065	46,581	47,206	48,725	51,082	51,391	54,435
Statistical Record								
Return on Assets %	1.46	1.44	1.44	1.55	1.42	1.32	1.32	1.24
Return on Equity %	19.23	18.75	18.29	19.20	18.38	18.46	17.25	13.84
Net Interest Margin %	68.68	72.58	72.06	66.36	53.06	44.98	53.33	51.45
Efficiency Ratio %	38.50	41.38	40.92	37.33	32.01	29.79	35.70	37.80
Loans to Deposits	0.83	0.83	0.83	0.80	0.79	0.75	0.73	0.65
Price Range	38.19-32.02	38.19-31.38	32.57-25.08	31.85-24.02	29.19-20.95	23.20-17.00	23.37-18.43	27.67-18.90
P/E Ratio	17.68-14.82	18.01-14.80	16.53-12.73	17.12-12.91	17.91-12.85	15.89-11.64	17.44-13.76	28.23-19.29
Average Yield %	2.66	2.62	2.73	2.48	2.64	3.02	2.52	2.18

Address: 300 Park Blvd., Suite 400, P.O. Box 459, Itasca, IL 60143-9768
Telephone: 630-875-7450
Web Site: www.firstmidwest.com

Officers: Robert P. O'Meara - Chmn. John M. O'Meara - Pres., C.E.O. **Transfer Agents:** Mellon Investor Services, Ridgefield Park, NJ

Investor Contact: 630-875-7345
No of Institutions: 132
Shares: 20,414,588 **% Held:** 44.63

FIRST OAK BROOK BANCSHARES, INC.

Exchange	Symbol	Price	52Wk Range	Yield	P/E
NMS	FOBB	$27.59 (5/31/2005)	33.47-27.40	2.61	14.75

*7 Year Price Score 141.14 *NYSE Composite Index=100 *12 Month Price Score 90.61

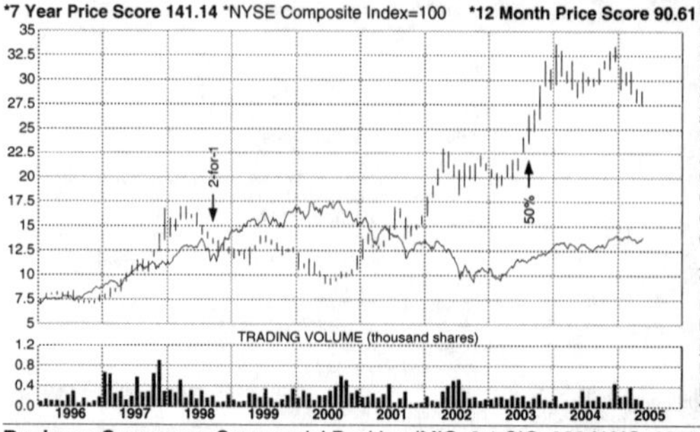

Interim Earnings (Per Share)

Qtr.	Mar	Jun	Sep	Dec
2002	0.41	(0.25)	0.42	0.49
2003	0.47	0.47	0.47	0.47
2004	0.48	0.48	0.46	0.50
2005	0.43	...	...	...

Interim Dividends (Per Share)

Amt	Decl	Ex	Rec	Pay
0.16Q	7/20/2004	10/6/2004	10/8/2004	10/22/2004
0.16Q	10/19/2004	1/6/2005	1/10/2005	1/21/2005
0.18Q	1/25/2005	4/7/2005	4/11/2005	4/22/2005
0.18Q	4/19/2005	7/7/2005	7/11/2005	7/22/2005

Indicated Div: $0.72

Valuation Analysis

Forecast P/E 14.90 (6/2/2005)

Market Cap $269.5 Million Book Value 128.0 Million

Price/Book 2.11 Price/Sales 2.50

Dividend Achiever Status

Rank 33 **10 Year Growth Rate** 21.06%

Total Years of Dividend Growth 13

Business Summary: Commercial Banking (MIC: 8.1 SIC: 022 NAIC: 22110)

First Oak Brook Bancshares is a holding company. Through its Oak Brook Bank (the Bank) subsidiary, Co. provides general retail and commercial banking, primarily in the Chicago Metropolitan area. The services offered include demand, savings and time deposits, corporate treasury management services, merchant credit card processing, commercial lending products such as commercial loans, construction loans, mortgages and letters of credit, and personal lending products such as residential mortgages, home equity lines and vehicle loans. The Bank operates an investment management and trust department as well as an investment sales division. At Dec 31 2004, Co. had total assets of $2.08 billion.

Recent Developments: For the quarter ended Mar 31 2005, net income decreased 10.2% to $4,280 thousand from net income of $4,765 thousand in the year-earlier quarter. Net interest income was $12,815 thousand, down 2.3% from $13,118 thousand the year before. Provision for loan losses was nil versus $250 thousand in the prior-year quarter. Non-interest income rose 3.8% to $4,738 thousand, while non-interest expense advanced 8.8% to $11,318 thousand.

Prospects: Co.'s outlook appears mixed. On the positive side, Co.'s results for the quarter ended Mar 31 2005 included higher other income due to increased merchant credit card processing fees, mainly reflecting increased volume. Investment management and trust fees also improved. However, net interest income declined, reflecting a 38 basis point decrease in the net interest margin to 2.70%, partially offset by a 13.0% increase in average earning assets. Meanwhile, Co.'s branch expansion program appears on track, with four additional branches planned in Wheaton, Homer Glen, Northbrook, and Glencoe, IL. Co. stated that it continues to evaluate branch expansion opportunities in the Chicago area.

Financial Data

(US$ in Thousands)	3 Mos	12/31/2004	12/31/2003	12/31/2002	12/31/2001	12/31/2000	12/31/1999	12/31/1998
Earnings Per Share	1.87	1.91	1.87	1.07	1.41	1.13	1.05	0.93
Cash Flow Per Share	2.02	2.14	2.90	2.51	1.35	1.20	1.63	1.09
Tang Book Value Per Share	13.10	13.62	12.49	11.78	10.52	9.20	8.17	7.80
Dividends Per Share	0.640	0.620	0.448	0.350	0.300	0.287	0.267	0.230
Dividend Payout %	34.22	32.46	23.98	32.61	21.23	25.29	25.48	24.82
Income Statement								
Interest Income	22,874	86,711	79,935	82,567	86,358	84,183	69,460	61,696
Interest Expense	10,059	33,300	28,704	35,119	47,442	50,978	37,123	33,286
Net Interest Income	12,815	53,411	51,231	47,448	38,916	33,205	32,337	28,410
Provision for Losses	...	500	1,600	14,650	1,550	900	840	630
Non-Interest Income	4,738	18,532	18,435	17,450	14,442	10,482	8,966	7,991
Non-Interest Expense	11,318	43,732	41,503	35,741	31,928	27,117	25,640	22,423
Income Before Taxes	6,235	27,711	26,563	14,507	19,880	15,670	14,823	13,348
Income Taxes	1,955	8,639	8,128	4,006	6,232	4,621	4,277	3,907
Net Income	4,280	19,072	18,435	10,501	13,648	11,049	10,546	9,441
Average Shares	10,006	10,005	9,874	9,765	9,661	5,257	10,099	10,216
Balance Sheet								
Net Loans & Leases	1,093,890	1,063,109	907,309	904,730	909,663	819,338	715,141	627,542
Total Assets	2,058,152	2,082,524	1,847,815	1,597,496	1,386,551	1,249,272	1,146,356	1,009,275
Total Deposits	1,731,177	1,714,536	1,458,502	1,264,731	1,077,966	978,226	894,072	777,802
Total Liabilities	1,930,188	1,948,737	1,726,923	1,485,554	1,286,999	1,161,666	1,066,357	932,214
Stockholders' Equity	127,964	133,787	120,892	111,942	99,552	87,606	79,999	77,061
Shares Outstanding	9,768	9,820	9,680	9,501	9,465	9,518	9,796	9,874
Statistical Record								
Return on Assets %	0.93	0.97	1.07	0.70	1.04	0.92	0.98	1.03
Return on Equity %	14.37	14.94	15.84	9.93	14.58	13.15	13.43	12.70
Net Interest Margin %	56.02	61.60	64.09	57.47	45.06	39.44	46.55	46.05
Efficiency Ratio %	40.99	41.55	42.19	35.73	31.67	28.65	32.69	32.18
Loans to Deposits	0.63	0.62	0.62	0.72	0.84	0.84	0.80	0.81
Price Range	33.47-28.25	33.70-28.25	32.00-18.95	22.97-16.03	17.00-11.63	12.33-9.00	14.00-11.00	17.00-11.83
P/E Ratio	17.90-15.11	17.64-14.79	17.11-10.13	21.46-14.98	12.06-8.24	10.91-7.96	13.33-10.48	18.28-12.72
Average Yield %	2.10	2.02	1.88	1.72	2.11	2.79	2.11	1.58

Address: 1400 Sixteenth Street, Oak Brook, IL 60523
Telephone: 630-571-1050
Web Site: www.firstoakbrook.com

Officers: Eugene P. Heytow - Chmn., C.E.O. Frank M. Paris - Vice-Chmn. **Transfer Agents:** Oak Brook Bank

Investor Contact: 630-571-1050
No of Institutions: 42
Shares: 2,166,109 **% Held:** 22.17

FIRST STATE BANCORPORATION

Exchange	Symbol	Price	52Wk Range	Yield	P/E
NMS	FSNM	$18.46 (5/31/2005)	19.32-14.51	1.52	17.92

***7 Year Price Score 140.41** *NYSE Composite Index=100 ***12 Month Price Score 101.99**

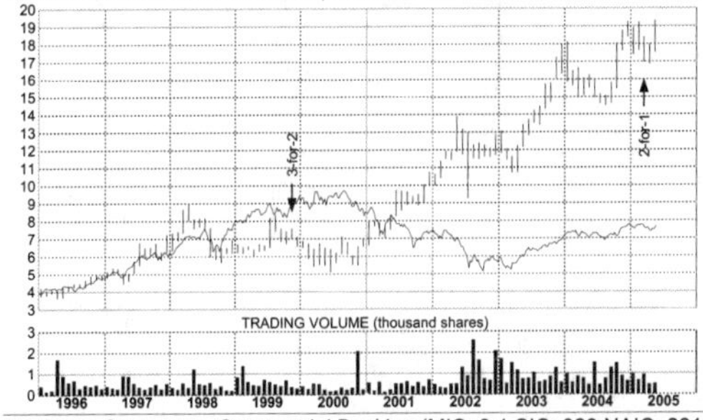

TRADING VOLUME (thousand shares)

Interim Earnings (Per Share)

Qtr.	Mar	Jun	Sep	Dec
2002	0.20	0.22	0.18	0.23
2003	0.23	0.25	0.27	0.23
2004	0.23	0.22	0.27	0.28
2005	0.28	...	...	...

Interim Dividends (Per Share)

Amt	Decl	Ex	Rec	Pay
0.06Q	10/15/2004	11/8/2004	11/10/2004	12/8/2004
2-for-1	1/21/2005	3/10/2005	2/9/2005	3/9/2005
0.07Q	1/21/2005	2/7/2005	2/9/2005	3/9/2005
0.07Q	4/15/2005	5/9/2005	5/11/2005	6/8/2005

Indicated Div: $0.28 (Div. Reinv. Plan)

Valuation Analysis

Forecast P/E	N/A		
Market Cap	$283.3 Million	Book Value	145.9 Million
Price/Book	1.94	Price/Sales	2.53

Dividend Achiever Status

Rank	10	**10 Year Growth Rate**	27.12%
Total Years of Dividend Growth			10

Business Summary: Commercial Banking (MIC: 8.1 SIC: 029 NAIC: 22110)

First State Bancorporation is a New Mexico-based bank holding company. Co. provides commercial banking services to businesses through its subsidiary bank, First State Bank N.M. Co. operates thirty branch offices, including twenty-four in New Mexico (three offices in Taos, nine offices in Albuquerque, four offices in Santa Fe, and one office each in Rio Rancho, Los Lunas, Bernalillo, Questa, Pojoaque, Placitas, Moriarty, and Belen), five in Colorado (Denver, Colorado Springs, Fort Collins, Littleton, and Longmont), and one in Utah (Salt Lake City). At Dec 31 2004, Co. had total assets and total deposits of $1.816 billion and $1.401 billion, respectively.

Recent Developments: For the quarter ended Mar 31 2005, net income increased 20.5% to $4,306,000 from net income of $3,574,000 in the year-earlier quarter. Net interest income was $19,341,000, up 16.2% from $16,645,000 the year before. Provision for loan losses was $1,075,000 versus $1,440,000 in the prior-year quarter, a decrease of 25.3%. Non-interest income fell 6.9% to $3,244,000 , while non-interest expense advanced 16.9% to $14,727,000 .

Prospects: Earnings growth for the first quarter of 2005 is benefiting primarily from Co.'s outstanding loan growth, which is occurring in all of its market areas, as well as net interest income. Net interest income increase in the first quarter of 16.3% over the first quarter of 2004 was due primarily to the increase in loan and investment volume made possible by the increase in deposits and an increase in Federal Home Loan Bank borrowings. Meanwhile, Co. is pleased with the positive trends in its asset quality numbers, exhibiting a significant improvement in the level of its non-performing assets, as well as minimal loan charge-offs during the quarter.

Financial Data (US$ in Thousands)	3 Mos	12/31/2004	12/31/2003	12/31/2002	12/31/2001	12/31/2000	12/31/1999	12/31/1998
Earnings Per Share	1.03	0.99	0.97	0.83	0.81	0.72	0.51	0.43
Cash Flow Per Share	0.93	1.07	2.59	1.12	0.45	0.28	0.99	0.86
Tang Book Value Per Share	6.69	6.60	5.87	5.05	5.93	5.20	4.25	4.24
Dividends Per Share	0.250	0.235	0.215	0.195	0.170	0.135	0.113	0.083
Dividend Payout %	24.15	23.74	22.05	23.49	21.12	18.62	22.44	19.53
Income Statement								
Interest Income	26,754	93,442	83,713	62,448	55,713	52,152	43,146	36,542
Interest Expense	7,413	23,875	22,629	18,384	20,478	20,198	14,686	13,142
Net Interest Income	19,341	69,567	61,084	44,064	35,235	31,953	28,460	23,401
Provision for Losses	1,075	4,500	5,543	2,589	2,386	2,475	3,075	2,322
Non-Interest Income	3,244	14,191	14,521	12,698	9,414	7,782	5,875	5,053
Non-Interest Expense	14,776	55,478	47,242	38,584	29,600	26,180	23,208	19,674
Income Before Taxes	6,734	23,780	22,820	15,589	12,663	11,080	8,052	6,458
Income Taxes	2,428	8,555	7,969	5,631	4,521	3,849	2,845	2,245
Net Income	4,306	15,225	14,851	9,958	8,142	7,232	5,206	4,212
Average Shares	15,563	15,443	15,196	11,995	10,098	9,993	10,285	10,529
Balance Sheet								
Net Loans & Leases	1,409,031	1,362,464	1,217,364	1,005,187	541,515	453,776	423,251	331,144
Total Assets	1,893,135	1,815,510	1,646,739	1,386,870	827,921	652,729	566,884	493,654
Total Deposits	1,413,952	1,401,303	1,195,875	1,079,684	685,022	528,408	463,536	409,021
Total Liabilities	1,747,209	1,671,201	1,514,298	1,269,402	769,577	601,411	522,457	449,500
Stockholders' Equity	145,926	144,309	132,441	117,468	58,345	51,318	44,427	44,154
Shares Outstanding	15,348	15,324	15,209	14,655	9,771	9,786	10,317	10,256
Statistical Record								
Return on Assets %	0.90	0.88	0.98	0.90	1.10	1.18	0.98	0.94
Return on Equity %	11.31	10.97	11.89	11.33	14.85	15.06	11.75	11.72
Net Interest Margin %	72.29	74.45	72.97	70.56	63.24	61.27	65.96	64.04
Efficiency Ratio %	49.26	51.54	48.09	51.35	45.45	43.68	47.34	47.30
Loans to Deposits	1.00	0.97	1.02	0.93	0.79	0.86	0.91	0.81

Address: 7900 Jefferson N.E., Albuquerque, NM 87109 **Telephone:** 505-241-7500 **Web Site:** www.fsbnm.com	**Officers:** Michael R. Stanford - Pres., C.E.O. H. Patrick Dee - Exec. V.P., C.O.O., Treas., Sec. **Transfer Agents:** American Stock Transfer & Trust Company	**Investor Contact:** 505-241-7500 **No of Institutions:** 64 **Shares:** 10,279,827 **% Held:** 67.17

FIRSTMERIT CORP

Exchange	Symbol	Price	52Wk Range	Yield	P/E
NMS	FMER	$25.50 (5/31/2005)	28.74-23.92	4.24	17.96

*7 Year Price Score 94.20 *NYSE Composite Index=100 *12 Month Price Score 94.20

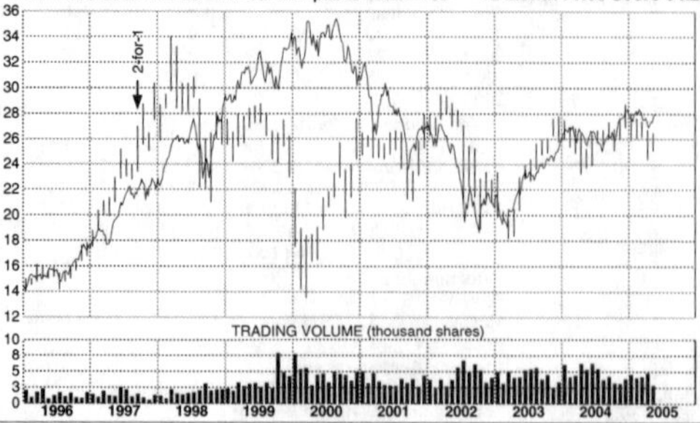

Interim Earnings (Per Share)

Qtr.	Mar	Jun	Sep	Dec
2002	0.51	0.49	0.38	0.43
2003	0.45	0.44	0.46	0.07
2004	0.15	0.36	0.37	0.33
2005	0.36	...	...	...

Interim Dividends (Per Share)

Amt	Decl	Ex	Rec	Pay
0.27Q	8/19/2004	8/26/2004	8/30/2004	9/20/2004
0.27Q	11/18/2004	11/24/2004	11/29/2004	12/20/2004
0.27Q	2/17/2005	2/24/2005	2/28/2005	3/21/2005
0.27Q	5/19/2005	5/26/2005	5/31/2005	6/20/2005

Indicated Div: $1.08

Valuation Analysis

Forecast P/E	15.94 (6/2/2005)		
Market Cap	$2.1 Billion	Book Value	946.7 Million
Price/Book	2.25	Price/Sales	3.17

Dividend Achiever Status

Rank	213	10 Year Growth Rate	7.97%
Total Years of Dividend Growth			22

Business Summary: Commercial Banking (MIC: 8.1 SIC: 022 NAIC: 22110)

FirstMerit is a multi-bank holding company with $10.12 billion in total assets and $7.37 billion in total deposits as of Dec 31 2004. Co., through its banking subsidiary, FirstMerit Bank, N.A., operates principally as a regional banking organization, providing banking, fiduciary, financial, insurance and investment services to corporate, institutional and individual customers throughout northeastern and central Ohio and western Pennsylvania counties. FirstMerit Bank, Co.'s largest subsidiary, is the parent company of 16 wholly-owned subsidiaries. At Dec 31 2004, FirstMerit Bank operated 162 full-service banking offices in 24 Ohio and western Pennsylvania counties.

Recent Developments: For the quarter ended Mar 31 2005, net income increased 136.8% to $30,088 thousand from net income of $12,706 thousand in the year-earlier quarter. Net interest income was $86,010 thousand, down 3.4% from $89,002 thousand the year before. Provision for loan losses was $11,614 thousand versus $40,390 thousand in the prior-year quarter, a decrease of 71.2%. Non-interest income fell 0.3% to $44,939 thousand, while non-interest expense declined 1.2% to $75,911 thousand.

Prospects: Co.'s earnings are being positively affected by a substantial decline in its provision for loan losses as a result of lower credit-related charges due to improved asset quality and the strengthening allowance for loan losses. Meanwhile, economic activity appears to be improving in Co.'s Northeast Ohio markets. Production is rising in the manufacturing sector and, as a result, Co.'s commercial loan portfolio is growing. Co. is optimistic about the positive effects of its actions taken over the last two years as the regional economy continues to improve. Co. is seeing progress in controlling its expenses and expects efficiency to improve throughout the remainder of 2005.

Financial Data (US$ in Thousands)	3 Mos	12/31/2004	12/31/2003	12/31/2002	12/31/2001	12/31/2000	12/31/1999	12/31/1998
Earnings Per Share	1.42	1.21	1.42	1.81	1.35	1.80	1.31	1.34
Cash Flow Per Share	1.21	2.19	3.63	10.73	5.80	0.02	1.52	0.24
Tang Book Value Per Share	9.60	9.95	9.94	9.68	9.06	10.48	9.39	10.39
Dividends Per Share	1.070	1.060	1.020	0.980	0.930	0.860	0.760	0.660
Dividend Payout %	75.35	87.60	71.83	54.14	68.89	47.78	58.02	49.25
Income Statement								
Interest Income	127,841	497,395	567,269	648,013	726,899	791,495	684,851	503,097
Interest Expense	41,831	146,590	173,656	226,417	335,443	415,251	300,865	197,651
Net Interest Income	86,010	350,805	393,613	421,596	391,456	376,244	383,986	305,446
Provision for Losses	11,614	73,923	102,211	98,628	61,807	32,708	37,430	28,383
Non-Interest Income	44,939	174,285	210,146	186,402	182,419	163,891	154,710	110,480
Non-Interest Expense	75,911	311,929	326,952	287,030	328,597	275,192	316,506	242,723
Income Before Taxes	43,424	139,238	174,596	222,340	183,471	232,235	184,760	144,820
Income Taxes	13,336	36,024	52,939	67,974	60,867	72,448	59,043	47,342
Net Income	30,088	103,214	120,969	154,366	116,305	159,787	119,870	97,478
Average Shares	84,497	84,995	84,929	85,317	86,288	88,861	91,523	72,703
Balance Sheet								
Net Loans & Leases	6,433,431	6,335,787	6,454,046	7,091,515	7,262,085	7,128,800	6,909,284	4,918,447
Total Assets	10,274,154	10,122,627	10,473,635	10,688,206	10,193,374	10,215,203	10,115,477	7,127,365
Total Deposits	7,324,551	7,365,447	7,502,784	7,711,259	7,539,400	7,614,932	6,860,147	5,461,563
Total Liabilities	9,327,423	9,141,370	9,486,460	9,723,549	9,282,567	9,300,314	9,260,452	6,358,729
Stockholders' Equity	946,731	981,257	987,175	964,657	910,807	914,889	833,575	768,636
Shares Outstanding	83,611	84,190	84,724	84,505	84,991	87,032	88,375	74,009
Statistical Record								
Return on Assets %	1.16	1.00	1.14	1.48	1.14	1.57	1.39	1.57
Return on Equity %	12.38	10.46	12.40	16.46	12.74	18.23	14.96	15.01
Net Interest Margin %	67.28	70.53	69.39	65.06	53.85	47.54	56.07	60.71
Efficiency Ratio %	43.94	46.44	42.06	34.40	36.14	28.80	37.70	39.56
Loans to Deposits	0.88	0.86	0.86	0.92	0.96	0.94	1.01	0.90
Price Range	28.74-23.23	28.74-23.23	27.81-18.16	29.49-18.89	27.94-21.10	27.63-13.50	28.78-22.94	34.00-21.00
P/E Ratio	20.24-16.36	23.75-19.20	19.58-12.79	16.29-10.44	20.70-15.63	15.35-7.50	21.97-17.51	25.37-15.67
Average Yield %	4.09	4.08	4.42	3.87	3.71	4.24	2.87	2.37

Address: III Cascade Plaza, 7th Floor, Akron, OH 44308-1103
Telephone: 330-996-6300
Web Site: www.firstmerit.com

Officers: John R. Cochran - Chmn., C.E.O. Sid A. Bostic - Pres., C.O.O. **Transfer Agents:** American Stock Transfer & Trust Co., New York, NY

Investor Contact: 330-996-6300
No of Institutions: 138
Shares: 36,514,836 **% Held:** 43.40

FOREST CITY ENTERPRISES, INC.

Exchange	Symbol	Price	52Wk Range	Yield	P/E
NYS	FCE A	$63.35 (5/31/2005)	65.51-50.25	0.63	37.93

*7 Year Price Score 151.21 *NYSE Composite Index=100 *12 Month Price Score 107.00

TRADING VOLUME (thousand shares)

Interim Earnings (Per Share)

Qtr.	Apr	Jul	Oct	Jan
2000-01	0.61	1.03	0.29	0.09
2001-02	0.20	0.33	1.38	0.23
2002-03	0.20	0.25	0.18	0.34
2003-04	0.29	0.13	0.52	(0.10)
2004-05	0.14	0.68	0.73	0.11

Interim Dividends (Per Share)

Amt	Decl	Ex	Rec	Pay
0.10Q	9/8/2004	11/29/2004	12/1/2004	12/15/2004
0.20Q	12/9/2004	12/30/2004	1/3/2005	1/18/2005
0.10Q	12/9/2004	2/25/2005	3/1/2005	3/15/2005
0.10Q	3/24/2005	5/27/2005	6/1/2005	6/15/2005

Indicated Div: $0.40 (Div. Reinv. Plan)

Valuation Analysis

Forecast P/E	N/A		
Market Cap	$3.2 Billion	Book Value	804.5 Million
Price/Book	3.96	Price/Sales	3.06

Dividend Achiever Status

Rank	20	10 Year Growth Rate	23.94%
Total Years of Dividend Growth			10

Business Summary: Property, Real Estate & Development (MIC: 8.3 SIC: 512 NAIC: 36220)

Forest City Enterprises is engaged in the ownership, development, management and acquisition of commercial and residential real estate properties in 19 states and the District of Columbia. Co. operates through three strategic business units. The Commercial Group owns, develops, acquires and operates regional malls, specialty/urban retail centers, office buildings, hotels and mixed-use projects. The Residential Group owns, develops, acquires and operates residential rental properties. The Land Development Group acquires and sells land and developed lots to residential, commercial and industrial customers. It also owns and develops land into master-planned communities and mixed-use projects.

Recent Developments: For the year ended Jan 31 2005, income from continuing operations increased 18.4% to $40,056 thousand from income of $33,834 thousand a year earlier. Net income increased 99.7% to $85,206 thousand from net income of $42,669 thousand a year earlier. Revenues were $1,041,851 thousand, up 22.8% from $848,121 thousand the year before.

Prospects: Co. is benefiting from improved occupancy in its retail, office and residential properties. Co. is continuing to expand in its core high-growth urban markets where it has gained access to large, complex commercial, residential and mixed-use projects. Among the projects scheduled to open in 2005 is the final phase of Co.'s University Park at MIT biotechnology, life sciences mixed use development in Cambridge, MA with the completion of the development's final two apartment buildings. Co. also plans to open three new retail centers in 2005 in Southern California, Aurora, CO and near Chicago, IL. Co. also expects to open three residential projects in the Los Angeles, CA area during 2005.

Financial Data (US$ in Thousands)	01/31/2005	01/31/2004	01/31/2003	01/31/2002	01/31/2001	01/31/2000	01/31/1999	01/31/1998
Earnings Per Share	1.67	0.84	0.97	2.17	2.01	0.90	1.21	0.47
Cash Flow Per Share	7.48	2.98	4.33	1.69	4.57	2.82	2.08	1.46
Tang Book Value Per Share	15.98	14.98	14.22	13.39	10.13	8.58	7.38	6.27
Dividends Per Share	0.580	0.300	0.220	0.177	0.147	0.120	0.100	0.080
Dividend Payout %	34.73	35.71	22.68	8.14	7.28	13.33	8.29	16.90
Income Statement								
Property Income	1,041,851	898,339	791,806	738,508	658,369	...	...	...
Non-Property Income	...	123,249	135,744	168,062	136,416	...	...	...
Total Revenue	1,041,851	1,021,588	927,550	906,570	794,785	793,071	696,649	632,669
Depn & Amortn	176,416	127,631	115,001	97,842	98,364	88,144	87,068	74,793
Interest Expense	248,328	198,122	177,237	178,580	182,544	159,719	149,960	136,322
Income Before Taxes	102,476	77,052	81,998	159,957	117,348	64,849	66,081	3,385
Income Taxes	37,326	28,799	31,826	63,487	22,312	24,319	27,674	2,202
Net Income	85,206	42,669	48,831	103,029	91,637	40,802	54,750	20,539
Average Shares	50,923	50,572	50,178	47,386	45,500	45,229	45,261	43,446
Balance Sheet								
Total Assets	7,289,260	5,895,072	5,077,209	4,417,646	4,030,470	3,814,474	3,437,110	2,963,353
Long-Term Obligations	5,386,591	4,010,827	3,371,757	2,894,998	2,849,812	2,749,380	2,478,872	2,132,931
Total Liabilities	6,388,962	5,097,687	4,292,171	3,687,256	3,495,744	3,427,968	3,105,002	2,681,408
Stockholders' Equity	804,525	748,911	705,972	662,513	456,636	386,506	332,108	281,945
Shares Outstanding	50,351	49,986	49,655	49,463	45,096	45,046	44,974	44,967
Statistical Record								
Return on Assets %	1.29	0.78	1.03	2.44	2.33	1.13	1.71	0.72
Return on Equity %	10.94	5.87	7.14	18.41	21.68	11.36	17.83	8.67
Net Margin %	8.18	4.18	5.26	11.36	11.53	5.14	7.86	3.25
Price Range	58.35-50.00	52.00-30.95	40.27-29.00	40.90-27.27	27.71-16.67	18.92-13.50	20.38-11.88	20.83-13.21

Address: Terminal Tower, 50 Public Square, Suite 1100, Cleveland, OH 44113
Telephone: 216-621-6060
Web Site: www.fceinc.com

Officers: Albert B. Ratner - Co-Chmn. Samuel H. Miller - Co-Chmn., Treas. **Transfer Agents:** National City Bank

Investor Contact: 216-416-3215
No of Institutions: 107
Shares: 25,853,152 **% Held:** 69.88

FRANKLIN ELECTRIC CO., INC.

Exchange	Symbol	Price	52Wk Range	Yield	P/E
NMS	FELE	$38.42 (5/31/2005)	44.11-32.44	1.04	22.87

*7 Year Price Score 146.05 *NYSE Composite Index=100 *12 Month Price Score 92.44

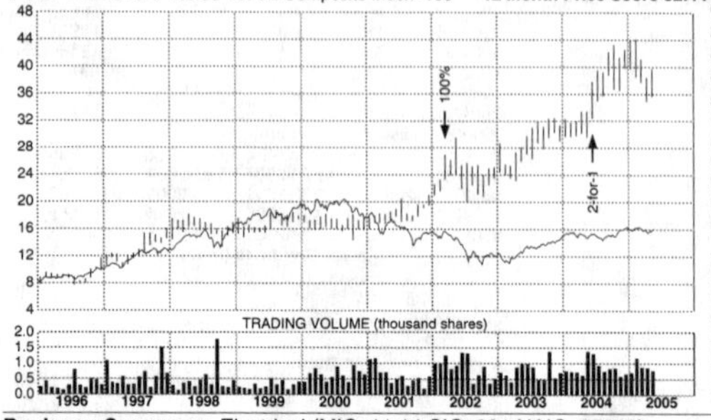

TRADING VOLUME (thousand shares)

Interim Earnings (Per Share)

Qtr.	Mar	Jun	Sep	Dec
2002	0.16	0.40	0.42	0.44
2003	0.18	0.41	0.47	0.47
2004	0.23	0.48	0.48	0.47
2005	0.25	...	...	...

Interim Dividends (Per Share)

Amt	Decl	Ex	Rec	Pay
0.08Q	7/23/2004	8/3/2004	8/5/2004	8/19/2004
0.08Q	10/22/2004	11/2/2004	11/4/2004	11/18/2004
0.08Q	2/1/2005	2/8/2005	2/10/2005	2/24/2005
0.10Q	4/29/2005	5/10/2005	5/12/2005	5/26/2005

Indicated Div: $0.40

Valuation Analysis

Forecast P/E 19.30 (6/1/2005)

Market Cap $853.7 Million Book Value 238.2 Million

Price/Book 3.58 Price/Sales 2.10

Dividend Achiever Status

Rank 82 **10 Year Growth Rate** 15.64%

Total Years of Dividend Growth 11

Business Summary: Electrical (MIC: 11.14 SIC: 621 NAIC: 35312)

Franklin Electric is engaged in the design, manufacture and distribution of groundwater and fuel pumping systems, electronic controls and related parts and equipment. Co.'s motors and pumps are used principally in submersible applications for pumping fresh water, fuel, wastewater and other liquids in a variety of applications including residential, industrial, agriculture, fueling, off-shore drilling, and mining. Co. also manufactures other industrial electric motors, which are used in a wide variety of applications, and manufactures electronic drives and controls for the motors that control functionality and provide protection from various hazards, such as electric surges and over-heating.

Recent Developments: For the quarter ended Apr 2 2005, net income increased 13.5% to $5,811 thousand from net income of $5,121 thousand in the year-earlier quarter. Revenues were $82,434 thousand, up 2.8% from $80,207 thousand the year before. Operating income was $9,002 thousand versus an income of $8,077 thousand in the prior-year quarter, an increase of 11.5%. Total direct expense was $56,955 thousand versus $56,587 thousand in the prior-year quarter, an increase of 0.7%. Total indirect expense was $16,477 thousand versus $15,543 thousand in the prior-year quarter, an increase of 6.0%.

Prospects: Strong earnings reflect an improved sales mix combined with contributions from cost-reduction programs, more than offsetting lower volume. As part of Co.'s global manufacturing realignment program, the ramp up of production at the Mexico four-inch motor manufacturing plant and the new six-inch motor manufacturing facility in the Czech Republic are on schedule. Meanwhile, Co. is seeing benefits from the consolidation of operations at its new Fueling facility in Madison, WI. Co. anticipates total pre-tax restructuring charges of about $10.0 million as the realignment program is implemented from the first quarter of 2004 to the fourth quarter of 2005, of which $5.7 million has been incurred.

Financial Data

(US$ in Thousands)	3 Mos	01/01/2005	01/03/2004	12/28/2002	12/29/2001	12/30/2000	01/01/2000	01/02/1999
Earnings Per Share	1.68	1.65	1.52	1.42	1.20	0.98	1.15	1.00
Cash Flow Per Share	2.74	2.62	2.14	2.69	1.84	0.86	1.64	1.36
Tang Book Value Per Share	8.17	8.03	6.26	5.28	5.10	4.56	4.45	4.11
Dividends Per Share	0.320	0.310	0.275	0.255	0.235	0.215	0.193	0.165
Dividend Payout %	19.02	18.79	18.03	18.02	19.67	21.99	16.74	16.42
Income Statement								
Total Revenue	82,434	404,305	359,502	354,872	322,908	325,731	293,236	272,533
EBITDA	13,108	74,665	66,182	64,672	57,238	47,859	51,173	48,072
Depn & Amortn	3,944	15,143	13,748	12,878	12,660	10,839	7,460	6,687
Income Before Taxes	8,992	59,034	51,327	50,477	43,385	35,909	42,396	40,021
Income Taxes	3,181	20,951	16,847	18,273	16,235	13,683	15,591	15,237
Net Income	5,811	38,083	34,480	32,204	27,150	22,226	26,805	24,784
Average Shares	23,200	23,100	22,626	22,732	22,740	22,736	23,292	24,680
Balance Sheet								
Current Assets	169,948	166,142	128,041	113,009	109,583	101,961	104,243	106,283
Total Assets	331,771	333,473	281,971	258,583	195,643	197,179	176,101	167,590
Current Liabilities	48,900	54,445	45,401	50,247	40,425	47,064	47,357	44,405
Long-Term Obligations	13,626	13,752	14,960	25,946	14,465	15,874	17,057	18,089
Total Liabilities	93,598	99,140	89,033	105,445	72,374	81,181	79,808	75,993
Stockholders' Equity	238,173	234,333	192,938	153,138	123,269	115,998	96,293	91,597
Shares Outstanding	22,220	22,041	21,828	21,648	21,336	22,016	21,652	22,296
Statistical Record								
Return on Assets %	12.64	12.41	12.55	14.22	13.86	11.94	15.64	15.03
Return on Equity %	17.92	17.88	19.60	23.37	22.76	21.00	28.61	26.95
EBITDA Margin %	15.90	18.47	18.41	18.22	17.73	14.69	17.45	17.64
Net Margin %	7.05	9.42	9.59	9.07	8.41	6.82	9.14	9.09
Asset Turnover	1.33	1.32	1.31	1.57	1.65	1.75	1.71	1.65
Current Ratio	3.48	3.05	2.82	2.25	2.71	2.17	2.20	2.39
Debt to Equity	0.06	0.06	0.08	0.17	0.12	0.14	0.18	0.20
Price Range	44.11-29.57	43.30-29.57	32.50-23.14	29.50-19.98	21.02-16.00	18.19-14.36	18.72-14.75	18.13-13.38
P/E Ratio	26.26-17.60	26.24-17.92	21.38-15.22	20.77-14.07	17.52-13.33	18.56-14.65	16.28-12.83	18.13-13.38
Average Yield %	0.84	0.87	0.98	1.08	1.30	1.28	1.15	1.02

Address: 400 East Spring Street, Bluffton, IN 46714-3798
Telephone: 260-824-2900
Web Site: www.franklin-electric.com

Officers: R. Scott Trumbull - Chmn., C.E.O. Gregg C. Sengstack - Sr. V.P., C.F.O., Sec. **Transfer Agents:** Illinois Stock Transfer Company, Chicago, IL

Investor Contact: 219-824-2900
No of Institutions: 84
Shares: 12,186,530 **% Held:** 55.29

FRANKLIN RESOURCES, INC.

Exchange	Symbol	Price	52Wk Range	Yield	P/E
NYS	BEN	$72.14 (5/31/2005)	73.24-47.37	0.55	22.54

*7 Year Price Score 128.29 *NYSE Composite Index=100 *12 Month Price Score 107.94

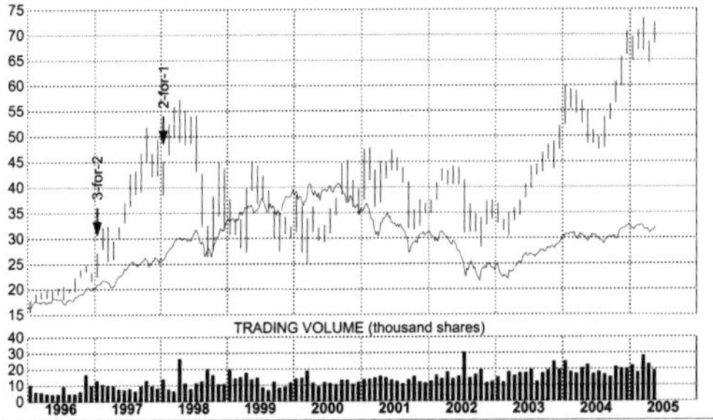

Interim Earnings (Per Share)

Qtr.	Dec	Mar	Jun	Sep
2001-02	0.45	0.46	0.48	0.26
2002-03	0.43	0.43	0.52	0.60
2003-04	0.69	0.68	0.69	0.74
2004-05	0.92	0.85	...	...

Interim Dividends (Per Share)

Amt	Decl	Ex	Rec	Pay
0.085Q	9/24/2004	9/30/2004	10/4/2004	10/15/2004
0.10Q	12/16/2004	12/29/2004	12/31/2004	1/14/2005
0.10Q	3/15/2005	3/29/2005	3/31/2005	4/15/2005
2.00Q	3/15/2005	3/29/2005	3/31/2005	4/15/2005

Indicated Div: $0.40 (Div. Reinv. Plan)

Valuation Analysis

Forecast P/E	18.74 (5/28/2005)		
Market Cap	$18.1 Billion	Book Value	5.1 Billion
Price/Book	3.58	Price/Sales	4.77

Dividend Achiever Status

Rank	133	10 Year Growth Rate	12.29%
Total Years of Dividend Growth			15

Business Summary: Wealth Management (MIC: 8.8 SIC: 282 NAIC: 23930)

Franklin Resources is a bank holding company and a financial services company. Through its wholly-owned direct and indirect subsidiary companies, Co. provides a range of investment advisory, investment management and related services to open-end and closed-end investment companies, institutional accounts, high net-worth families, individuals and separate accounts in the United States and internationally. Co. also provides investment management and related services to a number of closed-end investment companies. As of Sep 30 2004, Co.'s subsidiaries had $361.90 billion in assets under management.

Recent Developments: For the quarter ended Mar 31 2005, net income increased 28.1% to $221,274 thousand from net income of $172,791 thousand in the year-earlier quarter. Revenues were $1,051,181 thousand, up 19.6% from $878,995 thousand the year before. Net investment income fell 8.2% to $1,361 thousand from $1,483 thousand a year ago.

Prospects: Going forward, earnings and revenues should continue to benefit from increases in assets under management, which is a key driver of results for fund firms. As of Mar 31 2005, assets under management by Co.'s subsidiaries were $412.10 billion compared with $351.60 billion the previous year. Simple monthly average assets under management during the second quarter of fiscal 2005 were $407.40 billion versus $345.70 billion in the corresponding prior-year quarter. Separately, during the second quarter, Co. raised approximately $450.0 million from the launch of the Franklin India Flexi Cap Fund, a diversified equity fund that invests in Indian stocks across the entire market capitalization range.

Financial Data (US$ in Thousands)	6 Mos	3 Mos	09/30/2004	09/30/2003	09/30/2002	09/30/2001	09/30/2000	09/30/1999
Earnings Per Share	3.20	3.02	2.80	1.97	1.65	1.91	2.28	1.69
Cash Flow Per Share	4.54	4.30	3.78	2.16	2.82	2.19	2.84	2.32
Tang Book Value Per Share	11.99	13.11	12.23	9.31	8.69	7.63	7.37	5.79
Dividends Per Share	0.355	0.34	0.33	0.295	0.275	0.255	0.235	0.215
Dividend Payout %	11.09	11.26	11.79	14.97	16.67	13.35	10.31	12.72
Income Statement								
Total Revenue	2,037,203	986,022	3,438,208	2,624,448	2,518,532	2,354,843	2,340,140	2,262,497
Income Before Taxes	637,713	335,649	993,866	700,203	578,275	637,790	739,591	574,084
Income Taxes	176,450	95,660	291,981	197,373	145,552	153,069	177,502	147,373
Net Income	461,263	239,989	706,664	502,830	432,723	484,721	562,089	426,711
Average Shares	263,386	262,629	252,152	254,681	262,054	253,663	246,624	252,757
Balance Sheet								
Total Assets	8,699,455	8,451,248	8,228,135	6,970,749	6,422,738	6,265,650	4,042,443	3,666,790
Total Liabilities	3,548,510	3,019,346	3,045,262	2,660,641	2,155,792	2,287,754	1,076,950	1,009,796
Stockholders' Equity	5,061,287	5,339,332	5,106,784	4,310,108	4,266,946	3,977,896	2,965,493	2,656,994
Shares Outstanding	251,071	250,242	249,680	245,931	258,555	260,797	243,730	251,006
Statistical Record								
Return on Assets %	9.94	9.74	9.27	7.51	6.82	9.40	14.54	11.94
Return on Equity %	16.69	15.55	14.97	11.73	10.50	13.96	19.94	17.28
Price Range	73.24-47.37	70.75-47.37	60.05-43.56	46.80-28.18	44.13-30.97	47.83-31.90	44.72-25.19	45.00-27.25
P/E Ratio	22.89-14.80	23.43-15.69	21.45-15.56	23.76-14.30	26.75-18.77	25.04-16.70	19.61-11.05	26.63-16.12
Average Yield %	0.59	0.58	0.64	0.80	0.73	0.62	0.67	0.60

Address: One Franklin Parkway, San Mateo, CA 94403
Telephone: 650-312-2000
Web Site: www.frk.com

Officers: Charles B. Johnson - Chmn. Harmon E. Burns - Vice-Chmn. **Transfer Agents:** Bank of New York

Investor Contact: 800-632-2350
No of Institutions: 345
Shares: 117,255,456 **% Held:** 46.83

FREDDIE MAC

Exchange	Symbol	Price	52Wk Range	Yield	P/E
NYS	FRE	$65.04 (5/31/2005)	73.70-58.06	2.15	9.74

***7 Year Price Score 99.20** *NYSE Composite Index=100 ***12 Month Price Score 92.94**

Interim Earnings (Per Share)

Qtr.	Mar	Jun	Sep	Dec
2000	0.81	0.83	0.86	0.89
2001	1.13	1.24	1.40	1.87
2002	1.94	1.50	2.13	8.61
2003	—	—	6.68	—

Interim Dividends (Per Share)

Amt	Decl	Ex	Rec	Pay
0.30Q	6/4/2004	6/10/2004	6/14/2004	6/30/2004
0.30Q	9/10/2004	9/16/2004	9/20/2004	9/30/2004
0.30Q	12/3/2004	12/9/2004	12/13/2004	12/31/2004
0.35Q	3/4/2005	3/10/2005	3/14/2005	3/31/2005

Indicated Div: $1.40 (Div. Reinv. Plan)

Valuation Analysis

Forecast P/E	17.41 (6/1/2005)		
Market Cap	$44.8 Billion	Book Value	31.5 Billion
Price/Book	1.42	Price/Sales	1.17

Dividend Achiever Status

Rank	73	**10 Year Growth Rate**	16.53%
Total Years of Dividend Growth			14

Business Summary: Credit & Lending (MIC: 8.6 SIC: 111 NAIC: 22292)

Freddie Mac purchases conventional residential mortgages from mortgage lending institutions and finances most of its purchases with sales of guaranteed mortgage securities called Mortgage Participation Certificates for which Co. ultimately assumes the risk of borrower default. Co. also maintains an investment portfolio that consists principally of federal funds sold, reverse repurchase agreements and tax-advantaged and other short-term investments. Co.'s financial performance is driven primarily by the growth of its total servicing portfolio, the mix of sold versus retained portfolios, the spreads earned on the sold and retained portfolios and mortgage default costs.

Recent Developments: For the year ended Dec 31 2004, net income fell 41.3% to $2.83 billion compared with $4.82 billion in the previous year. Results for 2004 and 2003 included losses on investment activity of $348.0 million and $1.11 billion, and losses on debt retirement of $327.0 million and $1.78 billion, respectively. Results also included a loss of $4.48 billion in 2004 and a gain of $39.0 million in 2003 on derivatives. Net interest income decreased 3.8% to $9.14 billion from $9.50 billion a year earlier. Total interest income declined 4.0% to $35.60 billion, while total interest expense inched up 0.2% to $9.14 billion.

Prospects: Co. is making considerable progress in increasing its market share, streamlining operations and seizing business opportunities. While operating in a challenging, lower-growth environment, Co. believes it can continue to produce value for investors and home owners. For 2005, Co. expects to report net interest income materially lower than 2004, primarily due to compression in net interest margins on its existing portfolio and lower nominal margins on floating-rate mortgage-related security purchases. However, this decrease should be significantly offset by lower losses in non-interest income/loss, assuming current forward rates are realized.

Financial Data

(US$ in Thousands)	12/31/2003	12/31/2002	12/31/2001	12/31/2000	12/31/1999	12/31/1998	12/31/1997	12/31/1996
Earnings Per Share	6.68	14.18	5.64	3.40	2.96	2.31	1.88	1.65
Cash Flow Per Share	6.52	24.53	25.61	20.95	(17.82)	(11.01)	7.95	(2.51)
Tang Book Value Per Share	39.03	38.87	15.50	16.81	11.98	11.55	8.74	9.62
Dividends Per Share	1.040	0.880	0.800	0.680	0.600	0.480	0.400	0.350
Dividend Payout %	15.57	6.21	14.18	20.00	20.27	20.78	21.28	21.21
Income Statement								
Interest Income	37,098,000	38,476,000	34,288,000	28,350,000	22,753,000	16,638,000	13,001,000	10,783,000
Interest Expense	26,509,000	26,564,000	28,808,000	25,512,000	20,213,000	14,711,000	11,370,000	9,241,000
Net Interest Income	10,589,000	11,912,000	5,480,000	2,838,000	2,540,000	1,927,000	1,631,000	1,542,000
Provision for Losses	10,000	128,000	45,000	40,000	60,000	190,000	310,000	320,000
Non-Interest Income	1,102,000	(68,000)	1,639,000	1,489,000	1,405,000	1,307,000	1,298,000	1,249,000
Non-Interest Expense	2,211,000	1,737,000	1,020,000	883,000	834,000	791,000	755,000	758,000
Income Before Taxes	7,018,000	14,803,000	6,300,000	3,534,000	3,161,000	2,356,000	1,964,000	1,797,000
Income Taxes	2,202,000	4,713,000	1,927,000	995,000	943,000	656,000	569,000	539,000
Net Income	4,816,000	10,090,000	4,147,000	2,547,000	2,223,000	1,700,000	1,395,000	1,243,000
Average Shares	688,675	695,116	696,876	696,448	700,211	684,658	692,000	710,000
Balance Sheet								
Net Loans & Leases	660,357,000	589,722,000	494,259,000	385,117,000	322,569,000	255,348,000	164,250,000	137,520,000
Total Assets	803,449,000	752,249,000	617,340,000	459,297,000	386,684,000	321,421,000	194,597,000	173,866,000
Total Liabilities	770,033,000	718,610,000	598,367,000	443,865,000	374,602,000	309,978,000	186,154,000	166,271,000
Stockholders' Equity	31,487,000	31,330,000	15,373,000	14,837,000	11,525,000	10,835,000	7,521,000	6,731,000
Shares Outstanding	688,573	687,376	695,304	692,584	695,091	695,179	679,000	695,000
Statistical Record								
Return on Assets %	0.62	1.47	0.77	0.60	0.63	0.66	0.76	0.80
Return on Equity %	15.33	43.21	27.45	19.27	19.88	18.52	19.58	19.69
Net Interest Margin %	28.54	30.96	15.98	10.01	11.16	11.58	12.55	14.30
Efficiency Ratio %	5.79	4.52	2.84	2.96	3.45	4.41	5.28	6.30
Price Range	64.73-47.35	68.60-53.98	70.79-60.00	69.00-37.69	64.63-45.75	65.13-39.50	43.38-27.03	28.66-19.44
P/E Ratio	9.69-7.09	4.84-3.81	12.55-10.64	20.29-11.08	21.83-15.46	28.19-17.10	23.07-14.38	17.37-11.78
Average Yield %	1.88	1.41	1.22	1.41	1.08	0.98	1.18	1.54

Address: 8200 Jones Branch Drive, McLean, VA 22102-3110 **Telephone:** 703-903-2000 **Web Site:** www.freddiemac.com	**Officers:** Richard F. Syron - Chmn., C.E.O. Eugene M. McQuade - Pres., C.O.O. **Transfer Agents:** EquiServe Trust Company, N.A., Jersey City, NJ	**Investor Contact:** 800-373-3343 **No of Institutions:** 527 **Shares:** 615,126,976 **% Held:** 88.65

FULLER (H.B.) COMPANY

Exchange	Symbol	Price	52Wk Range	Yield	P/E
NYS	FUL	$32.40 (5/31/2005)	32.40-25.34	1.51	24.92

*7 Year Price Score 95.13 *NYSE Composite Index=100 *12 Month Price Score 105.15

Interim Earnings (Per Share)

Qtr.	Feb	May	Aug	Nov
2001-02	0.02	0.28	0.32	0.36
2002-03	0.11	0.34	0.43	0.47
2003-04	0.16	0.41	0.33	0.34
2004-05	0.22	...	...	...

Interim Dividends (Per Share)

Amt	Decl	Ex	Rec	Pay
0.115Q	7/9/2004	7/20/2004	7/22/2004	8/5/2004
0.115Q	9/30/2004	10/12/2004	10/14/2004	10/28/2004
0.115Q	1/28/2005	2/9/2005	2/11/2005	2/25/2005
0.123Q	4/14/2005	4/26/2005	4/28/2005	5/12/2005

Indicated Div: $0.49 (Div. Reinv. Plan)

Valuation Analysis

Forecast P/E	21.61 (5/28/2005)		
Market Cap	$932.7 Million	Book Value	556.5 Million
Price/Book	1.68	Price/Sales	0.64

Dividend Achiever Status

Rank	274	10 Year Growth Rate	4.76%
Total Years of Dividend Growth			37

Business Summary: Chemicals (MIC: 11.1 SIC: 891 NAIC: 25520)

H.B. Fuller and its subsidiaries manufacture and market adhesives and specialty chemical products globally, with sales operations in 34 countries in North America, Europe, Latin America and the Asia/Pacific region. Co.'s products, in thousands of formulations, are sold to customers in a wide range of industries. Also, Co. is a producer and supplier of specialty chemical products for a variety of applications such as ceramic tile installation, HVAC insulation installation, powder coatings applied to metal surfaces such as office furniture, appliances and lawn and garden equipment, specialty hot melt adhesives for packaging applications, and liquid paint sold through retail outlets.

Recent Developments: For the quarter ended Feb 26 2005, net income jumped 40.9% to $6.5 million compared with $4.6 million in the year-earlier quarter. Results for 2005 and 2004 included gains of $1.8 million and $34,000, respectively, from sales of fixed assets. Net revenue advanced 10.8% to $353.0 million from $318.6 million a year earlier. The improvement in revenues was primarily attributed to pricing increases of 4.4% and growth in volumes of 1.4%, while acquisitions added 2.7% and positive currency effects contributed 2.3%. Gross profit climbed 5.7% to $90.7 million, or 25.7% of net revenue, from $85.8 million, or 26.9% of net revenue.

Prospects: Top-line growth is being driven by improved pricing and increased sales volume, along with contributions from recent acquisitions and favorable foreign currency exchange rates. Meanwhile, gross margins are being negatively affected by the continued escalation of raw material prices. Going forward, Co. plans to focus on passing along the raw material increases it is facing, in an effort to continue the positive trend in its operating income. Separately, Co. expects to complete the formation of its joint ventures with Sekisui Chemical Company in Japan and China during the second quarter of 2005. The two will merge their Japanese adhesives businesses to form Sekisui-Fuller Company, Ltd.

Financial Data

(US$ in Thousands)	3 Mos	11/27/2004	11/29/2003	11/30/2002	12/01/2001	12/02/2000	11/27/1999	11/28/1998
Earnings Per Share	1.30	1.23	1.35	0.98	1.57	1.74	1.55	0.57
Cash Flow Per Share	4.23	4.35	2.12	2.94	3.22	2.76	4.13	1.90
Tang Book Value Per Share	15.49	15.24	14.52	12.59	12.37	11.07	9.88	8.51
Dividends Per Share	0.460	0.458	0.448	0.438	0.427	0.417	0.407	0.393
Dividend Payout %	35.34	37.20	33.15	44.64	27.23	23.99	26.29	68.26
Income Statement								
Total Revenue	352,987	1,409,606	1,287,331	1,256,210	1,274,059	1,352,562	1,364,458	1,347,241
EBITDA	25,748	103,549	104,218	97,203	117,871	129,070	125,202	82,327
Depn & Amortn	13,918	56,030	54,136	57,544	54,401	52,165	50,776	49,541
Income Before Taxes	8,500	48,298	50,808	40,312	63,470	76,905	74,426	32,786
Income Taxes	2,720	14,713	14,307	12,973	19,833	28,455	31,807	18,826
Net Income	6,501	35,603	38,619	28,176	44,439	49,163	43,370	15,990
Average Shares	28,962	28,909	28,694	28,601	28,330	28,206	27,956	27,688
Balance Sheet								
Current Assets	513,758	553,650	448,492	408,874	403,873	435,064	440,143	457,900
Total Assets	1,087,820	1,135,359	1,007,588	961,439	966,173	1,010,361	1,025,615	1,046,169
Current Liabilities	245,564	293,449	200,026	214,846	204,163	226,725	265,920	285,160
Long-Term Obligations	137,747	138,149	161,047	161,763	203,001	250,464	263,714	300,074
Total Liabilities	531,355	582,300	498,250	513,109	532,147	605,651	649,235	704,765
Stockholders' Equity	556,465	553,059	509,338	448,330	434,026	404,710	376,380	341,404
Shares Outstanding	28,787	28,641	28,435	28,362	28,280	28,240	28,080	27,965
Statistical Record								
Return on Assets %	3.57	3.33	3.93	2.93	4.51	4.75	4.20	1.63
Return on Equity %	6.99	6.72	8.09	6.40	10.63	12.38	12.12	4.71
EBITDA Margin %	7.29	7.35	8.10	7.74	9.25	9.54	9.18	6.11
Net Margin %	1.84	2.53	3.00	2.24	3.49	3.63	3.18	1.19
Asset Turnover	1.38	1.32	1.31	1.31	1.29	1.31	1.32	1.38
Current Ratio	2.09	1.89	2.24	1.90	1.98	1.92	1.66	1.61
Debt to Equity	0.25	0.25	0.32	0.36	0.47	0.62	0.70	0.88
Price Range	29.10-24.84	30.19-24.84	29.50-20.00	32.50-24.54	30.95-16.59	34.25-14.34	36.09-19.19	32.41-17.25
P/E Ratio	22.38-19.11	24.54-20.20	21.85-14.81	33.16-25.04	19.71-10.57	19.68-8.24	23.29-12.38	56.85-30.26
Average Yield %	1.69	1.67	1.83	1.53	1.85	1.92	1.43	1.51

Address: 1200 Willow Lake Boulevard, St. Paul, Vadnais Heights, MN 55110-5101 **Telephone:** 651-236-5900 **Web Site:** www.hbfuller.com	**Officers:** Albert P. L. Stroucken - Chmn., Pres., C.E.O. John A. Feenan - Sr. V.P., C.F.O. **Transfer Agents:** Wells Fargo Shareowner Services, Minnesota, MN	**Investor Contact:** 651-236-5150 **No of Institutions:** 128 **Shares:** 21,249,476 **% Held:** 74.16

FULTON FINANCIAL CORP. (PA)

Exchange	Symbol	Price	52Wk Range	Yield	P/E
NMS	FULT	$21.73 (5/31/2005)	23.49-19.76	2.67	16.84

*7 Year Price Score 114.88 *NYSE Composite Index=100 *12 Month Price Score 96.58

Interim Earnings (Per Share)

Qtr.	Mar	Jun	Sep	Dec
2002	0.28	0.18	0.30	0.31
2003	0.30	0.30	0.30	0.30
2004	0.31	0.31	0.32	0.33
2005	0.33	...	...	...

Interim Dividends (Per Share)

Amt	Decl	Ex	Rec	Pay
0.165Q	10/19/2004	12/17/2004	12/21/2004	1/14/2005
0.165Q	1/18/2005	3/18/2005	3/22/2005	4/15/2005
25%	4/13/2005	6/9/2005	5/17/2005	6/8/2005
0.145Q	4/13/2005	6/15/2005	6/17/2005	7/15/2005

Indicated Div: $0.58 (Div. Reinv. Plan)

Valuation Analysis

Forecast P/E	15.74 (6/4/2005)		
Market Cap	$2.7 Billion	Book Value	1.2 Billion
Price/Book	2.21	Price/Sales	4.13

Dividend Achiever Status

Rank	167	10 Year Growth Rate	10.34%
Total Years of Dividend Growth			31

Business Summary: Commercial Banking (MIC: 8.1 SIC: 021 NAIC: 22110)

Fulton Financial, with $11.16 billion in assets at Dec 31 2004, is a financial holding company. As of Dec 31 2004, Co. operated 218 banking offices in Delaware, Maryland, New Jersey, Pennsylvania and Virginia through the following affiliates: Fulton Bank, Lebanon Valley Farmers Bank, Swineford National Bank, Lafayette Ambassador Bank, FNB Bank, Hagerstown Trust, Delaware National Bank, The Bank, The Peoples Bank of Elkton, Skylands Community Bank, Premier Bank, Resource Bank and First Washington State Bank. Co.'s financial services affiliates include Fulton Financial Advisors and Fulton Insurance Services Group. Residential mortgage lending is offered by all banks through Fulton Mortgage.

Recent Developments: For the quarter ended Mar 31 2005, net income increased 15.9% to $41,531 thousand from net income of $35,846 thousand in the year-earlier quarter. Net interest income was $98,248 thousand, up 18.4% from $82,967 thousand the year before. Provision for loan losses was $800 thousand versus $1,740 thousand in the prior-year quarter, a decrease of 54.0%. Non-interest income rose 11.9% to $35,853 thousand, while non-interest expense advanced 18.4% to $73,731 thousand.

Prospects: Strong loan growth is being driven by the acquisitions of Resource Bank in April 2004 and First Washington State Bank in December 2004, along with a higher rate of commercial loans and mortgages. Results are also benefiting from increases in both net interest income and net interest margin, due partially to higher interest rates, and continued excellent asset quality. Separately, on Jan 11 2005, Co. announced that it has entered into a definitive agreement to acquire Somerville, NJ-based SVB Financial Services, Inc. for approximately $89.0 million. The transaction is expected to be completed in the third quarter of 2005.

Financial Data

(US$ in Thousands)	3 Mos	12/31/2004	12/31/2003	12/31/2002	12/31/2001	12/31/2000	12/31/1999	12/31/1998
Earnings Per Share	1.29	1.27	1.22	1.17	0.99	1.00	0.92	0.84
Cash Flow Per Share	1.11	1.22	1.67	0.84	0.92	1.15	1.22	0.55
Tang Book Value Per Share	6.73	6.79	7.20	7.10	6.48	6.53	5.91	5.78
Dividends Per Share	0.660	0.647	0.593	0.532	0.481	0.430	0.386	0.351
Dividend Payout %	51.16	50.97	48.66	45.43	48.35	42.95	41.89	41.86
Income Statement								
Interest Income	140,810	493,643	435,531	469,288	518,178	462,581	418,914	409,292
Interest Expense	42,562	135,994	131,094	158,219	227,962	210,481	174,827	177,805
Net Interest Income	98,248	357,649	304,437	311,069	290,216	252,100	244,087	231,487
Provision for Losses	800	4,717	9,705	11,900	14,585	8,645	8,216	5,582
Non-Interest Income	35,853	138,864	136,987	115,783	100,994	69,611	62,822	60,641
Non-Interest Expense	73,731	273,615	234,176	225,536	216,669	165,022	160,988	158,203
Income Before Taxes	59,570	218,181	197,543	189,416	159,956	148,044	137,705	128,343
Income Taxes	18,039	65,264	59,363	56,468	46,367	44,240	40,479	39,832
Net Income	41,531	152,917	138,180	132,948	113,589	103,804	97,226	88,511
Average Shares	127,431	120,641	113,135	113,898	114,592	103,685	105,385	105,574
Balance Sheet								
Net Loans & Leases	7,657,174	7,494,920	6,082,294	5,245,148	5,301,148	4,806,498	4,364,776	3,972,976
Total Assets	11,418,278	11,158,351	9,767,288	8,387,778	7,770,711	6,571,155	6,070,019	5,838,663
Total Deposits	7,981,147	7,895,524	6,751,783	6,245,528	5,986,804	4,934,405	4,546,813	4,592,969
Total Liabilities	10,182,759	9,916,061	8,820,352	7,524,036	6,959,257	5,891,819	5,455,725	5,230,329
Stockholders' Equity	1,235,519	1,242,290	946,936	863,742	811,454	679,336	614,294	608,334
Shares Outstanding	125,872	125,700	113,820	111,462	113,833	104,041	104,000	105,269
Statistical Record								
Return on Assets %	1.51	1.46	1.52	1.65	1.58	1.64	1.63	1.72
Return on Equity %	14.39	13.93	15.26	15.87	15.24	16.00	15.90	16.34
Net Interest Margin %	69.77	72.45	69.90	66.29	56.01	54.50	58.27	56.56
Efficiency Ratio %	41.74	43.26	40.90	38.55	34.99	31.01	33.42	33.67
Loans to Deposits	0.96	0.95	0.90	0.84	0.89	0.97	0.96	0.87
Price Range	23.49-19.48	23.49-19.48	20.86-16.02	18.40-15.28	16.54-13.30	16.50-10.49	14.23-11.31	17.99-10.77
P/E Ratio	18.21-15.10	18.50-15.34	17.10-13.13	15.73-13.06	16.71-13.44	16.50-10.49	15.47-12.30	21.41-12.82
Average Yield %	3.10	3.09	3.16	3.15	3.14	3.18	2.94	2.42

Address: One Penn Square, P.O. Box 4887, Lancaster, PA 17604
Telephone: 717-291-2411
Web Site: www.fult.com

Officers: Rufus A. Fulton Jr. - Chmn., C.E.O. R. Scott Smith Jr. - Pres., C.O.O. **Transfer Agents:** Stock Transfer Department, Lancaster, PA

Investor Contact: 717-291-2739
No of Institutions: 118
Shares: 23,818,104 **% Held:** 18.91

GALLAGHER (ARTHUR J.) & CO.

Exchange	Symbol	Price	52Wk Range	Yield	P/E
NYS	AJG	$27.62 (5/31/2005)	33.96-27.06	4.06	35.87

*7 Year Price Score 108.71 *NYSE Composite Index=100 *12 Month Price Score 89.32

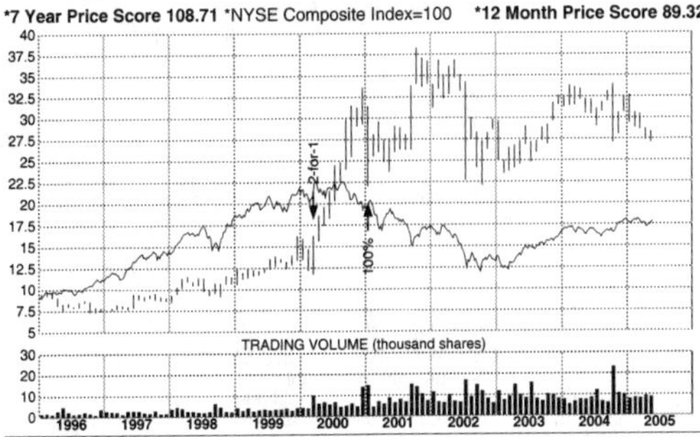

Interim Earnings (Per Share)

Qtr.	Mar	Jun	Sep	Dec
2002	0.37	0.37	0.26	0.36
2003	0.13	0.39	0.52	0.53
2004	0.41	0.49	0.57	0.51
2005	(0.80)	...	...	...

Interim Dividends (Per Share)

Amt	Decl	Ex	Rec	Pay
0.25Q	7/22/2004	9/28/2004	9/30/2004	10/15/2004
0.25Q	10/21/2004	12/29/2004	12/31/2004	1/14/2005
0.28Q	1/19/2005	3/29/2005	3/31/2005	4/15/2005
0.28Q	5/17/2005	6/28/2005	6/30/2005	7/15/2005

Indicated Div: $1.12

Valuation Analysis

Forecast P/E	13.73 (5/28/2005)		
Market Cap	$2.6 Billion	Book Value	682.7 Million
Price/Book	3.77	Price/Sales	1.73

Dividend Achiever Status

Rank	75	10 Year Growth Rate	16.04%
Total Years of Dividend Growth			20

Business Summary: Insurance (MIC: 8.2 SIC: 411 NAIC: 24210)

Arthur J. Gallagher & Co. is engaged in providing insurance brokerage, risk management and related services to clients in the U.S. and abroad. Co.'s principal activity is the negotiation and placement of insurance for its clients. Co. also specializes in furnishing risk management services. Risk management involves assisting clients in analyzing risks and determining whether proper protection is best obtained through the purchase of insurance or through retention of all or a portion of those risks, and the adoption of corporate risk management policies and cost-effective loss control and prevention programs. Co. also has a financial services group that manages its investment portfolio.

Recent Developments: For the quarter ended Mar 31 2005, loss from continuing operations was $73,800 thousand versus income of $38,800 thousand in the year-earlier quarter. Net loss was $74,000 thousand from net income of $38,900 thousand in the year-earlier quarter. Revenues were $348,900 thousand, up 4.8% from $332,900 thousand the year before.

Prospects: Growth in results reflects Co.'s strength in selling insurance products and completing acquisitions. Risk management in particular continues to show excellent results. Separately, on Apr 29 2005, Co. announced the acquisition of Chris Schroeder Insurance of Milwaukee, WI., is a property/casualty retail insurance broker offering risk management, commercial, and personal lines insurance services to their Midwest client base. Chris Schroeder Insurance is a cultural fit to Co.'s Milwaukee operations, and their specializations should help to expand its higher education, religious and non-profit niche strategy.

Financial Data (US$ in Thousands)	3 Mos	12/31/2004	12/31/2003	12/31/2002	12/31/2001	12/31/2000	12/31/1999	12/31/1998
Earnings Per Share	0.77	1.99	1.57	1.41	1.39	1.05	0.88	0.78
Cash Flow Per Share	2.46	3.02	2.54	1.71	1.54	1.73	0.87	0.81
Tang Book Value Per Share	3.32	4.20	4.40	4.44	3.60	3.75	3.14	2.69
Dividends Per Share	1.030	1.000	0.720	0.600	0.520	0.460	0.400	0.350
Dividend Payout %	133.77	50.25	45.86	42.55	37.41	43.81	45.45	45.16
Income Statement								
Total Revenue	348,900	1,480,300	1,263,800	1,101,222	910,043	740,596	605,836	540,655
Income Before Taxes	(125,100)	235,500	193,300	185,342	141,853	125,394	104,235	84,529
Income Taxes	(51,300)	47,000	47,100	55,603	16,597	37,618	36,482	28,028
Net Income	(74,000)	188,500	146,200	129,739	125,256	87,776	67,753	56,501
Average Shares	94,800	94,500	93,300	91,861	90,127	83,924	77,132	72,824
Balance Sheet								
Total Assets	3,227,700	3,237,900	2,901,600	2,463,574	1,471,823	1,062,298	884,146	746,010
Total Liabilities	2,545,000	2,476,900	2,282,500	1,935,419	1,100,210	747,926	641,679	543,542
Stockholders' Equity	682,700	761,000	619,100	528,155	371,613	314,372	242,467	202,468
Shares Outstanding	93,200	92,100	90,000	88,548	85,111	79,497	73,680	70,580
Statistical Record								
Return on Assets %	2.48	6.12	5.45	6.59	9.89	8.99	8.31	8.14
Return on Equity %	11.36	27.24	25.49	28.84	36.52	31.44	30.46	30.84
Price Range	33.96-27.06	33.96-27.06	32.65-23.45	36.86-22.10	38.30-22.00	33.66-11.75	16.19-10.59	11.59-8.44
P/E Ratio	44.10-35.14	17.07-13.60	20.80-14.94	26.14-15.67	27.55-15.83	32.05-11.19	18.39-12.04	14.86-10.82
Average Yield %	3.32	3.17	2.63	1.94	1.77	2.13	3.17	3.36

Address: Two Pierce Place, Itasca, IL 60143-3141
Telephone: 630-773-3800
Web Site: www.ajg.com

Officers: Robert E. Gallagher - Chmn. J. Patrick Gallagher Jr. - Pres., C.E.O. **Transfer Agents:** Computershare Investor Services, Chicago, IL

No of Institutions: 219
Shares: 57,923,652 **% Held:** 62.88

GANNETT CO., INC.

Exchange	Symbol	Price	52Wk Range	Yield	P/E
NYS	GCI	$74.46 (5/31/2005)	87.87-74.46	1.45	14.92

*7 Year Price Score 100.31 *NYSE Composite Index=100 *12 Month Price Score 91.52

Interim Earnings (Per Share)

Qtr.	Mar	Jun	Sep	Dec
2002	0.91	1.13	0.99	1.29
2003	0.93	1.20	1.03	1.31
2004	1.00	1.30	1.18	1.45
2005	1.05	...	...	...

Interim Dividends (Per Share)

Amt	Decl	Ex	Rec	Pay
0.27Q	8/4/2004	9/8/2004	9/10/2004	10/1/2004
0.27Q	10/26/2004	12/15/2004	12/17/2004	1/3/2005
0.27Q	2/22/2005	3/2/2005	3/4/2005	4/1/2005
0.27Q	4/14/2005	6/1/2005	6/3/2005	7/1/2005

Indicated Div: $1.08 (Div. Reinv. Plan)

Valuation Analysis

Forecast P/E	14.51 (5/28/2005)		
Market Cap	$18.6 Billion	Book Value	7.9 Billion
Price/Book	2.36	Price/Sales	2.49

Dividend Achiever Status

Rank	282	10 Year Growth Rate	4.37%
Total Years of Dividend Growth			33

Business Summary: Media (MIC: 13.1 SIC: 711 NAIC: 11110)

Gannett is a news and information company that publishes newspapers and operates broadcasting stations. Co. is also engaged in marketing, commercial printing, a newswire service, data services, and news programming. Co. has operations in 43 states, the District of Columbia, Guam, the U.K., and in certain European and Asian markets. Co. is the largest U.S. newspaper group in terms of circulation, with 101 daily newspapers, including USA Today, more than 750 non-daily publications and USA Weekend, a weekly newspaper magazine. In the U.K., Co.'s subsidiary Newsquest publishes nearly 300 titles, including 17 daily newspapers. Co. owns and operates 21 television stations in major markets.

Recent Developments: For the quarter ended Mar 27 2005, net income decreased 3.2% to $265,737 thousand from net income of $274,408 thousand in the year-earlier quarter. Revenues were $1,792,097 thousand, up 3.6% from $1,729,684 thousand the year before. Operating income was $455,494 thousand versus an income of $445,849 thousand in the prior-year quarter, an increase of 2.2%. Total direct expense was $974,425 thousand versus $939,448 thousand in the prior-year quarter, an increase of 3.7%. Total indirect expense was $362,178 thousand versus $344,387 thousand in the prior-year quarter, an increase of 5.2%.

Prospects: Co. is enjoying gains in operating revenue, cash flow and earnings per share. On a segment basis, Co. newspaper segment is generating solid quarterly revenue growth, despite much softer advertising demand, reflecting in part, the impact of an earlier Easter in 2005 and tougher comparisons throughout the first quarter. Meanwhile, USA Today continues to post strong results in both print and on-line. However, Co.'s results in its broadcasting segment are being hampered by substantially lower level of political advertising and the absence of the Super Bowl on its six CBS affiliates. Also, Co. results are being negatively affected by higher newsprint and interest expense.

Financial Data

(US$ in Thousands)	3 Mos	12/26/2004	12/28/2003	12/29/2002	12/30/2001	12/31/2000	12/26/1999	12/27/1998
Earnings Per Share	4.99	4.92	4.46	4.31	3.12	6.41	3.40	3.50
Cash Flow Per Share	6.47	6.01	5.50	3.88	4.96	1.85	4.12	3.44
Tang Book Value Per Share	N.M.	N.M.	N.M.	N.M.	N.M.	N.M.	N.M.	0.66
Dividends Per Share	1.060	1.040	0.980	0.940	0.900	0.860	0.820	0.780
Dividend Payout %	21.24	21.14	21.97	21.81	28.85	13.42	24.12	22.29
Income Statement								
Total Revenue	1,792,097	7,381,283	6,711,115	6,422,249	6,344,245	6,222,318	5,260,190	5,121,291
EBITDA	509,278	2,375,506	2,205,909	2,129,883	2,031,552	2,176,774	1,896,158	2,039,713
Depn & Amortn	64,703	244,021	231,532	222,444	443,777	375,915	280,091	310,206
Income Before Taxes	399,637	1,995,386	1,840,313	1,764,528	1,370,597	1,608,840	1,527,187	1,669,413
Income Taxes	133,900	678,200	629,100	604,400	539,400	636,900	607,800	669,500
Net Income	265,737	1,317,186	1,211,213	1,160,128	831,197	1,719,077	957,928	999,913
Average Shares	254,270	267,590	271,872	269,286	266,833	268,118	281,608	285,711
Balance Sheet								
Current Assets	1,341,893	1,370,695	1,223,261	1,133,079	1,178,198	1,302,336	1,075,222	906,385
Total Assets	15,263,578	15,399,251	14,706,239	13,733,014	13,096,101	12,980,411	9,006,446	6,979,480
Current Liabilities	1,050,982	1,005,450	961,837	958,625	1,127,737	1,174,001	883,778	727,967
Long-Term Obligations	4,707,625	4,607,743	3,834,511	4,547,265	5,080,025	5,747,856	2,463,250	1,306,859
Total Liabilities	7,288,231	7,143,888	6,190,819	6,821,219	7,360,179	7,877,001	4,376,800	2,999,656
Stockholders' Equity	7,884,767	8,164,002	8,422,981	6,911,795	5,735,922	5,103,410	4,629,646	3,979,824
Shares Outstanding	249,571	254,344	272,417	267,909	265,797	264,271	277,926	279,001
Statistical Record								
Return on Assets %	8.69	8.77	8.54	8.67	6.39	15.38	12.02	14.46
Return on Equity %	15.89	15.93	15.84	18.40	15.38	34.75	22.31	26.88
EBITDA Margin %	28.42	32.18	32.87	33.16	32.02	34.98	36.05	39.83
Net Margin %	14.83	17.84	18.05	18.06	13.10	27.63	18.21	19.52
Asset Turnover	0.49	0.49	0.47	0.48	0.49	0.56	0.66	0.74
Current Ratio	1.28	1.36	1.27	1.18	1.04	1.11	1.22	1.25
Debt to Equity	0.60	0.56	0.46	0.66	0.89	1.13	0.53	0.33
Price Range	91.00-78.43	91.00-78.99	88.93-67.68	79.87-63.39	71.10-55.55	83.25-48.69	79.31-61.81	74.69-48.94
P/E Ratio	18.24-15.72	18.50-16.05	19.94-15.17	18.53-14.71	22.79-17.80	12.99-7.60	23.33-18.18	21.34-13.98
Average Yield %	1.27	1.22	1.27	1.28	1.40	1.40	1.17	1.22

Address: 7950 Jones Branch Drive, McLean, VA 22107-0910 **Telephone:** 703-854-6000 **Web Site:** www.gannett.com	**Officers:** Douglas H. McCorkindale - Chmn., Pres., C.E.O. Gracia C. Martore - Sr. V.P., C.F.O. **Transfer Agents:** Wells Fargo Bank Minnesota, N.A., St. Paul, MN	**Investor Contact:** 703-854-6918 **No of Institutions:** 610 **Shares:** 193,011,616 **% Held:** 76.53

GENERAL DYNAMICS CORP.

Exchange	Symbol	Price	52Wk Range	Yield	P/E
NYS	GD	$107.98 (5/31/2005)	109.83-94.05	1.48	16.82

Interim Earnings (Per Share)

Qtr.	Mar	Jun	Sep	Dec
2002	1.13	1.29	1.32	0.78
2003	1.11	1.22	1.32	1.40
2004	1.34	1.49	1.60	1.66
2005	1.66	...	...	...

Interim Dividends (Per Share)

Amt	Decl	Ex	Rec	Pay
0.36Q	6/2/2004	6/30/2004	7/2/2004	8/6/2004
0.36Q	8/4/2004	10/6/2004	10/8/2004	11/12/2004
0.36Q	12/1/2004	1/12/2005	1/14/2005	2/4/2005
0.40Q	3/2/2005	4/5/2005	4/7/2005	5/6/2005

Indicated Div: $1.60

Valuation Analysis

Forecast P/E	15.42 (6/1/2005)		
Market Cap	$21.6 Billion	Book Value	7.4 Billion
Price/Book	2.93	Price/Sales	1.12

Dividend Achiever Status

Rank	220	**10 Year Growth Rate**	7.57%
Total Years of Dividend Growth			13

Business Summary: Shipping (MIC: 15.3 SIC: 731 NAIC: 36611)

General Dynamics is a major defense contractor operating in four business segments. Information Systems and Technology provides defense and commercial customers with infrastructure and systems integration skills required to process, communicate and manage information. Marine Systems provides the U.S. Navy with combat vessels. Aerospace designs and develops technologically advanced business jet aircraft. Combat Systems provides systems integration, design, and production for armored vehicles, armaments, munitions and components. Other businesses consist of a coal mining operation, an aggregates operation and a leasing operation for liquefied natural gas tankers.

Recent Developments: For the quarter ended Apr 3 2005, net income increased 24.9% to $336,000 thousand from net income of $269,000 thousand in the year-earlier quarter. Revenues were $4,819,000 thousand, up 3.7% from $4,646,000 thousand the year before. Operating income was $448,000 thousand versus an income of $436,000 thousand in the prior-year quarter, an increase of 2.8%. Total indirect expense was $4,371,000 thousand versus $4,210,000 thousand in the prior-year quarter, an increase of 3.8%.

Prospects: Co. is benefiting from gains in three of its four primary business groups, with notable favorable margin improvement in its Aerospace and Information Systems and Technology sectors. However, these results are being partially offset by the negative impact of an additional charge Co. had to take against the commercial tanker program at NASSCO. Looking ahead, Co. should be well-positioned to benefit from a stronger backlog. Accordingly, Co. has revised its 2005 earnings outlook, as it now expects full-year 2005 earnings from continuing operations of $6.95 per share, approximately 16.0% above the $5.97 earnings per share recorded for continuing operations in 2004.

Financial Data

(US$ in Thousands)	3 Mos	12/31/2004	12/31/2003	12/31/2002	12/31/2001	12/31/2000	12/31/1999	12/31/1998
Earnings Per Share	6.42	6.09	5.04	4.52	4.65	4.48	4.36	2.86
Cash Flow Per Share	9.15	9.01	8.71	5.59	5.48	5.34	5.08	2.94
Tang Book Value Per Share	0.03	N.M.	N.M.	5.62	3.84	6.43	3.27	5.46
Dividends Per Share	1.440	1.400	1.260	1.180	1.100	1.020	0.940	0.865
Dividend Payout %	22.42	22.99	25.00	26.11	23.66	22.77	21.56	30.24
Income Statement								
Total Revenue	4,819,000	19,178,000	16,617,000	13,829,000	12,163,000	10,356,000	8,959,000	4,970,000
EBITDA	534,000	2,259,000	1,747,000	1,842,000	1,751,000	1,548,000	1,360,000	671,000
Depn & Amortn	87,000	326,000	277,000	213,000	271,000	226,000	200,000	126,000
Income Before Taxes	413,000	1,785,000	1,372,000	1,584,000	1,424,000	1,262,000	1,126,000	549,000
Income Taxes	69,000	582,000	375,000	533,000	481,000	361,000	246,000	185,000
Net Income	336,000	1,227,000	1,004,000	917,000	943,000	901,000	880,000	364,000
Average Shares	202,024	201,467	199,152	202,852	202,907	201,262	202,057	127,000
Balance Sheet								
Current Assets	7,720,000	7,287,000	6,394,000	5,098,000	4,893,000	3,551,000	3,491,000	1,873,000
Total Assets	17,905,000	17,544,000	16,183,000	11,731,000	11,069,000	7,987,000	7,774,000	4,572,000
Current Liabilities	5,583,000	5,374,000	5,616,000	4,582,000	4,579,000	2,901,000	3,453,000	1,461,000
Long-Term Obligations	3,290,000	3,291,000	3,296,000	718,000	724,000	162,000	169,000	249,000
Total Liabilities	10,509,000	10,355,000	10,262,000	6,532,000	6,541,000	4,167,000	4,603,000	2,353,000
Stockholders' Equity	7,396,000	7,189,000	5,921,000	5,199,000	4,528,000	3,820,000	3,171,000	2,219,000
Shares Outstanding	200,375	201,033	197,966	200,993	200,746	200,502	201,013	127,000
Statistical Record								
Return on Assets %	7.50	7.26	7.19	8.04	9.90	11.40	14.26	8.40
Return on Equity %	19.05	18.67	18.06	18.85	22.59	25.71	32.65	17.61
EBITDA Margin %	11.08	11.78	10.51	13.32	14.40	14.95	15.18	13.50
Net Margin %	6.97	6.40	6.04	6.63	7.75	8.70	9.82	7.32
Asset Turnover	1.12	1.13	1.19	1.21	1.28	1.31	1.45	1.15
Current Ratio	1.38	1.36	1.14	1.11	1.07	1.22	1.01	1.28
Debt to Equity	0.44	0.46	0.56	0.14	0.16	0.04	0.05	0.11
Price Range	109.83-91.00	109.83-86.10	90.39-52.37	110.58-74.57	94.99-61.00	78.00-37.00	74.81-46.94	61.25-40.38
P/E Ratio	17.11-14.17	18.03-14.14	17.93-10.39	24.46-16.50	20.43-13.12	17.41-8.26	17.16-10.77	21.42-14.12
Average Yield %	1.43	1.44	1.72	1.34	1.43	1.76	1.53	1.80

Address: 2941 Fairview Park Drive, Suite 100, Falls Church, VA 22042-4153 **Telephone:** 703-876-3000 **Web Site:** www.generaldynamics.com	**Officers:** Nicholas D. Chabraja - Chmn., C.E.O. Michael W. Toner - Exec. V.P., Group Exec., Marine Systems **Transfer Agents:** EquiServe Trust Company, N.A., Jersey City, NJ	**Investor Contact:** 703-876-3195 **No of Institutions:** 533 **Shares:** 155,012,944 **% Held:** 77.46

GENERAL ELECTRIC CO.

Exchange	Symbol	Price	52Wk Range	Yield	P/E
NYS	GE	$36.48 (5/31/2005)	37.48-31.00	2.41	22.24

***7 Year Price Score 83.21** *NYSE Composite Index=100 ***12 Month Price Score 100.99**

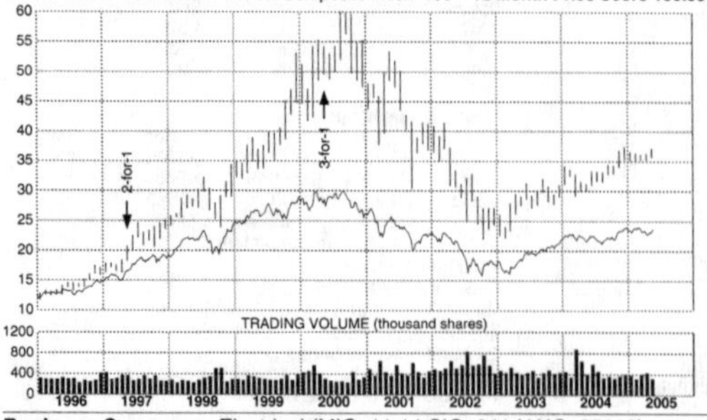

TRADING VOLUME (thousand shares)

Interim Earnings (Per Share)

Qtr.	Mar	Jun	Sep	Dec
2002	0.25	0.44	0.41	0.31
2003	0.30	0.38	0.36	0.45
2004	0.32	0.38	0.38	0.51
2005	0.37	...	...	...

Interim Dividends (Per Share)

Amt	Decl	Ex	Rec	Pay
0.20Q	6/11/2004	6/24/2004	6/28/2004	7/26/2004
0.20Q	9/17/2004	9/23/2004	9/27/2004	10/25/2004
0.22Q	12/10/2004	12/22/2004	12/27/2004	1/25/2005
0.22Q	2/11/2005	2/24/2005	2/28/2005	4/25/2005

Indicated Div: $0.88 (Div. Reinv. Plan)

Valuation Analysis

Forecast P/E	20.41 (5/28/2005)		
Market Cap	$386.9 Billion	Book Value	112.9 Billion
Price/Book	3.43	Price/Sales	2.44

Dividend Achiever Status

Rank	124	**10 Year Growth Rate**	12.79%
Total Years of Dividend Growth			29

Business Summary: Electrical (MIC: 11.14 SIC: 641 NAIC: 35110)

General Electric is engaged in developing, manufacturing and marketing a wide variety of products for the generation, transmission, distribution, control and utilization of electricity. Co.'s operating segments include: Commercial Finance, Consumer Finance, Energy, Healthcare, Infrastructure, Transportation, NBC, Advanced Materials, Consumer and Industrial, Equipment Services and Insurance. Co.'s products include major appliances; lighting products; industrial automation products; medical diagnostic imaging equipment; motors; electrical distribution and control equipment; locomotives; power generation and delivery products; nuclear power support services and fuel assemblies.

Recent Developments: For the quarter ended Mar 31 2005, net income increased 17.8% to $3,965 million from net income of $3,366 million in the year-earlier quarter. Revenues were $39,726 million, up 18.3% from $33,592 million the year before. Total direct expense was $19,562 million versus $16,206 million in the prior-year quarter, an increase of 20.7%. Total indirect expense was $10,071 million versus $9,074 million in the prior-year quarter, an increase of 11.0%.

Prospects: Co.'s businesses and its end-use markets are continuing to see strong growth. Co. is exceeding the high end of its initial expectations and is building solid momentum for 2005. For example, nine of Co.'s eleven businesses are delivering at least double-digit earnings growth and are achieving favorable revenue growth. Separately, Co. announced that it plans to sell up to 82.0 million shares of class A common stock of Genworth Financial, Inc. through a secondary public offering and a sale of Citigroup Global Markets Inc. Upon completion of these proposed transactions, Co. will own approximately 51.0% of Genworth's common stock if the underwriters' over-allotment option is exercised in full.

Financial Data

(US$ in Thousands)	3 Mos	12/31/2004	12/31/2003	12/31/2002	12/31/2001	12/31/2000	12/31/1999	12/31/1998
Earnings Per Share	1.64	1.59	1.49	1.41	1.37	1.27	1.07	0.93
Cash Flow Per Share	3.62	3.50	3.02	2.96	3.24	2.29	2.50	1.97
Tang Book Value Per Share	2.47	2.55	2.40	1.76	2.33	2.32	1.68	1.55
Dividends Per Share	0.840	0.820	0.770	0.730	0.660	0.570	0.487	0.417
Dividend Payout %	51.22	51.57	51.68	51.77	48.18	44.88	45.36	44.64
Income Statement								
Total Revenue	39,726,000	152,363,000	134,187,000	131,698,000	125,913,000	129,853,000	111,630,000	100,469,000
EBITDA	7,387,000	28,491,000	26,860,000	24,889,000	26,790,000	26,182,000	22,268,000	19,337,000
Depn & Amortn	2,288,000	8,385,000	6,956,000	5,998,000	7,089,000	7,736,000	6,691,000	5,860,000
Income Before Taxes	5,099,000	20,106,000	19,904,000	18,891,000	19,701,000	18,446,000	15,577,000	13,477,000
Income Taxes	1,134,000	3,513,000	4,315,000	3,758,000	5,573,000	5,711,000	4,860,000	4,181,000
Net Income	3,965,000	16,593,000	15,002,000	14,118,000	13,684,000	12,735,000	10,717,000	9,296,000
Average Shares	10,641,000	10,445,000	10,075,000	10,028,000	10,052,000	10,057,000	9,996,000	9,990,000
Balance Sheet								
Current Assets	172,422,000	39,339,000	32,148,000	28,838,000	27,237,000	25,509,000	24,092,000	18,590,000
Total Assets	752,223,000	750,330,000	647,483,000	575,244,000	495,023,000	437,006,000	405,200,000	355,935,000
Current Liabilities	204,644,000	206,280,000	176,530,000	181,827,000	198,904,000	156,112,000	161,216,000	141,579,000
Long-Term Obligations	212,928,000	213,161,000	170,004,000	140,632,000	79,806,000	82,132,000	71,427,000	59,663,000
Total Liabilities	620,763,000	623,663,000	562,523,000	506,065,000	434,984,000	381,578,000	357,429,000	312,780,000
Stockholders' Equity	112,872,000	110,284,000	79,180,000	63,706,000	54,824,000	50,492,000	42,557,000	38,880,000
Shares Outstanding	10,605,920	10,586,358	10,063,120	9,969,894	9,925,938	9,932,006	9,854,529	9,813,000
Statistical Record								
Return on Assets %	2.45	2.37	2.45	2.64	2.94	3.02	2.82	2.82
Return on Equity %	17.37	17.47	21.00	23.82	25.99	27.30	26.32	25.36
EBITDA Margin %	18.59	18.70	20.02	18.90	21.28	20.16	19.95	19.25
Net Margin %	9.98	10.89	11.18	10.72	10.87	9.81	9.60	9.25
Asset Turnover	0.22	0.22	0.22	0.25	0.27	0.31	0.29	0.30
Current Ratio	0.84	0.19	0.18	0.16	0.14	0.16	0.15	0.13
Debt to Equity	1.89	1.93	2.15	2.21	1.46	1.63	1.68	1.53
Price Range	37.48-29.95	37.48-29.18	32.11-22.17	41.55-22.00	53.40-30.37	60.00-41.71	53.17-32.00	34.42-23.85
P/E Ratio	22.85-18.26	23.57-18.35	21.55-14.88	29.47-15.60	38.98-22.17	47.24-32.84	49.69-29.91	37.01-25.65
Average Yield %	2.49	2.49	2.75	2.34	1.52	1.10	1.27	1.48

Address: 3135 Easton Turnpike, Fairfield, CT 06828-0001
Telephone: 203-373-2211
Web Site: www.ge.com

Officers: Jeffrey R. Immelt - Chmn., C.E.O. William M. Castell - Vice-Chmn. **Transfer Agents:** GE Share Owner Services, c/o The Bank of New York, New York, NY

Investor Contact: 203-373-2816
No of Institutions: 1242
Shares: 5,686,059,008 **% Held:** 53.64

GENERAL GROWTH PROPERTIES, INC. (DE)

Exchange	Symbol	Price	52Wk Range	Yield	P/E
NYS	GGP	$38.93 (5/31/2005)	39.88-28.70	3.70	38.93

***7 Year Price Score 166.34** *NYSE Composite Index=100 ***12 Month Price Score 108.98**

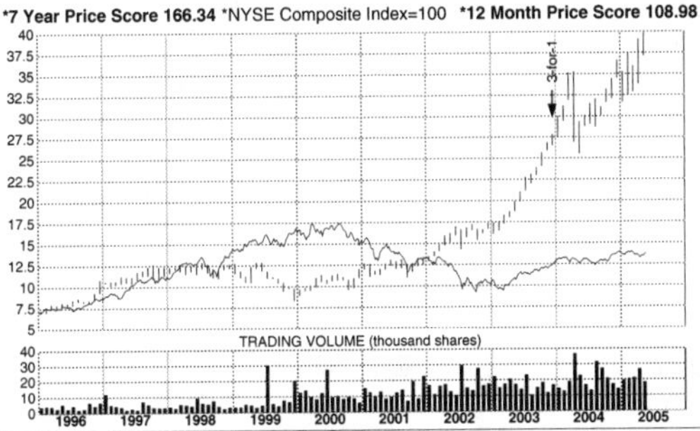

TRADING VOLUME (thousand shares)

Interim Earnings (Per Share)

Qtr.	Mar	Jun	Sep	Dec
2002	0.17	0.19	0.24	0.39
2003	0.24	0.23	0.29	1.12
2004	0.27	0.23	0.29	0.42
2005	0.06	...	...	...

Interim Dividends (Per Share)

Amt	Decl	Ex	Rec	Pay
0.30Q	7/2/2004	7/13/2004	7/15/2004	7/30/2004
0.36Q	8/20/2004	10/13/2004	10/15/2004	10/29/2004
0.36Q	1/7/2005	1/12/2005	1/17/2005	1/31/2005
0.36Q	4/4/2005	4/13/2005	4/15/2005	4/29/2005

Indicated Div: $1.44 (Div. Reinv. Plan)

Valuation Analysis

Forecast P/E	N/A		
Market Cap	$9.2 Billion	Book Value	2.1 Billion
Price/Book	4.35	Price/Sales	4.29

Dividend Achiever Status

Rank	184	10 Year Growth Rate	9.39%
Total Years of Dividend Growth			11

Business Summary: Property, Real Estate & Development (MIC: 8.3 SIC: 798 NAIC: 25930)

General Growth Properties is a self-administered and self-managed real estate investment trust primarily engaged in the ownership, operation, management, leasing, acquisition, development expansion and financing of operating properties in the U.S. The Retail and Other segment consists of retail centers, office and industrial buildings and mixed-use and other properties. The Community Development segment includes land development and sales for residential, commercial and other uses primarily in master-planned communities in and around Columbia, MD; Summerlin, NV and Houston, TX.

Recent Developments: For the quarter ended Mar 31 2005, net income decreased 77.9% to $13,065 thousand from net income of $59,123 thousand in the year-earlier quarter. Revenues were $709,533 thousand, up 97.2% from $359,826 thousand the year before. Operating income was $240,965 thousand versus an income of $152,520 thousand in the prior-year quarter, an increase of 58.0%.

Prospects: The first quarter of 2005 was Co.'s first full quarter of combined operations following the acquisition of The Rouse Company. Although Co. has already captured some efficiencies, there are still significant benefits it expects to obtain throughout the remainder of 2005 and in 2006 from the expanded platform that it can offer to all of its constituents. Co.'s real estate property net operating income is up substantially year over year, primarily due to the acquisition. Meanwhile, Co.'s overall average rent per square foot for new/renewal leases continue to increase. As a result, Co. expects funds from operations for full-year 2005 to be at least $3.13 per share.

Financial Data (US$ in Thousands)	3 Mos	12/31/2004	12/31/2003	12/31/2002	12/31/2001	12/31/2000	12/31/1999	12/31/1998
Earnings Per Share	1.00	1.21	1.22	0.98	0.43	0.73	0.55	0.49
Cash Flow Per Share	3.20	3.41	2.88	2.47	1.31	1.98	1.61	0.93
Tang Book Value Per Share	8.94	9.13	7.69	6.39	6.37	5.98	5.98	5.01
Dividends Per Share	1.320	1.260	1.020	0.890	0.747	0.680	0.647	0.470
Dividend Payout %	132.00	104.13	83.61	90.51	175.00	93.58	116.87	96.58
Income Statement								
Property Income	667,483	1,588,496	1,150,315	871,559	713,316	682,109	595,142	416,105
Non-Property Income	42,050	214,349	120,413	108,907	90,393	16,658	17,200	10,471
Total Revenue	709,533	1,802,845	1,270,728	980,466	803,709	698,767	612,342	426,576
Depn & Amortn	165,301	377,056	240,234	185,124	152,878	126,689	112,874	75,227
Interest Expense	245,028	472,185	278,543	218,935	214,277	218,075	185,984	125,851
Income Taxes	(1,307)	2,383	...	...	...	...	...	...
Net Income	13,065	267,852	263,411	209,258	92,310	137,948	101,125	66,445
Average Shares	236,588	220,149	215,079	212,553	158,721	156,288	138,093	109,146
Balance Sheet								
Total Assets	25,750,014	25,718,625	9,582,897	7,280,822	5,646,807	5,284,104	4,954,895	4,027,474
Long-Term Obligations	20,392,810	20,310,947	6,649,490	4,592,311	3,398,207	3,244,126	3,119,534	2,648,776
Total Liabilities	22,862,722	22,621,032	7,008,664	4,900,850	3,570,562	3,478,028	3,333,097	2,804,836
Stockholders' Equity	2,124,639	2,143,150	1,670,409	1,196,525	1,183,386	938,418	927,758	585,707
Shares Outstanding	237,597	234,724	217,293	187,191	185,771	156,843	155,092	117,003
Statistical Record								
Return on Assets %	1.24	1.51	3.12	3.24	1.69	2.69	2.25	2.17
Return on Equity %	11.70	14.01	18.38	17.59	8.70	14.74	13.36	12.26
Net Margin %	1.84	14.86	20.73	21.34	11.49	19.74	16.51	15.58
Price Range	37.54-25.51	36.63-25.51	27.89-16.09	17.33-12.91	13.39-11.00	12.06-8.94	12.85-8.35	12.90-10.96
P/E Ratio	37.54-25.51	30.27-21.08	22.86-13.19	17.69-13.17	31.15-25.58	16.52-12.24	23.37-15.19	26.32-22.36
Average Yield %	4.15	4.07	4.78	5.71	6.10	6.47	5.85	3.90

Address: 110 North Wacker Drive, Suite 3100, Chicago, IL 60606
Telephone: 312-960-5000
Web Site: www.generalgrowth.com

Officers: Matthew Bucksbaum - Chmn. Robert Michaels - Pres., C.O.O. **Transfer Agents:** Mellon Investor Services, LLC, South Hackensack, NJ

No of Institutions: 262
Shares: 180,730,880 **% Held:** 82.64

GENUINE PARTS CO.

Exchange	Symbol	Price	52Wk Range	Yield	P/E
NYS	GPC	$42.96 (5/31/2005)	44.70-36.28	2.91	18.76

*7 Year Price Score 114.36 *NYSE Composite Index=100 *12 Month Price Score 102.01

Interim Earnings (Per Share)

Qtr.	Mar	Jun	Sep	Dec
2002	(1.76)	0.55	0.54	0.51
2003	0.39	0.52	0.51	0.49
2004	0.57	0.58	0.56	0.54
2005	0.61	...	...	...

Interim Dividends (Per Share)

Amt	Decl	Ex	Rec	Pay
0.30Q	8/16/2004	9/8/2004	9/10/2004	10/1/2004
0.30Q	11/15/2004	12/8/2004	12/10/2004	1/3/2005
0.313Q	2/21/2005	3/9/2005	3/11/2005	4/1/2005
0.313Q	4/18/2005	6/8/2005	6/10/2005	7/1/2005

Indicated Div: $1.25 (Div. Reinv. Plan)

Valuation Analysis

Forecast P/E	17.53 (6/2/2005)		
Market Cap	$7.5 Billion	Book Value	2.6 Billion
Price/Book	2.92	Price/Sales	0.81

Dividend Achiever Status

Rank	275	10 Year Growth Rate	4.75%
Total Years of Dividend Growth			48

TRADING VOLUME (thousand shares)

Business Summary: Retail - Automotive (MIC: 5.7 SIC: 013 NAIC: 23120)

Genuine Parts is a service distribution and sales organization. Co.'s Automotive Parts group distributes automotive replacement parts and accessory items to independent and company-owned NAPA auto parts stores. The Industrial Parts group's Motion Industries distributes industrial bearings and power transmission replacement parts, including hydraulic and pneumatic products, material handling equipment and agricultural and irrigation equipment. The Office Products group's S.P. Richards Company distributes a line of office and business-related products. The Electrical and Electronic Materials Group's EIS distributes a range of materials and products for electrical and electronic apparatus.

Recent Developments: For the quarter ended Mar 31 2005, net income increased 6.4% to $106.6 million compared with $100.2 million in the equivalent 2004 quarter. Revenues were $2.34 billion, up 6.6% from $2.20 billion the year before. The improvement in sales was primarily driven by Co.'s internal growth initiatives across all of its businesses, as well as by favorable economic conditions. Gross margin advanced 7.2% to $736.5 million, or 31.4% of net sales, from $686.9 million, or 31.3%, in the year-earlier quarter. Operating profit as a percentage of sales was 8.2% compared with 8.5% for the same period of the previous year.

Prospects: Co.'s balance sheet remains in good condition and the combination of working capital initiatives and solid earnings growth is enabling it to continue to generate positive cash flows. In an effort to grow sales and earnings, Co. will continue to focus on the introduction of new product lines, sales to new markets and cost saving initiatives. Meanwhile, Co. believes the market conditions remains strong in the industries it serves and will continue to focus on its marketing plans and sales initiatives. As a result, Co. expects to be well positioned for improved performance throughout full-year 2005.

Financial Data

(US$ in Thousands)	3 Mos	12/31/2004	12/31/2003	12/31/2002	12/31/2001	12/31/2000	12/31/1999	12/31/1998
Earnings Per Share	2.29	2.25	1.91	(0.16)	1.71	2.20	2.11	1.98
Cash Flow Per Share	3.38	3.17	2.31	1.56	1.93	1.79	2.05	1.58
Tang Book Value Per Share	14.39	14.21	12.95	11.88	10.97	10.50	9.80	9.52
Dividends Per Share	1.212	1.200	1.180	1.160	1.140	1.100	1.040	1.000
Dividend Payout %	52.95	53.33	61.78	...	66.67	50.00	49.29	50.51
Income Statement								
Total Revenue	2,342,201	9,097,267	8,449,300	8,258,927	8,220,668	8,369,857	7,981,687	6,614,032
EBITDA	189,281	698,126	640,756	675,887	581,806	739,053	718,034	658,422
Depn & Amortn	17,071	62,207	69,013	70,151	85,793	92,303	89,967	69,305
Income Before Taxes	172,210	635,919	571,743	605,736	496,013	646,750	628,067	589,117
Income Taxes	65,612	240,367	218,101	238,236	198,866	261,427	250,445	233,323
Net Income	106,598	395,552	334,101	(27,590)	297,147	385,323	377,622	355,794
Average Shares	176,036	175,660	174,480	175,104	173,633	175,327	179,238	180,081
Balance Sheet								
Current Assets	3,689,502	3,633,484	3,417,626	3,335,775	3,146,212	3,019,481	2,895,203	2,683,357
Total Assets	4,530,972	4,455,247	4,116,497	4,019,843	4,206,646	4,142,114	3,929,672	3,600,380
Current Liabilities	1,180,326	1,132,715	1,016,931	1,069,718	919,181	988,313	916,012	818,409
Long-Term Obligations	500,000	500,000	625,108	674,796	835,580	770,581	702,417	588,640
Total Liabilities	1,962,372	1,910,870	1,804,214	1,889,834	1,861,523	1,881,308	1,752,155	1,547,048
Stockholders' Equity	2,568,600	2,544,377	2,312,283	2,130,009	2,345,123	2,260,806	2,177,517	2,053,332
Shares Outstanding	174,450	174,964	174,045	174,380	173,473	172,389	177,275	179,505
Statistical Record								
Return on Assets %	9.24	9.20	8.21	N.M.	7.12	9.52	10.03	11.20
Return on Equity %	16.29	16.24	15.04	N.M.	12.90	17.32	17.85	18.19
EBITDA Margin %	8.08	7.67	7.58	8.18	7.08	8.83	9.00	9.95
Net Margin %	4.55	4.35	3.95	N.M.	3.61	4.60	4.73	5.38
Asset Turnover	2.13	2.12	2.08	2.01	1.97	2.07	2.12	2.08
Current Ratio	3.13	3.21	3.36	3.12	3.42	3.06	3.16	3.28
Debt to Equity	0.19	0.20	0.27	0.32	0.36	0.34	0.32	0.29
Price Range	44.70-32.72	44.06-32.13	33.66-27.43	38.08-27.64	37.44-24.26	26.44-18.63	35.75-23.13	38.13-29.38
P/E Ratio	19.52-14.29	19.58-14.28	17.62-14.36	...	21.89-14.19	12.02-8.47	16.94-10.96	19.26-14.84
Average Yield %	3.04	3.20	3.74	3.48	3.78	4.98	3.49	2.95

Address: 2999 Circle 75 Parkway, Atlanta, GA 30339
Telephone: 770-953-1700
Web Site: www.genpt.com

Officers: Larry L. Prince - Chmn. Thomas C. Gallagher - Pres., C.E.O. **Transfer Agents:** Sun Trust Bank, Atlanta, GA

Investor Contact: 770-953-1700
No of Institutions: 332
Shares: 119,532,656 **% Held:** 68.41

GLACIER BANCORP, INC.

Exchange	Symbol	Price	52Wk Range	Yield	P/E
NMS	GBCI	$23.35 (5/31/2005)	28.35-20.76	2.47	15.99

***7 Year Price Score 154.61** *NYSE Composite Index=100 ***12 Month Price Score 91.68**

Interim Earnings (Per Share)

Qtr.	Mar	Jun	Sep	Dec
2002	0.23	0.27	0.29	0.29
2003	0.32	0.33	0.31	0.31
2004	0.34	0.34	0.38	0.37
2005	0.37	...	...	...

Interim Dividends (Per Share)

Amt	Decl	Ex	Rec	Pay
0.136Q	9/29/2004	10/7/2004	10/12/2004	10/21/2004
0.136Q	12/29/2004	1/7/2005	1/11/2005	1/20/2005
0.144Q	3/11/2005	4/8/2005	4/12/2005	4/21/2005
5-for-4	4/26/2005	5/27/2005	5/10/2005	5/26/2005

Indicated Div: $0.58 (Div. Reinv. Plan)

Valuation Analysis

Forecast P/E	14.62 (6/2/2005)		
Market Cap	$720.4 Million	Book Value	273.4 Million
Price/Book	2.63	Price/Sales	3.82

Dividend Achiever Status

Rank	96	**10 Year Growth Rate**	14.61%
Total Years of Dividend Growth			13

Business Summary: Other Depository Banking (MIC: 8.5 SIC: 035 NAIC: 22120)

Glacier Bancorp is the parent holding company of its nine wholly-owned subsidiaries, Glacier Bank, First Security Bank of Missoula, Western Security Bank, Mountain West Bank in Idaho, Big Sky Western Bank, Valley Bank of Helena, Glacier Bank of Whitefish and Glacier Capital Trust I & II. Co. provides commercial banking services from 55 banking offices throughout Montana, Idaho and Utah. Co. offers a range of banking products and services, including transaction and savings deposits, commercial, consumer and real estate loans, mortgage origination services, and retail brokerage services. As of Dec 31 2004, Co. had total assets of $3.01 billion and total deposits of $1.73 billion.

Recent Developments: For the quarter ended Mar 31 2005, net income increased 8.6% to $11,520 thousand from net income of $10,610 thousand in the year-earlier quarter. Net interest income was $28,456 thousand, up 7.8% from $26,389 thousand the year before. Provision for loan losses was $1,490 thousand versus $830 thousand in the prior-year quarter, an increase of 79.5%. Non-interest income rose 22.9% to $9,108 thousand, while non-interest expense advanced 9.5% to $19,074 thousand.

Prospects: On Apr 1 2005, Co. announced the completion of the acquisition of Citizens Bank Holding Company and its commercial bank subsidiary, Citizens Community Bank. Citizens has assets of approximately $113.0 million, with three banking offices in Pocatello and Idaho Falls and a loan production office in Rexberg, ID. Citizens will operate as a separately chartered community banking subsidiary of Co. Separately, Co.'s subsidiary, Mountain West Bank of Coeur d'Alene entered into a agreement to acquire Zions First National Bank's branch in Bonners Ferry, ID with total deposits of approximately $23.0 million. The transaction is expected to close before mid 2005.

Financial Data

(US$ in Thousands)	3 Mos	12/31/2004	12/31/2003	12/31/2002	12/31/2001	12/31/2000	12/31/1999	12/31/1998
Earnings Per Share	1.46	1.43	1.24	1.08	0.78	0.70	0.67	0.62
Cash Flow Per Share	1.91	2.28	3.16	0.56	(1.04)	1.94	1.65	0.50
Tang Book Value Per Share	6.68	7.43	6.45	5.80	4.66	4.66	3.98	4.15
Dividends Per Share	0.542	0.534	0.459	0.372	0.349	0.360	0.332	0.246
Dividend Payout %	37.20	37.32	36.97	34.43	44.78	51.09	49.39	39.99
Income Statement								
Interest Income	40,507	147,285	130,830	133,989	137,920	78,837	58,921	51,081
Interest Expense	12,051	39,892	38,478	47,522	65,546	37,357	25,592	22,204
Net Interest Income	28,456	107,393	92,352	86,467	72,374	41,480	33,329	28,877
Provision for Losses	1,490	4,195	3,809	5,745	4,525	1,864	1,506	1,490
Non-Interest Income	9,108	34,565	33,562	25,917	23,251	13,294	11,064	11,259
Non-Interest Expense	19,074	72,133	65,944	57,813	57,385	31,327	24,077	21,606
Income Before Taxes	17,000	65,630	56,161	48,826	33,715	21,583	18,810	17,040
Income Taxes	5,480	21,014	18,153	16,424	12,026	7,580	6,631	6,296
Net Income	11,520	44,616	38,008	32,402	21,689	14,003	12,179	10,744
Average Shares	31,305	31,144	30,656	29,982	27,742	19,841	18,172	17,448
Balance Sheet								
Net Loans & Leases	1,860,295	1,687,329	1,413,392	1,248,666	1,294,924	726,503	590,278	494,249
Total Assets	3,306,440	3,010,737	2,739,633	2,281,344	2,085,747	1,056,712	884,117	666,651
Total Deposits	1,976,681	1,729,708	1,597,625	1,459,923	1,446,064	720,570	576,282	444,459
Total Liabilities	3,032,991	2,740,553	2,501,794	2,069,095	1,908,764	958,599	805,304	591,714
Stockholders' Equity	273,449	270,184	237,839	212,249	176,983	98,113	78,813	74,937
Shares Outstanding	30,853	30,686	30,254	29,709	29,002	19,674	18,056	17,413
Statistical Record								
Return on Assets %	1.48	1.55	1.51	1.48	1.38	1.44	1.57	1.72
Return on Equity %	17.30	17.52	16.89	16.65	15.77	15.79	15.84	15.97
Net Interest Margin %	70.25	72.92	70.59	64.53	52.48	52.61	56.57	56.53
Efficiency Ratio %	38.44	39.67	40.11	36.15	35.61	34.00	34.40	34.66
Loans to Deposits	0.94	0.98	0.88	0.86	0.90	1.01	1.02	1.11
Price Range	28.35-19.64	28.35-18.89	21.11-13.71	14.40-11.12	12.22-7.31	8.53-6.40	12.69-8.17	12.90-9.14
P/E Ratio	19.42-13.45	19.83-13.21	17.02-11.05	13.33-10.30	15.66-9.37	12.18-9.14	18.95-12.19	20.80-14.74
Average Yield %	2.30	2.38	2.73	2.88	3.55	4.92	3.28	2.18

Address: 49 Commons Loop, Kalispell, MT 59901-2679 **Telephone:** 406-756-4200 **Web Site:** www.glacierbancorp.com	**Officers:** John S. MacMillan - Chmn. Michael J. Blodnick - Pres., C.E.O. **Transfer Agents:** TrustCorp, Great Falls, MT	**No of Institutions:** 102 **Shares:** 11,224,778 **% Held:** 45.57

GOLDEN WEST FINANCIAL CORP.

Exchange	Symbol	Price	52Wk Range	Yield	P/E
NYS	GDW	$62.62 (5/31/2005)	66.94-50.58	0.38	14.63

*7 Year Price Score 156.02 *NYSE Composite Index=100 *12 Month Price Score 102.98

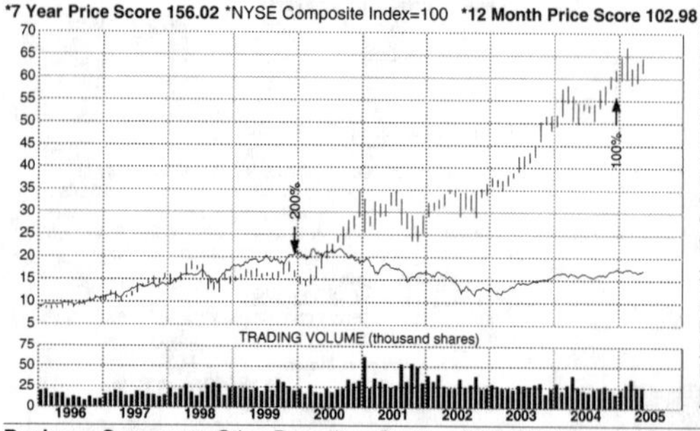

TRADING VOLUME (thousand shares)

Interim Earnings (Per Share)

Qtr.	Mar	Jun	Sep	Dec
2002	0.76	0.72	0.78	0.80
2003	0.83	0.88	0.92	0.94
2004	0.96	1.02	1.04	1.10
2005	1.12	...	...	...

Interim Dividends (Per Share)

Amt	Decl	Ex	Rec	Pay
0.05Q	7/26/2004	8/11/2004	8/15/2004	9/10/2004
0.06Q	10/21/2004	11/10/2004	11/15/2004	12/10/2004
0.06Q	1/27/2005	2/11/2005	2/15/2005	3/10/2005
0.06Q	4/26/2005	5/11/2005	5/15/2005	6/10/2005

Indicated Div: $0.24

Valuation Analysis

Forecast P/E	13.47 (6/2/2005)		
Market Cap	$19.2 Billion	Book Value	7.6 Billion
Price/Book	2.54	Price/Sales	3.95

Dividend Achiever Status

Rank	85	10 Year Growth Rate	15.43%
Total Years of Dividend Growth			21

Business Summary: Other Depository Banking (MIC: 8.5 SIC: 035 NAIC: 22120)

Golden West Financial is a savings and loan holding company with assets totaling $106.89 billion as of Dec 31 2004. Through its financial institution subsidiaries, Co. is a residential mortgage portfolio lender and its primary source of revenue is interest from loans and mortgage-backed securities. Co.'s principal operating subsidiary is World Savings Bank. World Savings Bank has a subsidiary, World Savings Bank, FSB (Texas). As of Dec 31 2004, Co. operated 276 savings branches in ten states and had lending operations in 38 states under the World name.

Recent Developments: For the quarter ended Mar 31 2005, net income increased 16.2% to $348,250 thousand from net income of $299,724 thousand in the year-earlier quarter. Net interest income was $704,564 thousand, up 13.8% from $619,254 thousand the year before. The improvement in net interest income reflected loan portfolio growth, partially offset by an average primary spread that decreased to 2.46% from 2.90% for the three months ended Mar 31 2004. Provision for loan losses was $884 thousand versus $241 thousand in the prior-year quarter, an increase of 266.8%. Non-interest income rose 38.1% to $82,613 thousand, while non-interest expense advanced 12.4% to $224,239 thousand.

Prospects: Results are benefiting from strong mortgage originations and retail savings growth. In the first quarter of 2005, new loan volume totaled $11.20 billion, up 19.0% from $9.40 billion reported one year earlier. This growth is significant by reflecting that the larger Co.'s mortgage portfolio, the greater its ability to generate profits. Strong loan growth is easily exceeding the payoffs of existing mortgages. Meanwhile, customers responded enthusiastically to Co.'s promoted products and rates it offered in the first quarter. As a result, deposit inflows amounted to $2.60 billion nearly four times the $657.0 million recorded in the first three months of 2004.

Financial Data

(US$ in Thousands)	3 Mos	12/31/2004	12/31/2003	12/31/2002	12/31/2001	12/31/2000	12/31/1999	12/31/1998
Earnings Per Share	4.28	4.13	3.57	3.06	2.54	1.71	1.44	1.25
Cash Flow Per Share	6.45	5.48	8.71	4.41	4.00	2.04	1.54	1.89
Tang Book Value Per Share	24.67	23.73	19.55	16.37	13.77	11.64	9.90	9.16
Dividends Per Share	0.220	0.210	0.177	0.151	0.130	0.110	0.096	0.086
Dividend Payout %	5.14	5.08	4.97	4.94	5.13	6.45	6.71	6.85
Income Statement								
Interest Income	1,311,485	4,178,856	3,528,344	3,497,034	4,209,612	3,796,540	2,825,845	2,962,553
Interest Expense	606,921	1,560,251	1,319,960	1,566,740	2,578,280	2,645,372	1,822,360	1,995,231
Net Interest Income	704,564	2,618,605	2,208,384	1,930,294	1,631,332	1,151,168	1,003,485	967,322
Provision for Losses	884	3,401	11,864	21,170	22,265	9,195	(2,089)	11,260
Non-Interest Income	82,613	293,923	313,330	247,000	236,739	160,820	143,302	137,613
Non-Interest Expense	224,239	840,126	720,515	601,494	513,802	424,847	386,147	354,507
Income Before Taxes	562,054	2,069,001	1,789,335	1,554,630	1,332,004	877,946	762,729	739,168
Income Taxes	213,804	789,280	683,236	596,351	513,181	332,155	282,750	292,077
Net Income	348,250	1,279,721	1,106,099	958,279	812,805	545,791	479,979	434,580
Average Shares	311,539	310,119	309,974	313,364	320,716	320,555	333,902	346,923
Balance Sheet								
Net Loans & Leases	105,682,092	100,559,179	74,205,578	58,268,899	41,065,375	33,762,643	27,919,817	25,721,288
Total Assets	112,587,849	106,888,541	82,549,890	68,405,828	58,586,271	55,703,969	42,142,205	38,468,729
Total Deposits	55,593,265	52,965,311	46,726,965	41,038,797	34,472,585	30,047,919	27,714,910	26,219,095
Total Liabilities	105,008,351	99,613,665	76,602,622	63,380,578	54,302,081	52,016,682	38,947,351	35,344,411
Stockholders' Equity	7,579,498	7,274,876	5,947,268	5,025,250	4,284,190	3,687,287	3,194,854	3,124,318
Shares Outstanding	307,248	306,524	304,238	307,042	311,063	316,820	322,715	341,166
Statistical Record								
Return on Assets %	1.33	1.35	1.47	1.51	1.42	1.11	1.19	1.11
Return on Equity %	19.22	19.30	20.16	20.59	20.39	15.82	15.19	14.93
Net Interest Margin %	53.72	62.66	62.59	55.20	38.75	30.32	35.51	32.65
Efficiency Ratio %	16.08	18.78	18.76	16.07	11.56	10.74	13.01	11.44
Loans to Deposits	1.90	1.90	1.59	1.42	1.19	1.12	1.01	0.98
Price Range	66.94-49.88	61.90-49.33	51.73-34.84	36.49-28.95	35.00-23.57	34.72-13.59	19.01-14.64	19.04-12.06
P/E Ratio	15.64-11.66	14.99-11.94	14.49-9.76	11.92-9.46	13.78-9.28	20.30-7.95	13.20-10.16	15.23-9.65
Average Yield %	0.39	0.38	0.42	0.46	0.45	0.52	0.59	0.55

Address: 1901 Harrison Street, Oakland, CA 94612 **Telephone:** 510-446-3420 **Web Site:** www.gdw.com	**Officers:** Herbert M. Sandler - Co-Chmn., Co-C.E.O. Marion O. Sandler - Co-Chmn., Co-C.E.O. **Transfer Agents:** Mellon Investor Services, LLC, San Francisco, CA	**Investor Contact:** 510-446-3614 **No of Institutions:** 331 **Shares:** 213,251,632 **% Held:** 69.48

GRAINGER (W.W.) INC.

Exchange	Symbol	Price	52Wk Range	Yield	P/E
NYS	GWW	$54.39 (5/31/2005)	66.62-50.65	1.77	16.84

*7 Year Price Score 109.93 *NYSE Composite Index=100 *12 Month Price Score 93.36

Interim Earnings (Per Share)

Qtr.	Mar	Jun	Sep	Dec
2002	0.61	0.57	0.64	0.67
2003	0.57	0.60	0.62	0.67
2004	0.69	0.72	0.74	0.98
2005	0.79	...	...	...

Interim Dividends (Per Share)

Amt	Decl	Ex	Rec	Pay
0.20Q	7/28/2004	8/5/2004	8/9/2004	9/1/2004
0.20Q	10/27/2004	11/4/2004	11/8/2004	12/1/2004
0.20Q	1/31/2005	2/3/2005	2/7/2005	3/1/2005
0.24Q	4/27/2005	5/5/2005	5/9/2005	6/1/2005

Indicated Div: $0.96

Valuation Analysis

Forecast P/E	16.23 (6/1/2005)		
Market Cap	$4.9 Billion	Book Value	2.1 Billion
Price/Book	2.32	Price/Sales	0.96

Dividend Achiever Status

Rank	227	10 Year Growth Rate	7.25%
Total Years of Dividend Growth			33

Business Summary: Engineering Services (MIC: 12.1 SIC: 063 NAIC: 23610)

W.W. Grainger is a broad-line supplier of facilities maintenance and other related products to customers in North America through a network of 582 branches, 17 distribution centers and multiple Web sites. Operations are divided into three business segments. The Branch-based Distribution unit provides product applications for facility maintenance and other product needs. Co.'s Lab Safety segment is a direct marketer of safety and other industrial products to U.S. and Canadian businesses. Co.'s Integrated Supply segment offers customers on-site outsourcing services, including business process re-engineering, inventory and tool crib management, purchasing management and information management.

Recent Developments: For the quarter ended Mar 31 2005, net income increased 16.4% to $72,792 thousand from net income of $62,559 thousand in the year-earlier quarter. Revenues were $1,334,880 thousand, up 8.7% from $1,227,799 thousand the year before. Operating income was $108,676 thousand versus an income of $100,748 thousand in the prior-year quarter, an increase of 7.9%. Total direct expense was $836,004 thousand versus $780,334 thousand in the prior-year quarter, an increase of 7.1%. Total indirect expense was $390,200 thousand versus $346,717 thousand in the prior-year quarter, an increase of 12.5%.

Prospects: Co.'s market expansion program remains on track and is contributing to its growth rate. Also, Co. is continuing to see improvements in product availability resulting from its logistics network. During the first quarter, Co. continued to invest in its security action plan system. The team has virtually completed development and that additional testing has been built into the plan. Co. now expects to begin implementation in the first half of 2006. When complete, the new system will provide Co. with a single, uniform platform that will help it better serve customers. Co. reiterated its projected earnings per share guidance of $3.20 to $3.45 for 2005.

Financial Data

(US$ in Thousands)	3 Mos	12/31/2004	12/31/2003	12/31/2002	12/31/2001	12/31/2000	12/31/1999	12/31/1998
Earnings Per Share	3.23	3.13	2.46	2.24	1.84	2.05	1.92	2.44
Cash Flow Per Share	3.61	4.49	4.34	3.30	5.48	2.98	0.32	3.48
Tang Book Value Per Share	21.43	20.44	18.20	16.59	15.09	14.08	13.47	11.39
Dividends Per Share	0.800	0.785	0.735	0.715	0.695	0.670	0.630	0.585
Dividend Payout %	24.77	25.08	29.88	31.92	37.77	32.68	32.81	23.98
Income Statement								
Total Revenue	1,334,880	5,049,785	4,667,014	4,643,898	4,754,317	4,977,044	4,533,853	4,341,269
EBITDA	139,773	541,407	474,011	492,915	408,336	461,000	415,967	484,804
Depn & Amortn	26,434	98,256	90,253	93,488	103,209	106,893	98,227	78,865
Income Before Taxes	115,296	445,139	381,090	397,837	297,280	331,595	303,750	400,847
Income Taxes	42,504	158,216	154,119	162,349	122,750	138,692	123,019	162,343
Net Income	72,792	286,923	226,971	211,567	174,530	192,903	180,731	238,504
Average Shares	92,460	91,673	92,394	94,303	94,727	94,223	94,315	97,846
Balance Sheet								
Current Assets	1,784,480	1,754,713	1,633,413	1,484,947	1,392,611	1,483,002	1,471,145	1,206,365
Total Assets	2,853,065	2,809,573	2,624,678	2,437,448	2,331,246	2,459,601	2,564,826	2,103,902
Current Liabilities	647,921	662,434	706,640	586,266	553,811	747,324	870,534	664,493
Long-Term Obligations	...	...	4,895	119,693	118,219	125,258	124,928	122,883
Total Liabilities	731,348	741,603	779,543	769,750	728,057	922,215	1,084,297	825,161
Stockholders' Equity	2,121,717	2,067,970	1,845,135	1,667,698	1,603,189	1,537,386	1,480,529	1,278,741
Shares Outstanding	90,684	90,597	91,020	91,568	93,344	93,932	93,381	93,505
Statistical Record								
Return on Assets %	10.73	10.53	8.97	8.87	7.29	7.66	7.74	11.63
Return on Equity %	14.93	14.62	12.92	12.94	11.11	12.75	13.10	18.54
EBITDA Margin %	10.47	10.72	10.16	10.61	8.59	9.26	9.17	11.17
Net Margin %	5.45	5.68	4.86	4.56	3.67	3.88	3.99	5.49
Asset Turnover	1.86	1.85	1.84	1.95	1.98	1.98	1.94	2.12
Current Ratio	2.75	2.65	2.31	2.53	2.51	1.98	1.69	1.82
Debt to Equity	...	...	N.M.	0.07	0.07	0.08	0.08	0.10
Price Range	66.62-47.81	66.62-45.17	53.11-41.93	59.27-39.82	48.52-30.23	56.00-24.63	58.06-37.13	54.47-37.63
P/E Ratio	20.63-14.80	21.28-14.43	21.59-17.04	26.46-17.78	26.37-16.43	27.32-12.01	30.24-19.34	22.32-15.42
Average Yield %	1.39	1.46	1.56	1.42	1.72	1.75	1.34	1.24

Address: 100 Grainger Parkway, Lake Forest, IL 60045-5201
Telephone: 847-535-1000
Web Site: www.grainger.com

Officers: Richard L. Keyser - Chmn., C.E.O. James T. Ryan - Exec. V.P., Mktg., Sales, & Services **Transfer Agents:** BankBoston, N.A. c/o EquiServe, Boston, MA

Investor Contact: 847-535-1000
No of Institutions: 325
Shares: 61,781,460 **% Held:** 68.14

GRANITE CONSTRUCTION INC.

Exchange	Symbol	Price	52Wk Range	Yield	P/E
NYS	GVA	$23.45 (5/31/2005)	27.87-17.33	1.71	16.51

Interim Earnings (Per Share)

Qtr.	Mar	Jun	Sep	Dec
2002	(0.04)	0.41	0.57	0.27
2003	0.25	0.26	0.63	0.34
2004	(0.23)	0.34	0.80	0.48
2005	(0.20)	...	...	...

Interim Dividends (Per Share)

Amt	Decl	Ex	Rec	Pay
0.10Q	7/23/2004	9/28/2004	9/30/2004	10/15/2004
0.10Q	12/3/2004	12/28/2004	12/30/2004	1/14/2005
0.10Q	3/9/2005	3/29/2005	3/31/2005	4/15/2005
0.10Q	5/23/2005	6/28/2005	6/30/2005	7/15/2005

Indicated Div: $0.40

Valuation Analysis

Forecast P/E	15.87 (5/28/2005)		
Market Cap	$978.2 Million	Book Value	536.8 Million
Price/Book	1.82	Price/Sales	0.44

Dividend Achiever Status

Rank	34	10 Year Growth Rate	21.04%
Total Years of Dividend Growth			10

Business Summary: Construction - Public Infrastructure (MIC: 3.1 SIC: 611 NAIC: 37310)

Granite Construction is a heavy civil construction contractor that serves both public and private sector clients in the U.S. Within the public sector, Co. primarily concentrates on infrastructure projects, including the construction of roads, highways, bridges, mass transit facilities and airports. Within the private sector, Co. performs site preparation services for buildings, plants, subdivisions and other facilities. Co.'s operations are divided into two segments. The Branch Division is comprised of branch offices that serve local markets, while the Heavy Construction Division is composed of regional offices and pursues major infrastructure projects throughout the nation.

Recent Developments: For the quarter ended Mar 31 2005, net loss decreased 9.2% to $8,267 thousand from net loss of $9,109 thousand in the year-earlier quarter. Revenues were $420,934 thousand, up 24.9% from $337,018 thousand the year before. Operating loss was $11,904 thousand versus a loss of $12,530 thousand in the prior-year quarter, a decrease of 5.0%. Total direct expense was $393,994 thousand versus $326,334 thousand in the prior-year quarter, an increase of 20.7%. Total indirect expense was $77,714 thousand versus $59,758 thousand in the prior-year quarter, an increase of 30.0%.

Prospects: Co. is encouraged with the strength of its private development market, which is supporting its construction business in the West and driving demand for its construction materials. Co. expects this trend to continue in 2005. Meanwhile, bottom-line results from Co.'s Heavy Construction Division are being hampered by profit forecasts on several projects that were revised downward as a result of increased estimated costs to complete. While this segment still has some underperforming projects yet to complete, Co. believes that its focus on improving gross margins, coupled with a healthy backlog of $2.60 billion, should lead to improved financial results going forward.

Financial Data

(US$ in Thousands)	3 Mos	12/31/2004	12/31/2003	12/31/2002	12/31/2001	12/31/2000	12/31/1999	12/31/1998
Earnings Per Share	1.42	1.39	1.48	1.21	1.24	1.38	1.31	1.13
Cash Flow Per Share	1.72	1.96	1.93	2.60	3.13	1.89	2.56	2.41
Tang Book Value Per Share	12.87	13.23	12.16	11.03	10.19	9.24	8.09	7.26
Dividends Per Share	0.400	0.400	0.38	0.320	0.307	0.287	0.26	0.187
Dividend Payout %	28.17	28.78	25.68	26.45	24.76	20.80	19.85	16.55
Income Statement								
Total Revenue	420,934	2,136,212	1,844,491	1,764,742	1,547,994	1,348,325	1,328,774	1,226,100
EBITDA	4,501	162,623	171,324	146,319	134,510	140,703	133,349	116,116
Depn & Amortn	16,538	68,470	71,644	64,466	54,990	50,525	47,197	41,410
Income Before Taxes	(11,909)	94,924	97,525	82,739	81,497	92,870	86,043	75,011
Income Taxes	(3,692)	28,477	35,304	29,951	30,969	37,055	33,127	28,504
Net Income	(8,267)	57,007	60,504	49,279	50,528	55,815	52,916	46,507
Average Shares	40,485	41,031	40,808	40,723	40,711	40,409	40,444	41,008
Balance Sheet								
Current Assets	772,728	825,338	618,651	547,895	586,916	411,628	402,321	370,808
Total Assets	1,233,228	1,277,954	1,060,410	983,819	929,684	711,142	679,572	626,571
Current Liabilities	448,728	469,411	348,704	327,499	338,503	231,577	258,664	228,360
Long-Term Obligations	139,705	148,503	126,708	132,380	131,391	63,891	64,853	69,137
Total Liabilities	674,374	727,480	555,519	528,950	511,182	333,378	351,840	325,289
Stockholders' Equity	536,849	550,474	504,891	454,869	418,502	377,764	327,732	301,282
Shares Outstanding	41,715	41,612	41,528	41,257	41,089	40,881	40,493	41,473
Statistical Record								
Return on Assets %	5.00	4.86	5.92	5.15	6.16	8.00	8.10	7.89
Return on Equity %	11.26	10.77	12.61	11.28	12.69	15.78	16.83	16.65
EBITDA Margin %	1.07	7.61	9.29	8.29	8.69	10.44	10.04	9.47
Net Margin %	N.M.	2.67	3.28	2.79	3.26	4.14	3.98	3.79
Asset Turnover	1.92	1.82	1.80	1.84	1.89	1.93	2.03	2.08
Current Ratio	1.72	1.76	1.77	1.67	1.73	1.78	1.56	1.62
Debt to Equity	0.26	0.27	0.25	0.29	0.31	0.17	0.20	0.23
Price Range	27.87-17.33	27.87-17.33	24.25-13.89	25.30-13.98	30.50-19.33	20.50-11.75	24.67-11.38	22.58-9.56
P/E Ratio	19.63-12.20	20.05-12.47	16.39-9.39	20.91-11.55	24.60-15.59	14.86-8.51	18.83-8.68	19.99-8.46
Average Yield %	1.73	1.78	1.99	1.57	1.23	1.78	1.44	1.16

Address: 585 W. Beach Street, Box 50085, Watsonville, CA 95077-5085 **Telephone:** 831-761-7500 **Web Site:** www.graniteconstruction.com	**Officers:** David H. Watts - Chmn. William G. Dorey - Pres., C.E.O.	**Investor Contact:** 831-761-4741 **No of Institutions:** 133 **Shares:** 26,544,416 **% Held:** 63.79

HARLEY-DAVIDSON, INC.

Exchange	Symbol	Price	52Wk Range	Yield	P/E
NYS	HDI	$49.03 (5/31/2005)	62.97-45.42	1.31	15.87

***7 Year Price Score 118.97** *NYSE Composite Index=100 ***12 Month Price Score 83.87**

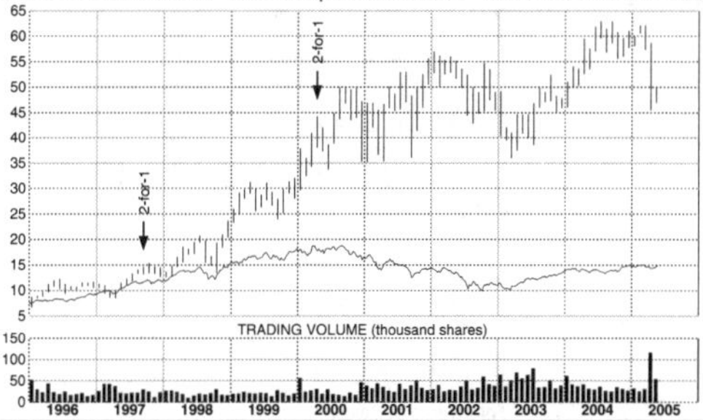

TRADING VOLUME (thousand shares)

Interim Earnings (Per Share)

Qtr.	Mar	Jun	Sep	Dec
2002	0.39	0.47	0.54	0.49
2003	0.61	0.66	0.62	0.60
2004	0.68	0.83	0.77	0.71
2005	0.77	...	...	...

Interim Dividends (Per Share)

Amt	Decl	Ex	Rec	Pay
0.10Q	8/4/2004	9/13/2004	9/15/2004	9/29/2004
0.125Q	12/9/2004	12/15/2004	12/17/2004	12/29/2004
0.125Q	2/15/2005	3/4/2005	3/8/2005	3/25/2005
0.16Q	4/30/2005	6/10/2005	6/14/2005	6/24/2005

Indicated Div: $0.64 (Div. Reinv. Plan)

Valuation Analysis

Forecast P/E	15.53 (5/28/2005)		
Market Cap	$14.0 Billion	Book Value	3.3 Billion
Price/Book	4.27	Price/Sales	2.58

Dividend Achiever Status

Rank	9	**10 Year Growth Rate**	27.74%
Total Years of Dividend Growth			11

Business Summary: Automotive (MIC: 15.1 SIC: 751 NAIC: 36991)

Harley-Davidson is a motorcycle manufacturer. Co.'s Motorcycles and Related Products segment designs, manufactures and sells primarily heavyweight touring, custom and performance motorcycles as well as a full line of motorcycle parts, accessories, clothing and collectibles. Co.'s motorcycle brands include Harley-Davidson® and Buell®. The Financial Services segment, consisting of Co.'s subsidiary Harley-Davidson Financial Services, Inc. (HDFS) and its subsidiaries, provides financing and servicing of wholesale inventory receivables and retail loans, primarily for the purchase of motorcycles. HDFS conducts business in the U.S., Canada and Europe.

Recent Developments: For the quarter ended Mar 27 2005, net income increased 11.1% to $227,215 thousand from net income of $204,580 thousand in the year-earlier quarter. Revenues were $1,324,276 thousand, up 6.3% from $1,246,195 thousand the year before. Operating income was $345,142 thousand versus an income of $312,922 thousand in the prior-year quarter, an increase of 10.3%. Total direct expense was $806,434 thousand versus $755,753 thousand in the prior-year quarter, an increase of 6.7%.

Prospects: Co. is continuing to benefit from increasing sales of motorcycles, parts and accessories and general merchandise. Worldwide retail sales of Harley-Davidson motorcycles is being driven by strong performances in Europe and Japan. At the same time, U.S. retail sales of Harley-Davidson motorcyles has been relatively flat versus 2004, falling short of Co.'s expectations. As a result, Co. is limiting its short-term production growth to maintain demand in excess of supply. For full-year 2005, Co. is now targeting shipments of 329,000 units compared with 317,000 units in 2004 and sees earnings growth in the range of 5.0% to 8.0% instead of its previous forecast for mid-teens earnings growth.

Financial Data

(US$ in Thousands)	3 Mos	12/31/2004	12/31/2003	12/31/2002	12/31/2001	12/31/2000	12/31/1999	12/31/1998
Earnings Per Share	3.09	3.00	2.50	1.90	1.43	1.13	0.86	0.69
Cash Flow Per Share	2.30	3.28	3.10	2.58	2.50	1.86	1.37	1.04
Tang Book Value Per Share	11.28	10.73	9.63	7.21	5.64	4.47	3.65	3.20
Dividends Per Share	0.450	0.405	0.195	0.135	0.115	0.098	0.087	0.077
Dividend Payout %	14.57	13.50	7.80	7.11	8.04	8.63	10.12	11.23
Income Statement								
Total Revenue	1,324,276	5,320,452	4,903,733	4,302,470	3,544,959	2,943,543	2,480,624	2,084,167
EBITDA	398,467	1,570,497	1,339,865	1,045,064	809,038	664,321	526,601	419,823
Depn & Amortn	53,325	214,112	196,918	175,778	153,061	133,348	113,822	87,422
Income Before Taxes	352,271	1,379,486	1,166,035	885,827	673,455	548,556	420,793	336,229
Income Taxes	125,056	489,720	405,107	305,610	235,709	200,843	153,592	122,729
Net Income	227,215	889,766	760,928	580,217	437,746	347,713	267,201	213,500
Average Shares	294,161	296,852	304,470	305,158	306,248	307,470	309,714	309,406
Balance Sheet								
Current Assets	3,283,740	3,266,272	2,729,127	2,066,586	1,665,264	1,297,264	948,994	844,963
Total Assets	5,305,773	5,483,293	4,923,088	3,861,217	3,118,495	2,436,404	2,112,077	1,920,209
Current Liabilities	1,065,885	1,172,696	955,773	990,052	716,110	497,743	518,154	468,515
Long-Term Obligations	800,000	800,000	670,000	380,000	380,000	355,000	280,000	280,000
Total Liabilities	2,034,936	2,264,822	1,965,396	1,628,302	1,362,212	1,030,749	950,997	890,298
Stockholders' Equity	3,270,837	3,218,471	2,957,692	2,232,915	1,756,283	1,405,655	1,161,080	1,029,911
Shares Outstanding	284,663	294,310	301,510	302,662	302,789	302,070	302,722	305,862
Statistical Record								
Return on Assets %	18.30	17.05	17.32	16.63	15.76	15.25	13.25	12.13
Return on Equity %	30.30	28.73	29.32	29.09	27.69	27.02	24.39	23.00
EBITDA Margin %	30.09	29.52	27.32	24.29	22.82	22.57	21.23	20.14
Net Margin %	17.16	16.72	15.52	13.49	12.35	11.81	10.77	10.24
Asset Turnover	1.08	1.02	1.12	1.23	1.28	1.29	1.23	1.18
Current Ratio	3.08	2.79	2.86	2.09	2.33	2.61	1.83	1.80
Debt to Equity	0.24	0.25	0.23	0.17	0.22	0.25	0.24	0.27
Price Range	62.97-52.54	62.97-46.00	52.45-35.95	57.00-42.83	55.66-35.19	50.00-29.63	32.03-23.22	23.69-12.56
P/E Ratio	20.38-17.00	20.99-15.33	20.98-14.38	30.00-22.54	38.92-24.61	44.25-26.22	37.25-27.00	34.33-18.21
Average Yield %	0.76	0.71	0.44	0.27	0.25	0.24	0.31	0.45

Address: 3700 West Juneau Avenue, Milwaukee, WI 53208
Telephone: 414-342-4680
Web Site: www.harley-davidson.com

Officers: Jeffrey L. Bleustein - Chmn. James A. McCaslin - Pres., C.O.O. **Transfer Agents:** Computershare Investor Services, LLC, Chicago, IL

Investor Contact: 877-437-8625
No of Institutions: 551
Shares: 198,876,896 **% Held:** 68.11

HARLEYSVILLE GROUP, INC. (PA)

Exchange	Symbol	Price	52Wk Range	Yield	P/E
NMS	HGIC	$20.31 (5/31/2005)	24.96-18.03	3.35	14.72

*7 Year Price Score 83.77 *NYSE Composite Index=100 *12 Month Price Score 93.36

Interim Earnings (Per Share)

Qtr.	Mar	Jun	Sep	Dec
2002	0.44	0.01	0.50	0.58
2003	(0.11)	0.33	(1.16)	(0.66)
2004	0.55	0.32	0.29	0.38
2005	0.39	...	...	...

Interim Dividends (Per Share)

Amt	Decl	Ex	Rec	Pay
0.17Q	6/8/2004	6/14/2004	6/15/2004	6/30/2004
0.17Q	8/3/2004	9/13/2004	9/15/2004	9/30/2004
0.17Q	11/9/2004	12/13/2004	12/15/2004	12/30/2004
0.17Q	2/23/2005	3/11/2005	3/15/2005	3/30/2005

Indicated Div: $0.68 (Div. Reinv. Plan)

Valuation Analysis

Forecast P/E 11.96 (5/28/2005)

Market Cap $615.5 Million Book Value 580.9 Million

Price/Book 1.06 Price/Sales 0.65

Dividend Achiever Status

Rank 222 **10 Year Growth Rate** 7.50%

Total Years of Dividend Growth 18

Business Summary: Insurance (MIC: 8.2 SIC: 331 NAIC: 24126)

Harleysville Group is an insurance holding company that engages, through its subsidiaries, in the property and casualty insurance business on a regional basis. Co. and Harleysville Mutual Insurance Company, which owned about 56.0% of Co.'s outstanding shares as of Dec 31 2004, operate together as a network of regional insurance companies that underwrite an array of personal and commercial coverages. The personal lines of insurance include both auto and homeowners, and the commercial lines include auto, commercial multi-peril and workers compensation. These insurance coverages are marketed primarily in the Eastern and Midwestern U.S. through about 1,600 insurance agencies.

Recent Developments: For the quarter ended Mar 31 2005, net income decreased 27.4% to $11,982 thousand from net income of $16,493 thousand in the year-earlier quarter. Revenues were $232,724 thousand, down 5.3% from $245,642 thousand the year before. Net premiums earned were $206,680 thousand versus $206,948 thousand in the prior-year quarter, a decrease of 0.1%. Net investment income rose 0.5% to $21,761 thousand from $21,642 thousand a year ago.

Prospects: Despite signs of an increasingly competitive market, Co. indicated that it remains on track to achieve its goals of a combined ratio under 100.0% in 2006. Premiums earned for the three months ended Mar 31 2005 decreased to $206.7 million from $206.9 million for the three months ended Mar 31 2004, primarily due to a decrease of $5.3 million in premiums earned for personal lines partially offset by an increase of $5.0 million in commercial lines premiums earned. The reduction in personal lines volume was driven mainly by a reduction in personal automobile business from the continued implementation of more stringent underwriting processes.

Financial Data

(US$ in Thousands)	3 Mos	12/31/2004	12/31/2003	12/31/2002	12/31/2001	12/31/2000	12/31/1999	12/31/1998
Earnings Per Share	1.38	1.55	(1.59)	1.53	1.46	1.67	1.35	2.15
Cash Flow Per Share	4.43	3.84	4.49	3.81	1.56	0.13	2.90	2.82
Tang Book Value Per Share	19.17	19.47	19.16	21.13	20.05	19.54	18.29	18.17
Dividends Per Share	0.680	0.680	0.670	0.630	0.580	0.550	0.520	0.480
Dividend Payout %	49.28	43.87	...	41.18	39.73	32.93	38.52	22.33
Income Statement								
Premium Income	206,680	837,665	823,407	764,636	729,889	688,330	707,200	664,604
Total Revenue	232,724	953,392	924,965	847,736	827,751	802,571	824,756	779,311
Benefits & Claims	147,868	605,660	727,875	521,617	519,822	492,801	523,002	464,480
Income Before Taxes	14,456	55,637	(89,450)	56,482	51,800	57,705	47,752	80,441
Income Taxes	2,474	8,759	(41,821)	10,227	8,307	9,013	4,935	17,028
Net Income	11,982	46,878	(47,629)	46,255	43,493	48,692	39,913	63,413
Average Shares	30,399	30,154	29,985	30,295	29,818	29,136	29,565	29,519
Balance Sheet								
Total Assets	2,705,101	2,718,063	2,680,389	2,311,524	2,045,290	2,021,862	2,020,056	1,934,497
Total Liabilities	2,124,214	2,130,139	2,107,642	1,679,412	1,454,992	1,455,281	1,493,162	1,404,839
Stockholders' Equity	580,887	587,924	572,747	632,112	590,298	566,581	526,894	529,658
Shares Outstanding	30,306	30,191	29,900	29,917	29,444	29,001	28,812	29,150
Statistical Record								
Return on Assets %	1.57	1.73	N.M.	2.12	2.14	2.40	2.02	3.39
Return on Equity %	7.24	8.06	N.M.	7.57	7.52	8.88	7.56	12.99
Loss Ratio %	71.54	72.30	88.40	68.22	71.22	71.59	73.95	69.89
Net Margin %	5.15	4.92	(5.15)	5.46	5.25	6.07	4.84	8.14
Price Range	24.96-18.03	24.96-17.84	27.50-18.99	31.44-19.90	30.00-20.40	29.81-11.81	25.81-13.13	28.22-18.88
P/E Ratio	18.09-13.07	16.10-11.51	...	20.55-13.01	20.55-13.97	17.85-7.07	19.12-9.72	13.13-8.78
Average Yield %	3.30	3.37	2.86	2.43	2.28	3.09	2.79	2.06

Address: 355 Maple Avenue, Harleysville, PA 19438-2297 **Telephone:** 215-256-5000 **Web Site:** www.harleysvillegroup.com	**Officers:** William W. Scranton III - Chmn. Michael L. Browne - Pres., C.E.O. **Transfer Agents:** Mellon Investor Services, Ridgefield Park, NJ	**Investor Contact:** 215-256-5020 **No of Institutions:** 55 **Shares:** 6,439,946 **% Held:** 21.26

HARLEYSVILLE NATIONAL CORP.

Exchange	Symbol	Price	52Wk Range	Yield	P/E
NMS	HNBC	$23.07 (5/31/2005)	28.45-19.66	3.12	15.80

*7 Year Price Score 122.91 *NYSE Composite Index=100 *12 Month Price Score 85.55

Interim Earnings (Per Share)

Qtr.	Mar	Jun	Sep	Dec
2002	0.30	0.32	0.34	0.29
2003	0.33	0.35	0.35	0.31
2004	0.34	0.37	0.38	0.37
2005	0.34	...	...	...

Interim Dividends (Per Share)

Amt	Decl	Ex	Rec	Pay
0.18Q	11/15/2004	11/23/2004	11/26/2004	12/15/2004
0.04Q	11/15/2004	11/23/2004	11/26/2004	12/15/2004
0.18Q	2/14/2005	2/24/2005	2/28/2005	3/15/2005
0.18Q	5/12/2005	5/26/2005	5/31/2005	6/15/2005

Indicated Div: $0.72 (Div. Reinv. Plan)

Valuation Analysis

Forecast P/E	N/A		
Market Cap	$605.4 Million	Book Value	268.7 Million
Price/Book	2.25	Price/Sales	3.71

Dividend Achiever Status

Rank	95	10 Year Growth Rate	14.67%
Total Years of Dividend Growth			18

Business Summary: Commercial Banking (MIC: 8.1 SIC: 021 NAIC: 22110)

Harleysville National Corporation, is the parent bank holding company of Harleysville National Bank and Trust Company, Citizen's National Bank and Security National Bank. Through its banking subsidiaries, Co. is engaged in the full-service commercial banking and trust business, including accepting time and demand deposits, making secured and unsecured commercial and consumer loans, financing commercial transactions, making construction and mortgage loans and performing corporate pension and personal investment and trust services. Co. operates 45 branch offices located in ten counties throughout Eastern Pennsylvania. As of Dec 31 2004, Co. had total assets of $3.02 billion.

Recent Developments: For the quarter ended Mar 31 2005, net income increased 2.9% to $9,165,000 from net income of $8,907,000 in the year-earlier quarter. Net interest income was $21,670,000, up 7.1% from $20,230,000 the year before. Provision for loan losses was $750,000 versus $489,000 in the prior-year quarter, an increase of 53.4%. Non-interest income rose 20.1% to $6,943,000 , while non-interest expense advanced 12.2% to $15,503,000 .

Prospects: On Apr 5 2005, Co.'s subsidiary, Harleysville National Bank, announced that is has completed the sale of its McAdoo Pennsylvania branch to The Legacy Bank. The sale of the branch includes approximately $13.8 million in deposits as well as certain loans and other assets. Meanwhile, Co. will continue to place emphasis on building Millennium Wealth Management & Private Banking's full line of trust, wealth management and private banking products and services. Also, Co. will continue to improve results, which includes favorable noninterest income being generated.

Financial Data

(US$ in Thousands)	3 Mos	12/31/2004	12/31/2003	12/31/2002	12/31/2001	12/31/2000	12/31/1999	12/31/1998
Earnings Per Share	1.46	1.44	1.37	1.27	1.12	1.00	0.97	0.88
Cash Flow Per Share	2.03	1.92	1.89	1.29	1.70	1.37	1.24	0.95
Tang Book Value Per Share	8.84	8.90	9.07	8.26	7.46	6.73	5.57	5.65
Dividends Per Share	0.733	0.715	0.623	0.537	0.472	0.410	0.371	0.329
Dividend Payout %	50.23	49.67	45.42	42.23	42.21	40.92	38.03	37.45
Income Statement								
Interest Income	35,272	127,729	119,200	132,630	138,679	131,811	106,117	87,597
Interest Expense	13,602	42,638	40,079	52,610	64,937	65,774	46,873	37,809
Net Interest Income	21,670	85,091	79,121	80,020	73,742	66,037	59,244	49,788
Provision for Losses	750	2,555	3,200	4,370	3,930	2,312	1,907	2,140
Non-Interest Income	6,943	28,158	27,638	22,523	22,225	12,206	10,092	9,810
Non-Interest Expense	15,503	59,561	59,629	56,297	55,043	44,677	38,438	32,573
Income Before Taxes	12,360	51,133	43,930	41,876	36,994	31,254	28,991	24,885
Income Taxes	3,195	12,566	8,597	8,949	8,174	5,650	6,644	6,109
Net Income	9,165	38,567	35,333	32,927	28,820	25,604	22,347	18,776
Average Shares	26,967	26,726	25,855	25,856	25,854	25,575	22,936	21,371
Balance Sheet								
Net Loans & Leases	1,844,019	1,826,111	1,391,638	1,316,102	1,301,051	1,196,845	1,047,768	829,937
Total Assets	3,002,572	3,024,515	2,510,939	2,490,864	2,208,971	1,935,213	1,635,679	1,332,389
Total Deposits	2,237,567	2,212,563	1,979,081	1,979,822	1,746,862	1,489,050	1,231,265	1,033,968
Total Liabilities	2,733,848	2,753,983	2,283,886	2,284,658	2,019,622	1,761,677	1,506,019	1,209,578
Stockholders' Equity	268,724	270,532	227,053	206,206	189,349	173,536	129,660	122,811
Shares Outstanding	26,240	26,277	25,037	24,974	25,196	25,520	22,906	21,386
Statistical Record								
Return on Assets %	1.40	1.39	1.41	1.40	1.39	1.43	1.51	1.53
Return on Equity %	15.33	15.46	16.31	16.65	15.88	16.84	17.70	16.14
Net Interest Margin %	61.44	66.62	66.38	60.33	53.17	50.10	55.83	56.84
Efficiency Ratio %	36.72	38.21	40.61	36.28	34.21	31.02	33.08	33.44
Loans to Deposits	0.82	0.83	0.70	0.66	0.74	0.80	0.85	0.80
Price Range	28.45-20.79	29.69-21.24	30.92-18.54	20.50-16.02	18.82-12.43	12.59-8.21	13.16-10.88	14.32-10.70
P/E Ratio	19.49-14.24	20.62-14.75	22.57-13.53	16.14-12.62	16.80-11.09	12.59-8.21	13.57-11.22	16.27-12.15
Average Yield %	2.98	2.81	2.78	2.95	3.10	3.99	3.20	2.52

Address: 483 Main Street, Harleysville, PA 19438
Telephone: 215-256-8851
Web Site: www.harleysvillebank.com

Officers: Walter E. Daller Jr. - Chmn. Gregg J. Wagner - Pres., C.E.O. **Transfer Agents:** American Stock Transfer & Trust Company, New York, NY

Investor Contact: 888-462-2100
No of Institutions: 57
Shares: 4,340,168 **% Held:** 16.55

HARSCO CORP.

Exchange	Symbol	Price	52Wk Range	Yield	P/E
NYS	HSC	$58.03 (5/31/2005)	60.74-42.05	2.07	19.03

Interim Earnings (Per Share)

Qtr.	Mar	Jun	Sep	Dec
2002	0.35	0.64	0.63	0.59
2003	0.31	0.63	0.69	0.62
2004	0.41	0.74	0.93	0.83
2005	0.55	...	...	...

Interim Dividends (Per Share)

Amt	Decl	Ex	Rec	Pay
0.275Q	6/22/2004	7/13/2004	7/15/2004	8/16/2004
0.275Q	9/28/2004	10/13/2004	10/15/2004	11/15/2004
0.30Q	11/16/2004	1/12/2005	1/14/2005	2/15/2005
0.30Q	3/10/2005	4/13/2005	4/15/2005	5/16/2005

Indicated Div: $1.20 (Div. Reinv. Plan)

Valuation Analysis

Forecast P/E	18.30 (5/28/2005)		
Market Cap	$2.4 Billion	Book Value	912.7 Million
Price/Book	2.64	Price/Sales	0.93

Dividend Achiever Status

Rank	277	10 Year Growth Rate	4.62%
Total Years of Dividend Growth			10

Business Summary: Metal Products (MIC: 11.4 SIC: 449 NAIC: 32312)

Harsco is a diversified multinational provider of industrial services and engineered products. Operations are divided into three primary segments. The Mill Services segment includes the MultiServ division and provides outsourced, on-site mill services to the global steel and metals industries. The Access Services segment includes the SGB Group and Patent Construction Systems divisions and provides scaffolding, shoring, forming and other access solutions. The Gas Technologies segment's manufacturing and service facilities in the United States, Europe, Australia, Malaysia and China comprise an integrated manufacturing network for gas containment and control products.

Recent Developments: For the quarter ended Mar 31 2005, income from continuing operations increased 36.8% to $23,053 thousand from income of $16,857 thousand in the year-earlier quarter. Net income increased 36.2% to $23,055 thousand from net income of $16,924 thousand in the year-earlier quarter. Revenues were $640,061 thousand, up 15.1% from $556,273 thousand the year before. Operating income was $47,276 thousand versus an income of $36,956 thousand in the prior-year quarter, an increase of 27.9%. Total direct expense was $493,647 thousand versus $428,988 thousand in the prior-year quarter, an increase of 15.1%. Total indirect expense was $99,138 thousand versus $90,329 thousand in the prior-year quarter, an increase of 9.8%.

Prospects: Co.'s favorable results are being fueled by strength from its Access Services and Engineered Products and Services businesses. In fact, Co. noted that three of its four major operating groups achieved solid growth in both sales and operating income for the first quarter ended Mar 31 2005. Consequently, Co. has sharpened its full year 2005 guidance for earnings from continuing operations to $3.10 to $3.15 per diluted share, from the previous range of $3.05 to $3.15 per diluted share. Co. noted that this guidance includes the effect of the change in its outlook for its full year 2005 effective tax rate to 32.0% from the previously estimated 31.0%.

Financial Data

(US$ in Thousands)	3 Mos	12/31/2004	12/31/2003	12/31/2002	12/31/2001	12/31/2000	12/31/1999	12/31/1998
Earnings Per Share	3.05	2.91	2.25	2.21	1.79	2.42	2.21	2.34
Cash Flow Per Share	6.90	6.56	6.46	6.29	6.03	6.47	5.23	4.15
Tang Book Value Per Share	11.72	11.61	9.03	6.59	8.32	7.66	9.77	9.74
Dividends Per Share	1.125	1.100	1.050	1.000	0.960	0.940	0.900	0.880
Dividend Payout %	36.89	37.80	46.67	45.25	53.63	38.84	40.72	37.61
Income Statement								
Total Revenue	640,061	2,502,059	2,118,516	1,976,732	2,108,474	2,004,741	1,720,811	1,735,394
EBITDA	96,615	394,348	343,148	331,995	338,294	351,807	305,589	323,282
Depn & Amortn	49,260	184,371	168,935	155,661	176,531	159,099	135,853	131,381
Income Before Taxes	37,489	171,239	135,902	136,699	113,795	148,591	147,430	179,775
Income Taxes	12,109	49,034	41,708	42,240	36,982	46,805	51,599	67,361
Net Income	23,055	121,211	92,217	90,106	71,725	96,803	90,713	107,513
Average Shares	41,978	41,598	40,973	40,680	40,066	40,022	41,017	45,910
Balance Sheet								
Current Assets	917,691	924,924	764,351	702,402	716,067	726,415	612,955	587,441
Total Assets	2,365,846	2,389,756	2,138,035	1,999,297	2,090,766	2,180,948	1,659,823	1,623,581
Current Liabilities	580,716	578,397	495,075	473,850	474,674	536,179	430,516	474,822
Long-Term Obligations	570,921	594,747	584,425	605,613	720,197	774,450	418,504	309,131
Total Liabilities	1,453,179	1,475,566	1,361,047	1,354,757	1,404,593	1,506,769	1,009,702	938,282
Stockholders' Equity	912,667	914,190	776,988	644,540	686,173	674,179	650,121	685,299
Shares Outstanding	41,595	41,431	40,866	40,539	39,984	39,805	40,071	42,250
Statistical Record								
Return on Assets %	5.61	5.34	4.46	4.41	3.36	5.03	5.53	6.93
Return on Equity %	15.04	14.30	12.97	13.54	10.55	14.58	13.59	14.66
EBITDA Margin %	15.09	15.76	16.20	16.80	16.04	17.55	17.76	18.63
Net Margin %	3.60	4.84	4.35	4.56	3.40	4.83	5.27	6.20
Asset Turnover	1.14	1.10	1.02	0.97	0.99	1.04	1.05	1.12
Current Ratio	1.58	1.60	1.54	1.48	1.51	1.35	1.42	1.24
Debt to Equity	0.63	0.65	0.75	0.94	1.05	1.15	0.64	0.45
Price Range	60.74-40.37	56.01-40.37	44.27-27.74	44.00-24.86	35.91-23.82	31.75-17.69	34.13-23.44	46.69-24.31
P/E Ratio	19.91-13.24	19.25-13.87	19.68-12.33	19.91-11.25	20.06-13.31	13.12-7.31	15.44-10.61	19.95-10.39
Average Yield %	2.30	2.38	2.96	2.98	3.29	3.61	3.10	2.23

Address: 350 Poplar Church Road, Camp Hill, PA 17011
Telephone: 717-763-7064
Web Site: www.harsco.com

Officers: Derek C. Hathaway - Chmn., Pres., C.E.O. D. H. Butler - Sr. V.P. **Transfer Agents:** Mellon Investor Services

Investor Contact: 717-975-5677
No of Institutions: 195
Shares: 26,520,620 **% Held:** 63.90

HAVERTY FURNITURE COS., INC.

Exchange	Symbol	Price	52Wk Range	Yield	P/E
NYS	HVT A	$14.15 (5/31/2005)	20.35-13.37	1.63	16.26

Interim Earnings (Per Share)

Qtr.	Mar	Jun	Sep	Dec
2002	0.30	0.17	0.27	0.36
2003	0.22	0.10	0.33	0.48
2004	0.27	0.16	0.19	0.38
2005	0.14	...	...	...

Interim Dividends (Per Share)

Amt	Decl	Ex	Rec	Pay
0.058Q	7/29/2004	8/11/2004	8/13/2004	8/27/2004
0.058Q	10/28/2004	11/9/2004	11/12/2004	11/26/2004
0.058Q	3/1/2005	3/9/2005	3/11/2005	3/28/2005
0.058Q	5/19/2005	5/26/2005	5/31/2005	6/15/2005

Indicated Div: $0.23

Valuation Analysis

Forecast P/E	14.35 (5/28/2005)		
Market Cap	$321.7 Million	Book Value	275.1 Million
Price/Book	1.17	Price/Sales	0.40

Dividend Achiever Status

Rank	244	**10 Year Growth Rate**	6.16%
Total Years of Dividend Growth			34

Business Summary: Retail - Furniture & Home Furnishings (MIC: 5.9 SIC: 712 NAIC: 42110)

Haverty Furniture Companies is a specialty retailer of residential furniture and accessories with 117 stores in 16 states as of Dec 31 2004. Co. offers nationally well-known brand names of merchandise, such as Broyhill, Lane, Bernhardt, La-Z-Boy, Sealy, Serta and Tempur-Pedic, primarily in the middle to upper-middle price ranges. Co. also carries merchandise that bears the Havertys brands (Havertys Collections® and Havertys Premium Collections®). Co. offers a revolving charge credit plan with credit limits determined through its on-line credit approval system and an additional credit program outsourced to a third party finance company.

Recent Developments: For the quarter ended Mar 31 2005, net income decreased 47.5% to $3,174 thousand from net income of $6,047 thousand in the year-earlier quarter. Revenues were $208,623 thousand, up 8.9% from $191,605 thousand the year before. Total direct expense was $103,024 thousand versus $92,339 thousand in the prior-year quarter, an increase of 11.6%. Total indirect expense was $100,095 thousand versus $89,133 thousand in the prior-year quarter, an increase of 12.3%.

Prospects: Co.'s outlook appears mixed. On one hand, Co.'s recent bottom line results were lackluster, a result primarily of the last major phase of its distribution transition that included closing and consolidating six warehouses into its new Florida Distribution Center. Co. also experienced increased costs during the quarter related to ongoing operations for fuel, insurance and professional service fees. On the positive side, comparable-store sales increased 4.7% for the quarter ended Mar 31 2005, and top line growth was decent. Looking ahead, Co. expects gross margins to improve in the last half of 2005, due to new merchandising programs, exclusive products and fewer closeouts.

Financial Data

(US$ in Thousands)	3 Mos	12/31/2004	12/31/2003	12/31/2002	12/31/2001	12/31/2000	12/31/1999	12/31/1998
Earnings Per Share	0.87	0.99	1.13	1.10	1.06	1.15	1.19	0.72
Cash Flow Per Share	1.96	2.70	3.73	3.94	1.43	0.80	3.15	2.42
Tang Book Value Per Share	12.10	12.08	11.28	10.30	9.45	8.64	7.81	7.08
Dividends Per Share	0.250	0.250	0.235	0.220	0.210	0.203	0.190	0.165
Dividend Payout %	28.74	25.25	20.80	20.00	19.81	17.61	15.97	22.92
Income Statement								
Total Revenue	208,623	784,162	744,635	703,959	678,112	680,917	618,796	540,298
EBITDA	10,334	58,802	59,796	61,367	63,160	71,306	69,116	53,750
Depn & Amortn	5,272	19,145	17,199	15,903	16,239	15,738	14,844	14,272
Income Before Taxes	5,062	36,174	38,725	38,903	36,340	43,861	42,870	26,295
Income Taxes	1,888	13,420	14,444	14,588	13,630	16,010	15,470	9,460
Net Income	3,174	22,754	25,331	24,315	22,710	24,495	27,400	16,835
Average Shares	27,331	23,083	22,437	22,145	21,502	21,203	22,982	23,404
Balance Sheet								
Current Assets	222,371	230,422	256,485	263,825	305,755	295,992	271,678	278,177
Total Assets	451,847	457,566	433,202	404,839	460,905	448,163	404,648	392,901
Current Liabilities	115,074	126,096	104,196	101,520	123,903	95,520	98,434	70,467
Long-Term Obligations	42,335	44,228	65,402	69,821	131,599	170,369	134,687	161,778
Total Liabilities	176,792	183,610	180,466	179,958	259,507	268,788	235,855	234,843
Stockholders' Equity	275,055	273,956	252,736	224,881	201,398	179,375	168,793	158,058
Shares Outstanding	22,737	22,674	22,409	21,832	21,302	20,773	21,610	22,330
Statistical Record								
Return on Assets %	4.49	5.09	6.05	5.62	5.00	5.73	6.87	4.21
Return on Equity %	7.41	8.62	10.61	11.41	11.93	14.03	16.77	10.60
EBITDA Margin %	4.95	7.50	8.03	8.72	9.31	10.47	11.17	9.95
Net Margin %	1.52	2.90	3.40	3.45	3.35	3.60	4.43	3.12
Asset Turnover	1.82	1.76	1.78	1.63	1.49	1.59	1.55	1.35
Current Ratio	1.93	1.83	2.46	2.60	2.47	3.10	2.76	3.95
Debt to Equity	0.15	0.16	0.26	0.31	0.65	0.95	0.80	1.02
Price Range	21.60-15.38	23.49-16.10	24.30-9.75	21.25-10.05	16.40-10.00	13.19-9.56	18.50-9.63	12.72-6.38
P/E Ratio	24.83-17.68	23.73-16.26	21.50-8.63	19.32-9.14	15.47-9.43	11.47-8.32	15.55-8.09	17.66-8.85
Average Yield %	1.41	1.30	1.46	1.41	1.49	1.77	1.36	1.69

Address: 780 Johnson Ferry Road, Suite 800, Atlanta, GA 30342 **Telephone:** 404-443-2900 **Web Site:** www.havertys.com	**Officers:** Clarence H. Ridley - Chmn. Clarence H. Smith - Pres., C.E.O. **Transfer Agents:** SunTrust Bank, Atlanta, GA	**Investor Contact:** 404-443-2900 **No of Institutions:** 5 **Shares:** 393,516 **% Held:** 9.12

HEALTH CARE PROPERTY INVESTORS, INC.

Exchange	Symbol	Price	52Wk Range	Yield	P/E
NYS	HCP	$27.19 (5/31/2005)	28.85-23.22	6.18	25.18

Interim Earnings (Per Share)

Qtr.	Mar	Jun	Sep	Dec
2002	0.21	0.29	0.27	0.20
2003	0.18	0.17	0.30	0.32
2004	0.31	0.27	0.22	0.31
2005	0.28	...	...	...

Interim Dividends (Per Share)

Amt	Decl	Ex	Rec	Pay
0.417Q	7/23/2004	8/2/2004	8/4/2004	8/19/2004
0.417Q	10/27/2004	11/4/2004	11/8/2004	11/19/2004
0.42Q	1/31/2005	2/3/2005	2/7/2005	2/18/2005
0.42Q	4/25/2005	5/3/2005	5/5/2005	5/19/2005

Indicated Div: $1.68 (Div. Reinv. Plan)

Valuation Analysis

Forecast P/E	14.58 (6/1/2005)		
Market Cap	$3.7 Billion	Book Value	1.4 Billion
Price/Book	2.58	Price/Sales	8.29

Dividend Achiever Status

Rank	258	10 Year Growth Rate	5.37%
Total Years of Dividend Growth			19

Business Summary: Property, Real Estate & Development (MIC: 8.3 SIC: 798 NAIC: 25930)

Health Care Property Investors is a real estate investment trust that, together with its consolidated subsidiaries and joint ventures, invests in healthcare-related facilities throughout the U.S. Co. develops, acquires and manages health care real estate, and provide mortgage financing to health care providers. Co. invests directly by structuring sale-leaseback transactions, and through joint ventures. As of Dec 31 2004 Co.'s portfolio, consisting of interests in 527 properties in 43 states, included: 29 hospitals; 171 skilled nursing facilities; 119 assisted living and continuing care retirement communities; 184 medical office buildings; and, 24 other health care facilities.

Recent Developments: For the quarter ended Mar 31 2005, income from continuing operations increased 7.7% to $37,599 thousand from income of $34,919 thousand in the year-earlier quarter. Net income decreased 7.2% to $43,458 thousand from net income of $46,835 thousand in the year-earlier quarter. Revenues were $108,396 thousand, up 14.1% from $94,986 thousand the year before.

Prospects: Co. is continuing to make portfolio investments. On Apr 28 2005, Co. acquired five medical office buildings for approximately $81.0 million including assumed debt valued at $29.0 million. The initial yield is 7.0% with two properties in lease up. The yield following lease up is expected to be 8.2%. The buildings include approximately 537,000 rentable square feet and are 88.0% occupied. Separately, Co. recently acquired five assisted living facilities for $58.0 million through a sale-leaseback transaction. These facilities have an initial lease term of 15 years, with two ten-year renewal options. The initial annual lease rate is approximately 9.0% with Consumer Price Index-based escalators.

Financial Data

(US$ in Thousands)	3 Mos	12/31/2004	12/31/2003	12/31/2002	12/31/2001	12/31/2000	12/31/1999	12/31/1998
Earnings Per Share	1.08	1.11	0.97	0.96	0.89	1.06	1.13	1.27
Cash Flow Per Share	2.08	2.06	2.06	1.94	1.86	2.01	1.78	1.83
Tang Book Value Per Share	8.26	8.49	8.82	8.46	8.62	8.55	9.00	6.58
Dividends Per Share	1.673	1.670	1.660	1.630	1.550	1.470	1.390	1.310
Dividend Payout %	154.86	150.45	171.13	168.91	174.16	138.03	123.56	103.15
Income Statement								
Property Income	102,515	388,631	348,649	331,737	310,602	306,830	199,570	138,439
Non-Property Income	5,881	40,053	51,534	27,839	21,858	22,977	25,223	23,110
Total Revenue	108,396	428,684	400,183	359,576	332,460	329,807	224,793	161,549
Depn & Amortn	26,143	99,342	87,551	82,259	84,098	72,590	44,789	29,577
Interest Expense	23,238	89,136	90,749	77,952	78,489	86,747	57,701	36,753
Net Income	43,458	169,040	158,585	137,380	121,166	133,767	96,225	87,167
Average Shares	134,529	133,362	126,130	116,294	107,950	102,200	69,722	67,328
Balance Sheet								
Total Assets	3,048,133	3,102,634	3,035,957	2,748,417	2,431,153	2,398,703	2,469,390	1,356,612
Long-Term Obligations	1,432,751	1,486,206	1,407,284	1,333,848	1,057,752	1,158,928	1,179,507	709,045
Total Liabilities	1,512,469	1,561,411	1,595,340	1,467,528	1,184,429	1,254,148	1,269,133	761,193
Stockholders' Equity	1,413,821	1,419,442	1,440,617	1,280,889	1,246,724	1,144,555	1,200,257	595,419
Shares Outstanding	134,318	133,658	131,039	118,939	112,773	101,747	102,842	61,974
Statistical Record								
Return on Assets %	5.61	5.49	5.48	5.30	5.02	5.48	5.03	7.59
Return on Equity %	11.59	11.79	11.65	10.87	10.13	11.38	10.72	16.80
Net Margin %	40.09	39.43	39.63	38.21	36.45	40.56	42.81	53.96
Price Range	28.85-21.68	29.09-21.68	25.63-16.68	22.43-18.11	19.51-14.78	15.25-11.84	16.47-10.97	19.63-14.44
P/E Ratio	26.71-20.07	26.21-19.53	26.42-17.19	23.36-18.86	21.92-16.61	14.39-11.17	14.57-9.71	15.45-11.37
Average Yield %	6.57	6.43	8.01	8.00	8.87	10.77	10.09	7.57

Address: 4675 MacArthur Court, Suite 900, Newport Beach, CA 92660 **Telephone:** 949-221-0600 **Web Site:** www.hcpi.com	**Officers:** Kenneth B. Roath - Chmn. James F. Flaherty III - Pres., C.E.O. **Transfer Agents:** The Bank of New York, New York, NY	**Investor Contact:** 949-221-0600 **No of Institutions:** 228 **Shares:** 63,382,500 **% Held:** 47.24

HEALTHCARE REALTY TRUST, INC.

Exchange	Symbol	Price	52Wk Range	Yield	P/E
NYS	HR	$39.09 (5/31/2005)	42.06-35.55	6.70	26.06

*7 Year Price Score 122.43 *NYSE Composite Index=100 *12 Month Price Score 96.00

Interim Earnings (Per Share)

Qtr.	Mar	Jun	Sep	Dec
2001	0.47	0.44	0.45	0.45
2002	0.44	0.50	0.44	0.17
2003	0.45	0.42	0.42	0.40
2004	0.42	0.37	0.31	...

Interim Dividends (Per Share)

Amt	Decl	Ex	Rec	Pay
0.64Q	7/27/2004	8/12/2004	8/16/2004	9/2/2004
0.645Q	10/26/2004	11/10/2004	11/15/2004	12/2/2004
0.65Q	1/25/2005	2/10/2005	2/14/2005	3/3/2005
0.655Q	4/26/2005	5/12/2005	5/16/2005	6/2/2005

Indicated Div: $2.62 (Div. Reinv. Plan)

Valuation Analysis

Forecast P/E 14.76 (6/3/2005)
Market Cap $1.9 Billion Book Value 1.0 Billion
Price/Book 1.81 Price/Sales 8.65

Dividend Achiever Status

Rank 289 **10 Year Growth Rate** 3.84%
Total Years of Dividend Growth 11

Business Summary: Property, Real Estate & Development (MIC: 8.3 SIC: 798 NAIC: 25930)

Healthcare Realty Trust is a self-managed and self-administered real estate investment trust (REIT) that integrates owning, acquiring, managing and developing real estate properties and mortgages associated with the delivery of healthcare services throughout the U.S. Co. focuses predominantly on outpatient healthcare facilities, which are designed to provide medical services outside of traditional impatient hospital or nursing home settings. As of Dec 31 2003, Co. had investments of $1.70 billion in 218 properties and mortgages located in 30 states, and affiliated with 61 healthcare-related entities.

Recent Developments: On Apr 1 2005, Co. announced that it will not file its Form 10-K on time. Co.'s auditors have not completed the year-end audit for 2004. Co. is working with KPMG LLP to finish the audit and file its Form 10-K as promptly as possible. For the year ended Dec 31 2004, income from continuing operations declined 8.2% to $57.6 million compared with $62.8 million in the previous year. Earnings for 2004 and 2003 excluded income from discontinued operations of $5.8 million and $62.8 million, respectively. Results for 2004 included a charge for an adjustment to amortization of deferred compensation of $2.4 million. Total revenues advanced 23.3% to $227.2 million from $184.2 million a year earlier.

Prospects: Results are being negatively affected by the application of Financial Accounting Standards Board (FASB) Statement No. 141 in accounting for the acquisition of real estate operations. FASB Statement No. 141 requires that the purchase price of these real estate operations be allocated between the land, the physical building as if the building was vacant when acquired and the lease intangible assets acquired. The purchase price allocated to the lease intangible assets is amortized over the remaining lease term, typically one to five years. This has reduced net income more notably in 2004 than prior years due to Co.'s increased volume of acquisitions, which totaled $299.0 million during 2004.

Financial Data (US$ in Thousands)	9 Mos	6 Mos	3 Mos	12/31/2003	12/31/2002	12/31/2001	12/31/2000	12/31/1999
Earnings Per Share	1.50	1.61	1.66	1.69	1.55	1.81	1.82	1.99
Cash Flow Per Share	2.55	2.36	1.95	2.36	2.66	2.29	3.16	2.34
Tang Book Value Per Share	21.61	20.54	20.79	21.07	21.72	24.41	25.00	25.44
Dividends Per Share	2.530	2.510	2.490	2.470	2.390	2.310	2.230	2.150
Dividend Payout %	169.16	156.34	150.42	146.15	154.19	127.62	122.53	108.04
Income Statement								
Property Income	147,812	99,367	47,956	177,470	177,800	173,461	167,465	156,733
Non-Property Income	22,781	7,580	3,708	14,527	16,727	21,077	27,873	30,524
Total Revenue	170,593	106,947	51,664	191,997	194,527	194,538	195,338	187,257
Depn & Amortn	40,006	24,763	11,935	46,162	46,558	45,129	42,938	42,378
Interest Expense	32,470	20,755	8,973	34,601	34,195	38,110	42,995	38,603
Net Income	47,375	33,437	17,812	70,507	70,091	79,887	79,801	86,027
Average Shares	45,692	42,414	42,379	41,780	41,606	40,463	40,301	39,810
Balance Sheet								
Total Assets	1,807,296	1,691,697	1,647,813	1,525,710	1,489,546	1,555,910	1,587,076	1,607,964
Long-Term Obligations	720,865	764,198	716,872	590,281	545,063	505,222	536,781	563,884
Total Liabilities	776,984	807,220	752,998	623,432	581,347	543,823	579,039	590,061
Stockholders' Equity	1,030,312	884,477	894,815	902,278	908,199	1,012,087	1,008,037	1,017,903
Shares Outstanding	47,682	43,065	43,046	42,823	41,823	41,465	40,314	40,004
Statistical Record								
Return on Assets %	3.85	4.26	4.44	4.68	4.60	5.08	4.98	5.34
Return on Equity %	6.60	7.59	7.74	7.79	7.30	7.91	7.86	8.45
Net Margin %	27.77	31.27	34.48	36.72	36.03	41.06	40.85	45.94
Price Range	43.66-31.98	43.66-29.15	42.83-24.42	36.45-24.42	32.15-27.28	28.25-21.38	21.44-15.50	22.81-14.69
P/E Ratio	29.11-21.32	27.12-18.11	25.80-14.71	21.57-14.45	20.74-17.60	15.61-11.81	11.78-8.52	11.46-7.38
Average Yield %	6.84	7.06	7.43	8.06	7.94	9.14	12.24	10.90

Address: 3310 West End Avenue, Suite 700, Nashville, TN 37203 **Telephone:** 615-269-8175 **Web Site:** www.healthcarerealty.com	**Officers:** David R. Emery - Chmn., C.E.O. Scott W. Holmes - Sr. V.P., C.F.O. **Transfer Agents:** EquiServe , Providence, RI	**Investor Contact:** 781-575-3400 **No of Institutions:** 166 **Shares:** 25,833,666 **% Held:** 54.17

HELMERICH & PAYNE, INC.

Exchange	Symbol	Price	52Wk Range	Yield	P/E
NYS	HP	$41.47 (5/31/2005)	42.15-24.01	0.80	39.12

*7 Year Price Score 115.18 *NYSE Composite Index=100 *12 Month Price Score 118.23

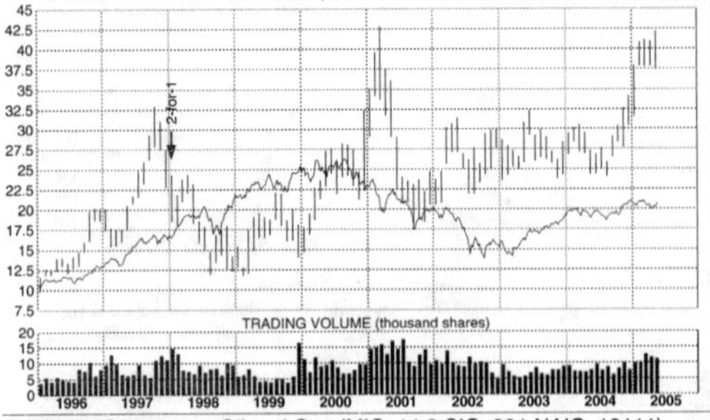

TRADING VOLUME (thousand shares)

Interim Earnings (Per Share)

Qtr.	Dec	Mar	Jun	Sep
2001-02	0.31	0.22	0.56	0.17
2002-03	0.01	0.05	0.16	0.13
2003-04	0.11	0.12	0.09	(0.23)
2004-05	0.77	0.43	...	...

Interim Dividends (Per Share)

Amt	Decl	Ex	Rec	Pay
0.08Q	6/5/2002	8/13/2002	8/15/2002	9/3/2002
0.00Q	9/20/2002	10/1/2002	9/27/2002	9/30/2002
0.08Q	12/4/2002	2/12/2003	2/14/2003	3/3/2003
0.08Q	3/5/2003	5/13/2003	5/15/2003	6/2/2003

Indicated Div: $0.33

Valuation Analysis

Forecast P/E 21.85 (5/28/2005)

Market Cap	$2.1 Billion	Book Value	989.7 Million
Price/Book	2.14	Price/Sales	3.07

Dividend Achiever Status

Rank 300 **10 Year Growth Rate** 2.87%

Total Years of Dividend Growth 28

Business Summary: Oil and Gas (MIC: 14.2 SIC: 381 NAIC: 13111)

Helmerich & Payne is primarily engaged in contract drilling of oil and gas wells for others. Co.'s contract drilling business is composed of three business segments: U.S. land drilling, U.S. offshore platform drilling and international drilling. Co.s U.S. drilling is conducted primarily in Oklahoma, Texas, Wyoming, Colorado, and Louisiana, and offshore from platforms in the Gulf of Mexico and California. Co. also operates in Venezuela, Ecuador, Colombia, Argentina, Bolivia, Equatorial Guinea, Chad and Hungary. In addition, Co. provides drilling consulting services for one customer in Russia. Co. is also engaged in the ownership, development, and operation of commercial real estate.

Recent Developments: For the quarter ended Mar 31 2005, net income increased 269.5% to $22,350 thousand from net income of $6,048 thousand in the year-earlier quarter. Revenues were $370,900 thousand, up 29.7% from $286,048 thousand the year before. Operating income was $37,586 thousand versus an income of $4,883 thousand in the prior-year quarter, an increase of 669.7%. Total direct expense was $114,321 thousand versus $104,950 thousand in the prior-year quarter, an increase of 8.9%. Total indirect expense was $33,543 thousand versus $33,191 thousand in the prior-year quarter, an increase of 1.1%.

Prospects: Co.'s U.S. land business is continuing to improve, fueled by strong energy prices. Customers are paying more for rigs across the industry and appear to be attracted to the performance and drilling efficiency offered by Co.'s fleet. Co.'s U.S. platform business is steady, while its international results are being hampered by Venezuelan currency revaluation costs, reduction in operating income in Bolivia and Equatorial Guinea, and expenses associated with terminating operations in Chad and Hungary. Separately, Co.has entered a new three-year contract to operate 10 new FlexRig4s® for Williams Production RMT Company, with the first rig scheduled for completion in November 2005.

Financial Data

(US$ in Thousands)	6 Mos	3 Mos	09/30/2004	09/30/2003	09/30/2002	09/30/2001	09/30/2000	09/30/1999
Earnings Per Share	1.06	0.75	0.09	0.35	1.26	2.84	1.64	0.86
Cash Flow Per Share	3.46	2.83	2.68	1.93	3.05	5.57	4.06	3.22
Tang Book Value Per Share	19.34	17.94	18.12	18.29	17.90	20.59	19.12	17.09
Dividends Per Share	0.328	0.325	0.323	0.320	0.305	0.300	0.285	0.280
Dividend Payout %	30.90	43.41	358.33	91.43	24.21	10.56	17.38	32.56
Income Statement								
Total Revenue	360,129	174,679	620,928	515,284	510,928	826,854	631,095	564,319
EBITDA	156,328	92,308	115,130	128,924	154,769	323,857	252,225	182,152
Depn & Amortn	47,223	23,265	94,435	82,693	62,569	88,787	112,386	110,733
Income Before Taxes	102,550	65,734	8,000	33,942	91,220	235,102	136,763	64,938
Income Taxes	42,283	27,130	4,365	14,649	40,573	93,027	57,684	25,706
Net Income	61,660	39,310	4,359	17,873	63,517	144,254	82,300	42,788
Average Shares	51,891	51,256	50,833	50,596	50,345	50,772	50,035	49,817
Balance Sheet								
Current Assets	392,932	352,239	245,886	197,531	178,751	331,412	265,144	160,624
Total Assets	1,510,157	1,473,092	1,406,844	1,415,835	1,227,313	1,364,507	1,259,492	1,109,699
Current Liabilities	55,721	58,342	59,903	88,618	72,899	121,221	78,894	71,904
Long-Term Obligations	200,000	200,000	200,000	200,000	100,000	50,000	50,000	50,000
Total Liabilities	520,457	512,923	492,734	498,584	332,143	338,030	303,789	261,590
Stockholders' Equity	989,700	960,169	914,110	917,251	895,170	1,026,477	955,703	848,109
Shares Outstanding	51,163	53,529	50,445	50,140	50,010	49,852	49,980	49,625
Statistical Record								
Return on Assets %	3.67	2.61	0.31	1.35	4.90	10.99	6.93	3.89
Return on Equity %	5.64	4.03	0.47	1.97	6.61	14.56	9.10	5.21
EBITDA Margin %	43.41	52.84	18.54	25.02	30.29	39.17	39.97	32.28
Net Margin %	17.12	22.50	0.70	3.47	12.43	17.45	13.04	7.58
Asset Turnover	0.47	0.45	0.44	0.39	0.39	0.63	0.53	0.51
Current Ratio	7.05	6.04	4.10	2.23	2.45	2.73	3.36	2.23
Debt to Equity	0.20	0.21	0.22	0.22	0.11	0.05	0.05	0.06
Price Range	41.10-24.01	34.16-24.01	30.61-23.77	32.34-23.57	31.42-18.40	42.84-17.38	28.19-14.00	22.10-11.76
P/E Ratio	38.77-22.65	45.55-32.01	340.11-264.11	92.40-67.34	24.93-14.60	15.08-6.12	17.19-8.54	25.70-13.68
Average Yield %	1.09	1.16	1.20	1.17	1.24	1.05	1.34	1.70

Address: 1437 South Boulder Avenue, Suite 1400, Tulsa, OK 74119
Telephone: 918-742-5531
Web Site: www.hpinc.com

Officers: W. H. Helmerich III - Chmn. Hans C. Helmerich - Pres., C.E.O. **Transfer Agents:** UMB Bank, Kansas City, MO

Investor Contact: 918-742-5531
No of Institutions: 186
Shares: 38,779,360 **% Held:** 76.41

HERSHEY COMPANY (THE)

Exchange	Symbol	Price	52Wk Range	Yield	P/E
NYS	HSY	$64.21 (5/31/2005)	66.65-44.16	1.37	27.09

*7 Year Price Score 136.89 *NYSE Composite Index=100 *12 Month Price Score 113.87

Interim Earnings (Per Share)

Qtr.	Mar	Jun	Sep	Dec
2002	0.32	0.23	0.45	0.48
2003	0.36	0.27	0.55	0.55
2004	0.41	0.56	0.66	0.68
2005	0.47	...	...	...

Interim Dividends (Per Share)

Amt	Decl	Ex	Rec	Pay
0.22Q	7/28/2004	8/23/2004	8/25/2004	9/15/2004
0.22Q	10/5/2004	11/22/2004	11/24/2004	12/15/2004
0.22Q	2/15/2005	2/23/2005	2/25/2005	3/15/2005
0.22Q	4/19/2005	5/23/2005	5/25/2005	6/15/2005

Indicated Div: $0.88 (Div. Reinv. Plan)

Valuation Analysis

Forecast P/E	27.65 (5/28/2005)		
Market Cap	$15.7 Billion	Book Value	970.7 Million
Price/Book	16.16	Price/Sales	3.44

Dividend Achiever Status

Rank	168	**10 Year Growth Rate**	10.33%
Total Years of Dividend Growth			30

Business Summary: Food (MIC: 4.1 SIC: 066 NAIC: 11320)

Hershey is engaged in the manufacture, distribution and sale of consumer food products including: chocolate and non-chocolate confectionery products sold in the form of bar goods, bagged items and boxed items; and grocery products sold in the form of baking ingredients, chocolate drink mixes, peanut butter, dessert toppings and beverages. Co.'s products are marketed in over 90 countries worldwide under more than 50 brands. Principal confectionery brands include: Hershey's®, Reese's®, Mr. Goodbar®, Jolly Rancher®, Kit Kat®, Milk Duds®, Whoppers®, York®, Twizzlers®, Super Bubble®, Ice Breakers®, Breath Savers® and Care*free®.

Recent Developments: For the quarter ended Apr 3 2005, net income increased 10.3% to $118,221 thousand from net income of $107,147 thousand in the year-earlier quarter. Revenues were $1,126,414 thousand, up 11.2% from $1,013,089 thousand the year before. Operating income was $205,873 thousand versus an income of $183,324 thousand in the prior-year quarter, an increase of 12.3%. Total direct expense was $695,131 thousand versus $625,632 thousand in the prior-year quarter, an increase of 11.1%. Total indirect expense was $225,410 thousand versus $204,133 thousand in the prior-year quarter, an increase of 10.4%.

Prospects: Strong sales growth, combined with cost controls, have led to a continuation of Co.'s momentum into the first quarter of 2005. Consistent with Co.'s strategy, new product innovation across both confectionery and snacks more than offset anticipated shortfalls from a shorter seasonal period. Looking to the remainder of 2005, by capitalizing on Co.'s brand position and its value chain capabilities, it will strengthen its confectionery leadership while gaining critical mass in relevant snack categories. As such, for the full year, Co. expects organic sales to be above its ongoing 3.0% to 4.0% expectations with diluted earnings per share to be at the top of its stated range of 9.0% to 11.0%.

Financial Data

(US$ in Thousands)	3 Mos	12/31/2004	12/31/2003	12/31/2002	12/31/2001	12/31/2000	12/31/1999	12/31/1998
Earnings Per Share	2.37	2.30	1.73	1.47	0.75	1.21	1.63	1.17
Cash Flow Per Share	2.99	3.13	2.26	2.29	2.59	1.50	1.17	1.36
Tang Book Value Per Share	1.57	2.03	3.29	3.55	2.16	2.57	2.34	1.79
Dividends Per Share	0.858	0.835	0.723	0.630	0.583	0.540	0.500	0.460
Dividend Payout %	36.12	36.30	41.76	42.86	77.67	44.63	30.67	39.32
Income Statement								
Total Revenue	1,126,414	4,429,248	4,172,551	4,120,317	4,557,241	4,220,976	3,970,924	4,435,615
EBITDA	255,123	1,091,842	976,923	876,195	603,128	798,614	965,453	800,824
Depn & Amortn	49,250	189,665	180,567	177,908	190,494	175,964	163,308	158,161
Income Before Taxes	186,469	835,644	732,827	637,565	343,541	546,639	727,874	557,006
Income Taxes	68,248	244,765	267,875	233,987	136,385	212,096	267,564	216,118
Net Income	118,221	590,879	457,584	403,578	207,156	334,543	460,310	340,888
Average Shares	250,308	256,827	264,532	275,429	275,392	276,730	282,600	291,126
Balance Sheet								
Current Assets	1,120,065	1,182,441	1,131,569	1,263,618	1,167,541	1,295,348	1,279,980	1,133,966
Total Assets	3,748,774	3,797,531	3,582,540	3,480,551	3,247,430	3,447,764	3,346,652	3,404,098
Current Liabilities	1,341,145	1,285,382	585,810	546,846	606,444	766,901	712,829	814,824
Long-Term Obligations	690,312	690,602	968,499	851,800	876,972	877,654	878,213	879,103
Total Liabilities	2,778,052	2,708,229	2,302,674	2,108,848	2,100,226	2,272,728	2,248,025	2,361,797
Stockholders' Equity	970,722	1,089,302	1,279,866	1,371,703	1,147,204	1,175,036	1,098,627	1,042,301
Shares Outstanding	244,284	246,587	259,059	268,440	332,145	272,563	276,919	286,294
Statistical Record								
Return on Assets %	16.32	15.97	12.96	12.00	6.19	9.82	13.64	10.18
Return on Equity %	52.66	49.74	34.51	32.04	17.84	29.35	43.00	35.98
EBITDA Margin %	22.65	24.65	23.41	21.27	13.23	18.92	24.31	18.05
Net Margin %	10.50	13.34	10.97	9.79	4.55	7.93	11.59	7.69
Asset Turnover	1.23	1.20	1.18	1.22	1.36	1.24	1.18	1.32
Current Ratio	0.84	0.92	1.93	2.31	1.93	1.69	1.80	1.39
Debt to Equity	0.71	0.63	0.76	0.62	0.76	0.75	0.80	0.84
Price Range	64.42-40.90	56.58-37.42	39.26-30.65	39.74-28.68	34.66-28.50	32.81-18.88	32.00-23.16	38.03-29.91
P/E Ratio	27.18-17.26	24.60-16.27	22.69-17.72	27.04-19.51	46.21-38.00	27.12-15.60	19.63-14.21	32.51-25.56
Average Yield %	1.69	1.82	2.05	1.86	1.85	2.20	1.82	1.36

Address: 100 Crystal A Drive, Hershey, PA 17033
Telephone: 717-534-6799
Web Site: www.hersheys.com

Officers: Richard H. Lenny - Chmn., Pres., C.E.O. David J. West - Sr. V.P., C.F.O. **Transfer Agents:** Mellon Investor Services, LLC, Ridgefield Park, NJ

Investor Contact: 800-539-0291
No of Institutions: 422
Shares: 104,753,056 **% Held:** 56.63

HIBERNIA CORP.

Exchange	Symbol	Price	52Wk Range	Yield	P/E
NYS	HIB	$32.15 (5/31/2005)	32.95-23.23	2.49	16.16

*7 Year Price Score 134.56 *NYSE Composite Index=100 *12 Month Price Score 110.24

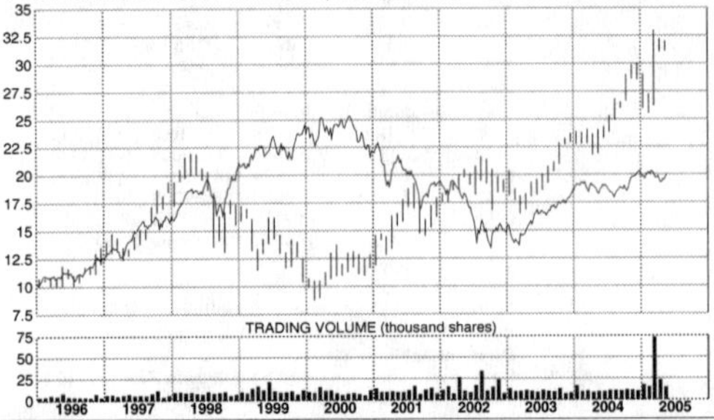

TRADING VOLUME (thousand shares)

Interim Earnings (Per Share)

Qtr.	Mar	Jun	Sep	Dec
2002	0.37	0.39	0.40	0.41
2003	0.36	0.39	0.44	0.45
2004	0.42	0.47	0.49	0.49
2005	0.54	...	...	...

Interim Dividends (Per Share)

Amt	Decl	Ex	Rec	Pay
0.20Q	7/21/2004	7/29/2004	8/2/2004	8/20/2004
0.20Q	10/27/2004	11/4/2004	11/8/2004	11/22/2004
0.20Q	1/25/2005	2/2/2005	2/4/2005	2/22/2005
0.20Q	4/20/2005	4/28/2005	5/2/2005	5/20/2005

Indicated Div: $0.80 (Div. Reinv. Plan)

Valuation Analysis

Forecast P/E	15.88 (6/2/2005)		
Market Cap	$5.0 Billion	Book Value	2.0 Billion
Price/Book	2.52	Price/Sales	3.40

Dividend Achiever Status

Rank	91	10 Year Growth Rate	14.87%
Total Years of Dividend Growth			11

Business Summary: Commercial Banking (MIC: 8.1 SIC: 021 NAIC: 22110)

Hibernia is a financial holding company. As of Dec 31 2004, Co. had assets of $22.31 billion and deposits of $17.38 billion with 314 locations in 34 Louisiana parishes and 34 Texas counties and two mortgage loan production and retail brokerage services offices in southern Mississippi. Co. conducts its banking business through its subsidiary, Hibernia National Bank. Co. offers financial products and services, including retail, small business, commercial, international, mortgage and private banking; leasing; investment banking; corporate finance; treasury management; merchant processing; property and casualty, life, and health insurance; trust and investment management; and retail brokerage.

Recent Developments: For the quarter ended Mar 31 2005, net income increased 29.9% to $85,776 thousand from net income of $66,021 thousand in the year-earlier quarter. Net interest income was $198,648 thousand, up 11.3% from $178,443 thousand the year before. Provision for loan losses was $15,700 thousand versus $12,000 thousand in the prior-year quarter, an increase of 30.8%. Non-interest income rose 41.8% to $113,536 thousand, while non-interest expense advanced 16.8% to $258,253 thousand.

Prospects: On Mar 6 2005, a definitive agreement was announced under which Capital One Financial Corp. will acquire Co. in a stock and cash transaction valued at approximately $5.30 billion. Upon closing, Co. will become a subsidiary of Capital One. Under the agreement, Co.'s shareholders will have the right, subject to proration, to elect to receive cash or Capital One common stock, having a value equal to $15.35 plus the value at closing of 0.2261 Capital One shares. The transaction is expected to close in the third quarter of 2005. Separately, Co.'s Texas expansion program continues to gain momentum with five new locations opening in high-growth markets in the first quarter of 2005.

Financial Data

(US$ in Thousands)	3 Mos	12/31/2004	12/31/2003	12/31/2002	12/31/2001	12/31/2000	12/31/1999	12/31/1998
Earnings Per Share	1.99	1.86	1.64	1.56	1.35	1.04	1.06	1.10
Cash Flow Per Share	4.08	3.97	4.96	3.24	(0.53)	1.86	3.07	1.56
Tang Book Value Per Share	10.39	10.12	9.26	8.51	9.81	8.83	7.96	7.79
Dividends Per Share	0.780	0.760	0.630	0.570	0.530	0.490	0.435	0.375
Dividend Payout %	39.20	40.86	38.41	36.54	39.26	47.12	41.04	34.09
Income Statement								
Interest Income	283,576	1,002,433	910,305	987,094	1,159,400	1,217,319	1,055,325	953,722
Interest Expense	84,928	251,760	239,552	282,857	494,729	606,760	470,520	423,188
Net Interest Income	198,648	750,673	670,753	704,237	664,671	610,559	584,805	530,534
Provision for Losses	15,700	48,250	60,050	80,625	97,250	120,650	87,800	26,000
Non-Interest Income	113,536	387,426	350,083	352,905	318,124	248,685	214,703	184,935
Non-Interest Expense	165,026	640,131	564,383	593,697	548,295	476,078	440,921	416,584
Income Before Taxes	131,458	449,718	396,403	382,820	337,250	262,516	270,787	272,885
Income Taxes	45,930	174,263	154,304	132,963	118,452	91,883	95,684	94,256
Net Income	85,776	292,954	258,336	249,857	218,798	170,633	175,103	178,629
Average Shares	158,198	157,498	157,600	160,057	159,236	158,020	158,902	156,165
Balance Sheet								
Net Loans & Leases	15,552,299	15,491,642	12,669,711	11,279,447	11,045,216	11,946,425	10,700,604	9,878,206
Total Assets	22,233,660	22,308,088	18,560,442	17,392,661	16,618,176	16,698,046	15,314,179	14,011,531
Total Deposits	17,574,412	17,378,946	14,159,519	13,481,022	12,953,112	12,692,732	11,855,903	10,603,006
Total Liabilities	20,239,430	20,366,191	16,782,957	15,711,799	15,058,397	15,218,395	13,938,664	12,693,430
Stockholders' Equity	1,994,230	1,941,897	1,777,485	1,680,862	1,559,779	1,479,651	1,375,515	1,318,101
Shares Outstanding	156,400	155,245	155,261	157,412	159,066	157,729	160,324	156,400
Statistical Record								
Return on Assets %	1.53	1.43	1.44	1.47	1.31	1.06	1.19	1.43
Return on Equity %	16.35	15.71	14.94	15.42	14.40	11.92	13.00	15.08
Net Interest Margin %	70.05	74.89	73.68	71.34	57.33	50.16	55.41	55.63
Efficiency Ratio %	41.56	46.06	44.78	44.31	37.11	32.47	34.72	36.59
Loans to Deposits	0.88	0.89	0.89	0.84	0.85	0.94	0.90	0.93
Price Range	32.95-21.72	29.98-21.72	23.69-16.47	21.60-16.80	19.23-11.88	13.75-8.75	17.38-10.38	21.94-13.06
P/E Ratio	16.56-10.91	16.12-11.68	14.45-10.04	13.85-10.77	14.24-8.80	13.22-8.41	16.39-9.79	19.94-11.88
Average Yield %	2.96	3.03	3.18	2.95	3.34	4.33	3.12	2.05

Address: 313 Carondelet Street, New Orleans, LA 70130
Telephone: 504-533-2831
Web Site: www.hibernia.com

Officers: E. R. Campbell - Vice-Chmn. Paul J. Bonitatibus - Pres., Consumer & Buss. Banking
ransfer Agents: Mellon Investor Services, Ridgefield Park, NJ

Investor Contact: 504-533-2180
No of Institutions: 223
Shares: 80,749,664 **% Held:** 52.04

HILB ROGAL & HOBBS CO

Exchange	Symbol	Price	52Wk Range	Yield	P/E
NYS	HRH	$34.09 (5/31/2005)	38.20-31.65	1.35	14.69

*7 Year Price Score 122.14 *NYSE Composite Index=100 *12 Month Price Score 98.47

Interim Earnings (Per Share)

Qtr.	Mar	Jun	Sep	Dec
2002	0.60	0.40	0.53	0.48
2003	0.51	0.52	0.50	0.53
2004	0.67	0.56	0.58	0.42
2005	0.76	...	...	...

Interim Dividends (Per Share)

Amt	Decl	Ex	Rec	Pay
0.105Q	7/20/2004	9/13/2004	9/15/2004	9/30/2004
0.105Q	11/30/2004	12/13/2004	12/15/2004	12/31/2004
0.105Q	2/7/2005	3/11/2005	3/15/2005	3/31/2005
0.115Q	5/3/2005	6/13/2005	6/15/2005	6/30/2005

Indicated Div: $0.46

Valuation Analysis

Forecast P/E	13.65 (6/2/2005)		
Market Cap	$1.2 Billion	Book Value	520.1 Million
Price/Book	2.34	Price/Sales	1.89

Dividend Achiever Status

Rank	267	10 Year Growth Rate	5.01%
Total Years of Dividend Growth			18

Business Summary: Insurance (MIC: 8.2 SIC: 411 NAIC: 24210)

Hilb, Rogal & Hamilton serves as an intermediary between its clients and insurance companies that underwrite client risks. Co. assists clients in managing their risks in areas such as property and casualty, executive and employee benefits and other areas of specialized exposure. Co. has offices located throughout the U.S. and London, England. Co.'s client base ranges from personal to large national accounts and is primarily comprised of middle-market and top-tier commercial and industrial accounts. Co. also advises clients on risk management and employee benefits and provides claims administration and loss control consulting services to clients.

Recent Developments: For the quarter ended Mar 31 2005, net income increased 14.4% to $27,722,000 from net income of $24,234,000 in the year-earlier quarter. Results for 2004 included pre-tax integration costs of $991,000. Revenues were $183,345,000, up 15.9% from $158,227,000 the year before. Commissions and fees advanced 15.3% to $180,257,000 from $156,396,000 the previous year. Investment income totaled $1,073,000 compared with $555,000 the prior year. Other revenues rose 57.9% to $2,015,000 from $1,276,000 a year earlier. Income before taxes grew 14.3% to $46,117,000 from $40,332,000 the year before.

Prospects: Top-line growth is being driven by higher commissions and fees stemming from recent acquisitions and increased contingent commissions, partially offset by a continued softening of premium rates. Despite strong increases in new business, Co.'s organic growth is being constrained by lower premium rates on renewals of property and casualty business, a reduction in the commission rates for two lines of business, and variability in timing of renewals and new business sold. Meanwhile, earnings are being negatively affected by significantly higher legal, compliance and claims expenses. Co. is taking aggressive steps to manage costs in an effort to boost profitability.

Financial Data (US$ in Thousands)	3 Mos	12/31/2004	12/31/2003	12/31/2002	12/31/2001	12/31/2000	12/31/1999	12/31/1998
Earnings Per Share	2.32	2.23	2.06	2.01	1.07	0.77	0.72	0.59
Cash Flow Per Share	3.39	3.19	3.19	2.51	2.27	1.83	0.67	0.79
Dividends Per Share	0.420	0.407	0.367	0.357	0.347	0.338	0.328	0.318
Dividend Payout %	18.10	18.27	17.84	17.79	32.48	43.83	45.49	53.81
Income Statement								
Total Revenue	183,345	619,603	563,647	452,726	330,267	262,119	227,226	175,364
Income Before Taxes	46,117	137,977	124,901	103,257	56,730	39,737	33,069	25,364
Income Taxes	18,395	56,563	49,947	42,082	24,381	17,610	13,583	10,418
Net Income	27,722	81,414	74,954	65,119	32,349	21,802	19,486	14,945
Average Shares	36,510	36,493	36,304	29,240	27,411	29,783	28,014	25,417
Balance Sheet								
Total Assets	1,249,187	1,277,999	1,049,227	833,024	499,301	353,371	317,981	188,066
Total Liabilities	729,081	770,843	614,960	522,376	356,500	265,149	246,806	142,355
Stockholders' Equity	520,106	507,156	434,267	310,648	142,801	88,222	71,176	45,710
Shares Outstanding	35,679	35,886	35,446	33,484	28,310	26,560	26,117	24,234
Statistical Record								
Return on Assets %	7.40	6.98	7.96	9.78	7.59	6.48	7.70	8.09
Return on Equity %	17.30	17.25	20.12	28.72	28.00	27.28	33.34	30.80
Price Range	38.75-31.65	38.75-31.49	43.85-28.34	45.40-27.75	31.08-16.97	20.97-12.91	14.56-7.78	9.94-7.75
P/E Ratio	16.70-13.64	17.38-14.12	21.29-13.76	22.59-13.81	29.05-15.86	27.23-16.76	20.23-10.81	16.84-13.14
Average Yield %	1.20	1.16	1.12	0.93	1.56	1.98	3.02	3.52

Address: 4951 Lake Brook Drive, Suite 500, Glen Allen, VA 23060
Telephone: 804-747-6500
Web Site: www.hrh.com

Officers: Martin L. Vaughan III - Chmn., C.E.O. Robert B. Lockhart - Pres., C.O.O. **Transfer Agents:** Mellon Investor Services, LLC, Ridgefield Park, NJ

Investor Contact: 804-747-6500
No of Institutions: 150
Shares: 34,825,512 **% Held:** 96.25

HILLENBRAND INDUSTRIES, INC.

Exchange	Symbol	Price	52Wk Range	Yield	P/E
NYS	HB	$50.46 (5/31/2005)	60.45-47.70	2.22	15.87

*7 Year Price Score 95.56 *NYSE Composite Index=100 *12 Month Price Score 95.08

Interim Earnings (Per Share)

Qtr.	Dec	Mar	Jun	Sep
2001-02	1.00	0.85	0.52	(2.53)
2002-03	0.12	1.00	1.00	0.09
2003-04	0.91	(0.76)	0.62	0.99
2004-05	0.70	0.87	...	...

Interim Dividends (Per Share)

Amt	Decl	Ex	Rec	Pay
0.27Q	9/9/2004	9/14/2004	9/16/2004	9/30/2004
0.28Q	12/2/2004	12/15/2004	12/17/2004	12/31/2004
0.28Q	2/10/2005	3/15/2005	3/17/2005	3/31/2005
0.28Q	5/11/2005	6/14/2005	6/16/2005	6/30/2005

Indicated Div: $1.12 (Div. Reinv. Plan)

Valuation Analysis

Forecast P/E	16.39 (6/1/2005)		
Market Cap	$3.1 Billion	Book Value	1.1 Billion
Price/Book	2.73	Price/Sales	1.63

Dividend Achiever Status

Rank	237	10 Year Growth Rate	6.70%
Total Years of Dividend Growth			34

Business Summary: Hospitals & Health Care (MIC: 9.3 SIC: 599 NAIC: 39995)

Hillenbrand Industries is a holding company for its two major operating businesses serving the health care and funeral services industries in the United States and abroad. Hill-Rom is a manufacturer of equipment for the health care industry, a provider of associated systems for wound, pulmonary and circulatory care and provides biomedical equipment rentals and other services to enhance the operational efficiency and asset utilization of health care facilities. Batesville Casket serves the funeral services industry and is a manufacturer of caskets and cremation-related products.

Recent Developments: For the quarter ended Mar 31 2005, income from continuing operations increased 1.5% to $53,600 thousand from income of $52,800 thousand in the year-earlier quarter. Net income was $54,000 thousand from net loss of $47,900 thousand in the year-earlier quarter. Revenues were $500,700 thousand, up 6.2% from $471,600 thousand the year before. Operating income was $85,400 thousand versus an income of $101,500 thousand in the prior-year quarter, a decrease of 15.9%. Total direct expense was $264,600 thousand versus $232,100 thousand in the prior-year quarter, an increase of 14.0%. Total indirect expense was $150,700 thousand versus $138,000 thousand in the prior-year quarter, an increase of 9.2%.

Prospects: Looking ahead, Co. is targeting full-year 2005 total revenues of between $1.94 billion and $1.97 billion, including health care sale and rentals revenues at Hill-Rom in the range of $1.28 billion to $1.31 billion and funeral services sales at Batesville Casket of between $657.0 million and $662.0 million. Meanwhile, Co. anticipates gross margins in the range of 46.9% to 47.2% during 2005, along with earnings from continuing operations of between $3.00 and $3.15 per share. Co. is experiencing margin pressures stemming from lower core product demand and higher than anticipated costs at Hill-Rom's rental business.

Financial Data

(US$ in Thousands)	6 Mos	3 Mos	09/30/2004	09/30/2003	09/30/2002	12/01/2001	12/02/2000	11/27/1999
Earnings Per Share	3.18	1.56	1.75	2.22	(0.16)	2.71	2.44	1.87
Cash Flow Per Share	6.00	7.03	5.58	6.06	6.31	7.10	4.63	2.27
Tang Book Value Per Share	9.66	9.38	8.81	15.79	12.72	13.24	10.42	10.17
Dividends Per Share	1.100	1.090	1.080	1.000	0.977	0.840	0.800	0.780
Dividend Payout %	34.59	69.95	61.71	45.05	...	31.00	32.79	41.71
Income Statement								
Total Revenue	975,500	475,000	1,829,000	2,042,000	1,757,000	2,107,000	2,096,000	2,047,000
EBITDA	220,400	102,000	387,000	374,000	43,000	246,000	267,000	222,000
Depn & Amortn	57,800	29,000	64,000	73,000	64,000	...	...	...
Income Before Taxes	154,200	69,000	308,000	282,000	(35,000)	223,000	240,000	195,000
Income Taxes	57,100	25,000	120,000	100,000	(25,000)	53,000	86,000	71,000
Net Income	97,600	44,000	110,000	138,000	(10,000)	170,000	154,000	124,000
Average Shares	62,389	62,689	62,725	62,184	62,921	62,814	62,913	66,295
Balance Sheet								
Current Assets	807,400	781,000	739,000	708,000	958,000	868,000	724,000	782,000
Total Assets	2,054,600	2,034,000	1,992,000	5,412,000	5,442,000	5,049,000	4,597,000	4,433,000
Current Liabilities	309,500	302,000	313,000	367,000	551,000	320,000	282,000	371,000
Long-Term Obligations	352,000	356,000	360,000	155,000	322,000	305,000	302,000	302,000
Total Liabilities	917,600	906,000	896,000	4,253,000	4,443,000	4,023,000	3,766,000	3,595,000
Stockholders' Equity	1,137,000	1,128,000	1,096,000	1,159,000	999,000	1,026,000	831,000	838,000
Shares Outstanding	61,581	62,028	61,953	61,814	61,702	62,466	62,404	63,546
Statistical Record								
Return on Assets %	4.99	2.62	2.96	2.54	N.M.	3.53	3.36	2.85
Return on Equity %	18.24	8.41	9.73	12.79	N.M.	18.36	18.16	13.89
EBITDA Margin %	22.59	21.47	21.16	18.32	2.45	11.68	12.74	10.85
Net Margin %	10.01	9.26	6.01	6.76	N.M.	8.07	7.35	6.06
Asset Turnover	0.48	0.51	0.49	0.38	0.40	0.44	0.46	0.47
Current Ratio	2.61	2.59	2.36	1.93	1.74	2.71	2.57	2.11
Debt to Equity	0.31	0.32	0.33	0.13	0.32	0.30	0.36	0.36
Price Range	70.22-47.70	70.22-47.70	70.22-49.76	57.64-46.91	65.99-48.75	58.10-43.88	51.00-29.06	57.94-26.38
P/E Ratio	22.08-15.00	45.01-30.58	40.13-28.43	25.96-21.13	...	21.44-16.19	20.90-11.91	30.98-14.10
Average Yield %	1.95	1.85	1.80	1.95	1.69	1.62	2.28	1.89

Address: 700 State Route 46 East, Batesville, IN 47006-8835
Telephone: 812-934-7000
Web Site: www.hillenbrand.com

Officers: Ray J. Hillenbrand - Chmn. Rolf A. Classon - Vice-Chmn., Interim C.E.O. **Transfer Agents:** Computershare Investor Services, Chicago, IL

Investor Contact: 812-934-8400
No of Institutions: 193
Shares: 31,425,330 **% Held:** 50.80

HNI CORP

Exchange	Symbol	Price	52Wk Range	Yield	P/E
NYS	HNI	$51.59 (5/31/2005)	52.95-37.57	1.20	25.04

*7 Year Price Score 127.94 *NYSE Composite Index=100 *12 Month Price Score 112.97

Interim Earnings (Per Share)

Qtr.	Mar	Jun	Sep	Dec
2002	0.27	0.34	0.46	0.48
2003	0.27	0.35	0.59	0.47
2004	0.38	0.44	0.65	0.50
2005	0.47	...	...	...

Interim Dividends (Per Share)

Amt	Decl	Ex	Rec	Pay
0.14Q	8/2/2004	8/10/2004	8/12/2004	9/1/2004
0.14Q	11/12/2004	11/18/2004	11/22/2004	12/1/2004
0.155Q	2/16/2005	2/23/2005	2/25/2005	3/1/2005
0.155Q	5/3/2005	5/11/2005	5/13/2005	6/1/2005

Indicated Div: $0.62

Valuation Analysis

Forecast P/E	21.56 (6/1/2005)		
Market Cap	$2.8 Billion	Book Value	674.8 Million
Price/Book	4.21	Price/Sales	1.29

Dividend Achiever Status

Rank	176	10 Year Growth Rate	9.79%
Total Years of Dividend Growth			16

Business Summary: Chemicals (MIC: 11.1 SIC: 522 NAIC: 37214)

HNI manufactures and markets office furniture and hearth products. Co.'s office furniture products are in four categories: storage, seating, office systems, and desks and related products. The office products are sold to dealers, wholesalers, warehouse clubs, retail superstores, end-user customers, and federal and state governments. Co.'s hearth products include wood-burning, pellet-burning, gas-burning and electric factory-built fireplaces, fireplace inserts, stoves, gas logs, and accessories. The hearth products are sold through a national system of dealers, wholesalers, large regional contractors and Co.-owned retail outlets. Co. has locations in the U.S., Canada and Mexico.

Recent Developments: For the quarter ended Apr 2 2005, net income increased 16.6% to $26,122 thousand from net income of $22,411 thousand in the year-earlier quarter. Revenues were $562,261 thousand, up 21.2% from $464,037 thousand the year before. Operating income was $40,445 thousand versus an income of $34,662 thousand in the prior-year quarter, an increase of 16.7%. Total direct expense was $366,416 thousand versus $294,275 thousand in the prior-year quarter, an increase of 24.5%. Total indirect expense was $155,400 thousand versus $135,100 thousand in the prior-year quarter, an increase of 15.0%.

Prospects: Co. is enjoying strong top-line growth in both its office furniture and hearth products segments. Sales are benefiting from contributions from several acquisitions during the first quarter of 2005, along with price increases that were recently implemented to offset rising steel, and other raw material costs. These price increases are expected to be fully effective during the second quarter of 2005. Meanwhile, strong earnings growth in the office furniture segment is being driven by improving economic conditions and strong industry growth. However, operating performance in the hearth products segment is being hurt by retail softness in certain markets and higher operating expenses.

Financial Data

(US$ in Thousands)	3 Mos	01/01/2005	01/03/2004	12/28/2002	12/29/2001	12/30/2000	01/01/2000	01/02/1999
Earnings Per Share	2.06	1.97	1.68	1.55	1.26	1.77	1.44	1.72
Cash Flow Per Share	3.53	3.41	2.39	3.45	3.87	3.42	2.57	2.39
Tang Book Value Per Share	8.12	8.04	8.89	7.79	6.45	5.97	6.45	5.77
Dividends Per Share	0.575	0.560	0.520	0.500	0.480	0.440	0.380	0.320
Dividend Payout %	27.86	28.43	30.95	32.26	38.10	24.86	26.39	18.60
Income Statement								
Total Revenue	562,261	2,093,447	1,755,728	1,692,622	1,792,438	2,046,286	1,789,281	1,696,433
EBITDA	57,327	245,115	222,733	211,445	204,477	257,080	211,896	232,176
Depn & Amortn	16,882	66,703	72,772	68,755	81,385	79,046	65,453	52,999
Income Before Taxes	40,500	178,869	150,931	140,554	116,261	165,964	137,575	170,109
Income Taxes	14,378	65,287	52,826	49,194	41,854	59,747	50,215	63,796
Net Income	26,122	113,582	98,105	91,360	74,407	106,217	87,360	106,313
Average Shares	55,551	57,577	58,545	59,040	59,087	60,140	60,855	61,650
Balance Sheet								
Current Assets	403,011	374,579	462,122	405,054	319,657	330,141	316,556	290,329
Total Assets	1,047,120	1,021,657	1,021,826	1,020,552	961,891	1,022,470	906,723	864,469
Current Liabilities	267,075	266,250	245,816	298,680	230,443	264,868	225,123	217,438
Long-Term Obligations	26,693	3,645	4,126	9,837	80,830	128,285	124,173	135,563
Total Liabilities	372,308	352,494	311,937	373,659	369,211	449,128	405,452	402,447
Stockholders' Equity	674,812	669,163	709,889	646,893	592,680	573,342	501,271	462,022
Shares Outstanding	55,037	55,303	58,238	58,373	58,672	59,796	60,171	61,290
Statistical Record								
Return on Assets %	11.62	11.15	9.45	9.24	7.52	11.04	9.89	13.17
Return on Equity %	16.87	16.52	14.23	14.78	12.80	19.82	18.19	25.27
EBITDA Margin %	10.20	11.71	12.69	12.49	11.41	12.56	11.84	13.69
Net Margin %	4.65	5.43	5.59	5.40	4.15	5.19	4.88	6.27
Asset Turnover	2.17	2.05	1.69	1.71	1.81	2.13	2.03	2.10
Current Ratio	1.51	1.41	1.88	1.36	1.39	1.25	1.41	1.34
Debt to Equity	0.04	0.01	0.01	0.02	0.14	0.22	0.25	0.29
Price Range	45.39-36.80	45.71-35.40	43.87-24.67	30.64-23.37	28.82-19.96	27.81-16.00	29.75-18.88	36.88-20.00
P/E Ratio	22.03-17.86	23.20-17.97	26.11-14.68	19.77-15.08	22.87-15.84	15.71-9.04	20.66-13.11	21.44-11.63
Average Yield %	1.41	1.39	1.57	1.83	1.95	1.87	1.63	1.12

Address: 414 East Third Street, P.O. Box 1109, Muscatine, IA 52761-0071 **Telephone:** 563-264-7400 **Web Site:** www.honi.com	**Officers:** Stan A. Askren - Chmn., C.E.O., Pres. David C. Burdakin - Exec. V.P. **Transfer Agents:** Computershare Investor Services, LLC, Chicago, IL	**Investor Contact:** 563-264-7400 **No of Institutions:** 131 **Shares:** 27,155,284 **% Held:** 49.28

HOLLY CORP.

Exchange	Symbol	Price	52Wk Range	Yield	P/E
NYS	HOC	$38.23 (5/31/2005)	39.40-17.40	0.84	14.82

*7 Year Price Score 231.34 *NYSE Composite Index=100 *12 Month Price Score 127.76

Interim Earnings (Per Share)

Qtr.	Mar	Jun	Sep	Dec
2003			1.44	
2004	0.44	1.56	0.36	0.24
2005	0.41	...	...	...

Interim Dividends (Per Share)

Amt	Decl	Ex	Rec	Pay
100%	8/2/2004	8/31/2004	8/16/2004	8/30/2004
0.08Q	8/2/2004	9/16/2004	9/20/2004	10/4/2004
0.08Q	12/10/2004	12/23/2004	12/28/2004	1/4/2005
0.08Q	3/14/2005	3/23/2005	3/28/2005	4/4/2005

Indicated Div: $0.32

Valuation Analysis

Forecast P/E 14.13 (6/1/2005)

Market Cap $1.2 Billion Book Value 358.4 Million

Price/Book 3.39 Price/Sales 0.50

Dividend Achiever Status

Rank 156 **10 Year Growth Rate** 10.95%

Total Years of Dividend Growth 11

TRADING VOLUME (thousand shares)

Business Summary: Oil and Gas (MIC: 14.2 SIC: 911 NAIC: 24110)

Holly is an indepedent petroleum refiner. The Refining segment refines crude oil and markets wholesale refined products, such as gasoline, diesel fuel and jet fuel, and includes refineries in New Mexico, Utah, and Montana. Co. also owns and operates or owns interests in thirteen refined products storage terminals in New Mexico, Texas, Utah, Montana, Washington, Idaho and Arizona. Also, Co. owns or leases about 1,000 miles of pipeline located principally in west Texas and New Mexico. The Pipeline Transportation segment uses 780 miles of the pipeline and owns a 70.0% interest in Rio Grande Pipeline Company, which transports liquid petroleum gases to Mexico.

Recent Developments: For the quarter ended Mar 31 2005, net income decreased 6.4% to $13,066 thousand from net income of $13,962 thousand in the year-earlier quarter. Revenues were $651,725 thousand, up 40.7% from $463,057 thousand the year before. Operating income was $25,909 thousand versus an income of $25,066 thousand in the prior-year quarter, an increase of 3.4%. Total direct expense was $556,193 thousand versus $374,895 thousand in the prior-year quarter, an increase of 48.4%. Total indirect expense was $69,623 thousand versus $63,096 thousand in the prior-year quarter, an increase of 10.3%.

Prospects: Co.'s refinery margins that started 2005 at seasonally reduced levels, particularly at the Woods Cross Refinery, have rebounded nicely and are at considerably higher levels. Moreover, Co. is benefiting from its 80.0% sour crude oil capabilities and will move forward in its efforts to further increase its capacity to process sour crude oil. Also, Co. will continue to explore operational improvement initiatives and deploy capital to improve the profitability of its existing operations. Going forward, Co. will continue to look for opportunities for strategic acquisition and organic growth, where it can leverage its strong financial condition.

Financial Data

(US$ in Thousands)	3 Mos	12/31/2004	12/31/2003	12/31/2002	07/31/2002	07/31/2001	07/31/2000	07/31/1999
Earnings Per Share	2.58	2.61	1.44	0.17	1.00	2.38	0.35	0.60
Cash Flow Per Share	4.44	5.27	2.28	(0.20)	1.36	3.48	1.45	1.44
Tang Book Value Per Share	10.73	10.35	8.32	7.23	7.34	6.52	4.29	3.90
Dividends Per Share	0.305	0.290	0.220	0.215	0.205	0.185	0.170	0.160
Dividend Payout %	11.84	11.11	15.28	126.47	20.40	7.76	47.89	26.45
Income Statement								
Total Revenue	651,725	2,246,373	1,403,244	448,637	888,906	1,142,130	965,946	597,986
EBITDA	33,441	178,102	112,312	20,842	80,020	151,689	51,283	67,296
Depn & Amortn	11,819	40,481	36,275	11,726	27,699	27,327	27,496	26,358
Income Before Taxes	21,246	138,469	74,359	8,517	50,896	121,895	18,634	33,159
Income Taxes	8,180	54,590	28,306	3,114	18,867	48,445	7,189	13,222
Net Income	13,066	83,879	46,053	5,403	32,029	73,450	11,445	19,937
Average Shares	32,252	32,170	32,032	31,804	31,942	30,774	32,260	33,016
Balance Sheet								
Current Assets	694,800	572,906	336,406	254,347	278,844	284,130	267,104	194,778
Total Assets	1,267,000	982,713	708,892	515,793	502,306	490,429	464,362	390,982
Current Liabilities	545,342	424,264	364,667	241,902	218,971	226,399	266,741	180,927
Long-Term Obligations	147,055	25,000	8,571	17,143	25,714	34,286	42,857	56,595
Total Liabilities	727,328	485,247	425,808	287,299	273,750	288,695	334,781	262,102
Stockholders' Equity	358,390	339,916	268,609	228,494	228,556	201,734	129,581	128,880
Shares Outstanding	31,754	31,294	31,028	31,035	31,122	30,961	30,203	33,016
Statistical Record								
Return on Assets %	8.42	9.89	7.52	0.76	6.45	15.39	2.67	5.38
Return on Equity %	25.87	27.49	18.53	1.77	14.89	44.34	8.83	16.39
EBITDA Margin %	5.13	7.93	8.00	4.65	9.00	13.28	5.31	11.25
Net Margin %	2.00	3.73	3.28	1.20	3.60	6.43	1.18	3.33
Asset Turnover	2.47	2.65	2.29	0.63	1.79	2.39	2.25	1.61
Current Ratio	1.27	1.35	0.92	1.05	1.27	1.25	1.00	1.08
Debt to Equity	0.41	0.07	0.03	0.08	0.11	0.17	0.33	0.44
Price Range	39.17-15.93	28.43-13.60	14.99-10.00	11.49-7.50	10.57-7.33	12.49-3.00	3.81-2.34	6.50-3.11
P/E Ratio	15.18-6.17	10.89-5.21	10.41-6.94	67.59-44.12	10.57-7.33	5.25-1.26	10.89-6.70	10.83-5.18
Average Yield %	1.27	1.48	1.72	2.36	2.27	3.29	5.24	4.18

Address: 100 Crescent Court, Suite 1600, Dallas, TX 75201-6927
Telephone: 214-871-3555
Web Site: www.hollycorp.com

Officers: C. Lamar Norsworthy III - Chmn., C.E.O. Matthew P. Clifton - Pres. **Transfer Agents:** American Stock Transfer & Trust Company, New York, NY

No of Institutions: 106
Shares: 21,641,492 **% Held:** 68.50

HOME DEPOT, INC.

Exchange	Symbol	Price	52Wk Range	Yield	P/E
NYS	HD	$39.35 (5/31/2005)	43.79-32.88	1.02	17.41

*7 Year Price Score 85.03 *NYSE Composite Index=100 *12 Month Price Score 93.98

Interim Earnings (Per Share)

Qtr.	Apr	Jul	Oct	Jan
2000-01	0.27	0.36	0.28	0.20
2001-02	0.27	0.39	0.33	0.30
2002-03	0.36	0.50	0.40	0.30
2003-04	0.39	0.56	0.50	0.42
2004-05	0.49	0.70	0.60	0.48

Interim Dividends (Per Share)

Amt	Decl	Ex	Rec	Pay
0.085Q	8/6/2004	8/31/2004	9/2/2004	9/16/2004
0.085Q	11/18/2004	11/30/2004	12/2/2004	12/16/2004
0.10Q	2/24/2005	3/8/2005	3/10/2005	3/24/2005
0.10Q	5/25/2005	6/7/2005	6/9/2005	6/23/2005

Indicated Div: $0.40 (Div. Reinv. Plan)

Valuation Analysis

Forecast P/E	13.69 (6/1/2005)		
Market Cap	$86.0 Billion	Book Value	24.2 Billion
Price/Book	3.56	Price/Sales	1.18

Dividend Achiever Status

Rank	14	10 Year Growth Rate	25.57%
Total Years of Dividend Growth			17

Business Summary: Retail - Hardware (MIC: 5.6 SIC: 211 NAIC: 44110)

The Home Depot is a home improvement retailer. As of Jan 30 2005, Co. operated 1,818 Home Depot® stores located throughout the U.S., Canada and Mexico. Home Depot stores sell a wide assortment of building materials, home improvement and lawn and garden products and provide a number of services. Home Depot stores average about 106,000 square feet of enclosed space, with approximately 22,000 additional square feet in the outside garden area. Co. also operated 54 EXPO Design Center® stores that sell products and services primarily for home decorating and remodeling projects, 11 Home Depot Landscape Supply stores, five Home Depot Supply stores, and two stores called The Home Depot Floor Store.

Recent Developments: For the year ended Jan 30 2005, net income increased 16.2% to $5,001,000 thousand from net income of $4,304,000 thousand a year earlier. Revenues were $73,094,000 thousand, up 12.8% from $64,816,000 thousand the year before. Operating income was $7,926,000 thousand versus an income of $6,846,000 thousand in the prior year, an increase of 15.8%. Total direct expense was $48,664,000 thousand versus $44,236,000 thousand in the prior year, an increase of 10.0%. Total indirect expense was $16,504,000 thousand versus $13,734,000 thousand in the prior year, an increase of 20.2%.

Prospects: On May 17 2005, Co. announced its intent to close and dispose of its interest in the underlying real estate of 15 EXPO Design Center stores. Co. also plans to convert five EXPO stores to The Home Depot store format. Co. stated that the remaining 34 EXPO stores are profitable and will continue operating. During the quarter ended May 1 2005 Co.'s Builder Solutions Group, an installer of flooring and countertops to professional homebuilders, acquired Grand Floor Design, mainly a flooring installation company with 11 locations in Northern California and Nevada, and, in Apr 2005, announced its intent to acquire Landmark Interiors Inc., a design center serving homebuilders in the Phoenix market.

Financial Data (US$ in Thousands)	01/30/2005	02/01/2004	02/02/2003	02/03/2002	01/28/2001	01/30/2000	01/31/1999	02/01/1998
Earnings Per Share	2.26	1.88	1.56	1.29	1.10	1.00	0.71	0.52
Cash Flow Per Share	3.14	2.87	2.06	2.51	1.21	1.09	0.87	0.47
Tang Book Value Per Share	10.42	9.56	8.39	7.53	6.32	5.22	3.83	3.17
Dividends Per Share	0.325	0.260	0.210	0.170	0.160	0.113	0.077	0.063
Dividend Payout %	14.38	13.83	13.46	13.18	14.55	11.33	10.80	12.26
Income Statement								
Total Revenue	73,094,000	64,816,000	58,247,000	53,553,000	45,738,000	38,434,000	30,219,000	24,156,000
EBITDA	9,245,000	7,922,000	6,733,000	5,696,000	4,792,000	4,258,000	3,034,000	2,179,000
Depn & Amortn	1,319,000	1,076,000	903,000	764,000	601,000	463,000	373,000	283,000
Income Before Taxes	7,912,000	6,843,000	5,872,000	4,957,000	4,217,000	3,804,000	2,654,000	1,898,000
Income Taxes	2,911,000	2,539,000	2,208,000	1,913,000	1,636,000	1,484,000	1,040,000	738,000
Net Income	5,001,000	4,304,000	3,664,000	3,044,000	2,581,000	2,320,000	1,614,000	1,160,000
Average Shares	2,216,000	2,289,000	2,344,000	2,353,000	2,352,000	2,342,000	2,320,000	2,286,000
Balance Sheet								
Current Assets	14,190,000	13,328,000	11,917,000	10,361,000	7,777,000	6,390,000	4,933,000	4,460,000
Total Assets	38,907,000	34,437,000	30,011,000	26,394,000	21,385,000	17,081,000	13,465,000	11,229,000
Current Liabilities	10,529,000	9,554,000	8,035,000	6,501,000	4,385,000	3,656,000	2,857,000	2,456,000
Long-Term Obligations	2,148,000	856,000	1,321,000	1,250,000	1,545,000	750,000	1,566,000	1,303,000
Total Liabilities	14,749,000	12,030,000	10,209,000	8,312,000	6,381,000	4,740,000	4,725,000	4,131,000
Stockholders' Equity	24,158,000	22,407,000	19,802,000	18,082,000	15,004,000	12,341,000	8,740,000	7,098,000
Shares Outstanding	2,185,000	2,257,000	2,293,000	2,345,888	2,323,747	2,304,317	2,213,178	2,196,324
Statistical Record								
Return on Assets %	13.67	13.39	13.03	12.54	13.46	15.23	13.11	11.31
Return on Equity %	21.54	20.45	19.40	18.10	18.93	22.07	20.44	17.82
EBITDA Margin %	12.65	12.22	11.56	10.64	10.48	11.08	10.04	9.02
Net Margin %	6.84	6.64	6.29	5.68	5.64	6.04	5.34	4.80
Asset Turnover	2.00	2.02	2.07	2.21	2.38	2.52	2.45	2.36
Current Ratio	1.35	1.40	1.48	1.59	1.77	1.75	1.73	1.82
Debt to Equity	0.09	0.04	0.07	0.07	0.10	0.06	0.18	0.18
Price Range	43.79-32.88	37.52-20.70	52.07-20.53	53.45-32.80	68.50-34.88	68.75-36.17	41.04-20.60	20.25-11.11
P/E Ratio	19.38-14.55	19.96-11.01	33.38-13.16	41.43-25.43	62.27-31.70	68.75-36.17	57.81-29.02	38.94-21.37
Average Yield %	0.86	0.83	0.60	0.37	0.31	0.25	0.27	0.40

Address: 2455 Paces Ferry Road N.W., Atlanta, GA 30339-4024	**Officers:** Robert L. Nardelli - Chmn. Pres., C.E.O. Carol B. Tome - Exec. V.P., C.F.O.	**Investor Contact:** 770-384-4388
Telephone: 770-433-8211	**Transfer Agents:** EquiServe Trust Company, N.A., Providence, RI	**No of Institutions:** 972
Web Site: www.homedepot.com		**Shares:** 1,341,788,288 **% Held:** 61.10

HOME PROPERTIES INC

Exchange	Symbol	Price	52Wk Range	Yield	P/E
NYS	HME	$41.20 (5/31/2005)	43.92-37.12	6.12	42.04

Interim Earnings (Per Share)

Qtr.	Mar	Jun	Sep	Dec
2002	0.24	0.39	0.49	(0.17)
2003	0.14	0.31	0.30	0.28
2004	0.14	0.26	0.09	0.69
2005	(0.06)	...	...	...

Interim Dividends (Per Share)

Amt	Decl	Ex	Rec	Pay
0.62Q	8/3/2004	8/12/2004	8/16/2004	8/27/2004
0.63Q	11/2/2004	11/12/2004	11/16/2004	11/26/2004
0.63Q	2/7/2005	2/15/2005	2/17/2005	2/28/2005
0.63Q	5/6/2005	5/13/2005	5/17/2005	5/27/2005

Indicated Div: $2.52

Valuation Analysis

Forecast P/E	21.82 (5/28/2005)		
Market Cap	$1.3 Billion	Book Value	662.2 Million
Price/Book	1.96	Price/Sales	2.78

Dividend Achiever Status

Rank	15	**10 Year Growth Rate**	25.35%
Total Years of Dividend Growth			10

Business Summary: Property, Real Estate & Development (MIC: 8.3 SIC: 798 NAIC: 25930)

Home Properties is a self-administered and self-managed real estate investment trust that owns, operates, acquires and rehabilitates apartment communities. Co.'s properties are regionally focused in certain Northeast, Mid-Atlantic, Midwest and Southeast Florida markets of the U.S. Co. conducts its business through Home Properties, L.P., a New York limited partnership in which Co. held a 67.7% partnership interest as of Dec 31 2004 and two management companies, Home Properties Management, Inc. and Home Properties Resident Services, Inc. As of Dec 31 2004, Co. operated 169 communities with 47,378 apartment units.

Recent Developments: For the quarter ended Mar 31 2005, income from continuing operations decreased 21.2% to $5,134 thousand from income of $6,518 thousand in the year-earlier quarter. Net income decreased 99.6% to $28 thousand from net income of $6,478 thousand in the year-earlier quarter. Revenues were $118,787 thousand, up 7.7% from $110,271 thousand the year before. Operating income was $6,732 thousand versus an income of $9,345 thousand in the prior-year quarter, a decrease of 28.0%.

Prospects: Co. is encouraged by occupancy for the month of March that was higher than for the quarter as whole, consistent with the trend of improving occupancy it anticipates with its guidance for 2005 operating results. Separately, during the first quarter of 2005, Co. announced the acquisition of three apartment communities in three unrelated transactions. The acquisitions consisted of one apartment community in Maryland with a total of 204 units and two apartment communities in New Jersey with 346 units combined for total consideration of $40.0 million. For full-year 2005, Co. expects funds from operations to range from $2.83 to $2.97 per diluted share.

Financial Data

(US$ in Thousands)	3 Mos	12/31/2004	12/31/2003	12/31/2002	12/31/2001	12/31/2000	12/31/1999	12/31/1998
Earnings Per Share	0.98	1.18	1.03	0.96	2.11	1.41	1.34	1.33
Cash Flow Per Share	4.49	4.82	4.99	5.51	6.71	6.15	4.84	4.36
Tang Book Value Per Share	18.36	19.48	20.53	20.67	21.10	19.50	21.03	20.52
Dividends Per Share	2.500	2.490	2.450	2.410	2.310	2.160	1.970	1.830
Dividend Payout %	255.10	211.02	237.86	251.04	109.48	153.19	147.01	137.59
Income Statement								
Property Income	118,131	455,023	429,618	392,620	362,233	310,249	224,469	141,171
Non-Property Income	656	3,307	4,886	2,942	5,290	8,799	9,994	8,072
Total Revenue	118,787	458,330	434,504	395,562	367,523	319,048	234,463	149,243
Depn & Amortn	24,756	95,228	79,279	68,799	65,521	52,995	38,066	24,405
Interest Expense	24,943	90,506	85,110	77,314	66,446	56,792	39,558	23,980
Income Before Taxes	6,732	...	...	...	...	...	...	...
Net Income	28	47,022	41,798	44,939	64,506	41,456	26,282	18,688
Average Shares	32,227	33,314	29,575	26,335	22,227	20,755	18,800	14,022
Balance Sheet								
Total Assets	2,808,831	2,816,796	2,513,317	2,456,266	2,063,789	1,871,888	1,503,617	1,012,235
Long-Term Obligations	1,688,986	1,644,722	1,380,696	1,300,807	960,358	832,783	618,901	418,942
Total Liabilities	1,851,713	1,785,599	1,441,510	1,396,963	1,052,606	882,083	706,614	445,570
Stockholders' Equity	662,232	720,422	741,263	726,242	620,596	569,528	497,123	361,956
Shares Outstanding	31,442	32,625	31,966	27,027	24,010	21,565	19,598	17,635
Statistical Record								
Return on Assets %	1.44	1.76	1.68	1.99	3.28	2.45	2.09	2.40
Return on Equity %	5.73	6.42	5.70	6.67	10.84	7.75	6.12	7.28
Net Margin %	0.02	10.26	9.62	11.36	17.55	12.99	11.21	12.52
Price Range	43.92-36.85	43.92-36.85	40.92-31.19	37.94-28.90	33.14-26.13	31.56-25.56	29.06-22.38	27.94-21.56
P/E Ratio	44.82-37.60	37.22-31.23	39.73-30.28	39.52-30.10	15.71-12.38	22.38-18.13	21.69-16.70	21.01-16.21
Average Yield %	6.24	6.23	6.76	7.16	7.81	7.68	7.54	7.09

Address: 850 Clinton Square, Rochester, NY 14604 **Telephone:** 585-546-4900 **Web Site:** www.homeproperties.com	**Officers:** Norman P. Leenhouts - Co-Chmn. Nelson B. Leenhouts - Co-Chmn. **Transfer Agents:** Mellon Investor Services LLC, Ridgefield Park, NJ	**Investor Contact:** 716-546-4900 **No of Institutions:** 127 **Shares:** 25,809,158 **% Held:** 82.15

HORMEL FOODS CORP.

Exchange	Symbol	Price	52Wk Range	Yield	P/E
NYS	HRL	$29.62 (5/31/2005)	33.08-26.00	1.76	17.32

*7 Year Price Score 116.77 *NYSE Composite Index=100 *12 Month Price Score 100.08

Interim Earnings (Per Share)

Qtr.	Jan	Apr	Jul	Oct
2001-02	0.36	0.23	0.27	0.49
2002-03	0.34	0.24	0.25	0.50
2003-04	0.37	0.38	0.40	0.50
2004-05	0.46	...	...	...

Interim Dividends (Per Share)

Amt	Decl	Ex	Rec	Pay
0.113Q	9/20/2004	10/20/2004	10/23/2004	11/15/2004
0.13Q	11/22/2004	1/19/2005	1/22/2005	2/15/2005
0.13Q	3/29/2005	4/20/2005	4/23/2005	5/15/2005
0.13Q	5/23/2005	7/20/2005	7/23/2005	8/15/2005

Indicated Div: $0.52 (Div. Reinv. Plan)

Valuation Analysis

Forecast P/E	16.94 (6/1/2005)		
Market Cap	$4.1 Billion	Book Value	1.5 Billion
Price/Book	2.82	Price/Sales	0.85

Dividend Achiever Status

Rank	247	10 Year Growth Rate	6.05%
Total Years of Dividend Growth			37

Business Summary: Food (MIC: 4.1 SIC: 011 NAIC: 11611)

Hormel Foods is primarily engaged in the production of a variety of meat and food products and the marketing of those products throughout the United States. Although pork and turkey remain the major raw materials for Co. products, Co. has emphasized for several years the manufacture and distribution of branded, consumer packaged items rather than the commodity fresh meat business. Co.'s business is reported in five segments: Grocery Products, Refrigerated Foods, Jennie-O Turkey Store, Specialty Foods, and All Other. Co.'s products primarily consist of meat and other food products. The meat products are sold fresh, frozen, cured, smoked, cooked and canned.

Recent Developments: For the quarter ended Jan 30 2005, net income increased 24.4% to $64,474 thousand from net income of $51,826 thousand in the year-earlier quarter. Revenues were $1,271,431 thousand, up 12.0% from $1,135,533 thousand the year before. Operating income was $104,601 thousand versus an income of $85,224 thousand in the prior-year quarter, an increase of 22.7%. Total direct expense was $959,618 thousand versus $863,757 thousand in the prior-year quarter, an increase of 11.1%. Total indirect expense was $210,139 thousand versus $188,258 thousand in the prior-year quarter, an increase of 11.6%.

Prospects: Looking ahead, Co. is boosting its full-year 2005 earnings projection to the range of $1.70 to $1.80 per share from its previous guidance of between $1.65 and $1.75 per share. Results are expected to benefit from Co.'s recent acquisition activity. On Mar 21 2005, Co. announced that it has completed its acquisition of Lloyd's Barbeque Company from General Mills, Inc. terms of the transaction were not disclosed. Also, on Mar 30 2005, Co. announced that it has acquired, for the purchase price of about $42.5 million, Mark-Lynn Foods Inc., a privately held manufacturer and distributor of foodservice products. Both acquisitions are expected to be immediately accretive to Co.'s earnings.

Financial Data
(US$ in Thousands)

	3 Mos	10/30/2004	10/25/2003	10/26/2002	10/27/2001	10/28/2000	10/30/1999	10/31/1998
Earnings Per Share	1.71	1.65	1.33	1.35	1.30	1.20	1.11	0.93
Cash Flow Per Share	2.43	2.09	1.83	2.36	2.32	1.08	1.65	1.51
Tang Book Value Per Share	6.50	6.43	5.36	5.41	4.45	5.64	5.20	4.82
Dividends Per Share	0.468	0.450	0.420	0.390	0.370	0.350	0.330	0.320
Dividend Payout %	27.33	27.27	31.58	28.89	28.46	29.17	29.73	34.59
Income Statement								
Total Revenue	1,271,431	4,779,875	4,200,328	3,910,314	4,124,112	3,675,132	3,357,757	3,261,045
EBITDA	135,366	486,452	409,215	408,633	403,160	345,173	329,875	291,301
Depn & Amortn	26,160	94,745	88,020	83,238	90,193	65,886	64,656	60,273
Income Before Taxes	102,432	364,565	289,331	293,970	285,014	264,381	251,473	217,336
Income Taxes	37,958	132,902	103,552	104,648	102,573	94,164	88,035	78,045
Net Income	64,474	231,663	185,779	189,322	182,441	170,217	163,438	139,291
Average Shares	139,626	140,179	139,710	140,292	140,125	141,523	147,010	150,406
Balance Sheet								
Current Assets	943,332	1,029,403	823,974	962,170	883,281	711,109	800,143	717,365
Total Assets	2,605,404	2,533,968	2,393,121	2,220,196	2,162,698	1,641,940	1,685,585	1,555,892
Current Liabilities	488,424	464,366	441,990	410,111	420,203	342,625	385,407	267,651
Long-Term Obligations	361,495	361,510	395,273	409,648	462,407	145,928	184,723	204,874
Total Liabilities	1,154,843	1,134,720	1,140,386	1,104,941	1,166,817	768,063	844,443	742,577
Stockholders' Equity	1,450,561	1,399,248	1,252,735	1,115,255	995,881	873,877	841,142	813,315
Shares Outstanding	138,175	137,875	138,596	138,411	138,663	138,569	142,724	146,992
Statistical Record								
Return on Assets %	9.57	9.25	8.08	8.66	9.62	10.26	10.11	8.89
Return on Equity %	17.47	17.19	15.73	17.98	19.57	19.90	19.81	16.97
EBITDA Margin %	10.65	10.18	9.74	10.45	9.78	9.39	9.82	8.93
Net Margin %	5.07	4.85	4.42	4.84	4.42	4.63	4.87	4.27
Asset Turnover	1.92	1.91	1.83	1.79	2.17	2.21	2.08	2.08
Current Ratio	1.93	2.22	1.86	2.35	2.10	2.08	2.08	2.68
Debt to Equity	0.25	0.26	0.32	0.37	0.46	0.17	0.22	0.25
Price Range	31.87-26.00	31.63-23.80	24.98-20.18	28.03-20.50	26.39-16.75	22.28-14.13	22.63-14.78	19.50-13.09
P/E Ratio	18.64-15.20	19.17-14.42	18.78-15.17	20.76-15.19	20.30-12.88	18.57-11.77	20.38-13.32	20.97-14.08
Average Yield %	1.61	1.60	1.85	1.58	1.73	2.00	1.77	1.97

Address: 1 Hormel Place, Austin, MN 55912-3680
Telephone: 507-437-5611
Web Site: www.hormel.com

Officers: Joel W. Johnson - Chmn., C.E.O. Jeffrey M. Ettinger - Pres., C.O.O. **Transfer Agents:** Wells Fargo Bank Minnesota, N.A., South St. Paul, MN

Investor Contact: 507-437-5007
No of Institutions: 182
Shares: 36,831,756 **% Held:** 26.66

HUDSON UNITED BANCORP

Exchange	Symbol	Price	52Wk Range	Yield	P/E
NYS	HU	$34.15 (5/31/2005)	41.64-31.74	4.33	12.15

Interim Earnings (Per Share)

Qtr.	Mar	Jun	Sep	Dec
2002	0.93	0.56	0.60	0.63
2003	0.63	0.65	0.68	0.54
2004	0.69	0.70	0.72	0.73
2005	0.66	...	...	...

Interim Dividends (Per Share)

Amt	Decl	Ex	Rec	Pay
0.35Q	7/28/2004	8/11/2004	8/13/2004	9/1/2004
0.35Q	10/22/2004	11/9/2004	11/12/2004	12/1/2004
0.37Q	1/25/2005	2/16/2005	2/18/2005	3/1/2005
0.37Q	4/29/2005	5/11/2005	5/13/2005	6/1/2005

Indicated Div: $1.48 (Div. Reinv. Plan)

Valuation Analysis

Forecast P/E	12.22 (6/1/2005)		
Market Cap	$1.5 Billion	Book Value	530.9 Million
Price/Book	2.90	Price/Sales	2.65

Dividend Achiever Status

Rank	90	10 Year Growth Rate	15.17%
Total Years of Dividend Growth			14

Business Summary: Commercial Banking (MIC: 8.1 SIC: 022 NAIC: 22110)

Hudson United Bancorp is a bank holding company. Co. directly owns Hudson United Bank, a full-service commercial bank that operated more than 200 offices, as of Dec 31 2004, throughout the state of New Jersey; in the Hudson Valley area of New York State; in New York City; in southern Connecticut; and in the Philadelphia, PA area. Co. also directly owns seven additional subsidiaries, which are HUBCO Capital Trust I, HUBCO Capital Trust II, JBI Capital Trust I, Hudson United Capital Trust I, Hudson United Capital Trust II, Hudson United Statutory Trust I and Jefferson Delaware Inc. As of Dec 31 2004, Co. had total deposits of $6.34 billion and total assets of $9.08 billion.

Recent Developments: For the quarter ended Mar 31 2005, net income decreased 4.0% to $29,731,000 from net income of $30,982,000 in the year-earlier quarter. Net interest income was $7,729,700, down 0.6% from $7,779,100 the year before. Provision for loan losses was $450,000 versus $560,000 in the prior-year quarter, a decrease of 19.6%. Non-interest income fell 11.3% to $31,551,000, while non-interest expense declined 3.0% to $64,002,000.

Prospects: Net interest margin is being hampered by significant interest rate competition for branch and public sector deposits. Meanwhile, results are being negatively affected by the delay in the sale of an OREO property foreclosed by Co. during December 2004. The sale is expected to close in the second quarter of 2005, with Co. being reimbursed for all operating expenses of the property which aggregated $0.01 per diluted share for the first quarter of 2005. Separately, a reduction in service fees was recognized in February. Co. has taken immediate actions to readjust fees, which is expected to favorably impact earnings going forward.

Financial Data

(US$ in Thousands)	3 Mos	12/31/2004	12/31/2003	12/31/2002	12/31/2001	12/31/2000	12/31/1999	12/31/1998
Earnings Per Share	2.81	2.85	2.50	2.72	2.00	0.92	1.18	0.49
Cash Flow Per Share	3.21	3.13	4.00	6.00	0.73	3.44	2.81	5.37
Tang Book Value Per Share	9.51	9.51	7.91	7.38	6.50	5.58	7.07	8.25
Dividends Per Share	1.400	1.360	1.180	1.100	1.010	0.932	0.883	0.778
Dividend Payout %	49.82	47.72	47.20	40.44	50.50	101.28	74.68	157.32
Income Statement								
Interest Income	110,866	414,434	394,129	430,003	470,363	608,309	644,576	468,547
Interest Expense	33,569	98,782	94,871	129,246	184,997	288,583	301,510	214,353
Net Interest Income	77,297	315,652	299,258	300,757	285,366	319,726	343,066	254,194
Provision for Losses	4,500	14,850	26,000	51,333	34,147	24,000	52,200	14,374
Non-Interest Income	31,551	156,327	133,045	185,122	109,425	31,095	88,698	33,299
Non-Interest Expense	64,588	283,706	256,295	247,126	227,240	250,031	271,287	232,096
Income Before Taxes	39,760	173,423	150,008	187,420	133,404	76,790	108,277	41,023
Income Taxes	10,029	45,340	37,687	64,214	38,943	26,969	38,939	17,872
Net Income	29,731	128,083	112,321	123,206	94,461	49,821	69,338	23,151
Average Shares	45,119	44,944	44,892	45,349	47,160	54,186	58,566	47,241
Balance Sheet								
Net Loans & Leases	4,747,652	4,766,385	4,591,909	4,267,546	4,374,556	5,182,343	5,571,759	3,333,311
Total Assets	8,850,443	9,079,042	8,100,658	7,651,261	6,999,535	6,817,226	9,686,286	6,778,661
Total Deposits	6,254,058	6,344,198	6,243,359	6,199,701	5,983,545	5,813,267	6,455,345	5,051,390
Total Liabilities	8,319,577	8,547,392	7,642,468	7,218,735	6,615,631	6,448,753	9,167,120	6,321,846
Stockholders' Equity	530,866	531,650	458,190	432,526	383,904	368,473	519,166	456,815
Shares Outstanding	45,030	44,982	44,798	45,023	45,814	47,964	57,085	45,786
Statistical Record								
Return on Assets %	1.51	1.49	1.43	1.68	1.37	0.60	0.84	0.47
Return on Equity %	24.78	25.81	25.22	30.18	25.11	11.19	14.21	7.20
Net Interest Margin %	69.72	76.16	75.93	69.94	60.67	52.56	53.22	54.25
Efficiency Ratio %	45.35	49.71	48.62	40.17	39.19	39.10	37.00	46.25
Loans to Deposits	0.76	0.75	0.74	0.69	0.73	0.89	0.86	0.66
Price Range	41.64-33.09	41.64-33.09	40.39-29.80	32.85-23.30	29.33-20.00	25.11-16.42	31.77-22.73	33.53-19.09
P/E Ratio	14.82-11.78	14.61-11.61	16.16-11.92	12.08-8.57	14.66-10.00	27.30-17.85	26.93-19.26	68.42-38.95
Average Yield %	3.78	3.64	3.43	3.71	4.06	4.54	3.14	2.76

Address: 1000 Macarthur Boulevard, Mahwah, NJ 07430	**Officers:** Kenneth T. Neilson - Chmn., Pres., C.E.O. James Mayo - Exec. V.P., Oper. & Technology	**Investor Contact:** 201-236-2803
Telephone: 201-236-2600	**ransfer Agents:** American Stock Transfer Company, New York, NY	**No of Institutions:** 159
Web Site: www.hudsonunitedbank.com		**Shares:** 23,208,880 **% Held:** 51.57

ILLINOIS TOOL WORKS, INC.

Exchange	Symbol	Price	52Wk Range	Yield	P/E
NYS	ITW	$84.43 (5/31/2005)	95.99-82.08	1.33	18.72

*7 Year Price Score 114.92 *NYSE Composite Index=100 *12 Month Price Score 91.53

Interim Earnings (Per Share)

Qtr.	Mar	Jun	Sep	Dec
2002	(0.08)	0.87	0.80	0.72
2003	0.63	0.90	0.87	0.92
2004	0.93	1.16	1.09	1.20
2005	1.06	...	...	...

Interim Dividends (Per Share)

Amt	Decl	Ex	Rec	Pay
0.28Q	8/6/2004	9/28/2004	9/30/2004	10/18/2004
0.28Q	10/29/2004	12/29/2004	12/31/2004	1/24/2005
0.28Q	2/16/2005	3/29/2005	3/31/2005	4/18/2005
0.28Q	5/6/2005	6/28/2005	6/30/2005	7/18/2005

Indicated Div: $1.12 (Div. Reinv. Plan)

Valuation Analysis

Forecast P/E	16.57 (5/28/2005)		
Market Cap	$24.5 Billion	Book Value	7.7 Billion
Price/Book	3.18	Price/Sales	2.03

Dividend Achiever Status

Rank	107	**10 Year Growth Rate**	13.99%
Total Years of Dividend Growth			42

Business Summary: Plastics (MIC: 11.7 SIC: 089 NAIC: 26199)

Illinois Tool Works is a global manufacturer of engineered products and specialty systems primarily serving the construction, automotive, food institutional and retail, and general industrial markets. Co.'s North America and International Engineered Products segments manufacture short lead-time plastic and metal components and fasteners and specialty products. The North America and International Specialty Systems segments design and manufacture longer lead-time machinery and related consumables and specialty equipment. The Leasing and Investments segment makes investments in mortgage entities, leases of telecommunications, aircraft and other equipment, properties, and a venture capital fund.

Recent Developments: For the quarter ended Mar 31 2005, net income increased 7.6% to $312,306 thousand from net income of $290,196 thousand in the year-earlier quarter. Revenues were $3,074,291 thousand, up 13.4% from $2,710,349 thousand the year before. Operating income was $477,889 thousand versus an income of $447,642 thousand in the prior-year quarter, an increase of 6.8%. Total direct expense was $2,022,337 thousand versus $1,750,343 thousand in the prior-year quarter, an increase of 15.5%. Total indirect expense was $574,065 thousand versus $512,364 thousand in the prior-year quarter, an increase of 12.0%.

Prospects: Co.'s North American Specialty Systems revenues are benefiting from increases in several business units including welding, food equipment, marking and decorating, and industrial packaging. Co.'s International Specialty Systems are also being positively affected by strength in industrial packaging in Europe and Asia, food equipment and welding. Separately, Co. is using its strong free cash flow generation to fund acquisition activity and forecasts acquired revenues of $600.0 million to $800.0 million of annualized revenues in 2005. Looking ahead, Co. expects operating results to improve modestly as the year progresses. For 2005, Co. expects earnings to range from $5.06 to $5.20 per share.

Financial Data

(US$ in Thousands)	3 Mos	12/31/2004	12/31/2003	12/31/2002	12/31/2001	12/31/2000	12/31/1999	12/31/1998
Earnings Per Share	4.51	4.39	3.32	2.31	2.63	3.15	2.76	2.67
Cash Flow Per Share	5.20	5.05	4.46	4.21	4.44	3.71	3.45	2.89
Tang Book Value Per Share	15.06	15.17	16.44	13.13	10.83	9.55	9.27	8.59
Dividends Per Share	1.080	1.040	0.940	0.900	0.840	0.760	0.660	0.540
Dividend Payout %	23.95	23.69	28.31	38.96	31.94	24.13	23.91	20.22
Income Statement								
Total Revenue	3,074,291	11,731,425	10,035,623	9,467,740	9,292,791	9,983,577	9,333,185	5,647,889
EBITDA	553,969	2,396,308	1,922,705	1,790,193	1,669,032	1,948,078	1,745,946	1,263,783
Depn & Amortn	72,636	353,283	302,090	305,752	386,308	413,370	343,284	199,712
Income Before Taxes	462,606	1,999,405	1,576,114	1,433,560	1,230,849	1,478,180	1,352,712	1,059,584
Income Taxes	150,300	659,800	535,900	501,750	428,400	520,200	511,600	386,800
Net Income	312,306	1,338,694	1,023,680	712,592	805,659	957,980	841,112	672,784
Average Shares	293,600	304,851	308,750	308,045	306,306	304,414	304,649	252,443
Balance Sheet								
Current Assets	4,856,242	4,322,198	4,783,202	3,878,809	3,163,244	3,329,061	3,272,931	1,834,473
Total Assets	12,005,915	11,351,934	11,193,321	10,623,101	9,822,349	9,603,456	9,060,259	6,118,162
Current Liabilities	2,371,318	1,850,971	1,488,903	1,567,162	1,518,158	1,817,610	2,045,361	1,222,009
Long-Term Obligations	967,857	921,098	920,360	1,460,381	1,267,141	1,549,038	1,360,746	947,008
Total Liabilities	4,297,222	3,724,324	3,319,035	3,974,030	3,781,611	4,202,469	4,244,836	2,780,127
Stockholders' Equity	7,708,693	7,627,610	7,874,286	6,649,071	6,040,738	5,400,987	4,815,423	3,338,035
Shares Outstanding	290,398	292,228	308,636	306,582	304,926	305,448	300,568	250,128
Statistical Record								
Return on Assets %	11.45	11.84	9.38	6.97	8.29	10.24	11.08	11.69
Return on Equity %	17.07	17.22	14.10	11.23	14.08	18.70	20.63	21.90
EBITDA Margin %	18.02	20.43	19.16	18.91	17.96	19.51	18.71	22.38
Net Margin %	10.16	11.41	10.20	7.53	8.67	9.60	9.01	11.91
Asset Turnover	1.02	1.04	0.92	0.93	0.96	1.07	1.23	0.98
Current Ratio	2.05	2.34	3.21	2.48	2.08	1.83	1.60	1.50
Debt to Equity	0.13	0.12	0.12	0.22	0.21	0.29	0.28	0.28
Price Range	95.99-78.87	95.99-73.42	84.15-55.15	77.38-55.73	71.20-49.15	68.31-51.06	81.75-58.00	71.81-45.38
P/E Ratio	21.28-17.49	21.87-16.72	25.35-16.61	33.50-24.13	27.07-18.69	21.69-16.21	29.62-21.01	26.90-16.99
Average Yield %	1.19	1.18	1.39	1.33	1.34	1.30	0.93	0.89

Address: 3600 West Lake Avenue, Glenview, IL 60025-5811
Telephone: 847-724-7500
Web Site: www.itw.com

Officers: W. James Farrell - Chmn., C.E.O. Frank S. Ptak - Vice-Chmn. **Transfer Agents:** Computershare Investor Service, L.L.C., Chicago, IL

No of Institutions: 584
Shares: 223,237,536 **% Held:** 76.38

INDEPENDENT BANK CORPORATION (IONIA, MI)

Exchange	Symbol	Price	52Wk Range	Yield	P/E
NMS	IBCP	$28.14 (5/31/2005)	31.49-24.05	2.70	14.51

*7 Year Price Score 146.37 *NYSE Composite Index=100 *12 Month Price Score 97.40

Interim Earnings (Per Share)

Qtr.	Mar	Jun	Sep	Dec
2002	0.34	0.35	0.35	0.39
2003	0.45	0.45	0.51	0.46
2004	0.42	0.44	0.48	0.50
2005	0.52	...	...	...

Interim Dividends (Per Share)

Amt	Decl	Ex	Rec	Pay
0.16Q	6/15/2004	7/1/2004	7/6/2004	7/30/2004
0.17Q	9/24/2004	10/1/2004	10/5/2004	10/29/2004
0.17Q	11/23/2004	1/3/2005	1/5/2005	1/31/2005
0.19Q	2/9/2005	4/1/2005	4/5/2005	4/29/2005

Indicated Div: $0.76 (Div. Reinv. Plan)

Valuation Analysis

Forecast P/E	N/A		
Market Cap	$598.6 Million	Book Value	239.1 Million
Price/Book	2.50	Price/Sales	2.79

Dividend Achiever Status

Rank	68	10 Year Growth Rate	16.87%
Total Years of Dividend Growth			16

32.5 30 27.5 25 22.5 20 17.5 15 12.5 10 7.5 5 2.5
5% 3-for-2 5% 3-for-2 5% 5% 5% 5% 5% 3-for-2 10%
TRADING VOLUME (thousand shares)
3 2 1 0
1996 1997 1998 1999 2000 2001 2002 2003 2004 2005

Business Summary: Commercial Banking (MIC: 8.1 SIC: 022 NAIC: 22110)

Independent Bank is a bank holding company. Co.'s commercial banking activities include providing checking and savings accounts, commercial lending, direct and indirect consumer financing, mortgage lending, insurance premium and automobile warranty financing and safe deposit box services. Co. also offers title insurance services and provides investment and insurance services through a third party agreement with PrimeVest Financial Services, Inc. Co.'s principal markets are the rural and suburban communities across lower Michigan. As of Dec 31 2004, Co. had four main offices, 88 branches, 4 drive-thru facilities and 14 loan production offices. At Dec 31 2004, total assets were $3.09 billion.

Recent Developments: For the quarter ended Mar 31 2005, net income increased 33.9% to $11,301 thousand from net income of $8,443 thousand in the year-earlier quarter. Net interest income was $33,521 thousand, up 32.1% from $25,375 thousand the year before. Provision for loan losses was $1,606 thousand versus $801 thousand in the prior-year quarter, an increase of 100.5%. Non-interest income rose 30.8% to $9,725 thousand, while non-interest expense advanced 26.0% to $26,026 thousand.

Prospects: Co. is pleased with its results for the quarter ended Mar 31 2005 and thus has reaffirmed its diluted earnings per share outlook of between $2.10 and $2.20 for full year 2005. Co. attributed its recent earnings improvement mainly to increases in net interest income, service charges on deposits and real estate mortgage loan servicing fees. Co. noted the latter factor was due primarily to a decline in the impairment reserve on capitalized mortgage loan servicing rights. Loans, excluding loans held for sales, rose to $2.32 billion at Mar 31 2005 from $2.23 billion at Dec 31 2004. The increase in loans reflected growth in commercial loans, real estate mortgage loans and finance receivables.

Financial Data

(US$ in Thousands)	3 Mos	12/31/2004	12/31/2003	12/31/2002	12/31/2001	12/31/2000	12/31/1999	12/31/1998
Earnings Per Share	1.94	1.84	1.87	1.44	1.15	0.93	0.39	0.69
Cash Flow Per Share	2.74	3.14	7.12	(0.72)	(1.00)	1.44	2.13	(0.03)
Tang Book Value Per Share	8.12	7.71	7.05	7.04	6.42	6.38	5.30	4.71
Dividends Per Share	0.660	0.65	0.56	0.416	0.346	0.309	0.274	0.244
Dividend Payout %	34.02	35.33	29.95	28.93	30.00	33.25	70.26	35.36
Income Statement								
Interest Income	47,657	162,547	139,366	129,815	141,359	138,415	125,510	86,073
Interest Expense	14,136	45,014	44,113	48,008	62,460	67,865	58,730	36,840
Net Interest Income	33,521	117,533	95,253	81,807	78,899	70,550	66,780	49,233
Provision for Losses	1,606	4,309	4,032	3,562	3,737	3,287	2,661	3,043
Non-Interest Income	9,725	37,798	42,604	30,911	27,085	18,961	17,323	13,845
Non-Interest Expense	26,026	98,668	82,506	68,293	68,526	58,949	69,480	45,688
Income Before Taxes	15,614	52,354	51,319	40,863	33,721	27,275	11,962	14,347
Income Taxes	4,313	13,796	13,727	11,396	9,288	7,266	3,293	4,126
Net Income	11,301	38,558	37,592	29,467	24,398	20,009	8,669	10,221
Average Shares	21,671	20,900	20,059	20,516	21,174	21,525	21,985	14,893
Balance Sheet								
Net Loans & Leases	2,299,695	2,200,553	1,649,665	1,364,737	1,368,517	1,365,682	1,277,656	812,890
Total Assets	3,187,347	3,094,027	2,358,557	2,057,562	1,888,457	1,783,791	1,725,205	1,085,258
Total Deposits	2,348,057	2,176,947	1,702,806	1,535,603	1,387,367	1,389,900	1,310,602	830,514
Total Liabilities	2,948,223	2,863,735	2,196,341	1,919,515	1,756,554	1,655,455	1,611,459	1,015,553
Stockholders' Equity	239,124	230,292	162,216	138,047	131,903	128,336	113,746	69,705
Shares Outstanding	21,271	21,194	19,568	19,604	20,555	20,113	21,459	14,806
Statistical Record								
Return on Assets %	1.48	1.41	1.70	1.49	1.33	1.14	0.62	0.99
Return on Equity %	20.12	19.59	25.04	21.83	18.75	16.49	9.45	15.82
Net Interest Margin %	70.34	72.31	68.35	63.02	55.81	50.97	53.21	57.20
Efficiency Ratio %	45.36	49.25	45.34	42.49	40.68	37.46	48.64	45.73
Loans to Deposits	0.98	1.01	0.97	0.89	0.99	0.98	0.97	0.98
Price Range	31.49-23.86	30.60-23.86	30.50-17.74	20.32-15.02	16.74-10.24	10.86-5.66	10.47-6.94	15.04-9.47
P/E Ratio	16.23-12.30	16.63-12.97	16.31-9.48	14.11-10.43	14.56-8.90	11.67-6.09	26.85-17.79	21.79-13.73
Average Yield %	2.41	2.64	2.32	2.32	2.58	3.94	3.15	1.99

Address: 230 West Main Street, P.O. Box 491, Ionia, MI 48846
Telephone: 616-527-9450
Web Site: www.ibcp.com

Officers: Charles C. Van Loan - Chmn. Michael M. Magee Jr. - Pres., C.E.O. **Transfer Agents:** EquiServe Trust Company, N.A., Providence, RI

Investor Contact: 616-527-9450
No of Institutions: 79
Shares: 7,056,115 **% Held:** 33.20

IRWIN FINANCIAL CORP. (COLUMBUS, IN)

Exchange	Symbol	Price	52Wk Range	Yield	P/E
NYS	IFC	$20.99 (5/31/2005)	28.65-19.72	1.91	11.79

*7 Year Price Score 100.97 *NYSE Composite Index=100 *12 Month Price Score 82.49

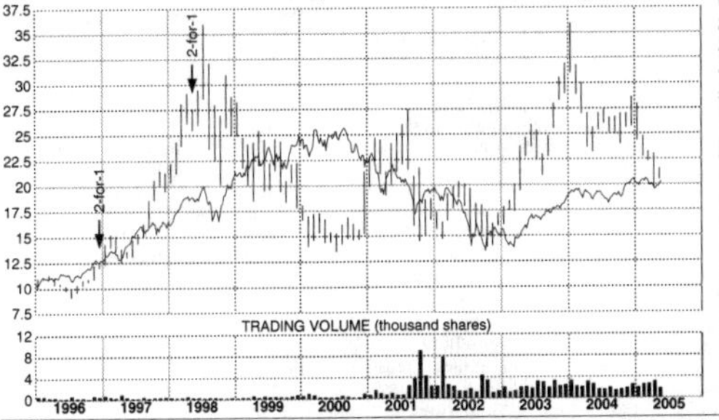

TRADING VOLUME (thousand shares)

Interim Earnings (Per Share)

Qtr.	Mar	Jun	Sep	Dec
2002	0.39	0.28	0.29	0.93
2003	0.41	0.45	1.03	0.56
2004	0.67	0.60	0.57	0.48
2005	0.13	...	...	...

Interim Dividends (Per Share)

Amt	Decl	Ex	Rec	Pay
0.08Q	8/26/2004	9/8/2004	9/10/2004	9/24/2004
0.08Q	12/1/2004	12/14/2004	12/16/2004	12/30/2004
0.10Q	2/10/2005	3/9/2005	3/11/2005	3/25/2005
0.10Q	5/4/2005	6/8/2005	6/10/2005	6/24/2005

Indicated Div: $0.40 (Div. Reinv. Plan)

Valuation Analysis

Forecast P/E	12.13 (5/28/2005)		
Market Cap	$598.6 Million	Book Value	503.8 Million
Price/Book	1.19	Price/Sales	0.99

Dividend Achiever Status

Rank	116	10 Year Growth Rate	13.52%
Total Years of Dividend Growth			15

Business Summary: Commercial Banking (MIC: 8.1 SIC: 022 NAIC: 22110)

Irwin Financial is a diversified financial services engaged in mortgage banking, commercial banking, home equity lending, commercial finance, and venture capital. The mortgage banking business originates, purchases, sells, and services residential mortgage loans. The commercial banking business provides credit, cash management and personal banking products primarily to small businesses and business owners. Irwin Home Equity originates, purchases, securitizes and services home equity loans and lines of credit. Co.'s commercial finance business originates small-ticket equipment leases. Irwin Ventures invests in early stage companies in the financial services industry.

Recent Developments: For the quarter ended Mar 31 2005, net income decreased 82.2% to $3,625,000 from net income of $20,341,000 in the year-earlier quarter. Net interest income was $60,213,000, up 1.7% from $59,203,000 the year before. Provision for loan losses was $3,291,000 versus $8,146,000 in the prior-year quarter, a decrease of 59.6%. Non-interest income fell 43.9% to $46,220,000, while non-interest expense declined 2.3% to $98,099,000.

Prospects: Results continue to be adversely affected by the decline in Co.'s mortgage banking business. It has been difficult to reduce the size of operations after the refinance boom between 2001 and 2003 in a rapid enough fashion to align with the reduced margins of the past several quarters. Co. has implemented a number of actions intended to return the mortgage banking business to profitability. These steps include a strategic paring of Co.'s production operation to focus on its traditional strengths in first-time and emerging market homebuyers and selective servicing sales. Meanwhile, Co. continues to have strong origination in its home equity sector and steady growth in its commercial portfolios.

Financial Data

(US$ in Thousands)	3 Mos	12/31/2004	12/31/2003	12/31/2002	12/31/2001	12/31/2000	12/31/1999	12/31/1998
Earnings Per Share	1.78	2.32	2.45	1.89	2.00	1.67	1.51	1.38
Cash Flow Per Share	(2.84)	0.55	21.38	(24.11)	(12.84)	(4.87)	21.38	(18.60)
Tang Book Value Per Share	4.09	17.67	15.36	12.98	10.84	8.97	7.55	6.70
Dividends Per Share	0.340	0.320	0.280	0.270	0.260	0.240	0.200	0.160
Dividend Payout %	19.10	13.79	11.43	14.29	13.00	14.37	13.25	11.59
Income Statement								
Interest Income	88,166	344,303	370,984	311,442	268,233	184,530	126,613	122,386
Interest Expense	27,953	92,225	99,099	97,795	121,084	93,534	54,794	59,202
Net Interest Income	60,213	252,078	271,885	213,647	147,149	90,996	71,819	63,184
Provision for Losses	3,291	14,195	47,583	43,996	17,505	5,403	4,443	5,995
Non-Interest Income	46,220	287,050	329,299	257,433	271,391	211,711	204,069	243,729
Non-Interest Expense	98,099	407,235	435,199	340,853	327,420	237,962	214,111	245,436
Income Before Taxes	5,043	117,698	118,402	86,231	73,615	59,342	57,334	55,482
Income Taxes	1,418	47,794	45,585	33,398	28,624	23,676	19,481	20,354
Net Income	3,625	69,904	72,817	53,328	45,516	...	37,853	35,128
Average Shares	28,791	31,278	30,850	29,675	24,173	21,593	21,886	22,139
Balance Sheet								
Net Loans & Leases	3,442,269	3,405,997	3,096,769	2,764,340	2,115,464	1,221,793	724,869	547,103
Total Assets	5,565,481	5,239,341	4,988,359	4,884,722	3,439,795	2,422,429	1,680,847	1,946,179
Total Deposits	3,770,415	3,395,263	2,899,662	2,694,344	2,309,018	1,443,330	870,318	1,009,211
Total Liabilities	5,061,632	4,736,697	4,556,099	4,523,311	3,207,472	2,232,504	1,473,480	1,752,947
Stockholders' Equity	503,849	502,644	432,260	360,555	232,323	189,925	159,296	145,233
Shares Outstanding	28,519	28,452	28,134	27,771	21,305	21,025	21,104	21,672
Statistical Record								
Return on Assets %	0.99	1.36	1.48	1.28	1.55	...	2.09	2.04
Return on Equity %	11.12	14.91	18.37	17.99	21.56	...	24.86	25.71
Net Interest Margin %	68.30	73.21	73.29	68.60	54.86	49.31	56.72	51.63
Efficiency Ratio %	73.00	64.50	62.15	59.92	60.68	60.05	64.75	67.04
Loans to Deposits	0.91	1.00	1.07	1.03	0.92	0.85	0.83	0.54
Price Range	28.65-22.27	35.95-23.20	31.99-16.10	20.36-13.90	27.50-14.51	21.38-13.50	28.31-17.81	36.00-20.13
P/E Ratio	16.10-12.51	15.50-10.00	13.06-6.57	10.77-7.35	13.75-7.25	12.80-8.08	18.75-11.80	26.09-14.58
Average Yield %	1.33	1.18	1.20	1.58	1.22	1.52	0.90	0.60

Address: 500 Washington Street, Columbus, IN 47201
Telephone: 812-376-1909
Web Site: www.irwinfinancial.com

Officers: William I. Miller - Chmn., C.E.O. Thomas D. Washburn - Exec. V.P. **Transfer Agents:** Mellon Investor Services, LLC, Ridgefield Park, NJ

Investor Contact: 812-376-1020
No of Institutions: 103
Shares: 13,609,156 **% Held:** 47.74

JACK HENRY & ASSOCIATES, INC.

Exchange	Symbol	Price	52Wk Range	Yield	P/E
NMS	JKHY	$17.69 (5/31/2005)	21.76-17.15	1.02	22.97

*7 Year Price Score 96.03 *NYSE Composite Index=100 *12 Month Price Score 89.41

Interim Earnings (Per Share)

Qtr.	Sep	Dec	Mar	Jun
2001-02	0.16	0.14	0.15	0.17
2002-03	0.13	0.13	0.14	0.15
2003-04	0.15	0.16	0.18	0.19
2004-05	0.18	0.19	0.21	...

Interim Dividends (Per Share)

Amt	Decl	Ex	Rec	Pay
0.04Q	8/30/2004	9/3/2004	9/8/2004	9/21/2004
0.04Q	10/27/2004	11/12/2004	11/16/2004	11/30/2004
0.045Q	1/31/2005	2/10/2005	2/14/2005	3/1/2005
0.045Q	5/2/2005	5/5/2005	5/9/2005	5/24/2005

Indicated Div: $0.18 (Div. Reinv. Plan)

Valuation Analysis

Forecast P/E	18.22 (6/1/2005)		
Market Cap	$1.6 Billion	Book Value	502.9 Million
Price/Book	3.21	Price/Sales	3.11

Dividend Achiever Status

Rank	62	10 Year Growth Rate	17.28%
Total Years of Dividend Growth			13

Business Summary: IT & Technology (MIC: 10.2 SIC: 373 NAIC: 41512)

Jack Henry & Associates offers a suite of integrated computer systems that provide data processing and management information to banks, credit unions and other financial institutions in the U.S. Co.'s core proprietary applications include: Silverlake System®, typically for banks with total assets up to $30.00 billion; CIF 20/20®, used primarily by banks with total assets up to $300.0 million and Core Director®, which is used by banks employing client-server technology. Also, Co. offers Episys™, used primarily by credit unions with total assets greater than $25.0 million and Cruise™, which is mainly used by credit unions with total assets under $25.0 million.

Recent Developments: For the quarter ended Mar 31 2005, net income increased 19.1% to $19,429 thousand from net income of $16,316 thousand in the year-earlier quarter. Revenues were $134,382 thousand, up 12.3% from $119,708 thousand the year before. Operating income was $31,026 thousand versus an income of $25,499 thousand in the prior-year quarter, an increase of 21.7%. Total direct expense was $77,105 thousand versus $72,389 thousand in the prior-year quarter, an increase of 6.5%. Total indirect expense was $26,251 thousand versus $21,820 thousand in the prior-year quarter, an increase of 20.3%.

Prospects: License and support and service revenues continue to grow at a reasonable level with the only decreased revenue component being hardware. This shift in revenues is having a positive impact on Co.'s margins. Moreover, the acquisitions that Co. has completed over the last 12 months continue to show significant promise, but several of these will take additional time to increase their revenues to generate margins equal to its traditional expectations. Therefore, some of these recent acquisitions will continue to put pressure on Co.'s margins in the short-term.

Financial Data

(US$ in Thousands)	9 Mos	6 Mos	3 Mos	06/30/2004	06/30/2003	06/30/2002	06/30/2001	06/30/2000
Earnings Per Share	0.77	0.74	0.71	0.68	0.55	0.62	0.61	0.40
Cash Flow Per Share	1.25	1.27	1.28	1.26	1.13	1.01	0.84	0.60
Tang Book Value Per Share	2.35	2.25	3.17	3.06	2.78	2.54	2.20	0.48
Dividends Per Share	0.165	0.160	0.155	0.150	0.140	0.130	0.110	0.090
Dividend Payout %	21.43	21.68	21.88	22.06	25.45	20.97	18.03	22.50
Income Statement								
Total Revenue	394,438	260,056	124,096	467,415	404,627	396,657	345,468	225,300
EBITDA	113,658	73,001	35,180	132,346	107,465	114,116	108,345	68,285
Depn & Amortn	28,448	18,817	8,957	33,540	30,194	27,470	21,888	15,473
Income Before Taxes	86,072	54,985	26,679	99,705	77,791	88,473	86,923	51,765
Income Taxes	32,277	20,619	10,005	37,390	28,394	31,408	31,292	17,415
Net Income	53,795	34,366	16,674	62,315	49,397	57,065	55,631	34,018
Average Shares	93,421	92,957	92,485	91,859	89,270	92,367	91,344	85,278
Balance Sheet								
Current Assets	129,670	144,752	227,035	259,058	217,262	179,977	172,050	104,000
Total Assets	660,100	661,588	633,293	653,614	548,575	486,142	433,121	321,082
Current Liabilities	113,471	138,868	135,657	173,240	146,780	112,656	107,018	151,140
Long-Term Obligations	...	...	...	...	...	...	228	320
Total Liabilities	157,226	179,226	174,060	210,696	183,352	145,403	130,617	166,537
Stockholders' Equity	502,874	482,362	459,233	442,918	365,223	340,739	302,504	154,545
Shares Outstanding	91,374	90,865	90,426	90,204	88,156	88,950	88,846	82,715
Statistical Record								
Return on Assets %	11.83	11.26	11.04	10.34	9.55	12.42	14.75	13.68
Return on Equity %	15.43	15.32	15.38	15.38	13.99	17.74	24.34	25.22
EBITDA Margin %	28.82	28.07	28.35	28.31	26.56	28.77	31.36	30.31
Net Margin %	13.64	13.21	13.44	13.33	12.21	14.39	16.10	15.10
Asset Turnover	0.86	0.83	0.82	0.78	0.78	0.86	0.92	0.91
Current Ratio	1.14	1.04	1.67	1.50	1.48	1.60	1.61	0.69
Price Range	21.76-17.26	20.90-17.26	21.97-17.26	21.97-16.53	17.79-8.31	31.51-16.09	31.47-18.88	25.97-8.13
P/E Ratio	28.26-22.42	28.24-23.32	30.94-24.31	32.31-24.31	32.35-15.11	50.82-25.95	51.59-30.94	64.92-20.31
Average Yield %	0.86	0.84	0.81	0.79	1.07	0.56	0.43	0.64

Address: 663 Highway 60, P.O. Box 807, Monett, MO 65708
Telephone: 417-235-6652
Web Site: www.jackhenry.com

Officers: Michael E. Henry - Chmn. John W. Henry - Vice-Chmn., Sr. V.P. **Transfer Agents:** Boston Equiserve, Boston, MA

Investor Contact: 417-235-6652
No of Institutions: 154
Shares: 48,127,356 **% Held:** 52.79

JEFFERSON-PILOT CORP.

Exchange	Symbol	Price	52Wk Range	Yield	P/E
NYS	JP	$50.40 (5/31/2005)	52.64-46.56	3.31	11.97

*7 Year Price Score 96.39 *NYSE Composite Index=100 *12 Month Price Score 96.94

Interim Earnings (Per Share)

Qtr.	Mar	Jun	Sep	Dec
2002	0.92	0.83	0.81	0.47
2003	0.76	0.98	0.88	0.82
2004	0.90	1.02	0.97	1.05
2005	1.17	...	...	...

Interim Dividends (Per Share)

Amt	Decl	Ex	Rec	Pay
0.38Q	8/2/2004	11/17/2004	11/19/2004	12/5/2004
0.38Q	11/1/2004	2/16/2005	2/18/2005	3/5/2005
0.417Q	2/14/2005	5/18/2005	5/20/2005	6/5/2005
0.417Q	5/2/2005	8/17/2005	8/19/2005	9/5/2005

Indicated Div: $1.67 (Div. Reinv. Plan)

Valuation Analysis

Forecast P/E	12.18 (6/1/2005)		
Market Cap	$6.9 Billion	Book Value	3.8 Billion
Price/Book	1.79	Price/Sales	1.65

Dividend Achiever Status

Rank	147	10 Year Growth Rate	11.44%
Total Years of Dividend Growth			37

Business Summary: Insurance (MIC: 8.2 SIC: 311 NAIC: 24113)

Jefferson-Pilot is a holding company. Life insurance, annuities, disability and dental insurance are currently marketed to individuals and businesses in the U.S. through Co.'s principal life insurance subsidiaries. Jefferson Pilot Securities Corp. is a registered non-clearing broker/dealer that sells variable life and annuity products and other investment products, including mutual funds, stocks, bonds and other investments. Broadcasting operations are conducted by Jefferson-Pilot Communications Company and consist of radio and television broadcasting, through facilities located in strategically selected markets in the Southeastern and Western U.S., and sports program production.

Recent Developments: For the quarter ended Mar 31 2005, net income increased 29.8% to $161,000 thousand from net income of $124,000 thousand in the year-earlier quarter. Revenues were $1,037,000 thousand, up 5.3% from $985,000 thousand the year before. Net premiums earned were $331,000 thousand versus $280,000 thousand in the prior-year quarter, an increase of 18.2%.

Prospects: Results are benefiting from solid sales of individual life insurance in Co.'s Individual Products segment. Meanwhile, Co.'s communications earnings are being positively affected by the strength of the Sports and Entertainment business. Co.'s overall earnings growth is being driven by its focus on fundamentals such as claims management in its group insurance business, both in the acquired Canada life business and its historical business. In addition, Co. has taken actions in its individual life line to appropriately balance profitability and policyholder value. Co.'s distribution expansion initiatives in the individual life and group businesses are driving strong sales in both lines.

Financial Data (US$ in Thousands)	3 Mos	12/31/2004	12/31/2003	12/31/2002	12/31/2001	12/31/2000	12/31/1999	12/31/1998
Earnings Per Share	4.21	3.92	3.44	3.04	3.34	3.29	2.95	2.61
Cash Flow Per Share	4.63	7.16	3.79	2.91	4.86	3.23	3.05	2.73
Tang Book Value Per Share	25.89	26.47	24.85	22.61	20.53	18.38	15.80	17.77
Dividends Per Share	1.520	1.470	1.293	1.183	1.072	0.960	0.857	0.768
Dividend Payout %	36.10	37.50	37.57	38.90	32.09	29.21	29.07	29.45
Income Statement								
Premium Income	331,000	1,293,000	951,000	1,564,000	1,424,000	1,365,000	903,000	1,049,000
Total Revenue	1,037,000	4,102,000	3,573,000	3,480,000	3,330,000	3,238,000	2,561,000	2,610,000
Benefits & Claims	537,000	2,287,000	2,005,000	1,999,000	1,796,000	1,660,000	1,208,000	1,307,000
Income Before Taxes	243,000	840,000	738,000	710,000	800,000	814,000	751,000	670,000
Income Taxes	82,000	277,000	246,000	235,000	263,000	277,000	256,000	226,000
Net Income	161,000	546,000	492,000	475,000	538,000	537,000	495,000	444,000
Average Shares	136,600	139,213	142,867	148,222	153,411	155,922	159,348	160,578
Balance Sheet								
Total Assets	35,151,000	35,105,000	32,696,000	30,609,000	28,996,000	27,321,000	26,446,000	24,338,000
Total Liabilities	31,320,000	31,171,000	28,890,000	26,769,000	25,305,000	23,862,000	23,393,000	20,983,000
Stockholders' Equity	3,831,000	3,934,000	3,806,000	3,540,000	3,391,000	3,159,000	2,753,000	3,052,000
Shares Outstanding	135,938	136,819	140,610	142,799	150,007	154,305	155,016	158,844
Statistical Record								
Return on Assets %	1.68	1.61	1.55	1.59	1.91	1.99	1.95	1.87
Return on Equity %	14.95	14.07	13.40	13.71	16.43	18.12	17.05	15.35
Loss Ratio %	162.24	176.88	210.83	127.81	126.12	121.61	133.78	124.59
Net Margin %	15.53	13.31	13.77	13.65	16.16	16.58	19.33	17.01
Price Range	55.89-46.56	55.89-46.56	50.65-36.20	52.60-36.53	48.95-39.60	50.29-33.63	52.92-41.21	52.21-32.89
P/E Ratio	13.28-11.06	14.26-11.88	14.72-10.52	17.30-12.02	14.66-11.86	15.29-10.22	17.94-13.97	20.00-12.60
Average Yield %	3.05	2.91	3.03	2.65	2.37	2.28	1.85	1.94

Address: 100 North Greene Street, Greensboro, NC 27401 **Telephone:** 336-691-3000 **Web Site:** www.jpfinancial.com	**Officers:** Dennis R. Glass - Pres., C.E.O. Theresa M. Stone - Exec. V.P., C.F.O. **Transfer Agents:** Wachovia Bank, Charlotte, NC	**Investor Contact:** 336-691-3379 **No of Institutions:** 343 **Shares:** 71,519,616 **% Held:** 52.36

JOHNSON CONTROLS INC

Exchange	Symbol	Price	52Wk Range	Yield	P/E
NYS	JCI	$56.66 (5/31/2005)	63.83-51.27	1.76	15.27

***7 Year Price Score 126.57** *NYSE Composite Index=100 ***12 Month Price Score 93.30**

Interim Earnings (Per Share)

Qtr.	Dec	Mar	Jun	Sep
2001-02	0.64	0.60	0.93	1.01
2002-03	0.74	0.70	1.00	1.16
2003-04	0.86	0.82	1.15	1.41
2004-05	0.87	0.28	...	...

Interim Dividends (Per Share)

Amt	Decl	Ex	Rec	Pay
0.225Q	7/28/2004	9/8/2004	9/10/2004	9/30/2004
0.25Q	11/17/2004	12/13/2004	12/15/2004	1/3/2005
0.25Q	1/26/2005	3/9/2005	3/11/2005	3/31/2005
0.25Q	5/25/2005	6/8/2005	6/10/2005	6/30/2005

Indicated Div: $1.00 (Div. Reinv. Plan)

Valuation Analysis

Forecast P/E	12.49 (6/2/2005)		
Market Cap	$10.9 Billion	Book Value	5.7 Billion
Price/Book	1.91	Price/Sales	0.39

Dividend Achiever Status

Rank	179	**10 Year Growth Rate**	9.60%
Total Years of Dividend Growth			29

Business Summary: Miscellaneous Business Services (MIC: 12.8 SIC: 531 NAIC: 61790)

Johnson Controls is a global company engaged in the supply of automotive systems and facility management and control products and systems and services. The Controls Group is a major worldwide supplier of installed control systems and technical and facility management services designed to improve the comfort, fire-safety, security, productivity, energy efficiency, and cost-effectiveness of non-residential buildings. The Automotive Group designs and manufactures products and systems for passenger cars and light trucks, including vans, pick-up trucks and sport/crossover utility vehicles.

Recent Developments: For the three months ended Mar 31 2005, income from continuing operations decreased 63.5% to $53,800 thousand from income of $147,500 thousand in the year-earlier quarter. Net income increased 28.4% to $202,500 thousand from net income of $157,700 thousand in the year-earlier quarter. Revenues were $6,289,800 thousand, up 13.3% from $5,549,200 thousand the year before. Gross profit rose 4.0% to $850,900 thousand from $817,800 thousand in 2004. Operating income was $60,000 thousand versus $244,600 thousand in the prior-year quarter, a decrease of 75.5%.

Prospects: Co. increased its full-year 2005 guidance for consolidated sales growth to 10.0% to 12.0% from 8.0% to 10.0% above the pro forma 2004 amount of $25.40 billion, primarily due to an assumption of a euro/dollar exchange rate of $1.30. The automotive and controls groups are each expected to achieve revenue growth in the same 10.0% to 12.0% range. Full year operating income before special items is projected to rise 10.0% to 12.0% to a range of $1.30 billion to $1.40 billion. On a GAAP basis, including an expected $210.0 million restructuring charge, operating income is projected to be $1.10 billion to $1.20 billion.

Financial Data

(US$ in Thousands)	6 Mos	3 Mos	09/30/2004	09/30/2003	09/30/2002	09/30/2001	09/30/2000	09/30/1999
Earnings Per Share	4.47	4.24	4.24	3.60	3.17	2.56	2.54	2.24
Cash Flow Per Share	6.79	7.71	7.91	4.30	5.59	5.60	4.34	5.95
Tang Book Value Per Share	8.95	7.98	5.81	3.80	2.24	3.51	1.82	0.22
Dividends Per Share	0.950	0.925	0.900	0.720	0.660	0.620	0.560	0.500
Dividend Payout %	21.25	21.81	21.23	20.00	20.79	24.27	22.00	22.32
Income Statement								
Total Revenue	13,921,000	6,975,500	26,553,400	22,646,000	20,103,400	18,427,200	17,154,600	16,139,400
EBITDA	643,000	421,100	1,925,300	1,718,800	1,632,800	1,493,000	1,429,000	1,351,500
Depn & Amortn	332,000	164,500	616,400	557,800	516,400	515,900	461,800	445,600
Income Before Taxes	256,900	230,100	1,212,100	1,057,500	1,006,000	867,100	855,700	769,900
Income Taxes	13,800	48,600	315,700	327,800	347,600	335,500	338,900	311,700
Net Income	370,900	168,400	817,500	682,900	600,500	478,300	472,400	419,600
Average Shares	194,200	193,600	192,600	189,200	188,200	186,000	183,800	184,200
Balance Sheet								
Current Assets	6,907,600	6,856,100	6,376,800	5,620,300	4,946,200	4,544,000	4,277,200	3,848,500
Total Assets	15,518,300	15,676,600	15,090,800	13,127,300	11,165,300	9,911,500	9,428,000	8,614,200
Current Liabilities	6,331,200	6,623,400	6,601,600	5,584,100	4,806,200	4,579,700	4,510,000	4,266,600
Long-Term Obligations	1,664,600	1,668,500	1,630,600	1,776,600	1,826,600	1,394,800	1,315,300	1,283,300
Total Liabilities	9,826,700	10,095,000	9,884,500	8,866,000	7,665,600	6,926,100	6,851,900	6,344,200
Stockholders' Equity	5,691,600	5,581,600	5,206,300	4,261,300	3,499,700	2,985,400	2,576,100	2,270,000
Shares Outstanding	192,037	191,174	190,320	180,310	177,760	174,997	171,978	170,790
Statistical Record								
Return on Assets %	5.85	5.59	5.78	5.62	5.70	4.95	5.22	5.07
Return on Equity %	16.56	16.13	17.22	17.60	18.52	17.20	19.44	19.93
EBITDA Margin %	4.62	6.04	7.25	7.59	8.12	8.10	8.33	8.37
Net Margin %	2.66	2.41	3.08	3.02	2.99	2.60	2.75	2.60
Asset Turnover	1.86	1.84	1.88	1.86	1.91	1.91	1.90	1.95
Current Ratio	1.09	1.04	0.97	1.01	1.03	0.99	0.95	0.90
Debt to Equity	0.29	0.30	0.31	0.42	0.52	0.47	0.51	0.57
Price Range	63.83-51.16	63.83-51.16	60.90-47.30	50.34-35.26	46.52-32.75	40.77-23.84	35.19-23.50	37.56-20.97
P/E Ratio	14.28-11.45	15.05-12.07	14.36-11.16	13.98-9.79	14.68-10.33	15.93-9.31	13.85-9.25	16.77-9.36
Average Yield %	1.66	1.62	1.62	1.71	1.61	1.88	1.99	1.59

Address: 5757 North Green Bay Avenue, P.O. Box 591, Milwaukee, WI 53201
Telephone: 414-524-1200
Web Site: www.johnsoncontrols.com

Officers: John M. Barth - Chmn., Pres., C.E.O. Stephen A. Roell - Vice-Chmn., Exec. V.P. **Transfer Agents:** Firstar Trust Company, Milwaukee, WI

Investor Contact: 414-524-2363
No of Institutions: 422
Shares: 122,556,016 **% Held:** 64.11

JOHNSON & JOHNSON

Exchange	Symbol	Price	52Wk Range	Yield	P/E
NYS	JNJ	$67.10 (5/31/2005)	69.40-54.49	1.97	22.90

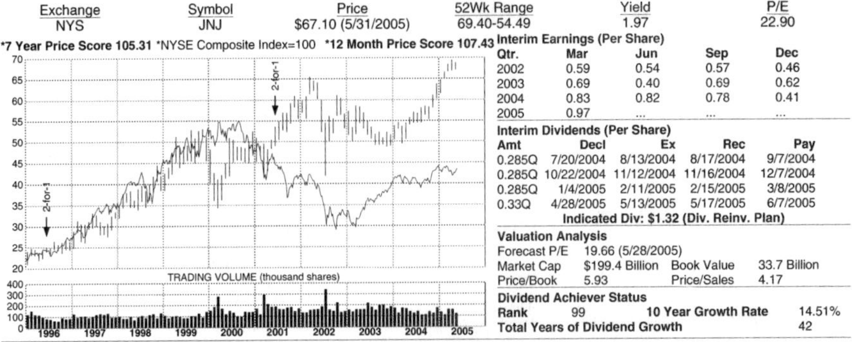

Interim Earnings (Per Share)

Qtr.	Mar	Jun	Sep	Dec
2002	0.59	0.54	0.57	0.46
2003	0.69	0.40	0.69	0.62
2004	0.83	0.82	0.78	0.41
2005	0.97	...	...	...

Interim Dividends (Per Share)

Amt	Decl	Ex	Rec	Pay
0.285Q	7/20/2004	8/13/2004	8/17/2004	9/7/2004
0.285Q	10/22/2004	11/12/2004	11/16/2004	12/7/2004
0.285Q	1/4/2005	2/11/2005	2/15/2005	3/8/2005
0.33Q	4/28/2005	5/13/2005	5/17/2005	6/7/2005

Indicated Div: $1.32 (Div. Reinv. Plan)

Valuation Analysis

Forecast P/E	19.66 (5/28/2005)		
Market Cap	$199.4 Billion	Book Value	33.7 Billion
Price/Book	5.93	Price/Sales	4.17

Dividend Achiever Status

Rank	99	**10 Year Growth Rate**	14.51%
Total Years of Dividend Growth			42

Business Summary: Pharmaceuticals (MIC: 9.1 SIC: 834 NAIC: 25412)

Johnson & Johnson is engaged in the manufacture and sale of a broad range of products in the health care field. The Pharmaceutical segment includes prescription drugs in the antifungal, anti-infective, cardiovascular, contraceptive, dermatology, gastrointestinal, hematology, immunology, neurology, oncology, pain management, psychotropic and urology fields. The Medical Devices and Diagnostics segment includes products used by or under the direction of health care professionals. The Consumer segment manufactures and markets products used in the baby and child care, skin care, oral and wound care and women's health care fields, as well over-the-counter pharmaceutical and nutritional products.

Recent Developments: For the quarter ended Apr 3 2005, net income increased 17.4% to $2,927 million from net income of $2,493 million in the year-earlier quarter. Revenues were $12,832 million, up 11.0% from $11,559 million the year before. Total direct expense was $3,482 million versus $3,367 million in the prior-year quarter, an increase of 3.4%. Total indirect expense was $5,390 million versus $4,735 million in the prior-year quarter, an increase of 13.8%.

Prospects: On Apr 19 2005, Co. announced a definitive agreement under which Ortho-McNeil Pharmaceutical, a subsidiary of Co., would acquire Peninsula Pharmaceuticals, a privately-held biopharmaceutical company focused on developing and commercializing antibiotics to treat life-threatening infections. The cash-for-stock transaction is valued at about $245.0 million and is expected to close in the second quarter. Separately, in Apr 2005, Co. announced the completion of its acquisition of TransForm Pharmaceuticals, which specializes in the discovery of superior formulations and novel crystalline forms of drug molecules.

Financial Data

(US$ in Thousands)	3 Mos	01/02/2005	12/28/2003	12/29/2002	12/30/2001	12/31/2000	01/02/2000	01/03/1999
Earnings Per Share	2.93	2.84	2.40	2.16	1.84	1.70	1.47	1.12
Cash Flow Per Share	3.70	3.69	3.58	2.73	2.93	2.37	2.05	1.79
Tang Book Value Per Share	7.35	6.72	5.17	4.53	4.97	4.15	3.11	2.37
Dividends Per Share	1.140	1.095	0.925	0.795	0.700	0.620	0.545	0.485
Dividend Payout %	38.96	38.56	38.54	36.81	38.04	36.47	37.07	43.50
Income Statement								
Total Revenue	12,832,000	47,348,000	41,862,000	36,298,000	33,004,000	29,139,000	27,471,000	23,657,000
EBITDA	4,577,000	14,933,000	12,192,000	10,900,000	9,200,000	7,904,000	7,148,000	5,363,000
Depn & Amortn	515,000	2,103,000	1,854,000	1,705,000	1,605,000	1,515,000	1,444,000	1,246,000
Income Before Taxes	4,062,000	12,838,000	10,308,000	9,291,000	7,898,000	6,622,000	5,753,000	4,269,000
Income Taxes	1,135,000	4,329,000	3,111,000	2,694,000	2,230,000	1,822,000	1,586,000	1,210,000
Net Income	2,927,000	8,509,000	7,197,000	6,597,000	5,668,000	4,800,000	4,167,000	3,059,000
Average Shares	3,023,700	3,003,500	3,008,100	3,054,100	3,099,300	2,834,800	2,836,400	2,743,200
Balance Sheet								
Current Assets	28,766,000	27,320,000	22,995,000	19,266,000	18,473,000	15,450,000	13,200,000	11,132,000
Total Assets	54,446,000	53,317,000	48,263,000	40,556,000	38,488,000	31,321,000	29,163,000	26,211,000
Current Liabilities	12,981,000	13,927,000	13,448,000	11,449,000	8,044,000	7,140,000	7,454,000	8,162,000
Long-Term Obligations	2,459,000	2,565,000	2,955,000	2,022,000	2,217,000	2,037,000	2,450,000	1,269,000
Total Liabilities	20,792,000	21,504,000	21,394,000	17,859,000	14,255,000	12,513,000	12,950,000	12,621,000
Stockholders' Equity	33,654,000	31,813,000	26,869,000	22,697,000	24,233,000	18,808,000	16,213,000	13,590,000
Shares Outstanding	2,972,386	2,971,023	2,967,973	2,968,295	3,047,215	2,781,874	2,779,366	2,688,000
Statistical Record								
Return on Assets %	17.00	16.48	16.25	16.74	16.28	15.92	15.09	12.63
Return on Equity %	28.26	28.53	29.12	28.19	26.41	27.49	28.04	23.20
EBITDA Margin %	35.67	31.54	29.12	30.03	27.88	27.13	26.02	22.67
Net Margin %	22.81	17.97	17.19	18.17	17.17	16.47	15.17	12.93
Asset Turnover	0.93	0.92	0.95	0.92	0.95	0.97	0.99	0.98
Current Ratio	2.22	1.96	1.71	1.68	2.30	2.16	1.77	1.36
Debt to Equity	0.07	0.08	0.11	0.09	0.09	0.11	0.15	0.09
Price Range	68.44-50.87	63.76-49.50	58.67-48.73	65.49-41.85	60.97-41.63	52.53-34.25	53.06-38.50	44.50-32.00
P/E Ratio	23.36-17.36	22.45-17.43	24.45-20.30	30.32-19.38	33.14-22.62	30.90-20.15	36.10-26.19	39.73-28.57
Average Yield %	1.93	1.96	1.76	1.38	1.35	1.39	1.16	1.29

Address: One Johnson & Johnson Plaza, New Brunswick, NJ 08933
Telephone: 732-524-0400
Web Site: www.jnj.com

Officers: William C. Weldon - Chmn., C.E.O. Robert J. Darretta - Vice-Chmn., C.F.O. **Transfer Agents:** EquiServe Trust Company, N.A., Providence, RI

Investor Contact: 800-950-5089
No of Institutions: 1222
Shares: 1,860,316,544 **% Held:** 62.56

KEYCORP (NEW)

Exchange	Symbol	Price	52Wk Range	Yield	P/E
NYS	KEY	$32.76 (5/31/2005)	34.46-29.09	3.97	13.94

*7 Year Price Score 103.98 *NYSE Composite Index=100 *12 Month Price Score 98.24

Interim Earnings (Per Share)

Qtr.	Mar	Jun	Sep	Dec
2002	0.56	0.57	0.57	0.58
2003	0.51	0.53	0.53	0.55
2004	0.59	0.58	0.61	0.52
2005	0.64	...	...	...

Interim Dividends (Per Share)

Amt	Decl	Ex	Rec	Pay
0.31Q	7/23/2004	8/27/2004	8/31/2004	9/15/2004
0.31Q	11/18/2004	11/26/2004	11/30/2004	12/13/2004
0.325Q	1/20/2005	2/25/2005	3/1/2005	3/15/2005
0.325Q	5/5/2005	5/26/2005	5/31/2005	6/15/2005

Indicated Div: $1.30 (Div. Reinv. Plan)

Valuation Analysis

Forecast P/E	12.60 (6/2/2005)		
Market Cap	$13.3 Billion	Book Value	7.2 Billion
Price/Book	1.86	Price/Sales	2.33

Dividend Achiever Status

Rank	235	10 Year Growth Rate	6.84%
Total Years of Dividend Growth			25

Business Summary: Commercial Banking (MIC: 8.1 SIC: 021 NAIC: 22110)

KeyCorp is a multi-line financial services company, with assets of $90.70 billion as of Dec 31 2004. Co. provides investment management, retail and commercial banking, consumer finance, and investment banking products and services to individuals and companies throughout the United States and, for certain businesses, internationally. As of Dec 31 2004, Co. operates nationwide through 935 KeyCenters and offices, a network of 2,194 ATMs, telephone banking centers, and a Web site named Key.com that provides account access and financial products 24 hours a day.

Recent Developments: For the three months ended Mar 31 2005, net income increased 5.6% to $264,000 thousand from net income of $250,000 thousand a year earlier. Net interest income was $694,000 thousand, up 5.0% from $661,000 thousand the year before. Provision for loan losses was $44,000 thousand versus $81,000 thousand in the prior year, a decrease of 45.7%. Non-interest income climbed 5.3% to $454,000 thousand, while non-interest expense advanced 10.9% to $731,000 thousand.

Prospects: Solid revenue growth and positive trends in asset quality continue to drive Co.'s improved operating performance. For example, Co.'s taxable-equivalent revenue is benefiting from stronger demand for commercial loans and growth in fee income. Also, improvements in Co.'s asset quality is being supported by a decrease in non-performing loans that are at the lowest level in the last ten years. Meanwhile, the stronger economy continues to contribute to these positive changes and they reflect strategic business mix changes being made to improve Co.'s risk profile. Going forward, Co. expects earnings to range from $2.55 to $2.65 per share for full-year 2005.

Financial Data

(US$ in Thousands)	3 Mos	12/31/2004	12/31/2003	12/31/2002	12/31/2001	12/31/2000	12/31/1999	12/31/1998
Earnings Per Share	2.35	2.30	2.12	2.27	0.31	2.30	2.45	2.23
Cash Flow Per Share	4.34	3.95	2.97	3.43	3.99	3.65	4.14	4.08
Tang Book Value Per Share	14.03	13.91	13.88	13.35	11.85	12.42	11.14	10.30
Dividends Per Share	1.255	1.240	1.220	1.200	1.180	1.120	1.040	0.940
Dividend Payout %	53.40	53.91	57.55	52.86	380.65	48.70	42.45	42.15
Income Statement								
Interest Income	1,073,000	3,818,000	3,970,000	4,366,000	5,627,000	6,277,000	5,695,000	5,525,000
Interest Expense	379,000	1,181,000	1,245,000	1,617,000	2,802,000	3,547,000	2,908,000	2,841,000
Net Interest Income	694,000	2,637,000	2,725,000	2,749,000	2,825,000	2,730,000	2,787,000	2,684,000
Provision for Losses	44,000	185,000	501,000	553,000	1,350,000	490,000	348,000	297,000
Non-Interest Income	454,000	1,746,000	1,760,000	1,769,000	1,725,000	2,194,000	2,294,000	1,575,000
Non-Interest Expense	731,000	2,810,000	2,742,000	2,653,000	2,941,000	2,917,000	3,049,000	2,483,000
Income Before Taxes	373,000	1,388,000	1,242,000	1,312,000	259,000	1,517,000	1,684,000	1,479,000
Income Taxes	109,000	434,000	339,000	336,000	102,000	515,000	577,000	483,000
Net Income	264,000	954,000	903,000	976,000	132,000	1,002,000	1,107,000	996,000
Average Shares	413,762	415,430	426,157	430,703	429,573	435,573	452,363	447,437
Balance Sheet								
Net Loans & Leases	67,204,000	67,326,000	61,305,000	61,005,000	61,632,000	65,904,000	63,292,000	61,112,000
Total Assets	90,263,000	90,739,000	84,487,000	85,202,000	80,938,000	87,270,000	83,395,000	80,020,000
Total Deposits	57,127,000	57,842,000	50,858,000	49,346,000	44,795,000	48,649,000	43,233,000	42,583,000
Total Liabilities	83,101,000	83,622,000	77,518,000	78,367,000	74,783,000	80,647,000	77,006,000	73,853,000
Stockholders' Equity	7,162,000	7,117,000	6,969,000	6,835,000	6,155,000	6,623,000	6,389,000	6,167,000
Shares Outstanding	407,297	407,569	416,494	423,943	424,005	423,254	443,427	452,452
Statistical Record								
Return on Assets %	1.11	1.09	1.06	1.17	0.16	1.17	1.35	1.30
Return on Equity %	13.67	13.51	13.08	15.03	2.07	15.36	17.63	17.55
Net Interest Margin %	64.68	69.07	68.64	62.96	50.20	43.49	48.94	48.58
Efficiency Ratio %	47.87	50.50	47.85	43.24	40.00	34.44	38.16	34.97
Loans to Deposits	1.18	1.16	1.21	1.24	1.38	1.35	1.46	1.44
Price Range	34.46-28.43	34.46-28.43	29.32-22.52	29.00-21.30	28.44-20.75	28.25-15.69	36.94-21.19	43.13-24.94
P/E Ratio	14.66-12.10	14.98-12.36	13.83-10.62	12.78-9.38	91.73-66.94	12.28-6.82	15.08-8.65	19.34-11.18
Average Yield %	3.96	3.97	4.71	4.66	4.75	5.36	3.48	2.77

Address: 127 Public Square, Cleveland, OH 44114-1306
Telephone: 216-689-6300
Web Site: www.key.com

Officers: Henry L. Meyer III - Chmn., Pres., C.E.O. Thomas C. Stevens - Vice-Chmn., Chief Admin. Officer, Sec. **Transfer Agents:** Computershare Investor Services, Chicago, IL

Investor Contact: 216-689-4520
No of Institutions: 411
Shares: 199,256,560 % **Held:** 49.04

KIMBERLY-CLARK CORP.

Exchange	Symbol	Price	52Wk Range	Yield	P/E
NYS	KMB	$64.33 (5/31/2005)	68.15-58.04	2.80	17.72

***7 Year Price Score 99.16** *NYSE Composite Index=100 ***12 Month Price Score 96.65**

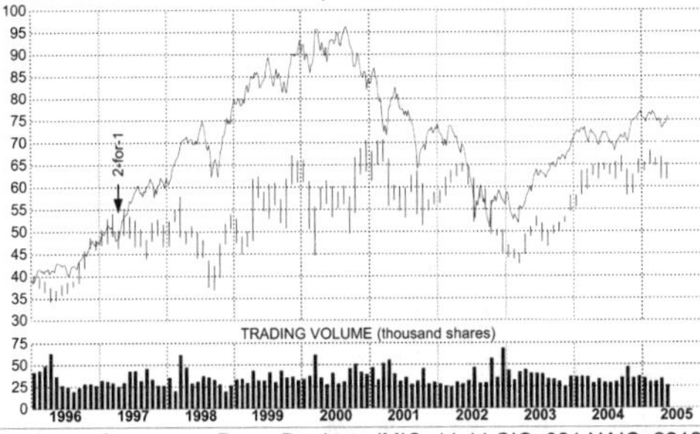

Interim Earnings (Per Share)

Qtr.	Mar	Jun	Sep	Dec
2002	0.84	0.81	0.85	0.72
2003	0.78	0.82	0.83	0.91
2004	0.91	0.90	0.89	0.91
2005	0.93	...	...	...

Interim Dividends (Per Share)

Amt	Decl	Ex	Rec	Pay
0.40Q	8/2/2004	9/8/2004	9/10/2004	10/4/2004
0.40Q	11/16/2004	12/8/2004	12/10/2004	1/4/2005
0.45Q	2/23/2005	3/2/2005	3/4/2005	4/4/2005
0.45Q	4/28/2005	6/8/2005	6/10/2005	7/5/2005

Indicated Div: $1.80 (Div. Reinv. Plan)

Valuation Analysis

Forecast P/E 16.93 (6/2/2005)

Market Cap $30.8 Billion Book Value N/A

Price/Book N/A Price/Sales N/A

Dividend Achiever Status

Rank 250 **10 Year Growth Rate** 5.82%

Total Years of Dividend Growth 30

Business Summary: Paper Products (MIC: 11.11 SIC: 621 NAIC: 22121)

Kimberly-Clark is engaged in the manufacturing and marketing of health and hygiene products. The Personal Care segment manufactures disposable diapers, training and youth pants and swimpants and feminine and incontinence care products. The Consumer Tissue segment manufactures facial and bathroom tissue, paper towels and napkins for household use. The Business-to-Business segment manufactures facial and bathroom tissue, paper towels, napkins, wipers, drapes, infection control products, and sterilization wrap for away-from-home use. Brands include Huggies, Pull-Ups, Little Swimmers, GoodNites, Kotex, Lightdays, Depend, Kleenex, Scott, Cottonelle, Viva, Scottex, Kimberly-Clark and Kimwipes.

Recent Developments: For the three months ended Mar 31 2005, net income totaled $450,100 thousand, up 1.4% compared with income of $443,800 thousand, before a $15,500 thousand gain from discontinued operations, in the corresponding quarter a year earlier. Revenues were $3,905,800 thousand, up 5.2% from $3,711,500 thousand the year before. Gross profit increased 4.1% to $1,306,600 thousand, or 33.5% of revenues, compared with $1,255,700 thousand, or 33.8% of revenues, the previous year. Operating income was $637,600 thousand versus $623,400 thousand in the prior year, an increase of 2.3%.

Prospects: Based on Co.'s results in the first quarter and its plans for the balance of the 2005, it remains comfortable with its previous guidance for 2005. Specifically, Co. is targeting sales growth of 3.0% to 5.0%, consistent with its long-term objective. Co. expects the gain to come largely from volume improvements, driven by strong innovation and marketing programs. Co. expects its top-line growth and continued success in reducing costs will help it achieve operating profit growth of 3.0% to 6.0% despite inflationary cost pressures. Co. expects 2005 earnings of $3.70 to $3.85 per share, representing mid- to high single-digit growth from a year ago.

Financial Data

(US$ in Thousands)	3 Mos	12/31/2004	12/31/2003	12/31/2002	12/31/2001	12/31/2000	12/31/1999	12/31/1998
Earnings Per Share	...	3.61	3.33	3.22	3.02	3.31	3.09	2.11
Cash Flow Per Share	...	5.49	5.15	4.69	4.26	3.94	3.98	3.62
Tang Book Value Per Share	...	8.13	8.21	6.65	7.10	7.04	7.12	6.13
Dividends Per Share	...	1.600	1.360	1.200	1.120	1.080	1.040	1.000
Dividend Payout %	...	44.32	40.84	37.27	37.09	32.63	33.66	47.39
Income Statement								
Total Revenue	...	15,083,200	14,348,000	13,566,300	14,524,400	13,982,000	13,006,800	12,297,800
EBITDA	...	3,148,300	3,065,700	3,182,400	3,077,800	3,307,200	3,063,400	2,379,900
Depn & Amortn	...	800,300	758,800	718,600	739,600	673,400	628,000	579,400
Income Before Taxes	...	2,203,400	2,157,000	2,297,400	2,164,400	2,436,000	2,251,700	1,626,100
Income Taxes	...	483,900	514,200	666,600	645,700	758,500	730,200	561,900
Net Income	...	1,800,200	1,694,200	1,674,600	1,609,900	1,800,600	1,668,100	1,165,800
Average Shares	...	499,200	508,600	520,000	533,200	543,800	540,100	553,100
Balance Sheet								
Current Assets	...	4,961,900	4,438,100	4,273,900	3,922,200	3,789,900	3,561,800	3,366,900
Total Assets	...	17,018,000	16,779,900	15,585,800	15,007,600	14,479,800	12,815,500	11,510,300
Current Liabilities	...	4,537,200	3,918,700	4,038,300	4,168,300	4,573,900	3,845,800	3,790,700
Long-Term Obligations	...	2,298,000	2,733,700	2,844,000	2,424,000	2,000,600	1,926,600	2,068,200
Total Liabilities	...	9,665,600	9,445,700	9,382,000	8,822,300	8,712,500	7,722,400	7,623,100
Stockholders' Equity	...	6,629,500	6,766,300	5,650,300	5,646,900	5,767,300	5,093,100	3,887,200
Shares Outstanding	...	482,903	501,589	510,800	521,000	533,400	540,600	538,300
Statistical Record								
Return on Assets %	...	10.62	10.47	10.95	10.92	13.16	13.71	10.24
Return on Equity %	...	26.80	27.29	29.65	28.21	33.07	37.15	29.10
EBITDA Margin %	...	20.87	21.37	23.46	21.19	23.65	23.55	19.35
Net Margin %	...	11.94	11.81	12.34	11.08	12.88	12.82	9.48
Asset Turnover	...	0.89	0.89	0.89	0.99	1.02	1.07	1.08
Current Ratio	...	1.09	1.13	1.06	0.94	0.83	0.93	0.89
Debt to Equity	...	0.35	0.40	0.50	0.43	0.35	0.38	0.53
Price Range	68.15-58.04	66.98-55.52	58.10-42.66	65.34-45.28	70.58-51.36	70.59-44.61	67.10-44.98	57.95-36.75
P/E Ratio	...	18.56-15.38	17.45-12.81	20.29-14.06	23.37-17.01	21.33-13.48	21.72-14.56	27.46-17.42
Average Yield %	...	2.56	2.76	2.08	1.86	1.85	1.87	2.10

Address: P.O. Box 619100, Dallas, TX 75261-9100
Telephone: 972-281-1200
Web Site: www.kimberly-clark.com

Officers: Thomas J. Falk - Chmn., Pres., C.E.O. Robert E. Abernathy - Group Pres. **Transfer Agents:** EquiServe Trust Company, N.A., Providence, RI

Investor Contact: 800-639-1352
No of Institutions: 689
Shares: 341,758,240 **% Held:** 71.01

KIMCO REALTY CORP.

Exchange	Symbol	Price	52Wk Range	Yield	P/E
NYS	KIM	$57.76 (5/31/2005)	58.94-44.71	4.22	22.05

*7 Year Price Score 136.72 *NYSE Composite Index=100 *12 Month Price Score 102.30

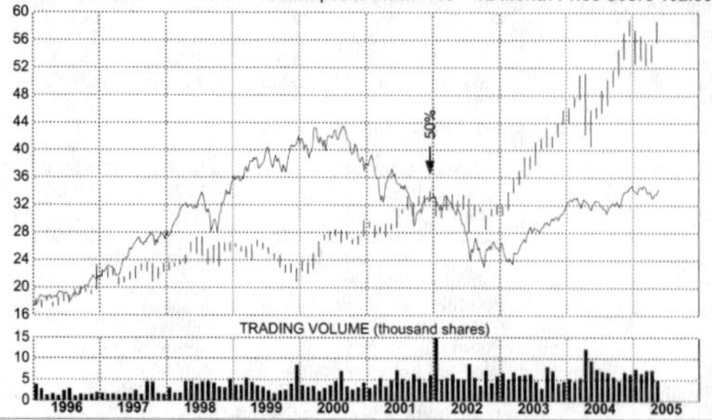

TRADING VOLUME (thousand shares)

Interim Earnings (Per Share)

Qtr.	Mar	Jun	Sep	Dec
2002	0.53	0.54	0.53	0.56
2003	0.63	0.46	0.80	0.72
2004	0.61	0.61	0.67	0.63
2005	0.71	...	...	...

Interim Dividends (Per Share)

Amt	Decl	Ex	Rec	Pay
0.57Q	6/15/2004	7/1/2004	7/6/2004	7/15/2004
0.57Q	9/15/2004	10/1/2004	10/5/2004	10/15/2004
0.61Q	10/26/2004	12/30/2004	1/3/2005	1/18/2005
0.61Q	3/15/2005	4/1/2005	4/5/2005	4/15/2005

Indicated Div: $2.44 (Div. Reinv. Plan)

Valuation Analysis

Forecast P/E	15.20 (6/2/2005)		
Market Cap	$6.5 Billion	Book Value	2.3 Billion
Price/Book	2.86	Price/Sales	12.78

Dividend Achiever Status

Rank	174	10 Year Growth Rate	9.88%
Total Years of Dividend Growth			12

Business Summary: Property, Real Estate & Development (MIC: 8.3 SIC: 798 NAIC: 25930)

Kimco Realty, a self-administered real estate investment trust, is an owner and operator of neighborhood and community shopping centers. As of Feb 4 2005, Co.'s portfolio was comprised of 773 property interests including 696 operating properties mainly consisting of neighborhood and community shopping centers, 32 retail store leases, 35 ground-up development projects and 10 parcels of undeveloped land totaling about 113.4 million square feet of leasable space located in 42 states, Canada and Mexico. Co.'s ownership interests in real estate consist of its consolidated portfolio, portfolios where it owns an economic interest, and other properties or portfolios where it also retains management.

Recent Developments: For the three months ended Mar 31 2005, Co. reported income from continuing operations of $82,685 thousand, up 12.0% compared with income of $73,858 thousand a year earlier. Net income increased 21.6% to $86,780 thousand from net income of $71,389 thousand a year earlier. Results for 2005 and 2004 included gains of $5,219 thousand and $3,899 thousand, respectively, from the sale of development properties. Revenues from rental properties was $132,043 thousand, down 5.1% from $139,137 thousand the year before.

Prospects: Citing its recent operating results, on Apr 25 2005 Co. raised the lower end of its range of guidance for funds from operations (FFO) from $3.77 to $3.78. Co. now anticipates a range for FFO per share of $3.78 to $3.83 for the year ending Dec 31 2005. Meanwhile, Co. has accelerated its redevelopment plans on a number of properties. Co. has 30 existing major capital projects, including three developments, underway in the parent portfolio representing about $230.0 million of new investment and 36 projects that are in preliminary stages. In its joint venture programs, 15 projects are in active redevelopment totaling about $45.0 million of new investment and 22 projects in preliminary stages.

Financial Data

(US$ in Thousands)	3 Mos	12/31/2004	12/31/2003	12/31/2002	12/31/2001	12/31/2000	12/31/1999	12/31/1998
Earnings Per Share	2.64	2.51	2.62	2.16	2.16	1.91	1.64	1.29
Cash Flow Per Share	3.28	3.27	2.88	2.67	2.98	2.70	2.61	2.11
Tang Book Value Per Share	20.17	19.89	19.30	18.23	18.28	17.98	17.59	17.56
Dividends Per Share	2.280	2.160	2.080	1.920	1.773	1.580	1.313	1.147
Dividend Payout %	90.84	82.44	96.30	88.89	92.83	96.34	101.78	96.39
Income Statement								
Property Income	132,043	516,967	479,664	450,829	468,616	459,407	433,880	338,798
Total Revenue	132,043	516,967	479,664	450,829	468,616	459,407	433,880	338,798
Depn & Amortn	26,183	102,872	89,068	76,674	74,209	71,129	67,416	51,348
Interest Expense	28,640	107,726	102,709	86,896	...	...	...	...
Income Before Taxes	58,858	226,397	200,889	261,474	255,914	...	176,778	...
Income Taxes	2,637	3,919	1,516	12,904	19,376	...	...	...
Net Income	86,780	297,137	307,879	245,668	236,538	205,025	176,778	122,266
Average Shares	117,155	113,572	108,770	105,969	101,163	93,653	91,466	75,960
Balance Sheet								
Total Assets	4,838,622	4,749,597	4,603,925	3,756,878	3,384,779	3,171,348	3,007,476	3,051,178
Long-Term Obligations	2,213,444	509,697	468,698	274,732	292,829	245,413	212,321	434,311
Total Liabilities	2,444,012	2,406,306	2,368,162	1,755,610	1,486,320	1,453,242	1,388,912	1,453,204
Stockholders' Equity	2,282,071	2,236,400	2,135,846	1,907,328	1,890,084	1,704,339	1,605,435	1,585,019
Shares Outstanding	113,087	112,426	110,623	104,601	103,352	94,717	91,193	90,200
Statistical Record								
Return on Assets %	6.51	6.34	7.36	6.88	7.22	6.62	5.84	5.56
Return on Equity %	14.07	13.55	15.23	12.94	13.16	12.36	11.08	10.50
Net Margin %	65.72	57.48	64.19	54.49	50.48	44.63	40.74	36.09
Price Range	58.94-40.55	58.94-40.55	45.86-30.50	33.61-28.01	34.00-27.27	29.75-22.04	26.92-20.83	27.38-22.42
P/E Ratio	22.33-15.36	23.48-16.16	17.50-11.64	15.56-12.97	15.74-12.62	15.58-11.54	16.41-12.70	21.22-17.38
Average Yield %	4.66	5.66	6.75	6.27	6.85	6.62	5.27	5.20

Address: 3333 New Hyde Park Road, Suite 100, New Hyde Park, NY 11042-0020
Telephone: 516-869-9000
Web Site: www.kimcorealty.com

Officers: Milton Cooper - Chmn., C.E.O. Michael J. Flynn - Vice-Chmn., Pres., C.O.O. **Transfer Agents:** The Bank of New York, New York, NY

Investor Contact: 516-869-9000
No of Institutions: 220
Shares: 64,649,968 **% Held:** 57.47

LA-Z-BOY INC.

Exchange	Symbol	Price	52Wk Range	Yield	P/E
NYS	LZB	$13.35 (5/31/2005)	19.23-11.81	3.30	N/A

*7 Year Price Score 69.18 *NYSE Composite Index=100 *12 Month Price Score 83.23

Interim Earnings (Per Share)

Qtr.	Jul	Oct	Jan	Apr
2001-02	0.05	0.20	0.35	0.41
2002-03	(0.68)	0.50	0.41	0.44
2003-04	0.11	0.28	0.29	(0.78)
2004-05	(0.07)	0.17	0.21	...

Interim Dividends (Per Share)

Amt	Decl	Ex	Rec	Pay
0.11Q	8/10/2004	8/26/2004	8/30/2004	9/10/2004
0.11Q	11/9/2004	11/23/2004	11/26/2004	12/10/2004
0.11Q	2/8/2005	2/23/2005	2/25/2005	3/10/2005
0.11Q	5/10/2005	5/25/2005	5/27/2005	6/10/2005

Indicated Div: $0.44 (Div. Reinv. Plan)

Valuation Analysis

Forecast P/E	12.12 (6/1/2005)		
Market Cap	$696.4 Million	Book Value	526.2 Million
Price/Book	1.32	Price/Sales	0.34

Dividend Achiever Status

Rank	238	10 Year Growth Rate	6.61%
Total Years of Dividend Growth			23

Business Summary: Chemicals (MIC: 11.1 SIC: 511 NAIC: 37121)

La-Z-Boy is a furniture manufacturer and import distributor. Co. is comprised of two business groups: upholstery and casegoods. The upholstery segment includes recliners, sofas, chairs, sleeper sofas, loveseats and ottomans. The casegoods segment includes tables, chairs, dressers, headboards and accent pieces. In addition to upholstery and wood, Co. markets contract furniture to the hospitality, healthcare and assisted living industries. Brand names include La-Z-Boy, England, Sam Moore, Bauhaus, Pennsylvania House, Clayton Marcus, Kincaid, Hammary, Alexvale, American Drew, La-Z-Boy Contract Furniture, American of Martinsville, Drew and Lea.

Recent Developments: For the quarter ended Jan 22 2005, net income decreased 27.4% to $11,092 thousand from net income of $15,279 thousand in the year-earlier quarter. Revenues were $518,160 thousand, up 5.3% from $492,167 thousand the year before. Operating income was $20,254 thousand versus an income of $26,040 thousand in the prior-year quarter, a decrease of 22.2%. Total direct expense was $791,990 thousand versus $768,218 thousand in the prior-year quarter, an increase of 3.1%. Total indirect expense was $101,911 thousand versus $82,018 thousand in the prior-year quarter, an increase of 24.3%.

Prospects: On Apr 29 2005, Co. announced that it has completed the sale of its La-Z-Boy office contract unit to the Lange family, owners of Best Home Furnishings, Inc. of Ferdinand, IN. The transaction will help Co. focus on growing its core home furninshings business. Separately, on Feb 21 2005, Co. announced that it has acquired the Chicagoland-area La-Z-Boy Furniture Galleries operation, which consists of 13 stores. Terms of the transaction were not disclosed. Co. estimates the market to represent a potential of over 20 stores, which will be developed over the next few years.

Financial Data (US$ in Thousands)	9 Mos	6 Mos	3 Mos	04/24/2004	04/26/2003	04/27/2002	04/28/2001	04/29/2000
Earnings Per Share	(0.47)	(0.39)	(0.28)	(0.11)	0.63	1.01	1.13	1.60
Cash Flow Per Share	0.58	0.68	2.10	2.49	2.19	2.20	1.92	1.06
Tang Book Value Per Share	8.24	8.10	8.01	8.19	8.36	8.15	7.40	6.70
Dividends Per Share	0.430	0.420	0.410	0.400	0.400	0.360	0.350	0.320
Dividend Payout %	...	...	...	...	63.49	35.64	30.97	20.00
Income Statement								
Total Revenue	1,518,201	1,000,041	466,371	1,998,876	2,111,830	2,153,952	2,256,197	1,717,420
EBITDA	54,021	26,292	3,435	62,653	196,202	141,625	173,922	178,334
Depn & Amortn	21,154	14,000	6,908	29,112	30,695	43,988	45,697	30,342
Income Before Taxes	25,367	7,476	(5,682)	22,288	154,997	88,936	112,044	140,313
Income Taxes	9,640	2,841	(2,159)	19,760	58,899	27,185	43,708	52,699
Net Income	16,429	5,337	(3,523)	(5,796)	36,316	61,751	68,336	87,614
Average Shares	52,193	52,101	51,967	53,679	57,435	61,125	60,692	54,860
Balance Sheet								
Current Assets	636,704	676,729	624,921	653,674	679,494	671,692	708,776	692,369
Total Assets	1,027,495	1,061,957	1,011,199	1,047,496	1,123,066	1,160,776	1,222,503	1,218,297
Current Liabilities	209,042	250,412	206,367	283,321	214,587	226,893	249,915	237,006
Long-Term Obligations	229,158	231,652	232,833	181,807	222,371	139,386	199,419	236,094
Total Liabilities	501,342	543,669	498,815	525,168	513,127	447,254	527,357	555,205
Stockholders' Equity	526,153	518,288	512,384	522,328	609,939	713,522	695,146	663,092
Shares Outstanding	52,166	52,087	52,002	52,031	55,027	59,953	60,501	61,328
Statistical Record								
Return on Assets %	N.M.	N.M.	N.M.	N.M.	3.19	5.20	5.61	9.33
Return on Equity %	N.M.	N.M.	N.M.	N.M.	5.50	8.79	10.09	15.99
EBITDA Margin %	3.56	2.63	0.74	3.13	9.29	6.58	7.71	10.38
Net Margin %	1.08	0.53	N.M.	N.M.	1.72	2.87	3.03	5.10
Asset Turnover	2.00	1.91	1.95	1.85	1.85	1.81	1.85	1.83
Current Ratio	3.05	2.70	3.03	2.31	3.17	2.96	2.84	2.92
Debt to Equity	0.44	0.45	0.45	0.35	0.36	0.20	0.29	0.36
Price Range	23.50-12.95	23.50-13.00	24.12-16.63	24.12-18.90	30.04-16.45	30.88-15.16	18.50-13.44	24.44-13.69
P/E Ratio	...	...	...	...	47.68-26.11	30.57-15.01	16.37-11.89	15.27-8.55
Average Yield %	2.43	2.20	1.98	1.86	1.74	1.71	2.21	1.67

Address: 1284 North Telegraph Road, Monroe, MI 48162
Telephone: 734-241-1444
Web Site: www.la-z-boy.com

Officers: Patrick H. Norton - Chmn. Kurt L. Darrow - Pres., C.E.O. **Transfer Agents:** EquiServe Trust Company, N.A., Providence, RI

Investor Contact: 734-241-4414
No of Institutions: 134
Shares: 34,490,600 **% Held:** 66.12

LANCASTER COLONY CORP.

Exchange	Symbol	Price	52Wk Range	Yield	P/E
NMS	LANC	$43.94 (5/31/2005)	44.63-38.26	2.28	17.16

*7 Year Price Score 106.07 *NYSE Composite Index=100 *12 Month Price Score 97.71

Interim Earnings (Per Share)

Qtr.	Sep	Dec	Mar	Jun
2001-02	0.55	0.47	0.78	0.69
2002-03	0.56	1.43	0.50	0.62
2003-04	0.55	0.74	0.45	0.50
2004-05	0.52	1.08	0.46	...

Interim Dividends (Per Share)

Amt	Decl	Ex	Rec	Pay
0.23Q	8/25/2004	9/8/2004	9/10/2004	9/30/2004
0.25Q	11/15/2004	12/8/2004	12/10/2004	12/30/2004
0.25Q	2/23/2005	3/8/2005	3/10/2005	3/31/2005
0.25Q	5/25/2005	6/8/2005	6/10/2005	6/30/2005

Indicated Div: $1.00 (Div. Reinv. Plan)

Valuation Analysis

Forecast P/E	18.16 (6/1/2005)		
Market Cap	$1.5 Billion	Book Value	589.2 Million
Price/Book	2.57	Price/Sales	1.34

Dividend Achiever Status

Rank	153	10 Year Growth Rate	11.09%
Total Years of Dividend Growth			35

Business Summary: Food (MIC: 4.1 SIC: 038 NAIC: 11412)

Lancaster Colony is a diversified manufacturer and marketer of consumer products. The Specialty Foods segment manufactures and sells salad dressings and sauces, fruit glazes, vegetable dips and fruit dips, frozen unbaked pies, frozen hearth-baked breads, yeast dinner rolls and sweet rolls, dry egg noodles, frozen specialty noodles and pastas, croutons and related products, and caviar. The Glassware and Candles segment produces machine pressed and machine blown consumer glassware and industrial glass products, and candles, candle accessories, and other home fragrance products. The Automotive segment manufactures and sells a line of rubber, vinyl and carpeted floor mats, and other products.

Recent Developments: For the quarter ended Mar 31 2005, net income increased 0.4% to $16,112,000 from net income of $16,045,000 in the year-earlier quarter. Revenues were $276,822,000 , up 2.7% from $269,463,000 the year before. Operating income was $24,599,000 versus an income of $25,403,000 in the prior-year quarter, a decrease of 3.2%. Total direct expense was $225,522,000 versus $219,659,000 in the prior-year quarter, an increase of 2.7%. Total indirect expense was $26,701,000 versus $24,401,000 in the prior-year quarter, an increase of 9.4%.

Prospects: Co.'s outlook appears mixed. On the positive side, Co. is experiencing modest top line growth across its three business segments. However, substantial increases in raw material costs have contributed to lower operating profit from Co.'s Automotive segment. Looking forward, Co. could benefit from the launch of several new food items, including T. Marzetti's recently repackaged line of produce dressings and new microwavable products being introduced under the Sister Schubert's brand. Also, in the quarter ended June 30 2005, Co. expects to begin production of aluminum automotive accessories supporting a large, new original equipment manufacturer program.

Financial Data

(US$ in Thousands)	9 Mos	6 Mos	3 Mos	06/30/2004	06/30/2003	06/30/2002	06/30/2001	06/30/2000
Earnings Per Share	2.56	2.55	2.20	2.24	3.11	2.49	2.37	2.51
Cash Flow Per Share	3.73	3.84	3.28	3.34	4.31	4.35	3.36	3.24
Tang Book Value Per Share	14.67	14.90	14.24	14.16	13.20	11.71	10.38	10.03
Dividends Per Share	0.960	0.940	0.920	0.890	0.780	0.710	0.670	0.630
Dividend Payout %	37.50	36.93	41.78	39.73	25.08	28.51	28.27	25.10
Income Statement								
Total Revenue	855,655	578,833	281,484	1,096,953	1,106,800	1,129,687	1,098,464	1,104,258
EBITDA	141,065	107,133	37,925	159,731	212,470	184,683	182,652	196,117
Depn & Amortn	25,093	16,865	8,499	31,267	31,669	35,287	35,528	34,340
Income Before Taxes	115,972	90,268	29,426	128,464	180,801	149,342	145,885	160,189
Income Taxes	43,363	33,771	11,048	48,462	68,255	57,402	55,649	60,925
Net Income	72,609	56,497	18,378	80,002	112,546	91,940	89,238	99,264
Average Shares	34,799	35,144	35,408	35,778	36,243	36,910	37,636	39,554
Balance Sheet								
Current Assets	464,183	485,693	464,767	451,005	414,385	366,100	317,605	315,895
Total Assets	717,532	743,311	725,420	712,887	667,716	618,705	571,937	531,844
Current Liabilities	95,050	104,070	105,421	92,731	84,923	89,304	92,294	96,475
Long-Term Obligations	...	...	...	...	...	...	1,095	3,040
Total Liabilities	128,304	137,766	139,574	126,102	120,051	117,428	112,036	116,361
Stockholders' Equity	589,228	605,545	585,846	586,785	547,665	501,277	459,901	415,483
Shares Outstanding	34,424	34,977	35,198	35,472	35,770	36,598	37,253	37,962
Statistical Record								
Return on Assets %	12.64	12.42	11.02	11.56	17.50	15.44	16.17	18.30
Return on Equity %	15.39	15.22	13.68	14.07	21.46	19.13	20.39	23.84
EBITDA Margin %	16.49	18.51	13.47	14.56	19.20	16.35	16.63	17.76
Net Margin %	8.49	9.76	6.53	7.29	10.17	8.14	8.12	8.99
Asset Turnover	1.58	1.54	1.56	1.58	1.72	1.90	1.99	2.04
Current Ratio	4.88	4.67	4.41	4.86	4.88	4.10	3.44	3.27
Debt to Equity	...	...	...	...	...	...	N.M.	0.01
Price Range	44.63-38.20	46.11-38.20	46.11-38.20	46.11-38.20	46.74-32.68	40.16-26.10	33.46-19.50	36.25-19.50
P/E Ratio	17.43-14.92	18.08-14.98	20.96-17.36	20.58-17.05	15.03-10.51	16.13-10.48	14.12-8.23	14.44-7.77
Average Yield %	2.30	2.24	2.21	2.15	2.00	2.06	2.46	2.06

Address: 37 West Broad Street, Columbus, OH 43215 **Telephone:** 614-224-7141 **Web Site:** www.lancastercolony.com	**Officers:** John B. Gerlach Jr. - Chmn., Pres., C.E.O. John L. Boylan - V.P., C.F.O., Treas., Asst. Sec. **ransfer Agents:**American Stock Transfer and Trust Company, New York, NY	**No of Institutions:** 145 **Shares:** 15,726,959 **% Held:** 45.08

LEGG MASON, INC.

Exchange	Symbol	Price	52Wk Range	Yield	P/E
NYS	LM	$82.18 (5/31/2005)	84.12-48.97	0.73	23.28

*7 Year Price Score 156.16 *NYSE Composite Index=100 *12 Month Price Score 109.51

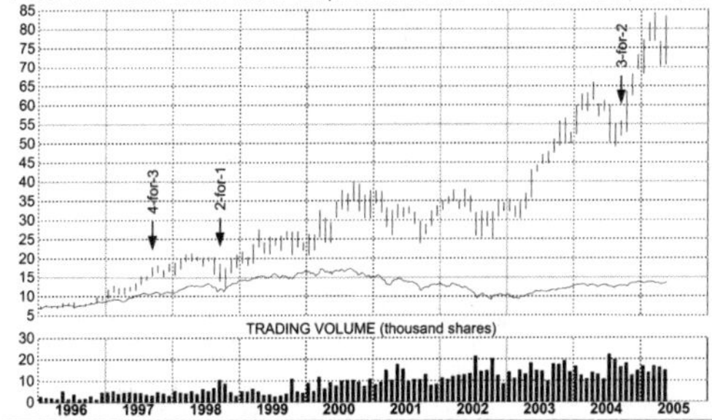

TRADING VOLUME (thousand shares)

Interim Earnings (Per Share)

Qtr.	Jun	Sep	Dec	Mar
2001-02	0.35	0.30	0.40	0.45
2002-03	0.47	0.44	0.47	0.47
2003-04	0.55	0.62	0.71	0.81
2004-05	0.76	0.81	0.98	0.98

Interim Dividends (Per Share)

Amt	Decl	Ex	Rec	Pay
3-for-2	7/20/2004	9/27/2004	9/8/2004	9/24/2004
0.15Q	10/19/2004	12/6/2004	12/8/2004	1/3/2005
0.15Q	1/18/2005	3/1/2005	3/3/2005	4/4/2005
0.15Q	4/19/2005	6/3/2005	6/7/2005	7/5/2005

Indicated Div: $0.60

Valuation Analysis

Forecast P/E	19.11 (6/2/2005)		
Market Cap	$8.7 Billion	Book Value	2.2 Billion
Price/Book	4.02	Price/Sales	3.67

Dividend Achiever Status

Rank	77	**10 Year Growth Rate**	15.94%
Total Years of Dividend Growth			21

Business Summary: Finance Intermediaries & Services (MIC: 8.7 SIC: 211 NAIC: 23120)

Legg Mason is a holding company. Through its subsidiaries, Co. provides asset management, securities brokerage, investment banking and other related financial services to individuals, institutions, corporations, governments and government agencies. Co. operates through three segments: Asset Management, Private Client and Capital Markets. Co.'s asset management business provides investment advisory services to institutional and individual clients and company-sponsored investment funds. Co.'s Private Client and Capital Markets business segments conduct activities primarily through Legg Mason Wood Walker, Inc., a full service broker-dealer, investment advisor and investment banking firm.

Recent Developments: For the twelve months ended Mar 31 2005, net income totaled $408,431 thousand compared with income of $290,608 thousand, before a $7,156 thousand gain from discontinued operations, in the corresponding period a year earlier. Revenues were $2,408,708 thousand, up 24.1% from $1,941,112 thousand the year before. Investment advisory and related fees increased 36.1% to $1,656,330 thousand from $1,217,030 thousand, while commissions rose 4.3% to $358,342 thousand versus $343,519 thousand the year before. Principal transactions slipped 2.4% to $161,533 thousand from $165,481 thousand in 2004.

Prospects: Co. is continuing to experience growth in its assets under management, which climbed approximately 30.0% in fiscal 2005 versus the prior year. In fact, each of Co.'s three asset management divisions, Institutional, Mutual Funds and Wealth Management, is experiencing solid growth in assets under management and net revenues. Meanwhile, Co.'s Investment banking net interest profit is increasing, primarily as a result of substantially higher interest rates earned on customer margin account balances and firm investments. Co.'s securities brokerage revenues are benefiting from increases in distribution fees from non-proprietary mutual funds, despite a decrease in institutional fixed income volume.

Financial Data

(US$ in Thousands)	9 Mos	6 Mos	3 Mos	03/31/2004	03/31/2003	03/31/2002	03/31/2001	03/31/2000
Earnings Per Share	3.35	3.09	2.90	2.71	1.85	1.49	1.53	1.55
Cash Flow Per Share	3.98	5.55	2.71	1.88	3.09	0.88	2.34	1.93
Tang Book Value Per Share	6.68	3.23	2.39	6.50	3.32	1.52	8.26	7.07
Dividends Per Share	0.500	0.400	0.373	0.347	0.280	0.253	0.227	0.193
Dividend Payout %	14.91	12.94	12.86	12.80	15.14	16.98	14.84	12.45
Income Statement								
Total Revenue	1,798,721	1,140,443	554,927	2,004,267	1,615,382	1,578,612	1,536,253	1,370,804
Income Before Taxes	468,659	287,381	138,701	472,309	308,321	253,249	265,820	239,141
Income Taxes	177,873	109,305	52,287	181,701	117,412	100,313	109,590	96,616
Net Income	290,786	178,076	86,414	297,764	190,909	152,936	156,230	142,525
Average Shares	116,401	114,742	115,569	110,769	103,140	102,393	101,874	91,180
Balance Sheet								
Total Assets	7,733,227	7,027,971	7,496,423	7,262,981	6,067,450	5,939,614	4,687,626	4,785,053
Total Liabilities	5,569,888	5,299,649	5,847,490	5,703,371	4,819,493	4,855,066	3,759,906	4,033,124
Stockholders' Equity	2,163,339	1,728,322	1,648,933	1,559,610	1,247,957	1,084,548	927,720	751,929
Shares Outstanding	105,923	100,765	100,740	99,823	97,241	96,665	94,274	87,898
Statistical Record								
Return on Assets %	5.25	5.17	4.74	4.46	3.18	2.88	3.30	3.44
Return on Equity %	20.92	22.41	21.86	21.15	16.37	15.20	18.60	21.76
Price Range	73.26-48.97	66.07-48.13	66.07-43.30	63.22-32.49	37.98-25.44	37.87-23.83	39.96-23.96	32.67-20.83
P/E Ratio	21.87-14.62	21.38-15.58	22.78-14.93	23.33-11.99	20.53-13.75	25.41-16.00	26.12-15.66	21.08-13.44
Average Yield %	0.84	0.53	0.73	0.75	0.89	0.82	0.70	0.83

Address: 100 Light Street, Baltimore, MD 21202
Telephone: 410-539-0000
Web Site: www.leggmason.com

Officers: Raymond A. Mason - Chmn., Pres., C.E.O. Timothy C. Scheve - Sr. Exec. V.P. **Transfer Agents:** Wachovia Bank, N.A., Charlotte, NC

Investor Contact: 410-539-0000
No of Institutions: 319
Shares: 80,293,304 **% Held:** 73.84

LEGGETT & PLATT, INC.

Exchange	Symbol	Price	52Wk Range	Yield	P/E
NYS	LEG	$26.64 (5/31/2005)	30.56-23.56	2.40	17.76

*7 Year Price Score 108.22 *NYSE Composite Index=100 *12 Month Price Score 97.04

TRADING VOLUME (thousand shares)

Interim Earnings (Per Share)

Qtr.	Mar	Jun	Sep	Dec
2002	0.28	0.35	0.29	0.25
2003	0.25	0.24	0.26	0.30
2004	0.32	0.39	0.41	0.33
2005	0.37	...	...	...

Interim Dividends (Per Share)

Amt	Decl	Ex	Rec	Pay
0.15Q	8/4/2004	9/13/2004	9/15/2004	10/15/2004
0.15Q	11/4/2004	12/13/2004	12/15/2004	1/14/2005
0.15Q	2/24/2005	3/11/2005	3/15/2005	4/15/2005
0.16Q	5/4/2005	6/13/2005	6/15/2005	7/15/2005

Indicated Div: $0.64

Valuation Analysis

Forecast P/E	16.32 (5/28/2005)		
Market Cap	$5.1 Billion	Book Value	2.3 Billion
Price/Book	2.17	Price/Sales	0.97

Dividend Achiever Status

Rank	61	**10 Year Growth Rate**	17.36%
Total Years of Dividend Growth			33

Business Summary: Chemicals (MIC: 11.1 SIC: 515 NAIC: 37121)

Leggett & Platt is a diversified manufacturer that conceives, designs and produces a wide range of engineered components and products that are used in homes, offices, retail stores and automobiles. Products include manufactured components for residential furniture and bedding, retail store fixtures and point-of-purchase displays, components for office furniture, non-automotive aluminum die castings, drawn steel wire, automotive seat support and lumbar systems, carpet underlay, adjustable beds, and bedding industry machinery for wire forming, sewing and quilting. Co.'s business is organized into 29 business units, which are organized into 10 groups that comprise five business segments.

Recent Developments: For the quarter ended Mar 31 2005, net income increased 15.9% to $72,800 thousand from net income of $62,800 thousand in the year-earlier quarter. Revenues were $1,301,300 thousand, up 9.6% from $1,187,200 thousand the year before. Operating income was $117,300 thousand versus an income of $103,300 thousand in the prior-year quarter, an increase of 13.6%. Total direct expense was $1,068,900 thousand versus $972,100 thousand in the prior-year quarter, an increase of 10.0%. Total indirect expense was $112,600 thousand versus $112,000 thousand in the prior-year quarter, an increase of 0.5%.

Prospects: Co. stated that earnings growth in 2005 should primarily be influenced by three factors: organic sales growth, the direction of raw material costs, and the extent of improvement in the Fixture and Display (F&D) operations. For planning purposes, Co. is assuming 2005 total sales growth of between 6.0% and 10.0%, with same location sales posting 4.0% to 6.0% growth, and acquisitions contributing the balance. Co. also expects costs for steel to stabilize. In contrast, Co. noted that costs for oil-related materials, including fuel and chemicals, have been increasing and are expected to escalate further. Thus, Co.'s earnings guidance for the full year 2005 remains at $1.50 to $1.70 per share.

Financial Data

(US$ in Thousands)	3 Mos	12/31/2004	12/31/2003	12/31/2002	12/31/2001	12/31/2000	12/31/1999	12/31/1998
Earnings Per Share	1.50	1.45	1.05	1.17	0.94	1.32	1.45	1.24
Cash Flow Per Share	1.80	1.75	2.01	2.29	2.68	2.21	1.87	1.80
Tang Book Value Per Share	6.48	6.37	5.62	5.36	4.81	4.58	4.50	4.59
Dividends Per Share	0.590	0.580	0.540	0.500	0.480	0.420	0.360	0.315
Dividend Payout %	39.33	40.00	51.43	42.74	51.06	31.82	24.83	25.40
Income Statement								
Total Revenue	1,301,300	5,085,500	4,388,200	4,271,800	4,113,800	4,276,300	3,779,000	3,370,400
EBITDA	160,700	638,900	522,300	565,200	547,800	654,100	651,800	557,000
Depn & Amortn	43,400	177,200	167,000	164,600	196,600	173,300	149,300	127,900
Income Before Taxes	107,700	422,600	315,100	363,500	297,300	418,600	462,600	395,600
Income Taxes	34,900	137,200	109,200	130,400	109,700	154,500	172,100	147,600
Net Income	72,800	285,400	205,900	233,100	187,600	264,100	290,500	248,000
Average Shares	196,500	196,875	196,953	199,795	200,434	200,388	200,938	200,669
Balance Sheet								
Current Assets	1,803,100	2,064,800	1,819,400	1,488,000	1,421,900	1,405,300	1,256,200	1,137,100
Total Assets	3,922,800	4,197,200	3,889,700	3,501,100	3,412,900	3,373,200	2,977,500	2,535,300
Current Liabilities	674,900	959,600	625,900	598,000	457,000	476,600	431,500	401,400
Long-Term Obligations	776,400	779,400	1,012,200	808,600	977,600	988,400	787,400	574,100
Total Liabilities	1,598,100	1,884,100	1,775,700	1,524,200	1,546,300	1,579,400	1,331,300	1,098,500
Stockholders' Equity	2,324,700	2,313,100	2,114,000	1,976,900	1,866,600	1,793,800	1,646,200	1,436,800
Shares Outstanding	189,629	190,886	192,102	194,498	196,298	196,097	196,880	197,683
Statistical Record								
Return on Assets %	7.45	7.04	5.57	6.74	5.53	8.29	10.54	10.69
Return on Equity %	13.16	12.86	10.07	12.13	10.25	15.31	18.85	19.00
EBITDA Margin %	12.35	12.56	11.90	13.23	13.32	15.30	17.25	16.53
Net Margin %	5.59	5.61	4.69	5.46	4.56	6.18	7.69	7.36
Asset Turnover	1.31	1.25	1.19	1.24	1.21	1.34	1.37	1.45
Current Ratio	2.67	2.15	2.91	2.49	3.11	2.95	2.91	2.83
Debt to Equity	0.33	0.34	0.48	0.41	0.52	0.55	0.48	0.40
Price Range	30.56-22.02	30.56-21.35	23.57-17.40	27.16-18.90	24.23-17.00	22.25-14.25	27.88-18.81	28.44-17.13
P/E Ratio	20.37-14.68	21.08-14.72	22.45-16.57	23.21-16.15	25.78-18.09	16.86-10.80	19.22-12.97	22.93-13.81
Average Yield %	2.19	2.25	2.58	2.13	2.26	2.35	1.58	1.30

Address: No. 1 Leggett Road, Carthage, MO 64836
Telephone: 417-358-8131
Web Site: www.leggett.com

Officers: Felix E. Wright - Chmn., C.E.O. David S. Haffner - Pres., C.O.O. **Transfer Agents:** U.M.B. Bank, Kansas City, MO

Investor Contact: 417-358-8131
No of Institutions: 270
Shares: 121,353,464 **% Held:** 63.59

LEXINGTON CORPORATE PROPERTIES TRUST

Exchange	Symbol	Price	52Wk Range	Yield	P/E
NYS	LXP	$23.03 (5/31/2005)	23.99-19.01	6.25	34.89

*7 Year Price Score 124.82 *NYSE Composite Index=100 *12 Month Price Score 102.44

TRADING VOLUME (thousand shares)

Interim Earnings (Per Share)

Qtr.	Mar	Jun	Sep	Dec
2002	0.29	0.29	0.28	0.24
2003	0.29	0.06	0.24	0.30
2004	0.24	0.27	0.19	0.09
2005	0.11	...	...	...

Interim Dividends (Per Share)

Amt	Decl	Ex	Rec	Pay
0.35Q	7/15/2004	7/28/2004	7/30/2004	8/13/2004
0.35Q	10/14/2004	10/27/2004	10/29/2004	11/15/2004
0.36Q	1/13/2005	1/27/2005	1/31/2005	2/14/2005
0.36Q	4/15/2005	4/27/2005	4/30/2005	5/16/2005

Indicated Div: $1.44

Valuation Analysis

Forecast P/E	11.91 (5/28/2005)		
Market Cap	$1.1 Billion	Book Value	861.7 Million
Price/Book	1.31	Price/Sales	7.22

Dividend Achiever Status

Rank	299	10 Year Growth Rate	2.92%
Total Years of Dividend Growth			10

Business Summary: Property, Real Estate & Development (MIC: 8.3 SIC: 798 NAIC: 25930)

Lexington Corporate Properties Trust is a self-managed and self-administered real estate investment trust that acquires, owns and manages a geographically diverse portfolio of net leased office, industrial and retail properties and provides investment advisory and asset management services to institutional investors in the net lease area. As of Dec 31 2004, Co.'s real property portfolio consisted of 154 properties or interests located in 37 states, including warehousing, distribution and manufacturing facilities, office buildings and retail properties. Co. manages its real estate and credit risk through geographic, industry, tenant and lease maturity diversification.

Recent Developments: For the quarter ended Mar 31 2005, income from continuing operations decreased 23.9% to $8,530,000 from income of $11,207,000 in the year-earlier quarter. Net income decreased 20.5% to $9,526,000 from net income of $11,978,000 in the year-earlier quarter. Revenues were $38,642,000 , up 14.4% from $33,773,000 the year before.

Prospects: On Apr 13 2005, Co. announced that it closed on the acquisition of a portfolio of twenty-seven properties from affiliates of Wells Real Estate Investment Trust, Inc. and Wells-affiliated joint venture partners for an aggregate purchase price of approximately $786.0 million. Meanwhile, Co.'s funds from operations per share are being positively affected by extremely high cash balances of approximately $150.0 million, substantially all of which were invested in the Wells acquisition. Accordingly, Co. expects to report strong growth in funds from operations per share during the balance of 2005.

Financial Data (US$ in Thousands)	3 Mos	12/31/2004	12/31/2003	12/31/2002	12/31/2001	12/31/2000	12/31/1999	12/31/1998
Earnings Per Share	0.66	0.80	0.88	1.09	0.77	1.10	1.08	0.78
Cash Flow Per Share	1.92	1.95	2.11	2.15	2.28	2.41	2.36	1.90
Tang Book Value Per Share	14.88	12.03	12.02	11.09	9.89	8.78	8.87	9.14
Dividends Per Share	1.410	1.400	1.340	1.320	1.270	1.220	1.200	1.170
Dividend Payout %	213.64	175.00	152.27	121.10	164.94	110.91	111.11	150.00
Income Statement								
Property Income	37,459	146,340	111,658	93,884	78,402	76,824	75,760	62,846
Non-Property Income	1,183	4,885	8,862	6,735	4,460	3,181	1,540	2,271
Total Revenue	38,642	151,225	120,520	100,619	82,862	80,005	77,300	65,117
Depn & Amortn	11,913	41,710	29,572	23,375	19,952	19,010	18,991	16,070
Income Before Taxes	8,082	41,860	34,812	...	...	27,967	...	...
Income Taxes	96	1,181	...	...	...	...	...	...
Net Income	9,526	44,807	33,649	30,595	18,062	21,952	21,347	15,737
Average Shares	48,429	52,048	39,493	32,602	19,862	24,714	24,945	21,983
Balance Sheet								
Total Assets	1,704,343	1,697,086	1,207,411	902,471	822,153	668,377	656,481	647,007
Long-Term Obligations	758,487	765,144	455,940	460,517	445,771	345,505	301,333	302,252
Total Liabilities	842,597	793,037	564,534	508,840	469,403	400,502	385,203	367,482
Stockholders' Equity	861,746	847,290	579,848	332,976	266,713	174,885	176,797	180,775
Shares Outstanding	49,133	48,621	40,682	30,030	24,507	17,151	17,193	17,103
Statistical Record								
Return on Assets %	2.67	3.08	3.19	3.55	2.42	3.30	3.28	2.83
Return on Equity %	5.34	6.26	7.37	10.20	8.18	12.45	11.94	8.66
Net Margin %	24.65	29.63	27.92	30.41	21.80	27.44	27.62	24.17
Price Range	23.56-17.30	23.23-17.30	20.85-15.63	16.75-14.25	15.56-11.94	12.25-9.00	12.88-9.00	16.25-10.88
P/E Ratio	35.70-26.21	29.04-21.63	23.69-17.76	15.37-13.07	20.21-15.50	11.14-8.18	11.92-8.33	20.83-13.94
Average Yield %	6.69	6.70	7.41	8.40	9.13	11.11	10.67	8.55

Address: One Penn Plaza, Suite 4015, New York, NY 10119-4015 **Telephone:** 212-692-7200 **Web Site:** www.lxp.com	**Officers:** E. Robert Roskind - Chmn. T. Wilson Eglin - Pres., C.E.O., C.O.O. **Transfer Agents:**	**No of Institutions:** 125 **Shares:** 26,244,256 **% Held:** 53.60

LIBERTY PROPERTY TRUST

Exchange	Symbol	Price	52Wk Range	Yield	P/E
NYS	LRY	$41.29 (5/31/2005)	43.20-38.19	5.91	21.17

Interim Earnings (Per Share)

Qtr.	Mar	Jun	Sep	Dec
2002	0.53	0.55	0.52	0.43
2003	0.53	0.57	0.49	0.46
2004	0.45	0.44	0.46	0.53
2005	0.52	...	...	...

Interim Dividends (Per Share)

Amt	Decl	Ex	Rec	Pay
0.605Q	6/16/2004	6/29/2004	7/1/2004	7/15/2004
0.61Q	9/16/2004	9/29/2004	10/1/2004	10/15/2004
0.61Q	12/14/2004	12/29/2004	1/1/2005	1/15/2005
0.61Q	2/7/2005	3/30/2005	4/1/2005	4/15/2005

Indicated Div: $2.44

Valuation Analysis

Forecast P/E	16.11 (6/1/2005)		
Market Cap	$3.6 Billion	Book Value	1.6 Billion
Price/Book	2.22	Price/Sales	5.38

Dividend Achiever Status

Rank	47	**10 Year Growth Rate**	18.88%
Total Years of Dividend Growth			10

Business Summary: Property, Real Estate & Development (MIC: 8.3 SIC: 798 NAIC: 25930)

Liberty Property Trust is a self-administered and self- managed real estate investment trust. Co. provides leasing, property management, development, acquisition and other tenant-related services for its industrial and office properties. Co.'s industrial properties consist of warehouse, distribution, service, assembly, light manufacturing and research and development facilities. Co.'s office properties are multi-story and single-story office buildings located principally in suburban mixed-use developments or office parks. As of Dec 31 2004, Co.'s portfolio consisted of 443 industrial and 280 office properties totaling approximately 61.7 million square feet.

Recent Developments: For the quarter ended Mar 31 2005, income from continuing operations increased 7.4% to $38,988 thousand from income of $36,311 thousand in the year-earlier quarter. Net income increased 17.9% to $45,601 thousand from net income of $38,671 thousand in the year-earlier quarter. Revenues were $171,400 thousand, up 7.0% from $160,162 thousand the year before. Operating income was $73,768 thousand versus an income of $69,533 thousand in the prior-year quarter, an increase of 6.1%.

Prospects: Real estate conditions are gradually improving as reflected by Co.'s recent activity. Co.'s development pipeline has grown significantly, with the initiation of a large office and a large industrial project. In the first quarter of 2005, Co. commenced construction on Comcast Center, a 1.2 million square-foot office building in Philadelphia, PA. Comcast Center is 43.0% pre-leased to Comcast Corp. and represents a projected investment of $437.0 million. In addition, Co. commenced construction on four additional properties including a 1.0 million square foot distribution center in Lehigh Valley, PA. Meanwhile, Co. continues to execute its acquisitions strategy according to plan.

Financial Data

(US$ in Thousands)	3 Mos	12/31/2004	12/31/2003	12/31/2002	12/31/2001	12/31/2000	12/31/1999	12/31/1998
Earnings Per Share	1.95	1.88	2.05	2.02	2.15	2.17	1.95	1.59
Cash Flow Per Share	3.43	3.45	3.32	3.93	4.27	3.56	3.19	3.59
Tang Book Value Per Share	18.64	18.63	18.61	17.69	17.68	17.59	17.53	17.46
Dividends Per Share	2.435	2.430	2.410	2.380	2.320	2.180	1.940	1.740
Dividend Payout %	124.87	129.26	117.56	117.82	107.91	100.46	99.49	109.43
Income Statement								
Property Income	121,819	655,355	625,032	597,430	580,308	528,589	466,522	382,980
Non-Property Income	49,581	...	...	8,599	6,857	4,374	5,976	4,113
Total Revenue	171,400	655,355	625,032	606,029	587,165	532,963	472,498	387,093
Depn & Amortn	36,538	141,015	127,115	114,870	106,642	97,360	89,415	72,394
Interest Expense	33,188	123,352	123,907	116,625	112,006	108,295	99,663	78,617
Income Before Taxes	42,031	...	...	...	...	...	...	...
Income Taxes	534	...	...	...	...	...	...	...
Net Income	45,601	161,443	163,610	161,665	166,537	159,271	141,324	108,615
Average Shares	87,274	86,024	79,868	76,272	73,580	68,173	66,727	61,315
Balance Sheet								
Total Assets	4,276,479	4,162,827	3,834,008	3,627,061	3,552,825	3,396,355	3,118,133	2,933,371
Long-Term Obligations	2,252,660	2,133,171	1,885,866	1,866,187	1,753,131	1,703,896	1,491,238	1,423,843
Total Liabilities	2,458,214	2,358,702	2,081,444	2,067,033	1,935,009	1,876,781	1,636,015	1,565,081
Stockholders' Equity	1,613,100	1,596,259	1,544,897	1,351,589	1,423,422	1,320,805	1,294,607	1,267,036
Shares Outstanding	86,545	85,675	83,012	76,425	73,661	68,212	66,971	65,645
Statistical Record								
Return on Assets %	4.12	4.03	4.39	4.50	4.79	4.88	4.67	4.32
Return on Equity %	10.57	10.25	11.30	11.65	12.14	12.15	11.03	9.77
Net Margin %	26.61	24.63	26.18	26.68	28.36	29.88	29.91	28.06
Price Range	45.35-35.05	45.47-35.05	38.90-29.31	35.17-27.60	31.10-25.75	28.97-22.00	25.38-20.38	28.56-20.81
P/E Ratio	23.26-17.97	24.19-18.64	18.98-14.30	17.41-13.66	14.47-11.98	13.35-10.14	13.01-10.45	17.96-13.09
Average Yield %	6.05	6.04	7.10	7.60	8.15	8.50	8.34	6.93

Address: 65 Valley Stream Parkway, Suite 100, Malvern, PA 19355
Telephone: 610-648-1700
Web Site: www.libertyproperty.com

Officers: William P. Hankowsky - Chmn., Pres., C.E.O., Chief Invest. Officer George J. Alburger Jr. - Exec. V.P., C.F.O. **Transfer Agents:** EquiServe Trust Company, N.A., Providence, RI

Investor Contact: 610-648-1704
No of Institutions: 217
Shares: 71,947,704 **% Held:** 83.50

LILLY (ELI) & CO.

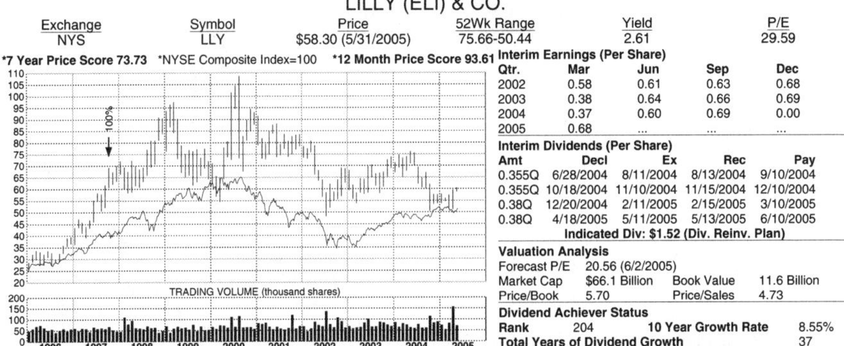

Exchange	Symbol	Price	52Wk Range	Yield	P/E
NYS	LLY	$58.30 (5/31/2005)	75.66-50.44	2.61	29.59

Interim Earnings (Per Share)

Qtr.	Mar	Jun	Sep	Dec
2002	0.58	0.61	0.63	0.68
2003	0.38	0.64	0.66	0.69
2004	0.37	0.60	0.69	0.00
2005	0.68	...	...	...

Interim Dividends (Per Share)

Amt	Decl	Ex	Rec	Pay
0.355Q	6/28/2004	8/11/2004	8/13/2004	9/10/2004
0.355Q	10/18/2004	11/10/2004	11/15/2004	12/10/2004
0.38Q	12/20/2004	2/11/2005	2/15/2005	3/10/2005
0.38Q	4/18/2005	5/11/2005	5/13/2005	6/10/2005

Indicated Div: $1.52 (Div. Reinv. Plan)

Valuation Analysis

Forecast P/E	20.56 (6/2/2005)		
Market Cap	$66.1 Billion	Book Value	11.6 Billion
Price/Book	5.70	Price/Sales	4.73

Dividend Achiever Status

Rank	204	**10 Year Growth Rate**	8.55%
Total Years of Dividend Growth			37

Business Summary: Pharmaceuticals (MIC: 9.1 SIC: 834 NAIC: 25412)

Eli Lilly is engaged primarily in the discovery, development, manufacture, and sale of pharmaceutical products. Co. also has an animal health segment. Neuroscience products include Zyprexa®, Strattera®, Prozac®, Cymbalta®, Permax®, Symbyax®, Sarafem®, and Yentreve™. Endocrine products include Humalog® and Humalog Mix 75/25®, Humulin®, Actos®, Evista®, Humatrope®, and Forteo®. Oncology products include Gemzar® and Alimta®. Cardiovascular agents include ReoPro® and Xigris®. Anti-infective products include Ceclor® and Vancocin®. Other pharmaceutical products include Cialis®.

Recent Developments: For the quarter ended Mar 31 2005, net income increased 84.0% to $736,600 thousand from net income of $400,400 thousand in the year-earlier quarter. Revenues were $3,497,400 thousand, up 3.6% from $3,376,900 thousand the year before. Total direct expense was $859,000 thousand versus $751,700 thousand in the prior-year quarter, an increase of 14.3%. Total indirect expense was $1,792,600 thousand versus $2,072,800 thousand in the prior-year quarter, a decrease of 13.5%.

Prospects: On Apr 18 2005, Co. provided full year 2005 earnings per share guidance of $2.80 to $2.90. Co. also expects 2005 sales to grow 8.0% to 10.0%, with sales accelerating in the second half. Further, Co. sees full year 2005 gross margins as a percent of sales declining by about 50 basis points to 75 basis points. Separately, on Apr 29 2005, Co. and Amylin Pharmaceuticals, Inc. announced that the FDA has approved BYETTA™ (exenatide) injection as adjunctive therapy to improve blood sugar control in patients with type 2 diabetes who have not achieved adequate control on metformin and/or a sulfonylurea, two common oral diabetes medications. BYETTA will be available to pharmacies by June 1 2005.

Financial Data (US$ in Thousands)	3 Mos	12/31/2004	12/31/2003	12/31/2002	12/31/2001	12/31/2000	12/31/1999	12/31/1998
Earnings Per Share	1.97	1.66	2.37	2.50	2.55	2.79	2.46	1.87
Cash Flow Per Share	2.85	2.64	3.39	1.92	3.40	3.44	2.41	2.40
Tang Book Value Per Share	10.24	9.65	8.69	7.37	6.32	5.37	4.49	2.86
Dividends Per Share	1.445	1.420	1.340	1.240	1.120	1.040	0.920	0.800
Dividend Payout %	73.35	85.54	56.54	49.60	43.92	37.28	37.40	42.78
Income Statement								
Total Revenue	3,497,400	13,857,900	12,582,500	11,077,500	11,542,500	10,862,200	10,002,900	9,236,800
EBITDA	1,103,100	3,539,400	3,810,200	3,950,700	4,007,000	4,294,500	3,685,100	3,155,400
Depn & Amortn	158,700	597,500	548,500	493,000	454,900	435,800	439,700	490,400
Income Before Taxes	944,400	2,941,900	3,261,700	3,457,700	3,552,100	3,858,700	3,245,400	2,665,000
Income Taxes	207,800	1,131,800	700,900	749,800	742,700	800,900	698,700	568,700
Net Income	736,600	1,810,100	2,560,800	2,707,900	2,780,000	3,057,800	2,721,000	2,097,900
Average Shares	1,089,200	1,088,936	1,082,230	1,085,088	1,090,793	1,097,725	1,106,055	1,121,486
Balance Sheet								
Current Assets	11,257,300	12,835,800	8,758,700	7,804,100	6,938,900	7,943,000	7,055,500	5,406,800
Total Assets	23,239,700	24,867,000	21,678,100	19,042,000	16,434,100	14,690,800	12,825,200	12,595,500
Current Liabilities	5,381,700	7,593,700	5,550,600	5,063,500	5,203,000	4,960,700	3,935,400	4,607,200
Long-Term Obligations	4,357,000	4,491,900	4,687,800	4,358,200	3,132,100	2,633,700	2,811,900	2,185,500
Total Liabilities	11,641,900	13,947,100	11,913,300	10,768,400	9,330,100	8,643,900	7,812,200	8,165,900
Stockholders' Equity	11,597,800	10,919,900	9,764,800	8,273,600	7,104,000	6,046,900	5,013,000	4,429,600
Shares Outstanding	1,133,093	1,131,942	1,123,725	1,122,443	1,123,348	1,125,560	1,090,238	1,019,090
Statistical Record								
Return on Assets %	9.40	7.76	12.58	15.27	17.86	22.16	21.41	16.67
Return on Equity %	19.37	17.45	28.39	35.22	42.28	55.14	57.63	46.23
EBITDA Margin %	31.54	25.54	30.28	35.66	34.72	39.54	36.84	34.16
Net Margin %	21.06	13.06	20.35	24.45	24.08	28.15	27.20	22.71
Asset Turnover	0.61	0.59	0.62	0.62	0.74	0.79	0.79	0.73
Current Ratio	2.09	1.69	1.58	1.54	1.33	1.60	1.79	1.17
Debt to Equity	0.38	0.41	0.48	0.53	0.44	0.44	0.56	0.49
Price Range	76.26-50.44	76.26-50.44	73.89-53.70	80.69-48.15	91.50-72.59	108.56-54.50	97.44-61.50	90.88-58.25
P/E Ratio	38.71-25.60	45.94-30.39	31.18-22.66	32.28-19.26	35.88-28.47	38.91-19.53	39.61-25.00	48.60-31.15
Average Yield %	2.32	2.15	2.11	1.91	1.40	1.32	1.21	1.12

Address: Lilly Corporate Center, Indianapolis, IN 46285 **Telephone:** 317-276-2000 **Web Site:** www.lilly.com	**Officers:** Sidney Taurel - Chmn., Pres., C.E.O. Charles E. Golden - Exec. V.P., C.F.O. **Transfer Agents:**Norwest Shareowner Services, South St. Paul, MN	**Investor Contact:** 317-276-2506 **No of Institutions:** 731 **Shares:** 766,607,360 **% Held:** 67.68

LINCOLN NATIONAL CORP. (ID)

Exchange	Symbol	Price	52Wk Range	Yield	P/E
NYS	LNC	$45.53 (5/31/2005)	49.30-41.71	3.21	10.74

*7 Year Price Score 94.21 *NYSE Composite Index=100 *12 Month Price Score 93.57

Interim Earnings (Per Share)

Qtr.	Mar	Jun	Sep	Dec
2002	0.49	0.81	(0.68)	0.34
2003	0.23	0.80	0.74	1.08
2004	0.72	1.04	1.12	1.07
2005	1.01	...	...	...

Interim Dividends (Per Share)

Amt	Decl	Ex	Rec	Pay
0.35Q	9/9/2004	10/6/2004	10/8/2004	11/1/2004
0.365Q	11/11/2004	1/6/2005	1/10/2005	2/1/2005
0.365Q	3/10/2005	4/7/2005	4/11/2005	5/1/2005
0.365Q	5/12/2005	7/7/2005	7/11/2005	8/1/2005

Indicated Div: $1.46 (Div. Reinv. Plan)

Valuation Analysis

Forecast P/E	11.23 (6/1/2005)		
Market Cap	$7.9 Billion	Book Value	6.0 Billion
Price/Book	1.31	Price/Sales	1.46

Dividend Achiever Status

Rank	256	**10 Year Growth Rate**	5.49%
Total Years of Dividend Growth			21

Business Summary: Insurance (MIC: 8.2 SIC: 311 NAIC: 24113)

Lincoln National is a holding company, which operates multiple insurance and investment management businesses through subsidiary companies. Through its business segments, Co. sells a wide range of wealth protection and accumulation products. These products include fixed annuities, variable annuities, universal life insurance, variable universal life insurance, term life insurance, other individual insurance coverages, retail mutual funds, 529 college savings plans and managed accounts. Co. has four business segments: Lincoln Retirement, Life Insurance, Investment Management and Lincoln UK.

Recent Developments: For the quarter ended Mar 31 2005, net income increased 37.2% to $178,936 thousand from net income of $130,457 thousand in the year-earlier quarter. Revenues were $1,313,239 thousand, up 4.3% from $1,259,030 thousand the year before. Net premiums earned were $70,368 thousand versus $75,563 thousand in the prior-year quarter, a decrease of 6.9%.

Prospects: Co. is optimistic regarding its 2005 prospects. For the retirement segment, Co. expects income from operations to benefit from continued positive variable flows recognizing adjustments for equity markets and spread compression guidance. Also, Co. expects life insurance income from operations to build from results reported in the first quarter of 2005 after factoring in greater than expected mortality and related deferred acquisition costs of approximately $3.0 million. For investment management, Co. expects income from operations to build assuming the effect of positive equity markets are offset by the acquisition costs related to significant deposit growth.

Financial Data

(US$ in Thousands)	3 Mos	12/31/2004	12/31/2003	12/31/2002	12/31/2001	12/31/2000	12/31/1999	12/31/1998
Earnings Per Share	4.24	3.95	2.85	0.49	3.05	3.19	2.30	2.51
Cash Flow Per Share	6.49	6.29	5.89	2.68	6.64	10.35	8.27	6.63
Tang Book Value Per Share	21.62	22.26	18.77	15.62	14.11	11.06	5.59	10.16
Dividends Per Share	1.415	1.400	1.340	1.280	1.220	1.160	1.100	1.040
Dividend Payout %	33.37	35.44	47.02	261.22	40.00	36.36	47.83	41.43
Income Statement								
Premium Income	70,368	298,904	280,951	315,943	1,704,002	1,813,111	1,881,515	1,620,629
Total Revenue	1,313,239	5,371,274	5,283,881	4,635,462	6,380,638	6,851,507	6,803,700	6,087,063
Benefits & Claims	572,645	2,303,652	2,428,523	2,859,505	3,409,740	3,557,160	3,805,024	3,328,865
Income Before Taxes	237,803	1,035,658	1,047,563	1,624	764,139	836,291	569,964	697,398
Income Taxes	58,867	304,147	280,408	(89,966)	158,362	214,898	109,610	187,623
Net Income	178,936	707,009	511,936	91,590	590,211	621,393	460,354	509,775
Average Shares	176,628	179,017	179,441	185,596	193,303	194,920	200,417	203,262
Balance Sheet								
Total Assets	116,352,181	116,219,265	106,744,868	93,133,422	98,001,304	99,844,059	103,095,733	93,836,260
Total Liabilities	110,309,253	110,043,676	100,933,243	87,837,155	92,737,820	94,889,975	98,831,865	88,448,319
Stockholders' Equity	6,042,928	6,175,589	5,811,625	5,296,267	5,263,484	4,954,084	4,263,868	5,387,941
Shares Outstanding	173,682	173,557	178,212	177,307	186,943	190,748	195,494	202,112
Statistical Record								
Return on Assets %	0.67	0.63	0.51	0.10	0.60	0.61	0.47	0.60
Return on Equity %	12.40	11.76	9.22	1.73	11.55	13.45	9.54	9.83
Loss Ratio %	813.79	770.70	864.39	905.07	200.10	196.19	202.23	205.41
Net Margin %	13.63	13.16	9.69	1.98	9.25	9.07	6.77	8.37
Price Range	49.95-41.71	49.95-40.17	41.32-25.17	53.50-25.17	52.55-39.10	56.13-23.19	57.31-36.50	48.78-34.38
P/E Ratio	11.78-9.84	12.65-10.17	14.50-8.83	109.18-51.37	17.23-12.82	17.59-7.27	24.92-15.87	19.43-13.70
Average Yield %	3.09	3.11	4.03	3.25	2.66	2.92	2.35	2.50

Address: 1500 Market Street, Suite 3900, Philadelphia, PA 19102-2112 **Telephone:** 215-448-1400 **Web Site:** www.lfg.com	**Officers:** Jon A. Boscia - Chmn., C.E.O. Casey J. Trumble - Sr. V.P. **Transfer Agents:** First Chicago Trust Company of New York, Jersey City, NJ	**Investor Contact:** 215-448-1422 **No of Institutions:** 393 **Shares:** 125,705,912 **% Held:** 72.10

LINEAR TECHNOLOGY CORP.

Exchange	Symbol	Price	52Wk Range	Yield	P/E
NMS	LLTC	$37.50 (5/31/2005)	40.31-34.42	1.07	27.99

***7 Year Price Score 88.57** *NYSE Composite Index=100 ***12 Month Price Score 95.25**

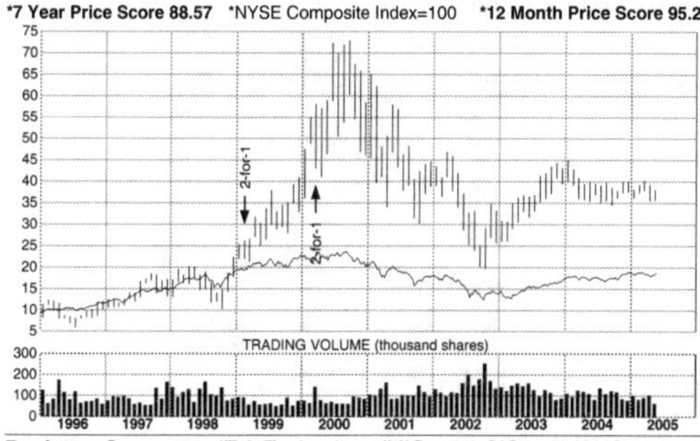

TRADING VOLUME (thousand shares)

Interim Earnings (Per Share)

Qtr.	Sep	Dec	Mar	Jun
2001-02	0.14	0.14	0.16	0.17
2002-03	0.17	0.18	0.19	0.21
2003-04	0.22	0.23	0.27	0.31
2004-05	0.33	0.33	0.39	...

Interim Dividends (Per Share)

Amt	Decl	Ex	Rec	Pay
0.08Q	7/21/2004	7/28/2004	7/30/2004	8/18/2004
0.08Q	10/12/2004	10/20/2004	10/22/2004	11/10/2004
0.10Q	1/18/2005	1/26/2005	1/28/2005	2/16/2005
0.10Q	4/19/2005	4/27/2005	4/29/2005	5/18/2005

Indicated Div: $0.40

Valuation Analysis

Forecast P/E	26.37 (6/1/2005)		
Market Cap	$11.6 Billion	Book Value	2.0 Billion
Price/Book	5.79	Price/Sales	11.37

Dividend Achiever Status

Rank	13	10 Year Growth Rate	26.19%
Total Years of Dividend Growth			12

Business Summary: IT & Technology (MIC: 10.2 SIC: 674 NAIC: 34413)

Linear Technology, together with its consolidated subsidiaries, designs, manufactures and markets a broad line of standard high performance linear integrated circuits. Applications for Co.'s products include telecommunications, cellular telephones, networking products, notebook computers, computer peripherals, video/multimedia, industrial instrumentation, security monitoring devices, high-end consumer products such as digital cameras and MP3 players, complex medical devices, automotive electronics, factory automation, process control, and military and space systems.

Recent Developments: For the quarter ended Apr 3 2005, net income increased 42.2% to $121,633 thousand from net income of $85,549 thousand in the year-earlier quarter. Revenues were $290,734 thousand, up 39.0% from $209,133 thousand the year before. Operating income was $165,960 thousand versus an income of $114,351 thousand in the prior-year quarter, an increase of 45.1%. Total direct expense was $56,600 thousand versus $47,596 thousand in the prior-year quarter, an increase of 18.9%. Total indirect expense was $68,174 thousand versus $47,186 thousand in the prior-year quarter, an increase of 44.5%.

Prospects: Co.'s near-term outlook appears challenging. Co. stated that many of its customers are cautious given the general concerns in the macroeconomic environment. For the quarter ended June 2005, Co. expects end demand to be relatively stable with bookings increasing slightly over the prior quarter. Co. noted that additional royalty revenue under its recent license agreement, which is not expected to be material, does not commence until the Sep 2005 quarter. However, Co. expects sequential product revenues in the June 2005 quarter to increase 2.0% to 3.0% over the quarter ended Apr 3 2005. Thus, Co. expect total revenue for the June 2005 quarter in the range of $255.0 million to $258.0 million.

Financial Data

(US$ in Thousands)	9 Mos	6 Mos	3 Mos	06/27/2004	06/29/2003	06/30/2002	07/01/2001	07/02/2000
Earnings Per Share	1.34	1.22	1.14	1.02	0.74	0.60	1.29	0.88
Cash Flow Per Share	1.55	1.60	1.66	1.47	0.91	0.81	1.77	1.40
Tang Book Value Per Share	6.47	6.25	6.03	5.87	5.80	5.63	5.59	4.20
Dividends Per Share	0.340	0.320	0.300	0.280	0.210	0.170	0.130	0.090
Dividend Payout %	25.38	26.18	26.26	27.45	28.38	28.33	10.08	10.23
Income Statement								
Total Revenue	793,883	503,149	253,028	807,281	606,573	512,282	972,625	705,917
EBITDA	484,672	305,305	155,964	485,530	340,411	271,360	582,073	399,354
Depn & Amortn	36,718	23,311	11,467	48,800	45,900	46,261	35,788	24,958
Income Before Taxes	468,468	294,706	149,965	462,213	333,226	278,350	610,651	417,254
Income Taxes	140,541	88,412	46,489	134,042	96,635	80,721	183,195	129,348
Net Income	327,927	206,294	103,476	328,171	236,591	197,629	427,456	287,906
Average Shares	315,617	315,797	316,918	321,456	321,375	328,538	332,527	328,002
Balance Sheet								
Current Assets	1,986,354	1,924,662	1,891,638	1,832,095	1,776,000	1,727,581	1,727,848	1,310,103
Total Assets	2,257,726	2,195,638	2,151,146	2,087,703	2,056,879	1,988,433	2,017,074	1,507,256
Current Liabilities	192,439	193,966	219,912	202,614	162,029	168,997	202,224	168,677
Total Liabilities	263,265	267,586	294,342	277,098	241,950	206,979	235,117	185,059
Stockholders' Equity	1,994,461	1,928,052	1,856,804	1,810,605	1,814,929	1,781,454	1,781,957	1,322,197
Shares Outstanding	308,195	308,271	307,902	308,548	312,706	316,150	318,908	315,167
Statistical Record								
Return on Assets %	19.28	17.75	16.93	15.88	11.73	9.89	24.32	22.18
Return on Equity %	21.88	20.17	19.34	18.15	13.19	11.12	27.62	25.42
EBITDA Margin %	61.05	60.68	61.64	60.14	56.12	52.97	59.85	56.57
Net Margin %	41.31	41.00	40.90	40.65	39.00	38.58	43.95	40.78
Asset Turnover	0.47	0.43	0.41	0.39	0.30	0.26	0.55	0.54
Current Ratio	10.32	9.92	8.60	9.04	10.96	10.22	8.54	7.77
Price Range	40.31-34.42	44.95-34.42	44.95-34.42	44.95-32.38	36.77-19.61	48.24-28.58	72.94-33.95	72.31-27.89
P/E Ratio	30.08-25.69	36.84-28.21	39.43-30.19	44.07-31.75	49.69-26.50	80.40-47.63	56.54-26.32	82.17-31.69
Average Yield %	0.90	0.84	0.77	0.71	0.71	0.42	0.24	0.21

Address: 1630 McCarthy Boulevard, Milpitas, CA 95035 **Telephone:** 408-432-1900 **Web Site:** www.linear.com	**Officers:** Robert H. Swanson Jr. - Chmn. David B. Bell - Pres. **Transfer Agents:** EquiServe Trust Company	**Investor Contact:** 408-432-1900 **No of Institutions:** 397 **Shares:** 264,479,552 **% Held:** 86.13

LOWE'S COS., INC.

Exchange	Symbol	Price	52Wk Range	Yield	P/E
NYS	LOW	$57.21 (5/31/2005)	60.25-46.49	0.42	21.11

*7 Year Price Score 129.22 *NYSE Composite Index=100 *12 Month Price Score 96.47

Interim Earnings (Per Share)

Qtr.	Apr	Jul	Oct	Jan
2000-01	0.25	0.36	0.27	0.19
2001-02	0.29	0.42	0.32	0.28
2002-03	0.44	0.59	0.43	0.40
2003-04	0.53	0.75	0.56	0.50
2004-05	0.57	0.89	0.66	0.60

Interim Dividends (Per Share)

Amt	Decl	Ex	Rec	Pay
0.04Q	9/13/2004	10/13/2004	10/15/2004	10/29/2004
0.04Q	12/6/2004	1/12/2005	1/14/2005	1/28/2005
0.04Q	3/21/2005	4/13/2005	4/15/2005	4/29/2005
0.06Q	5/27/2005	7/13/2005	7/15/2005	7/29/2005

Indicated Div: $0.24 (Div. Reinv. Plan)

Valuation Analysis

Forecast P/E	14.99 (6/3/2005)		
Market Cap	$44.3 Billion	Book Value	11.5 Billion
Price/Book	3.84	Price/Sales	1.21

Dividend Achiever Status

Rank	127	10 Year Growth Rate	12.70%
Total Years of Dividend Growth			43

Business Summary: Retail - Hardware (MIC: 5.6 SIC: 211 NAIC: 44110)

Lowe's Companies is a major retailer of home improvement products, with specific emphasis on retail do-it-yourself customers, do-it-for-me customers who utilize Co.'s installation services, and commercial business customers. Co. offers an array of products and services for home decorating, maintenance, repair, remodeling and maintenance of commercial buildings. As of Jan 28 2005, Co. operated 1,087 stores in 48 states representing 124.0 million square feet of retail selling space. Co.'s typical home improvement store stocks more than 40,000 items, with hundreds of thousands of items available through its Special Order Sales system.

Recent Developments: For the three months ended Apr 29 2005, net earnings increased 30.5% to $590.0 million compared with $452.0 million in the corresponding year-earlier period. Net sales advanced 14.2% to $9.91 billion from $8.68 billion the previous year. Gross margin was $3.42 billion, or 34.5% of net sales, versus $2.87 billion, or 33.1% of net sales, the year before. Selling, general and administrative expenses amounted to $2.14 billion compared with $1.85 billion in the prior-year period. During the quarter ended Apr 29 2005, Co. opened 27 stores, including 2 relocations.

Prospects: Co.'s outlook appears decent, supported in part by recent comparable store sales gains of 3.8% for the first quarter ended Apr 29 2005. Looking ahead, Co. expects to open 150 stores in 2005 reflecting total square footage growth of 13.0% to 14.0%. Additionally, Co. expects total sales for fiscal year 2005 to grow approximately 17.0%, with comparable store sales increasing about 5.0%. Operating margin, which is defined as gross margin less selling, general and administrative expense and depreciation, is expected to increase about 20 basis points. Diluted earnings per share of $3.25 to $3.34 are expected for the fiscal year ending Feb 3 2006. Co. noted that fiscal year 2005 is a 53-week year.

Financial Data

(US$ in Thousands)	01/28/2005	01/30/2004	01/31/2003	02/01/2002	02/02/2001	01/28/2000	01/29/1999	01/30/1998
Earnings Per Share	2.71	2.34	1.85	1.30	1.05	0.88	0.68	0.52
Cash Flow Per Share	3.91	3.88	3.47	2.09	1.45	1.54	0.99	0.96
Tang Book Value Per Share	14.91	13.09	10.62	8.60	7.17	6.14	4.45	3.71
Dividends Per Share	0.150	0.110	0.085	0.077	0.070	0.063	0.059	0.055
Dividend Payout %	5.55	4.70	4.59	5.96	6.64	7.14	8.64	10.68
Income Statement								
Total Revenue	36,464,000	30,838,000	26,491,000	22,111,108	18,778,559	15,905,595	12,244,882	10,136,890
EBITDA	4,632,000	3,959,000	3,186,000	2,331,890	1,811,776	1,485,791	1,105,371	865,186
Depn & Amortn	920,000	781,000	645,000	534,102	409,511	337,822	272,214	241,072
Income Before Taxes	3,536,000	2,998,000	2,359,000	1,624,251	1,281,440	1,063,117	758,422	558,547
Income Taxes	1,360,000	1,136,000	888,000	600,989	471,569	390,322	276,000	201,063
Net Income	2,176,000	1,877,000	1,471,000	1,023,262	809,871	672,795	482,422	357,484
Average Shares	808,000	806,000	800,000	794,597	768,950	767,708	707,590	697,518
Balance Sheet								
Current Assets	6,974,000	6,687,000	5,568,000	4,920,392	4,175,013	3,709,541	2,585,683	2,109,602
Total Assets	21,209,000	19,042,000	16,109,000	13,736,219	11,375,754	9,012,323	6,344,651	5,219,277
Current Liabilities	5,719,000	4,368,000	3,578,000	3,016,830	2,928,585	2,385,954	1,765,344	1,449,320
Long-Term Obligations	3,060,000	3,678,000	3,736,000	3,734,011	2,697,669	1,726,579	1,283,092	1,045,570
Total Liabilities	9,674,000	8,733,000	7,807,000	7,061,777	5,880,869	4,316,852	3,208,699	2,618,668
Stockholders' Equity	11,535,000	10,309,000	8,302,000	6,674,442	5,494,885	4,695,471	3,135,952	2,600,609
Shares Outstanding	773,800	787,300	781,900	775,714	766,484	764,718	705,286	701,264
Statistical Record								
Return on Assets %	10.84	10.71	9.88	8.17	7.82	8.79	8.37	7.43
Return on Equity %	19.98	20.23	19.70	16.86	15.64	17.23	16.87	14.88
EBITDA Margin %	12.70	12.84	12.03	10.55	9.65	9.34	9.03	8.54
Net Margin %	5.97	6.09	5.55	4.63	4.31	4.23	3.94	3.53
Asset Turnover	1.82	1.76	1.78	1.77	1.81	2.08	2.12	2.11
Current Ratio	1.22	1.53	1.56	1.63	1.43	1.55	1.46	1.46
Debt to Equity	0.27	0.36	0.45	0.56	0.49	0.37	0.41	0.40
Price Range	60.25-46.49	60.05-34.01	48.10-33.50	47.50-25.00	31.75-18.72	32.56-21.50	29.16-12.47	12.64-8.09
P/E Ratio	22.23-17.15	25.66-14.53	26.00-18.11	36.54-19.23	30.24-17.83	37.00-24.43	42.88-18.34	24.31-15.56
Average Yield %	0.28	0.23	0.20	0.22	0.30	0.23	0.31	0.55

Address: 1000 Lowe's Boulevard, Mooresville, NC 28117	**Officers:** Robert A. Niblock - Chmn., Pres., C.E.O. Dale C. Pond - Sr. Exec. V.P., Merchandising & Mktg.	**Investor Contact:** 704-758-2033
Telephone: 704-758-1000	**ransfer Agents:**EquiServe Trust Company, NA, Canton, MA	**No of Institutions:** 700
Web Site: www.lowes.com		**Shares:** 604,269,376 **% Held:** 78.29

LSI INDUSTRIES INC.

Exchange	Symbol	Price	52Wk Range	Yield	P/E
NMS	LYTS	$13.59 (5/31/2005)	13.92-8.49	2.94	23.43

Interim Earnings (Per Share)

Qtr.	Sep	Dec	Mar	Jun
2001-02	0.19	0.23	0.13	0.16
2002-03	0.11	0.14	0.02	(0.81)
2003-04	0.13	0.20	0.05	0.05
2004-05	0.17	0.24	0.12	...

Interim Dividends (Per Share)

Amt	Decl	Ex	Rec	Pay
0.072Q	8/12/2004	9/2/2004	9/7/2004	9/14/2004
0.072Q	10/27/2004	11/5/2004	11/9/2004	11/16/2004
0.10Q	1/26/2005	2/4/2005	2/8/2005	2/15/2005
0.10Q	4/28/2005	5/6/2005	5/10/2005	5/17/2005

Indicated Div: $0.40

Valuation Analysis

Forecast P/E 17.10 (5/28/2005)
Market Cap $268.4 Million Book Value 134.9 Million
Price/Book 1.99 Price/Sales 0.97

Dividend Achiever Status

Rank 42 **10 Year Growth Rate** 19.60%
Total Years of Dividend Growth 11

Business Summary: Electrical (MIC: 11.14 SIC: 648 NAIC: 35129)

LSI Industries is a provider of comprehensive corporate visual image solutions through the combination of extensive screen and digital graphics capabilities, a wide variety of high quality indoor and outdoor lighting products, and related professional services. Co. is also a provider of corporate visual image solutions to the petroleum/convenience store industry. Co. also provides graphics and lighting products and professional services on a stand-alone basis. Co.'s business is organized in two segments: the Lighting Segment and the Graphics Segment.

Recent Developments: For the quarter ended Mar 31 2005, net income increased 163.3% to $2,422 thousand from net income of $920 thousand in the year-earlier quarter. Revenues were $67,814 thousand, up 31.7% from $51,500 thousand the year before. Operating income was $3,214 thousand versus an income of $1,477 thousand in the prior-year quarter, an increase of 117.6%. Total direct expense was $52,435 thousand versus $39,690 thousand in the prior-year quarter, an increase of 32.1%. Total indirect expense was $12,165 thousand versus $10,333 thousand in the prior-year quarter, an increase of 17.7%.

Prospects: Co. continues to penetrate new segments of the commercial industrial lighting market through increased promotional efforts and new product introductions. During the third quarter, Co. continued to expand its architectural outdoor lighting product line with the release of a new decorative low-voltage line and the expansion of its family of architectural wall mounted products. In addition, Co. is experiencing positive initial customer response to its recently launched Encore™ products for the petroleum/convenience store market. For the fiscal year ending Jun 30 2005, Co. anticipates net sales in the range of $277.0 million to $282.0 million and earnings of between $0.68 and $0.70 per share.

Financial Data

(US$ in Thousands)	9 Mos	6 Mos	3 Mos	06/30/2004	06/30/2003	06/30/2002	06/30/2001	06/30/2000
Earnings Per Share	0.58	0.51	0.47	0.43	(0.54)	0.70	0.50	0.89
Cash Flow Per Share	0.95	0.56	0.53	0.61	0.67	1.39	(0.14)	1.03
Tang Book Value Per Share	5.74	5.70	5.52	5.41	5.20	4.95	4.37	4.96
Dividends Per Share	0.316	0.288	0.288	0.264	0.192	0.189	0.205	0.207
Dividend Payout %	54.48	56.53	61.56	61.40	...	26.89	40.96	23.20
Income Statement								
Total Revenue	210,448	142,634	68,335	241,405	213,133	259,261	233,940	235,601
EBITDA	21,480	16,524	7,098	19,959	17,068	29,480	22,852	34,052
Depn & Amortn	5,262	3,520	1,773	5,925	5,702	6,096	5,558	5,511
Income Before Taxes	16,052	12,870	5,263	13,797	11,247	22,860	17,317	29,409
Income Taxes	5,522	4,762	1,947	5,107	3,454	8,674	6,716	11,130
Net Income	10,530	8,108	3,316	8,690	(10,748)	14,186	9,878	17,279
Average Shares	20,109	20,047	19,993	20,038	19,922	20,058	19,730	19,413
Balance Sheet								
Current Assets	93,303	99,394	100,985	97,123	83,505	86,176	91,780	87,080
Total Assets	168,109	175,390	177,588	174,732	162,776	189,842	181,759	146,783
Current Liabilities	28,749	29,667	29,786	32,399	23,872	30,383	29,661	25,941
Long-Term Obligations	3,000	9,959	15,014	11,554	13,999	17,688	23,638	1,498
Total Liabilities	33,175	41,073	46,701	45,869	37,871	50,493	54,566	28,571
Stockholders' Equity	134,934	134,317	130,887	128,863	124,905	139,349	127,193	118,212
Shares Outstanding	19,750	19,772	19,773	19,733	19,702	19,720	19,572	19,296
Statistical Record								
Return on Assets %	6.98	5.93	5.45	5.14	N.M.	7.64	6.01	12.11
Return on Equity %	8.86	7.72	7.27	6.83	N.M.	10.64	8.05	15.60
EBITDA Margin %	10.21	11.58	10.39	8.27	8.01	11.37	9.77	14.45
Net Margin %	5.00	5.68	4.85	3.60	N.M.	5.47	4.22	7.33
Asset Turnover	1.65	1.52	1.45	1.43	1.21	1.40	1.42	1.65
Current Ratio	3.25	3.35	3.39	3.00	3.50	2.84	3.09	3.36
Debt to Equity	0.02	0.07	0.11	0.09	0.11	0.13	0.19	0.01
Price Range	12.90-8.49	14.37-8.49	14.37-8.49	14.37-8.73	14.79-6.94	17.29-10.77	14.29-7.87	13.52-7.17
P/E Ratio	22.24-14.64	28.18-16.65	30.57-18.06	33.42-20.30	...	24.70-15.39	28.58-15.73	15.19-8.05
Average Yield %	2.95	2.59	2.51	2.28	2.18	1.37	1.88	1.90

Address: 10000 Alliance Road, Cincinnati, OH 45242
Telephone: 513-793-3200
Web Site: www.lsi-industries.com

Officers: Robert J. Ready - Chmn., Pres., C.E.O. James P. Sferra - Exec. V.P., Manufacturing, Sec.

Investor Contact: 513-793-3200
No of Institutions: 68
Shares: 12,126,823 **% Held:** 61.33

M & T BANK CORP

Exchange	Symbol	Price	52Wk Range	Yield	P/E
NYS	MTB	$102.14 (5/31/2005)	108.01-87.08	1.76	16.16

*7 Year Price Score 122.71 *NYSE Composite Index=100 *12 Month Price Score 100.22

Interim Earnings (Per Share)

Qtr.	Mar	Jun	Sep	Dec
2002	1.25	1.26	1.23	1.32
2003	1.23	1.10	1.28	1.36
2004	1.30	1.53	1.56	1.61
2005	1.62	...	...	...

Interim Dividends (Per Share)

Amt	Decl	Ex	Rec	Pay
0.40Q	7/27/2004	8/31/2004	9/2/2004	9/30/2004
0.40Q	10/27/2004	11/29/2004	12/1/2004	12/31/2004
0.40Q	2/17/2005	2/24/2005	2/28/2005	3/31/2005
0.45Q	4/19/2005	5/27/2005	6/1/2005	6/30/2005

Indicated Div: $1.80 (Div. Reinv. Plan)

Valuation Analysis

Forecast P/E	15.24 (6/2/2005)		
Market Cap	$11.6 Billion	Book Value	5.7 Billion
Price/Book	2.05	Price/Sales	3.49

Dividend Achiever Status

Rank	31	10 Year Growth Rate	21.95%
Total Years of Dividend Growth			24

TRADING VOLUME (thousand shares)

Business Summary: Commercial Banking (MIC: 8.1 SIC: 022 NAIC: 22110)

M&T Bank, with assets of $52.94 billion as of Dec 31 2004, is a bank holding company with two wholly-owned bank subsidiaries, M&T Bank and M&T Bank, National Association. Co. provides individuals, corporations and other businesses, and institutions with commercial and retail banking services, including loans and deposits, trust, mortgage banking, asset management, insurance and other financial services. Banking activities are focused on consumers in New York, Pennsylvania, Maryland and the District of Columbia and on small and medium-size businesses in those areas. Banking services are also provided in Delaware, Virginia and West Virginia, and certain subsidiaries operate in other states.

Recent Developments: For the quarter ended Mar 31 2005, net income increased 18.7% to $189,290 thousand from net income of $159,490 thousand in the year-earlier quarter. Net interest income was $442,055 thousand, up 5.4% from $419,303 thousand the year before. Provision for loan losses was $24,000 thousand versus $20,000 thousand in the prior-year quarter, an increase of 20.0%. Non-interest income rose 2.7% to $234,258 thousand, while non-interest expense declined 5.8% to $367,337 thousand.

Prospects: Co. is encouraged by the recent growth experienced in its commercial loan portfolios. Meanwhile, Co.'s credit quality trends continue to be favorable, with relatively low levels of non-performing loans and net charge-offs. In addition, Co. continues to see solid results at residential mortgage banking business. Looking ahead to full-year 2005, Co. expects earnings to be in the range of $6.60 to $6.80 per diluted share. Separately, on Mar 17 2005, Co. announced that it has changed the name of its commercial property and casualty insurance agency from Matthews, Bartlett & Dedecker, Inc. to M&T Insurance Agency, Inc. in order to more closely affiliate the agency with M&T Bank.

Financial Data

(US$ in Thousands)	3 Mos	12/31/2004	12/31/2003	12/31/2002	12/31/2001	12/31/2000	12/31/1999	12/31/1998
Earnings Per Share	6.32	6.00	4.95	5.07	3.82	3.44	3.28	2.62
Cash Flow Per Share	6.53	6.14	10.94	6.90	1.61	4.29	7.78	0.48
Tang Book Value Per Share	22.99	23.08	21.42	21.36	17.84	16.10	14.88	13.72
Dividends Per Share	1.600	1.600	1.200	1.050	1.000	0.625	0.450	0.380
Dividend Payout %	25.32	26.67	24.24	20.71	26.18	18.17	13.71	14.53
Income Statement								
Interest Income	638,321	2,298,732	2,126,565	1,842,099	2,101,885	1,772,784	1,478,631	1,351,794
Interest Expense	196,266	564,160	527,810	594,514	943,597	918,597	719,234	687,503
Net Interest Income	442,055	1,734,572	1,598,755	1,247,585	1,158,288	854,187	759,397	664,291
Provision for Losses	24,000	95,000	131,000	122,000	103,500	38,000	44,500	43,200
Non-Interest Income	234,258	942,969	831,095	511,931	477,426	324,672	282,375	270,595
Non-Interest Expense	367,337	1,516,018	1,448,180	921,032	948,318	694,453	578,958	566,123
Income Before Taxes	284,976	1,066,523	850,670	716,484	583,896	446,406	418,314	325,563
Income Taxes	95,686	344,002	276,728	231,392	205,821	160,250	152,688	117,589
Net Income	189,290	722,521	573,942	485,092	378,075	286,156	265,626	207,974
Average Shares	117,184	120,406	115,932	95,663	99,024	83,171	80,900	79,500
Balance Sheet								
Net Loans & Leases	38,441,350	37,771,613	35,158,377	25,291,312	24,762,752	22,368,111	17,090,606	15,485,183
Total Assets	53,887,218	52,938,721	49,826,081	33,174,525	31,450,196	28,949,456	22,409,115	20,583,891
Total Deposits	36,293,407	35,429,473	33,114,944	21,664,923	21,580,400	20,232,673	15,373,620	14,737,152
Total Liabilities	48,213,613	47,209,107	44,108,871	29,992,702	28,510,745	26,248,971	20,612,069	18,981,525
Stockholders' Equity	5,673,605	5,729,614	5,717,210	3,181,823	2,939,451	2,700,485	1,797,046	1,602,366
Shares Outstanding	113,978	115,227	120,106	92,028	93,683	93,244	77,238	76,980
Statistical Record								
Return on Assets %	1.44	1.40	1.38	1.50	1.25	1.11	1.24	1.20
Return on Equity %	13.19	12.59	12.90	15.85	13.41	12.69	15.63	15.80
Net Interest Margin %	69.25	75.46	75.18	67.73	55.11	48.18	51.36	49.14
Efficiency Ratio %	42.10	46.77	48.96	39.13	36.77	33.11	32.88	34.89
Loans to Deposits	1.06	1.07	1.06	1.17	1.15	1.11	1.11	1.05
Price Range	108.01-83.37	108.01-83.37	98.55-75.69	89.94-68.00	81.23-61.09	68.00-36.40	56.66-41.00	57.52-41.00
P/E Ratio	17.09-13.19	18.00-13.90	19.91-15.29	17.74-13.41	21.26-15.99	19.77-10.58	17.27-12.50	21.96-15.65
Average Yield %	1.65	1.69	1.39	1.30	1.39	1.34	0.91	0.77

Address: One M&T Plaza, 5th Floor, Buffalo, NY 14203
Telephone: 716-842-5445
Web Site: www.mandtbank.com

Officers: Robert G. Wilmers - Chmn., Pres., CEO Carl L. Campbell - Vice-Chmn. **Transfer Agents:** Registrar and Transfer Company, Cranford, NJ

No of Institutions: 256
Shares: 73,741,136 **% Held:** 64.08

MACERICH CO. (THE)

Exchange	Symbol	Price	52Wk Range	Yield	P/E
NYS	MAC	$63.03 (5/31/2005)	64.66-44.70	4.13	45.35

***7 Year Price Score 154.05** *NYSE Composite Index=100 ***12 Month Price Score 102.10**

Interim Earnings (Per Share)

Qtr.	Mar	Jun	Sep	Dec
2002	0.50	(0.04)	0.32	0.85
2003	0.37	0.55	0.69	0.45
2004	0.31	0.29	0.29	0.51
2005	0.30	...	...	...

Interim Dividends (Per Share)

Amt	Decl	Ex	Rec	Pay
0.61Q	7/30/2004	8/18/2004	8/20/2004	9/10/2004
0.65Q	10/29/2004	11/10/2004	11/15/2004	12/9/2004
0.65Q	2/7/2005	2/18/2005	2/23/2005	3/8/2005
0.65Q	4/28/2005	5/18/2005	5/20/2005	6/10/2005

Indicated Div: $2.60

Valuation Analysis

Forecast P/E	14.56 (6/2/2005)		
Market Cap	$3.7 Billion	Book Value	897.4 Million
Price/Book	4.15	Price/Sales	6.48

Dividend Achiever Status

Rank	154	**10 Year Growth Rate**	11.04%
Total Years of Dividend Growth			10

Business Summary: Property, Real Estate & Development (MIC: 8.3 SIC: 798 NAIC: 25930)

Macerich is a self-administered and self-managed real estate investment trust involved in the acquisition, ownership, development, redevelopment, management and leasing of regional and community shopping centers located throughout the U.S. Co. is the sole general partner of, and owns a majority of the ownership interests in, The Macerich Partnership, L.P., a Delaware limited partnership. As of Dec 31 2004, The Macerich Partnership owned or had an ownership interest in 60 regional shopping centers, 18 community shopping centers and six development/redevelopment properties aggregating approximately 62.5 million square feet of gross leasable area .

Recent Developments: For the quarter ended Mar 31 2005, income totaled $23,422 thousand, before a $1,275 thousand gain from discontinued operations, compared with income of $22,835 thousand, before an $1,893 thousand gain from discontinued operations, in the year-earlier quarter. Results for 2005 included a $1,308 thousand gain from the sale of assets, while results for 2004 included a $405 thousand loss from the early extinguishment of debt. Revenues were $151,379 thousand, up 22.1% from $123,991 thousand the year before.

Prospects: Co. is benefiting from stronger retail sales growth and continued high occupancy levels. Also, Co is enjoying solid growth in funds from operations, fueled by solid same center performance and the positive impact of recent acquisitions. During the quarter, Co. acquired interests in two additional properties including Metrocenter and Kierland Commons, which should further strengthen its presence in the rapidly growing Phoenix, AZ market. Going forward, Co. has revised its 2005 year-end diluted earnings per share guidance to be in the range of $1.23 to $1.33.

Financial Data

(US$ in Thousands)	3 Mos	12/31/2004	12/31/2003	12/31/2002	12/31/2001	12/31/2000	12/31/1999	12/31/1998
Earnings Per Share	1.39	1.40	2.09	1.62	1.72	1.11	2.99	1.06
Cash Flow Per Share	3.00	3.31	4.88	5.52	4.16	3.55	4.10	2.77
Tang Book Value Per Share	12.83	12.83	14.42	15.49	10.27	10.78	18.20	17.03
Dividends Per Share	2.520	2.480	2.320	2.220	2.140	2.060	1.965	1.865
Dividend Payout %	181.29	177.14	111.00	137.04	124.42	185.59	65.72	175.94
Income Statement								
Property Income	141,024	528,099	468,255	366,883	323,038	311,919	318,800	279,306
Non-Property Income	10,355	19,169	17,749	12,041	11,535	8,173	8,644	4,555
Total Revenue	151,379	547,268	486,004	378,924	334,573	320,092	327,444	283,861
Depn & Amortn	36,972	145,573	106,794	77,767	66,016	61,680	61,574	52,506
Interest Expense	42,564	146,327	132,512	122,934	109,646	108,447	113,348	91,433
Income Before Taxes	23,422	...	...	...	...	...	...	...
Net Income	20,498	91,633	128,034	81,382	77,723	56,929	129,011	44,075
Average Shares	73,284	73,099	75,198	50,066	44,963	45,050	60,893	43,628
Balance Sheet								
Total Assets	4,661,984	4,637,096	4,145,593	3,662,080	2,294,502	2,337,242	2,404,293	2,322,056
Long-Term Obligations	2,339,165	2,337,120	1,916,798	1,743,108	1,364,660	1,403,595	1,400,456	1,370,118
Total Liabilities	3,450,970	3,403,314	2,855,559	2,395,449	1,584,226	1,607,134	1,626,408	1,579,119
Stockholders' Equity	897,371	913,533	953,485	797,798	348,954	362,272	620,286	577,413
Shares Outstanding	59,087	58,785	57,902	51,490	33,981	33,612	34,072	33,902
Statistical Record								
Return on Assets %	2.07	2.08	3.28	2.73	3.36	2.39	5.46	2.30
Return on Equity %	9.95	9.79	14.62	14.19	21.86	11.56	21.54	11.11
Net Margin %	13.54	16.74	26.34	21.48	23.23	17.79	39.40	15.53
Price Range	64.66-39.75	64.66-39.75	44.50-28.82	31.48-26.30	26.60-18.75	24.75-18.44	27.06-17.81	30.00-23.25
P/E Ratio	46.52-28.60	46.19-28.39	21.29-13.79	19.43-16.23	15.47-10.90	22.30-16.61	9.05-5.96	28.30-21.93
Average Yield %	4.74	4.86	6.46	7.59	9.26	9.69	8.37	6.82

Address: 401 Wilshire Boulevard, Suite 700, Santa Monica, CA 90401 **Telephone:** 310-394-6000 **Web Site:** www.macerich.com	**Officers:** Mace Siegel - Chmn. Dana K. Anderson - Vice-Chmn.	**No of Institutions:** 172 **Shares:** 53,902,936 **% Held:** 90.94

MAF BANCORP, INC.

Exchange	Symbol	Price	52Wk Range	Yield	P/E
NMS	MAFB	$42.56 (5/31/2005)	47.00-38.50	2.16	14.19

***7 Year Price Score 121.27** *NYSE Composite Index=100 ***12 Month Price Score 93.30**

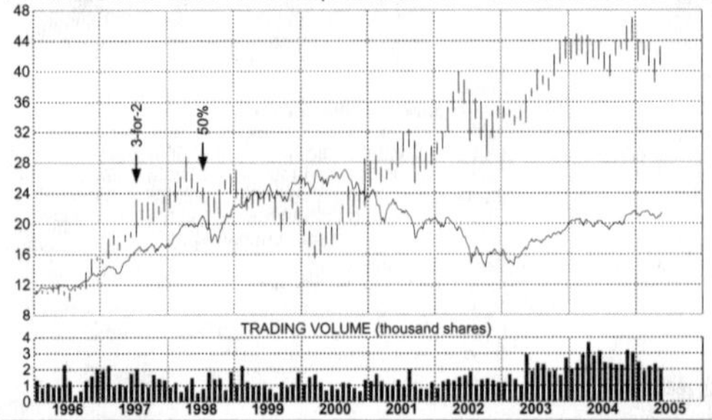

Interim Earnings (Per Share)

Qtr.	Mar	Jun	Sep	Dec
2002	0.70	0.68	0.86	0.86
2003	0.81	0.82	0.79	0.84
2004	0.73	0.77	0.77	0.74
2005	0.72	...	...	...

Interim Dividends (Per Share)

Amt	Decl	Ex	Rec	Pay
0.21Q	7/28/2004	9/13/2004	9/15/2004	10/4/2004
0.21Q	11/18/2004	12/14/2004	12/16/2004	1/3/2005
0.23Q	1/28/2005	3/15/2005	3/17/2005	4/4/2005
0.23Q	4/27/2005	6/10/2005	6/14/2005	7/1/2005

Indicated Div: $0.92

Valuation Analysis

Forecast P/E 13.37 (6/2/2005)
Market Cap $1.4 Billion Book Value 953.1 Million
Price/Book 1.45 Price/Sales 2.75

Dividend Achiever Status

Rank 2 **10 Year Growth Rate** 38.01%
Total Years of Dividend Growth 10

TRADING VOLUME (thousand shares)

Business Summary: Other Depository Banking (MIC: 8.5 SIC: 035 NAIC: 22120)

MAF Bancorp is a savings and loan holding company. Through its wholly-owned subsidiary, Mid America Bank. Co. is engaged in providing general banking services including customer deposits and accounts, consumer loans and lending services and other related activities. The Bank also makes multi-family mortgage, residential construction, land acquisition and development loans. In addition, the Bank provides insurance services; general title services and the residential real estate development business. The Bank operates through a network of 72 branches in Illinois and Wisconsin with total assets of $9.68 billion as of Dec 31 2004.

Recent Developments: For the quarter ended Mar 31 2005, net income decreased 2.5% to $24,177 thousand from net income of $24,794 thousand in the year-earlier quarter. Net interest income was $67,539 thousand, up 5.5% from $64,029 thousand the year before. Provision for loan losses was Nil versus $300 thousand in the prior-year quarter. Non-interest income fell 12.6% to $17,835 thousand, while non-interest expense advanced 3.1% to $73,740 thousand.

Prospects: Co. is experiencing an unfavorable decline in its net interest margin due to deposits and other borrowings being repriced faster than asset yields due to the rise in short-term interest rates. The rise in cost of deposits reflects higher rates on money market accounts and certificates of deposits, driven by the higher short-term interest rates and more aggressive deposit pricing as Co. competes for deposit growth in its markets. Furthermore, Co. expects that the flatter yield curve and increased competition for deposits to pressure its net interest margin throughout full-year 2005.

Financial Data

(US$ in Thousands)	3 Mos	12/31/2004	12/31/2003	12/31/2002	12/31/2001	12/31/2000	12/31/1999	12/31/1998
Earnings Per Share	3.00	3.01	3.26	3.11	2.56	2.40	2.07	1.65
Cash Flow Per Share	4.84	2.40	8.14	2.18	(3.68)	0.53	7.31	(0.30)
Tang Book Value Per Share	18.74	18.95	18.17	16.62	14.37	13.80	12.20	11.31
Dividends Per Share	0.860	0.840	0.720	0.600	0.460	0.390	0.340	0.257
Dividend Payout %	28.67	27.91	22.09	19.29	17.97	16.25	16.43	15.56
Income Statement								
Interest Income	111,524	421,173	316,430	329,490	345,736	343,103	285,092	247,096
Interest Expense	43,985	159,885	136,952	171,465	214,489	217,173	168,401	150,575
Net Interest Income	67,539	261,288	179,478	158,025	131,247	125,930	116,691	96,521
Provision for Losses	...	1,215	...	300	...	1,500	1,100	800
Non-Interest Income	17,835	76,286	71,633	56,363	47,118	37,443	34,844	25,717
Non-Interest Expense	48,155	184,048	120,197	99,342	83,424	73,003	67,680	58,943
Income Before Taxes	37,219	152,311	130,914	114,746	94,941	88,870	82,755	62,495
Income Taxes	13,042	50,789	47,481	40,775	35,466	32,311	31,210	23,793
Net Income	24,177	101,522	83,433	73,971	59,475	56,559	51,545	38,246
Average Shares	33,685	33,706	25,592	23,748	23,195	23,586	24,930	23,198
Balance Sheet								
Net Loans & Leases	6,803,170	6,842,259	6,324,596	4,363,152	4,286,470	4,287,040	3,871,968	3,229,670
Total Assets	9,715,529	9,681,384	8,933,585	5,937,181	5,595,039	5,195,588	4,658,065	4,121,087
Total Deposits	6,014,946	5,935,708	5,580,455	3,751,237	3,557,997	2,974,213	2,699,242	2,656,872
Total Liabilities	8,762,459	8,706,998	8,031,981	5,435,723	5,159,166	4,807,859	4,305,144	3,776,407
Stockholders' Equity	953,070	974,386	901,604	501,458	435,873	387,729	352,921	344,680
Shares Outstanding	32,558	33,273	33,063	23,252	22,982	23,110	23,911	24,970
Statistical Record								
Return on Assets %	1.07	1.09	1.12	1.28	1.10	1.14	1.17	1.01
Return on Equity %	10.80	10.79	11.89	15.78	14.44	15.23	14.78	12.58
Net Interest Margin %	60.56	62.04	56.72	47.96	37.96	36.70	40.93	39.06
Efficiency Ratio %	37.23	37.00	30.97	25.75	21.24	19.18	21.15	21.61
Loans to Deposits	1.13	1.15	1.13	1.16	1.20	1.44	1.43	1.22
Price Range	47.00-39.30	47.00-39.30	44.53-32.87	39.95-28.76	32.35-24.81	28.50-15.50	27.00-19.00	28.83-19.38
P/E Ratio	15.67-13.10	15.61-13.06	13.66-10.08	12.85-9.25	12.64-9.69	11.88-6.46	13.04-9.18	17.47-11.74
Average Yield %	2.01	1.95	1.91	1.76	1.63	1.94	1.50	1.06

Address: 55th Street & Holmes Avenue, Clarendon Hills, IL 60514-1500
Telephone: 630-325-7300
Web Site: www.mafbancorp.com

Officers: Allen H. Koranda - Chmn., C.E.O. Kenneth Koranda - Vice-Chmn., Pres.

Investor Contact: 630-325-7300
No of Institutions: 129
Shares: 14,733,597 **% Held:** 45.05

MARSH & MCLENNAN COS., INC.

Exchange	Symbol	Price	52Wk Range	Yield	P/E
NYS	MMC	$29.04 (5/31/2005)	46.86-24.10	2.34	N/A

*7 Year Price Score 70.99 *NYSE Composite Index=100 *12 Month Price Score 79.16

Interim Earnings (Per Share)

Qtr.	Mar	Jun	Sep	Dec
2002	0.73	0.60	0.55	0.57
2003	0.81	0.66	0.65	0.69
2004	0.83	0.73	0.04	(1.27)
2005	0.25	...	...	...

Interim Dividends (Per Share)

Amt	Decl	Ex	Rec	Pay
0.34Q	9/14/2004	10/13/2004	10/15/2004	11/15/2004
0.17Q	3/1/2005	3/11/2005	3/15/2005	3/30/2005
0.17Q	3/17/2005	4/5/2005	4/7/2005	5/13/2005
0.17Q	5/19/2005	7/5/2005	7/7/2005	8/15/2005

Indicated Div: $0.68 (Div. Reinv. Plan)

Valuation Analysis

Forecast P/E	16.55 (6/2/2005)		
Market Cap	$15.4 Billion	Book Value	5.0 Billion
Price/Book	3.06	Price/Sales	1.27

Dividend Achiever Status

Rank	160	10 Year Growth Rate	10.79%
Total Years of Dividend Growth			43

Business Summary: Insurance (MIC: 8.2 SIC: 411 NAIC: 24210)

Marsh & McLennan Companies is engaged in the worldwide business of providing retail and wholesale insurance services, principally as a broker or consultant for insurers, insurance underwriters and other brokers. Co.'s subsidiaries include Marsh, a risk and insurance services firm; Putnam Investments, one of the largest investment management companies in the U.S.; and Mercer Consulting Group, a major global provider of consulting services. Other subsidiaries render advisory services in the area of employee benefits and compensation consulting, management consulting, economic consulting and environmental consulting.

Recent Developments: For the quarter ended Mar 31 2005, net income decreased 70.0% to $134,000 thousand from net income of $446,000 thousand in the year-earlier quarter. Revenues were $3,182,000 thousand, down 0.4% from $3,196,000 thousand the year before. Service revenue slipped 1.2% to $3,125,000 thousand from $3,163,000 thousand the prior year, while investment income advanced 72.7% to $57,000 thousand from $33,000 thousand the previous year. Operating income totaled $272,000 thousand, down 64.8% versus $773,000 thousand a year earlier.

Prospects: Co. is taking steps to simplify its management structure, as well as improve efficiencies and account profitability. These efforts are expected to expand margins and drive earnings growth in 2006. Meanwhile, Co.'s risk consulting and technology segment is benefiting from sharply higher demand for its technology services. In addition, Co. is making significant progress in expanding its outsourcing capabilities and range of investment advice and services, including the combination of its existing benefits administration operations with Putnam Investments' defined contribution administration activities. Also, Co. continues to see a moderation in net redemptions at Putnam.

Financial Data

(US$ in Thousands)	3 Mos	12/31/2004	12/31/2003	12/31/2002	12/31/2001	12/31/2000	12/31/1999	12/31/1998
Earnings Per Share	(0.25)	0.33	2.81	2.45	1.70	2.05	1.31	1.49
Cash Flow Per Share	3.07	3.92	3.50	2.37	2.50	2.50	1.90	2.21
Dividends Per Share	1.160	1.30	1.18	1.090	1.030	0.950	0.850	0.733
Dividend Payout %	...	393.94	41.99	44.49	60.77	46.34	64.89	49.22
Income Statement								
Total Revenue	3,182,000	12,159,000	11,588,000	10,440,000	9,943,000	10,157,000	9,157,000	7,190,000
Income Before Taxes	212,000	450,000	2,335,000	2,133,000	1,590,000	1,955,000	1,247,000	1,305,000
Income Taxes	74,000	259,000	770,000	747,000	599,000	753,000	521,000	509,000
Net Income	134,000	176,000	1,540,000	1,365,000	974,000	1,181,000	726,000	796,000
Average Shares	536,000	535,000	548,000	557,000	572,000	568,000	544,000	528,000
Balance Sheet								
Total Assets	17,547,000	18,337,000	15,053,000	13,855,000	13,293,000	13,769,000	13,021,000	11,871,000
Total Liabilities	12,519,000	13,281,000	9,602,000	8,837,000	8,120,000	8,541,000	8,851,000	8,212,000
Stockholders' Equity	5,028,000	5,056,000	5,451,000	5,018,000	5,173,000	5,228,000	4,170,000	3,659,000
Shares Outstanding	530,234	526,809	526,736	538,199	548,654	552,052	534,051	514,000
Statistical Record								
Return on Assets %	N.M.	1.05	10.65	10.06	7.20	8.79	5.83	8.05
Return on Equity %	N.M.	3.34	29.42	26.79	18.73	25.06	18.55	23.21
Price Range	47.00-24.10	49.30-24.10	54.74-38.52	56.85-35.53	58.56-40.25	67.44-36.50	48.16-28.72	32.00-22.25
P/E Ratio	...	149.39-73.03	19.48-13.71	23.20-14.50	34.45-23.68	32.90-17.80	36.76-21.92	21.48-14.93
Average Yield %	3.05	3.54	2.53	2.23	2.04	1.75	2.30	2.60

Address: 1166 Avenue Of The Americas, New York, NY 10036
Telephone: 212-345-5000
Web Site: www.mmc.com

Officers: Michael G. Cherkasky - Pres., C.E.O. Sandra S. Wijnberg - Sr. V.P., C.F.O. **Transfer Agents:** The Bank of New York, New York, NY

Investor Contact: 212-345-5475
No of Institutions: 426
Shares: 418,338,752 **% Held:** 79.09

MARSHALL & ILSLEY CORP.

Exchange	Symbol	Price	52Wk Range	Yield	P/E
NYS	MI	$43.51 (5/31/2005)	44.43-37.32	2.21	15.27

*7 Year Price Score 118.33 *NYSE Composite Index=100 *12 Month Price Score 99.56

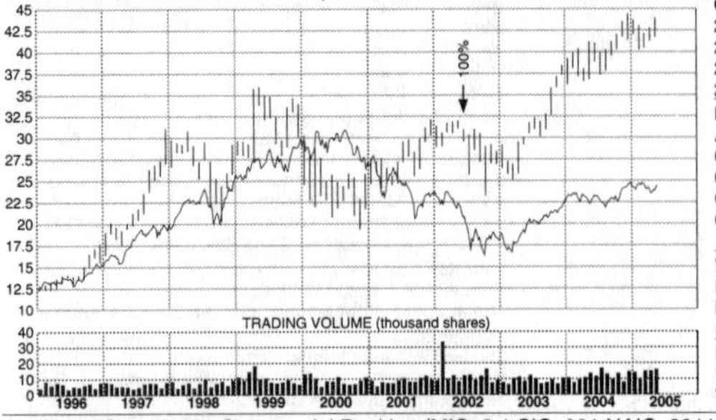

Interim Earnings (Per Share)

Qtr.	Mar	Jun	Sep	Dec
2002	0.53	0.54	0.54	0.55
2003	0.56	0.59	0.61	0.61
2004	0.65	0.67	0.69	0.76
2005	0.73	...	...	...

Interim Dividends (Per Share)

Amt	Decl	Ex	Rec	Pay
0.21Q	8/19/2004	8/27/2004	8/31/2004	9/10/2004
0.21Q	10/21/2004	11/26/2004	11/30/2004	12/10/2004
0.21Q	2/17/2005	2/25/2005	3/1/2005	3/11/2005
0.24Q	4/26/2005	5/25/2005	5/27/2005	6/10/2005

Indicated Div: $0.96 (Div. Reinv. Plan)

Valuation Analysis

Forecast P/E	14.41 (6/2/2005)		
Market Cap	$10.0 Billion	Book Value	4.0 Billion
Price/Book	2.47	Price/Sales	3.01

Dividend Achiever Status

Rank	164	10 Year Growth Rate	10.63%
Total Years of Dividend Growth			32

Business Summary: Commercial Banking (MIC: 8.1 SIC: 021 NAIC: 22110)

Marshall & Ilsley, a multibank holding company with assets of $40.40 billion as of Dec 31 2004, is headquartered in Milwaukee, WI. Co. has 196 banking offices in Wisconsin, 34 locations throughout Arizona, 12 offices in Minnesota, six offices in Missouri, two offices in Florida, one office in Nevada and one office in Illinois, as well as on the Internet. Co. also provides trust services, residential mortgage banking, capital markets, brokerage and insurance, commercial leasing and commercial mortgage banking. Co.'s principal subsidiary is Metavante Corporation, a provider of integrated financial transaction processing, outsourcing services, software, and consulting services.

Recent Developments: For the quarter ended Mar 31 2005, net income increased 16.1% to $169,580 thousand from net income of $146,109 thousand in the year-earlier quarter. Net interest income was $291,781 thousand, up 4.7% from $278,636 thousand the year before. Provision for loan losses was $8,126 thousand versus $9,027 thousand in the prior-year quarter, a decrease of 10.0%. Non-interest income rose 30.7% to $409,534 thousand, while non-interest expense advanced 20.5% to $436,446 thousand.

Prospects: Co.'s near-term prospects remain relatively favorable, supported by solid earnings growth. The improvement in earnings is primarily attributed to an increase in total loan growth and a decrease in non-performing loans compared with the previous year. Co. expects loan growth to continue with the strengthening economy as well as it ability to lower provision for loan and lease losses. Meanwhile, Co.'s balance sheet continues to gain momentum despite returns on average assets and equity. As of Mar 31 2005, Co.'s assets totalled $41.60 billion, compared to $35.50 billion at Mar 31 2004.

Financial Data

(US$ in Thousands)	3 Mos	12/31/2004	12/31/2003	12/31/2002	12/31/2001	12/31/2000	12/31/1999	12/31/1998
Earnings Per Share	2.85	2.77	2.38	2.16	1.54	1.45	1.57	1.30
Cash Flow Per Share	4.53	4.51	4.57	4.41	1.13	4.79	2.97	1.28
Tang Book Value Per Share	8.18	7.76	9.96	8.61	9.16	9.22	8.27	8.99
Dividends Per Share	0.840	0.810	0.700	0.625	0.568	0.517	0.470	0.430
Dividend Payout %	29.47	29.24	29.41	28.94	36.73	35.81	29.94	32.95
Income Statement								
Interest Income	485,607	1,665,790	1,529,920	1,567,336	1,709,107	1,747,982	1,496,584	1,434,044
Interest Expense	193,826	533,798	472,634	561,038	866,328	1,074,976	791,303	757,974
Net Interest Income	291,781	1,131,992	1,057,286	1,006,298	842,779	673,006	705,281	676,070
Provision for Losses	8,126	37,963	62,993	74,416	54,115	30,352	25,419	27,090
Non-Interest Income	409,534	1,446,495	1,215,801	1,082,688	1,002,812	928,352	845,774	756,333
Non-Interest Expense	436,446	1,595,558	1,451,707	1,295,978	1,290,431	1,100,656	997,697	940,028
Income Before Taxes	256,743	944,966	758,387	718,592	501,045	470,350	527,939	465,285
Income Taxes	87,163	317,880	214,282	238,265	163,124	152,948	173,428	163,962
Net Income	169,580	627,086	544,105	480,327	337,485	315,123	354,511	301,323
Average Shares	231,610	226,551	228,285	222,048	218,264	217,766	226,010	230,480
Balance Sheet								
Net Loans & Leases	30,089,372	29,097,000	24,800,756	23,570,437	19,027,174	17,351,972	16,109,199	13,770,114
Total Assets	41,640,521	40,437,402	34,372,643	32,874,642	27,253,734	26,077,739	24,369,723	21,566,293
Total Deposits	25,701,708	26,455,087	22,270,105	20,393,706	16,493,047	19,248,627	16,435,182	15,919,919
Total Liabilities	37,618,119	36,547,588	31,043,950	29,837,974	24,760,766	23,835,550	22,252,797	19,322,514
Stockholders' Equity	4,022,402	3,889,814	3,328,693	3,036,668	2,492,968	2,242,189	2,116,926	2,243,779
Shares Outstanding	228,742	227,340	223,226	226,232	207,897	205,693	211,632	212,206
Statistical Record								
Return on Assets %	1.69	1.67	1.62	1.60	1.27	1.25	1.54	1.47
Return on Equity %	17.52	17.33	17.10	17.37	14.25	14.42	16.26	14.47
Net Interest Margin %	60.09	67.96	69.11	64.20	49.31	38.50	47.13	47.14
Efficiency Ratio %	48.76	51.27	52.87	48.90	47.58	41.13	42.59	42.92
Loans to Deposits	1.17	1.10	1.11	1.16	1.15	0.90	0.98	0.86
Price Range	44.43-36.60	44.43-36.18	38.40-25.07	31.95-23.25	32.06-24.02	31.41-19.31	35.97-27.38	31.06-20.25
P/E Ratio	15.59-12.84	16.04-13.06	16.13-10.53	14.79-10.76	20.82-15.60	21.66-13.32	22.91-17.44	23.89-15.58
Average Yield %	2.07	2.04	2.26	2.11	2.06	2.16	1.50	1.60

Address: 770 North Water Street, Milwaukee, WI 53202 **Telephone:** 414-765-7700 **Web Site:** www.micorp.com	**Officers:** Dennis J. Kuester - Chmn., Pres., C.E.O. John M. Presley - Sr. V.P., C.F.O. **Transfer Agents:** Continental Stock Transfer & Trust Company, New York, NY	**No of Institutions:** 293 **Shares:** 96,873,776 **% Held:** 42.58

MARTIN MARIETTA MATERIALS, INC.

Exchange	Symbol	Price	52Wk Range	Yield	P/E
NYS	MLM	$61.05 (5/31/2005)	61.76-41.76	1.31	20.69

*7 Year Price Score 100.95 *NYSE Composite Index=100 *12 Month Price Score 110.75

Interim Earnings (Per Share)

Qtr.	Mar	Jun	Sep	Dec
2002	(0.22)	1.09	0.80	0.10
2003	(0.43)	0.81	0.93	0.60
2004	(0.14)	0.92	1.11	0.77
2005	0.15	...	...	...

Interim Dividends (Per Share)

Amt	Decl	Ex	Rec	Pay
0.20Q	8/18/2004	8/30/2004	9/1/2004	9/30/2004
0.20Q	11/18/2004	11/29/2004	12/1/2004	12/31/2004
0.20Q	2/3/2005	2/25/2005	3/1/2005	3/31/2005
0.20Q	5/24/2005	5/27/2005	6/1/2005	6/30/2005

Indicated Div: $0.80

Valuation Analysis

Forecast P/E	18.86 (5/28/2005)		
Market Cap	$2.8 Billion	Book Value	1.1 Billion
Price/Book	2.54	Price/Sales	1.58

Dividend Achiever Status

Rank	121	10 Year Growth Rate	13.20%
Total Years of Dividend Growth			10

Business Summary: Construction - Public Infrastructure (MIC: 3.1 SIC: 611 NAIC: 37310)

Martin Marietta Materials is principally engaged in the aggregates business used in the construction of highways, and in domestic commercial and residential construction. As of Dec 31 2004, Co.'s aggregates and asphalt products and ready-mixed concrete were sold from a network of 308 quarries, distribution facilities and plants to customers in 28 states, Canada and the Caribbean. Also, Co. has a Specialty Products segment that produces magnesia-based chemicals products used in industrial, agricultural and environmental applications; dolomitic lime sold for the steel industry; and structural composite products used in a variety of industries.

Recent Developments: For the quarter ended Mar 31 2005, income$8,300 thousand versus loss of $3,893 thousand in the year-earlier quarter. Net income was $7,077 thousand from net loss of $6,545 thousand in the year-earlier quarter. Revenues were $392,003 thousand, up 15.2% from $340,147 thousand the year before. Operating income was $18,851 thousand versus an income of $4,322 thousand in the prior-year quarter, an increase of 336.2%. Total direct expense was $342,860 thousand versus $304,278 thousand in the prior-year quarter, an increase of 12.7%. Total indirect expense was $30,292 thousand versus $31,547 thousand in the prior-year quarter, a decrease of 4.0%.

Prospects: Co.'s aggregates products business is benefiting from increased demand, strong pricing and benefits from cost controls. Shipments are particular strong across the Southeast and the Southwest, as highway and commercial demand has ramped up and residential demand remains robust. Also, business activity for Co.'s Specialty Products segment, which includes Magnesia Specialties and Structural Composites, remains positive. For fiscal 2005, Co. expects net earnings per diluted share to range from $2.90 to $3.25. For the second quarter of 2005, earnings per diluted share are expected to be in the range of $0.95 to $1.10.

Financial Data

(US$ in Thousands)	3 Mos	12/31/2004	12/31/2003	12/31/2002	12/31/2001	12/31/2000	12/31/1999	12/31/1998
Earnings Per Share	2.95	2.66	1.91	1.77	2.19	2.39	2.68	2.48
Cash Flow Per Share	6.66	5.53	5.67	4.18	5.28	4.54	4.79	4.79
Tang Book Value Per Share	11.33	11.99	10.83	9.70	8.55	9.70	7.86	6.25
Dividends Per Share	0.780	0.760	0.690	0.580	0.560	0.540	0.520	0.500
Dividend Payout %	26.44	28.57	36.13	32.77	25.57	22.59	19.40	20.16
Income Statement								
Total Revenue	392,003	1,759,613	1,711,453	1,692,437	1,718,050	1,517,517	1,258,827	1,057,691
EBITDA	53,639	359,849	324,324	326,994	359,866	347,089	358,478	296,666
Depn & Amortn	32,400	132,173	139,606	138,696	154,635	136,373	124,754	98,765
Income Before Taxes	10,449	184,722	142,131	144,270	158,439	168,821	194,313	174,142
Income Taxes	2,149	56,543	41,047	46,455	53,077	56,794	68,532	58,529
Net Income	7,077	129,163	93,623	86,305	105,362	112,027	125,781	115,613
Average Shares	47,737	48,534	49,136	48,858	48,066	46,948	46,947	46,707
Balance Sheet								
Current Assets	585,543	624,253	621,519	526,149	496,232	425,001	403,365	369,388
Total Assets	2,354,128	2,355,852	2,330,093	2,258,530	2,224,580	1,841,439	1,742,574	1,588,589
Current Liabilities	198,721	203,813	220,164	197,827	192,037	189,113	182,696	152,233
Long-Term Obligations	710,346	713,661	717,073	733,471	797,385	601,580	602,011	602,113
Total Liabilities	1,235,557	1,202,425	1,200,246	1,175,520	1,202,368	978,153	968,568	920,890
Stockholders' Equity	1,118,571	1,153,427	1,129,847	1,083,010	1,022,212	863,286	774,006	667,699
Shares Outstanding	46,610	47,306	48,670	48,847	48,559	46,783	46,715	46,642
Statistical Record								
Return on Assets %	6.18	5.50	4.08	3.85	5.18	6.23	7.55	8.58
Return on Equity %	12.93	11.28	8.46	8.20	11.18	13.65	17.45	18.81
EBITDA Margin %	13.68	20.45	18.95	19.32	20.95	22.87	28.48	28.05
Net Margin %	1.81	7.34	5.47	5.10	6.13	7.38	9.99	10.93
Asset Turnover	0.78	0.75	0.75	0.76	0.85	0.84	0.76	0.79
Current Ratio	2.95	3.06	2.82	2.66	2.58	2.25	2.21	2.43
Debt to Equity	0.64	0.62	0.63	0.68	0.78	0.70	0.78	0.90
Price Range	57.84-41.66	53.66-41.66	47.78-26.15	48.12-27.45	51.27-36.00	54.25-32.25	67.75-36.00	62.19-36.00
P/E Ratio	19.61-14.12	20.17-15.66	25.02-13.69	27.19-15.51	23.41-16.44	22.70-13.49	25.28-13.43	25.08-14.52
Average Yield %	1.63	1.66	1.97	1.56	1.27	1.27	1.03	1.11

Address: 2710 Wycliff Road, Raleigh, NC 27607-3033
Telephone: 919-781-4550
Web Site: www.martinmarietta.com

Officers: Stephen P. Zelnak Jr. - Chmn., Pres., C.E.O. Philip J. Sipling - Exec. V.P.

Investor Contact: 919-783-4658
No of Institutions: 178
Shares: 42,391,688 **% Held:** 89.88

MASCO CORP.

Exchange	Symbol	Price	52Wk Range	Yield	P/E
NYS	MAS	$32.02 (5/31/2005)	38.03-28.68	2.50	15.03

*7 Year Price Score 113.99 *NYSE Composite Index=100 *12 Month Price Score 93.16

Interim Earnings (Per Share)

Qtr.	Mar	Jun	Sep	Dec
2002	0.31	0.43	0.24	0.37
2003	0.32	0.46	0.65	0.20
2004	0.36	0.58	0.80	0.23
2005	0.52	...	...	...

Interim Dividends (Per Share)

Amt	Decl	Ex	Rec	Pay
0.16Q	6/25/2004	7/7/2004	7/9/2004	8/9/2004
0.18Q	9/13/2004	10/6/2004	10/8/2004	11/8/2004
0.18Q	12/8/2004	1/5/2005	1/7/2005	2/7/2005
0.20Q	3/22/2005	4/6/2005	4/8/2005	5/9/2005

Indicated Div: $0.80 (Div. Reinv. Plan)

Valuation Analysis

Forecast P/E 13.19 (6/1/2005)
Market Cap $13.9 Billion Book Value 5.0 Billion
Price/Book 2.78 Price/Sales 1.14

Dividend Achiever Status

Rank 236 **10 Year Growth Rate** 6.70%
Total Years of Dividend Growth 46

Business Summary: Metal Products (MIC: 11.4 SIC: 432 NAIC: 37122)

Masco is engaged in the manufacture and sale of cabinets and related products, plumbing products, architectural coatings and other specialty home improvement and building products. These products are sold to the home improvement and home construction markets through mass merchandisers, hardware stores, home centers, builders, distributors and other outlets for consumers and builders. Co.'s brand names and tradenames include the following: Kraftmaid®, Merillat®, Tvilum-Scanbirkt™, Bluestone™, Moores™, Newform™, Mill's Pride®, Quality Cabinets®, Delta®, Peerless®, Newport Brass®, Behr®, Premium Plus®, Masterchem®, Franklin Brass®, Ginger®, Bath Unlimited®, Milgard®, Griffin™, and Cambrian™.

Recent Developments: For the quarter ended Mar 31 2005, income from continuing operations decreased 12.0% to $212,000 thousand from income of $241,000 thousand in the year-earlier quarter. Net income increased 37.5% to $231,000 thousand from net income of $168,000 thousand in the year-earlier quarter. Revenues were $2,969,000 thousand, up 5.8% from $2,806,000 thousand the year before. Operating income was $343,000 thousand versus an income of $387,000 thousand in the prior-year quarter, a decrease of 11.4%. Total direct expense was $2,128,000 thousand versus $1,955,000 thousand in the prior-year quarter, an increase of 8.8%. Total indirect expense was $498,000 thousand versus $464,000 thousand in the prior-year quarter, an increase of 7.3%.

Prospects: Results are being adversely affected by lower-than-expected consumer spending on certain of Co.'s products sold through retail markets, product mix, as well as increases in commodity, energy, and freight costs, much of which have not yet been recovered due to the lag in implementing selling price increases to customers. Co. expects these conditions to continue at least through the second quarter of 2005. If higher energy costs and recent trends indicating lower consumer confidence and the related slowing in sales of certain retail products continue, Co. believes that 2005 results may be nearer to the low end of earnings guidance for continuing operations of $2.40 to $2.50 per share.

Financial Data

(US$ in Thousands)	3 Mos	12/31/2004	12/31/2003	12/31/2002	12/31/2001	12/31/2000	12/31/1999	12/31/1998
Earnings Per Share	2.13	1.96	1.64	1.15	0.42	1.31	1.28	1.39
Cash Flow Per Share	3.40	3.26	2.97	2.53	2.10	1.66	1.13	1.26
Tang Book Value Per Share	0.74	1.54	1.35	1.31	1.30	2.78	3.14	4.99
Dividends Per Share	0.680	0.660	0.580	0.545	0.525	0.490	0.450	0.430
Dividend Payout %	31.92	33.67	35.37	47.39	125.00	37.40	35.16	30.94
Income Statement								
Total Revenue	2,969,000	12,074,000	10,936,000	9,419,400	8,358,000	7,243,000	6,307,000	4,345,000
EBITDA	380,000	1,958,000	1,702,000	1,462,440	773,860	1,262,630	1,153,790	930,220
Depn & Amortn	...	229,000	232,000	200,600	269,500	238,300	181,800	136,300
Income Before Taxes	321,000	1,518,000	1,216,000	1,031,000	300,700	893,400	904,100	755,000
Income Taxes	104,000	569,000	463,000	348,900	102,200	301,700	334,500	279,000
Net Income	231,000	893,000	806,000	589,700	198,500	591,700	569,600	476,000
Average Shares	443,000	456,000	491,000	514,100	474,900	451,800	446,200	343,700
Balance Sheet								
Current Assets	4,302,000	4,402,000	3,804,000	3,949,770	2,626,920	2,308,160	2,109,780	1,862,620
Total Assets	12,135,000	12,541,000	12,149,000	12,050,430	9,183,330	7,744,000	6,634,920	5,167,350
Current Liabilities	2,976,000	2,147,000	2,099,000	1,932,450	1,236,560	1,078,050	846,430	846,580
Long-Term Obligations	3,407,000	4,187,000	3,848,000	4,316,470	3,627,630	3,018,240	2,431,270	1,391,420
Total Liabilities	7,127,000	7,118,000	6,693,000	6,756,590	5,063,500	4,317,940	3,498,420	2,438,770
Stockholders' Equity	5,008,000	5,423,000	5,456,000	5,293,840	4,119,830	3,426,060	3,136,500	2,728,580
Shares Outstanding	435,020	446,720	458,380	488,890	459,050	444,750	443,510	339,330
Statistical Record								
Return on Assets %	7.84	7.21	6.66	5.55	2.35	8.21	9.65	10.02
Return on Equity %	18.87	16.37	15.00	12.53	5.26	17.98	19.42	19.20
EBITDA Margin %	12.80	16.22	15.56	15.53	9.26	17.43	18.29	21.41
Net Margin %	7.78	7.40	7.37	6.26	2.37	8.17	9.03	10.96
Asset Turnover	1.00	0.98	0.90	0.89	0.99	1.00	1.07	0.91
Current Ratio	1.45	2.05	1.81	2.04	2.12	2.14	2.49	2.20
Debt to Equity	0.68	0.77	0.71	0.82	0.88	0.88	0.78	0.51
Price Range	38.03-26.94	36.80-26.02	28.31-16.82	29.08-17.68	26.49-18.00	25.69-14.81	33.50-23.00	32.50-21.13
P/E Ratio	17.85-12.65	18.78-13.28	17.26-10.26	25.29-15.37	63.07-42.86	19.61-11.31	26.17-17.97	23.38-15.20
Average Yield %	2.07	2.13	2.50	2.24	2.24	2.46	1.55	1.55

Address: 21001 Van Born Road, Taylor, MI 48180
Telephone: 313-274-7400
Web Site: www.masco.com

Officers: Richard A. Manoogian - Chmn., C.E.O. Alan H. Barry - Pres., C.O.O. **Transfer Agents:** Bank of New York, New York, NY

Investor Contact: 313-274-7400
No of Institutions: 450
Shares: 362,221,728 **% Held:** 81.36

MATTHEWS INTERNATIONAL CORP

Exchange	Symbol	Price	52Wk Range	Yield	P/E
NMS	MATW	$36.99 (5/31/2005)	38.00-30.69	0.49	20.32

Interim Earnings (Per Share)

Qtr.	Dec	Mar	Jun	Sep
2001-02	0.25	0.30	0.33	0.32
2002-03	0.29	0.36	0.38	0.36
2003-04	0.35	0.42	0.44	0.51
2004-05	0.39	0.47	...	...

Interim Dividends (Per Share)

Amt	Decl	Ex	Rec	Pay
0.04Q	7/20/2004	7/28/2004	7/30/2004	8/13/2004
0.045Q	10/14/2004	10/27/2004	10/29/2004	11/12/2004
0.045Q	1/20/2005	1/27/2005	1/31/2005	2/14/2005
0.045Q	4/19/2005	4/27/2005	4/29/2005	5/13/2005

Indicated Div: $0.18

Valuation Analysis

Forecast P/E	20.05 (5/28/2005)		
Market Cap	$1.2 Billion	Book Value	321.6 Million
Price/Book	3.68	Price/Sales	2.07

Dividend Achiever Status

Rank	11	10 Year Growth Rate	27.10%
Total Years of Dividend Growth			10

Business Summary: Consumer Accessories (MIC: 4.6 SIC: 995 NAIC: 39995)

Matthews International is a designer, manufacturer and marketer principally of memorialization products and brand products and services. Memorialization products consist primarily of bronze memorials and memorialization products, caskets and cremation equipment for the cemetery and funeral home industries. Brand products and services include graphics imaging products and services, merchandising solutions and marking products. Co.'s products and operations are comprised of six business segments: Bronze, York Casket, Cremation, Graphics Imaging, Marking Products and Merchandising Solutions.

Recent Developments: For the quarter ended Mar 31 2005, net income increased 10.6% to $15,263,000 from net income of $13,801,000 in the year-earlier quarter. Revenues were $156,243,000 , up 25.0% from $124,987,000 the year before. Operating income was $26,385,000 versus an income of $24,166,000 in the prior-year quarter, an increase of 9.2%. Total direct expense was $101,857,000 versus $77,355,000 in the prior-year quarter, an increase of 31.7%. Total indirect expense was $28,001,000 versus $23,466,000 in the prior-year quarter, an increase of 19.3%.

Prospects: Top-line growth is being driven by contributions from recent acquisitions and the favorable impact of foreign currency exchange rates. Meanwhile, Co. is experiencing lower profitability in its graphics imaging business stemming from weak demand in the U.S. and lower margins in Europe. Separately, Co. remains concerned with the continued high cost of bronze and steel. While recent cost initiatives and productivity improvements have mitigated some of this impact, the higher costs will be a challenge for the remainder of the fiscal year. For fiscal 2005, Co. is targeting earnings in the range of $1.80 to $1.85 per share.

Financial Data

(US$ in Thousands)	6 Mos	3 Mos	09/30/2004	09/30/2003	09/30/2002	09/30/2001	09/30/2000	09/30/1999
Earnings Per Share	1.82	1.76	1.72	1.39	1.10	1.01	0.88	0.77
Cash Flow Per Share	2.19	2.63	2.58	1.85	1.80	1.26	1.22	0.83
Tang Book Value Per Share	2.82	2.90	2.81	2.75	0.74	1.29	2.52	1.96
Dividends Per Share	0.170	0.165	0.160	0.110	0.105	0.100	0.095	0.090
Dividend Payout %	9.34	9.40	9.30	7.91	9.55	9.90	10.80	11.69
Income Statement								
Total Revenue	304,949	148,706	508,801	458,865	428,086	283,282	262,365	239,329
EBITDA	55,994	25,936	109,459	91,078	80,484	66,037	59,434	52,753
Depn & Amortn	9,832	4,928	15,628	14,872	13,856	12,932	12,007	10,609
Income Before Taxes	45,141	20,525	91,833	73,354	62,457	51,458	45,938	41,277
Income Taxes	(17,153)	7,800	35,638	28,461	24,225	19,859	18,015	16,261
Net Income	27,988	12,725	56,195	44,893	35,006	31,599	27,923	25,016
Average Shares	32,533	32,741	32,688	32,314	31,795	31,320	31,703	32,482
Balance Sheet								
Current Assets	188,436	197,367	202,478	166,054	156,020	102,328	94,833	96,891
Total Assets	522,556	536,554	530,542	436,741	422,601	288,952	220,665	225,678
Current Liabilities	102,303	104,558	111,572	76,323	87,186	66,539	46,832	62,291
Long-Term Obligations	46,979	52,723	54,389	57,023	96,487	40,726	13,908	14,144
Total Liabilities	200,994	211,689	218,292	180,513	241,226	145,236	93,810	111,056
Stockholders' Equity	321,562	324,865	312,250	256,228	181,375	143,716	126,856	114,622
Shares Outstanding	31,951	32,211	32,410	32,162	31,167	30,273	31,007	31,319
Statistical Record								
Return on Assets %	12.07	11.79	11.59	10.45	9.84	12.40	12.48	12.12
Return on Equity %	19.45	19.29	19.72	20.52	21.54	23.36	23.06	22.85
EBITDA Margin %	18.36	17.44	21.51	19.85	18.80	23.31	22.65	22.04
Net Margin %	9.18	8.56	11.04	9.78	8.18	11.15	10.64	10.45
Asset Turnover	1.17	1.11	1.05	1.07	1.20	1.11	1.17	1.16
Current Ratio	1.84	1.89	1.81	2.18	1.79	1.54	2.02	1.56
Debt to Equity	0.15	0.16	0.17	0.22	0.53	0.28	0.11	0.12
Price Range	38.00-28.87	38.00-28.87	36.08-26.33	28.46-21.71	28.67-21.23	22.30-13.06	15.06-10.06	16.13-12.44
P/E Ratio	20.88-15.86	21.59-16.40	20.98-15.31	20.47-15.62	26.06-19.30	22.08-12.93	17.12-11.43	20.94-16.15
Average Yield %	0.50	0.50	0.51	0.46	0.43	0.58	0.74	0.63

Address: Two Northshore Center, Pittsburgh, PA 15212-5851	**Officers:** David M. Kelly - Chmn., Pres., C.E.O. Joseph C. Bartolacci - Exec. V.P., Pres., York Casket Division	**Investor Contact:** 412-442-8200
Telephone: 412-442-8200	**Transfer Agents:**	**No of Institutions:** 105
Web Site: www.matw.com	Computershare Investor Services LLC, Chicago, IL	**Shares:** 21,252,600 **% Held:** 65.98

MAY DEPARTMENT STORES CO. (THE)

Exchange	Symbol	Price	52Wk Range	Yield	P/E
NYS	MAY	$38.16 (5/31/2005)	38.73-23.95	2.57	22.45

***7 Year Price Score 83.73** *NYSE Composite Index=100 ***12 Month Price Score 117.88**

Interim Earnings (Per Share)

Qtr.	Apr	Jul	Oct	Jan
2000-01	0.35	0.41	0.27	1.59
2001-02	0.34	0.35	0.16	1.36
2002-03	0.23	0.22	0.05	1.26
2003-04	0.23	(0.39)	0.15	1.42
2004-05	0.24	0.33	0.02	1.11

Interim Dividends (Per Share)

Amt	Decl	Ex	Rec	Pay
0.242Q	8/20/2004	8/30/2004	9/1/2004	9/15/2004
0.242Q	11/12/2004	11/29/2004	12/1/2004	12/15/2004
0.245Q	2/10/2005	2/25/2005	3/1/2005	3/15/2005
0.245Q	3/18/2005	5/27/2005	6/1/2005	6/15/2005

Indicated Div: $0.98 (Div. Reinv. Plan)

Valuation Analysis

Forecast P/E	18.16 (6/1/2005)		
Market Cap	$11.2 Billion	Book Value	4.5 Billion
Price/Book	2.50	Price/Sales	0.77

Dividend Achiever Status

Rank	291	**10 Year Growth Rate**	3.72%
Total Years of Dividend Growth			29

Business Summary: Retail - General (MIC: 5.2 SIC: 311 NAIC: 52111)

The May Department Stores operated 491 department stores in 39 states and the District of Columbia as of Jan 29 2005 under the following names: Lord & Taylor, Marshall Field's, Filene's, Kaufmann's, Robinsons-May, Meier & Frank, Hecht's, Strawbridge's, Foley's, Famous-Barr, L.S. Ayers, and The Jones Store. Co. is also a major retailer of bridal gowns and bridal-related merchandise through David's Bridal, Inc. and Priscilla of Boston, Inc., and provides tuxedo rental services through After Hours Formalwear, Inc. At Jan 29 2005, Co. operated 239 David's Bridal stores in 45 states and Puerto Rico, 449 After Hours Formalwear stores in 31 states, and 11 Priscilla of Boston stores in nine states.

Recent Developments: For the year ended Jan 29 2005, net income increased 20.7% to $524 million from net income of $434 million a year earlier. Revenues were $14,441 million, up 8.2% from $13,343 million the year before. Total direct expense was $10,212 million versus $9,378 million in the prior year, an increase of 8.9%. Total indirect expense was $3,040 million versus $3,008 million in the prior year, an increase of 1.1%.

Prospects: On Feb 28 2005, Co. announced that it has entered into an agreement to be acquired by Federated Department Stores, Inc. for approximately $17.00 billion, including the assumption of about $6.00 billion of debt. The transaction is expected to close in the third quarter of 2005, subject to regulatory and shareholder approvals. Meanwhile, results are being hampered by sluggish sales of Co.'s proprietary ladies' and men's apparel brands. Separately, the integration of Marshall Field's continues on schedule with all system conversions being completed in April 2005.

Financial Data

(US$ in Thousands)	01/29/2005	01/31/2004	02/01/2003	02/02/2002	02/03/2001	01/29/2000	01/30/1999	01/31/1998
Earnings Per Share	1.70	1.41	1.76	2.21	2.62	2.60	2.30	2.06
Cash Flow Per Share	4.64	5.79	5.08	5.57	4.32	4.62	4.40	4.39
Tang Book Value Per Share	4.23	8.72	8.39	7.76	8.53	9.51	8.67	8.82
Dividends Per Share	0.970	0.960	0.950	0.940	0.930	0.890	0.847	0.800
Dividend Payout %	57.06	68.09	53.98	42.53	35.50	34.23	36.81	38.83
Income Statement								
Total Revenue	14,441,000	13,343,000	13,491,000	14,175,000	14,511,000	13,866,000	13,413,000	12,685,000
EBITDA	1,825,000	1,521,000	1,722,000	2,052,000	2,258,000	2,279,000	2,112,000	1,990,000
Depn & Amortn	636,000	564,000	557,000	559,000	511,000	469,000	439,000	412,000
Income Before Taxes	803,000	639,000	820,000	1,144,000	1,402,000	1,523,000	1,395,000	1,279,000
Income Taxes	279,000	205,000	278,000	438,000	544,000	596,000	546,000	500,000
Net Income	524,000	434,000	542,000	703,000	858,000	927,000	849,000	775,000
Average Shares	308,000	307,000	307,900	317,600	327,700	355,600	367,400	373,600
Balance Sheet								
Current Assets	5,577,000	5,143,000	4,722,000	4,925,000	5,270,000	5,115,000	4,987,000	4,878,000
Total Assets	15,163,000	12,097,000	11,936,000	11,920,000	11,574,000	10,935,000	10,533,000	9,930,000
Current Liabilities	3,469,000	2,685,000	2,666,000	2,538,000	2,214,000	2,415,000	2,059,000	1,866,000
Long-Term Obligations	5,662,000	3,797,000	4,035,000	4,403,000	4,534,000	3,560,000	3,825,000	3,512,000
Total Liabilities	10,688,000	7,906,000	7,901,000	8,079,000	7,719,000	6,858,000	6,697,000	6,121,000
Stockholders' Equity	4,475,000	4,191,000	4,035,000	3,841,000	3,855,000	4,077,000	3,836,000	3,809,000
Shares Outstanding	293,100	288,800	288,300	287,200	298,200	325,500	334,700	346,500
Statistical Record								
Return on Assets %	3.86	3.62	4.56	6.00	7.50	8.66	8.32	7.78
Return on Equity %	12.13	10.58	13.80	18.32	21.28	23.49	22.27	20.84
EBITDA Margin %	12.64	11.40	12.76	14.48	15.56	16.44	15.75	15.69
Net Margin %	3.63	3.25	4.02	4.96	5.91	6.69	6.33	6.11
Asset Turnover	1.06	1.11	1.13	1.21	1.27	1.30	1.31	1.27
Current Ratio	1.61	1.92	1.77	1.94	2.38	2.12	2.42	2.61
Debt to Equity	1.27	0.91	1.00	1.15	1.18	0.87	1.00	0.92
Price Range	36.31-23.95	33.61-18.01	37.60-20.43	41.25-27.98	38.95-19.63	45.00-29.56	47.08-33.50	37.96-29.33
P/E Ratio	21.36-14.09	23.84-12.77	21.36-11.61	18.67-12.66	14.87-7.49	17.31-11.37	20.47-14.57	18.43-14.24
Average Yield %	3.35	3.91	3.22	2.71	3.41	2.34	2.06	2.36

Address: 611 Olive Street, St. Louis, MO 63101-1799
Telephone: 314-342-6300
Web Site: www.mayco.com

Officers: John L. Dunham - Interim Chmn., Pres., C.E.O. William P. McNamara - Vice-Chmn. **Transfer Agents:** The Bank of New York, New York, NY

Investor Contact: 314-342-6413
No of Institutions: 333
Shares: 262,135,616 **% Held:** 89.78

MBIA INC.

Exchange	Symbol	Price	52Wk Range	Yield	P/E
NYS	MBI	$55.93 (5/31/2005)	64.83-50.50	2.00	9.92

*7 Year Price Score 105.99 *NYSE Composite Index=100 *12 Month Price Score 91.58

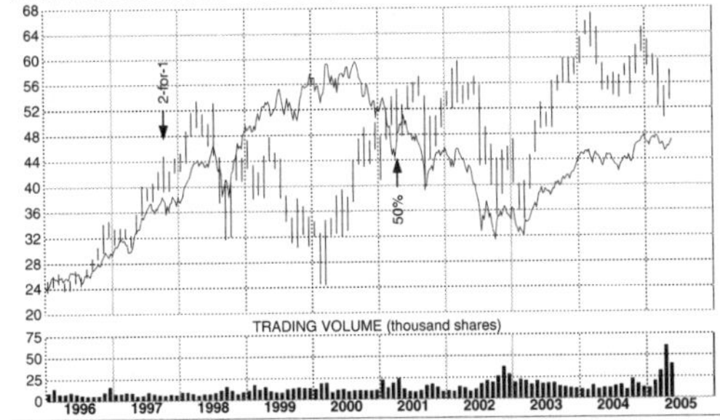

Interim Earnings (Per Share)

Qtr.	Mar	Jun	Sep	Dec
2002	1.03	0.97	1.11	0.81
2003	1.54	1.51	1.31	1.25
2004	1.42	1.48	1.29	1.44
2005	1.43	...	...	...

Interim Dividends (Per Share)

Amt	Decl	Ex	Rec	Pay
0.24Q	6/11/2004	6/23/2004	6/25/2004	7/15/2004
0.24Q	9/10/2004	9/22/2004	9/24/2004	10/15/2004
0.24Q	12/10/2004	12/21/2004	12/23/2004	1/18/2005
0.28Q	3/10/2005	3/23/2005	3/28/2005	4/15/2005

Indicated Div: $1.12

Valuation Analysis

Forecast P/E	9.87 (5/28/2005)		
Market Cap	$7.6 Billion	Book Value	6.4 Billion
Price/Book	1.19	Price/Sales	3.72

Dividend Achiever Status

Rank	177	10 Year Growth Rate	9.74%
Total Years of Dividend Growth			17

Business Summary: Insurance (MIC: 8.2 SIC: 351 NAIC: 24130)

MBIA is engaged in providing financial guarantee insurance, investment management services and municipal and other services to public finance clients and structured finance clients on a global basis. Financial guarantee insurance provides an unconditional and irrevocable guarantee of the payment of the principal of, and interest or other amounts owing on, insured obligations when due. Co. conducts its financial guarantee business through its wholly-owned subsidiary, MBIA Insurance Corporation. Co. also owns MBIA Assurance S.A., a French insurance company, which writes financial guarantee insurance in the member countries of the European Union.

Recent Developments: For the quarter ended Mar 31 2005, net income decreased 3.9% to $200,504 thousand from net income of $208,617 thousand in the year-earlier quarter. Revenues were $8,342 thousand, up 166.8% from $-12,485 thousand the year before. Net premiums earned were $206,238 thousand versus $201,870 thousand in the prior-year quarter, an increase of 2.2%. Net investment income fell 2.2% to $119,146 thousand from $121,841 thousand a year ago.

Prospects: Co. continues to post solid operating results despite the challenging environment for business production. For 2005, Co. anticipates operating earnings per share, excluding refundings, will increase by between 10.0% and 12.0%, but then return to the 12.0% to 14.0% growth range in 2006-2007. In addition, Co. expects operating return on equity (ROE) will be at the lower end of the 12.0% to 14.0% range in 2005 due to its strong capital position and the projected decline in refunding volume. Looking ahead, Co. anticipates operating ROE will improve and be within the 12.0% to 14.0% range in 2006 and 2007.

Financial Data (US$ in Thousands)	3 Mos	12/31/2004	12/31/2003	12/31/2002	12/31/2001	12/31/2000	12/31/1999	12/31/1998
Earnings Per Share	5.64	5.63	5.61	3.92	3.82	3.55	2.13	2.88
Cash Flow Per Share	6.76	6.34	6.82	5.95	4.87	4.32	2.97	4.59
Tang Book Value Per Share	46.60	46.63	42.88	37.32	31.56	27.86	22.79	24.59
Dividends Per Share	1.000	0.960	0.800	0.680	0.600	0.547	0.537	0.527
Dividend Payout %	17.73	17.05	14.26	17.35	15.71	15.38	25.23	18.29
Income Statement								
Premium Income	206,238	822,467	732,997	588,509	523,870	446,353	442,796	424,550
Total Revenue	538,452	2,001,369	1,688,881	1,217,358	1,135,785	1,024,570	964,421	921,047
Benefits & Claims	20,385	81,880	72,888	61,688	56,651	51,291	198,454	34,683
Income Before Taxes	277,706	1,129,913	1,148,640	792,581	790,984	714,857	387,883	565,038
Income Taxes	77,202	317,185	335,055	205,763	207,826	186,220	67,353	132,310
Net Income	200,504	815,304	813,585	579,087	570,091	528,637	320,530	432,728
Average Shares	140,442	144,799	144,980	147,574	149,282	148,668	150,603	150,244
Balance Sheet								
Total Assets	33,756,665	33,027,410	30,267,734	18,852,101	16,199,685	13,894,338	12,263,899	11,796,564
Total Liabilities	27,320,654	26,448,339	24,008,719	13,358,750	11,417,047	9,670,925	8,750,798	8,004,347
Stockholders' Equity	6,436,011	6,579,071	6,259,015	5,493,351	4,782,638	4,223,413	3,513,101	3,792,217
Shares Outstanding	136,412	139,391	143,875	144,773	148,434	147,845	149,328	149,322
Statistical Record								
Return on Assets %	2.50	2.57	3.31	3.30	3.79	4.03	2.66	4.01
Return on Equity %	12.44	12.67	13.85	11.27	12.66	13.63	8.78	12.65
Loss Ratio %	9.88	9.96	9.94	10.48	10.81	11.49	44.82	8.17
Net Margin %	37.24	40.74	48.17	47.57	50.19	51.60	33.24	46.98
Price Range	64.86-52.28	67.13-53.67	60.08-34.64	59.65-35.32	57.25-39.21	49.96-24.42	47.71-30.38	53.46-31.67
P/E Ratio	11.50-9.27	11.92-9.53	10.71-6.17	15.22-9.01	14.99-10.26	14.07-6.88	22.40-14.26	18.56-11.00
Average Yield %	1.71	1.61	1.61	1.37	1.18	1.44	1.38	1.17

Address: 113 King Street, Armonk, NY 10504
Telephone: 914-273-4545
Web Site: www.mbia.com

Officers: Joseph W. Brown Jr. - Chmn., C.E.O. Gary C. Dunton - Pres., C.O.O. **Transfer Agents:** Wells Fargo Shareowner Services, St. Paul, MN

Investor Contact: 914-765-3648
No of Institutions: 374
Shares: 133,741,544 **% Held:** 97.17

MBNA CORP.

Exchange	Symbol	Price	52Wk Range	Yield	P/E
NYS	KRB	$21.09 (5/31/2005)	28.49-18.45	2.66	12.55

***7 Year Price Score 105.48** *NYSE Composite Index=100 ***12 Month Price Score 82.18**

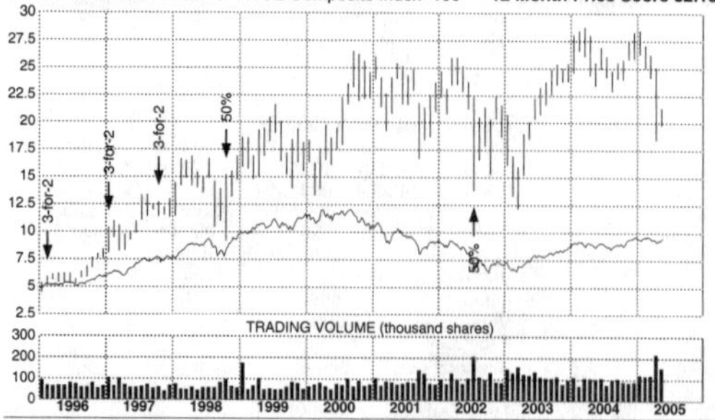

Interim Earnings (Per Share)

Qtr.	Mar	Jun	Sep	Dec
2002	0.28	0.35	0.30	0.41
2003	0.33	0.42	0.51	0.54
2004	0.40	0.51	0.56	0.59
2005	0.02	...	...	...

Interim Dividends (Per Share)

Amt	Decl	Ex	Rec	Pay
0.12Q	7/22/2004	9/13/2004	9/15/2004	10/1/2004
0.12Q	10/21/2004	12/13/2004	12/15/2004	1/1/2005
0.14Q	1/20/2005	3/11/2005	3/15/2005	4/1/2005
0.14Q	4/21/2005	6/13/2005	6/15/2005	7/1/2005

Indicated Div: $0.56

Valuation Analysis

Forecast P/E	N/A		
Market Cap	$26.7 Billion	Book Value	12.7 Billion
Price/Book	2.10	Price/Sales	2.19

Dividend Achiever Status

Rank	60	10 Year Growth Rate	17.44%
Total Years of Dividend Growth			13

Business Summary: Commercial Banking (MIC: 8.1 SIC: 021 NAIC: 22110)

MBNA is a registered bank holding company, with assets of $61.71 billion as of Dec 31 2004. Co. is the parent of MBNA America Bank, N.A., which has two wholly-owned foreign bank subsidiaries, MBNA Europe Bank and MBNA Canada Bank. MBNA.com, provides credit card, consumer loan, retail deposit, travel and shopping services. Co. is an independent credit card lender and an issuer of affinity credit cards, marketed primarily to members of associations and customers of financial institutions. Co. offers credit cards in the U.S., the U.K., Ireland, Canada and Spain. In addition to its credit card lending, Co. also makes other consumer loans and offers insurance and deposit products.

Recent Developments: For the quarter ended Mar 31 2005, net income decreased 93.9% to $31,730 thousand from net income of $519,708 thousand in the year-earlier quarter. Net interest income was $666,114 thousand, down 0.3% from $667,805 thousand the year before. Provision for loan losses was $287,228 thousand versus $365,161 thousand in the prior-year quarter, a decrease of 21.3%. Non-interest income fell 8.2% to $1,782,335 thousand, while non-interest expense advanced 47.5% to $2,126,702 thousand.

Prospects: On May 3 2005, Co. announced that it completed the acquisition of Nexstar Financial Corporation, of St. Charles, MO. Nexstar provides mortgage outsourcing services to many of the nation's banks, credit unions, and other financial institutions. Financial terms of the acquisition were not disclosed. Meanwhile, Co. is implementing programs to offset the higher payment rates in the U.S. Card business, and has made progress with product introductions, diversification strategies, and improvements in credit quality and operating efficiency. Co.'s focus on improved operating efficiency is expected to continue generating better-than-anticipated results.

Financial Data

(US$ in Thousands)	3 Mos	12/31/2004	12/31/2003	12/31/2002	12/31/2001	12/31/2000	12/31/1999	12/31/1998
Earnings Per Share	1.68	2.05	1.79	1.34	1.28	1.02	0.81	0.65
Cash Flow Per Share	5.16	3.62	3.03	3.60	2.14	(0.20)	1.17	0.45
Tang Book Value Per Share	7.28	7.63	6.20	4.63	4.08	3.03	3.49	2.12
Dividends Per Share	0.500	0.480	0.360	0.273	0.240	0.213	0.187	0.160
Dividend Payout %	29.76	23.41	20.11	20.40	18.75	20.91	23.14	24.74
Income Statement								
Interest Income	1,068,957	4,068,619	3,858,884	3,678,070	3,205,102	2,775,679	2,262,271	1,966,172
Interest Expense	402,843	1,531,818	1,508,511	1,603,495	1,814,065	1,691,727	1,328,506	1,223,833
Net Interest Income	666,114	2,536,801	2,350,373	2,074,575	1,391,037	1,083,952	933,765	742,339
Provision for Losses	287,228	1,146,855	1,392,701	1,340,157	1,140,615	409,017	408,914	310,039
Non-Interest Income	1,782,335	8,258,386	7,825,480	6,752,923	6,939,619	5,093,174	4,207,821	3,228,969
Non-Interest Expense	2,126,702	5,516,703	5,124,147	4,701,925	4,474,831	3,647,702	3,077,708	2,407,204
Income Before Taxes	34,519	4,131,629	3,659,005	2,785,416	2,715,210	2,120,407	1,654,964	1,254,065
Income Taxes	2,789	1,454,333	1,320,901	1,019,462	1,020,919	807,875	630,541	477,799
Net Income	31,730	2,677,296	2,338,104	1,765,954	1,694,291	1,312,532	1,024,423	776,266
Average Shares	1,292,143	1,297,178	1,295,142	1,277,787	1,314,229	1,269,796	1,255,557	1,184,131
Balance Sheet								
Net Loans & Leases	30,743,505	32,622,292	19,323,656	16,585,582	13,870,193	11,296,336	7,615,134	11,559,188
Total Assets	61,426,108	61,714,140	59,113,355	52,856,746	45,447,945	38,678,096	30,859,132	25,806,260
Total Deposits	31,152,050	31,239,504	31,836,081	30,616,216	27,094,745	24,343,595	18,714,753	15,407,040
Total Liabilities	48,721,140	48,390,888	48,000,315	43,755,427	37,649,227	32,050,818	26,659,689	23,415,225
Stockholders' Equity	12,704,968	13,323,252	11,113,040	9,101,319	7,798,718	6,627,278	4,199,443	2,391,035
Shares Outstanding	1,267,661	1,277,671	1,277,597	1,277,671	1,277,671	1,277,705	1,202,671	1,127,693
Statistical Record								
Return on Assets %	3.57	4.42	4.18	3.59	4.03	3.76	3.62	3.30
Return on Equity %	18.13	21.85	23.13	20.90	23.49	24.18	31.09	35.60
Net Interest Margin %	62.31	62.35	60.91	56.40	43.40	39.05	41.28	37.76
Efficiency Ratio %	74.59	44.75	43.85	45.08	44.11	46.36	47.57	46.34
Loans to Deposits	0.99	1.04	0.61	0.54	0.51	0.46	0.41	0.75
Price Range	28.49-22.92	28.78-22.92	25.45-12.15	25.97-13.80	26.04-16.70	26.54-13.33	21.67-13.96	16.92-9.17
P/E Ratio	16.96-13.64	14.04-11.18	14.22-6.79	19.38-10.30	20.35-13.05	26.02-13.07	26.75-17.23	26.03-14.10
Average Yield %	1.95	1.86	1.74	1.26	1.06	1.06	1.07	1.11

Address: 1100 North King Street, Wilmington, DE 19884-0141
Telephone: 302-456-8588
Web Site: www.mbna.com

Officers: Randolph D. Lerner Esq. - Chmn. Richard K. Struthers - Vice-Chmn., Chief Loan Officer
ransfer Agents: National City Bank, Cleveland, OH

Investor Contact: 800-362-6255
No of Institutions: 637
Shares: 954,726,272 **% Held:** 74.72

MBT FINANCIAL CORP.

Exchange	Symbol	Price	52Wk Range	Yield	P/E
NMS	MBTF	$19.12 (5/31/2005)	24.95-17.13	3.35	15.17

*7 Year Price Score 101.14 *NYSE Composite Index=100 *12 Month Price Score 92.11

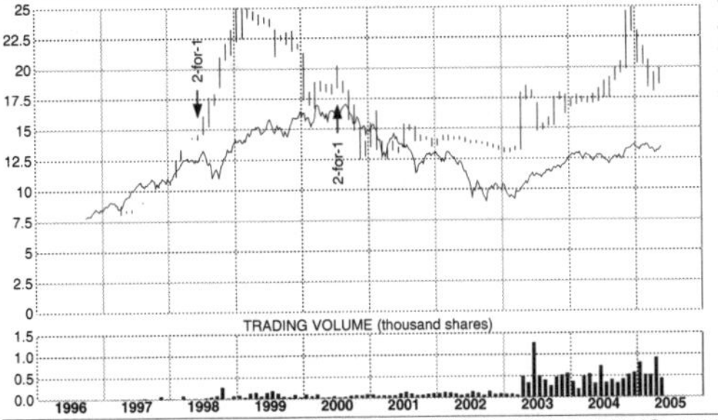

TRADING VOLUME (thousand shares)

Interim Earnings (Per Share)

Qtr.	Mar	Jun	Sep	Dec
2002	0.21	0.31	0.29	0.31
2003	0.26	0.30	0.10	0.34
2004	0.31	0.32	0.35	0.31
2005	0.28	...	...	...

Interim Dividends (Per Share)

Amt	Decl	Ex	Rec	Pay
0.16Q	8/26/2004	9/22/2004	9/24/2004	10/15/2004
0.16Q	11/18/2004	12/21/2004	12/24/2004	1/14/2005
0.16Q	2/28/2005	3/22/2005	3/25/2005	4/15/2005
0.16Q	5/26/2005	6/17/2005	6/21/2005	7/15/2005

Indicated Div: $0.64

Valuation Analysis

Forecast P/E	15.10 (5/28/2005)		
Market Cap	$330.3 Million	Book Value	153.6 Million
Price/Book	2.15	Price/Sales	3.46

Dividend Achiever Status

Rank	18	10 Year Growth Rate	24.17%
Total Years of Dividend Growth			11

Business Summary: Commercial Banking (MIC: 8.1 SIC: 022 NAIC: 22110)

MBT Financial is a bank holding company. Through its wholly-owned subsidiary, Monroe Bank & Trust, Co. provides customary retail and commercial banking and trust services to its customers, including checking and savings accounts, time deposits, safe deposit facilities, commercial loans, personal loans, real estate mortgage loans, installment loans, IRAs, ATM and night depository facilities, treasury management services, telephone and internet banking, personal trust, employee benefit and investment management services. As of Dec 31 2004, Co. operated 21 offices in Monroe County, MI and four offices in Wayne County, MI and had total assets of $1.55 billion.

Recent Developments: For the quarter ended Mar 31 2005, net income decreased 9.6% to $4,879,000 from net income of $5,400,000 in the year-earlier quarter. Net interest income was $12,622,000, down 0.1% from $12,640,000 the year before. Provision for loan losses was unchanged at $600,000 versus the prior-year quarter. Non-interest income rose 6.8% to $3,446,000 , while non-interest expense advanced 10.6% to $8,729,000 .

Prospects: Near-term earnings are being adversely affected by the compression of net interest margin as well as increased non-interest expenses. Co. believes that its fundamental strengths will lead to improved financial performance. Co. is encouraged by increases in its non-interest income, particularly from the strength in its trust services. Although Co.'s spending has increased due to its expansion into the Downriver market in southern Wayne County and its new headquarters building, it remains committed to controlling expenses. Co. continues to focus on strategies to grow future earnings, such as geographic expansion, new products, investments in technology and asset quality improvement.

Financial Data (US$ in Thousands)	3 Mos	12/31/2004	12/31/2003	12/31/2002	12/31/2001	12/31/2000	12/31/1999	12/31/1998
Earnings Per Share	1.26	1.29	1.01	1.12	1.10	1.06	0.85	0.83
Cash Flow Per Share	1.49	1.56	1.29	1.33	1.73	0.74	...	...
Tang Book Value Per Share	8.89	8.89	8.20	8.72	8.19	7.55	6.97	6.55
Dividends Per Share	0.630	0.620	0.580	0.540	0.500	0.370	0.360	0.290
Dividend Payout %	50.00	48.06	57.43	48.21	45.45	34.91	42.11	34.94
Income Statement								
Interest Income	20,919	79,703	77,774	84,604	101,324	99,570	83,179	77,766
Interest Expense	8,297	26,998	27,467	34,387	49,535	49,681	38,290	34,203
Net Interest Income	12,622	52,705	50,307	50,217	51,789	49,889	44,888	43,563
Provision for Losses	600	2,491	8,005	6,101	7,400	6,298	9,388	3,218
Non-Interest Income	3,446	13,209	12,762	11,466	10,234	8,690	6,902	6,784
Non-Interest Expense	8,729	32,616	30,179	26,989	24,809	23,094	20,144	25,448
Income Before Taxes	6,739	31,374	25,926	29,917	30,231	29,205	22,277	21,862
Income Taxes	1,860	8,775	6,611	8,114	8,307	8,031	5,207	5,302
Net Income	4,879	22,599	19,315	21,804	21,924	21,174	17,069	16,561
Average Shares	17,593	17,527	19,072	19,459	19,933	20,000	20,000	20,000
Balance Sheet								
Net Loans & Leases	927,623	932,081	849,350	761,405	774,825	801,523	693,482	679,906
Total Assets	1,551,607	1,552,279	1,457,788	1,409,694	1,394,168	1,379,386	1,216,477	1,075,268
Total Deposits	1,099,393	1,100,711	1,039,117	1,010,960	998,880	994,596	944,076	917,045
Total Liabilities	1,397,989	1,396,933	1,314,342	1,242,695	1,232,438	1,228,431	1,076,829	944,051
Stockholders' Equity	153,618	155,346	143,446	167,000	161,730	150,955	139,647	131,217
Shares Outstanding	17,273	17,465	17,491	19,160	19,752	20,000	20,000	20,000
Statistical Record								
Return on Assets %	1.49	1.50	1.35	1.56	1.58	1.63	...	...
Return on Equity %	14.60	15.09	12.44	13.27	14.02	14.53	...	...
Net Interest Margin %	60.34	66.13	64.68	59.35	51.11	50.10	53.97	56.02
Efficiency Ratio %	35.83	35.10	33.33	28.09	22.24	21.33	22.36	30.10
Loans to Deposits	0.84	0.85	0.82	0.75	0.78	0.81	0.73	0.74
Price Range	24.95-17.00	24.95-16.51	18.55-13.00	14.45-13.20	16.50-12.50	21.63-12.50	25.00-21.00	23.25-10.50
P/E Ratio	19.80-13.49	19.34-12.80	18.37-12.87	12.90-11.79	15.00-11.36	20.40-11.79	29.41-24.71	28.01-12.65
Average Yield %	3.20	3.29	3.72	3.88	3.54	2.14	1.55	1.62

Address: 102 E. Front Street, Monroe, MI 48161
Telephone: 734-241-3431
Web Site: www.MBandT.com

Officers: William D. McIntyre Jr. - Chmn. H. Douglas Chaffin - Pres., C.E.O. **Transfer Agents:** American Stock Transfer & Trust Company, New York, NY

Investor Contact: 734-241-3431
No of Institutions: 42
Shares: 4,371,481 **% Held:** 25.00

MCCORMICK & CO., INC.

Exchange	Symbol	Price	52Wk Range	Yield	P/E
NYS	MKC	$33.84 (5/31/2005)	39.06-32.25	1.89	22.41

Interim Earnings (Per Share)

Qtr.	Feb	May	Aug	Nov
2001-02	0.24	0.24	0.25	0.54
2002-03	0.25	0.28	0.36	0.59
2003-04	0.27	0.30	0.33	0.62
2004-05	0.26	...	...	...

Interim Dividends (Per Share)

Amt	Decl	Ex	Rec	Pay
0.14Q	6/22/2004	6/30/2004	7/2/2004	7/16/2004
0.14Q	9/28/2004	10/6/2004	10/8/2004	10/22/2004
0.16Q	11/23/2004	12/29/2004	12/31/2004	1/21/2005
0.16Q	3/23/2005	3/31/2005	4/4/2005	4/15/2005

Indicated Div: $0.64

Valuation Analysis

Forecast P/E	N/A		
Market Cap	$4.6 Billion	Book Value	904.5 Million
Price/Book	5.06	Price/Sales	1.79

Dividend Achiever Status

Rank	197	10 Year Growth Rate	8.84%
Total Years of Dividend Growth			18

Business Summary: Food (MIC: 4.1 SIC: 099 NAIC: 11942)

McCormick & Company is a specialty food company. Co. manufactures, markets and distributes spices, herbs, seasonings and other flavors to the food industry. Co.'s consumer segment sells seasoning blends, spices, herbs, extracts, sauces, marinades and specialty foods to the consumer food market under a variety of brands, including "McCormick" and "Zatarain's" in the U.S., "Ducros" and "Silvo" in continental Europe, "Club House" in Canada and "Schwartz" in the U.K. Co.'s industrial segment sells blended seasonings, spices and herbs, condiments, compound flavors and extracts, and coating systems to food processors, restaurants, distributors, warehouse clubs and institutional operations.

Recent Developments: For the three months ended Feb 28 2005, net income decreased 5.4% to $36.0 million compared with $38.1 million in the comparable year-earlier period. Results for 2005 and 2004 included special charges of $1.3 million and $69,000, respectively. Net sales rose 5.5% to $603.6 million from $572.4 million the previous year. Co. stated that higher volume, pricing and product mix contributed 3.0% of the increase, of which 2.0% was attributable to its 2004 acquisition of Silvo. Favorable foreign exchange rates added 2.0%. Gross profit amounted to $228.2 million, or 37.8% of net sales, versus $221.7 million, or 38.7% of net sales.

Prospects: Top-line growth is being driven by additional sales from recent acquisitions, favorable foreign currency exchange rates, new product launches and more effective marketing, partially offset by a reduction in inventory levels by certain retail customers and difficult market conditions in Co.'s European consumer business. Meanwhile, Co. is targeting earnings per share of $0.30 for the second quarter of 2005. Looking ahead, Co. is projecting fiscal 2005 sales growth of between 4.0% and 7.0%, along with earnings in the range of $1.70 to $1.74 per share. Results are expected to benefit from cost savings of about $25.0 million in 2005 and gross margin improvement during the second half of the year.

Financial Data

(US$ in Thousands)	3 Mos	11/30/2004	11/30/2003	11/30/2002	11/30/2001	11/30/2000	11/30/1999	11/30/1998
Earnings Per Share	1.51	1.52	1.48	1.26	1.04	0.99	0.71	0.70
Cash Flow Per Share	2.53	2.54	1.40	1.60	1.48	1.46	1.61	0.98
Tang Book Value Per Share	0.56	0.45	0.28	0.62	N.M.	N.M.	1.70	1.57
Dividends Per Share	0.580	0.560	0.460	0.420	0.400	0.380	0.340	0.320
Dividend Payout %	38.41	36.84	31.08	33.33	38.28	38.38	47.55	45.39
Income Statement								
Total Revenue	603,623	2,526,200	2,269,600	2,320,000	2,218,500	2,123,500	2,006,900	1,881,100
EBITDA	75,653	406,800	373,900	345,200	315,700	287,000	239,800	244,200
Depn & Amortn	17,641	72,000	65,300	66,800	73,000	61,300	57,400	54,800
Income Before Taxes	46,928	293,800	270,000	234,800	190,400	186,000	150,000	152,500
Income Taxes	15,017	89,000	83,400	74,300	62,900	66,600	60,100	54,900
Net Income	36,035	214,500	210,800	179,800	146,600	137,500	103,300	103,800
Average Shares	140,457	141,300	142,600	142,300	140,200	139,200	144,000	147,600
Balance Sheet								
Current Assets	775,484	864,000	762,100	724,600	635,800	620,000	490,600	503,800
Total Assets	2,276,675	2,369,600	2,148,200	1,930,800	1,772,000	1,659,900	1,188,800	1,259,100
Current Liabilities	850,674	772,700	712,700	673,400	713,700	1,027,200	470,600	518,000
Long-Term Obligations	295,524	465,000	448,600	453,900	454,100	160,200	241,400	250,400
Total Liabilities	1,339,922	1,448,900	1,370,800	1,338,500	1,308,900	1,300,600	806,400	871,000
Stockholders' Equity	904,547	889,700	755,200	592,300	463,100	359,300	382,400	388,100
Shares Outstanding	135,213	135,500	137,200	140,000	138,400	136,600	140,800	145,000
Statistical Record								
Return on Assets %	9.57	9.47	10.34	9.71	8.54	9.63	8.44	8.25
Return on Equity %	24.38	26.01	31.29	34.07	35.65	36.98	26.81	26.57
EBITDA Margin %	12.53	16.10	16.47	14.88	14.23	13.52	11.95	12.98
Net Margin %	5.97	8.49	9.29	7.75	6.61	6.48	5.15	5.52
Asset Turnover	1.15	1.12	1.11	1.25	1.29	1.49	1.64	1.50
Current Ratio	0.91	1.12	1.07	1.08	0.89	0.60	1.04	0.97
Debt to Equity	0.33	0.52	0.59	0.77	0.98	0.45	0.63	0.65
Price Range	39.06-31.00	37.41-28.84	30.21-22.10	26.93-20.36	23.00-17.13	18.63-12.03	17.25-13.38	18.03-13.19
P/E Ratio	25.87-20.53	24.61-18.97	20.41-14.93	21.37-16.16	22.11-16.47	18.81-12.15	24.30-18.84	25.76-18.84
Average Yield %	1.65	1.68	1.79	1.78	1.95	2.48	2.16	2.05

Address: 18 Loveton Circle, P.O Box 6000, Sparks, MD 21152
Telephone: 410-771-7301
Web Site: www.mccormick.com

Officers: Robert J. Lawless - Chmn., Pres., C.E.O. Francis A. Contino - Exec. V.P., Strategic Planning, C.F.O. **Transfer Agents:** Wells Fargo Bank Minnesota, N.A., St. Paul, MN

Investor Contact: 410-771-7244
No of Institutions: 293
Shares: 80,867,136 **% Held:** 66.94

MCDONALD'S CORP

Exchange	Symbol	Price	52Wk Range	Yield	P/E
NYS	MCD	$30.94 (5/31/2005)	34.21-25.75	1.78	15.87

*7 Year Price Score 87.92 *NYSE Composite Index=100 *12 Month Price Score 99.43

Interim Earnings (Per Share)

Qtr.	Mar	Jun	Sep	Dec
2002	0.20	0.39	0.38	(0.26)
2003	0.26	0.37	0.43	0.10
2004	0.40	0.47	0.61	0.31
2005	0.56	...	...	...

Interim Dividends (Per Share)

Amt	Decl	Ex	Rec	Pay
0.225A	10/29/2001	11/13/2001	11/15/2001	12/3/2001
0.235A	10/22/2002	11/13/2002	11/15/2002	12/2/2002
0.40A	9/24/2003	11/12/2003	11/14/2003	12/1/2003
0.55A	9/14/2004	11/10/2004	11/15/2004	12/1/2004

Indicated Div: $0.55 (Div. Reinv. Plan)

Valuation Analysis

Forecast P/E	15.95 (6/1/2005)		
Market Cap	$39.2 Billion	Book Value	14.6 Billion
Price/Book	2.68	Price/Sales	2.01

Dividend Achiever Status

Rank	70	**10 Year Growth Rate**	16.75%
Total Years of Dividend Growth			28

Business Summary: Hospitality & Tourism (MIC: 5.1 SIC: 812 NAIC: 22211)

McDonald's develops, licenses, leases and services a worldwide system of restaurants in more than 100 countries. Co.'s menu includes hamburgers, cheeseburgers, the Big Mac, Quarter Pounder with Cheese, Big N' Tasty, Filet-O-Fish, Chicken McNuggets, several chicken sandwiches, french fries, salads, milk shakes, McFlurry desserts, ice cream sundaes and cones, pies, cookies and beverages. As of Dec 31 2004, there were approx.18,000 units operated by franchisees, more than 8,000 units operated by Co., and about 4,000 units operated by affiliates. Co. also operates Boston Market and Chipotle Mexican Grill in the U.S. and has a minority ownership interest in U.K.-based Pret A Manger.

Recent Developments: For the quarter ended Mar 31 2005, net income increased 42.3% to $727,900 thousand from net income of $511,500 thousand in the year-earlier quarter. Revenues were $4,802,800 thousand, up 9.2% from $4,399,700 thousand the year before. Operating income was $909,600 thousand versus an income of $858,400 thousand in the prior-year quarter, an increase of 6.0%. Total direct expense was $3,109,100 thousand versus $2,827,400 thousand in the prior-year quarter, an increase of 10.0%. Total indirect expense was $800,500 thousand versus $724,800 thousand in the prior-year quarter, an increase of 10.4%.

Prospects: Co. is enjoying strong sales at its U.S. restaurants due to strong sales of new menu items. Co. recently introduced a new, stronger coffee blend, one of several additions to its U.S. menu that have helped boost top-line growth. In addition, Co. is experiencing positive customer response to healthier menu items such as salads and apple slices, as well as new chicken offerings like fried chicken strips. co. plans to test espresso drinks in some of its U.S. restaurants this summer. Meanwhile, sales in Germany and the U.K. are being positively affected by new, lower-priced and premium menu offerings and Co.'s efforts to boost the McDonald's brand image.

Financial Data

(US$ in Thousands)	3 Mos	12/31/2004	12/31/2003	12/31/2002	12/31/2001	12/31/2000	12/31/1999	12/31/1998
Earnings Per Share	1.95	1.79	1.15	0.70	1.25	1.46	1.39	1.10
Cash Flow Per Share	3.02	3.09	2.57	2.27	2.08	2.07	2.22	2.03
Tang Book Value Per Share	10.12	9.74	8.18	6.88	6.30	5.95	6.20	6.26
Dividends Per Share	0.550	0.550	0.400	0.235	0.225	0.215	0.195	0.176
Dividend Payout %	28.21	30.73	34.78	33.57	18.00	14.73	14.03	16.02
Income Statement								
Total Revenue	4,802,800	19,064,700	17,140,500	15,405,700	14,870,000	14,243,000	13,259,300	12,421,400
EBITDA	1,236,500	4,761,800	3,882,600	3,087,000	3,868,400	4,322,900	4,236,700	3,602,300
Depn & Amortn	316,500	1,201,000	1,148,200	1,050,800	1,086,300	1,010,700	956,300	881,100
Income Before Taxes	830,200	3,202,400	2,346,400	1,662,100	2,329,700	2,882,300	2,884,100	2,307,400
Income Taxes	102,300	923,900	838,200	670,000	693,100	905,000	936,200	757,300
Net Income	727,900	2,278,500	1,471,400	893,500	1,636,600	1,977,300	1,947,900	1,550,100
Average Shares	1,289,000	1,273,700	1,276,500	1,281,500	1,309,300	1,356,500	1,404,200	1,405,700
Balance Sheet								
Current Assets	2,797,500	2,857,800	1,885,400	1,715,400	1,819,300	1,662,400	1,572,300	1,309,400
Total Assets	27,234,000	27,837,500	25,525,100	23,970,500	22,534,500	21,683,500	20,983,200	19,784,400
Current Liabilities	2,669,200	3,520,500	2,485,800	2,422,300	2,248,300	2,360,900	3,274,300	2,497,100
Long-Term Obligations	8,155,200	8,357,300	9,342,500	9,703,600	8,555,500	7,843,900	5,632,400	6,188,600
Total Liabilities	12,596,400	13,636,000	13,543,200	13,689,600	13,046,100	12,479,100	11,344,100	10,319,700
Stockholders' Equity	14,637,600	14,201,500	11,981,900	10,280,900	9,488,400	9,204,400	9,639,100	9,464,700
Shares Outstanding	1,267,500	1,269,900	1,261,900	1,268,200	1,280,700	1,304,900	1,350,800	1,356,200
Statistical Record								
Return on Assets %	9.41	8.52	5.95	3.84	7.40	9.24	9.56	8.15
Return on Equity %	18.48	17.36	13.22	9.04	17.51	20.93	20.39	16.93
EBITDA Margin %	25.75	24.98	22.65	20.04	26.01	30.35	31.95	29.00
Net Margin %	15.16	11.95	8.58	5.80	11.01	13.88	14.69	12.48
Asset Turnover	0.73	0.71	0.69	0.66	0.67	0.67	0.65	0.65
Current Ratio	1.05	0.81	0.76	0.71	0.81	0.70	0.48	0.52
Debt to Equity	0.56	0.59	0.78	0.94	0.90	0.85	0.58	0.65
Price Range	34.21-25.31	32.66-24.64	26.56-12.38	30.65-15.48	34.69-25.00	42.75-27.00	48.38-37.66	39.16-22.69
P/E Ratio	17.54-12.98	18.25-13.77	23.10-10.77	43.79-22.11	27.75-20.00	29.28-18.49	34.80-27.09	35.60-20.63
Average Yield %	1.89	1.98	1.98	0.97	0.79	0.64	0.46	0.57

Address: McDonald's Plaza, Oak Brook, IL 60523
Telephone: 630-623-3000
Web Site: www.mcdonalds.com

Officers: Andrew J. McKenna - Chmn. Jim Skinner - Vice-Chmn., C.E.O. **Transfer Agents:** First Chicago Trust Company, Jersey City, NJ

Investor Contact: 630-623-7428
No of Institutions: 698
Shares: 900,201,088 **% Held:** 70.76

MCGRATH RENTCORP

Exchange	Symbol	Price	52Wk Range	Yield	P/E
NMS	MGRC	$23.05 (5/31/2005)	24.35-14.89	2.43	18.29

*7 Year Price Score 141.14 *NYSE Composite Index=100 *12 Month Price Score 108.08

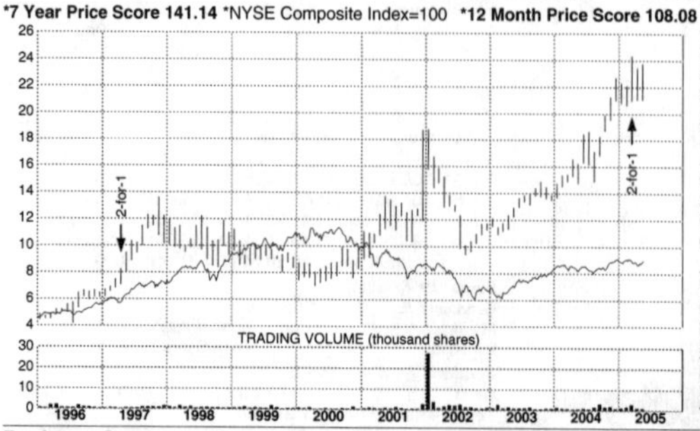

Interim Earnings (Per Share)

Qtr.	Mar	Jun	Sep	Dec
2002	(0.10)	(0.05)	0.34	0.30
2003	0.20	0.20	0.25	0.28
2004	0.23	0.25	0.38	0.35
2005	0.29	...	...	...

Interim Dividends (Per Share)

Amt	Decl	Ex	Rec	Pay
0.11Q	12/6/2004	1/12/2005	1/14/2005	1/31/2005
2-for-1	2/24/2005	3/28/2005	3/11/2005	3/25/2005
0.14Q	2/24/2005	4/13/2005	4/15/2005	4/29/2005
0.14Q	5/19/2005	7/13/2005	7/15/2005	7/29/2005

Indicated Div: $0.56

Valuation Analysis

Forecast P/E	14.21 (6/1/2005)		
Market Cap	$567.3 Million	Book Value	171.6 Million
Price/Book	3.31	Price/Sales	2.51

Dividend Achiever Status

Rank	91	10 Year Growth Rate	14.87%
Total Years of Dividend Growth			14

TRADING VOLUME (thousand shares)

Business Summary: General Construction Supplies & Services (MIC: 3.3 SIC: 359 NAIC: 32490)

McGrath RentCorp is comprised of three business segments: Mobile Modular Management Corporation (MMMC), its modular building rental division; RenTelco, its electronic test equipment rental division; and Enviroplex, its 81.0%-owned portable classroom manufacturing business. MMMC rents and sells modular buildings and accessories to fulfill customers' temporary and permanent space needs in California, Texas and Florida. RenTelco rents and sells electronic test and measurement equipment nationally and internationally from its Dallas, TX and Montreal, Canada facilities. Enviroplex sells its portable classrooms directly to the California public school districts.

Recent Developments: For the quarter ended Mar 31 2005, net income increased 25.1% to $7,177,000 from net income of $5,738,000 in the year-earlier quarter. Revenues were $52,938,000 , up 77.2% from $29,879,000 the year before. Operating income was $13,432,000 versus an income of $10,091,000 in the prior-year quarter, an increase of 33.1%. Total direct expense was $29,945,000 versus $13,731,000 in the prior-year quarter, an increase of 118.1%. Total indirect expense was $9,561,000 versus $6,057,000 in the prior-year quarter, an increase of 57.9%.

Prospects: In 2005, Co. is continuing its focus on lowering its depreciation expense as a percentage of rental revenues by targeting underutilized equipment for sale. Also, Co. is working hard at refining and executing its business development strategies with a high focus on the deployment of the most effective marketing mediums to reach each of its target customer bases. If Co. is successful in these efforts, it believes it will see increasing profitability for TRS-RenTelco in 2005. Separately, Co. reconfirmed its 2005 full-year earnings per share to be in a range of $1.45 to $1.55 per diluted share.

Financial Data

(US$ in Thousands)	3 Mos	12/31/2004	12/31/2003	12/31/2002	12/31/2001	12/31/2000	12/31/1999	12/31/1998
Earnings Per Share	1.26	1.21	0.93	0.50	1.07	1.10	0.84	0.83
Cash Flow Per Share	2.98	2.55	1.98	2.10	2.41	2.02	2.01	1.97
Tang Book Value Per Share	6.97	6.80	5.94	5.57	5.33	4.49	3.80	3.77
Dividends Per Share	0.440	0.430	0.390	0.340	0.310	0.270	0.230	0.190
Dividend Payout %	34.78	35.54	42.16	68.00	28.97	24.66	27.38	22.75
Income Statement								
Total Revenue	52,938	202,520	130,971	145,086	159,394	164,158	129,962	135,428
EBITDA	25,571	88,577	55,400	43,107	81,677	82,232	67,038	66,030
Depn & Amortn	12,139	34,501	14,692	17,872	29,632	25,716	21,474	18,794
Income Before Taxes	11,713	48,888	38,040	21,253	44,967	47,676	38,958	40,910
Income Taxes	4,451	18,843	15,178	8,459	17,807	19,762	14,874	16,010
Net Income	7,177	29,997	22,692	12,633	26,678	27,244	22,466	23,895
Average Shares	25,147	24,804	24,518	25,238	24,990	24,856	26,766	28,698
Balance Sheet								
Current Assets	51,750	54,035	32,203	33,253	36,900	46,330	25,585	22,668
Total Assets	484,515	474,280	323,858	313,134	354,884	357,246	297,722	278,676
Current Liabilities	198,199	39,460	28,695	29,889	30,745	37,012	24,811	22,964
Long-Term Obligations	...	151,888	47,266	55,523	104,140	126,876	110,300	97,000
Total Liabilities	312,938	307,392	179,880	174,115	223,289	248,288	202,319	173,282
Stockholders' Equity	171,577	166,888	143,978	139,019	131,595	108,958	95,403	105,394
Shares Outstanding	24,613	24,543	24,244	24,980	24,670	24,250	25,092	27,940
Statistical Record								
Return on Assets %	7.79	7.50	7.12	3.78	7.49	8.30	7.80	9.00
Return on Equity %	19.71	19.25	16.04	9.34	22.18	26.59	22.38	23.42
EBITDA Margin %	48.30	43.74	42.30	29.71	51.24	50.09	51.58	48.76
Net Margin %	13.56	14.81	17.33	8.71	16.74	16.60	17.29	17.64
Asset Turnover	0.56	0.51	0.41	0.43	0.45	0.50	0.45	0.51
Current Ratio	0.26	1.37	1.12	1.11	1.20	1.25	1.03	0.99
Debt to Equity	...	0.91	0.33	0.40	0.79	1.16	1.16	0.92
Price Range	24.35-14.76	22.75-13.63	14.88-10.90	18.82-9.40	18.77-9.06	9.94-7.00	11.25-8.06	12.25-8.38
P/E Ratio	19.33-11.71	18.80-11.26	16.00-11.73	37.64-18.80	17.54-8.47	9.03-6.36	13.39-9.60	14.76-10.09
Average Yield %	2.33	2.51	3.01	2.65	2.60	3.24	2.47	1.86

Address: 5700 Las Positas Road, Livermore, CA 94551-7800
Telephone: 925-606-9200
Web Site: www.mgrc.com

Officers: Robert P. McGrath - Chmn. Dennis C. Kakures - Pres., C.E.O. **Transfer Agents:** U.S. Stock Transfer, Glendale, CA

Investor Contact: 206-652-9704
No of Institutions: 78
Shares: 7,236,015 **% Held:** 58.90

MCGRAW-HILL COS., INC. (THE)

Exchange	Symbol	Price	52Wk Range	Yield	P/E
NYS	MHP	$43.66 (5/31/2005)	47.95-36.55	1.51	22.16

*7 Year Price Score 119.63 *NYSE Composite Index=100 *12 Month Price Score 99.31

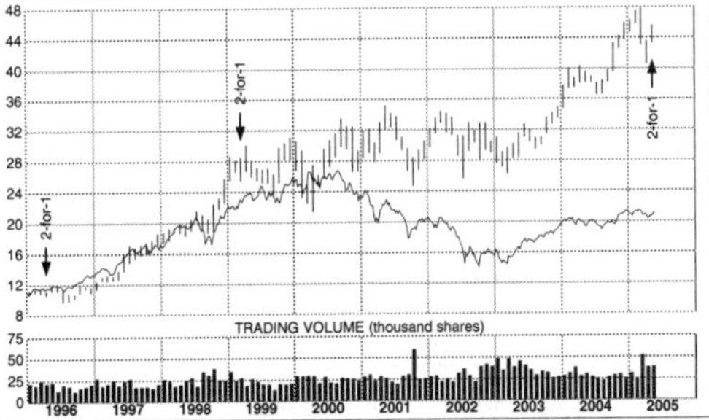

TRADING VOLUME (thousand shares)

Interim Earnings (Per Share)

Qtr.	Mar	Jun	Sep	Dec
2002	0.07	0.35	0.71	0.34
2003	0.25	0.37	0.76	0.41
2004	0.20	0.43	0.84	0.49
2005	0.20	...	...	...

Interim Dividends (Per Share)

Amt	Decl	Ex	Rec	Pay
0.15Q	10/28/2004	11/23/2004	11/26/2004	12/10/2004
0.165Q	1/26/2005	2/22/2005	2/24/2005	3/10/2005
2-for-1	4/27/2005	5/18/2005	5/6/2005	5/17/2005
0.165Q	4/27/2005	5/24/2005	5/26/2005	6/10/2005

Indicated Div: $0.66 (Div. Reinv. Plan)

Valuation Analysis

Forecast P/E	20.36 (5/28/2005)		
Market Cap	$16.4 Billion	Book Value	2.7 Billion
Price/Book	5.96	Price/Sales	3.05

Dividend Achiever Status

Rank	221	10 Year Growth Rate	7.54%
Total Years of Dividend Growth			31

Business Summary: Non-Media Publishing (MIC: 13.3 SIC: 731 NAIC: 11130)

McGraw-Hill, a multimedia publishing and information services company, serves worldwide markets in education, finance and business information. Co. provides information in print through books, newsletters, and magazines, including Business Week; on-line over electronic networks; over the air by television, satellite and FM sideband; and on software, videotape, facsimile and compact disks. Among Co.'s business units are Standard & Poor's Financial Information Services and Standard & Poor's Ratings Services divisions. Operations consist of three business segments: McGraw-Hill Education, Financial Services and Information and Media Services.

Recent Developments: For the quarter ended Mar 31 2005, net income increased 4.0% to $78,735 thousand from net income of $75,679 thousand in the year-earlier quarter. Revenues were $1,029,006 thousand, up 11.9% from $919,867 thousand the year before. Operating income was $125,674 thousand versus an income of $91,048 thousand in the prior-year quarter, an increase of 38.0%. Total direct expense was $430,727 thousand versus $386,360 thousand in the prior-year quarter, an increase of 11.5%. Total indirect expense was $472,605 thousand versus $442,459 thousand in the prior-year quarter, an increase of 6.8%.

Prospects: In 2005, Co. expects to continue its growth in higher education both domestically and abroad, as the McGraw-Hill Education segment should, at current growth rates, outpace the market in higher education. Separately, Co. expects to achieve double-digit top- and bottom-line growth for the Financial Services segment, despite a projected 20.0% decline in the issuance of residential mortgage-backed securities in the U.S. market. Meanwhile, broadcasting remains an event-driven business and will be challenged by an off year in the political advertising cycle. The Broadcasting Group is negotiating new affiliation agreements with the ABC network and anticipates reduced network compensation in 2005.

Financial Data (US$ in Thousands)	3 Mos	12/31/2004	12/31/2003	12/31/2002	12/31/2001	12/31/2000	12/31/1999	12/31/1998
Earnings Per Share	1.97	1.96	1.79	1.48	0.96	1.03	1.07	0.83
Cash Flow Per Share	3.25	2.79	3.63	2.96	2.76	1.81	1.80	1.91
Tang Book Value Per Share	0.89	2.72	2.24	0.94	0.09	0.16	1.12	0.74
Dividends Per Share	0.615	0.600	0.540	0.510	0.490	0.470	0.430	0.391
Dividend Payout %	31.22	30.61	30.17	34.46	51.04	45.63	40.19	46.86
Income Statement								
Total Revenue	1,029,006	5,250,538	4,827,857	4,787,668	4,645,535	4,280,968	3,991,997	3,729,145
EBITDA	184,010	1,299,458	1,255,027	1,055,960	850,485	973,891	877,683	738,081
Depn & Amortn	58,336	124,768	117,653	128,378	180,357	153,708	137,696	129,698
Income Before Taxes	124,976	1,168,905	1,130,277	905,065	615,058	767,342	697,974	560,422
Income Taxes	46,241	412,495	442,466	328,305	238,027	295,426	272,210	218,565
Net Income	78,735	755,823	687,650	576,760	377,031	403,794	425,764	333,141
Average Shares	386,600	385,824	384,010	389,146	391,746	392,144	397,114	398,208
Balance Sheet								
Current Assets	2,016,053	2,447,830	2,256,152	1,674,307	1,812,947	1,801,690	1,553,725	1,428,761
Total Assets	5,454,592	5,862,989	5,394,068	5,032,182	5,161,191	4,931,444	4,088,797	3,788,144
Current Liabilities	1,811,250	1,968,662	1,993,734	1,775,291	1,876,393	1,780,785	1,525,453	1,291,451
Long-Term Obligations	357	513	389	458,923	833,571	817,529	354,775	452,097
Total Liabilities	2,711,420	2,878,476	2,837,017	2,866,360	3,307,306	3,170,400	2,397,304	2,236,336
Stockholders' Equity	2,743,172	2,984,513	2,557,051	2,165,822	1,853,885	1,761,044	1,691,493	1,551,808
Shares Outstanding	374,600	379,626	380,792	383,665	386,436	388,570	391,417	394,222
Statistical Record								
Return on Assets %	14.66	13.39	13.19	11.32	7.47	8.93	10.81	8.87
Return on Equity %	28.71	27.20	29.12	28.70	20.86	23.33	26.25	22.31
EBITDA Margin %	17.88	24.75	26.00	22.06	18.31	22.75	21.99	19.79
Net Margin %	7.65	14.40	14.24	12.05	8.12	9.43	10.67	8.93
Asset Turnover	1.04	0.93	0.93	0.94	0.92	0.95	1.01	0.99
Current Ratio	1.11	1.24	1.13	0.94	0.97	1.01	1.02	1.11
Debt to Equity	N.M.	N.M.	N.M.	0.21	0.45	0.46	0.21	0.29
Price Range	47.95-36.55	45.93-34.75	34.96-26.25	34.45-25.57	35.23-24.65	33.56-21.38	31.13-23.81	25.77-17.36
P/E Ratio	24.34-18.55	23.43-17.73	19.53-14.66	23.27-17.28	36.69-25.68	32.58-20.75	29.09-22.25	31.04-20.91
Average Yield %	1.49	1.53	1.76	1.63	1.62	1.69	1.58	1.94

Address: 1221 Avenue Of The Americas, New York, NY 10020-1095
Telephone: 212-512-2000
Web Site: www.mcgraw-hill.com

Officers: Harold McGraw III - Chmn., Pres., C.E.O. Robert J. Bahash - Exec. V.P., C.F.O. **Transfer Agents:** Mellon Investor Services, South Hackensack, NJ

Investor Contact: 212-512-4321
No of Institutions: 520
Shares: 140,519,552 **% Held:** 73.85

MDU RESOURCES GROUP INC.

Exchange	Symbol	Price	52Wk Range	Yield	P/E
NYS	MDU	$28.79 (5/31/2005)	28.79-23.32	2.50	15.65

*7 Year Price Score 119.05 *NYSE Composite Index=100 *12 Month Price Score 102.37

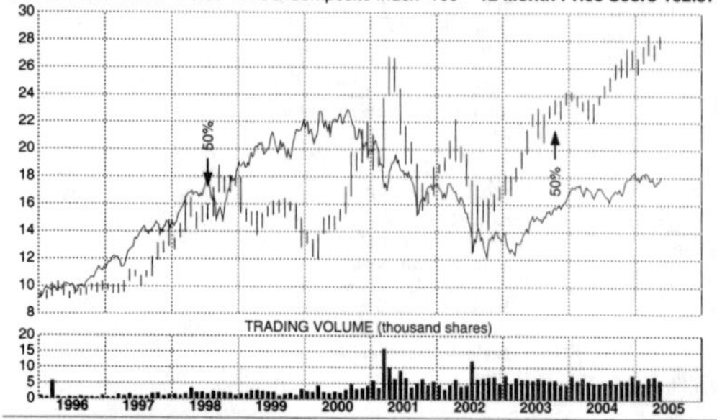

Interim Earnings (Per Share)

Qtr.	Mar	Jun	Sep	Dec
2002	0.23	0.23	0.50	0.42
2003	0.18	0.39	0.58	0.40
2004	0.20	0.50	0.60	0.45
2005	0.29	...	...	...

Interim Dividends (Per Share)

Amt	Decl	Ex	Rec	Pay
0.18Q	8/12/2004	9/7/2004	9/9/2004	10/1/2004
0.18Q	11/11/2004	12/7/2004	12/9/2004	1/1/2005
0.18Q	2/17/2005	3/8/2005	3/10/2005	4/1/2005
0.18Q	5/12/2005	6/7/2005	6/9/2005	7/1/2005

Indicated Div: $0.72 (Div. Reinv. Plan)

Valuation Analysis

Forecast P/E	14.30 (6/1/2005)		
Market Cap	$3.4 Billion	Book Value	1.7 Billion
Price/Book	2.03	Price/Sales	1.21

Dividend Achiever Status

Rank	286	10 Year Growth Rate	4.02%
Total Years of Dividend Growth			14

TRADING VOLUME (thousand shares)

Business Summary: Construction - Public Infrastructure (MIC: 3.1 SIC: 611 NAIC: 37310)

MDU Resources Group is a diversified natural resource company. Co.'s electric and natural gas distribution segments include the operations of Montana- Dakota and Great Plains Natural Gas Co. WBI Holdings is comprised of Co.'s pipeline and energy services and the natural gas and oil production segments. Knife River mines aggregates and markets crushed stone, sand, gravel and related construction materials. Utility Services specializes in electrical line construction, pipeline construction, inside electrical wiring and cabling, and the manufacture and distribution of specialty equipment. Centennial Resources owns, builds and operates electric generating facilities.

Recent Developments: For the quarter ended Mar 31 2005, net income increased 46.0% to $34,420 thousand from net income of $23,580 thousand in the year-earlier quarter. Revenues were $604,295 thousand, up 17.2% from $515,459 thousand the year before. Operating income was $65,113 thousand versus an income of $44,023 thousand in the prior-year quarter, an increase of 47.9%. Total direct expense was $459,674 thousand versus $400,040 thousand in the prior-year quarter, an increase of 14.9%. Total indirect expense was $79,508 thousand versus $71,396 thousand in the prior-year quarter, an increase of 11.4%.

Prospects: Recent higher earnings contributions from its natural gas and oil production, utility services, natural gas distribution and pipeline and energy services businesses reinforce Co.'s favorable near-term outlook. Thus, on Apr 19 2005 Co. increased its full-year 2005 earnings per share guidance to between $1.80 and $2.00, up from its previous guidance of $1.70 to $1.90. Co.'s long-term compound annual growth goals on earnings per share from operations are in the range of 6.0% to 9.0%. Separately, on Apr 25 2005, Co. announced that it has signed an agreement to acquire natural gas and oil properties from a Houston-based independent producer for an aggregate cash purchase price of $145.0 million.

Financial Data

(US$ in Thousands)	3 Mos	12/31/2004	12/31/2003	12/31/2002	12/31/2001	12/31/2000	12/31/1999	12/31/1998
Earnings Per Share	1.84	1.76	1.55	1.38	1.53	1.20	1.01	0.44
Cash Flow Per Share	4.08	3.71	3.75	3.08	3.45	2.25	1.89	1.83
Tang Book Value Per Share	12.20	12.21	9.20	8.25	10.60	9.03	7.83	6.92
Dividends Per Share	0.710	0.700	0.660	0.627	0.600	0.573	0.547	0.522
Dividend Payout %	38.59	39.77	42.58	45.41	39.30	47.78	53.95	118.69
Income Statement								
Total Revenue	604,295	2,719,257	2,352,189	2,031,537	2,223,632	1,873,671	1,279,809	896,627
EBITDA	120,417	567,248	522,616	437,650	440,006	339,599	251,214	159,651
Depn & Amortn	52,839	208,770	188,337	157,961	139,917	110,888	81,818	77,786
Income Before Taxes	54,561	301,041	281,485	234,674	254,190	180,678	133,390	51,592
Income Taxes	20,141	93,974	98,572	86,230	98,341	69,650	49,310	17,485
Net Income	34,420	207,067	175,324	148,444	155,849	111,028	84,080	34,107
Average Shares	118,773	117,411	112,460	106,863	101,803	92,085	82,305	76,255
Balance Sheet								
Net PPE	2,622,001	2,572,705	2,222,293	1,924,886	1,809,318	1,601,014	1,248,176	1,120,615
Total Assets	3,787,340	3,733,521	3,380,592	2,937,249	2,623,071	2,312,959	1,766,303	1,488,713
Long-Term Obligations	907,061	873,441	939,450	819,558	783,709	728,166	563,545	413,264
Total Liabilities	2,111,993	2,052,508	1,929,956	1,638,504	1,498,300	1,416,899	1,081,770	922,871
Stockholders' Equity	1,675,347	1,681,013	1,450,636	1,298,745	1,124,771	896,060	684,533	565,842
Shares Outstanding	118,398	118,226	113,357	111,063	104,665	97,542	85,557	79,549
Statistical Record								
Return on Assets %	6.02	5.81	5.55	5.34	6.31	5.43	5.17	2.62
Return on Equity %	13.62	13.19	12.75	12.25	15.42	14.01	13.45	7.04
EBITDA Margin %	19.93	20.86	22.22	21.54	19.79	18.12	19.63	17.81
Net Margin %	5.70	7.61	7.45	7.31	7.01	5.93	6.57	3.80
PPE Turnover	1.15	1.13	1.13	1.09	1.30	1.31	1.08	0.91
Asset Turnover	0.78	0.76	0.74	0.73	0.90	0.92	0.79	0.69
Debt to Equity	0.54	0.52	0.65	0.63	0.70	0.81	0.82	0.73
Price Range	28.47-22.06	27.46-22.06	24.25-16.69	22.23-12.47	26.82-15.20	22.00-12.00	17.96-12.83	18.83-12.67
P/E Ratio	15.47-11.99	15.60-12.53	15.65-10.77	16.11-9.03	17.53-9.93	18.33-10.00	17.78-12.71	42.80-28.79
Average Yield %	2.80	2.86	3.15	3.55	2.96	3.61	3.57	3.28

Address: Schuchart Building, 918 East Divide Avenue, P.O. Box 5650, Bismarck, ND 58506-5650
Telephone: 701-222-7900
Web Site: www.mdu.com

Officers: Martin A. White - Chmn., C.E.O. Terry D. Hildestad - Pres., C.O.O. **Transfer Agents:** Wells Fargo Bank Minnesota, N.A. Shareowner Services, St. Paul, MN

Investor Contact: 800-437-8000x7621
No of Institutions: 206
Shares: 43,367,128 **% Held:** 36.66

MEDIA GENERAL, INC.

Exchange	Symbol	Price	52Wk Range	Yield	P/E
NYS	MEG	$61.10 (5/31/2005)	70.53-53.97	1.37	N/A

***7 Year Price Score 101.12** *NYSE Composite Index=100 ***12 Month Price Score 96.90**

Interim Earnings (Per Share)

Qtr.	Mar	Jun	Sep	Dec
2002	(5.21)	0.70	0.41	0.93
2003	0.30	0.75	0.16	1.29
2004	0.38	0.78	0.66	1.55
2005	(13.25)	...	...	...

Interim Dividends (Per Share)

Amt	Decl	Ex	Rec	Pay
0.20Q	7/29/2004	8/25/2004	8/27/2004	9/15/2004
0.20Q	9/30/2004	11/23/2004	11/26/2004	12/15/2004
0.21Q	1/27/2005	2/24/2005	2/28/2005	3/15/2005
0.21Q	4/28/2005	5/26/2005	5/31/2005	6/15/2005

Indicated Div: $0.84

Valuation Analysis

Forecast P/E	20.19 (6/1/2005)		
Market Cap	$1.5 Billion	Book Value	864.7 Million
Price/Book	1.69	Price/Sales	1.61

Dividend Achiever Status

Rank	244	**10 Year Growth Rate**	6.16%
Total Years of Dividend Growth			10

Business Summary: Media (MIC: 13.1 SIC: 711 NAIC: 11110)

Media General is an independent, publicly-owned communications company with interests in newspapers, television stations, interactive media, and diversified information services. Co.'s publishing assets include The Tampa Tribune, the Richmond Times-Dispatch, the Winston-Salem Journal, and 22 other daily newspapers in Virginia, North Carolina, Florida, Alabama and South Carolina, as well as nearly 100 other periodicals and a 20.0% interest in The Denver Post. Co. has 26 network-affiliated television stations and operates more than 50 on-line enterprises. Operations consist of the Publishing, Broadcast and Interactive Media segments.

Recent Developments: For the quarter ended Mar 27 2005, net loss was $316,156 thousand versus net income of $9,100 thousand in the year-earlier quarter. Revenues were $217,907 thousand, up 4.7% from $208,156 thousand the year before. Operating income was $20,946 thousand versus an income of $22,525 thousand in the prior-year quarter, a decrease of 7.0%. Total direct expense was $97,529 thousand versus $93,096 thousand in the prior-year quarter, an increase of 4.8%. Total indirect expense was $99,432 thousand versus $92,535 thousand in the prior-year quarter, an increase of 7.5%.

Prospects: For the second quarter of 2005, the Publishing Division revenues are expected to show increases similar to the first quarter, with continued strength in classified advertising, especially help wanted. For the Broadcast Division, while time sales are expected to be slightly higher than the second quarter year over year, driven mostly by local transactional sales, segment profit will be down from last year. The major contributing factor will be the expense necessary to generate new revenue growth to offset the absence of Political and Olympics revenue.

Financial Data

(US$ in Thousands)	3 Mos	12/26/2004	12/28/2003	12/29/2002	12/30/2001	12/31/2000	12/26/1999	12/27/1998
Earnings Per Share	(10.26)	3.38	2.50	(3.14)	0.79	2.22	32.78	2.63
Cash Flow Per Share	7.07	5.94	5.34	7.54	5.49	(15.33)	4.70	5.29
Tang Book Value Per Share	N.M.	N.M.	N.M.	N.M.	N.M.	N.M.	11.92	N.M.
Dividends Per Share	0.810	0.800	0.760	0.720	0.680	0.640	0.600	0.560
Dividend Payout %	...	23.67	30.40	...	86.08	28.83	1.83	21.29
Income Statement								
Total Revenue	217,907	900,420	837,423	836,800	807,176	830,601	795,408	973,978
EBITDA	39,308	219,003	187,074	201,519	198,925	250,777	259,496	277,425
Depn & Amortn	17,172	60,643	58,804	65,495	113,732	105,293	97,532	100,201
Income Before Taxes	14,641	127,278	93,846	88,150	30,946	102,926	115,410	111,175
Income Taxes	5,344	47,093	34,800	34,731	13,022	39,369	45,463	40,301
Net Income	(316,156)	80,185	58,685	(72,917)	18,204	53,719	881,316	70,874
Average Shares	23,857	23,729	23,408	23,236	22,956	24,189	26,885	26,914
Balance Sheet								
Current Assets	154,904	170,847	162,621	160,552	163,038	172,880	796,734	176,226
Total Assets	1,951,715	2,368,812	2,386,755	2,347,011	2,534,059	2,561,282	2,340,374	1,917,346
Current Liabilities	101,423	126,871	114,403	111,501	100,497	114,541	629,188	147,097
Long-Term Obligations	538,786	533,280	627,289	642,937	777,662	822,077	46,838	928,101
Total Liabilities	1,086,976	1,185,043	1,279,294	1,287,757	1,370,391	1,389,360	1,009,472	1,439,997
Stockholders' Equity	864,739	1,183,769	1,107,461	1,059,254	1,163,668	1,171,922	1,330,902	477,349
Shares Outstanding	23,970	23,786	23,545	23,208	22,976	22,714	26,468	26,771
Statistical Record								
Return on Assets %	N.M.	3.38	2.49	N.M.	0.72	2.16	41.51	3.81
Return on Equity %	N.M.	7.02	5.43	N.M.	1.56	4.22	97.74	15.87
EBITDA Margin %	18.04	24.32	22.34	24.08	24.64	30.19	32.62	28.48
Net Margin %	N.M.	8.91	7.01	N.M.	2.26	6.47	110.80	7.28
Asset Turnover	0.42	0.38	0.35	0.34	0.32	0.33	0.37	0.52
Current Ratio	1.53	1.35	1.42	1.44	1.62	1.51	1.27	1.20
Debt to Equity	0.62	0.45	0.57	0.61	0.67	0.70	0.04	1.94
Price Range	72.40-53.97	72.40-53.97	67.88-47.53	69.49-47.38	53.50-34.09	54.19-33.98	55.50-44.38	51.38-34.25
P/E Ratio	...	21.42-15.97	27.15-19.01	...	67.72-43.15	24.41-15.31	1.69-1.35	19.53-13.02
Average Yield %	1.29	1.27	1.31	1.26	1.45	1.36	1.19	1.21

Address: 333 East Franklin Street, Richmond, VA 23219	**Officers:** J. Stewart Bryan III - Chmn., C.E.O. Marshall N. Morton - Vice-Chmn., C.F.O. **Transfer Agents:**	**Investor Contact:** 804-649-6000
Telephone: 804-649-6000		**No of Institutions:** 136
Web Site: www.mediageneral.com		**Shares:** 16,547,891 **% Held:** 70.74

MEDTRONIC, INC.

Exchange	Symbol	Price	52Wk Range	Yield	P/E
NYS	MDT	$53.75 (5/31/2005)	54.92-47.01	0.62	30.54

***7 Year Price Score 99.80** *NYSE Composite Index=100 ***12 Month Price Score 99.18**

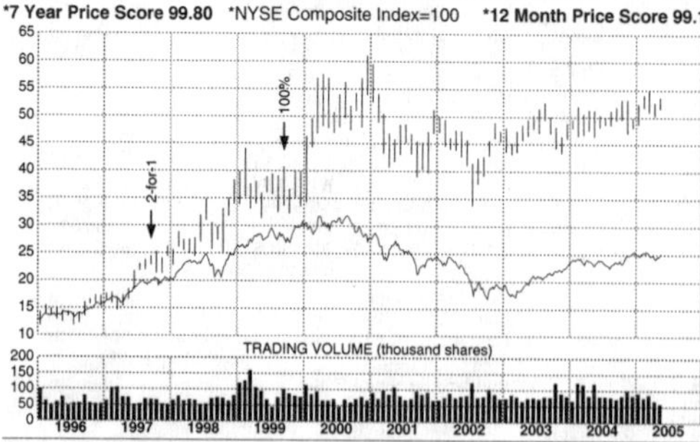

Interim Earnings (Per Share)

Qtr.	Jul	Oct	Jan	Apr
2001-02	0.25	0.05	0.26	0.24
2002-03	0.31	0.25	0.35	0.39
2003-04	0.37	0.39	0.38	0.47
2004-05	0.43	0.44	0.45	...

Interim Dividends (Per Share)

Amt	Decl	Ex	Rec	Pay
0.084Q	6/24/2004	6/30/2004	7/2/2004	7/30/2004
0.084Q	8/26/2004	9/29/2004	10/1/2004	10/29/2004
0.084Q	10/21/2004	1/5/2005	1/7/2005	1/28/2005
0.084Q	1/20/2005	3/30/2005	4/1/2005	4/29/2005

Indicated Div: $0.34 (Div. Reinv. Plan)

Valuation Analysis

Forecast P/E	24.95 (6/1/2005)		
Market Cap	$65.0 Billion	Book Value	10.2 Billion
Price/Book	6.35	Price/Sales	6.65

Dividend Achiever Status

Rank	35	**10 Year Growth Rate**	20.89%
Total Years of Dividend Growth			27

Business Summary: Medical Instruments & Equipment (MIC: 9.6 SIC: 845 NAIC: 34510)

Medtronic operates in five business segments that manufacture and sell device-based medical therapies. Cardiac Rhythm Management offers physicians and their patients a variety of products to treat heart rhythm disorders. Cardiac Surgery offers a broad range of products for use by cardiac surgeons in the operating room. The Vascular segment offers minimally invasive products for the treatment of coronary vascular disease. The Neurological and Diabetes segment offers products for the treatment of neurological disorders. The Spinal and Ear, Nose & Throat segment offers a range of products and therapies to treat a variety of disorders of the cranium, spine, ear, nose and throat.

Recent Developments: For the quarter ended Jan 28 2005, net income increased 17.3% to $544,100 thousand from net income of $463,900 thousand in the year-earlier quarter. Revenues were $2,530,700 thousand, up 15.4% from $2,193,800 thousand the year before. Total direct expense was $605,600 thousand versus $538,400 thousand in the prior-year quarter, an increase of 12.5%. Total indirect expense was $1,079,500 thousand versus $908,400 thousand in the prior-year quarter, an increase of 18.8%.

Prospects: Co. is enjoying solid growth in its two largest product lines, implantable cardioverter defibrillators and spinal products. Also, a long-standing legal dispute in Co.'s Spinal business was concluded with the acquisition of Karlin Technology, Inc. for approximately $1.35 billion in May 2005. Looking ahead, Co. plans to benefit from a number of new product launches that should help support continued strong growth across its business. In addition, Co. projects revenue of between $11.10 billion and $11.60 billion, and diluted earnings in the range of $2.10 to $2.15 per share for fiscal 2006.

Financial Data

(US$ in Thousands)	9 Mos	6 Mos	3 Mos	04/30/2004	04/25/2003	04/26/2002	04/27/2001	04/30/2000
Earnings Per Share	1.76	1.69	1.64	1.60	1.30	0.80	0.85	0.90
Cash Flow Per Share	2.44	2.49	2.39	2.31	1.71	1.32	1.54	0.87
Tang Book Value Per Share	4.06	3.86	3.50	3.18	2.21	1.10	3.53	2.61
Dividends Per Share	0.324	0.313	0.301	0.290	0.250	0.230	0.200	0.160
Dividend Payout %	18.38	18.44	18.32	18.13	19.23	28.75	23.57	17.78
Income Statement								
Total Revenue	7,276,600	4,745,900	2,346,100	9,087,200	7,665,200	6,410,800	5,551,800	5,014,600
EBITDA	2,579,500	1,712,900	851,900	3,236,700	2,756,600	1,860,600	1,772,500	1,856,900
Depn & Amortn	339,300	223,700	110,100	442,600	408,100	329,800	297,300	243,300
Income Before Taxes	2,264,600	1,500,600	746,100	2,796,900	2,341,300	1,524,200	1,549,400	1,629,000
Income Taxes	655,100	435,200	216,400	837,600	741,500	540,200	503,400	530,500
Net Income	1,609,500	1,065,400	529,700	1,959,300	1,599,800	984,000	1,046,000	1,098,500
Average Shares	1,219,100	1,220,700	1,220,200	1,225,200	1,227,900	1,224,400	1,226,000	1,220,800
Balance Sheet								
Current Assets	6,728,200	6,369,600	5,873,700	5,312,700	4,605,500	3,488,000	3,756,800	3,013,400
Total Assets	15,695,400	15,180,300	14,557,000	14,110,800	12,320,800	10,904,500	7,038,900	5,669,400
Current Liabilities	2,655,900	2,487,600	4,298,300	4,240,600	1,813,300	3,984,900	1,359,300	991,500
Long-Term Obligations	1,974,900	1,974,800	1,600	1,100	1,980,300	9,500	13,300	14,100
Total Liabilities	5,463,300	5,255,000	5,108,900	5,033,800	4,414,400	4,473,400	1,529,400	1,177,900
Stockholders' Equity	10,232,100	9,925,300	9,448,100	9,077,000	7,906,400	6,431,100	5,509,500	4,491,500
Shares Outstanding	1,209,520	1,208,725	1,210,281	1,209,459	1,218,128	1,215,208	1,209,514	1,197,698
Statistical Record								
Return on Assets %	14.72	14.73	14.77	14.59	13.81	11.00	16.60	20.79
Return on Equity %	22.66	22.69	22.78	22.70	22.38	16.53	21.09	26.90
EBITDA Margin %	35.45	36.09	36.31	35.62	35.96	29.02	31.93	37.03
Net Margin %	22.12	22.45	22.58	21.56	20.87	15.35	18.84	21.91
Asset Turnover	0.67	0.67	0.68	0.68	0.66	0.72	0.88	0.95
Current Ratio	2.53	2.56	1.37	1.25	2.54	0.88	2.76	3.04
Debt to Equity	0.19	0.20	N.M.	N.M.	0.25	N.M.	N.M.	N.M.
Price Range	53.28-46.40	53.19-43.36	52.65-43.36	52.65-43.36	48.95-33.74	51.24-38.99	61.00-40.71	57.69-31.31
P/E Ratio	30.27-26.36	31.47-25.66	32.10-26.44	32.91-27.10	37.65-25.95	64.05-48.74	71.76-47.89	64.10-34.79
Average Yield %	0.65	0.64	0.62	0.60	0.57	0.51	0.39	0.40

Address: 710 Medtronic Parkway, Minneapolis, MN 55432
Telephone: 763-514-4000
Web Site: www.medtronic.com

Officers: Arthur D. Collins Jr. - Chmn., C.E.O. William A. Hawkins - Pres., C.O.O. **Transfer Agents:** Wells Fargo Bank Minnesota N.A., St. Paul, MN

Investor Contact: 763-505-2692
No of Institutions: 897
Shares: 829,222,464 **% Held:** 68.56

MERCANTILE BANKSHARES CORP.

Exchange	Symbol	Price	52Wk Range	Yield	P/E
NMS	MRBK	$52.13 (5/31/2005)	52.90-44.36	2.92	17.61

***7 Year Price Score** 110.69 *NYSE Composite Index=100 ***12 Month Price Score** 100.36

Interim Earnings (Per Share)

Qtr.	Mar	Jun	Sep	Dec
2002	0.66	0.67	0.69	0.70
2003	0.71	0.72	0.63	0.63
2004	0.69	0.71	0.71	0.76
2005	0.78	...	...	...

Interim Dividends (Per Share)

Amt	Decl	Ex	Rec	Pay
0.35Q	9/14/2004	9/21/2004	9/23/2004	9/30/2004
0.35Q	12/14/2004	12/21/2004	12/23/2004	12/31/2004
0.35Q	3/8/2005	3/22/2005	3/24/2005	3/31/2005
0.38Q	5/6/2005	5/12/2005	5/16/2005	6/30/2005

Indicated Div: $1.52 (Div. Reinv. Plan)

Valuation Analysis

Forecast P/E	N/A		
Market Cap	$4.1 Billion	Book Value	1.9 Billion
Price/Book	2.13	Price/Sales	4.60

Dividend Achiever Status

Rank	158	**10 Year Growth Rate**	10.83%
Total Years of Dividend Growth			28

Business Summary: Commercial Banking (MIC: 8.1 SIC: 022 NAIC: 22110)

Mercantile Bankshares, with assets of $14.43 billion and deposits of $10.80 billion as of Dec 31 2004, is a bank holding company comprised of 13 banks and a mortgage banking company with a network of 226 banking offices. Ten banks are located in Maryland, two are in Virginia and one is in southern Delaware. Mercantile-Safe Deposit and Trust is Co.'s largest bank and operates 26 offices in Maryland and one commercial office in Pennsylvania. The banks are engaged in the general commercial and retail banking business, including acceptance of demand, savings and time deposits and the making of various types of loans. Co. provides mortgages through its banks and through Mercantile Mortgage, LLC.

Recent Developments: For the quarter ended Mar 31 2005, net income increased 12.4% to $62,627 thousand from net income of $55,697 thousand in the year-earlier quarter. Net interest income was $143,083 thousand, up 9.7% from $130,405 thousand the year before. Provision for loan losses was $756 thousand versus $2,426 thousand in the prior-year quarter, a decrease of 68.8%. Non-interest income rose 8.9% to $57,869 thousand, while non-interest expense advanced 7.2% to $100,153 thousand.

Prospects: Co. is experiencing good loan growth, an expanding net interest margin and solid overall revenue growth. In addition, Co. is seeing marked improvement in its credit quality. Co. also is having some success in controlling expense growth and plans to continue to focus on this issue going forward. Co.'s loan growth is solid in all categories, except for consumer loans which are up only marginally versus the prior year. Meanwhile, the strongest loan growth is in average construction loans. Separately, the improvement in the net interest margin is primarily due to increases in non-interest bearing funds. Due to these factors, Co. is enjoying strong earnings growth.

Financial Data (US$ in Thousands)	**3 Mos**	**12/31/2004**	**12/31/2003**	**12/31/2002**	**12/31/2001**	**12/31/2000**	**12/31/1999**	**12/31/1998**
Earnings Per Share	2.96	2.87	2.68	2.72	2.55	2.51	2.25	2.04
Cash Flow Per Share	3.71	3.14	2.71	4.83	1.32	3.08	2.28	2.37
Tang Book Value Per Share	17.46	17.17	15.83	17.64	16.03	15.03	13.51	13.36
Dividends Per Share	1.400	1.380	1.290	1.180	1.100	1.020	0.940	0.860
Dividend Payout %	47.30	48.08	48.13	43.38	43.14	40.64	41.78	42.16
Income Statement								
Interest Income	179,245	659,037	596,575	586,386	649,766	646,495	559,168	555,392
Interest Expense	36,162	113,256	117,245	144,582	231,525	237,110	190,082	202,027
Net Interest Income	143,083	545,781	479,330	441,804	418,241	409,385	369,086	353,365
Provision for Losses	756	7,221	12,105	16,378	13,434	17,231	12,056	11,489
Non-Interest Income	57,869	213,929	176,591	143,750	145,490	125,541	121,991	108,693
Non-Interest Expense	100,153	391,958	337,447	272,608	263,959	243,505	230,420	219,005
Income Before Taxes	100,043	360,531	306,369	296,568	286,338	274,190	248,601	231,564
Income Taxes	37,416	131,124	109,555	106,330	105,043	98,960	90,864	84,436
Net Income	62,627	229,407	196,814	190,238	181,295	175,230	157,737	147,128
Average Shares	79,875	79,854	73,421	70,067	71,199	69,719	70,020	72,237
Balance Sheet								
Net Loans & Leases	10,264,205	10,079,431	9,116,823	7,173,426	6,764,783	6,554,682	5,600,945	5,108,467
Total Assets	14,627,833	14,425,690	13,695,472	10,790,376	9,928,786	8,938,030	7,895,024	7,609,563
Total Deposits	10,971,276	10,799,199	10,262,553	8,260,940	7,447,372	6,796,541	5,925,083	5,958,346
Total Liabilities	12,689,317	12,508,007	11,854,031	9,466,018	8,698,580	7,764,729	6,920,984	6,610,204
Stockholders' Equity	1,938,516	1,917,683	1,841,441	1,324,358	1,230,206	1,173,301	974,040	999,359
Shares Outstanding	79,316	79,300	79,772	68,836	69,775	71,098	68,646	71,027
Statistical Record								
Return on Assets %	1.64	1.63	1.61	1.84	1.92	2.08	2.03	1.99
Return on Equity %	12.35	12.17	12.43	14.89	15.09	16.28	15.99	15.21
Net Interest Margin %	79.83	82.81	80.35	75.34	64.37	63.32	66.01	63.62
Efficiency Ratio %	42.24	44.90	43.64	37.34	33.19	31.54	33.83	32.98
Loans to Deposits	0.94	0.93	0.89	0.87	0.91	0.96	0.95	0.86
Price Range	52.90-40.50	52.90-40.50	45.59-32.75	45.20-32.65	43.74-34.06	44.69-23.84	39.88-30.38	39.94-26.38
P/E Ratio	17.87-13.68	18.43-14.11	17.01-12.22	16.62-12.00	17.15-13.36	17.80-9.50	17.72-13.50	19.58-12.93
Average Yield %	2.92	2.98	3.24	2.91	2.78	3.14	2.69	2.49

Address: Two Hopkins Plaza, Baltimore, MD 21203 **Telephone:** 410-237-5900 **Web Site:** www.mercantile.com	**Officers:** Edward J. Kelly III - Chmn., Pres., C.E.O. Jay M. Wilson - Vice-Chmn. **Transfer Agents:** American Stock Transfer & Trust Company, New York, NY	**No of Institutions:** 194 **Shares:** 31,527,428 **% Held:** 39.79

MERCK & CO., INC

Exchange	Symbol	Price	52Wk Range	Yield	P/E
NYS	MRK	$32.44 (5/31/2005)	48.37-26.00	4.69	12.92

Interim Earnings (Per Share)

Qtr.	Mar	Jun	Sep	Dec
2002	0.71	0.77	0.83	0.83
2003	0.76	0.83	0.82	0.62
2004	0.73	0.79	0.60	0.50
2005	0.62	...	...	...

Interim Dividends (Per Share)

Amt	Decl	Ex	Rec	Pay
0.38Q	7/27/2004	9/1/2004	9/3/2004	10/1/2004
0.38Q	11/23/2004	12/1/2004	12/3/2004	1/3/2005
0.38Q	2/22/2005	3/2/2005	3/4/2005	4/1/2005
0.38Q	5/24/2005	6/1/2005	6/3/2005	7/1/2005

Indicated Div: $1.52 (Div. Reinv. Plan)

Valuation Analysis

Forecast P/E	12.99 (5/28/2005)		
Market Cap	$71.5 Billion	Book Value	17.6 Billion
Price/Book	4.05	Price/Sales	3.16

Dividend Achiever Status

Rank	172	10 Year Growth Rate	10.09%
Total Years of Dividend Growth			21

Business Summary: Pharmaceuticals (MIC: 9.1 SIC: 834 NAIC: 25412)

Merck & Co. is a research-driven pharmaceutical company that discovers, develops, manufactures and markets products designed to improve human and animal health, directly and through joint ventures. Co.'s products include therapeutic and preventive agents, generally sold by prescription, for the treatment of human disorders. Among these are Zocor for cholesterol modification; Cozaar, Hyzaar and Vasotec for hypertension/heart failure; Fosamax, for treatment and prevention of osteoporosis; Singulair, for treatment of asthma and for relief of symptoms of seasonal allergic rhinitis; Arcoxia, anti-inflammatory/analgesic agents that inhibit the COX-2 enzyme responsible for pain and inflammation.

Recent Developments: For the quarter ended Mar 31 2005, net income decreased 15.4% to $1,370,100 thousand from net income of $1,618,600 thousand in the year-earlier quarter. Revenues were $5,362,200 thousand, down 4.8% from $5,630,800 thousand the year before. Total direct expense was $1,271,400 thousand versus $1,148,200 thousand in the prior-year quarter, an increase of 10.7%. Total indirect expense was $2,459,900 thousand versus $2,607,700 thousand in the prior-year quarter, a decrease of 5.7%.

Prospects: Co.'s overall sales are lower due to the voluntary withdrawal of Vioxx from the market. This is being partially offset by growth in sales of Co.'s newer franchises and higher alliance revenues. Meanwhile, Co.'s better-than-anticipated operating performance reflects cost management, favorable foreign exchange and overall revenue levels. Separately, Co. announced that the U.S. Food and Drug Administration recently accepted the supplemental New Drug Application for Singulair for use in the prevention of exercise-induced bronchospasm in patients 15 years of age and older. Looking ahead to full-year 2005, Co. expects earnings to range from $2.44 to $2.52 per share, before non-recurring items.

Financial Data

(US$ in Thousands)	3 Mos	12/31/2004	12/31/2003	12/31/2002	12/31/2001	12/31/2000	12/31/1999	12/31/1998
Earnings Per Share	2.51	2.61	3.03	3.14	3.14	2.90	2.45	2.15
Cash Flow Per Share	3.77	3.95	3.77	4.22	3.97	3.32	2.61	2.24
Tang Book Value Per Share	7.22	7.03	6.13	4.88	3.77	3.23	2.43	1.91
Dividends Per Share	1.510	1.500	1.460	1.420	1.380	1.260	1.120	0.990
Dividend Payout %	60.16	57.47	48.18	45.22	43.95	43.45	45.71	46.05
Income Statement								
Total Revenue	5,362,200	22,938,600	22,485,900	51,790,300	47,715,700	40,363,200	32,714,000	26,898,200
EBITDA	2,291,200	9,418,800	10,408,000	11,673,400	11,841,000	11,115,200	9,716,500	9,046,100
Depn & Amortn	379,800	1,450,700	1,314,200	1,488,300	1,463,800	1,277,300	1,144,800	1,015,100
Income Before Taxes	1,920,700	7,974,500	9,051,600	10,213,600	10,402,600	9,824,100	8,619,500	8,133,100
Income Taxes	550,600	2,161,100	2,462,000	3,064,100	3,120,800	3,002,400	2,729,000	2,884,900
Net Income	1,370,100	5,813,400	6,830,900	7,149,500	7,281,800	6,821,700	5,890,500	5,248,200
Average Shares	2,210,400	2,226,400	2,253,100	2,277,000	2,322,300	2,353,200	2,404,600	2,441,100
Balance Sheet								
Current Assets	15,760,000	13,475,200	11,527,200	14,833,900	12,961,600	13,353,400	11,259,200	10,228,500
Total Assets	43,117,100	42,572,800	40,587,500	47,561,200	44,006,700	39,910,400	35,634,900	31,853,400
Current Liabilities	10,902,700	11,744,100	9,569,600	12,375,200	11,544,200	9,709,600	8,758,800	6,068,800
Long-Term Obligations	5,655,600	4,691,500	5,096,000	4,879,000	4,798,600	3,600,700	3,143,900	3,220,800
Total Liabilities	25,468,100	25,284,600	25,011,100	29,360,700	27,956,600	25,078,000	22,393,300	19,051,600
Stockholders' Equity	17,649,000	17,288,200	15,576,400	18,200,500	16,050,100	14,832,400	13,241,600	12,801,800
Shares Outstanding	2,205,404	2,208,639	2,221,764	2,244,983	2,272,729	2,307,599	2,329,078	2,360,453
Statistical Record								
Return on Assets %	13.13	13.94	15.50	15.62	17.35	18.01	17.46	18.20
Return on Equity %	32.81	35.28	40.45	41.75	47.16	48.47	45.24	41.30
EBITDA Margin %	42.73	41.06	46.29	22.54	24.82	27.54	29.70	33.63
Net Margin %	25.55	25.34	30.38	13.80	15.26	16.90	18.01	19.51
Asset Turnover	0.53	0.55	0.51	1.13	1.14	1.07	0.97	0.93
Current Ratio	1.45	1.15	1.20	1.20	1.12	1.38	1.29	1.69
Debt to Equity	0.32	0.27	0.33	0.27	0.30	0.24	0.24	0.25
Price Range	48.37-26.00	49.08-26.00	59.85-40.60	60.92-36.96	88.02-54.11	89.80-51.05	81.75-57.67	75.18-48.68
P/E Ratio	19.27-10.36	18.80-9.96	19.75-13.40	19.40-11.77	28.03-17.23	30.96-17.60	33.37-23.54	34.97-22.64
Average Yield %	3.96	3.57	2.84	2.77	2.05	1.81	1.62	1.63

Address: P.O. Box 100, One Merck Drive, Whitehouse Station, NJ 08889-0100 **Telephone:** 908-423-1000 **Web Site:** www.merck.com	**Officers:** Richard T. Clark - Pres., C.E.O. Judy C. Lewent - Exec. V.P., C.F.O. **Transfer Agents:** Wells Fargo Bank Minnesota, N.A., South St. Paul, MN	**Investor Contact:** 908-423-5881 **No of Institutions:** 920 **Shares:** 1,265,310,336 **% Held:** 57.30

MERCURY GENERAL CORP.

Exchange	Symbol	Price	52Wk Range	Yield	P/E
NYS	MCY	$55.20 (5/31/2005)	59.98-46.98	3.12	10.87

*7 Year Price Score 114.86 *NYSE Composite Index=100 *12 Month Price Score 97.30

Interim Earnings (Per Share)

Qtr.	Mar	Jun	Sep	Dec
2002	0.53	0.02	0.34	0.32
2003	0.77	0.80	0.91	0.90
2004	1.26	1.43	1.19	1.36
2005	1.10	...	...	...

Interim Dividends (Per Share)

Amt	Decl	Ex	Rec	Pay
0.37Q	8/2/2004	9/13/2004	9/15/2004	9/30/2004
0.37Q	10/29/2004	12/13/2004	12/15/2004	12/29/2004
0.43Q	1/28/2005	3/11/2005	3/15/2005	3/31/2005
0.43Q	5/2/2005	6/13/2005	6/15/2005	6/30/2005

Indicated Div: $1.72

Valuation Analysis

Forecast P/E	11.17 (6/1/2005)		
Market Cap	$3.0 Billion	Book Value	1.5 Billion
Price/Book	2.03	Price/Sales	1.09

Dividend Achiever Status

Rank	84	10 Year Growth Rate	15.51%
Total Years of Dividend Growth			18

Business Summary: Insurance (MIC: 8.2 SIC: 331 NAIC: 24126)

Mercury General and its subsidiaries are engaged primarily in writing all risk classifications of automobile insurance. The percentage of gross automobile insurance premiums written during 2004 by state was 76.2% in California, 9.6% in Florida, 4.6% in New Jersey, 4.3% in Texas and 5.3% in all other states. Co. also writes homeowners insurance, mechanical breakdown insurance, commercial and dwelling fire insurance and commercial property insurance. Co. offers automobile policyholders the following types of coverage: bodily injury liability, underinsured and uninsured motorist, personal injury protection, property damage liability, comprehensive, collision and other hazards.

Recent Developments: For the quarter ended Mar 31 2005, net income decreased 12.2% to $60,424 thousand from net income of $68,816 thousand in the year-earlier quarter. Revenues were $719,338 thousand, up 15.2% from $624,456 thousand the year before. Net premiums earned were $684,714 thousand versus $591,937 thousand in the prior-year quarter, an increase of 15.7%. Net investment income rose 11.9% to $28,785 thousand from $25,728 thousand a year ago.

Prospects: Notwithstanding its recent results for the quarter ended Mar 31 2005, which were hurt by increased rainfall in the state of California, Co.'s prospects appears encouraging. Company-wide net premiums written for the quarter ended Mar 31 2005 were $729.8 million, 15.8% higher than first quarter 2004 net premiums written of $630.3 million. California net premiums written were $526.1 million in the quarter, an increase of 5.2% over 2004. Non-California net premiums written were $203.8 million in the quarter, a 56.5% increase over 2004. Co. noted that non-California net premiums written represented 27.9% of its total first quarter 2005 net premiums written, up from 20.7% the year before.

Financial Data (US$ in Thousands)	3 Mos	12/31/2004	12/31/2003	12/31/2002	12/31/2001	12/31/2000	12/31/1999	12/31/1998
Earnings Per Share	5.08	5.24	3.38	1.21	1.94	2.02	2.44	3.21
Cash Flow Per Share	9.18	8.58	8.17	6.31	3.68	2.82	3.46	3.50
Tang Book Value Per Share	27.21	26.77	23.07	20.21	19.71	19.06	16.71	16.78
Dividends Per Share	1.540	1.480	1.320	1.200	1.060	0.960	0.840	0.700
Dividend Payout %	30.31	28.24	39.05	99.17	54.64	47.52	34.43	21.81
Income Statement								
Premium Income	684,714	2,528,636	2,145,047	1,741,527	1,380,561	1,249,259	1,188,307	1,121,584
Total Revenue	719,338	2,668,157	2,265,517	1,786,271	1,506,980	1,366,018	1,280,676	1,222,123
Benefits & Claims	448,246	1,582,254	1,452,051	1,268,243	1,010,439	901,781	789,103	684,468
Income Before Taxes	83,845	407,843	245,801	60,668	124,809	128,555	168,539	235,280
Income Taxes	23,421	121,635	61,480	(5,437)	19,470	19,189	34,830	57,754
Net Income	60,424	286,208	184,321	66,105	105,339	109,366	133,709	177,526
Average Shares	54,716	54,633	54,547	54,502	54,382	54,258	54,815	55,354
Balance Sheet								
Total Assets	3,756,149	3,609,743	3,119,766	2,645,296	2,316,540	2,142,263	1,906,367	1,877,025
Total Liabilities	2,271,980	2,150,195	1,864,263	1,546,510	1,246,829	1,109,358	996,776	959,650
Stockholders' Equity	1,484,169	1,459,548	1,255,503	1,098,786	1,069,711	1,032,905	909,591	917,375
Shares Outstanding	54,540	54,514	54,424	54,361	54,276	54,193	54,425	54,684
Statistical Record								
Return on Assets %	7.92	8.48	6.39	2.66	4.72	5.39	7.07	9.86
Return on Equity %	19.87	21.03	15.66	6.10	10.02	11.23	14.64	20.68
Loss Ratio %	65.46	62.57	67.69	72.82	73.19	72.19	66.41	61.03
Net Margin %	8.40	10.73	8.14	3.70	6.99	8.01	10.44	14.53
Price Range	59.98-46.98	59.98-46.44	48.58-34.30	50.63-37.37	43.85-32.21	43.88-21.25	45.50-21.06	69.44-33.25
P/E Ratio	11.81-9.25	11.45-8.86	14.37-10.15	41.84-30.88	22.60-16.60	21.72-10.52	18.65-8.63	21.63-10.36
Average Yield %	2.91	2.90	3.07	2.74	2.83	3.44	2.59	1.36

Address: 4484 Wilshire Boulevard, Los Angeles, CA 90010
Telephone: 323-937-1060
Web Site: www.mercuryinsurance.com

Officers: George Joseph - Chmn., C.E.O. Gabriel Tirador - Pres., C.O.O. **Transfer Agents:** The Bank of New York, New York, NY

Investor Contact: 800-900-6729
No of Institutions: 160
Shares: 21,217,010 **% Held:** 38.90

MEREDITH CORP.

Exchange	Symbol	Price	52Wk Range	Yield	P/E
NYS	MDP	$49.60 (5/31/2005)	55.75-44.81	1.13	20.33

***7 Year Price Score 111.19** *NYSE Composite Index=100 ***12 Month Price Score 90.75**

Interim Earnings (Per Share)

Qtr.	Sep	Dec	Mar	Jun
2001-02	0.17	0.17	0.35	1.10
2002-03	(1.36)	0.38	0.50	0.58
2003-04	0.39	0.39	0.65	0.71
2004-05	0.50	0.54	0.69	...

Interim Dividends (Per Share)

Amt	Decl	Ex	Rec	Pay
0.12Q	8/11/2004	8/27/2004	8/31/2004	9/15/2004
0.12Q	11/8/2004	11/26/2004	11/30/2004	12/15/2004
0.14Q	1/31/2005	2/24/2005	2/28/2005	3/15/2005
0.14Q	5/11/2005	5/26/2005	5/31/2005	6/15/2005

Indicated Div: $0.56

Valuation Analysis

Forecast P/E 17.59 (6/2/2005)

Market Cap $2.5 Billion Book Value 621.3 Million

Price/Book 3.94 Price/Sales 2.05

Dividend Achiever Status

Rank 169 **10 Year Growth Rate** 10.31%

Total Years of Dividend Growth 11

Business Summary: Media (MIC: 13.1 SIC: 721 NAIC: 11120)

Meredith is engaged in magazine and book publishing, television broadcasting, integrated marketing, and interactive media. The publishing segment consists of 17 magazine brands, including Better Homes and Gardens, Ladies' Home Journal, and American Baby, as well as 160 special interest publications; book publishing with nearly 300 books in print; integrated marketing relationships; a consumer database; an Internet presence, including 24 web sites and strategic alliances with Internet destinations; brand licensing relationships; and other related operations. The broadcasting segment includes the operations of 12 network-affiliated television stations located across the continental U.S.

Recent Developments: For the three months ended Mar 31 2005, net earnings increased 12.8% to $35.2 million compared with $31.2 million in the corresponding year-earlier period. Total revenues advanced 2.0% to $305.5 million from $299.6 million the previous year. Advertising revenue decreased 1.6% to $178.6 million from $181.5 million last year. Circulation revenue rose 3.2% to $65.0 million versus $63.0 million in prior-year period. All other revenue increased 12.4% to $61.9 million from $55.1 million the year before. Income from operations was $62.3 million, 10.2% higher than the year-ago period.

Prospects: Co. continues to deliver strong year-over-year earnings growth. For the fourth quarter of fiscal 2005, Publishing advertising revenue is expected to increase in the mid-single digits. Meanwhile, Broadcast pacings are currently up in the low-single digits versus the prior year. For the fourth quarter, Co. expects earnings per share of approximately $0.83 per share. These results include investment spending in Publishing to launch Meredith Hispanic Ventures, incremental direct mail investment and a mid-teen increase in paper prices from the fourth quarter of fiscal 2004. For fiscal year 2005, Co. expects earnings of about $2.50 per share.

Financial Data

(US$ in Thousands)	9 Mos	6 Mos	3 Mos	06/30/2004	06/30/2003	06/30/2002	06/30/2001	06/30/2000
Earnings Per Share	2.44	2.39	2.25	2.14	0.10	1.79	1.39	1.35
Cash Flow Per Share	3.51	3.27	3.82	3.40	3.47	2.83	2.74	2.88
Dividends Per Share	0.500	0.480	0.455	0.430	0.370	0.350	0.330	0.310
Dividend Payout %	20.49	20.06	20.26	20.09	370.00	19.55	23.74	22.96
Income Statement								
Total Revenue	888,933	583,416	288,863	1,161,652	1,080,104	987,829	1,053,213	1,097,165
EBITDA	181,010	109,873	55,203	269,428	244,554	275,431	243,800	248,951
Depn & Amortn	26,034	17,199	8,445	66,314	68,786	93,770	95,699	87,614
Income Before Taxes	140,239	82,772	41,803	180,613	148,559	149,072	116,200	127,586
Income Taxes	54,272	32,033	16,179	69,897	57,491	57,691	44,928	56,556
Net Income	86,860	51,632	25,624	110,716	5,319	91,381	71,272	71,030
Average Shares	50,990	51,469	51,658	51,689	51,093	50,921	51,354	52,774
Balance Sheet								
Current Assets	287,316	310,481	329,690	314,014	268,429	272,211	291,082	288,799
Total Assets	1,479,698	1,507,255	1,490,561	1,465,927	1,436,721	1,460,264	1,437,747	1,439,773
Current Liabilities	438,606	435,079	440,426	370,961	297,199	307,406	371,406	358,701
Long-Term Obligations	145,000	175,000	175,000	225,000	375,000	385,000	400,000	455,000
Total Liabilities	858,398	885,945	908,369	877,197	935,956	952,547	989,839	1,017,264
Stockholders' Equity	621,300	621,310	582,192	588,730	500,765	507,717	447,908	379,844
Shares Outstanding	49,395	49,979	49,999	50,484	50,149	49,575	49,791	49,209
Statistical Record								
Return on Assets %	8.58	8.39	7.89	7.61	0.37	6.31	4.95	4.95
Return on Equity %	21.35	21.57	21.19	20.27	1.05	19.12	17.22	19.14
EBITDA Margin %	20.36	18.83	19.11	23.19	22.64	27.88	23.15	22.69
Net Margin %	9.77	8.85	8.87	9.53	0.49	9.25	6.77	6.47
Asset Turnover	0.82	0.81	0.80	0.80	0.75	0.68	0.73	0.76
Current Ratio	0.66	0.71	0.75	0.85	0.90	0.89	0.78	0.81
Debt to Equity	0.23	0.28	0.30	0.38	0.75	0.76	0.89	1.20
Price Range	55.75-45.89	55.75-48.81	55.75-46.17	55.75-44.00	47.58-34.09	44.75-27.20	38.52-27.19	41.94-22.44
P/E Ratio	22.85-18.81	23.33-20.42	24.78-20.52	26.05-20.56	475.80-340.90	25.00-15.20	27.71-19.56	31.06-16.62
Average Yield %	0.97	0.93	0.90	0.87	0.89	0.94	1.00	0.92

Address: 1716 Locust Street, Des Moines, IA 50309-3023
Telephone: 515-284-3000
Web Site: www.meredith.com

Officers: William T. Kerr - Chmn., C.E.O. Stephen M. Lacy - Pres., C.O.O. **Transfer Agents:** Boston EquiServe, Boston, MA

Investor Contact: 800-284-4236
No of Institutions: 185
Shares: 34,631,904 **% Held:** 85.89

MERIDIAN BIOSCIENCE INC.

Exchange	Symbol	Price	52Wk Range	Yield	P/E
NMS	VIVO	$18.25 (5/31/2005)	19.78-10.06	2.63	27.24

*7 Year Price Score 152.59 *NYSE Composite Index=100 *12 Month Price Score 110.35

TRADING VOLUME (thousand shares)

Interim Earnings (Per Share)

Qtr.	Dec	Mar	Jun	Sep
2001-02	0.08	0.10	0.11	0.06
2002-03	0.10	0.13	0.12	0.12
2003-04	0.12	0.15	0.14	0.19
2004-05	0.14	0.20	...	...

Interim Dividends (Per Share)

Amt	Decl	Ex	Rec	Pay
0.10Q	7/22/2004	7/29/2004	8/2/2004	8/9/2004
0.10Q	11/17/2004	11/23/2004	11/26/2004	12/6/2004
0.12Q	1/20/2005	1/28/2005	2/1/2005	2/8/2005
0.12Q	4/20/2005	4/28/2005	5/2/2005	5/9/2005

Indicated Div: $0.48 (Div. Reinv. Plan)

Valuation Analysis

Forecast P/E	26.82 (6/1/2005)		
Market Cap	$286.4 Million	Book Value	44.7 Million
Price/Book	6.41	Price/Sales	3.45

Dividend Achiever Status

Rank	56	10 Year Growth Rate	17.81%
Total Years of Dividend Growth			12

Business Summary: Biotechnology (MIC: 9.2 SIC: 835 NAIC: 25413)

Meridian Bioscience is an integrated life science company whose principal businesses are the development, manufacture, sale and distribution of diagnostic test kits, primarily for certain respiratory, gastrointestinal, viral and parasitic infectious diseases; the manufacture and distribution of bulk antigens and reagents used by researchers and other diagnostic manufacturers; and the contract manufacture of proteins and other biologicals for use by biopharmaceutical and biotechnology companies engaged in research for new drugs and vaccines. Co. has three operating segments: US Diagnostics, European Diagnostics, and Life Science.

Recent Developments: For the quarter ended Mar 31 2005, net income increased 39.6% to $3,196,000 from net income of $2,289,000 in the year-earlier quarter. Revenues were $23,686,000 , up 13.1% from $20,940,000 the year before. Operating income was $5,198,000 versus an income of $3,981,000 in the prior-year quarter, an increase of 30.6%. Total direct expense was $10,109,000 versus $8,907,000 in the prior-year quarter, an increase of 13.5%. Total indirect expense was $8,379,000 versus $8,052,000 in the prior-year quarter, an increase of 4.1%.

Prospects: Co.'s outlook appears constructive, reflecting its broad-based product portfolio, new product introductions, and its Jan 2005 acquisition of O.E.M. Concepts. So, for the fiscal year ended Sep 30 2005, Co. expects net sales to be in the range of $84.0 to $88.0 million and per share diluted earnings to be between $0.66 and $0.70. The revenue for O.E.M. Concepts is expected to be in the $3.0 million to $3.5 million range for the eight months of fiscal 2005 post acquisition; earnings per share accretion after giving effect to purchase accounting adjustments, is expected to be between $0.01 and $0.02 per share. Co. noted that the O.E.M. estimates are not included in its aforementioned guidance.

Financial Data

(US$ in Thousands)	6 Mos	3 Mos	09/30/2004	09/30/2003	09/30/2002	09/30/2001	09/30/2000	09/30/1999
Earnings Per Share	0.67	0.62	0.60	0.47	0.34	(0.70)	0.49	0.16
Cash Flow Per Share	1.02	0.85	0.85	0.84	0.78	0.60	0.36	0.63
Tang Book Value Per Share	1.49	1.49	1.22	0.83	0.58	0.49	0.84	0.66
Dividends Per Share	0.420	0.400	0.390	0.340	0.275	0.255	0.230	0.200
Dividend Payout %	62.69	64.69	65.00	72.34	80.88	...	46.94	125.00
Income Statement								
Total Revenue	42,528	18,842	79,606	65,864	59,104	56,527	57,096	54,351
EBITDA	10,845	4,426	18,540	17,047	13,898	(7,780)	13,491	12,632
Depn & Amortn	2,031	935	3,819	3,780	3,719	4,746	4,811	5,673
Income Before Taxes	8,313	3,207	13,195	11,591	8,243	(14,906)	6,938	5,321
Income Taxes	3,007	1,097	4,010	4,573	3,212	(4,631)	(173)	2,935
Net Income	5,306	2,110	9,185	7,018	5,031	(10,275)	7,111	2,386
Average Shares	16,108	15,551	15,259	14,950	14,760	14,589	14,652	14,580
Balance Sheet								
Current Assets	39,760	38,837	36,111	33,161	30,375	32,502	40,166	31,972
Total Assets	79,903	71,801	69,322	66,420	65,095	65,982	84,769	72,389
Current Liabilities	21,287	17,351	16,650	15,330	15,249	16,368	17,303	13,517
Long-Term Obligations	9,162	14,708	17,093	21,505	23,626	24,349	27,105	21,366
Total Liabilities	35,191	34,703	36,390	38,936	40,714	43,038	48,158	38,485
Stockholders' Equity	44,712	37,098	32,932	27,484	24,381	22,944	36,611	33,904
Shares Outstanding	15,695	15,242	14,962	14,720	14,624	14,590	14,587	14,429
Statistical Record								
Return on Assets %	14.24	13.66	13.50	10.67	7.68	N.M.	9.02	3.63
Return on Equity %	27.84	28.66	30.32	27.06	21.26	N.M.	20.11	6.96
EBITDA Margin %	25.50	23.49	23.29	25.88	23.51	N.M.	23.63	23.24
Net Margin %	12.48	11.20	11.54	10.66	8.51	N.M.	12.45	4.39
Asset Turnover	1.14	1.15	1.17	1.00	0.90	0.75	0.72	0.83
Current Ratio	1.87	2.24	2.17	2.16	1.99	1.99	2.32	2.37
Debt to Equity	0.20	0.40	0.52	0.78	0.97	1.06	0.74	0.63
Price Range	19.78-9.92	18.55-9.92	13.32-9.76	11.06-5.61	7.55-4.54	7.88-2.31	10.94-6.06	8.56-5.00
P/E Ratio	29.52-14.81	29.92-16.00	22.20-16.27	23.53-11.94	22.21-13.35	...	22.32-12.37	53.52-31.25
Average Yield %	3.11	3.28	3.56	4.08	4.40	5.16	3.06	2.87

Address: 3471 River Hills Drive, Cincinnati, OH 45244 **Telephone:** 513-271-3700 **Web Site:** www.meridianbioscience.com	**Officers:** William J. Motto - Chmn., C.E.O. John A. Kraeutler - Pres., C.O.O. **Transfer Agents:** Computershare Investor Services LLC, OH	**Investor Contact:** 513-271-3700 **No of Institutions:** 59 **Shares:** 4,817,945 **% Held:** 30.78

MGE ENERGY INC

Exchange	Symbol	Price	52Wk Range	Yield	P/E
NMS	MGEE	$36.00 (5/31/2005)	36.87-29.39	3.80	25.35

*7 Year Price Score 113.12 *NYSE Composite Index=100 *12 Month Price Score 97.07

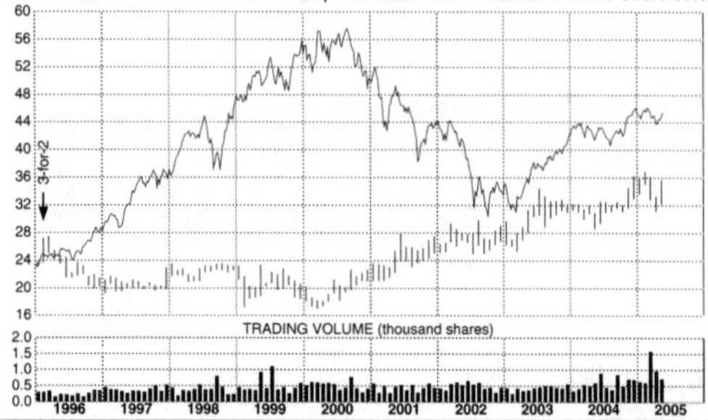

TRADING VOLUME (thousand shares)

Interim Earnings (Per Share)

Qtr.	Mar	Jun	Sep	Dec
2002	0.64	0.26	0.60	0.19
2003	0.53	0.33	0.56	0.29
2004	0.74	0.30	0.48	0.24
2005	0.40	...	...	...

Interim Dividends (Per Share)

Amt	Decl	Ex	Rec	Pay
0.342Q	8/20/2004	8/30/2004	9/1/2004	9/15/2004
0.342Q	11/19/2004	11/29/2004	12/1/2004	12/15/2004
0.342Q	2/18/2005	2/25/2005	3/1/2005	3/15/2005
0.342Q	5/10/2005	5/27/2005	6/1/2005	6/15/2005

Indicated Div: $1.37 (Div. Reinv. Plan)

Valuation Analysis

Forecast P/E	N/A		
Market Cap	$736.3 Million	Book Value	341.2 Million
Price/Book	2.16	Price/Sales	1.72

Dividend Achiever Status

Rank	314	**10 Year Growth Rate**	0.87%
Total Years of Dividend Growth			29

Business Summary: Electricity (MIC: 7.1 SIC: 931 NAIC: 21121)

MGE Energy is the holding company for Madison Gas & Electric, which is a public utility that generates and distributes electricity to nearly 134,000 customers in Dane County, WI as of Dec 31 2004. Co. also purchases, transports and distributes natural gas to more than 133,000 customers in the Wisconsin cities of Elroy, Fitchburg, Lodi, Madison, Middleton, Monona, Prairie du Chien, Verona, and Viroqua; 24 villages and all or parts of 45 townships. Co. has a 22.0% ownership interest in two, 512-megawatt coal-burning units at the Columbia Energy Center in Columbia, WI. The units burn low-sulfur coal obtained from the Powder River Basin coal fields located in Wyoming and Montana.

Recent Developments: For the quarter ended Mar 31 2005, net income decreased 40.4% to $8,215 thousand from net income of $13,791 thousand in the year-earlier quarter. Revenues were $138,909 thousand, up 2.7% from $135,281 thousand the year before. Operating income was $15,062 thousand versus an income of $23,972 thousand in the prior-year quarter, a decrease of 37.2%. Total direct expense was $113,725 thousand versus $101,938 thousand in the prior-year quarter, an increase of 11.6%. Total indirect expense was $10,122 thousand versus $9,371 thousand in the prior-year quarter, an increase of 8.0%.

Prospects: Earnings are being negatively affected by a 7-week planned major outage at Co.'s Columbia plant, which occurred during the first quarter of 2005 and caused higher maintenance and replacement purchased power costs. Co. anticipates that the majority of these costs will be recovered through existing rates over the remainder of 2005. Separately, Co. is recovering in electric rates the revenue associated with the West Campus Cogeneration plant that has been constructed on the University of Wisconsin campus. Co. has deferred the recognition of approximately $2.5 million in revenues at Mar 31 2005. This revenue will be recognized from the commercial operation date throughout the remainder of 2005.

Financial Data

(US$ in Thousands)	3 Mos	12/31/2004	12/31/2003	12/31/2002	12/31/2001	12/31/2000	12/31/1999	12/31/1998
Earnings Per Share	1.42	1.77	1.71	1.69	1.62	1.67	1.48	1.38
Cash Flow Per Share	3.14	3.25	3.83	3.28	4.44	2.91	3.75	4.38
Tang Book Value Per Share	16.68	16.59	14.34	12.94	12.67	12.05	11.49	11.34
Dividends Per Share	1.363	1.360	1.348	1.338	1.328	1.318	1.308	1.298
Dividend Payout %	96.01	76.84	78.85	79.19	81.99	78.93	88.37	94.07
Income Statement								
Total Revenue	138,909	424,881	401,547	347,096	333,711	324,108	274,034	249,752
EBITDA	22,940	90,861	85,145	89,307	...	...	...	...
Depn & Amortn	6,634	24,931	22,828	28,842	36,459	36,548	37,053	34,759
Income Before Taxes	13,488	54,496	50,541	47,920	...	...	...	...
Income Taxes	5,273	20,656	19,901	18,727	2,105	...	...	...
Net Income	8,215	33,840	30,640	29,193	27,245	27,355	23,746	22,230
Average Shares	20,421	19,119	17,894	17,311	16,819	16,382	16,084	16,080
Balance Sheet								
Net PPE	620,742	607,398	537,511	460,328	401,249	441,654	394,825	367,302
Total Assets	803,902	827,371	721,687	628,895	541,451	571,604	495,510	466,265
Long-Term Obligations	202,271	202,257	202,204	192,149	157,600	183,437	148,599	159,761
Total Liabilities	462,679	489,174	458,617	401,525	167,559	371,292	161,225	283,990
Stockholders' Equity	341,223	338,197	263,070	227,370	216,292	200,312	185,686	182,275
Shares Outstanding	20,453	20,389	18,343	17,574	17,071	16,618	16,161	16,080
Statistical Record								
Return on Assets %	3.70	4.36	4.54	4.99	4.90	5.11	4.94	4.74
Return on Equity %	9.09	11.23	12.49	13.16	13.08	14.13	12.91	12.24
EBITDA Margin %	16.51	21.39	21.20	25.73	...	...	...	...
Net Margin %	5.91	7.96	7.63	8.41	8.16	8.44	8.67	8.90
PPE Turnover	0.73	0.74	0.80	0.81	0.79	0.77	0.72	0.68
Asset Turnover	0.56	0.55	0.59	0.59	0.60	0.61	0.57	0.53
Debt to Equity	0.59	0.60	0.77	0.85	0.73	0.92	0.80	0.88
Price Range	36.87-28.57	36.30-28.57	34.45-25.27	29.84-25.01	27.80-21.06	22.75-17.00	23.38-17.25	23.56-20.88
P/E Ratio	25.96-20.12	20.51-16.14	20.15-14.78	17.66-14.80	17.16-13.00	13.62-10.18	15.79-11.66	17.07-15.13
Average Yield %	4.17	4.28	4.50	4.97	5.53	6.70	6.29	5.79

Address: 133 South Blair Street, Madison, WI 53703 **Telephone:** 608-252-7000 **Web Site:** www.mgeenergy.com	**Officers:** Gary J. Wolter - Chmn., Pres., C.E.O. David C. Mebane - Vice-Chmn. **Transfer Agents:** Continental Stock Transfer & Trust Company, New York, NY	**Investor Contact:** 608-252-7907 **No of Institutions:** 74 **Shares:** 4,429,191 **% Held:** 21.68

MIDLAND CO.

Exchange	Symbol	Price	52Wk Range	Yield	P/E
NMS	MLAN	$31.95 (5/31/2005)	34.26-25.65	0.70	10.54

***7 Year Price Score 139.88** *NYSE Composite Index=100 ***12 Month Price Score 104.30**

Interim Earnings (Per Share)

Qtr.	Mar	Jun	Sep	Dec
2002	0.44	0.33	(0.15)	0.44
2003	0.56	(0.60)	0.23	0.56
2004	0.90	0.58	0.12	1.23
2005	1.10	...	...	...

Interim Dividends (Per Share)

Amt	Decl	Ex	Rec	Pay
0.051Q	7/29/2004	9/17/2004	9/21/2004	10/5/2004
0.051Q	10/28/2004	12/20/2004	12/22/2004	1/5/2005
0.056Q	1/27/2005	3/18/2005	3/22/2005	4/5/2005
0.056Q	4/28/2005	6/20/2005	6/22/2005	7/6/2005

Indicated Div: $0.23 (Div. Reinv. Plan)

Valuation Analysis

Forecast P/E	10.79 (6/1/2005)		
Market Cap	$602.6 Million	Book Value	439.7 Million
Price/Book	1.37	Price/Sales	0.77

Dividend Achiever Status

Rank	219	**10 Year Growth Rate**	7.80%
Total Years of Dividend Growth			18

Business Summary: Insurance (MIC: 8.2 SIC: 399 NAIC: 24128)

Midland is a provider of specialty insurance products and services through two wholly owned subsidiaries. American Modern specializes in writing physical damage insurance and related coverages on manufactured housing, as well as other areas of insurance, including coverage for site-built homes, motorcycles, watercraft, snowmobiles, recreational vehicles, physical damage on long-haul trucks, extended service contracts, credit life and related products as well as collateral protection and mortgage fire products sold to financial institutions and their customers. Co.'s other subsidiary, M/G Transport, charters barges and brokers freight for the movement of commodities on the inland waterways.

Recent Developments: For the quarter ended Mar 31 2005, net income increased 27.9% to $21,550 thousand from net income of $16,848 thousand in the year-earlier quarter. Revenues were $190,366 thousand, down 0.1% from $190,621 thousand the year before. Net investment income rose 13.9% to $9,926 thousand from $8,714 thousand a year ago.

Prospects: Results are being positively affected by solid underwriting results from the manufactured housing sector, as well as strong underwriting results in several specialty lines such as motorcycle, mortgage fire and watercraft. Meanwhile, Co. is focused on improving its policyholder retention and increasing its policies in force. Looking ahead, Co. is projecting full-year 2005 revenue growth in the low single digit range, along with net income, excluding capital gains and losses, in the range of $2.75 to $3.00 per share. In addition, Co. anticipates a property and casualty combined ratio of between 94.5% and 96.0% for 2005, assuming normal weather conditions.

Financial Data

(US$ in Thousands)	3 Mos	12/31/2004	12/31/2003	12/31/2002	12/31/2001	12/31/2000	12/31/1999	12/31/1998
Earnings Per Share	3.03	2.83	1.30	1.06	1.51	1.89	1.65	1.43
Cash Flow Per Share	4.19	4.76	4.42	2.46	2.79	4.01	3.99	3.34
Tang Book Value Per Share	23.31	22.98	20.18	17.59	16.53	15.73	13.56	13.30
Dividends Per Share	0.210	0.205	0.190	0.175	0.160	0.150	0.135	0.125
Dividend Payout %	6.93	7.24	14.62	16.51	10.56	7.94	8.18	8.74
Income Statement								
Premium Income	168,833	691,364	652,128	584,342	515,408	464,904	407,784	377,986
Total Revenue	190,366	783,841	718,187	636,690	586,543	534,422	469,126	442,362
Benefits & Claims	62,939	348,611	392,232	341,015	292,188	240,680	204,365	210,015
Income Before Taxes	31,380	77,104	30,232	25,741	36,704	50,669	43,713	37,527
Income Taxes	9,830	22,866	6,956	5,437	9,482	15,206	12,534	10,595
Net Income	21,550	54,238	23,276	18,841	27,222	35,463	31,179	26,932
Average Shares	19,508	19,190	17,937	17,789	17,990	18,758	18,926	18,824
Balance Sheet								
Total Assets	1,333,197	1,364,684	1,179,505	1,090,674	1,053,942	993,850	888,057	837,220
Total Liabilities	893,521	932,408	823,447	781,766	762,066	710,673	630,055	588,388
Stockholders' Equity	439,676	432,276	356,058	308,908	291,876	283,177	258,002	248,832
Shares Outstanding	18,862	18,807	17,643	17,566	17,660	18,000	19,032	18,704
Statistical Record								
Return on Assets %	4.63	4.25	2.05	1.76	2.66	3.76	3.61	3.37
Return on Equity %	14.12	13.72	7.00	6.27	9.47	13.07	12.30	12.08
Loss Ratio %	37.28	50.42	60.15	58.36	56.69	51.77	50.12	55.56
Net Margin %	11.32	6.92	3.24	2.96	4.64	6.64	6.65	6.09
Price Range	34.26-24.95	32.74-23.04	24.29-16.32	25.23-16.44	23.60-13.25	15.69-9.25	14.38-9.63	15.83-9.71
P/E Ratio	11.31-8.23	11.57-8.14	18.68-12.55	23.81-15.51	15.63-8.77	8.30-4.89	8.71-5.83	11.07-6.79
Average Yield %	0.73	0.76	0.91	0.84	0.86	1.21	1.12	0.98

Address: 7000 Midland Blvd., Amelia, OH 45102-2607
Telephone: 513-943-7100
Web Site: www.midlandcompany.com

Officers: John P. Hayden III - Chmn., C.O.O. John W. Hayden - Pres., C.E.O. **Transfer Agents:** National City Bank

Investor Contact: 513-943-7100
No of Institutions: 66
Shares: 7,404,085 **% Held:** 39.26

MINE SAFETY APPLIANCES CO

Exchange	Symbol	Price	52Wk Range	Yield	P/E
NYS	MSA	$45.81 (5/31/2005)	51.57-29.42	1.22	22.79

*7 Year Price Score 228.30 *NYSE Composite Index=100 *12 Month Price Score 91.05

TRADING VOLUME (thousand shares)

Interim Earnings (Per Share)

Qtr.	Mar	Jun	Sep	Dec
2002	0.22	0.26	0.16	0.32
2003	0.33	0.36	0.66	0.40
2004	0.43	0.48	0.50	0.46
2005	0.57	...	...	...

Interim Dividends (Per Share)

Amt	Decl	Ex	Rec	Pay
0.10Q	7/28/2004	8/18/2004	8/20/2004	9/10/2004
0.10Q	10/26/2004	11/17/2004	11/19/2004	12/10/2004
0.10Q	1/18/2005	2/16/2005	2/18/2005	3/10/2005
0.14Q	5/10/2005	5/18/2005	5/20/2005	6/10/2005

Indicated Div: $0.56

Valuation Analysis

Forecast P/E	19.36 (5/28/2005)		
Market Cap	$1.7 Billion	Book Value	340.8 Million
Price/Book	4.89	Price/Sales	1.87

Dividend Achiever Status

Rank	117	10 Year Growth Rate	13.48%
Total Years of Dividend Growth			34

Business Summary: Apparel (MIC: 4.4 SIC: 326 NAIC: 23840)

Mine Safety Appliances develops, manufactures and supplies sophisticated products that protect people's health and safety. Safety products integrate any combination of electronics, mechanical systems and advanced materials to protect users against hazardous or life threatening situations. Co.'s safety products are used by workers around the world in the fire service, homeland security, construction and other industries, as well as the military. This product offering includes self-contained breathing apparatus, gas masks, gas detection instruments, head protection, respirators and thermal imaging devices. Also, Co. provides consumer and contractor safety products through retail channels.

Recent Developments: For the quarter ended Mar 31 2005, net income increased 32.3% to $21,353 thousand from net income of $16,138 thousand in the year-earlier quarter. Revenues were $229,380 thousand, up 17.5% from $195,276 thousand the year before. Total direct expense was $134,680 thousand versus $112,687 thousand in the prior-year quarter, an increase of 19.5%. Total indirect expense was $59,853 thousand versus $56,076 thousand in the prior-year quarter, an increase of 6.7%.

Prospects: Co. is encouraged to see substantial growth in all of its segments. North American segment sales benefited primarily from strong shipments of Advanced Combat Helmets to the U.S. military. In the U.S., Co. is working to further strengthen its position in the military and homeland security markets. In addition, Co. is focused on growing its European and International businesses through global new product development, selected acquisitions, and major sales and marketing efforts in promising new geographical markets, particularly in Eastern Europe and Asia.

Financial Data

(US$ in Thousands)	3 Mos	12/31/2004	12/31/2003	12/31/2002	12/31/2001	12/31/2000	12/31/1999	12/31/1998
Earnings Per Share	2.01	1.86	1.75	0.95	0.87	0.63	0.39	0.46
Cash Flow Per Share	1.67	1.45	1.10	1.35	0.86	1.41	1.01	0.54
Tang Book Value Per Share	7.92	8.69	7.03	6.62	5.96	6.28	6.18	6.07
Dividends Per Share	0.400	0.370	1.717	0.217	0.180	0.158	0.151	0.148
Dividend Payout %	19.90	19.89	98.10	22.81	20.69	25.18	39.08	32.44
Income Statement								
Total Revenue	229,380	857,513	698,197	566,697	545,666	502,833	498,051	497,207
EBITDA	40,115	139,364	96,967	69,608	79,357	58,607	46,810	50,606
Depn & Amortn	6,486	25,496	23,208	21,525	26,471	24,557	23,625	22,398
Income Before Taxes	33,629	113,868	73,759	48,083	52,886	34,050	23,185	28,208
Income Taxes	12,276	42,821	24,835	16,870	21,255	10,811	6,859	9,933
Net Income	21,353	71,047	65,267	35,077	31,631	23,239	15,134	18,275
Average Shares	37,382	38,130	37,264	36,885	36,237	37,068	39,015	40,023
Balance Sheet								
Current Assets	384,083	397,660	323,242	282,944	217,686	201,153	203,090	229,209
Total Assets	716,687	734,110	643,885	579,765	520,698	489,683	451,741	456,716
Current Liabilities	151,808	127,067	114,715	99,700	82,500	86,978	80,005	110,006
Long-Term Obligations	54,283	54,463	59,915	64,350	67,381	71,806	36,550	11,919
Total Liabilities	375,891	356,499	336,027	290,703	267,194	263,218	209,284	213,870
Stockholders' Equity	340,796	377,611	307,858	289,062	253,504	226,465	242,457	242,846
Shares Outstanding	36,411	37,341	36,927	36,621	36,302	35,482	38,625	39,411
Statistical Record								
Return on Assets %	11.05	10.28	10.67	6.37	6.26	4.92	3.33	4.23
Return on Equity %	23.02	20.67	21.87	12.93	13.18	9.88	6.24	7.55
EBITDA Margin %	17.49	16.25	13.89	12.28	14.54	11.66	9.40	10.18
Net Margin %	9.31	8.29	9.35	6.19	5.80	4.62	3.04	3.68
Asset Turnover	1.29	1.24	1.14	1.03	1.08	1.07	1.10	1.15
Current Ratio	2.53	3.13	2.82	2.84	2.64	2.31	2.54	2.08
Debt to Equity	0.16	0.14	0.19	0.22	0.27	0.32	0.15	0.05
Price Range	51.57-25.56	51.57-23.42	28.21-10.23	16.83-9.17	16.98-7.58	8.67-6.33	8.06-5.89	9.52-6.44
P/E Ratio	25.66-12.72	27.73-12.59	16.12-5.85	17.72-9.65	19.52-8.72	13.76-10.05	20.66-15.10	20.70-14.01
Average Yield %	1.01	1.06	10.91	1.70	1.69	2.13	2.14	1.90

Address: 121 Gamma Drive, RIDC Industrial Park, O'Hara Township, Pittsburgh, PA 15238 **Telephone:** 412-967-3000 **Web Site:** www.msanet.com	**Officers:** John T. Ryan III - Chmn., C.E.O. D. L. Zeitler - V.P., Treas., C.F.O. **Transfer Agents:** Wells Fargo Shareowner Services, South St.Paul, MN	**No of Institutions:** 130 **Shares:** 16,351,942 **% Held:** 44.97

MYERS INDUSTRIES INC.

Exchange	Symbol	Price	52Wk Range	Yield	P/E
NYS	MYE	$11.15 (5/31/2005)	14.61-9.36	1.79	15.70

***7 Year Price Score 99.90** *NYSE Composite Index=100 ***12 Month Price Score 91.30**

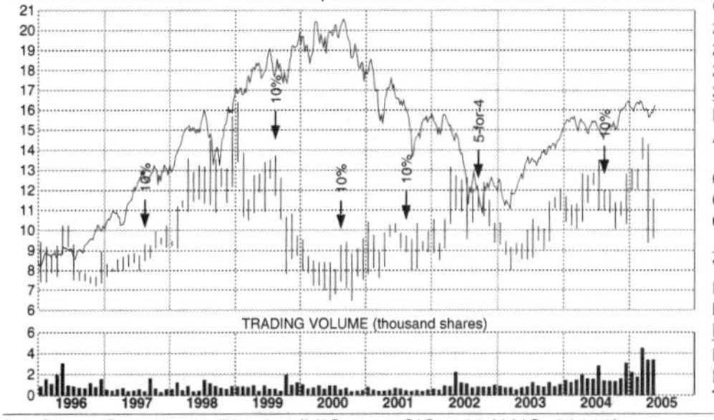

Interim Earnings (Per Share)

Qtr.	Mar	Jun	Sep	Dec
2002	0.31	0.20	0.09	0.12
2003	0.22	0.10	0.05	0.13
2004	0.26	0.18	0.11	0.20
2005	0.22	...	...	...

Interim Dividends (Per Share)

Amt	Decl	Ex	Rec	Pay
10%	6/28/2004	8/11/2004	8/13/2004	8/31/2004
0.05Q	9/21/2004	12/8/2004	12/10/2004	1/3/2005
0.05Q	2/17/2005	3/2/2005	3/4/2005	4/1/2005
0.05Q	4/20/2005	6/8/2005	6/10/2005	7/1/2005

Indicated Div: $0.20 (Div. Reinv. Plan)

Valuation Analysis

Forecast P/E	14.81 (6/1/2005)		
Market Cap	$386.7 Million	Book Value	343.5 Million
Price/Book	1.13	Price/Sales	0.45

Dividend Achiever Status

Rank	159	**10 Year Growth Rate**	10.80%
Total Years of Dividend Growth			28

TRADING VOLUME (thousand shares)

Business Summary: Plastics (MIC: 11.7 SIC: 089 NAIC: 26199)

Myers Industries is an international manufacturer of polymer products for industrial, agricultural, automotive, commercial, and consumer markets. Principal products include plastic horticultural pots, trays, and flower planters. Other principal product lines include plastic storage and organization containers, plastic storage tanks, plastic and rubber OEM parts, rubber tire repair products, and custom plastic and rubber products. Co. is also a wholesale distributor of tools, equipment, and supplies for the tire, wheel, and undervehicle service industry. Co.'s distribution products range from tire balancers and alignment systems to valve caps and other consumable service supplies.

Recent Developments: For the quarter ended Mar 31 2005, net income decreased 12.3% to $7,769,314 from net income of $8,856,171 in the year-earlier quarter. Revenues were $236,225,160 , up 27.3% from $185,518,527 the year before. Total direct expense was $172,398,322 versus $124,460,575 in the prior-year quarter, an increase of 38.5%. Total indirect expense was $47,894,958 versus $43,906,135 in the prior-year quarter, an increase of 9.1%.

Prospects: Co.'s outlook is mixed. On the positive side, Co. is experiencing increased demand for its products, as evidenced by the solid top line gains across its business segments for the quarter ended Mar 31 2005. However, Co. noted that its modest success with product price increases and internal cost reduction could not offset higher costs for plastic raw materials, which resulted in lower earnings. According to Co., resin costs were up more than 50.0% on average compared with last year. In response, Co. continues to implement price increases throughout its product lines and is committed to further strengthening cost management and efficiency initiatives to help offset higher raw material prices.

Financial Data

(US$ in Thousands)	3 Mos	12/31/2004	12/31/2003	12/31/2002	12/31/2001	12/31/2000	12/31/1999	12/31/1998
Earnings Per Share	0.71	0.76	0.49	0.73	0.47	0.73	0.93	0.86
Cash Flow Per Share	1.33	1.37	1.54	1.99	2.35	2.05	1.71	1.26
Tang Book Value Per Share	1.81	1.73	2.05	1.48	0.82	0.51	0.25	4.86
Dividends Per Share	0.195	0.191	0.182	0.178	0.167	0.151	0.138	0.120
Dividend Payout %	27.46	25.12	37.04	24.50	35.80	20.64	14.78	14.01
Income Statement								
Total Revenue	236,225	803,070	661,092	607,991	607,950	652,660	580,761	392,020
EBITDA	25,653	91,226	71,276	87,884	89,844	106,097	76,748	66,891
Depn & Amortn	9,721	39,175	36,555	35,714	43,905	42,828	7,241	17,518
Income Before Taxes	12,096	38,729	24,647	40,361	27,240	40,910	54,301	48,485
Income Taxes	4,327	13,019	8,321	16,401	12,049	16,909	23,125	19,806
Net Income	7,769	25,710	16,326	23,960	15,191	24,001	31,176	28,679
Average Shares	34,663	33,846	33,138	32,969	32,727	32,811	33,552	33,500
Balance Sheet								
Current Assets	298,368	284,072	207,933	201,140	196,619	219,307	206,991	153,650
Total Assets	787,898	785,603	621,627	602,482	582,166	624,797	600,410	306,708
Current Liabilities	139,267	136,252	94,175	117,369	104,899	115,583	102,244	51,234
Long-Term Obligations	276,170	275,252	211,003	212,223	247,145	284,273	280,104	48,832
Total Liabilities	444,400	439,599	327,102	346,793	364,640	410,894	392,663	104,019
Stockholders' Equity	343,498	346,004	294,524	255,690	217,526	213,903	207,747	202,689
Shares Outstanding	34,682	34,645	33,201	33,078	32,790	32,654	33,254	33,560
Statistical Record								
Return on Assets %	3.31	3.64	2.67	4.05	2.52	3.91	6.87	10.81
Return on Equity %	7.67	8.01	5.93	10.13	7.04	11.35	15.19	15.12
EBITDA Margin %	10.86	11.36	10.78	14.45	14.78	16.26	13.22	17.06
Net Margin %	3.29	3.20	2.47	3.94	2.50	3.68	5.37	7.32
Asset Turnover	1.15	1.14	1.08	1.03	1.01	1.06	1.28	1.48
Current Ratio	2.14	2.08	2.21	1.71	1.87	1.90	2.02	3.00
Debt to Equity	0.80	0.80	0.72	0.83	1.14	1.33	1.35	0.24
Price Range	14.61-10.07	13.50-10.06	12.05-8.00	13.16-8.51	10.41-7.60	9.59-6.45	16.39-7.81	15.68-9.08
P/E Ratio	20.58-14.18	17.76-13.24	24.60-16.33	18.03-11.66	22.16-16.18	13.13-8.83	17.63-8.40	18.23-10.56
Average Yield %	1.63	1.67	1.87	1.66	1.81	1.87	1.18	1.00

Address: 1293 South Main Street, Akron, OH 44301
Telephone: 330-253-5592
Web Site: www.myersind.com

Officers: Stephen E. Myers - Chmn. Milton I. Wiskind - Vice-Chmn., Sec. **Transfer Agents:** National City Bank, Cleveland, Ohio

Investor Contact: 330-253-5592
No of Institutions: 97
Shares: 16,550,943 **% Held:** 47.75

NACCO INDUSTRIES INC.

Exchange	Symbol	Price	52Wk Range	Yield	P/E
NYS	NC	$102.50 (5/31/2005)	114.67-78.15	1.81	14.62

*7 Year Price Score 122.46 *NYSE Composite Index=100 *12 Month Price Score 100.94

TRADING VOLUME (thousand shares)

Interim Earnings (Per Share)

Qtr.	Mar	Jun	Sep	Dec
2002	0.77	0.34	0.98	3.08
2003	0.50	1.17	1.43	3.34
2004	(0.55)	0.78	1.63	3.97
2005	0.63	...	...	...

Interim Dividends (Per Share)

Amt	Decl	Ex	Rec	Pay
0.453Q	8/11/2004	8/30/2004	9/1/2004	9/15/2004
0.453Q	11/10/2004	11/29/2004	12/1/2004	12/15/2004
0.453Q	2/9/2005	2/25/2005	3/1/2005	3/15/2005
0.465Q	5/11/2005	5/27/2005	6/1/2005	6/15/2005

Indicated Div: $1.86

Valuation Analysis

Forecast P/E N/A

Market Cap $843.0 Million Book Value 682.1 Million

Price/Book 1.24 Price/Sales 0.29

Dividend Achiever Status

Rank 183 **10 Year Growth Rate** 9.51%

Total Years of Dividend Growth 21

Business Summary: Industrial Machinery and Equipment (MIC: 11.5 SIC: 537 NAIC: 33924)

NACCO Industries is a holding company with three principal businesses. NACCO Materials Handling Group (NMHG) designs, engineers, manufactures, sells, services and leases a full line of lift trucks and replacement parts marketed worldwide under the Hyster™ and Yale™ brand names. NACCO Housewares Group consists of Hamilton Beach/Procter-Silex, Inc., a manufacturer and marketer of small household appliances and commercial products for restaurants, bars and hotels, and The Kitchen Collection, Inc., a national specialty retailer of brand-name kitchenware and electrical appliances. The North American Coal Corporation mines and markets lignite coal primarily as fuel for power generators.

Recent Developments: For the quarter ended Mar 31 2005, net income was $5,200 thousand versus net loss of $4,500 thousand in the year-earlier quarter. Revenues were $727,800 thousand, up 18.5% from $614,200 thousand the year before. Operating income was $12,200 thousand versus an income of $5,300 thousand in the prior-year quarter, an increase of 130.2%. Total direct expense was $617,200 thousand versus $509,800 thousand in the prior-year quarter, an increase of 21.1%. Total indirect expense was $106,800 thousand versus $107,600 thousand in the prior-year quarter, a decrease of 0.7%.

Prospects: Global lift truck markets continued to grow in the first quarter of 2005. However, despite the stronger lift truck markets, Co. expects 2005 to be challenging for its NACCO Materials Handling Group as it works to moderate the effect of increases in material costs, which are largely related to supplier price increases for steel. Meanwhile, Co.'s North American Coal unit anticipates that both the consolidated mines and the unconsolidated project mines will continue to perform well throughout the remainder of 2005. Nevertheless, results are expected to continue to be adversely affected temporarily by moderately increased costs related to certain adverse geological conditions.

Financial Data

(US$ in Thousands)	3 Mos	12/31/2004	12/31/2003	12/31/2002	12/31/2001	12/31/2000	12/31/1999	12/31/1998
Earnings Per Share	7.01	5.83	6.44	5.17	(4.40)	8.29	6.51	12.53
Cash Flow Per Share	9.66	15.33	15.03	18.20	16.61	16.24	15.84	17.71
Tang Book Value Per Share	20.37	21.01	14.67	5.73	1.98	9.44	11.51	9.52
Dividends Per Share	1.748	1.675	1.260	0.970	0.930	0.890	0.850	0.810
Dividend Payout %	24.93	28.73	19.57	18.76	...	10.74	13.06	6.46
Income Statement								
Total Revenue	727,800	2,782,600	2,472,600	2,285,000	2,637,900	2,871,300	2,602,800	2,536,200
EBITDA	32,000	162,600	184,400	182,800	128,000	213,100	233,600	289,300
Depn & Amortn	17,200	62,900	68,400	70,200	116,500	106,000	103,700	88,700
Income Before Taxes	3,200	52,300	65,000	59,700	(45,400)	60,000	86,600	166,000
Income Taxes	(1,900)	5,300	15,800	11,300	(9,900)	22,300	31,700	60,700
Net Income	5,200	47,900	52,800	42,400	(36,000)	67,700	53,100	102,300
Average Shares	8,219	8,214	8,204	8,198	8,190	8,167	8,154	8,166
Balance Sheet								
Current Assets	1,009,600	996,800	812,900	739,500	770,000	815,700	772,200	703,200
Total Assets	2,043,500	2,038,600	1,839,800	1,780,800	2,161,900	2,193,900	2,013,000	1,898,300
Current Liabilities	678,500	672,000	589,800	545,500	874,300	650,200	583,100	548,600
Long-Term Obligations	413,300	407,400	363,200	416,100	519,400	732,700	615,500	569,600
Total Liabilities	1,361,400	1,350,600	1,202,800	1,221,400	1,632,600	1,587,500	1,450,800	1,380,000
Stockholders' Equity	682,100	688,000	637,000	559,400	529,300	606,400	562,200	518,300
Shares Outstanding	8,224	8,214	8,206	8,201	8,195	8,171	9,804	8,120
Statistical Record								
Return on Assets %	2.97	2.46	2.92	2.15	N.M.	3.21	2.72	5.64
Return on Equity %	8.78	7.21	8.83	7.79	N.M.	11.55	9.83	21.69
EBITDA Margin %	4.40	5.84	7.46	8.00	4.85	7.42	8.97	11.41
Net Margin %	0.71	1.72	2.14	1.86	N.M.	2.36	2.04	4.03
Asset Turnover	1.49	1.43	1.37	1.16	1.21	1.36	1.33	1.40
Current Ratio	1.49	1.48	1.38	1.36	0.88	1.25	1.32	1.28
Debt to Equity	0.61	0.59	0.57	0.74	0.98	1.21	1.09	1.10
Price Range	114.67-78.15	111.70-77.15	93.77-37.99	75.25-36.65	81.47-42.63	55.56-33.75	96.25-45.13	172.50-78.94
P/E Ratio	16.36-11.15	19.16-13.23	14.56-5.90	14.56-7.09	...	6.70-4.07	14.78-6.93	13.77-6.30
Average Yield %	1.85	1.86	2.01	1.79	1.47	2.09	1.17	0.69

Address: 5875 Landerbrook Drive, Mayfield Heights, OH 44124-4017
Telephone: 440-449-9600
Web Site: www.naccoind.com

Officers: Alfred M. Rankin Jr. - Chmn., Pres., C.E.O. J. C. Butler Jr. - V.P., Corp. Devel., Treas. **Transfer Agents:** National City Bank, Cleveland, OH

Investor Contact: 440-449-9676
No of Institutions: 81
Shares: 4,059,093 **% Held:** 61.43

NATIONAL CITY CORP

Exchange	Symbol	Price	52Wk Range	Yield	P/E
NYS	NCC	$34.56 (5/31/2005)	39.44-32.51	4.05	8.88

***7 Year Price Score 105.65** *NYSE Composite Index=100 ***12 Month Price Score 90.65**

Interim Earnings (Per Share)

Qtr.	Mar	Jun	Sep	Dec
2002	0.73	0.63	0.61	0.62
2003	0.81	0.99	0.62	1.01
2004	1.16	0.83	0.86	1.46
2005	0.74	...	...	...

Interim Dividends (Per Share)

Amt	Decl	Ex	Rec	Pay
0.35Q	7/1/2004	7/8/2004	7/12/2004	8/1/2004
0.35Q	10/1/2004	10/6/2004	10/11/2004	11/1/2004
0.35Q	1/3/2005	1/11/2005	1/13/2005	2/1/2005
0.35Q	4/1/2005	4/7/2005	4/11/2005	5/1/2005

Indicated Div: $1.40 (Div. Reinv. Plan)

Valuation Analysis

Forecast P/E N/A

Market Cap	$22.0 Billion	Book Value	12.6 Billion
Price/Book	1.74	Price/Sales	2.07

Dividend Achiever Status

Rank	205	10 Year Growth Rate	8.55%
Total Years of Dividend Growth			12

Business Summary: Commercial Banking (MIC: 8.1 SIC: 021 NAIC: 22110)

National City is a financial holding company with total assets of $139.28 billion as of Dec 31 2004. Co. operates through a distribution network in Ohio, Indiana, Illinois, Kentucky, Michigan, Missouri, and Pennsylvania and also conducts selected consumer lending businesses and other financial services on a nationwide basis. Its primary businesses include commercial and retail banking, consumer finance, asset management, and mortgage financing and servicing. As of Dec 31 2004, operations were primarily conducted through more than 1,200 branch banking offices located within its seven-state footprint and over 490 retail and wholesale mortgage offices located throughout the United States.

Recent Developments: For the quarter ended Mar 31 2005, net income decreased 31.8% to $484,142 thousand from net income of $710,368 thousand in the year-earlier quarter. Net interest income was $1,170,879 thousand, up 14.9% from $1,018,627 thousand the year before. Provision for loan losses was $70,447 thousand versus $82,507 thousand in the prior-year quarter, a decrease of 14.6%. Non-interest income fell 29.4% to $789,281 thousand, while non-interest expense advanced 17.1% to $1,155,344 thousand.

Prospects: Co.'s prospects appear satisfactory, reflecting in part improving loan demand. For example, average portfolio loans for the quarter ended Mar 31 2005 were $101.14 billion, a 27.9% increase from last year and 2.2% higher than the preceding quarter. Co. attributed the improvement in the loan portfolio to growth in commercial, home equity and consumer loans from new business and acquisitions. Separately, on Jan 15 2005, Co. completed the acquisition of Charter One Vendor Finance for a cash payment of $310.0 million. Charter One Vendor Finance serves vendors, such as manufacturers, value-added resellers, and select specialized lessors, in middle- and large-ticket equipment and software markets.

Financial Data

(US$ in Thousands)	3 Mos	12/31/2004	12/31/2003	12/31/2002	12/31/2001	12/31/2000	12/31/1999	12/31/1998
Earnings Per Share	3.89	4.31	3.43	2.59	2.27	2.13	2.22	1.61
Cash Flow Per Share	5.01	7.78	20.92	(10.25)	(19.67)	1.94	3.19	(2.78)
Tang Book Value Per Share	11.56	14.36	13.47	11.70	12.15	11.06	9.39	10.69
Dividends Per Share	1.370	1.340	1.250	1.200	1.160	1.140	1.060	0.940
Dividend Payout %	35.22	31.09	36.44	46.33	51.10	53.52	47.75	58.39
Income Statement								
Interest Income	1,764,821	6,096,907	5,997,822	5,915,920	6,414,752	6,566,583	5,912,609	5,756,677
Interest Expense	593,942	1,593,335	1,629,816	1,910,541	2,975,903	3,608,221	2,912,587	2,845,029
Net Interest Income	1,170,879	4,503,572	4,368,006	4,005,379	3,438,849	2,958,362	3,000,022	2,911,648
Provision for Losses	70,447	323,272	638,418	681,918	605,295	286,795	249,674	201,400
Non-Interest Income	789,281	4,463,022	3,596,001	2,811,999	2,677,823	2,484,234	2,380,769	2,314,142
Non-Interest Expense	1,155,344	4,565,382	4,088,123	3,729,634	3,344,876	3,183,909	2,982,504	3,377,113
Income Before Taxes	734,369	4,077,940	3,237,466	2,405,826	2,166,501	1,971,892	2,148,613	1,647,277
Income Taxes	250,227	1,298,006	1,120,402	812,228	778,393	669,515	743,128	576,596
Net Income	484,142	2,779,934	2,117,064	1,593,598	1,388,108	1,302,377	1,405,485	1,070,681
Average Shares	652,487	645,510	616,410	616,174	611,936	612,625	632,452	665,720
Balance Sheet								
Net Loans & Leases	101,607,418	98,949,373	78,153,524	71,035,824	67,043,315	64,675,857	59,233,441	57,040,923
Total Assets	140,836,129	139,280,377	113,933,460	118,258,415	105,816,700	88,534,609	87,121,499	88,245,632
Total Deposits	80,689,736	85,954,607	63,930,030	65,118,768	63,129,932	55,256,422	50,066,310	58,246,909
Total Liabilities	128,192,640	126,476,848	104,604,789	109,950,403	98,435,477	81,764,788	81,393,766	81,232,724
Stockholders' Equity	12,643,489	12,803,529	9,328,671	8,308,012	7,381,223	6,769,821	5,727,733	7,012,908
Shares Outstanding	636,712	646,749	605,996	611,491	607,354	609,188	607,058	652,654
Statistical Record								
Return on Assets %	2.03	2.19	1.82	1.42	1.43	1.48	1.60	1.50
Return on Equity %	22.70	25.05	24.01	20.31	19.62	20.79	22.06	18.96
Net Interest Margin %	66.35	73.87	72.83	67.71	53.61	45.05	50.74	50.58
Efficiency Ratio %	45.23	43.23	42.61	42.73	36.79	35.18	35.96	41.84
Loans to Deposits	1.26	1.15	1.22	1.09	1.06	1.17	1.18	0.98
Price Range	39.44-33.00	39.44-32.36	34.58-26.75	33.69-24.68	32.51-24.50	29.38-16.00	37.81-22.13	38.75-28.75
P/E Ratio	10.14-8.48	9.15-7.51	10.08-7.80	13.01-9.53	14.32-10.79	13.79-7.51	17.03-9.97	24.07-17.86
Average Yield %	3.78	3.71	4.03	4.06	4.06	5.53	3.40	2.79

Address: 1900 East Ninth Street, Cleveland, OH 44114-3484
Telephone: 216-222-2000
Web Site: www.nationalcity.com

Officers: David A. Daberko - Chmn., C.E.O. Jeffrey D. Kelly - Vice-Chmn., C.F.O. **Transfer Agents:** National City Bank, Corporate Trust Operations, Cleveland, OH

Investor Contact: 800-622-4204
No of Institutions: 505
Shares: 316,090,784 **% Held:** 48.87

NATIONAL FUEL GAS CO.

Exchange	Symbol	Price	52Wk Range	Yield	P/E
NYS	NFG	$28.00 (5/31/2005)	29.40-24.31	4.00	14.66

***7 Year Price Score 99.90** *NYSE Composite Index=100 ***12 Month Price Score 98.15**

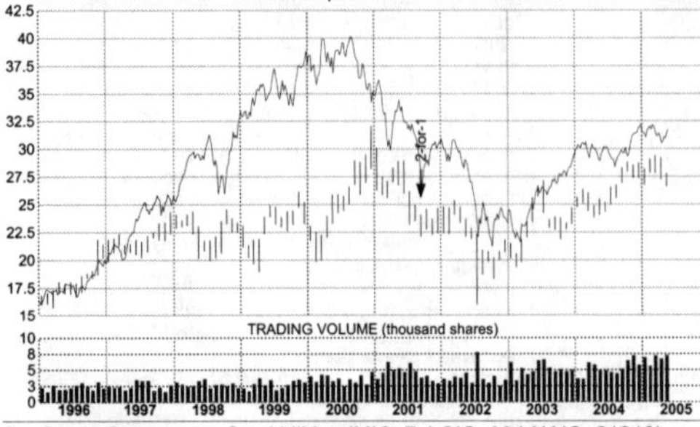

Interim Earnings (Per Share)

Qtr.	Dec	Mar	Jun	Sep
2001-02	0.41	0.77	0.22	0.06
2002-03	(0.57)	0.99	0.03	0.71
2003-04	0.60	0.93	0.39	0.09
2004-05	0.60	0.83	...	...

Interim Dividends (Per Share)

Amt	Decl	Ex	Rec	Pay
0.28Q	6/10/2004	6/28/2004	6/30/2004	7/15/2004
0.28Q	9/9/2004	9/28/2004	9/30/2004	10/15/2004
0.28Q	12/9/2004	12/29/2004	12/31/2004	1/15/2005
0.28Q	3/10/2005	3/29/2005	3/31/2005	4/15/2005

Indicated Div: $1.12 (Div. Reinv. Plan)

Valuation Analysis

Forecast P/E	15.03 (6/1/2005)		
Market Cap	$2.3 Billion	Book Value	1.3 Billion
Price/Book	1.76	Price/Sales	1.15

Dividend Achiever Status

Rank	292	**10 Year Growth Rate**	3.50%
Total Years of Dividend Growth			33

TRADING VOLUME (thousand shares)

Business Summary: Gas Utilities (MIC: 7.4 SIC: 924 NAIC: 21210)

National Fuel Gas is a diversified energy holding company. Through its subsidiaries, Co. operates in six business segments. The Utility segment operations are carried out by National Fuel Gas Distribution Corporation, which sells natural gas to approx. 732,000 customers in western New York and northwestern Pennsylvania. Other business segments include the Exploration and Production segment, the Energy Marketing segment, the International segment, the Pipeline and Storage segment, and the Timber segment. As of Sept 30, 2004, proved developed reserves for crude oil and natural gas were 42,944,000 barrels and 203,845,000,000 cubic ft., respectively.

Recent Developments: For the quarter ended Mar 31 2005, net income decreased 8.3% to $70,683 thousand from net income of $77,055 thousand in the year-earlier quarter. Revenues were $791,329 thousand, down 1.3% from $801,678 thousand the year before. Operating income was $138,282 thousand versus an income of $148,555 thousand in the prior-year quarter, a decrease of 6.9%. Total direct expense was $582,928 thousand versus $589,645 thousand in the prior-year quarter, a decrease of 1.1%. Total indirect expense was $70,119 thousand versus $63,478 thousand in the prior-year quarter, an increase of 10.5%.

Prospects: Earnings are being hurt by declining sales and increasing operating expenses in Co.'s Utility segment. However, rate increases in both its New York and Pennsylvania territories should have a positive impact on results in fiscal 2006. Meanwhile, Co's Exploration and Production segment's initial production volumes from the Sukunka region in Canada are encouraging. Following strong production from the third well in the region, Co. is looking forward to the results from a fourth well. Separately, Co. anticipates earnings for the third quarter of fiscal 2005 to be in the range of $0.22 to $0.30 per share. Looking ahead, Co. expects full-year 2005 earnings of between $1.75 and $1.85 per share.

Financial Data

(US$ in Thousands)	6 Mos	3 Mos	09/30/2004	09/30/2003	09/30/2002	09/30/2001	09/30/2000	09/30/1999
Earnings Per Share	1.91	2.00	2.01	2.20	1.46	0.82	1.61	1.48
Cash Flow Per Share	4.98	4.81	5.40	4.04	4.33	5.24	3.04	3.52
Tang Book Value Per Share	15.33	15.49	14.49	13.29	12.44	12.63	12.55	12.09
Dividends Per Share	1.120	1.110	1.100	1.060	1.025	0.985	0.945	0.915
Dividend Payout %	58.64	55.51	54.73	48.18	70.21	120.12	58.88	62.03
Income Statement								
Total Revenue	1,335,587	544,258	2,031,393	2,035,471	1,464,496	2,100,352	1,425,277	1,263,274
EBITDA	343,552	149,312	541,384	617,064	...	...	...	...
Depn & Amortn	96,285	46,940	189,538	195,226	180,668	174,914	142,170	129,690
Income Before Taxes	205,898	81,410	261,256	316,782	...	...	...	...
Income Taxes	81,436	30,035	92,737	128,161	...	...	...	...
Net Income	121,120	50,438	166,586	178,944	117,682	65,499	127,207	115,037
Average Shares	84,770	84,638	82,900	81,357	80,534	80,361	79,166	78,084
Balance Sheet								
Net PPE	3,059,803	3,038,048	3,006,764	2,999,087	2,844,745	2,780,713	2,683,391	2,353,894
Total Assets	4,026,179	3,885,612	3,711,798	3,727,915	3,401,309	3,445,566	3,236,888	2,842,586
Long-Term Obligations	1,126,401	1,130,290	1,133,317	1,147,779	1,145,341	1,046,694	953,622	822,743
Total Liabilities	2,695,777	2,545,727	2,458,097	2,590,525	2,394,451	2,442,911	2,249,451	1,903,293
Stockholders' Equity	1,330,402	1,339,885	1,253,701	1,137,390	1,006,858	1,002,655	987,437	939,293
Shares Outstanding	83,508	83,214	82,990	81,438	80,264	79,406	78,659	77,674
Statistical Record								
Return on Assets %	4.10	4.32	4.47	5.02	3.44	1.96	4.17	4.16
Return on Equity %	12.64	13.26	13.90	16.69	11.71	6.58	13.17	12.68
EBITDA Margin %	25.72	27.43	26.65	30.32	...	...	...	...
Net Margin %	9.07	9.27	8.20	8.79	8.04	3.12	8.93	9.11
PPE Turnover	0.67	0.67	0.67	0.70	0.52	0.77	0.56	0.55
Asset Turnover	0.52	0.53	0.54	0.57	0.43	0.63	0.47	0.46
Debt to Equity	0.85	0.84	0.90	1.01	1.14	1.04	0.97	0.88
Price Range	29.40-23.83	28.85-23.83	28.33-21.86	27.17-18.33	25.37-15.97	32.06-22.12	28.98-19.84	24.94-18.94
P/E Ratio	15.39-12.48	14.43-11.91	14.09-10.88	12.35-8.33	17.38-10.94	39.10-26.98	18.00-12.33	16.85-12.80
Average Yield %	4.17	4.24	4.41	4.73	4.54	3.68	3.92	4.01

Address: 6363 Main Street, Williamsville, NY 14221 **Telephone:** 716-857-7000 **Web Site:** www.nationalfuelgas.com	**Officers:** Philip C. Ackerman - Chmn., Pres., C.E.O. Ronald J. Tanski - Treas. **Transfer Agents:** The Bank of New York, New York, NY	**Investor Contact:** 716-857-6987 **No of Institutions:** 223 **Shares:** 37,019,200 **% Held:** 44.49

NATIONAL PENN BANCSHARES, INC. (BOYERTOWN, PENN.)

Exchange	Symbol	Price	52Wk Range	Yield	P/E
NMS	NPBC	$23.68 (5/31/2005)	29.63-21.92	3.38	15.48

***7 Year Price Score 117.41** *NYSE Composite Index=100 ***12 Month Price Score 91.48**

TRADING VOLUME (thousand shares)

Interim Earnings (Per Share)

Qtr.	Mar	Jun	Sep	Dec
2002	0.32	0.33	0.33	0.33
2003	0.34	0.35	0.36	0.37
2004	0.37	0.38	0.39	0.33
2005	0.40	...	...	...

Interim Dividends (Per Share)

Amt	Decl	Ex	Rec	Pay
5-for-4	8/25/2004	10/1/2004	9/10/2004	9/30/2004
0.20Q	10/28/2004	11/3/2004	11/6/2004	11/17/2004
0.20Q	1/26/2005	2/2/2005	2/5/2005	2/17/2005
0.20Q	4/27/2005	5/4/2005	5/7/2005	5/17/2005

Indicated Div: $0.80 (Div. Reinv. Plan)

Valuation Analysis

Forecast P/E	N/A		
Market Cap	$818.3 Million	Book Value	426.5 Million
Price/Book	1.92	Price/Sales	3.13

Dividend Achiever Status

Rank	143	**10 Year Growth Rate**	11.63%
Total Years of Dividend Growth			26

Business Summary: Commercial Banking (MIC: 8.1 SIC: 021 NAIC: 22110)

National Penn Bancshares, with total assets of $4.48 billion at Dec 31 2004, is a bank holding company. As of Dec 31 2004, Co. operated 73 community banking offices throughout nine counties in southeastern Pennsylvania and one office in Cecil County, MD, through National Penn Bank, providing commercial banking products, primarily loans and deposits. Trust and investment management services are provided through Investors Trust Company and FirstService Capital; mortgage banking activities are provided through National Penn Mortgage Company; commercial equipment leases are offered through National Penn Leasing Company; and insurance products are provided through National Penn Insurance Agency.

Recent Developments: For the quarter ended Mar 31 2005, net income increased 23.2% to $14,010 thousand from net income of $11,368 thousand in the year-earlier quarter. Net interest income was $36,986 thousand, up 17.7% from $31,425 thousand the year before. Provision for loan losses was $750 thousand versus $1,763 thousand in the prior-year quarter, a decrease of 57.5%. Non-interest income rose 29.7% to $13,959 thousand, while non-interest expense advanced 21.8% to $31,093 thousand.

Prospects: Co. is seeing strong earnings reflecting its increased asset size following the acquisition of Peoples First, Inc. Earnings are also benefiting from non-interest income growth as a result of higher insurance commissions and related fees and increases in service charges and other fees. Co.'s strategic focus in 2005 is to complete the integration of the operations of Krombolz Agency and other acquired insurance agencies with National Penn Insurance Agency to form a single unit. Separately, Co. is converting its Investors Trust Company subsidiary into a limited purpose national trust bank to provide a single entity to offer wealth management products and services under the National Penn brand.

Financial Data

(US$ in Thousands)	3 Mos	12/31/2004	12/31/2003	12/31/2002	12/31/2001	12/31/2000	12/31/1999	12/31/1998
Earnings Per Share	1.53	1.44	1.42	1.31	1.18	1.10	1.01	0.97
Cash Flow Per Share	2.06	2.08	2.65	2.22	1.70	1.25	1.91	0.35
Tang Book Value Per Share	6.39	6.45	6.81	8.18	7.13	6.69	5.87	6.33
Dividends Per Share	0.784	0.776	0.718	0.646	0.599	0.543	0.505	0.463
Dividend Payout %	51.17	53.89	50.40	49.28	50.94	49.45	49.76	47.63
Income Statement								
Interest Income	56,937	198,775	165,648	173,010	188,497	184,652	164,270	131,910
Interest Expense	19,951	60,493	51,099	63,446	92,512	99,702	82,753	67,002
Net Interest Income	36,986	138,282	114,549	109,564	95,985	84,950	81,517	64,908
Provision for Losses	750	4,800	9,371	14,000	9,000	5,600	5,960	5,100
Non-Interest Income	13,959	46,774	41,285	39,847	34,502	27,164	23,338	16,997
Non-Interest Expense	31,093	117,491	103,033	89,831	80,723	70,777	65,724	51,283
Income Before Taxes	19,102	62,765	43,430	45,580	40,764	35,737	33,171	25,522
Income Taxes	5,092	14,851	8,697	9,346	8,030	6,500	5,762	5,039
Net Income	14,010	47,914	43,354	36,234	32,734	29,237	27,409	20,483
Average Shares	35,323	33,351	30,513	27,628	27,869	26,667	26,939	21,119
Balance Sheet								
Net Loans & Leases	2,860,753	2,805,048	2,192,090	1,842,987	1,814,162	1,683,198	1,536,404	1,220,673
Total Assets	4,554,837	4,478,793	3,512,574	2,858,262	2,727,482	2,512,508	2,242,432	1,811,594
Total Deposits	2,969,549	3,143,193	2,435,296	2,112,640	2,076,795	1,814,253	1,593,254	1,208,061
Total Liabilities	4,128,344	4,050,668	3,194,761	2,635,902	2,531,800	2,335,080	2,094,736	1,681,138
Stockholders' Equity	426,493	428,125	317,813	222,360	195,682	177,428	147,696	130,456
Shares Outstanding	34,556	34,510	30,355	27,168	27,461	26,530	25,176	20,607
Statistical Record								
Return on Assets %	1.24	1.20	1.36	1.30	1.25	1.23	1.35	1.22
Return on Equity %	13.39	12.81	16.05	17.34	17.55	17.94	19.71	16.15
Net Interest Margin %	64.96	69.57	69.15	63.33	50.92	46.01	49.62	49.21
Efficiency Ratio %	43.86	47.85	49.79	42.20	36.20	33.41	35.03	34.44
Loans to Deposits	0.96	0.89	0.90	0.87	0.87	0.93	0.96	1.01
Price Range	29.63-21.92	29.63-21.92	27.36-17.71	20.81-15.96	17.61-13.30	16.86-12.41	17.95-13.58	21.41-12.98
P/E Ratio	19.37-14.33	20.58-15.22	19.27-12.47	15.88-12.19	14.93-11.27	15.32-11.28	17.77-13.44	22.07-13.38
Average Yield %	3.13	3.09	3.21	3.46	3.83	3.90	3.24	2.72

Address: Philadelphia and Reading Avenues, Boyertown, PA 19512
Telephone: 610-367-6001
Web Site: www.nationalpennbancshares.com

Officers: Wayne R. Weidner - Chmn., C.E.O. Glenn E. Moyer - Pres. **Transfer Agents:** Mellon Investor Services, L.L.C., Ridgefield Park, NJ

Investor Contact: 610-369-6291
No of Institutions: 57
Shares: 4,076,053 **% Held:** 11.76

NICOR INC.

Exchange	Symbol	Price	52Wk Range	Yield	P/E
NYS	GAS	$39.50 (5/31/2005)	39.65-32.68	4.71	17.56

*7 Year Price Score 87.77 *NYSE Composite Index=100 *12 Month Price Score 99.98

Interim Earnings (Per Share)

Qtr.	Mar	Jun	Sep	Dec
2002	0.90	0.46	0.68	0.95
2003	1.04	0.54	0.01	0.79
2004	0.44	0.44	(0.26)	1.08
2005	0.99	...	...	...

Interim Dividends (Per Share)

Amt	Decl	Ex	Rec	Pay
0.465Q	7/15/2004	9/28/2004	9/30/2004	11/1/2004
0.465Q	11/18/2004	12/29/2004	12/31/2004	2/1/2005
0.465Q	3/17/2005	3/29/2005	3/31/2005	5/1/2005
0.465Q	4/21/2005	6/28/2005	6/30/2005	8/1/2005

Indicated Div: $1.86 (Div. Reinv. Plan)

Valuation Analysis

Forecast P/E	18.32 (6/1/2005)		
Market Cap	$1.7 Billion	Book Value	776.4 Million
Price/Book	2.25	Price/Sales	0.62

Dividend Achiever Status

Rank	285	10 Year Growth Rate	4.05%
Total Years of Dividend Growth			17

Business Summary: Gas Utilities (MIC: 7.4 SIC: 924 NAIC: 21210)

NICOR is engaged in the purchase, storage, distribution, transportation, sale, and gathering of natural gas. Co.'s natural gas unit, Northern Illinois Gas, is the largest gas distribution company in Illinois and one of the biggest in the nation. As of Dec 31 2004, Northern Illinois served more than 2.1 million customers in the northern third of the state, generally outside of Chicago. Co. also owns Tropical Shipping Co., a transporter of containerized freight in the Bahamas and Caribbean. Co.'s shipments consist primarily of southbound cargo such as food, building materials and other necessities for developers, manufacturers and residents, as well as tourist-related shipments.

Recent Developments: For the quarter ended Mar 31 2005, net income increased 123.0% to $43,700 thousand from net income of $19,600 thousand in the year-earlier quarter. Revenues were $1,179,800 thousand, up 5.7% from $1,115,700 thousand the year before. Operating income was $69,800 thousand versus an income of $34,300 thousand in the prior-year quarter, an increase of 103.5%. Total direct expense was $905,600 thousand versus $856,100 thousand in the prior-year quarter, an increase of 5.8%. Total indirect expense was $204,400 thousand versus $225,300 thousand in the prior-year quarter, a decrease of 9.3%.

Prospects: Results are being positively affected by higher earnings from Co.'s shipping business in the Caribbean and Bahamas stemming from improved economic conditions throughout the regions and continued hurricane restoration activity. Meanwhile, lower profitability in Co.'s wholesale natural gas marketing business, reflecting higher operating and maintenance costs, is being partially offset by improved operating results from Co.'s energy-related products and services businesses. Looking ahead, Co. is projecting full-year 2005 diluted earnings per common share in the range of $1.90 to $2.10.

Financial Data

(US$ in Thousands)	3 Mos	12/31/2004	12/31/2003	12/31/2002	12/31/2001	12/31/2000	12/31/1999	12/31/1998
Earnings Per Share	2.25	1.70	2.38	2.88	3.17	1.00	2.62	2.42
Cash Flow Per Share	9.14	7.18	(0.29)	6.08	10.89	4.97	4.35	7.69
Tang Book Value Per Share	17.59	16.99	17.13	16.55	16.39	15.56	16.80	15.97
Dividends Per Share	1.860	1.860	1.860	1.840	1.760	1.660	1.560	1.480
Dividend Payout %	82.67	109.41	78.15	63.89	55.52	166.00	59.54	61.16
Income Statement								
Total Revenue	1,179,800	2,739,700	2,662,700	1,897,400	2,544,100	2,298,100	1,615,200	1,465,100
EBITDA	115,900	310,800	366,500	379,100	410,800	254,000	375,500	360,600
Depn & Amortn	43,000	166,600	161,700	155,000	148,800	144,300	140,300	136,500
Income Before Taxes	60,700	105,300	169,400	185,600	217,100	61,100	190,100	177,500
Income Taxes	17,000	30,200	59,600	57,600	73,400	14,400	65,700	61,100
Net Income	43,700	75,100	105,300	128,000	143,700	46,700	124,400	116,400
Average Shares	44,300	44,300	44,200	44,300	45,200	46,300	47,400	48,100
Balance Sheet								
Net PPE	2,557,400	2,549,800	2,484,200	1,796,800	1,768,600	1,729,600	1,735,200	1,731,800
Total Assets	3,833,000	3,975,200	3,797,200	2,899,400	2,574,800	2,885,400	2,451,800	2,364,600
Long-Term Obligations	495,400	495,300	495,100	396,200	446,400	347,100	436,100	557,300
Total Liabilities	3,056,600	3,226,100	3,042,600	2,171,000	1,847,200	2,177,600	1,664,100	1,605,600
Stockholders' Equity	776,400	749,100	754,600	728,400	727,600	707,800	787,700	759,000
Shares Outstanding	44,136	44,102	44,040	44,011	44,397	45,491	46,890	47,514
Statistical Record								
Return on Assets %	2.67	1.93	3.14	4.68	5.26	1.75	5.17	4.89
Return on Equity %	12.96	9.96	14.20	17.58	20.02	6.23	16.09	15.49
EBITDA Margin %	9.82	11.34	13.76	19.98	16.15	11.05	23.25	24.61
Net Margin %	3.70	2.74	3.95	6.75	5.65	2.03	7.70	7.94
PPE Turnover	1.11	1.09	1.24	1.06	1.45	1.32	0.93	0.85
Asset Turnover	0.75	0.70	0.80	0.69	0.93	0.86	0.67	0.62
Debt to Equity	0.64	0.66	0.66	0.54	0.61	0.49	0.55	0.73
Price Range	39.65-32.22	39.65-32.22	39.10-23.85	48.96-22.75	41.66-34.12	43.56-29.81	42.88-31.31	44.00-37.25
P/E Ratio	17.62-14.32	23.32-18.95	16.43-10.02	17.00-7.90	13.14-10.76	43.56-29.81	16.36-11.95	18.18-15.39
Average Yield %	5.20	5.28	5.58	4.89	4.58	4.75	4.16	3.64

Address: 1844 Ferry Road, Naperville, IL 60563-9600 **Telephone:** 630-305-9500 **Web Site:** www.nicor.com	**Officers:** Thomas L. Fisher - Chmn., C.E.O. Russ M. Strobel - Pres. **Transfer Agents:** ComputerShare Investor Services, Chicago, IL	**No of Institutions:** 197 **Shares:** 27,584,366 **% Held:** 62.53

NORDSON CORP.

Exchange	Symbol	Price	52Wk Range	Yield	P/E
NMS	NDSN	$31.06 (5/31/2005)	43.74-31.06	2.06	16.70

***7 Year Price Score 116.54** *NYSE Composite Index=100 ***12 Month Price Score 86.50**

TRADING VOLUME (thousand shares)

Interim Earnings (Per Share)

Qtr.	Jan	Apr	Jul	Oct
2001-02	0.17	0.23	0.21	0.05
2002-03	0.15	0.24	0.26	0.39
2003-04	0.27	0.46	0.47	0.53
2004-05	0.39	0.47	...	...

Interim Dividends (Per Share)

Amt	Decl	Ex	Rec	Pay
0.16Q	8/4/2004	8/25/2004	8/27/2004	9/15/2004
0.16Q	11/9/2004	12/13/2004	12/15/2004	1/4/2005
0.16Q	2/22/2005	3/4/2005	3/8/2005	3/22/2005
0.16Q	5/24/2005	6/3/2005	6/7/2005	6/21/2005

Indicated Div: $0.64 (Div. Reinv. Plan)

Valuation Analysis

Forecast P/E	14.86 (6/2/2005)		
Market Cap	$1.1 Billion	Book Value	425.7 Million
Price/Book	2.66	Price/Sales	1.39

Dividend Achiever Status

Rank	207	**10 Year Growth Rate**	8.36%
Total Years of Dividend Growth			24

Business Summary: Industrial Machinery and Equipment (MIC: 11.5 SIC: 569 NAIC: 33999)

Nordson is a producer of precision dispensing equipment that apply adhesives, sealants and coatings to a broad range of consumer and industrial products during manufacturing operations, helping customers meet quality, productivity and environmental targets. Co. also produces technology-based systems for curing and surface-treatment processes, as well as life sciences applications. Equipment ranges from manual, stand-alone units for low-volume operations to microprocessor-based automated systems for high-speed, high-volume production lines.

Recent Developments: For the second quarter ended May 1 2005, net income increased 4.8% to $17.5 million compared with $16.7 million in the corresponding year-earlier period. Net sales advanced 5.6% to $207.6 million from $196.6 million the previous year. Operating profit amounted to $28.2 million versus $28.1 million the year before. On a geographic basis, sales volume was up 11.0% in the United States and 3.0% in the Americas. Sales volume decreased 1.0% and 8.0% in Europe and Japan respectively, while volume was up 5.0% in the Asia Pacific Region. Backlog as of May 1 2005 was approximately $95.0 million, an increase of $16.0 million from the beginning of the fiscal year calculated at constant exchange rates.

Prospects: Co.'s outlook appears mixed. On one hand, Co.'s results may be further restrained by the effect of a softening business environment in both Europe and Japan, which had an influence on the performance of its Adhesive System businesses during the quarter ended Mar 31 2005. However, Co. noted that the Adhesive System businesses are posting solid results in the United States, and it is encouraged with the continued strong pace of order activity in the United States, especially within its Advanced Technology segment. Accordingly, Co. continues to expect sales volume growth for fiscal year 2005, exclusive of acquisitions, to be in the 4.0% to 5.0% range.

Financial Data

(US$ in Thousands)	3 Mos	10/31/2004	11/02/2003	11/03/2002	10/28/2001	10/29/2000	10/31/1999	11/01/1998
Earnings Per Share	1.85	1.73	1.04	0.66	0.74	1.67	1.42	0.63
Cash Flow Per Share	2.58	3.09	2.60	3.84	2.25	2.63	2.47	2.13
Tang Book Value Per Share	2.09	1.50	N.M.	N.M.	N.M.	4.73	2.45	3.90
Dividends Per Share	0.630	0.625	0.605	0.570	0.560	0.520	0.480	0.440
Dividend Payout %	34.00	36.13	58.17	86.36	75.68	31.14	33.80	70.40
Income Statement								
Total Revenue	190,166	793,544	667,347	647,756	731,416	740,568	700,465	660,900
EBITDA	30,966	136,136	99,780	84,144	108,166	125,398	110,982	73,577
Depn & Amortn	6,387	26,876	29,240	29,487	40,961	30,325	29,300	25,003
Income Before Taxes	21,283	93,828	52,477	32,944	37,716	83,408	71,438	38,927
Income Taxes	6,917	30,494	17,317	10,872	13,106	28,776	23,932	18,102
Net Income	14,366	63,334	35,160	22,072	24,610	54,632	47,506	20,825
Average Shares	37,200	36,546	33,899	33,690	33,050	32,767	33,048	33,322
Balance Sheet								
Current Assets	368,134	363,111	277,370	274,573	362,177	369,238	341,316	328,476
Total Assets	845,861	839,387	766,806	764,472	862,453	610,040	591,790	538,944
Current Liabilities	170,029	195,749	211,662	252,647	355,653	253,008	251,940	207,082
Long-Term Obligations	147,612	152,479	176,725	174,895	191,773	60,800	65,975	70,444
Total Liabilities	420,132	436,054	466,697	495,582	598,727	362,817	370,392	324,169
Stockholders' Equity	425,729	403,333	300,109	268,890	263,726	247,223	221,398	214,775
Shares Outstanding	36,449	36,278	34,035	33,613	33,137	32,449	49,012	33,480
Statistical Record								
Return on Assets %	8.43	7.91	4.60	2.67	3.35	9.12	8.43	4.01
Return on Equity %	17.80	18.06	12.39	8.15	9.66	23.38	21.84	9.59
EBITDA Margin %	16.28	17.16	14.95	12.99	14.79	16.93	15.84	11.13
Net Margin %	7.55	7.98	5.27	3.41	3.36	7.38	6.78	3.15
Asset Turnover	1.01	0.99	0.87	0.78	1.00	1.24	1.24	1.27
Current Ratio	2.17	1.85	1.31	1.09	1.02	1.46	1.35	1.59
Debt to Equity	0.35	0.38	0.59	0.65	0.73	0.25	0.30	0.33
Price Range	43.74-32.51	43.74-28.23	28.11-20.72	33.32-21.45	31.75-21.14	32.56-18.09	32.38-22.13	26.75-21.31
P/E Ratio	23.64-17.57	25.28-16.32	27.03-19.92	50.48-32.50	42.91-28.57	19.50-10.83	22.80-15.58	42.46-33.83
Average Yield %	1.69	1.72	2.42	2.17	2.10	2.10	1.77	1.83

Address: 28601 Clemens Road, Westlake, OH 44145-4551
Telephone: 440-892-1580
Web Site: www.nordson.com

Officers: Edward P. Campbell - Chmn., C.E.O. Peter S. Hellman - Pres., C.F.O., Chief Admin. Officer
ransfer Agents: National City Bank, Cleveland, OH

Investor Contact: 440-414-5344
No of Institutions: 143
Shares: 16,712,405 **% Held:** 45.85

NORTH FORK BANCORPORATION, INC.

Exchange	Symbol	Price	52Wk Range	Yield	P/E
NYS	NFB	$27.26 (5/31/2005)	30.54-24.59	3.23	13.98

Interim Earnings (Per Share)

Qtr.	Mar	Jun	Sep	Dec
2002	0.41	0.43	0.44	0.45
2003	0.45	0.41	0.42	0.45
2004	0.45	0.45	0.47	0.48
2005	0.55	...	...	...

Interim Dividends (Per Share)

Amt	Decl	Ex	Rec	Pay
0.22Q	9/28/2004	10/27/2004	10/29/2004	11/15/2004
3-for-2	9/28/2004	11/16/2004	10/29/2004	11/15/2004
0.22Q	12/14/2004	1/26/2005	1/28/2005	2/15/2005
0.22Q	3/22/2005	4/27/2005	4/29/2005	5/16/2005

Indicated Div: $0.88 (Div. Reinv. Plan)

Valuation Analysis

Forecast P/E	11.65 (6/1/2005)		
Market Cap	$13.0 Billion	Book Value	9.0 Billion
Price/Book	1.44	Price/Sales	5.44

Dividend Achiever Status

Rank	7	10 Year Growth Rate	30.89%
Total Years of Dividend Growth			10

Business Summary: Commercial Banking (MIC: 8.1 SIC: 022 NAIC: 22110)

North Fork Bancorporation is a bank holding company with assets of $60.76 billion as of Dec 31 2004. Co.'s principal bank subsidiary, North Fork Bank, operated 355 retail bank branches in New York, New Jersey and Connecticut. Co. also operates a nationwide mortgage business, GreenPoint Mortgage Funding Inc., headquartered in Novato, CA. Through non-bank subsidiaries, Co. offers financial products and services including asset management, securities brokerage, and the sale of alternative investment products. Co. also operates a second subsidiary bank, Superior Savings of New England, N.A., that is focused on telephonic and media-based generation of deposits principally in the Northeast U.S.

Recent Developments: For the quarter ended Mar 31 2005, net income increased 152.7% to $259,035 thousand from net income of $102,519 thousand in the year-earlier quarter. Net interest income was $47,131,9thousand, up 127.9% from $20,682,9thousand the year before. Provision for loan losses was $900,0thousand versus $650,0thousand in the prior-year quarter, an increase of 38.5%. Non-interest income rose 338.3% to $182,885 thousand, while non-interest expense advanced 182.1% to $246,653 thousand.

Prospects: Results are being positively affected by acquisitions completed during 2004 as well as sustained organic growth. On Feb 22 2005, Co completed its conversion of GreenPoint's operating systems to North Fork Bank systems and is beginning to realize cost savings. Co. expects that the $100.0 million of cost savings from the GreenPoint acquisition will be fully realized by the third quarter of 2005. Meanwhile, during the second quarter of 2005, Co. commenced a program to bulk sell non-performing mortgages, which is expected to result in fewer non-performing mortgage loans going forward.

Financial Data

(US$ in Thousands)	3 Mos	12/31/2004	12/31/2003	12/31/2002	12/31/2001	12/31/2000	12/31/1999	12/31/1998
Earnings Per Share	1.95	1.85	1.73	1.72	1.37	0.93	1.08	0.79
Cash Flow Per Share	0.81	(0.66)	1.72	2.17	1.77	1.04	0.80	1.18
Tang Book Value Per Share	5.65	5.49	4.61	4.58	4.13	3.59	2.80	3.53
Dividends Per Share	0.840	0.820	0.720	0.653	0.540	0.480	0.383	0.417
Dividend Payout %	43.15	44.32	41.54	37.98	39.51	51.80	35.49	52.97
Income Statement								
Interest Income	691,212	1,578,152	1,110,260	1,189,338	1,109,880	1,072,600	817,746	753,100
Interest Expense	219,893	402,931	294,746	347,560	423,361	480,608	368,440	328,456
Net Interest Income	471,319	1,175,221	815,514	841,778	686,519	591,992	449,306	424,644
Provision for Losses	9,000	27,189	26,250	25,000	17,750	17,000	6,000	15,500
Non-Interest Income	182,885	248,503	155,811	124,139	108,895	102,513	73,017	64,318
Non-Interest Expense	246,653	555,802	345,870	305,186	271,582	301,534	177,294	230,381
Income Before Taxes	398,551	840,733	599,205	635,731	506,082	375,971	339,029	243,081
Income Taxes	139,516	287,737	202,840	218,838	174,598	141,206	118,660	75,106
Net Income	259,035	552,996	396,365	416,893	331,484	234,765	220,369	167,975
Average Shares	473,314	299,219	228,774	242,473	242,072	252,795	203,797	212,647
Balance Sheet								
Net Loans & Leases	36,992,537	30,242,237	12,222,540	11,254,144	10,295,890	9,305,060	6,548,535	5,642,534
Total Assets	60,780,400	60,667,055	20,961,641	21,413,101	17,232,103	14,840,962	12,108,116	10,679,556
Total Deposits	36,537,733	34,812,428	15,116,115	13,192,530	11,303,306	9,169,195	6,544,750	6,427,622
Total Liabilities	51,772,209	51,785,976	19,483,152	19,899,048	15,550,731	13,382,705	11,290,092	9,649,017
Stockholders' Equity	9,008,191	8,881,079	1,478,489	1,514,053	1,437,008	1,213,918	618,710	831,250
Shares Outstanding	476,926	472,842	228,782	238,135	244,333	241,246	192,662	211,608
Statistical Record								
Return on Assets %	1.71	1.35	1.87	2.16	2.07	1.74	1.93	1.92
Return on Equity %	13.40	10.65	26.49	28.25	25.01	25.55	30.40	23.44
Net Interest Margin %	68.19	74.47	73.45	70.78	61.86	55.19	54.94	56.39
Efficiency Ratio %	28.22	30.43	27.32	23.23	22.28	25.66	19.90	28.18
Loans to Deposits	1.01	0.87	0.81	0.85	0.91	1.01	1.00	0.88
Price Range	30.54-23.57	30.54-23.57	27.21-19.13	28.21-21.15	22.32-15.33	16.63-9.67	15.96-11.42	18.22-10.88
P/E Ratio	15.66-12.09	16.51-12.74	15.73-11.06	16.40-12.30	16.29-11.19	17.88-10.39	14.78-10.57	23.07-13.77
Average Yield %	3.06	2.99	3.14	2.66	2.87	4.05	2.75	2.73

Address: 275 Broadhollow Road, Melville, NY 11747
Telephone: 631-844-1004
Web Site: www.northforkbank.com

Officers: John A. Kanas - Chmn., Pres., C.E.O. John Bohlsen - Vice-Chmn. **Transfer Agents:** EquiServe Trust Company, N.A.

Investor Contact: 631-501-4618
No of Institutions: 407
Shares: 271,929,472 **% Held:** 57.21

NORTHERN TRUST CORP.

Exchange	Symbol	Price	52Wk Range	Yield	P/E
NMS	NTRS	$46.03 (5/31/2005)	49.25-38.87	1.82	19.67

*7 Year Price Score 77.03 *NYSE Composite Index=100 *12 Month Price Score 100.38

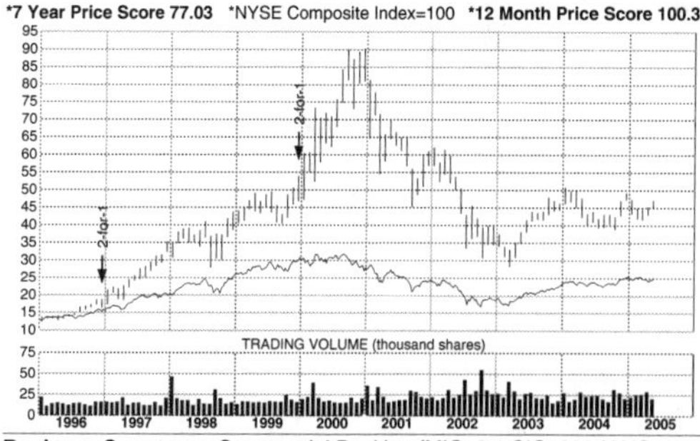

TRADING VOLUME (thousand shares)

Interim Earnings (Per Share)

Qtr.	Mar	Jun	Sep	Dec
2002	0.56	0.56	0.43	0.43
2003	0.42	0.30	0.51	0.57
2004	0.57	0.59	0.52	0.60
2005	0.63	...	...	...

Interim Dividends (Per Share)

Amt	Decl	Ex	Rec	Pay
0.19Q	7/19/2004	9/8/2004	9/10/2004	10/1/2004
0.21Q	11/16/2004	12/8/2004	12/10/2004	1/3/2005
0.21Q	2/15/2005	3/8/2005	3/10/2005	4/1/2005
0.21Q	4/19/2005	6/8/2005	6/10/2005	7/1/2005

Indicated Div: $0.84

Valuation Analysis

Forecast P/E	18.05 (6/2/2005)		
Market Cap	$10.1 Billion	Book Value	3.4 Billion
Price/Book	2.99	Price/Sales	3.42

Dividend Achiever Status

Rank	121	10 Year Growth Rate	13.20%
Total Years of Dividend Growth			19

Business Summary: Commercial Banking (MIC: 8.1 SIC: 022 NAIC: 22110)

Northern Trust is a multibank holding company. Co.'s principal subsidiary is The Northern Trust Company, an Illinois banking corporation. Co. also owns national bank subsidiaries in Arizona, California, Colorado, Florida and Texas; a federal savings bank with offices in ten states; trust companies in New York and Connecticut; and various other nonbank subsidiaries. Co. offers financial services including fiduciary, banking, investment and financial consulting services for individuals as well as credit operating, trust and investment management services for corporations. Total assets for Co. were $45.30 billion as of Dec 31 2004.

Recent Developments: For the quarter ended Mar 31 2005, net income increased 9.1% to $139,100 thousand from net income of $127,500 thousand in the year-earlier quarter. Net interest income was $157,400 thousand, an increase of 13.6% from $138,500 thousand the year before. Provision for loan losses was Nil versus $5,000 thousand in the prior-year quarter. Non-interest income rose 5.4% to $449,400 thousand, while non-interest expense advanced 3.2% to $515,800 thousand.

Prospects: On Mar 31 2005, Co. announced that it completed the acquisition of Baring Asset Management's Financial Services Group from ING Group N.V. Under the terms of the agreement, Co. paid approximately $500.0 million and acquired a fund services group with approximately $70.00 billion in funds under administration, $33.00 billion in custody and $33.00 billion in trust assets. The acquisition should enhance Co.'s ability to serve its existing global fund manager clients. Meanwhile, Co. is enjoying favorable revenue and earnings growth. This performance is being supported by positive fee income, strong net interest income growth, and effective cost management.

Financial Data

(US$ in Thousands)	3 Mos	12/31/2004	12/31/2003	12/31/2002	12/31/2001	12/31/2000	12/31/1999	12/31/1998
Earnings Per Share	2.34	2.27	1.80	1.97	2.11	2.08	1.74	1.52
Cash Flow Per Share	2.89	2.97	2.32	3.17	3.28	1.67	2.74	2.26
Tang Book Value Per Share	15.37	15.04	13.88	13.04	11.97	10.54	9.25	8.18
Dividends Per Share	0.800	0.780	0.700	0.680	0.635	0.560	0.495	0.435
Dividend Payout %	34.19	34.36	38.89	34.52	30.09	26.92	28.45	28.62
Income Statement								
Interest Income	343,500	1,118,200	1,055,700	1,238,300	1,681,500	2,011,100	1,568,600	1,503,100
Interest Expense	186,100	557,100	507,500	636,500	1,086,200	1,442,500	1,049,800	1,025,900
Net Interest Income	157,400	561,100	548,200	601,800	595,300	568,600	518,800	477,200
Provision for Losses	...	(15,000)	2,500	37,500	66,500	24,000	12,500	9,000
Non-Interest Income	449,400	1,710,900	1,542,200	1,536,800	1,580,000	1,537,000	1,235,200	1,071,600
Non-Interest Expense	395,000	1,532,500	1,456,800	1,432,100	1,376,900	1,351,500	1,125,000	997,100
Income Before Taxes	211,800	754,500	631,100	669,000	731,900	730,100	616,500	542,700
Income Taxes	72,700	249,700	207,800	221,900	244,400	245,000	211,500	188,800
Net Income	139,100	505,600	404,800	447,100	487,500	485,100	405,000	353,900
Average Shares	221,657	223,135	224,067	225,834	228,971	230,613	229,874	229,734
Balance Sheet								
Net Loans & Leases	18,937,700	17,812,000	17,664,600	17,902,600	17,818,300	17,981,700	15,223,600	13,500,100
Total Assets	47,761,300	45,276,700	41,450,200	39,478,200	39,664,500	36,022,300	28,708,200	27,870,000
Total Deposits	35,096,700	31,057,600	26,270,000	26,062,100	25,019,300	22,827,900	21,371,000	18,202,700
Total Liabilities	44,399,900	41,981,100	38,394,900	36,478,400	36,891,000	33,560,100	26,533,500	25,929,700
Stockholders' Equity	3,361,400	3,295,600	3,055,300	2,999,800	2,773,500	2,462,200	2,174,700	1,940,300
Shares Outstanding	218,635	219,067	220,118	220,800	221,647	222,232	222,161	222,430
Statistical Record								
Return on Assets %	1.18	1.16	1.00	1.13	1.29	1.49	1.43	1.33
Return on Equity %	15.96	15.88	13.37	15.49	18.62	20.87	19.68	19.24
Net Interest Margin %	45.82	50.18	51.93	48.60	35.40	28.27	33.07	31.75
Efficiency Ratio %	49.82	54.17	56.08	51.61	42.22	38.09	40.12	38.73
Loans to Deposits	0.54	0.57	0.67	0.69	0.71	0.79	0.71	0.74
Price Range	49.25-38.87	50.76-38.87	48.02-28.27	62.02-30.74	81.30-45.25	90.19-47.19	53.83-40.44	43.81-27.88
P/E Ratio	21.05-16.61	22.36-17.12	26.68-15.71	31.48-15.60	38.53-21.45	43.36-22.69	30.94-23.24	28.82-18.34
Average Yield %	1.85	1.76	1.77	1.47	1.02	0.78	1.09	1.19

Address: 50 South La Salle Street, Chicago, IL 60675
Telephone: 312-630-6000
Web Site: www.northerntrust.com

Officers: William A. Osborn - Chmn., C.E.O., Pres. Perry R. Pero - Vice-Chmn., Corp. Risk Management
ransfer Agents: Wells Fargo Shareowners Services, St. Paul, MN

Investor Contact: 312-444-7811
No of Institutions: 368
Shares: 143,983,552 **% Held:** 65.84

NUCOR CORP.

Exchange	Symbol	Price	52Wk Range	Yield	P/E
NYS	NUE	$52.96 (5/31/2005)	63.83-31.90	1.13	6.23

*7 Year Price Score 155.25 *NYSE Composite Index=100 *12 Month Price Score 105.03

Interim Earnings (Per Share)

Qtr.	Mar	Jun	Sep	Dec
2002	0.13	0.38	0.25	0.28
2003	0.12	0.06	0.10	0.13
2004	0.71	1.59	2.59	2.12
2005	2.20	...	...	...

Interim Dividends (Per Share)

Amt	Decl	Ex	Rec	Pay
0.13Q	9/9/2004	9/28/2004	9/30/2004	11/11/2004
0.13Q	12/7/2004	12/29/2004	12/31/2004	2/11/2005
0.15Q	2/24/2005	3/29/2005	3/31/2005	5/11/2005
0.25Q	2/24/2005	3/29/2005	3/31/2005	5/11/2005

Indicated Div: $0.60 (Div. Reinv. Plan)

Valuation Analysis

Forecast P/E	6.75 (5/28/2005)		
Market Cap	$8.5 Billion	Book Value	3.8 Billion
Price/Book	2.24	Price/Sales	0.68

Dividend Achiever Status

Rank	59	10 Year Growth Rate	17.53%
Total Years of Dividend Growth			32

Business Summary: Metal Works (MIC: 11.3 SIC: 312 NAIC: 31111)

Nucor is engaged in the manufacture and sale of steel and steel products. Co.'s principal products from the steel mills segment are hot- and cold-rolled steel, while the steel products segment produces steel joists and joist girders, steel deck, cold finished steel, steel fasteners, metal building systems and light gauge steel framing. Steel joists and hoist girders, and steel deck are sold to general contractors and fabricators domestically. Cold finished steel and steel fasteners are sold primarily to distributors and manufacturers, and hot-rolled steel and cold-rolled steel are sold primarily to steel services centers, fabricators and manufacturers in the U.S.

Recent Developments: For the quarter ended Apr 2 2005, net income increased 213.2% to $354,666,000 from net income of $113,238,000 in the year-earlier quarter. Revenues were $3,322,621,000 , up 45.3% from $2,286,416,000 the year before. Total direct expense was $2,620,628,000 versus $2,016,369,000 in the prior-year quarter, an increase of 30.0%. Total indirect expense was $125,429,000 versus $77,399,000 in the prior-year quarter, an increase of 62.1%.

Prospects: Co.'s near-term prospects appear favorable, supported by an increase in average sales price per ton. However, sales growth is being partially offset by lower total steel shipments and total tons shipped to outside customers that remained flat from the prior year. Meanwhile, Co. expects diluted earnings for the second quarter of 2005 to range from $1.95 to $2.15 per share. Separately, Co. announced that it entered into an agreement to purchase substantially all of the assets of Marion Steel Company for a cash purchase price of approximately $113.0 million. The transaction should be complete by mid-June of 2005, and is expected to be immediately accretive to earnings.

Financial Data

(US$ in Thousands)	3 Mos	12/31/2004	12/31/2003	12/31/2002	12/31/2001	12/31/2000	12/31/1999	12/31/1998
Earnings Per Share	8.50	7.02	0.40	1.03	0.72	1.90	1.40	1.50
Cash Flow Per Share	8.88	6.48	3.16	3.18	3.19	5.01	3.47	3.65
Tang Book Value Per Share	23.63	21.67	14.90	14.86	14.16	13.73	12.96	11.86
Dividends Per Share	0.765	0.470	0.400	0.380	0.340	0.300	0.260	0.240
Dividend Payout %	9.00	6.70	100.00	36.71	46.90	15.79	18.57	16.00
Income Statement								
Total Revenue	3,322,621	11,376,828	6,265,823	4,801,777	4,139,249	4,586,146	4,009,346	4,151,232
EBITDA	641,756	2,136,933	455,616	551,440	469,449	736,857	630,731	664,595
Depn & Amortn	91,290	383,305	364,112	307,101	289,063	259,365	256,637	253,119
Income Before Taxes	550,466	1,731,276	66,877	230,053	173,861	478,308	379,189	415,309
Income Taxes	195,800	609,791	4,096	67,973	60,900	167,400	134,600	151,600
Net Income	354,666	1,121,485	62,781	162,080	112,961	310,908	244,589	263,709
Average Shares	161,246	159,754	156,833	156,499	155,566	163,554	174,574	175,756
Balance Sheet								
Current Assets	3,611,341	3,174,948	1,620,560	1,424,139	1,373,666	1,381,447	1,538,509	1,129,467
Total Assets	6,613,134	6,133,207	4,492,353	4,381,001	3,759,348	3,721,788	3,729,848	3,226,546
Current Liabilities	1,203,615	1,065,790	629,595	591,536	484,159	558,068	531,031	486,897
Long-Term Obligations	923,550	923,550	903,550	878,550	460,450	460,450	390,450	215,450
Total Liabilities	2,827,519	2,677,222	2,150,275	2,058,012	1,557,888	1,590,836	1,467,600	1,153,994
Stockholders' Equity	3,785,615	3,455,985	2,342,078	2,322,989	2,201,460	2,130,952	2,262,248	2,072,552
Shares Outstanding	160,195	159,512	157,180	156,360	155,415	155,165	174,494	174,705
Statistical Record								
Return on Assets %	23.84	21.05	1.42	3.98	3.02	8.32	7.03	8.49
Return on Equity %	43.72	38.58	2.69	7.16	5.21	14.12	11.28	13.36
EBITDA Margin %	19.31	18.78	7.27	11.48	11.34	16.07	15.73	16.01
Net Margin %	10.67	9.86	1.00	3.38	2.73	6.78	6.10	6.35
Asset Turnover	2.17	2.14	1.41	1.18	1.11	1.23	1.15	1.34
Current Ratio	3.00	2.98	2.57	2.41	2.84	2.48	2.90	2.32
Debt to Equity	0.24	0.27	0.39	0.38	0.21	0.22	0.17	0.10
Price Range	63.83-28.63	55.08-26.67	28.95-17.99	34.58-18.95	28.00-17.25	27.97-15.00	30.31-20.88	30.03-17.97
P/E Ratio	7.51-3.37	7.85-3.80	72.38-44.97	33.57-18.40	38.89-23.96	14.72-7.89	21.65-14.91	20.02-11.98
Average Yield %	1.71	1.24	1.71	1.41	1.48	1.47	1.06	1.02

Address: 2100 Rexford Road, Charlotte, NC 28211	**Officers:** Peter C. Browning - Chmn. Daniel R. DiMicco - Vice-Chmn., Pres., C.E.O.	**Investor Contact:** 704-366-7000
Telephone: 704-366-7000	**Transfer Agents:** American Stock Transfer & Trust Company, New York, NY	**No of Institutions:** 349
Web Site: www.nucor.com		**Shares:** 141,438,624 **% Held:** 88.53

NUVEEN INVESTMENTS INC

Exchange	Symbol	Price	52Wk Range	Yield	P/E
NYS	JNC	$36.05 (5/31/2005)	42.21-24.76	2.00	21.46

*7 Year Price Score 135.23 *NYSE Composite Index=100 *12 Month Price Score 100.21

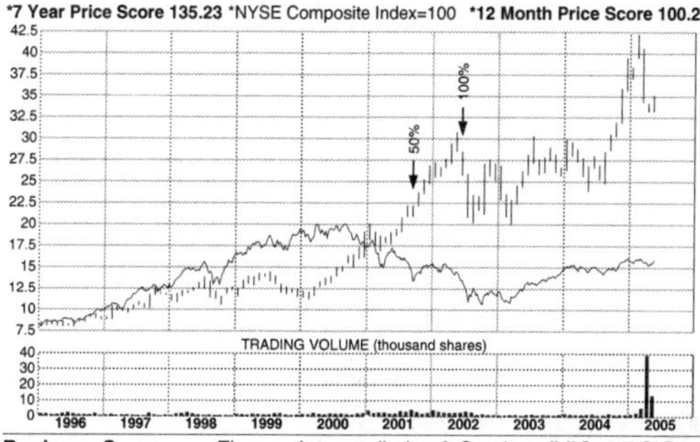

TRADING VOLUME (thousand shares)

Interim Earnings (Per Share)

Qtr.	Mar	Jun	Sep	Dec
2002	0.30	0.31	0.33	0.35
2003	0.34	0.36	0.39	0.42
2004	0.42	0.38	0.41	0.45
2005	0.44	...	...	...

Interim Dividends (Per Share)

Amt	Decl	Ex	Rec	Pay
0.18Q	8/5/2004	8/30/2004	9/1/2004	9/15/2004
0.18Q	11/12/2004	11/29/2004	12/1/2004	12/15/2004
0.18Q	2/14/2005	2/25/2005	3/1/2005	3/15/2005
0.18Q	5/17/2005	5/27/2005	6/1/2005	6/15/2005

Indicated Div: $0.72

Valuation Analysis

Forecast P/E	18.93 (6/2/2005)		
Market Cap	$3.4 Billion	Book Value	629.6 Million
Price/Book	5.39	Price/Sales	6.51

Dividend Achiever Status

Rank	132	10 Year Growth Rate	12.46%
Total Years of Dividend Growth			12

Business Summary: Finance Intermediaries & Services (MIC: 8.7 SIC: 211 NAIC: 23110)

Nuveen Investments is engaged in asset management and related research as well as the development, marketing and distribution of investment products and services for the affluent, high-net-worth and institutional market segments. Co. distributes its investment products and services, including closed-end exchange-traded funds, mutual funds and individually managed accounts, through unaffiliated intermediary firms including broker-dealers, commercial banks, affiliates of insurance providers, financial planners, accountants, consultants and investment advisors. Co. also provides managed account services to several institutional market segments and channels.

Recent Developments: For the three months ended Mar 31 2005, net income increased 14.0% to $43,193 thousand from net income of $37,877 thousand in the year-earlier quarter. Revenues were $134,868 thousand, up 12.7% from $119,694 thousand the year before. Investment advisory fees from assets under management grew 16.8% to $131,209 thousand versus $112,355 thousand last year, driven by an increase in fees across all product lines. Total operating expenses rose 13.6% to $65,845 thousand compared with $57,965 thousand the year before, reflecting higher compensation and benefits expenses.

Prospects: On Mar 25 2005, Co. and The St. Paul Travelers Companies, Inc. (STA) announced that STA is implementing a program to sell its equity interest in Co. Under the program, STA will sell 39.6 million Nuveen shares, through a public secondary offering. Also, Co. intends to repurchase $600.0 million of its shares from STA at the price of the secondary offering. Lastly, STA will enter into forward sale agreements with affiliates of Merrill Lynch and Morgan Stanley, with respect to its remaining equity interest in Co., or approximately 13.5 million shares. The objective is for STA to sell its entire interest in Co., resulting in Co. becoming a fully independent, publicly traded company.

Financial Data
(US$ in Thousands)

	3 Mos	12/31/2004	12/31/2003	12/31/2002	12/31/2001	12/31/2000	12/31/1999	12/31/1998
Earnings Per Share	1.68	1.63	1.50	1.29	1.13	1.05	0.95	0.81
Cash Flow Per Share	2.12	2.19	2.26	2.34	2.20	1.27	1.39	1.37
Tang Book Value Per Share	0.05	N.M.	N.M.	N.M.	0.01	2.07	1.58	1.07
Dividends Per Share	0.720	0.690	0.560	0.500	0.467	0.407	0.377	0.327
Dividend Payout %	42.86	42.33	37.33	38.76	41.30	38.85	39.65	40.33
Income Statement								
Total Revenue	134,868	505,637	452,028	396,447	371,103	358,393	338,760	307,535
Income Before Taxes	69,892	252,507	235,288	206,860	189,554	177,366	161,011	137,737
Income Taxes	26,699	96,099	91,292	80,675	74,856	70,700	63,701	54,092
Net Income	43,193	156,408	143,996	126,185	114,698	106,666	97,310	83,645
Average Shares	98,913	96,121	95,944	98,042	101,688	101,979	102,429	103,281
Balance Sheet								
Total Assets	1,088,429	1,071,593	954,393	841,042	696,611	576,039	540,965	467,961
Total Liabilities	456,991	483,513	486,212	452,216	284,721	128,138	149,903	118,853
Stockholders' Equity	629,605	585,478	463,953	385,763	406,265	402,901	346,062	304,108
Shares Outstanding	94,119	92,905	92,506	92,726	95,142	93,941	93,189	94,068
Statistical Record								
Return on Assets %	15.76	15.40	16.04	16.41	18.03	19.05	19.29	17.42
Return on Equity %	28.86	29.73	33.89	31.86	28.35	28.41	29.93	28.98
Price Range	42.21-23.89	39.47-23.89	30.30-19.99	30.79-20.18	26.86-16.83	19.17-11.19	14.46-11.50	13.83-10.52
P/E Ratio	25.13-14.22	24.21-14.66	20.20-13.33	23.86-15.64	23.77-14.90	18.25-10.65	15.22-12.11	17.08-12.99
Average Yield %	2.28	2.37	2.18	1.93	2.26	2.86	2.88	2.70

Address: 333 West Wacker Drive, Chicago, IL 60606
Telephone: 312-917-7700
Web Site: www.nuveen.com

Officers: Timothy R. Schwertfeger - Chmn., C.E.O. John P. Amboian - Pres. **Transfer Agents:** The Bank of New York, New York, NY

No of Institutions: 93
Shares: 88,244,904 **% Held:** N/A

OLD NATIONAL BANCORP

Exchange	Symbol	Price	52Wk Range	Yield	P/E
NYS	ONB	$19.83 (5/31/2005)	25.41-18.71	3.83	20.66

Interim Earnings (Per Share)

Qtr.	Mar	Jun	Sep	Dec
2002	0.40	0.40	0.49	0.38
2003	0.37	0.39	0.16	0.07
2004	0.28	0.16	0.26	0.27
2005	0.27	...	...	...

Interim Dividends (Per Share)

Amt	Decl	Ex	Rec	Pay
0.181Q	10/28/2004	11/29/2004	12/1/2004	12/15/2004
5%	12/9/2004	1/3/2005	1/5/2005	1/26/2005
0.19Q	1/27/2005	2/25/2005	3/1/2005	3/15/2005
0.19Q	4/21/2005	5/27/2005	6/1/2005	6/15/2005

Indicated Div: $0.76 (Div. Reinv. Plan)

Valuation Analysis

Forecast P/E	N/A		
Market Cap	$1.4 Billion	Book Value	670.6 Million
Price/Book	2.03	Price/Sales	2.33

Dividend Achiever Status

Rank	226	10 Year Growth Rate	7.28%
Total Years of Dividend Growth			21

Business Summary: Commercial Banking (MIC: 8.1 SIC: 021 NAIC: 22110)

Old National Bancorp, with total assets of $8.90 billion as of Dec 31 2004, is a financial holding company headquartered in Evansville, IN with banking activity in Indiana, Illinois, Kentucky, Tennessee, and Ohio. As of Dec 31 2004, Co. operated over 120 banking offices serving customers in both urban and rural markets. Co.'s banking centers provide a wide range of financial services, such as commercial, real estate, and consumer loans; lease financing; checking, savings, time deposits; and letters of credit. Co.'s non-bank affiliates provide additional financial or support services incidental to its operations, including issuance and reinsurance of credit life services.

Recent Developments: For the quarter ended Mar 31 2005, income from continuing operations increased 4.6% to $19,440 thousand from income of $18,590 thousand in the year-earlier quarter. Net income decreased 5.4% to $18,456 thousand from net income of $19,509 thousand in the year-earlier quarter. Net interest income was $58,638 thousand, down 9.9% from $65,099 thousand the year before. Provision for loan losses was $5,100 thousand versus $7,500 thousand in the prior-year quarter, a decrease of 32.0%. Non-interest income fell 4.7% to $35,726 thousand, while non-interest expense declined 10.5% to $66,077 thousand.

Prospects: On May 2 2005, Co. announced that it has acquired J.W.F. Insurance Companies, Inc., which does business as the J.W. Flynn Company, and J.W.F. Specialty Company, Inc. a related alternative risk services company. The acquisition will boost Co.'s insurance business annual revenue to approximately $43.0 million. Meanwhile, Co. is pleased with the internal progress it is making in sharpening its strategic focus. Although it is not yet fully reflected in its earnings, changes in deposit mix, reduction in expenses, and improvement in credit quality are the result of this progress. Looking ahead, Co. expects full-year 2005 earnings to range from $1.22 to $1.28 per share.

Financial Data

(US$ in Thousands)	3 Mos	12/31/2004	12/31/2003	12/31/2002	12/31/2001	12/31/2000	12/31/1999	12/31/1998
Earnings Per Share	0.96	0.97	1.00	1.67	1.29	0.85	1.38	1.04
Cash Flow Per Share	0.70	1.27	2.91	0.99	1.48	1.44	1.67	1.37
Tang Book Value Per Share	7.83	7.48	7.58	8.40	9.03	8.54	8.16	8.58
Dividends Per Share	0.733	0.724	0.689	0.622	0.559	0.533	0.495	0.436
Dividend Payout %	76.04	74.62	68.93	37.27	43.46	62.87	35.89	41.92
Income Statement								
Interest Income	102,768	417,198	469,748	547,383	629,707	638,275	488,923	437,909
Interest Expense	44,130	166,391	197,741	257,954	338,408	368,404	250,536	223,059
Net Interest Income	58,638	250,807	272,007	289,429	291,299	269,871	238,387	214,850
Provision for Losses	5,100	22,400	85,000	33,500	28,700	29,803	11,489	11,420
Non-Interest Income	35,726	182,163	192,149	154,497	112,967	101,713	67,508	54,557
Non-Interest Expense	66,077	329,692	285,040	257,845	254,812	265,537	185,564	158,125
Income Before Taxes	23,187	74,643	79,440	152,581	120,754	76,244	108,842	99,862
Income Taxes	3,747	7,072	9,027	34,649	27,710	14,548	26,148	28,144
Net Income	18,456	67,571	70,413	117,932	93,044	61,696	86,795	61,864
Average Shares	68,787	70,024	70,173	70,673	72,037	73,173	63,654	60,730
Balance Sheet								
Net Loans & Leases	4,854,032	4,879,093	5,465,546	5,681,893	6,058,613	6,274,480	4,780,888	4,112,804
Total Assets	8,793,047	8,898,304	9,353,896	9,612,556	9,080,473	8,767,748	6,982,932	6,165,968
Total Deposits	6,361,663	6,414,263	6,493,092	6,439,280	6,616,440	6,583,906	5,071,298	4,443,472
Total Liabilities	8,122,458	8,195,096	8,638,406	8,871,846	8,441,238	8,141,407	6,490,188	5,671,388
Stockholders' Equity	670,589	703,208	715,490	740,710	639,235	626,341	492,744	494,580
Shares Outstanding	68,717	69,287	69,903	70,401	70,816	73,308	60,354	57,662
Statistical Record								
Return on Assets %	0.74	0.74	0.74	1.26	1.04	0.78	1.32	1.04
Return on Equity %	9.43	9.50	9.67	17.09	14.70	11.00	17.58	12.73
Net Interest Margin %	57.06	60.12	57.90	52.88	46.26	42.28	48.76	49.06
Efficiency Ratio %	47.71	55.01	43.06	36.74	34.31	35.88	33.35	32.11
Loans to Deposits	0.76	0.76	0.84	0.88	0.92	0.95	0.94	0.93
Price Range	25.41-19.83	25.41-20.02	21.73-19.22	22.89-19.70	23.51-16.92	27.23-18.46	27.42-20.71	27.72-21.32
P/E Ratio	26.47-20.66	26.20-20.64	21.73-19.22	13.71-11.80	18.22-13.12	32.03-21.72	19.87-15.01	26.65-20.50
Average Yield %	3.20	3.19	3.35	2.93	2.71	2.34	2.12	1.87

Address: 1 Main Street, Evansville, IN 47708 **Telephone:** 812-464-1294 **Web Site:** www.oldnational.com	**Officers:** Larry E. Dunigan - Chmn. Robert G. Jones - Pres., C.E.O. **Transfer Agents:** Old National Bancorp, Evansville, IN	**Investor Contact:** 812-464-1366 **No of Institutions:** 90 **Shares:** 20,485,482 **% Held:** 29.65

OLD REPUBLIC INTERNATIONAL CORP.

Exchange	Symbol	Price	52Wk Range	Yield	P/E
NYS	ORI	$24.86 (5/31/2005)	25.79-22.31	2.74	10.32

Interim Earnings (Per Share)

Qtr.	Mar	Jun	Sep	Dec
2002	0.53	0.59	0.53	0.51
2003	0.57	0.67	0.65	0.62
2004	0.57	0.65	0.59	0.55
2005	0.62	...	...	...

Interim Dividends (Per Share)

Amt	Decl	Ex	Rec	Pay
0.13Q	5/14/2004	6/2/2004	6/4/2004	6/15/2004
0.13Q	8/12/2004	9/1/2004	9/3/2004	9/15/2004
0.13Q	12/2/2004	12/8/2004	12/10/2004	12/15/2004
0.17Q	5/12/2005	6/1/2005	6/3/2005	6/15/2005

Indicated Div: $0.68 (Div. Reinv. Plan)

Valuation Analysis

Forecast P/E	9.84 (6/1/2005)		
Market Cap	$4.5 Billion	Book Value	3.9 Billion
Price/Book	1.17	Price/Sales	1.28

Dividend Achiever Status

Rank	113	10 Year Growth Rate	13.70%
Total Years of Dividend Growth			23

Business Summary: Insurance (MIC: 8.2 SIC: 351 NAIC: 24130)

Old Republic International is an insurance holding company. Through its general insurance group, Co. assumes risks and provides related risk management and marketing services pertaining to a large variety of property and liability commercial insurance coverages. Co.'s mortgage guaranty group protects mortgage lenders and investors from default related losses on residential mortgage loans made primarily to homebuyers with down payments of less than 20.0% of the property value. Co.'s title insurance group insures real estate purchasers and investors against losses from defects, liens and encumbrances affecting the insured title and not excluded or excepted from the coverage of the policy.

Recent Developments: For the quarter ended Mar 31 2005, net income increased 7.4% to $114,300 thousand from net income of $106,400 thousand in the year-earlier quarter. Revenues were $880,600 thousand, up 7.1% from $822,400 thousand the year before. Net premiums earned were $717,100 thousand versus $660,700 thousand in the prior-year quarter, an increase of 8.5%. Net investment income rose 7.4% to $75,700 thousand from $70,500 thousand a year ago.

Prospects: Co. is continuing to experience growth in earnings from strong performances at its general insurance and mortgage guaranty insurance groups. These segments are generating greater underwriting income, as well as moderate growth of investment income. Co.'s overall revenues are being positively affected by improved underwriting and investment income in its general and mortgage guaranty businesses, which is more than offsetting weaker revenues from its title insurance business. Co.'s positive underwriting results at its general insurance group is due to a stable pricing environment controlled production and administrative expenses for the majority of coverages.

Financial Data

(US$ in Thousands)	3 Mos	12/31/2004	12/31/2003	12/31/2002	12/31/2001	12/31/2000	12/31/1999	12/31/1998
Earnings Per Share	2.41	2.36	2.51	2.15	1.92	1.65	1.17	1.55
Cash Flow Per Share	4.32	4.53	4.16	3.71	2.95	1.92	1.42	1.62
Tang Book Value Per Share	21.24	20.85	19.26	17.00	15.19	13.38	9.35	11.51
Dividends Per Share	0.520	0.503	1.113	0.420	0.393	0.367	0.327	0.258
Dividend Payout %	21.58	21.31	44.36	19.50	20.49	22.27	28.00	16.60
Income Statement								
Premium Income	717,100	2,804,800	2,582,100	2,135,400	1,786,800	1,550,300	1,567,200	1,568,100
Total Revenue	880,600	3,491,600	3,285,800	2,756,400	2,373,400	2,070,600	2,102,100	2,171,700
Benefits & Claims	345,700	1,305,600	1,097,600	975,300	861,000	760,300	829,900	781,700
Income Before Taxes	168,500	650,900	680,000	560,900	503,900	426,400	317,000	466,700
Income Taxes	54,200	215,900	219,900	167,700	159,700	131,000	92,900	145,900
Net Income	114,300	435,000	459,800	392,900	346,900	297,500	226,800	323,700
Average Shares	184,688	184,607	183,302	182,323	180,491	180,295	194,680	208,725
Balance Sheet								
Total Assets	10,679,500	10,570,800	9,712,300	8,715,400	7,920,200	7,281,400	6,938,400	7,019,700
Total Liabilities	6,798,600	6,705,100	6,158,600	5,559,500	5,136,100	4,842,000	4,739,200	4,714,200
Stockholders' Equity	3,880,900	3,865,600	3,553,600	3,155,800	2,783,700	2,438,700	2,198,400	2,304,200
Shares Outstanding	182,700	185,429	184,471	185,687	183,253	182,167	235,018	200,104
Statistical Record								
Return on Assets %	4.29	4.28	4.99	4.72	4.56	4.17	3.25	4.64
Return on Equity %	11.73	11.69	13.71	13.23	13.29	12.80	10.07	14.53
Loss Ratio %	48.21	46.55	42.51	45.67	48.19	49.04	52.95	49.85
Net Margin %	12.98	12.46	13.99	14.25	14.62	14.37	10.79	14.91
Price Range	25.79-21.37	27.19-21.37	25.79-16.53	23.15-16.85	20.04-15.10	21.33-7.17	15.04-8.25	21.25-12.00
P/E Ratio	10.70-8.87	11.52-9.06	10.27-6.58	10.77-7.84	10.44-7.86	12.93-4.34	12.86-7.05	13.71-7.74
Average Yield %	2.18	2.09	5.17	2.06	2.16	2.86	2.88	1.50

Address: 307 North Michigan Avenue, Chicago, IL 60601 **Telephone:** 312-346-8100 **Web Site:** www.oldrepublic.com	**Officers:** Aldo C. Zucaro - Chmn., Pres., C.E.O. Karl W. Mueller - Sr. V.P., C.F.O. **Transfer Agents:** EquiServe, First Chicago Trust Division, Jersey City, NJ	**No of Institutions:** 239 **Shares:** 126,357,096 **% Held:** 69.19

OTTER TAIL CORP.

Exchange	Symbol	Price	52Wk Range	Yield	P/E
NMS	OTTR	$25.46 (5/31/2005)	27.36-23.85	4.40	15.91

*7 Year Price Score 91.01 *NYSE Composite Index=100 *12 Month Price Score 94.57

Interim Earnings (Per Share)

Qtr.	Mar	Jun	Sep	Dec
2002	0.40	0.41	0.50	0.49
2003	0.38	0.32	0.46	0.36
2004	0.31	0.30	0.42	0.55
2005	0.33	...	...	...

Interim Dividends (Per Share)

Amt	Decl	Ex	Rec	Pay
0.275Q	8/2/2004	8/11/2004	8/13/2004	9/10/2004
0.275Q	11/1/2004	11/10/2004	11/15/2004	12/10/2004
0.28Q	1/31/2005	2/11/2005	2/15/2005	3/10/2005
0.28Q	4/12/2005	5/11/2005	5/13/2005	6/10/2005

Indicated Div: $1.12 (Div. Reinv. Plan)

Valuation Analysis

Forecast P/E	13.81 (6/1/2005)		
Market Cap	$742.0 Million	Book Value	434.9 Million
Price/Book	1.71	Price/Sales	0.82

Dividend Achiever Status

Rank	304	10 Year Growth Rate	2.49%
Total Years of Dividend Growth			29

Business Summary: Electricity (MIC: 7.1 SIC: 911 NAIC: 21121)

Otter Tail is a diversified operating company. The Electric segment includes the production, transmission, distribution and sale of electric energy in Minnesota, North Dakota and South Dakota under the name Otter Tail Power Co. The Plastics segment consists of businesses producing polyvinyl chloride and polyethylene pipe. The Manufacturing segment consists of businesses producing waterfront equipment, wind towers, automotive frame-straightening equipment and fabricated steel products and providing contract machining, and metal parts stamping and fabrication. Health Services segment consists of businesses involved in the sale of diagnostic medical equipment and patient monitoring equipment.

Recent Developments: For the quarter ended Mar 31 2005, income from continuing operations increased 34.2% to $11,016 thousand from income of $8,210 thousand in the year-earlier quarter. Net income increased 20.7% to $9,971 thousand from net income of $8,259 thousand in the year-earlier quarter. Revenues were $233,838 thousand, up 16.0% from $201,653 thousand the year before. Operating income was $21,030 thousand versus an income of $16,128 thousand in the prior-year quarter. Total direct expense was $198,700 thousand versus $172,453 thousand in the prior-year quarter, an increase of 15.2%. Total indirect expense was $14,108 thousand versus $13,072 thousand in the prior-year quarter, an increase of 7.9%.

Prospects: Co. is seeing strong earnings growth as gains in its non-electric businesses more than offset declines in the electric segment. This reduction in wholesale electric results primarily reflects uncertainty in wholesale electric markets with the introduction of the Midwest Independent Transmission System Operator markets. Co.'s non-electric performance is benefiting from strength in its plastics segment and manufacturing operations. Improvement in Co.'s health services segment and contributions from its new food ingredient processing segment are also contributing to higher earnings. For full-year 2005, Co. expects earnings from continuing operations to range from $1.50 to $1.70 per share.

Financial Data

(US$ in Thousands)	3 Mos	12/31/2004	12/31/2003	12/31/2002	12/31/2001	12/31/2000	12/31/1999	12/31/1998
Earnings Per Share	1.60	1.58	1.51	1.79	1.68	1.60	1.79	1.37
Cash Flow Per Share	2.07	2.29	3.00	3.05	3.15	2.52	3.29	2.71
Tang Book Value Per Share	10.94	10.95	9.88	9.51	9.31	9.06	9.32	8.58
Dividends Per Share	1.105	1.100	1.080	1.060	1.040	1.020	0.990	0.960
Dividend Payout %	69.06	69.62	71.52	59.22	61.90	63.75	55.31	70.33
Income Statement								
Total Revenue	233,838	882,324	753,239	710,116	654,132	559,445	464,577	431,078
EBITDA	32,659	119,600	118,414	126,652	121,777	112,571	118,459	96,372
Depn & Amortn	11,435	44,344	45,962	42,613	42,100	38,249	34,796	34,965
Income Before Taxes	16,639	56,984	54,586	66,189	63,686	57,739	68,892	45,841
Income Taxes	5,623	17,004	14,930	20,061	20,083	17,515	23,915	15,140
Net Income	9,971	42,195	39,656	46,128	43,603	40,224	44,977	34,520
Average Shares	29,230	26,207	25,826	25,397	24,832	23,928	23,831	23,596
Balance Sheet								
Net PPE	682,976	682,098	633,325	587,886	542,977	515,929	502,956	500,186
Total Assets	1,168,019	1,134,148	986,423	878,736	782,541	722,115	680,788	655,612
Long-Term Obligations	260,334	261,810	265,193	258,229	227,360	191,493	176,437	181,046
Total Liabilities	733,145	689,438	637,036	549,771	487,733	429,236	401,595	409,705
Stockholders' Equity	434,874	444,710	349,387	328,965	294,808	292,879	279,193	245,907
Shares Outstanding	29,145	28,976	25,723	25,592	24,653	23,852	23,849	23,760
Statistical Record								
Return on Assets %	4.06	3.97	4.25	5.55	5.80	5.72	6.73	5.27
Return on Equity %	11.32	10.60	11.69	14.79	14.84	14.02	17.13	14.48
EBITDA Margin %	13.97	13.56	15.72	17.84	18.62	20.12	25.50	22.36
Net Margin %	4.26	4.78	5.26	6.50	6.67	7.19	9.68	8.01
PPE Turnover	1.38	1.34	1.23	1.26	1.24	1.10	0.93	0.85
Asset Turnover	0.85	0.83	0.81	0.85	0.87	0.80	0.70	0.66
Debt to Equity	0.60	0.59	0.76	0.78	0.77	0.65	0.63	0.74
Price Range	27.36-23.85	27.36-23.85	28.50-24.00	34.12-23.80	30.69-23.88	29.00-17.81	22.63-17.00	20.78-15.63
P/E Ratio	17.10-14.91	17.32-15.09	18.87-15.89	19.06-13.30	18.27-14.21	18.13-11.13	12.64-9.50	15.17-11.41
Average Yield %	4.32	4.24	4.02	3.70	3.76	4.72	4.91	5.16

Address: 215 South Cascade Street, P.O. Box 496, Fergus Falls, MN 56538-0496
Telephone: 800-664-1259
Web Site: www.ottertail.com

Officers: John C. MacFarlane - Chmn. John D. Erickson - Pres., C.E.O. **Transfer Agents:** Wells Fargo Bank, Minnesota, N.A., St. Paul, MN

No of Institutions: 81
Shares: 8,032,788 **% Held:** 27.57

PACIFIC CAPITAL BANCORP

Exchange	Symbol	Price	52Wk Range	Yield	P/E
NMS	PCBC	$33.80 (5/31/2005)	34.54-26.30	2.37	14.76

***7 Year Price Score 131.85** *NYSE Composite Index=100 ***12 Month Price Score 97.74**

TRADING VOLUME (thousand shares)

Interim Earnings (Per Share)

Qtr.	Mar	Jun	Sep	Dec
2002	0.57	0.32	0.38	0.32
2003	0.79	0.29	0.29	0.28
2004	0.93	0.36	0.32	0.31
2005	1.30	...	...	...

Interim Dividends (Per Share)

Amt	Decl	Ex	Rec	Pay
0.18Q	7/1/2004	7/16/2004	7/20/2004	8/10/2004
0.18Q	10/1/2004	10/22/2004	10/26/2004	11/16/2004
0.18Q	1/3/2005	1/21/2005	1/25/2005	2/15/2005
0.20Q	4/1/2005	4/15/2005	4/19/2005	5/10/2005

Indicated Div: $0.80

Valuation Analysis

Forecast P/E	N/A		
Market Cap	$1.5 Billion	Book Value	504.7 Million
Price/Book	3.07	Price/Sales	3.26

Dividend Achiever Status

Rank	65	**10 Year Growth Rate**	17.09%
Total Years of Dividend Growth			35

Business Summary: Commercial Banking (MIC: 8.1 SIC: 022 NAIC: 22110)

Pacific Capital Bancorp is the parent of Pacific Capital Bank, N.A., a nationally chartered bank with four brands: Santa Barbara Bank and Trust, First National Bank of Central California, South Valley National Bank and San Benito Bank. The banks provide commercial banking services to households, professionals, and small- to medium-sized businesses. Co. also offers products related to income tax returns filed electronically. As of Dec 31 2004, Co. had assets of $6.02 billion and deposits of $4.51 billion. Pacific Capital Bank, N.A. is a 45-branch community bank network serving the California central coast counties of Monterey, Santa Cruz, San Benito, Santa Barbara, Ventura and Santa Clara.

Recent Developments: For the quarter ended Mar 31 2005, net income increased 39.5% to $59,406 thousand from net income of $42,591 thousand in the year-earlier quarter. Net interest income was $122,383 thousand, up 42.5% from $85,868 thousand the year before. Provision for loan losses was $39,012 thousand versus $7,584 thousand in the prior-year quarter, an increase of 414.4%. Non-interest income rose 77.9% to $65,158 thousand, while non-interest expense advanced 13.6% to $53,508 thousand.

Prospects: Co.'s near-term prospect appears favorable, supported by continued strong performances by both the core bank and its seasonal Refund Anticipation Loan (RAL) and Refund Transfer (RT) business. Consumer demand for RALs and RTs remains healthy and is helping to drive an increase in income. Going forward, Co. increased its full-year 2005 diluted earnings estimate to range from $2.30 to $2.38 per share from a previous estimate in the range of $2.02 to $2.12 per share. Co. believes it can continue to generate solid results throughout 2005, although Co. expects to receive about $100.0 million in commercial real estate loan payoffs in the second quarter that will impact its level of loan growth.

Financial Data

(US$ in Thousands)	3 Mos	12/31/2004	12/31/2003	12/31/2002	12/31/2001	12/31/2000	12/31/1999	12/31/1998
Earnings Per Share	2.29	1.92	1.64	1.61	1.19	1.09	1.01	0.68
Cash Flow Per Share	3.10	2.48	2.66	1.94	2.05	1.01	0.55	1.34
Tang Book Value Per Share	8.52	7.54	8.08	7.31	6.99	6.29	5.37	4.97
Dividends Per Share	0.705	0.690	0.600	0.517	0.495	0.450	0.405	0.343
Dividend Payout %	30.79	35.94	36.53	32.24	41.71	41.45	40.22	50.41
Income Statement								
Interest Income	145,266	326,181	272,189	266,746	291,108	290,916	211,643	193,516
Interest Expense	22,883	69,211	53,933	62,799	97,226	110,526	67,856	68,113
Net Interest Income	122,383	256,970	218,256	203,947	193,882	180,390	143,787	125,403
Provision for Losses	39,012	12,809	18,286	19,727	26,671	14,440	6,375	9,123
Non-Interest Income	65,158	75,635	81,745	73,784	65,726	49,388	41,618	35,972
Non-Interest Expense	53,508	179,906	163,702	143,288	143,150	131,957	110,389	103,710
Income Before Taxes	95,021	139,890	118,013	114,716	89,787	83,381	68,641	48,542
Income Taxes	35,615	51,946	42,342	39,865	33,676	31,925	24,367	18,975
Net Income	59,406	87,944	75,671	74,851	56,111	51,456	44,274	29,567
Average Shares	46,123	45,911	46,082	46,653	47,358	47,304	44,071	43,461
Balance Sheet								
Net Loans & Leases	4,164,562	4,008,317	3,131,329	2,965,999	2,750,220	2,481,979	1,953,193	1,553,485
Total Assets	6,181,827	6,024,785	4,859,630	4,219,213	3,960,929	3,677,625	2,879,282	2,649,418
Total Deposits	4,558,016	4,512,290	3,854,717	3,516,077	3,365,575	3,102,819	2,440,181	2,329,676
Total Liabilities	5,677,096	5,565,103	4,460,582	3,848,138	3,635,053	3,381,364	2,644,709	2,435,418
Stockholders' Equity	504,731	459,682	399,048	371,075	325,876	296,261	234,573	214,000
Shares Outstanding	45,811	45,719	45,284	46,066	46,590	47,077	43,651	43,038
Statistical Record								
Return on Assets %	1.77	1.61	1.67	1.83	1.47	1.57	1.60	1.39
Return on Equity %	22.12	20.43	19.65	21.48	18.04	19.33	19.74	17.80
Net Interest Margin %	84.25	78.78	80.19	76.46	66.60	62.01	67.94	64.80
Efficiency Ratio %	25.43	44.77	46.25	42.08	40.12	38.78	43.59	45.19
Loans to Deposits	0.91	0.89	0.81	0.84	0.82	0.80	0.80	0.67
Price Range	34.54-25.87	34.54-25.87	28.66-19.03	21.75-15.37	17.13-14.31	17.30-13.18	19.44-11.60	18.56-12.45
P/E Ratio	15.08-11.30	17.99-13.47	17.48-11.60	13.51-9.55	14.39-12.02	15.87-12.10	19.25-11.49	27.30-18.30
Average Yield %	2.39	2.37	2.47	2.81	3.12	2.96	2.52	2.33

Address: 1021 Anacapa Street, 3rd Floor, Santa Barbara, CA 93101
Telephone: 805-564-6300
Web Site: www.pcbancorp.com

Officers: David W. Spainhour - Chmn. D. Vernon Horton - Vice-Chmn. **Transfer Agents:** Norwest Shareowner Services, South St. Paul, MN

Investor Contact: 805-564-6298
No of Institutions: 105
Shares: 13,675,030 **% Held:** 29.95

PARK NATIONAL CORP.

Exchange	Symbol	Price	52Wk Range	Yield	P/E
ASE	PRK	$103.25 (5/31/2005)	141.25-99.04	3.49	16.26

*7 Year Price Score 109.17 *NYSE Composite Index=100 *12 Month Price Score 85.10

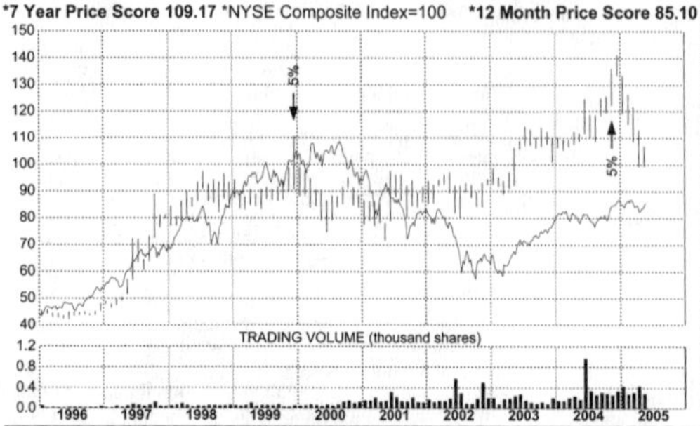

Interim Earnings (Per Share)

Qtr.	Mar	Jun	Sep	Dec
2002	1.46	1.50	1.51	1.38
2003	1.60	1.72	1.39	1.26
2004	1.58	1.67	1.63	1.44
2005	1.61	...	...	...

Interim Dividends (Per Share)

Amt	Decl	Ex	Rec	Pay
5%	11/15/2004	11/29/2004	12/1/2004	12/15/2004
0.90Q	11/15/2004	12/15/2004	12/17/2004	1/3/2005
0.90Q	1/18/2005	2/17/2005	2/22/2005	3/10/2005
0.90Q	4/18/2005	5/20/2005	5/24/2005	6/10/2005

Indicated Div: $3.60 (Div. Reinv. Plan)

Valuation Analysis

Forecast P/E	15.91 (6/2/2005)		
Market Cap	$1.5 Billion	Book Value	556.3 Million
Price/Book	2.66	Price/Sales	4.46

Dividend Achiever Status

Rank	129	**10 Year Growth Rate**	12.58%
Total Years of Dividend Growth			17

Business Summary: Commercial Banking (MIC: 8.1 SIC: 021 NAIC: 22110)

Park National, with $5.41 billion in total assets at Dec 31 2004, is a bank holding company. Through its subsidiaries, Co. engages in general commercial banking and trust business in small and medium population Ohio communities. Co.'s subsidiaries provide the following services: the acceptance and servicing of demand, savings and time deposit accounts; commercial, industrial, consumer and real estate lending, including installment loans, credit cards, home equity lines of credit and commercial and auto leasing; trust services; cash management; safe deposit operations; electronic funds transfers; and online Internet banking with bill pay service.

Recent Developments: For the quarter ended Mar 31 2005, net income increased 1.6% to $23,342 thousand from net income of $22,978 thousand in the year-earlier quarter. Net interest income was $54,445 thousand, up 3.5% from $52,616 thousand the year before. Provision for loan losses was $1,082 thousand versus $1,465 thousand in the prior-year quarter, a decrease of 26.1%. Non-interest income rose 8.7% to $14,112 thousand, while non-interest expense advanced 9.1% to $34,404 thousand.

Prospects: Co. is benefiting from strong results. For example, average interest earning assets advanced 10.3% to $5.14 billion for the first quarter of 2005, primarily due to the acquisitions of First Federal and First Clermont, whose interest earning assets totaled $416.0 million at the time of acquisition. Further, deposits increased by $25.0 million during the first quarter and appear to be on pace to grow by about 2.5% in 2005. The net interest margin for the first quarter of 2005 was 4.35%. However, Co. expects that due to the slower expected growth in loans, the net interest margin will be slightly less than 4.35% for the remaining three quarters of 2005.

Financial Data

(US$ in Thousands)	3 Mos	12/31/2004	12/31/2003	12/31/2002	12/31/2001	12/31/2000	12/31/1999	12/31/1998
Earnings Per Share	6.35	6.32	5.97	5.86	5.31	4.86	4.45	4.02
Cash Flow Per Share	5.22	6.03	6.86	10.94	6.67	5.11	5.78	4.16
Tang Book Value Per Share	38.79	39.28	37.57	35.17	32.00	28.25	23.43	22.38
Dividends Per Share	3.476	3.414	3.210	2.962	2.752	2.533	2.252	1.850
Dividend Payout %	54.75	54.02	53.75	50.57	51.79	52.16	50.63	46.05
Income Statement								
Interest Income	74,959	270,993	264,629	287,920	320,348	249,332	191,920	185,946
Interest Expense	20,514	58,702	61,992	82,588	127,404	110,437	76,063	78,295
Net Interest Income	54,445	212,291	202,637	205,332	192,944	138,895	115,857	107,651
Provision for Losses	1,082	8,600	12,595	15,043	13,059	8,729	6,969	6,798
Non-Interest Income	14,112	51,848	55,523	50,850	45,238	29,691	23,088	23,969
Non-Interest Expense	34,404	126,290	122,376	119,964	114,207	82,919	67,540	64,309
Income Before Taxes	33,071	129,249	123,189	121,175	110,916	76,938	64,436	60,513
Income Taxes	9,729	37,742	36,311	35,596	32,554	21,533	18,689	18,941
Net Income	23,342	91,507	86,878	85,579	78,362	55,405	45,747	41,572
Average Shares	14,475	14,486	14,551	14,605	14,753	11,420	10,301	10,348
Balance Sheet								
Net Loans & Leases	3,179,592	3,052,280	2,667,661	2,630,159	2,735,849	2,229,259	1,792,682	1,603,523
Total Assets	5,676,842	5,412,584	5,034,956	4,446,625	4,569,515	3,211,068	2,634,337	2,460,779
Total Deposits	3,838,563	3,689,861	3,414,249	3,495,135	3,314,203	2,415,575	2,015,147	1,939,778
Total Liabilities	5,120,539	4,850,023	4,491,915	3,937,333	4,101,169	2,891,316	2,394,757	2,225,089
Stockholders' Equity	556,303	562,561	543,041	509,292	468,346	319,752	239,580	235,690
Shares Outstanding	14,342	14,320	14,455	14,481	14,637	11,317	10,226	10,532
Statistical Record								
Return on Assets %	1.72	1.75	1.83	3.77	2.01	1.89	1.80	1.75
Return on Equity %	16.48	16.51	16.51	34.73	19.89	19.76	19.25	18.16
Net Interest Margin %	72.63	78.34	76.57	71.32	60.23	55.71	60.37	57.89
Efficiency Ratio %	38.63	39.12	38.22	35.41	31.24	29.72	31.41	30.64
Loans to Deposits	0.83	0.83	0.78	0.75	0.83	0.92	0.89	0.83
Price Range	141.25-107.52	141.25-105.33	114.29-88.86	97.24-80.01	97.62-71.52	98.93-74.76	110.48-83.16	97.28-77.10
P/E Ratio	22.24-16.93	22.35-16.67	19.14-14.88	16.59-13.65	18.38-13.47	20.36-15.38	24.83-18.69	24.20-19.18
Average Yield %	2.90	2.92	3.11	3.28	3.24	2.88	2.52	2.12

Address: 50 North Third Street, Newark, OH 43055
Telephone: 740-349-8451
Web Site: www.parknationalcorp.com

Officers: C. Daniel DeLawder - Chmn., C.E.O. Harry O. Egger - Vice Chmn. **Transfer Agents:** First-Knox National Bank, Mount Vernon, OH

Investor Contact: 740-349-3927
No of Institutions: 84
Shares: 3,811,200 **% Held:** 26.59

PARKER HANNIFIN CORP.

Exchange	Symbol	Price	52Wk Range	Yield	P/E
NYS	PH	$60.33 (5/31/2005)	77.81-53.57	1.33	12.75

*7 Year Price Score 121.32 *NYSE Composite Index=100 *12 Month Price Score 90.88

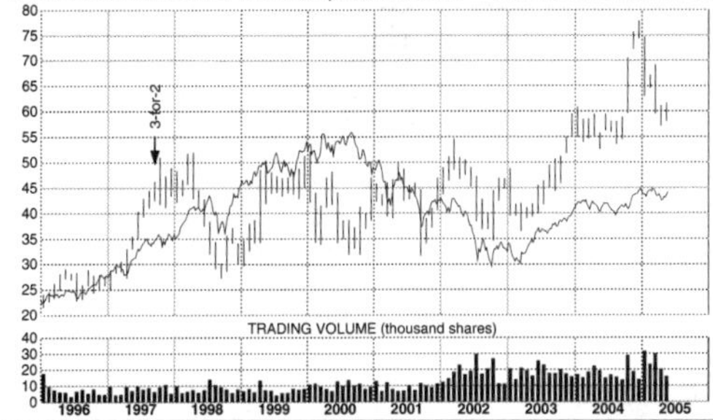

Interim Earnings (Per Share)

Qtr.	Sep	Dec	Mar	Jun
2001-02	0.52	0.25	0.45	(0.11)
2002-03	0.52	0.32	0.42	0.42
2003-04	0.48	0.47	0.90	1.06
2004-05	1.11	1.41	1.15	...

Interim Dividends (Per Share)

Amt	Decl	Ex	Rec	Pay
0.19Q	7/23/2004	8/18/2004	8/20/2004	9/3/2004
0.19Q	10/27/2004	11/16/2004	11/18/2004	12/3/2004
0.20Q	1/27/2005	2/15/2005	2/17/2005	3/4/2005
0.20Q	4/21/2005	5/17/2005	5/19/2005	6/3/2005

Indicated Div: $0.80 (Div. Reinv. Plan)

Valuation Analysis

Forecast P/E	11.83 (6/1/2005)		
Market Cap	$7.3 Billion	Book Value	3.5 Billion
Price/Book	2.10	Price/Sales	0.90

Dividend Achiever Status

Rank	255	10 Year Growth Rate	5.51%
Total Years of Dividend Growth			48

Business Summary: Metal Products (MIC: 11.4 SIC: 491 NAIC: 32911)

Parker-Hannifin is a manufacturer of motion-control products, including fluid power systems, electromechanical controls and related components. Co. operates in two main business segments: The Industrial segment includes several business units that manufacture motion-control and fluid power system components for builders and users of various types of manufacturing, packaging, processing, transportation, agricultural, construction, and military vehicles and equipment. The Aerospace segment produces hydraulic, fuel and pneumatic systems and components for domestic commercial, military and general aviation aircraft, as well as naval vessels and land-based weapons systems.

Recent Developments: For the quarter ended Mar 31 2005, income from continuing operations increased 34.5% to $142,175 thousand from income of $105,740 thousand in the year-earlier quarter. Net income increased 29.2% to $139,370 thousand from net income of $107,848 thousand in the year-earlier quarter. Revenues were $2,141,708 thousand, up 14.0% from $1,879,057 thousand the year before. Total direct expense was $1,712,884 thousand versus $1,526,297 thousand in the prior-year quarter, an increase of 12.2%. Total indirect expense was $218,207 thousand versus $195,452 thousand in the prior-year quarter, an increase of 11.6%.

Prospects: On May 4 2005, Co.'s Parker Aerospace segment acquired the engineering research and development company Mechatronic Systems LLC. Mechatronic specializes in the development of high-temperature electronic control and power drive and high-temperature electric machines. Separately, Co. announced it has entered into a joint venture agreement with Tianjin Tejing Hydraulics Company, LTD, to produce hydraulic components and systems in China. Co. will be the major partner in the new venture known as Parker Tejing Hydraulics (Tianjin) Co., Ltd. Meanwhile, Co. is on track to achieve record results in fiscal year 2005 with earnings expected to range from $4.72 to $4.92 per diluted share.

Financial Data

(US$ in Thousands)	9 Mos	6 Mos	3 Mos	06/30/2004	06/30/2003	06/30/2002	06/30/2001	06/30/2000
Earnings Per Share	4.73	4.47	3.53	2.91	1.68	1.12	2.96	3.31
Cash Flow Per Share	5.66	5.34	5.71	5.61	4.79	5.47	4.66	4.86
Tang Book Value Per Share	14.81	14.30	15.13	14.08	11.45	12.27	13.43	14.94
Dividends Per Share	0.770	0.760	0.760	0.760	0.740	0.720	0.700	0.680
Dividend Payout %	16.28	17.00	21.50	26.12	44.05	64.29	23.65	20.54
Income Statement								
Total Revenue	6,004,563	3,862,855	1,947,192	7,106,907	6,410,610	6,149,122	5,979,604	5,355,337
EBITDA	783,686	510,162	268,593	820,249	638,121	582,118	888,485	827,778
Depn & Amortn	196,051	131,272	63,669	252,785	259,178	281,598	264,527	206,408
Income Before Taxes	537,015	345,386	188,679	494,068	297,382	218,036	533,596	562,187
Income Taxes	150,454	101,000	55,896	148,285	101,110	87,886	189,426	193,955
Net Income	443,280	303,910	132,783	345,783	196,272	130,150	340,792	368,232
Average Shares	120,769	121,122	119,712	119,006	116,894	116,060	115,064	111,224
Balance Sheet								
Current Assets	2,611,057	2,552,896	2,676,920	2,536,933	2,396,807	2,235,618	2,196,362	2,153,113
Total Assets	6,755,425	6,681,094	6,339,810	6,256,904	5,985,633	5,752,583	5,337,661	4,646,299
Current Liabilities	1,243,222	1,205,878	1,223,041	1,259,741	1,423,727	1,359,837	1,413,129	1,186,303
Long-Term Obligations	966,814	988,828	955,145	953,804	966,332	1,088,883	857,078	701,762
Total Liabilities	3,294,374	3,293,692	3,223,345	3,274,450	3,464,722	3,169,067	2,808,746	2,336,841
Stockholders' Equity	3,461,051	3,387,402	3,116,465	2,982,454	2,520,911	2,583,516	2,528,915	2,309,458
Shares Outstanding	120,187	120,171	119,474	119,483	118,165	118,024	117,309	116,387
Statistical Record								
Return on Assets %	8.76	8.59	6.89	5.63	3.34	2.35	6.83	8.79
Return on Equity %	18.20	17.60	14.77	12.53	7.69	5.09	14.09	17.64
EBITDA Margin %	13.05	13.21	13.79	11.54	9.95	9.47	14.86	15.46
Net Margin %	7.38	7.87	6.82	4.87	3.06	2.12	5.70	6.88
Asset Turnover	1.24	1.24	1.22	1.16	1.09	1.11	1.20	1.28
Current Ratio	2.10	2.12	2.19	2.01	1.68	1.64	1.55	1.81
Debt to Equity	0.28	0.29	0.31	0.32	0.38	0.42	0.34	0.30
Price Range	77.81-52.58	77.81-52.58	60.92-44.70	60.92-41.71	48.80-34.65	54.63-31.65	50.03-31.94	52.13-33.94
P/E Ratio	16.45-11.12	17.41-11.76	17.26-12.66	20.93-14.33	29.05-20.63	48.78-28.26	16.90-10.79	15.75-10.25
Average Yield %	1.22	1.26	1.36	1.43	1.77	1.59	1.72	1.55

Address: 6035 Parkland Boulevard, Cleveland, OH 44124-4141
Telephone: 216-896-3000
Web Site: www.phstock.com

Officers: Duane E. Collings - Chmn. Donald E. Washkewicz - Pres., C.E.O. **Transfer Agents:** National City Bank, Cleveland, Ohio

Investor Contact: 216-896-2240
No of Institutions: 320
Shares: 95,226,240 **% Held:** 79.24

PAYCHEX INC

Exchange	Symbol	Price	52Wk Range	Yield	P/E
NMS	PAYX	$28.88 (5/31/2005)	38.84-28.88	1.80	33.58

*7 Year Price Score 88.81 *NYSE Composite Index=100 *12 Month Price Score 93.06

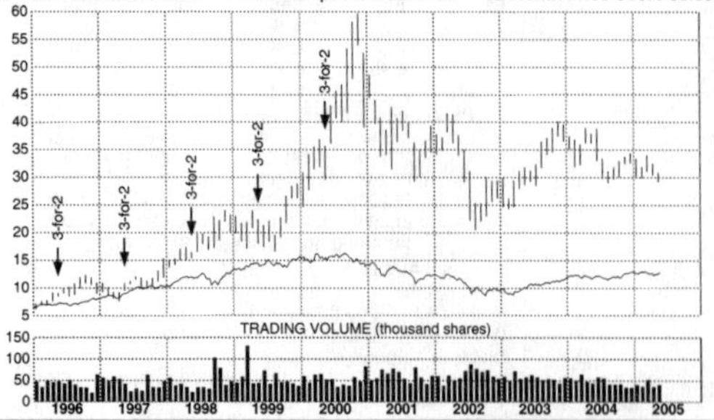

Interim Earnings (Per Share)

Qtr.	Aug	Nov	Feb	May
2001-02	0.19	0.18	0.18	0.19
2002-03	0.20	0.20	0.19	0.19
2003-04	0.21	0.21	0.21	0.16
2004-05	0.23	0.23	0.24	...

Interim Dividends (Per Share)

Amt	Decl	Ex	Rec	Pay
0.12Q	7/8/2004	7/29/2004	8/2/2004	8/16/2004
0.13Q	10/6/2004	10/28/2004	11/1/2004	11/15/2004
0.13Q	1/14/2005	1/28/2005	2/1/2005	2/15/2005
0.13Q	4/8/2005	4/28/2005	5/2/2005	5/16/2005

Indicated Div: $0.52 (Div. Reinv. Plan)

Valuation Analysis

Forecast P/E	26.65 (6/1/2005)		
Market Cap	$10.9 Billion	Book Value	1.3 Billion
Price/Book	8.21	Price/Sales	7.83

Dividend Achiever Status

Rank	4	10 Year Growth Rate	35.37%
Total Years of Dividend Growth			16

Business Summary: Accounting & Management Consulting Services (MIC: 12.2 SIC: 721 NAIC: 41214)

Paychex is a provider of payroll and human resource and employee benefits outsourcing services for small- to medium-sized businesses. Co.'s payroll processing services includes the calculation, preparation, and delivery of employee payroll checks; production of internal accounting records and management reports; and the preparation of federal, state, and local payroll tax returns. Co.'s other products and services include tax filing and payment, employee payment, time and attendance systems, regulatory compliance (new-hire reporting and garnishment processing), retirement services administration, employee benefits administration, and workers' compensation insurance.

Recent Developments: For the quarter ended Feb 28 2005, Co. reported net income of $92.8 million, up 15.3% from $80.5 million in the equivalent quarter a year earlier. Total revenues rose 9.1% to $373.9 million from $342.6 million in the comparable period the year before. Services revenues rose 8.8% to $357.1 million from $328.1 million, while interest on funds held for clients rose 15.5% to $16.8 million. Operating income increased 16.2% to $135.4 million from $116.5 million the year before.

Prospects: Co. is seeing positive year-over-year growth in Payroll services revenue due to organic client base growth, increased use of ancillary services and price increases. Meanwhile, increases in human resource and benefits services revenue reflect growth in clients for Co.'s retirement services, growth in client employees served by Paychex Administrative Services and Professional Employer Organization bundled services, as well as contributions from the acquisition of Stromberg time and attendance products. For fiscal 2005, Co. expects total revenue growth of 9.0% to 11.0% to be accompanied by net income growth in the range of 17.0% to 19.0% based on current economic and interest rate conditions.

Financial Data

(US$ in Thousands)	9 Mos	6 Mos	3 Mos	05/31/2004	05/31/2003	05/31/2002	05/31/2001	05/31/2000
Earnings Per Share	0.86	0.83	0.81	0.80	0.78	0.73	0.68	0.51
Cash Flow Per Share	1.14	1.07	1.06	1.03	0.99	0.81	0.82	0.67
Tang Book Value Per Share	2.25	2.13	2.03	1.88	1.55	2.43	2.00	1.50
Dividends Per Share	0.500	0.490	0.480	0.470	0.440	0.420	0.330	0.220
Dividend Payout %	58.14	59.20	59.43	58.75	56.41	57.53	48.53	43.14
Income Statement								
Total Revenue	1,066,121	692,260	344,975	1,294,347	1,099,079	954,910	869,857	728,119
EBITDA	434,448	299,143	142,868	489,115	465,596	411,086	375,841	295,377
Depn & Amortn	43,500	43,577	14,200	55,800	64,555	47,392	39,139	36,484
Income Before Taxes	399,057	260,576	130,927	449,784	431,544	395,009	363,981	275,372
Income Taxes	131,689	85,990	43,206	146,834	138,092	120,478	109,112	85,365
Net Income	267,368	174,586	87,721	302,950	293,452	274,531	254,869	190,007
Average Shares	379,814	379,696	379,706	379,524	378,083	378,002	377,510	375,081
Balance Sheet								
Current Assets	3,965,113	3,370,041	3,272,342	3,280,447	3,032,642	2,814,574	2,791,273	2,362,575
Total Assets	4,629,165	4,035,097	3,938,755	3,950,203	3,690,783	2,953,075	2,907,196	2,455,577
Current Liabilities	3,256,693	2,707,413	2,650,741	2,721,903	2,587,525	2,023,406	2,143,842	1,886,945
Total Liabilities	3,297,774	2,745,362	2,683,383	2,750,230	2,613,412	2,029,094	2,149,354	1,892,145
Stockholders' Equity	1,331,391	1,289,735	1,255,372	1,199,973	1,077,371	923,981	757,842	563,432
Shares Outstanding	378,458	378,337	378,196	377,968	376,698	375,859	373,647	371,769
Statistical Record								
Return on Assets %	7.38	8.20	8.20	7.91	8.83	9.37	9.51	8.75
Return on Equity %	26.02	25.82	26.17	26.53	29.33	32.65	38.58	37.93
EBITDA Margin %	40.75	43.21	41.41	37.79	42.36	43.05	43.21	40.57
Net Margin %	25.08	25.22	25.43	23.41	26.70	28.75	29.30	26.10
Asset Turnover	0.31	0.35	0.35	0.34	0.33	0.33	0.32	0.34
Current Ratio	1.22	1.24	1.23	1.21	1.17	1.39	1.30	1.25
Price Range	38.97-29.04	39.57-29.04	40.14-29.04	40.14-28.52	35.00-20.55	42.00-29.28	59.69-31.44	36.88-16.58
P/E Ratio	45.31-33.77	47.67-34.99	49.56-35.85	50.17-35.65	44.87-26.35	57.53-40.11	87.78-46.24	72.30-32.52
Average Yield %	1.51	1.43	1.35	1.33	1.61	1.14	0.75	0.84

Address: 911 Panorama Trail South, Rochester, NY 14625-2396
Telephone: 585-385-6666
Web Site: www.paychex.com

Officers: B. Thomas Golisano - Chmn., Pres., C.E.O. John M. Morphy - Sr. V.P., C.F.O., Sec. **Transfer Agents:** American Stock Transfer & Trust Co. New York. NY

Investor Contact: 585-383-3406
No of Institutions: 383
Shares: 226,369,376 **% Held:** 59.83

PENNROCK FINANCIAL SERVICES CORP.

Exchange	Symbol	Price	52Wk Range	Yield	P/E
NMS	PRFS	$34.61 (5/31/2005)	41.77-26.16	2.75	22.04

***7 Year Price Score 133.73** *NYSE Composite Index=100 ***12 Month Price Score 101.27**

Interim Earnings (Per Share)

Qtr.	Mar	Jun	Sep	Dec
2002	0.43	0.41	0.39	0.48
2003	0.46	0.48	0.42	0.45
2004	0.53	0.40	0.47	0.23
2005	0.47	...	...	...

Interim Dividends (Per Share)

Amt	Decl	Ex	Rec	Pay
0.20Q	9/14/2004	9/24/2004	9/28/2004	10/12/2004
0.22Q	12/14/2004	12/23/2004	12/28/2004	1/11/2005
0.22Q	3/8/2005	3/18/2005	3/22/2005	4/5/2005
0.238Q	5/10/2005	5/20/2005	5/24/2005	6/28/2005

Indicated Div: $0.95 (Div. Reinv. Plan)

Valuation Analysis

Forecast P/E	24.72 (6/2/2005)		
Market Cap	$266.5 Million	Book Value	105.6 Million
Price/Book	2.52	Price/Sales	3.89

Dividend Achiever Status

Rank	166	**10 Year Growth Rate**	10.34%
Total Years of Dividend Growth			18

Business Summary: Commercial Banking (MIC: 8.1 SIC: 021 NAIC: 22110)

PennRock Financial Services is a financial holding company that operates through its subsidiaries to deliver financial and related services to its customers. Through its Blue Ball National Bank subsidiary, Co. provides a range of general commercial and retail banking services to its customers, including several types of checking and savings accounts, certificates of deposit, and commercial, consumer and mortgage loans through 19 full service community offices in Lancaster, Berks and Chester Counties in southeastern and south-central Pennsylvania, as of Dec 31 2004. Co. also provides personal and corporate trust and agency services to individuals, corporations and others.

Recent Developments: For the quarter ended Mar 31 2005, net income decreased 10.5% to $3,685 thousand from net income of $4,119 thousand in the year-earlier quarter. Net interest income was $9,559 thousand, an increase of 5.9% from $9,023 thousand the year before. Provision for loan losses was Nil versus $398 thousand in the prior-year quarter. Non-interest income fell 26.8% to $2,964 thousand, while non-interest expense advanced 5.6% to $7,880 thousand.

Prospects: Co. is benefiting from strong loan growth largely due to an increase in deposits and borrowed funds and decrease in securities available for sale. Co.'s significant increase in loans is expected to have a positive effect on future earnings. Meanwhile, Co. continues to work to complete the affiliation with CommunityBanks, Inc., while continuing its existing operations. The combined organization is expected to present new opportunities and benefits to both shareholders and customers. The organization will include 69 banking offices in 11 counties throughout Pennsylvania and upper Maryland, and completion is expected for mid-year 2005.

Financial Data

(US$ in Thousands)	3 Mos	12/31/2004	12/31/2003	12/31/2002	12/31/2001	12/31/2000	12/31/1999	12/31/1998
Earnings Per Share	1.57	1.63	1.81	1.71	1.58	1.26	1.41	1.25
Cash Flow Per Share	1.35	1.40	2.98	1.28	0.97	1.57	1.99	0.58
Tang Book Value Per Share	12.26	12.03	12.85	11.44	10.27	9.62	7.85	8.77
Dividends Per Share	0.840	0.820	0.754	0.702	0.630	0.551	0.488	0.472
Dividend Payout %	53.50	50.31	41.64	41.05	39.89	43.75	34.64	37.74
Income Statement								
Interest Income	15,286	55,340	53,394	57,142	62,274	64,234	54,783	50,643
Interest Expense	5,727	18,651	17,825	23,283	32,366	37,073	28,137	25,458
Net Interest Income	9,559	36,689	35,569	33,859	29,908	27,161	26,646	25,185
Provision for Losses	...	565	1,917	1,750	1,548	3,076	1,026	1,225
Non-Interest Income	2,964	12,235	13,750	11,144	11,030	7,315	6,159	5,087
Non-Interest Expense	7,880	31,616	29,678	27,447	25,282	20,280	18,566	17,451
Income Before Taxes	4,643	16,743	17,724	15,806	14,108	11,120	13,213	11,596
Income Taxes	958	4,062	3,724	2,580	2,041	1,574	2,503	1,981
Net Income	3,685	12,681	14,000	13,226	12,067	9,546	10,710	9,615
Average Shares	7,778	7,757	7,741	7,728	7,663	7,576	7,586	7,694
Balance Sheet								
Net Loans & Leases	817,675	764,317	703,259	595,765	551,107	495,167	454,551	402,890
Total Assets	1,206,939	1,175,084	1,108,740	1,008,589	948,938	910,950	842,446	730,531
Total Deposits	846,159	828,734	784,042	743,262	663,694	682,994	631,415	550,046
Total Liabilities	1,101,379	1,071,594	1,010,733	921,611	870,534	838,352	783,213	663,620
Stockholders' Equity	105,560	103,490	98,007	86,978	78,404	72,598	59,233	66,911
Shares Outstanding	7,700	7,679	7,625	7,600	7,631	7,544	7,549	7,631
Statistical Record								
Return on Assets %	1.06	1.11	1.32	1.35	1.30	1.09	1.36	1.39
Return on Equity %	11.86	12.55	15.14	15.99	15.98	14.44	16.98	15.00
Net Interest Margin %	62.53	66.30	66.62	59.25	48.03	42.28	48.64	49.73
Efficiency Ratio %	43.18	46.79	44.20	40.19	34.49	28.34	30.47	31.31
Loans to Deposits	0.97	0.92	0.90	0.80	0.83	0.72	0.72	0.73
Price Range	41.77-26.16	41.77-26.16	33.49-21.47	29.09-18.15	19.01-10.72	13.77-10.63	18.89-13.58	21.65-15.15
P/E Ratio	26.61-16.66	25.63-16.05	18.50-11.86	17.01-10.61	12.03-6.79	10.93-8.43	13.40-9.63	17.32-12.12
Average Yield %	2.64	2.68	2.77	2.90	4.19	4.53	2.91	2.48

Address: 1060 Main St., Blue Ball, PA 17506 **Telephone:** 717-354-4541 **Web Site:** www.pennrock.com	**Officers:** Dennis L. Dinger - Chmn. Glen H. Weaver - Pres. **Transfer Agents:** American Stock Transfer & Trust Co.	**Investor Contact:** 717-354-4541 **No of Institutions:** 36 **Shares:** 821,092 **% Held:** 10.69

PENTAIR, INC.

Exchange	Symbol	Price	52Wk Range	Yield	P/E
NYS	PNR	$44.51 (5/31/2005)	46.03-30.90	1.17	26.18

*7 Year Price Score 153.65 *NYSE Composite Index=100 *12 Month Price Score 105.03

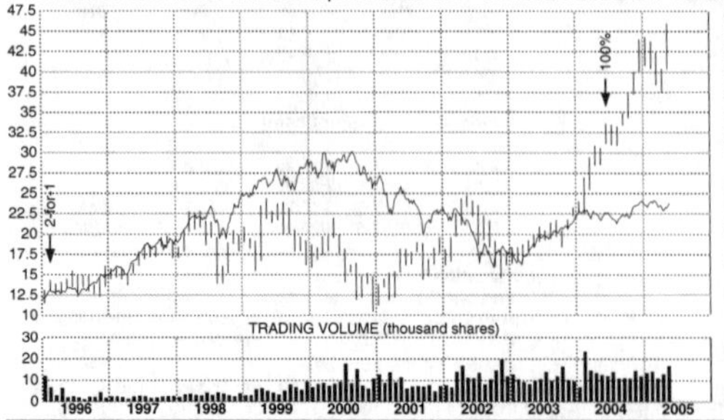

Interim Earnings (Per Share)

Qtr.	Mar	Jun	Sep	Dec
2002	0.22	0.43	0.38	0.28
2003	0.28	0.44	0.39	0.32
2004	0.40	0.55	0.47	0.26
2005	0.42	...	...	...

Interim Dividends (Per Share)

Amt	Decl	Ex	Rec	Pay
100%	5/17/2004	6/9/2004	6/1/2004	6/8/2004
0.11Q	10/14/2004	10/27/2004	10/29/2004	11/12/2004
0.13Q	12/10/2004	1/26/2005	1/28/2005	2/11/2005
0.13Q	4/14/2005	4/27/2005	4/29/2005	5/13/2005

Indicated Div: $0.52 (Div. Reinv. Plan)

Valuation Analysis

Forecast P/E	21.12 (6/1/2005)		
Market Cap	$4.5 Billion	Book Value	1.5 Billion
Price/Book	3.05	Price/Sales	1.61

Dividend Achiever Status

Rank	188	10 Year Growth Rate	9.10%
Total Years of Dividend Growth			28

TRADING VOLUME (thousand shares)

Business Summary: Industrial Machinery and Equipment (MIC: 11.5 SIC: 553 NAIC: 33210)

Pentair is a diversified industrial manufacturer operating through two business segments. Co.'s Water segment manufactures and markets products and systems used in the movement, treatment, storage and enjoyment of water. Co.'s Enclosures segment designs, manufactures and markets standard, modified and custom enclosures that protect sensitive controls and components for markets that include industrial machinery, data communications, networking, telecommunications, test and measurement, automotive, medical, security, defense, and general electronics.

Recent Developments: For the quarter ended Apr 2 2005, net income increased 7.7% to $43,305 thousand from net income of $40,210 thousand in the year-earlier quarter. Revenues were $709,635 thousand, up 45.3% from $488,453 thousand the year before. Operating income was $76,373 thousand versus an income of $50,110 thousand in the prior-year quarter, an increase of 52.4%. Total direct expense was $505,497 thousand versus $348,380 thousand in the prior-year quarter, an increase of 45.1%. Total indirect expense was $127,765 thousand versus $89,963 thousand in the prior-year quarter, an increase of 42.0%.

Prospects: Looking ahead, Co.will continue to focus on capturing solid internal growth in both the Water and Enclosures businesses through growth initiatives. Also, Co. will attempt to duplicate these efforts in its European markets. Meanwhile, Co. will look to continue to more than offset material cost inflation with pricing and productivity and production, the integration of the former WICOR businesses and continue to pursue acquisition opportunities in both Water and Enclosures. Going forward, Co. is raising the low end of its previous 2005 earnings guidance from $1.95 to $2.00 per share, while maintaining the high end of the range at $2.10.

Financial Data

(US$ in Thousands)	3 Mos	12/31/2004	12/31/2003	12/31/2002	12/31/2001	12/31/2000	12/31/1999	12/31/1998
Earnings Per Share	1.70	1.68	1.42	1.30	0.34	0.57	1.17	1.23
Cash Flow Per Share	1.84	2.65	2.69	2.75	2.37	1.90	1.67	1.76
Tang Book Value Per Share	N.M.	N.M.	N.M.	N.M.	N.M.	N.M.	N.M.	2.35
Dividends Per Share	0.458	0.430	0.410	0.370	0.350	0.330	0.320	0.300
Dividend Payout %	26.84	25.60	28.87	28.35	104.48	57.39	27.47	24.39
Income Statement								
Total Revenue	709,635	2,278,129	2,724,365	2,580,783	2,615,944	2,748,013	2,367,753	1,937,578
EBITDA	93,736	301,805	322,483	295,725	259,125	301,058	302,976	261,580
Depn & Amortn	17,363	54,563	62,929	59,733	104,349	99,028	88,645	68,388
Income Before Taxes	65,097	210,032	218,618	192,447	93,288	127,131	166,529	170,944
Income Taxes	21,792	73,008	74,330	62,545	35,772	45,263	63,220	64,104
Net Income	43,305	171,225	141,352	129,902	32,869	55,887	103,309	106,840
Average Shares	102,742	101,706	99,620	99,488	98,594	97,290	88,574	86,298
Balance Sheet								
Current Assets	937,103	825,137	829,451	810,808	835,603	1,091,802	1,150,478	748,569
Total Assets	3,228,922	3,120,575	2,780,677	2,514,450	2,372,198	2,644,025	2,802,966	1,554,666
Current Liabilities	480,309	526,879	497,451	476,200	428,433	648,792	760,947	394,793
Long-Term Obligations	848,006	724,148	732,862	673,911	714,977	781,834	857,296	288,026
Total Liabilities	1,757,443	1,672,781	1,519,199	1,408,726	1,357,196	1,633,434	1,809,761	845,301
Stockholders' Equity	1,471,479	1,447,794	1,261,478	1,105,724	1,015,002	1,010,591	993,205	709,365
Shares Outstanding	100,967	100,967	99,005	98,444	98,221	97,423	96,634	77,007
Statistical Record								
Return on Assets %	5.71	5.79	5.34	5.32	1.31	2.05	4.74	7.06
Return on Equity %	12.61	12.61	11.94	12.25	3.25	5.56	12.14	15.95
EBITDA Margin %	13.21	13.25	11.84	11.46	9.91	10.96	12.80	13.50
Net Margin %	6.10	7.52	5.19	5.03	1.26	2.03	4.36	5.51
Asset Turnover	0.91	0.77	1.03	1.06	1.04	1.01	1.09	1.28
Current Ratio	1.95	1.57	1.67	1.70	1.95	1.68	1.51	1.90
Debt to Equity	0.58	0.50	0.58	0.61	0.70	0.77	0.86	0.41
Price Range	44.32-28.48	44.03-22.52	23.29-16.40	24.81-14.67	19.64-11.25	22.00-10.50	24.44-15.47	22.88-13.94
P/E Ratio	26.07-16.75	26.21-13.40	16.40-11.55	19.08-11.28	57.76-33.09	38.60-18.42	20.89-13.22	18.60-11.33
Average Yield %	1.28	1.35	2.09	1.85	2.19	2.00	1.57	1.55

Address: 5500 Wayzata Boulevard, Suite 800, Golden Valley, MN 55416-1261
Telephone: 763-545-1730
Web Site: www.pentair.com

Officers: Randall J. Hogan - Chmn., Pres., C.E.O. Richard J. Cathcart - Vice-Chmn. **Transfer Agents:** Wells Fargo Bank Minnesota, N.A.

Investor Contact: 651-639-5278
No of Institutions: 245
Shares: 65,498,712 **% Held:** 64.67

PEOPLES BANCORP, INC.

Exchange	Symbol	Price	52Wk Range	Yield	P/E
NMS	PEBO	$28.20 (5/31/2005)	32.12-24.00	2.70	17.09

***7 Year Price Score 116.83** *NYSE Composite Index=100 ***12 Month Price Score 97.08**

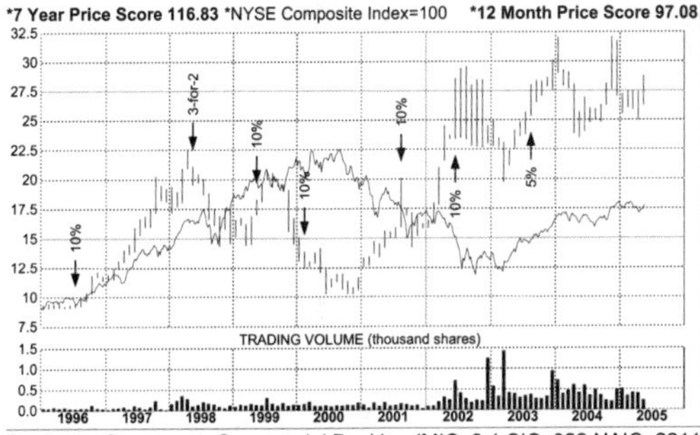

Interim Earnings (Per Share)

Qtr.	Mar	Jun	Sep	Dec
2002	0.54	0.54	0.54	0.57
2003	0.49	0.51	0.55	(0.03)
2004	0.50	0.47	0.48	0.26
2005	0.44	...	...	...

Interim Dividends (Per Share)

Amt	Decl	Ex	Rec	Pay
0.18Q	8/13/2004	9/13/2004	9/15/2004	10/1/2004
0.18Q	11/10/2004	12/13/2004	12/15/2004	1/3/2005
0.19Q	2/10/2005	3/11/2005	3/15/2005	4/1/2005
0.19Q	5/13/2005	6/13/2005	6/15/2005	7/1/2005

Indicated Div: $0.76

Valuation Analysis

Forecast P/E	14.61 (6/2/2005)		
Market Cap	$293.1 Million	Book Value	172.6 Million
Price/Book	1.70	Price/Sales	2.60

Dividend Achiever Status

Rank	118	**10 Year Growth Rate**	13.43%
Total Years of Dividend Growth			12

Business Summary: Commercial Banking (MIC: 8.1 SIC: 022 NAIC: 22110)

Peoples Bancorp is a holding company. Through its principal operating subsidiary, Co. provides a a range of financial products and services to its customers, which include interest-bearing and non-interest-bearing demand deposit accounts, savings and money market accounts, certificates of deposit, commercial, installment, and real estate mortgage loans, credit and debit cards, corporate and personal trust services, and safe deposit rental facilities. Co. also offers a range of life, health, property and casualty insurance products and provides custom-tailored solutions for asset management needs. As of Dec 31 2004, Co. had total assets of $1.81 billion and total deposits of $1.07 billion.

Recent Developments: For the quarter ended Mar 31 2005, net income decreased 12.6% to $4,692 thousand from net income of $5,366 thousand in the year-earlier quarter. Net interest income was $12,712 thousand, down 6.2% from $13,548 thousand the year before. Provision for loan losses was $941 thousand versus $794 thousand in the prior-year quarter, an increase of 18.5%. Non-interest income rose 50.8% to $7,368 thousand, while non-interest expense advanced 23.9% to $12,747 thousand.

Prospects: Earnings are being negatively affected by reduced levels of net interest income, partially offset by higher revenues stemming from acquisitions of insurance agencies completed during 2004. In addition, results are being hampered by increased salaries and benefits expenses, professional fees, and marketing costs, resulting from Co.'s efforts to promote new deposit products and increase brand awareness in various markets. Separately, Co. is experiencing strong e-banking revenues due to higher debit card activity and additional cards issued to customers.

Financial Data

(US$ in Thousands)	3 Mos	12/31/2004	12/31/2003	12/31/2002	12/31/2001	12/31/2000	12/31/1999	12/31/1998
Earnings Per Share	1.65	1.71	1.52	2.19	1.47	1.33	1.20	1.11
Cash Flow Per Share	4.24	3.11	2.71	3.03	2.73	1.92	1.60	1.50
Tang Book Value Per Share	9.84	10.00	11.52	11.85	11.43	10.09	9.58	9.75
Dividends Per Share	0.730	0.720	0.645	0.558	0.488	0.441	0.392	0.343
Dividend Payout %	44.24	42.11	42.45	25.49	33.15	33.14	32.52	30.98
Income Statement								
Interest Income	22,643	87,030	91,655	82,968	86,107	85,129	72,346	63,645
Interest Expense	9,931	35,160	38,050	32,970	42,974	44,839	34,258	30,497
Net Interest Income	12,712	51,870	53,605	49,998	43,133	40,290	38,088	33,148
Provision for Losses	941	2,546	3,601	4,067	2,659	2,322	1,878	2,325
Non-Interest Income	7,368	22,208	17,538	15,236	10,650	8,928	7,529	7,238
Non-Interest Expense	12,747	47,198	45,903	35,967	33,412	31,062	28,197	23,276
Income Before Taxes	6,392	24,334	21,639	25,200	17,712	15,834	15,542	14,785
Income Taxes	1,700	6,059	5,385	6,858	5,377	4,708	4,824	4,740
Net Income	4,692	18,275	16,254	18,752	12,335	11,126	10,718	10,045
Average Shares	10,558	10,710	10,660	8,557	8,403	8,385	8,923	9,099
Balance Sheet								
Net Loans & Leases	997,798	1,008,298	900,423	837,805	760,499	726,035	649,569	558,408
Total Assets	1,791,629	1,809,086	1,736,104	1,394,361	1,193,966	1,135,834	1,075,450	880,284
Total Deposits	1,103,133	1,069,421	1,028,530	955,877	814,368	757,621	728,207	714,168
Total Liabilities	1,618,991	1,633,668	1,565,224	1,218,088	1,071,056	1,023,619	973,590	794,270
Stockholders' Equity	172,638	175,418	170,880	147,183	93,854	83,194	72,874	86,014
Shares Outstanding	10,393	10,435	10,603	9,829	8,213	8,245	7,608	8,821
Statistical Record								
Return on Assets %	1.00	1.03	1.04	1.45	1.06	1.00	1.10	1.23
Return on Equity %	10.11	10.53	10.22	15.56	13.93	14.22	13.49	12.19
Net Interest Margin %	56.14	59.60	58.49	60.26	50.09	47.33	52.65	52.08
Efficiency Ratio %	42.47	43.21	42.04	36.62	34.53	33.02	35.30	32.84
Loans to Deposits	0.90	0.94	0.88	0.88	0.93	0.96	0.89	0.78
Price Range	32.12-23.47	32.12-23.47	30.10-19.68	29.56-15.84	20.09-12.59	15.38-10.23	20.66-14.39	22.60-14.31
P/E Ratio	19.47-14.22	18.78-13.73	19.80-12.95	13.50-7.23	13.66-8.57	11.57-7.69	17.22-11.99	20.36-12.89
Average Yield %	2.76	2.66	2.57	2.38	3.21	3.63	2.24	1.86

Address: 138 Putnam Street, P.O. Box 738, Marietta, OH 45750-0738
Telephone: 740-373-3155
Web Site: www.peoplesbancorp.com

Officers: Robert E. Evans - Chmn. Joseph H. Wesel - Vice-Chmn. **Transfer Agents:** Register and Transfer Company

Investor Contact: 740-374-6136
No of Institutions: 57
Shares: 4,159,935 **% Held:** 40.01

PEOPLE'S BANK

Exchange	Symbol	Price	52Wk Range	Yield	P/E
NMS	PBCT	$28.31 (5/31/2005)	29.50-19.27	3.11	23.79

***7 Year Price Score 159.56** *NYSE Composite Index=100 ***12 Month Price Score 110.64**

TRADING VOLUME (thousand shares)

Interim Earnings (Per Share)

Qtr.	Mar	Jun	Sep	Dec
2002			0.40	
2003	0.12	0.11	0.11	0.12
2004	0.85	...	...	...

Interim Dividends (Per Share)

Amt	Decl	Ex	Rec	Pay
0.193Q	10/21/2004	10/28/2004	11/1/2004	11/15/2004
0.193Q	1/20/2005	1/28/2005	2/1/2005	2/15/2005
3-for-2	4/14/2005	5/16/2005	5/1/2005	5/15/2005
0.22Q	4/21/2005	4/27/2005	5/1/2005	5/15/2005

Indicated Div: $0.88 (Div. Reinv. Plan)

Valuation Analysis

Forecast P/E	0.00 (6/2/2005)		
Market Cap	$4.0 Billion	Book Value	1.2 Billion
Price/Book	3.43	Price/Sales	5.66

Dividend Achiever Status

Rank	53	**10 Year Growth Rate**	18.39%
Total Years of Dividend Growth			11

Business Summary: Commercial Banking (MIC: 8.1 SIC: 022 NAIC: 22110)

People's Bank is a state-chartered stock savings bank offering a range of financial services to individual, corporate and municipal customers, primarily in Connecticut. Co. provides traditional banking services of accepting deposits and originating loans, as well as specialized financial services through its subsidiaries, including: brokerage, financial advisory services and life insurance; equipment leasing and financing; asset management; and insurance services. As of Dec 31 2004, Co. operated 8 financial centers, 73 traditional branches, 66 supermarket branches, and 8 limited-service branches. At Dec 31 2004, Co. had total assets of $10.72 billion.

Recent Developments: For the three months ended Mar 31 2005, income from continuing operations was $29.8 million compared with a loss of $77.8 million in the corresponding year-earlier period. Results for 2005 included liability restructuring costs of $133.4 million. Net interest income increased 24.4% to $91.2 million from $73.3 million the previous year. Provision for loan losses amounted to $1.3 million for 2004 versus a recovery of $100,000 in the year-ago period. Total non-interest income advanced 7.8% to $37.3 million compared with $34.6 million the year before.

Prospects: Co.'s results for the first quarter ended Mar 31 2005 were aided by solid loan growth across its commercial and consumer businesses. For instance, for the first quarter of 2005, Co.'s average commercial banking, home equity and residential mortgage loan portfolios advanced 11.8% from first quarter of 2004. Co.'s results have also benefited from its sharp focus on expenses, as evidenced by the reduction in operating expenses versus the year-ago quarter. Looking ahead, Co. has indicated that it will expand its statewide branch network in 2005, notably in Fairfield County, which it views as a particularly attractive market.

Financial Data

(US$ in Thousands)	3 Mos	12/31/2003	12/31/2002	12/31/2001	12/31/2000	12/31/1999	12/31/1998	12/31/1997
Earnings Per Share	1.19	0.46	0.40	0.55	0.79	0.80	0.64	0.67
Cash Flow Per Share	1.01	1.05	0.26	0.67	1.56	1.27	0.89	1.06
Tang Book Value Per Share	7.45	6.37	5.95	5.92	5.49	4.71	5.00	5.16
Dividends Per Share	0.693	0.680	0.631	0.596	0.533	0.458	0.373	0.299
Dividend Payout %	58.27	148.54	157.78	108.94	67.80	56.91	58.33	44.59
Income Statement								
Interest Income	107,200	514,700	614,200	727,100	766,800	666,800	593,100	524,800
Interest Expense	33,900	194,300	263,000	373,100	381,700	328,900	305,900	271,800
Net Interest Income	73,300	320,400	351,200	354,000	385,100	337,900	287,200	253,000
Provision for Losses	(100)	48,600	77,700	101,100	59,900	54,500	45,800	39,900
Non-Interest Income	34,500	251,000	247,900	320,500	293,000	300,800	310,500	250,000
Non-Interest Expense	227,700	435,900	441,000	440,500	452,700	413,800	378,500	319,000
Income Before Taxes	(119,800)	86,900	80,400	132,900	165,500	170,400	173,400	144,100
Income Taxes	(41,700)	23,100	25,000	46,200	57,100	58,400	81,700	51,700
Net Income	119,200	63,800	55,400	75,800	108,400	112,000	91,700	92,400
Average Shares	140,625	139,275	138,825	138,600	138,150	139,500	143,707	138,150
Balance Sheet								
Net Loans & Leases	7,164,600	8,121,800	7,336,200	6,931,000	7,344,700	6,969,600	6,481,100	5,389,600
Total Assets	10,669,100	11,671,500	12,260,600	11,890,600	11,570,900	10,738,100	9,918,700	8,184,000
Total Deposits	8,793,100	8,714,000	8,426,100	7,983,400	7,761,300	7,191,100	6,937,500	5,818,400
Total Liabilities	9,510,400	10,669,500	11,321,000	10,955,600	10,689,100	9,956,400	9,066,400	7,474,100
Stockholders' Equity	1,158,700	1,002,000	939,600	935,000	881,800	781,700	852,300	709,900
Shares Outstanding	140,400	139,500	138,825	138,375	137,925	137,475	143,361	137,610
Statistical Record								
Return on Assets %	1.07	0.53	0.46	0.65	0.97	1.08	1.01	1.17
Return on Equity %	11.06	6.57	5.91	8.34	13.00	13.71	11.74	13.92
Net Interest Margin %	68.38	62.25	57.18	48.69	50.22	50.67	48.42	48.21
Efficiency Ratio %	160.69	56.93	51.15	42.05	42.72	42.77	41.89	41.17
Loans to Deposits	0.81	0.93	0.87	0.87	0.95	0.97	0.93	0.93
Price Range	20.66-11.22	15.06-10.88	12.40-9.22	12.56-9.34	11.92-7.56	14.19-8.89	18.28-8.50	16.89-8.43
P/E Ratio	17.36-9.43	32.74-23.66	31.00-23.06	22.83-16.98	15.08-9.56	17.74-11.11	28.56-13.28	25.21-12.58
Average Yield %	4.80	5.34	5.83	5.61	5.86	3.80	2.59	2.49

Address: 850 Main Street, Bridgeport, CT 06604
Telephone: 203-338-7171
Web Site: www.peoples.com

Officers: John A. Klein - Chmn., Pres., C.E.O. Jacinta A. Coleman - Exec. V.P., Chief Info. Off. **Transfer Agents:** Mellon Investor Services, LLC, Ridgefield Park, NJ

Investor Contact: 203-338-4114
No of Institutions: 142
Shares: 19,869,704 **% Held:** 21.57

PEOPLES ENERGY CORP.

Exchange	Symbol	Price	52Wk Range	Yield	P/E
NYS	PGL	$42.75 (5/31/2005)	45.28-38.96	5.10	23.75

*7 Year Price Score 97.80 *NYSE Composite Index=100 *12 Month Price Score 94.39

Interim Earnings (Per Share)

Qtr.	Dec	Mar	Jun	Sep
2001-02	0.87	1.55	0.04	0.05
2002-03	0.87	1.77	0.22	0.02
2003-04	0.85	1.46	0.15	(0.28)
2004-05	0.59	1.34	...	...

Interim Dividends (Per Share)

Amt	Decl	Ex	Rec	Pay
0.54Q	6/2/2004	6/18/2004	6/22/2004	7/15/2004
0.54Q	8/4/2004	9/20/2004	9/22/2004	10/15/2004
0.54Q	12/3/2004	12/20/2004	12/22/2004	1/14/2005
0.545Q	2/4/2005	3/18/2005	3/22/2005	4/15/2005

Indicated Div: $2.18 (Div. Reinv. Plan)

Valuation Analysis

Forecast P/E	16.42 (6/1/2005)		
Market Cap	$1.6 Billion	Book Value	877.8 Million
Price/Book	1.85	Price/Sales	0.65

Dividend Achiever Status

Rank	308	10 Year Growth Rate	1.82%
Total Years of Dividend Growth			21

Business Summary: Gas Utilities (MIC: 7.4 SIC: 924 NAIC: 21210)

Peoples Energy is a holding company. Co.'s regulated utility subsidiaries include The Peoples Gas Light and Coke Company (Peoples Gas) and North Shore Gas Company (North Shore Gas). As of Sep 30 2004, Peoples Gas and North Shore Gas purchased, stored, distributed, sold and transported natural gas to approximately 1.0 million customers through a 6,000-mile distribution system serving Chicago and 54 communities in northeastern Illinois. The customer base includes residential, commercial and industrial sales and transportation accounts. Other businesses of Co. include oil and gas production, power generation, midstream services and retail energy services.

Recent Developments: For the quarter ended Mar 31 2005, net income decreased 6.8% to $51,172 thousand from net income of $54,904 thousand in the year-earlier quarter. Revenues were $1,026,906 thousand, up 10.8% from $927,021 thousand the year before. Operating income was $90,745 thousand versus an income of $94,941 thousand in the prior-year quarter, a decrease of 4.4%. Total indirect expense was $939,449 thousand versus $833,569 thousand in the prior-year quarter, an increase of 12.7%.

Prospects: Despite the favorable effect of restructuring to lower labor-related costs and the positive growth from Co.'s Midwest-based energy businesses, Co. will not be able to overcome the approximately $0.20 per share negative effects of the warm winter, as well as shortfalls in its oil and gas production volumes. Accordingly, Co. has lowered its fiscal 2005 earnings estimate to a range to $2.30 to $2.45 per share on a GAAP basis, which includes a restructuring charge of approximately $0.22 per share. Meanwhile, Co. expects production in its Oil and Gas segment to rise during the second half of fiscal 2005.

Financial Data (US$ in Thousands)	6 Mos	3 Mos	09/30/2004	09/30/2003	09/30/2002	09/30/2001	09/30/2000	09/30/1999
Earnings Per Share	1.80	1.90	2.18	2.87	2.51	2.74	2.44	2.61
Cash Flow Per Share	5.94	5.06	5.41	5.71	9.26	4.79	1.44	5.18
Tang Book Value Per Share	23.12	23.34	23.06	23.11	22.74	22.66	21.86	21.66
Dividends Per Share	2.165	2.160	2.150	2.110	2.070	2.030	1.990	1.950
Dividend Payout %	120.28	113.45	98.62	73.52	82.47	74.09	81.56	74.71
Income Statement								
Total Revenue	1,764,317	737,411	2,260,199	2,138,394	1,482,534	2,270,218	1,417,533	1,194,381
EBITDA	201,111	79,068	293,035	329,330	295,174	315,568	283,615	268,259
Depn & Amortn	62,075	31,742	125,212	116,773	98,852	95,046	100,935	83,531
Income Before Taxes	113,682	34,816	119,397	163,116	135,392	148,471	129,761	145,217
Income Taxes	40,034	12,340	37,833	59,182	46,321	51,417	43,346	52,581
Net Income	73,648	22,476	81,564	103,934	89,071	97,020	86,415	92,636
Average Shares	38,093	37,993	37,490	36,193	35,492	35,439	35,413	35,490
Balance Sheet								
Net PPE	1,909,190	1,903,172	1,904,185	1,838,173	1,773,901	1,753,912	1,645,340	1,519,836
Total Assets	3,322,160	3,320,292	3,094,790	2,928,538	2,723,647	2,994,054	2,501,918	2,100,164
Long-Term Obligations	895,647	897,207	897,377	744,345	554,014	644,308	419,663	521,734
Total Liabilities	2,444,358	2,436,499	2,224,707	2,080,539	1,917,323	2,188,537	1,724,836	1,331,434
Stockholders' Equity	877,802	883,793	870,083	847,999	806,324	805,517	777,082	768,730
Shares Outstanding	37,968	37,867	37,733	36,689	35,459	35,544	35,544	35,489
Statistical Record								
Return on Assets %	2.13	2.22	2.70	3.68	3.12	3.53	3.75	4.63
Return on Equity %	7.73	8.26	9.47	12.57	11.05	12.26	11.15	12.27
EBITDA Margin %	11.40	10.72	12.97	15.40	19.91	13.90	20.01	22.46
Net Margin %	4.17	3.05	3.61	4.86	6.01	4.27	6.10	7.76
PPE Turnover	1.31	1.26	1.20	1.18	0.84	1.34	0.89	0.81
Asset Turnover	0.77	0.73	0.75	0.76	0.52	0.83	0.61	0.60
Debt to Equity	1.02	1.02	1.03	0.88	0.69	0.80	0.54	0.68
Price Range	45.28-38.96	45.91-38.96	45.91-38.92	45.12-31.68	42.62-29.83	46.56-31.81	39.44-26.81	40.00-32.31
P/E Ratio	25.16-21.64	24.16-20.51	21.06-17.85	15.72-11.04	16.98-11.88	16.99-11.61	16.16-10.99	15.33-12.38
Average Yield %	5.10	5.07	5.14	5.45	5.56	5.22	6.06	5.28

Address: 130 East Randolph Drive, 24th Floor, Chicago, IL 60601-6207
Telephone: 312-240-4000
Web Site: www.peoplesenergy.com

Officers: Thomas M. Patrick - Chmn., Pres., C.E.O. William E. Morrow - Exec. V.P., Opers. **Transfer Agents:** LaSalle Bank, N.A., Chicago, IL

Investor Contact: 312-240-4730
No of Institutions: 177
Shares: 19,643,184 **% Held:** 51.81

PEPSICO INC.

Exchange	Symbol	Price	52Wk Range	Yield	P/E
NYS	PEP	$56.26 (5/31/2005)	57.12-47.85	1.85	22.33

***7 Year Price Score 104.78** *NYSE Composite Index=100 ***12 Month Price Score 102.38**

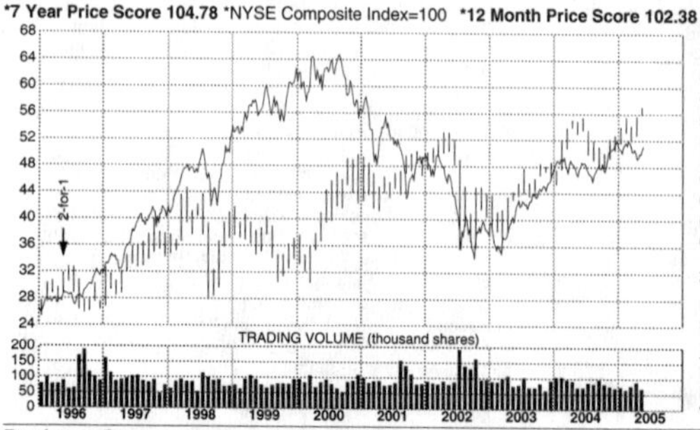

TRADING VOLUME (thousand shares)

Interim Earnings (Per Share)

Qtr.	Mar	Jun	Aug	Dec
2002	0.36	0.49	0.54	0.46
2003	0.45	0.58	0.62	0.41
2004	0.46	0.61	0.79	0.58
2005	0.53	...	...	...

Interim Dividends (Per Share)

Amt	Decl	Ex	Rec	Pay
0.23Q	7/23/2004	9/8/2004	9/10/2004	9/30/2004
0.23Q	11/19/2004	12/8/2004	12/10/2004	1/3/2005
0.23Q	1/27/2005	3/9/2005	3/11/2005	3/31/2005
0.26Q	5/4/2005	6/8/2005	6/10/2005	6/30/2005

Indicated Div: $1.04 (Div. Reinv. Plan)

Valuation Analysis

Forecast P/E	15.59 (6/2/2005)		
Market Cap	$94.3 Billion	Book Value	14.0 Billion
Price/Book	6.75	Price/Sales	3.17

Dividend Achiever Status

Rank	201	10 Year Growth Rate	8.66%
Total Years of Dividend Growth			33

Business Summary: Food (MIC: 4.1 SIC: 086 NAIC: 12111)

PepsiCo is a global snack and beverage company. Co. manufactures, markets and sells a variety of salty, convenient, sweet and grain-based snacks, carbonated and non-carbonated beverages and foods. Co.'s Frito-Lay North America division's brands include Lay's potato chips, Fritos corn chips, Quaker Chewy granola bars and Rold Gold pretzels. PepsiCo Beverages North America brands include Pepsi, Mountain Dew, Sierra Mist, Mug, SoBe, Gatorade, Tropicana Pure Premium and Propel. PepsiCo International brands include Sabritas in Mexico, Walkers in the UK, and Smith's in Australia. Quaker Foods North America's products include Quaker oatmeal and Cap'n Crunch and Life ready-to-eat cereals.

Recent Developments: For the first quarter ended Mar 19 2005, net income advanced 13.4% to $912.0 million compared with $804.0 million in the corresponding prior-year quarter. Net revenues increased 7.4% to $6.59 billion from $6.13 billion a year earlier. Frito-Lay North America revenue grew 5.5% to $2.26 billion, while Pepsico Beverages North America revenue rose 3.8% to $1.78 billion. Pepsico International revenue climbed 12.2% to $2.12 billion, and Quaker Foods North America revenue was up 10.3% to $417.0 million. Cost of sales rose 7.4% to $3.02 billion from $2.81 billion the year before. Operating profit amounted to $1.25 billion versus $1.13 billion in the previous year, an increase of 10.6%.

Prospects: Results are benefiting from strong earnings growth in Co.'s international operations, fueled by robust demand for both snacks and drinks in India, China, Russia and Brazil. Looking ahead, Co. is targeting full-year 2005 earnings of at least $2.60 per share. Separately, on May 2 2005, Co. announced that it has entered into an agreement to acquire Punica Getranke GmbH, a major manufacturer and distributor of fruit juices and juice drinks in Germany, from Sunny Delight Beverages Co. The acquisition will significantly expand Co.'s juice business in Continental Europe. Terms of the transaction were not disclosed.

Financial Data

(US$ in Thousands)	3 Mos	12/25/2004	12/27/2003	12/28/2002	12/29/2001	12/30/2000	12/25/1999	12/26/1998
Earnings Per Share	2.52	2.44	2.05	1.85	1.47	1.48	1.37	1.31
Cash Flow Per Share	3.04	2.99	2.53	2.65	2.39	2.66	2.07	2.18
Tang Book Value Per Share	5.08	4.84	3.82	2.37	2.17	1.91	1.47	N.M.
Dividends Per Share	0.920	0.850	0.630	0.595	0.575	0.555	0.535	0.515
Dividend Payout %	36.57	34.84	30.73	32.16	39.12	37.50	39.05	39.31
Income Statement								
Total Revenue	6,585,000	29,261,000	26,971,000	25,112,000	26,935,000	20,438,000	20,367,000	22,348,000
EBITDA	1,594,000	6,848,000	6,269,000	6,077,000	5,189,000	4,209,000	4,843,000	3,818,000
Depn & Amortn	282,000	1,209,000	1,165,000	1,067,000	1,008,000	854,000	942,000	1,234,000
Income Before Taxes	1,285,000	5,546,000	4,992,000	4,868,000	4,029,000	3,210,000	3,656,000	2,263,000
Income Taxes	373,000	1,372,000	1,424,000	1,555,000	1,367,000	1,027,000	1,606,000	270,000
Net Income	912,000	4,212,000	3,568,000	3,313,000	2,662,000	2,183,000	2,050,000	1,993,000
Average Shares	1,713,000	1,729,000	1,739,000	1,789,000	1,807,000	1,475,000	1,496,000	1,519,000
Balance Sheet								
Current Assets	8,876,000	8,639,000	6,930,000	6,413,000	5,853,000	4,604,000	4,173,000	4,362,000
Total Assets	28,671,000	27,987,000	25,327,000	23,474,000	21,695,000	18,339,000	17,551,000	22,660,000
Current Liabilities	7,194,000	6,752,000	6,415,000	6,052,000	4,998,000	3,935,000	3,788,000	7,914,000
Long-Term Obligations	2,390,000	2,397,000	1,702,000	2,187,000	2,651,000	2,346,000	2,812,000	4,028,000
Total Liabilities	14,758,000	14,464,000	13,453,000	14,183,000	13,021,000	11,090,000	10,670,000	16,259,000
Stockholders' Equity	13,968,000	13,572,000	11,896,000	9,298,000	8,648,000	7,249,000	6,881,000	6,401,000
Shares Outstanding	1,677,000	1,679,000	1,705,000	1,722,000	1,756,000	1,446,000	1,455,000	1,471,000
Statistical Record								
Return on Assets %	15.98	15.84	14.66	14.71	13.34	11.97	10.22	9.35
Return on Equity %	32.69	33.17	33.76	37.02	33.58	30.40	30.95	29.97
EBITDA Margin %	24.21	23.40	23.24	24.20	19.26	20.59	23.78	17.08
Net Margin %	13.85	14.39	13.23	13.19	9.88	10.68	10.07	8.92
Asset Turnover	1.10	1.10	1.11	1.11	1.35	1.12	1.02	1.05
Current Ratio	1.23	1.28	1.08	1.06	1.17	1.17	1.10	0.55
Debt to Equity	0.17	0.18	0.14	0.24	0.31	0.32	0.41	0.63
Price Range	55.55-47.85	55.55-45.39	48.71-37.30	53.12-35.50	50.28-41.26	49.75-30.50	41.81-30.50	44.69-27.88
P/E Ratio	22.04-18.99	22.77-18.60	23.76-18.20	28.71-19.19	34.20-28.07	33.61-20.61	30.52-22.26	34.11-21.28
Average Yield %	1.76	1.66	1.43	1.29	1.25	1.36	1.46	1.37

Address: 700 Anderson Hill Road, Purchase, NY 10577-1444
Telephone: 914-253-2000
Web Site: www.pepsico.com

Officers: Steven S. Reinemund - Chmn., C.E.O. Indra K. Nooyi - Pres., C.F.O. **Transfer Agents:** The Bank of New York

Investor Contact: 914-253-3035
No of Institutions: 1011
Shares: 1,087,719,936 **% Held:** 64.82

PFIZER INC

Exchange	Symbol	Price	52Wk Range	Yield	P/E
NYS	PFE	$27.90 (5/31/2005)	36.14-23.86	2.72	23.25

***7 Year Price Score 70.51** *NYSE Composite Index=100 ***12 Month Price Score 92.03**

TRADING VOLUME (thousand shares)

Interim Earnings (Per Share)

Qtr.	Mar	Jun	Sep	Dec
2002	0.37	0.32	0.38	0.46
2003	0.76	(0.48)	0.29	0.08
2004	0.30	0.38	0.44	0.37
2005	0.04	...	...	...

Interim Dividends (Per Share)

Amt	Decl	Ex	Rec	Pay
0.17Q	6/24/2004	8/11/2004	8/13/2004	9/3/2004
0.17Q	10/28/2004	11/9/2004	11/12/2004	12/3/2004
0.19Q	12/13/2004	2/9/2005	2/11/2005	3/8/2005
0.19Q	4/28/2005	5/11/2005	5/13/2005	6/7/2005

Indicated Div: $0.76 (Div. Reinv. Plan)

Valuation Analysis

Forecast P/E	14.32 (6/1/2005)		
Market Cap	$207.4 Billion	Book Value	67.5 Billion
Price/Book	3.07	Price/Sales	3.97

Dividend Achiever Status

Rank	78	**10 Year Growth Rate**	15.81%
Total Years of Dividend Growth			37

Business Summary: Pharmaceuticals (MIC: 9.1 SIC: 834 NAIC: 25412)

Pfizer is a research-based, global pharmaceutical company that discovers, develops, manufactures and markets medicines for humans and animals as well as consumer healthcare products. The products include Norvasc, for the treatment of hypertension and angina, Zyrtec, an anti-allergy medicine, Viagra, an oral medication for the treatment of erectile dysfunction, Zoloft, a selective serotonin re-uptake inhibitor for the treatment of depression. The animal health segment includes anti-parasitic, anti-infective and anti-inflammatory medicines, and vaccines. The consumer healthcare segment includes Nicorette, for tobacco dependence and Benadryl antihistamine for allergies.

Recent Developments: For the quarter ended Apr 3 2005, income from continuing operations decreased 88.3% to $272 million from income of $2,318 million in the year-earlier quarter. Net income decreased 87.1% to $301 million from net income of $2,331 million in the year-earlier quarter. Revenues were $13,091 million, up 4.8% from $12,487 million the year before. Total direct expense was $2,191 million versus $1,794 million in the prior-year quarter, an increase of 22.1%. Total indirect expense was $7,990 million versus $7,564 million in the prior-year quarter, an increase of 5.6%.

Prospects: Top-line growth is being fueled by strong sales of Co.'s cholesterol-lowering drug Lipitor and antibiotic Zithromax. These gains were partially offset by sharply lower sales from Co.'s pain relievers Bextra and Celebrex. For 2005, Co. is targeting earnings of about $1.98 per share. Meanwhile, Co. is taking aggressive steps to stimulate long-term earnings growth. Co. is implementing a series of initiatives, including staff reductions, changes to purchase arrangements and plant closings, expected to cut $4.00 billion in costs by 2008 as part of a program to drive a return to double-digit earnings growth in 2006 and 2007.

Financial Data (US$ in Thousands)	3 Mos	12/31/2004	12/31/2003	12/31/2002	12/31/2001	12/31/2000	12/31/1999	12/31/1998
Earnings Per Share	1.20	1.49	0.54	1.46	1.22	0.59	0.82	0.85
Cash Flow Per Share	2.39	2.16	1.63	1.60	1.49	0.99	0.81	0.77
Tang Book Value Per Share	1.70	1.48	0.85	3.04	2.64	2.26	2.11	2.06
Dividends Per Share	0.700	0.680	0.600	0.520	0.440	0.360	0.307	0.253
Dividend Payout %	58.09	45.64	111.11	35.62	36.07	61.02	37.40	29.80
Income Statement								
Total Revenue	13,091,000	52,516,000	45,188,000	32,373,000	32,259,000	29,574,000	16,204,000	13,544,000
EBITDA	4,276,000	19,101,000	7,265,000	12,701,000	11,124,000	6,577,000	4,912,000	3,034,000
Depn & Amortn	1,366,000	5,093,000	4,078,000	1,036,000	1,068,000	968,000	542,000	489,000
Income Before Taxes	2,910,000	14,007,000	3,263,000	11,796,000	10,329,000	5,781,000	4,448,000	2,594,000
Income Taxes	2,635,000	2,665,000	1,621,000	2,609,000	2,561,000	2,049,000	1,244,000	642,000
Net Income	301,000	11,361,000	3,910,000	9,126,000	7,788,000	3,726,000	3,179,000	3,351,000
Average Shares	7,474,001	7,614,001	7,286,001	6,240,999	6,360,999	6,367,999	3,884,000	3,945,000
Balance Sheet								
Current Assets	42,353,000	39,694,000	29,741,000	24,781,000	18,450,000	17,187,000	11,191,000	9,931,000
Total Assets	122,935,000	123,684,000	116,775,000	46,356,000	39,153,000	33,510,000	20,574,000	18,302,000
Current Liabilities	28,948,000	26,458,000	23,657,000	18,555,000	13,640,000	11,981,000	9,185,000	7,192,000
Long-Term Obligations	6,432,000	7,279,000	5,755,000	3,140,000	2,609,000	1,123,000	525,000	527,000
Total Liabilities	55,403,000	55,406,000	51,398,000	26,406,000	20,860,000	17,434,000	11,687,000	9,492,000
Stockholders' Equity	67,532,000	68,278,000	65,377,000	19,950,000	18,293,000	16,076,000	8,887,000	8,810,000
Shares Outstanding	7,435,345	7,473,001	7,629,001	6,161,999	6,276,999	6,313,999	3,847,000	3,883,000
Statistical Record								
Return on Assets %	7.46	9.42	4.79	21.35	21.44	13.74	16.35	19.92
Return on Equity %	13.39	16.95	9.16	47.73	45.32	29.77	35.93	40.03
EBITDA Margin %	32.66	36.37	16.08	39.23	34.48	22.24	30.31	22.40
Net Margin %	2.30	21.63	8.65	28.19	24.14	12.60	19.62	24.74
Asset Turnover	0.43	0.44	0.55	0.76	0.89	1.09	0.83	0.81
Current Ratio	1.46	1.50	1.26	1.34	1.35	1.43	1.22	1.38
Debt to Equity	0.10	0.11	0.09	0.16	0.14	0.07	0.06	0.06
Price Range	37.62-23.86	38.85-24.29	36.18-28.56	42.15-25.92	46.13-35.67	49.00-30.00	50.04-31.71	42.04-24.65
P/E Ratio	31.35-19.88	26.07-16.30	67.00-52.89	28.87-17.75	37.81-29.24	83.05-50.85	61.03-38.67	49.46-29.00
Average Yield %	2.31	2.06	1.88	1.49	1.06	0.87	0.80	0.75

Address: 235 East 42nd Street, New York, NY 10017-5755
Telephone: 212-573-2323
Web Site: www.pfizer.com

Officers: Henry A. McKinnell - Chmn., Pres., C.E.O. Jeffery B. Kindler - Exec. V.P., Gen. Couns. **Transfer Agents:** EquiServe Trust Company, N.A., Jersey City, NJ

No of Institutions: 1274
Shares: 4,571,825,664 **% Held:** 61.29

PIEDMONT NATURAL GAS CO., INC.

Exchange	Symbol	Price	52Wk Range	Yield	P/E
NYS	PNY	$24.46 (5/31/2005)	24.54-20.30	3.76	20.91

***7 Year Price Score 111.38** *NYSE Composite Index=100 ***12 Month Price Score 99.72**

Interim Earnings (Per Share)

Qtr.	Jan	Apr	Jul	Oct
2001-02	0.63	0.64	(0.14)	(0.18)
2002-03	0.87	0.47	(0.14)	(0.07)
2003-04	1.09	0.54	(0.11)	(0.19)
2004-05	0.93	...	...	...

Interim Dividends (Per Share)

Amt	Decl	Ex	Rec	Pay
0.215Q	8/27/2004	9/22/2004	9/24/2004	10/15/2004
100%	8/27/2004	11/1/2004	10/11/2004	10/29/2004
0.215Q	12/10/2004	12/20/2004	12/22/2004	1/14/2005
0.23Q	3/4/2005	3/22/2005	3/24/2005	4/15/2005

Indicated Div: $0.92 (Div. Reinv. Plan)

Valuation Analysis

Forecast P/E	18.88 (6/1/2005)		
Market Cap	$1.9 Billion	Book Value	910.2 Million
Price/Book	2.06	Price/Sales	1.18

Dividend Achiever Status

Rank	262	**10 Year Growth Rate**	5.22%
Total Years of Dividend Growth			25

Business Summary: Gas Utilities (MIC: 7.4 SIC: 924 NAIC: 21210)

Piedmont Natural Gas is an energy services company primarily engaged in the distribution of natural gas to 960,000 residential, commercial and industrial customers in portions of North Carolina, South Carolina and Tennessee, including 60,000 customers served by municipalities who are its wholesale customers. Co.'s subsidiaries are invested in joint venture, energy-related businesses, including unregulated retail natural gas marketing, interstate natural gas storage, intrastate natural gas transportation and regulated natural gas distribution. Also, Co. sells residential and commercial gas appliances in Tennessee.

Recent Developments: For the quarter ended Jan 31 2005, net income decreased 4.5% to $71,277 thousand from net income of $74,622 thousand in the year-earlier quarter. Revenues were $680,556 thousand, up 10.0% from $618,785 thousand the year before. Operating income was $78,919 thousand versus an income of $77,349 thousand in the prior-year quarter, an increase of 2.0%. Total direct expense was $477,936 thousand versus $422,305 thousand in the prior-year quarter, an increase of 13.2%. Total indirect expense was $123,701 thousand versus $119,131 thousand in the prior-year quarter, an increase of 3.8%.

Prospects: Based on strong margin improvement and slower growth in operations and maintenance expenses, Co.'s outlook for 2005 appears optimistic. Accordingly, Co. reaffirmed its fiscal year 2005 earnings guidance of $1.23 to $1.30 per diluted share. The 2005 earnings guidance assumes normal weather for the remainder of the fiscal year, a stable economy and wholesale natural gas prices in the range of prices that prevailed during fiscal year 2004. No general rate case activity is expected that would impact 2005 earnings in any of Co.'s jurisdictions.

Financial Data

(US$ in Thousands)	3 Mos	10/31/2004	10/31/2003	10/31/2002	10/31/2001	10/31/2000	10/31/1999	10/31/1998
Earnings Per Share	1.17	1.27	1.11	0.94	1.01	1.00	0.93	0.98
Cash Flow Per Share	0.94	2.07	1.49	1.66	2.49	0.86	0.51	2.02
Tang Book Value Per Share	11.23	10.52	8.61	8.91	8.63	8.26	7.86	7.45
Dividends Per Share	0.860	0.853	0.823	0.792	0.760	0.720	0.680	0.640
Dividend Payout %	73.57	67.13	74.10	83.86	75.25	71.64	73.12	65.31
Income Statement								
Total Revenue	680,556	1,529,739	1,220,822	832,028	1,107,856	830,377	686,470	765,277
Depn & Amortn	22,064	86,786	63,611	57,837	52,511	51,532	47,359	45,555
Income Taxes	46,576	63,147	8,524	9,010	7,300	...	...	...
Net Income	71,277	95,188	74,362	62,217	65,485	64,031	58,207	60,313
Average Shares	76,925	74,797	67,006	65,874	64,840	63,558	62,484	61,434
Balance Sheet								
Net PPE	1,856,230	1,850,796	1,813,414	1,159,601	1,115,862	1,071,983	1,046,975	990,640
Total Assets	2,576,278	2,335,877	2,296,406	1,445,088	1,393,658	1,445,003	1,288,657	1,162,844
Long-Term Obligations	660,000	660,000	460,000	462,000	509,000	451,000	423,000	371,000
Total Liabilities	1,666,095	1,480,979	1,666,211	855,492	833,279	917,631	796,910	704,576
Stockholders' Equity	910,183	854,898	630,195	589,596	560,379	527,372	491,747	458,268
Shares Outstanding	76,757	76,670	67,310	66,180	64,926	63,828	62,589	61,476
Statistical Record								
Return on Assets %	3.64	4.10	3.97	4.38	4.61	4.67	4.75	5.34
Return on Equity %	10.26	12.78	12.19	10.82	12.04	12.53	12.25	13.74
Net Margin %	10.47	6.22	6.09	7.48	5.91	7.71	8.48	7.88
PPE Turnover	0.86	0.83	0.82	0.73	1.01	0.78	0.67	0.79
Asset Turnover	0.63	0.66	0.65	0.59	0.78	0.61	0.56	0.68
Debt to Equity	0.73	0.77	0.73	0.78	0.91	0.86	0.86	0.81
Price Range	23.92-19.30	22.84-19.30	20.38-16.45	18.98-14.18	19.69-14.72	16.50-11.88	18.00-14.44	18.22-13.59
P/E Ratio	20.44-16.50	17.98-15.20	18.36-14.82	20.19-15.09	19.49-14.57	16.50-11.88	19.35-15.52	18.59-13.87
Average Yield %	3.98	4.06	4.44	4.56	4.51	5.01	4.14	4.00

Address: 1915 Rexford Road, Charlotte, NC 28211 **Telephone:** 704-364-3120 **Web Site:** www.piedmontng.com	**Officers:** Thomas E. Skains - Chmn., Pres., C.E.O. David J. Dzuricky - Sr. V.P., C.F.O. **Transfer Agents:** American Stock Transfer & Trust Company, New York, NY	**Investor Contact:** 704-731-4438 **No of Institutions:** 162 **Shares:** 30,268,712 **% Held:** 39.47

PIER 1 IMPORTS INC.

Exchange	Symbol	Price	52Wk Range	Yield	P/E
NYS	PIR	$16.79 (5/31/2005)	19.78-14.35	2.38	24.69

Interim Earnings (Per Share)

Qtr.	May	Aug	Nov	Feb
2000-01	0.17	0.18	0.24	0.38
2001-02	0.13	0.14	0.26	0.51
2002-03	0.23	0.23	0.33	0.57
2003-04	0.21	0.20	0.35	0.53
2004-05	0.13	0.12	0.22	0.21

Interim Dividends (Per Share)

Amt	Decl	Ex	Rec	Pay
0.10Q	6/25/2004	8/2/2004	8/4/2004	8/18/2004
0.10Q	9/30/2004	11/1/2004	11/3/2004	11/17/2004
0.10Q	12/9/2004	1/31/2005	2/2/2005	2/16/2005
0.10Q	3/31/2005	5/2/2005	5/4/2005	5/18/2005

Indicated Div: $0.40 (Div. Reinv. Plan)

Valuation Analysis

Forecast P/E	20.18 (6/1/2005)		
Market Cap	$1.4 Billion	Book Value	664.4 Million
Price/Book	2.18	Price/Sales	0.76

Dividend Achiever Status

Rank	20	**10 Year Growth Rate**	23.94%
Total Years of Dividend Growth			13

Business Summary: Retail - Furniture & Home Furnishings (MIC: 5.9 SIC: 712 NAIC: 42110)

Pier 1 Imports is a retailer of decorative home furnishings, furniture, dining and kitchen goods, bath and bedding accessories and other specialty items for the home. As of Feb 28 2004, Co. operated 1,015 Pier 1 Imports® stores in the U.S. and 68 stores in Canada, and also supported eight franchised stores in the U.S. In addition, Co. operated 29 stores located in the U.K. under the name The Pier® and 40 Cargokids® stores located in the U.S. Co. also supplies merchandise, and licenses the Pier 1 Imports name to Sears Mexico and Sears Puerto Rico, which sells Pier 1 merchandise in a store within a store format in 20 Sears Mexico stores and in seven Sears Puerto Rico stores.

Recent Developments: For the year ended Feb 26 2005, net income decreased 48.8% to $60,457 thousand from net income of $118,001 thousand a year earlier. Revenues were $1,897,853 thousand, up 1.6% from $1,868,243 thousand the year before. Operating income was $95,762 thousand versus an income of $186,157 thousand in the prior year, a decrease of 48.6%. Total direct expense was $1,170,588 thousand versus $1,086,623 thousand in the prior year, an increase of 7.7%. Total indirect expense was $631,503 thousand versus $595,463 thousand in the prior year, an increase of 6.1%.

Prospects: Fiscal 2006 first quarter comparable-store sales are projected to be down 8.0% to 12.0% from the previous year, with diluted losses per share for the first quarter currently projected to be in a range of $0.03 to $0.10 per share. First quarter's negative projections reflect a conservative forecast and an up-front investment in the business through increased marketing, payroll and other costs to support Co.'s major initiatives, which are expected to improve store traffic and sales over the next few months. Historically, Co.'s first-quarter sales and profits are the smallest of the year.

Financial Data (US$ in Thousands)	**02/26/2005**	**02/28/2004**	**03/01/2003**	**03/02/2002**	**03/03/2001**	**02/26/2000**	**02/27/1999**	**02/28/1998**
Earnings Per Share	0.68	1.29	1.36	1.04	0.97	0.75	0.77	0.72
Cash Flow Per Share	1.64	2.00	1.90	2.59	1.12	1.25	0.98	1.06
Tang Book Value Per Share	7.70	7.74	7.10	6.27	5.53	4.70	4.14	3.86
Dividends Per Share	0.400	0.300	0.210	0.160	0.150	0.120	0.117	0.088
Dividend Payout %	58.82	23.26	15.44	15.38	15.46	16.00	15.15	12.19
Income Statement								
Total Revenue	1,897,853	1,868,243	1,754,867	1,548,556	1,411,498	1,231,095	1,138,590	1,075,405
EBITDA	157,073	253,614	254,133	204,118	196,554	165,503	168,656	156,661
Depn & Amortn	58,588	64,606	46,432	42,821	43,184	39,973	31,130	23,946
Income Before Taxes	96,841	187,316	205,374	158,997	150,240	118,612	129,610	124,011
Income Taxes	36,384	69,315	75,988	58,788	55,590	43,887	49,253	45,964
Net Income	60,457	118,001	129,386	100,209	94,650	74,725	80,357	78,047
Average Shares	88,838	91,624	95,305	96,185	97,952	103,297	108,864	112,880
Balance Sheet								
Current Assets	660,690	698,151	663,601	605,153	477,066	415,280	381,943	402,381
Total Assets	1,075,749	1,052,173	967,487	862,672	735,710	670,710	653,991	653,410
Current Liabilities	289,009	279,888	243,589	208,396	144,110	175,966	129,832	121,590
Long-Term Obligations	19,000	19,000	25,000	25,356	25,000	25,000	96,008	114,881
Total Liabilities	411,380	368,542	323,551	277,016	203,831	230,047	250,097	260,679
Stockholders' Equity	664,369	683,631	643,936	585,656	531,879	440,663	403,894	392,731
Shares Outstanding	86,320	88,306	90,734	93,417	96,160	93,830	97,672	101,854
Statistical Record								
Return on Assets %	5.70	11.72	14.18	12.57	13.24	11.31	12.33	12.79
Return on Equity %	8.99	17.83	21.10	17.98	19.15	17.74	20.23	21.87
EBITDA Margin %	8.28	13.58	14.48	13.18	13.93	13.44	14.81	14.57
Net Margin %	3.19	6.32	7.37	6.47	6.71	6.07	7.06	7.26
Asset Turnover	1.79	1.86	1.92	1.94	1.97	1.86	1.75	1.76
Current Ratio	2.29	2.49	2.72	2.90	3.31	2.36	2.94	3.31
Debt to Equity	0.03	0.03	0.04	0.04	0.05	0.06	0.24	0.29
Price Range	25.00-15.43	26.19-14.85	23.95-15.20	20.24-8.13	14.00-7.88	12.25-5.38	20.63-6.31	18.63-7.39
P/E Ratio	36.76-22.69	20.30-11.51	17.61-11.18	19.46-7.82	14.43-8.12	16.33-7.17	26.79-8.20	25.87-10.26
Average Yield %	2.11	1.46	1.08	1.20	1.36	1.52	0.92	0.73

Address: 301 Commerce Street, Suite 600, Fort Worth, TX 76102
Telephone: 817-252-8000
Web Site: www.pier1.com

Officers: Marvin J. Girouard - Chmn., C.E.O. Charles H. Turner - Exec. V.P., Fin., C.F.O., Treas. **Transfer Agents:** Mellon Investor Services, Ridgefield Park, NJ

Investor Contact: 817-252-7835
No of Institutions: 176
Shares: 73,132,072 **% Held:** 84.69

PINNACLE WEST CAPITAL CORP.

Exchange	Symbol	Price	52Wk Range	Yield	P/E
NYS	PNW	$44.12 (5/31/2005)	45.41-39.72	4.31	17.17

*7 Year Price Score 94.77 *NYSE Composite Index=100 *12 Month Price Score 98.34

TRADING VOLUME (thousand shares)

Interim Earnings (Per Share)

Qtr.	Mar	Jun	Sep	Dec
2002	0.63	0.89	1.19	(1.37)
2003	0.28	0.61	1.20	0.54
2004	0.33	0.78	1.15	0.37
2005	0.27	...	...	...

Interim Dividends (Per Share)

Amt	Decl	Ex	Rec	Pay
0.45Q	7/16/2004	7/29/2004	8/2/2004	9/1/2004
0.475Q	10/20/2004	10/28/2004	11/1/2004	12/1/2004
0.475Q	1/19/2005	1/28/2005	2/1/2005	3/1/2005
0.475Q	3/23/2005	4/28/2005	5/2/2005	6/1/2005

Indicated Div: $1.90 (Div. Reinv. Plan)

Valuation Analysis

Forecast P/E	14.71 (6/2/2005)		
Market Cap	$4.3 Billion	Book Value	3.0 Billion
Price/Book	1.45	Price/Sales	1.47

Dividend Achiever Status

Rank	209	10 Year Growth Rate	8.26%
Total Years of Dividend Growth			11

Business Summary: Electricity (MIC: 7.1 SIC: 911 NAIC: 21121)

Pinnacle West Capital is a holding company whose principal asset is Arizona Public Service (APS). APS is an electric utility that provides retail and wholesale electric service to substantially all of the state of Arizona, with the major exceptions of the Tucson metropolitan area and about one-half of the Phoenix metropolitan area. Through its marketing and trading operation, APS also generates, sells and delivers wholesale electricity. Co.'s other major subsidiaries are Pinnacle West Energy, which owns and operates generating plants; APS Energy Services, which provides competitive energy services; and SunCor, which is engaged in real estate development activities.

Recent Developments: For the quarter ended Mar 31 2005, income from continuing operations decreased 23.2% to $23,656 thousand from income of $30,791 thousand in the year-earlier quarter. Net income decreased 22.2% to $24,448 thousand from net income of $31,426 thousand in the year-earlier quarter. Revenues were $615,087 thousand, up 8.6% from $566,345 thousand the year before. Operating income was $85,256 thousand versus an income of $84,198 thousand in the prior-year quarter, an increase of 1.3%. Total direct expense was $392,036 thousand versus $341,451 thousand in the prior-year quarter, an increase of 14.8%. Total indirect expense was $137,795 thousand versus $140,696 thousand in the prior-year quarter.

Prospects: Co.'s earnings reflect a strong core business performance and rising demand for electricity in the growing Arizona market. Results are benefiting from higher retail sales at Arizona Public Service (APS) due to customer growth, lower replacement power costs due to fewer unplanned outages, lower gas and power prices and the absence of regulatory asset amortization. Meanwhile, the recent approval of Co.'s rate settlement provides a regulatory structure, which places all of its Arizona power plants in its rate base, while strengthening and clarifying APS's responsibility to provide for the energy needs of its customers.

Financial Data

(US$ in Thousands)	3 Mos	12/31/2004	12/31/2003	12/31/2002	12/31/2001	12/31/2000	12/31/1999	12/31/1998
Earnings Per Share	2.57	2.66	2.63	1.76	3.68	3.56	1.97	2.85
Cash Flow Per Share	8.83	9.19	9.88	10.26	6.74	8.23	7.50	7.15
Tang Book Value Per Share	30.43	32.14	31.00	18.99	29.46	28.09	26.00	25.50
Dividends Per Share	1.850	1.825	1.725	1.625	1.525	1.425	1.325	1.225
Dividend Payout %	71.98	68.61	65.59	92.33	41.44	40.03	67.26	42.98
Income Statement								
Total Revenue	615,087	2,899,725	2,817,852	2,637,279	4,551,373	3,690,175	2,423,353	2,130,586
EBITDA	179,288	962,819	959,530	953,567	1,125,127	1,100,278	1,005,493	970,569
Depn & Amortn	96,332	431,551	466,900	456,071	456,265	424,493	416,939	412,535
Income Before Taxes	38,388	364,075	336,136	353,253	540,902	526,184	437,837	407,485
Income Taxes	14,732	128,857	105,560	138,100	213,535	223,852	168,065	164,593
Net Income	24,448	243,195	240,579	149,408	312,166	302,332	167,887	242,892
Average Shares	92,045	91,532	91,405	84,964	84,930	84,935	85,008	85,345
Balance Sheet								
Net PPE	7,561,527	7,535,487	7,480,090	6,479,398	5,907,315	5,133,193	4,778,515	4,730,563
Total Assets	10,017,214	9,896,747	9,536,378	8,425,806	7,981,748	7,149,151	6,608,506	6,824,546
Long-Term Obligations	2,576,360	2,584,985	2,897,725	2,881,695	2,673,078	1,955,083	2,206,052	2,048,961
Total Liabilities	7,024,172	6,946,551	6,706,599	5,739,653	5,482,425	4,766,437	4,402,773	4,661,195
Stockholders' Equity	2,993,042	2,950,196	2,829,779	1,732,900	2,499,323	2,382,714	2,205,733	2,163,351
Shares Outstanding	98,350	91,793	91,287	91,255	84,824	84,824	84,824	84,824
Statistical Record								
Return on Assets %	2.42	2.50	2.68	1.82	4.13	4.38	2.50	3.55
Return on Equity %	8.04	8.39	10.55	7.06	12.79	13.14	7.69	11.59
EBITDA Margin %	29.15	33.20	34.05	36.16	24.72	29.82	41.49	45.55
Net Margin %	3.97	8.39	8.54	5.67	6.86	8.19	6.93	11.40
PPE Turnover	0.39	0.39	0.40	0.43	0.82	0.74	0.51	0.45
Asset Turnover	0.31	0.30	0.31	0.32	0.60	0.53	0.36	0.31
Debt to Equity	0.86	0.88	1.02	1.66	1.07	0.82	1.00	0.95
Price Range	45.41-36.85	45.41-36.85	40.24-29.07	46.16-22.49	50.37-38.10	51.88-25.94	42.88-30.44	48.88-39.75
P/E Ratio	17.67-14.34	17.07-13.85	15.30-11.05	26.23-12.78	13.69-10.35	14.57-7.29	21.76-15.45	17.15-13.95
Average Yield %	4.44	4.48	4.90	4.46	3.45	3.77	3.49	2.82

Address: 400 North Fifth Street, P.O. Box 53999, Phoenix, AZ 85072-3999
Telephone: 602-250-1000
Web Site: www.pinnaclewest.com

Officers: William J. Post - Chmn., C.E.O. Jack E. Davis - Pres., C.O.O **Transfer Agents:** Pinnacle West Capital Corporation, Phoenix, AZ

Investor Contact: 602-250-5668
No of Institutions: 227
Shares: 67,711,352 **% Held:** 73.53

PITNEY BOWES, INC.

Exchange	Symbol	Price	52Wk Range	Yield	P/E
NYS	PBI	$44.61 (5/31/2005)	47.30-41.05	2.78	20.75

*7 Year Price Score 90.73 *NYSE Composite Index=100 *12 Month Price Score 97.71

Interim Earnings (Per Share)

Qtr.	Mar	Jun	Sep	Dec
2002	0.53	0.59	0.61	0.24
2003	0.48	0.50	0.50	0.62
2004	0.54	0.58	0.58	0.35
2005	0.64	...	...	...

Interim Dividends (Per Share)

Amt	Decl	Ex	Rec	Pay
0.305Q	7/12/2004	8/18/2004	8/20/2004	9/12/2004
0.305Q	11/8/2004	11/17/2004	11/19/2004	12/12/2004
0.31Q	2/2/2005	2/16/2005	2/18/2005	3/12/2005
0.31Q	4/11/2005	5/18/2005	5/20/2005	6/12/2005

Indicated Div: $1.24 (Div. Reinv. Plan)

Valuation Analysis

Forecast P/E	16.97 (6/1/2005)		
Market Cap	$10.3 Billion	Book Value	1.3 Billion
Price/Book	7.76	Price/Sales	2.01

Dividend Achiever Status

Rank	195	**10 Year Growth Rate**	8.90%
Total Years of Dividend Growth			21

Business Summary: Office Equipment Supplies (MIC: 11.12 SIC: 579 NAIC: 23420)

Pitney Bowes provides integrated mail and document management applications for organizations of all sizes. The Global Mailstream Solutions segment includes the rental of postage meters and the sale, rental and financing of mailing equipment, including mail finishing and mail creation equipment. The Global Enterprise Solutions segment includes Pitney Bowes Management Services and Document Messaging Technologies. In this segment, Co. sells, rents or finances its products. The Capital Services segment consists of financing for non-Pitney Bowes equipment, and primarily includes interest and fee-based income generated by external financing arrangements.

Recent Developments: For the quarter ended Mar 31 2005, net income increased 18.2% to $149,604 thousand from net income of $126,594 thousand in the year-earlier quarter. Revenues were $1,317,788 thousand, up 12.4% from $1,171,922 thousand the year before. Total direct expense was $599,110 thousand versus $532,590 thousand in the prior-year quarter, an increase of 12.5%. Total indirect expense was $434,093 thousand versus $411,866 thousand in the prior-year quarter, an increase of 5.4%.

Prospects: Co. anticipates second quarter revenue growth in the range of 9.0% to 11.0% and adjusted diluted earnings per share in the range of $0.64 to $0.66. Co. is not able to give quarterly guidance inclusive of restructuring charges at this time because the timing of some of the restructuring activities is uncertain. Meanwhile, Co. is increasing its revenue and adjusted earnings guidance for full-year 2005. Co. expects 2005 revenue growth in the range of 8.0% to 10.0% and diluted earnings per share in the range of $2.51 to $2.64. Excluding net restructuring charges and charitable contributions, adjusted diluted earnings per share is expected to be in the range of $2.64 to $2.72.

Financial Data (US$ in Thousands)	3 Mos	12/31/2004	12/31/2003	12/31/2002	12/31/2001	12/31/2000	12/31/1999	12/31/1998
Earnings Per Share	2.15	2.05	2.11	1.97	1.97	2.41	2.34	2.06
Cash Flow Per Share	3.74	4.08	3.64	2.10	4.22	3.39	3.67	2.79
Tang Book Value Per Share	N.M.	N.M.	N.M.	0.10	1.05	4.34	5.28	5.26
Dividends Per Share	1.225	1.220	1.200	1.180	1.160	1.140	1.020	0.900
Dividend Payout %	56.98	59.51	56.87	59.90	58.88	47.30	43.59	43.69
Income Statement								
Total Revenue	1,317,788	4,957,440	4,576,853	4,409,758	4,122,474	3,880,868	4,432,608	4,220,517
EBITDA	308,969	1,170,394	1,164,632	1,047,899	1,268,006	1,316,382	1,576,001	1,374,743
Depn & Amortn	81,200	302,200	278,600	249,300	317,449	321,157	412,104	361,333
Income Before Taxes	227,769	699,448	721,091	619,445	766,384	802,848	984,572	864,177
Income Taxes	78,165	218,922	226,244	181,739	252,064	239,723	325,413	296,236
Net Income	149,604	480,526	498,117	475,750	488,343	622,546	636,212	576,394
Average Shares	233,476	234,133	236,165	241,483	247,615	258,602	272,006	279,656
Balance Sheet								
Current Assets	2,716,434	2,693,086	2,513,175	2,552,625	2,556,608	2,626,708	3,342,574	2,508,963
Total Assets	9,818,720	9,820,580	8,891,388	8,732,314	8,318,471	7,901,266	8,222,672	7,661,039
Current Liabilities	2,893,277	3,294,477	2,646,969	3,350,309	3,083,042	2,881,577	2,872,764	2,721,812
Long-Term Obligations	3,176,025	2,798,894	2,840,943	2,316,844	2,419,150	1,881,947	1,997,856	1,712,937
Total Liabilities	8,186,148	8,220,499	7,494,026	7,568,987	7,117,116	6,306,291	6,287,062	5,702,940
Stockholders' Equity	1,322,572	1,290,081	1,087,362	853,327	891,355	1,284,975	1,625,610	1,648,002
Shares Outstanding	230,026	230,318	232,288	235,373	242,028	248,800	264,694	270,378
Statistical Record								
Return on Assets %	5.30	5.12	5.65	5.58	6.02	7.70	8.01	7.41
Return on Equity %	40.82	40.31	51.33	54.54	44.88	42.66	38.87	32.74
EBITDA Margin %	23.45	23.61	25.45	23.76	30.76	33.92	35.55	32.57
Net Margin %	11.35	9.69	10.88	10.79	11.85	16.04	14.35	13.66
Asset Turnover	0.54	0.53	0.52	0.52	0.51	0.48	0.56	0.54
Current Ratio	0.94	0.82	0.95	0.76	0.83	0.91	1.16	0.92
Debt to Equity	2.40	2.17	2.61	2.72	2.71	1.46	1.23	1.04
Price Range	47.30-41.05	46.88-39.23	42.44-29.90	43.92-28.80	43.33-31.78	52.45-24.89	69.41-40.74	64.47-41.96
P/E Ratio	22.00-19.09	22.87-19.14	20.11-14.17	22.29-14.62	21.99-16.13	21.77-10.33	29.66-17.41	31.30-20.37
Average Yield %	2.77	2.83	3.26	3.11	3.09	3.01	1.73	1.80

Address: 1 Elmcroft Road, Stamford, CT 06926-0700
Telephone: 203-356-5000
Web Site: www.pb.com

Officers: Michael J. Critelli - Chmn., C.E.O. Murray D. Martin - Pres., C.O.O. **Transfer Agents:** First Chicago Trust Company of New York, Jersey City, NJ

No of Institutions: 419
Shares: 173,743,856 **% Held:** 75.27

POPULAR INC.

Exchange	Symbol	Price	52Wk Range	Yield	P/E
NMS	BPOP	$23.55 (5/31/2005)	28.87-21.01	2.72	12.02

Interim Earnings (Per Share)

Qtr.	Mar	Jun	Sep	Dec
2002	0.32	0.36	0.33	0.30
2003	0.37	0.50	0.48	0.39
2004	0.44	0.47	0.42	0.47
2005	0.60	...	...	...

Interim Dividends (Per Share)

Amt	Decl	Ex	Rec	Pay
0.16Q	8/17/2004	9/9/2004	9/13/2004	10/1/2004
0.16Q	11/24/2004	12/8/2004	12/10/2004	1/3/2005
0.16Q	2/16/2005	3/9/2005	3/11/2005	4/1/2005
0.16Q	5/11/2005	6/8/2005	6/10/2005	7/1/2005

Indicated Div: $0.64 (Div. Reinv. Plan)

Valuation Analysis

Forecast P/E	12.39 (6/2/2005)		
Market Cap	$6.3 Billion	Book Value	3.1 Billion
Price/Book	2.05	Price/Sales	2.09

Dividend Achiever Status

Rank	69	**10 Year Growth Rate**	16.79%
Total Years of Dividend Growth			12

Business Summary: Commercial Banking (MIC: 8.1 SIC: 022 NAIC: 22110)

Popular is a diversified holding company incorporated under the laws of the Commonwealth of Puerto Rico. As of Dec 31 2004, Co. had total assets of $44.40 billion. Co.'s principal subsidiary, Banco Popular de Puerto Rico, is a consumer-oriented bank operating 192 branches and over 560 automated teller machines in Puerto Rico. The bank also operates seven branches in the U.S. Virgin Islands, one branch in the British Islands and one branch in New York. Co. has three other principal subsidiaries; Popular Securities, Inc., Popular International Bank, Inc. and EVERTEC, Inc.

Recent Developments: For the quarter ended Mar 31 2005, net income increased 37.4% to $162,879 thousand from net income of $118,504 thousand in the year-earlier quarter. Net interest income was $357,286 thousand, up 8.0% from $330,714 thousand the year before. Provision for loan losses was $44,336 thousand versus $44,678 thousand in the prior-year quarter, a decrease of 0.8%. Non-interest income rose 41.6% to $205,589 thousand, while non-interest expense advanced 12.5% to $472,750 thousand.

Prospects: Results are benefiting from strong net interest income growth, which is being driven by an increase in average earning assets stemming from growth in commercial loans, mortgage loans and consumer loans. Also, loan growth is being fueled by the recent acquisitions of Quaker City Bank and Kislak Financial Corporation. Separately, during the first quarter of 2005, Co. announced that it has entered into a five-year agreement to be the official bank of the New York Mets. The agreement includes substantial advertising and community outreach opportunities for Banco Popular, including the operation of ATM's at Shea Stadium.

Financial Data

(US$ in Thousands)	3 Mos	12/31/2004	12/31/2003	12/31/2002	12/31/2001	12/31/2000	12/31/1999	12/31/1998
Earnings Per Share	1.96	1.79	1.74	1.30	1.09	0.98	0.92	0.82
Cash Flow Per Share	3.92	0.54	2.12	1.43	1.62	1.51	2.02	0.03
Tang Book Value Per Share	8.66	9.26	8.84	8.28	7.02	5.93	4.63	4.92
Dividends Per Share	0.640	0.615	0.505	0.400	0.380	0.320	0.300	0.250
Dividend Payout %	32.65	34.36	29.11	30.65	35.02	32.49	32.61	30.30
Income Statement								
Interest Income	633,280	2,216,265	2,034,238	2,023,797	2,095,862	2,150,157	1,851,670	1,651,703
Interest Expense	275,994	840,754	749,550	843,468	1,018,877	1,167,396	897,932	778,691
Net Interest Income	357,286	1,375,511	1,284,688	1,180,329	1,076,985	982,761	953,738	873,012
Provision for Losses	44,336	178,657	195,939	205,570	213,250	194,640	148,948	137,213
Non-Interest Income	205,589	608,771	626,010	523,678	465,516	465,098	372,916	291,246
Non-Interest Expense	316,834	1,171,012	1,113,083	1,029,002	920,137	877,471	837,482	720,354
Income Before Taxes	201,705	634,613	601,676	469,435	409,114	375,748	340,224	307,019
Income Taxes	42,433	144,705	130,326	117,255	105,280	100,797	85,120	74,671
Net Income	162,879	489,908	470,915	351,932	304,538	276,103	257,558	232,348
Average Shares	267,428	266,674	265,595	267,830	272,476	271,814	271,171	271,064
Balance Sheet								
Net Loans & Leases	27,752,475	27,554,452	21,922,058	18,116,395	16,892,431	14,942,531	13,996,446	12,167,387
Total Assets	45,167,838	44,401,576	36,434,715	33,660,352	30,744,676	28,057,051	25,460,539	23,160,357
Total Deposits	21,728,677	20,593,160	18,097,828	17,614,740	16,370,042	14,804,907	14,173,715	13,672,214
Total Liabilities	42,102,736	41,296,853	33,680,193	31,248,311	28,470,949	26,062,480	23,776,942	21,423,653
Stockholders' Equity	3,065,000	3,104,621	2,754,417	2,410,879	2,272,818	1,993,644	1,660,986	1,709,113
Shares Outstanding	266,795	266,582	265,783	264,878	272,724	271,997	271,171	271,064
Statistical Record								
Return on Assets %	1.28	1.21	1.34	1.09	1.04	1.03	1.06	1.09
Return on Equity %	17.77	16.68	18.23	15.03	14.28	15.07	15.28	14.47
Net Interest Margin %	56.42	62.06	63.15	58.32	51.39	45.71	51.51	52.86
Efficiency Ratio %	37.77	41.45	41.84	40.39	35.92	33.55	37.65	37.08
Loans to Deposits	1.28	1.34	1.21	1.03	1.03	1.01	0.99	0.89
Price Range	28.87-20.04	28.87-20.04	23.79-15.98	17.93-13.75	18.13-12.63	13.97-9.31	18.94-12.72	18.38-11.52
P/E Ratio	14.73-10.22	16.13-11.20	13.67-9.18	13.79-10.58	16.63-11.58	14.25-9.50	20.58-13.82	22.41-14.04
Average Yield %	2.61	2.62	2.62	2.55	2.54	2.79	1.97	1.63

Address: Popular Center Building, 209 Munoz Rivera Avenue, Hato Rey, San Juan, PR 00918
Telephone: 809-765-9800
Web Site: www.popularinc.com

Officers: Richard L. Carrion - Chmn., Pres., C.E.O. Antonion Luis Ferre - Vice-Chmn. **Transfer Agents:** Banco Popular de Puerto Rico, San Juan, Puerto Rico

Investor Contact: 787-765-9800x6102
No of Institutions: 136
Shares: 66,302,636 **% Held:** 24.85

PPG INDUSTRIES, INC.

Exchange	Symbol	Price	52Wk Range	Yield	P/E
NYS	PPG	$65.39 (5/31/2005)	73.80-56.63	2.88	17.25

***7 Year Price Score 103.52** *NYSE Composite Index=100 ***12 Month Price Score 100.93**

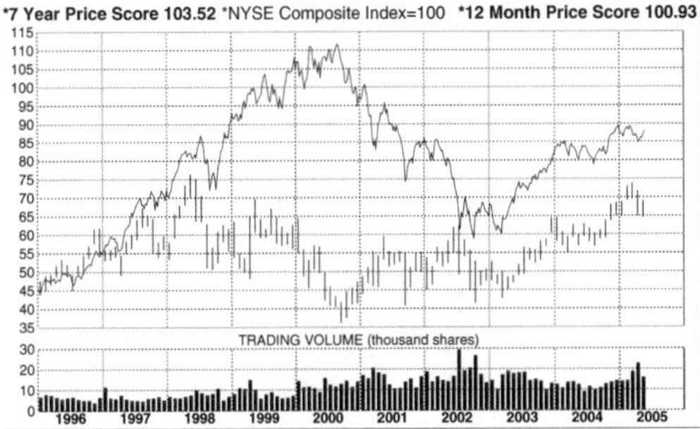

TRADING VOLUME (thousand shares)

Interim Earnings (Per Share)

Qtr.	Mar	Jun	Sep	Dec
2002	0.02	(2.30)	0.87	0.55
2003	0.46	0.89	0.83	0.71
2004	0.67	1.06	1.12	1.06
2005	0.55	...	...	...

Interim Dividends (Per Share)

Amt	Decl	Ex	Rec	Pay
0.45Q	7/15/2004	8/6/2004	8/10/2004	9/10/2004
0.45Q	10/22/2004	11/8/2004	11/10/2004	12/10/2004
0.45Q	1/20/2005	2/17/2005	2/22/2005	3/11/2005
0.47Q	4/21/2005	5/6/2005	5/10/2005	6/10/2005

Indicated Div: $1.88 (Div. Reinv. Plan)

Valuation Analysis

Forecast P/E	13.19 (6/1/2005)		
Market Cap	$11.2 Billion	Book Value	3.5 Billion
Price/Book	3.16	Price/Sales	1.15

Dividend Achiever Status

Rank	273	10 Year Growth Rate	4.80%
Total Years of Dividend Growth			33

Business Summary: Chemicals (MIC: 11.1 SIC: 851 NAIC: 25510)

PPG Industries is comprised of three basic business segments: coatings, glass and chemicals. Within these business segments, Co. has focused resources on industrial, aerospace, packaging, architectural, automotive original and refinish coatings; flat glass, automotive original and replacement glass, and continuous-strand fiber glass; and chlor-alkali and specialty chemicals. The coatings businesses operate production facilities around the world. Co.'s principal glass production facilities are in North America and Europe. The chemicals businesses operate production facilities around the world including five plants in the United States and one each in Canada and Mexico.

Recent Developments: For the quarter ended Mar 31 2005, net income decreased 20.2% to $95,000 thousand from net income of $119,000 thousand in the year-earlier quarter. Revenues were $2,493,000 thousand, up 10.1% from $2,264,000 thousand the year before. Total direct expense was $1,558,000 thousand versus $1,438,000 thousand in the prior-year quarter, an increase of 8.3%. Total indirect expense was $769,000 thousand versus $601,000 thousand in the prior-year quarter, an increase of 28.0%.

Prospects: Co.'s strong earnings performance reflects the strength of its chlor-alkali business coupled with improvements in glass. This is enabling Co. to more than offset rising raw material costs for its coatings business. At this point, Co. continues to see sales throughout its businesses and pricing is up in most of its businesses, particularly chlor-alkali. In addition, Co.'s optical products business is positioned for continued growth with the introduction of its fifth-generation Transitions photochromic lenses. Separately, on May 4 2005, Co. announced an agreement to acquire International Polarizer Holdings Trust, a polarized film manufacturer, to expand its presence in optical materials.

Financial Data (US$ in Thousands)	3 Mos	12/31/2004	12/31/2003	12/31/2002	12/31/2001	12/31/2000	12/31/1999	12/31/1998
Earnings Per Share	3.79	3.95	2.89	(0.41)	2.29	3.57	3.23	4.48
Cash Flow Per Share	5.96	5.91	6.61	5.16	6.30	5.04	5.19	...
Tang Book Value Per Share	10.89	10.81	7.37	3.48	9.12	8.61	8.30	13.17
Dividends Per Share	1.800	1.790	1.730	1.700	1.680	1.600	1.520	1.420
Dividend Payout %	47.49	45.32	59.86	...	73.36	44.82	47.06	31.70
Income Statement								
Total Revenue	2,493,000	9,513,000	8,756,000	8,067,000	8,169,000	8,629,000	7,995,000	7,510,000
EBITDA	240,000	1,529,000	1,334,000	489,000	1,267,000	1,629,000	1,517,000	1,775,000
Depn & Amortn	95,000	388,000	394,000	398,000	447,000	447,000	419,000	383,000
Income Before Taxes	145,000	1,063,000	843,000	(28,000)	666,000	1,017,000	973,000	1,294,000
Income Taxes	34,000	322,000	293,000	(7,000)	247,000	369,000	377,000	466,000
Net Income	95,000	683,000	494,000	(69,000)	387,000	620,000	568,000	801,000
Average Shares	174,200	173,000	170,900	169,900	168,300	172,300	175,500	178,700
Balance Sheet								
Current Assets	4,209,000	4,054,000	3,537,000	2,945,000	2,703,000	3,093,000	3,062,000	2,660,000
Total Assets	9,022,000	8,932,000	8,424,000	7,863,000	8,452,000	9,125,000	8,914,000	7,387,000
Current Liabilities	2,321,000	2,221,000	2,139,000	1,920,000	1,955,000	2,543,000	2,384,000	1,912,000
Long-Term Obligations	1,137,000	1,184,000	1,339,000	1,699,000	1,699,000	1,810,000	1,836,000	1,081,000
Total Liabilities	5,358,000	5,264,000	5,376,000	5,582,000	5,250,000	5,900,000	5,710,000	4,420,000
Stockholders' Equity	3,549,000	3,572,000	2,911,000	2,150,000	3,080,000	3,097,000	3,106,000	2,880,000
Shares Outstanding	171,661	172,001	170,926	169,442	168,713	168,222	173,988	175,000
Statistical Record								
Return on Assets %	7.43	7.85	6.07	N.M.	4.40	6.86	6.97	...
Return on Equity %	20.09	21.01	19.52	N.M.	12.53	19.94	18.98	...
EBITDA Margin %	9.63	16.07	15.24	6.06	15.51	18.88	18.97	23.64
Net Margin %	3.81	7.18	5.64	N.M.	4.74	7.19	7.10	10.67
Asset Turnover	1.11	1.09	1.08	0.99	0.93	0.95	0.98	...
Current Ratio	1.81	1.83	1.65	1.53	1.38	1.22	1.28	1.39
Debt to Equity	0.32	0.33	0.46	0.79	0.55	0.58	0.59	0.38
Price Range	73.80-56.63	68.55-55.18	64.42-42.64	62.44-41.41	59.54-40.71	64.38-36.13	69.69-48.06	76.31-50.50
P/E Ratio	19.47-14.94	17.35-13.97	22.29-14.75	...	26.00-17.78	18.03-10.12	21.58-14.88	17.03-11.27
Average Yield %	2.83	2.94	3.31	3.24	3.27	3.39	2.57	2.27

Address: One PPG Place, Pittsburgh, PA 15272
Telephone: 412-434-3131
Web Site: www.ppg.com

Officers: Raymond W. LeBoeuf - Chmn., C.E.O. Charles E. Bunch - Pres., C.O.O. **Transfer Agents:** Mellon Investor Services LLC, Ridgefield Park, NJ

Investor Contact: 412-434-3318
No of Institutions: 409
Shares: 105,218,784 **% Held:** 61.11

PRAXAIR, INC.

Exchange	Symbol	Price	52Wk Range	Yield	P/E
NYS	PX	$46.87 (5/31/2005)	48.88-36.81	1.54	21.40

*7 Year Price Score 136.67 *NYSE Composite Index=100 *12 Month Price Score 104.73

Interim Earnings (Per Share)

Qtr.	Mar	Jun	Sep	Dec
2002	0.39	0.46	0.40	0.42
2003	0.40	0.46	0.46	0.47
2004	0.49	0.53	0.53	0.54
2005	0.59	...	...	...

Interim Dividends (Per Share)

Amt	Decl	Ex	Rec	Pay
0.15Q	7/27/2004	9/2/2004	9/7/2004	9/15/2004
0.15Q	10/26/2004	12/3/2004	12/7/2004	12/15/2004
0.18Q	1/25/2005	3/3/2005	3/7/2005	3/15/2005
0.18Q	4/26/2005	6/3/2005	6/7/2005	6/15/2005

Indicated Div: $0.72 (Div. Reinv. Plan)

Valuation Analysis

Forecast P/E 19.14 (6/1/2005)

Market Cap	$15.2 Billion	Book Value	3.7 Billion
Price/Book	4.15	Price/Sales	2.20

Dividend Achiever Status

Rank 80 **10 Year Growth Rate** 15.67%

Total Years of Dividend Growth 12

Business Summary: Chemicals (MIC: 11.1 SIC: 813 NAIC: 25120)

Praxair is a major supplier of industrial gases in North and South America, Asia and Europe. Co.'s primary products are atmospheric gases (oxygen, nitrogen, argon, and rare gases) and process gases (carbon dioxide, helium, hydrogen, electronic gases, specialty gasses and acetylene). Co. also designs, engineers, and builds equipment that produces industrial gases for internal use and external sales. Co.'s surface technology segment, operated through Praxair Surface Technologies, Inc., supplies wear-resistant and high-temperature corrosion-resistant metallic and ceramic coatings and powders.

Recent Developments: For the quarter ended Mar 31 2005, net income increased 18.9% to $195,000 thousand from net income of $164,000 thousand in the year-earlier quarter. Revenues were $1,827,000 thousand, up 19.3% from $1,531,000 thousand the year before. Operating income was $309,000 thousand versus an income of $260,000 thousand in the prior-year quarter, an increase of 18.8%. Total direct expense was $1,109,000 thousand versus $908,000 thousand in the prior-year quarter, an increase of 22.1%. Total indirect expense was $427,000 thousand versus $362,000 thousand in the prior-year quarter, an increase of 18.0%.

Prospects: Co. is projecting second-quarter 2005 earnings in the range of $0.60 to $0.62 per diluted share. Looking ahead, Co. is targeting full-year 2005 sales growth of between 12.0% and 15.0% year over year, along with diluted earnings in the range of $2.40 to $2.48 per share. Continued strong operating results in 2005 are expected to be driven by Co.'s growing hydrogen and energy businesses, contributions from its recently acquired business in Germany, a strong pipeline of new contracts and projects under construction, and increased price realization. Separately, Co. anticipates full-year 2005 capital expenditures of between $750.0 million and $800.0 million.

Financial Data

(US$ in Thousands)	3 Mos	12/31/2004	12/31/2003	12/31/2002	12/31/2001	12/31/2000	12/31/1999	12/31/1998
Earnings Per Share	2.19	2.10	1.77	1.24	1.31	1.13	1.33	1.30
Cash Flow Per Share	4.17	3.80	3.48	3.07	3.16	2.82	2.99	2.95
Tang Book Value Per Share	6.30	6.08	6.00	4.02	4.00	3.95	3.70	3.36
Dividends Per Share	0.630	0.600	0.458	0.380	0.340	0.310	0.280	0.250
Dividend Payout %	28.77	28.57	25.85	30.65	25.86	27.56	21.05	19.23
Income Statement								
Total Revenue	1,827,000	6,594,000	5,613,000	5,128,000	5,158,000	5,043,000	4,639,000	4,833,000
EBITDA	471,000	1,681,000	1,439,000	1,406,000	1,299,000	1,178,000	1,276,000	1,323,000
Depn & Amortn	162,000	578,000	517,000	483,000	499,000	471,000	445,000	467,000
Income Before Taxes	267,000	948,000	771,000	717,000	576,000	483,000	627,000	596,000
Income Taxes	69,000	232,000	174,000	158,000	135,000	103,000	152,000	127,000
Net Income	195,000	697,000	585,000	409,000	430,000	363,000	431,000	425,000
Average Shares	329,669	331,403	330,991	329,490	327,014	322,184	324,444	326,712
Balance Sheet								
Current Assets	1,773,000	1,744,000	1,449,000	1,286,000	1,276,000	1,361,000	1,335,000	1,394,000
Total Assets	9,832,000	9,878,000	8,305,000	7,401,000	7,715,000	7,762,000	7,722,000	8,096,000
Current Liabilities	1,827,000	1,875,000	1,117,000	1,100,000	1,194,000	1,439,000	1,725,000	1,289,000
Long-Term Obligations	2,841,000	2,876,000	2,661,000	2,510,000	2,725,000	2,641,000	2,111,000	2,895,000
Total Liabilities	5,960,000	6,045,000	5,022,000	4,897,000	5,077,000	5,247,000	4,998,000	5,202,000
Stockholders' Equity	3,651,000	3,608,000	3,088,000	2,340,000	2,477,000	2,357,000	2,290,000	2,332,000
Shares Outstanding	323,482	323,620	326,085	324,536	324,285	318,758	318,095	315,142
Statistical Record								
Return on Assets %	8.02	7.65	7.45	5.41	5.56	4.68	5.45	5.34
Return on Equity %	21.45	20.76	21.55	16.98	17.79	15.58	18.65	19.08
EBITDA Margin %	25.78	25.49	25.64	27.42	25.18	23.36	27.51	27.37
Net Margin %	10.67	10.57	10.42	7.98	8.34	7.20	9.29	8.79
Asset Turnover	0.76	0.72	0.71	0.68	0.67	0.65	0.59	0.61
Current Ratio	0.97	0.93	1.30	1.17	1.07	0.95	0.77	1.08
Debt to Equity	0.78	0.80	0.86	1.07	1.10	1.12	0.92	1.24
Price Range	48.31-34.93	45.97-34.70	38.20-25.33	30.30-22.81	27.64-18.65	27.25-15.84	29.06-16.16	26.78-15.63
P/E Ratio	22.06-15.95	21.89-16.52	21.58-14.31	24.43-18.39	21.10-14.24	24.12-14.02	21.85-12.15	20.60-12.02
Average Yield %	1.52	1.52	1.48	1.37	1.44	1.54	1.26	1.15

Address: 39 Old Ridgebury Rd., Danbury, CT 06810-5113 **Telephone:** 203-837-2000 **Web Site:** www.praxair.com	**Officers:** Dennis H. Reilley - Chmn., Pres., C.E.O. Stephen F. Angel - Exec. V.P. **Transfer Agents:** Registrar and Transfer Company, Cranford, NJ	**Investor Contact:** 203-837-2210 **No of Institutions:** 462 **Shares:** 253,320,864 **% Held:** 78.58

PROCTER & GAMBLE CO.

Exchange	Symbol	Price	52Wk Range	Yield	P/E
NYS	PG	$55.15 (5/31/2005)	56.73-50.97	2.03	21.21

*7 Year Price Score 109.04 *NYSE Composite Index=100 *12 Month Price Score 98.18

Interim Earnings (Per Share)

Qtr.	Sep	Dec	Mar	Jun
2001-02	0.40	0.47	0.37	0.32
2002-03	0.52	0.53	0.46	0.34
2003-04	0.63	0.65	0.55	0.50
2004-05	0.73	0.74	0.63	...

Interim Dividends (Per Share)

Amt	Decl	Ex	Rec	Pay
0.25Q	7/13/2004	7/21/2004	7/23/2004	8/16/2004
0.25Q	10/12/2004	10/20/2004	10/22/2004	11/15/2004
0.25Q	1/11/2005	1/19/2005	1/21/2005	2/15/2005
0.28Q	4/11/2005	4/20/2005	4/22/2005	5/16/2005

Indicated Div: $1.12 (Div. Reinv. Plan)

Valuation Analysis

Forecast P/E	19.03 (6/1/2005)		
Market Cap	$137.6 Billion	Book Value	18.7 Billion
Price/Book	7.34	Price/Sales	2.48

Dividend Achiever Status

Rank	146	10 Year Growth Rate	11.47%
Total Years of Dividend Growth			51

Business Summary: Chemicals (MIC: 11.1 SIC: 841 NAIC: 25611)

Procter & Gamble manufactures and markets consumer branded products. Fabric and Home Care includes laundry detergent, fabric conditioners and dish care. Baby and Family Care includes diapers, wipes and bibs. Beauty Care includes hair care/hair color, and cosmetics. Health Care includes oral care, pet health, and pharmaceuticals. Snacks and Beverages includes coffee, snacks and beverages. Co. markets approximately 300 consumer products in more than 160 countries around the world. Co.'s key brands include Tide, Downy, Lenor, Joy, Gain, Ace, Swiffer, Pantene, Olay, Head & Shoulders, Herbal Essences, Max Factor, Pampers, Charmin, Crest, Iams, Eukanuba, Scope, Pringles, and Folgers.

Recent Developments: For the quarter ended Mar 31 2005, net income increased 12.6% to $1,720 million from net income of $1,528 million in the year-earlier quarter. Revenues were $14,287 million, up 9.7% from $13,029 million the year before. Operating income was $2,688 million versus an income of $2,303 million in the prior-year quarter, an increase of 16.7%. Total direct expense was $7,033 million versus $6,394 million in the prior-year quarter, an increase of 10.0%. Total indirect expense was $4,566 million versus $4,332 million in the prior-year quarter, an increase of 5.4%.

Prospects: Co.'s results are benefiting from a combination of higher demand and improved pricing. For instance, unit volume for the quarter ended Mar 31 2005 rose 6.0%, while organic volume, which excludes the effect of acquisitions and divestitures, grew 7.0%. Also, organic sales for the quarter ended Mar 31 2005 grew 8.0%, with pricing adding 1.0% to sales growth primarily reflecting increases that partially recovered commodity costs in the family care, coffee and pet health and nutrition categories. Thus, on Apr 28 2005 Co. raised its fiscal year earnings per share guidance range to $2.64 to $2.65. Meanwhile, Co. continues the integration planning process with The Gillette Company.

Financial Data (US$ in Thousands)	9 Mos	6 Mos	3 Mos	06/30/2004	06/30/2003	06/30/2002	06/30/2001	06/30/2000
Earnings Per Share	2.60	2.50	2.41	2.32	1.85	1.54	1.03	1.24
Cash Flow Per Share	3.60	3.70	3.80	3.62	3.35	2.98	2.23	1.78
Tang Book Value Per Share	N.M.	N.M.	N.M.	N.M.	0.42	N.M.	0.78	0.68
Dividends Per Share	1.000	0.978	0.955	0.933	0.820	0.760	0.700	0.640
Dividend Payout %	38.54	39.04	39.58	40.19	44.44	49.19	67.63	51.82
Income Statement								
Total Revenue	42,483,000	28,196,000	13,744,000	51,407,000	43,377,000	40,238,000	39,244,000	39,951,000
EBITDA	10,328,000	7,105,000	3,532,000	11,712,000	9,794,000	8,679,000	7,681,000	8,449,000
Depn & Amortn	1,403,000	928,000	480,000	1,733,000	1,703,000	1,693,000	2,271,000	2,191,000
Income Before Taxes	8,322,000	5,796,000	2,871,000	9,350,000	7,530,000	6,383,000	4,616,000	5,536,000
Income Taxes	2,562,000	1,756,000	870,000	2,869,000	2,344,000	2,031,000	1,694,000	1,994,000
Net Income	5,760,000	4,040,000	2,001,000	6,481,000	5,186,000	4,352,000	2,922,000	3,542,000
Average Shares	2,718,700	2,741,000	2,756,000	2,790,100	2,802,600	2,809,800	2,811,200	2,854,400
Balance Sheet								
Current Assets	21,591,000	20,996,000	18,716,000	17,115,000	15,220,000	12,166,000	10,889,000	10,069,000
Total Assets	63,076,000	63,032,000	59,203,000	57,048,000	43,706,000	40,776,000	34,387,000	34,194,000
Current Liabilities	25,322,000	23,903,000	21,902,000	22,147,000	12,358,000	12,704,000	9,846,000	10,065,000
Long-Term Obligations	12,936,000	13,385,000	13,731,000	12,554,000	11,475,000	11,201,000	9,792,000	8,916,000
Total Liabilities	44,346,000	43,148,000	40,844,000	39,770,000	27,520,000	27,070,000	22,377,000	21,907,000
Stockholders' Equity	18,730,000	19,884,000	18,359,000	17,278,000	16,186,000	13,706,000	12,010,000	12,287,000
Shares Outstanding	2,494,400	2,522,600	2,536,700	2,543,800	2,594,400	2,601,600	2,591,400	2,611,800
Statistical Record								
Return on Assets %	12.20	11.85	12.22	12.83	12.28	11.58	8.52	10.65
Return on Equity %	38.54	36.02	37.51	38.63	34.70	33.85	24.05	29.02
EBITDA Margin %	24.31	25.20	25.70	22.78	22.58	21.57	19.57	21.15
Net Margin %	13.56	14.33	14.56	12.61	11.96	10.82	7.45	8.87
Asset Turnover	0.95	0.92	0.96	1.02	1.03	1.07	1.14	1.20
Current Ratio	0.85	0.88	0.85	0.77	1.23	0.96	1.11	1.00
Debt to Equity	0.69	0.67	0.75	0.73	0.71	0.82	0.82	0.73
Price Range	56.73-50.97	56.73-49.05	56.73-46.41	55.96-43.35	46.50-37.23	47.20-32.00	38.96-27.08	58.44-26.61
P/E Ratio	21.82-19.60	22.69-19.62	23.54-19.26	24.12-18.69	25.14-20.12	30.65-20.78	37.82-26.29	47.13-21.46
Average Yield %	1.85	1.83	1.84	1.89	1.87	1.90	2.12	1.48

Address: One Procter & Gamble Plaza, Cincinnati, OH 45202
Telephone: 513-983-1100
Web Site: www.pg.com

Officers: Alan G. Lafley - Chmn., Pres., C.E.O. Bruce L. Byrnes - Vice-Chmn. **Transfer Agents:** The Procter and Gamble Company, Cincinnati, OH

No of Institutions: 1061
Shares: 1,381,813,504 **% Held:** 54.78

PROGRESS ENERGY, INC.

Exchange	Symbol	Price	52Wk Range	Yield	P/E
NYS	PGN	$44.23 (5/31/2005)	45.87-40.70	5.34	14.50

***7 Year Price Score 90.62** *NYSE Composite Index=100 ***12 Month Price Score 95.84**

Interim Earnings (Per Share)

Qtr.	Mar	Jun	Sep	Dec
2002	0.62	0.56	0.70	0.54
2003	0.89	0.64	1.34	0.41
2004	0.45	0.63	1.24	0.80
2005	0.38	...	...	...

Interim Dividends (Per Share)

Amt	Decl	Ex	Rec	Pay
0.575Q	9/17/2004	10/6/2004	10/11/2004	11/1/2004
0.59Q	12/8/2004	1/6/2005	1/10/2005	2/1/2005
0.59Q	3/16/2005	4/7/2005	4/11/2005	5/2/2005
0.59Q	5/11/2005	7/7/2005	7/11/2005	8/1/2005

Indicated Div: $2.36 (Div. Reinv. Plan)

Valuation Analysis

Forecast P/E	14.44 (6/1/2005)		
Market Cap	$11.0 Billion	Book Value	7.8 Billion
Price/Book	1.42	Price/Sales	1.13

Dividend Achiever Status

Rank	298	**10 Year Growth Rate**	3.07%
Total Years of Dividend Growth			16

Business Summary: Electricity (MIC: 7.1 SIC: 911 NAIC: 21121)

Progress Energy is a utility holding company with over 24,000 megawatts of generating capacity as of Dec 31 2004. Co.'s utility segment includes two major electric utilities, Progress Energy Carolinas and Progress Energy Florida. At Dec 31 2004, Co.'s electric utilities served more than 2.9 million customers in North Carolina, South Carolina and Florida. Co.'s Competitive Commercial Operations segment provides non-regulated electricity generation. The Fuels segment is involved in natural gas drilling and production, coal mining and terminal services and fuel delivery. The Rail Services segment engages in rail and railcar services. Other activities include Co.'s telecommunication services.

Recent Developments: For the quarter ended Mar 31 2005, income from continuing operations increased 6.1% to $105,000 thousand from income of $99,000 thousand in the year-earlier quarter. Net income decreased 13.9% to $93,000 thousand from net income of $108,000 thousand in the year-earlier quarter. Revenues grew 9.6% to $2,198,000 thousand from $2,006,000 thousand the year before. Operating income decreased 9.0% to $253,000 thousand versus $278,000 thousand in the prior-year quarter. Total direct expense was $1,549,000 thousand versus $1,350,000 thousand in the prior-year quarter, an increase of 14.7%. Total indirect expense was $396,000 thousand versus $378,000 thousand in the prior-year quarter.

Prospects: Earnings are being negatively affected by mild weather conditions, increased costs and lower sales at Co.'s synthetic fuel unit, partially offset by increased utility growth and usage, higher wholesale sales due to new utility contracts, and rising coal and natural gas prices. Separately, on Mar 28 2005, Co. announced that it has completed its sale of Progress Rail Services Corp. to subsidiaries of One Equity Partners LLC, a private equity affiliate of J.P. Morgan Chase & Co., for $405.0 million. Proceeds from the sale will be used to reduce debt. Looking ahead, Co. is projecting full-year 2005 earnings from continuing operations of between $2.90 and $3.20 per share.

Financial Data

(US$ in Thousands)	3 Mos	12/31/2004	12/31/2003	12/31/2002	12/31/2001	12/31/2000	12/31/1999	12/31/1998
Earnings Per Share	3.05	3.12	3.28	2.42	2.64	3.03	2.55	2.75
Cash Flow Per Share	6.16	6.62	7.54	7.36	7.06	5.46	5.61	6.39
Tang Book Value Per Share	14.51	14.48	13.78	12.43	10.58	8.60	19.57	19.49
Dividends Per Share	2.315	2.300	2.240	2.180	2.120	1.030	2.015	1.955
Dividend Payout %	75.90	73.72	68.29	90.08	80.30	33.99	79.02	71.09
Income Statement								
Total Revenue	2,198,000	9,772,000	8,743,000	7,945,120	8,461,459	4,118,873	3,357,615	3,130,045
EBITDA	531,000	2,137,000	2,462,000	2,112,404	2,241,745	1,751,386	1,397,927	1,399,790
Depn & Amortn	276,000	653,000	1,146,000	1,099,128	1,189,171	834,950	588,123	578,348
Income Before Taxes	96,000	851,000	702,000	394,361	389,967	681,135	640,676	656,732
Income Taxes	(1,000)	115,000	(109,000)	(157,808)	(151,643)	202,774	258,421	257,494
Net Income	93,000	759,000	782,000	528,386	541,610	478,361	382,255	399,238
Average Shares	245,000	243,100	237,000	218,166	204,683	157,169	148,344	143,941
Balance Sheet								
Net PPE	14,122,000	16,373,000	16,592,000	12,540,505	11,987,961	11,166,360	7,004,795	6,299,540
Total Assets	25,696,000	25,993,000	26,202,000	21,352,704	20,739,791	20,091,012	9,494,019	8,347,406
Long-Term Obligations	8,998,000	18,772,000	9,934,000	9,747,293	9,483,745	5,890,099	3,028,561	2,614,414
Total Liabilities	17,940,000	27,518,000	18,665,000	14,582,864	14,643,427	14,573,980	6,021,996	5,338,725
Stockholders' Equity	7,756,000	7,726,000	7,537,000	6,769,840	6,096,364	5,517,032	3,472,023	3,008,681
Shares Outstanding	249,000	247,000	246,000	237,992	218,725	206,089	159,599	151,338
Statistical Record								
Return on Assets %	2.88	2.90	3.29	2.51	2.65	3.22	4.29	4.82
Return on Equity %	9.73	9.92	10.93	8.21	9.33	10.61	11.80	13.56
EBITDA Margin %	24.16	21.87	28.16	26.59	26.49	42.52	41.63	44.72
Net Margin %	4.23	7.77	8.94	6.65	6.40	11.61	11.38	12.76
PPE Turnover	0.68	0.59	0.60	0.65	0.73	0.45	0.50	0.50
Asset Turnover	0.38	0.37	0.37	0.38	0.41	0.28	0.38	0.38
Debt to Equity	1.16	2.43	1.32	1.44	1.56	1.07	0.87	0.87
Price Range	47.37-40.48	47.78-40.48	47.38-38.32	52.38-33.58	48.44-39.61	49.19-28.56	47.50-29.50	49.06-39.50
P/E Ratio	15.53-13.27	15.31-12.97	14.45-11.68	21.64-13.88	18.35-15.00	16.23-9.43	18.63-11.57	17.84-14.36
Average Yield %	5.37	5.27	5.29	4.79	4.98	2.88	5.21	4.48

Address: 410 South Wilmington Street, Raleigh, NC 27601-1748
Telephone: 919-546-6111
Web Site: www.progress-energy.com

Officers: Robert B. McGehee - Chmn., C.E.O. William D. Johnson - Pres., C.O.O. **Transfer Agents:** EquiServe Trust Company, N.A., Providence, RI

Investor Contact: 919-546-7474
No of Institutions: 355
Shares: 131,480,336 **% Held:** 52.90

PROGRESSIVE CORP.

Exchange	Symbol	Price	52Wk Range	Yield	P/E
NYS	PGR	$96.07 (5/31/2005)	96.97-74.07	0.12	12.67

*7 Year Price Score 142.94 *NYSE Composite Index=100 *12 Month Price Score 102.21

Interim Earnings (Per Share)

Qtr.	Mar	Jun	Sep	Dec
2002	0.78	0.71	0.80	0.69
2003	1.32	1.29	1.45	1.63
2004	2.09	1.76	1.77	2.01
2005	2.04	...	...	...

Interim Dividends (Per Share)

Amt	Decl	Ex	Rec	Pay
0.03Q	8/20/2004	9/8/2004	9/10/2004	9/30/2004
0.03Q	10/15/2004	12/8/2004	12/10/2004	12/31/2004
0.03Q	1/31/2005	3/9/2005	3/11/2005	3/31/2005
0.03Q	4/15/2005	6/8/2005	6/10/2005	6/30/2005

Indicated Div: $0.12

Valuation Analysis

Forecast P/E	13.62 (6/2/2005)		
Market Cap	$19.2 Billion	Book Value	5.3 Billion
Price/Book	3.62	Price/Sales	1.37

Dividend Achiever Status

Rank	278	10 Year Growth Rate	4.62%
Total Years of Dividend Growth			35

Business Summary: Insurance (MIC: 8.2 SIC: 331 NAIC: 24126)

Progressive is an insurance holding company. As of Dec 31 2004, Co. owned 70 subsidiaries and had 1 mutual insurance company affiliate. The insurance subsidiaries and affiliate provide personal automobile insurance and other specialty property-casualty insurance and related services throughout the United States. Co.'s Personal Lines segment writes insurance for private passenger automobiles and recreation vehicles through both an independent agency channel and a direct channel. Co.'s Commercial Auto segment writes insurance for automobiles and trucks owned by small businesses primarily through the independent agency channel.

Recent Developments: For the quarter ended Mar 31 2005, net income decreased 10.3% to $412,700 thousand from net income of $460,000 thousand in the year-earlier quarter. Total revenues were $3,491,800 thousand, up 6.4% from $3,280,300 thousand the year before. Net premiums earned climbed 8.3% to $3,350,000 thousand, while investment income rose 4.8% to $120,400 thousand. Total expenses grew 10.6% to $2,877,100 thousand from $2,601,600 thousand in the previous year.

Prospects: Underwriting margins are benefiting from favorable reserve development stemming from actuarial adjustments and claims settling for less than reserved. In addition, Co.continues to experience low accident frequency and the quality of Co.'s claims processes continues to rise. Separately, as of May 9 2005, Co. operated a total of 21 centers that provide concierge-level claims service, including one facility that opened in May 2005. Co. recently announced it plans to significantly expand this service and is looking for additional sites. Co. expects to more than double the number of sites over the next two years, with approximately 50 additional facilities opened over the next several years.

Financial Data

(US$ in Thousands)	3 Mos	12/31/2004	12/31/2003	12/31/2002	12/31/2001	12/31/2000	12/31/1999	12/31/1998
Earnings Per Share	7.58	7.63	5.69	2.99	1.83	0.21	1.32	2.04
Cash Flow Per Share	12.16	12.47	11.24	8.73	5.58	3.73	3.54	2.84
Tang Book Value Per Share	26.53	25.73	23.25	17.28	14.76	13.01	12.55	11.76
Dividends Per Share	0.115	0.110	0.100	0.097	0.093	0.090	0.087	0.083
Dividend Payout %	1.52	1.44	1.76	3.23	5.11	43.54	6.57	4.09
Income Statement								
Premium Income	3,350,000	13,169,900	11,341,000	8,883,500	7,161,800	6,348,400	5,683,600	4,948,000
Total Revenue	3,491,800	13,782,100	11,892,000	9,294,400	7,488,200	6,771,000	6,124,200	5,292,400
Benefits & Claims	2,168,600	8,555,000	7,640,400	6,299,100	5,264,100	5,279,400	4,256,400	3,376,300
Income Before Taxes	614,700	2,450,800	1,859,700	981,400	587,600	31,800	412,200	661,100
Income Taxes	202,000	802,100	604,300	314,100	176,200	(14,300)	117,000	204,400
Net Income	412,700	1,648,700	1,255,400	667,300	411,400	46,100	295,200	456,700
Average Shares	201,900	216,200	220,500	223,200	225,299	222,900	223,800	224,100
Balance Sheet								
Total Assets	17,723,200	17,184,300	16,281,500	13,564,400	11,122,400	10,051,600	9,704,700	8,463,100
Total Liabilities	12,428,400	12,028,900	11,250,900	9,796,400	7,871,700	7,181,800	6,951,900	5,906,000
Stockholders' Equity	5,294,800	5,155,400	5,030,600	3,768,000	3,250,700	2,869,800	2,752,800	2,557,100
Shares Outstanding	199,600	200,400	216,400	218,000	220,200	220,500	219,300	217,500
Statistical Record								
Return on Assets %	9.18	9.83	8.41	5.41	3.89	0.47	3.25	5.70
Return on Equity %	29.56	32.28	28.54	19.01	13.44	1.64	11.12	19.46
Loss Ratio %	64.73	64.96	67.37	70.91	73.50	83.16	74.89	68.24
Net Margin %	11.82	11.96	10.56	7.18	5.49	0.68	4.82	8.63
Price Range	96.97-74.07	96.97-74.07	83.59-46.55	59.49-46.15	50.28-28.00	36.67-16.42	56.92-23.69	56.69-31.98
P/E Ratio	12.79-9.77	12.71-9.71	14.69-8.18	19.90-15.43	27.48-15.30	174.60-78.17	43.12-17.95	27.79-15.68
Average Yield %	0.13	0.13	0.15	0.18	0.23	0.35	0.22	0.19

Address: 6300 Wilson Mills Road, Mayfield Village, OH 44143
Telephone: 440-461-5000
Web Site: www.progressive.com

Officers: Peter B. Lewis - Chmn. Glenn M. Renwick - Pres., C.E.O. **Transfer Agents:** Corporate Trust Customer Service, National City Bank, Cleveland, OH

Investor Contact: 440-446-7165
No of Institutions: 331
Shares: 146,056,352 **% Held:** 72.99

PROLOGIS

Exchange	Symbol	Price	52Wk Range	Yield	P/E
NYS	PLD	$40.84 (5/31/2005)	43.33-31.08	3.62	36.14

*7 Year Price Score 130.96 *NYSE Composite Index=100 *12 Month Price Score 101.20

TRADING VOLUME (thousand shares)

Interim Earnings (Per Share)

Qtr.	Mar	Jun	Sep	Dec
2002	0.31	0.31	0.14	0.44
2003	0.21	0.26	(0.04)	0.73
2004	0.23	0.42	0.42	0.00
2005	0.29	...	...	...

Interim Dividends (Per Share)

Amt	Decl	Ex	Rec	Pay
0.365Q	8/2/2004	8/13/2004	8/17/2004	8/31/2004
0.365Q	11/1/2004	11/12/2004	11/16/2004	11/30/2004
0.37Q	2/1/2005	2/11/2005	2/15/2005	2/28/2005
0.37Q	5/2/2005	5/12/2005	5/16/2005	5/31/2005

Indicated Div: $1.48

Valuation Analysis

Forecast P/E	N/A		
Market Cap	$7.6 Billion	Book Value	3.1 Billion
Price/Book	2.46	Price/Sales	12.67

Dividend Achiever Status

Rank	202	10 Year Growth Rate	8.64%
Total Years of Dividend Growth			10

Business Summary: Property, Real Estate & Development (MIC: 8.3 SIC: 531 NAIC: 25930)

Prologis is a real estate investment trust that is a global provider of integrated distribution facilities and services. The Property Operations segment is engaged in long-term ownership, management and leasing of industrial distribution properties. Co. held 1,936 operating properties aggregating 282.8 million square feet in North America, 11 countries in Europe and in Japan, at Dec 31 2004. The Corporate Distribution Facilities Services segment is engaged in the development of distribution properties with the intent to contribute the property to a property fund or to sell the property to a third party.

Recent Developments: For the quarter ended Mar 31 2005, income from continuing operations increased 54.9% to $71,036 thousand from income of $45,872 thousand in the year-earlier quarter. Net income increased 12.9% to $61,428 thousand from net income of $54,417 thousand in the year-earlier quarter. Revenues were $153,355 thousand, up 2.3% from $149,886 thousand the year before. Operating income was $97,468 thousand versus an income of $77,785 thousand in the prior-year quarter, an increase of 25.3%.

Prospects: Co.'s near-term outlook appears positive, supported by further improvement in global market activity, which has led to record leasing activity and further acceleration in Co.'s development starts and continued growth of its property fund business. Also, Co. overall property operations are stronger, with improving or stable rental rates and positive net absorption in virtually every global market. As a result, Co. believes that it is well-positioned to meet its previously stated 2005 guidance of $1.30 billion to $1.40 billion in new starts for the full year.

Financial Data

(US$ in Thousands)	3 Mos	12/31/2004	12/31/2003	12/31/2002	12/31/2001	12/31/2000	12/31/1999	12/31/1998
Earnings Per Share	1.13	1.08	1.16	1.20	0.52	0.96	0.81	0.51
Cash Flow Per Share	2.53	2.63	1.82	2.12	2.01	2.05	1.78	1.96
Tang Book Value Per Share	14.71	14.82	14.35	13.96	12.94	13.53	13.86	12.83
Dividends Per Share	1.465	1.460	1.440	1.420	1.380	1.340	1.300	1.240
Dividend Payout %	129.65	135.19	124.14	118.33	265.38	139.58	160.48	243.12
Income Statement								
Property Income	136,697	598,139	674,939	576,252	570,213	558,191	538,504	362,296
Non-Property Income	16,658	...	59,166	98,749	(47,088)	85,330	28,888	10,499
Total Revenue	153,355	598,139	734,105	675,001	523,125	643,521	567,392	372,795
Depn & Amortn	44,961	180,347	170,861	158,042	148,698	156,080	156,887	102,790
Interest Expense	36,608	153,334	155,475	152,958	163,629	172,191	171,691	103,700
Income Before Taxes	73,048	277,104	266,049	277,050	132,869	219,608	183,746	...
Income Taxes	2,012	43,562	15,374	28,169	4,725	5,130	1,472	...
Net Income	61,428	232,795	250,675	248,881	128,144	214,478	180,834	111,329
Average Shares	196,180	191,801	187,222	184,869	175,197	164,401	152,739	122,028
Balance Sheet								
Total Assets	7,439,389	7,097,799	6,369,202	5,923,525	5,603,941	5,946,334	5,848,040	4,330,729
Long-Term Obligations	2,439,666	3,366,285	2,990,669	2,731,978	2,578,340	2,677,736	2,554,808	1,655,745
Total Liabilities	4,280,753	3,929,033	3,270,757	2,994,571	2,882,303	2,972,333	2,832,232	2,023,066
Stockholders' Equity	3,092,086	3,102,493	3,060,668	2,886,487	2,675,999	2,927,371	2,953,736	2,256,368
Shares Outstanding	186,410	185,788	180,182	178,145	175,888	165,287	161,825	123,416
Statistical Record								
Return on Assets %	3.44	3.45	4.08	4.32	2.22	3.63	3.55	3.02
Return on Equity %	7.90	7.53	8.43	8.95	4.57	7.27	6.94	5.26
Net Margin %	40.06	38.92	34.15	36.87	24.50	33.33	31.87	29.86
Price Range	43.33-28.39	43.33-28.39	32.26-23.85	26.00-21.03	23.15-19.70	24.50-17.81	22.00-17.06	26.38-20.00
P/E Ratio	38.35-25.12	40.12-26.29	27.81-20.56	21.67-17.53	44.52-37.88	25.52-18.55	27.16-21.06	51.72-39.22
Average Yield %	4.05	4.21	5.20	5.98	6.47	6.36	6.57	5.27

Address: 14100 East 35th Place, Aurora, CO 80011
Telephone: 303-375-9292
Web Site: www.prologis.com

Officers: K. Dane Brooksher - Chmn. Walter C. Rakowich - Pres., C.O.O. **Transfer Agents:** Equiserve Trust Company N.A.

Investor Contact: 303-576-2622
No of Institutions: 281
Shares: 166,423,248 **% Held:** 89.33

PROTECTIVE LIFE CORP.

Exchange	Symbol	Price	52Wk Range	Yield	P/E
NYS	PL	$40.19 (5/31/2005)	43.33-35.84	1.94	11.96

*7 Year Price Score 107.27 *NYSE Composite Index=100 *12 Month Price Score 95.11

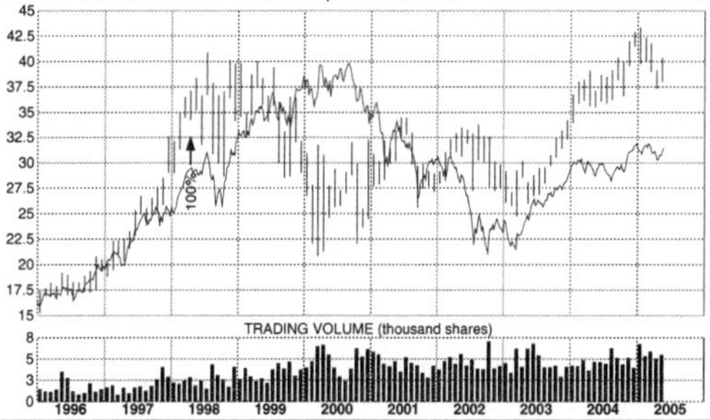

Interim Earnings (Per Share)

Qtr.	Mar	Jun	Sep	Dec
2002	0.60	0.77	0.73	0.43
2003	0.53	0.85	0.74	0.95
2004	0.78	0.86	0.94	0.72
2005	0.84	...	...	...

Interim Dividends (Per Share)

Amt	Decl	Ex	Rec	Pay
0.175Q	8/2/2004	8/18/2004	8/20/2004	9/1/2004
0.175Q	11/2/2004	11/17/2004	11/19/2004	12/1/2004
0.175Q	2/7/2005	2/16/2005	2/18/2005	3/1/2005
0.195Q	5/2/2005	5/18/2005	5/20/2005	6/1/2005

Indicated Div: $0.78 (Div. Reinv. Plan)

Valuation Analysis

Forecast P/E	11.50 (6/3/2005)		
Market Cap	$2.8 Billion	Book Value	2.1 Billion
Price/Book	1.32	Price/Sales	1.39

Dividend Achiever Status

Rank	181	10 Year Growth Rate	9.56%
Total Years of Dividend Growth			15

TRADING VOLUME (thousand shares)

Business Summary: Insurance (MIC: 8.2 SIC: 311 NAIC: 24113)

Protective Life is a holding company whose subsidiaries provide financial services through the production, distribution, and administration of insurance and investment products. Co. markets individual life insurance, credit life and disability insurance, guaranteed investment contracts, guaranteed funding agreements, fixed and variable annuities, and extended service contracts throughout the United States. Co. also maintains a separate division devoted to the acquisition of insurance policies from other companies. Co.'s operating segments are Life Marketing, Acquisitions, Annuities, Stable Value Products and Asset Protection.

Recent Developments: For the quarter ended Mar 31 2005, net income increased 21.4% to $60,083 thousand from net income of $49,504 thousand in the year-earlier quarter. Revenues were $540,109 thousand, up 4.2% from $518,194 thousand the year before. Net premiums earned were $187,230 thousand versus $194,457 thousand in the prior-year quarter, a decrease of 3.7%.

Prospects: Co. is positive regarding its outlook for 2005. For the quarter ended Mar 31 2005, Co. experienced higher sales results from its Life Marketing segment as a result of increasing momentum in universal life sales. However, segment operating earnings were affected by factors that included less favorable mortality and higher expenses. Meanwhile, results from the Annuity segment improved over last year due to higher sales of both fixed and variable annuity products. Also, the Stable Value segment posted solid operating earnings gains as a result of growth in account balances and strong spreads. Lastly, Co. indicated that the underlying trends in its Asset Protection segment continue to improve.

Financial Data

(US$ in Thousands)	3 Mos	12/31/2004	12/31/2003	12/31/2002	12/31/2001	12/31/2000	12/31/1999	12/31/1998
Earnings Per Share	3.36	3.30	3.07	2.52	1.47	2.32	2.29	2.04
Cash Flow Per Share	17.32	10.60	11.22	12.90	17.02	13.28	5.94	5.92
Tang Book Value Per Share	29.85	30.52	28.33	24.37	19.72	13.38	10.03	11.51
Dividends Per Share	0.700	0.685	0.630	0.590	0.550	0.510	0.470	0.430
Dividend Payout %	20.83	20.76	20.52	23.41	37.41	21.98	20.52	21.08
Income Statement								
Premium Income	187,230	698,652	735,877	783,132	618,669	833,658	761,284	662,795
Total Revenue	540,109	1,988,575	1,957,525	1,920,678	1,614,217	1,733,967	1,533,882	1,366,415
Benefits & Claims	300,434	1,130,437	1,151,574	1,162,231	972,624	989,565	864,582	785,765
Income Before Taxes	91,870	385,201	325,412	267,203	209,596	253,795	255,775	220,724
Income Taxes	31,787	134,820	108,362	88,444	68,538	90,858	92,079	77,845
Net Income	60,083	234,580	217,050	177,355	102,943	153,476	151,327	130,781
Average Shares	71,273	71,064	70,644	70,462	69,950	66,281	66,161	64,088
Balance Sheet								
Total Assets	27,863,074	27,211,378	24,573,991	21,953,004	19,718,824	15,145,633	12,994,164	11,989,495
Total Liabilities	25,738,672	25,045,051	22,571,847	20,232,302	18,318,680	13,841,575	11,938,941	10,800,301
Stockholders' Equity	2,124,402	2,166,327	2,002,144	1,720,702	1,400,144	1,114,058	865,223	944,194
Shares Outstanding	69,615	69,449	68,991	68,675	68,555	64,557	64,502	64,435
Statistical Record								
Return on Assets %	0.90	0.90	0.93	0.85	0.59	1.09	1.21	1.16
Return on Equity %	11.07	11.22	11.66	11.37	8.19	15.47	16.73	15.36
Loss Ratio %	160.46	161.80	156.49	148.41	157.21	118.70	113.57	118.55
Net Margin %	11.12	11.80	11.09	9.23	6.38	8.85	9.87	9.57
Price Range	43.33-35.49	42.92-33.84	34.22-24.71	33.75-27.20	34.51-25.55	32.25-20.81	40.00-28.50	40.88-28.63
P/E Ratio	12.90-10.56	13.01-10.25	11.15-8.05	13.39-10.79	23.48-17.38	13.90-8.97	17.47-12.45	20.04-14.03
Average Yield %	1.79	1.81	2.16	1.93	1.82	1.90	1.35	1.23

Address: 2801 Highway 280 South, Birmingham, AL 35223
Telephone: 205-268-1000
Web Site: www.protective.com

Officers: John D. Johns - Chmn., Pres., C.E.O. Allen W. Ritchie - Exec. V.P., C.F.O. **Transfer Agents:** Bank of New York, New York, NY

Investor Contact: 205-268-1000
No of Institutions: 218
Shares: 53,405,848 **% Held:** 76.72

QUESTAR CORP.

Exchange	Symbol	Price	52Wk Range	Yield	P/E
NYS	STR	$63.04 (5/31/2005)	63.04-36.59	1.43	21.89

Interim Earnings (Per Share)

Qtr.	Mar	Jun	Sep	Dec
2002	0.42	0.36	0.28	0.82
2003	0.77	0.24	0.34	0.71
2004	0.89	0.50	0.43	0.85
2005	1.10	...	...	...

Interim Dividends (Per Share)

Amt	Decl	Ex	Rec	Pay
0.215Q	8/10/2004	8/18/2004	8/20/2004	9/13/2004
0.215Q	10/21/2004	11/17/2004	11/19/2004	12/13/2004
0.215Q	2/8/2005	2/16/2005	2/18/2005	3/14/2005
0.225Q	5/17/2005	5/25/2005	5/27/2005	6/13/2005

Indicated Div: $0.90 (Div. Reinv. Plan)

Valuation Analysis

Forecast P/E	18.36 (6/1/2005)		
Market Cap	$5.3 Billion	Book Value	1.4 Billion
Price/Book	3.80	Price/Sales	2.65

Dividend Achiever Status

Rank	284	**10 Year Growth Rate**	4.17%
Total Years of Dividend Growth			25

Business Summary: Gas Utilities (MIC: 7.4 SIC: 923 NAIC: 21210)

Questar is a natural gas-focused energy company that is involved in a range of natural gas activities through its Market Resources and Regulated Services groups. Market Resources is engaged in gas and oil development and production; cost-of-service gas development; gas gathering and processing; and wholesale gas and hydrocarbon liquids marketing, risk management, and gas storage. Regulated Services, through its two primary subsidiaries, Questar Pipeline Company and Questar Gas Company, conducts interstate gas transmission and storage activities and retail gas distribution services.

Recent Developments: For the quarter ended Mar 31 2005, net income increased 25.0% to $95,171 thousand from net income of $76,133 thousand in the year-earlier quarter. Revenues were $680,324 thousand, up 20.7% from $563,616 thousand the year before. Operating income was $163,701 thousand versus an income of $136,790 thousand in the prior-year quarter, an increase of 19.7%. Total direct expense was $428,635 thousand versus $344,688 thousand in the prior-year quarter, an increase of 24.4%. Total indirect expense was $87,988 thousand versus $82,138 thousand in the prior-year quarter, an increase of 7.1%.

Prospects: Co. is pleased with its operating performance, supported by solid production, higher realized gas and oil prices and improved gas-processing margins. However, Co.'s pace of production for 2005 has been slower than anticipated due to adverse effect of bad weather, a shortage of rigs, and land access-related delays. Co. will continue to work through these issues, and still expects full-year 2005 production to be within the previous guidance range of 112 billion cubic feet equivalent (bcfe) to 114 bcfe, which is 8.0% to 10.0% higher than the prior year. Meanwhile, Co. expects 2005 earnings to range from $3.15 to $3.30 per share compared with its previous guidance of $3.10 to $3.30 per share.

Financial Data

(US$ in Thousands)	3 Mos	12/31/2004	12/31/2003	12/31/2002	12/31/2001	12/31/2000	12/31/1999	12/31/1998
Earnings Per Share	2.88	2.67	2.06	1.88	1.94	1.94	1.20	0.93
Cash Flow Per Share	6.82	6.93	5.40	5.68	4.60	3.23	2.60	3.46
Tang Book Value Per Share	15.61	16.06	14.12	12.81	12.14	12.01	11.37	10.62
Dividends Per Share	0.860	0.850	0.780	0.725	0.705	0.685	0.670	0.652
Dividend Payout %	29.86	31.84	37.86	38.56	36.34	35.31	55.83	70.16
Income Statement								
Total Revenue	680,324	1,901,431	1,463,188	1,200,667	1,439,350	1,266,153	924,219	906,256
EBITDA	212,276	587,148	485,609	456,388	405,498	389,723	291,322	234,593
Depn & Amortn	61,100	228,267	203,850	194,369	159,042	147,645	144,704	128,664
Income Before Taxes	151,176	358,881	281,759	262,019	246,456	242,078	146,618	105,929
Income Taxes	56,005	129,580	102,563	91,126	88,270	85,367	47,788	29,030
Net Income	95,171	229,301	173,616	155,596	158,186	156,711	98,830	76,899
Average Shares	86,728	85,722	84,190	82,573	81,658	80,915	82,676	82,817
Balance Sheet								
Net PPE	3,039,901	2,984,660	2,768,529	2,617,798	2,565,098	1,953,993	1,786,914	1,747,641
Total Assets	3,664,732	3,646,658	3,309,055	3,067,850	3,235,711	2,539,045	2,237,997	2,161,281
Long-Term Obligations	933,197	933,195	950,189	1,145,180	997,423	714,537	735,043	615,770
Total Liabilities	2,256,703	2,207,100	2,047,790	1,929,089	2,154,930	1,547,979	1,312,152	1,283,323
Stockholders' Equity	1,408,029	1,439,558	1,261,265	1,138,761	1,080,781	991,066	925,845	877,958
Shares Outstanding	84,826	84,441	83,233	82,053	81,523	80,818	81,418	82,632
Statistical Record								
Return on Assets %	7.15	6.58	5.45	4.94	5.48	6.54	4.49	3.75
Return on Equity %	18.24	16.93	14.47	14.02	15.27	16.31	10.96	8.92
EBITDA Margin %	31.20	30.88	33.19	38.01	28.17	30.78	31.52	25.89
Net Margin %	13.99	12.06	11.87	12.96	10.99	12.38	10.69	8.49
PPE Turnover	0.70	0.66	0.54	0.46	0.64	0.68	0.52	0.55
Asset Turnover	0.58	0.55	0.46	0.38	0.50	0.53	0.42	0.44
Debt to Equity	0.66	0.65	0.75	1.01	0.92	0.72	0.79	0.70
Price Range	60.95-34.36	51.51-34.09	35.35-26.66	29.27-19.40	33.51-18.70	31.50-13.81	19.88-14.94	22.34-16.25
P/E Ratio	21.16-11.93	19.29-12.77	17.16-12.94	15.57-10.32	17.27-9.64	16.24-7.12	16.56-12.45	24.03-17.47
Average Yield %	1.92	2.10	2.49	2.91	2.73	3.23	3.72	3.29

Address: 180 East 100 South Street, Salt Lake City, UT 84145-0433 **Telephone:** 801-324-5000 **Web Site:** www.questar.com	**Officers:** Keith O. Rattie - Chmn., Pres., C.E.O. Alan K. Allred - Exec. V.P. **Transfer Agents:** Wells Fargo Bank Minnesota, N.A., South St. Paul, MN	**Investor Contact:** 801-324-5497 **No of Institutions:** 266 **Shares:** 51,790,372 **% Held:** 61.14

RAVEN INDUSTRIES, INC.

Exchange	Symbol	Price	52Wk Range	Yield	P/E
NMS	RAVN	$25.48 (5/31/2005)	26.56-16.00	1.10	26.27

*7 Year Price Score 227.65 *NYSE Composite Index=100 *12 Month Price Score 102.89

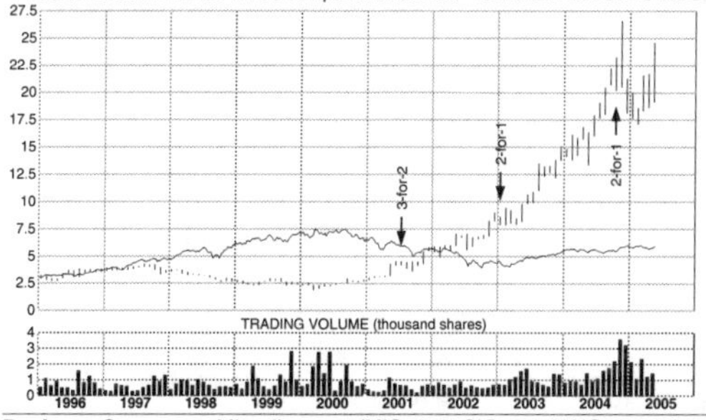

TRADING VOLUME (thousand shares)

Interim Earnings (Per Share)

Qtr.	Apr	Jul	Oct	Jan
2000-01	0.07	0.06	0.08	0.10
2001-02	0.12	0.11	0.13	0.11
2002-03	0.18	0.12	0.17	0.12
2003-04	0.23	0.17	0.21	0.14
2004-05	0.29	0.20	0.28	0.20

Interim Dividends (Per Share)

Amt	Decl	Ex	Rec	Pay
0.055Q	8/20/2004	9/22/2004	9/24/2004	10/15/2004
0.055Q	11/19/2004	12/21/2004	12/23/2004	1/14/2005
0.07Q	3/14/2005	3/23/2005	3/28/2005	4/15/2005
0.07Q	5/26/2005	6/22/2005	6/24/2005	7/15/2005

Indicated Div: $0.28 (Div. Reinv. Plan)

Valuation Analysis

Forecast P/E	25.11 (6/1/2005)		
Market Cap	$458.6 Million	Book Value	66.1 Million
Price/Book	6.94	Price/Sales	2.73

Dividend Achiever Status

Rank	8	10 Year Growth Rate	29.59%
Total Years of Dividend Growth			17

Business Summary: Miscellaneous (MIC: 8.11 SIC: 672 NAIC: 34412)

Raven Industries is an industrial manufacturing company that operates through four business segments consisting of three Co. divisions and one subsidiary. The Engineered Films Division produces rugged reinforced plastic sheeting and high-altitude research balloons for public and commercial research. The Electronics Systems Division provides electronic manufacturing services. The Flow Controls Division develops global positioning systems-based control systems, computerized control hardware and software for precision farming, and systems for the precision application of insecticides, fertilizer and road de-icers. Aerostar International Inc. produces custom-shaped advertising inflatables.

Recent Developments: For the year ended Jan 31 2005, net income increased 29.3% to $17,891 thousand from net income of $13,836 thousand a year earlier. Revenues were $168,086 thousand, up 17.8% from $142,727 thousand the year before. Operating income was $27,862 thousand versus an income of $21,626 thousand in the prior year, an increase of 28.8%. Total direct expense was $124,886 thousand versus $108,968 thousand in the prior year, an increase of 14.6%. Total indirect expense was $15,338 thousand versus $12,133 thousand in the prior year, an increase of 26.4%.

Prospects: Co. is benefiting from strong revenue and operating income growth in all of its businesses, with the expectation of its Aerostar segment, which is being affected by lower shipments of cargo parachutes. In particular, Co. is seeing considerable growth in its Engineered Films Division, largely due to increased shipments of pit liners for oil exploration. Meanwhile, Co.'s Autoboom product line, which was acquired in February from Montgomery Industries, is performing well, and benefiting Co.'s Flow Controls Division. For 2005, Co. is seeing opportunities to replace the high level of disaster film shipped in the last half of 2004.

Financial Data

(US$ in Thousands)	01/31/2005	01/31/2004	01/31/2003	01/31/2002	01/31/2001	01/31/2000	01/31/1999	01/31/1998
Earnings Per Share	0.97	0.75	0.60	0.47	0.31	0.26	0.22	0.28
Cash Flow Per Share	1.04	1.09	0.70	0.99	0.46	0.40	0.29	0.32
Tang Book Value Per Share	3.33	3.25	2.83	2.82	2.53	1.94	2.21	2.13
Dividends Per Share	0.845	0.170	0.140	0.128	0.117	0.110	0.103	0.093
Dividend Payout %	87.11	22.67	23.33	27.42	37.63	42.58	47.69	33.94
Income Statement								
Total Revenue	168,086	142,727	120,903	118,515	132,858	147,906	152,798	149,619
EBITDA	31,831	25,931	21,283	16,839	14,849	15,805	15,256	18,000
Depn & Amortn	3,841	4,145	3,966	3,145	3,667	4,884	5,133	5,137
Income Before Taxes	27,955	21,716	17,254	13,565	10,924	10,503	9,649	12,540
Income Taxes	10,064	7,880	6,069	4,718	4,513	3,741	3,467	4,478
Net Income	17,891	13,836	11,185	8,847	6,411	6,762	6,182	8,062
Average Shares	18,410	18,489	18,695	18,983	20,675	26,232	28,542	29,346
Balance Sheet								
Current Assets	61,592	55,710	49,351	45,308	52,236	55,371	60,861	57,831
Total Assets	88,509	79,508	72,816	67,836	65,656	74,047	83,674	82,590
Current Liabilities	20,950	11,895	13,167	13,810	13,935	14,702	16,792	19,375
Long-Term Obligations	...	57	151	280	2,013	3,024	4,572	1,128
Total Liabilities	22,427	13,037	14,580	15,804	17,667	19,528	21,381	21,027
Stockholders' Equity	66,082	66,471	58,236	52,032	47,989	54,519	62,293	61,563
Shares Outstanding	17,999	18,041	18,132	18,422	18,956	28,164	28,164	28,944
Statistical Record								
Return on Assets %	21.24	18.17	15.90	13.25	9.15	8.57	7.44	9.88
Return on Equity %	26.92	22.19	20.29	17.69	12.47	11.58	9.98	13.63
EBITDA Margin %	18.94	18.17	17.60	14.21	11.18	10.69	9.98	12.03
Net Margin %	10.64	9.69	9.25	7.46	4.83	4.57	4.05	5.39
Asset Turnover	2.00	1.87	1.72	1.78	1.90	1.88	1.84	1.83
Current Ratio	2.94	4.68	3.75	3.28	3.75	3.77	3.62	2.98
Debt to Equity	...	N.M.	N.M.	0.01	0.04	0.06	0.07	0.02
Price Range	26.56-13.34	15.07-7.84	9.00-4.89	5.88-3.02	3.04-1.85	3.00-2.25	3.75-2.58	4.29-3.27
P/E Ratio	27.38-13.75	20.09-10.45	15.00-8.15	12.50-6.43	9.81-5.98	11.54-8.65	17.05-11.74	15.33-11.68
Average Yield %	4.60	1.52	2.08	2.99	4.69	4.32	3.30	2.41

Address: 205 East 6th Street, P.O. Box 5107, Sioux Falls, SD 57117-5107
Telephone: 605-336-2750
Web Site: www.ravenind.com

Officers: Ronald M. Moquist - Pres., C.E.O. Thomas Iacarella - V.P., C.F.O., Treas., Sec. **Transfer Agents:** Wells Fargo Bank N.A., St. Paul, MN

Investor Contact: 605-336-2750
No of Institutions: 64
Shares: 7,815,264 **% Held:** 43.34

REALTY INCOME CORP.

Exchange	Symbol	Price	52Wk Range	Yield	P/E
NYS	O	$24.62 (5/31/2005)	26.07-19.76	5.39	21.79

Interim Earnings (Per Share)

Qtr.	Mar	Jun	Sep	Dec
2002	0.24	0.24	0.28	0.26
2003	0.23	0.26	0.26	0.34
2004	0.29	0.27	0.28	0.31
2005	0.27	...	...	...

Interim Dividends (Per Share)

Amt	Decl	Ex	Rec	Pay
0.11M	2/16/2005	2/25/2005	3/1/2005	3/15/2005
0.111M	3/22/2005	3/30/2005	4/1/2005	4/15/2005
0.111M	4/13/2005	4/28/2005	5/2/2005	5/16/2005
0.111M	5/10/2005	5/27/2005	6/1/2005	6/15/2005

Indicated Div: $1.33

Valuation Analysis

Forecast P/E	15.24 (6/2/2005)		
Market Cap	$2.0 Billion	Book Value	909.1 Million
Price/Book	2.16	Price/Sales	10.84

Dividend Achiever Status

Rank	49	10 Year Growth Rate	18.62%
Total Years of Dividend Growth			10

Business Summary: Property, Real Estate & Development (MIC: 8.3 SIC: 798 NAIC: 25930)

Realty Income is a real estate investment trust engaged in acquiring and owning freestanding retail properties. As of Dec 31 2004, Co. owned 1,533 retail properties, located in 48 states with more than 11.9 million square feet of leasable space. Co. is a fully integrated, self-administered real estate company with in-house acquisition, leasing, legal, retail and real estate research, portfolio management and capital markets expertise. In addition, Co.'s wholly-owned subsidiary, Crest Net Lease, Inc., focuses on acquiring and subsequently marketing net-leased properties for sale.

Recent Developments: For the quarter ended Mar 31 2005, income from continuing operations increased 12.0% to $21,734 thousand from income of $19,398 thousand in the year-earlier quarter. Net income decreased 5.4% to $23,503 thousand from net income of $24,851 thousand in the year-earlier quarter. Revenues were $46,743 thousand, up 12.8% from $41,456 thousand the year before. Total costs and expenses climbed 13.4% to $25,009 thousand from $22,058 thousand in the previous year.

Prospects: Co. is continuing to grow its revenues along with the growth in its real estate portfolio. During the first quarter of 2005, Co. and its Crest Net Lease subsidiary invested $92.5 million in 34 new properties and properties under development. Co. invested $83.3 million in 31 new properties and properties under development in 12 states with an initial average contractual lease yield of 8.6%. The new properties are 100.0% leased under net-lease agreements with an initial average lease length of 16.1 years. Co. is targeting total acquisitions of $250.0 million in 2005. Looking ahead to full-year 2005, Co. expects funds from operations to range from $1.59 to $1.62 per share.

Financial Data

(US$ in Thousands)	3 Mos	12/31/2004	12/31/2003	12/31/2002	12/31/2001	12/31/2000	12/31/1999	12/31/1998
Earnings Per Share	1.13	1.15	1.08	1.01	0.99	0.84	0.77	0.78
Cash Flow Per Share	2.03	2.27	1.04	1.84	1.54	1.06	1.35	1.21
Tang Book Value Per Share	11.21	11.31	10.69	10.11	8.46	7.49	7.76	8.02
Dividends Per Share	1.281	1.251	1.184	1.154	1.124	1.184	1.048	0.988
Dividend Payout %	113.89	108.80	110.12	113.67	113.51	140.09	136.04	126.60
Income Statement								
Property Income	46,706	174,446	149,279	137,138	122,061	117,190	104,270	84,876
Non-Property Income	37	1,109	6,835	3,842	4,210	1,120	240	256
Total Revenue	46,743	175,555	156,114	140,980	126,271	118,310	104,510	85,132
Depn & Amortn	11,358	41,779	34,416	31,428	29,426	29,003	25,952	21,935
Interest Expense	9,058	34,132	26,974	23,536	26,466	31,547	24,473	13,723
Income Taxes	198	...	...	...	...	...	...	...
Net Income	23,503	103,397	86,435	78,667	67,558	54,788	46,241	41,304
Average Shares	79,659	78,598	71,222	67,976	58,562	53,401	53,652	53,276
Balance Sheet								
Total Assets	1,523,222	1,442,315	1,360,257	1,080,230	1,003,708	934,766	905,404	759,234
Long-Term Obligations	583,100	503,600	506,400	339,700	315,300	404,000	349,200	294,800
Total Liabilities	614,083	528,580	532,491	357,775	331,915	419,197	370,573	309,025
Stockholders' Equity	909,139	913,735	827,766	722,455	671,793	515,569	534,831	450,209
Shares Outstanding	79,582	79,301	75,818	69,749	65,658	53,127	53,644	53,634
Statistical Record								
Return on Assets %	6.90	7.36	7.08	7.55	6.97	5.94	5.56	6.18
Return on Equity %	11.31	11.84	11.15	11.28	11.38	10.40	9.39	9.35
Net Margin %	50.28	58.90	55.37	55.80	53.50	46.31	44.25	48.52
Price Range	26.07-18.13	26.07-18.13	20.49-16.53	18.46-14.65	14.99-12.22	12.75-9.63	12.50-10.25	13.63-11.78
P/E Ratio	23.08-16.04	22.67-15.76	18.97-15.31	18.28-14.50	15.14-12.34	15.18-11.46	16.23-13.31	17.47-15.10
Average Yield %	5.74	5.76	6.22	6.92	8.11	10.43	9.14	7.69

Address: 220 West Crest Street, Escondido, CA 92025-1707 **Telephone:** 760-741-2111 **Web Site:** www.realtyincome.com	**Officers:** William E. Clark - Chmn. Thomas A. Lewis - Vice-Chmn., C.E.O. **Transfer Agents:** The Bank of New York	**No of Institutions:** 106 **Shares:** 19,524,616 **% Held:** 24.53

REGENCY CENTERS CORP.

Exchange	Symbol	Price	52Wk Range	Yield	P/E
NYS	REG	$55.85 (5/31/2005)	56.46-39.80	3.94	24.60

Interim Earnings (Per Share)

Qtr.	Mar	Jun	Sep	Dec
2002	0.42	0.38	0.46	0.58
2003	0.30	0.42	0.51	0.89
2004	0.35	0.41	0.58	0.73
2005	0.55	...	...	...

Interim Dividends (Per Share)

Amt	Decl	Ex	Rec	Pay
0.53Q	7/28/2004	8/9/2004	8/11/2004	8/25/2004
0.53Q	10/27/2004	11/8/2004	11/10/2004	11/24/2004
0.55Q	2/1/2005	2/11/2005	2/15/2005	3/1/2005
0.55Q	5/3/2005	5/16/2005	5/18/2005	6/1/2005

Indicated Div: $2.20

Valuation Analysis

Forecast P/E	15.51 (6/2/2005)		
Market Cap	$3.5 Billion	Book Value	1.5 Billion
Price/Book	2.35	Price/Sales	8.75

Dividend Achiever Status

Rank	281	**10 Year Growth Rate**	4.42%
Total Years of Dividend Growth			10

Business Summary: Property, Real Estate & Development (MIC: 8.3 SIC: 798 NAIC: 25930)

Regency Centers is a self-administered, self-managed real estate investment trust. Co. is a national owner, operator, and developer focused on grocery-anchored, neighborhood retail centers. As of Dec 31 2004, Co. owned 291 retail properties in 23 states, including those held in joint ventures, totaling 33.8 million square feet. Geographically, 19.3% of Co.'s gross leasable area is located in California, 17.7% in Florida, 11.7% in Texas, 10.0% in Georgia, 5.5% in Ohio, and 35.8% spread throughout 18 other states. Co. owns and operates its shopping centers through its operating partnership, Regency Centers, L.P. in which it owns 98.0% of the operating partnership units, as of Dec 31 2004.

Recent Developments: For the quarter ended Mar 31 2005, income from continuing operations increased 38.4% to $29,146,000 from income of $21,060,000 in the year-earlier quarter. Net income increased 68.1% to $38,348,000 from net income of $22,817,000 in the year-earlier quarter. Revenues were $101,688,000, up 10.0% from $92,453,000 the year before. Total operating expenses grew 13.0% to $55,164 thousand from $48,810 thousand in the previous year.

Prospects: Co. is pleased with its operating performance, supported by strong fundamentals in each key area of its business, including its operating portfolio, development and capital recycling and joint ventures. Separately, Co. had 32 properties under development at Mar 31 2005 for an estimated total net investment at completion of $552.0 million. The in-process developments are 56.0% funded and 75.0% leased, including tenant-owned GLA. The expected return on these in-process developments is 10.3%. With Co.'s high probability exceeding $500.0 million, new development starts are still expected to be in the range of $300.0 million to $350.0 million for 2005.

Financial Data

(US$ in Thousands)	3 Mos	12/31/2004	12/31/2003	12/31/2002	12/31/2001	12/31/2000	12/31/1999	12/31/1998
Earnings Per Share	2.27	2.08	2.12	1.84	1.69	1.49	1.61	1.75
Cash Flow Per Share	2.66	2.99	3.84	2.97	3.20	3.14	2.83	2.58
Tang Book Value Per Share	20.42	20.45	19.96	20.34	20.56	20.93	20.41	19.68
Dividends Per Share	2.140	2.120	2.080	2.040	2.000	1.920	1.840	1.760
Dividend Payout %	94.27	101.92	98.11	110.87	118.34	128.86	114.29	100.57
Income Statement								
Property Income	95,979	371,091	359,926	354,183	353,615	331,218	278,960	130,487
Non-Property Income	5,709	20,857	17,695	26,020	34,934	30,365	22,927	12,809
Total Revenue	101,688	391,948	377,621	380,203	388,550	361,583	301,887	143,296
Depn & Amortn	22,850	83,675	76,122	76,016	68,642	60,039	49,168	24,224
Interest Expense	21,076	81,196	86,373	83,620	74,416	71,971	60,067	28,786
Income Before Taxes	...	135,613	144,146	117,873	137,417	122,336	107,968	56,239
Net Income	38,348	136,327	130,789	110,525	100,664	87,611	89,846	50,590
Average Shares	62,562	61,481	61,242	60,438	59,274	56,754	55,502	26,898
Balance Sheet								
Total Assets	3,195,566	3,243,824	3,098,229	3,061,859	3,109,314	3,035,144	2,654,936	1,240,107
Long-Term Obligations	175,000	1,493,090	1,452,777	1,333,524	1,396,721	1,307,072	1,011,967	548,126
Total Liabilities	1,560,840	1,610,743	1,562,530	1,419,280	1,478,812	1,390,795	1,068,805	571,173
Stockholders' Equity	1,501,708	1,498,717	1,280,978	1,221,720	1,219,051	1,225,415	1,247,249	550,741
Shares Outstanding	63,087	62,808	59,907	59,557	57,601	56,898	59,423	27,988
Statistical Record								
Return on Assets %	4.83	4.29	4.25	3.58	3.28	3.07	4.61	4.90
Return on Equity %	10.95	9.78	10.45	9.06	8.24	7.07	9.99	9.51
Net Margin %	37.71	34.78	34.64	29.07	25.91	24.23	29.76	35.30
Price Range	55.40-35.11	55.40-35.11	40.20-30.60	32.40-26.80	27.75-22.94	24.00-18.44	22.94-18.75	27.75-20.50
P/E Ratio	24.41-15.47	26.63-16.88	18.96-14.43	17.61-14.57	16.42-13.57	16.11-12.37	14.25-11.65	15.86-11.71
Average Yield %	4.62	4.79	5.94	6.84	8.02	8.92	8.81	7.23

Address: 121 West Forsyth Street, Suite 200, Jacksonville, FL 32202 **Telephone:** 904-598-7000 **Web Site:** www.regencyrealty.com	**Officers:** Martin E. Stein Jr. - Chmn., C.E.O. Mary Lou Fiala - Pres., C.O.O. **Transfer Agents:**	**Investor Contact:** 904-598-7000 **No of Institutions:** 158 **Shares:** 59,345,844 **% Held:** 94.09

REGIONS FINANCIAL CORP

Exchange	Symbol	Price	52Wk Range	Yield	P/E
NYS	RF	$33.68 (5/31/2005)	35.79-29.57	4.04	17.27

*7 Year Price Score N/A *NYSE Composite Index=100 *12 Month Price Score N/A

TRADING VOLUME (thousand shares)

Interim Earnings (Per Share)

Qtr.	Mar	Jun	Sept	Dec
2002	0.66	0.67	0.70	0.69
2003	0.71	0.73	0.73	0.73
2004	0.75	0.58	0.55	0.31
2005	0.51	...	...	...

Interim Dividends (Per Share)

Amt	Decl	Ex	Rec	Pay
0.333Q	7/16/2004	7/29/2004	8/2/2004	8/16/2004
0.333Q	10/21/2004	10/28/2004	11/1/2004	11/15/2004
0.34Q	1/21/2005	1/28/2005	2/1/2005	2/15/2005
0.34Q	4/21/2005	4/28/2005	5/2/2005	5/16/2005

Indicated Div: $1.36

Valuation Analysis

Forecast P/E	N/A		
Market Cap	$15.6 Billion	Book Value	10.6 Billion
Price/Book	1.47	Price/Sales	N/A

Dividend Achiever Status

Rank	136	10 Year Growth Rate	12.05%
Total Years of Dividend Growth			33

Business Summary: Commercial Banking (MIC: 8.1 SIC: 712 NAIC: 51111)

Regions Financial is a financial holding company which operates primarily within the southeastern United States. Co.'s operations consist of banking, brokerage and investment services, mortgage banking, insurance brokerage, credit life insurance, commercial accounts receivable factoring and specialty financing. At Dec. 31, 2004, Co. had total consolidated assets of $84.11 billion and total consolidated deposits of approximately $58.67 billion. As of Dec. 31, 2004, Co. operated 1,323 full service banking offices in Alabama, Arkansas, Florida, Georgia, Illinois, Indiana, Iowa, Kentucky, Louisiana, Mississippi, Missouri, North Carolina, South Carolina, Tennessee and Texas.

Recent Developments: For the quarter ended Mar 31 2005, net income increased 43.4% to $241,641 thousand from net income of $168,535 thousand in the year-earlier quarter. Net interest income was $810,339 thousand, up 72.0% from $471,215 thousand the year before. Provision for loan losses was $30,000 thousand versus $15,000 thousand in the prior-year quarter, an increase of 100.0%. Non-interest income rose 17.0% to $418,802 thousand, while non-interest expense advanced 49.3% to $721,838 thousand.

Prospects: On May 3 2005, Co. announced that it has completed the conversion of more than 130 former Union Planters Bank branch locations in Arkansas, Texas, Louisiana, north Alabama, south Kentucky and eastern and middle Tennessee. The customer systems conversion was the first bank branch integration since Co. acquired Union Planters Corp. on Jul 1 2004. The second bank conversion event, set for Aug 2005, will involve more than 200 Union Planters Bank branches in Mississippi, southern Alabama, west Tennessee and the greater Memphis, TN, area. The remaining Union Planters branches in south Florida and the Midwest are scheduled for technical conversion by year-end 2005.

Financial Data

(US$ in Thousands)	3 Mos	12/31/2004	12/31/2003	12/31/2002	12/31/2001	12/31/2000	12/31/1999	12/31/1998
Earnings Per Share	1.95	2.19	2.90	2.72	2.24	2.38	2.35	1.88
Cash Flow Per Share	...	2.90	4.17	1.50	(0.14)	4.31	4.51	(1.38)
Tang Book Value Per Share	10.53	10.73	20.06	18.88	17.54	15.73	13.89	13.61
Dividends Per Share	1.41	1.49	1.240	1.160	1.120	1.080	1.000	0.920
Dividend Payout %	...	68.04	42.76	42.65	50.00	45.38	42.55	48.94
Income Statement								
Interest Income	991,976	2,955,685	2,219,130	2,536,989	3,055,637	3,234,243	2,854,686	2,597,786
Interest Expense	311,405	842,651	744,532	1,039,401	1,630,144	1,845,446	1,428,831	1,272,968
Net Interest Income	680,571	2,113,034	1,474,598	1,497,588	1,425,493	1,388,797	1,425,855	1,324,818
Provision for Losses	30,000	128,500	121,500	127,500	165,402	127,099	113,658	60,505
Non-Interest Income	418,802	1,654,354	1,398,757	1,258,878	981,885	601,210	537,141	474,697
Non-Interest Expense	721,838	2,463,306	1,827,316	1,747,405	1,524,025	1,121,182	1,064,312	1,103,708
Income Before Taxes	347,535	1,175,582	911,572	869,240	717,951	741,726	785,026	635,302
Income Taxes	105,894	351,817	259,731	249,338	209,017	214,203	259,640	213,590
Net Income	241,641	823,765	651,841	619,902	508,934	527,523	525,386	421,712
Average Shares	470,759	373,732	225,118	227,639	227,063	221,989	223,967	223,781
Balance Sheet								
Net Loans & Leases	57,204,471	56,772,233	31,730,266	30,548,610	30,466,181	30,999,955	27,806,300	24,050,175
Total Assets	84,283,632	84,106,438	48,597,996	47,938,840	45,382,712	43,688,293	42,714,395	36,831,940
Total Deposits	59,587,671	58,667,023	32,732,535	32,926,201	31,548,323	32,022,491	29,989,094	28,350,066
Total Liabilities	73,638,489	73,356,981	44,145,881	43,760,418	41,346,947	40,230,349	39,649,283	33,831,539
Stockholders' Equity	10,645,143	10,749,457	4,452,115	4,178,422	4,035,765	3,457,944	3,065,112	3,000,401
Shares Outstanding	463,228	466,241	221,967	221,336	230,081	219,769	220,635	220,454
Statistical Record								
Return on Assets %	1.14	1.24	1.35	1.33	1.14	1.22	1.32	1.41
Return on Equity %	9.08	10.81	15.11	15.09	13.58	16.13	17.32	17.17
Net Interest Margin %	68.61	71.49	66.45	59.03	46.65	42.94	49.95	51.00
Efficiency Ratio %	51.17	53.43	50.51	46.03	37.75	29.23	31.38	35.92
Loans to Deposits	0.96	0.97	0.97	0.93	0.97	0.97	0.93	0.85
Price Range	35.79-29.57	35.79-29.57	37.85-30.49	36.13-27.10	32.35-26.34	27.81-18.44	41.44-23.38	45.25-30.25
P/E Ratio	18.35-15.16	16.34-13.50	13.05-10.51	13.28-9.96	14.44-11.76	11.69-7.75	17.63-9.95	24.07-16.09
Average Yield %	3.04	2.01	3.58	3.45	3.77	4.82	2.89	2.33

Address: 417 North 20th Street, Birmingham, AL 35203
Telephone: 205-944-1300
Web Site: www.regions.com

Officers: Carl E. Jones Jr. - Chmn., C.E.O. Richard D. Horsley - Vice-Chmn., C.O.O. **Transfer Agents:**

Investor Contact: 205-326-7090
No of Institutions: 332
Shares: 123,185,336 **% Held:** 26.51

REPUBLIC BANCORP, INC.

Exchange	Symbol	Price	52Wk Range	Yield	P/E
NMS	RBNC	$13.87 (5/31/2005)	15.90-12.04	3.17	15.24

***7 Year Price Score 127.55** *NYSE Composite Index=100 ***12 Month Price Score 92.62**

Interim Earnings (Per Share)

Qtr.	Mar	Jun	Sep	Dec
2002	0.20	0.20	0.22	0.13
2003	0.21	0.21	0.25	0.15
2004	0.23	0.23	0.27	0.17
2005	0.24	...	...	...

Interim Dividends (Per Share)

Amt	Decl	Ex	Rec	Pay
10%	10/22/2004	11/3/2004	11/5/2004	12/3/2004
0.11Q	11/18/2004	12/8/2004	12/10/2004	1/4/2005
0.11Q	2/18/2005	3/9/2005	3/11/2005	4/4/2005
0.11Q	4/27/2005	6/8/2005	6/10/2005	7/5/2005

Indicated Div: $0.44 (Div. Reinv. Plan)

Valuation Analysis

Forecast P/E	19.38 (4/15/2004)		
Market Cap	$974.7 Million	Book Value	404.9 Million
Price/Book	2.41	Price/Sales	2.88

Dividend Achiever Status

Rank	98	**10 Year Growth Rate**	14.52%
Total Years of Dividend Growth			12

Business Summary: Commercial Banking (MIC: 8.1 SIC: 021 NAIC: 22110)

Republic Bancorp, with total assets of $5.72 billion and total deposits of $3.05 billion as of Dec 31 2004, is a bank holding company. Through its wholly-owned subsidiary, Republic Bank, a Michigan banking corporation, Co. has three primary lines of business: commercial banking, retail banking and mortgage banking. Republic Bank offers financial products to consumers and businesses through its 95 retail, commercial and mortgage banking branches located in Michigan, Ohio and Indiana and a loan production office in Massachusetts. Co. also operated a network of 97 ATMs as of Dec 31 2004.

Recent Developments: For the quarter ended Mar 31 2005, net income increased 6.2% to $17,307 thousand from net income of $16,299 thousand in the year-earlier quarter. Net interest income was $38,328 thousand, up 6.8% from $35,879 thousand the year before. Provision for loan losses was $1,500 thousand versus $2,500 thousand in the prior-year quarter, a decrease of 40.0%. Non-interest income rose 2.1% to $11,038 thousand, while non-interest expense advanced 8.8% to $22,872 thousand.

Prospects: Co. is benefiting from solid performance from its three business lines. Total assets continue to grow driven by increases in all three targeted loan portfolios. Installment loans are being positively affected by strong demand for home equity loans. Meanwhile, Co.'s commercial loan portfolio is seeing growth due to demand for commercial real estate mortgages. Co. is experiencing strong originations of single-family residential mortgages and its residential real estate mortgage loan portfolio growth is primarily the reflects its retention of adjustable-rate mortgage loans. Co.'s net interest income is being positively affected by the growth in its loan portfolios.

Financial Data

(US$ in Thousands)	3 Mos	12/31/2004	12/31/2003	12/31/2002	12/31/2001	12/31/2000	12/31/1999	12/31/1998
Earnings Per Share	0.91	0.94	0.86	0.79	0.65	0.63	0.20	0.54
Cash Flow Per Share	2.32	1.15	8.13	1.89	(6.95)	1.64	3.90	(6.53)
Tang Book Value Per Share	5.76	5.82	5.29	4.79	4.27	3.36	2.73	2.16
Dividends Per Share	0.406	0.383	0.305	0.262	0.238	0.216	0.205	0.181
Dividend Payout %	44.79	40.72	35.36	33.00	36.42	34.44	100.15	33.33
Income Statement								
Interest Income	75,841	282,379	265,680	284,704	333,376	348,328	299,662	146,005
Interest Expense	37,513	132,529	123,183	137,024	189,767	213,680	171,396	86,364
Net Interest Income	38,328	149,850	142,497	147,680	143,609	134,648	128,266	59,641
Provision for Losses	1,500	8,500	12,000	16,000	8,700	6,500	11,650	4,000
Non-Interest Income	11,038	47,319	60,779	56,027	71,384	70,838	137,731	137,441
Non-Interest Expense	22,872	94,075	104,654	100,515	132,213	127,641	225,968	157,466
Income Before Taxes	24,994	94,594	86,622	87,192	74,080	71,345	28,379	35,616
Income Taxes	7,687	27,910	25,896	24,687	22,515	22,945	10,745	12,726
Net Income	17,307	66,684	60,726	62,505	51,565	48,400	17,634	22,890
Average Shares	71,201	71,273	70,588	71,420	73,231	73,058	73,696	42,329
Balance Sheet								
Net Loans & Leases	4,446,301	4,422,157	4,117,243	3,620,466	3,429,224	3,743,226	3,346,297	1,201,979
Total Assets	5,923,692	5,713,977	5,353,688	4,778,195	4,740,605	4,610,641	4,301,615	2,195,612
Total Deposits	2,992,746	3,046,211	2,815,269	2,788,272	2,753,468	2,728,526	2,613,050	1,378,691
Total Liabilities	5,518,744	5,304,339	4,984,268	4,395,467	4,356,969	4,287,058	4,005,360	2,044,268
Stockholders' Equity	404,948	409,638	369,420	332,728	304,917	294,864	266,441	150,417
Shares Outstanding	70,274	70,425	69,879	69,503	70,763	72,361	72,933	42,079
Statistical Record								
Return on Assets %	1.18	1.20	1.20	1.31	1.10	1.08	0.54	1.13
Return on Equity %	17.10	17.07	17.30	19.60	17.19	17.20	8.46	16.26
Net Interest Margin %	50.54	53.07	53.63	51.87	43.08	38.66	42.80	40.85
Efficiency Ratio %	26.33	28.53	32.06	29.50	32.66	30.45	51.66	55.55
Loans to Deposits	1.49	1.45	1.46	1.30	1.25	1.37	1.28	0.87
Price Range	15.90-11.64	15.90-11.64	12.71-9.59	11.53-8.44	10.91-7.34	7.85-4.70	8.57-6.42	9.67-6.77
P/E Ratio	17.47-12.79	16.91-12.38	14.78-11.15	14.60-10.69	16.78-11.30	12.47-7.45	42.86-32.10	17.90-12.54
Average Yield %	2.96	2.88	2.77	2.60	2.56	3.72	2.77	2.12

Address: 1070 East Main Street, P.O. Box 70, Owosso, MI 48867 **Telephone:** 989-725-7337 **Web Site:** www.republicbancorp.com	**Officers:** Jerry D. Campbell - Chmn. George J. Butvilas - Vice-Chmn. **Transfer Agents:** EquiServe Trust Company, N.A., Providence, RI	**Investor Contact:** 989-725-7337 **No of Institutions:** 122 **Shares:** 31,209,184 **% Held:** 44.28

RLI CORP.

Exchange	Symbol	Price	52Wk Range	Yield	P/E
NYS	RLI	$43.74 (5/31/2005)	45.43-35.52	1.46	13.34

*7 Year Price Score 137.84 *NYSE Composite Index=100 *12 Month Price Score 104.26

Interim Earnings (Per Share)

Qtr.	Mar	Jun	Sep	Dec
2002	0.45	0.48	0.28	0.54
2003	0.56	0.60	0.98	0.62
2004	0.65	0.71	0.32	1.13
2005	1.12	...	...	...

Interim Dividends (Per Share)

Amt	Decl	Ex	Rec	Pay
0.13Q	8/3/2004	9/28/2004	9/30/2004	10/15/2004
0.14Q	11/19/2004	12/29/2004	12/31/2004	1/14/2005
0.14Q	2/3/2005	3/29/2005	3/31/2005	4/15/2005
0.16Q	5/5/2005	6/28/2005	6/30/2005	7/15/2005

Indicated Div: $0.64 (Div. Reinv. Plan)

Valuation Analysis

Forecast P/E	14.11 (6/2/2005)		
Market Cap	$1.1 Billion	Book Value	631.3 Million
Price/Book	1.76	Price/Sales	1.92

Dividend Achiever Status

Rank	171	**10 Year Growth Rate**	10.16%
Total Years of Dividend Growth			28

Business Summary: Insurance (MIC: 8.2 SIC: 331 NAIC: 24126)

RLI is a holding company that underwrites selected property and casualty insurance through its insurance subsidiaries. Co. conducts its operations principally through three insurance companies. RLI Insurance Company, Co.'s principal subsidiary, writes multiple lines insurance on an admitted basis in all 50 states, the District of Columbia and Puerto Rico. Mt. Hawley Insurance Company, a subsidiary of RLI Insurance, writes surplus lines insurance in all 50 states, the District of Columbia, Puerto Rico, the Virgin Islands and Guam. RLI Indemnity Company, a subsidiary of Mt. Hawley, has authority to write multiple lines insurance on an admitted basis in 48 states and the District of Columbia.

Recent Developments: For the first quarter ended Mar 31 2005, net earnings advanced 73.0% to $29.3 million compared with $16.9 million in the corresponding prior-year quarter. Total revenue rose 0.7% to $141.6 million from $140.6 million a year earlier. Net investment income climbed 18.7% to $14.6 million, and net realized investment gains grew 22.5% to $3.0 million. Net premiums earned decreased 1.5% to $124.0 million. Total costs and expenses fell 14.2% to $101.4 million from $118.1 million the year before.

Prospects: Co.'s outlook appears satisfactory, reflecting in part profitable underwriting results reported across each of its segments for the first quarter ended Mar 31 2005. However, Co. noted that the marketplace continues to soften in many coverage areas. Separately, during the first quarter ended Mar 31 2005, Co. announced the opening of a marine insurance division in New York, NY. Co. stated that the new division will focus on marine classes of cargo, hull, protection and indemnity, primary and excess liabilities, yachts and other marine coverages. The division plans to have a presence in several other current RLI offices.

Financial Data

(US$ in Thousands)	3 Mos	12/31/2004	12/31/2003	12/31/2002	12/31/2001	12/31/2000	12/31/1999	12/31/1998
Earnings Per Share	3.28	2.80	2.76	1.75	1.55	1.45	1.54	1.33
Cash Flow Per Share	7.36	7.47	7.60	8.12	3.97	2.70	2.88	1.12
Tang Book Value Per Share	23.80	23.60	20.98	17.37	15.36	14.99	13.11	14.12
Dividends Per Share	0.540	0.510	0.400	0.345	0.315	0.295	0.275	0.255
Dividend Payout %	16.46	18.21	14.49	19.71	20.32	20.42	17.86	19.25
Income Statement								
Premium Income	124,040	511,348	463,597	348,065	273,008	231,603	195,274	142,324
Total Revenue	141,636	578,800	519,886	382,153	309,354	263,496	225,756	168,114
Benefits & Claims	56,519	306,131	278,990	203,122	155,876	124,586	96,457	64,728
Income Before Taxes	41,540	100,342	94,278	48,728	41,018	38,293	43,035	37,721
Income Taxes	12,233	27,306	22,987	12,876	10,771	9,600	11,584	9,482
Net Income	29,307	73,036	71,291	35,852	31,047	28,693	31,451	28,239
Average Shares	26,213	26,093	25,846	20,512	20,004	19,890	20,444	21,276
Balance Sheet								
Total Assets	2,519,636	2,468,775	2,134,364	1,719,327	1,390,970	1,281,323	1,170,363	1,012,685
Total Liabilities	1,888,296	1,845,114	1,580,230	1,262,772	1,055,538	954,669	877,294	718,726
Stockholders' Equity	631,340	623,661	554,134	456,555	335,432	326,654	293,069	293,959
Shares Outstanding	25,430	25,315	25,165	24,681	19,825	19,607	19,746	20,811
Statistical Record								
Return on Assets %	3.63	3.16	3.70	2.31	2.32	2.33	2.88	2.93
Return on Equity %	14.15	12.37	14.11	9.05	9.38	9.23	10.72	10.08
Loss Ratio %	45.57	59.87	60.18	58.36	57.10	53.79	49.40	45.48
Net Margin %	20.69	12.62	13.71	9.38	10.04	10.89	13.93	16.80
Price Range	44.99-33.55	43.20-33.55	38.10-25.40	29.60-22.25	23.00-19.40	22.34-13.25	19.38-13.97	22.65-15.41
P/E Ratio	13.72-10.23	15.43-11.98	13.80-9.20	16.91-12.71	14.84-12.52	15.41-9.14	12.58-9.07	17.03-11.58
Average Yield %	1.39	1.34	1.28	1.33	1.50	1.66	1.64	1.30

Address: 9025 North Lindbergh Drive, Peoria, IL 61615-1499
Telephone: 309-692-1000
Web Site: www.rlicorp.com

Officers: Jonathan E. Michael - Pres., C.E.O. Joseph E. Dondanville - Sr. V.P., C.F.O. **Transfer Agents:** Wells Fargo Shareholder Services, St. Paul, MN

Investor Contact: 309-693-5880
No of Institutions: 119
Shares: 18,816,248 **% Held:** 74.08

ROHM & HAAS CO.

Exchange	Symbol	Price	52Wk Range	Yield	P/E
NYS	ROH	$46.65 (5/31/2005)	49.62-37.23	2.49	19.36

*7 Year Price Score 104.19 *NYSE Composite Index=100 *12 Month Price Score 101.65

Interim Earnings (Per Share)

Qtr.	Mar	Jun	Sep	Dec
2002	0.36	0.40	0.33	(0.17)
2003	0.33	(0.02)	0.45	0.49
2004	0.51	0.52	0.61	0.58
2005	0.70	...	...	...

Interim Dividends (Per Share)

Amt	Decl	Ex	Rec	Pay
0.25Q	7/26/2004	8/11/2004	8/13/2004	9/1/2004
0.25Q	9/24/2004	11/3/2004	11/5/2004	12/1/2004
0.25Q	2/7/2005	2/16/2005	2/18/2005	3/1/2005
0.29Q	5/2/2005	5/11/2005	5/13/2005	6/1/2005

Indicated Div: $1.16 (Div. Reinv. Plan)

Valuation Analysis

Forecast P/E	16.43 (6/1/2005)		
Market Cap	$10.6 Billion	Book Value	3.9 Billion
Price/Book	2.73	Price/Sales	1.41

Dividend Achiever Status

Rank	224	10 Year Growth Rate	7.29%
Total Years of Dividend Growth			27

Business Summary: Chemicals (MIC: 11.1 SIC: 821 NAIC: 25211)

Rohm & Haas is a global specialty materials company that operates through six reportable segments: coatings, adhesives and sealants, electronic materials, performance chemicals, salt and monomers. Coatings is Co.'s largest segment in terms of sales, and is comprised of three businesses including architectural functional coatings, powder coatings and automotive coatings. Co. operates approximately 100 manufacturing and 37 research facilities in 27 countries, and serves several industries, including construction and building, electronics, household products and personal care, packaging, food and retail, and automotive.

Recent Developments: For the quarter ended Mar 31 2005, net income increased 39.5% to $159,000 thousand from net income of $114,000 thousand in the year-earlier quarter. Revenues were $2,022,000 thousand, up 10.4% from $1,832,000 thousand the year before. Total direct expense was $1,412,000 thousand versus $1,304,000 thousand in the prior-year quarter, an increase of 8.3%. Total indirect expense was $351,000 thousand versus $328,000 thousand in the prior-year quarter, an increase of 7.0%.

Prospects: Co. is experiencing solid earnings growth and improved margins as a result of the successful implementation of price increases to recover the extraordinary run-up in raw material and energy costs. Looking ahead, Co. continues to expect modest overall volume growth for the year. Co. remains focused on improving its sales mix through the introduction of new and improved products, implementing selective price increases to offset continuing escalations in raw material and energy costs, improving its manufacturing efficiency and streamlining its processes. As a result, Co. expects full-year 2005 sales in excess of $8.00 billion and earnings in the range of $2.65 to $2.90 per share.

Financial Data

(US$ in Thousands)	3 Mos	12/31/2004	12/31/2003	12/31/2002	12/31/2001	12/31/2000	12/31/1999	12/31/1998
Earnings Per Share	2.41	2.22	1.26	(2.57)	1.79	1.61	1.27	2.45
Cash Flow Per Share	3.99	3.95	4.51	4.41	3.17	3.50	4.24	3.88
Tang Book Value Per Share	1.92	1.37	0.13	N.M.	N.M.	N.M.	N.M.	9.06
Dividends Per Share	1.000	0.970	0.860	0.820	0.800	0.780	0.740	0.693
Dividend Payout %	41.49	43.69	68.25	...	44.69	48.45	58.27	28.30
Income Statement								
Total Revenue	2,022,000	7,300,000	6,421,000	5,727,000	5,666,000	6,879,000	5,339,000	3,720,000
EBITDA	384,000	1,319,000	1,014,000	903,000	672,000	1,428,000	1,061,000	992,000
Depn & Amortn	119,000	481,000	478,000	457,000	562,000	613,000	451,000	271,000
Income Before Taxes	230,000	714,000	415,000	320,000	(64,000)	581,000	464,000	700,000
Income Taxes	70,000	207,000	127,000	102,000	6,000	227,000	215,000	247,000
Net Income	159,000	497,000	280,000	(570,000)	395,000	354,000	249,000	440,000
Average Shares	226,500	224,200	222,400	221,900	220,200	220,500	218,981	179,700
Balance Sheet								
Current Assets	2,861,000	3,247,000	2,527,000	2,543,000	2,421,000	2,781,000	2,497,000	1,287,000
Total Assets	9,624,000	10,095,000	9,445,000	9,706,000	10,350,000	11,267,000	11,256,000	3,648,000
Current Liabilities	1,588,000	1,740,000	1,797,000	1,621,000	1,624,000	2,194,000	2,510,000	875,000
Long-Term Obligations	2,089,000	2,563,000	2,468,000	2,872,000	2,720,000	3,225,000	3,122,000	409,000
Total Liabilities	5,654,000	6,294,000	6,075,000	6,576,000	6,517,000	7,591,000	7,762,000	2,068,000
Stockholders' Equity	3,859,000	3,697,000	3,357,000	3,119,000	3,815,000	3,653,000	3,475,000	1,561,000
Shares Outstanding	226,231	225,260	222,453	221,131	220,427	219,937	218,981	154,000
Statistical Record								
Return on Assets %	5.65	5.07	2.92	N.M.	3.65	3.13	3.34	11.66
Return on Equity %	14.86	14.05	8.65	N.M.	10.58	9.91	9.89	26.21
EBITDA Margin %	18.99	18.07	15.79	15.77	11.86	20.76	19.87	26.67
Net Margin %	7.86	6.81	4.36	N.M.	6.97	5.15	4.66	11.83
Asset Turnover	0.78	0.75	0.67	0.57	0.52	0.61	0.72	0.99
Current Ratio	1.80	1.87	1.41	1.57	1.49	1.27	0.99	1.47
Debt to Equity	0.54	0.69	0.74	0.92	0.71	0.88	0.90	0.26
Price Range	49.62-36.16	45.17-36.16	42.92-26.67	42.27-30.55	38.27-26.12	47.88-26.00	49.13-28.75	38.54-26.75
P/E Ratio	20.59-15.00	20.35-16.29	34.06-21.17	...	21.38-14.59	29.74-16.15	38.68-22.64	15.73-10.92
Average Yield %	2.38	2.39	2.53	2.25	2.35	2.26	1.96	2.10

Address: 100 Independence Mall West, Philadelphia, PA 19106-2399
Telephone: 215-592-3000
Web Site: www.rohmhaas.com

Officers: Raj L. Gupta - Chmn., C.E.O., Pres. Alan E. Barton - V.P., Coatings, Business Unit Director, Architectural Functional Coatings **Transfer Agents:** EquiServe Trust Company, N.A., Providence, RI

Investor Contact: 215-592-3052
No of Institutions: 275
Shares: 124,569,768 **% Held:** 55.10

ROPER INDUSTRIES, INC

Exchange	Symbol	Price	52Wk Range	Yield	P/E
NYS	ROP	$69.90 (5/31/2005)	71.91-50.82	0.61	26.38

***7 Year Price Score 135.77** *NYSE Composite Index=100 ***12 Month Price Score 108.23**

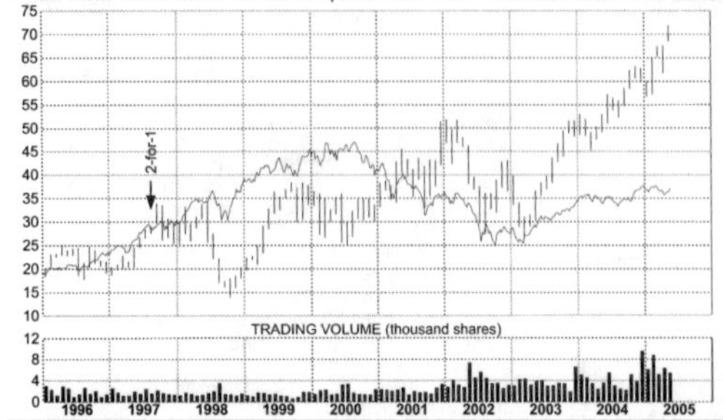

TRADING VOLUME (thousand shares)

Interim Earnings (Per Share)

Qtr.	Mar	Jun	Sep	Dec
2003			1.41	
2004	0.49	0.63	0.73	0.64
2005	0.65	...	...	...

Interim Dividends (Per Share)

Amt	Decl	Ex	Rec	Pay
0.096Q	8/17/2004	10/13/2004	10/15/2004	10/29/2004
0.106Q	11/18/2004	1/12/2005	1/14/2005	1/31/2005
0.106Q	3/3/2005	4/13/2005	4/15/2005	4/29/2005
0.106Q	5/25/2005	7/13/2005	7/15/2005	7/29/2005

Indicated Div: $0.42

Valuation Analysis

Forecast P/E	21.04 (6/1/2005)		
Market Cap	$3.0 Billion	Book Value	1.1 Billion
Price/Book	2.63	Price/Sales	2.75

Dividend Achiever Status

Rank	50	**10 Year Growth Rate**	18.59%
Total Years of Dividend Growth			12

Business Summary: Industrial Machinery and Equipment (MIC: 11.5 SIC: 561 NAIC: 33911)

Roper Industries is a diversified industrial company that designs, manufactures and distributes energy systems and controls, scientific and industrial imaging products and software, industrial technology products and instrumentation and radio frequency (RF) products and services. Co. markets these products and services to selected segments of a broad range of markets, including RF applications, water and wastewater, oil and gas, research, power generation, general industry, and fifteen other niche markets. Co. operates through five business segments: Instrumentation, Industrial Technology, Energy Systems and Controls, Scientific and Industrial Imaging, and RF Technology.

Recent Developments: For the quarter ended Mar 31 2005, net income increased 54.5% to $28,011 thousand from net income of $18,134 thousand in the year-earlier quarter. Revenues were $333,837 thousand, up 51.3% from $220,640 thousand the year before. Operating income was $51,864 thousand versus an income of $32,972 thousand in the prior-year quarter, an increase of 57.3%. Total direct expense was $171,213 thousand versus $111,202 thousand in the prior-year quarter, an increase of 54.0%. Total indirect expense was $110,760 thousand versus $76,466 thousand in the prior-year quarter, an increase of 44.8%.

Prospects: Co.'s results are benefiting from contributions from its new Radio Frequency (RF) segment businesses, TransCore and Inovonics, the latter of which was acquired on Feb 28 2005. Co. stated that it is making progress on its RF technology and market initiatives and remains excited about the growing potential for RF applications into targeted markets, such as security and asset tracking. Also, Co.'s Instrumentation, Industrial Technology, and Energy Systems & Controls segments posted solid top line growth and higher profit for the quarter ended Mar 31 2005. Thus, Co. has raised its full year 2005 diluted earnings per share guidance to a range of $3.15 to $3.35 from $3.10 to $3.30.

Financial Data

(US$ in Thousands)	3 Mos	12/31/2004	12/31/2003	12/31/2002	10/31/2002	10/31/2001	10/31/2000	10/31/1999
Earnings Per Share	2.65	2.48	1.41	0.03	1.26	1.77	1.58	1.53
Cash Flow Per Share	4.19	4.42	2.26	0.20	2.79	3.33	2.21	1.75
Tang Book Value Per Share	N.M.	N.M.	N.M.	N.M.	N.M.	N.M.	N.M.	0.56
Dividends Per Share	0.395	0.385	0.350	0.330	0.330	0.300	0.280	0.260
Dividend Payout %	14.91	15.52	24.82	1,100.00	26.19	16.95	17.72	16.99
Income Statement								
Total Revenue	333,837	969,764	657,356	83,885	627,030	586,506	503,813	407,256
EBITDA	69,604	199,262	98,442	7,367	129,368	129,811	111,712	95,504
Depn & Amortn	17,728	36,699	15,768	2,620	15,176	27,455	22,298	15,966
Income Before Taxes	41,499	133,716	66,290	1,769	95,686	86,439	75,931	72,284
Income Taxes	13,488	39,864	18,229	529	29,663	30,600	26,653	24,938
Net Income	28,011	93,852	45,239	853	40,053	55,839	49,278	47,346
Average Shares	43,157	37,832	31,992	31,854	31,815	31,493	31,182	30,992
Balance Sheet								
Current Assets	533,989	556,160	381,192	247,565	247,622	233,053	213,955	161,819
Total Assets	2,356,074	2,366,404	1,514,995	824,966	828,973	762,122	596,902	420,163
Current Liabilities	232,575	253,550	161,497	121,344	130,237	103,880	84,492	72,243
Long-Term Obligations	844,539	855,364	630,186	308,684	311,590	323,830	234,603	109,659
Total Liabilities	1,223,091	1,252,318	859,214	443,985	452,961	438,616	326,711	188,195
Stockholders' Equity	1,132,983	1,114,086	655,781	380,981	376,012	323,506	270,191	231,968
Shares Outstanding	42,601	42,416	36,042	31,370	31,363	30,879	30,599	30,282
Statistical Record								
Return on Assets %	5.35	4.82	3.87	0.09	5.03	8.22	9.66	11.81
Return on Equity %	11.32	10.58	8.73	0.21	11.45	18.81	19.57	22.07
EBITDA Margin %	20.85	20.55	14.98	8.78	20.63	22.13	22.17	23.45
Net Margin %	8.39	9.68	6.88	1.02	6.39	9.52	9.78	11.63
Asset Turnover	0.56	0.50	0.56	0.09	0.79	0.86	0.99	1.02
Current Ratio	2.30	2.19	2.36	2.04	1.90	2.24	2.53	2.24
Debt to Equity	0.75	0.77	0.96	0.81	0.83	1.00	0.87	0.47
Price Range	67.55-47.45	63.31-45.27	51.58-26.75	43.15-36.46	51.80-27.36	45.50-30.06	38.31-25.00	38.38-15.94
P/E Ratio	25.49-17.91	25.53-18.25	36.58-18.97	N.M.	41.11-21.71	25.71-16.98	24.25-15.82	25.08-10.42
Average Yield %	0.69	0.71	0.89	0.84	0.80	0.79	0.86	0.93

Address: 2160 Satellite Boulevard, Suite 200, Duluth, GA 30097
Telephone: 770-495-5100
Web Site: www.roperind.com

Officers: Brian D. Jellison - Chmn., Pres., C.E.O. Shanler D. Cronk - V.P., Sec., Couns. **Transfer Agents:** Wachovia Bank, N.A., Charlotte, NC

No of Institutions: 209
Shares: 36,014,016 **% Held:** 84.78

ROSS STORES, INC.

Exchange	Symbol	Price	52Wk Range	Yield	P/E
NMS	ROST	$28.19 (5/31/2005)	30.41-21.15	0.71	24.95

*7 Year Price Score 138.92 *NYSE Composite Index=100 *12 Month Price Score 100.39

TRADING VOLUME (thousand shares)

Interim Earnings (Per Share)

Qtr.	Apr	Jul	Oct	Jan
2000-01	0.23	0.22	0.18	0.28
2001-02	0.22	0.22	0.22	0.31
2002-03	0.29	0.31	0.28	0.37
2003-04	0.32	0.35	0.33	0.47
2004-05	0.32	0.22	0.26	0.34

Interim Dividends (Per Share)

Amt	Decl	Ex	Rec	Pay
0.043Q	8/19/2004	8/31/2004	9/2/2004	10/1/2004
0.043Q	11/17/2004	12/6/2004	12/8/2004	1/3/2005
0.05Q	2/3/2005	2/23/2005	2/25/2005	4/1/2005
0.05Q	5/19/2005	6/9/2005	6/13/2005	7/1/2005

Indicated Div: $0.20

Valuation Analysis

Forecast P/E 15.61 (6/3/2005)

Market Cap	$4.1 Billion	Book Value	765.6 Million
Price/Book	5.40	Price/Sales	0.98

Dividend Achiever Status

Rank	23	**10 Year Growth Rate**	23.62%
Total Years of Dividend Growth			10

Business Summary: Retail - Apparel and Accessory Stores (MIC: 5.8 SIC: 651 NAIC: 48140)

Ross Stores operates a chain of off-price retail apparel and home accessories stores, which target value conscious men and women between the ages of 25 and 54, primarily in middle income households. The decisions of Co., from merchandising, purchasing and pricing, to the location of its stores, are aimed at this customer base. Co. offers brand name and designer merchandise at low everyday prices, generally 20% to 60% below regular prices of most department and specialty stores, in an organized and easy-to-shop environment. As of Jan 29 2005, Co. operated 639 Ross Dress for Less stores and ten dd's DISCOUNTSsm stores in 26 states and Guam, which are supported by four distribution centers.

Recent Developments: For the quarter ended Apr 30 2005, net income advanced 4.0% to $50.0 million compared with $48.1 million in the equivalent 2004 quarter. Sales grew 13.3% to $1.12 billion from $991.9 million a year earlier. Comparable store sales for the same period grew 3.0% from the prior year. Cost of goods sold, including related buying, distribution and occupancy costs as a percent of sales was 76.5% versus 75.7% the year before. A combination of higher markdowns and higher distribution center costs contributed to lower gross margin, which declined about 75 basis points during the quarter.

Prospects: Operating margins are being pressured by the combination of higher markdowns and increased distribution costs as a percentage of sales. Looking ahead, Co. is projecting second-quarter earnings for fiscal 2005 in the range of $0.30 to $0.32 per share, along with a same-store sales increase of between 2.0% and 3.0%, compared with a 3.0% decline in the prior-year period. In addition, Co. is forecasting capital expenditures of approximately $185.0 million for fiscal 2005, which will be used to fund fixtures and leasehold improvements to open both new Ross stores and dd's DISCOUNTSsm stores.

Financial Data

(US$ in Thousands)	01/29/2005	01/31/2004	02/01/2003	02/02/2002	02/03/2001	01/29/2000	01/30/1999	01/31/1998
Earnings Per Share	1.13	1.47	1.26	0.95	0.91	0.82	0.70	0.59
Cash Flow Per Share	2.03	2.08	2.13	1.52	0.85	1.02	1.07	0.60
Tang Book Value Per Share	5.22	5.00	4.15	3.45	2.90	2.67	2.30	1.99
Dividends Per Share	0.170	0.115	0.095	0.085	0.075	0.065	0.055	0.045
Dividend Payout %	15.04	7.82	7.54	8.90	8.24	7.93	7.86	7.66
Income Statement								
Total Revenue	4,239,990	3,920,583	3,531,349	2,986,596	2,709,039	2,468,638	2,182,361	1,988,692
EBITDA	360,500	451,028	396,797	320,378	307,715	294,344	262,922	235,002
Depn & Amortn	80,600	76,739	66,176	62,621	55,063	48,187	43,248	39,478
Income Before Taxes	278,985	374,551	330,342	254,589	249,186	246,479	219,415	195,789
Income Taxes	109,083	146,465	129,164	99,544	97,432	96,373	85,572	78,315
Net Income	169,902	228,102	201,178	155,045	151,754	150,106	133,843	117,474
Average Shares	150,380	155,151	159,492	162,420	166,674	183,342	191,400	200,008
Balance Sheet								
Current Assets	1,122,721	1,120,538	922,420	714,991	631,069	613,194	573,934	498,424
Total Assets	1,735,999	1,657,210	1,361,345	1,082,725	975,047	947,678	870,306	737,953
Current Liabilities	711,561	711,844	626,684	489,588	434,065	422,470	403,139	323,746
Long-Term Obligations	50,000	50,000	25,000	...	30,000	...	...	...
Total Liabilities	970,430	901,791	718,157	538,270	507,500	474,247	445,603	357,272
Stockholders' Equity	765,569	755,419	643,188	544,455	467,547	473,431	424,703	380,681
Shares Outstanding	146,717	151,208	154,982	157,920	161,054	177,548	185,000	191,668
Statistical Record								
Return on Assets %	10.04	15.15	16.51	15.11	15.53	16.56	16.69	16.86
Return on Equity %	22.40	32.71	33.97	30.73	31.73	33.52	33.33	33.20
EBITDA Margin %	8.50	11.50	11.24	10.73	11.36	11.92	12.05	11.82
Net Margin %	4.01	5.82	5.70	5.19	5.60	6.08	6.13	5.91
Asset Turnover	2.51	2.60	2.90	2.91	2.77	2.72	2.72	2.85
Current Ratio	1.58	1.57	1.47	1.46	1.45	1.45	1.42	1.54
Debt to Equity	0.07	0.07	0.04	...	0.06	...	...	...
Price Range	32.85-21.15	28.79-16.48	23.44-16.38	18.16-9.04	12.03-6.28	13.00-6.13	12.42-6.11	10.45-5.05
P/E Ratio	29.07-18.72	19.59-11.21	18.60-13.00	19.12-9.52	13.22-6.90	15.85-7.47	17.75-8.73	17.72-8.55
Average Yield %	0.64	0.51	0.48	0.65	0.87	0.62	0.56	0.57

Address: 8333 Central Ave., Newark, CA 94560-3433
Telephone: 510-505-4400
Web Site: www.rossstores.com

Officers: Norman A. Ferber - Chmn. Lawrence M. Higby - Chmn. Emeritus **Transfer Agents:** Bank of New York

No of Institutions: 231
Shares: 130,979,072 **% Held:** 89.23

RPM INTERNATIONAL INC (DE)

Exchange	Symbol	Price	52Wk Range	Yield	P/E
NYS	RPM	$17.60 (5/31/2005)	19.83-14.02	3.41	18.14

***7 Year Price Score 112.94** *NYSE Composite Index=100 ***12 Month Price Score 97.47**

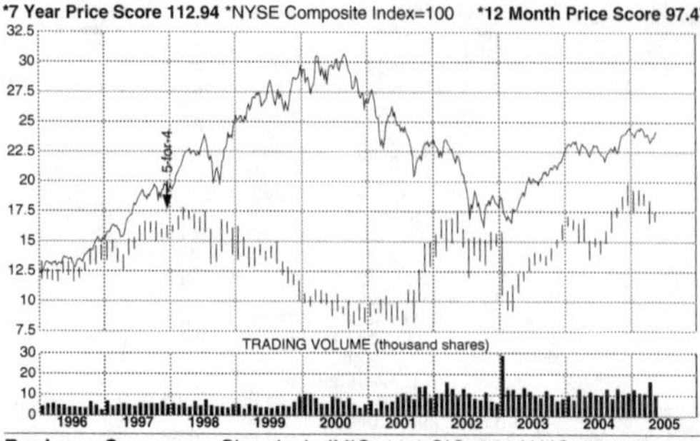

TRADING VOLUME (thousand shares)

Interim Earnings (Per Share)

Qtr.	Aug	Nov	Feb	May
2001-02	0.36	0.24	0.03	0.34
2002-03	0.38	0.26	0.04	(0.38)
2003-04	0.41	0.30	0.05	0.46
2004-05	0.47	0.08	(0.04)	...

Interim Dividends (Per Share)

Amt	Decl	Ex	Rec	Pay
0.14Q	7/2/2004	7/8/2004	7/12/2004	7/30/2004
0.15Q	10/8/2004	10/14/2004	10/18/2004	10/29/2004
0.15Q	1/3/2005	1/12/2005	1/14/2005	1/31/2005
0.15Q	4/1/2005	4/13/2005	4/15/2005	4/29/2005

Indicated Div: $0.60 (Div. Reinv. Plan)

Valuation Analysis

Forecast P/E	12.57 (6/2/2005)		
Market Cap	$2.1 Billion	Book Value	1.0 Billion
Price/Book	2.00	Price/Sales	0.83

Dividend Achiever Status

Rank	261	**10 Year Growth Rate**	5.33%
Total Years of Dividend Growth			31

Business Summary: Chemicals (MIC: 11.1 SIC: 851 NAIC: 25510)

RPM International manufactures and markets specialty paints, protective coatings and roofing systems, sealants and adhesives, focusing on the maintenance and improvement needs of both the industrial and consumer markets. Co.'s family of products includes those marketed under brand names such as CARBOLINE, DAP, DAY-GLO, FLECTO, RUST-OLEUM, STONHARD, TREMCO and ZINSSER. As of May 31 2004, Co. marketed its products in over 140 countries and territories and operated manufacturing facilities in 74 locations in the U.S., Argentina, Belgium, Brazil, Canada, China, Colombia, Germany, Italy, Mexico, New Zealand, The Netherlands, Poland, South Africa, the United Arab Emirates and the United Kingdom.

Recent Developments: For the third quarter ended Feb 28 2005, Co. reported a net loss of $4.8 million compared with net income of $6.0 million in the corresponding prior-year quarter. Results for 2005 included asbestos charges of $15.0 million. Net sales advanced 8.9% to $516.3 million from $474.0 million a year earlier, primarily reflecting growth in industrial and consumer segment sales due improved demand and favorable foreign currency exchange, as well as contributions from acquisitions. Gross profit increased 3.6% to $211.1 million from $203.8 million the year before.

Prospects: Co.'s outlook appears mixed. On the positive side, Co. noted that its strategies to drive organic growth are paying off as numerous new products and services continue to gain market acceptance. However, Co. continues to see higher raw material costs. Also, during the quarter ended Feb 28 2005, Co. elected to take an additional $15.0 million pre-tax asbestos charge, bringing its balance sheet reserves for asbestos liability to $96.3 million. Co. believes this level sufficiently supports a conservatively estimated valuation of existing claims in light of its more aggressive defense strategy which, according to Co., entails higher legal costs but has produced ultimately lower resolution costs.

Financial Data

(US$ in Thousands)	9 Mos	6 Mos	3 Mos	05/31/2004	05/31/2003	05/31/2002	05/31/2001	05/31/2000
Earnings Per Share	0.97	1.06	1.28	1.22	0.30	0.97	0.62	0.38
Cash Flow Per Share	1.21	1.60	1.44	1.32	1.39	1.83	0.73	0.95
Tang Book Value Per Share	0.81	0.96	0.71	0.38	N.M.	0.01	N.M.	N.M.
Dividends Per Share	0.580	0.570	0.560	0.550	0.515	0.500	0.498	0.485
Dividend Payout %	59.79	53.80	43.86	45.08	171.67	51.55	80.24	127.63
Income Statement								
Total Revenue	1,801,319	1,284,982	661,513	2,341,572	2,083,489	1,986,126	2,007,762	1,954,131
EBITDA	163,873	146,835	108,720	307,201	131,205	249,458	246,021	201,280
Depn & Amortn	48,930	32,736	16,275	60,640	56,640	54,870	79,331	77,726
Income Before Taxes	89,458	97,214	84,475	217,616	47,853	154,124	101,487	71,761
Income Taxes	30,632	33,616	29,989	75,730	12,526	52,570	38,526	30,769
Net Income	58,826	63,598	54,486	141,886	35,327	101,554	62,961	40,992
Average Shares	119,152	118,284	117,078	116,710	115,986	105,131	102,212	107,384
Balance Sheet								
Current Assets	1,108,972	1,157,348	1,011,211	994,617	928,094	801,314	819,420	785,092
Total Assets	2,485,473	2,539,000	2,369,008	2,353,119	2,247,211	2,036,403	2,078,490	2,099,203
Current Liabilities	419,601	445,566	689,713	477,493	427,650	364,714	375,768	376,202
Long-Term Obligations	835,625	837,926	490,284	718,929	724,846	707,921	955,399	959,330
Total Liabilities	1,450,501	1,480,799	1,350,717	1,377,827	1,370,203	1,178,297	1,438,780	1,453,479
Stockholders' Equity	1,034,972	1,058,201	1,018,291	975,292	877,008	858,106	639,710	645,724
Shares Outstanding	117,452	117,146	116,271	116,122	115,496	114,696	102,211	103,134
Statistical Record								
Return on Assets %	4.75	5.10	6.44	6.15	1.65	4.94	3.01	2.13
Return on Equity %	11.30	12.23	15.45	15.28	4.07	13.56	9.80	5.89
EBITDA Margin %	9.10	11.43	16.44	13.12	6.30	12.56	12.25	10.30
Net Margin %	3.27	4.95	8.24	6.06	1.70	5.11	3.14	2.10
Asset Turnover	1.05	1.02	1.05	1.02	0.97	0.97	0.96	1.02
Current Ratio	2.64	2.60	1.47	2.08	2.17	2.20	2.18	2.09
Debt to Equity	0.81	0.79	0.48	0.74	0.83	0.82	1.49	1.49
Price Range	19.83-13.50	18.83-13.50	17.10-13.06	17.10-12.55	16.06-9.20	17.61-8.05	10.63-7.75	15.00-9.56
P/E Ratio	20.44-13.92	17.76-12.74	13.36-10.20	14.02-10.29	53.53-30.67	18.15-8.30	17.14-12.50	39.47-25.16
Average Yield %	3.50	3.57	3.70	3.73	3.88	3.84	5.37	4.13

Address: P.O. Box 777, 2628 Pearl Road, Medina, OH 44258
Telephone: 330-273-5090
Web Site: www.rpminc.com

Officers: Thomas C. Sullivan - Chmn. Frank C. Sullivan - Pres., C.E.O. **Transfer Agents:** National City Bank, Cleveland, OH

Investor Contact: 330-273-8820
No of Institutions: 218
Shares: 58,972,744 **% Held:** 50.32

S & T BANCORP, INC. (INDIANA, PA.)

Exchange	Symbol	Price	52Wk Range	Yield	P/E
NMS	STBA	$35.15 (5/31/2005)	38.40-29.33	3.19	17.06

*7 Year Price Score 118.80 *NYSE Composite Index=100 *12 Month Price Score 95.25

TRADING VOLUME (thousand shares)

Interim Earnings (Per Share)

Qtr.	Mar	Jun	Sep	Dec
2002	0.43	0.44	0.46	0.48
2003	0.47	0.48	0.50	0.49
2004	0.48	0.51	0.50	0.54
2005	0.51	...	...	...

Interim Dividends (Per Share)

Amt	Decl	Ex	Rec	Pay
0.27Q	6/21/2004	6/28/2004	6/30/2004	7/23/2004
0.27Q	9/20/2004	9/29/2004	10/1/2004	10/25/2004
0.27Q	12/21/2004	12/29/2004	12/31/2004	1/25/2005
0.28Q	3/21/2005	3/30/2005	4/1/2005	4/25/2005

Indicated Div: $1.12

Valuation Analysis

Forecast P/E	16.35 (6/2/2005)		
Market Cap	$934.4 Million	Book Value	347.3 Million
Price/Book	2.69	Price/Sales	4.99

Dividend Achiever Status

Rank	106	10 Year Growth Rate	14.04%
Total Years of Dividend Growth			15

Business Summary: Commercial Banking (MIC: 8.1 SIC: 022 NAIC: 22110)

S&T Bancorp is a bank holding company with two wholly owned subsidiaries, S&T Bank and 9th Street Holdings, Inc. Co. owns a 50.0% interest in Commonwealth Trust Credit Life Insurance Company. S&T Bank is a full service bank providing service to its customers through a branch network of 51 offices located in Allegheny, Armstrong, Blair, Butler, Cambria, Clarion, Clearfield, Indiana, Jefferson and Westmoreland counties of Pennsylvania. S&T Bank's services include accepting time and demand deposit accounts, originating commercial and consumer loans, offering discount brokerage services, personal financial planning and credit card services. At Dec 31 2004, Co. had total assets of $2.99 billion.

Recent Developments: For the quarter ended Mar 31 2005, net income increased 6.7% to $13,820 thousand from net income of $12,956 thousand in the year-earlier quarter. Net interest income was $27,318 thousand, up 4.7% from $26,090 thousand the year before. Provision for loan losses was $800 thousand versus $1,500 thousand in the prior-year quarter, a decrease of 46.7%. Non-interest income rose 8.3% to $9,086 thousand, while non-interest expense advanced 9.1% to $15,999 thousand.

Prospects: Co.'s outlook appears satisfactory, reflecting in part recent year-over-year loan and deposit growth. Additionally, noninterest revenue, excluding investment security gains, has benefited from higher insurance revenue, primarily driven by stronger sales volume and the acquisition of Bennett Associates, Inc. and Cowher-Nehrig & Company insurance agencies during the first quarter of 2005. Wealth management revenues, debit and credit card income, and letters of credit fees also all increased during the first quarter of 2005 as compared with the first quarter of 2004.

Financial Data

(US$ in Thousands)	3 Mos	12/31/2004	12/31/2003	12/31/2002	12/31/2001	12/31/2000	12/31/1999	12/31/1998
Earnings Per Share	2.06	2.03	1.94	1.81	1.75	1.66	1.51	1.35
Cash Flow Per Share	2.08	2.34	1.92	1.89	2.85	1.58	0.75	1.38
Tang Book Value Per Share	11.05	11.12	10.48	9.47	11.01	10.28	8.88	9.38
Dividends Per Share	1.090	1.070	1.020	0.970	0.920	0.840	0.760	0.660
Dividend Payout %	52.91	52.71	52.58	53.59	52.57	50.60	50.33	48.89
Income Statement								
Interest Income	39,466	148,638	151,460	151,160	166,702	176,184	156,727	151,438
Interest Expense	12,148	40,890	47,066	56,300	76,713	86,141	69,942	69,156
Net Interest Income	27,318	107,748	104,394	94,860	89,989	90,043	86,785	82,282
Provision for Losses	800	4,400	7,300	7,800	5,000	4,000	4,000	10,550
Non-Interest Income	9,086	34,202	36,204	32,680	31,230	22,154	20,100	24,418
Non-Interest Expense	16,073	60,191	60,658	51,766	46,972	45,658	43,490	41,988
Income Before Taxes	19,531	77,359	72,640	67,974	69,247	62,539	59,395	54,162
Income Taxes	5,711	23,001	20,863	19,370	20,062	17,566	17,977	16,199
Net Income	13,820	54,358	51,777	48,604	47,298	44,973	41,418	37,963
Average Shares	26,951	26,799	26,723	26,784	27,051	27,073	27,366	28,055
Balance Sheet								
Net Loans & Leases	2,284,361	2,253,089	2,069,142	1,968,755	1,615,842	1,577,629	1,469,143	1,339,232
Total Assets	3,027,881	2,989,034	2,900,272	2,823,867	2,357,874	2,310,290	2,194,073	2,069,611
Total Deposits	2,168,932	2,176,263	1,962,253	1,926,119	1,611,317	1,525,332	1,435,065	1,380,063
Total Liabilities	2,680,602	2,639,905	2,567,554	2,517,753	2,064,547	2,033,193	1,954,373	1,809,974
Stockholders' Equity	347,279	349,129	332,718	306,114	293,327	277,097	239,700	259,637
Shares Outstanding	26,584	26,600	26,652	26,584	26,646	26,947	26,998	27,676
Statistical Record								
Return on Assets %	1.85	1.84	1.81	1.88	2.03	1.99	1.94	1.90
Return on Equity %	16.09	15.90	16.21	16.22	16.58	17.36	16.59	14.61
Net Interest Margin %	69.22	72.49	68.93	62.75	53.98	51.11	55.37	54.33
Efficiency Ratio %	33.10	32.92	32.32	28.16	23.73	23.02	24.59	23.88
Loans to Deposits	1.05	1.04	1.05	1.02	1.00	1.03	1.02	0.97
Price Range	38.40-28.42	38.40-28.42	31.25-25.05	28.03-23.30	25.30-20.31	23.44-16.75	29.00-19.13	29.00-21.19
P/E Ratio	18.64-13.80	18.92-14.00	16.11-12.91	15.49-12.87	14.46-11.61	14.12-10.09	19.21-12.67	21.48-15.69
Average Yield %	3.17	3.27	3.63	3.80	4.00	4.43	3.10	2.51

Address: 43 South Ninth Street, Indiana, PA 15701
Telephone: 724-465-1466
Web Site: www.stbank.com

Officers: James C. Miller - Chmn., C.E.O. Todd D. Brice - Pres. **Transfer Agents:** American Stock Transfer & Trust Company, New York, NY

Investor Contact: 724-465-1466
No of Institutions: 70
Shares: 7,594,324 **% Held:** 28.50

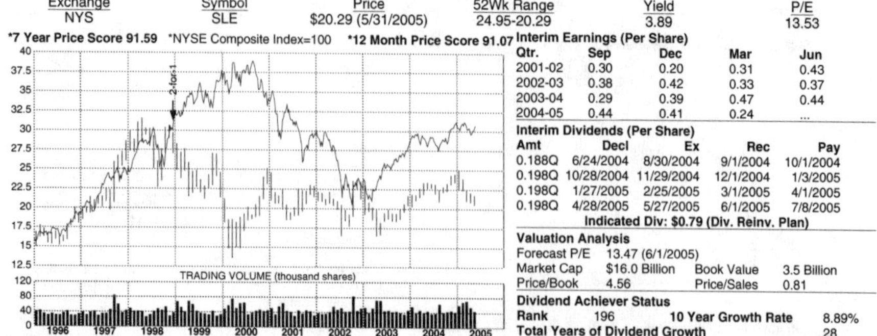

SARA LEE CORP.

Exchange	Symbol	Price	52Wk Range	Yield	P/E
NYS	SLE	$20.29 (5/31/2005)	24.95-20.29	3.89	13.53

***7 Year Price Score 91.59** *NYSE Composite Index=100 ***12 Month Price Score 91.07**

Interim Earnings (Per Share)

Qtr.	Sep	Dec	Mar	Jun
2001-02	0.30	0.20	0.31	0.43
2002-03	0.38	0.42	0.33	0.37
2003-04	0.29	0.39	0.47	0.44
2004-05	0.44	0.41	0.24	...

Interim Dividends (Per Share)

Amt	Decl	Ex	Rec	Pay
0.188Q	6/24/2004	8/30/2004	9/1/2004	10/1/2004
0.198Q	10/28/2004	11/29/2004	12/1/2004	1/3/2005
0.198Q	1/27/2005	2/25/2005	3/1/2005	4/1/2005
0.198Q	4/28/2005	5/27/2005	6/1/2005	7/8/2005

Indicated Div: $0.79 (Div. Reinv. Plan)

Valuation Analysis

Forecast P/E	13.47 (6/1/2005)		
Market Cap	$16.0 Billion	Book Value	3.5 Billion
Price/Book	4.56	Price/Sales	0.81

Dividend Achiever Status

Rank	196	**10 Year Growth Rate**	8.89%
Total Years of Dividend Growth			28

Business Summary: Food (MIC: 4.1 SIC: 013 NAIC: 11613)

Sara Lee is a global manufacturer and marketer of brand-name products for consumers throughout the world. As of July 3 2004, Co. has operations in 58 countries and markets products in nearly 200 nations. Co. has five reportable segments: Sara Lee Meats, Sara Lee Bakery, Beverage, Household Products and Branded Apparel. Co.'s products and services include fresh and frozen baked goods, processed meats, coffee and tea, beverage systems, intimate apparel, underwear, sportswear, legwear and other apparel, and personal, household and shoe care products.

Recent Developments: For the quarter ended Apr 2 2005, net income decreased 49.7% to $189 million from net income of $376 million in the year-earlier quarter. Revenues were $4,785 million, up 0.8% from $4,745 million the year before. Total direct expense was $3,018 million versus $2,888 million in the prior-year quarter, an increase of 4.5%. Total indirect expense was $2,898 million versus $2,970 million in the prior-year quarter, a decrease of 2.4%.

Prospects: Co. is experiencing decreasing unit volumes due to softness in regional white breads and planned exits of unprofitable, non-core businesses in Bakery, price increases in Beverage, and softness in Household Products and Branded Apparel. However, Co. is beginning to implement its announced transformation plan to improve results. Meanwhile, strategic investment brands such as Sara Lee, Senseo, Jimmy Dean and Hillshire Farm continue to be strong. For fiscal year 2005, Co. expects earnings to range from $1.39 to $1.41 per diluted share versus $1.59 per share in fiscal 2004, reflecting continuing higher raw material costs and a difficult European retail environment in the fourth quarter.

Financial Data

(US$ in Thousands)	9 Mos	6 Mos	3 Mos	07/03/2004	06/28/2003	06/29/2002	06/30/2001	07/01/2000
Earnings Per Share	1.50	1.73	1.71	1.59	1.50	1.23	2.65	1.34
Cash Flow Per Share	2.12	2.29	2.21	2.55	2.34	2.22	1.83	1.76
Dividends Per Share	0.770	0.760	0.750	0.563	0.615	0.595	0.570	0.530
Dividend Payout %	51.23	43.96	43.75	35.38	41.00	48.37	21.51	39.55
Income Statement								
Total Revenue	14,845,000	10,060,000	4,861,000	19,566,000	18,291,000	17,628,000	17,747,000	17,511,000
EBITDA	1,814,000	1,288,000	671,000	2,457,000	2,356,000	1,975,000	2,630,000	2,345,000
Depn & Amortn	554,000	380,000	190,000	734,000	674,000	582,000	599,000	602,000
Income Before Taxes	1,127,000	822,000	441,000	1,542,000	1,484,000	1,185,000	1,851,000	1,567,000
Income Taxes	260,000	144,000	89,000	270,000	263,000	175,000	248,000	409,000
Net Income	867,000	678,000	352,000	1,272,000	1,221,000	1,010,000	2,266,000	1,222,000
Average Shares	797,000	795,000	795,000	798,000	812,000	818,000	854,000	912,000
Balance Sheet								
Current Assets	5,665,000	6,138,000	5,439,000	5,746,000	5,953,000	4,986,000	5,083,000	5,974,000
Total Assets	14,793,000	15,488,000	14,550,000	14,883,000	15,084,000	13,753,000	10,167,000	11,611,000
Current Liabilities	4,501,000	4,912,000	5,044,000	5,423,000	5,199,000	5,463,000	4,958,000	6,759,000
Long-Term Obligations	4,361,000	4,487,000	4,136,000	4,171,000	5,157,000	4,326,000	2,640,000	2,248,000
Total Liabilities	11,292,000	11,878,000	11,528,000	11,935,000	13,032,000	12,011,000	9,045,000	10,377,000
Stockholders' Equity	3,501,000	3,610,000	3,022,000	2,948,000	2,052,000	1,742,000	1,122,000	1,234,000
Shares Outstanding	787,295	789,329	784,813	793,924	777,347	784,720	781,964	846,331
Statistical Record								
Return on Assets %	8.06	9.10	9.55	8.35	8.49	8.47	20.87	11.07
Return on Equity %	40.06	46.64	55.16	50.06	64.54	70.72	192.89	98.03
EBITDA Margin %	12.22	12.80	13.80	12.56	12.88	11.20	14.82	13.39
Net Margin %	5.84	6.74	7.24	6.50	6.68	5.73	12.77	6.98
Asset Turnover	1.32	1.29	1.35	1.28	1.27	1.48	1.63	1.59
Current Ratio	1.26	1.25	1.08	1.06	1.15	0.91	1.03	0.88
Debt to Equity	1.25	1.24	1.37	1.41	2.51	2.48	2.35	1.82
Price Range	24.95-20.92	24.49-20.31	23.44-18.68	23.44-18.36	23.75-16.50	23.04-19.04	25.19-18.44	27.06-13.63
P/E Ratio	16.63-13.95	14.16-11.74	13.71-10.92	14.74-11.55	15.83-11.00	18.73-15.48	9.50-6.96	20.20-10.17
Average Yield %	3.37	3.37	3.46	2.69	3.08	2.81	2.75	2.58

Address: Three First National Plaza, Suite 4600, Chicago, IL 60602-4260
Telephone: 312-726-2600
Web Site: www.saralee.com

Officers: C. Steven McMillan - Chmn. Brenda C. Barnes - Pres., C.E.O., C.O.O. **Transfer Agents:** Sara Lee Corporation, Chicago, IL

Investor Contact: 312-558-4947
No of Institutions: 553
Shares: 458,265,056 **% Held:** 58.06

SBC COMMUNICATIONS, INC.

Exchange	Symbol	Price	52Wk Range	Yield	P/E
NYS	SBC	$23.38 (5/31/2005)	27.20-22.96	5.52	16.12

Interim Earnings (Per Share)

Qtr.	Mar	Jun	Sep	Dec
2002	(0.02)	0.55	0.53	0.64
2003	1.50	0.42	0.37	0.28
2004	0.59	0.35	0.63	0.20
2005	0.27	...	...	...

Interim Dividends (Per Share)

Amt	Decl	Ex	Rec	Pay
0.313Q	6/25/2004	7/7/2004	7/10/2004	8/2/2004
0.313Q	9/24/2004	10/6/2004	10/8/2004	11/1/2004
0.323Q	12/10/2004	1/6/2005	1/10/2005	2/1/2005
0.323Q	3/11/2005	4/6/2005	4/8/2005	5/2/2005

Indicated Div: $1.29 (Div. Reinv. Plan)

Valuation Analysis

Forecast P/E	N/A		
Market Cap	$80.3 Billion	Book Value	40.4 Billion
Price/Book	1.99	Price/Sales	1.95

Dividend Achiever Status

Rank	272	**10 Year Growth Rate**	4.81%
Total Years of Dividend Growth			20

Business Summary: Communications (MIC: 10.1 SIC: 813 NAIC: 51112)

SBC Communications is a global provider of telecommunications services. Co.'s products and services include local exchange services, wireless communications, long-distance services, internet services, telecommunications equipment, and directory advertising and publishing. Co.'s principal wireline subsidiaries provide telecommunications services in thirteen states: Arkansas, California, Connecticut, Illinois, Indiana, Kansas, Michigan, Missouri, Nevada, Ohio, Oklahoma, Texas, and Wisconsin. As of Dec 31 2004, Co. had 52.0 million network access lines in service and maintained a 60.0% equity interest in Cingular Wireless, which serves more than 49.0 million wireless customers.

Recent Developments: For the quarter ended Mar 31 2005, net income decreased 54.3% to $885 million from net income of $1,937 million in the year-earlier quarter. Revenues were $10,248 million, up 2.4% from $10,012 million the year before. Operating income was $1,556 million versus an income of $1,516 million in the prior-year quarter, an increase of 2.6%. Total direct expense was $4,397 million versus $4,227 million in the prior-year quarter, an increase of 4.0%. Total indirect expense was $4,295 million versus $4,269 million in the prior-year quarter, an increase of 0.6%.

Prospects: Results are being positively affected by continued strong subscriber growth at Cingular Wireless, along with solid growth in its wireline operations, which is being driven by robust demand for Co.'s DSL/Internet services. Separately, on Apr 29 2005, Co. announced that it has received approvals from nine states, of the approximately 30 state approvals needed, for its proposed $16.00 billion acquisition of AT&T Corp. In addition, Co. expects to gain approvals from the U.S. Justice Department and Federal Communications Commission by October 2005, and may complete the acquisition by the end of 2005.

Financial Data

(US$ in Thousands)	3 Mos	12/31/2004	12/31/2003	12/31/2002	12/31/2001	12/31/2000	12/31/1999	12/31/1998
Earnings Per Share	1.45	1.77	2.56	1.69	2.13	2.32	2.36	2.03
Cash Flow Per Share	3.08	3.30	4.07	4.57	4.40	4.20	4.86	4.28
Tang Book Value Per Share	11.25	11.78	11.08	9.51	8.62	7.38	5.87	4.95
Dividends Per Share	1.260	1.250	1.367	1.066	1.023	1.005	0.965	0.925
Dividend Payout %	86.90	70.62	53.42	63.09	48.00	43.32	40.89	45.57
Income Statement								
Total Revenue	10,248,000	40,787,000	40,843,000	43,138,000	45,908,000	51,476,000	49,489,000	28,777,000
EBITDA	3,364,000	15,228,000	17,385,000	19,826,000	21,307,000	23,878,000	20,751,000	12,472,000
Depn & Amortn	1,819,000	7,532,000	7,846,000	8,548,000	9,033,000	9,677,000	8,468,000	5,105,000
Income Before Taxes	1,301,000	7,165,000	8,901,000	10,457,000	11,357,000	12,888,000	10,853,000	6,374,000
Income Taxes	416,000	2,186,000	2,930,000	2,984,000	4,097,000	4,921,000	4,280,000	2,306,000
Net Income	885,000	5,887,000	8,505,000	5,653,000	7,242,000	7,967,000	8,159,000	4,023,000
Average Shares	3,303,000	3,322,000	3,329,000	3,348,000	3,396,000	3,433,000	3,458,000	1,984,000
Balance Sheet								
Net PPE	49,311,000	50,046,000	52,128,000	48,490,000	49,827,000	47,195,000	46,571,000	29,920,000
Total Assets	106,946,000	108,844,000	100,166,000	95,057,000	96,322,000	98,651,000	83,215,000	45,066,000
Long-Term Obligations	20,937,000	21,231,000	16,060,000	18,536,000	17,133,000	15,492,000	17,475,000	11,612,000
Total Liabilities	66,542,000	68,340,000	61,918,000	61,858,000	63,831,000	68,188,000	56,489,000	32,286,000
Stockholders' Equity	40,404,000	40,504,000	38,248,000	33,199,000	32,491,000	30,463,000	26,726,000	12,780,000
Shares Outstanding	3,433,000	3,300,912	3,305,236	3,318,000	3,354,216	3,386,709	3,395,272	1,959,000
Statistical Record								
Return on Assets %	4.66	5.62	8.71	5.91	7.43	8.74	12.72	9.23
Return on Equity %	12.12	14.91	23.81	17.21	23.01	27.79	41.31	35.49
EBITDA Margin %	32.83	37.34	42.57	45.96	46.41	46.39	41.93	43.34
Net Margin %	8.64	14.43	20.82	13.10	15.78	15.48	16.49	13.98
PPE Turnover	0.82	0.80	0.81	0.88	0.95	1.09	1.29	1.01
Asset Turnover	0.40	0.39	0.42	0.45	0.47	0.56	0.77	0.66
Debt to Equity	0.52	0.52	0.42	0.56	0.53	0.51	0.65	0.91
Price Range	27.20-23.00	27.59-23.00	31.19-19.34	40.17-20.10	52.38-37.38	58.50-35.44	59.19-44.25	54.13-35.78
P/E Ratio	18.76-15.86	15.59-12.99	12.18-7.55	23.77-11.89	24.59-17.55	25.22-15.27	25.08-18.75	26.66-17.63
Average Yield %	5.04	4.95	5.77	3.48	2.37	2.19	1.84	2.21

Address: 175 E. Houston, San Antonio, TX 78205-2233 **Telephone:** 210-821-4105 **Web Site:** www.sbc.com	**Officers:** Edward E. Whitacre Jr. - Chmn., C.E.O. William M. Daley - Pres. **Transfer Agents:** EquiServe Trust Company, N.A., Jersey City, NJ	**Investor Contact:** 210-351-3990 **No of Institutions:** 805 **Shares:** 1,764,964,352 **% Held:** 53.43

SEI INVESTMENTS CO.

Exchange	Symbol	Price	52Wk Range	Yield	P/E
NMS	SEIC	$34.76 (5/31/2005)	43.09-27.40	0.63	21.07

***7 Year Price Score 106.21** *NYSE Composite Index=100 ***12 Month Price Score 94.29**

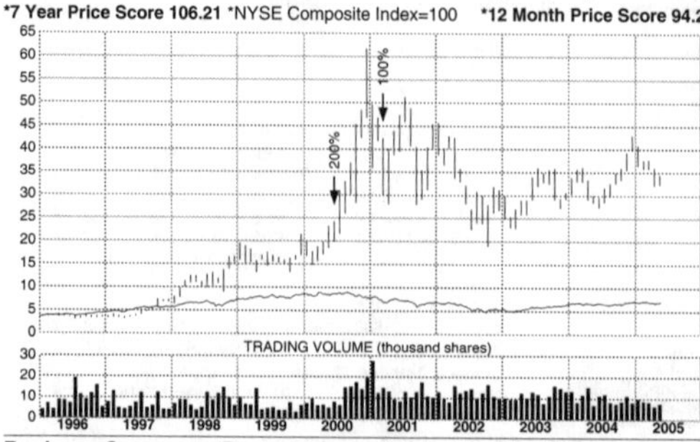

Interim Earnings (Per Share)

Qtr.	Mar	Jun	Sep	Dec
2002	0.30	0.31	0.32	0.32
2003	0.32	0.32	0.33	0.35
2004	0.37	0.39	0.43	0.41
2005	0.42	...	...	...

Interim Dividends (Per Share)

Amt	Decl	Ex	Rec	Pay
0.09S	12/16/2003	1/2/2004	1/6/2004	1/22/2004
0.10S	5/25/2004	6/4/2004	6/8/2004	6/24/2004
0.10S	12/14/2004	12/31/2004	1/4/2005	1/21/2005
0.11S	5/25/2005	6/6/2005	6/8/2005	6/24/2005

Indicated Div: $0.22

Valuation Analysis

Forecast P/E	19.92 (6/2/2005)		
Market Cap	$3.5 Billion	Book Value	403.6 Million
Price/Book	8.70	Price/Sales	4.94

Dividend Achiever Status

Rank	25	**10 Year Growth Rate**	23.33%
Total Years of Dividend Growth			13

Business Summary: Finance Intermediaries & Services (MIC: 8.7 SIC: 211 NAIC: 23120)

SEI Investments provides investment processing, fund processing, and investment management business outsourcing solutions to corporations, financial institutions, financial advisors, and affluent families primarily in the U.S., Canada, the U.K. and Continental Europe. Investment processing solutions use Co.'s proprietary software system to track investment activities in multiple types of investment accounts, including various trust and investment accounts, thereby allowing banks and trust companies to outsource trust and investment related activities. Co.'s business segments are: Private Banking and Trust, Investment Advisors, Enterprises, Money Managers, and Investments in New Businesses.

Recent Developments: For the quarter ended Mar 31 2005, net income increased 10.9% to $43,709 thousand from net income of $39,409 thousand in the year-earlier quarter. Revenues were $185,681 thousand, up 11.1% from $167,161 thousand the year before. The revenue growth was primarily driven by higher asset-based fees due to higher levels of assets under management and administration due to rising capital markets during 2004 and sales of new business. Income from operations increased 4.1% to $51,626 thousand from $49,573 thousand in the previous year.

Prospects: Co. continues to make significant investments in the development of its Global Wealth Management Platform. Co. believes the development of this platform is critical to the future expansion of its business and to the launch of a private bank operations outsourcing business in Europe. In addition, by having a single platform, Co. anticipates achieving significant development and operational leverage. Co. is currently in the development phase of the platform and expects these development expenditures will continue throughout 2005. Meanwhile, Co. is continuing to roll out its new SEI Wealth Network® franchise for qualified advisors of high-net-worth individuals.

Financial Data

(US$ in Thousands)	3 Mos	12/31/2004	12/31/2003	12/31/2002	12/31/2001	12/31/2000	12/31/1999	12/31/1998
Earnings Per Share	1.65	1.60	1.32	1.25	1.09	0.87	0.60	0.38
Cash Flow Per Share	1.66	1.80	1.69	1.62	1.61	1.39	0.87	0.93
Tang Book Value Per Share	3.32	3.41	3.27	2.54	2.38	1.70	0.60	0.40
Dividends Per Share	0.200	0.290	0.070	0.170	0.090	0.073	0.033	0.053
Dividend Payout %	12.12	18.13	5.30	13.60	8.26	8.43	5.54	14.04
Income Statement								
Total Revenue	185,681	692,269	636,233	620,819	658,013	598,806	456,192	366,119
EBITDA	71,562	278,322	238,823	238,171	213,178	172,797	125,052	86,588
Depn & Amortn	4,280	15,624	16,599	18,060	19,650	17,305	15,793	15,688
Income Before Taxes	68,833	265,131	224,284	223,048	198,324	159,618	109,169	69,883
Income Taxes	25,124	96,110	81,303	82,528	73,380	60,655	42,030	26,904
Net Income	43,709	169,021	142,981	140,520	124,944	98,963	68,431	43,689
Average Shares	104,695	105,866	108,137	112,803	114,810	113,820	113,826	114,756
Balance Sheet								
Current Assets	304,084	355,679	352,413	261,435	266,142	249,031	146,992	113,509
Total Assets	583,259	615,475	592,629	464,147	460,916	375,582	253,779	208,772
Current Liabilities	134,320	163,569	193,474	134,247	144,343	146,453	138,918	110,794
Long-Term Obligations	9,000	14,389	23,944	33,500	43,055	27,000	29,000	31,000
Total Liabilities	179,632	211,533	228,856	174,140	190,323	178,161	174,777	149,087
Stockholders' Equity	403,627	403,942	363,773	290,007	270,593	197,421	79,002	59,685
Shares Outstanding	101,058	102,175	104,869	109,180	109,180	108,560	106,152	107,166
Statistical Record								
Return on Assets %	29.92	27.90	27.06	30.38	29.87	31.36	29.59	23.14
Return on Equity %	44.44	43.91	43.74	50.13	53.39	71.41	98.68	82.36
EBITDA Margin %	38.54	40.20	37.54	38.36	32.40	28.86	27.41	23.65
Net Margin %	23.54	24.42	22.47	22.63	18.99	16.53	15.00	11.93
Asset Turnover	1.23	1.14	1.20	1.34	1.57	1.90	1.97	1.94
Current Ratio	2.26	2.17	1.82	1.95	1.84	1.70	1.06	1.02
Debt to Equity	0.02	0.04	0.07	0.12	0.16	0.14	0.37	0.52
Price Range	43.09-27.40	43.09-27.40	35.92-22.90	45.75-19.03	51.31-27.90	61.72-14.89	21.50-13.23	16.67-6.38
P/E Ratio	26.12-16.61	26.93-17.13	27.21-17.35	36.60-15.22	47.07-25.60	70.94-17.11	35.83-22.05	43.86-16.78
Average Yield %	0.58	0.87	0.24	0.53	0.23	0.26	0.20	0.46

Address: 1 Freedom Valley Drive, Oaks, PA 19456-1100
Telephone: 610-676-1000
Web Site: www.seic.com

Officers: Alfred P. West Jr. - Chmn., C.E.O. Carmen V. Romeo - Exec. V.P. **Transfer Agents:** American Stock Transfer & Trust Co., New York, NY

Investor Contact: 610-676-1000
No of Institutions: 216
Shares: 48,708,000 **% Held:** 47.83

SERVICEMASTER CO. (THE)

Exchange	Symbol	Price	52Wk Range	Yield	P/E
NYS	SVM	$13.00 (5/31/2005)	13.87-11.25	3.38	11.61

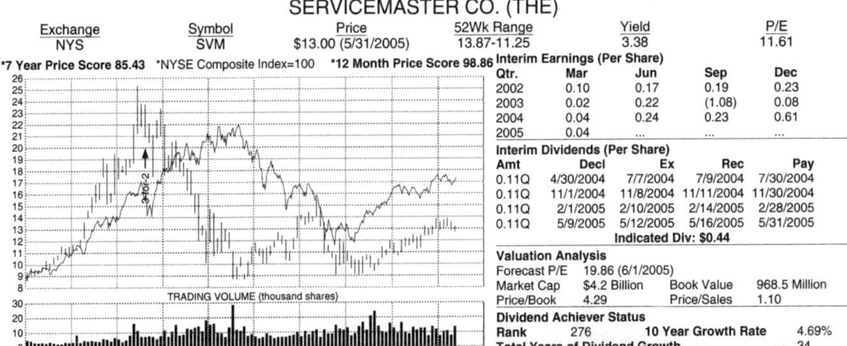

Interim Earnings (Per Share)

Qtr.	Mar	Jun	Sep	Dec
2002	0.10	0.17	0.19	0.23
2003	0.02	0.22	(1.08)	0.08
2004	0.04	0.24	0.23	0.61
2005	0.04	...	...	...

Interim Dividends (Per Share)

Amt	Decl	Ex	Rec	Pay
0.11Q	4/30/2004	7/7/2004	7/9/2004	7/30/2004
0.11Q	11/1/2004	11/8/2004	11/11/2004	11/30/2004
0.11Q	2/1/2005	2/10/2005	2/14/2005	2/28/2005
0.11Q	5/9/2005	5/12/2005	5/16/2005	5/31/2005

Indicated Div: $0.44

Valuation Analysis

Forecast P/E	19.86 (6/1/2005)		
Market Cap	$4.2 Billion	Book Value	968.5 Million
Price/Book	4.29	Price/Sales	1.10

Dividend Achiever Status

Rank	276	**10 Year Growth Rate**	4.69%
Total Years of Dividend Growth			34

Business Summary: Accounting & Management Consulting Services (MIC: 12.2 SIC: 741 NAIC: 61110)

ServiceMaster provides outsourcing services to residential and commercial customers. The TruGreen segment provides lawn care services and landscape maintenance services. The Terminix segment includes domestic termite and pest control services. The American Residential Services and American Mechanical Services (ARS/AMS) segment provides plumbing, drain cleaning, heating, ventilation, air conditioning and electrical services. The American Home Shield segment offers warranty contracts on home systems and appliances and home inspection services. The Other Operations segment includes ServiceMaster Clean, Merry Maids and Furniture Medic franchise operations.

Recent Developments: For the quarter ended Mar 31 2005, income from continuing operations decreased 6.5% to $10,718 thousand from income of $11,461 thousand in the year-earlier quarter. Net income decreased 5.6% to $10,572 thousand from net income of $11,199 thousand in the year-earlier quarter. Revenues were $782,309 thousand, up 3.4% from $756,891 thousand the year before. Operating income was $25,850 thousand versus an income of $31,103 thousand in the prior-year quarter, a decrease of 16.9%. Total direct expense was $556,323 thousand versus $545,056 thousand in the prior-year quarter, an increase of 2.1%. Total indirect expense was $200,136 thousand versus $180,732 thousand in the prior-year quarter, an increase of 10.7%.

Prospects: Co. continues to expect revenue growth to be in the mid-to-high single digit range in 2005 and that earnings per share will grow somewhat faster than revenues. In addition, excluding the impact of the Internal Revenue Service settlement, Co. expects cash from operating activities to increase and substantially exceed net income. Throughout the year, Co. expects to continue to overcome certain external factors that it does not directly control. However, Co. believes that challenges can be mitigated and in some cases use them to its competitive advantage through a combination of focused cost controls, strategic initiatives, and improved customer retention.

Financial Data

(US$ in Thousands)	3 Mos	12/31/2004	12/31/2003	12/31/2002	12/31/2001	12/31/2000	12/31/1999	12/31/1998
Earnings Per Share	1.12	1.11	(0.76)	0.52	0.51	0.57	0.55	0.64
Cash Flow Per Share	0.73	1.29	0.96	1.27	1.22	1.32	0.83	1.40
Dividends Per Share	0.435	0.430	0.420	0.410	0.400	0.380	0.360	0.330
Dividend Payout %	38.84	38.74	...	78.85	78.43	66.67	65.45	51.56
Income Statement								
Total Revenue	782,309	3,758,568	3,568,586	3,589,089	3,601,429	5,970,615	5,703,535	4,724,119
EBITDA	52,723	399,396	(103,521)	398,519	50,621	612,829	543,592	516,328
Depn & Amortn	19,545	55,596	55,861	57,434	126,937	157,691	138,444	104,605
Income Before Taxes	17,599	283,092	(224,637)	263,566	(201,373)	318,307	296,193	318,778
Income Taxes	6,881	(40,965)	(2,662)	93,468	(29,594)	133,319	122,630	128,786
Net Income	10,572	331,227	(224,687)	156,994	155,033	173,827	173,563	189,992
Average Shares	297,080	303,568	295,610	314,112	311,408	305,518	314,406	298,887
Balance Sheet								
Current Assets	930,401	978,752	890,774	919,174	1,150,658	984,759	959,238	670,202
Total Assets	3,097,459	3,140,202	2,956,426	3,414,938	3,674,739	3,967,668	3,870,215	2,914,851
Current Liabilities	928,357	1,027,927	818,240	839,064	814,401	833,414	845,804	753,697
Long-Term Obligations	853,503	781,841	785,490	804,340	1,105,518	1,756,757	1,697,582	1,076,167
Total Liabilities	2,128,930	2,048,667	2,039,600	2,095,929	2,351,101	2,806,080	2,664,499	1,958,365
Stockholders' Equity	968,529	991,535	816,517	1,218,700	1,220,961	1,161,588	1,205,716	956,486
Shares Outstanding	319,247	290,524	293,981	299,221	300,531	298,474	307,530	298,030
Statistical Record								
Return on Assets %	10.92	10.84	N.M.	4.43	4.06	4.42	5.12	7.05
Return on Equity %	38.20	36.54	N.M.	12.87	13.01	14.65	16.05	25.66
EBITDA Margin %	6.74	10.63	N.M.	11.10	1.41	10.26	9.53	10.93
Net Margin %	1.35	8.81	N.M.	4.37	4.30	2.91	3.04	4.02
Asset Turnover	1.25	1.23	1.12	1.01	0.94	1.52	1.68	1.75
Current Ratio	1.00	0.95	1.09	1.10	1.41	1.18	1.13	0.89
Debt to Equity	0.88	0.79	0.96	0.66	0.91	1.51	1.41	1.13
Price Range	13.87-11.25	13.87-10.71	11.97-9.05	15.49-9.11	14.10-10.05	14.75-8.75	22.06-10.13	25.38-17.33
P/E Ratio	12.38-10.04	12.50-9.65	...	29.79-17.52	27.65-19.71	25.88-15.35	40.11-18.41	39.65-27.08
Average Yield %	3.46	3.57	4.06	3.29	3.46	3.43	2.14	1.61

Address: 3250 Lacey Road, Suite 600, Downers Grove, IL 60515-1700
Telephone: 630-663-2000
Web Site: www. servicemaster.com

Officers: Johnathan P. Ward - Chmn. , C.E.O. Ernest J. Mrozek - Pres., C.O.O. **Transfer Agents:** Computershare Investor Services, Chicago, IL

Investor Contact: 630-271-1300
No of Institutions: 233
Shares: 169,521,568 **% Held:** 58.05

SHERWIN-WILLIAMS CO.

Exchange	Symbol	Price	52Wk Range	Yield	P/E
NYS	SHW	$44.45 (5/31/2005)	46.29-38.19	1.84	15.07

*7 Year Price Score 130.36 *NYSE Composite Index=100 *12 Month Price Score 99.00

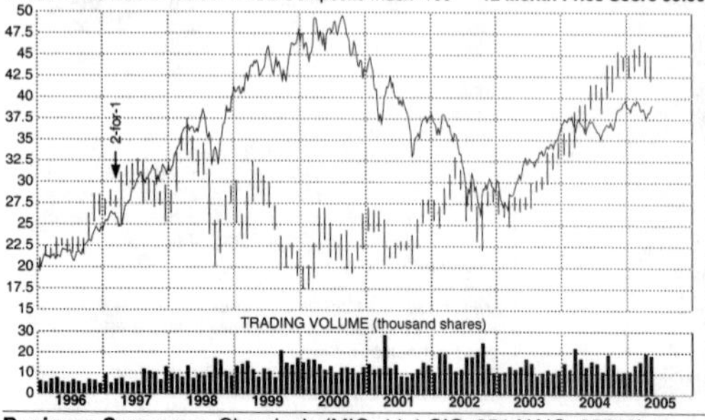

Interim Earnings (Per Share)

Qtr.	Mar	Jun	Sep	Dec
2002	(0.98)	0.70	0.73	0.38
2003	0.21	0.75	0.82	0.49
2004	0.35	0.87	0.92	0.58
2005	0.58	...	...	...

Interim Dividends (Per Share)

Amt	Decl	Ex	Rec	Pay
0.17Q	7/21/2004	8/18/2004	8/20/2004	9/3/2004
0.17Q	10/20/2004	11/9/2004	11/12/2004	11/26/2004
0.205Q	2/2/2005	2/24/2005	2/28/2005	3/14/2005
0.205Q	4/20/2005	5/18/2005	5/20/2005	6/10/2005

Indicated Div: $0.82 (Div. Reinv. Plan)

Valuation Analysis

Forecast P/E	14.06 (6/1/2005)		
Market Cap	$6.2 Billion	Book Value	1.6 Billion
Price/Book	3.88	Price/Sales	0.98

Dividend Achiever Status

Rank	186	10 Year Growth Rate	9.28%
Total Years of Dividend Growth			25

Business Summary: Chemicals (MIC: 11.1 SIC: 851 NAIC: 25510)

Sherwin-Williams manufactures, distributes and sells coatings and related products. The Paint Stores segment consisted of 2,983 specialty paint stores in the U.S., Canada, Virgin Islands, Puerto Rico and Mexico at Dec 31 2004. The Consumer segment manufactures and distributes a variety of paints, coatings and related products to third party customers and the Paint Stores segment. Automotive Finishes manufactures and distributes motor vehicle finish, refinish and touch-up products. International Coatings licenses, manufactures and distributes various paints, coatings and related products worldwide. Co.'s brands include Sherwin-Williams®, Dutch Boy®, Thompson's® WaterSeal®, Krylon® and Duron®.

Recent Developments: For the quarter ended Mar 31 2005, net income increased 61.8% to $83,294 thousand from net income of $51,468 thousand in the year-earlier quarter. Revenues were $1,538,545 thousand, up 16.6% from $1,319,522 thousand the year before. Total direct expense was $877,771 thousand versus $747,895 thousand in the prior-year quarter, an increase of 17.4%. Total indirect expense was $541,597 thousand versus $484,546 thousand in the prior-year quarter, an increase of 11.8%.

Prospects: Though significant raw material cost increases continue to adversely affect gross margins, Co. has implemented certain price increases and have taken actions, including tight control over expenses, which it believes will support earnings growth for the remainder of 2005. Meanwhile, Co.'s results are benefiting from contributions from the Duron and Paint Sundry Brands acquisitions. Co. continues to be encouraged by strong architectural paint sales. However, Co. is concerned about sluggish Consumer segment paint sales and selling prices not increasing on pace with raw material costs. For 2005. Co. expects low-to-mid teens sales growth and earnings in the range of $3.10 to $3.20 per share.

Financial Data

(US$ in Thousands)	3 Mos	12/31/2004	12/31/2003	12/31/2002	12/31/2001	12/31/2000	12/31/1999	12/31/1998
Earnings Per Share	2.95	2.72	2.26	0.84	1.68	0.10	1.80	1.57
Cash Flow Per Share	3.96	3.86	3.86	3.72	3.61	2.84	2.89	2.78
Tang Book Value Per Share	1.74	1.90	2.95	3.77	2.59	3.18	2.32	1.76
Dividends Per Share	0.715	0.680	0.620	0.600	0.580	0.540	0.480	0.450
Dividend Payout %	24.24	25.00	27.43	71.43	34.52	540.00	26.67	28.66
Income Statement								
Total Revenue	1,538,545	6,113,789	5,407,764	5,184,788	5,066,005	5,211,624	5,003,837	4,934,430
EBITDA	155,237	745,785	678,232	653,298	627,174	361,638	704,936	659,962
Depn & Amortn	35,630	125,642	116,564	115,659	148,098	156,206	153,650	147,888
Income Before Taxes	107,643	580,195	522,926	497,164	424,449	143,406	490,118	440,103
Income Taxes	24,109	185,662	190,868	186,463	161,291	127,380	186,258	167,239
Net Income	83,294	393,254	332,058	127,565	263,158	16,026	303,860	272,864
Average Shares	143,364	144,735	147,005	152,435	156,893	162,695	169,026	173,536
Balance Sheet								
Current Assets	1,962,821	1,781,928	1,715,144	1,505,993	1,506,945	1,551,539	1,597,377	1,547,290
Total Assets	4,480,702	4,274,151	3,682,608	3,432,312	3,627,925	3,750,670	4,052,090	4,065,462
Current Liabilities	1,778,641	1,520,137	1,154,170	1,083,496	1,141,353	1,115,243	1,189,862	1,111,973
Long-Term Obligations	487,943	488,239	502,992	506,682	503,517	623,587	624,365	730,283
Total Liabilities	2,887,036	2,626,905	2,223,751	2,090,422	2,140,161	2,278,806	2,353,558	2,349,522
Stockholders' Equity	1,593,666	1,647,246	1,458,857	1,341,890	1,487,764	1,471,864	1,698,532	1,715,940
Shares Outstanding	139,084	140,777	143,406	148,910	153,978	159,558	165,664	171,033
Statistical Record								
Return on Assets %	10.45	9.86	9.33	3.61	7.13	0.41	7.49	6.74
Return on Equity %	27.92	25.25	23.71	9.02	17.78	1.01	17.80	16.50
EBITDA Margin %	10.09	12.20	12.54	12.60	12.38	6.94	14.09	13.37
Net Margin %	5.41	6.43	6.14	2.46	5.19	0.31	6.07	5.53
Asset Turnover	1.56	1.53	1.52	1.47	1.37	1.33	1.23	1.22
Current Ratio	1.10	1.17	1.49	1.39	1.32	1.39	1.34	1.39
Debt to Equity	0.31	0.30	0.34	0.38	0.34	0.42	0.37	0.43
Price Range	46.29-36.06	45.48-33.06	34.74-24.82	33.00-22.06	28.02-20.31	27.00-17.44	32.44-19.00	37.50-20.06
P/E Ratio	15.69-12.22	16.72-12.15	15.37-10.98	39.29-26.26	16.68-12.09	270.00-174.38	18.02-10.56	23.89-12.78
Average Yield %	1.71	1.72	2.12	2.14	2.42	2.45	1.87	1.51

Address: 101 Prospect Avenue, N.W., Cleveland, OH 44115-1075
Telephone: 216-566-2000
Web Site: www.sherwin.com

Officers: Christopher M. Connor - Chmn., C.E.O. Sean P. Hennessy - Sr. V.P., Fin., C.F.O. **Transfer Agents:** The Bank of New York, New York, NY

Investor Contact: 216-566-2000
No of Institutions: 330
Shares: 91,697,040 **% Held:** 65.28

SHURGARD STORAGE CENTERS, INC. (WA)

Exchange	Symbol	Price	52Wk Range	Yield	P/E
NYS	SHU	$43.65 (5/31/2005)	44.76-36.42	5.13	53.23

*7 Year Price Score 115.95 *NYSE Composite Index=100 *12 Month Price Score 99.86

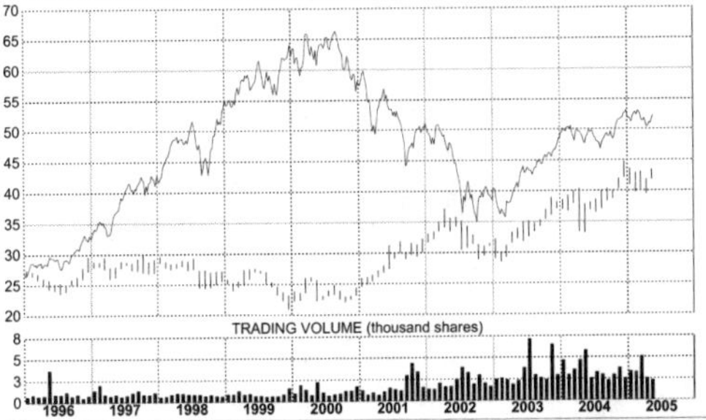

TRADING VOLUME (thousand shares)

Interim Earnings (Per Share)

Qtr.	Mar	Jun	Sep	Dec
2002	0.27	0.43	0.42	0.38
2003	0.30	0.21	0.28	(0.18)
2004	(0.05)	0.38	0.32	0.07
2005	0.05	...	...	...

Interim Dividends (Per Share)

Amt	Decl	Ex	Rec	Pay
0.55Q	7/23/2004	8/4/2004	8/6/2004	8/20/2004
0.55Q	11/5/2004	11/10/2004	11/15/2004	11/24/2004
0.55Q	2/15/2005	2/25/2005	3/1/2005	3/10/2005
0.56Q	5/6/2005	5/18/2005	5/20/2005	6/6/2005

Indicated Div: $2.24

Valuation Analysis

Forecast P/E 27.47 (6/1/2005)
Market Cap $2.0 Billion Book Value 879.2 Million
Price/Book 2.32 Price/Sales 4.63

Dividend Achiever Status

Rank 214 **10 Year Growth Rate** 7.94%
Total Years of Dividend Growth 10

Business Summary: Property, Real Estate & Development (MIC: 8.3 SIC: 798 NAIC: 25930)

Shurgard Storage Centers is an equity real estate investment trust that develops, acquires, invests in, operates and manages self storage centers and related operations located in markets throughout the U.S. and in Western Europe. Co. leases self-storage space to tenants primarily on a month-to-month basis. Co. also provide ancillary services at storage centers consisting primarily of truck rentals and sales of storage products. As of Dec 31 2004, Co. operated a network of 633 storage centers containing approximately 40.0 million net rentable square feet. Co. operates in Europe through its Shurgard Self Storage, SCA subsidiary, which is 87.2% owned.

Recent Developments: For the quarter ended Mar 31 2005, loss from continuing operations was $1,235 thousand versus income of $1,542 thousand in the year-earlier quarter. Net income was $5,256 thousand from net loss of $305 thousand in the year-earlier quarter. Revenues were $113,864 thousand, up 14.7% from $99,308 thousand the year before. Operating income was $20,016 thousand versus an income of $19,052 thousand in the prior-year quarter, an increase of 5.1%.

Prospects: Strong earnings are being driven by continuing growth in U.S. and European net operating income. Co. continues to see solid performance in most of its U.S. markets, although it is experiencing high growth in its indirect operating expenses reflecting the increase in accounting and related field positions. Meanwhile, Co.'s European operations are seeing strong revenue growth mainly due to increases in average occupancy in same-store locations. However, sluggish occupancy gains in certain areas has led Co. to moderate its new European store development pace to 15 from 20 openings for 2005. For full-year 2005, Co. expects funds from operation to range from $2.16 to $2.31 per share.

Financial Data (US$ in Thousands)	3 Mos	12/31/2004	12/31/2003	12/31/2002	12/31/2001	12/31/2000	12/31/1999	12/31/1998
Earnings Per Share	0.82	0.71	0.62	1.50	0.64	1.47	1.44	1.39
Cash Flow Per Share	2.48	2.61	3.05	3.69	3.80	2.78	3.05	2.76
Tang Book Value Per Share	15.50	16.10	17.47	16.21	15.90	18.28	18.72	19.27
Dividends Per Share	2.200	2.190	2.150	2.110	2.070	2.030	1.990	1.950
Dividend Payout %	268.29	308.45	346.77	140.67	323.44	138.10	138.19	140.29
Income Statement								
Total Revenue	113,864	425,661	302,314	264,113	232,590	195,867	173,154	159,254
EBITDA	40,153	183,347	141,282	150,406	133,486	...	...	...
Depn & Amortn	23,384	87,001	50,851	52,787	62,110	40,893	36,858	33,645
Income Before Taxes	(7,356)	13,470	39,249	65,594	34,814	...	...	...
Income Taxes	10	72	1,611	(314)	(1,545)	...	...	...
Net Income	5,256	45,295	37,638	67,632	34,914	52,632	50,673	44,734
Average Shares	46,514	46,626	41,209	35,401	31,086	29,761	29,130	28,724
Balance Sheet								
Current Assets	57,723	57,458	69,798	62,077	7,797	16,174	18,811	16,338
Total Assets	2,887,055	2,932,884	2,067,091	1,420,176	1,238,805	1,239,157	1,153,226	1,153,907
Current Liabilities	418,100	...	...	...	...	...	...	...
Long-Term Obligations	1,278,293	1,684,502	974,246	560,362	423,093	495,354	434,349	426,137
Total Liabilities	1,847,517	1,857,454	1,091,731	666,681	516,105	529,748	468,661	467,338
Stockholders' Equity	879,171	906,198	954,420	738,121	716,325	640,565	643,802	651,810
Shares Outstanding	46,658	46,624	45,747	35,934	33,778	29,774	29,248	28,831
Statistical Record								
Return on Assets %	1.83	1.81	2.16	5.09	2.82	4.39	4.39	4.24
Return on Equity %	5.64	4.86	4.45	9.30	5.15	8.17	7.82	7.09
EBITDA Margin %	35.26	43.07	46.73	56.95	57.39	...	...	...
Net Margin %	4.62	10.64	12.45	25.61	15.01	26.87	29.26	28.09
Asset Turnover	0.16	0.17	0.17	0.20	0.19	0.16	0.15	0.15
Current Ratio	0.14	...	...	...	...	...	...	...
Debt to Equity	1.45	1.86	1.02	0.76	0.59	0.77	0.67	0.65
Price Range	44.76-33.15	44.76-33.15	38.95-28.48	37.15-28.86	32.25-24.56	26.19-22.00	27.63-20.94	29.56-24.38
P/E Ratio	54.59-40.43	63.04-46.69	62.82-45.94	24.77-19.24	50.39-38.38	17.81-14.97	19.18-14.54	21.27-17.54
Average Yield %	5.59	5.69	6.41	6.44	7.26	8.64	7.90	7.14

Address: 1155 Valley Street, Suite 400, Seattle, WA 98109
Telephone: 206-624-8100
Web Site: www.shurgard.com

Officers: Charles K. Barbo - Chmn., C.E.O. David K. Grant - Pres., C.O.O., Interim C.F.O. **Transfer Agents:** American Stock Transfer & Trust Co. New York, NY.

No of Institutions: 131
Shares: 30,781,368 **% Held:** 66.21

SIGMA-ALDRICH CORP.

Exchange	Symbol	Price	52Wk Range	Yield	P/E
NMS	SIAL	$59.89 (5/31/2005)	64.50-53.92	1.27	17.01

*7 Year Price Score 119.66 *NYSE Composite Index=100 *12 Month Price Score 97.71

Interim Earnings (Per Share)

Qtr.	Mar	Jun	Sep	Dec
2002	0.54	(0.30)	0.63	0.91
2003	0.72	0.67	0.66	0.66
2004	0.89	0.85	0.81	0.79
2005	1.07	...	...	...

Interim Dividends (Per Share)

Amt	Decl	Ex	Rec	Pay
0.17Q	8/10/2004	8/30/2004	9/1/2004	9/15/2004
0.17Q	11/9/2004	11/29/2004	12/1/2004	12/15/2004
0.19Q	2/8/2005	2/25/2005	3/1/2005	3/15/2005
0.19Q	5/3/2005	5/27/2005	6/1/2005	6/15/2005

Indicated Div: $0.76

Valuation Analysis

Forecast P/E	16.75 (6/1/2005)		
Market Cap	$4.1 Billion	Book Value	1.3 Billion
Price/Book	3.29	Price/Sales	2.86

Dividend Achiever Status

Rank	87	10 Year Growth Rate	15.21%
Total Years of Dividend Growth			23

Business Summary: Biotechnology (MIC: 9.2 SIC: 169 NAIC: 24690)

Sigma-Aldrich develops, manufactures and distributes a broad range of biochemicals and organic chemicals. These chemical products and kits are used in scientific and genomic research, biotechnology, pharmaceutical development, the diagnosis of disease, and chemical manufacturing. Co. consists of three business units: Scientific Research, Biotechnology and Fine Chemicals. The Scientific Research unit sells biochemicals, organic chemicals, and reagents. The Biotechnology unit supplies immunochemical, cell culture, molecular biology, cell signaling and neuroscience biochemicals. The Fine Chemicals unit supplies organic chemicals and biochemicals.

Recent Developments: For the quarter ended Mar 31 2005, net income increased 19.7% to $74,600 thousand from net income of $62,300 thousand in the year-earlier quarter. Revenues were $399,800 thousand, up 8.6% from $368,100 thousand the year before. Total direct expense was $192,000 thousand versus $171,500 thousand in the prior-year quarter, an increase of 12.0%. Total indirect expense was $116,500 thousand versus $110,300 thousand in the prior-year quarter, an increase of 5.6%.

Prospects: Results are benefiting from Co.'s recent acquisition activity. On Apr 1 2005, Co. announced that it has completed its acquisition of the Proligo Group, a supplier of key genomics research tools, from Degussa AG. Separately, on Feb 28 2005, Co. announced that it has completed its acquisition of the JRH Biosciences division of CSL Limited for $370.0 million in cash. JRH is a global supplier of cell culture and sera products to the biopharmaceutical industry. Looking ahead, Co. anticipates full-year 2005 sales growth in the range of 17.0% to 20.0%, and diluted earnings per share of between $3.56 and $3.66.

Financial Data

(US$ in Thousands)	3 Mos	12/31/2004	12/31/2003	12/31/2002	12/31/2001	12/31/2000	12/31/1999	12/31/1998
Earnings Per Share	3.52	3.34	2.71	1.78	1.87	3.83	1.71	1.64
Cash Flow Per Share	4.66	4.68	4.38	4.83	2.13	1.38	2.29	1.61
Tang Book Value Per Share	13.20	15.34	12.83	10.90	9.34	9.72	11.89	10.96
Dividends Per Share	0.700	0.680	0.500	0.345	0.333	0.315	0.295	0.282
Dividend Payout %	19.89	20.36	18.45	19.38	17.78	8.22	17.25	17.23
Income Statement								
Total Revenue	399,800	1,409,200	1,298,146	1,206,982	1,179,447	1,096,270	1,037,945	1,194,290
EBITDA	109,200	392,400	352,216	352,302	289,548	277,043	270,636	304,417
Depn & Amortn	20,100	73,400	69,267	66,326	71,373	67,563	66,919	61,827
Income Before Taxes	89,100	311,800	272,823	272,139	201,633	202,909	203,717	242,590
Income Taxes	14,500	78,900	82,393	85,404	60,928	63,859	55,112	76,243
Net Income	74,600	232,900	193,102	130,714	140,705	320,198	172,270	166,347
Average Shares	69,700	69,800	71,126	73,412	75,175	83,585	100,984	101,188
Balance Sheet								
Current Assets	1,062,500	893,400	815,030	694,887	727,311	713,625	774,571	772,681
Total Assets	2,226,200	1,745,000	1,548,242	1,389,656	1,439,802	1,347,707	1,432,001	1,432,835
Current Liabilities	487,200	230,900	257,378	265,653	397,563	335,280	105,612	142,372
Long-Term Obligations	326,100	177,100	176,259	176,805	177,700	100,846	205	415
Total Liabilities	972,800	533,300	548,981	507,482	630,087	488,432	172,650	216,455
Stockholders' Equity	1,253,400	1,211,700	999,261	882,174	809,715	859,275	1,259,351	1,216,380
Shares Outstanding	68,900	68,700	69,101	71,253	73,014	76,216	98,292	100,623
Statistical Record								
Return on Assets %	12.96	14.11	13.15	9.24	10.10	22.98	12.03	12.43
Return on Equity %	21.32	21.01	20.53	15.45	16.86	30.14	13.92	14.61
EBITDA Margin %	27.31	27.85	27.13	29.19	24.55	25.27	26.07	25.49
Net Margin %	18.66	16.53	14.88	10.83	11.93	29.21	16.60	13.93
Asset Turnover	0.76	0.85	0.88	0.85	0.85	0.79	0.72	0.89
Current Ratio	2.18	3.87	3.17	2.62	1.83	2.13	7.33	5.43
Debt to Equity	0.26	0.15	0.18	0.20	0.22	0.12	N.M.	N.M.
Price Range	64.50-53.92	61.34-53.92	57.46-41.17	52.51-39.41	51.21-37.10	40.25-20.75	35.13-25.75	42.75-26.38
P/E Ratio	18.32-15.32	18.37-16.14	21.20-15.19	29.50-22.14	27.39-19.84	10.51-5.42	20.54-15.06	26.07-16.08
Average Yield %	1.20	1.19	0.98	0.73	0.77	1.01	0.96	0.82

Address: 3050 Spruce Street, St. Louis, MO 63103 **Telephone:** 314-771-5765 **Web Site:** www.sigma-aldrich.com	**Officers:** David R. Harvey - Chmn., C.E.O. Jai P. Nagarkatti - Pres., C.O.O. **Transfer Agents:** Computershare Investor Services, Chicago, IL	**Investor Contact:** 314-286-8004 **No of Institutions:** 287 **Shares:** 54,334,800 **% Held:** 78.92

SKY FINANCIAL GROUP, INC.

Exchange	Symbol	Price	52Wk Range	Yield	P/E
NMS	SKYF	$28.76 (5/31/2005)	29.01-23.23	3.06	17.86

Interim Earnings (Per Share)

Qtr.	Mar	Jun	Sep	Dec
2002	0.38	0.35	0.40	0.39
2003	0.41	0.42	0.46	0.44
2004	0.62	0.43	0.43	0.46
2005	0.29	...	...	...

Interim Dividends (Per Share)

Amt	Decl	Ex	Rec	Pay
0.21Q	9/2/2004	9/13/2004	9/15/2004	10/1/2004
0.22Q	11/17/2004	12/13/2004	12/15/2004	1/3/2005
0.22Q	3/1/2005	3/11/2005	3/15/2005	4/1/2005
0.22Q	5/3/2005	5/26/2005	5/31/2005	7/1/2005

Indicated Div: $0.88

Valuation Analysis

Forecast P/E	16.92 (6/2/2005)		
Market Cap	$3.0 Billion	Book Value	1.4 Billion
Price/Book	2.16	Price/Sales	3.42

Dividend Achiever Status

Rank	3	**10 Year Growth Rate**	36.44%
Total Years of Dividend Growth			10

Business Summary: Commercial Banking (MIC: 8.1 SIC: 021 NAIC: 22110)

Sky Financial Group is a financial holding company that owns and operates Sky Bank, which is primarily engaged in the commercial and consumer banking business that includes the acceptance of a variety of demand, savings and time deposits and the extension of commercial and consumer loans. Co. also operates businesses relating to insurance, brokerage, trust and other financial-related services. As of Dec 31 2004, Co. operated over 280 financial centers and over 300 ATMs serving Ohio, western Pennsylvania, southern Michigan, eastern Indiana and northern West Virginia. As of Dec 31 2004, Co. had total assets of $14.94 billion.

Recent Developments: For the first quarter ended Mar 31 2005, net income declined 21.2% to $31.5 million compared with income of $40.0 million, before income from discontinued operations of $18.7 million. Results for 2004 included a merger, integration and restructuring charge of $346,000. Net interest income advanced 21.8% to $124.0 million from $101.8 million a year earlier. Provision for credit losses grew to $30.8 million from $6.7 million the year before. Non-interest income climbed 18.6% to $51.5 million, while non-interest expense was up 25.2% to $98.3 million.

Prospects: Co.'s earnings in the first quarter of 2005 were adversely affected by a substantially higher provision for credit losses due to higher net charge-offs, primarily from two large commercial credits and the sale of a group of non-performing consumer loans. Co. does not see these higher credit losses as indicative of any systemic concern Going forward, Co. expects its profitability will return to previous levels and reflect the benefits of strong credit underwriting and a renewed emphasis on expense management. Including its first quarter results and the previously announced acquisition of Belmont Bancorp., Co. projects full-year 2005 earnings in the range of $1.68 to $1.71 per diluted share.

Financial Data (US$ in Thousands)	3 Mos	12/31/2004	12/31/2003	12/31/2002	12/31/2001	12/31/2000	12/31/1999	12/31/1998
Earnings Per Share	1.61	1.93	1.73	1.52	1.45	1.35	0.82	0.32
Cash Flow Per Share	2.33	2.37	3.02	2.10	0.59	1.61	2.36	(0.04)
Tang Book Value Per Share	8.20	8.65	8.24	7.81	7.92	7.31	6.61	6.31
Dividends Per Share	0.860	0.850	0.810	0.770	0.740	0.725	0.702	0.530
Dividend Payout %	53.42	44.04	46.82	50.66	51.03	53.74	85.86	164.58
Income Statement								
Interest Income	191,594	661,943	662,935	625,906	642,376	626,015	573,595	363,680
Interest Expense	67,587	210,632	242,732	264,221	316,779	322,219	269,950	176,556
Net Interest Income	124,007	451,311	420,203	361,685	325,597	303,796	303,645	187,124
Provision for Losses	30,823	37,660	42,712	43,577	34,635	22,250	20,712	24,968
Non-Interest Income	51,471	176,553	156,135	115,890	96,780	90,006	96,069	79,300
Non-Interest Expense	98,282	356,524	323,769	276,814	237,220	235,407	302,497	232,708
Income Before Taxes	46,373	260,544	235,072	191,175	179,982	168,097	104,778	26,662
Income Taxes	14,902	85,344	78,455	63,368	59,319	53,724	33,596	8,854
Net Income	31,471	194,355	156,617	127,807	120,663	114,373	71,182	17,808
Average Shares	107,591	100,568	90,404	84,096	83,028	84,967	86,773	55,280
Balance Sheet								
Net Loans & Leases	10,512,835	10,464,729	9,240,279	7,764,149	6,370,466	5,822,837	5,390,744	3,301,873
Total Assets	14,977,812	14,944,423	12,896,494	11,013,943	9,220,228	8,386,802	8,063,756	4,815,121
Total Deposits	10,441,292	10,351,591	8,514,852	7,615,420	6,542,177	5,891,932	5,758,691	3,832,662
Total Liabilities	13,571,036	13,473,468	11,897,918	10,181,510	8,571,784	7,777,112	7,497,425	4,471,279
Stockholders' Equity	1,406,776	1,470,955	998,576	832,433	648,444	609,690	566,331	343,842
Shares Outstanding	105,752	106,839	92,443	87,056	81,847	83,407	85,677	54,481
Statistical Record								
Return on Assets %	1.23	1.39	1.31	1.26	1.37	1.39	1.11	0.60
Return on Equity %	13.52	15.70	17.11	17.26	19.18	19.40	15.64	7.97
Net Interest Margin %	64.72	68.18	63.39	57.79	50.69	48.53	52.94	51.45
Efficiency Ratio %	40.43	42.52	39.53	37.32	32.09	32.88	45.17	52.53
Loans to Deposits	1.01	1.01	1.09	1.02	0.97	0.99	0.94	0.86
Price Range	29.01-23.23	29.01-23.23	25.95-19.03	23.52-17.71	20.80-15.69	18.30-12.67	24.82-17.17	28.64-19.53
P/E Ratio	18.02-14.43	15.03-12.04	15.00-11.00	15.47-11.65	14.34-10.82	13.55-9.39	30.27-20.94	89.51-61.04
Average Yield %	3.30	3.29	3.67	3.74	3.90	4.69	3.24	2.10

Address: 221 South Church Street, P.O. Box 428, Bowling Green, OH 43402
Telephone: 419-327-6300
Web Site: www.skyfi.com

Officers: Marty E. Adams - Chmn., Pres., C.E.O. Kevin T. Thompson - Exec. V.P., C.F.O. **Transfer Agents:** The Bank of New York, New York, NY

Investor Contact: 800-576-5007
No of Institutions: 138
Shares: 28,352,128 **% Held:** 26.60

SLM CORP.

Exchange	Symbol	Price	52Wk Range	Yield	P/E
NYS	SLM	$48.27 (5/31/2005)	54.97-36.99	1.82	12.41

***7 Year Price Score 145.57** *NYSE Composite Index=100 ***12 Month Price Score 102.19**

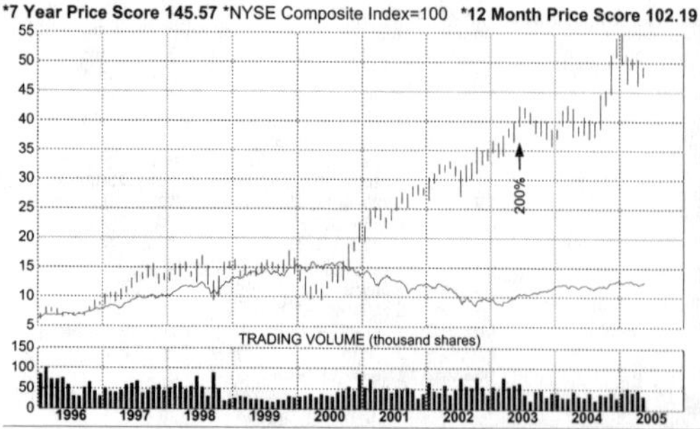

TRADING VOLUME (thousand shares)

Interim Earnings (Per Share)

Qtr.	Mar	Jun	Sep	Dec
2002	0.88	0.26	(0.14)	0.64
2003	0.88	0.80	1.04	0.58
2004	0.64	1.36	0.80	1.24
2005	0.49	...	...	...

Interim Dividends (Per Share)

Amt	Decl	Ex	Rec	Pay
0.19Q	7/30/2004	9/1/2004	9/3/2004	9/17/2004
0.19Q	10/29/2004	12/1/2004	12/3/2004	12/17/2004
0.19Q	1/27/2005	3/2/2005	3/4/2005	3/18/2005
0.22Q	5/19/2005	6/1/2005	6/3/2005	6/17/2005

Indicated Div: $0.88

Valuation Analysis

Forecast P/E	N/A		
Market Cap	$20.4 Billion	Book Value	3.1 Billion
Price/Book	6.65	Price/Sales	3.64

Dividend Achiever Status

Rank	51	**10 Year Growth Rate**	18.53%
Total Years of Dividend Growth			24

Business Summary: Credit & Lending (MIC: 8.6 SIC: 141 NAIC: 22291)

SLM is a holding company. Through its subsidiaries, Co. provides funding, delivery and servicing support for education loans in the United States primarily through its participation in the Federal Family Education Loan Program. Co. provides a range of financial services, processing capabilities and information technology to meet the needs of educational institutions, lenders, students and their families, guarantee agencies and the U.S. Department of Education. Co.'s primary business is to originate and hold student loans. Co. also provides fee-based related products and services and earns fees for student loan and guarantee servicing, and student loan default management and loan collections.

Recent Developments: For the quarter ended Mar 31 2005, net income decreased 23.4% to $223,384 thousand from net income of $291,465 thousand in the year-earlier quarter. Net interest income was $346,760 thousand, up 7.8% from $321,715 thousand the year before. Provision for loan losses was $46,523 thousand versus $39,818 thousand in the prior-year quarter, an increase of 16.8%. Non-interest income rose 21.6% to $374,098 thousand, while non-interest expense advanced 25.6% to $262,291 thousand.

Prospects: On Apr 8 2005, Co. announced that it is introducing an array of loan products, education resources and scholarships for community college students. Products include the Community College Loan, a new private, credit-based loan designed for students enrolled in an associate degree or eligible certificate program. Co. is also introducing the Continuing Education Loan for returning adults pursuing professional or technical training. Meanwhile, Co.'s results for the quarter ended Mar 31 2005 benefited from $6.80 billion in preferred-channel loan originations, an increase 16.0% from last year. Preferred-channel loan originations are loans funded by Co.'s owned brands and other lender partners.

Financial Data

(US$ in Thousands)	3 Mos	12/31/2004	12/31/2003	12/31/2002	12/31/2001	12/31/2000	12/31/1999	12/31/1998
Earnings Per Share	3.89	4.04	3.29	1.64	0.76	0.92	1.02	0.98
Cash Flow Per Share	0.80	(0.73)	1.49	1.65	1.76	1.55	0.70	0.25
Tang Book Value Per Share	4.47	4.42	4.18	2.72	3.23	2.54	1.43	1.33
Dividends Per Share	0.760	0.740	0.593	0.283	0.242	0.218	0.203	0.19
Dividend Payout %	19.54	18.32	18.03	17.24	31.80	2.370	19.90	19.39
Income Statement								
Interest Income	910,972	2,732,995	2,348,275	2,211,761	2,997,531	3,478,659	2,808,575	2,587,649
Interest Expense	564,212	1,433,696	1,021,906	1,202,620	2,124,115	2,836,871	2,114,785	1,924,997
Net Interest Income	346,760	1,299,299	1,326,369	1,009,141	873,416	641,788	693,790	662,652
Provision for Losses	46,523	111,066	147,480	116,624	65,991	32,119	34,358	28,619
Non-Interest Income	374,098	2,484,532	1,811,951	1,020,654	517,617	687,632	450,790	476,967
Non-Interest Expense	262,291	1,115,780	807,871	689,772	707,654	585,710	358,570	360,869
Income Before Taxes	412,044	2,556,985	2,182,969	1,223,399	617,388	711,591	751,652	750,131
Income Taxes	186,466	642,689	779,380	431,403	223,322	235,880	240,127	237,973
Net Income	223,384	1,913,270	1,533,560	791,996	383,996	465,017	500,831	501,464
Average Shares	463,014	475,787	463,335	474,519	490,200	493,065	489,474	510,198
Balance Sheet								
Net Loans & Leases	71,000,983	67,028,795	51,078,136	43,541,720	42,769,017	39,485,817	35,879,327	31,005,649
Total Assets	83,796,953	84,093,526	64,610,651	53,175,005	52,873,959	48,791,788	44,024,784	37,210,009
Total Liabilities	80,659,102	80,919,589	61,980,605	51,177,055	51,201,497	47,162,569	42,969,987	36,342,500
Stockholders' Equity	3,064,982	3,102,304	2,630,046	1,997,950	1,672,462	1,415,336	840,914	653,626
Shares Outstanding	421,981	423,632	447,678	457,740	466,485	492,434	472,729	492,381
Statistical Record								
Return on Assets %	2.35	2.57	2.60	1.49	0.76	1.00	1.23	1.30
Return on Equity %	63.60	66.57	66.27	43.16	24.87	41.11	67.02	75.51
Net Interest Margin %	38.06	47.54	56.48	45.63	29.14	18.45	24.70	25.61
Efficiency Ratio %	20.41	21.39	19.42	21.34	20.13	14.06	11.00	11.78
Price Range	54.97-36.99	54.24-36.99	42.64-33.85	35.63-26.38	29.13-19.38	22.67-9.44	17.88-13.38	17.00-9.33
P/E Ratio	14.13-9.51	13.43-9.16	12.96-10.29	21.73-16.09	38.33-25.49	24.64-10.26	17.52-13.11	17.35-9.52
Average Yield %	1.71	1.76	1.55	0.90	0.96	1.36	1.30	1.44

Address: 12061 Bluemont Way, Reston, VA 20190
Telephone: 703-810-3000
Web Site: www.salliemae.com

Officers: Edward A. Fox - Chmn. Thomas J. Fitzpatrick - C.E.O. **Transfer Agents:** The Bank of New York, New York, NY

Investor Contact: 703-984-6746
No of Institutions: 373
Shares: 391,912,480 **% Held:** 92.95

SMITH (A.O.) CORP

Exchange	Symbol	Price	52Wk Range	Yield	P/E
NYS	AOS	$31.36 (5/31/2005)	31.79-23.20	2.04	24.12

*7 Year Price Score 100.62 *NYSE Composite Index=100 *12 Month Price Score 102.21

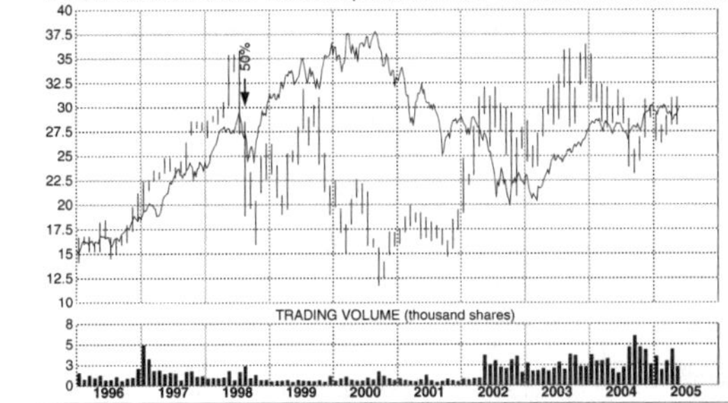

TRADING VOLUME (thousand shares)

Interim Earnings (Per Share)

Qtr.	Mar	Jun	Sep	Dec
2002	0.50	0.66	0.34	0.37
2003	0.46	0.67	0.20	0.43
2004	0.36	0.58	0.10	0.14
2005	0.48	...	...	...

Interim Dividends (Per Share)

Amt	Decl	Ex	Rec	Pay
0.16Q	7/13/2004	7/28/2004	7/30/2004	8/16/2004
0.16Q	10/12/2004	10/27/2004	10/29/2004	11/15/2004
0.16Q	1/14/2005	1/27/2005	1/31/2005	2/15/2005
0.16Q	4/12/2005	4/27/2005	4/29/2005	5/16/2005

Indicated Div: $0.64 (Div. Reinv. Plan)

Valuation Analysis

Forecast P/E	17.02 (6/1/2005)		
Market Cap	$930.8 Million	Book Value	601.1 Million
Price/Book	1.55	Price/Sales	0.57

Dividend Achiever Status

Rank	241	10 Year Growth Rate	6.40%
Total Years of Dividend Growth			12

Business Summary: Electrical (MIC: 11.14 SIC: 621 NAIC: 35312)

A.O. Smith is a manufacturer of electric motors and water heating equipment serving residential, commercial and industrial end markets primarily in the United States. The Electric Products segment manufactures hermetic motors, fractional horsepower alternating current and direct current motors, and integral horsepower motors. The Water Systems segment manufactures and markets a line of residential gas and electric water heaters, standard and specialty commercial water heating equipment, high-efficiency copper-tube boilers, and water systems tanks. Co. operates manufacturing facilities in the United States, Canada, Mexico, England, Ireland, Hungary, the Netherlands and China.

Recent Developments: For the quarter ended Mar 31 2005, net income increased 32.4% to $14,300 thousand from net income of $10,800 thousand in the year-earlier quarter. Revenues were $409,200 thousand, down 1.8% from $416,500 thousand the year before. Total direct expense was $321,100 thousand versus $338,300 thousand in the prior-year quarter, a decrease of 5.1%. Total indirect expense was $63,300 thousand versus $58,600 thousand in the prior-year quarter, an increase of 8.0%.

Prospects: Co. plans to close its facility located in Bray, Ireland that manufactures hermetic motors for commercial air conditioning and refrigeration equipment by the end of the second quarter of 2005. Co. will consolidate operations into existing plants in North America and China. Meanwhile, in an effort to met the increased demand for its residential and commercial water heaters in China, Co. plans to double the size of its operations in Nanjing, China. The first phase of the expansion is expected to be completed by the first half of 2006. Separately, Co. is projecting full-year 2005 earnings of between $1.45 and $1.65 per share, including a $0.35 per share restructuring charge.

Financial Data

(US$ in Thousands)	3 Mos	12/31/2004	12/31/2003	12/31/2002	12/31/2001	12/31/2000	12/31/1999	12/31/1998
Earnings Per Share	1.30	1.18	1.76	1.86	0.61	1.26	1.78	1.84
Cash Flow Per Share	3.13	2.29	0.87	4.16	2.11	3.27	2.06	3.29
Tang Book Value Per Share	9.70	9.35	9.07	6.95	6.30	8.64	7.69	10.93
Dividends Per Share	0.630	0.620	0.580	0.540	0.520	0.500	0.480	0.467
Dividend Payout %	48.46	52.54	32.95	29.03	85.25	39.68	26.97	25.36
Income Statement								
Total Revenue	409,200	1,653,100	1,530,700	1,469,100	1,151,156	1,247,945	1,039,281	917,569
EBITDA	37,800	114,900	141,200	141,678	84,345	130,704	125,836	107,195
Depn & Amortn	13,100	53,900	50,000	49,362	45,441	43,514	37,315	31,173
Income Before Taxes	21,300	47,500	79,000	78,390	22,486	65,088	77,092	72,963
Income Taxes	7,000	12,100	26,800	27,045	7,984	23,432	26,822	25,283
Net Income	14,300	35,400	52,200	51,345	14,502	29,753	42,422	44,491
Average Shares	30,004	29,912	29,710	27,649	23,914	23,691	23,787	24,184
Balance Sheet								
Current Assets	607,500	585,000	547,700	488,251	477,574	406,099	388,627	287,389
Total Assets	1,329,600	1,312,800	1,279,900	1,224,857	1,293,923	1,059,176	1,063,986	767,432
Current Liabilities	268,200	245,200	338,600	261,679	255,950	170,431	168,440	132,157
Long-Term Obligations	257,200	272,500	170,100	239,084	390,385	316,372	351,251	131,203
Total Liabilities	728,500	722,200	703,700	713,805	842,045	610,781	632,902	366,339
Stockholders' Equity	601,100	590,600	576,200	511,052	451,878	448,395	431,084	401,093
Shares Outstanding	29,681	29,665	29,246	29,039	23,786	23,549	23,394	23,252
Statistical Record								
Return on Assets %	2.94	2.72	4.17	4.08	1.23	2.80	4.63	6.00
Return on Equity %	6.53	6.05	9.60	10.66	3.22	6.75	10.20	11.11
EBITDA Margin %	9.24	6.95	9.22	9.64	7.33	10.47	12.11	11.68
Net Margin %	3.49	2.14	3.41	3.49	1.26	2.38	4.08	4.85
Asset Turnover	1.24	1.27	1.22	1.17	0.98	1.17	1.13	1.24
Current Ratio	2.27	2.39	1.62	1.87	1.87	2.38	2.31	2.17
Debt to Equity	0.43	0.46	0.30	0.47	0.86	0.71	0.81	0.33
Price Range	32.06-23.20	35.49-23.20	36.50-23.80	32.10-19.15	20.00-14.68	22.63-11.75	31.94-19.00	35.88-15.94
P/E Ratio	24.66-17.85	30.08-19.66	20.74-13.52	17.26-10.30	32.79-24.07	17.96-9.33	17.94-10.67	19.50-8.66
Average Yield %	2.24	2.13	1.91	2.02	2.96	2.83	1.95	1.71

Address: P.O. Box 245008, Milwaukee, WI 53224-9508
Telephone: 414-359-4000
Web Site: www.aosmith.com

Officers: Robert J. O'Toole - Chmn., C.E.O. Paul W. Jones - Pres., C.O.O. **Transfer Agents:** Wells Fargo Bank Minnesota, N.A., St. Paul, MN

Investor Contact: 414-359-4009
No of Institutions: 113
Shares: 18,085,448 **% Held:** 85.41

SONOCO PRODUCTS CO.

Exchange	Symbol	Price	52Wk Range	Yield	P/E
NYS	SON	$26.63 (5/31/2005)	30.07-24.55	3.45	17.87

*7 Year Price Score 97.56 *NYSE Composite Index=100 *12 Month Price Score 97.06

Interim Earnings (Per Share)

Qtr.	Mar	Jun	Sep	Dec
2002	0.35	0.39	0.30	0.36
2003	0.30	0.24	0.14	0.75
2004	0.38	0.35	0.42	0.35
2005	0.37	...	...	...

Interim Dividends (Per Share)

Amt	Decl	Ex	Rec	Pay
0.22Q	7/21/2004	8/18/2004	8/20/2004	9/10/2004
0.22Q	10/18/2004	11/17/2004	11/19/2004	12/10/2004
0.22Q	2/2/2005	2/16/2005	2/18/2005	3/10/2005
0.23Q	4/20/2005	5/18/2005	5/20/2005	6/10/2005

Indicated Div: $0.92 (Div. Reinv. Plan)

Valuation Analysis

Forecast P/E 14.88 (6/2/2005)

Market Cap $2.6 Billion Book Value 1.2 Billion

Price/Book 2.25 Price/Sales 0.80

Dividend Achiever Status

Rank 246 **10 Year Growth Rate** 6.12%

Total Years of Dividend Growth 21

TRADING VOLUME (thousand shares)

Business Summary: Paper Products (MIC: 11.11 SIC: 631 NAIC: 22130)

Sonoco Products is a manufacturer of industrial and consumer packaging products and provider of packaging services, with 322 locations in 35 countries as of Dec 31 2004. Each of Co.'s operating units has its own sales staff and maintains direct sales relationships with its customers. The industrial packaging segment includes engineered carriers, paper, molded & extruded plastics, wire & cable reels, and protective packaging. The consumer packaging segment includes rigid packaging, closures, printed flexible packaging, packaging services & folding cartons, glass covers & coasters, and artwork management.

Recent Developments: For the first quarter ended Mar 27 2005, net income decreased 4.1% to $37.0 million compared with $38.6 million in the corresponding prior-year quarter. Results for 2005 and 2004 included restructuring charges of $5.0 million and $1.3 million, respectively. Net sales advanced 17.1% to $814.4 million from $695.4 million a year earlier, primarily due to the acquisition of CorrFlex Graphics, LLC in May 2004 and contributions from a newly formed European joint venture. Sales also benefited from increased volume and higher average selling prices. Cost of sales grew 16.1% to $666.1 million from $573.8 million the year before.

Prospects: Co. results are being negatively affected by costs associated with the integration of Sonoco and Ahlstrom operations in Europe, continued weak general economic conditions in Europe and startup costs associated with Co.'s new rigid plastic container plant in Wisconsin. Looking ahead, Co. expects to benefit from continued improvement in its businesses serving consumer product customers, reflecting Co.'s strategy to achieve a greater balance of sales and earnings between consumer and industrial markets. Moreover, Co. expects to report diluted earnings for full-year 2005 in the range of $1.75 to $1.79 per share.

Financial Data

(US$ in Thousands)	3 Mos	12/31/2004	12/31/2003	12/31/2002	12/31/2001	12/31/2000	12/31/1999	12/31/1998
Earnings Per Share	1.49	1.53	1.43	1.39	0.96	1.66	1.83	1.73
Cash Flow Per Share	2.55	2.57	3.43	2.82	3.82	3.62	2.36	2.22
Tang Book Value Per Share	5.26	5.00	6.48	5.26	4.64	5.94	6.37	6.40
Dividends Per Share	0.880	0.870	0.840	0.830	0.800	0.790	0.750	0.704
Dividend Payout %	58.89	56.86	58.74	59.71	83.33	47.59	40.98	40.67
Income Statement								
Total Revenue	814,438	3,155,433	2,758,326	2,812,150	2,606,276	2,711,493	2,546,734	2,557,917
EBITDA	101,081	403,333	312,082	410,296	382,772	477,221	482,558	534,130
Depn & Amortn	38,604	163,928	153,538	159,256	158,574	150,816	145,846	145,669
Income Before Taxes	53,082	197,342	108,333	198,493	175,781	270,595	289,560	339,598
Income Taxes	19,179	58,858	37,698	70,614	82,958	111,999	108,585	153,989
Net Income	36,989	151,229	138,949	135,316	91,609	166,298	187,805	180,243
Average Shares	100,449	98,947	97,129	97,178	95,807	99,900	102,780	104,275
Balance Sheet								
Current Assets	970,001	922,112	755,265	663,267	665,169	695,793	723,081	661,416
Total Assets	3,063,999	3,041,319	2,520,633	2,390,094	2,352,197	2,212,611	2,297,020	2,082,983
Current Liabilities	648,478	639,886	679,594	600,027	460,270	437,080	416,631	436,069
Long-Term Obligations	807,489	813,207	473,220	699,346	885,961	812,085	819,540	686,826
Total Liabilities	1,887,477	1,888,440	1,506,473	1,522,669	1,548,075	1,411,140	1,395,800	1,261,391
Stockholders' Equity	1,176,522	1,152,879	1,014,160	867,425	804,122	801,471	901,220	821,592
Shares Outstanding	99,222	98,793	97,217	96,640	95,713	95,006	101,448	101,683
Statistical Record								
Return on Assets %	5.27	5.42	5.66	5.71	4.01	7.36	8.58	8.46
Return on Equity %	13.39	13.92	14.77	16.19	11.41	19.48	21.80	21.58
EBITDA Margin %	12.41	12.78	11.31	14.59	14.69	17.60	18.95	20.88
Net Margin %	4.54	4.79	5.04	4.81	3.51	6.13	7.37	7.05
Asset Turnover	1.17	1.13	1.12	1.19	1.14	1.20	1.16	1.20
Current Ratio	1.50	1.44	1.11	1.11	1.45	1.59	1.74	1.52
Debt to Equity	0.69	0.71	0.47	0.81	1.10	1.01	0.91	0.84
Price Range	30.07-23.93	29.70-22.86	24.73-19.47	29.70-19.81	26.58-19.69	23.00-16.88	29.94-21.06	38.92-22.44
P/E Ratio	20.18-16.06	19.41-14.94	17.29-13.62	21.37-14.25	27.69-20.51	13.86-10.17	16.36-11.51	22.50-12.97
Average Yield %	3.30	3.39	3.78	3.25	3.36	3.97	2.95	2.25

Address: One North Second Street, Hartsville, SC 29550-3305
Telephone: 843-383-7000
Web Site: www.sonoco.com

Officers: Harris E. DeLoach Jr. - Chmn., Pres., C.E.O. Charles L. Sullivan Jr. - Exec. V.P. **Transfer Agents:** EquiServe Trust Company, NA Providence, RI

Investor Contact: 843-383-7524
No of Institutions: 209
Shares: 53,082,464 **% Held:** 53.63

SOUTH FINANCIAL GROUP INC

Exchange	Symbol	Price	52Wk Range	Yield	P/E
NMS	TSFG	$27.15 (5/31/2005)	32.53-26.16	2.36	15.60

*7 Year Price Score 119.35 *NYSE Composite Index=100 *12 Month Price Score 91.48

Interim Earnings (Per Share)

Qtr.	Mar	Jun	Sep	Dec
2002	0.34	0.36	0.33	0.38
2003	0.42	0.48	0.50	0.50
2004	0.53	0.49	0.44	0.34
2005	0.47	...	...	...

Interim Dividends (Per Share)

Amt	Decl	Ex	Rec	Pay
0.15Q	5/6/2004	7/16/2004	7/20/2004	8/2/2004
0.15Q	8/19/2004	10/13/2004	10/15/2004	11/1/2004
0.16Q	12/15/2004	1/12/2005	1/15/2005	2/1/2005
0.16Q	2/16/2005	4/13/2005	4/15/2005	5/1/2005

Indicated Div: $0.64

Valuation Analysis

Forecast P/E	13.30 (6/2/2005)		
Market Cap	$1.9 Billion	Book Value	1.4 Billion
Price/Book	1.41	Price/Sales	2.84

Dividend Achiever Status

Rank	100	10 Year Growth Rate	14.50%
Total Years of Dividend Growth			10

Business Summary: Commercial Banking (MIC: 8.1 SIC: 022 NAIC: 22110)

South Financial Group is a financial institution holding company. Through its subsidiaries, Co. provide a full range of financial services, including cash management, insurance, investments, mortgage, and trust services. As of Dec 31 2004, Co. operated 76 branch offices in South Carolina, 54 in Florida, and 24 in North Carolina. Co.'s subsidiary banks include Carolina First Bank, headquartered in Greenville, SC, and Mercantile Bank, headquartered in Orlando, FL. Co.'s non-banking subsidiaries include American Pensions, Inc., Carolina First Community Development Corp., CF Investment Co., CF Technology Services Co., Gardner Associates, Inc. and South Financial Asset Management, Inc.

Recent Developments: For the quarter ended Mar 31 2005, net income increased 7.0% to $34,559 thousand from net income of $32,293 thousand in the year-earlier quarter. Net interest income was $152,511 thousand, up 26.1% from $120,985 thousand the year before. Provision for loan losses was $10,962 thousand versus $7,722 thousand in the prior-year quarter, an increase of 42.0%. Non-interest income fell 9.2% to $24,032 thousand, while non-interest expense advanced 16.1% to $66,510 thousand.

Prospects: On May 6 2005, Co. announced that it has completed its acquisition of Point Financial Corporation. The acquisition will help expand Co.'s market presence in South Florida and adds approximately $315.0 million in deposits, $302.0 million in loans, and ten branch offices. Separately, results may benefit from Co.'s efforts to increase its fee-based business. In April 2005, Co. acquired Koss Olinger, a Gainesville, FL-based group of companies with operations in wealth management and insurance, and entered into an agreement to acquire a Florida-based commercial insurance broker. Combined, Koss Olinger and the Florida insurance company are expected to add about $6.0 million in revenues.

Financial Data

(US$ in Thousands)	3 Mos	12/31/2004	12/31/2003	12/31/2002	12/31/2001	12/31/2000	12/31/1999	12/31/1998
Earnings Per Share	1.74	1.80	1.89	1.38	0.98	0.16	1.06	1.19
Cash Flow Per Share	3.22	3.54	3.73	7.14	3.84	1.15	(3.71)	4.32
Tang Book Value Per Share	10.77	11.08	10.61	8.55	8.76	8.51	11.52	9.72
Dividends Per Share	0.610	0.600	0.560	0.480	0.440	0.400	0.360	0.320
Dividend Payout %	35.06	33.33	29.63	34.78	44.90	250.00	33.96	26.89
Income Statement								
Interest Income	170,249	542,232	414,128	353,739	382,548	389,032	228,868	180,876
Interest Expense	66,348	175,504	141,537	135,487	197,324	214,403	107,124	91,740
Net Interest Income	103,901	366,728	272,591	218,252	185,224	174,629	121,744	89,136
Provision for Losses	10,962	34,987	20,581	22,266	22,045	23,378	15,846	11,129
Non-Interest Income	25,743	94,767	95,490	59,640	53,827	49,348	48,386	22,531
Non-Interest Expense	66,510	250,244	207,170	162,840	148,504	189,859	113,821	64,844
Income Before Taxes	52,172	176,264	140,330	92,786	68,502	10,740	40,463	35,694
Income Taxes	17,217	56,657	43,260	28,972	23,571	3,751	13,312	13,251
Net Income	34,559	119,117	95,058	59,158	41,892	6,989	27,151	22,443
Average Shares	73,021	66,235	50,328	42,714	42,823	43,550	25,597	18,870
Balance Sheet								
Net Loans & Leases	8,323,628	8,032,141	5,688,537	4,430,954	3,692,176	3,692,158	2,405,393	1,841,629
Total Assets	14,684,880	13,789,814	10,719,401	7,941,010	6,029,442	5,220,554	3,561,888	2,725,934
Total Deposits	8,154,575	7,665,537	6,028,649	4,592,510	3,605,255	3,894,662	2,514,994	2,125,236
Total Liabilities	13,300,481	12,389,211	9,739,532	7,207,799	5,534,245	4,751,901	3,152,071	2,381,571
Stockholders' Equity	1,384,399	1,400,603	979,869	646,799	458,174	468,653	409,817	344,363
Shares Outstanding	71,757	71,252	59,064	47,347	41,228	42,460	25,723	22,004
Statistical Record								
Return on Assets %	0.95	0.97	1.02	0.85	0.74	0.16	0.86	0.92
Return on Equity %	10.07	9.98	11.69	10.71	9.04	1.59	7.20	8.22
Net Interest Margin %	61.03	67.63	65.82	61.70	48.42	44.89	53.19	49.28
Efficiency Ratio %	33.94	39.28	40.65	39.39	34.03	43.31	41.05	31.88
Loans to Deposits	1.02	1.05	0.94	0.96	1.02	0.95	0.96	0.87
Price Range	32.53-26.00	32.53-26.00	29.25-19.46	23.46-17.61	19.95-12.25	18.25-9.25	29.94-15.88	29.81-17.44
P/E Ratio	18.70-14.94	18.07-14.44	15.48-10.30	17.00-12.76	20.36-12.50	114.06-57.81	28.24-14.98	25.05-14.65
Average Yield %	2.07	2.06	2.32	2.31	2.71	3.00	1.61	1.31

Address: 102 South Main Street, Greenville, SC 29601
Telephone: 864-255-7900
Web Site: www.thesouthgroup.com

Officers: William R. Timmons Jr. - Chmn. William S. Hummers III - Vice-Chmn., Exec. V.P., C.F.O.
ransfer Agents: Registrar and Transfer Company, Cranford, NY

Investor Contact: 800-951-2699*54919
No of Institutions: 143
Shares: 32,840,736 **% Held:** 45.81

SOUTHWEST BANCORP, INC.

Exchange	Symbol	Price	52Wk Range	Yield	P/E
NMS	OKSB	$18.10 (5/31/2005)	26.85-17.11	1.66	11.53

***7 Year Price Score 159.23** *NYSE Composite Index=100 ***12 Month Price Score 85.70**

Interim Earnings (Per Share)

Qtr.	Mar	Jun	Sep	Dec
2002	0.26	0.28	0.28	0.29
2003	0.29	0.33	0.28	0.32
2004	0.34	0.36	0.39	0.39
2005	0.43	...	...	...

Interim Dividends (Per Share)

Amt	Decl	Ex	Rec	Pay
0.07Q	8/27/2004	9/15/2004	9/17/2004	10/1/2004
0.07Q	11/23/2004	12/16/2004	12/20/2004	1/3/2005
0.075Q	2/25/2005	3/15/2005	3/17/2005	4/1/2005
0.075Q	5/27/2005	6/15/2005	6/17/2005	7/1/2005

Indicated Div: $0.30

Valuation Analysis

Forecast P/E 16.57 (6/2/2005)

Market Cap $220.7 Million Book Value 129.7 Million

Price/Book 1.70 Price/Sales 1.72

Dividend Achiever Status

Rank 76 **10 Year Growth Rate** 15.98%

Total Years of Dividend Growth 10

Business Summary: Other Depository Banking (MIC: 8.5 SIC: 035 NAIC: 22120)

Southwest Bancorp is a bank holding company. Co. provides commercial and consumer banking services through its banking subsidiaries, Stillwater National Bank & Trust Company and SNB Bank of Wichita, along with management consulting services through Business Consulting Group, Inc. and Healthcare Strategic Support, Inc. At Dec 31 2004, Co. operated twelve full-service banking offices, including three in Stillwater, OK, two located in Tulsa, Oklahoma, two each located in the Dallas and Austin, TX, and one each in Oklahoma City and Chickasha, OK, San Antonio, TX, and Wichita, KS. Co, also operated a loan production offices in Kansas City, KS, and on two universities in Stillwater and Tulsa, OK.

Recent Developments: For the quarter ended Mar 31 2005, net income increased 28.2% to $5,386 thousand from net income of $4,202 thousand in the year-earlier quarter. Net interest income was $21,092 thousand, up 35.0% from $15,618 thousand the year before. Provision for loan losses was $4,309 thousand versus $1,649 thousand in the prior-year quarter, an increase of 161.3%. Non-interest income rose 19.3% to $3,720 thousand, while non-interest expense advanced 15.5% to $12,027 thousand.

Prospects: Operating results are being positively affected by growth in loan operations and Co.'s focus on increasing net interest income by careful management of interest margins and funding. Also, other initiatives are contributing to Co.'s performance, including continued emphasis on appropriately pricing loan renewals, commercial loan participation sales, and service charge increases. Going forward, Co. will seek to continue to grow its earnings and banking assets from its operations in Oklahoma, Texas, and Kansas that specialize in serving medical, professional, business and commercial real estate customers and from its more traditional, banking operations.

Financial Data

(US$ in Thousands)	3 Mos	12/31/2004	12/31/2003	12/31/2002	12/31/2001	12/31/2000	12/31/1999	12/31/1998
Earnings Per Share	1.57	1.48	1.22	1.12	1.00	0.88	0.73	0.63
Cash Flow Per Share	(6.82)	(9.15)	(8.03)	1.54	1.35	0.88	1.00	1.06
Tang Book Value Per Share	10.64	10.41	9.20	8.35	6.95	6.44	5.52	5.07
Dividends Per Share	0.285	0.280	0.250	0.220	0.160	0.147	0.133	0.120
Dividend Payout %	18.15	18.92	20.49	19.73	16.00	16.67	18.26	19.05
Income Statement								
Interest Income	31,946	104,723	84,079	76,495	90,400	97,274	80,595	80,252
Interest Expense	10,854	32,246	28,611	30,606	48,867	57,155	42,495	42,274
Net Interest Income	21,092	72,477	55,468	45,889	41,533	40,119	38,100	37,978
Provision for Losses	4,309	12,982	8,522	5,443	4,000	3,550	2,495	3,380
Non-Interest Income	3,720	14,085	14,500	12,646	10,741	8,489	8,444	6,943
Non-Interest Expense	12,144	44,412	38,448	33,319	31,165	29,615	30,426	26,982
Income Before Taxes	8,359	29,168	22,998	19,773	17,109	15,443	13,623	14,559
Income Taxes	2,973	10,539	8,106	6,354	5,357	5,238	4,757	5,181
Net Income	5,386	18,629	14,892	13,419	11,752	10,205	8,866	9,378
Average Shares	12,628	12,548	12,159	12,052	11,728	11,585	12,164	11,742
Balance Sheet								
Net Loans & Leases	1,253,939	1,249,374	1,074,566	1,078,586	906,814	900,425	841,618	782,918
Total Assets	1,994,569	1,912,834	1,580,725	1,349,768	1,216,495	1,203,566	1,120,420	1,027,865
Total Deposits	1,628,934	1,500,058	1,204,125	1,021,757	904,796	945,102	871,235	843,061
Total Liabilities	1,864,835	1,786,850	1,470,790	1,253,396	1,131,370	1,130,327	1,056,166	970,064
Stockholders' Equity	129,734	125,984	109,935	96,372	85,125	73,239	64,254	57,801
Shares Outstanding	12,193	12,104	11,955	11,546	12,243	11,370	11,649	11,397
Statistical Record								
Return on Assets %	1.07	1.06	1.02	1.05	0.97	0.88	0.83	0.94
Return on Equity %	16.20	15.75	14.44	14.79	14.84	14.80	14.53	14.90
Net Interest Margin %	66.02	69.21	65.97	59.99	45.94	41.24	47.27	47.32
Efficiency Ratio %	34.05	37.38	39.00	37.38	30.81	28.00	34.17	30.94
Loans to Deposits	0.77	0.83	0.89	1.06	1.00	0.95	0.97	0.93
Price Range	26.85-16.40	26.85-16.22	18.90-11.25	13.62-8.80	9.57-5.58	7.00-4.50	8.98-6.50	10.83-6.58
P/E Ratio	17.10-10.45	18.14-10.96	15.49-9.22	12.16-7.86	9.57-5.58	7.95-5.11	12.30-8.90	17.20-10.45
Average Yield %	1.41	1.44	1.75	1.87	2.03	2.64	1.76	1.30

Address: 608 South Main Street, Stillwater, OK 74074
Telephone: 405-372-2230
Web Site: www.oksb.com

Officers: Robert B. Rodgers - Chmn. Rick J. Green - Vice-Chmn., Pres., C.E.O. **Transfer Agents:** Computershare Investor Services, Chicago, IL

Investor Contact: 405-372-2230
No of Institutions: 69
Shares: 5,758,135 **% Held:** 47.24

STANLEY WORKS

Exchange	Symbol	Price	52Wk Range	Yield	P/E
NYS	SWK	$44.61 (5/31/2005)	48.99-40.27	2.51	13.40

*7 Year Price Score 113.44 *NYSE Composite Index=100 *12 Month Price Score 95.91

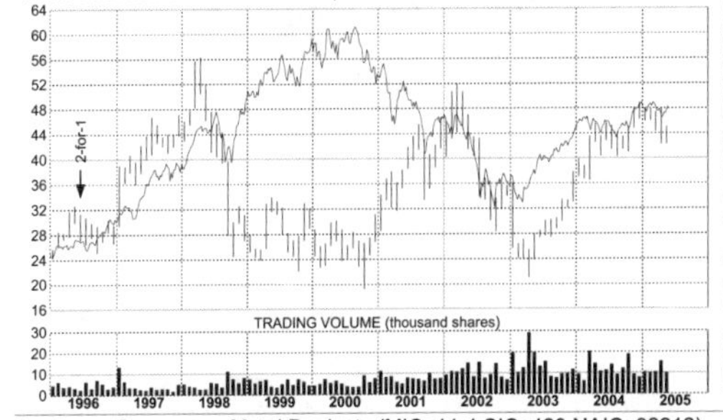

TRADING VOLUME (thousand shares)

Interim Earnings (Per Share)

Qtr.	Mar	Jun	Sep	Dec
2002	0.56	0.72	0.62	0.20
2003	0.22	0.14	0.51	0.41
2004	1.84	0.73	0.76	1.04
2005	0.78	...	...	...

Interim Dividends (Per Share)

Amt	Decl	Ex	Rec	Pay
0.28Q	7/22/2004	9/1/2004	9/3/2004	9/28/2004
0.28Q	10/14/2004	11/24/2004	11/29/2004	12/21/2004
0.28Q	2/23/2005	3/7/2005	3/9/2005	3/29/2005
0.28Q	4/27/2005	6/6/2005	6/8/2005	6/28/2005

Indicated Div: $1.12 (Div. Reinv. Plan)

Valuation Analysis

Forecast P/E	13.73 (6/1/2005)		
Market Cap	$3.7 Billion	Book Value	1.3 Billion
Price/Book	2.91	Price/Sales	1.20

Dividend Achiever Status

Rank	279	**10 Year Growth Rate**	4.58%
Total Years of Dividend Growth			37

Business Summary: Metal Products (MIC: 11.4 SIC: 423 NAIC: 32212)

Stanley Works is a worldwide producer of tools and door products for professional, industrial and consumer use and security products. The Consumer Products segment manufactures and markets hand tools, consumer mechanics tools and storage units, and hardware. The Industrial Tools segment manufactures and markets professional mechanics tools, pneumatic tools and fasteners, hydraulic tools and accessories, assembly tools and systems, and electronic measuring tools. The Security Solutions segment provides security services, and mechanical and electronic security products and systems, including automatic doors, door locking systems, commercial hardware and security access control systems.

Recent Developments: For the quarter ended Apr 2 2005, income from continuing operations increased 21.3% to $66,700 thousand from income of $55,000 thousand in the year-earlier quarter. Net income decreased 56.6% to $66,600 thousand from net income of $153,500 thousand in the year-earlier quarter. Revenues were $806,300 thousand, up 9.7% from $734,800 thousand the year before. Total direct expense was $517,400 thousand versus $466,900 thousand in the prior-year quarter, an increase of 10.8%. Total indirect expense was $185,200 thousand versus $166,700 thousand in the prior-year quarter, an increase of 11.1%.

Prospects: Co. is generating strong organic growth in key Industrial businesses, while laying the foundation for solid organic growth in its Consumer Products and Security Solutions segments during the remainder of the year. Co. is continuing to reposition for growth, both organically and through acquisitions in its Tools and Security growth platforms. Recent market share wins in Consumer Products, continuing strength in Industrial Tools markets and growing momentum in the access control business are all encouraging. Looking ahead to full-year 2005, Co. expects total sales growth of 8.0% to 10.0%, organic sales growth of 4.0% to 6.0% and earnings in the range of $3.20 to $3.30 per diluted share.

Financial Data

(US$ in Thousands)	3 Mos	01/01/2005	01/03/2004	12/28/2002	12/29/2001	12/30/2000	01/01/2000	01/02/1999
Earnings Per Share	3.33	4.36	1.27	2.10	1.81	2.22	1.67	1.53
Cash Flow Per Share	4.60	4.54	5.43	3.31	2.59	2.71	2.49	0.63
Tang Book Value Per Share	3.63	5.32	2.65	5.05	7.04	6.58	6.19	5.32
Dividends Per Share	1.100	1.080	1.030	0.990	0.940	0.900	0.870	0.830
Dividend Payout %	33.03	24.77	81.10	47.14	51.93	40.54	52.10	54.25
Income Statement								
Total Revenue	806,300	3,043,400	2,678,100	2,593,000	2,624,400	2,748,900	2,751,800	2,729,100
EBITDA	110,000	458,500	247,800	368,200	345,200	404,100	344,300	318,200
Depn & Amortn	23,400	95,000	86,500	71,200	82,900	83,300	85,600	79,700
Income Before Taxes	86,600	329,100	133,000	272,500	236,700	293,700	230,800	215,400
Income Taxes	19,900	88,900	36,300	87,500	78,400	99,300	80,800	77,600
Net Income	66,600	366,900	107,900	185,000	158,300	194,400	150,000	137,800
Average Shares	85,156	84,243	84,839	88,246	87,467	87,667	89,886	90,193
Balance Sheet								
Current Assets	1,434,600	1,371,900	1,200,700	1,190,400	1,141,400	1,094,300	1,091,000	1,086,400
Total Assets	2,952,800	2,850,600	2,423,800	2,418,200	2,055,700	1,884,800	1,890,600	1,932,900
Current Liabilities	886,700	818,800	753,500	680,900	825,500	707,300	693,000	702,100
Long-Term Obligations	474,500	481,800	534,500	564,300	196,800	248,700	290,000	344,800
Total Liabilities	1,685,300	1,629,300	1,565,200	1,434,400	1,223,400	1,148,300	1,155,200	1,263,500
Stockholders' Equity	1,267,500	1,221,300	858,600	983,800	832,300	736,500	735,400	669,400
Shares Outstanding	82,791	82,407	81,276	86,835	84,658	85,188	88,945	88,772
Statistical Record								
Return on Assets %	9.78	13.95	4.38	8.29	8.06	10.33	7.87	7.49
Return on Equity %	24.80	35.38	11.52	20.43	20.24	26.49	21.41	21.64
EBITDA Margin %	13.64	15.07	9.25	14.20	13.15	14.70	12.51	11.66
Net Margin %	8.26	12.06	4.03	7.13	6.03	7.07	5.45	5.05
Asset Turnover	1.07	1.16	1.09	1.16	1.34	1.46	1.44	1.48
Current Ratio	1.62	1.68	1.59	1.75	1.38	1.55	1.57	1.55
Debt to Equity	0.37	0.39	0.62	0.57	0.24	0.34	0.39	0.52
Price Range	48.99-40.27	48.99-36.50	37.87-21.00	51.98-28.38	46.60-28.50	31.19-19.25	33.94-22.13	56.38-24.50
P/E Ratio	14.71-12.09	11.24-8.37	29.82-16.54	24.75-13.51	25.75-15.75	14.05-8.67	20.32-13.25	36.85-16.01
Average Yield %	2.46	2.53	3.57	2.48	2.46	3.45	3.08	2.00

Address: 1000 Stanley Drive, New Britain, CT 06053
Telephone: 860-225-5111
Web Site: www.stanleyworks.com

Officers: John F. Lundgren - Chmn., C.E.O. Donald R. McIlnay - Pres. **Transfer Agents:** EquiServe Limited Partnership, Boston, MA

Investor Contact: 860-827-3833
No of Institutions: 268
Shares: 58,360,848 **% Held:** 70.64

STATE AUTO FINANCIAL CORP.

Exchange	Symbol	Price	52Wk Range	Yield	P/E
NMS	STFC	$27.00 (5/31/2005)	30.93-24.47	0.67	9.31

*7 Year Price Score 140.96 *NYSE Composite Index=100 *12 Month Price Score 92.42

Interim Earnings (Per Share)

Qtr.	Mar	Jun	Sep	Dec
2002	0.33	(0.04)	0.15	0.49
2003	0.53	0.21	0.38	0.46
2004	0.80	0.85	0.12	0.93
2005	1.00	...	...	...

Interim Dividends (Per Share)

Amt	Decl	Ex	Rec	Pay
0.045Q	8/9/2004	9/13/2004	9/15/2004	9/30/2004
0.045Q	11/10/2004	12/13/2004	12/15/2004	12/31/2004
0.045Q	3/4/2005	3/16/2005	3/19/2005	3/31/2005
0.045Q	5/11/2005	6/13/2005	6/15/2005	6/30/2005

Indicated Div: $0.18 (Div. Reinv. Plan)

Valuation Analysis

Forecast P/E	9.12 (6/1/2005)		
Market Cap	$1.1 Billion	Book Value	679.6 Million
Price/Book	1.60	Price/Sales	0.98

Dividend Achiever Status

Rank	165	10 Year Growth Rate	10.38%
Total Years of Dividend Growth			13

Business Summary: Insurance (MIC: 8.2 SIC: 331 NAIC: 24126)

State Auto Financial, through its principal insurance subsidiaries, State Auto Property and Casualty Insurance, Milbank Insurance, Farmers Casualty Insurance and State Auto Insurance, provides personal and commercial insurance. Co.'s principal lines of business include personal and commercial auto, homeowners, commercial multi-peril, workers' compensation, general liability and fire insurance. As of Dec 31 2004, Co. marketed its products through about 22,500 independent insurance agents associated with 3,250 agencies in 26 states and the District of Columbia. Co.'s products are marketed primarily in the central and eastern U.S., excluding New York, New Jersey and the New England States.

Recent Developments: For the quarter ended Mar 31 2005, net income increased 25.9% to $40,800 thousand from net income of $32,400 thousand in the year-earlier quarter. Revenues were $285,900 thousand, up 4.7% from $273,100 thousand the year before. Net premiums earned were $263,100 thousand versus $248,800 thousand in the prior-year quarter, an increase of 5.7%. Net investment income rose 8.6% to $19,000 thousand from $17,500 thousand a year ago.

Prospects: Co. is implementing a number of initiatives to stimulate sales in personal lines new business applications and is working with its independent agency partners to strengthen personal lines sales techniques and skills. Additionally, Co. continually reviews its insurance programs in order to provide insurance to a broader segment in the markets in which it operates. For example, Co. is expanding eligibility requirements for youthful operators within its standard segment and is selectively offering higher limits within the nonstandard segment. However, Co. continues to emphasize that it will not compromise underwriting profitability for top line growth.

Financial Data

(US$ in Thousands)	3 Mos	12/31/2004	12/31/2003	12/31/2002	12/31/2001	12/31/2000	12/31/1999	12/31/1998
Earnings Per Share	2.90	2.70	1.58	0.93	0.52	1.21	1.03	0.87
Cash Flow Per Share	4.81	3.69	3.51	3.25	1.64	2.28	1.20	1.35
Tang Book Value Per Share	16.86	16.41	13.71	11.89	10.23	9.95	8.22	8.06
Dividends Per Share	0.175	0.170	0.150	0.135	0.125	0.115	0.105	0.095
Dividend Payout %	6.03	6.30	9.49	14.52	24.04	9.50	10.19	10.92
Income Statement								
Premium Income	263,100	1,006,800	960,568	896,595	555,207	397,967	392,058	356,210
Total Revenue	285,900	1,092,400	1,041,696	967,479	623,272	462,774	440,871	402,059
Benefits & Claims	138,800	619,200	651,223	653,474	427,074	272,167	264,628	242,294
Income Before Taxes	57,800	151,600	83,277	37,790	17,976	61,444	56,985	49,605
Income Taxes	17,000	41,600	19,655	795	(2,639)	13,730	14,169	12,108
Net Income	40,800	110,000	63,622	36,995	20,615	47,714	42,816	37,497
Average Shares	40,900	40,800	40,153	39,743	39,681	39,120	41,526	42,901
Balance Sheet								
Total Assets	2,136,200	2,023,700	1,836,667	1,592,995	1,367,496	898,106	759,945	709,778
Total Liabilities	1,456,600	1,365,500	1,294,376	1,129,226	967,303	512,047	442,258	368,954
Stockholders' Equity	679,600	658,200	542,291	463,769	400,193	386,059	317,687	340,824
Shares Outstanding	40,300	40,100	39,559	39,001	38,937	38,554	38,321	42,027
Statistical Record								
Return on Assets %	5.83	5.68	3.71	2.50	1.82	5.74	5.83	6.23
Return on Equity %	18.71	18.28	12.65	8.56	5.24	13.52	13.00	13.24
Loss Ratio %	52.76	61.50	67.80	72.88	76.92	68.39	67.50	68.02
Net Margin %	14.27	10.07	6.11	3.82	3.31	10.31	9.71	9.33
Price Range	30.93-24.47	30.93-22.68	26.82-15.33	17.19-13.10	17.67-12.50	18.00-7.19	13.81-8.88	19.88-11.63
P/E Ratio	10.67-8.44	11.46-8.40	16.97-9.70	18.48-14.09	33.98-24.04	14.88-5.94	13.41-8.62	22.84-13.36
Average Yield %	0.63	0.62	0.70	0.87	0.81	1.03	0.93	0.62

Address: 518 East Broad Street, Columbus, OH 43215-3976 **Telephone:** 614-464-5000 **Web Site:** www.STFC.com	**Officers:** Robert H. Moone - Chmn., Pres., C.E.O. Mark A. Blackburn - Sr. V.P. **Transfer Agents:** National City Bank, Cleveland, OH	**Investor Contact:** 614-464-5078 **No of Institutions:** 68 **Shares:** 6,615,222 **% Held:** 16.50

STATE STREET CORP.

Exchange	Symbol	Price	52Wk Range	Yield	P/E
NYS	STT	$48.00 (5/31/2005)	50.01-40.68	1.42	20.08

***7 Year Price Score 89.11** *NYSE Composite Index=100 ***12 Month Price Score 96.94**

Interim Earnings (Per Share)

Qtr.	Mar	Jun	Sep	Dec
2002	0.54	0.54	0.56	1.46
2003	0.29	(0.07)	0.60	1.33
2004	0.63	0.65	0.52	0.55
2005	0.67	...	...	...

Interim Dividends (Per Share)

Amt	Decl	Ex	Rec	Pay
0.16Q	6/17/2004	6/29/2004	7/1/2004	7/15/2004
0.16Q	9/16/2004	9/29/2004	10/1/2004	10/15/2004
0.17Q	12/16/2004	12/30/2004	1/3/2005	1/18/2005
0.17Q	3/17/2005	3/30/2005	4/1/2005	4/15/2005

Indicated Div: $0.68 (Div. Reinv. Plan)

Valuation Analysis

Forecast P/E	17.30 (6/2/2005)		
Market Cap	$15.9 Billion	Book Value	6.0 Billion
Price/Book	2.64	Price/Sales	2.58

Dividend Achiever Status

Rank	82	**10 Year Growth Rate**	15.64%
Total Years of Dividend Growth			24

Business Summary: Commercial Banking (MIC: 8.1 SIC: 022 NAIC: 22110)

State Street is a bank holding company, with $94.04 billion in assets as of Dec 31 2004, that conducts business worldwide principally through its subsidiary, State Street Bank and Trust Company. Co. has two lines of business: Investment Servicing provides services for U.S. mutual funds, collective funds worldwide, corporate and public retirement plans, insurance companies, foundations, endowments, and other investment pools. Investment Management offers an array of services for managing financial assets, including investment management and investment research, primarily for institutional investors worldwide.

Recent Developments: For the quarter ended Mar 31 2005, net income increased 4.1% to $226,000 thousand from net income of $217,000 thousand in the year-earlier quarter. Net interest income was $212,000 thousand, up 4.4% from $203,000 thousand the year before. Total revenue climbed 7.3% to $1,308,000 thousand from $1,219,000 thousand in 2004. Non-interest income rose 8.3% to $1,097,000 thousand, while non-interest expense advanced 6.4% to $966,000 thousand.

Prospects: Co.'s outlook appears reasonable. On the positive side, servicing fees for the quarter ended Mar 31 2005 rose 7.9% to $599.0 million, which Co. attributed to new business from existing and new clients in 2005 and higher equity market valuations. Also, investment management fees, generated by State Street Global Advisors, were $177.0 million, up 20.4% from $147.0 million a year ago. Co. noted that management fees reflected continued new business and higher average month-end equity valuations. However, Co. stated that it is still dealing with some issues that will temper its results for the remainder of 2005, particularly rising interest rates and the ongoing repositioning of its real estate.

Financial Data

(US$ in Thousands)	3 Mos	12/31/2004	12/31/2003	12/31/2002	12/31/2001	12/31/2000	12/31/1999	12/31/1998
Earnings Per Share	2.39	2.35	2.15	3.10	1.90	1.81	1.89	1.33
Cash Flow Per Share	1.80	1.24	4.57	3.10	1.44	1.98	0.61	2.64
Tang Book Value Per Share	12.28	12.49	11.65	12.92	11.88	10.09	8.31	7.19
Dividends Per Share	0.660	0.640	0.560	0.480	0.405	0.425	0.300	0.260
Dividend Payout %	27.62	27.23	26.05	15.48	21.32	23.42	15.87	19.55
Income Statement								
Interest Income	603,000	1,787,000	1,539,000	1,974,000	2,855,000	3,256,000	2,437,000	2,237,000
Interest Expense	391,000	928,000	729,000	995,000	1,830,000	2,362,000	1,656,000	1,492,000
Net Interest Income	212,000	859,000	810,000	979,000	1,025,000	894,000	781,000	745,000
Provision for Losses	...	(18,000)	...	4,000	10,000	9,000	14,000	17,000
Non-Interest Income	1,096,000	4,074,000	3,924,000	3,421,000	2,782,000	2,665,000	3,707,000	3,021,000
Non-Interest Expense	966,000	3,759,000	3,622,000	2,841,000	2,867,000	2,644,000	2,336,000	2,068,000
Income Before Taxes	342,000	1,192,000	1,112,000	1,555,000	930,000	906,000	968,000	657,000
Income Taxes	116,000	394,000	390,000	540,000	302,000	311,000	349,000	221,000
Net Income	226,000	798,000	722,000	1,015,000	628,000	595,000	619,000	436,000
Average Shares	334,653	339,605	335,326	327,477	330,492	328,088	327,502	327,854
Balance Sheet								
Net Loans & Leases	4,830,000	4,611,000	4,960,000	4,113,000	5,283,000	5,216,000	4,245,000	6,225,000
Total Assets	100,094,000	94,040,000	87,534,000	85,794,000	69,896,000	69,298,000	60,896,000	47,082,000
Total Deposits	58,318,000	55,129,000	47,516,000	45,468,000	38,559,000	37,937,000	34,145,000	27,539,000
Total Liabilities	94,069,000	87,881,000	81,787,000	81,007,000	66,051,000	66,036,000	58,244,000	44,771,000
Stockholders' Equity	6,025,000	6,159,000	5,747,000	4,787,000	3,845,000	3,262,000	2,652,000	2,311,000
Shares Outstanding	331,277	333,645	334,474	324,927	323,670	323,422	319,180	321,390
Statistical Record								
Return on Assets %	0.84	0.88	0.83	1.30	0.90	0.91	1.15	1.03
Return on Equity %	13.49	13.37	13.71	23.52	17.67	20.07	24.94	20.25
Net Interest Margin %	35.16	48.07	52.63	49.59	35.90	27.46	32.05	33.30
Efficiency Ratio %	56.86	64.14	66.30	52.66	50.86	44.65	38.02	39.33
Loans to Deposits	0.08	0.08	0.10	0.09	0.14	0.14	0.12	0.23
Price Range	54.35-41.07	56.45-41.07	53.18-31.63	57.59-32.38	62.75-38.66	66.93-31.69	47.63-27.94	36.66-24.75
P/E Ratio	22.74-17.18	24.02-17.48	24.73-14.71	18.58-10.45	33.03-20.35	36.98-17.51	25.20-14.78	27.56-18.61
Average Yield %	1.44	1.33	1.32	1.04	0.80	0.81	0.80	0.81

Address: 225 Franklin Street, Boston, MA 02110 **Telephone:** 617-786-3000 **Web Site:** www.statestreet.com	**Officers:** Ronald E. Logue - Chmn., C.E.O. John R. Towers - Vice Chmn. **Transfer Agents:** EquiServe Trust Company, N.A., Providence, RI	**Investor Contact:** 617-664-3477 **No of Institutions:** 530 **Shares:** 258,557,184 **% Held:** 77.52

STERLING BANCORP

Exchange	Symbol	Price	52Wk Range	Yield	P/E
NYS	STL	$21.15 (5/31/2005)	28.44-20.95	3.59	16.79

*7 Year Price Score 139.58 *NYSE Composite Index=100 *12 Month Price Score 91.25

Interim Earnings (Per Share)

Qtr.	Mar	Jun	Sep	Dec
2002	0.27	0.27	0.29	0.31
2003	0.31	0.31	0.33	0.33
2004	0.33	0.35	0.36	0.25
2005	0.30	...	...	...

Interim Dividends (Per Share)

Amt	Decl	Ex	Rec	Pay
20%	11/18/2004	12/9/2004	11/29/2004	12/8/2004
0.19Q	11/18/2004	12/15/2004	12/17/2004	12/31/2004
0.19Q	2/17/2005	3/11/2005	3/15/2005	3/31/2005
0.19Q	5/5/2005	6/13/2005	6/15/2005	6/30/2005

Indicated Div: $0.76

Valuation Analysis

Forecast P/E 15.49 (6/2/2005)
Market Cap $386.9 Million Book Value 149.5 Million
Price/Book 2.59 Price/Sales 2.87

Dividend Achiever Status

Rank 28 **10 Year Growth Rate** 22.49%
Total Years of Dividend Growth 10

Business Summary: Commercial Banking (MIC: 8.1 SIC: 021 NAIC: 22110)

Sterling Bancorp is a financial holding company with assets of $1.87 billion and deposits of $1.34 billion as of Dec 31 2004. Co. offers a broad array of banking and financial services products such as business and consumer loans, commercial and residential mortgage lending and brokerage, asset-based financing, factoring/accounts receivable management services, trade financing, equipment leasing, deposit services, trust and estate administration and investment management services. Co. has operations in the metropolitan New York area, North Carolina and many mid-Atlantic states, and conducts business throughout the U.S.

Recent Developments: For the quarter ended Mar 31 2005, net income increased 10.8% to $5,766,723 from net income of $5,206,934 in the year-earlier quarter. Net interest income was $20,502,280, up 7.9% from $18,995,359 the year before. Provision for loan losses was $2,648,500 versus $2,426,500 in the prior-year quarter, an increase of 9.1%. Non-interest income fell 2.8% to $7,996,200, while non-interest expense advanced 5.2% to $26,883,236.

Prospects: Results are being positively affected by strong growth of both loans and deposits. In addition, results are benefiting from robust mortgage banking revenue growth, which is being fueled by Co.'s strategy of originating higher margin real estate loans that are more profitable and carry less risk. Meanwhile, net interest income growth is being driven by rising interest rates and growth in average loans outstanding, partially offset by purchases of mortgage-backed securities with a shorter average life, a flattening yield curve, and higher levels of interest-bearing deposits.

Financial Data

(US$ in Thousands)	3 Mos	12/31/2004	12/31/2003	12/31/2002	12/31/2001	12/31/2000	12/31/1999	12/31/1998
Earnings Per Share	1.26	1.29	1.27	1.14	1.00	0.88	0.75	0.64
Cash Flow Per Share	3.10	2.44	2.40	1.12	(0.22)	1.95	2.12	0.34
Tang Book Value Per Share	7.02	6.99	6.68	5.97	5.78	5.19	4.48	4.18
Dividends Per Share	0.697	0.665	0.570	0.427	0.342	0.274	0.222	0.184
Dividend Payout %	55.44	51.55	44.71	37.43	34.24	31.14	29.44	28.57
Income Statement								
Interest Income	26,204	97,799	91,582	94,197	95,865	97,125	79,787	73,961
Interest Expense	5,702	19,584	17,591	19,447	26,816	34,242	26,325	24,524
Net Interest Income	20,502	78,216	73,992	74,750	69,050	62,883	53,462	49,438
Provision for Losses	2,649	9,965	8,740	10,771	7,401	6,563	5,584	5,389
Non-Interest Income	7,996	34,718	32,556	29,256	24,123	22,373	17,944	16,448
Non-Interest Expense	16,976	65,613	58,910	59,157	53,696	50,280	41,583	38,298
Income Before Taxes	8,874	37,356	38,897	34,078	32,076	28,413	24,240	22,200
Income Taxes	3,107	12,752	14,693	12,300	12,689	11,854	9,676	9,403
Net Income	5,767	24,604	24,204	21,778	19,388	16,559	14,564	12,797
Average Shares	18,926	19,113	18,909	19,037	19,304	18,715	19,273	19,851
Balance Sheet								
Net Loans & Leases	959,826	1,005,958	886,097	777,766	794,649	738,213	677,979	630,050
Total Assets	1,901,252	1,871,112	1,758,746	1,561,122	1,482,871	1,270,749	1,218,887	1,044,445
Total Deposits	1,388,582	1,343,851	1,211,741	1,047,093	984,924	866,282	862,520	702,802
Total Liabilities	1,751,744	1,722,408	1,615,560	1,406,341	1,354,394	1,153,733	1,113,647	942,294
Stockholders' Equity	149,508	148,704	143,185	129,780	128,477	117,016	105,240	102,151
Shares Outstanding	18,292	18,237	17,925	17,794	18,161	17,998	18,219	18,772
Statistical Record								
Return on Assets %	1.31	1.35	1.46	1.43	1.41	1.33	1.29	1.24
Return on Equity %	16.05	16.81	17.73	16.87	15.79	14.86	14.04	13.14
Net Interest Margin %	78.24	79.98	80.79	79.35	72.03	64.74	67.01	66.84
Efficiency Ratio %	49.64	49.51	47.46	47.92	44.75	42.08	42.55	42.36
Loans to Deposits	0.69	0.75	0.73	0.74	0.81	0.85	0.79	0.90
Price Range	28.44-20.97	28.25-20.97	26.13-16.15	19.83-14.19	16.69-9.97	11.05-6.54	9.98-7.13	12.76-7.43
P/E Ratio	22.57-16.64	21.90-16.25	20.58-12.71	17.40-12.45	16.69-9.97	12.55-7.43	13.30-9.51	19.94-11.62
Average Yield %	2.90	2.79	2.85	2.53	2.59	3.45	2.63	1.75

Address: 650 Fifth Avenue, New York, NY 10019-6108 **Telephone:** 212-757-3300 **Web Site:** www.sterlingbancorp.com	**Officers:** Louis J. Cappelli - Chmn., C.E.O. John C. Millman - Pres. **Transfer Agents:** Mellon Shareholder Services, Ridgefield Park, NJ	**Investor Contact:** 212-757-3000 **No of Institutions:** 65 **Shares:** 8,491,292 **% Held:** 46.62

STERLING BANCSHARES, INC.

Exchange	Symbol	Price	52Wk Range	Yield	P/E
NMS	SBIB	$13.60 (5/31/2005)	15.00-12.30	1.76	22.67

*7 Year Price Score 106.88 *NYSE Composite Index=100 *12 Month Price Score 95.37

TRADING VOLUME (thousand shares)

Interim Earnings (Per Share)

Qtr.	Mar	Jun	Sep	Dec
2002	0.19	0.21	0.19	0.23
2003	0.25	0.10	0.61	0.13
2004	0.12	0.16	0.14	0.13
2005	0.17	...	...	...

Interim Dividends (Per Share)

Amt	Decl	Ex	Rec	Pay
0.05Q	7/26/2004	8/4/2004	8/6/2004	8/20/2004
0.05Q	10/25/2004	11/3/2004	11/5/2004	11/19/2004
0.06Q	1/31/2005	2/9/2005	2/12/2005	2/26/2005
0.06Q	4/26/2005	5/4/2005	5/6/2005	5/20/2005

Indicated Div: $0.24

Valuation Analysis

Forecast P/E	N/A		
Market Cap	$615.0 Million	Book Value	314.9 Million
Price/Book	1.95	Price/Sales	3.03

Dividend Achiever Status

Rank	104	10 Year Growth Rate	14.27%
Total Years of Dividend Growth			11

Business Summary: Commercial Banking (MIC: 8.1 SIC: 022 NAIC: 22110)

Sterling Bancshares is a bank holding company that provides commercial and retail banking to small- to mid-sized businesses and consumers primarily in the Houston, Dallas and San Antonio metropolitan areas through 36 banking offices of Sterling Bank. Co.'s commercial and consumer banking services include demand, savings and time deposits; commercial, real estate and consumer loans; merchant credit card services; letters of credit; and cash and asset management services. In addition, Co. facilitates sales of brokerage, mutual fund, alternative financing and insurance products through third party vendors. As of Dec 31 2003, Co. had total assets of $3.34 billion and deposits of $2.44 billion.

Recent Developments: For the quarter ended Mar 31 2005, net income increased 48.2% to $7,758 thousand from net income of $5,234 thousand in the year-earlier quarter. Net interest income was $36,739 thousand, up 11.3% from $33,021 thousand the year before. Provision for loan losses was $3,340 thousand versus $3,500 thousand in the prior-year quarter, a decrease of 4.6%. Non-interest income fell 4.4% to $6,565 thousand, while non-interest expense declined 1.1% to $28,732 thousand.

Prospects: Earnings are showing significant improvement as strengthening business conditions and Co.'s success in attracting new bankers and customers is leading to solid loan growth. While 2005 should present challenges, such as a relatively flat yield curve and increased competition in Texas, Co. expects to meet those challenges. Co. is focusing on meeting the needs of owner-operated businesses in the large and growing markets of Houston, San Antonio and Dallas. Co.'s net interest income is benefiting primarily from its loan growth, as well as an increasing net interest margin due to increases in overnight interest rates. Co. is seeing strong growth in commercial, industrial and construction lending.

Financial Data

(US$ in Thousands)	3 Mos	12/31/2004	12/31/2003	12/31/2002	12/31/2001	12/31/2000	12/31/1999	12/31/1998
Earnings Per Share	0.60	0.55	1.10	0.82	0.71	0.67	0.54	0.47
Cash Flow Per Share	2.97	2.88	18.84	(10.91)	(5.39)	(0.78)	0.57	0.23
Tang Book Value Per Share	5.54	5.52	5.09	3.67	3.27	3.89	3.29	2.95
Dividends Per Share	0.210	0.200	0.180	0.160	0.147	0.133	0.120	0.107
Dividend Payout %	35.00	36.36	16.36	19.51	20.66	20.00	22.22	22.54
Income Statement								
Interest Income	47,022	166,097	171,383	176,391	173,053	156,430	123,621	103,031
Interest Expense	10,283	30,713	26,769	29,719	50,052	58,109	35,132	29,681
Net Interest Income	36,739	135,384	144,614	146,672	123,001	98,321	88,489	73,350
Provision for Losses	3,340	12,250	17,698	14,018	11,684	9,100	8,643	5,892
Non-Interest Income	6,647	30,922	33,078	94,510	66,171	39,567	29,268	20,581
Non-Interest Expense	28,732	119,609	117,603	172,352	130,677	89,927	78,026	62,344
Income Before Taxes	11,314	34,447	42,391	54,812	46,811	38,861	31,088	25,695
Income Taxes	3,556	9,484	14,037	18,139	16,410	12,281	9,665	8,391
Net Income	7,758	24,963	49,110	36,551	30,401	26,580	21,423	17,304
Average Shares	45,597	45,278	44,648	44,756	43,044	39,832	39,505	36,484
Balance Sheet								
Net Loans & Leases	2,415,443	2,314,745	2,126,317	1,882,944	1,643,861	1,213,288	1,111,390	851,790
Total Assets	3,444,555	3,336,070	3,204,405	3,582,745	2,778,090	1,925,131	1,959,480	1,415,312
Total Deposits	2,493,863	2,443,967	2,418,369	2,532,902	2,268,980	1,577,735	1,415,551	1,251,685
Total Liabilities	3,129,647	3,022,898	2,831,809	3,248,344	2,498,989	1,735,195	1,794,886	1,275,105
Stockholders' Equity	314,908	313,172	292,596	249,327	217,369	159,134	134,543	111,509
Shares Outstanding	45,217	45,068	44,642	43,982	43,769	39,345	39,045	35,814
Statistical Record								
Return on Assets %	0.83	0.76	1.45	1.15	1.29	1.36	1.27	1.33
Return on Equity %	8.94	8.22	18.12	15.66	16.15	18.05	17.41	18.07
Net Interest Margin %	78.13	81.51	84.38	83.15	71.08	62.85	71.58	71.19
Efficiency Ratio %	53.54	60.71	57.52	63.62	54.63	45.88	51.03	50.44
Loans to Deposits	0.97	0.95	0.88	0.74	0.72	0.77	0.79	0.68
Price Range	15.00-12.17	15.00-11.92	14.00-11.12	15.30-10.60	16.15-10.83	13.42-5.81	10.04-6.83	12.17-7.96
P/E Ratio	25.00-20.28	27.27-21.67	12.73-10.11	18.66-12.93	22.74-15.26	20.02-8.68	18.60-12.65	25.89-16.93
Average Yield %	1.54	1.49	1.46	1.21	1.17	1.58	1.46	1.06

Address: 2550 North Loop West, Suite 600, Houston, TX 77092
Telephone: 713-466-8300
Web Site:

Officers: Steven F. Retzloff - Chmn. J. Downey Bridgwater - Pres., C.E.O. **Transfer Agents:** American Stock Transfer & Trust Company, New York, NY

Investor Contact: 888-577-7242
No of Institutions: 109
Shares: 25,178,740 **% Held:** 55.78

STERLING FINANCIAL CORP.

Exchange	Symbol	Price	52Wk Range	Yield	P/E
NMS	SLFI	$20.60 (5/31/2005)	24.31-18.22	2.52	14.01

*7 Year Price Score 127.29 *NYSE Composite Index=100 *12 Month Price Score 95.42

Interim Earnings (Per Share)

Qtr.	Mar	Jun	Sep	Dec
2002	0.27	0.29	0.30	0.32
2003	0.31	0.33	0.35	0.37
2004	0.35	0.37	0.38	0.40
2005	0.32	...	...	...

Interim Dividends (Per Share)

Amt	Decl	Ex	Rec	Pay
0.16Q	11/16/2004	12/13/2004	12/15/2004	1/3/2005
0.16Q	2/22/2005	3/11/2005	3/15/2005	4/1/2005
25%	4/26/2005	6/2/2005	5/13/2005	6/1/2005
0.13Q	5/24/2005	6/13/2005	6/15/2005	7/1/2005

Indicated Div: $0.52 (Div. Reinv. Plan)

Valuation Analysis

Forecast P/E 14.97 (6/2/2005)

Market Cap $597.9 Million Book Value 279.1 Million

Price/Book 2.14 Price/Sales 2.89

Dividend Achiever Status

Rank 203 **10 Year Growth Rate** 8.60%

Total Years of Dividend Growth 17

TRADING VOLUME (thousand shares)

Business Summary: Commercial Banking (MIC: 8.1 SIC: 021 NAIC: 22110)

Sterling Financial is a multi-bank financial holding company with $2.74 billion in assets as of Dec 31 2004. Co. provides a broad range of financial services to individuals and businesses through its banking and nonbanking subsidiaries, including personal and business banking, leasing, insurance and wealth management. As of Dec 31 2004, Co. operated 63 branch banking offices in south central Pennsylvania, northern Maryland and northern Delaware through its subsidiary banks, Bank of Lancaster County, N.A., Bank of Hanover and Trust Company, Pennsylvania State Bank, First National Bank of North East and Delaware Sterling Bank & Trust Company.

Recent Developments: For the quarter ended Mar 31 2005, net income increased 21.6% to $9,279,000 from net income of $7,629,000 in the year-earlier quarter. Net interest income was $27,576,000, up 22.2% from $22,567,000 the year before. Provision for loan losses was $357,000 versus $714,000 in the prior-year quarter, a decrease of 50.0%. Non-interest income rose 19.1% to $15,725,000 , while non-interest expense advanced 20.6% to $30,107,000 .

Prospects: Results are being positively affected by strong net interest income growth, which is being driven by Co.'s December 2004 acquisition of Pennsylvania State Bank and continued growth in interest earning assets, particularly higher yielding loans, including commercial loans and finance receivables. Meanwhile, results are benefiting from a decrease in the provision for loan losses reflecting improvements in asset quality ratios and in local and national economic conditions. Separately, non-interest income growth is being fueled by higher insurance commissions and fees at StoudtAdvisors, along with increased service charges stemming from Co.'s new product offerings.

Financial Data

(US$ in Thousands)	3 Mos	12/31/2004	12/31/2003	12/31/2002	12/31/2001	12/31/2000	12/31/1999	12/31/1998
Earnings Per Share	1.47	1.51	1.35	1.18	1.04	0.84	0.95	0.92
Cash Flow Per Share	2.64	2.43	3.00	2.85	1.16	1.89	2.85	0.11
Tang Book Value Per Share	6.47	8.14	8.49	8.45	7.78	7.11	6.45	6.46
Dividends Per Share	0.630	0.620	0.560	0.528	0.499	0.480	0.461	0.425
Dividend Payout %	42.97	41.06	41.48	44.90	48.15	56.82	48.72	46.37
Income Statement								
Interest Income	39,733	137,682	127,074	123,591	115,916	113,319	67,714	60,066
Interest Expense	12,157	40,265	41,156	48,617	57,274	58,501	29,797	27,925
Net Interest Income	27,576	97,417	85,918	74,974	58,642	54,818	37,917	32,141
Provision for Losses	357	4,438	3,697	2,095	1,217	605	420	896
Non-Interest Income	15,725	59,296	49,721	44,806	43,925	37,508	29,497	14,187
Non-Interest Expense	30,107	107,086	92,568	85,922	75,172	70,203	48,831	30,188
Income Before Taxes	12,837	45,189	39,374	31,763	26,178	21,518	18,163	15,244
Income Taxes	3,558	11,860	10,315	7,018	5,844	4,951	4,924	3,643
Net Income	9,279	33,329	29,059	24,745	20,334	16,567	13,239	11,601
Average Shares	29,344	22,121	21,448	21,028	19,656	19,619	13,960	12,652
Balance Sheet								
Net Loans & Leases	1,936,725	1,888,380	1,481,369	1,283,075	1,087,102	1,021,499	654,834	526,591
Total Assets	2,751,812	2,742,762	2,343,517	2,156,309	1,861,439	1,726,138	1,059,374	919,264
Total Deposits	2,057,969	2,015,394	1,778,587	1,702,302	1,535,649	1,420,300	892,432	781,383
Total Liabilities	2,472,683	2,460,818	2,123,506	1,959,476	1,709,328	1,586,791	969,356	837,951
Stockholders' Equity	279,129	281,944	220,011	196,833	152,111	139,347	90,018	81,313
Shares Outstanding	29,025	23,298	21,717	21,125	19,549	19,603	13,955	12,578
Statistical Record								
Return on Assets %	1.38	1.31	1.29	1.23	1.13	1.19	1.34	1.31
Return on Equity %	13.81	13.24	13.94	14.18	13.95	14.41	15.45	14.94
Net Interest Margin %	69.40	70.76	67.61	60.66	50.59	48.37	56.00	53.51
Efficiency Ratio %	54.29	54.36	52.36	51.02	47.03	46.55	50.23	40.66
Loans to Deposits	0.94	0.94	0.83	0.75	0.71	0.72	0.73	0.67
Price Range	24.31-18.22	24.31-17.76	18.84-13.91	17.11-11.52	12.95-7.74	14.43-6.57	16.85-11.54	19.27-11.08
P/E Ratio	16.54-12.39	16.10-11.76	13.95-10.30	14.50-9.76	12.46-7.45	17.18-7.83	17.74-12.15	20.95-12.05
Average Yield %	3.00	3.03	3.46	3.66	4.58	5.67	3.48	2.95

Address: 101 North Pointe Boulevard, Lancaster, PA 17601-4133
Telephone: 717-581-6030
Web Site: www.sterlingfi.com

Officers: John E. Stefan - Chmn. J. Roger Moyer Jr. - Pres., C.E.O. **Transfer Agents:** American Stock Transfer and Trust Company, New York, NY

Investor Contact: 717-735-5602
No of Institutions: 57
Shares: 3,290,883 **% Held:** 15.08

STRYKER CORP.

Exchange	Symbol	Price	52Wk Range	Yield	P/E
NYS	SYK	$48.65 (5/31/2005)	57.33-41.75	0.12	39.55

*7 Year Price Score 148.60 *NYSE Composite Index=100 *12 Month Price Score 95.69

Interim Earnings (Per Share)

Qtr.	Mar	Jun	Sep	Dec
2002	0.20	0.21	0.18	0.26
2003	0.26	0.27	0.27	0.33
2004	0.33	0.37	0.04	0.40
2005	0.42	...	...	...

Interim Dividends (Per Share)

Amt	Decl	Ex	Rec	Pay
0.06A	12/3/2002	12/27/2002	12/31/2002	1/31/2003
0.07A	12/2/2003	12/29/2003	12/31/2003	1/30/2004
2-for-1	4/21/2004	5/17/2004	5/3/2004	5/14/2004
0.09A	12/10/2004	12/29/2004	12/31/2004	1/31/2005

Indicated Div: $0.06

Valuation Analysis

Forecast P/E 27.95 (6/1/2005)

Market Cap	$19.6 Billion	Book Value	2.9 Billion
Price/Book	6.77	Price/Sales	4.43

Dividend Achiever Status

Rank	27	10 Year Growth Rate	23.11%
Total Years of Dividend Growth			12

Business Summary: Medical Instruments & Equipment (MIC: 9.6 SIC: 841 NAIC: 39112)

Stryker develops, manufactures and markets specialty surgical and medical products. Operations are divided into two reportable business segments: Orthopaedic Implants and MedSurg Equipment. The Orthopaedic Implants segment includes orthopaedic reconstructive (hip, knee and shoulder), trauma and spinal implants, bone cement and the bone growth factor osteogenic protein-1. The MedSurg Equipment segment includes powered surgical instruments, endoscopic products, hospital beds and stretchers and micro implant and surgical navigation systems. Co. also provides outpatient physical and occupational rehabilitative services in the U.S.

Recent Developments: For the quarter ended Mar 31 2005, net income increased 27.4% to $173,100 thousand from net income of $135,900 thousand in the year-earlier quarter. Revenues were $1,202,500 thousand, up 16.2% from $1,035,100 thousand the year before. Operating income was $246,200 thousand versus an income of $193,200 thousand in the prior-year quarter, an increase of 27.4%. Total direct expense was $429,100 thousand versus $368,200 thousand in the prior-year quarter, an increase of 16.5%. Total indirect expense was $527,200 thousand versus $473,700 thousand in the prior-year quarter, an increase of 11.3%.

Prospects: Results are benefiting from strong sales in Co.'s medical products segment, partially offset by slower sales of hip and knee implants. However, Co. expects a new generation of hip and knee products will fuel sales growth over the remainder of 2005. Co. is targeting full-year 2005 sales of approximately $4.90 billion and earnings of $1.74 per share. Separately, on Feb 23 2005, Co. announced that it has completed its acquisition of eTrauma.com, a privately-held developer of software for Picture Archive and Communications Systems (PACS), for $50.0 million in cash.

Financial Data

(US$ in Thousands)	3 Mos	12/31/2004	12/31/2003	12/31/2002	12/31/2001	12/31/2000	12/31/1999	12/31/1998
Earnings Per Share	1.23	1.14	1.12	0.85	0.66	0.55	0.05	0.10
Cash Flow Per Share	1.41	1.47	1.63	1.28	1.19	0.85	0.73	0.40
Tang Book Value Per Share	4.18	4.44	2.98	1.42	0.65	0.04	N.M.	N.M.
Dividends Per Share	0.090	0.090	0.070	0.060	0.050	0.040	0.033	0.030
Dividend Payout %	7.32	7.89	6.28	7.06	7.58	7.27	65.00	30.00
Income Statement								
Total Revenue	1,202,500	4,262,300	3,625,300	3,011,600	2,602,300	2,289,400	2,103,700	1,103,208
EBITDA	319,500	874,300	817,700	604,400	509,700	471,500	186,300	97,556
Depn & Amortn	73,900	150,500	142,600	57,400	36,100	40,000	33,900	37,596
Income Before Taxes	245,600	717,000	652,500	506,700	405,700	334,900	29,800	59,960
Income Taxes	72,500	251,300	199,000	161,100	133,900	113,900	10,400	20,390
Net Income	173,100	465,700	453,500	345,600	267,000	221,000	19,400	39,570
Average Shares	411,300	410,300	406,800	407,600	406,000	402,200	397,200	392,520
Balance Sheet								
Current Assets	2,081,800	2,142,600	1,397,600	1,151,300	993,100	997,000	1,110,400	1,311,843
Total Assets	4,068,200	4,083,800	3,159,100	2,815,500	2,423,600	2,430,800	2,580,500	2,885,852
Current Liabilities	950,400	1,113,500	850,500	707,500	533,400	617,400	669,600	699,455
Long-Term Obligations	700	700	18,800	491,000	720,900	876,500	1,181,100	1,487,971
Total Liabilities	1,172,300	1,331,800	1,004,300	1,317,300	1,367,400	1,575,900	1,909,000	2,233,777
Stockholders' Equity	2,895,900	2,752,000	2,154,800	1,498,200	1,056,200	854,900	671,500	652,075
Shares Outstanding	403,128	402,500	399,400	396,200	393,400	391,800	388,800	386,160
Statistical Record								
Return on Assets %	13.78	12.82	15.18	13.19	11.00	8.80	0.71	2.04
Return on Equity %	19.40	18.93	24.83	27.06	27.94	28.88	2.93	6.26
EBITDA Margin %	26.57	20.51	22.56	20.07	19.59	20.59	8.86	8.84
Net Margin %	14.40	10.93	12.51	11.48	10.26	9.65	0.92	3.59
Asset Turnover	1.21	1.17	1.21	1.15	1.07	0.91	0.77	0.57
Current Ratio	2.19	1.92	1.64	1.63	1.86	1.61	1.66	1.88
Debt to Equity	N.M.	N.M.	0.01	0.33	0.68	1.03	1.76	2.28
Price Range	57.33-41.75	57.33-41.75	42.51-30.12	33.62-22.72	30.75-22.06	27.00-12.75	17.92-11.19	13.77-7.86
P/E Ratio	46.61-33.94	50.29-36.62	37.95-26.89	39.55-26.73	46.60-33.42	49.09-23.18	358.44-223.75	137.66-78.59
Average Yield %	0.19	0.19	0.19	0.21	0.19	0.20	0.23	0.29

Address: 2725 Fairfield Road, Kalamazoo, MI 49002
Telephone: 269-385-2600
Web Site: www.stryker.com

Officers: John W. Brown - Chmn. Stephen P. MacMillan - Pres., C.E.O. **Transfer Agents:** National City Bank, Cleveland, OH

Investor Contact: 616-385-2600
No of Institutions: 524
Shares: 174,900,208 **% Held:** 43.41

SUN COMMUNITIES, INC.

Exchange	Symbol	Price	52Wk Range	Yield	P/E
NYS	SUI	$36.00 (5/31/2005)	40.74-34.45	7.00	N/A

*7 Year Price Score 93.15 *NYSE Composite Index=100 *12 Month Price Score 91.52

TRADING VOLUME (thousand shares)

Interim Earnings (Per Share)

Qtr.	Mar	Jun	Sep	Dec
2002	0.46	0.39	0.32	(0.42)
2003	0.35	0.25	0.34	0.34
2004	0.30	(2.57)	0.03	0.05
2005	0.04	...	...	...

Interim Dividends (Per Share)

Amt	Decl	Ex	Rec	Pay
0.61Q	7/1/2004	7/8/2004	7/12/2004	7/22/2004
0.61Q	10/1/2004	10/7/2004	10/12/2004	10/20/2004
0.61Q	1/3/2005	1/10/2005	1/12/2005	1/21/2005
0.63Q	3/22/2005	4/7/2005	4/11/2005	4/21/2005

Indicated Div: $2.52

Valuation Analysis

Forecast P/E	13.34 (6/1/2005)		
Market Cap	$660.1 Million	Book Value	188.4 Million
Price/Book	3.50	Price/Sales	3.26

Dividend Achiever Status

Rank	253	10 Year Growth Rate	5.66%
Total Years of Dividend Growth			10

Business Summary: Property, Real Estate & Development (MIC: 8.3 SIC: 798 NAIC: 25930)

Sun Communities is a real estate investment trust. Co. owns, operates, develops and finances manufactured housing communities concentrated in the midwestern and southeastern U.S. As of Dec 31 2004, Co. owned and operated a portfolio of 136 properties located in 18 states, including 124 manufactured housing communities, five recreational vehicle communities, and seven properties containing both manufactured housing and recreational vehicle sites. As of Dec 31 2004, Co.'s properties contained an aggregate of 46,856 developed sites comprised of 41,875 developed manufactured home sites and 4,981 recreational vehicle sites and an additional 7,277 manufactured home sites suitable for development.

Recent Developments: For the quarter ended Mar 31 2005, net income decreased 87.7% to $687 thousand from net income of $5,570 thousand in the year-earlier quarter. Revenues were $51,463 thousand, up 3.9% from $49,549 thousand the year before. Revenues consisted of income from rental property of $45,781 thousand, up 6.8% from $42,868 thousand a year earlier. Revenues from home sales were down 5.6% to $3,750 thousand from $3,974 thousand a year earlier. Income from operations amounted to $1,743 thousand compared with $7,389 thousand in the corresponding period in 2004.

Prospects: Top-line results are being positively affected by an increase in net leased sites and a declining annual rate of repossessions. During the first quarter of 2005, Co. achieved an increase of 289 revenue producing manufactured housing sales. In addition, Co. sold 111 homes and brokered 154 sales. In March 2005, Co. acquired a property located near Tampa, FL, comprised of 697 recreational vehicle sites and 31 manufactured home sites, for approximately $7.3 million. During 2005, Co. plans to invest between $2.0 million and $5.0 million in developments consisting of expansions to existing communities and the development of new communities.

Financial Data

(US$ in Thousands)	3 Mos	12/31/2004	12/31/2003	12/31/2002	12/31/2001	12/31/2000	12/31/1999	12/31/1998
Earnings Per Share	(2.45)	(2.21)	1.29	0.76	1.94	1.91	1.68	1.53
Cash Flow Per Share	3.44	3.15	3.48	2.90	3.82	3.27	3.58	3.12
Tang Book Value Per Share	10.27	11.49	17.20	17.67	18.56	19.19	19.38	19.72
Dividends Per Share	2.440	2.440	2.410	2.290	2.180	2.100	1.530	2.430
Dividend Payout %	...	...	186.82	301.32	112.37	109.95	91.07	158.82
Income Statement								
Property Income	45,781	167,835	159,115	151,612	139,022	132,440	125,424	114,346
Non-Property Income	5,682	33,018	30,023	10,684	14,532	14,105	8,992	6,242
Total Revenue	51,463	200,853	189,138	162,296	153,554	146,545	134,416	120,588
Depn & Amortn	14,788	51,670	46,302	39,756	34,581	943	29,416	25,642
Interest Expense	14,725	48,243	36,680	32,375	31,016	29,651	26,751	24,245
Income Before Taxes	...	(41,394)	25,362	23,118	47,246	46,304	37,435	32,054
Net Income	687	(40,468)	23,714	13,592	33,910	33,294	29,089	26,096
Average Shares	17,950	18,318	18,345	17,781	17,440	17,390	17,343	17,031
Balance Sheet								
Total Assets	1,332,547	1,403,167	1,221,574	1,163,976	994,449	966,628	911,083	821,439
Long-Term Obligations	1,073,822	1,078,442	674,328	604,373	402,198	452,508	358,473	339,164
Total Liabilities	1,116,134	1,110,378	798,161	691,954	521,810	489,651	432,391	389,852
Stockholders' Equity	188,363	211,746	326,610	319,532	329,641	336,034	338,358	340,364
Shares Outstanding	18,336	18,424	18,990	18,079	17,763	17,509	17,459	17,256
Statistical Record								
Return on Assets %	N.M.	N.M.	1.99	1.26	3.46	3.54	3.36	3.45
Return on Equity %	N.M.	N.M.	7.34	4.19	10.19	9.85	8.57	7.82
Net Margin %	1.33	(20.15)	12.54	8.37	22.08	22.72	21.64	21.64
Price Range	42.82-34.00	42.82-34.00	40.85-33.20	42.12-32.60	38.55-30.99	35.63-27.38	37.00-29.88	36.25-30.50
P/E Ratio	...	...	31.67-25.74	55.42-42.89	19.87-15.97	18.65-14.33	22.02-17.78	23.69-19.93
Average Yield %	6.46	6.31	6.36	6.00	6.26	6.68	4.56	7.18

Address: 27777 Franklin Road, Suite 200, Southfield, MI 48034
Telephone: 248-208-2500
Web Site: www.suncommunities.com

Officers: Gary A. Shiffman - Chmn., Pres., C.E.O. Jeffrey P. Jorissen - Sr. V.P., C.F.O., Treas., Sec.
ransfer Agents:

Investor Contact: 248-932-3100
No of Institutions: 93
Shares: 14,315,776 **% Held:** 77.71

SUNTRUST BANKS, INC.

Exchange	Symbol	Price	52Wk Range	Yield	P/E
NYS	STI	$73.61 (5/31/2005)	74.92-63.87	2.99	14.16

*7 Year Price Score 95.93 *NYSE Composite Index=100 *12 Month Price Score 100.20

Interim Earnings (Per Share)

Qtr.	Mar	Jun	Sep	Dec
2002	1.06	1.20	1.20	1.20
2003	1.17	1.17	1.18	1.21
2004	1.26	1.29	1.30	1.25
2005	1.36	...	...	...

Interim Dividends (Per Share)

Amt	Decl	Ex	Rec	Pay
0.50Q	8/10/2004	8/30/2004	9/1/2004	9/15/2004
0.50Q	11/10/2004	11/29/2004	12/1/2004	12/15/2004
0.55Q	2/8/2005	2/25/2005	3/1/2005	3/15/2005
0.55Q	4/19/2005	5/27/2005	6/1/2005	6/15/2005

Indicated Div: $2.20 (Div. Reinv. Plan)

Valuation Analysis

Forecast P/E	13.22 (6/2/2005)		
Market Cap	$26.6 Billion	Book Value	16.1 Billion
Price/Book	1.65	Price/Sales	3.12

Dividend Achiever Status

Rank	140	10 Year Growth Rate	11.72%
Total Years of Dividend Growth			19

Business Summary: Commercial Banking (MIC: 8.1 SIC: 021 NAIC: 22110)

SunTrust Banks, through its banking subsidiaries, provides deposit, credit, trust and investment services. Additional subsidiaries provide mortgage banking, insurance, asset management, brokerage and capital markets services. Co.'s customer base encompasses a range of individuals and families, high-net-worth clients, businesses and institutions. As of Dec 31 2004, Co. operates 1,710 retail and specialized service branches and 2,804 ATMs, located primarily in Florida, Georgia, Maryland, North Carolina, South Carolina, Tennessee, Virginia and the District of Columbia . At Dec 31 2004, Co. had total assets of $158.87 billion and total deposits of $103.36 billion.

Recent Developments: For the quarter ended Mar 31 2005, net income increased 36.1% to $492,294 thousand from net income of $361,835 thousand in the year-earlier quarter. Net interest income was $1,111,560 thousand, up 30.5% from $851,648 thousand the year before. Provision for loan losses was $10,556 thousand versus $53,837 thousand in the prior-year quarter, a decrease of 80.4%. Non-interest income rose 26.7% to $753,814 thousand, while non-interest expense advanced 27.4% to $1,133,906 thousand.

Prospects: On Apr 29 2005, Co. announced that it has completed the conversion of the former National Commerce Financial Corp. branches and customer accounts into the SunTrust banking franchise. Separately, Co. continues to build on the positive trends established in 2004. Co.'s results are benefiting from increasingly robust net interest income growth, excellent credit quality and a continuation of effective cost control. Factors driving net interest income growth include an improving net interest margin, strong loan growth particularly in residential real estate and home equity lending, and growth in low cost deposits.

Financial Data

(US$ in Thousands)	3 Mos	12/31/2004	12/31/2003	12/31/2002	12/31/2001	12/31/2000	12/31/1999	12/31/1998
Earnings Per Share	5.20	5.19	4.73	4.66	4.72	4.30	4.13	3.04
Cash Flow Per Share	1.18	3.77	14.85	(5.54)	(4.49)	1.72	11.23	(2.86)
Tang Book Value Per Share	22.62	22.50	28.43	26.56	26.67	25.07	23.24	22.99
Dividends Per Share	2.050	2.000	1.800	1.720	1.600	1.480	1.380	1.000
Dividend Payout %	39.42	38.54	38.05	36.91	33.90	34.42	33.41	32.89
Income Statement								
Interest Income	1,716,022	5,218,382	4,768,842	5,135,197	6,279,574	6,845,419	5,960,208	5,675,900
Interest Expense	604,462	1,533,227	1,448,539	1,891,488	3,026,974	3,736,981	2,814,752	2,746,779
Net Interest Income	1,111,560	3,685,155	3,320,303	3,243,709	3,252,600	3,108,438	3,145,456	2,929,121
Provision for Losses	10,556	135,537	313,550	469,792	275,165	133,974	170,437	214,602
Non-Interest Income	759,473	2,604,446	2,303,001	2,391,675	2,155,823	1,773,625	1,660,031	1,716,173
Non-Interest Expense	1,133,906	3,898,837	3,400,616	3,342,268	3,113,538	2,828,533	2,939,393	2,932,386
Income Before Taxes	720,912	2,257,026	1,909,138	1,823,324	2,019,720	1,919,556	1,695,657	1,498,306
Income Taxes	228,618	684,125	576,841	491,515	650,501	625,456	571,705	527,289
Net Income	492,294	1,572,901	1,332,297	1,331,809	1,375,537	1,294,100	1,326,600	971,017
Average Shares	363,138	303,309	281,434	286,052	291,584	300,956	317,079	319,711
Balance Sheet								
Net Loans & Leases	103,737,113	100,376,148	79,790,399	72,237,821	68,092,163	71,365,273	65,131,508	60,596,089
Total Assets	164,810,954	158,869,784	125,393,153	117,322,523	104,740,644	103,496,380	95,389,968	93,169,932
Total Deposits	107,534,884	103,361,251	81,189,519	79,706,628	67,536,422	69,533,337	60,100,529	59,033,283
Total Liabilities	148,706,695	142,882,885	115,661,987	108,553,027	96,381,076	95,257,172	87,763,106	84,991,288
Stockholders' Equity	16,104,259	15,986,899	9,731,166	8,769,496	8,359,568	8,239,208	7,626,862	8,178,644
Shares Outstanding	361,176	360,840	281,923	270,843	283,040	296,266	293,543	321,124
Statistical Record								
Return on Assets %	1.16	1.10	1.10	1.20	1.32	1.30	1.41	1.28
Return on Equity %	12.84	12.20	14.40	15.55	16.57	16.27	16.79	14.52
Net Interest Margin %	64.78	70.62	69.62	63.17	51.80	45.41	52.77	51.61
Efficiency Ratio %	45.81	49.84	48.09	44.40	36.91	32.82	38.57	39.67
Loans to Deposits	0.96	0.97	0.98	0.91	1.01	1.03	1.08	1.03
Price Range	74.35-61.80	76.41-61.80	71.55-51.56	70.00-51.79	71.81-58.10	68.81-42.56	79.81-62.25	87.44-54.94
P/E Ratio	14.30-11.88	14.72-11.91	15.13-10.90	15.02-11.11	15.21-12.31	16.00-9.90	19.33-15.07	28.76-18.07
Average Yield %	2.97	2.90	2.96	2.71	2.48	2.80	2.01	1.38

Address: 303 Peachtree Street, NE, Atlanta, GA 30308 **Telephone:** 404-588-7711 **Web Site:** www.suntrust.com	**Officers:** L. Phillip Humann - Chmn., Pres., C.E.O. James M. Wells III - Vice-Chmn., Pres., C.O.O. **ransfer Agents:**SunTrust Bank Atlanta, Atlanta, GA	**Investor Contact:** 404-658-4879 **No of Institutions:** 442 **Shares:** 186,107,008 **% Held:** 51.58

SUPERIOR INDUSTRIES INTERNATIONAL, INC.

Exchange	Symbol	Price	52Wk Range	Yield	P/E
NYS	SUP	$22.65 (5/31/2005)	33.97-20.33	2.83	15.10

*7 Year Price Score 73.02 *NYSE Composite Index=100 *12 Month Price Score 77.81

Interim Earnings (Per Share)

Qtr.	Mar	Jun	Sep	Dec
2002	0.65	0.78	0.65	0.83
2003	0.83	0.66	0.40	0.85
2004	0.51	0.51	0.20	0.45
2005	0.34	...	...	...

Interim Dividends (Per Share)

Amt	Decl	Ex	Rec	Pay
0.155Q	8/2/2004	9/29/2004	10/1/2004	10/15/2004
0.155Q	11/2/2004	1/5/2005	1/7/2005	1/21/2005
0.155Q	3/24/2005	4/6/2005	4/8/2005	4/22/2005
0.16Q	5/13/2005	6/29/2005	7/1/2005	7/15/2005

Indicated Div: $0.64

Valuation Analysis

Forecast P/E	20.51 (6/1/2005)		
Market Cap	$603.0 Million	Book Value	607.7 Million
Price/Book	0.99	Price/Sales	0.69

Dividend Achiever Status

Rank	97	10 Year Growth Rate	14.58%
Total Years of Dividend Growth			19

Business Summary: Automotive (MIC: 15.1 SIC: 714 NAIC: 36399)

Superior Industries International is principally engaged the design and manufacture of motor vehicle parts for sale to original equipment manufacturers (OEM). Co. supplies cast and forged aluminum wheels to automobile and light truck manufacturers, with wheel manufacturing operations in the United States, Mexico and Hungary. Co. is also engaged in the market for aluminum suspension and related underbody components. Co.'s OEM aluminum road wheels are sold for factory installation, as optional or standard equipment on many vehicle models, to Ford, GM, DaimlerChrysler, Audi, BMW, Isuzu, Jaguar, Land Rover, Mazda, MG Rover, Mitsubishi, Nissan, Subaru, Toyota and Volkswagen.

Recent Developments: For the quarter ended Mar 31 2005, net income decreased 34.7% to $8,931 thousand from net income of $13,667 thousand in the year-earlier quarter. Revenues were $211,915 thousand, down 9.5% from $234,191 thousand the year before. Operating income was $9,096 thousand versus an income of $18,689 thousand in the prior-year quarter, a decrease of 51.3%. Total direct expense was $197,761 thousand versus $209,620 thousand in the prior-year quarter, a decrease of 5.7%. Total indirect expense was $5,058 thousand versus $5,882 thousand in the prior-year quarter, a decrease of 14.0%.

Prospects: Co. is focusing on reducing its costs by enhancing efficiency and increasing automation in all of its plants, and reducing costs for the long run by taking advantage of global manufacturing opportunities. For example, Co. noted that its third facility in Mexico for cast aluminum wheel manufacturing is expected to commence in 2006. Co. is also moving forward with its plans to establish a joint venture manufacturing presence in China, and is evaluating opportunities in other parts of the developing world. Co. expects capital expenditures in 2005 and 2006 to approximate $125.0 million to 150.0 million. This estimate does not include the possibility of a joint venture wheel plant in Asia.

Financial Data (US$ in Thousands)	3 Mos	12/31/2004	12/31/2003	12/31/2002	12/31/2001	12/31/2000	12/31/1999	12/31/1998
Earnings Per Share	1.50	1.67	2.73	2.91	2.10	3.04	2.62	1.88
Cash Flow Per Share	3.08	2.89	2.87	3.64	2.29	3.67	3.23	2.88
Tang Book Value Per Share	22.83	22.66	22.12	19.96	17.30	15.45	13.35	11.42
Dividends Per Share	0.603	0.585	0.525	0.470	0.420	0.380	0.340	0.300
Dividend Payout %	40.17	35.03	19.23	16.15	20.00	12.50	12.98	15.96
Income Statement								
Total Revenue	211,915	901,755	840,349	782,599	643,395	644,899	571,782	539,431
EBITDA	10,704	102,618	144,265	149,470	108,529	142,107	131,590	103,212
Depn & Amortn	...	39,281	33,577	32,605	28,388	26,920	28,523	26,698
Income Before Taxes	11,829	66,109	113,415	120,384	84,189	122,510	108,518	80,801
Income Taxes	2,898	21,454	39,695	42,134	28,835	42,573	37,710	28,482
Net Income	8,931	44,655	73,720	78,250	55,354	79,937	70,808	52,319
Average Shares	26,642	26,809	27,033	26,907	26,361	26,255	27,056	27,818
Balance Sheet								
Current Assets	362,458	368,976	388,510	368,941	280,271	245,579	263,740	235,886
Total Assets	746,301	744,528	703,205	645,796	540,838	491,664	460,468	427,430
Current Liabilities	85,838	87,343	83,621	97,123	71,137	75,022	86,847	91,111
Long-Term Obligations	...	...	...	...	...	...	340	673
Total Liabilities	138,556	141,264	110,999	115,365	92,097	92,345	107,382	115,396
Stockholders' Equity	607,745	603,264	592,206	530,431	448,741	399,319	353,086	312,034
Shares Outstanding	26,621	26,621	26,768	26,573	25,932	25,840	26,454	27,312
Statistical Record								
Return on Assets %	5.39	6.15	10.93	13.19	10.72	16.75	15.95	12.92
Return on Equity %	6.62	7.45	13.13	15.98	13.05	21.19	21.29	17.46
EBITDA Margin %	5.05	11.38	17.17	19.10	16.87	22.04	23.01	19.13
Net Margin %	4.21	4.95	8.77	10.00	8.60	12.40	12.38	9.70
Asset Turnover	1.19	1.24	1.25	1.32	1.25	1.35	1.29	1.33
Current Ratio	4.22	4.22	4.65	3.80	3.94	3.27	3.04	2.59
Price Range	36.48-24.59	43.67-26.36	45.91-33.89	53.12-36.20	44.62-29.40	35.31-23.50	29.00-22.81	33.50-20.19
P/E Ratio	24.32-16.39	26.15-15.78	16.82-12.41	18.25-12.44	21.25-14.00	11.62-7.73	11.07-8.71	17.82-10.74
Average Yield %	2.03	1.78	1.27	1.06	1.13	1.28	1.29	1.10

Address: 7800 Woodley Avenue, Van Nuys, CA 91406 **Telephone:** 818-781-4973 **Web Site:** www.supind.com	**Officers:** Louis L. Borick - Chmn., C.E.O. Steven J. Borick - Pres., C.O.O. **Transfer Agents:** Registrar and Transfer Company, Cranford, NJ	**No of Institutions:** 127 **Shares:** 28,936,116 **% Held:** N/A

SUPERVALU INC.

Exchange	Symbol	Price	52Wk Range	Yield	P/E
NYS	SVU	$32.76 (5/31/2005)	34.88-25.95	1.86	12.09

***7 Year Price Score 120.50** *NYSE Composite Index=100 ***12 Month Price Score 101.73**

Interim Earnings (Per Share)

Qtr.	Jun	Aug	Nov	Feb
2001-02	0.45	0.39	0.44	0.25
2002-03	0.57	0.44	0.43	0.47
2003-04	0.55	0.46	0.36	0.69
Qtr.	**Jun**	**Sep**	**Nov**	**Feb**
2004-05	1.09	0.57	0.48	0.57

Interim Dividends (Per Share)

Amt	Decl	Ex	Rec	Pay
0.153Q	8/11/2004	8/30/2004	9/1/2004	9/15/2004
0.153Q	10/6/2004	11/29/2004	12/1/2004	12/15/2004
0.153Q	2/9/2005	2/25/2005	3/1/2005	3/15/2005
0.153Q	4/6/2005	5/27/2005	6/1/2005	6/15/2005

Indicated Div: $0.61 (Div. Reinv. Plan)

Valuation Analysis

Forecast P/E	12.62 (6/1/2005)		
Market Cap	$4.4 Billion	Book Value	2.5 Billion
Price/Book	1.77	Price/Sales	0.23

Dividend Achiever Status

Rank	303	**10 Year Growth Rate**	2.72%
Total Years of Dividend Growth			32

Business Summary: Retail - Food & Beverage (MIC: 5.3 SIC: 141 NAIC: 24410)

Supervalu is a major food retailer and distributor to independently-owned retail food stores. As of Feb 28 2004, Co. operated 1,225 Save-A-Lot extreme value stores, including 821 licensed Save-A-Lot locations, 280 Co.-owned stores and 124 Deals-Nothing Over a Dollar general merchandise stores; 258 regional supermarkets under the Cub Foods, Shop 'n Save, Shoppers Food Warehouse, bigg's, Farm Fresh, Scott's Foods, and Hornbacher's banners. Additionally, Co. is the primary supplier to approximately 2,500 retail grocery stores, as well as Co.'s 258 regional supermarkets, while serving as a secondary supplier to about 660 stores.

Recent Developments: For the year ended Feb 26 2005, net income increased 37.7% to $385,823 thousand from net income of $280,138 thousand a year earlier. Revenues were $19,543,240 thousand, down 3.3% from $20,209,679 thousand the year before. Operating income was $715,646 thousand versus an income of $601,398 thousand in the prior year, an increase of 19.0%. Total direct expense was $16,681,472 thousand versus $17,372,429 thousand in the prior year, a decrease of 4.0%. Total indirect expense was $2,146,122 thousand versus $2,235,852 thousand in the prior year, a decrease of 4.0%.

Prospects: On Apr 19 2005, Co. established preliminary full-year fiscal 2006 diluted earnings per share guidance of $2.30 to $2.45. Co.'s guidance includes costs of about $0.05 to $0.07 for new growth and return initiatives. Co.'s fiscal 2006 outlook also includes business assumptions such as, but not limited to: comparable store sales gains of 1.0%; store development plans including licensees of about 90 to 110 new extreme value food combination stores, about 100 extreme value combination store conversions, and about 10 to 12 new regional banner stores; total capital spending of $500.0 million to $550.0 million; and the fiscal 2006 divestiture of refrigeration case and system manufacturer Zero Zone.

Financial Data (US$ in Thousands)	02/26/2005	02/28/2004	02/22/2003	02/23/2002	02/24/2001	02/26/2000	02/27/1999	02/28/1998
Earnings Per Share	2.71	2.07	1.91	1.53	0.62	1.87	1.57	1.83
Cash Flow Per Share	5.88	6.11	4.30	5.93	4.94	2.65	4.66	3.08
Tang Book Value Per Share	6.52	4.84	3.24	2.90	1.64	1.58	6.09	5.80
Dividends Per Share	0.748	0.578	0.565	0.555	0.545	0.403	0.527	0.515
Dividend Payout %	27.58	27.90	29.58	36.27	87.90	21.52	33.60	28.22
Income Statement								
Total Revenue	19,543,240	20,209,679	19,160,368	20,908,522	23,194,279	20,339,079	17,420,507	17,201,378
EBITDA	1,018,685	902,987	866,999	857,227	688,971	859,908	651,691	728,855
Depn & Amortn	303,039	301,589	297,056	340,750	343,779	277,062	233,523	230,082
Income Before Taxes	600,864	454,880	408,004	343,703	154,357	447,454	316,261	384,780
Income Taxes	215,041	174,742	150,962	138,168	72,392	204,513	124,923	154,023
Net Income	385,823	280,138	257,042	205,535	81,965	242,941	191,338	230,757
Average Shares	144,924	135,418	134,877	133,978	132,829	130,090	121,961	126,550
Balance Sheet								
Current Assets	2,126,500	2,037,092	1,647,366	1,604,027	2,091,676	2,177,639	1,582,527	1,612,060
Total Assets	6,278,342	6,152,938	5,896,245	5,824,782	6,407,172	6,495,353	4,265,949	4,093,010
Current Liabilities	1,631,591	1,871,972	1,525,307	1,701,489	2,341,170	2,509,620	1,521,907	1,457,160
Long-Term Obligations	1,578,867	1,633,721	2,019,658	1,875,873	2,008,474	1,953,741	1,246,269	1,260,728
Total Liabilities	3,767,781	3,943,364	3,887,005	3,908,089	4,613,677	4,673,874	2,960,310	2,891,105
Stockholders' Equity	2,510,561	2,209,574	2,009,240	1,916,693	1,793,495	1,821,479	1,305,639	1,201,905
Shares Outstanding	135,478	134,760	133,688	132,889	132,374	134,662	120,109	120,368
Statistical Record								
Return on Assets %	6.22	4.57	4.40	3.37	1.27	4.53	4.59	5.42
Return on Equity %	16.39	13.07	13.13	11.11	4.55	15.58	15.30	18.09
EBITDA Margin %	5.21	4.47	4.52	4.10	2.97	4.23	3.74	4.24
Net Margin %	1.97	1.39	1.34	0.98	0.35	1.19	1.10	1.34
Asset Turnover	3.15	3.30	3.28	3.43	3.61	3.79	4.18	4.04
Current Ratio	1.30	1.09	1.08	0.94	0.89	0.87	1.04	1.11
Debt to Equity	0.63	0.74	1.01	0.98	1.12	1.07	0.95	1.05
Price Range	34.88-25.95	29.43-12.60	30.50-14.32	24.68-12.80	22.50-11.75	26.13-16.19	28.75-20.31	24.28-14.31
P/E Ratio	12.87-9.58	14.22-6.09	15.97-7.50	16.13-8.37	36.29-18.95	13.97-8.66	18.31-12.94	13.27-7.82
Average Yield %	2.47	2.55	2.63	2.91	3.25	1.88	2.19	2.74

Address: 11840 Valley View Road, Eden Prairie, MN 55344 **Telephone:** 952-828-4000 **Web Site:** www.supervalu.com	**Officers:** Jeffrey Noddle - Chmn., Pres., C.E.O. Pamela K. Knous - Exec. V.P., C.F.O. **Transfer Agents:** Wells Fargo Shareowner Services, St. Paul, MN	**Investor Contact:** 952-828-4000 **No of Institutions:** 269 **Shares:** 113,807,544 **% Held:** 84.24

SUSQUEHANNA BANCSHARES, INC

Exchange	Symbol	Price	52Wk Range	Yield	P/E
NMS	SUSQ	$22.76 (5/31/2005)	26.56-21.03	4.04	14.78

*7 Year Price Score 103.91 *NYSE Composite Index=100 *12 Month Price Score 90.92

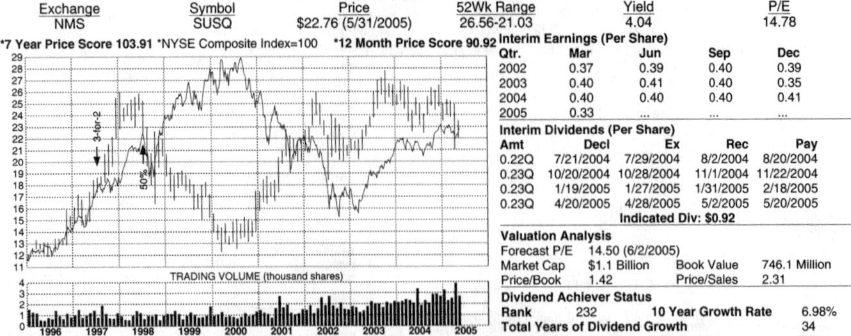

Interim Earnings (Per Share)

Qtr.	Mar	Jun	Sep	Dec
2002	0.37	0.39	0.40	0.39
2003	0.40	0.41	0.40	0.35
2004	0.40	0.40	0.40	0.41
2005	0.33	...	...	...

Interim Dividends (Per Share)

Amt	Decl	Ex	Rec	Pay
0.22Q	7/21/2004	7/29/2004	8/2/2004	8/20/2004
0.23Q	10/20/2004	10/28/2004	11/1/2004	11/22/2004
0.23Q	1/19/2005	1/27/2005	1/31/2005	2/18/2005
0.23Q	4/20/2005	4/28/2005	5/2/2005	5/20/2005

Indicated Div: $0.92

Valuation Analysis

Forecast P/E	14.50 (6/2/2005)		
Market Cap	$1.1 Billion	Book Value	746.1 Million
Price/Book	1.42	Price/Sales	2.31

Dividend Achiever Status

Rank	232	10 Year Growth Rate	6.98%
Total Years of Dividend Growth			34

Business Summary: Commercial Banking (MIC: 8.1 SIC: 021 NAIC: 22110)

Susquehanna Bancshares is a financial holding company that provides a range of retail and commercial banking and financial services through its subsidiaries in the mid-Atlantic region. In addition to its commercial banks that included an aggregate of 157 branches as of Dec 31 2004, Co. operates a trust and investment company, an asset management company, a property and casualty insurance brokerage company, a commercial leasing company and a vehicle leasing company. As of Dec 31 2004, Co. had total assets of $7.48 billion and deposits of $5.13 billion.

Recent Developments: For the quarter ended Mar 31 2005, net income decreased 3.3% to $15,403 thousand from net income of $15,926 thousand in the year-earlier quarter. Net interest income was $59,412 thousand, up 27.3% from $46,681 thousand the year before. Provision for loan losses was $2,750 thousand versus $1,700 thousand in the prior-year quarter, an increase of 61.8%. Non-interest income rose 3.3% to $27,970 thousand, while non-interest expense advanced 25.9% to $62,080 thousand.

Prospects: Despite a significant reduction in origination volumes at its auto lease subsidiary during the quarter ended Mar 31 2005 due to special financing offers provided by the major car manufacturers, Co. has maintained its full-year 2005 full diluted earnings per share range of $1.70 to $1.80. Separately, on Feb 1 2005, Co. announced its acquisition of Brandywine Benefits Corporation and Rockford Pensions, LLC (collectively Brandywine), a financial planning, consulting and administration firm specializing in retirement benefit plans for small- to medium-sized businesses. Brandywine serves over 250 customers in the mid-Atlantic states and generates approximately $1.6 million in annual revenues.

Financial Data

(US$ in Thousands)	3 Mos	12/31/2004	12/31/2003	12/31/2002	12/31/2001	12/31/2000	12/31/1999	12/31/1998
Earnings Per Share	1.54	1.60	1.56	1.55	1.41	1.40	1.17	1.26
Cash Flow Per Share	1.21	1.83	2.50	2.13	1.74	1.35	2.22	1.36
Tang Book Value Per Share	10.52	10.71	12.14	11.96	12.54	11.56	10.92	10.91
Dividends Per Share	0.900	0.890	0.860	0.810	0.770	0.700	0.620	0.570
Dividend Payout %	58.44	55.63	55.13	52.26	54.61	50.00	52.99	45.24
Income Statement								
Interest Income	91,902	321,759	286,020	316,713	341,295	353,416	299,770	292,766
Interest Expense	32,490	107,741	99,014	129,473	169,051	188,464	138,848	138,576
Net Interest Income	59,412	214,018	187,006	187,240	172,244	164,952	160,922	154,190
Provision for Losses	2,750	10,020	10,222	10,664	7,310	3,726	7,200	5,247
Non-Interest Income	27,970	114,590	101,750	94,150	84,166	74,010	39,979	30,921
Non-Interest Expense	62,080	219,042	189,430	181,663	167,763	155,581	131,882	113,206
Income Before Taxes	22,552	99,546	89,104	89,063	81,337	79,655	61,819	66,658
Income Taxes	7,149	29,366	26,731	27,342	25,621	24,693	18,422	21,084
Net Income	15,403	70,180	62,373	61,721	55,716	54,962	43,397	45,574
Average Shares	46,825	43,872	40,037	39,932	39,593	39,365	37,137	36,179
Balance Sheet								
Net Loans & Leases	4,937,762	5,198,915	4,220,600	3,791,282	3,481,800	3,396,423	2,957,919	2,738,379
Total Assets	7,253,296	7,475,073	5,953,107	5,544,647	5,051,092	4,792,856	4,310,606	4,064,827
Total Deposits	5,106,065	5,130,682	4,134,467	3,831,315	3,484,331	3,249,013	3,180,520	3,124,332
Total Liabilities	6,507,207	6,723,379	5,405,725	5,010,792	4,557,556	4,339,419	3,906,216	3,673,631
Stockholders' Equity	746,089	751,694	547,382	533,855	493,536	453,437	404,390	391,196
Shares Outstanding	46,650	46,592	39,861	39,638	39,344	39,221	37,022	35,857
Statistical Record								
Return on Assets %	1.05	1.04	1.08	1.17	1.13	1.20	1.04	1.20
Return on Equity %	10.67	10.78	11.54	12.02	11.77	12.78	10.91	12.35
Net Interest Margin %	64.65	66.52	65.38	59.12	50.47	46.67	53.68	52.67
Efficiency Ratio %	51.79	50.20	48.85	44.21	39.43	36.40	38.82	34.97
Loans to Deposits	0.97	1.01	1.02	0.99	1.00	1.05	0.93	0.88
Price Range	26.56-22.44	26.89-22.44	27.80-20.20	25.97-18.41	22.80-15.75	17.50-12.25	20.69-15.03	26.00-16.38
P/E Ratio	17.25-14.57	16.81-14.03	17.82-12.95	16.75-11.88	16.17-11.17	12.50-8.75	17.68-12.85	20.63-13.00
Average Yield %	3.67	3.58	3.60	3.60	4.00	4.97	3.50	2.51

Address: 26 North Cedar St., Lititz, PA 17543 **Telephone:** 717-626-4721 **Web Site:** www.susquehanna.net	**Officers:** William J. Reuter - Chmn., Pres., C.E.O. Gregory A. Duncan - Exec. V.P., C.O.O. **Transfer Agents:** The Bank of New York, New York, NY	**Investor Contact:** 717-625-6305 **No of Institutions:** 131 **Shares:** 17,818,346 **% Held:** 38.22

SYNOVUS FINANCIAL CORP.

Exchange	Symbol	Price	52Wk Range	Yield	P/E
NYS	SNV	$29.07 (5/31/2005)	29.45-24.49	2.51	20.19

Interim Earnings (Per Share)

Qtr.	Mar	Jun	Sep	Dec
2002	0.28	0.29	0.31	0.34
2003	0.30	0.32	0.33	0.34
2004	0.34	0.34	0.35	0.38
2005	0.37	...	...	...

Interim Dividends (Per Share)

Amt	Decl	Ex	Rec	Pay
0.173Q	8/19/2004	9/15/2004	9/17/2004	10/1/2004
0.173Q	11/16/2004	12/15/2004	12/17/2004	1/3/2005
0.183Q	2/23/2005	3/22/2005	3/24/2005	4/1/2005
0.183Q	5/24/2005	6/21/2005	6/23/2005	7/1/2005

Indicated Div: $0.73 (Div. Reinv. Plan)

Valuation Analysis

Forecast P/E	17.94 (6/2/2005)		
Market Cap	$9.0 Billion	Book Value	2.7 Billion
Price/Book	3.35	Price/Sales	3.24

Dividend Achiever Status

Rank	54	10 Year Growth Rate	18.29%
Total Years of Dividend Growth			28

Business Summary: Commercial Banking (MIC: 8.1 SIC: 021 NAIC: 22110)

Synovus Financial, with assets of $25.05 billion as of Dec 31 2004, is a registered bank holding company. Co. provides financial services including commercial and retail banking, financial management, insurance, mortgage and leasing services through affiliate banks and other offices in Georgia, Alabama, South Carolina, Florida and Tennessee. Co. also owns 81.0% of Total System Services, Inc.® (TSYS), which provides electronic payment processing services including consumer, debit, commercial, retail and stored value card processing and related services, as well as student loan processing.

Recent Developments: For the quarter ended Mar 31 2005, net income increased 12.1% to $116,734 thousand from net income of $104,162 thousand in the year-earlier quarter. Net interest income was $226,862 thousand, up 11.9% from $202,747 thousand the year before. Provision for loan losses was $19,283 thousand versus $15,724 thousand in the prior-year quarter, an increase of 22.6%. Non-interest income rose 12.7% to $425,110 thousand, while non-interest expense advanced 11.9% to $447,072 thousand.

Prospects: Stable credit quality and margins, continued strong loan growth, and successful expense controls lead Co. to believe that its Financial Services segment will continue to perform well. Also, Co. is optimistic that TSYS will perform within its range of guidance, supported by a promising economic climate and growing consumer confidence. As a result, Co. is increasing its expectations of earnings per share growth to a range of 13.0% to 16.0% for 2005 from its earlier guidance of 12.0% to 15.0% Going forward, Co. will look to focus on growing deposits, managing loan growth, quality and mix, maintaining a strong margin, expanding fee income and continuing to refine its processes.

Financial Data

(US$ in Thousands)	3 Mos	12/31/2004	12/31/2003	12/31/2002	12/31/2001	12/31/2000	12/31/1999	12/31/1998
Earnings Per Share	1.44	1.41	1.28	1.21	1.05	0.92	0.80	0.70
Cash Flow Per Share	2.19	2.60	2.40	2.43	0.61	1.60	1.62	0.60
Tang Book Value Per Share	5.56	7.04	6.50	6.40	5.75	4.98	4.35	3.96
Dividends Per Share	0.702	0.693	0.660	0.590	0.510	0.440	0.360	0.293
Dividend Payout %	48.78	49.16	51.56	48.76	48.57	47.83	45.00	41.89
Income Statement								
Interest Income	331,306	1,159,020	1,061,492	1,055,040	1,130,888	1,097,805	888,007	769,248
Interest Expense	104,444	298,341	298,428	337,536	501,097	535,473	374,713	328,722
Net Interest Income	226,862	860,679	763,064	717,504	629,791	562,332	513,294	440,526
Provision for Losses	19,283	75,319	71,777	65,327	51,673	44,341	34,007	26,660
Non-Interest Income	425,110	1,521,011	1,369,329	1,234,822	937,697	833,513	739,765	561,973
Non-Interest Expense	438,240	1,588,366	1,422,143	1,299,470	1,005,963	923,274	856,549	673,648
Income Before Taxes	185,617	689,281	611,501	563,880	489,993	411,735	349,315	291,632
Income Taxes	68,883	252,248	222,576	198,533	178,377	149,178	124,008	104,524
Net Income	116,734	437,033	388,925	365,347	311,616	262,557	225,307	187,108
Average Shares	313,900	310,330	304,928	301,197	295,850	286,882	283,355	269,151
Balance Sheet								
Net Loans & Leases	19,782,571	19,214,651	16,238,855	14,264,068	12,247,148	10,604,020	8,940,681	7,301,170
Total Assets	25,852,385	25,050,178	21,632,629	19,036,246	16,657,947	14,908,092	12,547,001	10,498,009
Total Deposits	19,114,272	18,577,468	15,941,609	13,928,834	12,146,198	11,161,710	9,440,087	8,542,798
Total Liabilities	22,978,495	22,241,605	19,245,752	16,878,294	14,864,363	13,410,031	11,256,047	9,375,315
Stockholders' Equity	2,698,871	2,641,289	2,245,039	2,040,853	1,694,946	1,417,171	1,226,669	1,070,601
Shares Outstanding	311,020	309,974	302,090	300,397	294,673	284,642	282,014	270,218
Statistical Record								
Return on Assets %	1.87	1.87	1.91	2.05	1.97	1.91	1.96	1.89
Return on Equity %	17.78	17.84	18.15	19.56	20.03	19.81	19.62	18.95
Net Interest Margin %	68.48	74.26	71.89	68.01	55.69	51.22	57.80	57.27
Efficiency Ratio %	57.94	59.27	58.50	56.75	48.63	47.81	52.62	50.60
Loans to Deposits	1.03	1.03	1.02	1.02	1.01	0.95	0.95	0.85
Price Range	28.89-23.31	28.92-22.67	29.04-17.31	31.74-16.81	34.45-23.02	27.19-14.50	25.00-17.50	25.83-18.06
P/E Ratio	20.06-16.19	20.51-16.08	22.69-13.52	26.23-13.89	32.81-21.92	29.55-15.76	31.25-21.88	36.90-25.80
Average Yield %	2.67	2.69	2.87	2.40	1.82	2.25	1.72	1.30

Address: 901 Front Avenue, P.O. Box 120, Columbus, GA 31902
Telephone: 706-649-2401
Web Site: www.synovus.com

Officers: James D. Yancey - Chmn., Pres., C.O.O. Richard E. Anthony - Pres. **Transfer Agents:** State Street Bank and Trust Company, Boston, MA

Investor Contact: 706-649-5220
No of Institutions: 239
Shares: 89,979,392 **% Held:** 28.95

SYSCO CORP.

Exchange	Symbol	Price	52Wk Range	Yield	P/E
NYS	SYY	$37.16 (5/31/2005)	38.20-29.89	1.61	25.81

***7 Year Price Score 118.28** *NYSE Composite Index=100 ***12 Month Price Score 100.73**

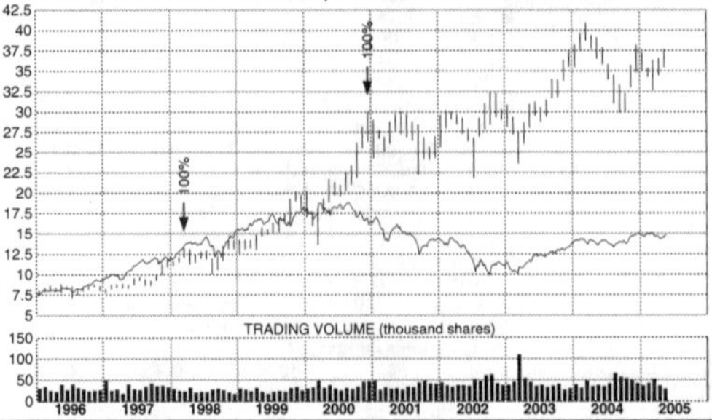

TRADING VOLUME (thousand shares)

Interim Earnings (Per Share)

Qtr.	Sep	Dec	Mar	Jun
2001-02	0.24	0.24	0.23	0.31
2002-03	0.28	0.28	0.26	0.37
2003-04	0.32	0.34	0.30	0.42
2004-05	0.35	0.36	0.34	...

Interim Dividends (Per Share)

Amt	Decl	Ex	Rec	Pay
0.13Q	9/3/2004	9/29/2004	10/1/2004	10/22/2004
0.15Q	11/12/2004	1/5/2005	1/7/2005	1/28/2005
0.15Q	2/18/2005	3/30/2005	4/1/2005	4/22/2005
0.15Q	5/13/2005	6/29/2005	7/1/2005	7/22/2005

Indicated Div: $0.60 (Div. Reinv. Plan)

Valuation Analysis

Forecast P/E	21.99 (6/1/2005)		
Market Cap	$23.5 Billion	Book Value	2.8 Billion
Price/Book	8.35	Price/Sales	0.79

Dividend Achiever Status

Rank	45	**10 Year Growth Rate**	19.17%
Total Years of Dividend Growth			28

Business Summary: Retail - Food & Beverage (MIC: 5.3 SIC: 141 NAIC: 24410)

Sysco is engaged in the marketing and distribution of food and related products to the foodservice or "food-prepared-away-from-home" industry. These services are performed for approximately 400,000 customers from 150 distribution facilities located throughout U.S. and Canada. Co.'s Broadline segment distributes a full line of food products and non-food products to both traditional and chain restaurant customers. The SYGMA segment distributes a full line of food products and non-food products to certain chain restaurant customer locations. The Other segment includes Co.'s specialty produce, custom-cut meat, Asian cuisine foodservice and lodging industry products segments.

Recent Developments: For the quarter ended Apr 2 2005, net income increased 11.4% to $218,220 thousand from net income of $195,824 thousand in the year-earlier quarter. Revenues were $7,437,453 thousand, up 5.9% from $7,025,585 thousand the year before. Total direct expense was $6,032,165 thousand versus $5,684,192 thousand in the prior-year quarter, an increase of 6.1%.

Prospects: Co. intends to continue to expand its market share. During the quarter ended Apr 2 2005, Co.'s FreshPoint subsidiary further expanded its distribution reach with the acquisition of a specialty produce distributor in Modesto, CA. In terms of internal growth activity, Co.'s broadline fold-out company in Post Falls, ID began distributing products in Apr 2005 to the Spokane, WA and surrounding foodservice markets. Co. defines fold-out companies as new operating companies created in established markets previously served by other SYSCO operating companies. Going forward, Co.'s goal is to open at least three fold-out companies per year.

Financial Data (US$ in Thousands)	9 Mos	6 Mos	3 Mos	07/03/2004	06/28/2003	06/29/2002	06/30/2001	07/01/2000
Earnings Per Share	1.44	1.41	1.39	1.37	1.18	1.01	0.88	0.67
Cash Flow Per Share	1.93	1.82	1.74	1.82	2.12	1.64	1.44	1.08
Tang Book Value Per Share	2.45	2.49	2.42	2.11	1.68	1.85	2.07	1.90
Dividends Per Share	0.560	0.390	0.520	0.500	0.400	0.320	0.260	0.170
Dividend Payout %	38.77	27.66	37.48	36.50	33.90	31.68	29.55	25.56
Income Statement								
Total Revenue	22,300,635	14,863,182	7,531,925	29,335,403	26,140,337	23,350,504	21,784,497	19,303,268
EBITDA	1,364,761	928,361	457,616	1,828,619	1,605,763	1,442,018	1,286,671	1,029,101
Depn & Amortn	230,964	150,294	74,065	283,595	273,142	278,251	248,240	220,661
Income Before Taxes	1,078,181	742,602	365,852	1,475,144	1,260,387	1,100,870	966,655	737,608
Income Taxes	401,404	284,045	139,938	567,930	482,099	421,083	369,746	283,979
Net Income	676,777	458,557	225,914	907,214	778,288	679,787	596,909	445,588
Average Shares	650,753	652,993	650,779	661,919	661,535	673,445	667,949	669,555
Balance Sheet								
Current Assets	3,996,142	3,931,578	4,012,781	3,851,411	3,629,534	3,185,289	2,984,882	2,733,215
Total Assets	8,167,236	8,100,887	8,105,806	7,847,632	6,936,521	5,989,753	5,468,521	4,813,955
Current Liabilities	3,333,839	3,169,956	3,170,343	3,126,634	2,701,129	2,239,357	2,089,895	1,782,935
Long-Term Obligations	1,032,822	1,101,852	1,082,345	1,231,493	1,249,467	1,176,307	961,421	1,023,642
Total Liabilities	5,351,456	5,257,663	5,343,900	5,283,126	4,738,990	3,857,234	3,321,001	3,052,387
Stockholders' Equity	2,815,780	2,843,224	2,761,906	2,564,506	2,197,531	2,132,519	2,147,520	1,761,568
Shares Outstanding	633,030	636,545	636,535	636,535	643,657	653,540	665,137	662,969
Statistical Record								
Return on Assets %	12.14	11.97	11.88	12.07	12.08	11.90	11.64	10.03
Return on Equity %	36.98	35.40	35.77	37.49	36.05	31.85	30.62	28.02
EBITDA Margin %	6.12	6.25	6.08	6.23	6.14	6.18	5.91	5.33
Net Margin %	3.03	3.09	3.00	3.09	2.98	2.91	2.74	2.31
Asset Turnover	3.86	3.84	3.82	3.90	4.06	4.09	4.25	4.34
Current Ratio	1.20	1.24	1.27	1.23	1.34	1.42	1.43	1.53
Debt to Equity	0.37	0.39	0.39	0.48	0.57	0.55	0.45	0.58
Price Range	39.37-29.89	40.90-29.89	40.90-29.92	40.90-28.75	32.34-21.81	30.15-22.22	30.03-19.59	21.69-13.63
P/E Ratio	27.34-20.76	29.01-21.20	29.42-21.53	29.85-20.99	27.41-18.48	29.85-22.00	34.13-22.27	32.37-20.34
Average Yield %	1.60	1.09	1.45	1.41	1.39	1.17	1.02	0.95

Address: 1390 Enclave Parkway, Houston, TX 77077-2099
Telephone: 281-584-1390
Web Site: www.sysco.com

Officers: Richard J. Schnieders - Chmn., C.E.O. Thomas E. Lankford - Pres., C.O.O. **Transfer Agents:** EquiServe Trust Company, N.A., Providence, RI

Investor Contact: 281-584-1458
No of Institutions: 670
Shares: 400,463,328 **% Held:** 62.88

T ROWE PRICE GROUP INC.

Exchange	Symbol	Price	52Wk Range	Yield	P/E
NMS	TROW	$59.66 (5/31/2005)	63.30-44.67	1.54	22.77

*7 Year Price Score 124.33 *NYSE Composite Index=100 *12 Month Price Score 100.67

TRADING VOLUME (thousand shares)

Interim Earnings (Per Share)

Qtr.	Mar	Jun	Sep	Dec
2002	0.41	0.40	0.34	0.37
2003	0.31	0.42	0.51	0.52
2004	0.58	0.60	0.62	0.71
2005	0.69	...	...	...

Interim Dividends (Per Share)

Amt	Decl	Ex	Rec	Pay
0.19Q	9/9/2004	9/23/2004	9/27/2004	10/8/2004
0.23Q	12/16/2004	12/22/2004	12/27/2004	1/10/2005
0.23Q	3/10/2005	3/22/2005	3/24/2005	4/8/2005
0.23Q	6/2/2005	6/22/2005	6/24/2005	7/8/2005

Indicated Div: $0.92

Valuation Analysis

Forecast P/E	N/A		
Market Cap	$7.8 Billion	Book Value	1.8 Billion
Price/Book	4.42	Price/Sales	5.83

Dividend Achiever Status

Rank	43	10 Year Growth Rate	19.31%
Total Years of Dividend Growth			18

Business Summary: Wealth Management (MIC: 8.8 SIC: 282 NAIC: 23930)

T. Rowe Price Group is a financial services holding company with total assets under management of $235.20 billion as of Dec 31 2004. Through its subsidiaries, Co. is engaged in providing investment advisory services to individual and institutional investors through the sponsored T. Rowe Price mutual funds and other investment portfolios. Co.'s assets under management are sourced approximately 20.0% to 30.0% from each of the following: third-party financial intermediaries that distribute its managed investment portfolios in the U.S. and foreign countries, individual U.S. investors, U.S. defined contribution retirement plans, and institutional investors in the U.S. and foreign countries.

Recent Developments: For the three months ended Mar 31 2005, net income declined 18.0% to $77.3 million compared with $94.3 million in the corresponding year-earlier period. Total revenues fell 14.4% to $306.5 million from $358.0 million the previous year. Operating expenses decreased 12.9% to $182.8 million versus $209.8 million the year before. Net operating income was to $122.9 million, 16.6% less than the prior-year period. As of Mar 31 2005, total assets under Co.'s management amounted to $235.90 billion, an increase of $670.0 million from $235.20 billion at Dec 31 2004.

Prospects: Co. believes its outlook remains strong. Although the year so far has been lackluster at best for the financial markets, Co. continues to be encouraged by business across its distribution channels and strong investment management results. Co.'s corporate earnings and cash flow remains healthy, providing substantial financial flexibility. Also, Co. remains debt free and has cash and net liquid investments of $650.0 million at Mar 31 2005. Meanwhile, Co. expects that its advertising and promotion expenditures in the second quarter of 2005 will decline about 15.0% to 20.0% from the first quarter of 2005 while its expenditures for the full year 2005 will be 10.0% to 15.0% higher than 2004.

Financial Data

(US$ in Thousands)	3 Mos	12/31/2004	12/31/2003	12/31/2002	12/31/2001	12/31/2000	12/31/1999	12/31/1998
Earnings Per Share	2.62	2.51	1.77	1.52	1.52	2.08	1.85	1.34
Cash Flow Per Share	3.32	2.93	2.41	2.19	2.36	2.66	2.46	1.95
Tang Book Value Per Share	8.37	7.96	5.31	3.82	3.35	2.42	6.41	5.11
Dividends Per Share	0.840	0.800	0.700	0.650	0.610	0.540	0.430	0.355
Dividend Payout %	32.06	31.87	39.55	42.76	40.13	25.96	23.24	26.49
Income Statement								
Total Revenue	357,071	1,280,349	998,855	925,829	1,027,496	1,212,327	1,036,379	886,142
Income Before Taxes	149,241	533,783	365,516	309,604	330,589	458,192	414,770	312,814
Income Taxes	54,944	196,523	138,029	115,350	135,078	174,818	155,166	118,676
Net Income	94,297	337,260	227,487	194,254	195,868	269,029	239,404	174,140
Average Shares	136,742	134,135	128,289	127,706	129,045	129,600	129,200	129,952
Balance Sheet								
Total Assets	2,003,706	1,928,825	1,546,577	1,370,433	1,313,115	1,469,459	998,039	796,784
Total Liabilities	249,381	231,525	217,497	236,593	235,290	478,394	227,855	182,480
Stockholders' Equity	1,754,325	1,697,300	1,329,080	1,133,840	1,077,825	991,065	770,184	614,304
Shares Outstanding	130,055	129,607	124,932	122,648	123,088	122,439	120,107	120,183
Statistical Record								
Return on Assets %	19.47	19.36	15.60	14.48	14.08	21.75	26.68	24.14
Return on Equity %	22.32	22.23	18.47	17.57	18.93	30.47	34.58	31.63
Price Range	63.30-44.67	63.13-44.67	47.41-24.30	41.99-21.45	42.69-25.70	48.63-30.19	40.88-26.44	42.44-22.75
P/E Ratio	24.16-17.05	25.15-17.80	26.79-13.73	27.63-14.11	28.08-16.91	23.38-14.51	22.09-14.29	31.67-16.98
Average Yield %	1.56	1.54	1.94	2.02	1.76	1.34	1.25	1.05

Address: 100 East Pratt Street, Baltimore, MD 21202 **Telephone:** 410-345-2000 **Web Site:** www.troweprice.com	**Officers:** George A. Roche - Chmn., Pres., Interim C.F.O. James S. Riepe - Vice-Chmn., V.P. **Transfer Agents:** Wells Fargo Bank Minnesota, N.A., St. Paul, MN	**Investor Contact:** 410-345-2124 **No of Institutions:** 314 **Shares:** 78,464,600 **% Held:** 60.23

TALBOTS, INC.

Exchange	Symbol	Price	52Wk Range	Yield	P/E
NYS	TLB	$29.65 (5/31/2005)	39.81-24.79	1.62	17.44

*7 Year Price Score 90.68 *NYSE Composite Index=100 *12 Month Price Score 93.89

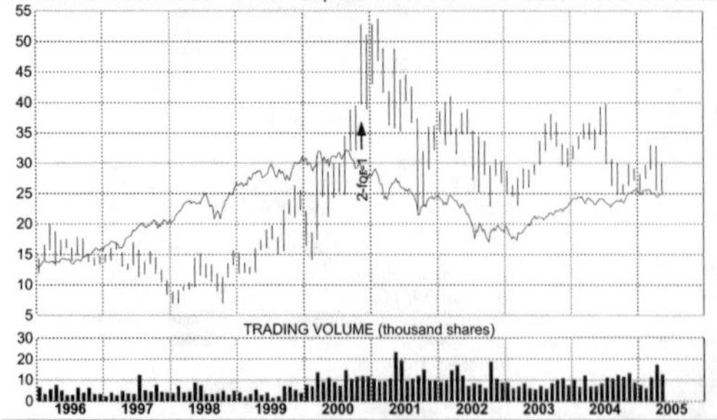

TRADING VOLUME (thousand shares)

Interim Earnings (Per Share)

Qtr.	Apr	Jul	Oct	Jan
2000-01	0.52	0.23	0.54	0.51
2001-02	0.62	0.28	0.58	0.52
2002-03	0.57	0.33	0.63	0.49
2003-04	0.51	0.32	0.60	0.38
2004-05	0.58	0.34	0.50	0.28

Interim Dividends (Per Share)

Amt	Decl	Ex	Rec	Pay
0.11Q	8/10/2004	9/2/2004	9/7/2004	9/20/2004
0.11Q	11/8/2004	12/2/2004	12/6/2004	12/20/2004
0.11Q	3/1/2005	3/10/2005	3/14/2005	3/28/2005
0.12Q	5/26/2005	6/2/2005	6/6/2005	6/20/2005

Indicated Div: $0.48

Valuation Analysis

Forecast P/E	N/A		
Market Cap	$1.6 Billion	Book Value	588.6 Million
Price/Book	2.73	Price/Sales	0.95

Dividend Achiever Status

Rank	67	10 Year Growth Rate	16.93%
Total Years of Dividend Growth			10

Business Summary: Retail - Apparel and Accessory Stores (MIC: 5.8 SIC: 621 NAIC: 48120)

Talbots is a specialty retailer and cataloger of women's, children's and men's classic apparel, accessories and shoes. Talbots offers sportswear, casual wear, dresses, coats, sweaters, accessories and shoes, consisting exclusively of Co.'s own branded merchandise in misses and petites female sizes. Talbots Kids offers clothing and accessories for infants, toddlers, boys and girls. As of Jan 29 2005, Co. operated 1,049 stores in U.S., Canada and U.K. This included 521 Talbots Misses stores, 285 Talbots Petites stores, 41 Talbots Accessories and Shoes stores, 71 Talbots Kids stores, 95 Talbots Woman stores, 11 Talbots Mens stores, one Talbots Collection store and 24 Talbots Outlet stores.

Recent Developments: For the three months ended Apr 30 2005, net income rose 3.1% to $34,519 thousand from net income of $33,464 thousand in the corresponding quarter of the previous year. Revenues were $446,531 thousand, up 8.3% from $412,181 thousand the year before. Operating income was 56,034 thousand versus an income of $53,914 thousand in the prior year, a decrease of 14.7%. Total direct expense was $264,279 thousand versus $237,068 thousand in the prior year, an increase of 11.4%. Total indirect expense was $126,218 thousand versus $121,199 thousand in the prior year, and increase of 4.1%.

Prospects: Regarding the 2005 spring season, Co. is pleased with its customers' early positive response to its new assortments, with February comparable store sales increasing 8.1% year over year. Co. is supporting its merchandise offerings with a comprehensive brand advertising campaign that includes national television and print advertising, complemented with a variety of special traffic driving events. For the full year 2005, Co. expects to open a total of approximately 50 new stores, on top of an increase of 75 new stores in fiscal 2004. In addition, Co.'s 2005 financial plan calls for a modest increase in reported earnings per diluted share compared with 2004.

Financial Data

(US$ in Thousands)	01/29/2005	01/31/2004	02/01/2003	02/02/2002	02/03/2001	01/29/2000	01/30/1999	01/31/1998
Earnings Per Share	1.70	1.81	2.01	2.00	1.80	1.85	1.15	0.18
Cash Flow Per Share	2.83	3.75	3.80	2.60	2.21	2.96	4.29	0.39
Tang Book Value Per Share	8.82	8.91	7.93	7.56	6.90	10.10	8.94	8.48
Dividends Per Share	0.430	0.390	0.350	0.310	0.270	0.230	0.220	0.210
Dividend Payout %	25.29	21.55	17.41	15.50	15.00	12.43	19.13	116.67
Income Statement								
Total Revenue	1,697,843	1,624,339	1,595,325	1,612,513	1,594,996	1,290,923	1,142,246	1,053,806
EBITDA	229,752	237,097	255,180	263,477	237,420	144,945	106,966	58,225
Depn & Amortn	87,637	67,509	59,113	53,461	45,830	43,377	40,035	41,172
Income Before Taxes	140,005	167,493	193,214	204,841	187,321	95,057	59,623	9,493
Income Taxes	44,639	62,810	72,455	77,840	72,119	36,597	22,955	3,655
Net Income	95,366	104,683	120,759	127,001	115,202	58,460	36,668	5,838
Average Shares	56,252	57,901	60,191	63,439	63,995	31,684	31,933	32,436
Balance Sheet								
Current Assets	527,397	496,154	435,898	432,769	506,405	369,786	339,915	360,402
Total Assets	1,062,130	958,392	871,925	831,064	858,596	693,904	657,064	676,433
Current Liabilities	202,638	166,142	147,941	130,292	188,040	143,931	138,394	215,301
Long-Term Obligations	100,000	100,000	100,000	100,000	100,000	100,000	100,000	50,000
Total Liabilities	473,542	342,266	304,249	263,188	307,825	262,572	254,991	279,967
Stockholders' Equity	588,588	616,126	567,676	567,876	550,771	431,332	402,073	396,466
Shares Outstanding	54,123	56,675	57,505	60,382	63,106	30,942	31,258	31,805
Statistical Record								
Return on Assets %	9.47	11.47	14.22	15.07	14.60	8.68	5.51	0.90
Return on Equity %	15.88	17.73	21.33	22.77	23.08	14.07	9.21	1.41
EBITDA Margin %	13.53	14.60	16.00	16.34	14.89	11.23	9.36	5.53
Net Margin %	5.62	6.44	7.57	7.88	7.22	4.53	3.21	0.55
Asset Turnover	1.69	1.78	1.88	1.91	2.02	1.92	1.72	1.63
Current Ratio	2.60	2.99	2.95	3.32	2.69	2.57	2.46	1.67
Debt to Equity	0.17	0.16	0.18	0.18	0.18	0.23	0.25	0.13
Price Range	39.81-24.79	38.15-23.02	41.02-22.90	53.75-22.33	53.50-14.13	26.38-11.81	15.69-6.97	17.00-6.97
P/E Ratio	23.42-14.58	21.08-12.72	20.41-11.39	26.88-11.16	29.72-7.85	14.26-6.39	13.64-6.06	94.44-38.72
Average Yield %	1.38	1.28	1.09	0.81	0.83	1.26	1.91	1.63

Address: One Talbots Drive, Hingham, MA 02043-1586
Telephone: 781-749-7600
Web Site: www.talbots.com

Officers: Arnold B. Zetcher - Chmn., Pres., C.E.O. Harold B. Bosworth - Exec. V.P., Chief Merchandise Off.

Investor Contact: 781-741-7775
No of Institutions: 113
Shares: 21,276,880 **% Held:** 39.31

TANGER FACTORY OUTLET CENTERS, INC.

Exchange	Symbol	Price	52Wk Range	Yield	P/E
NYS	SKT	$24.21 (5/31/2005)	26.48-18.69	5.33	201.75

*7 Year Price Score 138.07 *NYSE Composite Index=100 *12 Month Price Score 98.71

TRADING VOLUME (thousand shares)

Interim Earnings (Per Share)

Qtr.	Mar	Jun	Sep	Dec
2002	0.06	0.10	0.11	0.27
2003	0.10	0.10	0.17	0.23
2004	0.04	0.14	(0.07)	0.16
2005	(0.11)	...	...	...

Interim Dividends (Per Share)

Amt	Decl	Ex	Rec	Pay
0.313Q	10/14/2004	10/27/2004	10/29/2004	11/15/2004
100%	11/29/2004	12/29/2004	12/17/2004	12/28/2004
0.313Q	1/13/2005	1/27/2005	1/31/2005	2/15/2005
0.323Q	3/1/2005	4/27/2005	4/29/2005	5/16/2005

Indicated Div: $1.29 (Div. Reinv. Plan)

Valuation Analysis

Forecast P/E	12.41 (6/1/2005)		
Market Cap	$668.5 Million	Book Value	141.3 Million
Price/Book	4.73	Price/Sales	3.37

Dividend Achiever Status

Rank	295	10 Year Growth Rate	3.30%
Total Years of Dividend Growth			11

Business Summary: Property, Real Estate & Development (MIC: 8.3 SIC: 798 NAIC: 25930)

Tanger Factory Outlet Centers is a fully-integrated, self-administered and self-managed real estate investment trust, focusing exclusively on developing, acquiring, owning, operating and managing factory outlet centers. As of Dec 31 2004, Co. had ownership interests in or management responsibilities for 33 centers with a total gross leasable area of approximately 8.7 million square feet. These centers were approximately 97.0% occupied, contained over 1,900 stores and represented over 400 store brands. Co.'s factory outlet centers and other assets are held by, and all of its operations are conducted by, Tanger Properties Limited Partnership.

Recent Developments: For the quarter ended Mar 31 2005, income from continuing operations decreased 9.7% to $914 thousand from income of $1,012 thousand in the year-earlier quarter. Net loss was $2,929 thousand from net income of $1,012 thousand in the year-earlier quarter. Revenues were $47,991 thousand, up 6.9% from $44,907 thousand the year before. Operating income was $15,777 thousand versus an income of $16,170 thousand in the prior-year quarter, a decrease of 2.4%.

Prospects: Looking ahead, Co. is projecting full-year 2005 diluted earnings per share between $0.56 and $0.60, along with funds from operations in the range of $1.93 to $1.97 per diluted share. Meanwhile, as part of its long-term strategy to dispose of non-core assets and to upgrade its portfolio, Co. completed the sale of its 141,051 square foot outlet center located in Seymour, IN for a total cash sales price of $2.1 million. Separately, Co. continues its pre-development and leasing of four previously announced sites located in Pittsburgh, PA, Deer Park, NY, Charleston, SC and Wisconsin Dells, WI, with expected deliveries during 2006 and 2007.

Financial Data (US$ in Thousands)	3 Mos	12/31/2004	12/31/2003	12/31/2002	12/31/2001	12/31/2000	12/31/1999	12/31/1998
Earnings Per Share	0.12	0.26	0.58	0.54	0.34	0.16	0.87	0.62
Cash Flow Per Share	3.02	3.13	2.23	2.35	2.82	2.42	2.75	2.27
Tang Book Value Per Share	5.12	5.87	6.46	5.00	4.82	5.74	6.84	7.22
Dividends Per Share	1.250	1.245	1.229	1.224	1.219	1.214	1.208	1.175
Dividend Payout %	1,086.96	478.85	210.04	226.62	363.81	783.06	138.79	189.52
Income Statement								
Property Income	47,044	135,222	84,229	79,313	78,089	74,710	72,321	69,274
Non-Property Income	947	59,331	37,743	33,854	32,979	34,111	31,695	28,492
Total Revenue	47,991	194,553	121,972	113,167	111,068	108,821	104,016	97,766
Depn & Amortn	12,496	50,947	30,852	30,198	29,881	27,482	25,829	23,230
Interest Expense	8,228	35,117	26,486	28,460	30,134	27,565	24,239	22,028
Net Income	(2,929)	7,046	12,849	11,007	7,112	4,312	15,588	11,827
Average Shares	27,516	27,261	20,566	17,028	15,896	15,844	15,744	16,018
Balance Sheet								
Total Assets	924,712	936,378	987,437	477,675	476,272	487,408	490,069	471,795
Long-Term Obligations	492,938	488,007	540,319	345,005	358,195	346,843	329,647	302,485
Total Liabilities	528,472	516,951	562,689	363,410	378,395	369,434	349,015	322,432
Stockholders' Equity	141,300	161,133	167,418	90,635	76,371	90,877	107,764	114,039
Shares Outstanding	27,611	27,443	25,921	18,122	15,859	15,837	15,753	15,795
Statistical Record								
Return on Assets %	0.33	0.73	1.75	2.31	1.48	0.88	3.24	2.66
Return on Equity %	1.96	4.28	9.96	13.18	8.50	4.33	14.06	9.44
Net Margin %	(6.10)	3.62	10.53	9.73	6.40	3.96	14.99	12.10
Price Range	26.48-17.68	26.48-17.68	21.18-14.43	15.60-10.43	11.66-9.90	12.44-9.25	13.22-9.41	15.88-9.47
P/E Ratio	220.71-147.29	101.87-67.98	36.52-24.87	28.89-19.31	34.28-29.13	77.73-57.81	15.19-10.81	25.60-15.27
Average Yield %	5.63	5.77	7.16	9.02	11.27	11.19	10.49	8.55

Address: 3200 Northline Avenue, Suite 360, Greensboro, NC 27408
Telephone: 336-292-3010
Web Site: www.tangeroutlet.com

Officers: Stanley K. Tanger - Chmn., C.E.O. Steven B. Tanger - Pres., C.O.O. **Transfer Agents:** EquiServe Trust Company NA, Providence, RI

Investor Contact: 336-292-3010
No of Institutions: 103
Shares: 16,521,566 **% Held:** 60.20

TARGET CORP

Exchange	Symbol	Price	52Wk Range	Yield	P/E
NYS	TGT	$53.70 (5/31/2005)	53.70-40.42	0.60	15.30

*7 Year Price Score 118.74 *NYSE Composite Index=100 *12 Month Price Score 99.43

Interim Earnings (Per Share)

Qtr.	Apr	Jul	Oct	Jan
2000-01	0.26	0.28	0.24	0.60
2001-02	0.28	0.30	0.20	0.72
2002-03	0.38	0.38	0.30	0.75
2003-04	0.38	0.39	0.33	0.91
2004-05	0.48	1.54	0.60	0.89

Interim Dividends (Per Share)

Amt	Decl	Ex	Rec	Pay
0.08Q	6/9/2004	8/18/2004	8/20/2004	9/10/2004
0.08Q	9/8/2004	11/17/2004	11/20/2004	12/10/2004
0.08Q	1/13/2005	2/16/2005	2/20/2005	3/10/2005
0.08Q	3/10/2005	5/18/2005	5/20/2005	6/10/2005

Indicated Div: $0.32 (Div. Reinv. Plan)

Valuation Analysis

Forecast P/E	18.11 (6/2/2005)		
Market Cap	$47.8 Billion	Book Value	13.0 Billion
Price/Book	3.67	Price/Sales	1.02

Dividend Achiever Status

Rank	216	10 Year Growth Rate	7.92%
Total Years of Dividend Growth			33

Business Summary: Retail - General (MIC: 5.2 SIC: 331 NAIC: 52990)

Target is an operator of large-format general merchandise discount stores in the U.S. and an on-line business. Co.'s national discount store chain offers low prices with stores selling hardlines and fashion softgoods. Also, Co.'s credit card operations represent an integral component of its retail business. Co.'s principle competitors include national and local departments, specialty, off-price, discount, grocery and drug store chains, independent retail stores and Internet businesses that handle similar lines of merchandise. As of Dec 31 2004, Co. operated 1,308 stores in 47 states.

Recent Developments: For the three months ended Apr 30 2005, income from continuing operations increased 26.4% to $494,000 thousand from income of 392,000 thousand in the equivalent quarter of the previous year. Net income increased 14.6% to $494,000 thousand from net income of $432,000 thousand the year before. Revenues were $11,477,000 thousand, up 12.7% from $10,180,000 thousand a year earlier. Operating income was $796,000 thousand versus $630,000 thousand in the prior year, an increase of 26.6%. Total direct expense increased 11.6% to $7,556,000 thousand, while total indirect expense increased 14.2% to $3,014,000 thousand.

Prospects: Co. is experiencing strong growth and continued market share gains. Revenue growth is being driven primarily by increases in comparable-store sales, combined with contributions from new store expansion and Co.'s credit card operations. Also, Co.'s gross margin rate is showing considerable improvement primarily due to an increase in markup. Meanwhile, in connection with the 2004 sale of Mervyn's. Co. is supplying transition services for a fee until Aug 2007 or the date of which an alternative long-term solution for providing these services is in place.

Financial Data

(US$ in Thousands)	01/29/2005	01/31/2004	02/01/2003	02/02/2002	02/03/2001	01/29/2000	01/30/1999	01/31/1998
Earnings Per Share	3.51	2.01	1.81	1.50	1.38	1.23	0.99	0.80
Cash Flow Per Share	4.24	3.48	1.76	2.22	2.07	2.56	2.12	2.08
Tang Book Value Per Share	14.63	12.14	10.38	8.68	7.15	6.43	6.12	4.77
Dividends Per Share	0.300	0.260	0.240	0.220	0.210	0.200	0.180	0.165
Dividend Payout %	8.55	12.94	13.26	14.67	15.22	16.33	18.18	20.75
Income Statement								
Total Revenue	46,839,000	48,163,000	43,917,000	39,888,000	36,903,000	33,702,000	30,951,000	27,757,000
EBITDA	4,860,000	4,839,000	4,476,000	3,759,000	3,418,000	3,183,000	2,734,000	2,435,000
Depn & Amortn	1,259,000	1,320,000	1,212,000	1,079,000	940,000	854,000	780,000	693,000
Income Before Taxes	3,031,000	2,960,000	2,676,000	2,216,000	2,053,000	1,936,000	1,556,000	1,326,000
Income Taxes	1,146,000	1,119,000	1,022,000	842,000	789,000	751,000	594,000	524,000
Net Income	3,198,000	1,841,000	1,654,000	1,368,000	1,264,000	1,144,000	935,000	751,000
Average Shares	912,100	917,100	914,000	909,800	913,000	931,400	934,600	927,400
Balance Sheet								
Current Assets	13,922,000	12,928,000	11,935,000	9,648,000	7,304,000	6,483,000	6,005,000	5,561,000
Total Assets	32,293,000	31,392,000	28,603,000	24,154,000	19,490,000	17,143,000	15,666,000	14,191,000
Current Liabilities	8,220,000	8,314,000	7,523,000	7,054,000	6,301,000	5,850,000	5,057,000	4,556,000
Long-Term Obligations	9,034,000	10,217,000	10,186,000	8,088,000	5,634,000	4,521,000	4,452,000	4,425,000
Total Liabilities	19,264,000	20,327,000	19,160,000	16,294,000	12,971,000	11,281,000	10,355,000	9,731,000
Stockholders' Equity	13,029,000	11,065,000	9,443,000	7,860,000	6,519,000	5,862,000	5,311,000	4,460,000
Shares Outstanding	890,643	911,808	909,802	905,165	911,682	911,682	823,618	875,600
Statistical Record								
Return on Assets %	10.07	6.15	6.29	6.29	6.79	6.99	6.28	5.49
Return on Equity %	26.62	18.00	19.17	19.08	20.09	20.53	19.19	18.36
EBITDA Margin %	10.38	10.05	10.19	9.42	9.26	9.44	8.83	8.77
Net Margin %	6.83	3.82	3.77	3.43	3.43	3.39	3.02	2.71
Asset Turnover	1.48	1.61	1.67	1.83	1.98	2.06	2.08	2.03
Current Ratio	1.69	1.55	1.59	1.37	1.16	1.11	1.19	1.22
Debt to Equity	0.69	0.92	1.08	1.03	0.86	0.77	0.84	0.99
Price Range	52.43-38.59	41.54-26.06	45.72-26.15	44.41-26.68	38.59-22.75	37.88-27.63	31.88-16.88	18.42-9.41
P/E Ratio	14.94-10.99	20.67-12.97	25.26-14.45	29.61-17.79	27.97-16.49	30.79-22.46	32.20-17.05	23.03-11.76
Average Yield %	0.65	0.72	0.66	0.60	0.69	0.62	0.80	1.18

Address: 1000 Nicollet Mall, Minneapolis, MN 55403
Telephone: 612-304-6073
Web Site: www.target.com

Officers: Robert J. Ulrich - Chmn., C.E.O. Gerald L. Storch - Vice-Chmn. **Transfer Agents:** EquiServe, Jersey City, NJ

Investor Contact: 612-370-6736
No of Institutions: 714
Shares: 742,128,128 **% Held:** 82.88

TCF FINANCIAL CORP.

Exchange	Symbol	Price	52Wk Range	Yield	P/E
NYS	TCB	$25.88 (5/31/2005)	32.53-24.84	3.28	13.69

*7 Year Price Score 126.34 *NYSE Composite Index=100 *12 Month Price Score 86.93

Interim Earnings (Per Share)

Qtr.	Mar	Jun	Sep	Dec
2002	0.38	0.39	0.40	0.41
2003	0.41	0.42	0.26	0.42
2004	0.44	0.47	0.45	0.50
2005	0.47	...	...	...

Interim Dividends (Per Share)

Amt	Decl	Ex	Rec	Pay
100%	8/3/2004	9/7/2004	8/13/2004	9/3/2004
0.188Q	10/18/2004	11/3/2004	11/5/2004	11/30/2004
0.212Q	1/13/2005	2/2/2005	2/4/2005	2/28/2005
0.212Q	4/25/2005	5/4/2005	5/6/2005	5/31/2005

Indicated Div: $0.85 (Div. Reinv. Plan)

Valuation Analysis

Forecast P/E	13.32 (6/2/2005)		
Market Cap	$3.5 Billion	Book Value	926.3 Million
Price/Book	3.78	Price/Sales	3.09

Dividend Achiever Status

Rank	39	10 Year Growth Rate	19.62%
Total Years of Dividend Growth			13

Business Summary: Commercial Banking (MIC: 8.1 SIC: 021 NAIC: 22110)

TCF Financial, with total assets of $12.34 billion and total deposits of $7.96 billion as of Dec 31 2004, is a bank holding company. As of Dec 31 2004, Co. operated 430 retail banking branches, including 248 full-service supermarket branches, in Illinois, Indiana, Michigan, Minnesota, Wisconsin and Colorado. Co.'s products include commercial, small business, consumer and residential mortgage loans and deposit products, leasing and equipment finance, securities brokerage and investment and insurance services. Co. primarily focuses on serving lower- and middle-income customers and small- to medium-sized businesses in its markets.

Recent Developments: For the quarter ended Mar 31 2005, net income increased 4.6% to $63,465 thousand from net income of $60,661 thousand a year earlier. Net interest income was $129,053 thousand, up 8.9% from $118,493 thousand the year before. Provision for loan credits was $3,436 thousand versus losses of $1,160 thousand in the prior year. Non-interest income slipped 2.7 % to $112,148 thousand, while non-interest expense advanced 5.2% to $148,111 thousand.

Prospects: Co. is seeing solid earnings despite a difficult interest rate and competitive environment. While Co.'s total banking fees are flat, Co. is benefiting from improved margin, maintaining its credit quality and keeping expenses under control. In addition, Co. is enjoying strong growth in average home equity and commercial real estate loan balances and leasing and equipment finance average balances, as well as deposit balances in its Premier Checking, Plus eChecking and Premier Savings products. Meanwhile, Co. is continuing with new branch expansion program and expects to open 20 new traditional branches, seven new supermarket branches, and two new campus branches during the remainder of 2005.

Financial Data

(US$ in Thousands)	3 Mos	12/31/2004	12/31/2003	12/31/2002	12/31/2001	12/31/2000	12/31/1999	12/31/1998
Earnings Per Share	1.89	1.86	1.52	1.58	1.35	1.18	1.00	0.88
Cash Flow Per Share	2.70	3.23	3.10	2.21	0.96	1.28	2.43	1.11
Tang Book Value Per Share	5.40	5.50	5.09	5.15	4.95	4.64	3.89	3.87
Dividends Per Share	0.775	0.750	0.650	0.575	0.500	0.412	0.362	0.306
Dividend Payout %	41.01	40.32	42.62	36.51	37.04	35.11	36.25	34.80
Income Statement								
Interest Income	171,345	622,809	641,519	733,363	826,609	826,681	752,101	748,894
Interest Expense	42,292	130,918	160,374	234,138	345,387	388,145	327,888	323,160
Net Interest Income	129,053	491,891	481,145	499,225	481,222	438,536	424,213	425,734
Provision for Losses	(3,436)	10,947	12,532	22,006	20,878	14,772	16,923	23,280
Non-Interest Income	112,148	490,466	463,624	416,880	351,625	312,384	288,909	256,174
Non-Interest Expense	144,450	586,934	560,109	538,369	501,996	462,528	452,798	428,700
Income Before Taxes	96,526	384,476	327,783	357,692	329,834	302,838	273,091	265,249
Income Taxes	33,061	129,483	111,905	124,761	122,512	116,593	107,052	109,070
Net Income	63,465	254,993	215,878	232,931	207,322	186,245	166,039	156,179
Average Shares	134,391	137,174	141,540	147,881	153,685	158,777	166,142	177,832
Balance Sheet								
Net Loans & Leases	9,475,695	9,306,779	8,271,159	8,044,120	8,169,174	8,480,030	7,839,988	7,061,165
Total Assets	12,733,208	12,340,567	11,319,015	12,202,069	11,358,715	11,197,462	10,661,716	10,164,594
Total Deposits	8,395,013	7,962,195	7,611,749	7,709,988	7,098,958	6,891,824	6,584,835	6,715,146
Total Liabilities	11,806,865	11,382,149	10,398,157	11,225,049	10,441,682	10,287,242	9,852,734	9,319,092
Stockholders' Equity	926,343	958,418	920,858	977,020	917,033	910,220	808,982	845,502
Shares Outstanding	135,269	137,186	140,952	147,711	153,863	160,578	163,882	171,138
Statistical Record								
Return on Assets %	2.11	2.15	1.84	1.98	1.84	1.70	1.59	1.57
Return on Equity %	27.25	27.06	22.75	24.60	22.69	21.61	20.07	17.36
Net Interest Margin %	75.32	78.98	75.00	68.07	58.22	53.05	56.40	56.85
Efficiency Ratio %	50.95	52.72	50.68	46.80	42.61	40.61	43.50	42.65
Loans to Deposits	1.13	1.17	1.09	1.04	1.15	1.23	1.19	1.05
Price Range	32.53-24.40	32.53-24.15	26.78-18.52	27.20-17.61	25.35-16.85	22.66-9.31	15.13-11.00	18.38-8.28
P/E Ratio	17.21-12.91	17.49-12.98	17.62-12.19	17.21-11.14	18.78-12.48	19.20-7.89	15.13-11.00	20.88-9.41
Average Yield %	2.66	2.65	2.91	2.43	2.36	2.78	2.67	2.14

Address: 200 Lake Street East, Mail Code EX0-03-A, Wayzata, MN 55391-1693
Telephone: 612-661-6500
Web Site: www.tcfexpress.com

Officers: William A. Cooper - Chmn., C.E.O. Lynn A. Nagorske - Pres., C.O.O. **Transfer Agents:** EquiServe Trust Company, N.A., Providence, RI

Investor Contact: 952-745-2755
No of Institutions: 235
Shares: 84,175,984 **% Held:** 61.67

TD BANKNORTH INC

Exchange	Symbol	Price	52Wk Range	Yield	P/E
NYS	BNK	$29.98 (5/31/2005)	36.60-29.98	2.67	21.72

Interim Earnings (Per Share)

Qtr.	Mar	Jun	Sep	Dec
2001	0.39	0.43	0.45	0.41
2002	0.45	0.50	0.51	0.51
2003	0.51	0.53	0.55	0.56
2004	0.54	0.55	0.55	0.10
2005	0.18	...	...	...

Interim Dividends (Per Share)

Amt	Decl	Ex	Rec	Pay
0.20Q	7/27/2004	8/4/2004	8/6/2004	8/16/2004
0.20Q	10/26/2004	11/3/2004	11/5/2004	11/15/2004
0.20Q	1/25/2005	2/2/2005	2/4/2005	2/14/2005
0.20Q	5/3/2005	5/11/2005	5/13/2005	5/23/2005

Indicated Div: $0.80

Valuation Analysis

Forecast P/E	N/A		
Market Cap	$6.4 Billion	Book Value	3.2 Billion
Price/Book	2.02	Price/Sales	4.02

Dividend Achiever Status

Rank	36	10 Year Growth Rate	20.74%
Total Years of Dividend Growth			10

Business Summary: Commercial Banking (MIC: 8.1 SIC: 022 NAIC: 22110)

TD Banknorth is a banking and financial services company and a majority-owned subsidiary of TD Bank Financial Group. At Mar 31 2005, Co. had $32.10 billion in total assets and provided financial services to over 1.3 million households in the Northeast. Co.'s banking subsidiary, Banknorth, N.A., operates banking divisions in Connecticut , Maine, Massachusetts, New Hampshire, New York, and Vermont. Co. and Banknorth, N.A. also operate subsidiaries and divisions in insurance, wealth management, merchant services, mortgage banking, government banking and other financial services and offer investment products in association with PrimeVest Financial Services.

Recent Developments: For the first quarter ended Mar 31 2005, Co. reported net income of $34.1 million versus $90.3 million in the corresponding quarter of 2004. Net interest income was $255.1 million compared with $217.6 million in the equivalent period a year earlier. Provision for loan and lease losses was $2.1 million in 2005 and $9.5 million in 2004. Non-interest income amounted to $23.2 million, down 73.7% from $88.2 million a year earlier. Non-interest expense jumped to $223.1 million from $159.7 million the year before. Results for the prior year reflect the operations BankNorth Group, Inc., the predecessor to Co.

Prospects: The acquisition of 51.0% of the outstanding shares of Co. by the Toronto Dominion Bank's TD Bank Financial Group closed on Mar 1 2005. Following the transaction, Co. changed its name to TD Banknorth and reincorporate in Delaware. Co. expects the combination will provide it with greater resources to continue with its growth strategy in New England and beyond. Although the transaction was not predicated on synergies, Co. continues to identify both expense and revenue-related synergies, including potential synergies of $7.0 million in 2005 and $14.0 million in 2006.

Financial Data

(US$ in Thousands)	12/31/2004	12/31/2003	12/31/2002	12/31/2001	12/31/2000	12/31/1999	12/31/1998	12/31/1997
Earnings Per Share	1.75	2.15	1.99	1.68	1.32	1.37	1.12	1.29
Cash Flow Per Share	2.60	3.07	2.64	1.99	1.90	6.05	0.17	(3.90)
Tang Book Value Per Share	9.82	8.37	9.06	8.69	7.94	6.76	6.83	5.52
Dividends Per Share	0.790	0.700	0.580	0.525	0.500	0.470	0.440	0.380
Dividend Payout %	45.14	32.56	29.15	31.25	37.88	34.31	39.29	29.34
Income Statement								
Interest Income	1,257,005	1,192,969	1,235,117	1,263,789	1,330,287	907,935	712,956	442,212
Interest Expense	323,623	352,138	438,600	583,825	717,276	461,688	347,527	196,023
Net Interest Income	933,382	840,831	796,517	679,964	613,011	446,247	365,429	246,189
Provision for Losses	40,340	42,301	44,314	41,889	23,819	14,100	13,423	...
Non-Interest Income	339,799	367,159	274,508	240,505	211,188	129,188	104,795	56,938
Non-Interest Expense	765,101	641,270	579,392	509,396	511,853	346,874	309,919	188,006
Income Before Taxes	467,740	524,419	447,319	369,184	288,527	214,461	146,882	115,121
Income Taxes	163,097	173,660	148,681	126,202	96,793	72,039	46,292	41,720
Net Income	304,643	350,759	298,638	238,795	191,734	142,422	100,590	73,401
Average Shares	174,158	163,520	149,829	141,802	145,194	104,112	89,452	56,725
Balance Sheet								
Net Loans & Leases	18,349,842	16,113,675	13,847,735	12,525,493	10,692,112	6,736,788	6,098,487	4,421,280
Total Assets	28,687,810	26,453,735	23,418,941	21,076,586	18,233,810	13,919,528	10,102,459	6,795,337
Total Deposits	19,227,581	17,901,185	15,664,601	14,221,049	12,107,256	8,114,757	6,981,245	4,802,640
Total Liabilities	25,511,696	23,933,216	21,355,456	19,287,471	16,804,178	12,999,776	9,240,535	6,220,271
Stockholders' Equity	3,176,114	2,520,519	2,063,485	1,789,115	1,330,857	850,977	761,924	475,066
Shares Outstanding	179,297	162,187	150,578	151,220	141,244	102,181	87,545	55,474
Statistical Record								
Return on Assets %	1.10	1.41	1.34	1.21	1.19	1.19	1.19	1.20
Return on Equity %	10.67	15.30	15.50	15.31	17.53	17.66	16.26	16.10
Net Interest Margin %	74.25	70.48	64.49	53.80	46.08	49.15	51.26	55.67
Efficiency Ratio %	47.91	41.10	38.38	33.86	33.21	33.45	37.90	37.67
Loans to Deposits	0.95	0.90	0.88	0.88	0.88	0.83	0.87	0.92
Price Range	36.60-30.63	33.42-20.95	27.31-20.95	24.30-18.31	21.06-10.44	20.00-14.63	26.50-13.81	23.50-13.09
P/E Ratio	20.91-17.50	15.54-9.74	13.72-10.53	14.46-10.90	15.96-7.91	14.60-10.68	23.66-12.33	18.22-10.15
Average Yield %	2.37	2.65	2.40	2.46	3.17	2.65	2.18	2.11

Address: Two Portland Square, Portland, ME 04112-9540
Telephone: 207-761-8500
Web Site: www.banknorth.com

Officers: William J. Ryan - Chmn., Pres., C.E.O. Peter J. Verrill - Sr. Exec. V.P., C.O.O. **Transfer Agents:** American Stock Transfer &Trust Company

Investor Contact: 207-761-8517
No of Institutions: 312
Shares: 103,250,352 **% Held:** 55.10

TELEFLEX INCORPORATED

Exchange	Symbol	Price	52Wk Range	Yield	P/E
NYS	TFX	$55.95 (5/31/2005)	56.42-40.72	1.79	119.04

Interim Earnings (Per Share)

Qtr.	Mar	Jun	Sep	Dec
2002	0.77	0.84	0.66	0.88
2003	0.74	0.80	0.45	0.74
2004	0.73	0.84	0.43	(1.76)
2005	0.95	...	...	...

Interim Dividends (Per Share)

Amt	Decl	Ex	Rec	Pay
0.22Q	8/4/2004	8/23/2004	8/25/2004	9/15/2004
0.22Q	11/8/2004	11/22/2004	11/25/2004	12/15/2004
0.22Q	2/8/2005	2/23/2005	2/25/2005	3/15/2005
0.25Q	4/29/2005	5/23/2005	5/25/2005	6/15/2005

Indicated Div: $1.00 (Div. Reinv. Plan)

Valuation Analysis

Forecast P/E	16.46 (6/2/2005)		
Market Cap	$2.3 Billion	Book Value	1.1 Billion
Price/Book	2.01	Price/Sales	0.92

Dividend Achiever Status

Rank	126	**10 Year Growth Rate**	12.71%
Total Years of Dividend Growth			27

Business Summary: Medical Instruments & Equipment (MIC: 9.6 SIC: 841 NAIC: 39112)

Teleflex operates in three segments. Commercial Products designs and manufactures proprietary mechanical and electrical/electronic controls for the automotive market; mechanical, electrical and hydraulic controls, and electronics for the marine market; and proprietary products for fluid transfer and industrial applications. Medical Products manufactures and distributes a broad range of invasive disposable and reusable devices for selected medical care markets. Aerospace Products designs and manufactures cargo handling systems and containers for aviation, and provide surface treatments, repair services and manufactured components for the aerospace and turbine engine markets.

Recent Developments: For the quarter ended Mar 27 2005, income from continuing operations decreased 21.0% to $24,979 thousand from income of $31,595 thousand a year earlier. Net income increased 31.3% to $38,726 thousand from net income of $29,472 thousand a year earlier. Revenues were $626,029 thousand, up 7.9% from $579,689 thousand the year before. Operating income was $50,291 thousand versus an income of $53,620 thousand in the prior year, a decrease of 6.3%. Total direct expense was $452,054 thousand versus $415,299 thousand in the prior year, an increase of 8.8%. Total indirect expense was $116,390 thousand versus $110,770 thousand in the prior year, an increase of 5.0%.

Prospects: On Feb 28 2005, Co. announced that it has completed the sale of its Sermatech International business, which had revenues of approximately $85.0 million in 2004, to Arsenal Capital Partners. Looking ahead, Co. is projecting full-year 2005 earnings of between $2.76 and $3.00 per diluted share, including one-time charges. For 2005, operating margins are expected to be positively affected by cost benefits stemming from Co.'s ongoing restructuring and divestiture program, the integration of HudsonRCI, and the positive impact of portfolio changes in 2004.

Financial Data
(US$ in Thousands)

	3 Mos	12/26/2004	12/28/2003	12/29/2002	12/30/2001	12/31/2000	12/26/1999	12/27/1998
Earnings Per Share	0.47	0.24	2.73	3.15	2.86	2.83	2.47	2.15
Cash Flow Per Share	7.30	6.35	5.70	5.12	4.87	4.88	3.55	3.53
Tang Book Value Per Share	15.10	14.49	19.42	16.61	19.99	18.01	15.85	14.21
Dividends Per Share	0.880	0.860	0.780	0.710	0.660	0.580	0.505	0.445
Dividend Payout %	188.03	358.33	28.57	22.54	23.08	20.49	20.45	20.70
Income Statement								
Total Revenue	626,029	2,485,378	2,282,435	2,076,229	1,905,004	1,764,482	1,601,069	1,437,578
EBITDA	76,065	253,619	282,180	267,605	252,096	235,631	210,145	184,865
Depn & Amortn	25,774	114,133	104,352	95,117	92,401	77,417	67,389	60,105
Income Before Taxes	39,203	102,368	151,491	172,488	159,695	158,214	142,756	124,760
Income Taxes	9,526	14,351	42,388	47,222	47,384	48,990	47,536	42,210
Net Income	38,726	9,517	109,103	125,266	112,311	109,224	95,220	82,550
Average Shares	40,699	40,495	39,942	39,786	39,280	38,633	38,525	38,425
Balance Sheet								
Current Assets	1,163,922	1,148,442	1,006,187	837,895	747,477	662,038	604,940	616,942
Total Assets	2,570,006	2,634,436	2,110,613	1,813,384	1,635,020	1,401,288	1,263,444	1,215,917
Current Liabilities	485,791	535,247	612,671	498,483	495,426	383,872	329,412	311,479
Long-Term Obligations	654,090	685,912	229,882	240,123	228,180	220,557	246,191	275,581
Total Liabilities	1,376,622	1,459,225	1,048,311	901,103	856,877	710,866	660,880	681,467
Stockholders' Equity	1,131,284	1,109,733	1,062,302	912,281	778,143	690,422	602,564	534,450
Shares Outstanding	40,628	40,424	39,795	39,398	38,932	38,344	38,018	37,615
Statistical Record								
Return on Assets %	0.81	0.40	5.58	7.29	7.42	8.07	7.70	7.21
Return on Equity %	1.72	0.88	11.08	14.86	15.34	16.62	16.80	16.59
EBITDA Margin %	12.15	10.20	12.36	12.89	13.23	13.35	13.13	12.86
Net Margin %	6.19	0.38	4.78	6.03	5.90	6.19	5.95	5.74
Asset Turnover	1.05	1.05	1.17	1.21	1.26	1.30	1.30	1.26
Current Ratio	2.40	2.15	1.64	1.68	1.51	1.72	1.84	1.98
Debt to Equity	0.58	0.62	0.22	0.26	0.29	0.32	0.41	0.52
Price Range	52.60-40.72	54.82-40.72	49.95-34.24	58.57-40.92	50.98-35.71	44.69-26.94	50.38-29.69	45.50-30.00
P/E Ratio	111.91-86.64	228.42-169.67	18.30-12.54	18.59-12.99	17.83-12.49	15.79-9.52	20.39-12.02	21.16-13.95
Average Yield %	1.86	1.82	1.83	1.44	1.49	1.67	1.24	1.14

Address: 630 West Germantown Pike, Suite 450, Plymouth Meeting, PA 19462 **Telephone:** 610-834-6301 **Web Site:** www.teleflex.com	**Officers:** Lennox K. Black - Chmn. John J. Sickler - Vice-Chmn. **Transfer Agents:** American Stock Transfer & Trust Company, New York, NY	**Investor Contact:** 610-834-6362 **No of Institutions:** 203 **Shares:** 24,756,540 **% Held:** 61.09

TELEPHONE AND DATA SYSTEMS, INC.

Exchange	Symbol	Price	52Wk Range	Yield	P/E
ASE	TDS	$38.75 (5/31/2005)	44.31-34.46	0.90	45.59

***7 Year Price Score 91.31** *NYSE Composite Index=100 ***12 Month Price Score 97.86**

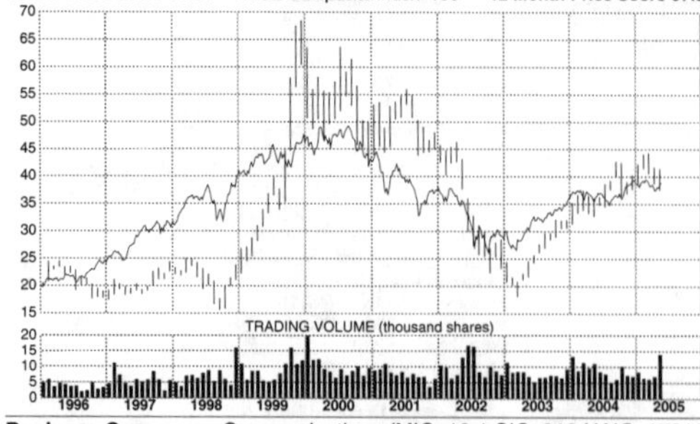

Interim Earnings (Per Share)

Qtr.	Mar	Jun	Sep	Dec
2002	0.23	(16.24)	(0.33)	(0.44)
2003	(0.09)	0.35	0.58	0.22
2004	0.34	0.72	0.43	(0.65)
2005	0.35	...	...	...

Interim Dividends (Per Share)

Amt	Decl	Ex	Rec	Pay
0.165Q	8/3/2004	9/14/2004	9/16/2004	9/30/2004
0.165Q	11/15/2004	12/14/2004	12/16/2004	12/30/2004
0.175Q	2/25/2005	3/14/2005	3/16/2005	3/31/2005
0.087Q	5/18/2005	6/14/2005	6/16/2005	6/30/2005

Indicated Div: $0.35 (Div. Reinv. Plan)

Valuation Analysis

Forecast P/E	24.75 (6/1/2005)		
Market Cap	$2.2 Billion	Book Value	3.2 Billion
Price/Book	0.70	Price/Sales	0.59

Dividend Achiever Status

Rank	243	10 Year Growth Rate	6.25%
Total Years of Dividend Growth			30

Business Summary: Communications (MIC: 10.1 SIC: 812 NAIC: 17212)

Telephone and Data Systems is a diversified telecommunications service company with wireless telephone and wireline telephone operations. At Dec 31 2004, Co. served approximately 6.1 million customers in 36 states, including 4.9 million wireless customers and 1.2 million wireline telephone equivalent access lines. Co. conducts substantially all of its wireless operations through its 82.0%-owned subsidiary, United States Cellular Corporation. Co. conducts its wireline telephone operations through its wholly owned subsidiary, TDS Telecommunications Corporation.

Recent Developments: For the quarter ended Mar 31 2005, net income increased 4.1% to $20,545 thousand from net income of $19,732 thousand in the year-earlier quarter. Revenues were $928,166 thousand, up 6.6% from $870,512 thousand the year before. Total direct expense was $852,726 thousand versus $797,345 thousand in the prior-year quarter, an increase of 6.9%. Total indirect expense was $518,862 thousand versus $485,952 thousand in the prior-year quarter, an increase of 6.8%.

Prospects: Co. anticipates full-year 2005 service revenues of approximately $2.90 billion at U.S. Cellular stemming from continued growth in U.S. Cellular's customer base and the continued marketing of data-related wireless services in its markets. U.S. Cellular plans to build out its network into unserved portions of its licensed areas, and expects to begin sales and marketing operations in the St. Louis area in the third quarter of 2005 and in other areas in subsequent years. Meanwhile, Co. is targeting full-year 2005 revenues of between $895.0 million and $915.0 million at TDS Telecom. Separately, Co. expects capital expenditures in the range of $720.0 million to $775.0 million during 2005.

Financial Data

(US$ in Thousands)	3 Mos	12/31/2004	12/31/2003	12/31/2002	12/31/2001	12/31/2000	12/31/1999	12/31/1998
Earnings Per Share	0.85	0.84	1.05	(16.79)	(3.38)	36.88	3.67	1.03
Cash Flow Per Share	13.64	13.01	15.95	13.53	9.30	12.57	7.81	5.84
Tang Book Value Per Share	40.95	19.39	17.23	14.78	31.34	43.70	18.80	13.99
Dividends Per Share	0.670	0.660	0.620	0.580	0.540	0.500	0.460	0.440
Dividend Payout %	78.82	78.57	59.05	...	...	1.36	12.53	42.72
Income Statement								
Total Revenue	928,166	3,720,389	3,445,216	2,985,366	2,588,542	2,326,856	1,963,098	1,805,725
EBITDA	...	946,385	892,361	(956,675)	331,090	807,412	964,309	628,896
Depn & Amortn	168,817	667,956	595,732	510,445	450,019	399,143	353,322	409,477
Income Before Taxes	...	149,346	178,392	(1,555,669)	(172,000)	346,433	542,327	133,705
Income Taxes	16,148	78,651	79,892	(577,000)	(44,908)	149,481	228,176	69,297
Net Income	20,545	49,004	61,490	(984,371)	(198,055)	2,237,002	229,961	64,408
Average Shares	57,823	57,567	57,875	58,644	58,661	60,636	62,736	60,982
Balance Sheet								
Net PPE	3,357,321	3,385,481	3,350,986	3,196,243	2,558,031	2,186,025	2,095,889	2,672,589
Total Assets	10,692,118	10,993,841	10,171,238	9,602,028	8,046,792	8,634,609	5,375,828	5,527,545
Long-Term Obligations	3,681,210	1,974,599	1,994,913	1,641,624	1,507,764	1,172,987	1,279,877	1,553,096
Total Liabilities	7,485,881	7,799,229	7,063,219	6,542,451	4,520,426	4,690,715	2,883,722	3,263,652
Stockholders' Equity	3,202,373	3,190,748	3,104,155	3,052,623	3,518,924	3,936,067	2,483,101	2,237,908
Shares Outstanding	57,550	57,436	57,034	58,678	58,569	58,688	61,133	61,177
Statistical Record								
Return on Assets %	0.48	0.46	0.62	N.M.	N.M.	31.85	4.22	1.23
Return on Equity %	1.57	1.55	2.00	N.M.	N.M.	69.51	9.74	3.06
EBITDA Margin %	...	25.44	25.90	N.M.	12.79	34.70	49.12	34.83
Net Margin %	2.21	1.32	1.78	(32.97)	(7.65)	96.14	11.71	3.57
PPE Turnover	1.13	1.10	1.05	1.04	1.09	1.08	0.82	0.70
Asset Turnover	0.36	0.35	0.35	0.34	0.31	0.33	0.36	0.34
Debt to Equity	1.15	0.62	0.64	0.54	0.43	0.30	0.52	0.69
Price Range	44.31-32.76	42.74-31.31	32.20-18.12	46.30-22.39	56.00-43.83	63.67-41.79	68.43-22.23	25.03-15.62
P/E Ratio	52.13-38.55	50.89-37.28	30.67-17.25	...	...	1.73-1.13	18.65-6.06	24.30-15.16
Average Yield %	1.74	1.79	2.40	1.69	1.09	0.93	1.18	2.07

Address: 30 North LaSalle Street, Suite 4000, Chicago, IL 60602
Telephone: 312-630-1900
Web Site: www.teldta.com

Officers: Walter C.D. Carlson - Chmn. LeRoy T. Carlson Jr. - Pres., C.E.O. **Transfer Agents:** Computershare Investor Services, Chicago, IL

Investor Contact: 312-592-5341
No of Institutions: 196
Shares: 45,644,212 **% Held:** 79.41

TENNANT CO.

Exchange	Symbol	Price	52Wk Range	Yield	P/E
NYS	TNC	$37.30 (5/31/2005)	42.07-34.83	2.36	23.76

*7 Year Price Score 91.18 *NYSE Composite Index=100 *12 Month Price Score 91.79

TRADING VOLUME (thousand shares)

Interim Earnings (Per Share)

Qtr.	Mar	Jun	Sep	Dec
2002	(0.15)	0.32	0.30	0.44
2003	0.28	0.36	0.36	0.56
2004	0.28	0.41	0.11	0.66
2005	0.39	...	...	...

Interim Dividends (Per Share)

Amt	Decl	Ex	Rec	Pay
0.22Q	8/18/2004	8/27/2004	8/31/2004	9/15/2004
0.22Q	11/10/2004	11/26/2004	11/30/2004	12/15/2004
0.22Q	2/16/2005	2/24/2005	2/28/2005	3/15/2005
0.22Q	5/5/2005	5/26/2005	5/31/2005	6/15/2005

Indicated Div: $0.88 (Div. Reinv. Plan)

Valuation Analysis

Forecast P/E 18.51 (6/1/2005)
Market Cap $335.9 Million Book Value 174.4 Million
Price/Book 1.93 Price/Sales 0.65

Dividend Achiever Status

Rank 301 **10 Year Growth Rate** 2.84%
Total Years of Dividend Growth 32

Business Summary: Purpose Machinery (MIC: 11.13 SIC: 589 NAIC: 33319)

Tennant designs, manufactures and markets cleaning products. Co.'s floor maintenance equipment, outdoor cleaning equipment, coatings and related products are used to clean factories, office buildings, parking lots and streets, airports, hospitals, schools, warehouses and shopping centers, among others. Customers include the building service contract cleaners to whom organizations outsource facilities maintenance, as well as user corporations, healthcare facilities, schools and federal, state and local governments that handle facilities maintenance themselves. Co. sells its products through its direct sales and service organization and through a network of authorized distributors worldwide.

Recent Developments: For the quarter ended Mar 31 2005, net income increased 38.6% to $3,543 thousand from net income of $2,557 thousand in the year-earlier quarter. Revenues were $125,958 thousand, up 5.8% from $119,102 thousand the year before. Operating income was $6,080 thousand versus an income of $4,292 thousand in the prior-year quarter, an increase of 41.7%. Total direct expense was $71,971 thousand versus $71,086 thousand in the prior-year quarter, an increase of 1.2%. Total indirect expense was $47,907 thousand versus $43,724 thousand in the prior-year quarter, an increase of 9.6%.

Prospects: Top-line results are being positively affected by higher sales in Co.'s international markets including Europe, Latin America, and the Middle East. This growth is being driven by increased demand for newly-introduced products, and growth in service, parts and consumables, along with favorable foreign currency exchange rates. Meanwhile, operating profitability is benefiting from a sales mix that includes a greater percentage of direct sales, improved operating efficiencies, as well as lower costs stemming from cost-reduction initiatives implemented in the third quarter of 2004. Looking ahead, Co. is projecting full-year 2005 earnings of between $1.80 and $2.10 per share.

Financial Data

(US$ in Thousands)	3 Mos	12/31/2004	12/31/2003	12/31/2002	12/31/2001	12/31/2000	12/31/1999	12/31/1998
Earnings Per Share	1.57	1.46	1.56	0.91	0.52	3.09	2.15	2.67
Cash Flow Per Share	2.99	4.07	3.40	2.14	3.76	4.27	4.21	4.53
Tang Book Value Per Share	16.63	16.55	16.43	15.19	15.18	15.16	13.06	12.68
Dividends Per Share	0.870	0.860	0.840	0.820	0.800	0.780	0.760	0.740
Dividend Payout %	55.41	58.90	53.85	90.11	153.85	25.24	35.35	27.72
Income Statement								
Total Revenue	125,958	507,785	453,962	424,183	422,970	454,044	429,407	389,388
EBITDA	9,044	34,019	35,754	31,335	31,916	61,628	50,350	55,163
Depn & Amortn	3,389	12,972	13,879	16,947	18,507	18,391	18,667	17,550
Income Before Taxes	5,808	21,379	22,483	14,898	13,749	44,044	30,586	39,092
Income Taxes	2,265	7,999	8,328	6,633	8,945	15,794	10,893	13,767
Net Income	3,543	13,380	14,155	8,265	4,804	28,250	19,693	25,325
Average Shares	9,129	9,150	9,064	9,048	9,203	9,135	9,140	9,500
Balance Sheet								
Current Assets	172,041	188,631	176,370	162,901	152,387	171,628	165,093	150,868
Total Assets	268,292	285,792	258,873	256,237	246,619	263,285	257,533	239,098
Current Liabilities	67,878	81,853	59,507	70,349	55,648	67,255	74,999	60,809
Long-Term Obligations	1,246	1,029	6,295	5,000	10,000	10,000	16,003	23,038
Total Liabilities	93,884	111,758	93,257	102,092	92,291	108,337	121,618	107,831
Stockholders' Equity	174,408	174,034	165,616	154,145	154,328	154,948	135,915	131,267
Shares Outstanding	9,005	9,003	8,994	8,981	9,036	9,052	8,989	9,123
Statistical Record								
Return on Assets %	5.40	4.90	5.50	3.29	1.88	10.82	7.93	10.71
Return on Equity %	8.43	7.86	8.85	5.36	3.11	19.37	14.74	19.09
EBITDA Margin %	7.18	6.70	7.88	7.39	7.55	13.57	11.73	14.17
Net Margin %	2.81	2.63	3.12	1.95	1.14	6.22	4.59	6.50
Asset Turnover	1.94	1.86	1.76	1.69	1.66	1.74	1.73	1.65
Current Ratio	2.53	2.30	2.96	2.32	2.74	2.55	2.20	2.48
Debt to Equity	0.01	0.01	0.04	0.03	0.06	0.06	0.12	0.18
Price Range	42.24-36.82	44.20-36.82	44.99-29.28	44.00-26.62	48.88-32.90	52.31-30.13	42.00-32.00	44.81-33.00
P/E Ratio	26.90-23.45	30.27-25.22	28.84-18.77	48.35-29.25	93.99-63.27	16.93-9.75	19.53-14.88	16.78-12.36
Average Yield %	2.19	2.15	2.30	2.24	2.01	2.06	2.18	1.88

Address: 701 North Lilac Drive, P.O. Box 1452, Minneapolis, MN 55440
Telephone: 763-540-1208
Web Site: www.tennantco.com

Officers: Janet M. Dolan - Pres., C.E.O. Eric A. Blanchard - V.P., Gen. Couns., Sec. **Transfer Agents:** Wells Fargo Bank Minnesota, N.A., St. Paul, MN

Investor Contact: 763-540-1553
No of Institutions: 71
Shares: 5,776,394 **% Held:** 64.14

TEPPCO PARTNERS, L.P.

Exchange	Symbol	Price	52Wk Range	Yield	P/E
NYS	TPP	$41.35 (5/31/2005)	45.29-37.35	6.41	24.32

***7 Year Price Score 117.18** *NYSE Composite Index=100 ***12 Month Price Score 101.59**

Interim Earnings (Per Share)

Qtr.	Mar	Jun	Sep	Dec
2002	0.46	0.39	0.48	0.47
2003	0.43	0.43	0.36	0.31
2004	0.46	0.43	0.29	0.43
2005	0.55	...	...	...

Interim Dividends (Per Share)

Amt	Decl	Ex	Rec	Pay
0.662Q	7/16/2004	7/28/2004	7/30/2004	8/6/2004
0.662Q	10/15/2004	10/27/2004	10/29/2004	11/5/2004
0.662Q	1/14/2005	1/27/2005	1/31/2005	2/7/2005
0.662Q	4/15/2005	4/27/2005	4/29/2005	5/6/2005

Indicated Div: $2.65

Valuation Analysis

Forecast P/E 20.88 (6/2/2005)

Market Cap $2.6 Billion | Book Value N/A

Price/Book N/A | Price/Sales 0.42

Dividend Achiever Status

Rank 208 | **10 Year Growth Rate** 8.33%

Total Years of Dividend Growth 12

Business Summary: Oil and Gas (MIC: 14.2 SIC: 613 NAIC: 86910)

TEPPCO Partners operates through three segments. The downstream segment includes transportation and storage of refined products, liquefied petroleum gases and petrochemicals. The upstream segment includes gathering, transportation, marketing and storage of crude oil, and distribution of lubrication oils and specialty chemicals. The midstream segment includes natural gas gathering services, fractionation of natural gas liquids (NGLs) and transportation of NGLs. Texas Eastern Products Pipeline Co., a subsidiary of Duke Energy Field Services (DEFS), serves as the general partner of TPP. Certain assets of the midstream segment are managed and operated by DEFS under an agreement with Co.

Recent Developments: For the quarter ended Mar 31 2005, net income increased 20.1% to $48,581 thousand from net income of $40,433 thousand a year earlier. Revenues were $1,387,209 thousand, up 15.8% from $1,182,113 thousand the year before. Operating income was $62,356 thousand versus an income of $53,901 thousand in the prior year, a increase of 15.6%. Total indirect expense was $1,464,249 thousand versus $1,264,160 thousand in the prior year, an increase of 15.8%.

Prospects: Co's outlook remains promising as it continues to enjoy a favorable business climate. In particular, Co.'s downstream segment is benefiting from increased refined products and propane deliveries and lower operating expenses. Also, Co.'s midstream sector is enjoying higher gas gathering volumes de to increased production and capacity expansions on the Jonah system and new supply connections on the Val Verde system. For 2005, Co. expects earnings before interest, taxes, depreciation and amortization to be in the range of $375.0 million to $395.0 million, and earnings in the range of $1.90 to $2.15 per unit.

Financial Data

(US$ in Thousands)	3 Mos	12/31/2004	12/31/2003	12/31/2002	12/31/2001	12/31/2000	12/31/1999	12/31/1998
Earnings Per Share	1.70	1.61	1.52	1.79	2.18	1.89	1.91	(0.60)
Cash Flow Per Share	3.79	4.21	4.00	4.77	4.31	3.21	3.13	3.14
Dividends Per Share	2.650	2.638	2.500	2.350	2.150	2.000	1.850	1.750
Dividend Payout %	155.88	163.82	164.47	131.28	98.62	105.82	96.86	...
Income Statement								
Total Revenue	1,526,605	5,958,192	4,255,832	3,242,163	3,556,413	3,087,941	1,934,883	429,638
Depn & Amortn	25,763	112,900	100,700	86,032	45,899	35,163	32,656	26,938
Net Income	48,581	142,381	125,769	117,862	109,131	77,376	72,120	(19,426)
Average Shares	62,999	62,999	59,765	49,202	39,258	33,594	45,058	74,933
Balance Sheet								
Net PPE	1,713,314	1,703,702	1,619,163	1,587,824	1,180,461	949,705	720,919	671,611
Total Assets	3,159,560	3,197,705	2,940,992	2,770,642	2,065,348	1,622,810	1,041,373	914,969
Long-Term Obligations	1,555,406	1,480,226	1,339,650	1,377,692	730,472	835,784	455,753	427,722
Total Liabilities	2,148,189	2,176,257	1,831,671	1,878,800	1,522,167	1,307,753	811,606	687,783
Shares Outstanding	62,998	62,998	62,998	53,809	40,500	32,700	29,000	29,000
Statistical Record								
Return on Assets %	4.90	4.63	4.40	4.87	5.92	5.79	7.37	N.M.
Net Margin %	3.18	2.39	2.96	3.64	3.07	2.51	3.73	(4.52)
PPE Turnover	3.70	3.58	2.65	2.34	3.34	3.69	2.78	0.69
Asset Turnover	2.01	1.94	1.49	1.34	1.93	2.31	1.98	0.54
Price Range	45.29-34.79	42.16-34.79	41.15-27.75	33.00-26.10	35.90-24.75	26.63-19.31	27.94-18.00	30.50-24.25
P/E Ratio	26.64-20.46	26.19-21.61	27.07-18.26	18.44-14.58	16.47-11.35	14.09-10.22	14.63-9.42	...
Average Yield %	6.69	6.73	7.26	7.80	7.32	8.72	7.79	6.35

Address: 2929 Allen Parkway, P.O. Box 2521, Houston, TX 77252-2521
Telephone: 713-759-3636
Web Site: www.teppco.com

Officers: Jim W. Mogg - Chmn. Barry R. Pearl - Pres., C.E.O., C.O.O. **Transfer Agents:** ChaseMellon Shareholder Services, L.L.C., Ridgefield Park, NJ

Investor Contact: 800-659-0059
No of Institutions: 135
Shares: 12,718,744 **% Held:** 20.19

TEXAS REGIONAL BANCSHARES, INC.

Exchange	Symbol	Price	52Wk Range	Yield	P/E
NMS	TRBS	$28.79 (5/31/2005)	35.88-27.26	1.39	15.31

*7 Year Price Score 153.82 *NYSE Composite Index=100 *12 Month Price Score 91.20

TRADING VOLUME (thousand shares)

Interim Earnings (Per Share)

Qtr.	Mar	Jun	Sep	Dec
2002	0.29	0.30	0.33	0.32
2003	0.35	0.52	0.35	0.36
2004	0.37	0.57	0.40	0.43
2005	0.48	...	...	...

Interim Dividends (Per Share)

Amt	Decl	Ex	Rec	Pay
50%	8/10/2004	8/31/2004	8/23/2004	8/30/2004
0.10Q	9/14/2004	9/29/2004	10/1/2004	10/15/2004
0.10Q	12/14/2004	12/29/2004	1/1/2005	1/14/2005
0.10Q	3/8/2005	3/30/2005	4/1/2005	4/15/2005

Indicated Div: $0.40

Valuation Analysis

Forecast P/E	N/A		
Market Cap	$1.4 Billion	Book Value	600.9 Million
Price/Book	2.38	Price/Sales	3.80

Dividend Achiever Status

Rank	16	10 Year Growth Rate	24.36%
Total Years of Dividend Growth			10

Business Summary: Commercial Banking (MIC: 8.1 SIC: 022 NAIC: 22110)

Texas Regional Bancshares is a bank holding company. Through its subsidiaries, Co. is engaged in providing an array of customary banking services to business customers and individuals. Co. operates sixty-seven full-service banking locations, including thirty throughout the Rio Grande Valley, one each in Bishop, Corpus Christi, Eagle Pass and Sugar Land, two banking offices in Houston and 31 banking locations in east Texas. Co. also provides travelers checks, money orders and safe deposit facilities, and offers trust services. At Dec 31 2004, Co. had total assets of $5.84 billion.

Recent Developments: For the quarter ended Mar 31 2005, net income increased 38.7% to $23,799 thousand from net income of $17,157 thousand in the year-earlier quarter. Net interest income was $57,680 thousand, up 33.8% from $43,104 thousand the year before. Provision for loan losses was $5,407 thousand versus $3,924 thousand in the prior-year quarter, an increase of 37.8%. Non-interest income rose 84.2% to $24,811 thousand, while non-interest expense advanced 49.4% to $49,710 thousand.

Prospects: Going forward, Co. should benefit from its expanded position into the Dallas market with the acquisition of Mercantile Bank & Trust, FSB. With the acquisition and the completion of the new facility in Weslaco, TX, Co.'s subsidiary bank, Texas State Bank, now operates 71 banking centers in the Dallas area, Greater Houston area, East Texas, the Rio Grande Valley and other areas of South Texas. Separately, Co.'s subsidiary bank, Texas State Bank, received a special after-tax distribution of approximately $3.4 million in proceeds from the January 2005 merger of PULSE EFT Association with Discover Financial Services.

Financial Data (US$ in Thousands)	3 Mos	12/31/2004	12/31/2003	12/31/2002	12/31/2001	12/31/2000	12/31/1999	12/31/1998
Earnings Per Share	1.88	1.59	1.40	1.24	0.98	0.88	0.78	0.57
Cash Flow Per Share	2.67	2.48	2.75	1.60	1.33	1.33	1.07	0.84
Tang Book Value Per Share	7.58	8.06	8.52	7.56	5.71	4.70	3.63	3.84
Dividends Per Share	0.383	0.367	0.320	0.271	0.242	0.266	0.189	0.213
Dividend Payout %	20.39	23.06	22.86	21.79	24.69	30.10	24.41	37.66
Income Statement								
Interest Income	80,976	272,057	208,777	201,705	183,302	181,537	143,841	125,649
Interest Expense	23,296	67,807	60,385	71,986	83,776	86,513	62,221	58,384
Net Interest Income	57,680	204,250	148,392	129,719	99,526	95,024	81,620	67,265
Provision for Losses	5,407	20,583	13,155	12,331	8,667	8,927	5,432	9,729
Non-Interest Income	24,811	67,880	39,415	35,218	27,717	21,562	17,398	14,753
Non-Interest Expense	49,941	142,810	91,890	76,159	59,344	53,544	45,888	41,102
Income Before Taxes	35,922	114,592	93,602	81,232	60,728	54,127	47,699	34,097
Income Taxes	12,123	37,934	31,293	27,385	21,306	18,825	16,849	11,623
Net Income	23,799	76,658	62,309	53,847	39,422	35,302	30,850	22,474
Average Shares	49,854	48,354	44,548	43,325	32,803	39,966	39,818	39,841
Balance Sheet								
Net Loans & Leases	3,796,466	3,705,495	2,488,460	2,239,414	1,688,951	1,568,369	1,358,048	1,076,269
Total Assets	6,089,473	5,839,347	4,217,936	3,835,187	2,590,812	2,426,097	2,120,690	1,762,329
Total Deposits	5,002,140	4,760,840	3,516,435	3,132,191	2,235,877	2,109,748	1,885,346	1,562,942
Total Liabilities	5,488,577	5,245,289	3,796,205	3,457,732	2,325,553	2,198,393	1,932,502	1,584,861
Stockholders' Equity	600,896	594,058	421,731	377,455	265,259	227,704	188,188	177,468
Shares Outstanding	49,592	48,354	44,205	43,705	40,185	39,824	39,543	39,236
Statistical Record								
Return on Assets %	1.44	1.52	1.55	1.68	1.57	1.55	1.59	1.42
Return on Equity %	14.43	15.05	15.59	16.76	15.99	16.93	16.87	13.91
Net Interest Margin %	71.23	75.08	71.08	64.31	54.30	52.34	56.74	53.53
Efficiency Ratio %	47.21	42.01	37.02	32.15	28.12	26.36	28.46	29.27
Loans to Deposits	0.76	0.78	0.71	0.71	0.76	0.74	0.72	0.69
Price Range	35.88-27.27	35.88-24.26	25.19-19.00	21.97-14.59	16.28-11.52	13.48-8.17	10.84-8.49	12.76-6.89
P/E Ratio	19.09-14.51	22.57-15.26	17.99-13.57	17.72-11.76	16.61-11.75	15.32-9.29	13.89-10.89	22.39-12.08
Average Yield %	1.26	1.25	1.42	1.43	1.67	2.70	1.93	2.04

Address: 3900 North 10th Street, 11th Floor, McAllen, TX 78502-5910
Telephone: 956-631-5400
Web Site: www.trbsinc.com

Officers: Glen E. Roney - Chmn., Pres., C.E.O. Paul S. Moxley - Sr. Exec. V.P. **Transfer Agents:**

Investor Contact: 956-632-7613
No of Institutions: 116
Shares: 24,526,134 **% Held:** 49.46

THE ST PAUL TRAVELERS COMPANIES INC

Exchange	Symbol	Price	52Wk Range	Yield	P/E
NYS	STA	$37.88 (5/31/2005)	41.59-30.99	2.43	45.64

***7 Year Price Score 84.62** *NYSE Composite Index=100 ***12 Month Price Score 95.59**

Interim Earnings (Per Share)

Qtr.	Mar	Jun	Sep	Dec
2002	0.63	(1.09)	0.27	1.10
2003	0.75	0.89	0.88	0.21
2004	1.34	(0.42)	0.50	0.44
2005	0.31	...	...	...

Interim Dividends (Per Share)

Amt	Decl	Ex	Rec	Pay
0.22Q	7/28/2004	9/8/2004	9/10/2004	9/30/2004
0.22Q	10/27/2004	12/8/2004	12/10/2004	12/31/2004
0.22Q	1/26/2005	3/8/2005	3/10/2005	3/31/2005
0.23Q	5/4/2005	6/8/2005	6/10/2005	6/30/2005

Indicated Div: $0.92

Valuation Analysis

Forecast P/E	8.36 (6/1/2005)		
Market Cap	$25.5 Billion	Book Value	20.7 Billion
Price/Book	1.23	Price/Sales	1.02

Dividend Achiever Status

Rank	231	10 Year Growth Rate	6.99%
Total Years of Dividend Growth			18

Business Summary: Insurance (MIC: 8.2 SIC: 331 NAIC: 24130)

The St. Paul Travelers Companies is a holding company principally engaged, through its subsidiaries, in providing commercial and personal property/casualty insurance products and services to businesses, government units, associations and individuals. The Commercial segment provides casualty products primarily to mid-sized businesses and property products to large, mid-sized and small businesses. The Specialty segment provides standard and specialized insurance coverages, including surety bonds, insurance products for the construction industry and professional liability and management liability coverages. The Personal segment writes property and casualty insurance covering personal risks.

Recent Developments: For the quarter ended Mar 31 2005, income from continuing operations increased 49.4% to $877,000 thousand from income of $587,000 thousand in the year-earlier quarter. Net income decreased 63.9% to $212,000 thousand from net income of $587,000 thousand in the year-earlier quarter. Revenues were $6,105,000 thousand, up 47.9% from $4,127,000 thousand the year before. Net premiums earned were $5,119,000 thousand versus $3,339,000 thousand in the prior-year quarter, an increase of 53.3%. Net investment income rose 23.6% to $765,000 thousand from $619,000 thousand a year ago.

Prospects: On Apr 6 2005, the secondary offering and related transactions for the sale of Co.'s equity investment in Nuveen Investments, Inc. were priced. Co. has received approximately $1.80 billion of cash and expects to receive an additional $400.0 million upon closing of the forward share repurchase contract with Nuveen, expected to occur in the third quarter of 2005. Separately, Co. is experiencing strong performances in all business segments. Retention levels are strong and operating margins are attractive, as Co.'s loss indications remain at low levels and its renewal price changes stay modestly positive. Going forward, Co. is continuing to actively seek profitable new underwriting business.

Financial Data

(US$ in Thousands)	3 Mos	12/31/2004	12/31/2003	12/31/2002	12/31/2001	12/31/2000	12/31/1999	12/31/1998
Earnings Per Share	0.83	1.53	2.72	0.92	(5.22)	4.24	3.41	0.32
Cash Flow Per Share	8.22	8.59	0.58	0.60	4.66	(2.59)	(0.22)	0.29
Tang Book Value Per Share	23.70	20.93	22.26	20.58	21.03	30.54	26.42	25.79
Dividends Per Share	1.090	1.160	1.160	1.160	1.120	1.080	1.040	1.000
Dividend Payout %	131.33	75.82	42.65	126.09	...	25.47	30.50	312.50
Income Statement								
Premium Income	5,119,000	19,038,000	7,039,000	7,390,000	7,296,000	5,898,000	5,290,000	6,944,575
Total Revenue	6,105,000	22,934,000	8,854,000	8,918,000	8,943,000	8,608,000	7,569,000	9,108,401
Benefits & Claims	3,223,000	15,439,000	5,188,000	5,995,000	7,479,000	4,407,000	4,087,000	5,876,317
Income Before Taxes	1,188,000	1,128,000	836,000	176,000	(1,431,000)	1,453,000	1,017,000	(46,287)
Income Taxes	311,000	138,000	137,000	(73,000)	(422,000)	440,000	238,000	(135,635)
Net Income	212,000	955,000	661,000	218,000	(1,088,000)	993,000	834,000	89,348
Average Shares	709,100	628,300	240,000	227,000	212,000	233,000	246,000	238,682
Balance Sheet								
Total Assets	111,534,000	111,815,000	39,563,000	39,920,000	38,321,000	41,075,000	38,873,000	38,322,708
Total Liabilities	90,802,000	90,614,000	33,338,000	33,285,000	32,314,000	33,511,000	31,976,000	31,183,621
Stockholders' Equity	20,732,000	21,201,000	6,225,000	5,746,000	5,114,000	7,227,000	6,472,000	6,636,387
Shares Outstanding	673,600	670,300	228,393	226,798	207,624	218,308	224,830	233,750
Statistical Record								
Return on Assets %	0.66	1.26	1.66	0.56	N.M.	2.48	2.16	0.30
Return on Equity %	3.47	6.95	11.04	4.01	N.M.	14.46	12.72	1.59
Loss Ratio %	62.96	81.10	73.70	81.12	102.51	74.72	77.26	84.62
Net Margin %	3.47	4.16	7.47	2.44	(12.17)	11.54	11.02	0.98
Price Range	42.99-30.99	43.35-30.99	39.65-29.33	50.12-24.20	52.12-35.50	56.38-21.75	36.75-25.56	47.09-29.00
P/E Ratio	51.80-37.34	28.33-20.25	14.58-10.78	54.48-26.30	...	13.30-5.13	10.78-7.50	147.17-90.63
Average Yield %	2.92	3.03	3.30	3.01	2.44	2.73	3.26	2.54

Address: 385 Washington Street, Saint Paul, MN 55102 **Telephone:** 651-310-7911 **Web Site:** www.stpaul.com	**Officers:** Jay S. Fishman - Chmn., Pres., C.E.O. John A. MacColl - Vice-Chmn., Gen. Couns. **Transfer Agents:** Wells Fargo Bank, Minnesota, N.A., St. Paul, MN	**No of Institutions:** 509 **Shares:** 566,497,408 **% Held:** 84.12

3M CO

Exchange	Symbol	Price	52Wk Range	Yield	P/E
NYS	MMM	$76.65 (5/31/2005)	90.01-75.23	2.19	19.76

*7 Year Price Score 122.46 *NYSE Composite Index=100 *12 Month Price Score 93.01

TRADING VOLUME (thousand shares)

Interim Earnings (Per Share)

Qtr.	Mar	Jun	Sep	Dec
2002	0.57	0.59	0.69	0.65
2003	0.64	0.78	0.83	0.77
2004	0.90	0.97	0.97	0.91
2005	1.03	...	...	...

Interim Dividends (Per Share)

Amt	Decl	Ex	Rec	Pay
0.36Q	8/9/2004	8/18/2004	8/20/2004	9/12/2004
0.36Q	11/8/2004	11/17/2004	11/19/2004	12/12/2004
0.42Q	2/14/2005	2/23/2005	2/25/2005	3/12/2005
0.42Q	5/11/2005	5/18/2005	5/20/2005	6/12/2005

Indicated Div: $1.68 (Div. Reinv. Plan)

Valuation Analysis

Forecast P/E	N/A		
Market Cap	$59.0 Billion	Book Value	10.3 Billion
Price/Book	5.73	Price/Sales	2.91

Dividend Achiever Status

Rank	266	**10 Year Growth Rate**	5.05%
Total Years of Dividend Growth			46

Business Summary: Chemicals (MIC: 11.1 SIC: 891 NAIC: 25520)

3M a diversified technology company with a global presence in the following markets: health care; industrial; display and graphics; consumer and office; safety, security and protection services; electronics and telecommunications; and transportation. As of Dec 31 2004, Co. had 15 sales offices in 12 states and operated 58 manufacturing facilities in 22 states. Internationally, Co. has 174 sales offices. Co. operates 74 manufacturing and converting facilities in 29 countries outside the United States. Scotch, Post-it, Scotchgard, Thinsulate, Scotch-Brite, Filtrete, Command and Vikuiti are trademarks of Co.

Recent Developments: For the quarter ended Mar 31 2005, net income increased 12.0% to $809 million from net income of $722 million in the year-earlier quarter. Revenues were $5,166 million, up 4.6% from $4,939 million the year before. Operating income was $1,224 million versus an income of $1,117 million in the prior-year quarter, an increase of 9.6%. Total direct expense was $2,537 million versus $2,436 million in the prior-year quarter, an increase of 4.1%. Total indirect expense was $1,405 million versus $1,386 million in the prior-year quarter, an increase of 1.4%.

Prospects: Despite recent lackluster economic growth in Western Europe and Japan and continued raw material pricing pressure, Co. expects to deliver higher organic growth rates the rest of 2005 through new product sales and growth drivers, like LCD films. Co. also expects to benefit from its strong presence in fast-growth markets like China and Eastern Europe. Accordingly, on Apr 18 2005, Co. reaffirmed its earnings guidance for 2005. For the year, Co. expects earnings to be within a range of $4.15 to $4.25 per share. Co. expects full-year local currency growth of 5.0% to 8.0%.

Financial Data

(US$ in Thousands)	3 Mos	12/31/2004	12/31/2003	12/31/2002	12/31/2001	12/31/2000	12/31/1999	12/31/1998
Earnings Per Share	3.88	3.75	3.02	2.50	1.79	2.23	2.17	1.44
Cash Flow Per Share	5.63	5.47	4.82	3.84	3.90	2.93	3.78	2.95
Tang Book Value Per Share	9.67	9.63	6.62	4.90	6.18	7.17	7.06	7.40
Dividends Per Share	1.500	1.440	1.320	1.240	1.200	1.160	1.120	1.100
Dividend Payout %	38.66	38.40	43.71	49.70	67.04	52.13	51.61	76.39
Income Statement								
Total Revenue	5,166,000	20,011,000	18,232,000	16,332,000	16,054,000	16,724,000	15,659,000	15,021,000
EBITDA	1,466,000	5,577,000	4,677,000	4,000,000	3,362,000	4,110,000	3,889,000	2,957,000
Depn & Amortn	242,000	999,000	964,000	954,000	1,089,000	1,025,000	900,000	866,000
Income Before Taxes	1,220,000	4,555,000	3,657,000	3,005,000	2,186,000	2,974,000	2,880,000	1,952,000
Income Taxes	396,000	1,503,000	1,202,000	966,000	702,000	1,025,000	1,032,000	685,000
Net Income	809,000	2,990,000	2,403,000	1,974,000	1,430,000	1,782,000	1,763,000	1,175,000
Average Shares	787,000	796,500	795,300	791,000	799,800	799,800	813,000	816,000
Balance Sheet								
Current Assets	8,922,000	8,720,000	7,720,000	6,059,000	6,296,000	6,379,000	6,066,000	6,318,000
Total Assets	20,755,000	20,708,000	17,600,000	15,329,000	14,606,000	14,522,000	13,896,000	14,153,000
Current Liabilities	6,237,000	6,071,000	5,082,000	4,457,000	4,509,000	4,754,000	3,819,000	4,386,000
Long-Term Obligations	707,000	798,000	1,805,000	2,140,000	1,520,000	971,000	1,480,000	1,614,000
Total Liabilities	10,465,000	10,330,000	9,715,000	9,336,000	8,520,000	7,991,000	7,607,000	8,217,000
Stockholders' Equity	10,290,000	10,378,000	7,885,000	5,993,000	6,086,000	6,531,000	6,289,000	5,936,000
Shares Outstanding	769,570	773,518	784,117	780,391	782,607	792,170	797,400	802,000
Statistical Record								
Return on Assets %	15.89	15.57	14.60	13.19	9.82	12.51	12.57	8.58
Return on Equity %	33.46	32.65	34.63	32.68	22.67	27.72	28.84	19.81
EBITDA Margin %	28.38	27.87	25.65	24.49	20.94	24.58	24.84	19.69
Net Margin %	15.66	14.94	13.18	12.09	8.91	10.66	11.26	7.82
Asset Turnover	1.04	1.04	1.11	1.09	1.10	1.17	1.12	1.10
Current Ratio	1.43	1.44	1.52	1.36	1.40	1.34	1.59	1.44
Debt to Equity	0.07	0.08	0.23	0.36	0.25	0.15	0.24	0.27
Price Range	90.01-75.29	90.01-74.87	85.25-60.51	65.49-51.85	62.75-43.49	60.97-39.50	51.41-34.94	48.72-34.03
P/E Ratio	23.20-19.40	24.00-19.97	28.23-20.03	26.20-20.74	35.06-24.30	27.34-17.71	23.69-16.10	33.83-23.63
Average Yield %	1.81	1.76	1.92	2.04	2.16	2.52	2.56	2.64

Address: 3M Center, St. Paul, MN 55144-1000
Telephone: 651-733-1110
Web Site: www.3m.com

Officers: W. James McNerney Jr. - Chmn., C.E.O. Joe E. Harlan - Exec. V.P., Electro & Communications
Business **Transfer Agents:**
Wells Fargo Shareowner Services, St. Paul, MN

Investor Contact: 651-733-8206
No of Institutions: 904
Shares: 538,560,960 **% Held:** 69.72

TOOTSIE ROLL INDUSTRIES INC

Exchange	Symbol	Price	52Wk Range	Yield	P/E
NYS	TR	$30.95 (5/31/2005)	32.64-27.41	0.90	24.56

*7 Year Price Score 83.53 *NYSE Composite Index=100 *12 Month Price Score 100.76

Interim Earnings (Per Share)

Qtr.	Mar	Jun	Sep	Dec
2002	0.23	0.22	0.48	0.30
2003	0.20	0.23	0.49	0.31
2004	0.21	0.22	0.50	0.30
2005	0.23	...	...	...

Interim Dividends (Per Share)

Amt	Decl	Ex	Rec	Pay
0.068Q	12/7/2004	12/15/2004	12/17/2004	1/4/2005
0.068Q	3/1/2005	3/9/2005	3/11/2005	4/1/2005
3%	3/1/2005	3/9/2005	3/11/2005	4/14/2005
0.07Q	5/31/2005	6/10/2005	6/14/2005	7/8/2005

Indicated Div: $0.28

Valuation Analysis

Forecast P/E	23.44 (6/1/2005)		
Market Cap	$1.7 Billion	Book Value	571.9 Million
Price/Book	2.90	Price/Sales	3.78

Dividend Achiever Status

Rank	108	10 Year Growth Rate	13.88%
Total Years of Dividend Growth			41

Business Summary: Food (MIC: 4.1 SIC: 064 NAIC: 11340)

Tootsie Roll Industries is engaged in the manufacture and sale of confectionery products. The majority of Co.'s products are sold under the registered trademarks TOOTSIE ROLL, TOOTSIE ROLL POPS, CHILD'S PLAY, CARAMEL APPLE POPS, CHARMS, BLOW-POP, BLUE RAZZ, ZIP-A-DEE-DOO-DA POPS, CELLA'S, MASON DOTS, MASON CROWS, JUNIOR MINT, CHARLESTON CHEW, SUGAR DADDY, SUGAR BABIES, ANDES, FLUFFY STUFF, DUBBLE BUBBLE, RAZZLES, CRY BABY and NIK-L-NIP. Co.'s products are marketed in a variety of packages designed to be suitable for display and sale in different types of retail outlets. Co.'s principal markets are in the United States, Canada and Mexico.

Recent Developments: For the quarter ended Apr 2 2005, net income increased 8.8% to $12,506,000 from net income of $11,493,000 in the year-earlier quarter. Revenues were $97,925,000 , up 22.3% from $80,046,000 the year before. Operating income was $17,159,000 versus an income of $16,060,000 in the prior-year quarter, an increase of 6.8%. Total direct expense was $58,476,000 versus $45,316,000 in the prior-year quarter, an increase of 29.0%. Total indirect expense was $22,290,000 versus $18,670,000 in the prior-year quarter, an increase of 19.4%.

Prospects: Co.'s results for the first quarter ended Apr 2 2005 benefited from higher reported net sales and resulting operating earnings from the inclusion of the Concord Confections business, which Co. acquired on Aug 30 2004. Separately, capital expenditures for first quarter 2005 and 2004 were $4.6 million and $3.2 million, respectively. Co. anticipates capital expenditures for the 2005 year to be generally in line with historical annualized spending after adjusting for the addition of the Concord Confections business, and are to be funded from its cash flow from operations and internal sources.

Financial Data

(US$ in Thousands)	3 Mos	12/31/2004	12/31/2003	12/31/2002	12/31/2001	12/31/2000	12/31/1999	12/31/1998
Earnings Per Share	1.26	1.23	1.22	1.22	1.23	1.44	1.38	1.33
Cash Flow Per Share	1.61	1.45	1.56	1.30	1.52	1.61	1.40	1.52
Tang Book Value Per Share	5.69	5.78	7.95	7.57	7.31	6.49	6.71	6.08
Dividends Per Share	0.272	0.270	0.262	0.254	0.247	0.233	0.200	0.161
Dividend Payout %	21.60	21.94	21.42	20.92	20.15	16.19	14.51	12.09
Income Statement								
Total Revenue	97,925	420,110	392,656	393,185	423,496	427,054	396,750	388,659
EBITDA	22,433	109,165	107,568	107,798	112,513	124,527	114,820	112,692
Depn & Amortn	4,067	13,565	13,913	12,354	17,926	13,489	10,369	12,807
Income Before Taxes	18,366	94,688	97,947	100,688	100,787	117,808	111,447	106,063
Income Taxes	5,860	30,514	32,933	34,300	35,100	42,071	40,137	38,537
Net Income	12,506	64,174	65,014	66,388	65,687	75,737	71,310	67,526
Average Shares	53,720	52,366	53,337	54,671	53,523	52,444	51,956	50,977
Balance Sheet								
Current Assets	183,081	192,693	243,705	224,948	246,096	203,211	224,532	228,539
Total Assets	794,217	811,753	665,297	646,080	618,676	562,442	529,416	487,423
Current Liabilities	81,875	82,317	62,887	63,096	57,846	57,446	56,109	53,384
Long-Term Obligations	7,500	93,167	7,500	7,500	7,500	7,500	7,500	7,500
Total Liabilities	222,308	241,574	128,716	119,340	110,215	103,746	98,770	90,966
Stockholders' Equity	571,909	570,179	536,581	526,740	508,461	458,696	430,646	396,457
Shares Outstanding	53,557	52,366	52,706	54,054	53,474	52,011	51,465	50,749
Statistical Record								
Return on Assets %	8.91	8.67	9.92	10.50	11.12	13.84	14.03	14.61
Return on Equity %	11.77	11.57	12.23	12.83	13.58	16.99	17.24	18.06
EBITDA Margin %	22.91	25.98	27.39	27.42	26.57	29.16	28.94	29.00
Net Margin %	12.77	15.28	16.56	16.88	15.51	17.73	17.97	17.37
Asset Turnover	0.60	0.57	0.60	0.62	0.72	0.78	0.78	0.84
Current Ratio	2.24	2.34	3.88	3.57	4.25	3.54	4.00	4.28
Debt to Equity	0.01	0.16	0.01	0.01	0.01	0.02	0.02	0.02
Price Range	35.44-27.41	35.45-27.41	33.81-24.26	42.62-26.22	42.80-30.26	40.04-23.53	38.01-24.24	37.30-22.87
P/E Ratio	28.13-21.75	28.82-22.29	27.71-19.88	34.94-21.49	34.79-24.60	27.81-16.34	27.54-17.57	28.04-17.20
Average Yield %	0.90	0.86	0.93	0.76	0.68	0.78	0.65	0.54

Address: 7401 South Cicero Avenue, Chicago, IL 60629 **Telephone:** 773-838-3400 **Web Site:** www.tootsie.com	**Officers:** Melvin J. Gordon - Chmn., C.E.O. Ellen R. Gordon - Pres., C.O.O. **Transfer Agents:** Mellon Investor Services, LLC, Ridgefield Park, NJ	**No of Institutions:** 134 **Shares:** 9,828,154 **% Held:** 18.25

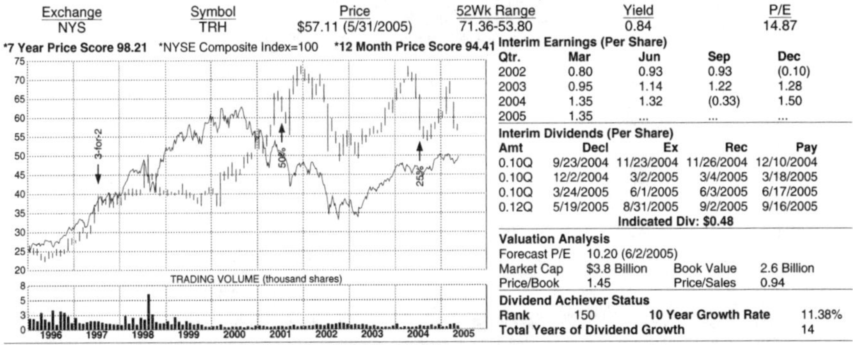

TRANSATLANTIC HOLDINGS, INC.

Exchange	Symbol	Price	52Wk Range	Yield	P/E
NYS	TRH	$57.11 (5/31/2005)	71.36-53.80	0.84	14.87

*7 Year Price Score 98.21 *NYSE Composite Index=100 *12 Month Price Score 94.41

Interim Earnings (Per Share)

Qtr.	Mar	Jun	Sep	Dec
2002	0.80	0.93	0.93	(0.10)
2003	0.95	1.14	1.22	1.28
2004	1.35	1.32	(0.33)	1.50
2005	1.35	...	...	...

Interim Dividends (Per Share)

Amt	Decl	Ex	Rec	Pay
0.10Q	9/23/2004	11/23/2004	11/26/2004	12/10/2004
0.10Q	12/2/2004	3/2/2005	3/4/2005	3/18/2005
0.10Q	3/24/2005	6/1/2005	6/3/2005	6/17/2005
0.12Q	5/19/2005	8/31/2005	9/2/2005	9/16/2005

Indicated Div: $0.48

Valuation Analysis

Forecast P/E	10.20 (6/2/2005)		
Market Cap	$3.8 Billion	Book Value	2.6 Billion
Price/Book	1.45	Price/Sales	0.94

Dividend Achiever Status

Rank	150	10 Year Growth Rate	11.38%
Total Years of Dividend Growth			14

Business Summary: Insurance (MIC: 8.2 SIC: 331 NAIC: 24126)

Transatlantic Holdings, through its wholly-owned subsidiaries Transatlantic Reinsurance Company, Trans Re Zurich and Putnam Reinsurance Company, offers reinsurance capacity for a full range of property and casualty products on a treaty and facultative basis, directly and through brokers, to insurance and reinsurance companies, in both the domestic and international markets. Co.'s principal lines of reinsurance include auto liability, other liability, medical malpractice, ocean marine and aviation, accident and health and surety and credit in the casualty lines, along with fire, homeowners multiple peril and auto physical damage in the property lines.

Recent Developments: For the quarter ended Mar 31 2005, net income decreased 0.3% to $89,363 thousand from net income of $89,653 thousand in the year-earlier quarter. Revenues were $981,720 thousand, up 1.0% from $972,444 thousand the year before. Net premiums earned were $887,913 thousand versus $893,147 thousand in the prior-year quarter, a decrease of 0.6%. Total expenses rose 1.3% to $868,859 thousand versus $856,958 thousand the year before.

Prospects: Co.'s outlook is mixed as recent operating results reflect the negative impact of higher catastrophe losses principally resulting from the European Windstorm Erwin, and a slight decline in net premiums written, following increased retentions by ceding companies and some slippage in market conditions. On the other side, Co. is seeing signs of improvement as net investments are up considerably year over year, bolstered by continued strong operating cash flows. Further, Co. believes its overall market conditions continue to be favorable, as it maintains its steadfast commitment to strict underwriting discipline.

Financial Data

(US$ in Thousands)	3 Mos	12/31/2004	12/31/2003	12/31/2002	12/31/2001	12/31/2000	12/31/1999	12/31/1998
Earnings Per Share	3.84	3.85	4.60	2.57	0.29	3.23	2.86	3.79
Cash Flow Per Share	12.98	13.73	14.06	9.15	3.71	(0.23)	2.98	3.50
Tang Book Value Per Share	39.38	39.30	36.24	31.03	28.26	28.47	25.22	24.77
Dividends Per Share	0.388	0.376	0.336	0.314	0.298	0.277	0.251	0.224
Dividend Payout %	10.10	9.77	7.30	12.21	103.33	8.60	8.75	5.92
Income Statement								
Premium Income	887,913	3,661,090	3,171,226	2,369,452	1,790,339	1,631,536	1,484,634	1,380,570
Total Revenue	981,720	3,990,057	3,452,140	2,615,527	2,030,182	1,866,021	1,715,373	1,602,570
Benefits & Claims	645,807	2,754,560	2,233,447	1,796,352	1,561,529	1,196,896	1,148,817	1,020,888
Income Before Taxes	112,861	276,212	386,674	188,320	(34,107)	267,982	236,097	323,351
Income Taxes	23,498	21,628	83,030	19,002	(52,999)	56,344	48,735	75,828
Net Income	89,363	254,584	303,644	169,318	18,892	211,638	187,362	247,523
Average Shares	66,232	66,189	65,952	65,943	65,920	65,595	65,403	65,371
Balance Sheet								
Total Assets	10,793,886	10,605,292	8,707,758	7,286,525	6,741,303	5,522,672	5,480,198	5,253,249
Total Liabilities	8,201,836	8,018,163	6,331,171	5,255,758	4,895,293	3,666,307	3,837,681	3,643,110
Stockholders' Equity	2,592,050	2,587,129	2,376,587	2,030,767	1,846,010	1,856,365	1,642,517	1,610,139
Shares Outstanding	65,818	65,827	65,585	65,451	65,319	65,200	65,114	65,000
Statistical Record								
Return on Assets %	2.53	2.63	3.80	2.41	0.31	3.84	3.49	4.91
Return on Equity %	10.12	10.23	13.78	8.73	1.02	12.06	11.52	16.69
Loss Ratio %	72.73	75.24	70.43	75.81	87.22	73.36	77.38	73.95
Net Margin %	9.10	6.38	8.80	6.47	0.93	11.34	10.92	15.45
Price Range	73.49-53.80	73.49-53.80	64.64-49.18	72.80-48.44	73.60-50.54	56.47-36.77	42.73-36.90	50.33-37.10
P/E Ratio	19.14-14.01	19.09-13.97	14.05-10.69	28.33-18.85	253.79-174.29	17.48-11.38	14.94-12.90	13.28-9.79
Average Yield %	0.62	0.59	0.59	0.51	0.48	0.61	0.63	0.54

Address: 80 Pine Street, New York, NY 10005 **Telephone:** 212-770-2000 **Web Site:** www.transre.com	**Officers:** Robert F. Orlich - Interim Chmn., Pres., C.E.O. Steven S. Skalicky - Exec. V.P., C.F.O. **ransfer Agents:** American Stock Transfer & Trust Company, New York, NY	**Investor Contact:** 212-770-2040 **No of Institutions:** 99 **Shares:** 62,118,812 **% Held:** 94.39

TRUSTMARK CORP.

Exchange	Symbol	Price	52Wk Range	Yield	P/E
NMS	TRMK	$28.57 (5/31/2005)	32.42-26.75	2.80	14.21

Interim Earnings (Per Share)

Qtr.	Mar	Jun	Sep	Dec
2002	0.48	0.50	0.49	0.48
2003	0.41	0.53	0.55	0.52
2004	0.46	0.57	0.48	0.49
2005	0.47	...	...	...

Interim Dividends (Per Share)

Amt	Decl	Ex	Rec	Pay
0.19Q	7/20/2004	8/30/2004	9/1/2004	9/15/2004
0.20Q	10/19/2004	11/29/2004	12/1/2004	12/15/2004
0.20Q	1/18/2005	2/25/2005	3/1/2005	3/15/2005
0.20Q	4/19/2005	5/27/2005	6/1/2005	6/15/2005

Indicated Div: $0.80

Valuation Analysis

Forecast P/E	14.02 (6/1/2005)		
Market Cap	$1.7 Billion	Book Value	731.5 Million
Price/Book	2.26	Price/Sales	3.26

Dividend Achiever Status

Rank	105	10 Year Growth Rate	14.22%
Total Years of Dividend Growth			31

Business Summary: Commercial Banking (MIC: 8.1 SIC: 021 NAIC: 22110)

Trustmark is a multi-bank holding company. Through its subsidiaries, Co. operates as a financial services organization providing banking and financial services to corporate, institutional and individual customers through over 145 offices in Florida, Mississippi, Tennessee, and Texas. The General Banking division provides traditional banking products and services, including loans and deposits. The Wealth Management division provides integrated financial services for affluent customers, such as trust and fiduciary services and brokerage services. The Insurance division provides a range of retail insurance products. Co. also operates a proprietary mutual fund family, The Performance Funds.

Recent Developments: For the quarter ended Mar 31 2005, net income increased 0.1% to $26,781 thousand from net income of $26,751 thousand in the year-earlier quarter. Net interest income was $6,840,9thousand, up 0.1% from $6,835,9thousand the year before. Provision for loan losses was $279,6thousand versus $105,2thousand in the prior-year quarter, an increase of 165.8%. Non-interest income rose 40.6% to $36,548 thousand, while non-interest expense advanced 15.5% to $61,142 thousand.

Prospects: Co.'s expansion efforts in Houston and the Florida Panhandle, along with solid performance in its Jackson and Memphis markets, are contributing to growth. Meanwhile, increasing contributions from wealth management and insurance services, combined with the solid profitability of Co.'s traditional banking franchise, is driving earnings improvement. Separately, higher interest rates have increased the value of Co.'s home mortgage servicing rights, which has allowed it to reverse a portion of previously taken mortgage servicing impairment charges. Additional impairment may be recovered if interest rates rise, refinancing slows and the expected life of home mortgage loans lengthens.

Financial Data

(US$ in Thousands)	3 Mos	12/31/2004	12/31/2003	12/31/2002	12/31/2001	12/31/2000	12/31/1999	12/31/1998
Earnings Per Share	2.01	2.00	2.00	1.94	1.72	1.50	1.36	1.14
Cash Flow Per Share	2.44	2.77	3.39	1.10	3.75	(1.76)	3.00	1.14
Tang Book Value Per Share	12.10	9.14	8.96	9.25	8.93	8.70	8.39	8.29
Dividends Per Share	0.780	0.770	0.685	0.615	0.555	0.510	0.440	0.352
Dividend Payout %	38.81	38.50	34.25	31.70	32.27	34.00	32.35	30.92
Income Statement								
Interest Income	95,922	364,355	359,388	405,952	477,820	488,759	448,509	420,100
Interest Expense	27,513	88,738	89,558	113,766	209,242	255,196	205,079	191,900
Net Interest Income	68,409	275,617	269,830	292,186	268,578	233,563	243,430	228,200
Provision for Losses	2,796	(3,055)	9,771	14,107	13,200	10,401	9,072	7,771
Non-Interest Income	36,548	124,028	157,543	141,870	131,990	124,540	101,943	89,060
Non-Interest Expense	61,142	225,309	236,120	233,841	215,941	189,377	187,071	180,391
Income Before Taxes	41,019	177,391	181,482	186,108	171,427	158,325	149,230	129,098
Income Taxes	14,238	60,682	62,952	64,968	60,146	54,124	51,236	45,784
Net Income	26,781	116,709	118,530	121,140	111,281	101,737	97,994	83,314
Average Shares	57,545	58,273	59,244	62,416	64,876	67,928	71,921	72,946
Balance Sheet								
Net Loans & Leases	5,389,107	5,265,298	4,845,776	4,542,595	4,448,832	4,078,083	3,949,085	3,636,168
Total Assets	8,179,993	8,052,957	7,914,321	7,138,706	7,180,339	6,886,988	6,743,404	6,355,190
Total Deposits	5,534,728	5,450,093	5,089,459	4,686,296	4,613,365	4,058,418	3,924,796	3,946,397
Total Liabilities	7,448,487	7,302,561	7,224,748	6,459,172	6,494,895	6,257,347	6,087,648	5,703,314
Stockholders' Equity	731,506	750,396	689,573	679,534	685,444	629,641	655,756	651,876
Shares Outstanding	57,858	57,858	58,246	60,516	63,705	64,755	70,423	72,531
Statistical Record								
Return on Assets %	1.43	1.46	1.57	1.69	1.58	1.49	1.50	1.40
Return on Equity %	16.10	16.17	17.31	17.75	16.92	15.79	14.99	13.38
Net Interest Margin %	71.32	75.65	75.08	71.98	56.21	47.79	54.28	54.32
Efficiency Ratio %	46.16	46.13	45.68	42.69	35.41	30.88	33.98	35.43
Loans to Deposits	0.97	0.97	0.95	0.97	0.96	1.00	1.01	0.92
Price Range	32.42-26.10	32.42-26.10	29.82-22.74	26.90-20.49	24.70-19.56	21.61-15.31	24.06-18.38	25.75-15.38
P/E Ratio	16.13-12.99	16.21-13.05	14.91-11.37	13.87-10.56	14.36-11.37	14.41-10.21	17.69-13.51	22.59-13.49
Average Yield %	2.67	2.60	2.61	2.53	2.48	2.72	1.99	1.67

Address: 248 East Capitol Street, Jackson, MS 39201 **Telephone:** 601-208-5111 **Web Site:** www.trustmark.com	**Officers:** Richard G. Hickson - Chmn., Pres., C.E.O. Louis E. Greer - Chief Acctg. Officer **Transfer Agents:** Trustmark National Bank, Jackson, MS	**Investor Contact:** 601-949-6898 **No of Institutions:** 97 **Shares:** 12,953,143 **% Held:** 22.65

UGI CORP.

Exchange	Symbol	Price	52Wk Range	Yield	P/E
NYS	UGI	$26.51 (5/31/2005)	26.78-15.30	2.55	14.10

***7 Year Price Score 153.10** *NYSE Composite Index=100 ***12 Month Price Score 121.04**

Interim Earnings (Per Share)

Qtr.	Dec	Mar	Jun	Sep
2001-02	0.29	0.64	0.05	(0.08)
2002-03	0.43	0.81	(0.03)	(0.07)
2003-04	0.44	0.74	0.08	(0.06)
2004-05	0.75	1.12	...	...

Interim Dividends (Per Share)

Amt	Decl	Ex	Rec	Pay
0.156Q	10/26/2004	11/26/2004	11/30/2004	1/1/2005
0.156Q	1/26/2005	2/24/2005	2/28/2005	4/1/2005
2-for-1	4/26/2005	5/25/2005	5/17/2005	5/24/2005
0.169Q	4/26/2005	6/13/2005	6/15/2005	7/1/2005

Indicated Div: $0.68 (Div. Reinv. Plan)

Valuation Analysis

Forecast P/E	15.92 (6/1/2005)		
Market Cap	$3.1 Billion	Book Value	1.0 Billion
Price/Book	2.99	Price/Sales	0.65

Dividend Achiever Status

Rank	302	**10 Year Growth Rate**	2.80%
Total Years of Dividend Growth			17

Business Summary: Gas Utilities (MIC: 7.4 SIC: 924 NAIC: 21210)

UGI is a holding company that distributes and markets energy products and related services through its subsidiaries and joint venture affiliates. Co. is a domestic and international distributor of propane and butane, (LPG); a provider of natural gas and electric service through regulated local distribution utilities; a generator of electricity through its ownership interests in electric generation facilities; a regional marketer of energy commodities; and a provider of heating and cooling services. Co.'s subsidiaries operate principally in the following five business segments: AmeriGas Propane; International Propane; Gas Utility; Electric Utility; and, Energy Services.

Recent Developments: For the quarter ended Mar 31 2005, net income increased 74.8% to $117,300 thousand from net income of $67,100 thousand in the year-earlier quarter. Revenues were $1,788,200 thousand, up 35.8% from $1,316,600 thousand the year before. Operating income was $287,700 thousand versus an income of $181,600 thousand in the prior-year quarter, an increase of 58.4%. Total direct expense was $1,195,100 thousand versus $914,400 thousand in the prior-year quarter, an increase of 30.7%. Total indirect expense was $313,100 thousand versus $215,500 thousand in the prior-year quarter, an increase of 45.3%.

Prospects: Co.'s results are being fueled by the positive effect of full ownership of Antargaz as well as higher operating income from all of its business units other than AmeriGas, which experienced warmer than normal weather. Antargaz was acquired by Co. in 2004 through the purchase of the remaining 80.5% ownership interests in AGZ Holding and is one of the largest distributors of liquefied petroleum gases in France. Looking ahead, Co. continues to expect to report fiscal year earnings of $3.45 to $3.55 per diluted share. Co. noted that the forecasted results do not include a loss on extinguishment of debt of up to $0.18 per diluted share due to an expected refinancing of long-term debt of AmeriGas.

Financial Data (US$ in Thousands)	6 Mos	3 Mos	09/30/2004	09/30/2003	09/30/2002	09/30/2001	09/30/2000	09/30/1999
Earnings Per Share	1.88	1.50	1.16	1.15	0.90	0.69	0.55	0.58
Cash Flow Per Share	3.30	2.41	2.72	2.95	2.99	2.50	1.62	1.48
Dividends Per Share	0.625	0.611	0.598	0.565	0.542	0.525	0.508	0.490
Dividend Payout %	33.24	40.84	51.73	49.34	60.19	76.46	92.99	84.48
Income Statement								
Total Revenue	3,151,300	1,363,100	3,784,700	3,026,100	2,213,700	2,468,100	1,761,700	1,383,600
EBITDA	463,100	191,300	426,100	373,000	326,600	309,000	282,400	274,800
Depn & Amortn	75,300	37,600	131,000	103,000	93,500	105,200	97,500	89,700
Income Before Taxes	321,000	120,200	176,000	160,800	124,000	99,000	86,400	100,500
Income Taxes	125,500	42,000	64,400	60,700	46,900	45,400	40,100	43,200
Net Income	195,500	78,200	111,600	98,900	75,500	56,500	44,700	55,700
Average Shares	105,086	105,200	96,682	86,472	83,814	82,119	81,765	96,048
Balance Sheet								
Net PPE	1,819,600	1,843,000	1,781,900	1,336,800	1,271,900	1,268,000	1,073,200	1,084,100
Total Assets	4,674,400	4,680,500	4,235,400	2,781,700	2,614,400	2,550,200	2,278,800	2,135,900
Long-Term Obligations	1,520,300	1,561,900	1,547,300	1,158,500	1,127,000	1,196,900	1,029,700	989,600
Total Liabilities	3,440,000	3,591,700	3,222,900	2,077,300	2,001,100	2,028,400	1,834,500	1,656,800
Stockholders' Equity	1,020,200	919,000	834,100	569,800	317,300	255,600	247,200	249,200
Shares Outstanding	115,152	103,100	102,422	85,398	83,103	81,889	80,981	81,811
Statistical Record								
Return on Assets %	4.45	3.90	3.17	3.67	2.92	2.34	2.02	2.65
Return on Equity %	21.02	19.67	15.86	22.30	26.36	22.47	17.96	18.08
EBITDA Margin %	14.70	14.03	11.26	12.33	14.75	12.52	16.03	19.86
Net Margin %	6.20	5.74	2.95	3.27	3.41	2.29	2.54	4.03
PPE Turnover	2.55	2.65	2.42	2.32	1.74	2.11	1.63	1.33
Asset Turnover	1.05	1.10	1.08	1.12	0.86	1.02	0.80	0.66
Debt to Equity	1.49	1.70	1.86	2.03	3.55	4.68	4.17	3.97
Price Range	23.49-14.95	20.56-14.95	18.63-14.47	17.45-11.74	12.22-8.87	9.70-7.23	8.08-6.08	8.40-5.31
P/E Ratio	12.49-7.95	13.71-9.96	16.06-12.47	15.17-10.21	13.57-9.85	14.05-10.48	14.70-11.06	14.48-9.16
Average Yield %	3.39	3.55	3.68	3.92	5.26	6.24	7.06	6.89

Address: 460 North Gulph Road, King of Prussia, PA 19406
Telephone: 610-337-1000
Web Site: www.ugicorp.com

Officers: Lon R. Greenberg - Chmn., C.E.O. John L. Walsh - Pres., C.O.O. **Transfer Agents:** Mellon Investor Services LLC, Ridgefield Park, NJ

Investor Contact: 610-337-1000
No of Institutions: 183
Shares: 33,683,752 **% Held:** 65.34

UNITED BANKSHARES, INC.

Exchange	Symbol	Price	52Wk Range	Yield	P/E
NMS	UBSI	$33.45 (5/31/2005)	39.18-30.00	3.11	14.80

*7 Year Price Score 110.02 *NYSE Composite Index=100 *12 Month Price Score 90.68

Interim Earnings (Per Share)

Qtr.	Mar	Jun	Sep	Dec
2002	0.50	0.51	0.52	0.53
2003	0.53	0.54	0.55	0.23
2004	0.53	0.55	0.56	0.58
2005	0.57	...	...	...

Interim Dividends (Per Share)

Amt	Decl	Ex	Rec	Pay
0.26Q	8/23/2004	9/8/2004	9/10/2004	10/1/2004
0.26Q	11/22/2004	12/8/2004	12/10/2004	1/3/2005
0.26Q	1/25/2005	3/9/2005	3/11/2005	4/1/2005
0.26Q	5/17/2005	6/8/2005	6/10/2005	7/1/2005

Indicated Div: $1.04 (Div. Reinv. Plan)

Valuation Analysis

Forecast P/E	14.31 (6/2/2005)		
Market Cap	$1.4 Billion	Book Value	626.7 Million
Price/Book	2.28	Price/Sales	4.03

Dividend Achiever Status

Rank	234	10 Year Growth Rate	6.86%
Total Years of Dividend Growth			23

Business Summary: Commercial Banking (MIC: 8.1 SIC: 021 NAIC: 22110)

United Bankshares is a bank holding company with total assets of $6.44 billion and total deposits of $4.30 billion as of Dec 31 2004. Co. has two banking subsidiaries "doing business" under the name of United Bank. These engage primarily in community banking. Banking services include the acceptance of deposits; the making and servicing of personal, commercial, floor plan and student loans; and the making of construction and real estate loans. Co. also owns non-bank subsidiaries which engage in other community banking services such as asset management, real property title insurance, investment banking, financial planning, and brokerage services.

Recent Developments: For the quarter ended Mar 31 2005, net income increased 5.3% to $24,760 thousand from net income of $23,504 thousand in the year-earlier quarter. Net interest income was $52,990 thousand, up 6.5% from $49,751 thousand the year before. Provision for loan losses was $1,111 thousand versus $1,357 thousand in the prior-year quarter, a decrease of 18.1%. Non-interest income fell 4.7% to $12,919 thousand, while non-interest expense declined 3.0% to $28,741 thousand.

Prospects: Co.'s earnings growth for the first quarter of 2005 was attributed primarily to increased net income. Co.'s net interest income is benefiting from an increase in its average earning assets as average loans continue to grow year-over-year. In addition the average yield on earnings assets is being positively affected by higher interest rates. These increases to net interest income are being partially offset by the higher cost of funds due to the higher interest rates. Separately, Co.'s non-interest income is down versus the prior year, primarily due a decline in fees from deposit services, partially offset by increases in revenues from its trust and brokerage services.

Financial Data

(US$ in Thousands)	3 Mos	12/31/2004	12/31/2003	12/31/2002	12/31/2001	12/31/2000	12/31/1999	12/31/1998
Earnings Per Share	2.26	2.22	1.85	2.06	1.90	1.40	1.61	1.02
Cash Flow Per Share	3.50	2.17	11.70	(2.28)	(1.38)	0.02	5.25	(2.33)
Tang Book Value Per Share	10.75	10.80	10.20	10.73	11.80	10.32	9.32	9.75
Dividends Per Share	1.030	1.020	1.000	0.950	0.910	0.840	0.820	0.745
Dividend Payout %	45.58	45.95	54.05	46.12	47.89	60.00	50.93	73.04
Income Statement								
Interest Income	79,276	293,350	297,508	339,478	360,610	377,847	354,665	325,647
Interest Expense	26,286	88,914	104,151	132,557	175,507	197,766	174,402	155,354
Net Interest Income	52,990	204,436	193,357	206,921	185,103	180,081	180,263	170,293
Provision for Losses	1,111	4,520	7,475	7,937	12,833	15,745	8,800	12,156
Non-Interest Income	12,919	54,231	103,316	73,479	62,205	33,786	51,078	41,752
Non-Interest Expense	28,741	137,061	176,678	144,130	115,745	110,422	117,519	137,964
Income Before Taxes	36,057	117,086	112,520	128,333	118,730	87,700	105,022	61,925
Income Taxes	11,297	33,771	33,755	39,400	38,739	28,724	34,774	17,523
Net Income	24,760	97,762	78,765	88,933	79,991	58,976	70,248	44,402
Average Shares	43,418	43,978	42,620	43,113	42,064	42,260	43,722	43,461
Balance Sheet								
Net Loans & Leases	4,347,523	4,374,911	4,045,587	3,525,774	3,454,926	3,151,962	3,130,497	2,613,202
Total Assets	6,311,308	6,435,971	6,378,999	5,792,019	5,631,775	4,904,547	5,069,160	4,567,899
Total Deposits	4,350,439	4,297,563	4,182,372	3,900,848	3,787,793	3,391,449	3,260,985	3,493,058
Total Liabilities	5,684,625	5,804,464	5,763,808	5,250,480	5,125,246	4,473,677	4,673,230	4,146,368
Stockholders' Equity	626,683	631,507	615,191	541,539	506,529	430,870	395,930	421,531
Shares Outstanding	42,790	43,008	43,689	42,031	42,926	41,765	42,487	43,256
Statistical Record								
Return on Assets %	1.55	1.52	1.29	1.56	1.52	1.18	1.46	1.22
Return on Equity %	15.81	15.64	13.62	16.97	17.07	14.23	17.19	12.67
Net Interest Margin %	66.84	69.69	64.99	60.95	51.33	47.66	50.83	52.29
Efficiency Ratio %	31.17	39.43	44.08	34.90	27.37	26.83	28.96	37.55
Loans to Deposits	1.00	1.02	0.97	0.90	0.91	0.93	0.96	0.75
Price Range	39.18-29.35	39.18-29.35	31.53-26.97	32.01-26.24	28.86-20.19	23.88-16.44	27.25-22.81	34.13-21.50
P/E Ratio	17.34-12.99	17.65-13.22	17.04-14.58	15.54-12.74	15.19-10.63	17.05-11.74	16.93-14.17	33.46-21.08
Average Yield %	3.06	3.11	3.38	3.23	3.65	4.25	3.27	2.84

Address: 300 United Center, 500 Virginia Street East, Charleston, WV 25301 **Telephone:** 304-424-8800 **Web Site:** www.ubsi-wv.com	**Officers:** Richard M. Adams - Chmn., C.E.O. Steven E. Wilson - C.F.O., Chief Acctg. Officer **Transfer Agents:** Mellon Investor Services LLC, Ridgefield Park, NJ	**Investor Contact:** 304-424-8704 **No of Institutions:** 122 **Shares:** 16,485,090 **% Held:** 38.46

UNITED DOMINION REALTY TRUST, INC.

Exchange	Symbol	Price	52Wk Range	Yield	P/E
NYS	UDR	$23.05 (5/31/2005)	24.80-19.08	5.21	39.74

***7 Year Price Score 128.26** *NYSE Composite Index=100 ***12 Month Price Score 100.23**

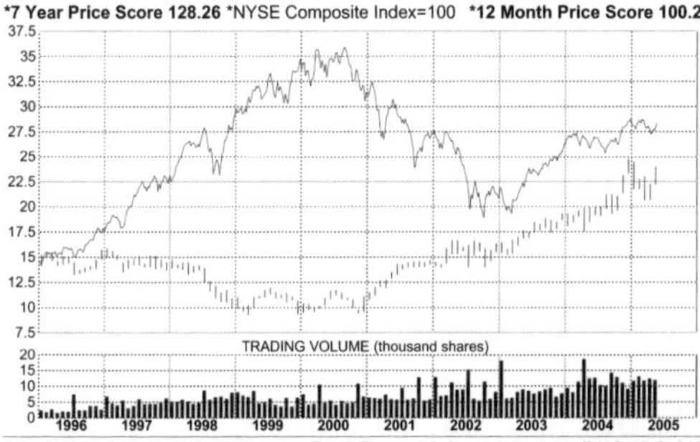

TRADING VOLUME (thousand shares)

Interim Earnings (Per Share)

Qtr.	Mar	Jun	Sep	Dec
2002	(0.08)	0.19	0.13	0.00
2003	0.06	0.02	0.01	0.12
2004	0.07	0.17	0.17	0.16
2005	0.08	...	...	...

Interim Dividends (Per Share)

Amt	Decl	Ex	Rec	Pay
0.292Q	9/24/2004	10/13/2004	10/15/2004	11/1/2004
0.292Q	12/9/2004	1/12/2005	1/14/2005	1/31/2005
0.30Q	3/17/2005	4/13/2005	4/15/2005	5/2/2005
0.30Q	5/5/2005	7/13/2005	7/15/2005	8/1/2005

Indicated Div: $1.20 (Div. Reinv. Plan)

Valuation Analysis

Forecast P/E	14.41 (6/2/2005)		
Market Cap	$3.2 Billion	Book Value	1.2 Billion
Price/Book	2.70	Price/Sales	4.87

Dividend Achiever Status

Rank	283	**10 Year Growth Rate**	4.34%
Total Years of Dividend Growth			23

Business Summary: Property, Real Estate & Development (MIC: 8.3 SIC: 798 NAIC: 25930)

United Dominion Realty Trust is a self-administered real estate investment trust that owns, acquires, renovates, develops and manages middle-market apartment communities nationwide. At Dec 31 2004, Co.'s apartment portfolio included 273 communities located in 43 markets, with a total of 78,855 completed apartment homes. In addition, Co. had three apartment communities under development. Co. focuses on the broad middle-market segment of the apartment market that generally consists of renters-by-necessity. This group includes young professionals, blue-collar families, single parent households, older singles, immigrants, non-related parties and families renting while waiting to purchase a home.

Recent Developments: For the quarter ended Mar 31 2005, income from continuing operations decreased 33.2% to $6,442 thousand from income of $9,645 thousand in the year-earlier quarter. Net income decreased 2.4% to $14,941 thousand from net income of $15,312 thousand in the year-earlier quarter. Revenues were $184,305 thousand, up 28.3% from $143,626 thousand the year before. Total expenses jumped 32.8% to $177,643 thousand versus $133,708 thousand in the prior year.

Prospects: Co. noted that the composition of its portfolio has changed significantly over the past three years. For example, as of Mar 31 2005 18.0% of Co.'s portfolio was considered non-mature, or communities that have not been owned or stabilized for more than five quarters. Looking ahead, Co.'s same community portfolio should benefit from an influx of acquired properties that are considered non-mature in California, Metropolitan Washington D.C. and Florida, which are high rent and high occupancy markets. The overall average monthly rental rate of Co.'s non-mature assets is about $1,000 per month. Separately, Co.'s funds from operations guidance for full year 2005 is $1.57 to $1.70 per diluted share.

Financial Data (US$ in Thousands)	3 Mos	12/31/2004	12/31/2003	12/31/2002	12/31/2001	12/31/2000	12/31/1999	12/31/1998
Earnings Per Share	0.58	0.56	0.21	0.24	0.27	0.41	0.54	0.49
Cash Flow Per Share	1.94	1.96	2.05	2.14	2.24	2.17	1.84	1.53
Tang Book Value Per Share	7.21	7.43	7.28	6.48	7.10	7.91	8.59	9.11
Dividends Per Share	1.170	1.163	1.133	1.103	1.077	1.067	1.058	1.040
Dividend Payout %	201.72	207.59	539.29	459.38	399.07	260.37	195.83	212.24
Income Statement								
Property Income	171,331	604,270	603,367	594,314	618,590	616,825	618,749	478,718
Non-Property Income	12,974	2,608	1,068	1,806	4,593	5,326	1,942	3,382
Total Revenue	184,305	606,878	604,435	596,120	623,183	622,151	620,691	482,100
Depn & Amortn	54,720	191,294	172,785	168,584	156,292	159,912	131,336	105,294
Interest Expense	39,160	124,087	117,185	130,956	144,379	156,040	153,748	106,238
Net Income	14,941	97,152	70,404	53,229	61,828	76,615	93,622	72,332
Average Shares	137,073	129,080	115,648	106,952	101,037	103,208	103,639	100,062
Balance Sheet								
Total Assets	4,354,016	4,332,001	3,543,643	3,276,136	3,348,091	3,453,957	3,688,317	3,762,940
Long-Term Obligations	2,941,114	2,879,982	2,132,037	2,057,640	2,064,197	1,992,330	2,127,305	2,117,749
Total Liabilities	3,105,346	3,052,957	2,286,001	2,205,649	2,229,701	2,146,739	2,283,938	2,273,377
Stockholders' Equity	1,168,728	1,195,451	1,163,436	1,001,271	1,042,725	1,218,892	1,310,212	1,374,121
Shares Outstanding	136,940	136,429	127,295	106,605	103,133	102,219	102,740	103,639
Statistical Record								
Return on Assets %	2.43	2.46	2.06	1.61	1.82	2.14	2.51	2.38
Return on Equity %	8.38	8.21	6.50	5.21	5.47	6.04	6.98	5.95
Net Margin %	8.11	16.01	11.65	8.93	9.92	12.31	15.08	15.00
Price Range	24.80-17.52	24.80-17.52	19.37-15.22	16.70-13.95	14.72-10.75	11.75-9.44	11.94-9.25	14.75-10.06
P/E Ratio	42.76-30.21	44.29-31.29	92.24-72.48	69.58-58.13	54.52-39.81	28.66-23.02	22.11-17.13	30.10-20.54
Average Yield %	5.60	5.80	6.53	7.18	8.10	10.22	9.86	8.11

Address: 400 East Cary St., Richmond, VA 23219 **Telephone:** 720-283-6120 **Web Site:** www.udrt.com	**Officers:** Robert C. Larson - Chmn. James D. Klingbeil - Vice-Chmn. **Transfer Agents:** ChaseMellon Shareholder Services, LLC, Pittsburgh, PA	**No of Institutions:** 210 **Shares:** 88,697,904 **% Held:** 64.73

UNITED TECHNOLOGIES CORP.

Exchange	Symbol	Price	52Wk Range	Yield	P/E
NYS	UTX	$106.70 (5/31/2005)	107.88-84.66	1.65	18.85

*7 Year Price Score 121.14 *NYSE Composite Index=100 *12 Month Price Score 102.25

Interim Earnings (Per Share)

Qtr.	Mar	Jun	Sep	Dec
2002	0.92	1.23	1.21	1.06
2003	1.00	1.26	1.27	1.16
2004	1.14	1.66	1.43	1.29
2005	1.28	...	...	...

Interim Dividends (Per Share)

Amt	Decl	Ex	Rec	Pay
0.35Q	10/13/2004	11/17/2004	11/19/2004	12/10/2004
0.44Q	2/7/2005	2/16/2005	2/18/2005	3/10/2005
0.44Q	4/13/2005	5/18/2005	5/20/2005	6/10/2005
100%	4/13/2005	6/13/2005	5/20/2005	6/10/2005

Indicated Div: $1.76 (Div. Reinv. Plan)

Valuation Analysis

Forecast P/E	17.49 (6/2/2005)		
Market Cap	$54.6 Billion	Book Value	14.7 Billion
Price/Book	3.72	Price/Sales	1.43

Dividend Achiever Status

Rank	148	**10 Year Growth Rate**	11.41%
Total Years of Dividend Growth			11

Business Summary: Aviation (MIC: 1.1 SIC: 724 NAIC: 36412)

United Technologies provides technology products and services to the building systems and aerospace industries. Co.'s principal businesses include: Otis, Carrier, Chubb, Pratt & Whitney, Hamilton Sundstrand and Sikorsky. Otis, Carrier and Chubb serve commercial and residential property customers. Carrier also serves commercial, industrial, transport refrigeration and food service equipment customers. Pratt & Whitney, Hamilton Sundstrand and Sikorsky Aircraft serve commercial and government customers in the aerospace industry and also industrial market customers. Products include elevators, HVAC equipment, security and fire systems, and commercial and military aerospace engines and products.

Recent Developments: For the quarter ended Mar 31 2005, net income increased 18.1% to $651 million from net income of $551 million a year earlier. Revenues were $9,407 million, up 8.8% from $8,646 million the year before. Operating income was $1,088 million versus an income of $920 million in the prior year, an increase of 18.2%. Total direct expense was $6,815 million versus $6,275 million in the prior year, an increase of 8.6%. Total indirect expense was $1,504 million versus $1,451 million in the prior year, an increase of 3.6%.

Prospects: On Apr 1 2005, Co. announced the completion of its Kidde global fire safety company acquisition and the renaming of Co.'s Chubb operating segment as UTC Fire & Security. Total consideration for the acquisition, including debt, was approximately $3.00 billion. Meanwhile, Co. is seeing strong revenues as a result of organic growth and contribution from the Linde commercial refrigeration business. Double-digit profit growth at Otis, Pratt & Whitney, Sikorsky, and UTC Fire & Security is fueling Co.'s margin expansion despite higher commodity costs. For 2005, Co. now expects revenues of about $43.00 billion and earnings ranging from $5.90 to $6.15 per share on a pre-split basis.

Financial Data

(US$ in Thousands)	3 Mos	12/31/2004	12/31/2003	12/31/2002	12/31/2001	12/31/2000	12/31/1999	12/31/1998
Earnings Per Share	5.66	5.52	4.69	4.42	3.83	3.55	3.01	2.52
Cash Flow Per Share	7.57	7.43	6.07	6.04	6.14	5.58	4.96	5.50
Tang Book Value Per Share	5.29	3.68	4.63	2.93	3.32	1.89	3.11	5.84
Dividends Per Share	1.490	1.400	1.135	0.980	0.900	0.825	0.760	0.695
Dividend Payout %	26.33	25.36	24.20	22.17	23.50	23.24	25.25	27.52
Income Statement								
Total Revenue	9,407,000	37,445,000	31,034,000	28,212,000	27,897,000	26,583,000	24,127,000	25,715,000
EBITDA	1,314,000	5,448,000	4,644,000	4,384,000	4,138,000	3,999,000	2,361,000	3,021,000
Depn & Amortn	226,000	978,000	799,000	727,000	905,000	859,000	844,000	854,000
Income Before Taxes	988,000	4,107,000	3,470,000	3,276,000	2,807,000	2,758,000	1,257,000	1,963,000
Income Taxes	277,000	1,085,000	941,000	887,000	755,000	853,000	325,000	623,000
Net Income	651,000	2,788,000	2,361,000	2,236,000	1,938,000	1,808,000	1,531,000	1,255,000
Average Shares	508,000	505,419	502,900	505,579	505,400	508,010	506,700	494,000
Balance Sheet								
Current Assets	15,746,000	15,522,000	12,364,000	11,751,000	11,263,000	10,662,000	10,627,000	9,355,000
Total Assets	40,535,000	40,035,000	34,648,000	29,090,000	26,969,000	25,364,000	24,366,000	18,375,000
Current Liabilities	12,753,000	12,947,000	10,295,000	7,903,000	8,371,000	9,344,000	9,215,000	7,735,000
Long-Term Obligations	4,223,000	4,231,000	4,257,000	4,632,000	4,237,000	3,476,000	3,086,000	1,575,000
Total Liabilities	25,835,000	26,027,000	22,941,000	20,735,000	18,600,000	17,702,000	17,249,000	13,997,000
Stockholders' Equity	14,700,000	14,008,000	11,707,000	8,355,000	8,369,000	7,662,000	7,117,000	4,378,000
Shares Outstanding	511,823	511,098	514,062	469,620	472,159	470,306	474,546	450,000
Statistical Record								
Return on Assets %	7.48	7.45	7.41	7.98	7.41	7.25	7.16	7.15
Return on Equity %	21.36	21.62	23.54	26.74	24.18	24.40	26.64	29.70
EBITDA Margin %	13.97	14.55	14.96	15.54	14.83	15.04	9.79	11.75
Net Margin %	6.92	7.45	7.61	7.93	6.95	6.80	6.35	4.88
Asset Turnover	1.00	1.00	0.97	1.01	1.07	1.07	1.13	1.47
Current Ratio	1.23	1.20	1.20	1.49	1.35	1.14	1.15	1.21
Debt to Equity	0.29	0.30	0.36	0.55	0.51	0.45	0.43	0.36
Price Range	105.52-81.50	105.52-81.50	95.54-54.15	77.25-49.19	87.21-41.64	79.75-48.06	74.69-52.31	55.88-34.25
P/E Ratio	18.64-14.40	19.12-14.76	20.37-11.55	17.48-11.13	22.77-10.87	22.46-13.54	24.81-17.38	22.17-13.59
Average Yield %	1.58	1.52	1.56	1.50	1.29	1.33	1.21	1.54

Address: One Financial Plaza, Hartford, CT 06103 **Telephone:** 860-728-7000 **Web Site:** www.utc.com	**Officers:** George David - Chmn., Pres., C.E.O. William H. Trachsel - Sr. V.P., Gen. Couns **Transfer Agents:** EquiServe Trust Company, N.A. of Providence, RI	**No of Institutions:** 801 **Shares:** 398,798,016 **% Held:** 77.92

UNIVERSAL CORP.

Exchange	Symbol	Price	52Wk Range	Yield	P/E
NYS	UVV	$44.40 (5/31/2005)	50.94-42.25	3.78	N/A

*7 Year Price Score 114.10 *NYSE Composite Index=100 *12 Month Price Score 94.64

TRADING VOLUME (thousand shares)

Interim Earnings (Per Share)

Qtr.	Sep	Dec	Mar	Jun
2002-03	1.09	1.04	0.94	1.26
2003-04	1.37	1.48	1.09	1.11
2004-05	0.80	0.54	1.08	...

Interim Dividends (Per Share)

Amt	Decl	Ex	Rec	Pay
0.39Q	8/5/2004	10/6/2004	10/11/2004	11/8/2004
0.42Q	11/4/2004	1/6/2005	1/10/2005	2/14/2005
0.42Q	2/3/2005	4/7/2005	4/11/2005	5/9/2005
0.42Q	5/12/2005	7/7/2005	7/11/2005	8/8/2005

Indicated Div: $1.68 (Div. Reinv. Plan)

Valuation Analysis

Forecast P/E	10.91 (6/2/2005)		
Market Cap	$1.1 Billion	Book Value	800.6 Million
Price/Book	1.42	Price/Sales	N/A

Dividend Achiever Status

Rank	268	**10 Year Growth Rate**	4.97%
Total Years of Dividend Growth			34

Business Summary: Trusts & Holding Entities (MIC: 8.9 SIC: 719 NAIC: 51112)

Universal is a holding company. Through its primary subsidiaries, Co. is a major independent leaf tobacco merchant and has operations in agri-products and the distribution of lumber and building products. Co.'s tobacco business includes the selecting, buying, shipping, processing, packing, storing, and financing of leaf tobacco for sale to manufacturers of tobacco products. Co.'s agri-products business involves selecting, buying and processing a number of products, including tea, rubber, sunflower seeds, nuts, dried fruit, and canned and frozen foods. Co. is also engaged in lumber and building products distribution and processing in the Netherlands and other countries in Europe.

Recent Developments: For the fiscal year ended Mar 31 2005, net income was $96.0 million compared with $95.8 million for the twelve months ended Mar 31 20004, which as been recast for the effect of last year's change in fiscal year. Results for 2005 included a charge of $14.9 million for announced European Union fines on Co's subsidiaries due to their tobacco buying practices in Spain. Results for the recast twelve months ended Mar 31 2004 included a $12.0 million charge related to the settlement of the DeLoach lawsuit in May 2003, $5.7 million in charges for rationalizing U.S. operations, and $10.8 million in charges for rejected tobacco. Sales and other operating revenues rose 13.5% to $3.28 billion.

Prospects: Co.'s results are being negatively affected by the changes in the monetary system in Zimbabwe, the effects of the change in its fiscal year end last year, the value-added tax provision in Brazil, and pricing pressures caused by larger crops and competitive pricing, particularly in South America and Africa. Meanwhile, Co.'s agri-products segment is benefiting from the acquisition of a controlling interest in nuts and dried fruits trading company, as well as higher volumes in rubber and canned meats. Meanwhile, Co.'s lumber and building products operations continue to perform well. Looking ahead, the larger tobacco crops may lead to certain market imbalances in fiscal 2006.

Financial Data

(US$ in Thousands)	9 Mos	6 Mos	3 Mos	03/31/2004	06/30/2003	06/30/2002	06/30/2001	06/30/2000
Earnings Per Share	2.42	2.43	3.37	3.94	4.34	4.00	4.08	3.77
Cash Flow Per Share	0.60	(6.90)	5.17	(1.39)	(1.76)	6.41	5.85	5.87
Tang Book Value Per Share	25.85	25.01	24.79	24.57	19.56	17.64	15.77	13.04
Dividends Per Share	1.560	1.530	1.500	1.470	1.400	1.320	1.260	1.220
Dividend Payout %	64.46	62.90	44.51	37.31	32.26	33.00	30.88	32.36
Income Statement								
Total Revenue	2,449,658	1,597,312	737,141	2,271,152	2,636,776	2,500,078	3,017,579	3,401,969
EBITDA	207,386	126,708	60,567	246,537	271,758	273,805	305,370	298,478
Depn & Amortn	54,554	34,779	16,433	48,867	53,504	54,987	56,399	52,022
Income Before Taxes	110,348	65,166	31,526	162,638	172,984	170,987	187,395	189,587
Income Taxes	49,259	31,303	12,453	59,329	53,094	59,821	66,336	68,221
Net Income	62,247	34,340	20,479	99,636	110,594	106,662	112,669	113,805
Average Shares	25,723	25,677	25,688	25,277	25,499	26,680	27,645	30,205
Balance Sheet								
Current Assets	1,759,433	1,846,530	1,795,725	1,526,669	1,374,997	1,105,037	1,132,646	1,088,150
Total Assets	2,789,673	2,842,616	2,748,326	2,482,773	2,243,074	1,844,415	1,782,373	1,748,104
Current Liabilities	982,613	993,307	1,012,608	739,110	824,281	673,431	581,765	883,234
Long-Term Obligations	741,519	851,735	769,348	770,296	614,994	435,592	515,349	223,262
Total Liabilities	1,957,033	2,034,694	1,949,355	1,722,940	1,622,796	1,256,420	1,230,244	1,250,325
Stockholders' Equity	800,611	774,693	766,699	759,833	620,278	587,995	552,129	497,779
Shares Outstanding	25,621	25,533	25,532	25,446	24,920	26,224	27,184	28,146
Statistical Record								
Return on Assets %	2.98	2.42	2.98	5.60	5.41	5.88	6.38	6.36
Return on Equity %	13.94	7.16	10.68	19.16	18.31	18.71	21.46	21.89
EBITDA Margin %	8.47	7.93	8.22	10.86	10.31	10.95	10.12	8.77
Net Margin %	2.54	2.15	2.78	4.39	4.19	4.27	3.73	3.35
Asset Turnover	1.22	1.21	1.07	1.28	1.29	1.38	1.71	1.90
Current Ratio	1.79	1.86	1.77	2.07	1.67	1.64	1.95	1.23
Debt to Equity	0.93	1.10	1.00	1.01	0.99	0.74	0.93	0.45
Price Range	53.01-42.25	53.01-40.78	53.01-40.78	52.32-40.78	43.01-31.81	43.05-31.74	41.30-20.63	31.00-13.56
P/E Ratio	21.90-17.46	21.81-16.78	15.73-12.10	13.28-10.35	9.91-7.33	10.76-7.93	10.12-5.06	8.22-3.60
Average Yield %	3.25	3.26	3.25	3.27	3.73	3.48	3.91	5.28

Address: 1501 North Hamilton Street, Richmond, VA 23230
Telephone: 804-359-9311
Web Site: www.universalcorp.com

Officers: Allen B. King - Chmn., Pres., C.E.O., C.O.O. Hartwell H. Roper - V.P., C.F.O. **Transfer Agents:** Wells Fargo Bank Minnesota, N.A., St. Paul, MN

Investor Contact: 804-359-9311
No of Institutions: 140
Shares: 21,857,908 **% Held:** 85.31

UNIVERSAL FOREST PRODUCTS INC.

Exchange	Symbol	Price	52Wk Range	Yield	P/E
NMS	UFPI	$39.80 (5/31/2005)	43.91-27.87	0.25	14.27

Interim Earnings (Per Share)

Qtr.	Mar	Jun	Sep	Dec
2002	0.32	0.82	0.58	0.26
2003	0.25	0.94	0.66	0.33
2004	0.30	1.06	0.78	0.46
2005	0.49	...	...	...

Interim Dividends (Per Share)

Amt	Decl	Ex	Rec	Pay
0.05S	10/15/2003	11/26/2003	12/1/2003	12/15/2003
0.05S	4/21/2004	5/27/2004	6/1/2004	6/15/2004
0.05S	10/22/2004	11/29/2004	12/1/2004	12/15/2004
0.05S	4/22/2005	5/27/2005	6/1/2005	6/15/2005

Indicated Div: $0.10

Valuation Analysis

Forecast P/E	N/A		
Market Cap	$721.2 Million	Book Value	369.4 Million
Price/Book	1.95	Price/Sales	0.29

Dividend Achiever Status

Rank	229	10 Year Growth Rate	7.18%
Total Years of Dividend Growth			11

Business Summary: Wood Products (MIC: 11.9 SIC: 421 NAIC: 21113)

Universal Forest Products engineers, manufactures, treats, distributes, and installs lumber, composite wood, plastic, and other building products for the do-it-yourself (DIY)/retail, site-built construction, manufactured housing, and industrial markets. Co.'s principal products include preservative-treated wood, remanufactured lumber, lattice, fence panels, deck components, specialty packaging, engineered trusses, wall panels, and other building products. As of Dec 25 2004, Co. operated 98 facilities located throughout the U.S., Canada, and Mexico.

Recent Developments: For the quarter ended Mar 26 2005, net income increased 65.8% to $9,229,000 from net income of $5,567,000 in the year-earlier quarter. Revenues were $537,160,000 , up 15.4% from $465,665,000 the year before. Operating income was $17,378,000 versus an income of $12,521,000 in the prior-year quarter, an increase of 38.8%. Total direct expense was $469,931,000 versus $409,304,000 in the prior-year quarter, an increase of 14.8%. Total indirect expense was $49,851,000 versus $43,840,000 in the prior-year quarter, an increase of 13.7%.

Prospects: Sales are being positively affected by an increase in unit sales as well as higher prices driven by the lumber market. Value-added sales increases are primarily due to increased sales of engineered wood components, turn-key framing services, and industrial packaging products. Site-built construction and industrial segments remain strong growth markets for Co. and it continues to consolidate these two large, fragmented markets. Looking ahead, Co. anticipates continued growth in its business in 2005 and reaffirms its annual targets of a 7.0% to 12.0% increase in unit sales and a 10.0% to 15.0% increase in net earnings compared with the corresponding period a year earlier.

Financial Data

(US$ in Thousands)	3 Mos	12/25/2004	12/27/2003	12/28/2002	12/29/2001	12/30/2000	12/25/1999	12/26/1998
Earnings Per Share	2.79	2.59	2.18	1.97	1.63	1.49	1.48	1.28
Cash Flow Per Share	3.48	2.79	3.97	0.93	3.96	3.28	1.58	3.35
Tang Book Value Per Share	13.15	12.50	9.71	7.45	6.06	6.60	6.01	4.65
Dividends Per Share	0.100	0.100	0.095	0.090	0.085	0.080	0.075	0.070
Dividend Payout %	3.58	3.86	4.36	4.57	5.21	5.37	5.07	5.47
Income Statement								
Total Revenue	537,160	2,453,281	1,898,830	1,639,899	1,530,353	1,389,443	1,435,055	1,238,907
EBITDA	26,596	128,532	107,563	97,832	90,233	84,084	80,953	67,254
Depn & Amortn	7,946	30,853	27,547	24,639	24,476	21,462	18,155	15,048
Income Before Taxes	15,024	83,059	65,792	62,115	54,300	50,375	51,537	43,034
Income Taxes	5,759	31,462	24,325	22,983	19,612	19,218	19,955	16,615
Net Income	9,229	48,603	40,119	36,637	33,142	30,438	31,448	26,419
Average Shares	18,972	18,771	18,379	18,619	20,377	20,477	21,186	20,613
Balance Sheet								
Current Assets	510,614	406,483	332,313	294,097	234,966	200,359	215,506	181,877
Total Assets	868,394	762,360	684,757	634,794	551,209	485,320	468,638	420,070
Current Liabilities	210,696	183,865	141,878	108,841	110,895	80,038	91,182	82,018
Long-Term Obligations	251,806	185,109	205,049	235,319	154,370	150,807	146,896	132,120
Total Liabilities	499,017	405,591	380,008	371,794	284,347	249,551	254,076	228,487
Stockholders' Equity	369,377	356,769	304,749	263,000	230,862	235,769	214,562	191,583
Shares Outstanding	18,121	18,002	17,813	17,741	17,787	19,719	20,212	20,710
Statistical Record								
Return on Assets %	6.27	6.74	6.10	6.20	6.41	6.28	7.10	8.16
Return on Equity %	15.36	14.73	14.17	14.88	14.24	13.30	15.53	17.23
EBITDA Margin %	4.95	5.24	5.66	5.97	5.90	6.05	5.64	5.43
Net Margin %	1.72	1.98	2.11	2.23	2.17	2.19	2.19	2.13
Asset Turnover	3.03	3.40	2.89	2.77	2.96	2.87	3.24	3.83
Current Ratio	2.42	2.21	2.34	2.70	2.12	2.50	2.36	2.22
Debt to Equity	0.68	0.52	0.67	0.89	0.67	0.64	0.68	0.69
Price Range	43.91-26.69	43.50-26.69	31.74-15.23	26.86-16.08	23.00-13.00	16.13-10.63	23.25-12.88	20.50-12.50
P/E Ratio	15.74-9.57	16.80-10.31	14.56-6.99	13.63-8.16	14.11-7.98	10.82-7.13	15.71-8.70	16.02-9.77
Average Yield %	0.29	0.31	0.42	0.42	0.48	0.62	0.42	0.43

Address: 2801 East Beltline N.E., Grand Rapids, MI 49525 **Telephone:** 616-364-6161 **Web Site:** www.ufpi.com	**Officers:** William G. Currie - Vice-Chmn., C.E.O. Michael R. Cole - C.F.O., Treas. **Transfer Agents:** American Stock Transfer & Trust Company, New York, NY	**No of Institutions:** 107 **Shares:** 13,278,792 **% Held:** 73.71

UNIVERSAL HEALTH REALTY INCOME TRUST

Exchange	Symbol	Price	52Wk Range	Yield	P/E
NYS	UHT	$36.97 (5/31/2005)	36.97-26.35	5.55	16.73

*7 Year Price Score 114.77 *NYSE Composite Index=100 *12 Month Price Score 102.98

Interim Earnings (Per Share)

Qtr.	Mar	Jun	Sep	Dec
2002	0.53	0.44	0.43	0.43
2003	0.48	0.45	0.45	0.68
2004	0.43	0.54	0.47	0.56
2005	0.64	...	...	...

Interim Dividends (Per Share)

Amt	Decl	Ex	Rec	Pay
0.50Q	9/1/2004	9/13/2004	9/15/2004	9/30/2004
0.505Q	12/1/2004	12/14/2004	12/16/2004	12/31/2004
0.505Q	3/1/2005	3/14/2005	3/16/2005	3/31/2005
0.555Q	4/21/2005	5/12/2005	5/16/2005	5/31/2005

Indicated Div: $2.05 (Div. Reinv. Plan)

Valuation Analysis

Forecast P/E	N/A		
Market Cap	$434.8 Million	Book Value	156.4 Million
Price/Book	2.78	Price/Sales	13.01

Dividend Achiever Status

Rank	307	10 Year Growth Rate	1.85%
Total Years of Dividend Growth			17

Business Summary: Property, Real Estate & Development (MIC: 8.3 SIC: 798 NAIC: 25930)

Universal Health Realty Income Trust is an organized Maryland real estate investment trust (REIT). As of Dec 31 2004, Co. had investments in 43 facilities located in 15 states consisting of investments in healthcare and human service related facilities including acute care hospitals, behavioral healthcare facilities, rehabilitation hospitals, sub-acute care facilities, surgery centers, pre-school and childcare centers and medical office buildings. Six of Co.'s hospital facilities and three medical office buildings are leased to subsidiaries of Universal Health Services, Inc. (UHS). As of Dec 31 2004, UHS owned 6.7% of Co.'s outstanding shares of beneficial interest.

Recent Developments: For the quarter ended Mar 31 2005, net income increased 50.2% to $7,580 thousand from net income of $5,048 thousand in the year-earlier quarter. Revenues were $8,491 thousand, up 24.1% from $6,842 thousand the year before. Operating income was $5,154 thousand versus an income of $4,600 thousand in the prior-year quarter, an increase of 12.0%.

Prospects: During the first quarter of 2005, Co. sold its two remaining acute care hospitals located in Puerto Rico and subsequent to quarter-end, Co. signed a definitive agreement to sell its 81.5% interest in Medi-Partenaires, an operating company that owns and operates 14 hospitals located in France. Co. expects its pre-tax sale proceeds after repayment of net debt to be approximately $295.0 million, which will result in an after-tax gain on the sale of approximately $100.0 million. The sale is subject to customary regulatory approvals and Co. expects the closing to occur in mid to late May 2005.

Financial Data

(US$ in Thousands)	3 Mos	12/31/2004	12/31/2003	12/31/2002	12/31/2001	12/31/2000	12/31/1999	12/31/1998
Earnings Per Share	2.21	2.00	2.07	1.84	1.74	1.81	1.56	1.76
Cash Flow Per Share	2.32	2.29	2.48	2.25	2.17	2.22	2.19	2.08
Tang Book Value Per Share	13.30	13.10	12.97	12.73	12.85	11.05	11.09	11.32
Dividends Per Share	2.010	2.000	1.960	1.920	1.875	1.840	1.810	1.755
Dividend Payout %	90.95	100.00	94.69	104.35	107.76	101.66	116.03	99.72
Income Statement								
Property Income	8,491	31,777	28,313	28,429	27,574	27,315	23,584	23,123
Non-Property Income	...	...	...	...	...	...	281	111
Total Revenue	8,491	31,777	28,313	28,429	27,574	27,315	23,865	23,234
Depn & Amortn	1,408	5,312	4,536	4,431	4,401	4,461	3,919	4,003
Interest Expense	1,083	3,357	2,497	2,403	3,896	6,114	4,004	3,490
Net Income	7,580	23,671	24,425	21,623	18,349	16,256	13,972	14,337
Average Shares	11,830	11,813	11,779	11,750	10,536	9,003	8,977	8,974
Balance Sheet								
Total Assets	199,238	204,583	194,291	185,117	187,904	183,658	178,821	169,406
Long-Term Obligations	26,138	46,210	...	...	1,446	1,359	1,289	1,216
Total Liabilities	42,549	50,291	42,093	36,255	37,870	84,401	79,146	68,058
Stockholders' Equity	156,447	154,053	152,198	148,862	150,034	99,257	99,675	101,348
Shares Outstanding	11,760	11,755	11,736	11,698	11,678	8,980	8,990	8,955
Statistical Record								
Return on Assets %	12.60	11.84	12.88	11.59	9.88	8.94	8.02	9.07
Return on Equity %	17.01	15.42	16.23	14.47	14.72	16.30	13.90	14.05
Net Margin %	89.27	74.49	86.27	76.06	66.54	59.51	58.55	61.71
Price Range	34.50-24.82	34.50-24.82	30.55-25.30	28.50-22.69	25.70-18.94	19.88-14.31	20.50-14.63	22.50-18.06
P/E Ratio	15.61-11.23	17.25-12.41	14.76-12.22	15.49-12.33	14.77-10.88	10.98-7.91	13.14-9.38	12.78-10.26
Average Yield %	6.77	6.66	7.19	7.59	8.48	10.90	9.70	8.75

Address: Universal Corporate Center, 367 South Gulph Road, King of Prussia, PA 19406-0958
Telephone: 610-265-0688
Web Site: www.uhrit.com

Officers: Alan B. Miller - Chmn., Pres., C.E.O. Charles F. Boyle - V.P., C.F.O., Contr. **Transfer Agents:** EquiServe Trust Company, N.A., Providence, RI

No of Institutions: 83
Shares: 4,236,722 **% Held:** 36.04

VALLEY NATIONAL BANCORP

Exchange	Symbol	Price	52Wk Range	Yield	P/E
NYS	VLY	$23.86 (5/31/2005)	27.09-23.00	3.69	16.12

*7 Year Price Score 104.40 *NYSE Composite Index=100 *12 Month Price Score 94.27

Interim Earnings (Per Share)

Qtr.	Mar	Jun	Sep	Dec
2002	0.35	0.36	0.36	0.35
2003	0.36	0.36	0.38	0.36
2004	0.37	0.35	0.38	0.38
2005	0.37	...	...	...

Interim Dividends (Per Share)

Amt	Decl	Ex	Rec	Pay
0.214Q	10/13/2004	12/1/2004	12/3/2004	1/3/2005
0.214Q	2/25/2005	3/3/2005	3/7/2005	4/1/2005
5%	4/6/2005	5/4/2005	5/6/2005	5/20/2005
0.22Q	5/25/2005	5/26/2005	5/31/2005	7/1/2005

Indicated Div: $0.88 (Div. Reinv. Plan)

Valuation Analysis

Forecast P/E	N/A		
Market Cap	$2.6 Billion	Book Value	820.9 Million
Price/Book	3.15	Price/Sales	4.21

Dividend Achiever Status

Rank	211	10 Year Growth Rate	8.14%
Total Years of Dividend Growth			13

Business Summary: Commercial Banking (MIC: 8.1 SIC: 021 NAIC: 22110)

Valley National Bancorp, with $10.80 billion in assets as of Dec 31 2004, is a bank holding company. Co.'s principal subsidiary is Valley National Bank (VNB). VNB is a national banking association, which provides a full range of commercial and retail banking services through 133 branch offices located in northern New Jersey and Manhattan. These services include the acceptance of demand, savings and time deposits; extension of consumer, real estate, small business administration and other commercial credits; title insurance; investment services; and full personal and corporate trust, as well as pension and fiduciary services.

Recent Developments: For the quarter ended Mar 31 2005, net income decreased 0.4% to $38,268 thousand from net income of $38,432 thousand in the year-earlier quarter. Net interest income was $94,593 thousand, up 4.9% from $90,217 thousand the year before. Provision for loan losses was $752 thousand versus $1,848 thousand in the prior-year quarter, a decrease of 59.3%. Non-interest income fell 15.8% to $19,358 thousand, while non-interest expense advanced 4.8% to $55,646 thousand.

Prospects: On Mar 31 2005, Co. completed its previously announced acquisition of Shrewsbury Bancorp. Shrewsbury is the holding company for Shrewsbury State Bank, a commercial bank with approximately $425.0 million in assets and 12 branch offices located in 10 communities in Monmouth County. Co. paid approximately $136.0 million in cash and stock for Shrewsbury. Co. estimates that the transaction will be accretive to earnings within one year of the closing. Meanwhile, Co.'s results remain favorable despite the absorbation of costs associated with external challenges and pressures arising from net interest margin compression.

Financial Data
(US$ in Thousands)

	3 Mos	12/31/2004	12/31/2003	12/31/2002	12/31/2001	12/31/2000	12/31/1999	12/31/1998
Earnings Per Share	1.48	1.49	1.47	1.43	1.20	1.15	1.14	1.10
Cash Flow Per Share	0.64	1.56	2.15	1.06	1.45	1.27	2.31	3.47
Tang Book Value Per Share	6.40	6.37	5.80	6.03	6.13	5.98	6.41	6.30
Dividends Per Share	0.857	0.847	0.807	0.766	0.721	0.676	0.638	0.579
Dividend Payout %	57.75	57.01	54.89	53.76	60.27	58.72	56.05	52.79
Income Statement								
Interest Income	139,163	518,926	497,498	517,419	553,486	460,853	427,535	389,656
Interest Expense	44,570	146,607	148,922	157,723	218,653	202,756	169,177	160,104
Net Interest Income	94,593	372,319	348,576	359,696	334,833	258,097	258,358	229,552
Provision for Losses	752	8,003	7,345	13,644	15,706	6,130	9,120	12,370
Non-Interest Income	19,358	84,328	108,197	81,238	68,476	50,883	47,252	43,073
Non-Interest Expense	55,646	220,049	216,278	207,994	188,248	141,013	137,946	134,757
Income Before Taxes	57,553	228,595	233,150	219,296	199,355	161,837	158,544	125,498
Income Taxes	19,285	74,197	79,735	64,680	64,151	55,064	52,220	28,150
Net Income	38,268	154,398	153,415	154,616	135,204	106,773	106,324	97,348
Average Shares	104,338	104,137	104,184	108,438	112,924	92,847	93,146	88,712
Balance Sheet								
Net Loans & Leases	7,251,506	6,868,616	6,107,759	5,698,401	5,268,004	4,607,679	4,499,632	3,927,982
Total Assets	11,407,946	10,763,391	9,880,740	9,134,674	8,583,765	6,425,837	6,360,394	5,541,207
Total Deposits	7,892,723	7,518,739	7,162,968	6,683,387	6,306,974	5,123,717	5,051,255	4,674,689
Total Liabilities	10,587,077	10,055,793	9,227,951	8,302,936	7,705,390	5,880,763	5,806,894	4,985,420
Stockholders' Equity	820,869	707,598	652,789	631,738	678,375	545,074	553,500	555,787
Shares Outstanding	108,469	103,798	103,536	104,792	110,651	91,220	86,378	88,168
Statistical Record								
Return on Assets %	1.43	1.49	1.61	1.75	1.80	1.67	1.79	1.83
Return on Equity %	20.60	22.64	23.89	23.60	22.10	19.39	19.17	18.88
Net Interest Margin %	67.97	71.75	70.07	69.52	60.50	56.00	60.43	58.91
Efficiency Ratio %	35.10	36.48	35.71	34.74	30.27	27.56	29.05	31.14
Loans to Deposits	0.92	0.91	0.85	0.85	0.84	0.90	0.89	0.84
Price Range	27.09-23.00	27.09-23.00	27.18-20.73	25.00-21.12	22.77-16.88	22.05-13.56	18.37-14.78	21.19-15.00
P/E Ratio	18.30-15.54	18.18-15.44	18.49-14.10	17.48-14.77	18.98-14.06	19.17-11.79	16.12-12.96	19.27-13.64
Average Yield %	3.45	3.39	3.31	3.25	3.68	3.98	3.87	3.21

Address: 1455 Valley Road, Wayne, NJ 07470
Telephone: 973-305-8800
Web Site: www.valleynationalbank.com

Officers: Gerald H. Lipkin - Chmn., Pres., C.E.O. Peter Crocitto - Exec. V.P. **Transfer Agents:** American Stock Transfer & Trust Company

Investor Contact: 973-305-8800
No of Institutions: 102
Shares: 12,477,423 **% Held:** 12.62

VALSPAR CORP.

Exchange	Symbol	Price	52Wk Range	Yield	P/E
NYS	VAL	$47.40 (5/31/2005)	50.75-41.15	1.69	18.37

***7 Year Price Score 105.61** *NYSE Composite Index=100 ***12 Month Price Score 91.25**

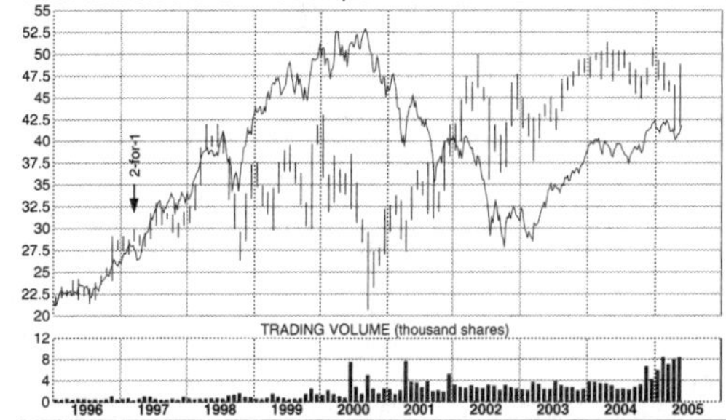

Interim Earnings (Per Share)

Qtr.	Jan	Apr	Jul	Oct
2001-02	0.25	0.67	0.74	0.68
2002-03	0.30	0.62	0.77	0.47
2003-04	0.35	0.74	0.85	0.77
2004-05	0.22	...	...	...

Interim Dividends (Per Share)

Amt	Decl	Ex	Rec	Pay
0.18Q	5/31/2004	6/29/2004	7/1/2004	7/15/2004
0.18Q	8/11/2004	9/29/2004	10/1/2004	10/15/2004
0.20Q	12/8/2004	12/29/2004	12/31/2004	1/14/2005
0.20Q	2/23/2005	3/30/2005	4/1/2005	4/15/2005

Indicated Div: $0.80 (Div. Reinv. Plan)

Valuation Analysis

Forecast P/E	17.96 (6/3/2005)		
Market Cap	$2.4 Billion	Book Value	1.0 Billion
Price/Book	2.36	Price/Sales	0.98

Dividend Achiever Status

Rank	162	10 Year Growth Rate	10.72%
Total Years of Dividend Growth			26

TRADING VOLUME (thousand shares)

Business Summary: Chemicals (MIC: 11.1 SIC: 851 NAIC: 25510)

Valspar is a global paint and coatings manufacturer. The Paints segment includes interior and exterior decorative paints, primers, varnishes and specialty decorative products, such as enamels, aerosols and faux finishes for the do-it-yourself and professional markets, as well as automotive refinish and high performance floor coatings. In the Coatings segment, the Industrial coatings product line includes decorative and protective coatings for wood, metal, plastic and glass. The Packaging coatings product line includes coatings and inks for rigid packaging containers. Other products include specialty polymers and colorants,as well as composites and furniture protection plans.

Recent Developments: For the three months ended Apr 29 2005, net income inched up to $39,241 thousand from net income of $39,089 thousand in the corresponding quarter of the previous year. Net sales were $705,942 thousand, up 10.5% from $638,387 thousand a year earlier. Operating income decreased 7.4% to $68,391 thousand versus income of $73,855 thousand the year before. Total direct expense was $497,813 thousand versus $432,420 thousand in the prior year, an increase of 15.1%. Total indirect expense was $139,738 thousand versus $132,112 thousand in the prior year, an increase of 5.7%.

Prospects: Co. has responded to increased raw material costs with across the board increases in selling prices and a continued focus on expense controls. Consequently, Co. stated that it has made considerable progress in restoring its margins and expects a significant improvement in its second half financial performance. Separately, on May 10 2005, Co. announced that it has agreed to acquire Samuel Cabot Incorporated, a privately owned manufacturer of premium quality exterior and interior stains and finishes. Cabot, based in Newburyport, MA, had 2004 sales of about $58.0 million. Terms of the transaction were not disclosed. Co. expects the acquisition will be slightly accretive to earnings in 2005.

Financial Data

(US$ in Thousands)	3 Mos	10/29/2004	10/31/2003	10/25/2002	10/26/2001	10/27/2000	10/29/1999	10/30/1998
Earnings Per Share	2.58	2.71	2.17	2.34	1.10	2.00	1.87	1.63
Cash Flow Per Share	4.09	4.81	4.88	4.33	4.30	2.19	2.95	2.63
Tang Book Value Per Share	N.M.	N.M.	N.M.	N.M.	N.M.	5.39	4.07	5.42
Dividends Per Share	0.740	0.720	0.600	0.560	0.540	0.520	0.460	0.420
Dividend Payout %	28.64	26.57	27.65	23.93	49.09	26.00	24.60	25.77
Income Statement								
Total Revenue	557,144	2,440,692	2,247,926	2,126,853	1,920,970	1,483,320	1,387,677	1,155,134
EBITDA	44,840	330,473	282,939	298,402	236,759	208,973	193,975	160,237
Depn & Amortn	15,739	60,537	55,622	51,143	73,050	45,238	39,800	30,742
Income Before Taxes	18,569	228,537	181,474	198,548	91,150	141,746	135,086	118,788
Income Taxes	6,871	85,701	68,960	78,427	39,650	55,280	52,944	46,658
Net Income	11,698	142,836	112,514	120,121	51,500	86,466	82,142	72,130
Average Shares	52,632	52,709	51,924	51,370	46,657	43,195	43,835	44,319
Balance Sheet								
Current Assets	846,983	802,315	738,831	701,788	661,494	533,864	514,928	426,069
Total Assets	2,695,201	2,634,258	2,496,524	2,419,552	2,226,070	1,125,030	1,110,720	801,680
Current Liabilities	823,991	718,211	531,063	503,895	475,067	334,288	374,712	267,984
Long-Term Obligations	465,246	549,073	749,199	885,819	1,006,217	300,300	298,874	164,768
Total Liabilities	1,658,445	1,633,895	1,627,207	1,682,299	1,571,505	687,459	716,964	461,492
Stockholders' Equity	1,036,756	1,000,363	869,317	737,253	654,565	437,571	393,756	340,188
Shares Outstanding	51,661	51,304	50,730	50,104	49,481	42,481	42,983	43,418
Statistical Record								
Return on Assets %	5.18	5.58	4.50	5.19	3.08	7.76	8.61	10.21
Return on Equity %	14.10	15.32	13.78	17.31	9.46	20.86	22.45	22.77
EBITDA Margin %	8.05	13.54	12.59	14.03	12.32	14.09	13.98	13.87
Net Margin %	2.10	5.85	5.01	5.65	2.68	5.83	5.92	6.24
Asset Turnover	0.95	0.95	0.90	0.92	1.15	1.33	1.46	1.63
Current Ratio	1.03	1.12	1.39	1.39	1.39	1.60	1.37	1.59
Debt to Equity	0.45	0.55	0.86	1.20	1.54	0.69	0.76	0.48
Price Range	51.35-44.87	51.35-44.87	47.95-37.69	49.91-33.21	37.49-25.45	43.06-20.60	39.56-28.06	42.00-26.31
P/E Ratio	19.90-17.39	18.95-16.56	22.10-17.37	21.33-14.19	34.08-23.14	21.53-10.30	21.16-15.01	25.77-16.14
Average Yield %	1.53	1.48	1.37	1.33	1.69	1.55	1.33	1.20

Address: 1101 Third Street South, Minneapolis, MN 55415 **Telephone:** 612-332-7371 **Web Site:** www.valspar.com	**Officers:** Richard M. Rompala - Chmn. William L. Mansfield - Pres., C.E.O. **Transfer Agents:** Mellon Investor Services LLC, Ridgefield Park, NJ	**No of Institutions:** 169 **Shares:** 29,379,078 **% Held:** 57.74

VECTREN CORP

Exchange	Symbol	Price	52Wk Range	Yield	P/E
NYS	VVC	$27.29 (5/31/2005)	27.86-23.43	4.32	18.95

*7 Year Price Score 101.14 *NYSE Composite Index=100 *12 Month Price Score 100.24

TRADING VOLUME (thousand shares)

Interim Earnings (Per Share)

Qtr.	Mar	Jun	Sep	Dec
2002	0.67	0.21	0.21	0.59
2003	0.82	0.06	0.10	0.60
2004	0.72	0.04	0.13	0.53
2005	0.74	...	...	...

Interim Dividends (Per Share)

Amt	Decl	Ex	Rec	Pay
0.285Q	7/28/2004	8/11/2004	8/13/2004	9/1/2004
0.295Q	10/28/2004	11/10/2004	11/15/2004	12/1/2004
0.295Q	1/26/2005	2/11/2005	2/15/2005	3/1/2005
0.295Q	4/27/2005	5/11/2005	5/13/2005	6/1/2005

Indicated Div: $1.18 (Div. Reinv. Plan)

Valuation Analysis

Forecast P/E 15.54 (6/1/2005)

Market Cap	$2.1 Billion	Book Value	1.1 Billion
Price/Book	1.83	Price/Sales	1.20

Dividend Achiever Status

Rank 287 **10 Year Growth Rate** 3.96%

Total Years of Dividend Growth 29

Business Summary: Electricity (MIC: 7.1 SIC: 932 NAIC: 21210)

Vectren is an energy and applied technology holding company. As of Dec 31 2004, Co.'s Indiana Gas Company, Inc. public utility provided energy delivery services to about 555,000 natural gas customers located in central and southern Indiana. Co.'s Southern Indiana Gas and Electric Company utility provided energy delivery services to approximately 136,000 electric customers and about 110,000 natural gas customers located near Evansville in southwestern Indiana. Co.'s Ohio operations provided energy delivery services to approximately 315,000 natural gas customers located near Dayton in west central Ohio. Co. is also involved in range of nonregulated activities.

Recent Developments: For the quarter ended Mar 31 2005, net income increased 2.4% to $56,100 thousand from net income of $54,800 thousand in the year-earlier quarter. Revenues were $677,200 thousand, up 4.9% from $645,300 thousand the year before. Operating income was $95,200 thousand versus an income of $86,000 thousand in the prior-year quarter, an increase of 10.7%. Total direct expense was $451,700 thousand versus $432,900 thousand in the prior-year quarter, an increase of 4.3%. Total indirect expense was $130,300 thousand versus $126,400 thousand in the prior-year quarter, an increase of 3.1%.

Prospects: On Apr 26 2005, Co. affirmed its fiscal 2005 earnings guidance of $1.70 to $1.90 per share. This projection is based on several factors, including normal weather for the balance of 2005, stable economic conditions, and continued growth from its nonregulated businesses. Co. noted that over the last nine months it has implemented new base rates for all three of its gas jurisdictions, which should support results going forward, and it continues to recover costs associated with its power generation environmental compliance expenditures. Meanwhile, Co.'s nonregulated group is benefiting from improved results from its coal mining group, mainly due to greater production and higher revenue per ton.

Financial Data (US$ in Thousands)	3 Mos	12/31/2004	12/31/2003	12/31/2002	12/31/2001	12/31/2000	12/31/1999	12/31/1998
Earnings Per Share	1.44	1.42	1.57	1.68	0.95	1.17	1.48	1.40
Cash Flow Per Share	3.56	3.18	2.51	4.32	2.75	0.66	2.43	...
Tang Book Value Per Share	12.21	11.70	11.46	9.83	9.68	8.69	11.58	...
Dividends Per Share	1.160	1.150	1.110	1.070	1.030	0.740	0.940	0.900
Dividend Payout %	80.56	80.99	70.70	63.69	108.42	63.25	63.51	64.29
Income Statement								
Total Revenue	677,200	1,689,800	1,587,700	1,804,300	2,170,000	1,648,690	1,068,417	997,706
EBITDA	141,100	357,200	344,200	341,100	293,700	270,070	267,236	251,209
Depn & Amortn	37,100	140,100	128,700	119,600	123,700	105,661	86,998	81,558
Income Before Taxes	83,900	147,000	149,000	153,400	87,400	107,276	137,376	129,350
Income Taxes	27,800	39,000	37,700	38,900	18,600	34,232	45,708	42,328
Net Income	56,100	107,900	111,200	114,000	63,600	72,040	90,748	86,600
Average Shares	76,100	75,900	70,800	67,900	66,900	61,380	61,430	61,578
Balance Sheet								
Net PPE	2,397,400	2,385,400	2,226,000	1,876,100	1,776,700	1,659,238	1,400,807	...
Total Assets	3,447,300	3,586,900	3,353,400	2,926,500	2,856,800	2,909,187	1,980,467	...
Long-Term Obligations	1,016,200	1,016,600	1,072,800	954,200	1,014,000	631,954	486,726	...
Total Liabilities	2,313,100	2,492,000	2,281,500	2,056,300	2,007,700	2,160,538	1,251,428	...
Stockholders' Equity	1,134,200	1,094,800	1,071,700	869,900	848,600	731,684	709,757	...
Shares Outstanding	75,900	75,900	75,600	67,900	67,700	61,419	61,305	...
Statistical Record								
Return on Assets %	3.26	3.10	3.54	3.94	2.21	2.94	...	...
Return on Equity %	9.73	9.93	11.45	13.27	8.05	9.97	...	...
EBITDA Margin %	20.84	21.14	21.68	18.90	13.53	16.38	25.01	25.18
Net Margin %	8.28	6.39	7.00	6.32	2.93	4.37	8.49	8.68
PPE Turnover	0.74	0.73	0.77	0.99	1.26	1.07	...	...
Asset Turnover	0.51	0.49	0.51	0.62	0.75	0.67	...	...
Debt to Equity	0.90	0.93	1.00	1.10	1.19	0.86	0.69	...
Price Range	27.86-22.90	27.08-22.90	26.00-20.01	25.87-18.69	24.19-19.90	26.50-15.13	24.63-17.75	26.38-19.88
P/E Ratio	19.35-15.90	19.07-16.13	16.56-12.75	15.40-11.13	25.46-20.95	22.65-12.93	16.64-11.99	18.84-14.20
Average Yield %	4.55	4.61	4.81	4.49	4.70	3.79	4.54	3.99

Address: 20 N.W. Fourth Street, Evansville, IN 47708
Telephone: 812-491-4000
Web Site: www.vectren.com

Officers: Niel C. Ellerbrook - Chmn., Pres., C.E.O. Jerome A. Benkert Jr. - Exec. V.P., C.F.O. **Transfer Agents:** National City Bank, Cleveland, OH

Investor Contact: 800-227-8625
No of Institutions: 170
Shares: 27,939,258 **% Held:** 36.72

VF CORP.

Exchange	Symbol	Price	52Wk Range	Yield	P/E
NYS	VFC	$56.43 (5/31/2005)	60.46-46.51	1.91	12.94

*7 Year Price Score 117.72 *NYSE Composite Index=100 *12 Month Price Score 103.67

Interim Earnings (Per Share)

Qtr.	Mar	Jun	Sep	Dec
2002	(4.11)	0.79	1.15	0.67
2003	0.83	0.68	1.14	0.96
2004	0.93	0.80	1.38	1.10
2005	1.07	...	...	...

Interim Dividends (Per Share)

Amt	Decl	Ex	Rec	Pay
0.26Q	7/21/2004	9/8/2004	9/10/2004	9/20/2004
0.27Q	10/21/2004	12/8/2004	12/10/2004	12/20/2004
0.27Q	2/8/2005	3/9/2005	3/11/2005	3/21/2005
0.27Q	4/26/2005	6/8/2005	6/10/2005	6/20/2005

Indicated Div: $1.08 (Div. Reinv. Plan)

Valuation Analysis

Forecast P/E	12.27 (6/1/2005)		
Market Cap	$6.3 Billion	Book Value	2.6 Billion
Price/Book	2.41	Price/Sales	1.02

Dividend Achiever Status

Rank	271	10 Year Growth Rate	4.91%
Total Years of Dividend Growth			32

Business Summary: Apparel (MIC: 4.4 SIC: 329 NAIC: 15228)

VF designs, manufactures and markets branded apparel and other products through its five business units: Jeanswear, Outdoor Apparel and Equipment, Intimate Apparel, Imagewear and Sportswear. Co.'s products and brands are sold through specialty store, department store, chain store and discount store channels, as well as through Co.-owned retail stores, and through licensees and distributors offering these products directly to consumers. Co.'s principal brands include: Lee®, Rustler®, Wrangler®, Riders®, H.I.S®, JanSport®, The North Face®, Eastpak®, Vans®, Napapijri®, Kipling®, Vanity Fair®, Vassarette®, Bestform®, Lily of France®, Lee Sport®, Bulwark®, Red Kap®, John Varvatos, and Nautica®.

Recent Developments: For the quarter ended Apr 2 2005, net income increased 18.3% to $122,868 thousand from net income of $103,874 thousand in the year-earlier quarter. Revenues were $1,563,643 thousand, up 9.1% from $1,432,669 thousand the year before. Operating income was $198,896 thousand versus an income of $172,559 thousand in the prior-year quarter, an increase of 15.3%. Total direct expense was $914,424 thousand versus $878,393 thousand in the prior-year quarter, an increase of 4.1%. Total indirect expense was $463,672 thousand versus $394,957 thousand in the prior-year quarter, an increase of 17.4%.

Prospects: On Apr 14 2005, Co. announced that it has completed the acquisition of Reef Holdings Corporation a provider of surf-inspired footwear. The Reef acquisition adds an authentic specialty surf brand to Co.'s Outdoor Coalition, and extends Co.'s presence in the action sports lifestyle market. Reef is expected to contribute about $45.0 million in sales and be neutral to earnings in 2005, and accretive to earnings in 2006. Meanwhile, Co.'s Outdoor, Imagewear and Sportswear businesses are each delivering strong increases in both sales and profits. For full-year 2005, Co. expects sales growth of 6.0% to 8.0%, excluding any additional acquisitions, and earnings per share growth of at least 8.0%.

Financial Data

(US$ in Thousands)	3 Mos	01/01/2005	01/03/2004	01/04/2003	12/29/2001	12/30/2000	01/01/2000	01/02/1999
Earnings Per Share	4.36	4.21	3.61	(1.38)	1.19	2.21	2.99	3.10
Cash Flow Per Share	5.97	6.66	5.06	5.82	6.18	3.90	3.58	3.59
Tang Book Value Per Share	8.35	6.57	8.61	10.91	9.97	12.56	10.08	9.33
Dividends Per Share	1.060	1.050	1.010	0.970	0.930	0.890	0.850	0.810
Dividend Payout %	24.31	24.94	27.98	...	78.15	40.27	28.43	26.13
Income Statement								
Total Revenue	1,563,643	6,054,536	5,207,459	5,083,523	5,518,805	5,747,879	5,551,616	5,478,807
EBITDA	224,914	907,324	756,437	733,054	518,289	685,987	825,498	848,854
Depn & Amortn	25,899	126,268	108,019	107,398	168,972	173,422	167,432	161,385
Income Before Taxes	183,357	712,120	598,506	561,728	262,801	431,533	595,576	631,598
Income Taxes	60,489	237,418	200,573	197,300	124,971	164,417	229,334	243,292
Net Income	122,868	474,702	397,933	(154,543)	137,830	260,334	366,242	388,306
Average Shares	114,926	112,730	110,323	112,336	114,764	117,218	122,258	124,995
Balance Sheet								
Current Assets	2,353,181	2,378,568	2,208,531	2,074,540	2,031,420	2,110,096	1,877,416	1,848,152
Total Assets	5,007,727	5,004,278	4,245,552	3,503,151	4,103,016	4,358,156	4,026,514	3,836,666
Current Liabilities	1,261,274	1,372,214	871,857	874,844	813,833	1,006,200	1,113,473	1,033,006
Long-Term Obligations	558,863	556,639	956,383	602,287	904,035	905,036	517,834	521,657
Total Liabilities	2,392,650	2,464,984	2,264,258	1,808,401	1,944,589	2,117,860	1,811,152	1,716,014
Stockholders' Equity	2,615,077	2,513,241	1,951,307	1,657,848	2,112,796	2,191,813	2,163,818	2,066,308
Shares Outstanding	111,830	111,388	108,170	108,525	109,998	86,807	116,204	119,466
Statistical Record								
Return on Assets %	10.53	10.29	10.30	N.M.	3.27	6.23	9.34	10.88
Return on Equity %	20.87	21.32	22.11	N.M.	6.42	11.99	17.36	19.80
EBITDA Margin %	14.38	14.99	14.53	14.42	9.39	11.93	14.87	15.49
Net Margin %	7.86	7.84	7.64	N.M.	2.50	4.53	6.60	7.09
Asset Turnover	1.32	1.31	1.35	1.32	1.31	1.37	1.42	1.53
Current Ratio	1.87	1.73	2.53	2.37	2.50	2.10	1.69	1.79
Debt to Equity	0.21	0.22	0.49	0.36	0.43	0.41	0.24	0.25
Price Range	60.46-43.90	55.38-42.36	44.05-32.85	45.33-32.09	41.99-28.61	36.56-22.00	54.25-28.00	53.81-34.00
P/E Ratio	13.87-10.07	13.15-10.06	12.20-9.10	...	35.29-24.04	16.54-9.95	18.14-9.36	17.36-10.97
Average Yield %	2.06	2.17	2.64	2.43	2.56	3.38	2.13	1.73

Address: 105 Corporate Center Boulevard, Greensboro, NC 27408	**Officers:** Mackey J. McDonald - Chmn., Pres., C.E.O. Bradley W. Batten - V.P., Contr., Chief Acctg. Officer	**Investor Contact:** 336-424-6000
Telephone: 336-424-6000	**ransfer Agents:**EquiServe Trust Company, Jersey City, NJ	**No of Institutions:** 277
Web Site: www.vfc.com		**Shares:** 98,244,488 **% Held:** 87.45

VULCAN MATERIALS CO.

Exchange	Symbol	Price	52Wk Range	Yield	P/E
NYS	VMC	$59.93 (5/31/2005)	60.38-44.59	1.94	19.03

*7 Year Price Score 104.33 *NYSE Composite Index=100 *12 Month Price Score 104.78

Interim Earnings (Per Share)

Qtr.	Mar	Jun	Sep	Dec
2002	0.11	0.64	0.75	0.36
2003	(0.17)	0.55	0.96	0.56
2004	0.14	0.85	0.96	0.82
2005	0.52	...	...	...

Interim Dividends (Per Share)

Amt	Decl	Ex	Rec	Pay
0.26Q	7/9/2004	8/24/2004	8/26/2004	9/10/2004
0.26Q	10/8/2004	11/22/2004	11/24/2004	12/10/2004
0.29Q	2/11/2005	2/23/2005	2/25/2005	3/10/2005
0.29Q	5/13/2005	5/25/2005	5/27/2005	6/10/2005

Indicated Div: $1.16 (Div. Reinv. Plan)

Valuation Analysis

Forecast P/E	19.17 (6/1/2005)		
Market Cap	$6.1 Billion	Book Value	2.0 Billion
Price/Book	3.06	Price/Sales	2.59

Dividend Achiever Status

Rank	193	10 Year Growth Rate	8.98%
Total Years of Dividend Growth			12

Business Summary: Earth & Rock Mining (MIC: 14.5 SIC: 422 NAIC: 12312)

Vulcan Materials and its subsidiaries are engaged in the production, distribution and sale of construction materials and industrial and specialty chemicals, including chloralkali. Co.'s construction materials business consists of the production, distribution and sale of construction aggregates and other construction materials and related services. Construction aggregates include crushed stone, sand and gravel, rock asphalt and recrushed concrete and are employed in all types of construction, including highway construction and maintenance. Other Construction Materials products and services include asphalt mix and related products and ready-mixed concrete.

Recent Developments: For the quarter ended Mar 31 2005, income from continuing operations increased 3.7% to $21,434 thousand from income of $20,673 thousand in the year-earlier quarter. Net income increased 262.5% to $54,351 thousand from net income of $14,995 thousand in the year-earlier quarter. Revenues were $528,616 thousand, up 11.4% from $474,399 thousand the year before. Total direct expense was $436,383 thousand versus $390,494 thousand in the prior-year quarter, an increase of 11.8%. Total indirect expense was $51,436 thousand versus $44,487 thousand in the prior-year quarter, an increase of 15.6%.

Prospects: Looking ahead, Co. is optimistic about opportunities for earnings growth in 2005. Demand in Co.'s markets is strong and pricing for aggregates continues to improve. Meanwhile, Co. expects higher unit costs for diesel and liquid asphalt to continue. Also, healthcare costs are expected to increase year-over-year, but the rate of increase should slow due to the changes Co. implemented last year in its plans. Moreover, Co. is raising its full year guidance for continuing operations to $2.95 to $3.20 per diluted share for 2005. Separately, Co. anticipate the completion of the sale of its Chemicals business around mid-year.

Financial Data

(US$ in Thousands)	3 Mos	12/31/2004	12/31/2003	12/31/2002	12/31/2001	12/31/2000	12/31/1999	12/31/1998
Earnings Per Share	3.15	2.77	1.90	1.66	2.17	2.16	2.35	2.50
Cash Flow Per Share	5.72	5.65	5.10	4.54	5.03	4.13	3.99	3.60
Tang Book Value Per Share	13.56	13.77	12.01	11.04	10.02	9.00	8.63	11.47
Dividends Per Share	1.070	1.040	0.980	0.940	0.900	0.840	0.780	0.693
Dividend Payout %	33.97	37.55	51.58	56.63	41.47	38.89	33.19	27.73
Income Statement								
Total Revenue	528,616	2,454,335	2,892,186	2,796,577	3,019,990	2,491,744	2,355,778	1,776,434
EBITDA	91,985	643,898	638,108	576,805	659,098	588,012	602,915	512,764
Depn & Amortn	52,661	233,651	277,091	267,676	278,209	232,365	207,108	137,792
Income Before Taxes	32,553	375,566	311,425	257,660	324,053	312,238	351,561	374,844
Income Taxes	11,119	114,353	87,971	67,247	101,373	92,345	111,868	118,936
Net Income	54,351	287,385	194,952	169,876	222,680	219,893	239,693	255,908
Average Shares	104,612	103,664	102,710	102,515	102,497	102,012	102,190	102,177
Balance Sheet								
Current Assets	1,410,444	1,417,959	1,050,242	789,688	729,952	694,504	624,724	576,381
Total Assets	3,713,531	3,665,133	3,636,860	3,448,221	3,398,224	3,228,574	2,839,493	1,658,611
Current Liabilities	719,252	426,689	542,952	297,709	344,495	572,231	386,642	211,462
Long-Term Obligations	728,302	604,522	607,654	857,757	906,299	685,361	698,862	76,533
Total Liabilities	2,076,609	1,651,158	1,742,037	1,658,577	1,793,950	1,757,078	1,515,840	504,911
Stockholders' Equity	2,001,073	2,013,975	1,802,836	1,696,986	1,604,274	1,471,496	1,323,653	1,153,700
Shares Outstanding	102,118	102,659	101,811	101,557	101,320	101,043	100,734	100,596
Statistical Record								
Return on Assets %	8.87	7.85	5.50	4.96	6.72	7.23	10.66	16.47
Return on Equity %	17.18	15.02	11.14	10.29	14.48	15.69	19.35	23.86
EBITDA Margin %	17.40	26.24	22.06	20.63	21.82	23.60	25.59	28.86
Net Margin %	10.28	11.71	6.74	6.07	7.37	8.82	10.17	14.41
Asset Turnover	0.64	0.67	0.82	0.82	0.91	0.82	1.05	1.14
Current Ratio	1.96	3.32	1.93	2.65	2.12	1.21	1.62	2.73
Debt to Equity	0.36	0.30	0.34	0.51	0.56	0.47	0.53	0.07
Price Range	59.65-42.35	54.95-42.35	48.25-29.06	49.55-32.37	55.10-38.15	48.50-36.69	50.50-34.88	44.06-31.63
P/E Ratio	18.94-13.44	19.84-15.29	25.39-15.29	29.85-19.50	25.39-17.58	22.45-16.98	21.49-14.84	17.63-12.65
Average Yield %	2.13	2.16	2.56	2.23	1.91	1.95	1.81	1.86

Address: 1200 Urban Center Drive, Birmingham, AL 35242
Telephone: 205-298-3000
Web Site: www.vulcanmaterials.com

Officers: Donald M. James - Chmn., C.E.O. Daniel F. Sansone - Sr. V.P., C.F.O., Treas. **Transfer Agents:** The Bank of New York, New York, NY

Investor Contact: 205-298-3220
No of Institutions: 246
Shares: 76,378,096 **% Held:** 74.21

WAL-MART STORES, INC.

Exchange	Symbol	Price	52Wk Range	Yield	P/E
NYS	WMT	$47.23 (5/31/2005)	57.70-46.81	1.27	19.60

Interim Earnings (Per Share)

Qtr.	Apr	Jul	Oct	Jan
2000-01	0.30	0.36	0.31	0.44
2001-02	0.30	0.36	0.33	0.49
2002-03	0.37	0.46	0.41	0.57
2003-04	0.42	0.56	0.46	0.63
2004-05	0.50	0.62	0.54	0.75

Interim Dividends (Per Share)

Amt	Decl	Ex	Rec	Pay
0.15Q	3/3/2005	3/16/2005	3/18/2005	4/4/2005
0.15Q	3/3/2005	5/18/2005	5/20/2005	6/6/2005
0.15Q	3/3/2005	8/17/2005	8/19/2005	9/6/2005
0.15Q	3/3/2005	12/14/2005	12/16/2005	1/3/2006

Indicated Div: $0.60 (Div. Reinv. Plan)

Valuation Analysis

Forecast P/E 15.94 (6/3/2005)
Market Cap $200.0 Billion Book Value 49.4 Billion
Price/Book 4.05 Price/Sales 0.69

Dividend Achiever Status

Rank 39 **10 Year Growth Rate** 19.62%
Total Years of Dividend Growth 29

Business Summary: Retail - General (MIC: 5.2 SIC: 331 NAIC: 52990)

Wal-Mart Stores operated 1,353 discount department stores, 1,713 Supercenters, 551 Sam's Clubs and 85 Neighborhood Markets in the U.S. as of Jan 31 2005. Co. also operated 679 Wal-Mart stores in Mexico, 282 in the U.K., 262 in Canada, 91 in Germany, 54 in Puerto Rico, 149 in Brazil, 16 in South Korea, and eleven in Argentina. Co. also operated 43 stores in China under joint venture agreements. Co.'s supercenters combine food, general merchandise, and services including pharmacy, dry cleaning, portrait studios, photo finishing, hair salons, and optical shops. In addition, Co. owns approximately 37.0% interest in Seiyu, Ltd., which operates over 403 stores throughout Japan.

Recent Developments: For the quarter ended April 30 2005, net income increased 13.6% to $2,461,000 thousand from net income of $2,166,000 thousand in the corresponding period of the previous year. Revenues were $70,908,000 thousand, up 9.5% from $65,443,000 thousand the year before. Operating income was $3,941,000 thousand versus an income of $3,605,000 thousand in the prior year, an increase of 9.3%. Total direct expense was $54,571,000 thousand versus $49,969,000 thousand in the prior year, an increase of 9.2%.

Prospects: Co.'s top-line results are being negatively hampered by a cooler and wetter spring than normal, as well as soaring gasoline prices, which is cutting into household budgets. Co. expects energy prices to continue to unfavorably weigh on second quarter results. In addition, rising costs for store labor, health care and utilities are negatively affecting bottom-line results. However, Co. expects trends to improve in the second half of the year and remains cautious about U.S. economic conditions. Meanwhile, Co. expects second quarter earnings to range from $0.63 to $0.67 per share. Moreover, Co. forecasts fiscal year earnings to range from $2.70 to $2.74 per share.

Financial Data

(US$ in Thousands)	01/31/2005	01/31/2004	01/31/2003	01/31/2002	01/31/2001	01/31/2000	01/31/1999	01/31/1998
Earnings Per Share	2.41	2.07	1.81	1.49	1.40	1.20	0.99	0.78
Cash Flow Per Share	3.52	3.67	2.83	2.30	2.15	1.84	1.70	1.58
Tang Book Value Per Share	9.12	7.83	6.78	5.95	4.99	3.69	4.18	4.13
Dividends Per Share	0.520	0.360	0.300	0.280	0.240	0.200	0.155	0.135
Dividend Payout %	21.58	17.39	16.57	18.79	17.14	16.67	15.66	17.31
Income Statement								
Total Revenue	287,989,000	258,681,000	246,525,000	219,812,000	193,295,000	166,809,000	139,208,000	119,299,000
EBITDA	21,496,000	18,877,000	17,076,000	15,367,000	14,358,000	12,480,000	9,992,000	8,137,000
Depn & Amortn	4,405,000	3,852,000	3,432,000	3,290,000	2,868,000	2,375,000	1,872,000	1,634,000
Income Before Taxes	16,105,000	14,193,000	12,719,000	10,751,000	10,116,000	9,083,000	7,323,000	5,719,000
Income Taxes	5,589,000	5,118,000	4,487,000	3,897,000	3,692,000	3,338,000	2,740,000	2,115,000
Net Income	10,267,000	9,054,000	8,039,000	6,671,000	6,295,000	5,377,000	4,430,000	3,526,000
Average Shares	4,266,000	4,372,999	4,445,999	4,480,999	4,483,999	4,473,999	4,484,999	4,532,999
Balance Sheet								
Current Assets	38,491,000	34,421,000	30,483,000	28,246,000	26,555,000	24,356,000	21,132,000	19,352,000
Total Assets	120,223,000	104,912,000	94,685,000	83,451,000	78,130,000	70,349,000	49,996,000	45,384,000
Current Liabilities	42,888,000	37,418,000	32,617,000	27,282,000	28,949,000	25,803,000	16,762,000	14,460,000
Long-Term Obligations	23,669,000	20,099,000	19,608,000	18,732,000	15,655,000	16,674,000	9,607,000	9,674,000
Total Liabilities	70,827,000	61,289,000	55,348,000	48,349,000	46,787,000	44,515,000	28,884,000	26,881,000
Stockholders' Equity	49,396,000	43,623,000	39,337,000	35,102,000	31,343,000	25,834,000	21,112,000	18,503,000
Shares Outstanding	4,234,000	4,310,999	4,394,999	4,452,999	4,469,999	4,456,999	4,447,999	4,481,999
Statistical Record								
Return on Assets %	9.10	9.07	9.03	8.26	8.46	8.94	9.29	8.30
Return on Equity %	22.01	21.83	21.60	20.08	21.96	22.91	22.37	19.78
EBITDA Margin %	7.46	7.30	6.93	6.99	7.43	7.48	7.18	6.82
Net Margin %	3.57	3.50	3.26	3.03	3.26	3.22	3.18	2.96
Asset Turnover	2.55	2.59	2.77	2.72	2.60	2.77	2.92	2.81
Current Ratio	0.90	0.92	0.93	1.04	0.92	0.94	1.26	1.34
Debt to Equity	0.48	0.46	0.50	0.53	0.50	0.65	0.46	0.52
Price Range	61.05-51.33	60.08-46.74	63.75-44.60	59.98-44.00	63.56-43.25	69.44-40.19	43.00-20.41	20.88-11.56
P/E Ratio	25.33-21.30	29.02-22.58	35.22-24.64	40.26-29.53	45.40-30.89	57.86-33.49	43.43-20.61	26.76-14.82
Average Yield %	0.95	0.66	0.55	0.53	0.45	0.40	0.50	0.80

Address: 702 S.W. Eighth Street, Bentonville, AR 72716 **Telephone:** 479-273-4000 **Web Site:** www.wal-mart.com	**Officers:** S. Robson Walton - Chmn. H. Lee Scott Jr. - Pres., C.E.O. **Transfer Agents:** EquiServe Trust Company, N.A., Providence, RI	**No of Institutions:** 999 **Shares:** 1,500,553,600 **% Held:** 35.43

WALGREEN CO.

Exchange	Symbol	Price	52Wk Range	Yield	P/E
NYS	WAG	$45.34 (5/31/2005)	46.47-34.38	0.46	31.27

*7 Year Price Score 105.50 *NYSE Composite Index=100 *12 Month Price Score 107.90

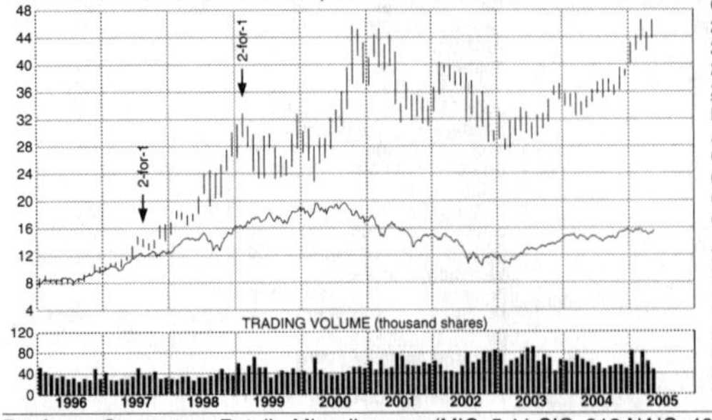

Interim Earnings (Per Share)

Qtr.	Nov	Feb	May	Aug
2001-02	0.18	0.32	0.25	0.24
2002-03	0.22	0.36	0.29	0.27
2003-04	0.25	0.42	0.33	0.32
2004-05	0.32	0.48	...	...

Interim Dividends (Per Share)

Amt	Decl	Ex	Rec	Pay
0.052Q	7/14/2004	8/18/2004	8/20/2004	9/11/2004
0.052Q	10/13/2004	11/10/2004	11/15/2004	12/11/2004
0.052Q	1/12/2005	2/16/2005	2/18/2005	3/12/2005
0.052Q	4/13/2005	5/18/2005	5/20/2005	6/11/2005

Indicated Div: $0.21 (Div. Reinv. Plan)

Valuation Analysis

Forecast P/E	29.85 (6/3/2005)		
Market Cap	$46.3 Billion	Book Value	8.7 Billion
Price/Book	5.35	Price/Sales	1.16

Dividend Achiever Status

Rank	212	10 Year Growth Rate	8.06%
Total Years of Dividend Growth			29

Business Summary: Retail - Miscellaneous (MIC: 5.11 SIC: 912 NAIC: 46110)
Walgreen is engaged in the operation of retail drugstores. Co.'s drugstores are engaged in the retail sale of prescription and non-prescription drugs and carry additional product lines such as general merchandise, cosmetics, toiletries, household items, food and beverages. Customer prescription purchases can be made at the drugstores as well as through the mail, by telephone and on the Internet. The total number of stores at Aug 31 2004 was 4,579 stores located in 44 states and Puerto Rico. In addition, Co. operates three mail service facilities.

Recent Developments: For the three months ended Feb 28 2005, net income increased 13.7% to $490,900 thousand from net income of $431,600 thousand in the corresponding quarter of the previous year. Revenues were $10,987,000 thousand, up 12.3% from $9,782,200 thousand the year before. Operating income jumped 13.2% to $782,300 thousand versus income of $690,700 thousand a year earlier. Total direct expense was $7,856,400 thousand versus $7,076,600 thousand in the prior year, an increase of 11.0%. Total indirect expense was 2,359,700 thousand versus $2,031,600 thousand in the prior year, an increase of 16.1%.

Prospects: In the second quarter of fiscal 2005, Co. benefited from strong sales and earnings growth supported by pharmacy results. Co.'s solid front-end and strong pharmacy sales continue to drive the business. Co.'s gross margins are being positively affected by growth in generic drug sales, better purchasing terms and digital photofinishing, even as other front-end categories experience lower margins due to more aggressive advertising. Co. opened 178 new stores in the first half of the year and expects to open a total of 450 new stores, with a net increase of 365 stores, in fiscal 2005. Meanwhile, Co. is continuing to incur significant costs related to digital photo lab conversions.

Financial Data (US$ in Thousands)	6 Mos	3 Mos	08/31/2004	08/31/2003	08/31/2002	08/31/2001	08/31/2000	08/31/1999
Earnings Per Share	1.45	1.39	1.32	1.14	0.99	0.86	0.76	0.62
Cash Flow Per Share	1.57	1.55	1.61	1.46	1.44	0.71	0.96	0.62
Tang Book Value Per Share	8.48	8.24	8.04	7.02	6.08	5.11	4.19	3.47
Dividends Per Share	0.201	0.191	0.182	0.156	0.145	0.140	0.135	0.130
Dividend Payout %	13.84	13.80	13.78	13.65	14.65	16.28	17.76	20.97
Income Statement								
Total Revenue	20,876,100	9,889,100	37,508,200	32,505,400	28,681,100	24,623,000	21,206,900	17,838,800
EBITDA	1,281,700	512,600	2,562,100	2,224,000	1,937,700	1,689,600	1,487,700	1,225,500
Depn & Amortn	...	...	403,100	346,100	307,300	269,200	230,100	210,100
Income Before Taxes	1,293,500	517,700	2,176,300	1,888,700	1,637,300	1,422,700	1,263,300	1,027,300
Income Taxes	474,000	185,000	816,100	713,000	618,100	537,100	486,400	403,200
Net Income	819,500	332,700	1,360,200	1,175,700	1,019,200	885,600	776,900	624,100
Average Shares	1,029,600	1,029,400	1,031,798	1,031,580	1,032,270	1,028,946	1,019,888	1,014,281
Balance Sheet								
Current Assets	8,266,200	8,385,100	7,764,400	6,358,100	5,166,500	4,393,900	3,550,100	3,221,700
Total Assets	14,174,000	14,149,700	13,342,100	11,405,900	9,878,800	8,833,800	7,103,700	5,906,700
Current Liabilities	4,306,800	4,645,000	4,077,900	3,420,500	2,955,200	3,011,600	2,303,700	1,923,800
Total Liabilities	5,508,800	5,731,600	5,114,100	4,210,200	3,648,600	3,626,600	2,869,700	2,422,400
Stockholders' Equity	8,665,200	8,418,100	8,228,000	7,195,700	6,230,200	5,207,200	4,234,000	3,484,300
Shares Outstanding	1,021,810	1,021,119	1,023,292	1,024,908	1,024,908	1,019,425	1,010,818	1,004,022
Statistical Record								
Return on Assets %	11.30	10.92	10.96	11.05	10.89	11.11	11.91	11.55
Return on Equity %	18.23	18.15	17.59	17.51	17.82	18.76	20.08	19.71
EBITDA Margin %	6.14	5.18	6.83	6.84	6.76	6.86	7.02	6.87
Net Margin %	3.93	3.36	3.63	3.62	3.55	3.60	3.66	3.50
Asset Turnover	3.01	2.94	3.02	3.05	3.07	3.09	3.25	3.30
Current Ratio	1.92	1.81	1.90	1.86	1.75	1.46	1.54	1.67
Price Range	44.17-32.45	39.48-32.45	37.74-30.57	35.96-27.35	40.24-30.98	45.63-31.43	36.00-22.75	32.88-19.19
P/E Ratio	30.46-22.38	28.40-23.35	28.59-23.16	31.54-23.99	40.65-31.29	53.05-36.55	47.37-29.93	53.02-30.95
Average Yield %	0.54	0.54	0.52	0.50	0.40	0.35	0.48	0.49

Address: 200 Wilmot Road, Deerfield, IL 60015
Telephone: 847-940-2500
Web Site: www.walgreens.com

Officers: David W. Bernauer - Chmn., C.E.O. Jeffrey A. Rein - Pres., C.O.O. **Transfer Agents:** Computershare Investor Services, Chicago, IL

Investor Contact: 847-914-2972
No of Institutions: 720
Shares: 596,883,392 **% Held:** 58.44

WASHINGTON FEDERAL INC.

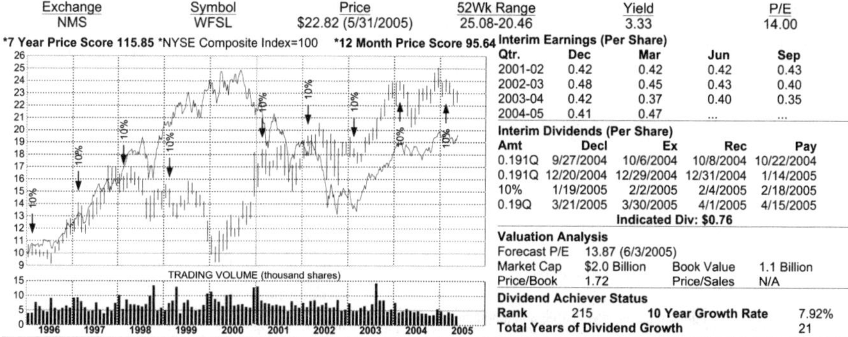

Exchange	Symbol	Price	52Wk Range	Yield	P/E
NMS	WFSL	$22.82 (5/31/2005)	25.08-20.46	3.33	14.00

*7 Year Price Score 115.85 *NYSE Composite Index=100 *12 Month Price Score 95.64

Interim Earnings (Per Share)

Qtr.	Dec	Mar	Jun	Sep
2001-02	0.42	0.42	0.42	0.43
2002-03	0.48	0.45	0.43	0.40
2003-04	0.42	0.37	0.40	0.35
2004-05	0.41	0.47	...	...

Interim Dividends (Per Share)

Amt	Decl	Ex	Rec	Pay
0.191Q	9/27/2004	10/6/2004	10/8/2004	10/22/2004
0.191Q	12/20/2004	12/29/2004	12/31/2004	1/14/2005
10%	1/19/2005	2/2/2005	2/4/2005	2/18/2005
0.19Q	3/21/2005	3/30/2005	4/1/2005	4/15/2005

Indicated Div: $0.76

Valuation Analysis

Forecast P/E	13.87 (6/3/2005)		
Market Cap	$2.0 Billion	Book Value	1.1 Billion
Price/Book	1.72	Price/Sales	N/A

Dividend Achiever Status

Rank	215	10 Year Growth Rate	7.92%
Total Years of Dividend Growth			21

Business Summary: Other Depository Banking (MIC: 8.5 SIC: 035 NAIC: 22120)

Washington Federal is a non-diversified unitary savings and loan holding company with total assets of $7.17 billion, as of Sep 30 2004. Co. conducts its operations through its federally insured savings and loan association subsidiary, Washington Federal Savings and Loan Association. Co.'s business consists primarily of attracting savings deposits from the general public and investing these funds in loans secured by first mortgage liens on single-family dwellings, including loans for the construction of such dwellings, and loans on multi-family dwellings. As of Sep 30 2004, Co. operated 120 offices located in eight states in the western United States.

Recent Developments: For the quarter ended Mar 31 2005, net income increased 26.0% to $40,961 thousand from net income of $32,520 thousand in the year-earlier quarter. Interest income advanced 18.9% to $122,180 thousand from $101,682 thousand in the prior year. Net interest income was $76,617 thousand, up 29.3% from $59,276 thousand the year before. Non-interest income fell 65.2% to $852 thousand, while non-interest expense advanced 21.6% to $13,964 thousand.

Prospects: Co.'s outlook appears encouraging, reflecting its recent results that reflected solid loan demand and strong asset quality. For instance, for the three months ended Mar 31 2005 Co.'s earnings benefited from year-over-year growth of 12.4% in its loan portfolio. Total interest income climbed 8.1% to $111.0 million from $102.7 million the year before, which more than offset a 25.4% increase in interest expense paid on customer accounts. Separately, during the three months ended Mar 31 2005, Co. opened two new branches; one in Las Vegas, NV and another in Klamath Falls, OR.

Financial Data

(US$ in Thousands)	6 Mos	3 Mos	09/30/2004	09/30/2003	09/30/2002	09/30/2001	09/30/2000	09/30/1999
Earnings Per Share	1.63	1.53	1.51	1.71	1.69	1.33	1.24	1.27
Cash Flow Per Share	1.73	1.78	1.60	1.42	1.61	1.47	0.99	1.03
Tang Book Value Per Share	12.58	12.44	12.26	11.56	10.94	10.89	8.55	8.04
Dividends Per Share	0.755	0.745	0.736	0.701	0.666	0.631	0.596	0.545
Dividend Payout %	46.32	48.69	48.80	40.97	39.39	47.41	48.00	42.79
Income Statement								
Interest Income	229,723	107,543	413,772	450,185	507,317	536,410	498,027	455,577
Interest Expense	87,709	42,146	169,753	194,884	234,941	320,120	299,511	244,490
Net Interest Income	142,014	65,397	244,019	255,301	272,376	216,290	198,516	211,087
Provision for Losses	...	...	(231)	1,500	7,000	1,850	...	684
Non-Interest Income	2,850	2,579	5,143	15,017	8,088	9,736	10,377	12,665
Non-Interest Expense	25,943	11,978	46,264	44,059	51,228	49,113	46,646	46,101
Income Before Taxes	119,720	56,216	203,712	224,565	222,354	175,464	163,179	177,081
Income Taxes	42,501	19,957	71,844	79,021	78,400	61,850	57,500	62,795
Net Income	77,219	36,259	131,868	145,544	143,954	113,614	105,679	114,286
Average Shares	87,464	87,440	87,130	84,981	85,333	85,258	85,220	89,877
Balance Sheet								
Net Loans & Leases	5,429,741	5,250,975	4,982,836	4,606,726	4,292,003	4,207,769	4,949,235	4,378,728
Total Assets	7,588,459	7,543,302	7,169,205	7,535,975	7,392,441	7,026,743	6,719,841	6,163,503
Total Deposits	4,687,448	4,626,855	4,569,245	4,520,051	4,452,250	4,251,113	3,375,036	3,291,857
Total Liabilities	6,438,948	6,407,195	6,049,017	6,480,379	6,431,723	6,152,734	5,960,676	5,413,480
Stockholders' Equity	1,149,511	1,136,107	1,120,188	1,055,596	960,718	874,009	759,165	750,023
Shares Outstanding	86,707	86,628	86,547	86,119	84,572	77,013	83,941	87,341
Statistical Record								
Return on Assets %	1.90	1.79	1.79	1.95	2.00	1.65	1.64	1.94
Return on Equity %	12.82	12.23	12.09	14.44	15.69	13.91	13.97	15.07
Net Interest Margin %	62.71	60.81	58.97	56.71	53.69	40.32	39.86	46.33
Efficiency Ratio %	11.40	10.88	11.04	9.47	9.94	8.99	9.17	9.85
Loans to Deposits	1.16	1.13	1.09	1.02	0.96	0.99	1.47	1.33
Price Range	25.08-20.24	25.08-20.24	23.96-20.24	21.83-15.51	20.59-15.03	18.88-12.30	14.75-9.28	15.87-12.81
P/E Ratio	15.39-12.41	16.39-13.23	15.87-13.40	12.76-9.07	12.19-8.89	14.19-9.25	11.89-7.48	12.50-10.08
Average Yield %	3.33	3.29	3.27	3.74	3.64	3.80	5.04	3.81

Address: 425 Pike Street, Seattle, WA 98101 **Telephone:** 206-624-7930 **Web Site:** www.washingtonfederal.com	**Officers:** Guy C. Pinkerton - Chmn. Roy M. Whitehead - Vice Chmn., Pres., C.E.O. **Transfer Agents:** American Stock Transfer & Trust Company , New York, NY	**Investor Contact:** 206-624-7930 **No of Institutions:** 151 **Shares:** 42,883,324 **% Held:** 49.50

WASHINGTON MUTUAL INC.

Exchange	Symbol	Price	52Wk Range	Yield	P/E
NYS	WM	$41.30 (5/31/2005)	42.99-37.63	4.55	13.41

*7 Year Price Score 108.90 *NYSE Composite Index=100 *12 Month Price Score 98.26

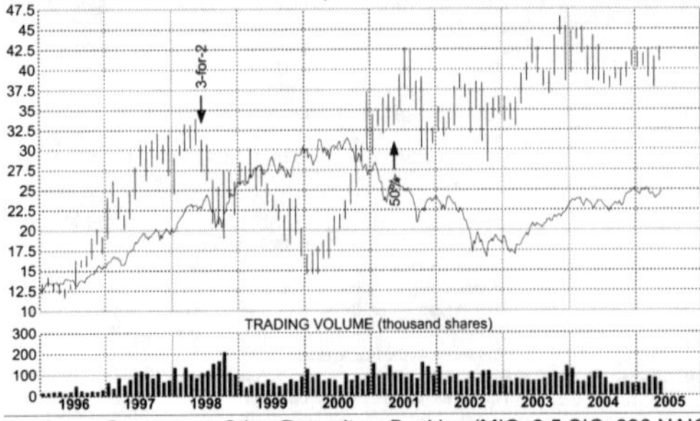

Interim Earnings (Per Share)

Qtr.	Mar	Jun	Sep	Dec
2002	0.98	1.01	1.01	1.04
2003	1.07	1.10	1.11	0.94
2004	1.18	0.55	0.76	0.76
2005	1.01	...	...	...

Interim Dividends (Per Share)

Amt	Decl	Ex	Rec	Pay
0.44Q	7/21/2004	7/28/2004	7/30/2004	8/13/2004
0.45Q	10/20/2004	10/27/2004	10/29/2004	11/15/2004
0.46Q	1/19/2005	1/27/2005	1/31/2005	2/15/2005
0.47Q	4/19/2005	4/27/2005	4/29/2005	5/13/2005

Indicated Div: $1.88 (Div. Reinv. Plan)

Valuation Analysis

Forecast P/E	11.32 (6/2/2005)		
Market Cap	$36.2 Billion	Book Value	21.8 Billion
Price/Book	1.66	Price/Sales	2.16

Dividend Achiever Status

Rank	48	10 Year Growth Rate	18.79%
Total Years of Dividend Growth			15

Business Summary: Other Depository Banking (MIC: 8.5 SIC: 036 NAIC: 22120)

Washington Mutual is a thrift holding company providing financial services to consumers and small businesses. Co. accepts deposits from the public, originates, purchases, services and sells home loans, makes consumer, home equity and commercial real estate loans, and, to a lesser extent, engages in certain commercial banking activities. Co. originates, purchases from correspondents, sells and services loans to subprime borrowers through its specialty mortgage finance operations. Co. also markets annuities and other insurance products, offers securities brokerage services and acts as the investment advisor to, and the distributor of, mutual funds. At Dec 31 2004, assets were $307.92 billion.

Recent Developments: For the quarter ended Mar 31 2005, net income decreased 13.8% to $902,000 thousand from net income of $1,047,000 thousand in the year-earlier quarter. Net interest income was $1,890,000 thousand, up 9.1% from $1,732,000 thousand the year before. Provision for loan losses was $16,000 thousand versus $56,000 thousand in the prior-year quarter, a decrease of 71.4%. Non-interest income fell 0.5% to $1,978,000 thousand, while non-interest expense declined 2.2% to $1,839,000 thousand.

Prospects: Co.'s prospects appear constructive, reflecting in part recent favorable business trends. For the quarter ended Mar 31 2005, Co. experienced gains in assets, deposits and checking accounts, as well as higher mortgage banking income. Total assets of $319.70 billion at Mar 31 2005 rose 3.8% from the fourth quarter of 2004 and 13.9% from last year, reflecting growth in all major categories of loans held in portfolio. Separately, Mortgage Banking segment loan volume in the first quarter of 2005 was $38.50 billion, down slightly from $41.78 billion at Dec 31 2004 and $43.72 billion last year. Co. attributed the decline to a slowdown in the mortgage market due to lower refinancing activity.

Financial Data

(US$ in Thousands)	3 Mos	12/31/2004	12/31/2003	12/31/2002	12/31/2001	12/31/2000	12/31/1999	12/31/1998
Earnings Per Share	3.08	3.26	4.21	4.05	3.59	2.36	2.11	1.71
Cash Flow Per Share	(14.20)	(22.78)	13.84	0.03	(12.68)	3.76	6.13	8.17
Tang Book Value Per Share	9.79	10.21	7.88	9.03	6.29	9.96	8.41	8.85
Dividends Per Share	1.780	1.740	1.400	1.060	0.897	0.760	0.653	0.547
Dividend Payout %	57.79	53.37	33.25	26.17	24.98	32.20	31.01	32.03
Income Statement								
Interest Income	3,360,000	11,350,000	12,163,000	14,247,000	15,065,000	13,783,000	12,062,198	11,221,468
Interest Expense	1,470,000	4,234,000	4,534,000	5,906,000	8,189,000	9,472,000	7,610,408	6,929,743
Net Interest Income	1,890,000	7,116,000	7,629,000	8,341,000	6,876,000	4,311,000	4,451,790	4,291,725
Provision for Losses	16,000	209,000	42,000	595,000	575,000	185,000	167,076	161,968
Non-Interest Income	1,408,000	4,612,000	5,850,000	4,790,000	2,627,000	1,984,000	1,508,997	1,577,019
Non-Interest Expense	1,839,000	7,535,000	7,408,000	6,382,000	4,617,000	3,126,000	2,909,551	3,337,319
Income Before Taxes	1,443,000	3,984,000	6,029,000	6,154,000	4,311,000	2,984,000	2,884,160	2,369,457
Income Taxes	541,000	1,505,000	2,236,000	2,258,000	1,579,000	1,085,000	1,067,096	882,525
Net Income	902,000	2,878,000	3,880,000	3,896,000	3,114,000	1,899,000	1,817,064	1,486,932
Average Shares	888,789	884,050	921,757	960,152	864,700	804,694	861,829	867,843
Balance Sheet								
Net Loans & Leases	212,834,000	205,770,000	174,394,000	145,875,000	131,587,000	118,612,000	113,497,225	108,370,906
Total Assets	319,696,000	307,918,000	275,178,000	268,298,000	242,506,000	194,716,000	186,513,630	165,493,281
Total Deposits	183,631,000	173,658,000	153,181,000	155,516,000	107,182,000	79,574,000	81,129,768	85,492,141
Total Liabilities	297,929,000	286,692,000	255,436,000	248,164,000	228,341,000	184,550,000	177,460,951	156,148,881
Stockholders' Equity	21,767,000	21,226,000	19,742,000	20,134,000	14,063,000	10,166,000	9,052,679	9,344,400
Shares Outstanding	877,286	874,261	880,985	944,046	873,089	809,783	857,383	890,112
Statistical Record								
Return on Assets %	0.91	0.98	1.43	1.53	1.42	0.99	1.03	1.13
Return on Equity %	12.97	14.01	19.46	22.79	25.70	19.71	19.75	20.29
Net Interest Margin %	56.25	62.70	62.72	58.55	45.64	31.28	36.91	38.25
Efficiency Ratio %	38.57	47.21	41.13	33.52	26.10	19.83	21.44	26.08
Loans to Deposits	1.16	1.18	1.14	0.94	1.23	1.49	1.40	1.27
Price Range	44.25-37.63	45.28-37.63	46.55-32.98	39.45-28.41	42.69-28.56	37.25-14.54	30.17-16.75	33.94-19.00
P/E Ratio	14.37-12.22	13.89-11.54	11.06-7.83	9.74-7.01	11.89-7.96	15.78-6.16	14.30-7.94	19.85-11.11
Average Yield %	4.43	4.27	3.57	3.00	2.55	3.50	2.74	1.98

Address: 1201 Third Avenue, Seattle, WA 98101
Telephone: 206-461-2000
Web Site: www.wamu.com

Officers: Kerry K. Killinger - Chmn., Pres., C.E.O. William A. Longbrake - Vice-Chmn. **Transfer Agents:** Mellon Investor Services, L.L.C., Ridgefield Park, NJ

Investor Contact: 206-461-3186
No of Institutions: 629
Shares: 616,269,184 **% Held:** 70.09

WASHINGTON REAL ESTATE INVESTMENT TRUST

Exchange	Symbol	Price	52Wk Range	Yield	P/E
NYS	WRE	$31.10 (5/31/2005)	34.43-27.48	5.18	16.99

*7 Year Price Score 114.52 *NYSE Composite Index=100 *12 Month Price Score 95.77

TRADING VOLUME (thousand shares)

Interim Earnings (Per Share)

Qtr.	Mar	Jun	Sep	Dec
2002	0.42	0.30	0.30	0.31
2003	0.28	0.29	0.28	0.28
2004	0.27	0.26	0.26	0.30
2005	1.01	...	...	...

Interim Dividends (Per Share)

Amt	Decl	Ex	Rec	Pay
0.393Q	8/4/2004	9/14/2004	9/16/2004	9/30/2004
0.393Q	11/17/2004	12/14/2004	12/16/2004	12/30/2004
0.393Q	2/17/2005	3/15/2005	3/17/2005	3/31/2005
0.403Q	5/4/2005	6/14/2005	6/16/2005	6/30/2005

Indicated Div: $1.61 (Div. Reinv. Plan)

Valuation Analysis

Forecast P/E	15.06 (6/2/2005)		
Market Cap	$1.3 Billion	Book Value	392.1 Million
Price/Book	3.33	Price/Sales	7.53

Dividend Achiever Status

Rank	259	10 Year Growth Rate	5.35%
Total Years of Dividend Growth			35

Business Summary: Property, Real Estate & Development (MIC: 8.3 SIC: 798 NAIC: 25930)

Washington Real Estate Investment Trust is a self-administered qualified equity real estate investment trust. Co.'s business consists of the ownership and operation of income-producing real estate properties principally in the Greater Washington, D.C.-Baltimore, MD area. Upon the purchase of a property, Co. begins a program of improving the real estate to increase the value and to improve the operations, with the goals of generating higher rental income and reducing expenses. As of Dec 31 2004, Co. owned a diversified portfolio of 69 properties consisting of 30 office buildings, eleven retail centers, nine multifamily buildings and 19 industrial/flex properties.

Recent Developments: For the three months ended Mar 31 2005, income from continuing operations slipped 5.2% to $9,911 thousand from $10,460 thousand the previous year. Net income increased 273.7% to $42,234 thousand from net income of $11,302 thousand in the year-earlier quarter. Revenues were $45,501 thousand, up 7.5% from $42,329 thousand the year before. Expenses grew 11.7% to $35,590 thousand from $31,869 thousand the prior year.

Prospects: On Apr 8 2005, Co. acquired the Coleman Building in Chantilly, VA for $10.0 million, completing its acquisition of the Dulles Business Park portfolio. Coleman is a single-story flex/warehouse building consisting of 59,767 rentable square feet and a surface parking lot with 228 spaces. The property is 64.0% leased to a single tenant with 21,539 square feet available. Separately, Co.'s net operating income from the Industrial, Multi-family and Retail sectors of its portfolio is showing positive year-over-year growth. Meanwhile, the Office sector is lagging, but this market is continuing to improve.

Financial Data

(US$ in Thousands)	3 Mos	12/31/2004	12/31/2003	12/31/2002	12/31/2001	12/31/2000	12/31/1999	12/31/1998
Earnings Per Share	1.83	1.09	1.13	1.32	1.38	1.26	1.24	1.15
Cash Flow Per Share	1.92	1.91	1.94	1.80	1.98	1.73	1.47	1.50
Tang Book Value Per Share	9.33	8.71	9.10	8.33	8.33	7.24	7.20	7.11
Dividends Per Share	1.570	1.550	1.470	1.390	1.310	1.230	1.158	1.110
Dividend Payout %	85.79	142.20	130.09	105.30	94.93	97.62	93.35	96.52
Income Statement								
Property Income	45,387	172,067	163,405	152,929	148,424	134,732	118,975	103,597
Non-Property Income	114	327	414	680	...	...	...	...
Total Revenue	45,501	172,394	163,819	153,609	148,424	134,732	118,975	103,597
Depn & Amortn	10,806	41,961	35,755	29,212	26,954	22,723	19,590	15,399
Interest Expense	8,588	34,500	30,040	27,849	27,071	25,531	22,271	17,106
Net Income	42,234	45,564	44,887	51,836	52,353	45,139	44,301	41,064
Average Shares	42,015	41,863	39,600	39,281	37,951	35,872	35,700	35,700
Balance Sheet								
Total Assets	1,036,831	1,012,393	927,129	755,997	707,935	632,047	608,480	558,707
Long-Term Obligations	517,775	493,429	517,182	351,951	359,726	351,260	297,038	238,912
Total Liabilities	643,101	644,755	546,780	428,266	382,717	371,833	349,769	303,447
Stockholders' Equity	392,088	366,009	378,748	326,177	323,607	258,656	257,189	253,733
Shares Outstanding	42,004	42,000	41,607	39,168	38,829	35,740	35,721	35,692
Statistical Record								
Return on Assets %	7.75	4.69	5.33	7.08	7.81	7.26	7.59	7.99
Return on Equity %	19.90	12.20	12.74	15.95	17.98	17.45	17.34	16.24
Net Margin %	92.82	26.43	27.40	33.75	35.27	33.50	37.24	39.64
Price Range	34.43-25.80	34.43-25.80	31.04-24.10	30.15-21.96	25.45-21.27	25.00-14.31	18.63-14.00	18.63-15.56
P/E Ratio	18.81-14.10	31.59-23.67	27.47-21.33	22.84-16.64	18.44-15.41	19.84-11.36	15.02-11.29	16.20-13.53
Average Yield %	5.24	5.16	5.33	5.31	5.59	6.89	7.11	6.53

Address: 6110 Executive Boulevard, Rockville, MD 20852-3927 **Telephone:** 301-984-9400 **Web Site:** www.writ.com	**Officers:** Edmund B. Cronin Jr. - Chmn., Pres., C.E.O. George F. McKenzie - Exec. V.P., Real Estate **ransfer Agents:**EquiServe Trust Company N.A., Providence, RI	**No of Institutions:** 142 **Shares:** 16,881,664 **% Held:** 40.19

WASHINGTON TRUST BANCORP, INC.

Exchange	Symbol	Price	52Wk Range	Yield	P/E
NMS	WASH	$28.20 (5/31/2005)	30.49-23.28	2.55	17.96

*7 Year Price Score 114.30 *NYSE Composite Index=100 *12 Month Price Score 93.65

Interim Earnings (Per Share)

Qtr.	Mar	Jun	Sep	Dec
2002	0.31	0.31	0.34	0.34
2003	0.36	0.34	0.35	0.36
2004	0.37	0.37	0.39	0.41
2005	0.40	...	...	...

Interim Dividends (Per Share)

Amt	Decl	Ex	Rec	Pay
0.17Q	6/17/2004	6/30/2004	7/2/2004	7/15/2004
0.17Q	9/17/2004	9/29/2004	10/1/2004	10/15/2004
0.17Q	12/16/2004	12/31/2004	1/4/2005	1/14/2005
0.18Q	3/17/2005	3/29/2005	3/31/2005	4/15/2005

Indicated Div: $0.72

Valuation Analysis

Forecast P/E	16.92 (6/2/2005)		
Market Cap	$374.8 Million	Book Value	149.2 Million
Price/Book	2.51	Price/Sales	2.91

Dividend Achiever Status

Rank	125	10 Year Growth Rate	12.77%
Total Years of Dividend Growth			12

Business Summary: Commercial Banking (MIC: 8.1 SIC: 022 NAIC: 22110)

Washington Trust Bancorp is a bank holding company, operating through its wholly owned subsidiary, The Washington Trust Company (the Bank). The Bank's market area includes Washington County and portions of Providence and Kent Counties in Rhode Island, as well as a part of New London County in Connecticut. The Bank provides a range of financial services, including: residential mortgages, commercial loans, commercial and consumer demand deposits, construction loans, consumer installment loans, home equity lines of credit, retirement accounts, merchant credit card services, cash management services, and trust and investment management services. At Dec 31 2004, Co. had assets of $2.31 billion.

Recent Developments: For the quarter ended Mar 31 2005, net income increased 9.2% to $5,410 thousand from net income of $4,955 thousand in the year-earlier quarter. Net interest income was $14,621 thousand, up 11.8% from $13,083 thousand the year before. Provision for loan losses was $300 thousand versus $120 thousand in the prior-year quarter, an increase of 150.0%. Non-interest income rose 2.3% to $6,079 thousand, while non-interest expense advanced 6.5% to $12,444 thousand.

Prospects: On Mar 21 2005, Co. announced that it has signed a definitive agreement to acquire Weston Financial Group, Inc., a registered investment advisor with assets under management in excess of $1.20 billion, for $20.0 million in cash. Weston specializes in providing financial planning and investment counseling services to high net worth individuals through third-party open-architecture wealth management products. Co. expects the acquisition to greatly increase the size and capabilities of its wealth management group, and expand its presence in the New England marketplace. Co. anticipates that the acquisition will most likely be completed in the third quarter of 2005.

Financial Data

(US$ in Thousands)	3 Mos	12/31/2004	12/31/2003	12/31/2002	12/31/2001	12/31/2000	12/31/1999	12/31/1998
Earnings Per Share	1.57	1.54	1.41	1.30	1.07	1.09	0.96	0.97
Cash Flow Per Share	2.06	2.02	2.42	1.60	0.79	1.46	2.17	1.19
Tang Book Value Per Share	9.44	9.64	8.60	7.93	8.15	7.43	7.08	7.30
Dividends Per Share	0.690	0.680	0.760	0.550	0.510	0.470	0.440	0.400
Dividend Payout %	43.95	44.16	53.90	42.31	47.66	43.12	45.83	41.24
Income Statement								
Interest Income	27,118	96,853	86,245	87,339	87,527	85,099	72,999	62,753
Interest Expense	12,497	42,412	37,446	43,057	48,160	47,231	37,392	32,606
Net Interest Income	14,621	54,441	48,799	44,282	39,367	37,868	35,607	30,147
Provision for Losses	300	610	460	400	550	1,150	1,840	1,800
Non-Interest Income	6,079	26,905	26,735	23,258	21,485	19,712	15,409	12,469
Non-Interest Expense	12,444	50,373	47,632	42,990	41,653	37,548	33,833	26,820
Income Before Taxes	7,956	30,363	27,442	24,150	18,649	18,882	15,343	13,996
Income Taxes	2,546	9,534	8,519	7,393	5,541	5,673	4,754	3,948
Net Income	5,410	20,829	18,923	16,757	13,108	13,209	10,589	10,048
Average Shares	13,617	13,542	13,393	12,932	12,202	12,102	11,082	10,354
Balance Sheet								
Net Loans & Leases	1,277,132	1,232,905	945,067	779,639	592,052	584,020	536,676	439,086
Total Assets	2,342,138	2,307,820	1,973,807	1,745,661	1,362,229	1,218,067	1,104,664	935,069
Total Deposits	1,529,047	1,457,885	1,206,141	1,110,493	816,876	735,684	660,753	575,323
Total Liabilities	2,192,913	2,155,968	1,835,752	1,616,940	1,264,292	1,128,881	1,027,417	862,003
Stockholders' Equity	149,225	151,852	138,055	128,721	97,937	89,186	77,247	73,066
Shares Outstanding	13,291	13,269	13,194	13,042	12,011	12,006	10,914	10,010
Statistical Record								
Return on Assets %	0.97	0.97	1.02	1.08	1.02	1.13	1.04	1.15
Return on Equity %	14.49	14.33	14.19	14.79	14.01	15.83	14.09	14.33
Net Interest Margin %	53.92	56.21	56.58	50.70	44.98	44.50	48.78	48.04
Efficiency Ratio %	37.49	40.70	42.16	38.87	38.21	35.82	38.27	35.65
Loans to Deposits	0.84	0.85	0.78	0.70	0.72	0.79	0.81	0.76
Price Range	30.49-23.28	30.49-23.28	29.19-19.45	23.69-18.00	22.25-13.75	17.75-13.50	21.50-14.75	27.17-18.63
P/E Ratio	19.42-14.83	19.80-15.12	20.70-13.79	18.22-13.85	20.79-12.85	16.28-12.39	22.40-15.36	28.01-19.20
Average Yield %	2.57	2.59	3.22	2.75	2.76	3.19	2.51	1.81

Address: 23 Broad Street, Westerly, RI 02891
Telephone: 401-348-1200
Web Site: www.washtrust.com

Officers: John C. Warren - Chmn., C.E.O. John F. Treanor - Pres., C.O.O.

No of Institutions: 62
Shares: 3,075,967 **% Held:** 23.13

WEBSTER FINANCIAL CORP.

Exchange	Symbol	Price	52Wk Range	Yield	P/E
NYS	WBS	$46.90 (5/31/2005)	51.33-43.67	2.13	15.74

*7 Year Price Score 121.65 *NYSE Composite Index=100 *12 Month Price Score 94.00

TRADING VOLUME (thousand shares)

Interim Earnings (Per Share)

Qtr.	Mar	Jun	Sep	Dec
2002	0.80	0.82	0.84	0.85
2003	0.86	0.88	0.89	0.84
2004	0.90	0.91	0.92	0.27
2005	1.08	...	...	...

Interim Dividends (Per Share)

Amt	Decl	Ex	Rec	Pay
0.23Q	7/20/2004	7/29/2004	8/2/2004	8/16/2004
0.23Q	10/19/2004	10/28/2004	11/1/2004	11/15/2004
0.23Q	2/1/2005	2/10/2005	2/14/2005	2/28/2005
0.25Q	4/18/2005	4/28/2005	5/2/2005	5/16/2005

Indicated Div: $1.00 (Div. Reinv. Plan)

Valuation Analysis

Forecast P/E 13.03 (6/2/2005)

Market Cap $2.5 Billion Book Value 1.6 Billion

Price/Book 1.61 Price/Sales 2.55

Dividend Achiever Status

Rank 120 **10 Year Growth Rate** 13.22%

Total Years of Dividend Growth 12

Business Summary: Other Depository Banking (MIC: 8.5 SIC: 035 NAIC: 22120)

Webster Financial is a holding company with $17.00 billion in assets as of Dec 31 2004. Through its subsidiaries, Co. is engaged in providing financial services to individuals, families and businesses, primarily in Connecticut and equipment financing, asset-based lending, mortgage origination and financial advisory services to public and private companies throughout the U.S. Co. provides business and consumer banking, mortgage origination and lending, trust and investment services and insurance services through 150 banking and other offices, 276 ATMs and its Internet website.

Recent Developments: For the quarter ended Mar 31 2005, net income increased 12.2% to $47,495 thousand from net income of $42,323 thousand in the year-earlier quarter. Net interest income was $92,364 thousand, up 15.5% from $79,976 thousand the year before. Provision for loan losses was $3,500 thousand versus $5,000 thousand in the prior-year quarter, a decrease of 30.0%. Non-interest income fell 3.1% to $53,028 thousand, while non-interest expense advanced 17.0% to $107,774 thousand.

Prospects: On Apr 18 2005, Co.'s subsidiary, Webster Bank, N.A. announced that it has completed the divestiture of the two branch offices of State Bank of Howards Grove, which operates under the trade name HSA Bank, to National Exchange Bank & Trust of Wisconsin. Co. is retaining the bank's HSA operation and HSA deposits, which totaled $169.0 million at Mar 31 2005. Meanwhile, Co. is enjoying the quality of its operating results and the progress toward achieving its strategic and financial goals. The strong performance includes improvement in the net interest margin, solid asset quality and expense control as Co. continues to invest in its de novo branching initiative.

Financial Data

(US$ in Thousands)	3 Mos	12/31/2004	12/31/2003	12/31/2002	12/31/2001	12/31/2000	12/31/1999	12/31/1998
Earnings Per Share	2.98	3.00	3.52	3.16	2.68	2.55	2.10	1.83
Cash Flow Per Share	3.48	7.08	10.93	(1.76)	0.23	4.63	3.76	1.70
Tang Book Value Per Share	15.79	15.85	17.76	16.18	13.97	11.53	10.98	12.77
Dividends Per Share	0.920	0.900	0.820	0.740	0.670	0.620	0.470	0.430
Dividend Payout %	30.87	30.00	23.30	23.42	25.00	24.31	22.38	23.50
Income Statement								
Interest Income	202,418	732,108	658,718	692,034	757,235	738,911	645,792	622,453
Interest Expense	74,186	263,947	245,199	286,306	389,756	412,395	342,279	377,018
Net Interest Income	128,232	468,161	413,519	405,728	367,479	326,516	303,513	245,435
Provision for Losses	3,500	18,000	25,000	29,000	14,400	11,800	9,000	6,800
Non-Interest Income	53,028	219,707	232,483	185,572	162,098	128,821	92,630	74,163
Non-Interest Expense	107,774	447,137	377,982	328,323	308,932	267,130	244,461	197,789
Income Before Taxes	69,986	222,731	243,020	233,977	206,245	176,407	142,682	115,009
Income Taxes	22,491	68,898	79,772	73,965	69,430	58,116	47,332	44,544
Net Income	47,495	153,833	163,248	152,732	133,188	118,291	95,350	70,465
Average Shares	54,217	51,352	46,362	48,392	42,742	46,427	45,393	38,571
Balance Sheet								
Net Loans & Leases	11,544,555	11,562,663	9,091,135	7,795,835	6,869,911	6,819,209	6,022,236	4,993,509
Total Assets	17,412,828	17,020,597	14,568,690	13,468,004	11,857,382	11,249,508	9,931,744	9,033,917
Total Deposits	11,031,835	10,571,288	8,372,135	7,606,122	7,066,471	6,941,522	6,191,091	5,651,273
Total Liabilities	15,839,657	15,467,046	13,406,218	12,301,714	10,691,338	10,159,557	9,096,500	8,279,461
Stockholders' Equity	1,563,594	1,543,974	1,152,895	1,035,458	1,006,467	890,374	635,667	554,879
Shares Outstanding	53,786	53,628	46,276	45,625	49,149	48,939	45,243	37,327
Statistical Record								
Return on Assets %	0.98	0.97	1.16	1.21	1.15	1.11	1.01	0.88
Return on Equity %	11.46	11.38	14.92	14.96	14.04	15.46	16.02	15.04
Net Interest Margin %	63.35	63.95	62.78	58.63	48.53	44.19	47.00	39.43
Efficiency Ratio %	42.19	46.98	42.41	37.41	33.60	30.78	33.11	28.39
Loans to Deposits	1.05	1.09	1.09	1.02	0.97	0.98	0.97	0.88
Price Range	51.33-42.56	51.65-42.56	46.50-33.93	39.96-30.65	37.06-26.44	29.63-20.13	32.00-21.88	36.25-18.88
P/E Ratio	17.22-14.28	17.22-14.19	13.21-9.64	12.65-9.70	13.83-9.86	11.62-7.89	15.24-10.42	19.81-10.31
Average Yield %	1.95	1.87	2.11	2.09	2.15	2.68	1.70	1.45

Address: Webster Plaza, Waterbury, CT 06702
Telephone: 203-578-2476
Web Site: www.websteronline.com

Officers: James C. Smith - Chmn., C.E.O. William T. Bromage - Pres., C.O.O. **Transfer Agents:** American Stock Transfer & Trust Co, New York, NY

Investor Contact: 203-578-2318
No of Institutions: 196
Shares: 31,902,744 **% Held:** 59.33

WEINGARTEN REALTY INVESTORS

Exchange	Symbol	Price	52Wk Range	Yield	P/E
NYS	WRI	$38.01 (5/31/2005)	40.90-29.53	4.63	23.76

*7 Year Price Score 130.82 *NYSE Composite Index=100 *12 Month Price Score 99.36

Interim Earnings (Per Share)

Qtr.	Mar	Jun	Sep	Dec
2002	0.31	0.34	0.43	0.34
2003	0.32	0.27	0.36	0.29
2004	0.32	0.42	0.33	0.47
2005	0.38	...	...	...

Interim Dividends (Per Share)

Amt	Decl	Ex	Rec	Pay
0.415Q	7/26/2004	9/1/2004	9/3/2004	9/15/2004
0.415Q	10/25/2004	12/1/2004	12/3/2004	12/15/2004
0.44Q	2/24/2005	3/3/2005	3/7/2005	3/15/2005
0.44Q	4/28/2005	6/2/2005	6/6/2005	6/15/2005

Indicated Div: $1.76 (Div. Reinv. Plan)

Valuation Analysis

Forecast P/E	13.98 (6/1/2005)		
Market Cap	$3.4 Billion	Book Value	1.1 Billion
Price/Book	3.10	Price/Sales	6.53

Dividend Achiever Status

Rank	265	10 Year Growth Rate	5.06%
Total Years of Dividend Growth			16

Business Summary: Property, Real Estate & Development (MIC: 8.3 SIC: 798 NAIC: 25930)

Weingarten Realty Investors is a self-administered and self-managed real estate investment trust that acquires, develops and manages real estate, primarily anchored neighborhood and community shopping centers and, to a lesser extent, industrial properties. As of Dec 31 2004, Co. owned or operated under long-term leases interests in 343 developed income-producing real estate projects. Co. owned 288 shopping centers located in the Houston metropolitan area and in other parts of Texas and in Arizona, Arkansas, California, Colorado, Florida, Georgia, Illinois, Kansas, Kentucky, Louisiana, Maine, Mississippi, Missouri, Nevada, New Mexico, North Carolina, Oklahoma, Tennessee and Utah.

Recent Developments: For the quarter ended Mar 31 2005, income from continuing operations increased 17.3% to $32,321 thousand from income of $27,545 thousand in the year-earlier quarter. Net income increased 28.7% to $36,562 thousand from net income of $28,409 thousand in the year-earlier quarter. Revenues were $133,330 thousand, up 14.9% from $116,006 thousand the year before. Operating income was $63,006 thousand versus an income of $54,554 thousand in the prior-year quarter, an increase of 15.5%.

Prospects: Co. attributes its strong performance to recent acquisitions, well-leased development projects coming on-line, and a healthy increase in cash flow from its existing portfolio. Co. has recently purchased three properties increasing building are by 759,000 square feet and representing a total investment of $112.0 million. The acquisitions include the 250,000 square foot Pinecrest Plaza Shopping Center in Pinehurst, NC, the 78,000 square foot Thompson Bridge Commons Shopping Center northeast of Atlanta in Gainesville, GA and the 430,000 square foot Best of the West Shopping Center in Las Vegas, NV. Over the remainder of 2005, Co. expects to open six retail developments currently in development.

Financial Data

(US$ in Thousands)	3 Mos	12/31/2004	12/31/2003	12/31/2002	12/31/2001	12/31/2000	12/31/1999	12/31/1998
Earnings Per Share	1.60	1.54	1.24	1.43	1.23	0.97	1.27	0.90
Cash Flow Per Share	2.37	2.44	2.08	2.16	2.03	2.20	1.97	1.62
Tang Book Value Per Share	12.26	12.30	10.03	11.95	11.92	10.39	10.75	8.88
Dividends Per Share	1.685	1.660	1.560	1.480	1.404	1.333	1.262	1.191
Dividend Payout %	105.31	107.79	125.81	103.26	114.49	136.99	99.65	132.02
Income Statement								
Property Income	132,169	492,036	410,490	359,044	309,457	264,552	225,244	194,624
Non-Property Income	1,161	10,255	8,670	6,366	5,435	8,822	5,012	3,501
Total Revenue	133,330	502,291	419,160	365,410	314,892	273,374	230,469	198,467
Depn & Amortn	30,753	117,053	94,455	79,344	68,316	58,518	49,612	41,946
Interest Expense	30,603	115,506	88,871	65,863	54,473	45,545	33,186	33,654
Net Income	36,562	141,381	116,280	131,867	108,542	79,001	96,130	60,365
Average Shares	93,092	89,511	81,574	80,040	72,553	60,594	60,502	60,455
Balance Sheet								
Total Assets	3,479,903	3,470,318	2,923,794	2,423,889	2,095,747	1,646,011	1,309,396	1,107,043
Long-Term Obligations	2,155,703	2,105,948	1,810,706	1,330,369	1,070,835	869,627	594,185	516,366
Total Liabilities	2,304,208	2,300,428	2,052,427	1,435,493	1,170,789	943,451	663,494	573,864
Stockholders' Equity	1,092,768	1,095,960	821,563	933,413	921,072	629,867	645,902	533,179
Shares Outstanding	89,134	89,066	81,888	78,114	77,280	60,572	60,063	60,014
Statistical Record								
Return on Assets %	4.50	4.41	4.35	5.84	5.80	5.33	7.96	5.88
Return on Equity %	14.81	14.71	13.25	14.22	14.00	12.35	16.31	13.08
Net Margin %	27.42	28.15	27.74	36.09	34.47	28.90	41.71	30.42
Price Range	40.90-27.55	40.90-27.55	30.70-23.80	25.76-20.57	22.40-17.80	19.89-15.42	20.28-16.61	20.61-16.25
P/E Ratio	25.56-17.22	26.56-17.89	24.76-19.19	18.01-14.38	18.21-14.48	20.50-15.89	15.97-13.08	22.90-18.06
Average Yield %	4.95	5.03	5.59	6.26	6.99	7.47	7.06	6.25

Address: 2600 Citadel Plaza Drive, P.O. Box 924133, Houston, TX 77292-4133
Telephone: 713-866-6000
Web Site: www.weingarten.com

Officers: Stanford Alexander - Chmn. Martin Debrovner - Vice-Chmn. **Transfer Agents:** Mellon Investor Services, LLC, Ridgefield Park, NJ

Investor Contact: 713-866-6050
No of Institutions: 210
Shares: 39,673,112 **% Held:** 44.61

WELLS FARGO & CO.

Exchange	Symbol	Price	52Wk Range	Yield	P/E
NYS	WFC	$60.41 (5/31/2005)	63.25-56.29	3.18	14.59

***7 Year Price Score 110.74** *NYSE Composite Index=100 ***12 Month Price Score 97.21**

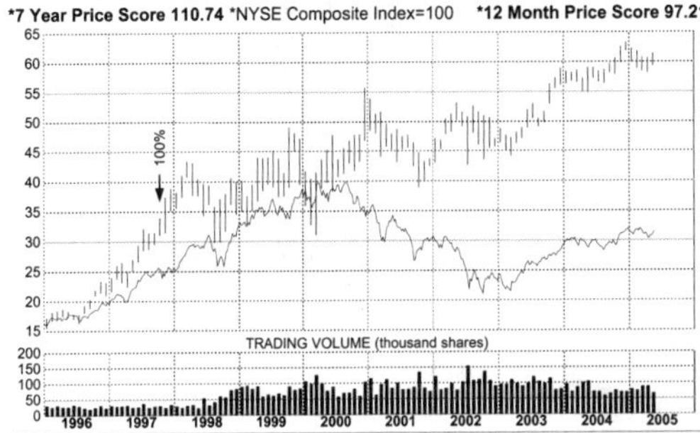

Interim Earnings (Per Share)

Qtr.	Mar	Jun	Sep	Dec
2002	0.64	0.82	0.84	0.86
2003	0.88	0.90	0.92	0.95
2004	1.03	1.00	1.02	1.04
2005	1.08	...	...	...

Interim Dividends (Per Share)

Amt	Decl	Ex	Rec	Pay
0.48Q	7/27/2004	8/4/2004	8/6/2004	9/1/2004
0.48Q	10/25/2004	11/3/2004	11/5/2004	12/1/2004
0.48Q	1/25/2005	2/2/2005	2/4/2005	3/1/2005
0.48Q	4/26/2005	5/4/2005	5/6/2005	6/1/2005

Indicated Div: $1.92 (Div. Reinv. Plan)

Valuation Analysis

Forecast P/E	N/A		
Market Cap	$102.2 Billion	Book Value	38.5 Billion
Price/Book	2.66	Price/Sales	2.89

Dividend Achiever Status

Rank	64	**10 Year Growth Rate**	17.14%
Total Years of Dividend Growth			17

TRADING VOLUME (thousand shares)

Business Summary: Commercial Banking (MIC: 8.1 SIC: 021 NAIC: 22110)

Wells Fargo is the fifth largest bank holding company in the U.S., based on total assets of $427.85 billion as of Dec 31 2004. Through its subsidiaries, Co. engages in banking and a variety of related financial services businesses. Retail, commercial and corporate banking services are provided through banking stores in 23 states. Other financial services are engaged in various businesses, principally wholesale banking, mortgage banking, consumer finance, equipment leasing, agricultural finance, commercial finance, securities brokerage and investment banking, insurance agency services, computer services, trust services, mortgage-backed securities servicing and venture capital investment.

Recent Developments: For the quarter ended Mar 31 2005, net income increased 5.0% to $1,856,000 thousand from net income of $1,767,000 thousand in the year-earlier quarter. Net interest income was $4,453,000 thousand, up 10.0% from $4,050,000 thousand the year before. Provision for loan losses was $585,000 thousand versus $404,000 thousand in the prior-year quarter, an increase of 44.8%. Non-interest income rose 17.4% to $3,636,000 thousand, while non-interest expense advanced 16.5% to $4,692,000 thousand.

Prospects: Top-line growth is being fueled by particularly strong growth in regional banking, institutional investments, debit cards, small business lending, insurance, corporate trust, consumer credit, consumer finance, home mortgage and corporate banking. In addition, Co. is enjoying commercial loan growth across virtually all customer segments. Despite increased competition in the commercial lending market, Co. continues to build volume through the addition of new customers and expanding relationships with existing customers. Separately, on Apr 11 2005, Co. completed the merger of certain Strong Funds and its own portfolios, creating a single fund family, the Wells Fargo Advantage Fundssm.

Financial Data (US$ in Thousands)	3 Mos	12/31/2004	12/31/2003	12/31/2002	12/31/2001	12/31/2000	12/31/1999	12/31/1998
Earnings Per Share	4.14	4.09	3.65	3.16	1.97	2.33	2.23	1.17
Cash Flow Per Share	14.23	11.84	18.56	(8.22)	(6.57)	0.52	8.17	(3.18)
Tang Book Value Per Share	10.83	10.86	9.56	8.90	6.02	5.84	5.11	4.84
Dividends Per Share	1.890	1.860	1.500	1.100	1.000	0.900	0.785	0.700
Dividend Payout %	45.65	45.48	41.10	34.81	50.76	38.63	35.20	59.83
Income Statement								
Interest Income	5,873,000	20,967,000	19,418,000	18,832,000	19,201,000	18,725,000	14,375,000	14,055,000
Interest Expense	1,420,000	3,817,000	3,411,000	3,977,000	6,741,000	7,860,000	5,020,000	5,065,000
Net Interest Income	4,453,000	17,150,000	16,007,000	14,855,000	12,460,000	10,865,000	9,355,000	8,990,000
Provision for Losses	585,000	1,717,000	1,722,000	1,733,000	1,780,000	1,329,000	1,045,000	1,545,000
Non-Interest Income	3,636,000	12,909,000	12,382,000	9,641,000	7,690,000	8,843,000	7,420,000	6,427,000
Non-Interest Expense	4,692,000	17,573,000	17,190,000	13,857,000	12,912,000	11,888,000	9,798,000	10,254,000
Income Before Taxes	2,812,000	10,769,000	9,477,000	8,854,000	5,479,000	6,549,000	5,948,000	3,293,000
Income Taxes	956,000	3,755,000	3,275,000	3,144,000	2,056,000	2,523,000	2,201,000	1,343,000
Net Income	1,856,000	7,014,000	6,202,000	5,434,000	3,423,000	4,026,000	3,747,000	1,950,000
Average Shares	1,715,700	1,713,400	1,697,500	1,718,000	1,726,900	1,718,400	1,665,200	1,641,800
Balance Sheet								
Net Loans & Leases	286,805,000	283,824,000	249,182,000	192,772,000	168,738,000	157,405,000	116,294,000	104,860,000
Total Assets	435,643,000	427,849,000	387,798,000	349,259,000	307,569,000	272,426,000	218,102,000	202,475,000
Total Deposits	273,163,000	274,858,000	247,527,000	216,916,000	187,266,000	169,559,000	132,708,000	136,788,000
Total Liabilities	397,166,000	389,983,000	353,329,000	279,040,903	280,355,000	245,938,000	195,971,000	181,716,000
Stockholders' Equity	38,477,000	37,866,000	34,469,000	30,358,000	27,214,000	26,488,000	22,131,000	20,759,000
Shares Outstanding	1,692,322	1,694,591	1,698,109	1,685,906	1,695,494	1,714,645	1,626,849	1,644,057
Statistical Record								
Return on Assets %	1.71	1.72	1.68	1.65	1.18	1.64	1.78	1.34
Return on Equity %	19.22	19.34	19.13	18.88	12.75	16.52	17.47	14.04
Net Interest Margin %	75.82	81.80	82.43	78.88	64.89	58.02	65.08	63.96
Efficiency Ratio %	49.34	51.87	54.06	48.67	48.02	43.12	44.96	50.06
Loans to Deposits	1.05	1.03	1.01	0.89	0.90	0.93	0.88	0.77
Price Range	63.25-54.79	63.25-54.79	58.94-44.15	53.21-42.63	53.94-38.85	55.75-31.00	49.06-32.75	43.44-29.75
P/E Ratio	15.28-13.23	15.46-13.40	16.15-12.10	16.84-13.49	27.38-19.72	23.93-13.30	22.00-14.69	37.13-25.43
Average Yield %	3.19	3.18	2.97	2.26	2.17	2.11	1.93	1.86

Address: 420 Montgomery Street, San Francisco, CA 94163
Telephone: 800-333-0343
Web Site: www.wellsfargo.com

Officers: Richard M. Kovacevich - Chmn., Pres., C.E.O. Howard I. Atkins - Exec. V.P., C.F.O.
ransfer Agents: Wells Fargo Shareowners Services, St. Paul, MN

Investor Contact: 415-396-0523
No of Institutions: 941
Shares: 1,117,872,128 **% Held:** 65.92

WESBANCO, INC.

Exchange	Symbol	Price	52Wk Range	Yield	P/E
NMS	WSBC	$29.57 (5/31/2005)	32.75-24.87	3.52	15.65

***7 Year Price Score 100.44** *NYSE Composite Index=100 ***12 Month Price Score 92.83**

TRADING VOLUME (thousand shares)

Interim Earnings (Per Share)

Qtr.	Mar	Jun	Sep	Dec
2002	0.42	0.41	0.43	0.44
2003	0.44	0.38	0.49	0.49
2004	0.49	0.48	0.50	0.43
2005	0.48	...	...	...

Interim Dividends (Per Share)

Amt	Decl	Ex	Rec	Pay
0.25Q	8/19/2004	9/8/2004	9/10/2004	10/1/2004
0.25Q	11/17/2004	12/8/2004	12/10/2004	1/3/2005
0.26Q	2/24/2005	3/9/2005	3/11/2005	4/1/2005
0.26Q	5/18/2005	6/8/2005	6/10/2005	7/1/2005

Indicated Div: $1.04 (Div. Reinv. Plan)

Valuation Analysis

Forecast P/E 15.46 (6/3/2005)

Market Cap $673.3 Million | Book Value 424.0 Million

Price/Book 1.59 | Price/Sales 3.05

Dividend Achiever Status

Rank 249 | **10 Year Growth Rate** 5.86%

Total Years of Dividend Growth 19

Business Summary: Commercial Banking (MIC: 8.1 SIC: 021 NAIC: 22110)

WesBanco is a bank holding company. Through its subsidiaries, Co. offers a range of financial services including retail banking, corporate banking, personal and corporate trust services, brokerage services, mortgage banking and insurance. Co. offers these services through two reportable segments, community banking and trust and investment services. As of Dec 31 2004, Co. operated a commercial bank, WesBanco Bank, through 80 offices, two loan production offices and 121 ATMs located in West Virginia, Ohio, and Western Pennsylvania. Co.'s additional services are offered through its non-banking subsidiaries. Co. also serves investment adviser to the WesMark Funds mutual fund family.

Recent Developments: For the quarter ended Mar 31 2005, net income increased 13.5% to $11,080 thousand from net income of $9,759 thousand in the year-earlier quarter. Net interest income was $45,517 thousand, up 19.9% from $37,972 thousand the year before. Provision for loan losses was $1,843 thousand versus $1,800 thousand in the prior-year quarter, an increase of 2.4%. Non-interest income rose 8.8% to $9,531 thousand, while non-interest expense advanced 28.5% to $19,052 thousand.

Prospects: Co.'s results are benefiting from an increase in its total assets due to the Winton Financial Corp. acquisition, as well as from higher revenues due to continuing growth in net interest income and non-interest income. Co.'s balance sheet growth continues to be led by loan growth in commercial and commercial real estate lending, which is seeing growth organically as well as by the additional loans acquired in the Winton and Western Ohio Financial Corp. acquisitions. Co. is also seeing improvement in its credit quality reflected by decreases in net charge-offs and lower provisions for loan losses. Going forward, Co. will focus on further integration of its recent acquisitions.

Financial Data

(US$ in Thousands)	3 Mos	12/31/2004	12/31/2003	12/31/2002	12/31/2001	12/31/2000	12/31/1999	12/31/1998
Earnings Per Share	1.89	1.90	1.80	1.70	1.60	1.41	1.37	1.36
Cash Flow Per Share	1.19	2.38	2.77	2.32	2.02	2.01	1.58	1.46
Tang Book Value Per Share	12.08	13.74	13.20	13.02	14.46	12.31	13.63	14.35
Dividends Per Share	1.010	1.000	0.960	0.935	0.920	0.895	0.880	0.840
Dividend Payout %	53.44	52.63	53.33	55.00	57.50	63.48	64.23	61.76
Income Statement								
Interest Income	54,884	169,436	165,516	176,155	163,939	163,079	155,861	162,718
Interest Expense	21,383	60,212	62,512	72,555	76,354	79,552	69,231	73,925
Net Interest Income	33,501	109,224	103,004	103,600	87,585	83,527	86,630	88,793
Provision for Losses	1,843	7,735	9,612	9,359	5,995	3,225	4,295	4,392
Non-Interest Income	9,399	35,541	33,230	27,852	24,588	23,376	24,581	25,715
Non-Interest Expense	27,129	89,872	81,810	76,647	64,894	64,483	67,813	68,308
Income Before Taxes	14,060	47,158	44,812	45,446	41,284	39,195	39,103	41,808
Income Taxes	2,980	8,976	8,682	10,620	12,282	12,271	11,465	13,495
Net Income	11,080	38,182	36,130	34,826	29,002	26,924	27,638	28,313
Average Shares	23,043	20,083	20,056	20,459	18,123	19,092	20,229	20,867
Balance Sheet								
Net Loans & Leases	2,925,869	2,455,880	1,905,562	1,791,081	1,513,387	1,568,281	1,493,941	1,344,640
Total Assets	4,557,613	4,011,399	3,445,006	3,297,231	2,474,454	2,310,137	2,269,726	2,242,712
Total Deposits	3,069,590	2,725,934	2,482,082	2,399,956	1,913,458	1,870,361	1,814,001	1,787,642
Total Liabilities	4,133,567	3,641,218	3,126,570	2,972,060	2,216,253	2,051,631	2,000,062	1,946,229
Stockholders' Equity	424,046	370,181	318,436	325,171	258,201	258,506	269,664	296,483
Shares Outstanding	22,769	20,837	19,741	20,461	17,854	20,996	19,789	20,660
Statistical Record								
Return on Assets %	1.00	1.02	1.07	1.21	1.21	1.17	1.22	1.40
Return on Equity %	10.54	11.06	11.23	11.94	11.23	10.17	9.76	10.37
Net Interest Margin %	61.04	64.46	62.23	58.81	53.43	51.22	55.58	54.57
Efficiency Ratio %	42.20	43.84	41.16	37.57	34.42	34.58	37.58	36.25
Loans to Deposits	0.95	0.90	0.77	0.75	0.79	0.84	0.82	0.75
Price Range	32.75-25.88	32.75-25.88	28.74-21.99	25.86-19.42	26.10-17.69	26.00-19.13	30.25-21.69	31.00-23.38
P/E Ratio	17.33-13.69	17.24-13.62	15.97-12.22	15.21-11.42	16.31-11.05	18.44-13.56	22.08-15.83	22.79-17.19
Average Yield %	3.50	3.44	3.85	4.02	4.23	3.93	3.14	3.05

Address: 1 Bank Plaza, Wheeling, WV 26003
Telephone: 304-234-9000
Web Site: www.wesbanco.com

Officers: Edward M. George - Chmn. Paul M. Limbert - Pres., C.E.O. **Transfer Agents:** WesBanco, Inc. c/o Corporate Trust Services, Cincinnati, OH

Investor Contact: 304-234-9000
No of Institutions: 73
Shares: 5,652,806 **% Held:** 24.42

WESCO FINANCIAL CORP.

Exchange	Symbol	Price	52Wk Range	Yield	P/E
ASE	WSC	$358.28 (5/31/2005)	417.00-339.99	0.40	47.52

*7 Year Price Score 102.97 *NYSE Composite Index=100 *12 Month Price Score 96.51

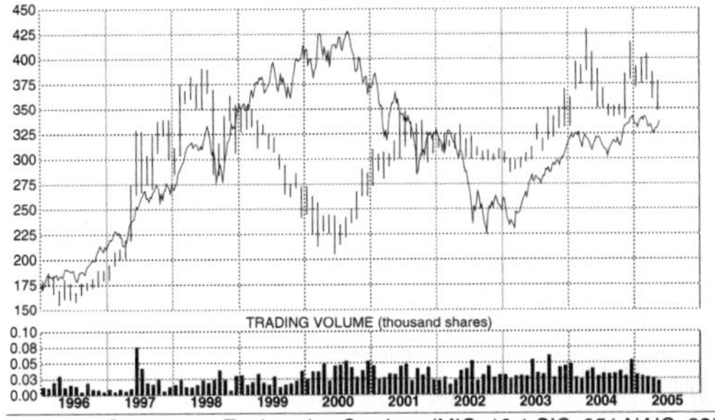

TRADING VOLUME (thousand shares)

Interim Earnings (Per Share)

Qtr.	Mar	Jun	Sep	Dec
2002	2.03	2.09	2.12	1.16
2003	1.76	6.45	1.00	1.28
2004	1.71	1.49	1.27	2.19
2005	2.59	...	...	...

Interim Dividends (Per Share)

Amt	Decl	Ex	Rec	Pay
0.345Q	7/22/2004	8/2/2004	8/4/2004	9/1/2004
0.345Q	9/16/2004	11/1/2004	11/3/2004	12/1/2004
0.355Q	1/21/2005	1/31/2005	2/2/2005	3/2/2005
0.355Q	3/10/2005	5/2/2005	5/4/2005	6/1/2005

Indicated Div: $1.42

Valuation Analysis

Forecast P/E	N/A		
Market Cap	$2.6 Billion	Book Value	2.1 Billion
Price/Book	1.19	Price/Sales	4.96

Dividend Achiever Status

Rank	294	10 Year Growth Rate	3.48%
Total Years of Dividend Growth			33

Business Summary: Engineering Services (MIC: 12.1 SIC: 051 NAIC: 23510)

Wesco Financial is engaged in three principal businesses: the insurance business, through Wesco-Financial Insurance Company, which engages in the property and casualty insurance business, and The Kansas Bankers Surety Company, which provides specialized insurance coverages for banks; the furniture rental business, through CORT Business Services Corporation, a provider of rental furniture, accessories and related services; and the steel service center business, through Precision Steel Warehouse, Inc. Co.'s operations also include, through MS Property Company, the ownership and management of commercial real estate property, and the development and liquidation of foreclosed real estate.

Recent Developments: For the quarter ended Mar 31 2005, net income increased 51.1% to $18,427 thousand from net income of $12,198 thousand in the year-earlier quarter. Revenues were $133,550 thousand, up 4.1% from $128,243 thousand the year before. Total direct expense was $44,307 thousand versus $46,336 thousand in the prior-year quarter, a decrease of 4.4%. Total indirect expense was $64,990 thousand versus $64,334 thousand in the prior-year quarter, an increase of 1.0%.

Prospects: Co.'s balance sheet position continues to be strong with relatively little debt. As of Dec 31 2004, Co.'s total assets were $2.57 billion, with cash and cash equivalents amounting to $1.16 billion, and notes payable of $29.2 million. Liquidity, which has traditionally been high, has risen further over the last couple of years due principally to sales, maturities and early redemption's of most of Co.'s mortgage-backed securities and other fixed-maturity investments and reinvestment of the proceeds in cash equivalents pending redeployment. Co. believes that its has adequate liquidity and capital resources to provide for any contingent needs that may arise.

Financial Data

(US$ in Thousands)	3 Mos	12/31/2004	12/31/2003	12/31/2002	12/31/2001	12/31/2000	12/31/1999	12/31/1998
Earnings Per Share	7.54	6.66	10.49	7.40	7.38	129.56	7.60	10.08
Cash Flow Per Share	16.17	17.29	17.28	26.47	23.11	(38.03)	3.29	1.85
Tang Book Value Per Share	264.26	259.89	254.44	237.64	231.46	241.16	262.20	308.20
Dividends Per Share	1.390	1.380	1.340	1.300	1.260	1.220	1.180	1.140
Dividend Payout %	18.44	20.72	12.77	17.57	17.07	0.94	15.53	11.31
Income Statement								
Total Revenue	133,550	509,313	614,317	575,677	561,079	1,823,964	145,706	176,179
EBITDA	24,253	105,507	153,119	134,825	151,061	1,470,830	79,342	107,390
Depn & Amortn	...	36,473	44,114	51,914	65,564	47,203	1,995	2,068
Income Before Taxes	24,036	68,235	108,256	80,917	81,328	1,418,392	74,798	102,306
Income Taxes	5,609	20,808	34,852	28,199	28,792	495,922	20,655	30,503
Net Income	18,427	47,427	74,711	52,718	52,536	922,470	54,143	71,803
Average Shares	7,119	7,119	7,119	7,119	7,119	7,119	7,119	7,120
Balance Sheet								
Current Assets	1,179,129	1,207,170	1,112,630	417,237	164,655	192,254	66,331	320,034
Total Assets	2,613,699	2,571,535	2,538,395	2,406,975	2,319,693	2,460,915	2,652,195	3,228,406
Current Liabilities	276,050	323,506	296,172	272,086	262,459	339,056	707,345	920,035
Long-Term Obligations	25,200	29,225	12,679	32,481	33,649	56,035	3,635	33,635
Total Liabilities	465,588	454,592	460,205	448,813	407,296	483,881	756,823	1,004,650
Stockholders' Equity	2,148,111	2,116,943	2,078,190	1,958,162	1,912,397	1,977,034	1,895,372	2,223,756
Shares Outstanding	7,119	7,119	7,119	7,119	7,119	7,119	7,119	7,120
Statistical Record								
Return on Assets %	2.07	1.85	3.02	2.23	2.20	35.98	1.84	2.47
Return on Equity %	2.53	2.25	3.70	2.72	2.70	47.51	2.63	3.60
EBITDA Margin %	18.16	20.72	24.93	23.42	26.92	80.64	54.45	60.96
Net Margin %	13.80	9.31	12.16	9.16	9.36	50.58	37.16	40.76
Asset Turnover	0.20	0.20	0.25	0.24	0.23	0.71	0.05	0.06
Current Ratio	4.27	3.73	3.76	1.53	0.63	0.57	0.09	0.35
Debt to Equity	0.01	0.01	0.01	0.02	0.02	0.03	N.M.	0.02
Price Range	429.75-339.99	429.75-332.00	370.01-286.00	334.00-298.00	347.90-273.00	290.00-205.00	354.75-241.50	391.00-284.00
P/E Ratio	57.00-45.09	64.53-49.85	35.27-27.26	45.14-40.27	47.14-36.99	2.24-1.58	46.68-31.78	38.79-28.17
Average Yield %	0.37	0.37	0.42	0.42	0.41	0.50	0.38	0.33

Address: 301 East Colorado Boulevard, Suite 300, Pasadena, CA 91101-1901 **Telephone:** 626-585-6700 **Web Site:** www.wescofinancial.com	**Officers:** Charles T. Munger - Chmn., C.E.O. Robert H. Bird - Pres. **Transfer Agents:** Mellon Investor Services, South Hackensack, NJ	**No of Institutions:** 78 **Shares:** 6,254,663 **% Held:** 87.85

WEST PHARMACEUTICAL SERVICES, INC.

Exchange	Symbol	Price	52Wk Range	Yield	P/E
NYS	WST	$27.84 (5/31/2005)	28.69-18.31	1.58	33.95

***7 Year Price Score 132.10** *NYSE Composite Index=100 ***12 Month Price Score 110.68**

Interim Earnings (Per Share)

Qtr.	Mar	Jun	Sep	Dec
2002	0.21	0.19	0.13	0.12
2003	0.13	0.24	0.14	0.58
2004	0.23	0.25	0.14	0.01
2005	0.42	...	...	...

Interim Dividends (Per Share)

Amt	Decl	Ex	Rec	Pay
100%	8/24/2004	9/30/2004	9/15/2004	9/29/2004
0.11Q	8/24/2004	10/18/2004	10/20/2004	11/3/2004
0.11Q	12/14/2004	1/14/2005	1/19/2005	2/2/2005
0.11Q	3/7/2005	4/18/2005	4/20/2005	5/4/2005

Indicated Div: $0.44 (Div. Reinv. Plan)

Valuation Analysis

Forecast P/E	18.36 (6/1/2005)		
Market Cap	$865.6 Million	Book Value	307.7 Million
Price/Book	2.81	Price/Sales	1.55

Dividend Achiever Status

Rank	240	**10 Year Growth Rate**	6.57%
Total Years of Dividend Growth			12

Business Summary: Rubber Products (MIC: 11.6 SIC: 069 NAIC: 26299)

West Pharmaceutical Services develops, manufactures and sells components and systems used for injectable drug delivery. These components include elastomeric stoppers and aluminum seals for vials, multi-piece tamper-resistant plastic and aluminum closures and components used in syringe, intravenous and blood collection systems. Co. also provides plastic systems and components for use in over the counter drugs, personal care and food and beverage applications. Co. operates in a single reportable segment referred to as the Pharmaceutical Systems segment. This reportable segment consists of three operating segments: the Americas, Europe/Asia and the Device Group.

Recent Developments: For the quarter ended Mar 31 2005, income from continuing operations increased 46.1% to $13,000 thousand from income of $8,900 thousand in the year-earlier quarter. Net income increased 90.0% to $13,300 thousand from net income of $7,000 thousand in the year-earlier quarter. Revenues were $149,500 thousand, up 14.6% from $130,400 thousand the year before. Operating income was $20,100 thousand versus an income of $13,600 thousand in the prior-year quarter, an increase of 47.8%. Total direct expense was $103,100 thousand versus $90,900 thousand in the prior-year quarter, an increase of 13.4%. Total indirect expense was $25,700 thousand versus $25,900 thousand in the prior-year quarter.

Prospects: On Apr 29 2005, Co. announced a definitive agreement to acquire the business assets of The Tech Group, Inc, a privately-owned company located in Scottsdale, AZ. The Tech Group manufactures plastic components and assemblies for the pharmaceutical, medical device, consumer products and personal care markets. Under the terms of the agreement, Co. will pay $140.0 million in cash for the assets, which include nine production facilities in Arizona, Michigan, Indiana, Puerto Rico, Mexico and Ireland. Co. expects the transaction to close during the second quarter of 2005. Meanwhile, Co. is benefiting from stronger sales, both in terms of total sales and profitable sales mix.

Financial Data

(US$ in Thousands)	3 Mos	12/31/2004	12/31/2003	12/31/2002	12/31/2001	12/31/2000	12/31/1999	12/31/1998
Earnings Per Share	0.82	0.63	1.10	0.64	(0.18)	0.06	1.28	0.20
Cash Flow Per Share	2.43	2.70	2.38	1.58	1.08	1.68	2.33	2.16
Tang Book Value Per Share	8.44	8.38	7.15	5.42	5.03	5.32	5.62	5.62
Dividends Per Share	0.430	0.425	0.405	0.385	0.365	0.345	0.325	0.305
Dividend Payout %	52.44	67.46	36.99	60.16	N.M.	627.27	25.29	152.50
Income Statement								
Total Revenue	149,500	541,600	490,700	419,700	396,900	430,100	469,100	449,700
EBITDA	30,100	81,500	87,500	59,700	73,300	52,200	102,600	67,300
Depn & Amortn	10,000	33,300	33,000	33,000	32,000	37,000	35,700	32,300
Income Before Taxes	18,100	41,200	47,000	17,200	27,800	2,100	56,500	27,800
Income Taxes	5,700	11,100	16,700	4,100	8,600	1,500	18,400	21,200
Net Income	13,300	19,400	31,900	18,400	(5,200)	1,600	38,700	6,700
Average Shares	31,775	30,842	29,092	28,868	28,696	28,818	30,096	33,008
Balance Sheet								
Current Assets	223,000	226,500	216,700	161,300	158,500	173,100	184,700	159,700
Total Assets	650,000	658,700	623,600	536,800	511,300	557,400	551,800	505,600
Current Liabilities	99,000	116,500	118,900	87,700	75,300	79,300	104,000	104,200
Long-Term Obligations	152,700	150,800	167,000	159,200	184,300	195,800	141,500	105,000
Total Liabilities	342,300	357,600	366,000	335,300	334,500	352,600	320,600	275,500
Stockholders' Equity	307,700	301,100	257,600	201,500	176,800	204,800	231,200	230,100
Shares Outstanding	31,091	30,709	29,264	28,960	28,688	28,620	29,328	30,052
Statistical Record								
Return on Assets %	4.10	3.02	5.50	3.51	N.M.	0.29	7.32	1.36
Return on Equity %	9.00	6.93	13.90	9.73	N.M.	0.73	16.78	2.64
EBITDA Margin %	20.13	15.05	17.83	14.22	18.47	12.14	21.87	14.97
Net Margin %	8.90	3.58	6.50	4.38	N.M.	0.37	8.25	1.49
Asset Turnover	0.89	0.84	0.85	0.80	0.74	0.77	0.89	0.91
Current Ratio	2.25	1.94	1.82	1.84	2.10	2.18	1.78	1.53
Debt to Equity	0.50	0.50	0.65	0.79	1.04	0.96	0.61	0.46
Price Range	26.96-18.31	25.03-16.55	17.80-8.50	16.05-8.28	14.03-11.45	15.84-9.94	20.13-15.44	17.84-12.91
P/E Ratio	32.88-22.32	39.73-26.26	16.18-7.73	25.07-12.93	N.M.	264.06-165.63	15.72-12.06	89.22-64.53
Average Yield %	1.97	2.13	3.06	3.01	2.86	2.86	1.83	2.04

Address: 101 Gordon Drive, P.O. Box 645, Lionville, PA 19341-0645 **Telephone:** 610-594-2900 **Web Site:** www.westpharma.com	**Officers:** Donald E. Morel Jr. - Chmn., Pres., C.E.O. William J. Federici - V.P., C.F.O. **Transfer Agents:** American Stock Transfer and Trust Company, New York, NY	**Investor Contact:** 610-594-3345 **No of Institutions:** 99 **Shares:** 23,318,968 **% Held:** 75.26

WESTAMERICA BANCORPORATION

Exchange	Symbol	Price	52Wk Range	Yield	P/E
NMS	WABC	$52.65 (5/31/2005)	61.05-48.98	2.28	18.22

Interim Earnings (Per Share)

Qtr.	Mar	Jun	Sep	Dec
2002	0.63	0.57	0.67	0.69
2003	0.69	0.71	0.72	0.73
2004	0.74	0.76	0.78	0.65
2005	0.70	...	...	...

Interim Dividends (Per Share)

Amt	Decl	Ex	Rec	Pay
0.28Q	7/22/2004	7/29/2004	8/2/2004	8/13/2004
0.28Q	10/28/2004	11/4/2004	11/8/2004	11/19/2004
0.30Q	1/26/2005	2/3/2005	2/7/2005	2/18/2005
0.30Q	4/28/2005	5/5/2005	5/9/2005	5/20/2005

Indicated Div: $1.20 (Div. Reinv. Plan)

Valuation Analysis

Forecast P/E 15.81 (6/2/2005)
Market Cap $1.7 Billion Book Value 437.6 Million
Price/Book 3.96 Price/Sales 6.82

Dividend Achiever Status

Rank 55 **10 Year Growth Rate** 18.20%
Total Years of Dividend Growth 15

Business Summary: Commercial Banking (MIC: 8.1 SIC: 021 NAIC: 22110)

Westamerica Bancorporation is a bank holding company that provides a full range of banking services to individual and corporate customers in northern and central California through its subsidiary bank, Westamerica Bank. Co. is a regional community bank with 91 branches two trust offices serving 22 California counties. At Dec 31 2004, Co. had total assets of $4.74 billion and total deposits of $3.58 billion. Co.'s focus is on serving the needs of small businesses. In addition, Co. also owns Community Banker Services Corporation, which is engaged in providing Co. and its subsidiaries data processing services and other support functions.

Recent Developments: For the quarter ended Mar 31 2005, net income decreased 6.5% to $22,733 thousand from net income of $24,314 thousand in the year-earlier quarter. Net interest income was $48,946 thousand, up 0.1% from $48,896 thousand the year before. Provision for loan losses was $300 thousand versus $750 thousand in the prior-year quarter, a decrease of 60.0%. Non-interest income fell 33.8% to $14,390 thousand, while non-interest expense advanced 0.6% to $25,140 thousand.

Prospects: On Mar 1 2005, Co. announced that it has completed its previously announced acquisition of Redwood Empire Bancorp in a cash and stock transaction valued at approximately $153.0 million. The acquisition expands Co.'s customer base in Sonoma and Mendocino counties of California, and is accretive to earnings. Meanwhile, Co. has completed the systems integration, and full integration is expected by Jun 30 2005. In addition, Co. expects to complete its branch consolidations in the second quarter and has entered into an agreement to sell one branch located in Lake County, which should be completed late in the second quarter of 2005.

Financial Data

(US$ in Thousands)	3 Mos	12/31/2004	12/31/2003	12/31/2002	12/31/2001	12/31/2000	12/31/1999	12/31/1998
Earnings Per Share	2.89	2.93	2.85	2.55	2.36	2.16	1.94	1.73
Cash Flow Per Share	3.48	3.56	3.51	2.69	2.80	2.55	2.48	1.51
Tang Book Value Per Share	8.52	11.33	10.54	10.22	9.19	9.32	8.10	9.25
Dividends Per Share	1.140	1.100	1.000	0.900	0.820	0.740	0.660	0.520
Dividend Payout %	39.45	37.54	35.09	35.29	34.75	34.26	34.02	30.06
Income Statement								
Interest Income	57,303	216,337	223,493	237,633	257,056	269,516	257,656	266,820
Interest Expense	8,357	21,106	27,197	39,182	68,887	88,614	78,456	86,665
Net Interest Income	48,946	195,231	196,296	198,451	188,169	180,902	179,200	180,155
Provision for Losses	300	2,700	3,300	3,600	3,600	3,675	4,780	5,180
Non-Interest Income	7,195	38,583	42,916	36,551	42,655	41,130	40,174	37,805
Non-Interest Expense	25,140	98,751	101,703	103,323	102,651	100,198	100,133	101,408
Income Before Taxes	30,701	132,363	134,209	128,079	124,573	118,159	114,461	111,372
Income Taxes	7,968	37,145	39,146	40,941	40,294	38,380	38,373	37,976
Net Income	22,733	95,218	95,063	87,138	84,279	79,779	76,088	73,396
Average Shares	32,680	32,461	33,369	34,225	35,748	36,936	39,194	42,524
Balance Sheet								
Net Loans & Leases	2,648,193	2,246,078	2,269,420	2,440,411	2,432,371	2,429,880	2,269,272	2,246,593
Total Assets	5,192,111	4,737,268	4,576,385	4,224,867	3,927,967	4,031,381	3,893,187	3,844,298
Total Deposits	3,938,843	3,583,619	3,463,991	3,294,065	3,234,635	3,236,744	3,065,344	3,189,005
Total Liabilities	4,754,536	4,378,659	4,236,014	3,883,368	3,613,608	3,693,634	3,592,595	3,475,702
Stockholders' Equity	437,575	358,609	340,371	341,499	314,359	337,747	300,592	368,596
Shares Outstanding	32,939	31,640	32,287	33,411	34,220	36,251	37,125	39,828
Statistical Record								
Return on Assets %	1.95	2.04	2.16	2.14	2.12	2.01	1.97	1.91
Return on Equity %	24.13	27.17	27.88	26.57	25.85	24.93	22.74	18.92
Net Interest Margin %	85.42	90.24	87.83	83.51	73.20	67.12	69.55	67.52
Efficiency Ratio %	38.98	38.74	38.18	37.68	34.25	32.25	33.62	33.29
Loans to Deposits	0.67	0.63	0.66	0.74	0.75	0.75	0.74	0.70
Price Range	61.05-47.58	61.05-47.58	53.28-38.70	45.67-35.57	42.00-32.55	43.75-21.00	37.50-26.63	37.00-24.25
P/E Ratio	21.12-16.46	20.84-16.24	18.69-13.58	17.91-13.95	17.80-13.79	20.25-9.72	19.33-13.72	21.39-14.02
Average Yield %	2.13	2.10	2.26	2.19	2.16	2.54	2.00	1.62

Address: 1108 Fifth Avenue, San Rafael, CA 94901
Telephone: 707-863-8000
Web Site: www.westamerica.com

Officers: David L. Payne - Chmn., Pres., C.E.O. Robert W. Entwisle - Sr. V.P., Banking Division
ransfer Agents: Computershare Investor Services LLC

No of Institutions: 133
Shares: 14,899,675 **% Held:** 45.14

WGL HOLDINGS, INC.

Exchange	Symbol	Price	52Wk Range	Yield	P/E
NYS	WGL	$32.54 (5/31/2005)	32.54-27.20	4.09	15.80

***7 Year Price Score 97.47** *NYSE Composite Index=100 ***12 Month Price Score 101.75**

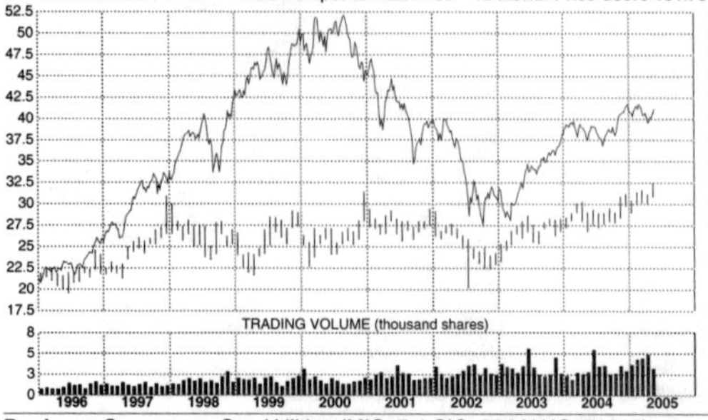

Interim Earnings (Per Share)

Qtr.	Dec	Mar	Jun	Sep
2001-02	0.62	0.94	(0.29)	(0.47)
2002-03	1.06	1.66	(0.05)	(0.37)
2003-04	0.81	1.60	(0.08)	(0.37)
2004-05	0.88	1.63	...	...

Interim Dividends (Per Share)

Amt	Decl	Ex	Rec	Pay
0.325Q	6/30/2004	7/7/2004	7/9/2004	8/1/2004
0.325Q	9/29/2004	10/6/2004	10/8/2004	11/1/2004
0.325Q	12/17/2004	1/6/2005	1/10/2005	2/1/2005
0.333Q	2/23/2005	4/6/2005	4/8/2005	5/1/2005

Indicated Div: $1.33 (Div. Reinv. Plan)

Valuation Analysis

Forecast P/E	16.66 (6/1/2005)		
Market Cap	$1.6 Billion	Book Value	945.5 Million
Price/Book	1.68	Price/Sales	0.73

Dividend Achiever Status

Rank	309	10 Year Growth Rate	1.60%
Total Years of Dividend Growth			28

Business Summary: Gas Utilities (MIC: 7.4 SIC: 924 NAIC: 21210)

WGL Holdings, through its subsidiaries, engages in the sale and distribution of natural gas and other energy-related products and services. Washington Gas Light Company is a regulated natural gas utility serving about 1.0 million customers in Washington, D.C., Virginia and Maryland as of Sep 30 2004. Hampshire Gas Company is a regulated natural gas storage business, serving Washington Gas Light. Washington Gas Energy Services, Inc. is an unregulated seller of natural gas and electricity both inside and outside Washington Gas Light's traditional service territory. Washington Gas Energy Systems, Inc. provides commercial energy services.

Recent Developments: For the quarter ended Mar 31 2005, net income increased 0.9% to $79,946 thousand from net income of $79,232 thousand in the year-earlier quarter. Revenues were $226,888 thousand, down 1.8% from $231,152 thousand the year before. Operating income was $87,059 thousand versus an income of $86,562 thousand in the prior-year quarter, an increase of 0.6%. Total direct expense was $465,514 thousand versus $421,165 thousand in the prior-year quarter, an increase of 10.5%. Total indirect expense was $373,545 thousand versus $356,332 thousand in the prior-year quarter, an increase of 4.8%.

Prospects: On Apr 27 2005, Washington Gas Light Company updated estimated costs to rehabilitate a portion of its distribution system in Prince George's County, MD, which is experiencing a higher than usual number of outdoor, underground natural gas leaks. The costs of this work are expected to be recorded as capital expenditures and estimated to be $87.0 million. The current estimate reflects the expectation that main replacements will be a larger portion of the total project cost versus encapsulating couplings on mains. This does not include any potential costs associated with paving, which could amount to as much as $50.0 million. For 2005, Co. expects earning to range from $1.94 to $2.04 per share.

Financial Data

(US$ in Thousands)	6 Mos	3 Mos	09/30/2004	09/30/2003	09/30/2002	09/30/2001	09/30/2000	09/30/1999
Earnings Per Share	2.06	2.01	1.98	2.30	0.80	1.75	1.79	1.47
Cash Flow Per Share	4.49	4.10	4.97	2.96	4.23	1.70	1.90	3.32
Tang Book Value Per Share	19.42	18.10	17.54	16.83	15.78	16.24	15.31	14.72
Dividends Per Share	1.300	1.295	1.290	1.275	1.265	1.250	1.230	1.210
Dividend Payout %	63.11	64.35	65.15	55.43	158.13	71.43	68.72	82.31
Income Statement								
Total Revenue	1,044,177	408,951	2,089,603	2,064,248	1,569,969	1,933,024	1,247,954	1,112,214
Depn & Amortn	45,563	22,798	95,348	88,375	77,021	72,362	68,908	65,193
Income Taxes	97,591	35,333	60,638	68,801	30,427	59,372	49,263	42,519
Net Income	123,078	43,132	(1,320)	113,662	40,441	83,765	84,574	68,768
Average Shares	48,996	48,936	48,847	48,756	48,563	47,120	46,473	45,984
Balance Sheet								
Net PPE	1,923,928	1,922,247	1,915,551	1,874,923	1,606,843	1,519,747	1,460,280	1,402,742
Total Assets	2,715,854	2,769,911	2,504,908	2,436,052	2,113,664	2,081,113	1,939,840	1,766,724
Long-Term Obligations	523,692	573,721	590,164	636,650	667,951	584,370	559,576	506,084
Total Liabilities	1,742,191	1,860,394	1,623,311	1,589,661	1,319,088	1,264,687	1,200,172	1,054,270
Stockholders' Equity	945,490	881,344	881,597	846,391	794,576	816,426	739,669	712,454
Shares Outstanding	48,692	48,692	48,652	48,611	48,564	48,542	46,469	46,473
Statistical Record								
Return on Assets %	0.11	0.01	N.M.	5.00	1.93	4.17	4.55	3.99
Return on Equity %	0.32	0.03	N.M.	13.85	5.02	10.77	11.62	10.20
Net Margin %	11.79	10.55	(0.06)	5.51	2.58	4.33	6.78	6.18
PPE Turnover	1.14	1.11	1.10	1.19	1.00	1.30	0.87	0.82
Asset Turnover	0.81	0.78	0.84	0.91	0.75	0.96	0.67	0.64
Debt to Equity	0.55	0.65	0.67	0.75	0.84	0.72	0.76	0.71
Price Range	31.71-26.78	31.22-26.78	30.28-26.27	28.64-22.38	29.45-20.16	31.44-25.19	29.25-22.63	28.50-21.63
P/E Ratio	15.39-13.00	15.53-13.32	15.29-13.27	12.45-9.73	36.81-25.20	17.96-14.39	16.34-12.64	19.39-14.71
Average Yield %	4.45	4.50	4.58	4.97	4.82	4.55	4.72	4.76

Address: 101 Constitution Avenue, N.W., Washington, DC 20080
Telephone: 703-750-2000
Web Site: www.wglholdings.com

Officers: James H. DeGraffenreidt Jr. - Chmn., C.E.O. Terry D. McCallister - Pres., C.O.O. **Transfer Agents:** The Bank of New York, New York, NY

No of Institutions: 158
Shares: 23,732,404 **% Held:** 48.74

WHITNEY HOLDING CORP.

Exchange	Symbol	Price	52Wk Range	Yield	P/E
NMS	WTNY	$31.71 (5/31/2005)	31.99-26.79	3.15	19.82

*7 Year Price Score 122.38 *NYSE Composite Index=100 *12 Month Price Score 101.02

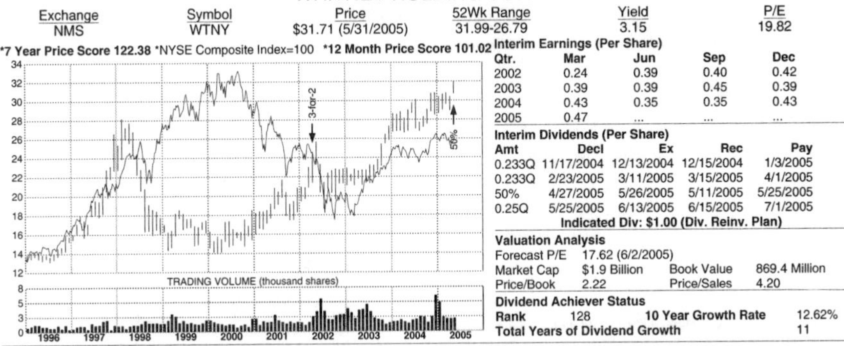

Interim Earnings (Per Share)

Qtr.	Mar	Jun	Sep	Dec
2002	0.24	0.39	0.40	0.42
2003	0.39	0.39	0.45	0.39
2004	0.43	0.35	0.35	0.43
2005	0.47	...	...	...

Interim Dividends (Per Share)

Amt	Decl	Ex	Rec	Pay
0.233Q	11/17/2004	12/13/2004	12/15/2004	1/3/2005
0.233Q	2/23/2005	3/11/2005	3/15/2005	4/1/2005
50%	4/27/2005	5/26/2005	5/11/2005	5/25/2005
0.25Q	5/25/2005	6/13/2005	6/15/2005	7/1/2005

Indicated Div: $1.00 (Div. Reinv. Plan)

Valuation Analysis

Forecast P/E	17.62 (6/2/2005)		
Market Cap	$1.9 Billion	Book Value	869.4 Million
Price/Book	2.22	Price/Sales	4.20

Dividend Achiever Status

Rank	128	10 Year Growth Rate	12.62%
Total Years of Dividend Growth			11

Business Summary: Commercial Banking (MIC: 8.1 SIC: 021 NAIC: 22110)

Whitney Holding, through its principal banking subsidiary, Whitney National Bank, serves the five-state Gulf Coast region stretching from Houston, TX, across southern Louisiana and the coastal region of Mississippi, to central and south Alabama, the western panhandle of Florida, and to the Tampa Bay metropolitan area of Florida. Co. serves commercial, small business and retail customers, and offers a range of transaction and savings deposit products and cash management services, secured and unsecured loan products, and letters of credit and similar financial guarantees. Co. also provides trust and investment management services to retirement benefit plans, corporations and individuals.

Recent Developments: For the quarter ended Mar 31 2005, net income increased 9.9% to $28,756 thousand from net income of $26,158 thousand in the year-earlier quarter. Net interest income was $88,419 thousand, up 14.5% from $77,190 thousand the year before. Provision for loan losses was $1,500 thousand versus a recovery of $2,000 thousand in the prior-year quarter, a decrease of 175.0%. Non-interest income rose 2.3% to $21,391 thousand, while non-interest expense advanced 6.8% to $66,261 thousand.

Prospects: On Apr 22 2005, Co. announced that it has completed its acquisition of Destin Bancshares, Inc. the parent company of Destin Bank, which operates ten banking centers in Florida and has approximately $500.0 million in assets. The acquisition boosts Co.'s presence in Florida to 23 branches and over $1.00 billion in total assets. Meanwhile, Co. continues to experience solid growth in its loan portfolio, driven primarily by increased commercial, commercial real estate and real estate construction lending stemming from both new customer development and demand from Co.'s established customer base. Also, results are benefiting from increased earnings assets, which is being funded by deposit growth.

Financial Data (US$ in Thousands)	3 Mos	12/31/2004	12/31/2003	12/31/2002	12/31/2001	12/31/2000	12/31/1999	12/31/1998
Earnings Per Share	1.60	1.57	1.63	1.59	1.27	1.31	1.20	1.00
Cash Flow Per Share	2.41	2.44	2.44	2.51	2.08	2.02	1.85	1.45
Tang Book Value Per Share	12.00	12.31	12.32	11.69	10.32	10.20	10.31	10.66
Dividends Per Share	0.907	0.893	0.820	0.740	0.684	0.640	0.587	0.533
Dividend Payout %	56.67	57.02	50.41	46.64	54.04	48.98	48.89	53.57
Income Statement								
Interest Income	102,189	360,772	338,069	370,909	441,145	417,687	349,813	336,113
Interest Expense	13,770	40,682	43,509	75,701	161,349	170,574	124,065	122,981
Net Interest Income	88,419	320,090	294,560	295,208	279,796	247,113	225,748	213,132
Provision for Losses	1,500	2,000	(3,500)	7,500	19,500	10,000	6,000	73
Non-Interest Income	21,391	82,523	89,504	85,185	91,209	71,625	66,663	60,771
Non-Interest Expense	66,261	260,278	242,923	230,926	239,104	208,903	194,163	195,993
Income Before Taxes	42,049	140,335	144,641	141,967	112,401	99,835	92,248	77,837
Income Taxes	13,293	43,198	46,099	46,644	36,581	32,807	29,828	25,158
Net Income	28,756	97,137	98,542	95,323	75,820	67,028	62,420	52,679
Average Shares	61,596	62,083	60,594	60,182	59,754	51,384	51,954	52,875
Balance Sheet								
Net Loans & Leases	5,588,111	5,571,931	4,823,135	4,389,297	4,482,905	4,245,501	3,628,581	3,230,299
Total Assets	8,275,949	8,222,624	7,754,982	7,097,881	7,243,650	6,242,076	5,454,388	5,211,919
Total Deposits	6,721,086	6,612,607	6,158,582	5,782,879	5,950,160	4,960,177	4,309,398	4,256,662
Total Liabilities	7,406,574	7,317,859	6,914,669	6,297,398	6,525,762	5,619,116	4,897,285	4,650,958
Stockholders' Equity	869,375	904,765	840,313	800,483	717,888	622,960	557,103	560,961
Shares Outstanding	60,920	62,101	60,671	60,101	59,500	52,541	50,791	52,634
Statistical Record								
Return on Assets %	1.24	1.21	1.33	1.33	1.12	1.14	1.17	1.11
Return on Equity %	11.46	11.10	12.01	12.56	11.31	11.33	11.17	10.13
Net Interest Margin %	86.52	88.72	87.13	79.59	63.42	59.16	64.53	63.41
Efficiency Ratio %	53.62	58.71	56.81	50.63	44.91	42.69	46.62	49.38
Loans to Deposits	0.83	0.84	0.78	0.76	0.75	0.86	0.84	0.76
Price Range	30.79-26.63	30.79-26.63	27.33-21.08	25.68-18.65	21.71-16.00	18.53-14.00	18.56-14.31	28.17-15.89
P/E Ratio	19.25-16.65	19.61-16.96	16.76-12.93	16.15-11.73	17.09-12.60	14.14-10.69	15.46-11.92	28.17-15.89
Average Yield %	3.15	3.16	3.55	3.39	3.68	4.09	3.54	2.44

Address: 228 St. Charles Avenue, New Orleans, LA 70130
Telephone: 504-586-7272
Web Site: www.whitneybank.com

Officers: William L. Marks - Chmn., C.E.O. R. King Milling - Pres. **Transfer Agents:** American Stock Transfer & Trust Company, New York, NY

Investor Contact: 504-552-4591
No of Institutions: 126
Shares: 16,069,000 **% Held:** 39.59

WILEY (JOHN) & SONS INC.

Exchange	Symbol	Price	52Wk Range	Yield	P/E
NYS	JW A	$38.75 (5/31/2005)	38.75-30.68	0.77	27.48

***7 Year Price Score 127.53** *NYSE Composite Index=100 ***12 Month Price Score 104.75**

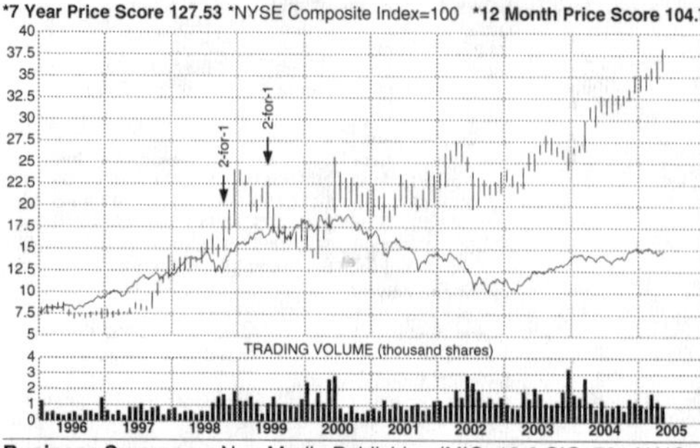

TRADING VOLUME (thousand shares)

Interim Earnings (Per Share)

Qtr.	Jul	Oct	Jan	Apr
2001-02	0.31	0.28	0.34	(0.02)
2002-03	0.32	0.55	0.39	0.13
2003-04	0.35	0.41	0.51	0.14
2004-05	0.32	0.42	0.53	...

Interim Dividends (Per Share)

Amt	Decl	Ex	Rec	Pay
0.075Q	6/17/2004	7/1/2004	7/6/2004	7/19/2004
0.075Q	9/15/2004	9/29/2004	10/1/2004	10/18/2004
0.075Q	12/16/2004	12/23/2004	12/28/2004	1/17/2005
0.075Q	3/9/2005	3/31/2005	4/4/2005	4/15/2005

Indicated Div: $0.30

Valuation Analysis

Forecast P/E	23.39 (6/3/2005)		
Market Cap	$2.3 Billion	Book Value	453.8 Million
Price/Book	5.10	Price/Sales	2.40

Dividend Achiever Status

Rank	102	**10 Year Growth Rate**	14.37%
Total Years of Dividend Growth			11

Business Summary: Non-Media Publishing (MIC: 13.3 SIC: 731 NAIC: 11130)

John Wiley & Sons is a publisher of print and electronic products, providing must-have content and services to customers worldwide. Core businesses include professional and consumer books and subscription services; scientific, technical, and medical journals, encyclopedias, books, and online products and services; and educational materials. Co. has publishing, marketing, and distribution centers in the United States, Canada, Europe, Asia, and Australia. In addition, Co. imports, adapts, markets and distributes books from other publishers. Co. also develops and markets computer software and electronic databases for educational use and professional research and training.

Recent Developments: For the quarter ended Jan 31 2005, net income increased 4.6% to $32,791 thousand from net income of $31,344 thousand in the year-earlier quarter. Revenues were $258,428 thousand, up 6.6% from $242,357 thousand the year before. Operating income was $50,425 thousand versus an income of $43,850 thousand in the prior-year quarter, an increase of 15.0%. Total direct expense was $85,708 thousand versus $81,979 thousand in the prior-year quarter, an increase of 4.5%. Total indirect expense was $122,295 thousand versus $116,528 thousand in the prior-year quarter, an increase of 4.9%.

Prospects: Co.'s near-term prospects appears favorable, supported by the solid performance of its Professional/Trade business and stronger growth in its international operations. The continued strength of Co.'s global Scientific, Technical and Medical business is also contributing to growth. However, Co. is experiencing unfavorable performance in its Higher Education business, which is below expectations due to the challenging market climate. Meanwhile, Co. anticipates full-year growth in revenue and earnings per diluted share of 4.0% to 6.0% in fiscal year 2005, excluding estimated expenses associated with Sarbanes-Oxley compliance of $0.03 per diluted share.

Financial Data

(US$ in Thousands)	9 Mos	6 Mos	3 Mos	04/30/2004	04/30/2003	04/30/2002	04/30/2001	04/30/2000
Earnings Per Share	1.41	1.38	1.38	1.41	1.38	0.91	0.93	0.81
Cash Flow Per Share	3.65	3.78	3.59	3.43	2.75	2.31	2.17	2.13
Dividends Per Share	0.290	0.280	0.270	0.260	0.200	0.180	0.160	0.142
Dividend Payout %	20.59	20.22	19.63	18.44	14.49	19.78	17.20	17.59
Income Statement								
Total Revenue	732,417	473,989	226,939	922,962	853,971	734,396	613,790	594,815
EBITDA	177,675	107,603	47,925	169,784	153,563	122,267	129,550	119,290
Depn & Amortn	56,349	36,702	18,335	39,515	33,040	33,669	31,298	28,269
Income Before Taxes	116,605	68,154	29,590	125,110	112,559	81,118	90,227	82,631
Income Taxes	37,471	21,811	9,706	36,270	25,284	23,802	31,309	30,243
Net Income	79,134	46,343	19,884	88,840	87,275	57,316	58,918	52,388
Average Shares	60,513	62,548	62,851	63,226	63,086	63,094	63,300	64,825
Balance Sheet								
Current Assets	413,789	267,776	298,132	324,006	283,844	275,259	189,535	177,111
Total Assets	1,108,349	957,275	989,193	1,014,582	955,972	896,145	588,002	569,337
Current Liabilities	358,667	226,637	265,836	306,365	323,265	320,393	246,761	254,050
Long-Term Obligations	200,000	200,000	200,000	200,000	200,000	235,000	65,000	95,000
Total Liabilities	654,532	522,601	559,860	599,518	611,968	619,495	367,979	396,599
Stockholders' Equity	453,817	434,674	429,333	415,064	344,004	276,650	220,023	172,738
Shares Outstanding	59,699	61,118	61,474	61,694	61,630	61,701	60,734	60,712
Statistical Record								
Return on Assets %	8.27	9.05	8.99	8.99	9.42	7.72	10.18	9.52
Return on Equity %	20.22	20.96	21.60	23.34	28.12	23.08	30.00	31.20
EBITDA Margin %	24.26	22.70	21.12	18.40	17.98	16.65	21.11	20.05
Net Margin %	10.80	9.78	8.76	9.63	10.22	7.80	9.60	8.81
Asset Turnover	0.89	0.98	0.96	0.93	0.92	0.99	1.06	1.08
Current Ratio	1.15	1.18	1.12	1.06	0.88	0.86	0.77	0.70
Debt to Equity	0.44	0.46	0.47	0.48	0.58	0.85	0.30	0.55
Price Range	35.25-26.28	33.05-24.24	32.77-24.24	31.58-24.07	27.30-19.61	27.46-18.65	25.69-17.56	22.75-13.88
P/E Ratio	25.00-18.64	23.95-17.57	23.75-17.57	22.40-17.07	19.78-14.21	30.18-20.49	27.62-18.88	28.09-17.13
Average Yield %	0.92	0.95	0.96	0.97	0.87	0.80	0.77	0.82

Address: 111 River Street, Hoboken, NJ 07030-5774
Telephone: 201-748-6000
Web Site: www.wiley.com

Officers: Peter Booth Wiley - Chmn. William J. Pesce - Pres., C.E.O. **Transfer Agents:** Registrar and Transfer Company

Investor Contact: 201-748-6000
No of Institutions: 121
Shares: 30,628,684 **% Held:** 62.84

WILMINGTON TRUST CORP.

Exchange	Symbol	Price	52Wk Range	Yield	P/E
NYS	WL	$35.83 (5/31/2005)	37.54-33.01	3.35	16.67

***7 Year Price Score 103.71** *NYSE Composite Index=100 ***12 Month Price Score 95.24**

Interim Earnings (Per Share)

Qtr.	Mar	Jun	Sep	Dec
2002	0.48	0.52	0.52	0.49
2003	0.44	0.49	0.52	0.57
2004	0.53	0.54	0.50	0.52
2005	0.59	...	...	...

Interim Dividends (Per Share)

Amt	Decl	Ex	Rec	Pay
0.285Q	4/16/2004	4/29/2004	5/3/2004	5/17/2004
0.285Q	10/22/2004	10/28/2004	11/1/2004	11/15/2004
0.285Q	1/21/2005	1/28/2005	2/1/2005	2/15/2005
0.30Q	4/22/2005	4/28/2005	5/2/2005	5/16/2005

Indicated Div: $1.20 (Div. Reinv. Plan)

Valuation Analysis

Forecast P/E	15.61 (6/2/2005)		
Market Cap	$2.4 Billion	Book Value	911.2 Million
Price/Book	2.66	Price/Sales	3.46

Dividend Achiever Status

Rank	217	**10 Year Growth Rate**	7.82%
Total Years of Dividend Growth			23

Business Summary: Commercial Banking (MIC: 8.1 SIC: 022 NAIC: 22110)

Wilmington Trust, with assets of $9.51 billion as of Dec 31 2004, is a financial services holding company with offices in California, Delaware, Florida, Georgia, Maryland, Nevada, New York, Pennsylvania, Tennessee, the Cayman and Channel Islands, Dublin, London, and Milan. Co. provides wealth management and specialized corporate services to clients throughout the United States and in more than 50 other countries, and commercial banking services throughout the Delaware Valley region. In addition, Co. is authorized to do business in Luxembourg and the Netherlands.

Recent Developments: For the quarter ended Mar 31 2005, net income increased 12.3% to $40,100 thousand from net income of $35,700 thousand in the year-earlier quarter. Net interest income was $77,600 thousand, up 8.1% from $71,800 thousand the year before. Provision for loan losses was $3,100 thousand versus $5,500 thousand in the prior-year quarter, a decrease of 43.6%. Non-interest income rose 7.0% to $139,900 thousand, while non-interest expense advanced 7.3% to $89,300 thousand.

Prospects: For the second quarter of fiscal 2005, Co. anticipates year-over-year loan growth in the range of 6.0% to 7.0%, assuming no significant change in the Delaware Valley economy. Meanwhile, net interest margin may fall below 3.60% in the second quarter, reflecting pricing pressures on retail deposits. Additionally, Co. is projecting an increase in Wealth Advisory revenues, assuming more stable financial markets. However, weakness in the capital markets sector continues to limit growth in Corporate Client revenue, which is expected to be unchanged versus the first quarter of 2005. Total expenses are expected to be between $90.0 million and $92.0 million.

Financial Data

(US$ in Thousands)	3 Mos	12/31/2004	12/31/2003	12/31/2002	12/31/2001	12/31/2000	12/31/1999	12/31/1998
Earnings Per Share	2.15	2.09	2.02	2.01	1.90	1.85	1.61	1.67
Cash Flow Per Share	3.24	2.97	2.99	2.66	4.14	2.28	2.54	2.12
Tang Book Value Per Share	7.87	7.78	8.08	7.31	7.25	6.48	5.17	6.07
Dividends Per Share	1.140	1.125	1.065	1.005	0.945	0.885	0.825	0.765
Dividend Payout %	53.02	53.83	52.72	50.00	49.74	47.84	51.40	45.81
Income Statement								
Interest Income	112,900	386,500	368,800	392,871	468,798	530,454	462,176	456,939
Interest Expense	35,300	92,100	91,700	116,341	209,985	275,315	216,263	219,242
Net Interest Income	77,600	294,400	277,100	276,530	258,813	255,139	245,913	237,697
Provision for Losses	3,100	15,600	21,600	22,013	19,850	21,900	17,500	20,000
Non-Interest Income	77,400	286,700	264,200	262,159	228,003	216,210	191,453	183,917
Non-Interest Expense	89,300	344,000	312,000	309,892	276,917	264,682	258,204	230,066
Income Before Taxes	62,600	221,500	207,700	206,784	190,049	184,767	161,662	171,548
Income Taxes	22,500	78,700	72,200	73,002	66,009	63,828	54,365	57,223
Net Income	40,100	141,900	134,400	133,157	125,170	120,939	107,297	114,325
Average Shares	68,229	67,755	66,536	66,301	65,942	65,360	66,766	68,550
Balance Sheet								
Net Loans & Leases	6,769,200	6,673,300	6,135,400	5,939,947	5,407,175	5,111,670	4,743,154	4,247,727
Total Assets	9,575,400	9,510,200	8,820,200	8,131,275	7,518,462	7,321,616	7,201,944	6,300,565
Total Deposits	6,891,100	6,871,900	6,577,200	6,337,093	5,590,785	5,286,016	5,369,484	4,536,763
Total Liabilities	8,664,000	8,604,800	8,019,200	7,390,001	6,835,932	6,729,716	6,703,713	5,754,356
Stockholders' Equity	911,200	905,300	800,800	741,269	682,530	591,900	498,231	546,209
Shares Outstanding	67,530	67,405	66,063	65,627	65,400	64,786	64,705	66,658
Statistical Record								
Return on Assets %	1.56	1.54	1.59	1.70	1.69	1.66	1.59	1.84
Return on Equity %	16.75	16.59	17.43	18.70	19.64	22.13	20.55	21.79
Net Interest Margin %	68.73	76.17	75.14	70.39	55.21	48.10	53.21	52.02
Efficiency Ratio %	46.93	51.10	49.29	47.31	39.74	35.45	39.50	35.90
Loans to Deposits	0.98	0.97	0.93	0.94	0.97	0.97	0.88	0.94
Price Range	38.04-33.52	38.30-33.95	36.21-26.35	34.58-25.30	33.42-25.65	31.56-20.75	31.25-23.00	34.00-23.25
P/E Ratio	17.69-15.59	18.33-16.24	17.93-13.04	17.20-12.59	17.59-13.50	17.06-11.22	19.41-14.29	20.36-13.92
Average Yield %	3.20	3.11	3.47	3.22	3.14	3.58	2.98	2.60

Address: Rodney Square North, 1100 North Market Street, Wilmington, DE 19890-0001
Telephone: 302-651-1000
Web Site: www.wilmingtontrust.com

Officers: Ted T. Cecala - Chmn., C.E.O. Robert V. A. Harra Jr. - Pres., C.O.O., Treas. **Transfer Agents:** National Bank Trust Company, Montreal, Quebec

Investor Contact: 302-651-8069
No of Institutions: 206
Shares: 27,485,836 **% Held:** 40.78

WOLVERINE WORLD WIDE, INC.

Exchange	Symbol	Price	52Wk Range	Yield	P/E
NYS	WWW	$22.98 (5/31/2005)	23.35-14.40	1.13	19.81

Interim Earnings (Per Share)

Qtr.	Mar	Jun	Aug	Dec
2003	0.12	0.15	0.27	0.31
2004	0.20	0.18	0.37	0.34
2005	0.27	...	...	...

Interim Dividends (Per Share)

Amt	Decl	Ex	Rec	Pay
0.065Q	12/15/2004	12/30/2004	1/3/2005	2/1/2005
50%	12/15/2004	2/2/2005	1/3/2005	2/1/2005
0.065Q	2/10/2005	3/30/2005	4/1/2005	5/2/2005
0.065Q	4/21/2005	6/29/2005	7/1/2005	8/1/2005

Indicated Div: $0.26

Valuation Analysis

Forecast P/E	17.95 (6/1/2005)		
Market Cap	$1.3 Billion	Book Value	461.7 Million
Price/Book	2.88	Price/Sales	1.31

Dividend Achiever Status

Rank	46	**10 Year Growth Rate**	19.12%
Total Years of Dividend Growth			11

Business Summary: Leather and Leather Products (MIC: 4.5 SIC: 149 NAIC: 16219)

Wolverine World Wide is a designer, manufacturer and marketer of a broad line of casual shoes, rugged outdoor and work footwear, and constructed slippers and moccasins. The products are marketed throughout the world under brand names including Bates®, CAT®, Harley-Davidson®, Hush Puppies®, HyTest®, Merrell®, Sebago®, Stanley® and Wolverine®. Co.'s footwear is distributed domestically through 70 Co.-owned retail stores and to numerous accounts including department stores, footwear chains, catalogs, specialty retailers, mass merchants and Internet retailers as of Jan 1 2005. Co.'s products are distributed worldwide in over 140 markets through licensees and distributors.

Recent Developments: For the quarter ended Mar 26 2005, net income increased 31.2% to $16,133 thousand from net income of $12,299 thousand in the year-earlier quarter. Revenues were $245,175 thousand, up 9.0% from $224,871 thousand the year before. Operating income was $24,252 thousand versus an income of $19,104 thousand in the prior-year quarter, an increase of 26.9%. Total direct expense was $148,769 thousand versus $139,430 thousand in the prior-year quarter, an increase of 6.7%. Total indirect expense was $72,154 thousand versus $66,337 thousand in the prior-year quarter, an increase of 8.8%.

Prospects: Due to strong first-quarter results and robust consumer demand, Co. is increasing its previously stated full-year 2005 estimates of revenue by $5.0 million to a range of $1.05 billion to $1.07 billion, along with its earnings per share estimates by approximately $0.03 per share to a range of $1.22 to $1.27. Top-line growth is being fueled by strong sales of Co.'s products sold under the Sebago®, Merrell®, Hush Puppies® and CAT® brands. Meanwhile, earnings are being positively affected by operating improvements in Europe and increased sales of higher-margin lifestyle products and favorable foreign currency exchange rates.

Financial Data

(US$ in Thousands)	3 Mos	01/01/2005	01/03/2004	12/28/2002	12/29/2001	12/30/2000	01/01/2000	01/02/1999
Earnings Per Share	1.16	1.09	0.85	0.77	0.71	0.17	0.52	0.65
Cash Flow Per Share	1.75	1.86	1.71	1.47	0.87	1.14	0.77	(0.07)
Tang Book Value Per Share	7.23	7.16	6.56	5.59	5.76	5.18	5.10	4.59
Dividends Per Share	0.195	0.195	0.147	0.117	0.107	0.113	0.080	0.073
Dividend Payout %	16.78	17.89	17.32	15.22	14.95	65.38	15.38	11.34
Income Statement								
Total Revenue	245,175	991,909	888,926	827,106	720,066	701,291	665,576	669,329
EBITDA	28,827	116,141	93,095	88,514	86,168	32,710	64,427	74,844
Depn & Amortn	4,442	19,071	17,947	16,860	17,621	17,695	14,881	13,036
Income Before Taxes	23,866	97,070	75,148	71,654	68,547	15,015	49,546	61,808
Income Taxes	7,733	30,879	23,262	23,599	23,307	4,325	17,166	20,157
Net Income	16,133	65,938	51,716	47,912	45,240	10,690	32,380	41,651
Average Shares	59,818	60,474	61,081	62,689	63,673	62,692	62,229	64,428
Balance Sheet								
Current Assets	442,102	430,855	386,636	363,345	374,802	325,086	349,301	340,978
Total Assets	649,799	639,571	578,881	531,994	543,678	494,568	534,395	521,478
Current Liabilities	114,089	110,251	85,766	80,177	74,521	54,004	48,539	51,268
Long-Term Obligations	36,848	32,169	43,903	57,885	75,818	87,878	134,831	157,089
Total Liabilities	187,492	180,714	148,473	162,754	169,526	157,330	202,290	221,158
Stockholders' Equity	461,740	458,291	430,094	369,097	374,152	337,238	332,105	300,320
Shares Outstanding	57,857	57,898	59,179	59,955	62,333	62,329	61,950	61,147
Statistical Record								
Return on Assets %	11.23	10.85	9.16	8.93	8.74	2.08	6.15	8.60
Return on Equity %	15.57	14.89	12.73	12.93	12.75	3.20	10.27	14.33
EBITDA Margin %	11.76	11.71	10.47	10.70	11.97	4.66	9.68	11.18
Net Margin %	6.58	6.65	5.82	5.79	6.28	1.52	4.86	6.22
Asset Turnover	1.63	1.63	1.57	1.54	1.39	1.37	1.26	1.38
Current Ratio	3.88	3.91	4.51	4.53	5.03	6.02	7.20	6.65
Debt to Equity	0.08	0.07	0.10	0.16	0.20	0.26	0.41	0.52
Price Range	23.35-14.40	21.48-13.57	14.19-9.59	12.83-8.60	12.80-8.37	11.04-5.75	9.33-6.00	20.33-5.63
P/E Ratio	20.13-12.41	19.71-12.45	16.69-11.29	16.66-11.17	18.03-11.79	64.95-33.82	17.95-11.54	31.28-8.65
Average Yield %	1.04	1.14	1.19	1.08	1.00	1.55	1.07	0.56

Address: 9341 Courtland Drive, Rockford, MI 49351 **Telephone:** 616-866-5500 **Web Site:** www.wolverineworldwide.com	**Officers:** Timothy J. O'Donovan - Chmn., Pres., C.E.O. Stephen L. Gulis Jr. - Exec. V.P., C.F.O., Treas. **Transfer Agents:** Computershare Investor Services, Chicago, IL	**Investor Contact:** 616-866-5589 **No of Institutions:** 156 **Shares:** 45,739,216 **% Held:** 64.31

WPS RESOURCES CORP.

Exchange	Symbol	Price	52Wk Range	Yield	P/E
NYS	WPS	$55.13 (5/31/2005)	56.08-44.99	4.03	12.79

*7 Year Price Score 116.78 *NYSE Composite Index=100 *12 Month Price Score 105.08

TRADING VOLUME (thousand shares)

Interim Earnings (Per Share)

Qtr.	Mar	Jun	Sep	Dec
2002	0.89	0.68	0.95	0.90
2003	1.02	0.08	1.04	0.71
2004	1.14	0.12	0.93	1.53
2005	1.73	...	...	...

Interim Dividends (Per Share)

Amt	Decl	Ex	Rec	Pay
0.555Q	7/8/2004	8/27/2004	8/31/2004	9/20/2004
0.555Q	10/14/2004	11/26/2004	11/30/2004	12/20/2004
0.555Q	2/10/2005	2/24/2005	2/28/2005	3/19/2005
0.555Q	4/14/2005	5/26/2005	5/31/2005	6/20/2005

Indicated Div: $2.22 (Div. Reinv. Plan)

Valuation Analysis

Forecast P/E	14.90 (6/1/2005)		
Market Cap	$2.1 Billion	Book Value	1.2 Billion
Price/Book	1.76	Price/Sales	0.42

Dividend Achiever Status

Rank	66	10 Year Growth Rate	17.07%
Total Years of Dividend Growth			46

Business Summary: Electricity (MIC: 7.1 SIC: 931 NAIC: 21121)

WPS Resources operates as a holding company with both regulated utility and non-regulated business units serving an 11,000 square mile service territory in northeastern Wisconsin and an adjacent portion of the Upper Peninsula of Michigan. Co.'s principal wholly-owned subsidiaries are: Wisconsin Public Service Corporation (WPSC), a regulated electric and gas utility in Wisconsin and Michigan; Upper Peninsula Power Company, a regulated electric utility in Michigan; and WPS Energy Service, Inc. and WPS Power Development, Inc., both non-regulated subsidiaries. As of Dec 31 2004, WPSC served 421,159 electric retail and 305,648 gas retail customers.

Recent Developments: For the quarter ended Mar 31 2005, net income increased 53.7% to $66,700 thousand from net income of $43,400 thousand in the year-earlier quarter. Revenues were $1,462,100 thousand, up 6.5% from $1,373,300 thousand the year before. Operating income was $85,000 thousand versus an income of $71,000 thousand in the prior-year quarter, an increase of 19.7%. Total direct expense was $1,336,000 thousand versus $1,264,800 thousand in the prior-year quarter, an increase of 5.6%. Total indirect expense was $41,100 thousand versus $37,500 thousand in the prior-year quarter, an increase of 9.6%.

Prospects: Going forward, Co. will continue to seek a balanced portfolio of utility and nonregulated growth and is placing emphasis on regulated growth, which limits its exposure to the risks of nonregulated markets. In Co.'s nonregulated business units, Co. continues to utilize financial tools commonly used in the industry to help mitigate risk. Also, Co.'s asset management strategy will continue to deliver shareholder return from certain asset transactions. Moreover, Co.'s long-term basic earnings per share growth rate target remains at 6.0% to 8.0% on an average annualized basis. Co. expects earnings from continuing operations to be between $3.62 and $3.86, assuming normal weather.

Financial Data

(US$ in Thousands)	3 Mos	12/31/2004	12/31/2003	12/31/2002	12/31/2001	12/31/2000	12/31/1999	12/31/1998
Earnings Per Share	4.31	3.72	2.85	3.42	2.74	2.53	2.24	1.76
Cash Flow Per Share	5.56	6.48	1.89	6.12	5.07	5.31	4.31	4.14
Tang Book Value Per Share	30.03	28.97	27.39	24.43	22.73	20.21	19.97	19.48
Dividends Per Share	2.210	2.200	2.160	2.120	2.080	2.040	2.000	1.960
Dividend Payout %	51.28	59.14	75.79	61.99	75.91	80.63	89.29	111.36
Income Statement								
Total Revenue	1,462,100	4,890,600	4,321,300	2,674,900	2,675,500	1,951,574	1,098,540	1,063,736
EBITDA	134,400	230,900	186,700	344,000	243,400	146,635	140,134	117,491
Depn & Amortn	40,700	44,700	42,400	148,600	102,100	19,746	14,949	16,257
Income Before Taxes	78,900	186,200	144,300	137,300	85,500	76,109	92,417	72,597
Income Taxes	16,400	30,000	33,700	24,800	4,800	6,005	29,741	23,445
Net Income	66,700	142,800	97,800	112,500	80,700	70,104	59,565	49,763
Average Shares	38,100	37,600	33,200	31,700	28,300	26,463	26,644	26,511
Balance Sheet								
Net PPE	2,061,000	2,002,600	1,828,700	1,610,200	1,463,600	1,198,324	1,150,902	1,010,158
Total Assets	4,685,100	4,445,600	4,292,300	3,207,900	2,870,000	2,816,142	1,816,548	1,510,387
Long-Term Obligations	864,900	865,700	871,900	824,400	727,800	587,017	510,917	343,037
Total Liabilities	3,498,200	3,302,700	3,238,000	2,324,000	2,053,000	2,099,242	1,105,470	891,997
Stockholders' Equity	1,186,900	1,142,900	1,054,300	833,900	767,000	593,945	587,493	568,390
Shares Outstanding	37,819	37,682	36,621	32,040	31,496	26,851	26,851	26,551
Statistical Record								
Return on Assets %	3.82	3.26	2.61	3.70	2.84	3.02	3.58	3.54
Return on Equity %	14.58	12.96	10.36	14.05	11.86	11.84	10.31	9.07
EBITDA Margin %	9.19	4.72	4.32	12.86	9.10	7.51	12.76	11.05
Net Margin %	4.56	2.92	2.26	4.21	3.02	3.59	5.42	4.68
PPE Turnover	2.56	2.55	2.51	1.74	2.01	1.66	1.02	1.12
Asset Turnover	1.14	1.12	1.15	0.88	0.94	0.84	0.66	0.76
Debt to Equity	0.73	0.76	0.83	0.99	0.95	0.99	0.87	0.60
Price Range	54.64-43.52	50.32-43.52	46.77-37.12	42.45-31.52	36.55-31.82	38.69-22.81	35.50-24.63	37.25-30.25
P/E Ratio	12.68-10.10	13.53-11.70	16.41-13.02	12.41-9.22	13.34-11.61	15.29-9.02	15.85-10.99	21.16-17.19
Average Yield %	4.60	4.68	5.27	5.55	6.08	6.89	6.74	5.88

Address: 700 North Adams Street, Green Bay, WI 54301
Telephone: 920-433-4901
Web Site: www.wpsr.com

Officers: Larry L. Weyers - Chmn., Pres., C.E.O. Thomas P. Meinz - Sr. V.P., Public Affairs **Transfer Agents:** American Stock Transfer & Trust Company, New York, NY

Investor Contact: 920-433-1857
No of Institutions: 171
Shares: 11,334,573 **% Held:** 30.43

WRIGLEY (WILLIAM) JR. CO.

Exchange	Symbol	Price	52Wk Range	Yield	P/E
NYS	WWY	$68.27 (5/31/2005)	70.65-59.78	1.64	29.94

Interim Earnings (Per Share)

Qtr.	Mar	Jun	Sep	Dec
2002	0.38	0.49	0.44	0.48
2003	0.43	0.56	0.50	0.49
2004	0.49	0.62	0.56	0.52
2005	0.58	...	...	...

Interim Dividends (Per Share)

Amt	Decl	Ex	Rec	Pay
0.235Q	8/18/2004	10/13/2004	10/15/2004	11/1/2004
0.235Q	10/26/2004	1/12/2005	1/14/2005	2/1/2005
0.28Q	1/26/2005	4/13/2005	4/15/2005	5/2/2005
0.28Q	5/20/2005	7/13/2005	7/15/2005	8/1/2005

Indicated Div: $1.12 (Div. Reinv. Plan)

Valuation Analysis

Forecast P/E	27.84 (6/1/2005)		
Market Cap	$15.4 Billion	Book Value	2.2 Billion
Price/Book	6.87	Price/Sales	4.06

Dividend Achiever Status

Rank	223	10 Year Growth Rate	7.47%
Total Years of Dividend Growth			24

Business Summary: Food (MIC: 4.1 SIC: 067 NAIC: 11340)

William Wrigley Jr. is a manufacturer and marketer of chewing gum and other confectionery products, both in the United States and abroad. Two domestic wholly-owned associated companies, L.A. Dreyfus Company and Northwestern Flavors, LLC, manufacture products, gum base and mint oil, respectively, other than chewing gum or confectionery products. As of Dec 31 2004, Co.'s brands were sold in over 180 countries and territories. Brand names include, among numerous others, Doublemint®, Eclipse®, Extra®, Orbit®, Wrigley's Spearmint®, Winterfresh®, Airwaves®, Alpine®, Big Red®, Cool Air®, Excel®, Freedent®, Juicy Fruit®, Hubba Bubba®, and P.K.®

Recent Developments: For the quarter ended Mar 31 2005, net income increased 18.0% to $131,014 thousand from net income of $110,983 thousand in the year-earlier quarter. Revenues were $950,390 thousand, up 17.0% from $812,151 thousand the year before. Operating income was $192,207 thousand versus an income of $161,669 thousand in the prior-year quarter, an increase of 18.9%. Total direct expense was $412,757 thousand versus $353,766 thousand in the prior-year quarter, an increase of 16.7%. Total indirect expense was $345,426 thousand versus $296,716 thousand in the prior-year quarter, an increase of 16.4%.

Prospects: Co.'s global sales are benefiting from strong performance of its core gum business, as well as contributions from its 2004 Joyco acquisition. U.S. sales growth is being fueled by volume gains, particularly of the Orbit®, Orbit® White, and Extra® brands. Sales are also seeing strong volume growth in Canada and Asia. Meanwhile, Co. has completed significant work on construction of a gum factory in Silao, Mexico to support business in Latin America and a new Global Innovation Center on Goose Island in Chicago, both of which are expected to open later in 2005. Separately, Co.'s previously announced purchase of certain confectionery assets of Kraft Foods is expected to be completed by mid-2005.

Financial Data

(US$ in Thousands)	3 Mos	12/31/2004	12/31/2003	12/31/2002	12/31/2001	12/31/2000	12/31/1999	12/31/1998
Earnings Per Share	2.28	2.19	1.98	1.78	1.61	1.45	1.33	1.31
Cash Flow Per Share	3.11	3.22	2.87	1.66	1.73	1.97	1.55	1.40
Tang Book Value Per Share	8.78	8.76	8.10	6.77	5.67	4.87	4.97	4.98
Dividends Per Share	0.940	0.925	0.865	0.805	0.745	0.700	0.665	0.650
Dividend Payout %	41.23	42.24	43.69	45.22	46.27	48.28	50.00	49.43
Income Statement								
Total Revenue	950,390	3,648,592	3,069,088	2,746,318	2,429,646	2,145,706	2,079,238	2,023,355
EBITDA	233,091	864,245	771,581	668,989	595,692	537,192	506,364	497,268
Depn & Amortn	39,712	143,749	120,040	85,568	68,326	57,880	61,225	55,774
Income Before Taxes	193,379	720,496	651,541	583,421	527,366	479,312	444,430	440,879
Income Taxes	62,365	227,542	205,647	181,896	164,380	150,370	136,247	136,378
Net Income	131,014	492,954	445,894	401,525	362,986	328,942	308,183	304,501
Average Shares	224,884	225,473	224,963	225,145	225,349	227,036	231,722	231,928
Balance Sheet								
Current Assets	1,631,250	1,505,910	1,290,591	1,006,292	913,843	828,715	803,746	843,172
Total Assets	3,303,660	3,166,703	2,520,410	2,108,296	1,765,648	1,574,740	1,547,745	1,520,855
Current Liabilities	799,038	717,970	464,794	386,087	332,324	288,210	251,825	218,626
Total Liabilities	1,067,270	988,019	699,589	585,720	489,451	441,843	408,970	363,823
Stockholders' Equity	2,236,390	2,178,684	1,820,821	1,522,576	1,276,197	1,132,897	1,138,775	1,157,032
Shares Outstanding	225,043	224,771	224,860	225,056	224,950	232,442	228,992	232,220
Statistical Record								
Return on Assets %	17.46	17.29	19.27	20.73	21.73	21.01	20.09	21.26
Return on Equity %	25.08	24.58	26.67	28.69	30.13	28.88	26.85	28.43
EBITDA Margin %	24.53	23.69	25.14	24.36	24.52	25.04	24.35	24.58
Net Margin %	13.79	13.51	14.53	14.62	14.94	15.33	14.82	15.05
Asset Turnover	1.29	1.28	1.33	1.42	1.45	1.37	1.36	1.41
Current Ratio	2.04	2.10	2.78	2.61	2.75	2.88	3.19	3.86
Price Range	70.65-58.66	69.73-55.23	58.11-51.18	58.35-44.52	52.92-43.34	47.91-30.31	50.00-33.66	51.66-36.56
P/E Ratio	30.99-25.73	31.84-25.22	29.35-25.85	32.78-25.01	32.87-26.92	33.04-20.91	37.59-25.31	39.43-27.91
Average Yield %	1.46	1.49	1.56	1.51	1.54	1.80	1.58	1.53

Address: 410 North Michigan Avenue, Chicago, IL 60611 **Telephone:** 312-644-2121 **Web Site:** www.wrigley.com	**Officers:** William Wrigley Jr. - Chmn., Pres., C.E.O. Peter R. Hempstead - Sr. V.P., Worldwide Strategy & New Bus. **Transfer Agents:** EquiServe Trust Company, N.A., Providence, RI	**Investor Contact:** 180-087-40474 **No of Institutions:** 406 **Shares:** 101,934,368 **% Held:** 53.28

Canadian Company Reports

AGF MANAGEMENT LTD

Exchange	Symbol	Price	52Wk Range	Yield	P/E
TSX	AGF NV	C$16.31 (5/31/2005)	18.84-15.35	3.68	20.14

***7 Year Price Score 86.33** *NYSE Composite Index=100 ***12 Month Price Score 95.61**

TRADING VOLUME (thousand shares)

Interim Earnings (Per Share) Can$

Qtr.	Feb	May	Aug	Nov
2001-02	0.37	0.40	0.34	0.19
2002-03	0.30	0.21	0.23	(0.28)
2003-04	0.26	0.37	0.30	(0.09)
2004-05	0.23	...	...	...

Interim Dividends (Per Share)

Amt	Decl	Ex	Rec	Pay
0.11Q	6/29/2004	7/8/2004	7/12/2004	7/22/2004
0.11Q	9/28/2004	10/6/2004	10/8/2004	10/20/2004
0.11Q	12/7/2004	12/15/2004	12/17/2004	1/6/2005
0.15Q	3/30/2005	4/8/2005	4/12/2005	4/22/2005

Indicated Div: C$0.60

Valuation Analysis

Forecast P/E	16.25 (6/1/2005)		
Market Cap	C$1.5 Billion	Book Value	929.2 Million
Price/Book	1.59	Price/Sales	2.32

Dividend Achiever Status

Rank	7	5 Year Growth Rate	22.28%
Total Years of Dividend Growth			8

Business Summary: Wealth Management (MIC: 8.8 SIC: 282 NAIC: 23930)

AGF Management is an integrated, global wealth management corporation. Through its subsidiaries, Co. is engaged in providing mutual fund management, private investment management for high-net-worth clients, trust products and services (including mortgage and investment lending and deposit-taking activities), investment advisory services, third-party fund administration services and investment industry software development for individual and institutional clients.

Recent Developments: For the three months ended Feb 28 2005, net income slipped 10.9% to C$21.2 million from C$23.8 million in the corresponding quarter a year earlier. Results for 2005 and 2004 included provision for loan losses of C$1.4 million and C$1.1 million, respectively. Revenue was C$157.4 million, down 1.1% compared with C$159.1 million in the prior-year period. Lower revenue from Co.'s investment management and fund administration operations was partially offset by increased revenues from its trust company operations. Total expenses increased 1.1% to C$127.0 million from C$125.6 million the previous year.

Prospects: On Mar 30 2005, Co. announced that it has entered into an agreement to acquire the mutual fund assets of ING Investment Management Inc., a subsidiary of ING Canada Inc. Terms of the transaction, which is expected to be completed on or about Jul 22 2005, subject to regulatory and ING Funds unitholder approvals, were not disclosed. Under the agreement, Co. will acquire 14 funds with approximately $240.0 million in assets, which will be merged into comparable AGF funds. The agreement includes the purchase of the ING Canadian Dividend Income Fund, which has assets of about $100.0 million and will continue to be subadvised by ING under the new name, AGF Dividend Income Fund.

Financial Data

(Can$ in Thousands)	3 Mos	11/30/2004	11/30/2003	11/30/2002	11/30/2001	11/30/2000	11/30/1999	11/30/1998
Earnings Per Share	0.81	0.84	0.47	1.30	1.77	1.07	0.76	0.59
Cash Flow Per Share	2.78	2.60	...	...	...	...	...	...
Tang Book Value Per Share	8.47	8.10	7.94	7.95	7.28	5.67	3.62	3.00
Dividends Per Share	0.440	0.410	0.295	0.255	0.220	0.180	0.150	0.130
Dividend Payout %	54.32	48.81	62.77	19.62	12.43	16.82	19.74	21.85
Income Statement								
Total Revenue	157,368	639,912	600,832	654,103	639,994	508,681	356,703	288,822
EBITDA	68,389	246,348	274,680	310,582	314,051	240,063	173,310	135,583
Depn & Amortn	38,034	161,466	157,457	147,181	165,645	92,224	70,276	52,717
Income Before Taxes	30,355	84,882	117,223	163,401	148,406	147,839	103,034	82,866
Income Taxes	9,178	7,595	73,207	43,645	(14,867)	59,987	41,324	34,089
Net Income	21,177	77,287	44,016	119,839	163,754	87,888	61,710	48,777
Average Shares	91,085	91,798	...	...	...	...	...	...
Balance Sheet								
Current Assets	164,129	202,014	80,738	84,296	79,508	127,227	85,622	76,009
Total Assets	2,275,313	2,167,846	1,966,996	1,974,920	1,546,090	1,278,289	643,745	539,021
Current Liabilities	117,269	148,417	105,854	102,220	118,954	224,412	44,360	40,961
Long-Term Obligations	93,724	69,706	114,114	225,403	165,481	278,051	72,048	81,422
Total Liabilities	1,346,075	1,253,480	1,063,686	1,087,354	781,383	806,241	359,501	305,638
Stockholders' Equity	929,238	914,366	903,310	887,566	764,707	472,048	284,244	233,383
Shares Outstanding	90,756	90,797	92,272	91,100	89,338	83,046	78,044	77,070
Statistical Record								
Return on Assets %	3.46	3.73	2.23	6.81	11.60	9.12	10.43	10.18
Return on Equity %	8.16	8.48	4.92	14.51	26.48	23.18	23.84	22.92
EBITDA Margin %	43.46	38.50	45.72	47.48	49.07	47.19	48.59	46.94
Net Margin %	13.46	12.08	7.33	18.32	25.59	17.28	17.30	16.89
Asset Turnover	0.30	0.31	0.30	0.37	0.45	0.53	0.60	0.60
Current Ratio	1.40	1.36	0.76	0.82	0.67	0.57	1.93	1.86
Debt to Equity	0.10	0.08	0.13	0.25	0.22	0.59	0.25	0.35
Price Range	19.87-15.35	19.87-15.35	19.17-12.11	28.18-11.75	28.90-18.20	28.20-10.50	14.00-9.03	14.05-6.88
P/E Ratio	24.53-18.95	23.65-18.27	40.79-25.77	21.68-9.04	16.33-10.28	26.36-9.81	18.42-11.88	23.81-11.65
Average Yield %	2.52	2.32	1.93	1.26	0.88	0.95	1.31	1.23

Address: Suite 3100, 66 Wellington Street West, Toronto-Dominion Bank Tower, toronto-Dominion Centre, Toronto.
Telephone: 416-367-1900
Web Site: www.agf.com

Officers: C. Warren Goldring - Chmn. W. Robert Farquharson CFA - Vice-Chmn. **Transfer Agents:** Computershare Trust Company of Canada

No of Institutions: 1
Shares: 186,850 **% Held:** 0.21

ATCO LTD.

Exchange	Symbol	Price	52Wk Range	Yield	P/E
TSX	ACO Y	C$64.75 (5/24/2005)	67.97-46.51	2.35	11.92

Interim Earnings (Per Share) Can$

Qtr.	Mar	Jun	Sep	Dec
2002	2.57	0.72	0.87	1.23
2003	1.51	0.67	0.75	1.42
2004	1.26	1.82	0.83	1.38
2005	1.40	...	...	...

Interim Dividends (Per Share)

Amt	Decl	Ex	Rec	Pay
0.35Q	7/30/2004	9/13/2004	9/15/2004	9/30/2004
0.35Q	11/16/2004	12/13/2004	12/15/2004	12/31/2004
0.38Q	2/25/2005	3/14/2005	3/16/2005	3/31/2005
0.38Q	5/13/2005	6/13/2005	6/15/2005	6/30/2005

Indicated Div: C$1.52

Valuation Analysis

Forecast P/E	14.16 (6/1/2005)		
Market Cap	C$1.9 Billion	Book Value	1.3 Billion
Price/Book	1.52	Price/Sales	0.66

Dividend Achiever Status

Rank	22	5 Year Growth Rate	11.84%
Total Years of Dividend Growth			11

Business Summary: Electricity (MIC: 7.1 SIC: 911 NAIC: 21122)

ATCO is a holding company. ATCO Power develops, builds, owns and operates independent power projects in Canada, Great Britain and Australia. ATCO Electric delivers electricity to customers in northern and east-central Alberta and parts of the Yukon and the Northwest Territories. ATCO Gas distributes natural gas throughout Alberta to industrial, residential and commercial customers. ATCO Pipelines transports natural gas throughout Alberta. ATCO Structures manufactures, sells and leases modular buildings. ATCO Noise Management provides complete noise reduction services for industrial facilities. ATCO Midstream owns natural gas gathering, processing, storage and liquids extraction facilities.

Recent Developments: For the first quarter ended Mar 31 2005, net income increased 11.5% to C$42.6 million compared with C$38.2 million in the corresponding prior-year quarter. Total revenues declined 33.6% to C$814.6 million from C$1.23 billion a year earlier. Utilities revenue dropped 51.3% to C$428.1 million, primarily due to lower sales of electricity and natural gas purchased for customers on a "no-margin" basis by ATCO Electric and ATCO Gas due to the transfer of Co.'s retail energy supply businesses to Direct Energy Marketing Limited. Power Generation revenue rose 12.6% to C$195.0 million, Global Enterprises revenue grew 6.6% to C$132.3 million and Industrials revenue climbed 19.5% to C$58.2 million.

Prospects: Co. earnings are benefiting from continuing strong activity in its ATCO Structures' operations in Canada and Australia, higher earnings in ATCO Power's U.K. operations due to improved performance and the settlement reached by Barking Power Limited with the administrators of TXU Europe, improved results at ATCO Midstream, and increased business activity, including work for new customers, at ATCO I-Tek. Separately, ATCO Gas and ATCO Electric expects to file general rate applications in the second quarter of 2005 requesting the Alberta Energy and Utilities Board increase customer rates to help offset higher gas and electric costs.

Financial Data

(Can$ in Thousands)	3 Mos	12/31/2004	12/31/2003	12/31/2002	12/31/2001	12/31/2000	12/31/1999	12/31/1998
Earnings Per Share	5.43	5.29	4.35	5.39	4.12	3.75	3.32	2.96
Cash Flow Per Share	24.49	23.30	17.30	12.41	...	...	...	...
Tang Book Value Per Share	40.27	39.25	35.66	32.65	28.26	25.14	22.34	19.93
Dividends Per Share	1.430	1.400	1.280	1.160	1.040	0.920	0.800	0.680
Dividend Payout %	26.34	26.47	29.43	21.52	25.24	24.53	24.10	22.97
Income Statement								
Total Revenue	814,600	3,349,100	3,929,700	3,196,300	3,754,300	3,076,000	2,374,800	2,071,400
EBITDA	232,100	836,200	742,300	790,400	691,800	685,400	633,700	589,200
Depn & Amortn	87,600	311,100	284,700	257,100	257,500	253,500	241,000	211,000
Income Before Taxes	144,500	525,100	457,600	533,300	434,300	431,900	392,700	378,200
Income Taxes	54,300	172,400	159,800	196,700	174,800	193,100	180,800	187,300
Net Income	42,600	159,400	131,200	163,000	124,400	112,700	100,700	88,900
Average Shares	30,304	30,113	30,172	30,257	29,731	29,723	29,931	30,044
Balance Sheet								
Net PPE	5,413,500	5,407,700	5,128,400	4,949,200	4,590,800	4,168,200	3,976,600	3,898,400
Total Assets	7,192,000	7,039,500	6,591,200	6,403,300	5,833,700	5,815,600	4,934,900	4,793,700
Long-Term Obligations	3,135,000	3,115,000	2,789,800	2,892,400	2,658,000	2,468,800	2,226,900	2,106,000
Total Liabilities	5,914,200	5,794,900	5,457,600	5,358,500	4,922,100	4,993,300	4,190,700	4,112,300
Stockholders' Equity	1,277,800	1,244,600	1,133,600	1,044,800	911,600	822,300	744,200	681,400
Shares Outstanding	29,962	29,896	29,796	29,816	29,733	29,722	29,791	30,048
Statistical Record								
Return on Assets %	2.33	2.33	2.02	2.66	2.14	2.09	2.07	1.93
Return on Equity %	13.42	13.37	12.05	16.66	14.35	14.35	14.13	13.74
EBITDA Margin %	28.49	24.97	18.89	24.73	18.43	22.28	26.68	28.44
Net Margin %	5.23	4.76	3.34	5.10	3.31	3.66	4.24	4.29
PPE Turnover	0.55	0.63	0.78	0.67	0.86	0.75	0.60	0.55
Asset Turnover	0.41	0.49	0.60	0.52	0.64	0.57	0.49	0.45
Debt to Equity	2.45	2.50	2.46	2.77	2.92	3.00	2.99	3.09
Price Range	63.80-46.15	59.25-46.15	49.18-41.75	55.00-41.00	52.70-42.00	48.00-29.05	43.85-32.50	38.00-30.50
P/E Ratio	11.75-8.50	11.20-8.72	11.31-9.60	10.20-7.61	12.79-10.19	12.80-7.75	13.21-9.79	12.84-10.30
Average Yield %	2.67	2.73	2.80	2.39	2.18	2.64	2.00	1.95

Address: 1600 ATCO Centre, 909 – 11th Avenue S.W., Calgary **Telephone:** 403-292-7500 **Web Site:** www.atco.com	**Officers:** Ronald D. Southern C.B.E. - Chmn. William L. Britton Q.C. - Vice-Chmn. **Transfer Agents:** CIBC Mellon Trust Company, Montreal, Quebec; Toronto, Ontario; Calgary, Alberta; Vancouver, British Columbia	**No of Institutions:** N/A **Shares:** N/A **% Held:** N/A

BANK OF MONTREAL

Exchange	Symbol	Price	52Wk Range	Yield	P/E
TSX	BMO	C$55.26 (5/31/2005)	59.10-52.48	3.33	11.96

***7 Year Price Score 124.08** *NYSE Composite Index=100 ***12 Month Price Score 98.13**

Interim Earnings (Per Share) Can$

Qtr.	Jan	Apr	Jul	Oct
2001-02	0.71	0.57	0.65	0.75
2002-03	0.75	0.77	0.95	0.97
2003-04	1.00	1.12	1.24	1.06
2004-05	1.16	1.16	...	...

Interim Dividends (Per Share)

Amt	Decl	Ex	Rec	Pay
0.44Q	8/24/2004	11/3/2004	11/5/2004	11/29/2004
0.44Q	11/23/2004	2/2/2005	2/4/2005	2/25/2005
0.46Q	2/22/2005	5/4/2005	5/6/2005	5/30/2005
0.46Q	5/24/2005	8/3/2005	8/5/2005	8/30/2005

Indicated Div: C$1.84 (Div. Reinv. Plan)

Valuation Analysis

Forecast P/E	12.31 (6/1/2005)		
Market Cap	C$27.7 Billion	Book Value	13.1 Billion
Price/Book	2.12	Price/Sales	2.06

Dividend Achiever Status

Rank	24	5 Year Growth Rate	11.08%
Total Years of Dividend Growth			12

Business Summary: Commercial Banking (MIC: 8.1 SIC: 029 NAIC: 22110)

Bank of Montreal is a North American financial services organization. With total assets of C$265 billion as at Oct 31 2004, Co. provides a range of retail banking, wealth management and investment banking products and solutions. Co. serves clients across Canada through its Canadian retail arm BMO Bank of Montreal and through BMO Nesbitt Burns investment firm. In the U.S., Co. serves clients through Chicago-based Harris, an integrated financial services organization that provides over 1.5 million personal, business, corporate and institutional clients with banking, lending, investing, financial planning, trust administration, portfolio management, family office and wealth transfer services.

Recent Developments: For the quarter ended Apr 30 2005, net income climbed 1.5% to C$600.0 million compared with C$591.0 million in the equivalent period of the previous year. Total interest income increased 16.8% to C$2.46 billion from C$2.11 billion in the year-earlier quarter. Net interest income grew 2.2% to C$1.18 billion from C$1.16 billion the year before. Provision for credit losses advanced 20.0% to C$6.0 million from C$5.0 million in 2004. Total non-interest income slipped 2.8% to C$1.22 billion from C$1.25 billion the year before. Total non-interest expense inched up to C$1.58 billion fromC $1.57 billion in the prior-year period.

Prospects: Co. remains committed to achieving its financial goals for 2005; however, achieving its target of improving cash productivity by 150 to 200 basis points should be challenging as Co. continues to invest in growing its businesses. Meanwhile, low interest rates continue to support personal and business spending, while the high Canadian dollar continues to restrict exports. Also, Co. expects short-term interest rates to remain stable until Fall, before rising modestly late in the year. The low interest rate environment should support growth in household and business lending for the remainder of 2005. Accordingly, the Canadian dollar should remain within a narrow range of C$0.79 to to C$0.81.

Financial Data

(Can$ in Thousands)	3 Mos	10/31/2004	10/31/2003	10/31/2002	10/31/2001	10/31/2000	10/31/1999	10/31/1998
Earnings Per Share	4.57	4.42	3.44	2.68	2.66	3.28	2.36	2.33
Cash Flow Per Share	8.12	4.96	(18.11)	(8.35)	20.83	(5.62)	...	...
Tang Book Value Per Share	20.76	20.28	18.24	21.07	19.69	19.63	17.44	16.38
Dividends Per Share	1.590	1.500	1.29	1.18	1.09	0.985	0.925	0.880
Dividend Payout %	34.81	33.94	37.50	44.03	40.98	30.03	39.19	37.77
Income Statement								
Interest Income	2,338,000	8,657,000	8,927,000	9,135,000	13,000,000	14,303,000	13,174,000	14,121,000
Interest Expense	1,140,000	3,735,000	4,028,000	4,306,000	8,501,000	10,099,000	8,895,000	10,097,000
Net Interest Income	1,198,000	4,922,000	4,899,000	4,829,000	4,499,000	4,204,000	4,279,000	4,024,000
Provision for Losses	43,000	(103,000)	455,000	820,000	980,000	358,000	320,000	130,000
Non-Interest Income	1,213,000	4,551,000	4,220,000	3,924,000	4,222,000	4,326,000	3,511,000	3,118,000
Income Before Taxes	835,000	3,419,000	2,577,000	1,903,000	2,070,000	2,914,000	2,182,000	2,179,000
Income Taxes	219,000	1,008,000	688,000	424,000	501,000	989,000	736,000	804,000
Net Income	602,000	2,351,000	1,825,000	1,417,000	1,471,000	1,857,000	1,382,000	1,350,000
Average Shares	512,941	515,045	507,009	499,464	523,561	542,170	545,146	538,000
Balance Sheet								
Net Loans & Leases	160,825,000	156,248,000	146,156,000	142,695,000	136,829,000	133,817,000	138,001,000	129,691,000
Total Assets	294,094,000	265,194,000	256,494,000	252,864,000	239,409,000	233,396,000	230,615,000	222,590,000
Total Deposits	182,332,000	175,190,000	171,551,000	161,838,000	154,290,000	156,697,000	156,874,000	143,983,000
Total Liabilities	281,016,000	252,005,000	244,012,000	240,970,000	228,727,000	221,455,000	219,634,000	211,982,000
Stockholders' Equity	13,078,000	13,189,000	12,482,000	11,894,000	10,682,000	11,941,000	10,981,000	10,608,000
Shares Outstanding	500,647	500,896	499,632	492,505	489,085	522,583	534,064	528,000
Statistical Record								
Return on Assets %	0.80	0.90	0.72	0.58	0.62	0.80	0.61	0.63
Return on Equity %	18.41	18.27	14.97	12.55	13.00	16.16	12.80	13.84
Net Interest Margin %	51.24	56.86	54.88	52.86	34.61	29.39	32.48	28.50
Loans to Deposits	0.88	0.89	0.85	0.88	0.89	0.85	0.88	0.90
Price Range	59.10-49.85	59.10-49.33	50.06-38.10	40.30-32.10	44.23-32.80	35.75-21.50	34.65-24.88	43.05-26.35
P/E Ratio	12.93-10.91	13.37-11.16	14.55-11.08	15.04-11.98	16.63-12.33	10.90-6.55	14.68-10.54	18.48-11.31
Average Yield %	2.90	2.77	3.03	3.24	281	3.50	3.14	2.50

Address: Corporate Secretary's Department, 100 King Street West, 1 First Canadian Place, 21st Floor, Toronto, M5X 1A1
Telephone: 416-867-6785
Web Site: www.bmo.com

Officers: F. Anthony Comper - Pres., C.E.O. William A. Downe - Dep. Chair, BMO Financial Group
ransfer Agents: Computershare Trust Company of Canada, Halifax, Montreal, Toronto, Winnipeg, Calgary and Vancouver

Investor Contact: 416-867-6656
No of Institutions: 67
Shares: 121,549,392 **% Held:** 24.24

BANK OF NOVA SCOTIA (TORONTO, CANADA)

Exchange	Symbol	Price	52Wk Range	Yield	P/E
TSX	BNS	C$39.75 (5/31/2005)	41.25-34.12	3.42	13.34

*7 Year Price Score 136.98 *NYSE Composite Index=100 *12 Month Price Score 100.19

Interim Earnings (Per Share) Can$

Qtr.	Jan	Apr	Jul	Oct
2001-02	0.03	0.56	0.53	0.55
2002-03	0.56	0.56	0.60	0.63
2003-04	0.67	0.75	0.71	0.69
2004-05	0.77	0.81	...	...

Interim Dividends (Per Share)

Amt	Decl	Ex	Rec	Pay
0.30Q	8/31/2004	10/1/2004	10/5/2004	10/27/2004
0.32Q	11/30/2004	12/31/2004	1/4/2005	1/27/2005
0.32Q	3/1/2005	4/1/2005	4/5/2005	4/27/2005
0.34Q	5/31/2005	6/30/2005	7/5/2005	7/27/2005

Indicated Div: C$1.36 (Div. Reinv. Plan)

Valuation Analysis

Forecast P/E	12.68 (6/4/2005)		
Market Cap	C$39.5 Billion	Book Value	15.9 Billion
Price/Book	2.48	Price/Sales	2.44

Dividend Achiever Status

Rank	10	5 Year Growth Rate	20.39%
Total Years of Dividend Growth			13

Business Summary: Commercial Banking (MIC: 8.1 SIC: 021 NAIC: 22110)

Bank of Nova Scotia is a diversified financial services institution that provides retail, commercial, corporate, investment and international banking services to individuals, small and medium-size businesses, corporations and governments across Canada and around the world. Operations are organized into three main operating segments, including domestic banking, international banking and Scotia Capital. As of Oct 31 2004, Co.'s total assets, assets under management and deposits amounted to C$279.21 billion, C$21.22 billion and C$195.19 billion, respectively. As of Oct 31 2004, Co. maintained a banking network of 1,871 branches and offices, and 4,219 automated teller machines.

Recent Developments: For the second quarter ended Apr 30 2005, net income increased 5.4% to C$826.0 million compared with C$784.0 million in the corresponding prior-year quarter. Net interest income was flat versus the year-earlier period at C$1.46 billion. Total interest income advanced 11.6% to C$3.37 billion, while total interest expense grew 22.2% to C$1.91 billion. Provision for credit losses fell 73.1% to C$35.0 million from C$130.0 million the year before. Non-interest income declined 9.0% to C$1.14 billion, while non-interest expense decreased 2.2% to C$1.49 billion.

Prospects: Lower loan losses combined with the continuing strength of Co.'s Domestic Banking, Scotia Capital and International Banking business lines. Co.'s Domestic Banking operations are seeing strong contributions from many areas, particularly mortgages and other areas of retail lending, where it is continuing to gain market share. Meanwhile, Co.'s International Banking operations are being positively affected by strong retail and commercial lending at Scotiabank Inverlat. Looking ahead to fiscal 2005, Co. anticipates achieving its financial targets, which include earnings growth in the range of 5.0% to 10.%.

Financial Data

(Can$ in Thousands)	6 Mos	3 Mos	10/31/2004	10/31/2003	10/31/2002	10/31/2001	10/31/2000	10/31/1999
Earnings Per Share	2.98	2.91	2.82	2.35	1.65	2.02	1.81	1.47
Cash Flow Per Share	(5.03)	(0.07)	0.97	(7.04)	(3.02)	(0.46)	(4.76)	2.23
Tang Book Value Per Share	14.92	14.44	14.06	13.12	12.79	12.89	11.25	9.74
Dividends Per Share	1.240	1.170	1.100	0.840	0.725	0.620	0.500	0.435
Dividend Payout %	41.61	40.18	39.01	35.82	43.94	30.62	27.62	29.69
Income Statement								
Interest Income	6,599,000	3,234,000	12,177,000	13,246,000	14,368,000	16,983,000	15,331,000	13,471,000
Interest Expense	3,714,000	1,807,000	6,312,000	7,096,000	7,693,000	10,783,000	10,132,000	8,799,000
Net Interest Income	2,885,000	1,427,000	5,865,000	6,150,000	6,675,000	6,200,000	5,199,000	4,672,000
Provision for Losses	109,000	74,000	390,000	893,000	2,029,000	1,425,000	765,000	635,000
Non-Interest Income	959,420	986,000	3,502,000	3,170,000	3,780,000	3,851,000	3,459,000	3,028,000
Income Before Taxes	2,076,000	1,007,000	3,933,000	3,541,000	2,614,000	3,184,000	2,980,000	2,464,000
Income Taxes	428,000	202,000	793,000	784,000	601,000	876,000	990,000	867,000
Net Income	1,614,000	788,000	2,931,000	2,477,000	1,797,000	2,169,000	1,926,000	1,551,000
Average Shares	1,011,000	1,021,000	1,026,000	1,025,738	1,025,504	1,017,990	1,041,938	986,272
Balance Sheet								
Net Loans & Leases	185,582,000	182,334,000	171,768,000	171,667,000	185,671,000	175,432,000	166,903,000	131,938,000
Total Assets	309,090,000	300,547,000	279,212,000	285,892,000	296,380,000	284,425,000	253,171,000	222,691,000
Total Deposits	214,782,000	206,866,000	195,196,000	192,672,000	195,618,000	186,195,000	173,900,000	156,618,000
Total Liabilities	293,146,000	285,329,000	263,977,000	271,278,000	281,603,000	269,817,000	240,196,000	211,285,000
Stockholders' Equity	15,944,000	15,218,000	15,235,000	14,614,000	14,777,000	14,608,000	12,975,000	11,406,000
Shares Outstanding	993,606	998,000	1,008,505	1,010,705	1,008,243	995,930	995,930	988,504
Statistical Record								
Return on Assets %	1.03	1.03	1.03	0.85	0.62	0.81	0.81	0.68
Return on Equity %	19.49	20.06	19.59	16.86	12.23	15.73	15.76	13.96
Net Interest Margin %	43.33	44.12	48.16	46.43	46.46	36.51	33.91	34.68
Loans to Deposits	0.86	0.88	0.88	0.89	0.95	0.94	0.96	0.84
Price Range	41.25-33.18	41.25-33.18	39.60-31.45	33.36-22.75	27.88-21.27	24.95-19.00	22.60-13.07	18.30-14.35
P/E Ratio	13.84-11.13	14.18-11.40	14.04-11.15	14.20-9.68	16.89-12.89	12.35-9.41	12.49-7.22	12.45-9.76
Average Yield %	3.28	3.20	3.15	2.99	2.94	2.84	2.92	2.66

Address: Scotia Plaza, 44 King Street West, Toronto
Telephone: 416-866-6161
Web Site: www.scotiabank.com

Officers: Sarabjit S. Marwah - Sr. Exec. V.P., C.F.O. Deborah M. Alexander - Exec. V.P., General Counsel & Sec. **Transfer Agents:** Computershare Investor Services plc, Bristol

Investor Contact: 416-866-5982
No of Institutions: 72
Shares: 303,132,992 **% Held:** 30.14

BMTC GROUP INC.

Exchange	Symbol	Price	52Wk Range	Yield	P/E
TSX	GBT SVA	C$12.20 (5/31/2005)	14.65-9.52	0.98	10.52

***7 Year Price Score N/A** *NYSE Composite Index=100 ***12 Month Price Score 106.00**

TRADING VOLUME (thousand shares)

Interim Earnings (Per Share) Can$

Qtr.	Mar	Jun	Sep	Dec
2002	0.04	0.14	0.27	0.35
2003	0.05	0.22	0.27	0.37
2004	0.06	0.41	0.43	0.28
2005	0.04	...	...	...

Interim Dividends (Per Share)

Amt	Decl	Ex	Rec	Pay
0.035S	11/22/2002	12/11/2002	12/15/2002	1/3/2003
0.035S	8/20/2003	8/27/2003	8/29/2003	9/4/2003
0.05S	8/13/2004	8/19/2004	8/23/2004	8/30/2004
0.06S	11/11/2004	12/16/2004	12/20/2004	1/3/2005

Indicated Div: C$0.12

Valuation Analysis

Forecast P/E N/A

Market Cap C$425.7 Million Book Value 117.5 Million

Price/Book 3.62 Price/Sales 0.53

Dividend Achiever Status

Rank 3 **5 Year Growth Rate** 29.46%

Total Years of Dividend Growth 13

Business Summary: Retail - Furniture & Home Furnishings (MIC: 5.9 SIC: 712 NAIC: 42110)

BMTC Group is a holding company. Through its subsidiaries, Co. is engaged in the retail sales of furniture and household and electronic appliances in Quebec. As of Dec 31 2004, Co.'s subsidiaries operated sales and distribution network comprised of twenty stores in the Quebec City, Repentigny, Laval, Ste-Therese, Ste-Foy, St-Georges, Three Rivers, Sherbrooke, Chicoutimi, Riviere-du-Loup, Rimouski and Gatineau regions Quebec. Co.'s network also includes two distribution and administrative centers in Montreal and Quebec.

Recent Developments: For the quarter ended Mar 31 2005, net income fell 33.2% to C$1.5 million compared with C$2.3 million in the corresponding period of the previous year. The result from costing of options had the effect of reducing the earnings per share by $0.06 compared with an increase in earnings of $0.03 per share for the corresponding 2004 period. Revenues advanced 3.0% to C$172.1 million from C$167.0 million the year before. Income before income taxes increased 35.8% to C$2.1 million from C$3.2 million a year earlier. Income taxes dropped 41.8% to C$558,000 versus C$959,000 the year before.

Prospects: Bottom-line results are being hampered by an increase in expense levels. However, Co.'s revenues are showing continued good growth. Separately, Co. has indicated that in the course of its redemption programs instituted on Jun 4 2004, it has redeemed a total of 1,102,624 Class A Subordinate Voting Shares with respect to which the average redemption price was $11.47 per share and 762,176 Class B Multiple Voting Shares with respect to which the average redemption price was $12.38 per share. As of May 11 2005, 21,917,384 Class A Subordinate Voting Shares and 12,976,116 Class B Multiple Voting Shares of Co. were outstanding.

Financial Data

(Can$ in Thousands)	3 Mos	12/31/2004	12/31/2003	12/31/2002	12/31/2001
Earnings Per Share	1.16	1.18	0.91	0.81	0.44
Cash Flow Per Share	0.60	0.09	3.03	0.77	0.67
Tang Book Value Per Share	3.37	3.55	2.98	3.01	2.48
Dividends Per Share	0.110	0.110	0.085	0.065	0.052
Dividend Payout %	9.48	9.32	9.34	8.07	11.93
Income Statement					
Total Revenue	172,095	801,846	802,870	807,937	642,532
EBITDA	2,350	69,250	59,095	61,253	37,582
Depn & Amortn	271	4,066	3,875	3,927	3,389
Income Before Taxes	2,079	65,184	55,220	57,326	34,193
Income Taxes	558	20,720	18,229	18,884	12,472
Net Income	1,521	44,464	36,991	38,442	21,721
Average Shares	36,118	37,754	40,458	47,758	49,416
Balance Sheet					
Current Assets	122,432	117,491	137,142	145,329	95,008
Total Assets	252,717	248,754	264,776	260,563	206,289
Current Liabilities	134,486	120,976	150,584	125,490	87,020
Total Liabilities	135,229	121,719	151,543	126,755	88,690
Stockholders' Equity	117,488	127,035	113,233	133,808	117,599
Shares Outstanding	34,893	35,750	38,000	44,400	47,339
Statistical Record					
Return on Assets %	17.68	17.27	14.08	16.47	10.53
Return on Equity %	39.99	36.91	29.95	30.58	18.48
EBITDA Margin %	1.37	8.64	7.36	7.58	5.85
Net Margin %	0.88	5.55	4.61	4.76	3.38
Asset Turnover	3.26	3.11	3.06	3.46	3.11
Current Ratio	0.91	0.97	0.91	1.16	1.09
Price Range	14.65-9.52	13.10-9.52	13.25-6.88	7.75-4.13	4.50-2.00
P/E Ratio	12.63-8.21	11.10-8.07	14.56-7.55	9.57-5.09	10.23-4.55
Average Yield %	0.96	0.97	0.90	1.06	1.79

Address: 8500 Place Marien, Montreal-East, Montreal
Telephone: 514-648-5757
Web Site: N.A.

Officers: Yves Des Groseillers - Pres., C.E.O. Charles Des Groseillers - Sec. **Transfer Agents:** National Bank Trust, Inc.

No of Institutions: N/A
Shares: N/A **% Held:** N/A

BUHLER INDUSTRIES, INC.

Exchange	Symbol	Price	52Wk Range	Yield	P/E
TSX	BUI	C$7.36 (5/31/2005)	7.61-6.50	1.90	15.33

Interim Earnings (Per Share) Can$

Qtr.	Dec	Mar	Jun	Sep
2001-02	0.13	0.16	0.22	0.07
2002-03	0.09	0.15	0.16	0.11
2003-04	0.09	0.16	0.17	0.08
2004-05	0.07	0.16	...	...

Interim Dividends (Per Share)

Amt	Decl	Ex	Rec	Pay
0.11A	12/3/2001	12/18/2001	12/20/2001	1/28/2002
0.12A	11/29/2002	12/24/2002	12/30/2002	1/29/2003
0.13A	11/10/2003	12/3/2003	12/5/2003	1/14/2004
0.14A	11/4/2004	12/1/2004	12/3/2004	1/14/2005

Indicated Div: C$0.14

Valuation Analysis
Forecast P/E 15.64 (6/1/2005)
Market Cap C$184.0 Million Book Value 94.3 Million
Price/Book 1.95 Price/Sales 0.87

Dividend Achiever Status
Rank 25 **5 Year Growth Rate** 10.20%
Total Years of Dividend Growth 8

Business Summary: Machinery Supply Retail (MIC: 12.9 SIC: 083 NAIC: 23820)

Buhler Industries is a manufacturer of agricultural equipment marketed throughout North America under the brand names: "Buhler," "Allied," "Farm King," "Inland" and "Buhler Versatile." Co.'s principal products are tractors, front-end loaders, grain augers, snow blowers, tillers, finishing mowers, feed processing equipment, hay & forage equipment and fibre reinforced plastic.

Recent Developments: For the second quarter ended Mar 31 2005, net earnings totaled C$4.1 million, up 4.2% compared with C$3.9 million in the corresponding quarter of the previous year. Results included pre-tax gains of C$36,000 in 2005 and C$239,000 in 2004 from the sale of capital assets. Revenue climbed 2.2% to C$64.0 million from C$62.6 million a year earlier. Gross profit totaled C$11.6 million, or 18.1% of revenue, compared with C$12.0 million, or 19.2% of revenue, in the prior year. Income from operations was C$7.3 million, essentially unchanged versus the year before.

Prospects: Gross profit margins are beginning to benefit from price increases that were implemented in January 2005. Over the remainder of fiscal 2005, Co. expects to sustain gross margins of about 18.0%. Meanwhile, Co. has seen significant profit slippage from increasing steel prices, which are anticipated to remain high for the remainder of the year. Co. continues to forecast flat or slightly improved revenues for fiscal 2005 due to the uncertain long term customer reaction to Co.'s recent price increases. In addition, Co. is projecting flat or lower earnings for the next three quarters.

Financial Data (Can$ in Thousands)	6 Mos	3 Mos	09/30/2004	09/30/2003	09/30/2002	09/30/2001	09/30/2000	09/30/1999
Earnings Per Share	0.48	0.48	0.50	0.51	0.58	0.30	0.30	0.23
Tang Book Value Per Share	3.77	3.61	3.68	3.08	2.70	2.28	2.13	1.93
Dividends Per Share	0.140	0.140	0.130	0.120	0.110	0.100	0.090	0.080
Dividend Payout %	29.17	29.27	26.00	23.53	18.97	33.33	30.00	34.78
Income Statement								
Total Revenue	109,800	45,811	206,130	181,162	232,619	187,633	116,700	79,961
EBITDA	9,374	3,123	20,040	21,874	26,202	14,518	15,882	14,488
Depn & Amortn	3,070	1,506	6,812	6,894	7,339	7,684	5,520	5,126
Income Before Taxes	6,695	1,851	13,556	14,277	18,494	5,802	9,691	8,928
Income Taxes	970	204	1,507	2,647	5,134	(1,313)	2,393	3,131
Net Income	5,725	1,647	12,049	11,630	13,360	7,115	7,298	5,797
Average Shares	...	...	...	...	...	...	24,225	24,459
Balance Sheet								
Current Assets	129,619	125,284	124,984	132,272	110,455	87,456	99,635	34,403
Total Assets	173,748	169,858	167,044	178,281	156,305	127,531	149,073	74,843
Current Liabilities	46,580	44,958	37,570	49,742	49,860	42,239	54,038	14,195
Long-Term Obligations	24,088	24,902	25,770	29,398	31,055	31,850	31,850	1,200
Total Liabilities	70,668	69,860	64,163	90,319	92,550	74,089	90,083	16,386
Stockholders' Equity	94,272	90,194	92,047	70,868	61,998	53,442	51,659	47,327
Shares Outstanding	25,000	25,000	25,000	23,000	23,000	23,483	24,225	24,459
Statistical Record								
Return on Assets %	6.87	6.61	6.96	6.95	9.41	5.14	6.50	8.53
Return on Equity %	13.05	14.44	14.75	17.51	23.15	13.54	14.71	12.59
EBITDA Margin %	8.54	6.82	9.72	12.07	11.26	7.74	13.61	18.12
Net Margin %	5.21	3.60	5.85	6.42	5.74	3.79	6.25	7.25
Asset Turnover	1.23	1.19	1.19	1.08	1.64	1.36	1.04	1.18
Current Ratio	2.78	2.79	3.33	2.66	2.22	2.07	1.84	2.42
Debt to Equity	0.26	0.28	0.28	0.41	0.50	0.60	0.62	0.03
Price Range	7.61-6.25	7.61-5.70	7.25-5.52	5.92-5.20	5.50-3.48	3.60-3.00	3.70-2.65	3.24-2.35
P/E Ratio	15.85-13.02	15.85-11.88	14.50-11.04	11.61-10.20	9.48-6.00	12.00-10.00	12.33-8.83	14.09-10.22
Average Yield %	2.02	2.11	2.07	2.16	2.47	2.92	2.94	2.90

Address: 1201 Regent Avenue West, Winnipeg **Telephone:** 204-661-8711 **Web Site:** www.buhler.com	**Officers:** John Buhler - Chmn., C.E.O. Craig P. Engel - Pres. **Transfer Agents:** Computershare Trust Company of Canada, Winnipeg, Manitoba	**No of Institutions:** N/A **Shares:** N/A **% Held:** N/A

CANADIAN IMPERIAL BANK OF COMMERCE

Exchange	Symbol	Price	52Wk Range	Yield	P/E
TSX	CM	C$58.23 (5/31/2005)	61.76-47.38	4.67	10.02

*7 Year Price Score 140.36 *NYSE Composite Index=100 *12 Month Price Score 103.51

TRADING VOLUME (thousand shares)

Interim Earnings (Per Share) Can$

Qtr.	Jan	Apr	Jul	Oct
2001-02	0.87	0.53	0.41	(0.40)
2002-03	1.11	0.76	2.02	1.29
2003-04	1.54	1.33	1.60	1.07
2004-05	1.94	1.20	...	...

Interim Dividends (Per Share)

Amt	Decl	Ex	Rec	Pay
0.60Q	8/25/2004	9/24/2004	9/28/2004	10/28/2004
0.65Q	12/2/2004	12/27/2004	12/29/2004	1/28/2005
0.65Q	2/24/2005	3/23/2005	3/28/2005	4/28/2005
0.68Q	5/25/2005	6/24/2005	6/28/2005	7/28/2005

Indicated Div: C$2.72

Valuation Analysis

Forecast P/E	12.27 (6/1/2005)		
Market Cap	C$19.7 Billion	Book Value	12.9 Billion
Price/Book	1.53	Price/Sales	1.15

Dividend Achiever Status

Rank	20	5 Year Growth Rate	12.89%
Total Years of Dividend Growth			5

Business Summary: Commercial Banking (MIC: 8.1 SIC: 029 NAIC: 22110)

Canadian Imperial Bank of Commerce (CIBC) is a diversified financial institution that operates three business lines: CIBC Retail Markets, CIBC Wealth Management and CIBC World Markets. CIBC Retail Markets provides financial services and products to personal and small business customers in Canada. CIBC Wealth Management provides branch-based advice, full-service brokerage, private wealth management, and online brokerage. CIBC World Markets is the wholesale banking arm of CIBC, providing a full range of integrated credit and capital markets products, investment banking and merchant banking to clients in key financial markets in North America and worldwide.

Recent Developments: For the quarter ended Apr 30 2005, net income declined 13.2% to C$440.0 million from C$507.0 million in the equivalent 2004 quarter. Total interest income grew 10.6% to C$2.73 billion. Net interest income decreased 2.9% to C$1.22 billion, primarily due to higher levels of securitized assets in cards, lower revenue from treasury activities, lower interest on income tax refunds and a reduction in non-core loans, partially offset by higher volumes and favorable lending spreads in personal banking, higher interest on investment securities, and volume growth in mortgages. Total non-interest income decreased 5.6% to C$2.66 billion, while total non-interest expense fell 2.0% to C$2.03 billion.

Prospects: Lending and deposit volumes should continue to grow given the outlook for low and stable interest rates. Capital markets volumes have declined somewhat from earlier in 2005 and the current outlook is for these lower volumes to continue through the third quarter. Co. is supporting growth in its core businesses through targeted investments, while eliminating duplication and streamlining processes. Co. remains firmly focused on strengthening client relationships while carefully managing costs and risk. Co. is confident that by working these objectives it should deliver attractive returns.

Financial Data (Can$ in Thousands)	6 Mos	3 Mos	10/31/2004	10/31/2003	10/31/2002	10/31/2001	10/31/2000	10/31/1999
Earnings Per Share	5.81	5.93	5.53	5.18	1.35	4.07	4.84	2.22
Cash Flow Per Share	3.27	13.52	13.52	(4.11)	24.69	3.50	(16.05)	...
Tang Book Value Per Share	27.55	27.24	26.19	25.19	21.92	26.44	25.17	22.68
Dividends Per Share	2.500	2.350	2.200	1.640	1.600	1.440	1.290	1.200
Dividend Payout %	43.03	39.66	39.78	31.66	118.52	35.38	26.65	54.05
Income Statement								
Interest Income	5,474,000	2,744,000	10,188,000	11,216,000	11,524,000	14,774,000	15,327,000	14,405,000
Interest Expense	2,928,000	1,422,000	4,822,000	5,546,000	6,014,000	10,225,000	11,045,000	9,997,000
Net Interest Income	2,546,000	1,322,000	5,366,000	5,670,000	5,510,000	4,549,000	4,282,000	4,408,000
Provision for Losses	337,000	178,000	628,000	1,143,000	1,500,000	1,100,000	1,220,000	750,000
Non-Interest Income	1,542,420	1,757,000	6,517,000	5,906,000	5,531,000	6,613,000	7,797,000	5,728,000
Income Before Taxes	1,629,000	1,000,000	3,004,000	2,305,000	412,000	1,836,000	2,763,000	1,388,000
Income Taxes	459,000	283,000	790,000	239,000	(279,000)	92,000	641,000	320,000
Net Income	1,147,000	707,000	2,199,000	2,063,000	653,000	1,686,000	2,060,000	1,029,000
Average Shares	344,289	350,201	359,776	362,307	363,227	388,236	404,569	422,486
Balance Sheet								
Net Loans & Leases	139,296,000	138,980,000	137,504,000	135,255,000	153,089,000	155,640,000	145,652,000	136,350,000
Total Assets	287,710,000	285,183,000	278,764,000	277,147,000	273,293,000	287,474,000	267,702,000	250,331,000
Total Deposits	196,484,000	193,301,000	190,577,000	188,130,000	196,630,000	194,352,000	179,632,000	160,041,000
Total Liabilities	274,850,000	272,780,000	265,541,000	263,369,000	260,960,000	275,574,000	256,333,000	239,273,000
Stockholders' Equity	12,860,000	12,403,000	13,223,000	13,778,000	12,333,000	11,900,000	11,369,000	11,058,000
Shares Outstanding	338,729	341,098	347,350	362,042	359,064	363,187	377,140	402,278
Statistical Record								
Return on Assets %	0.77	0.80	0.79	0.75	0.23	0.61	0.79	0.39
Return on Equity %	16.34	17.30	16.24	15.80	5.39	14.49	18.32	9.27
Net Interest Margin %	44.84	48.18	52.67	50.55	47.81	30.79	27.94	30.60
Loans to Deposits	0.71	0.72	0.72	0.72	0.78	0.80	0.81	0.85
Price Range	61.76-46.27	61.76-46.27	60.42-44.83	46.43-25.27	36.75-21.46	36.51-28.56	33.56-20.94	28.56-19.19
P/E Ratio	10.63-7.96	10.41-7.80	10.93-8.11	8.96-4.88	27.22-15.90	8.97-7.02	6.93-4.33	12.87-8.64
Average Yield %	4.58	4.45	4.37	4.71	5.09	4.43	4.76	5.09

Address: Commerce Court, Toronto
Telephone: 416-980-2211
Web Site: www.cibc.com

Officers: John S. Hunkin - C.E.O. Sonia Baxendale - Sr. Exec. V.P., CIBC Wealth Management **Transfer Agents:** CIBC Mellon Trust Company, Toronto, Canada

Investor Contact: 416-980-8306
No of Institutions: 66
Shares: 102,644,440 **% Held:** 29.48

CANADIAN NATIONAL RAILWAY CO.

Exchange	Symbol	Price	52Wk Range	Yield	P/E
TSX	CNR	C$76.80 (5/31/2005)	78.16-53.70	1.30	16.27

***7 Year Price Score 138.90** *NYSE Composite Index=100 ***12 Month Price Score 107.23**

Interim Earnings (Per Share) Can$

Qtr.	Mar	Jun	Sep	Dec
2002	0.77	0.69	0.88	(0.69)
2003	0.85	0.61	0.72	0.59
2004	0.73	1.13	1.26	1.29
2005	1.04	...	...	...

Interim Dividends (Per Share)

Amt	Decl	Ex	Rec	Pay
0.195Q	7/20/2004	9/8/2004	9/10/2004	9/30/2004
0.195Q	10/27/2004	12/8/2004	12/10/2004	12/31/2004
0.25Q	1/25/2005	3/8/2005	3/10/2005	3/31/2005
0.25Q	4/20/2005	6/7/2005	6/9/2005	6/30/2005

Indicated Div: C$1.00

Valuation Analysis

Forecast P/E	14.92 (6/1/2005)		
Market Cap	C$21.6 Billion	Book Value	9.3 Billion
Price/Book	2.32	Price/Sales	3.16

Dividend Achiever Status

Rank	17	5 Year Growth Rate	14.29%
Total Years of Dividend Growth			8

Business Summary: Rail Transport (MIC: 15.5 SIC: 011 NAIC: 82111)

Canadian National Railway is engaged in the rail transportation business. Co. spans Canada and mid-America, from the Atlantic and Pacific oceans to the Gulf of Mexico, serving the ports of Vancouver, Prince Rupert, B.C., Montreal, Halifax, New Orleans and Mobile, Alabama, and the cities of Toronto, Buffalo, Chicago, Detroit, Duluth, Minnesota/Superior, Wisconsin, Green Bay, Wisconsin, Minneapolis/St. Paul, Memphis, St. Louis and Jackson, Mississippi, with connections to all points in North America. Co.'s movement of goods includes petroleum and chemicals, grain and fertilizers, coal, metals and minerals, forest products, intermodal and automotive.

Recent Developments: For the three months ended Mar 31 2005, net income increased 42.4% to C$299.0 million compared with C$210.0 million in the comparable year-earlier period. Revenues grew 18.6% to C$1.71 billion from C$1.44 billion the previous year. Operating income was C$526.0 million versus C$395.0 million the year before. Co. attributed its improved performance to a number of factors including a solid economy, revenue gains from its 2004 acquisitions, a higher fuel surcharge, freight rate increases, and a return to more normal traffic levels following the first-quarter 2004 Canadian Auto Workers strike.

Prospects: Co.'s prospects appear encouraging, reflecting in part recent revenue increases from across each of its commodity groups, with the exception of automotive. Co. noted that it experienced particular strength during the quarter ended Mar 31 2005 in metals and minerals, forest products, and intermodal traffic. Separately, on Apr 6 2005, Co. announced orders for 75 high-horsepower locomotives. Co. expects delivery of the locomotives starting in the fourth quarter of 2005, with completion by mid-2006. Co. has also negotiated options, effective through the end of 2008, to acquire an additional 75 locomotives.

Financial Data

(Can$ in Thousands)	3 Mos	12/31/2004	12/31/2003	12/31/2002	12/31/2001	12/31/2000	12/31/1999	12/31/1998
Earnings Per Share	4.72	4.48	2.53	1.88	2.41	2.54	2.01	1.92
Cash Flow Per Share	8.57	7.48	5.23	3.98	4.28	3.85	4.32	4.51
Tang Book Value Per Share	33.17	25.95	22.81	22.37	20.88	18.79	17.06	17.54
Dividends Per Share	0.835	0.780	0.667	0.573	0.520	0.467	0.400	0.353
Dividend Payout %	17.69	17.41	26.39	30.50	21.55	18.37	19.87	18.40
Income Statement								
Total Revenue	1,706,000	6,548,000	5,884,000	6,110,000	5,652,000	5,446,000	5,261,000	4,121,000
EBITDA	679,000	2,731,000	1,867,000	1,698,000	1,900,000	1,930,000	1,775,000	859,000
Depn & Amortn	157,000	521,000	478,000	506,000	469,000	421,000	496,000	319,000
Income Before Taxes	447,000	1,928,000	1,072,000	839,000	1,119,000	1,214,000	971,000	298,000
Income Taxes	148,000	631,000	338,000	268,000	392,000	442,000	369,000	74,000
Net Income	299,000	1,297,000	734,000	571,000	727,000	772,000	602,000	266,000
Average Shares	287,500	289,600	290,700	304,200	301,500	304,200	295,950	274,500
Balance Sheet								
Total Assets	22,428,000	19,271,000	17,150,000	18,924,000	18,788,000	15,196,000	14,757,000	11,952,000
Long-Term Obligations	4,956,000	4,586,000	4,175,000	5,003,000	5,764,000	3,886,000	3,961,000	3,995,000
Total Liabilities	13,120,000	11,924,000	10,670,000	12,297,000	12,427,000	9,498,000	9,251,000	6,907,000
Stockholders' Equity	9,308,000	7,347,000	6,480,000	6,627,000	6,361,000	5,698,000	5,506,000	5,045,000
Shares Outstanding	280,600	283,100	284,100	296,250	289,050	285,900	303,600	287,700
Statistical Record								
Return on Assets %	6.37	7.10	4.07	3.03	4.28	5.14	4.51	2.80
Return on Equity %	15.23	18.71	11.20	8.79	12.06	13.74	11.41	6.29
EBITDA Margin %	39.80	41.71	31.73	27.79	33.62	35.44	33.74	20.84
Net Margin %	17.53	19.81	12.47	9.35	12.86	14.18	11.44	6.45
Asset Turnover	0.32	0.36	0.33	0.32	0.33	0.36	0.39	0.43
Price Range	78.16-50.85	75.20-50.10	54.99-39.69	56.07-38.61	52.21-28.67	32.97-22.43	36.33-23.07	31.78-21.37
P/E Ratio	16.56-10.77	16.79-11.18	21.73-15.69	29.82-20.54	21.66-11.89	12.98-8.83	18.08-11.48	16.55-11.13
Average Yield %	1.32	1.34	1.43	1.18	1.26	1.66	1.35	1.32

Address: 935 de La Gauchetiere Street West, Montreal **Telephone:** 514-399-4821 **Web Site:** www.cn.ca	**Officers:** David G.A. McLean - Chmn. E. Hunter Harrison - Pres. &, C.E.O. **Transfer Agents:** Computershare Trust Company of Canada, Montreal, QC; Toronto, ON; Calgary, AB; Vancouver, BC	**No of Institutions:** 174 **Shares:** 144,838,016 **% Held:** 51.16

CANADIAN UTILITIES LTD.

Exchange	Symbol	Price	52Wk Range	Yield	P/E
TSX	CU NV	C$64.15 (5/31/2005)	64.50-51.80	3.43	12.96

*7 Year Price Score 102.47 *NYSE Composite Index=100 *12 Month Price Score 103.21

Interim Earnings (Per Share) Can$

Qtr.	Mar	Jun	Sep	Dec
2002	2.27	0.67	0.70	1.15
2003	1.34	0.69	0.68	1.36
2004	1.16	1.58	0.70	1.42
2005	1.25	...	...	...

Interim Dividends (Per Share)

Amt	Decl	Ex	Rec	Pay
0.53Q	7/30/2004	8/10/2004	8/12/2004	9/1/2004
0.53Q	10/27/2004	11/8/2004	11/10/2004	12/1/2004
0.55Q	1/20/2005	2/7/2005	2/9/2005	3/1/2005
0.55Q	4/20/2005	5/9/2005	5/11/2005	6/1/2005

Indicated Div: C$2.20

Valuation Analysis

Forecast P/E	15.24 (6/1/2005)		
Market Cap	C$4.1 Billion	Book Value	2.8 Billion
Price/Book	1.45	Price/Sales	1.54

Dividend Achiever Status

Rank	30	**5 Year Growth Rate**	4.27%
Total Years of Dividend Growth			22

Business Summary: Electricity (MIC: 7.1 SIC: 939 NAIC: 21121)

Canadian Utilities is a holding company. Co.'s operating subsidiaries are engaged in regulated natural gas and electric energy operations, mainly in Alberta, and in related non-regulated operations. The Utilities segment includes the regulated distribution of natural gas, the regulated distribution and transmission of electric energy, the regulated transportation of natural gas, and the regulated transmission of distribution of water. Power Generation includes the non-regulated supply of electricity and cogeneration steam, and the regulated supply of electricity. Global Enterprises includes the non-regulated gathering, processing, storage, purchase and sale of natural gas and other services.

Recent Developments: For the three months ended Mar 31 2005, net earnings increased 6.6% to C$88.9 million compared with C$83.4 million in the corresponding year-earlier period. Revenues declined 36.3% to C$745.2 million from C$1.17 billion the previous year. Co. attributed the decrease in revenues primarily to lower sales of electricity and natural gas purchased for customers on a "no-margin" basis by ATCO Electric and ATCO Gas due to the transfer of the retail energy supply businesses in May 2004, and lower volumes of natural gas purchased and resold for natural gas liquids extraction in ATCO Midstream.

Prospects: Co.'s bottom line results are benefiting from increased earnings in its ATCO Power's United Kingdom operations, due to improved performance and the settlement reached by Barking Power Limited with the administrators of TXU Europe. Co. noted that ATCO Power has a 25.5% interest in Barking Power Limited. Co. expects the settlement to generate earnings of approximately C$69.0 million, which will be recognized over the remaining term of the TXU contract to Sep 30 2010, at approximately C$11.0 million per year. Co.'s recent results have also benefited from higher earnings in ATCO Midstream and increased business activity, including work for new customers, from its ATCO I-Tek unit.

Financial Data

(Can$ in Thousands)	3 Mos	12/31/2004	12/31/2003	12/31/2002	12/31/2001	12/31/2000	12/31/1999	12/31/1998
Earnings Per Share	4.95	4.86	4.07	4.79	3.72	3.58	3.16	3.00
Cash Flow Per Share	10.59	10.08	7.46	5.37	11.71	5.51	7.32	4.00
Tang Book Value Per Share	34.10	33.41	30.79	28.86	25.96	24.11	22.40	21.05
Dividends Per Share	2.140	2.120	2.040	1.960	1.880	1.800	1.720	1.640
Dividend Payout %	43.23	43.62	50.12	40.92	50.54	50.28	54.43	54.67
Income Statement								
Total Revenue	745,200	3,089,500	3,742,600	2,975,900	3,500,100	2,923,100	2,207,700	1,945,700
EBITDA	222,900	794,300	717,000	757,500	659,800	858,300	798,500	758,200
Depn & Amortn	81,900	291,500	268,900	244,400	241,700	238,700	229,500	204,100
Income Before Taxes	141,000	502,800	448,100	513,100	418,100	423,600	387,100	381,100
Income Taxes	52,100	158,000	155,700	189,900	164,000	179,400	172,100	180,500
Net Income	88,900	344,800	292,400	323,200	254,100	244,200	215,000	200,600
Average Shares	63,689	63,632	63,665	63,700	63,315	63,328	63,367	63,359
Balance Sheet								
Net PPE	5,042,400	5,045,300	4,809,400	4,657,000	4,362,900	4,007,000	3,847,700	3,802,000
Total Assets	6,594,300	6,463,100	6,070,500	5,934,400	5,392,300	5,390,100	4,528,600	4,437,200
Long-Term Obligations	2,948,500	2,931,900	2,611,400	2,738,000	2,534,300	2,422,600	2,192,300	2,085,400
Total Liabilities	3,794,400	3,708,900	3,482,400	3,617,800	3,412,000	3,527,100	2,739,000	2,636,300
Stockholders' Equity	2,799,900	2,754,200	2,588,100	2,316,600	2,316,800	1,863,000	1,789,600	1,800,900
Shares Outstanding	63,446	63,391	63,383	63,412	63,317	63,305	63,349	63,362
Statistical Record								
Return on Assets %	5.41	5.49	4.87	5.71	4.71	4.91	4.80	4.70
Return on Equity %	12.90	12.87	11.92	13.95	12.16	13.33	11.98	11.20
EBITDA Margin %	29.91	25.71	19.16	25.45	18.85	29.36	36.17	38.97
Net Margin %	11.93	11.16	7.81	10.86	7.26	8.35	9.74	10.31
PPE Turnover	0.53	0.63	0.79	0.66	0.84	0.74	0.58	0.53
Asset Turnover	0.41	0.49	0.62	0.53	0.65	0.59	0.49	0.46
Debt to Equity	1.05	1.06	1.01	1.18	1.09	1.30	1.23	1.16
Price Range	63.92-51.80	64.00-51.80	58.70-45.10	59.98-48.94	56.05-46.00	51.00-31.40	49.00-33.40	48.70-38.55
P/E Ratio	12.91-10.46	13.17-10.66	14.42-11.08	12.52-10.22	15.07-12.37	14.25-8.77	15.51-10.57	16.23-12.85
Average Yield %	3.72	3.70	3.81	3.56	3.67	4.53	3.97	3.65

Address: 1600, 909 - 11th Avenue S.W., Calgary **Telephone:** 403-292-7500 **Web Site:** www.canadian-utilities.com	**Officers:** R. D. Southern C.B.E - Chmn. W. L. Britton Q.C. - Vice-Chmn. **Transfer Agents:** CIBC Mellon Trust Company, Montreal, Toronto, Winnipeg, Calgary, Vancouver	**No of Institutions:** N/A **Shares:** N/A **% Held:** N/A

CI FUND MANAGEMENT INC

Exchange	Symbol	Price	52Wk Range	Yield	P/E
TSX	CIX	C$17.30 (5/31/2005)	18.20-15.33	3.47	18.02

Interim Earnings (Per Share) Can$

Qtr.	Aug	Nov	Feb	May
2001-02	(0.08)	(0.10)	(0.09)	(0.09)
2002-03	0.09	0.09	0.09	0.04
2003-04	0.19	0.06	0.29	0.26
2004-05	0.28	0.14	0.28	...

Interim Dividends (Per Share)

Amt	Decl	Ex	Rec	Pay
0.05M	1/11/2005	1/28/2005	2/1/2005	2/15/2005
0.05M	4/6/2005	4/27/2005	5/1/2005	5/13/2005
0.05M	4/6/2005	5/30/2005	6/1/2005	6/15/2005
0.05M	4/6/2005	6/28/2005	7/1/2005	7/15/2005

Indicated Div: C$0.60

Valuation Analysis

Forecast P/E	13.49 (6/4/2005)		
Market Cap	C$5.1 Billion	Book Value	1.5 Billion
Price/Book	3.29	Price/Sales	N/A

Dividend Achiever Status

Rank	1	5 Year Growth Rate	61.54
Total Years of Dividend Growth	7		

Business Summary: Wealth Management (MIC: 8.8 SIC: 282 NAIC: 23930)

CI Fund Management offers a broad range of investment products and services through its principal operating subsidiaries, CI Mutual Funds Inc. (CIMF), Assante Corporation and Skylon Advisors Inc. CIMF and Skylon are fund management companies that sponsor, manage, distribute and administer investment funds in Canada. Assante's subsidiaries include financial services distribution companies and a fund management company in the business of providing financial planning, investment advice, wealth management, estate and succession planning and insurance services and sponsoring, managing, distributing and administering investment funds in Canada.

Recent Developments: For the three months ended Feb 28 2005, net income totaled C$81.2 million, down 6.7% compared with C$87.0 million in the corresponding quarter a year earlier. Revenues advanced 9.3% to C$278.7 million from C$255.0 million the previous year. Revenues included gains from the sale of marketable securities of C$7.4 million in 2005 and C$126,000 in 2004. Management fees climbed 7.8% to C$221.9 million from C$205.8 million the year before. Administration fees grew 9.1% to C$28.9 million, while redemption fees rose 5.9% to C$12.2 million. Total expenses increased 27.0% to C$154.0 million from C$121.3 million the prior year, primarily reflecting higher selling, general and administrative costs.

Prospects: Results are beginning to benefit from improved global stock market performance during the last part of 2004 and through Co.'s third quarter of fiscal 2005. The positive performance of the equity markets is having a significant impact on the market value of Co.'s funds. Meanwhile, Co. is enjoying a decline in portfolio management expenses as a percentage of retail assets under management. This reduction is being driven by cost-efficiencies stemming from Co.'s efforts to rationalize its investment management activities, as well as efficiencies gained from market appreciation of managed assets and changes to existing contracts.

Financial Data

(Can$ in Thousands)	9 Mos	05/31/2004	05/31/2003	05/31/2002	05/31/2001	05/31/2000	05/31/1999	05/31/1998
Earnings Per Share	0.96	0.82	0.31	(0.35)	0.06	(0.01)	0.06	0.06
Cash Flow Per Share	...	1.37	0.79	...	...	...	...	...
Tang Book Value Per Share	2.00	2.08	1.29	0.33	0.90	0.63	0.88	0.95
Dividends Per Share	0.650	0.405	0.270	0.060	0.031	0.025	0.025	0.020
Dividend Payout %	67.71	49.39	87.10	...	51.67	...	41.67	33.33
Income Statement								
Total Revene	801,179	844,673	576,203	512,757	615,035	454,512	204,466	181,139
Income Before Taxes	318,531	391,744	119,982	58,783	124,335	108,151	21,119	16,336
Income Taxes	114,617	170,700	48,990	21,957	34,272	51,325	12,368	7,786
Net Income	203,914	221,044	70,992	(61,445)	11,499	(2,090)	8,746	8,551
Average Shares	294,581	268,103	228,447	182,098	190,240	...	...	...
Balance Sheet								
Total Assets	2,693,700	2,493,762	1,025,650	290,742	457,004	532,346	177,012	189,380
Total Liabilities	1,157,831	958,471	390,103	230,807	192,588	237,300	50,385	49,225
Stockholders' Equity	1,535,869	1,533,869	632,725	56,760	260,834	292,085	126,627	140,155
Shares Outstanding	292,476	295,199	235,525	170,785	180,684	182,829	144,220	147,486
Statistical Record								
Return on Assets %	10.09	12.53	10.79	...	2.32	...	4.77	5.97
Return on Equity %	17.70	20.35	20.59	...	4.16	...	6.56	8.73
Price Range	18.20-14.81	16.50-11.31	12.05-7.90	14.90-8.25	17.10-11.25	13.75-4.01	4.99-2.41	4.98-2.63
P/E Ratio	18.96-15.43	20.12-13.79	38.87-25.48	...	285.00-187.50	...	83.13-40.21	83.02-43.75
Average Yield %	3.94	2.91	2.71	0.51	0.22	0.34	0.67	0.53

Address: CI Place, 151 Yonge Street, Eleventh Floor, Toronto **Telephone:** 416-364-1145 **Web Site:** www.cifunds.com	**Officers:** G. Raymond Chang - Chmn. William T. Holland - Pres., C.E.O. **Transfer Agents:** Computershare Trust Company of Canada, Toronto, Ontario, Canada	**Investor Contact:** 416-364-1145 **No of Institutions:** 2 **Shares:** 1,164,300 **% Held:** 0.40

EMERA INC.

Exchange	Symbol	Price	52Wk Range	Yield	P/E
TSX	EMA	C$18.50 (5/31/2005)	19.93-16.40	4.81	15.81

***7 Year Price Score 95.71** *NYSE Composite Index=100 ***12 Month Price Score 95.94**

TRADING VOLUME (thousand shares)

Interim Earnings (Per Share) Can$

Qtr.	Mar	Jun	Sep	Dec
2002	0.33	0.16	0.17	0.17
2003	0.47	0.14	0.11	0.41
2004	0.41	0.27	0.20	0.28
2005	0.42	...	...	...

Interim Dividends (Per Share)

Amt	Decl	Ex	Rec	Pay
0.22Q	7/9/2004	7/28/2004	7/30/2004	8/16/2004
0.22Q	10/8/2004	10/27/2004	10/29/2004	11/15/2004
0.223Q	1/20/2005	1/28/2005	2/1/2005	2/15/2005
0.223Q	4/15/2005	4/28/2005	5/2/2005	5/16/2005

Indicated Div: C$0.89

Valuation Analysis

Forecast P/E	17.76 (6/1/2005)		
Market Cap	C$2.0 Billion	Book Value	1.4 Billion
Price/Book	1.48	Price/Sales	1.66

Dividend Achiever Status

Rank	34	**5 Year Growth Rate**	1.18%
Total Years of Dividend Growth			12

Business Summary: Electricity (MIC: 7.1 SIC: 911 NAIC: 21122)

Emera is an energy and services company, with its core business being electricity. Co. operates two regulated utility subsidiaries in northeast North America: Nova Scotia Power and Bangor Hydro-Electric - that together account for over 90.0% of Co.'s revenues. In addition, Co. owns a 12.9% equity interest in the Maritimes & Northeast Pipeline, which delivers Nova Scotia's offshore natural gas to markets in Maritime Canada and New England. Emera Fuels is a full service fuel oil company, and an extension of the Emera brand into complimentary businesses along the energy value chain.

Recent Developments: For the three months ended Mar 31 2005, net income rose 3.9% to C$48.3 million from C$46.5 million in the corresponding quarter in 2004. Nova Scotia Power segment earnings grew 5.2% to C$40.8 million, while earnings from the Bangor Hydro segment were down 29.3% to C$4.1 million. Total revenues slid 2.4% to C$338.9 million from C$347.4 million the year before. Electric revenue slipped 2.2% to C$299.0 million. Fuel oil revenue climbed 2.1% to C$29.2 million, while other revenue decreased 17.7% to C$10.7 million. Earnings from operations totaled C$95.1 million, down 17.4% compared with C$115.2 million in the prior year.

Prospects: On Mar 31 2005, the Nova Scotia Utility and Review Board (UARB) rendered its decision on Novia Scotia Power's (NSPI) 2005 rate application, granting an average rate increase of approximately 5.3%, effective Apr 1 2005. The decision should result in an increase in NSPI's revenue for 2005 of between C$30.0 million and C$35.0 million. However, NSPI's net earnings for 2005 are expected to decline between C$22.0 million and C$27.0 million year over year, reflecting UARB's disallowance of NSPI's proposal to defer C$13.0 million of fuel costs, and the effect of a lower allowed return on equity.

Financial Data

(Can$ in Thousands)	3 Mos	12/31/2004	12/31/2003	12/31/2002	12/31/2001	12/31/2000	12/31/1999	12/31/1998
Earnings Per Share	1.17	1.16	1.16	0.84	1.16	1.20	1.16	0.99
Cash Flow Per Share	2.44	2.79	2.22	2.61	...	...	...	...
Tang Book Value Per Share	11.53	11.29	11.06	11.08	10.64	11.11	10.75	10.50
Dividends Per Share	0.882	0.880	0.860	0.858	0.850	0.840	0.830	0.82
Dividend Payout %	75.43	75.86	74.14	102.08	73.28	70.00	71.55	82.83
Income Statement								
Total Revenue	338,900	1,222,000	1,231,300	1,226,900	1,003,900	896,500	824,600	773,100
EBITDA	136,100	491,200	483,200	394,500	382,400	379,500	373,500	350,900
Depn & Amortn	47,900	158,100	145,900	150,800	117,700	117,300	117,900	108,000
Income Before Taxes	57,900	206,300	203,700	98,300	141,200	126,800	119,100	110,200
Income Taxes	6,300	63,100	61,300	4,100	14,800	12,500	7,400	13,600
Net Income	48,300	129,800	129,200	83,600	114,200	104,400	100,400	85,400
Average Shares	122,500	123,400	123,800	99,000	111,200	87,200	...	...
Balance Sheet								
Net PPE	2,774,200	2,714,600	2,672,800	2,776,400	2,766,800	2,319,700	2,315,000	2,298,400
Total Assets	3,967,200	3,941,700	3,840,900	3,907,900	3,959,400	2,951,000	2,901,200	2,834,100
Long-Term Obligations	1,642,700	1,626,500	1,589,500	1,417,800	1,381,400	1,155,000	1,260,700	1,083,700
Total Liabilities	2,600,700	2,604,900	2,528,300	2,575,900	2,778,000	1,973,400	1,727,600	1,722,900
Stockholders' Equity	1,366,500	1,336,800	1,312,600	1,332,000	1,181,400	977,600	1,173,600	1,111,200
Shares Outstanding	109,104	108,870	108,262	107,800	98,000	87,350	87,050	86,800
Statistical Record								
Return on Assets %	3.33	3.33	3.33	2.13	3.31	3.56	3.50	2.99
Return on Equity %	9.72	9.77	9.77	6.65	10.58	9.68	8.79	7.75
EBITDA Margin %	40.16	40.20	39.24	32.15	38.09	42.33	45.29	45.39
Net Margin %	14.25	10.62	10.49	6.81	11.38	11.65	12.18	11.05
PPE Turnover	0.44	0.45	0.45	0.44	0.39	0.39	0.36	0.34
Asset Turnover	0.31	0.31	0.32	0.31	0.29	0.31	0.29	0.27
Debt to Equity	1.20	1.22	1.21	1.06	1.17	1.18	1.07	0.98
Price Range	19.93-16.40	19.80-16.40	17.94-14.38	17.82-15.65	18.07-15.70	18.20-11.70	19.05-13.20	20.05-14.95
P/E Ratio	17.03-14.02	17.07-14.14	15.47-12.40	21.21-18.63	15.58-13.53	15.17-9.75	16.42-11.38	20.25-15.10
Average Yield %	4.84	4.85	5.15	5.14	5.08	5.69	4.93	4.69

Address: 18th Floor, Barrington Tower Scotia Square, 1894 Barrington Street, Halifax
Telephone: 902-428-6494
Web Site: www.emera.com

Officers: Derek Oland - Chmn. David McD. Mann - Pres., C.E.O. **Transfer Agents:**
Computershare Trust Company of Canada, Halifax, Nova Scotia, Canada

Investor Contact: 902-428-6999
No of Institutions: N/A
Shares: N/A **% Held:** N/A

EMPIRE CO LTD

Exchange	Symbol	Price	52Wk Range	Yield	P/E
TSX	EMP NVA	C$40.00 (5/31/2005)	40.00-24.25	1.20	15.09

*7 Year Price Score 125.47 *NYSE Composite Index=100 *12 Month Price Score 117.88

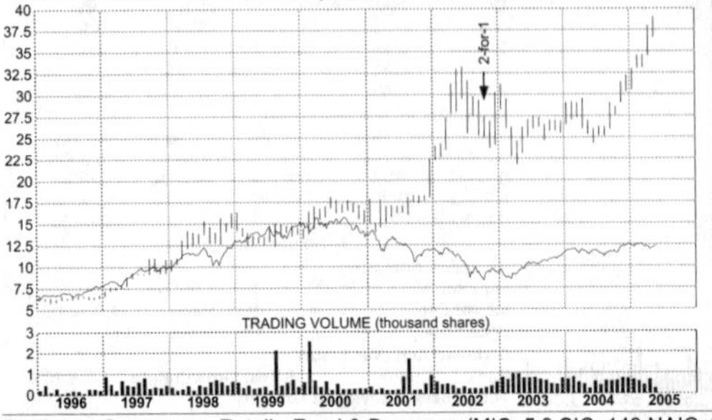

Interim Earnings (Per Share) Can$

Qtr.	Jul	Oct	Jan	Apr
2001-02	0.74	0.64	0.55	1.04
2002-03	0.60	0.59	0.60	0.55
2003-04	0.64	0.56	0.80	0.63
2004-05	0.67	0.61	0.72	...

Interim Dividends (Per Share)

Amt	Decl	Ex	Rec	Pay
0.12Q	6/24/2004	7/13/2004	7/15/2004	7/30/2004
0.12Q	9/9/2004	10/13/2004	10/15/2004	10/29/2004
0.12Q	12/10/2004	1/12/2005	1/14/2005	1/31/2005
0.12Q	3/9/2005	4/13/2005	4/15/2005	4/29/2005

Indicated Div: C$0.48

Valuation Analysis

Forecast P/E	12.62 (6/1/2005)		
Market Cap	C$2.6 Billion	Book Value	1.7 Billion
Price/Book	1.57	Price/Sales	0.22

Dividend Achiever Status

Rank	6	5 Year Growth Rate	25.74%
Total Years of Dividend Growth			10

TRADING VOLUME (thousand shares)

Business Summary: Retail - Food & Beverage (MIC: 5.3 SIC: 149 NAIC: 24490)

Empire operates principally in three business segments: food distribution, real estate and investments and theater operations. Through its subsidiary Sobeys Inc., Co. operates a national network of corporate and franchised stores under banners such as IGA, Sobeys and Price Chopper. Co.'s real estate operations are focused on the acquisition, development and management of a portfolio of properties primarily located in Atlantic Canada. In addition, Co. maintains a portfolio of short-term liquid equity investments and operates Empire Theatres Limited, a movie exhibitor in Atlantic Canada.

Recent Developments: For the third quarter ended Jan 29 2005, net earnings decreased 10.0% to C$47.7 million compared with C$53.0 million in the corresponding prior-year quarter. Results for 2004 and 2003 included capital gains of C$1.7 million and C$11.0 million, respectively. Revenue advanced 6.4% to C$2.98 billion from C$2.80 billion a year earlier. On a segment basis, Food Distribution sales rose 6.4% to C$2.92 billion, while Real Estate sales grew 8.5% to C$43.2 million. In the Food division, same-store sales were up 3.8% year over year. Operating income increased 2.8% to C$113.5 million from C$110.4 million the year before.

Prospects: On Apr 8 2005, Co. announced that it purchased 1.5 million common shares of Sobeys Inc. in a private transaction. Co. has increased its ownership of Sobeys to 44,672,536 common shares representing 68.4% of those outstanding. Separately, Co. is pleased with its consolidated operating results and the progress made by each of its operating businesses in executing against their respective plans. With respect to its food division, Co. continues to be pleased with same-store and total sales growth. The financial condition of Co. continues to improve. The ratio of funded debt to capital at the end of the third quarter equalled 40.0% versus 41.7% at the beginning of the fiscal year.

Financial Data

(Can$ in Thousands)	9 Mos	6 Mos	3 Mos	04/30/2004	04/30/2003	04/30/2002	04/30/2001	04/30/2000
Earnings Per Share	2.65	2.71	2.65	2.63	2.34	2.98	8.82	1.13
Cash Flow Per Share	7.53	7.35	6.78	7.08	5.41	...	...	...
Tang Book Value Per Share	15.34	14.77	14.45	13.83	21.54	19.21	16.82	8.72
Dividends Per Share	0.460	0.440	0.420	0.400	0.330	0.214	0.170	0.140
Dividend Payout %	17.38	16.24	15.83	15.21	14.10	7.18	1.93	12.44
Income Statement								
Total Revenue	9,075,000	6,096,500	3,073,700	11,284,000	10,624,200	9,926,500	11,538,600	11,164,495
EBITDA	506,200	332,900	169,900	607,100	595,600	532,000	1,023,500	498,636
Depn & Amortn	168,300	110,200	55,300	171,900	160,600	118,900	117,900	121,416
Income Before Taxes	274,500	179,700	92,700	343,600	342,100	301,500	763,500	217,709
Income Taxes	94,800	62,900	32,200	111,600	120,400	104,800	148,600	80,543
Net Income	132,000	84,300	44,300	173,100	153,900	195,900	580,000	86,812
Average Shares	65,756	65,766	65,796	65,772	65,781	65,700	65,626	75,572
Balance Sheet								
Current Assets	1,053,800	1,039,800	1,079,700	1,073,900	1,182,800	1,563,700	1,585,400	1,121,643
Total Assets	4,700,900	4,654,200	4,695,700	4,681,700	4,516,100	4,312,600	4,254,300	4,171,087
Current Liabilities	1,506,500	1,512,300	1,393,400	1,420,400	1,387,500	1,360,800	1,498,700	1,855,772
Long-Term Obligations	701,700	715,100	896,600	903,900	923,100	975,000	1,108,300	1,323,700
Total Liabilities	3,021,600	3,014,100	3,083,600	3,104,900	3,089,000	3,022,000	3,139,300	3,568,319
Stockholders' Equity	1,679,300	1,640,100	1,612,100	1,576,800	1,427,100	1,290,600	1,115,000	602,768
Shares Outstanding	...	...	65,735	65,754	65,758	66,607	65,657	65,549
Statistical Record								
Return on Assets %	3.82	3.91	3.79	3.75	3.49	4.57	13.77	2.11
Return on Equity %	10.81	11.37	11.36	11.49	11.33	16.29	67.53	12.92
EBITDA Margin %	5.58	5.46	5.53	5.38	5.61	5.36	8.87	4.47
Net Margin %	1.45	1.38	1.44	1.53	1.45	1.97	5.03	0.78
Asset Turnover	2.63	2.58	2.50	2.45	2.41	2.32	2.74	2.72
Current Ratio	0.70	0.69	0.77	0.76	0.85	1.15	1.06	0.60
Debt to Equity	0.42	0.44	0.56	0.57	0.65	0.76	0.99	2.20
Price Range	32.49-24.25	29.50-24.25	29.50-24.25	29.50-23.10	33.25-21.80	31.25-15.75	18.13-13.95	16.98-12.32
P/E Ratio	12.26-9.15	10.89-8.95	11.13-9.15	11.22-8.78	14.21-9.32	10.49-5.29	2.05-1.58	15.02-10.91
Average Yield %	1.66	1.64	1.57	1.50	1.20	1.06	1.04	0.98

Address: 115 King Street, Stellarton **Telephone:** 902-755-4440 **Web Site:** www.empireco.ca	**Officers:** Donald R. Sobey - Chmn. Paul D. Sobey - Pres., C.E.O. **Transfer Agents:** CIBC Mellon Trust Company of Canada, Stellarton, Nova Scotia	**No of Institutions:** N/A **Shares:** 9,500 **% Held:** 0.03

ENBRIDGE INC

Exchange	Symbol	Price	52Wk Range	Yield	P/E
TSX	ENB	C$33.40 (5/31/2005)	33.40-16.81	2.99	14.98

***7 Year Price Score N/A** *NYSE Composite Index=100 ***12 Month Price Score 98.92**

Interim Earnings (Per Share) Can$

Qtr.	Mar	Jun	Sep	Dec
2002	0.35	1.36	(0.01)	0.09
2003	0.32	1.34	0.27	0.08
2004	0.34	0.73	0.53	0.31
2005	0.65	...	...	...

Interim Dividends (Per Share)

Amt	Decl	Ex	Rec	Pay
0.229Q	7/29/2004	8/12/2004	8/16/2004	9/1/2004
0.229Q	11/4/2004	11/10/2004	11/15/2004	12/1/2004
0.25Q	1/26/2005	2/11/2005	2/15/2005	3/1/2005
0.25Q	5/5/2005	5/12/2005	5/16/2005	6/1/2005

Indicated Div: C$1.00 (Div. Reinv. Plan)

Valuation Analysis

Forecast P/E	20.86 (6/1/2005)		
Market Cap	C$11.6 Billion	Book Value	4.1 Billion
Price/Book	2.80	Price/Sales	1.60

Dividend Achiever Status

Rank	26	**5 Year Growth Rate**	8.90%
Total Years of Dividend Growth			9

Business Summary: Oil and Gas (MIC: 14.2 SIC: 619 NAIC: 86990)

Enbridge is engaged in the transportation and distribution of energy. Co. conducts its business through five operating segments: liquids pipelines, gas pipelines, sponsored investments, gas distribution and services, and international. Co.'s International business invests in energy transportation and related energy projects outside of Canada and the United States. This business also provides consulting and training services related to proprietary pipeline operating technologies and natural gas distribution.

Recent Developments: For the three months ended Mar 31 2005, net earnings were C$222.3 million, up 94.8% compared with C$114.1 million in the corresponding quarter a year earlier. Revenues increased 50.1% to C$2.18 billion from C$1.45 billion the previous year. Gas sales jumped 60.2% to C$1.55 billion from C$969.8 million the year before, while transportation revenue climbed 33.4% to C$545.5 million from C$409.0 million the prior year. Energy services revenue rose 10.6% to C$82.3 million. Operating income advanced 34.3% to C$383.3 million versus C$285.5 million in 2004.

Prospects: Results are being positively affected by a change in the year-end of Co.'s gas distribution operations and the elimination of seasonal distribution rates. Meanwhile, on Mar 28 2005, Co. announced that its wholly owned subsidiary, Enbridge (Offshore) Gas Transmission LLC has acquired the remaining 20.0% interest in the Garden Banks pipeline system, which is located in the Gulf of Mexico and interconnects with four interstate pipelines to move natural gas onshore. Co. plans to tie in other production to come on stream in late 2005 and 2006. The deep water Gulf of Mexico is expected to remain a strong production area for many years ahead.

Financial Data

(Can$ in Thousands)	3 Mos	12/31/2004	12/31/2003	12/31/2002	12/31/2001	12/31/2000	12/31/1999	12/31/1998
Earnings Per Share	2.23	1.92	2.00	1.78	1.44	1.27	0.95	0.83
Cash Flow Per Share	4.03	2.64	1.19	2.84	0.43	0.85	...	...
Tang Book Value Per Share	9.80	10.65	10.09	9.35	6.87	7.10	6.51	6.22
Dividends Per Share	0.936	0.915	0.830	0.760	0.700	0.635	0.598	0.560
Dividend Payout %	42.08	47.78	41.50	42.70	48.61	50.00	62.57	67.67
Income Statement								
Total Revenue	2,181,700	6,540,500	4,855,300	4,547,500	4,050,100	2,945,000	2,687,700	2,341,700
EBITDA	608,800	1,991,700	1,782,500	1,295,800	1,333,900	1,293,800	1,151,700	958,100
Depn & Amortn	143,300	525,000	443,000	403,900	392,500	453,500	383,800	309,000
Income Before Taxes	330,200	941,400	888,200	469,900	504,300	412,600	387,300	336,200
Income Taxes	107,900	289,200	187,400	102,100	66,700	1,900	87,500	95,300
Net Income	222,300	652,200	700,800	610,100	482,900	414,500	299,800	240,900
Average Shares	336,600	337,200	333,800	324,000	317,600	308,938	301,990	290,896
Balance Sheet								
Current Assets	1,957,100	2,349,000	2,052,700	1,442,000	2,281,700	1,334,300	1,107,200	1,094,000
Total Assets	15,919,100	14,905,100	13,823,300	12,987,400	13,127,700	10,568,200	9,208,200	8,347,200
Current Liabilities	1,766,900	2,744,400	2,349,800	1,716,500	3,200,300	1,259,900	910,500	1,286,700
Long-Term Obligations	6,514,800	6,718,500	5,995,500	6,040,300	5,922,800	5,592,700	5,284,800	4,502,300
Total Liabilities	11,773,700	10,926,900	9,697,300	9,155,000	10,095,600	7,804,800	6,707,600	6,285,800
Stockholders' Equity	4,145,400	3,978,200	4,126,000	3,832,400	3,032,100	2,763,400	2,500,600	2,061,400
Shares Outstanding	347,871	346,200	343,800	339,400	325,800	323,692	312,616	311,420
Statistical Record								
Return on Assets %	5.04	4.53	5.23	4.67	4.08	4.18	3.42	3.21
Return on Equity %	18.08	16.05	17.61	17.78	16.66	15.71	13.14	12.81
EBITDA Margin %	27.90	30.45	36.71	28.49	32.93	43.93	42.85	40.91
Net Margin %	10.19	9.97	14.43	13.42	11.92	14.07	11.15	10.29
Asset Turnover	0.49	0.45	0.36	0.35	0.34	0.30	0.31	0.31
Current Ratio	1.11	0.86	0.87	0.84	0.71	1.06	1.22	0.85
Debt to Equity	1.57	1.69	1.45	1.58	1.95	2.02	2.11	2.18
Price Range	32.25-23.63	29.85-23.63	27.07-20.54	24.63-20.60	22.63-17.02	21.85-12.05	18.10-14.32	17.81-16.09
P/E Ratio	14.46-10.59	15.55-12.30	13.54-10.27	13.83-11.57	15.71-11.82	17.20-9.49	19.05-15.08	21.46-19.38
Average Yield %	3.45	3.51	3.49	3.37	3.44	3.87	3.65	3.27

Address: 3000, 425-1st Street SW, Calgary **Telephone:** 403-231-3900 **Web Site:** www.enbridge.com	**Officers:** Donald J. Taylor - Chmn. Patrick D. Daniel - Pres., C.E.O. **Transfer Agents:** CIBC Mellon Trust Company, Toronto, Ontario, Canada	**No of Institutions:** 60 **Shares:** 41,226,748 **% Held:** 23.80

ENSIGN RESOURCE SERVICE GROUP INC.

Exchange	Symbol	Price	52Wk Range	Yield	P/E
TSX	ESI	C$28.63 (5/31/2005)	29.43-20.21	1.12	16.84

*7 Year Price Score 136.03 *NYSE Composite Index=100 *12 Month Price Score 105.98

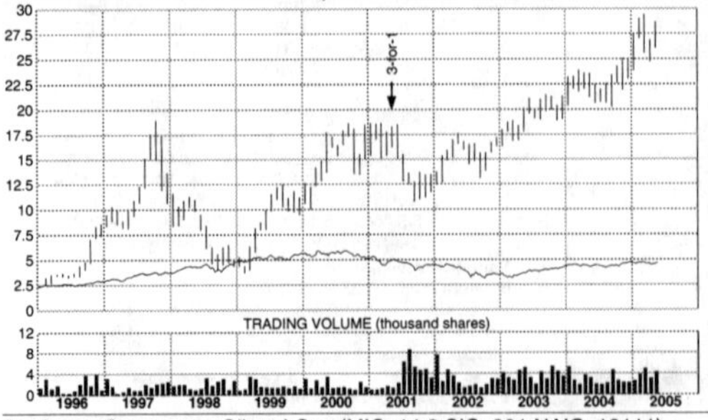

TRADING VOLUME (thousand shares)

Interim Earnings (Per Share) Can$

Qtr.	Mar	Jun	Sep	Dec
2002	0.39	0.04	0.11	0.15
2003	0.51	(0.09)	0.26	0.62
2004	0.70	0.13	0.23	0.48
2005	0.86	...	...	...

Interim Dividends (Per Share)

Amt	Decl	Ex	Rec	Pay
0.07Q	9/7/2004	9/16/2004	9/20/2004	10/1/2004
0.08Q	11/5/2004	12/15/2004	12/17/2004	1/4/2005
0.08Q	3/8/2005	3/18/2005	3/22/2005	4/1/2005
0.08Q	5/19/2005	6/16/2005	6/20/2005	7/4/2005

Indicated Div: C$0.32

Valuation Analysis

Forecast P/E	13.79 (6/1/2005)		
Market Cap	C$2.2 Billion	Book Value	713.4 Million
Price/Book	3.03	Price/Sales	1.93

Dividend Achiever Status

Rank	11	5 Year Growth Rate	20.01%
Total Years of Dividend Growth			5

Business Summary: Oil and Gas (MIC: 14.2 SIC: 381 NAIC: 13111)

Ensign Resource Services Group is the public holding company. Co.'s principal business activities include the provision of oilfield services in western Canada, in the Rocky Mountain region and the State of California in the U.S. through Caza Drilling Inc. and Caza Drilling (California) Inc., respectively, and in the international oilfield services market through Oil Drilling & Exploration Limited (ODE). ODE operates drilling rigs and workover rigs in Australia, New Zealand, Southeast Asia, Middle East, South America and North and South Africa. Co. also provides well servicing, production testing, wireline and oilfield equipment manufacturing services.

Recent Developments: For the quarter ended Mar 31 2005, net income grew 26.2% to C$67.3 million versus C$53.3 million in the equivalent 2004 quarter. The improvement in earnings was primarily attributed to higher demand for Co.'s oilfield services throughout North America. Revenue was C$400.3 million, up 18.0% from C$339.3 million a year earlier. Co.'s Canadian oilfield services division generated revenues of C$277.6 million, up 10.1% from C$252.2 million the year before. Revenues from Co.'s U.S oilfield services division was C$83.3 million, up 39.9% from the year before. Co.'s international oilfield services division posted revenues of C$39.4 million, up 43.0% from a year earlier.

Prospects: Strong demand for oilfield services is expected to persist in the near term. Although activity levels in Western Canada will likely decline in the second quarter due to "spring break-up", booking levels for Co.'s equipment over the summer months remains strong as operators strive to complete their budgeted drilling programs. In response to ongoing demand for oilfield services, Co. continues to expand its fleet of equipment. Co.'s expansion plan addresses the demand for oilfield services equipment, including new technology to service growth areas such as the shallow gas and coal-bed methane markets.

Financial Data

(Can$ in Thousands)	3 Mos	12/31/2004	12/31/2003	12/31/2002	12/31/2001	12/31/2000	12/31/1999	12/31/1998
Earnings Per Share	1.70	1.54	1.29	0.69	1.34	1.17	0.41	0.71
Cash Flow Per Share	2.04	2.33	1.95	1.20	...	...	...	...
Tang Book Value Per Share	9.44	8.61	7.50	6.37	5.85	4.62	3.56	3.70
Dividends Per Share	0.300	0.290	0.235	0.205	0.197	0.172	0.154	0.150
Dividend Payout %	17.65	18.83	18.22	29.71	14.68	14.67	37.60	21.23
Income Statement								
Total Revenue	400,313	1,059,494	928,960	651,768	767,669	672,041	372,322	418,919
EBITDA	122,541	222,120	177,516	121,865	193,971	155,564	75,275	105,915
Depn & Amortn	17,998	50,956	44,209	39,170	29,184	26,525	22,733	20,516
Income Before Taxes	104,543	171,164	133,307	82,695	164,787	129,039	52,542	85,399
Income Taxes	37,231	52,315	34,277	30,952	63,959	42,040	22,705	36,609
Net Income	67,312	118,849	99,030	51,743	100,828	86,999	29,837	48,790
Average Shares	77,835	77,101	76,565	75,254	75,044	74,346	75,315	71,172
Balance Sheet								
Current Assets	447,643	329,872	287,314	224,798	209,723	220,062	152,312	104,819
Total Assets	1,348,373	1,139,240	1,028,292	867,802	643,034	606,626	489,468	416,320
Current Liabilities	449,136	315,663	307,025	258,396	123,235	168,245	114,557	61,182
Long-Term Obligations	...	...	...	7,689	...	14,938	29,805	44,823
Total Liabilities	635,012	489,500	464,633	392,326	210,975	267,972	232,699	154,419
Stockholders' Equity	713,361	649,740	563,659	475,476	432,059	338,654	256,769	261,901
Shares Outstanding	75,555	75,450	75,164	74,609	73,821	73,253	72,040	70,707
Statistical Record								
Return on Assets %	10.73	10.94	10.45	6.85	16.14	15.83	6.59	12.96
Return on Equity %	19.92	19.54	19.06	11.40	26.16	29.14	11.51	23.77
EBITDA Margin %	30.61	20.96	19.11	18.70	25.27	23.15	20.22	25.28
Net Margin %	16.81	11.22	10.66	7.94	13.13	12.95	8.01	11.65
Asset Turnover	0.91	0.97	0.98	0.86	1.23	1.22	0.82	1.11
Current Ratio	1.00	1.05	0.94	0.87	1.70	1.31	1.33	1.71
Debt to Equity	...	...	...	0.02	...	0.04	0.12	0.17
Price Range	29.43-20.21	25.09-20.21	21.47-16.26	17.63-12.44	18.67-10.75	18.67-10.00	12.50-3.68	11.63-3.93
P/E Ratio	17.31-11.89	16.29-13.12	16.64-12.60	25.55-18.03	13.93-8.02	15.95-8.55	30.49-8.98	16.38-5.54
Average Yield %	1.28	1.30	1.23	1.33	1.32	1.14	1.78	1.96

Address: 900, 400 5th Avenue S.W., Calgary **Telephone:** 403-262-1361 **Web Site:** www.ensigngroup.com	**Officers:** N. Murray Edwards - Chmn. Selby Porter - Pres. **Transfer Agents:** Computershare Trust Company of Canada, Toronto, Ontario, Canada	**No of Institutions:** 4 **Shares:** 11,351,885 **% Held:** 15.05

FORTIS INC.

Exchange	Symbol	Price	52Wk Range	Yield	P/E
TSX	FTS	C$74.80 (5/31/2005)	75.50-57.51	3.05	17.12

*7 Year Price Score 125.97 *NYSE Composite Index=100 *12 Month Price Score 105.80

Interim Earnings (Per Share) Can$

Qtr.	Mar	Jun	Sep	Dec
2002	0.99	1.04	1.05	0.76
2003	1.14	1.19	1.03	0.75
2004	1.12	1.15	1.00	0.77
2005	1.45	...	...	...

Interim Dividends (Per Share)

Amt	Decl	Ex	Rec	Pay
0.54Q	9/23/2004	11/3/2004	11/5/2004	12/1/2004
0.57Q	12/1/2004	2/2/2005	2/4/2005	3/1/2005
0.57Q	3/1/2005	5/4/2005	5/6/2005	6/1/2005
0.57Q	5/10/2005	8/3/2005	8/5/2005	9/1/2005

Indicated Div: C$2.28

Valuation Analysis

Forecast P/E 17.42 (6/1/2005)

Market Cap C$1.9 Billion Book Value 1.2 Billion

Price/Book 1.66 Price/Sales 1.50

Dividend Achiever Status

Rank 31 **5 Year Growth Rate** 3.71%

Total Years of Dividend Growth 5

Business Summary: Electricity (MIC: 7.1 SIC: 911 NAIC: 21122)

Fortis is principally a diversified international electric utility holding company. Co. segments its utility operations by franchise area and, depending on regulatory requirements, by the nature of the assets. Co. also holds investments in commercial real estate and hotel properties which have been treated as a separate segment. Co. operates in the following four business segments: Regulated Utilities - Canada; Regulated Utilities - Caribbean; Non-regulated - Fortis Generation; and Non-regulated - Fortis Properties. As of Dec 31 2004, Co. served approximately 972,600 customers in Newfoundland, Prince Edward Island, Ontario, Alberta, British Columbia, Belize and Cayman Islands.

Recent Developments: For the quarter ended Mar 31 2005, net income advanced 93.3% to C$39.2 million compared with C$20.3 million in the corresponding period the year before. Results for 2005 included a gain on settlement of contractual matters of C$10.0 million. Operating revenues and equity income climbed 52.2% to C$381.8 million from C$250.8 million a year earlier. The improvement in results was primarily due to the earnings contributions from FortisAlberta and FortisBC, as well as the timing of recognition of earnings at Newfoundland Power. Co.'s Canadian utilities now provide electric distribution in five provinces. Operating income increased 68.1% to C$88.3 million from C$52.5 million the year before.

Prospects: Co.'s principal business of regulated electric utilities is capital intensive and it expects that most of its capital expenditures for the next five years will relate primarily to FortisAlberta and FortisBC. Consolidated utility capital expenditures for 2005 are expected to be over $400.0 million. Also, Co. expects to focus its capital on funding further acquisitions of electric utility assets. Co. will continue to pursue acquisition opportunities both in Canada and outside of Canada. In addition, Co. will pursue growth in its non-regulated businesses, including hydroelectric generation, hotels and real estate.

Financial Data

(Can$ in Thousands)	3 Mos	12/31/2004	12/31/2003	12/31/2002	12/31/2001	12/31/2000	12/31/1999	12/31/1998
Earnings Per Share	4.37	4.04	4.10	3.85	3.59	2.72	2.24	1.84
Cash Flow Per Share	13.33	12.77	9.28	8.26	...	...	...	...
Tang Book Value Per Share	24.27	19.58	30.33	29.02	27.78	25.44	23.32	22.86
Dividends Per Share	2.190	2.160	2.080	1.940	1.870	1.840	1.800	1.800
Dividend Payout %	50.11	53.47	50.73	50.39	52.09	67.65	80.36	97.83
Income Statement								
Total Revenue	381,789	1,146,129	843,080	715,465	628,254	584,575	505,218	472,725
EBITDA	102,578	269,447	182,014	235,760	144,277	107,834	105,901	89,659
Depn & Amortn	40,176	113,672	62,327	65,063	62,495	52,531	45,407	42,428
Income Before Taxes	62,402	155,775	119,687	99,969	81,782	53,065	57,519	47,231
Income Taxes	18,202	46,927	38,236	32,488	28,088	17,633	27,476	22,998
Average Shares	24,501	25,840	19,179	16,565	14,878	13,517	13,047	12,908
Balance Sheet								
Net PPE	2,389,101	2,688,136	1,609,477	1,506,289	1,284,595	1,114,411	989,748	780,582
Total Assets	3,999,522	3,837,996	2,210,581	1,986,999	1,624,752	1,478,596	1,243,608	1,037,192
Long-Term Obligations	1,901,082	1,878,639	1,031,358	942,300	796,092	728,350	537,828	474,275
Total Liabilities	2,844,547	2,837,884	1,472,924	1,402,546	1,175,823	1,066,456	898,742	698,515
Stockholders' Equity	1,154,975	1,000,112	737,657	584,453	448,929	412,140	344,866	338,677
Shares Outstanding	25,687	23,882	17,380	17,192	14,980	14,778	13,118	12,980
Statistical Record								
EBITDA Margin %	26.87	23.51	21.59	32.95	22.96	18.45	20.96	18.97
PPE Turnover	0.69	0.53	0.54	0.51	0.52	0.55	0.57	0.61
Asset Turnover	0.41	0.38	0.40	0.40	0.40	0.43	0.44	0.46
Debt to Equity	1.65	1.88	1.40	1.61	1.77	1.77	1.56	1.40
Price Range	75.50-57.51	70.70-57.51	60.78-49.00	53.00-44.25	46.95-34.60	36.50-28.00	39.50-29.75	47.85-35.40
P/E Ratio	17.28-13.16	17.50-14.24	14.82-11.95	13.77-11.49	13.08-9.64	13.42-10.29	17.63-13.28	26.01-19.24
Average Yield %	3.39	3.49	3.75	4.01	4.77	5.71	5.11	4.24

Address: The Fortis Building, Suite 1201, 139 Water Street, St. John's
Telephone: 709-737-2800
Web Site: www.fortisinc.com

Officers: Angus A. Bruneau - Chmn. H. Stanley Marshall - Pres., C.E.O. **Transfer Agents:** Computershare Trust Company of Canada, Toronto, Ontario, Canada

Investor Contact: 709-737-2800
No of Institutions: 2
Shares: 37,600 **% Held:** 0.16

GREAT-WEST LIFECO INC.

Exchange	Symbol	Price	52Wk Range	Yield	P/E
TSX	GWO	C$26.80 (5/31/2005)	29.15-23.85	2.91	14.64

*7 Year Price Score 130.60 *NYSE Composite Index=100 *12 Month Price Score 100.65

Interim Earnings (Per Share) Can$

Qtr.	Mar	Jun	Sep	Dec
2002	0.29	0.32	0.32	0.32
2003	0.34	0.35	0.37	0.39
2004	0.42	0.45	0.46	0.46
2005	0.47	...	...	...

Interim Dividends (Per Share)

Amt	Decl	Ex	Rec	Pay
2-for-1	9/29/2004	10/4/2004	10/6/2004	10/14/2004
0.181Q	10/28/2004	12/1/2004	12/3/2004	12/31/2004
0.195Q	2/17/2005	3/1/2005	3/3/2005	3/31/2005
0.195Q	5/5/2005	5/31/2005	6/2/2005	6/30/2005

Indicated Div: C$0.78

Valuation Analysis

Forecast P/E	13.68 (6/1/2005)		
Market Cap	C$23.9 Billion	Book Value	8.9 Billion
Price/Book	2.70	Price/Sales	1.04

Dividend Achiever Status

Rank	9	5 Year Growth Rate	20.92%
Total Years of Dividend Growth			12

Business Summary: Insurance (MIC: 8.2 SIC: 311 NAIC: 24113)

Great-West Lifeco is a financial services holding company providing life insurance, health insurance, retirement savings and reinsurance businesses. Co. has operations in Canada, Europe and United States. In Canada, The Great-West Life Assurance Company and its subsidiaries, London Life Insurance Company and The Canada Life Assurance Company offer financial and benefit plan solutions. In Europe, The Canada Life Assurance Company offers protection and wealth management products and reinsurance in the segment of Insurance & Annuities and Reinsurance. In the United States, Great-West Life & Annuity Insurance Company provide self-funded employee health plans and retirement income needs.

Recent Developments: For the three months ended Mar 31 2005, net income attributable to common shareholders increased 11.4% to C$419.0 million compared with C$376.0 million in the corresponding period a year earlier. Results for 2005 and 2004 included restructuring costs of C$7.0 million and C$9.0 million, respectively. Total revenues jumped to C$6.43 billion from C$5.30 billion, an increase of 21.4% from the year before. Net investment income decreased 4.9% to C$1.29 billion from C$1.36 billion, while fee and other income increased 15.4% to C$614.0 million from C$532.0 million the year before. Income before taxes rose 11.6% to C$604.0 million from C$541.0 million in 2004.

Prospects: Co. is seeing solid operating results in all major business segments and significant growth in net income attributable to common shareholders. For instance, in Canada, consolidated net earnings increased 27.0% year over year to C$186.0 million for the three months ended Mar 31 2005. In Europe, net earnings advanced 31.0% to C$101.0 million from C$77.0 million the year before. However, in the U.S., net earnings were C$144.0 million, down 9.4% compared with C$159.0 million in 2004. Assets under administration at Mar 31 2005 totaled C$167.00 billion, up C$2.10 billion from Dec 31 2004 levels.

Financial Data

(Can$ in Thousands)	3 Mos	12/31/2004	12/31/2003	12/31/2002	12/31/2001	12/31/2000	12/31/1999	12/31/1998
Earnings Per Share	1.83	1.78	1.46	1.25	0.68	0.86	0.71	0.58
Cash Flow Per Share	3.43	3.35	2.59	1.89	2.29	...	...	...
Tang Book Value Per Share	1.72	1.45	0.90	3.54	3.06	2.65	2.09	1.84
Dividends Per Share	0.719	0.685	0.563	0.472	0.390	0.325	0.265	1.377
Dividend Payout %	39.32	38.53	38.50	37.82	57.14	37.79	37.06	235.47
Income Statement								
Total Revenue	6,434,000	21,741,000	13,429,000	16,632,000	16,048,000	15,266,000	13,328,000	13,756,000
Income Before Taxes	604,000	2,362,000	1,906,000	1,426,000	1,053,000	1,253,000	1,118,000	942,000
Income Taxes	149,000	566,000	550,000	430,000	397,000	451,000	366,000	361,000
Net Income	426,000	1,660,000	1,236,000	962,000	546,000	674,000	569,000	473,000
Average Shares	899,072	900,140	817,946	745,215	754,728	747,097	747,781	746,000
Balance Sheet								
Total Assets	97,036,000	95,851,000	97,451,000	60,071,000	59,159,000	55,754,000	53,256,000	54,725,000
Total Liabilities	88,179,000	83,753,000	86,443,000	53,312,000	52,812,000	49,641,000	47,338,000	49,094,000
Stockholders' Equity	8,857,000	9,425,000	8,590,000	4,708,000	4,397,000	4,182,000	3,789,000	3,548,000
Shares Outstanding	891,219	890,592	893,123	732,753	738,919	744,809	748,760	746,000
Statistical Record								
Return on Assets %	1.73	1.71	1.57	1.61	0.95	1.23	1.05	0.89
Return on Equity %	19.11	18.38	18.59	21.13	12.73	16.87	15.51	14.10
Net Margin %	6.62	7.64	9.20	5.78	3.40	4.42	4.27	3.44
Price Range	29.15-23.85	26.70-22.13	22.81-17.51	19.90-16.25	20.02-15.48	21.00-8.38	15.50-8.90	13.50-9.00
P/E Ratio	15.93-13.03	15.00-12.43	15.62-11.99	15.92-13.00	29.44-22.76	24.42-9.74	21.83-12.54	23.28-15.52
Average Yield %	2.78	2.74	2.83	2.61	2.24	2.50	2.23	11.97

Address: 100 Osborne Street North, Winnipeg
Telephone: 204-946-1190
Web Site: www.greatwestlifeco.com

Officers: Robert Gratton - Chmn. Raymond L. McFeetors - Co-Pres., C.E.O. **Transfer Agents:** Computershare Trust Company of Canada, Toronto, Ontario; Calgary, Alberta; Montreal, Quebec; Vancouver, British Columbia and Winnipeg Manitoba

Investor Contact: 204-946-7341
No of Institutions: 4
Shares: 424,164 **% Held:** 0.05

HOME CAPITAL GROUP INC

Exchange	Symbol	Price	52Wk Range	Yield	P/E
TSX	HCG	C$33.74 (5/31/2005)	36.87-20.15	0.47	22.34

Interim Earnings (Per Share) Can$

Qtr.	Mar	Jun	Sep	Dec
2002	0.07	0.07	0.08	0.38
2003	0.09	0.10	0.12	0.56
2004	0.14	0.15	0.17	0.81
2005	0.39	...	...	...

Interim Dividends (Per Share)

Amt	Decl	Ex	Rec	Pay
0.03Q	8/4/2004	8/12/2004	8/16/2004	9/1/2004
0.03Q	10/21/2004	11/10/2004	11/15/2004	12/1/2004
0.04Q	1/25/2005	2/11/2005	2/15/2005	3/1/2005
0.04Q	4/27/2005	5/12/2005	5/16/2005	6/1/2005

Indicated Div: C$0.16

Valuation Analysis

Forecast P/E	20.60 (6/1/2005)		
Market Cap	C$1.1 Billion	Book Value	174.9 Million
Price/Book	6.53	Price/Sales	N/A

Dividend Achiever Status

Rank	1	5 Year Growth Rate	39.77%
Total Years of Dividend Growth			5

Business Summary: Finance Intermediaries & Services (MIC: 8.7 SIC: 163 NAIC: 22310)

Home Capital Group is a holding company. Through its subsidiary, Home Trust Company, Co. offers deposit, mortgage lending, retail credit and credit card issuing services. Co. provides residential first mortgages to borrowers that fail to meet all the major banks' lending requirements and also deposit investment services, including Certificates of Deposit, Guaranteed Investment Certificates, Registered Retirement Savings Plans and Registered Retirement Income. Co. offers the cash-secured Home Trust VISA Card and the Equity Plus VISA card. As of Dec 31 2004, Co. had total assets of C$2.57 billion and administered mortgage assets of C$500.7 million.

Recent Developments: For the first quarter ended Mar 31 2005, net income advanced 35.4% to C$13.6 million compared with C$10.0 million in the corresponding prior-year quarter. Net interest income increased 30.8% to C$23.1 million from C$17.7 million a year earlier. Interest and dividend income rose 27.4% to C$45.3 million, while interest expense grew 24.1% to C$22.2 million. Provision for credit losses climbed 31.2% to C$996,000 from C$759,000 the year before. Non-interest income increased 46.8% to C$10.6 million from C$7.2 million in the previous year. Non-interest expense climbed 30.6% to C$12.2 million from C$9.3 million in the 2004 period.

Prospects: Co. continues to benefit from an attractive economic environment in the regions where it conducts business. Forecasts for the remainder of 2005 foresee moderate economic growth across Canada, with sustained low interest rates supporting both new residential construction and resale markets. Co. remains strongly positioned to benefit from these economic conditions, as well as untapped opportunities in its target markets. Having achieved strong first quarter results, Co. is well positioned to meet its 2005 performance targets of 20.0% growth in net income, fully diluted earnings per share, combined total assets and securitized mortgages originated and managed by Co., and return on equity.

Financial Data

(Can$ in Thousands)	3 Mos	12/31/2004	12/31/2003	12/31/2002	12/31/2001	12/31/2000	12/31/1999	12/31/1998
Earnings Per Share	1.51	1.27	0.86	0.59	0.46	0.34	0.26	0.20
Cash Flow Per Share	2.52	2.19	1.65	1.14	0.96	...	...	...
Tang Book Value Per Share	5.17	4.80	3.61	2.82	2.30	1.59	1.29	1.05
Dividends Per Share	0.130	0.120	0.068	0.055	0.045	0.035	0.022	...
Dividend Payout %	8.58	9.45	7.85	9.24	9.89	10.29	8.65	...
Income Statement								
Interest Income	45,279	162,840	124,381	101,191	83,987	62,488	46,967	37,287
Interest Expense	22,164	77,768	65,104	55,329	51,293	41,360	30,234	23,450
Net Interest Income	23,155	85,072	59,277	45,862	32,694	21,128	16,733	13,837
Provision for Losses	996	4,465	4,286	3,588	2,448	...	...	...
Income Before Taxes	20,587	63,651	43,044	27,999	21,534	16,010	12,758	9,714
Income Taxes	7,011	19,100	13,538	7,404	6,674	5,558	4,677	3,646
Net Income	13,576	44,551	29,507	20,595	14,860	10,452	8,081	6,067
Average Shares	35,086	35,033	34,446	34,623	32,654	...	...	...
Balance Sheet								
Net Loans & Leases	2,332,814	2,224,411	1,608,301	1,171,102	958,564	773,404	639,986	471,841
Total Assets	2,708,595	2,568,513	1,897,176	1,394,289	1,136,220	881,925	738,135	538,876
Total Deposits	2,378,991	2,265,184	1,664,103	1,215,179	995,121	813,182	684,869	493,386
Total Liabilities	2,533,710	2,406,306	1,776,010	1,299,702	1,061,018	832,423	697,682	505,256
Stockholders' Equity	174,885	162,207	121,166	94,586	75,203	49,501	40,453	33,620
Shares Outstanding	33,854	33,777	33,534	33,517	32,695	29,608	29,507	29,567
Statistical Record								
Return on Assets %	2.05	1.99	1.79	1.63	1.47	1.29	1.27	1.25
Return on Equity %	31.49	31.36	27.35	24.26	23.83	23.17	21.82	20.70
Net Interest Margin %	51.14	52.24	47.66	45.32	38.93	33.81	35.63	37.11
Loans to Deposits	0.98	0.98	0.97	0.96	0.96	0.95	0.93	0.96
Price Range	36.87-20.15	32.35-16.38	17.09-7.09	7.75-5.41	5.63-2.92	3.17-1.65	2.30-1.63	2.20-1.02
P/E Ratio	24.42-13.34	25.47-12.89	19.88-8.24	13.14-9.17	12.23-6.36	9.34-4.85	8.85-6.25	11.00-5.13
Average Yield %	0.49	0.51	0.64	0.80	1.09	1.52	1.13	...

Address: Suite 1910, 145 King Street West, Toronto **Telephone:** 416-360-4663 **Web Site:** www.homecapital.com	**Officers:** William A. Dimma - Chmn. Gerald M. Soloway - Pres., C.E.O. **Transfer Agents:** Computershare Investor Services Inc., Toronto, Ontario, Canada	**No of Institutions:** 1 **Shares:** 278,651 **% Held:** 0.82

IMPERIAL OIL LTD.

Exchange	Symbol	Price	52Wk Range	Yield	P/E
TSX	IMO	C$87.00 (5/31/2005)	96.32-59.75	1.10	16.08

*7 Year Price Score 146.31 *NYSE Composite Index=100 *12 Month Price Score 117.12

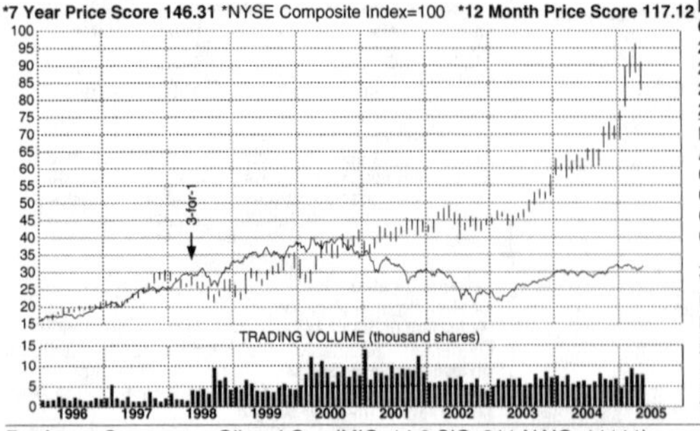

Interim Earnings (Per Share) Can$

Qtr.	Mar	Jun	Sep	Dec
2002	0.29	0.81	0.91	1.19
2003	1.42	1.38	1.01	0.71
2004	1.40	1.26	1.52	1.51
2005	1.12	...	...	...

Interim Dividends (Per Share)

Amt	Decl	Ex	Rec	Pay
0.22Q	8/17/2004	8/30/2004	9/1/2004	10/1/2004
0.22Q	11/17/2004	11/29/2004	12/1/2004	1/1/2005
0.22Q	2/16/2005	3/1/2005	3/3/2005	4/1/2005
0.24Q	5/26/2005	6/6/2005	6/8/2005	7/1/2005

Indicated Div: C$0.96 (Div. Reinv. Plan)

Valuation Analysis

Forecast P/E 14.85 (6/1/2005)

Market Cap C$30.1 Billion Book Value 6.3 Billion

Price/Book 4.75 Price/Sales 1.29

Dividend Achiever Status

Rank 32 **5 Year Growth Rate** 3.53%

Total Years of Dividend Growth 10

Business Summary: Oil and Gas (MIC: 14.2 SIC: 311 NAIC: 11111)

Imperial Oil is an integrated oil company. Co.'s operations are conducted in three main segments: natural resources include the exploration for, and production of, crude oil and natural gas; petroleum products consist of the transportation, refining and blending of crude oil and refined products; and chemicals consist of the manufacturing and marketing of various petrochemicals. In Canada, Co. is a major producer of crude oil and natural gas, and a refiner and marketer of petroleum products. Co. is also a supplier of petrochemicals. As of Dec 31 2004, proved reserves of crude oil, natural gas, and synthetic crude oil were 347 million barrels, 791 billion cubic feet, and 757 million barrels.

Recent Developments: For the three months ended Mar 31 2005, net income decreased 15.7% to C$393.0 million compared with C$466.0 million in the corresponding quarter of the previous year. Results for 2005 and 2004 included pre-tax costs of C$2.0 million for financing items. Total revenues improved 17.5% to C$5.96 billion from C$5.07 billion in the year-earlier period. The increase in revenues was largely due to strong light crude oil and natural gas prices and industry refining and petrochemical margins totalling about C$250.0 million, partially offset by lower Cold Lake bitumen realizations of about C$50.0 million and the impact of a higher Canadian dollar of about C$80.0 million.

Prospects: Co.'s earnings reflect the negative impact from lower volumes and higher maintenance costs associated with a major coker turnaround at Syncrude. However, Co.'s excellent 2004 operating performance is continuing in the current year with strong performances at Cold Lake, downstream and chemical facilities more than offsetting the natural decline in conventional crude oil and natural gas operations. Meanwhile, Co. will look to continue achieving improvements in the controllable aspects of its business, including cost management, volume performance and operating reliability.

Financial Data

(Can$ in Thousands)	3 Mos	12/31/2004	12/31/2003	12/31/2002	12/31/2001	12/31/2000	12/31/1999	12/31/1998
Earnings Per Share	5.41	5.69	4.52	3.19	3.16	3.40	1.35	1.26
Cash Flow Per Share	8.13	9.16	5.90	4.42	5.10	4.99	3.42	1.94
Tang Book Value Per Share	17.28	18.27	15.23	13.16	11.08	10.22	9.77	9.13
Dividends Per Share	0.880	0.880	0.870	0.840	0.825	0.780	0.750	0.738
Dividend Payout %	16.27	15.47	19.25	26.33	26.11	22.94	55.56	58.60
Income Statement								
Total Revenue	5,958,000	22,460,000	19,208,000	17,042,000	17,245,000	18,053,000	10,348,000	9,145,000
EBITDA	826,000	3,901,000	3,112,000	2,484,000	2,613,000	3,045,000	1,699,000	1,394,000
Depn & Amortn	238,000	903,000	750,000	703,000	716,000	724,000	667,000	647,000
Income Before Taxes	588,000	2,998,000	2,362,000	1,781,000	1,897,000	2,321,000	1,032,000	747,000
Income Taxes	195,000	965,000	680,000	571,000	653,000	901,000	450,000	193,000
Net Income	393,000	2,033,000	1,682,000	1,210,000	1,244,000	1,420,000	582,000	554,000
Average Shares	349,500	357,652	372,154	378,875	393,121	417,753	431,475	438,636
Balance Sheet								
Current Assets	3,815,000	3,897,000	2,628,000	2,980,000	2,685,000	3,476,000	2,388,000	2,037,000
Total Assets	14,004,000	13,992,000	12,361,000	11,868,000	10,761,000	11,222,000	9,687,000	9,429,000
Current Liabilities	5,164,000	4,658,000	3,390,000	2,743,000	3,027,000	3,417,000	2,239,000	1,938,000
Long-Term Obligations	48,000	367,000	859,000	1,466,000	906,000	928,000	1,239,000	1,312,000
Total Liabilities	7,675,000	7,354,000	6,583,000	6,656,000	6,332,000	6,901,000	4,372,000	4,220,000
Stockholders' Equity	6,329,000	6,638,000	5,778,000	5,212,000	4,429,000	4,321,000	4,438,000	4,180,000
Shares Outstanding	345,887	349,320	362,652	378,863	379,159	398,263	431,475	431,475
Statistical Record								
Return on Assets %	14.30	15.39	13.88	10.69	11.32	13.55	6.09	5.69
Return on Equity %	30.93	32.66	30.61	25.10	28.43	32.34	13.51	12.94
EBITDA Margin %	13.86	17.37	16.20	14.58	15.15	16.87	16.42	15.24
Net Margin %	6.60	9.05	8.76	7.10	7.21	7.87	5.62	6.06
Asset Turnover	1.74	1.70	1.59	1.51	1.57	1.72	1.08	0.94
Current Ratio	0.74	0.84	0.78	1.09	0.89	1.02	1.07	1.05
Debt to Equity	0.01	0.06	0.15	0.28	0.20	0.21	0.28	0.31
Price Range	93.92-58.65	73.65-57.20	58.22-43.45	49.30-39.50	45.65-34.75	42.25-26.85	35.70-22.00	30.67-21.15
P/E Ratio	17.36-10.84	12.94-10.05	12.88-9.61	15.45-12.38	14.45-11.00	12.43-7.90	26.44-16.30	24.34-16.79
Average Yield %	1.28	1.39	1.80	1.89	2.02	2.22	2.56	2.84

Address: 111 St. Clair Avenue West, Toronto **Telephone:** 416-968-8145 **Web Site:** www.imperialoil.ca	**Officers:** Tim J. Hearn - Chmn., Pres., C.E.O. Brian J. Fischer - Sr. V.P., Products Div., Chemicals Div. **ransfer Agents:**Mellon Investor Services LLC, Ridgefield Park, NJ	**Investor Contact:** 416-968-8145 **No of Institutions:** 119 **Shares:** 37,716,144 **% Held:** 10.80

IGM FINANCIAL INC

Exchange	Symbol	Price	52Wk Range	Yield	P/E
TSX	IGM	C$36.09 (5/31/2005)	39.45-31.96	3.57	15.83

*7 Year Price Score 120.19 *NYSE Composite Index=100 *12 Month Price Score 102.68

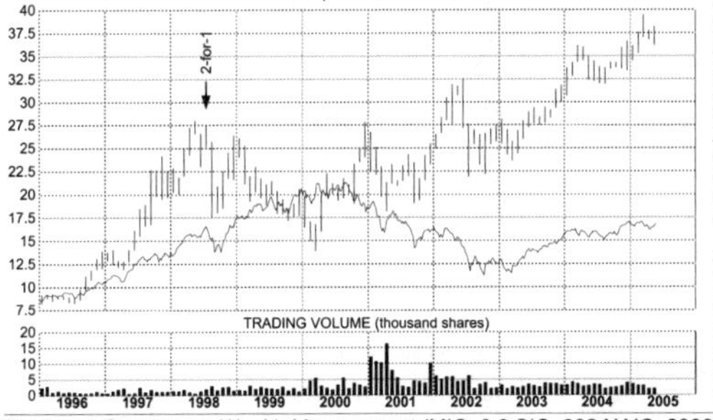

Interim Earnings (Per Share) Can$

Qtr.	Mar	Jun	Sep	Dec
2002	0.44	0.49	0.47	0.45
2003	0.45	0.49	0.00	0.00
2004	0.56	0.57	0.58	0.53
2005	0.60	...	...	...

Interim Dividends (Per Share)

Amt	Decl	Ex	Rec	Pay
0.30Q	7/29/2004	9/28/2004	9/30/2004	10/29/2004
0.30Q	10/29/2004	12/29/2004	12/31/2004	1/31/2005
0.323Q	2/18/2005	3/23/2005	3/28/2005	4/29/2005
0.323Q	5/6/2005	6/23/2005	6/27/2005	7/29/2005

Indicated Div: C$1.29

Valuation Analysis

Forecast P/E	14.27 (6/1/2005)		
Market Cap	C$9.6 Billion	Book Value	3.2 Billion
Price/Book	2.97	Price/Sales	4.40

Dividend Achiever Status

Rank	13	5 Year Growth Rate	18.90%
Total Years of Dividend Growth			13

Business Summary: Wealth Management (MIC: 8.8 SIC: 282 NAIC: 23930)

IGM Financial is a financial services company engaged in managing and distributing mutual funds and other managed assets products. As of Dec 31 2004, Co. has over 2 million clients and C$83.27 billion in mutual fund assets under management. Co.'s subsidiaries, Investors Group, Mackenzie Financial Corp and Investment Planning Counsel, offer their own products and services, including investment, retirement, tax and estate planning advice and service, mutual funds and managed asset funds, insurance and securities services, guaranteed investment certificates, banking products and mortgages. Co. offers products and services through more than 34,000 consultants and independent financial advisors.

Recent Developments: For the first quarter ended Mar 31 2005, net income advanced 8.7% to C$160.7 million compared with C$147.9 million in the corresponding prior-year quarter. Total fee and investment income grew 10.1% to C$573.1 million from C$520.4 million a year earlier. Management fees increased 7.0% to C$390.7 million, while administration fees inched up 1.9% to C$79.5 million. Distribution fees climbed 52.7% to C$53.3 million, and net investment income and other revenues rose 17.1% to C$49.6 million. Total operating expenses increased 11.9% to C$340.8 million from C$304.5 million the year before.

Prospects: During this year's Registered Retirement Savings Plan season, Canadians continued to choose mutual funds as a core component of their savings plans. Positive net sales and rising equity markets pushed Co.'s mutual funds under management to $85.25 billion at Mar 31 2005. Co.'s Investor Group operations benefited from higher mutual fund sales attributed in part to the growth in its consultant network, reflecting strong recruiting and retention. Meanwhile, Co.'s Mackenzie Financial operations are also contributing to improved results with increased mutual fund sales primarily due to its relationships with the advisor sales channel and a strong team of portfolio managers.

Financial Data

(Can$ in Thousands)	3 Mos	12/31/2004	12/31/2003	12/31/2002	12/31/2001	12/31/2000	12/31/1999	12/31/1998
Earnings Per Share	2.28	2.24	2.03	1.85	1.05	1.35	1.12	0.89
Cash Flow Per Share	1.79	1.83	1.68	1.35	...	...	...	...
Tang Book Value Per Share	N.M.	N.M.	N.M.	N.M.	N.M.	5.23	4.59	4.03
Dividends Per Share	1.198	1.150	0.990	0.860	0.730	0.610	0.490	0.380
Dividend Payout %	52.52	51.34	48.70	46.56	69.72	45.12	43.75	42.70
Income Statement								
Total Revenue	573,096	2,119,071	1,874,181	1,940,036	1,784,165	1,197,108	1,014,720	929,481
Income Before Taxes	232,321	883,216	858,979	827,670	598,449	506,233	414,138	324,171
Income Taxes	71,170	264,969	299,198	317,401	252,994	222,208	178,525	135,827
Net Income	160,695	617,096	559,781	511,759	272,994	284,025	235,613	188,344
Average Shares	266,415	266,010	265,174	264,873	247,932	210,012	210,854	211,396
Balance Sheet								
Total Assets	6,548,001	6,473,211	6,291,696	5,986,952	6,122,468	1,985,212	1,811,958	1,798,944
Total Liabilities	3,331,023	2,965,610	3,070,928	3,036,997	3,444,224	888,927	845,091	948,016
Stockholders' Equity	3,216,978	3,507,601	3,220,768	2,949,955	2,678,244	1,096,285	966,867	850,928
Shares Outstanding	264,628	264,598	264,089	263,845	263,081	209,742	210,453	211,283
Statistical Record								
Return on Assets %	9.70	9.64	9.12	8.45	6.73	14.92	13.05	10.57
Return on Equity %	19.24	18.29	18.14	18.19	14.47	27.46	25.92	23.57
Price Range	39.45-31.96	36.64-30.71	31.87-23.60	32.59-21.90	26.75-18.20	27.85-13.90	26.40-17.15	28.00-17.50
P/E Ratio	17.30-14.02	16.36-13.71	15.70-11.63	17.62-11.84	25.48-17.33	20.63-10.30	23.57-15.31	31.46-19.66
Average Yield %	3.46	3.39	3.57	3.14	3.27	3.04	2.41	1.64

Address: One Canada Centre, 447 Portage Avenue, Winnipeg
Telephone: 204-943-0361
Web Site: www.investorsgroup.com

Officers: R. Jeffrey Orr - Pres., C.E.O. Gregory D. Tretiak - Exec. V.P., Fin. **Transfer Agents:** Computershare Trust Company of Canada, Toronto, Ontario; Canada.

Investor Contact: 204-956-8532
No of Institutions: 3
Shares: 816,900 **% Held:** 0.31

LEON'S FURNITURE LTD.

Exchange	Symbol	Price	52Wk Range	Yield	P/E
TSX	LNF	C$37.99 (5/31/2005)	42.39-31.30	2.11	15.57

*7 Year Price Score 123.61 *NYSE Composite Index=100 *12 Month Price Score 104.02

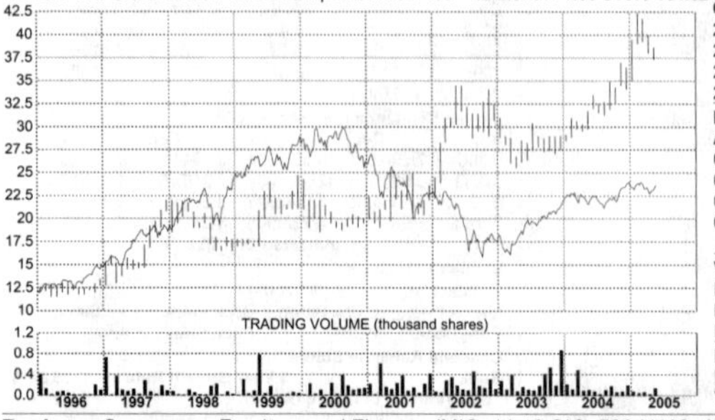

TRADING VOLUME (thousand shares)

Interim Earnings (Per Share) Can$

Qtr.	Mar	Jun	Sep	Dec
2002	0.34	0.35	0.53	0.71
2003	0.23	0.32	0.57	0.82
2004	0.39	0.40	0.73	0.90
2005	0.41	...	...	...

Interim Dividends (Per Share)

Amt	Decl	Ex	Rec	Pay
0.20Q	8/11/2004	9/13/2004	9/15/2004	10/15/2004
0.20Q	11/10/2004	12/10/2004	12/14/2004	1/14/2005
0.20Q	2/21/2005	3/2/2005	3/4/2005	4/6/2005
0.20Q	5/12/2005	6/6/2005	6/8/2005	7/8/2005

Indicated Div: C$0.80

Valuation Analysis

Forecast P/E N/A

Market Cap C$695.0 Million Book Value 254.2 Million

Price/Book 2.73 Price/Sales 1.35

Dividend Achiever Status

Rank 35 **5 Year Growth Rate** (3.44%)

Total Years of Dividend Growth 8

Business Summary: Furniture and Fixtures (MIC: 11.10 SIC: 599 NAIC: 37127)

Leon's Furniture is engaged in the manufacture and sale of furniture and other home furnishings. Co.'s product selection includes furniture, major appliances and consumer electronics. As of Dec 31, 2004, Co. had a total of 30 corporate and 27 franchise stores in Alberta, Saskatchewan, Manitoba, Ontario, Quebec, New Brunswick, Prince Edward Island, Nova Scotia and Newfoundland.

Recent Developments: For the three months ended Mar 31 2005, net income climbed 4.7% to C$7.8 million from C$7.5 million in the corresponding quarter a year earlier. Sales advanced 8.7% to C$113.6 million from C$104.5 million the year before. Same-store sales were up 3.3% year over year. Sales by franchisees rose 9.0% to C$34.5 million from C$31.6 million in 2005. Cost of sales, operating, administrative and selling expenses increased 8.8% to C$99.5 million from C$91.4 million a year earlier. Income before income taxes grew 4.2% to C$12.0 million from C$11.5 million the previous year.

Prospects: Top-line results are being positively affected by same-store sales growth and Co.'s aggressive marketing campaign, as well as the addition of sales from newly-opened stores. During the first quarter of 2005, Co. completed the renovation of its Windsor, Ontario store. Looking ahead, new warehouse showrooms are scheduled to open this summer in Quebec City and Hamilton, Ontario. Meanwhile, construction is expected to commence in 2005 on new stores located in Saskatoon, Saskatchewan and Vaughn, Ontario. In addition, Co. has secured properties in Newmarket, Ontario and the South Shore of Montreal for future stores.

Financial Data

(Can$ in Thousands)	3 Mos	12/31/2004	12/31/2003	12/31/2002	12/31/2001	12/31/2000	12/31/1999	12/31/1998
Earnings Per Share	2.44	2.41	1.94	1.93	1.79	1.78	1.73	1.27
Cash Flow Per Share	2.23	2.71	3.90	1.84	1.68	...	...	...
Tang Book Value Per Share	13.90	13.67	12.74	11.94	11.11	10.00	8.80	8.11
Dividends Per Share	0.74	0.68	0.48	0.96	0.400	1.130	0.81	0.27
Dividend Payout %	30.33	28.22	24.74	49.74	22.35	63.48	46.82	21.26
Income Statement								
Total Revenue	113,582	504,591	456,352	449,693	425,687	402,236	370,825	336,895
EBITDA	11,421	69,058	67,493	69,633	66,409	65,893	65,772	49,145
Depn & Amortn	163	1,404	9,881	8,552	7,742	6,933	6,401	5,649
Income Before Taxes	12,012	70,737	61,002	63,731	62,845	64,001	64,046	47,936
Income Taxes	4,186	24,633	22,150	25,211	26,522	27,301	27,880	21,530
Net Income	7,826	46,104	38,852	38,520	36,323	36,700	36,166	26,406
Average Shares	18,896	19,112	19,977	19,956	20,265	20,575	20,920	20,684
Balance Sheet								
Current Assets	165,674	191,814	180,277	179,845	171,906	167,145	168,556	156,584
Total Assets	341,094	368,121	334,578	320,439	295,675	280,656	268,581	245,270
Current Liabilities	70,014	100,976	96,867	87,605	77,414	78,232	90,232	81,325
Total Liabilities	86,845	118,254	96,969	87,804	77,553	78,311	90,268	81,353
Stockholders' Equity	254,249	249,867	237,609	232,635	218,122	202,345	178,313	163,197
Shares Outstanding	18,293	18,281	18,652	19,490	19,631	20,228	20,268	20,122
Statistical Record								
Return on Assets %	14.19	13.09	11.86	12.50	12.60	13.33	14.08	11.41
Return on Equity %	18.89	18.86	16.52	17.09	17.28	19.23	21.18	16.74
EBITDA Margin %	10.06	13.69	14.79	15.48	15.60	16.38	17.74	14.59
Net Margin %	6.89	9.14	8.51	8.57	8.53	9.12	9.75	7.84
Asset Turnover	1.57	1.43	1.39	1.46	1.48	1.46	1.44	1.46
Current Ratio	2.37	1.90	1.86	2.05	2.22	2.14	1.87	1.93
Price Range	42.39-29.50	37.00-28.40	31.00-25.50	34.50-22.20	25.00-19.00	24.25-18.50	24.70-17.00	22.00-16.50
P/E Ratio	17.37-12.09	15.35-11.78	15.98-13.14	17.88-11.50	13.97-10.61	13.62-10.39	14.28-9.83	17.32-12.99
Average Yield %	2.06	2.08	1.70	3.39	1.82	5.29	3.88	1.40

Address: 45 Gordon MacKay Road, P.O. Box 1100, Station "B", Weston
Telephone: 416-243-7880
Web Site: www.leons.ca

Officers: Anthony T. Leon - Chmn. Mark J. Leon - Vice-Chmn., C.E.O. **Transfer Agents:** CIBC Mellon Trust Co., Toronto, Ontario

No of Institutions: N/A
Shares: N/A **% Held:** N/A

LOBLAW COS. LTD.

Exchange	Symbol	Price	52Wk Range	Yield	P/E
TSX	L	C$72.51 (5/31/2005)	76.34-59.65	1.16	21.39

*7 Year Price Score 116.32 *NYSE Composite Index=100 *12 Month Price Score 105.31

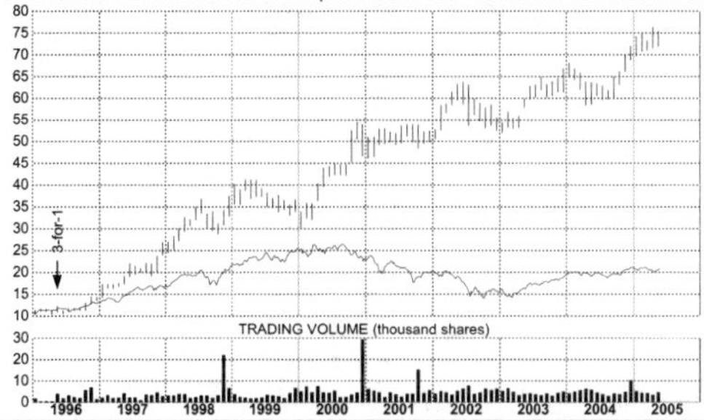

Interim Earnings (Per Share) Can$

Qtr.	Mar	Jun	Sep	Dec
2001	0.34	0.41	0.50	0.78
2002	0.46	0.53	0.68	0.95
2003	0.55	0.65	0.79	1.06
2004	0.64	0.71	0.94	1.22
2005	0.52	...	...	...

Interim Dividends (Per Share)

Amt	Decl	Ex	Rec	Pay
0.19Q	8/24/2004	9/13/2004	9/15/2004	10/1/2004
0.19Q	11/18/2004	12/13/2004	12/15/2004	12/30/2004
0.21Q	2/11/2005	3/11/2005	3/15/2005	4/1/2005
0.21Q	5/4/2005	6/13/2005	6/15/2005	7/1/2005

Indicated Div: C$0.84

Valuation Analysis

Forecast P/E	18.33 (6/4/2005)		
Market Cap	C$19.9 Billion	Book Value	5.1 Billion
Price/Book	3.88	Price/Sales	N/A

Dividend Achiever Status

Rank	4	5 Year Growth Rate	28.14%
Total Years of Dividend Growth			11

TRADING VOLUME (thousand shares)

Business Summary: Retail - General (MIC: 5.2 SIC: 399 NAIC: 52910)

Loblaw Companies is a holding company. Through its subsidiaries, Co. is engaged in food distribution and the provision of general merchandise products and services. Co. supplies the Canadian market through corporate, franchised and associated stores. The store network is supported by 32 warehouse facilities located across Canada. In addition, Co. makes available to consumers President's Choice financial services and products, including the President's Choice Financial MasterCard®, and PC Financial auto and home insurance, as well as a loyalty program.

Recent Developments: For the 12 weeks ended Mar 26 2005, net earnings were C$142.0 million compared with C$176.0 million in the corresponding year-earlier period. Results for 2005 included restructuring and other charges of C$55.0 million. Sales increased 7.9% to C$6.12 billion from C$5.68 billion the previous year. Same-store sales during the period increased 2.4%. Operating income amounted to C$259.0 million compared with C$306.0 million the year before. During the quarter ended Mar 26 2005, 14 new corporate and franchised stores were opened and 17 stores were closed resulting in a net increase of 400,000 square feet or 0.9%.

Prospects: Co. announced that it has commenced the reorganization of its supply chain network that will include the closure of a number of smaller, less efficient distribution centers over the next several years to be replaced by a network of significantly larger, more cost effective and productive facilities. Co. stated that the total restructuring cost to complete this initiative will be approximately $90.0 million, much of which will be recognized in 2005. Upon completion in late 2007, Co. expects to have a much more efficient supply chain network operating within a cost structure that provides significant annual savings to Co.

Financial Data

(Can$ in Thousands)	01/01/2005	01/03/2004	12/28/2002	12/29/2001	12/30/2000	01/01/2000	01/02/1999	01/03/1998
Earnings Per Share	3.51	3.05	2.62	2.03	1.70	1.37	1.06	0.88
Cash Flow Per Share	5.28	3.69	3.56	...	...	...	...	...
Tang Book Value Per Share	13.83	11.37	9.15	7.13	5.37	4.43	4.49	5.92
Dividends Per Share	0.760	0.600	0.480	0.400	0.350	0.220	0.200	0.150
Dividend Payout %	21.65	19.67	18.32	19.70	20.59	16.06	18.87	17.05
Income Statement								
Total Revenue	26,209,000	25,220,000	23,082,000	21,486,000	20,121,000	18,783,000	12,497,000	11,008,000
EBITDA	2,125,000	1,860,000	1,657,000	1,451,000	1,259,000	1,084,000	712,000	573,000
Depn & Amortn	473,000	393,000	354,000	315,000	283,000	273,000	183,000	147,000
Income Before Taxes	1,413,000	1,271,000	1,142,000	978,000	833,000	699,000	461,000	382,000
Income Taxes	445,000	426,000	414,000	372,000	317,000	280,000	199,000	169,000
Net Income	968,000	845,000	728,000	563,000	473,000	376,000	261,000	213,000
Average Shares	275,900	277,100	277,900	276,247	276,003	275,076	246,572	242,033
Balance Sheet								
Current Assets	3,451,000	3,485,000	3,526,000	3,086,000	2,916,000	2,415,000	2,249,000	1,681,000
Total Assets	13,046,000	12,177,000	11,110,000	10,008,000	9,025,000	7,979,000	7,105,000	4,013,000
Current Liabilities	3,213,000	3,114,000	3,154,000	2,796,000	3,207,000	2,812,000	2,956,000	1,479,000
Long-Term Obligations	3,935,000	3,956,000	3,420,000	3,333,000	2,377,000	1,979,000	1,364,000	915,000
Total Liabilities	7,632,000	7,445,000	6,986,000	6,439,000	5,901,000	5,075,000	4,510,000	2,518,000
Stockholders' Equity	5,414,000	4,732,000	4,124,000	3,569,000	3,124,000	2,904,000	2,595,000	1,495,000
Shares Outstanding	274,255	274,829	276,018	276,252	276,245	274,910	274,423	242,781
Statistical Record								
Return on Assets %	7.70	7.14	6.91	5.93	5.58	5.00	4.71	5.56
Return on Equity %	19.13	18.77	18.98	16.87	15.74	13.71	12.80	14.94
EBITDA Margin %	8.11	7.38	7.18	6.75	6.26	5.77	5.70	5.21
Net Margin %	3.69	3.35	3.15	2.62	2.35	2.00	2.09	1.93
Asset Turnover	2.08	2.13	2.19	2.26	2.37	2.50	2.25	2.87
Current Ratio	1.07	1.12	1.12	1.10	0.91	0.86	0.76	1.14
Debt to Equity	0.73	0.84	0.83	0.93	0.76	0.68	0.53	0.61
Price Range	72.02-58.40	67.85-51.95	63.81-50.50	54.05-46.10	54.50-30.30	41.25-33.00	37.50-24.50	26.85-14.75
P/E Ratio	20.52-16.64	22.25-17.03	24.35-19.27	26.63-22.71	32.06-17.82	30.11-24.09	35.38-23.11	30.51-16.76
Average Yield %	1.19	1.01	0.84	0.79	0.83	0.59	0.64	0.76

Address: 22 St. Clair Avenue East, Toronto
Telephone: 416-922-8500
Web Site: www.loblaw.com

Officers: W. Galen Weston - Chmn. John A. Lederer - Pres. **Transfer Agents:**
Computershare Trust Company of Canada, Toronto, Ontario, Canada

No of Institutions: 3
Shares: 176,098 **% Held:** 0.06

MELCOR DEVELOPMENTS LTD.

Exchange	Symbol	Price	52Wk Range	Yield	P/E
TSX	MRD	C$69.99 (5/31/2005)	69.99-44.50	2.14	11.44

***7 Year Price Score N/A** *NYSE Composite Index=100 ***12 Month Price Score 120.40**

TRADING VOLUME (thousand shares)

Interim Earnings (Per Share) Can$

Qtr.	Mar	Jun	Sep	Dec
2002	1.70	1.08	1.65	2.98
2003	1.18	0.71	2.07	1.90
2004	0.88	0.92	1.29	3.06
2005	0.85	...	...	...

Interim Dividends (Per Share)

Amt	Decl	Ex	Rec	Pay
0.55S	12/28/2003	12/10/2003	12/13/2003	12/30/2003
0.60S	4/28/2004	6/14/2004	6/16/2004	6/30/2004
0.60S	10/27/2004	12/13/2004	12/15/2004	12/30/2004
0.75S	5/3/2005	6/13/2005	6/15/2005	6/30/2005

Indicated Div: C$1.50

Valuation Analysis

Forecast P/E N/A

Market Cap C$209.6 Million Book Value 152.9 Million

Price/Book 1.37 Price/Sales 2.37

Dividend Achiever Status

Rank 23 **5 Year Growth Rate** 11.38%

Total Years of Dividend Growth 9

Business Summary: Property, Real Estate & Development (MIC: 8.3 SIC: 552 NAIC: 37210)

Melcor Developments is a real estate development company. Co. conducts business through four divisions. The Community Development division is engaged in the acquisition of land for development and sale for residential communities, multi-family sites and commercial sites. Co.'s development is concentrated in Alberta in the regions of Calgary, Edmonton, Red Deer and Lethbridge and the greater Tuscon, AZ area. The Property Development division develops income producing properties, which once completed and 75.0% leased, are transferred to the Investment Property division, which holds the properties as long-term investments. The Golf Courses division owns two public 18-hole golf courses.

Recent Developments: For the quarter ended Mar 31 2005, Co. reported net income decreased 6.4% to C$2.6 million compared with C$2.7 million in the corresponding period of the previous year. Revenues remained flat at C$15.6 million versus the prior-year quarter. On a segment basis, community development revenue fell 4.7% to C$12.3 million from C$12.8 million, while investment property revenue increased 20.5% to C$3.3 million from C$2.8 million in the year-earlier period. Recreation property revenue dropped 28.6% to C$15,000 from C$21,000 in 2003. General and administration expenses climbed 25.9% to C$2.2 million from C$1.8 million the year before.

Prospects: The real estate market in Co.'s territory remains strong as investment within Western Canada, aided by relatively low interest rates and high-energy prices, continue to stimulate the economy. Also, demand for Co.'s residential communities remains strong in all markets and leasing activity in new and existing properties is favorable. Meanwhile, Co. remains active in investigating real estate property acquisitions throughout Alberta and British Columbia's Okanagan Valley. During the first quarter of 2005, Co. acquired 145 acres of business industrial lands in Spruce Grove, Alberta, and obtained an option to acquire 120 acres of future residential land.

Financial Data

(Can$ in Thousands)	3 Mos	12/31/2004	12/31/2003	12/31/2002	12/31/2001	12/31/2000	12/31/1999	12/31/1998
Earnings Per Share	6.12	6.15	5.86	7.41	5.21	3.48	2.50	3.05
Cash Flow Per Share	5.66	7.86	6.05	9.21	5.81	...	...	...
Tang Book Value Per Share	51.07	50.27	45.65	41.45	35.04	30.57	27.57	25.83
Dividends Per Share	1.200	1.200	1.100	1.000	0.900	0.800	0.700	0.600
Dividend Payout %	19.61	19.51	18.77	13.50	17.27	22.99	28.00	19.67
Income Statement								
Total Revenue	15,593	88,339	80,035	110,565	82,607	61,221	46,563	57,661
EBITDA	3,713	28,223	26,203	35,253	24,258	17,144	12,454	16,276
Depn & Amortn	335	1,486	1,091	906	832	...	...	...
Income Before Taxes	3,730	28,323	27,501	36,063	24,842	18,293	14,112	17,613
Income Taxes	1,157	8,886	9,095	12,974	8,871	7,663	6,345	7,863
Net Income	2,573	19,437	18,406	23,089	15,971	10,630	7,767	9,659
Average Shares	...	3,161	3,139	3,115	3,065	...	...	...
Balance Sheet								
Current Assets	55,354	219,379	54,320	67,113	47,941	38,088	40,739	47,618
Total Assets	281,777	282,348	251,806	231,795	177,218	158,786	153,350	153,590
Current Liabilities	9,108	12,107	9,839	16,410	11,116	7,439	7,109	8,937
Long-Term Obligations	90,302	86,434	74,862	61,539	41,503	37,033	40,479	35,792
Total Liabilities	128,829	128,807	111,069	105,284	70,500	65,901	67,773	72,627
Stockholders' Equity	152,948	153,541	140,737	126,511	106,718	92,885	85,577	80,963
Shares Outstanding	2,994	3,054	3,082	3,052	3,045	3,038	3,104	3,134
Statistical Record								
Return on Assets %	7.27	7.26	7.61	11.29	9.51	6.79	5.06	6.86
Return on Equity %	12.99	13.17	13.77	19.80	16.00	11.88	9.33	12.51
EBITDA Margin %	23.81	31.95	32.74	31.88	29.37	28.00	26.75	28.23
Net Margin %	16.50	22.00	23.00	20.88	19.33	17.36	16.68	16.75
Asset Turnover	0.33	0.33	0.33	0.54	0.49	0.39	0.30	0.41
Current Ratio	6.08	18.12	5.52	4.09	4.31	5.12	5.73	5.33
Debt to Equity	0.59	0.56	0.53	0.49	0.39	0.40	0.47	0.44
Price Range	66.60-44.50	53.25-44.50	48.00-37.00	42.00-26.50	28.50-20.00	20.25-17.00	19.75-16.05	21.25-14.50
P/E Ratio	10.88-7.27	8.66-7.24	8.19-6.31	5.67-3.58	5.47-3.84	5.82-4.89	7.90-6.42	6.97-4.75
Average Yield %	2.36	2.52	2.73	2.86	3.72	4.41	3.93	3.31

Address: 900, 10310 Jasper Avenue, Edmonton
Telephone: 780-423-6931
Web Site: www.melcor.ca

Officers: Timothy C. Melton - Exec. Chmn. Ralph B. Young - Pres., C.E.O. **Transfer Agents:** CIBC Mellon Trust Company, Calgary and Toronto

No of Institutions: N/A
Shares: N/A **% Held:** N/A

METRO INC

Exchange	Symbol	Price	52Wk Range	Yield	P/E
TSX	MRU SVA	C$26.95 (5/31/2005)	29.00-17.30	1.48	14.65

Interim Earnings (Per Share) Can$

Qtr.	Dec	Mar	Jun	Sep
2001-02	0.29	0.30	0.45	0.36
2002-03	0.35	0.37	0.53	0.42
2003-04	0.38	0.36	0.51	0.47
2004-05	0.40	0.46	...	...

Interim Dividends (Per Share)

Amt	Decl	Ex	Rec	Pay
0.085Q	8/4/2004	8/12/2004	8/16/2004	8/31/2004
0.085Q	9/28/2004	11/4/2004	11/8/2004	11/29/2004
0.10Q	1/25/2005	2/4/2005	2/8/2005	3/1/2005
0.10Q	4/13/2005	5/5/2005	5/9/2005	5/30/2005

Indicated Div: C$0.40

Valuation Analysis

Forecast P/E	13.74 (6/1/2005)		
Market Cap	C$2.6 Billion	Book Value	897.5 Million
Price/Book	2.88	Price/Sales	0.42

Dividend Achiever Status

Rank	8	**5 Year Growth Rate**	21.20%
Total Years of Dividend Growth			9

Business Summary: Retail - Food & Beverage (MIC: 5.3 SIC: 141 NAIC: 24410)

Metro is a food retailer and distributor with operations focused in Quebec and Ontario. In addition, Co. is engaged in the distribution of pharmaceutical products and acts as a franchisor of the Brunet drugstores and Clini-Plus pharmacies. As of Sept 25 2004, Co. had a total of 445 stores.

Recent Developments: For the three months ended Mar 12 2005, net earnings increased 14.0% to C$44.7 million compared with C$39.2 million in the corresponding quarter of the previous year. Sales rose 4.1% to C$1.38 billion from C$1.32 billion in the year-earlier period, largely attributed to the purchase of 15 affiliated Metro supermarkets during the third quarter of the last fiscal year. Sales growth was partially offset by labor conflicts in corporate stores. Food sales rose 3.7% to C$1.26 billion, while pharmaceutical sales climbed 8.1% to C$120.0 million. Operating income advanced 10.6% to C$64.4 million versus C$58.2 million in 2004. Comparisons were made with restated prior-year figures.

Prospects: Despite continuing strong competition during the first half of the year, Co. merchandising strategies and retail investment program is enabling it to sustain sales growth in its food segment. Meanwhile, Co. is benefiting from major expansions and renovations that were completed in 13 stores, while nine new stores were opened. Co.'s ongoing conversion and new store opening program focused on the new Metro Plus store concept is seeing the opening of the 48th Metro Plus. Co. had 36 Metro Plus stores at the end of fiscal 2004, and expects to have 55 stores by the end of the current fiscal year.

Financial Data

(Can$ in Thousands)	6 Mos	3 Mos	09/25/2004	09/27/2003	09/28/2002	09/29/2001	09/30/2000	09/25/1999
Earnings Per Share	1.84	1.74	1.72	1.67	1.41	1.18	0.93	0.72
Cash Flow Per Share	2.44	2.08	3.18	2.00	2.26	N.A.	N.A.	N.A.
Tang Book Value Per Share	5.57	5.31	5.04	4.21	3.07	3.86	4.60	0.83
Dividends Per Share	0.355	0.340	0.325	0.265	0.210	0.172	0.145	0.125
Dividend Payout %	19.25	19.49	18.90	15.87	14.89	14.62	15.59	17.24
Income Statement								
Total Revenue	2,822,700	1,446,100	5,998,900	5,567,300	5,146,800	4,868,900	4,657,500	3,995,500
EBITDA	153,800	72,100	320,000	314,400	282,100	250,600	219,500	172,300
Depn & Amortn	34,300	17,000	71,700	64,900	57,600	61,400	52,500	44,300
Income Before Taxes	118,200	54,500	244,800	246,700	221,500	184,000	157,800	122,100
Income Taxes	34,900	15,900	76,000	80,400	77,800	61,200	60,500	45,700
Net Income	83,300	38,600	168,800	166,300	143,700	122,800	97,300	76,400
Average Shares	97,400	97,300	98,300	99,800	101,900	100,200	100,400	101,800
Balance Sheet								
Current Assets	591,200	673,600	607,300	647,800	556,600	504,500	421,800	382,800
Total Assets	1,579,000	1,648,200	1,560,000	1,507,100	1,329,100	1,186,000	1,059,700	996,200
Current Liabilities	592,600	683,800	623,900	678,700	568,100	492,100	447,600	425,000
Long-Term Obligations	10,600	10,600	9,400	8,800	25,000	55,300	88,600	144,200
Total Liabilities	681,500	771,000	707,900	755,200	684,900	628,000	598,000	603,900
Stockholders' Equity	897,500	877,200	852,100	751,900	644,200	558,000	461,700	392,300
Shares Outstanding	95,929	96,366	96,598	97,812	99,486	100,166	100,416	100,707
Statistical Record								
Return on Assets %	11.76	2.34	11.04	11.76	11.46	10.97	9.31	8.59
Return on Equity %	21.01	4.40	21.11	23.89	23.97	24.15	22.42	20.85
EBITDA Margin %	5.45	4.99	5.33	5.65	5.48	5.15	4.71	4.31
Net Margin %	2.95	2.67	2.81	2.99	2.79	2.52	2.09	1.91
Asset Turnover	4.07	3.80	3.92	3.94	4.10	4.35	4.46	4.49
Current Ratio	1.00	0.99	0.97	0.95	0.98	1.03	0.94	0.90
Debt to Equity	0.01	0.01	0.01	0.01	0.04	0.10	0.19	0.37
Price Range	28.10-17.30	23.34-17.30	22.25-17.30	20.00-16.10	22.20-16.95	18.50-9.25	9.85-7.47	11.50-8.63
P/E Ratio	15.27-9.40	13.41-9.94	12.94-10.06	11.98-9.64	15.74-12.02	15.68-7.84	10.59-8.04	15.97-11.98
Average Yield %	1.72	1.72	1.65	1.44	1.08	1.39	1.63	1.27

Address: 11011 Maurice-Duplessis Blvd., Montreal **Telephone:** 514-643-1055 **Web Site:** www.metro.ca	**Officers:** Maurice Jodoin - Chmn. Paul Gobeil - Vice-Chmn. **Transfer Agents:** National Bank Trust, Canada	**Investor Contact:** 514-643-1055 **No of Institutions:** N/A **Shares:** N/A **% Held:** N/A

NATIONAL BANK OF CANADA

Exchange	Symbol	Price	52Wk Range	Yield	P/E
TSX	NA	C$52.83 (5/31/2005)	55.24-42.31	3.33	11.61

***7 Year Price Score 135.86** *NYSE Composite Index=100 ***12 Month Price Score 105.83**

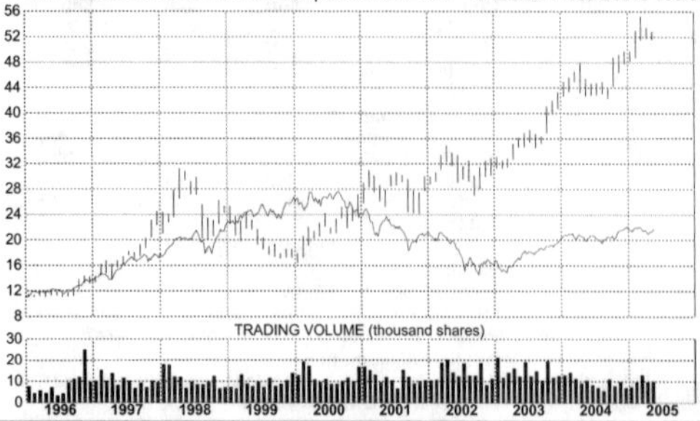

Interim Earnings (Per Share) Can$

Qtr.	Jan	Apr	Jul	Oct
2001-02	0.73	0.62	0.11	0.72
2002-03	0.88	0.72	0.88	0.86
2003-04	1.02	1.00	0.94	1.09
2004-05	1.37	1.15	...	...

Interim Dividends (Per Share)

Amt	Decl	Ex	Rec	Pay
0.38Q	8/26/2004	9/21/2004	9/23/2004	11/1/2004
0.42Q	12/2/2004	12/22/2004	12/27/2004	2/1/2005
0.42Q	2/22/2005	3/22/2005	3/24/2005	5/1/2005
0.44Q	5/26/2005	6/23/2005	6/27/2005	8/1/2005

Indicated Div: C$1.76

Valuation Analysis

Forecast P/E	11.71 (6/4/2005)		
Market Cap	C$8.8 Billion	Book Value	4.6 Billion
Price/Book	1.91	Price/Sales	1.78

Dividend Achiever Status

Rank	16	**5 Year Growth Rate**	15.20%
Total Years of Dividend Growth			9

Business Summary: Commercial Banking (MIC: 8.1 SIC: 021 NAIC: 22110)

National Bank of Canada is an integrated financial group. Co.'s Personal and Commercial segment comprises the branch network, intermediary services, credit cards, insurance, real estate and commercial banking services. Co.'s Wealth Management segment provides full-service retail brokerage, discount brokerage, mutual funds, trust services and portfolio management. Co.'s Financial Markets segment consists of corporate financing and lending, treasury operations, which include asset and liability management, and corporate brokerage. In addition, Co. has securitization operations. As of Oct 31 2004, Co. had assets of C$88.807 billion and total deposits of C$53.43 billion.

Recent Developments: For the second quarter ended Apr 30 2005, net income advanced 12.2% to C$202.0 million compared with C$180.0 million in the equivalent 2004 quarter. Net interest income climbed 16.6% to C$379.0 million from C$325.0 million a year earlier. Net income for the personal and commercial segment grew 16.1% to C$108.0 million, while net income for wealth management segment slid 3.1% to C$31.0 million. Net income from the financial markets segment increased 6.8% to C$63.0 million. Non-interest income decreased 6.8% to C$521.0 million versus C$559.0 million a year earlier, while non-interest expenses grew 3.7% to C$624.0 million. Provision for credit losses fell 94.7% to C$1.0 million.

Prospects: Co.'s Personal and Commercial segment growth is stemming from lower credit losses, particularly in the Commercial subsegment, while the Wealth Management segment is benefiting from revenue growth in full-service brokerage and private investment management, partially offset by lower portfolio management revenues. Moreover, Co.'s Financial Markets segment is benefiting from a decline in the provision for credit losses as well as gains in trading revenues and financial market fees for institutional brokerage activities. Going forward, Co. is stepping up the pace of investment in its technological infrastructure designed to create synergy within the banking network.

Financial Data

(Can$ in Thousands)	6 Mos	3 Mos	10/31/2004	10/31/2003	10/31/2002	10/31/2001	10/31/2000	10/31/1999
Earnings Per Share	4.55	4.39	4.05	3.34	2.18	2.76	2.52	2.21
Cash Flow Per Share	(38.05)	(14.75)	1.65	(26.57)	(7.85)	...	...	...
Tang Book Value Per Share	19.12	18.96	17.84	16.49	15.09	19.04	17.61	15.81
Dividends Per Share	1.600	1.510	1.420	1.080	0.930	0.820	0.750	0.700
Dividend Payout %	35.16	34.41	35.06	32.34	42.66	29.71	29.76	31.67
Income Statement								
Interest Income	1,450,000	716,000	2,605,000	2,529,000	2,591,000	3,381,000	3,856,000	3,493,000
Interest Expense	722,000	367,000	1,222,000	1,205,000	1,147,000	2,043,000	2,564,000	2,211,000
Net Interest Income	728,000	349,000	1,383,000	1,324,000	1,444,000	1,338,000	1,292,000	1,282,000
Provision for Losses	18,000	17,000	86,000	177,000	490,000	205,000	200,000	185,000
Non-Interest Income	389,420	420,000	2,117,000	1,989,000	1,531,000	1,703,000	1,737,000	1,120,000
Income Before Taxes	628,000	353,000	1,071,000	926,000	498,000	933,000	816,000	698,000
Income Taxes	173,000	107,000	318,000	277,000	150,000	278,000	259,000	238,000
Net Income	441,000	239,000	725,000	624,000	429,000	563,000	509,000	417,000
Average Shares	169,938	170,164	173,276	179,235	187,727	190,815	191,605	178,138
Balance Sheet								
Net Loans & Leases	50,389,000	47,860,000	41,498,000	42,336,000	40,812,000	44,469,000	46,739,000	43,891,000
Total Assets	99,917,000	91,703,000	88,807,000	82,423,000	74,611,000	75,763,000	75,827,000	69,801,000
Total Deposits	61,746,000	56,660,000	53,432,000	51,463,000	51,690,000	51,436,000	50,473,000	49,984,000
Total Liabilities	95,332,000	87,300,000	84,603,000	78,326,000	70,710,000	71,647,000	71,999,000	66,500,000
Stockholders' Equity	4,585,000	4,403,000	4,204,000	4,097,000	3,901,000	4,116,000	3,828,000	3,301,000
Shares Outstanding	165,744	168,049	167,430	174,619	182,596	190,331	189,474	188,728
Statistical Record								
Return on Assets %	0.87	0.90	0.84	0.79	0.57	0.74	0.70	0.59
Return on Equity %	18.42	18.12	17.42	15.60	10.70	14.17	14.24	13.91
Net Interest Margin %	51.63	48.74	53.09	52.35	55.73	39.57	33.51	36.70
Loans to Deposits	0.82	0.84	0.78	0.82	0.79	0.86	0.93	0.88
Price Range	55.24-42.31	49.75-42.31	48.78-40.17	41.19-29.39	34.93-24.12	31.00-23.00	25.25-16.40	26.25-17.15
P/E Ratio	12.14-9.30	11.33-9.64	12.04-9.92	12.33-8.80	16.02-11.06	11.23-8.33	10.02-6.51	11.88-7.76
Average Yield %	3.39	3.32	3.23	3.14	3.07	2.98	3.62	3.28

Address: National Bank Tower, 600 de La Gauchetiere West, 8th Floor, Montreal
Telephone: 514-394-5000
Web Site: www.nbc.ca

Officers: Real Raymond - Pres., C.E.O. Jean Turmel - Pres., Finl. Markets, Treasury, Invest. Bank **Transfer Agents:**National Bank Trust Inc.

Investor Contact: 514-394-6433
No of Institutions: 6
Shares: 1,045,545 **% Held:** 0.62

POWER CORP. OF CANADA

Exchange	Symbol	Price	52Wk Range	Yield	P/E
TSX	POW SV	C$31.31 (5/31/2005)	32.44-25.57	2.16	14.98

*7 Year Price Score 134.66 *NYSE Composite Index=100 *12 Month Price Score 102.78

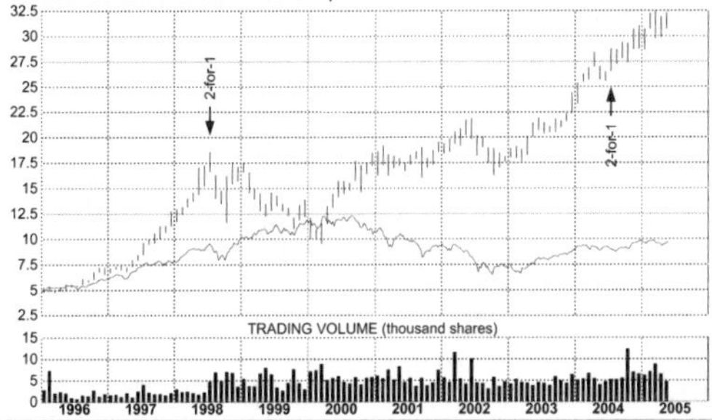

2-for-1

2-for-1

TRADING VOLUME (thousand shares)

Interim Earnings (Per Share) Can$

Qtr.	Mar	Jun	Sep	Dec
2002	0.37	0.41	0.28	0.32
2003	0.35	0.47	1.49	0.43
2004	0.45	0.60	0.49	0.49
2005	0.50	...	...	...

Interim Dividends (Per Share)

Amt	Decl	Ex	Rec	Pay
0.144Q	7/30/2004	9/2/2004	9/7/2004	9/30/2004
0.144Q	11/11/2004	12/6/2004	12/8/2004	12/31/2004
0.144Q	2/25/2005	3/8/2005	3/10/2005	3/31/2005
0.169Q	5/10/2005	6/7/2005	6/9/2005	6/30/2005

Indicated Div: C$0.68

Valuation Analysis

Forecast P/E	13.29 (6/1/2005)		
Market Cap	C$12.5 Billion	Book Value	6.7 Billion
Price/Book	1.86	Price/Sales	0.49

Dividend Achiever Status

Rank	14	5 Year Growth Rate	17.81%
Total Years of Dividend Growth			9

Business Summary: Other Depository Banking (MIC: 8.5 SIC: 099 NAIC: 51112)

Power Corp. of Canada is holding company whose principal asset is a 66.4% interest in Power Financial Corp. as of Dec 31 2004, which in turn holds controling interests in Great-West Lifeco Inc. (Lifeco) and IGM Financial Inc. Lifeco offers a range of life and health insurance, retirement and investment products, as well as reinsurance and specialty general insurance products. IGM Financial offers financial planning services and investment products, as well as investment advisory, management and administrative services for mutual funds. Co. also holds interest in Pargesa Holdings S.A., which holds interests in media, entertainment, energy, water, waste services, and specialty minerals.

Recent Developments: For the quarter ended Mar 31 2005, net earnings advanced 12.1% to C$232.0 million compared with C$207.0 million in the corresponding period of the previous year. Results for 2005 and 2004 included financing charges of C$86.0 million and C$90.0 million, respectively. Total revenues advanced 20.4% to C$7.09 billion from C$5.89 billion a year earlier. Premium income climbed 32.7% to C$4.53 billion from C$3.41 billion in 2004. Net investment income declined 4.1% to C$1.34 billion, while fees and media income grew 13.1% to C$1.22 billion. Total expenses grew 21.8% to C$6.29 billion from C$5.17 billion the year before.

Prospects: Growth in operating earnings reflects an increase in the contribution from subsidiaries, driven by the operating results at Power Financial Corporation, partly offset by a decrease in results from corporate activities. At Power Financial Corporation, growth in operating earnings reflects an increase in operating earnings of its subsidiaries and affiliate. Meanwhile, restructuring costs related to the acquisition of Canada Life Financial Corporation incurred for the three months ended Mar 31 2005 were $39.0 million. Of the $448.0 million total estimated restructuring costs, $384.0 million of these costs have been utilized with the remaining $64.0 million expected to be utilized in 2005.

Financial Data

(Can$ in Thousands)	3 Mos	12/31/2004	12/31/2003	12/31/2002	12/31/2001	12/31/2000	12/31/1999	12/31/1998
Earnings Per Share	2.09	2.03	2.74	1.38	1.35	1.47	1.18	0.94
Cash Flow Per Share	7.80	7.68	5.90	4.16	N.A.	N.A.	N.A.	N.A.
Tang Book Value Per Share	N.M.	N.M.	13.88	12.16	10.82	8.90	8.23	7.77
Dividends Per Share	0.575	0.553	0.469	0.397	0.338	0.287	0.244	0.219
Dividend Payout %	27.58	27.25	17.11	28.76	25.09	19.62	20.66	23.27
Income Statement								
Total Revenue	7,091,000	24,323,000	15,747,000	19,017,000	18,360,000	16,906,000	14,739,000	15,055,000
Income Before Taxes	802,000	3,266,000	3,509,000	2,222,000	2,022,000	1,994,000	1,707,000	1,441,000
Income Taxes	221,000	837,000	837,000	764,000	663,000	755,000	547,000	492,000
Net Income	232,000	949,000	1,268,000	645,000	618,000	657,000	533,000	420,000
Average Shares	452,900	452,400	452,200	451,600	450,000	440,312	...	...
Balance Sheet								
Total Assets	107,089,000	105,940,000	107,723,000	70,136,000	68,730,000	60,564,000	57,652,000	58,925,000
Total Liabilities	91,002,000	87,829,000	91,210,000	57,188,000	57,161,000	51,149,000	48,781,000	50,599,000
Stockholders' Equity	6,734,000	6,602,000	6,042,000	5,387,000	4,692,000	3,938,000	3,450,000	3,145,000
Shares Outstanding	399,046	396,091	393,859	395,408	393,362	391,920	393,032	395,796
Statistical Record								
Return on Assets %	0.90	0.89	1.43	0.93	0.96	1.11	0.91	0.73
Return on Equity %	15.03	14.97	22.19	12.80	14.32	17.74	16.16	14.52
Net Margin %	3.27	3.90	8.05	3.39	3.37	3.89	3.62	2.79
Price Range	32.44-25.57	31.00-23.32	24.45-17.60	21.93-16.27	19.55-16.00	18.52-9.55	17.55-11.00	18.60-11.63
P/E Ratio	15.52-12.24	15.27-11.49	8.92-6.42	15.89-11.79	14.48-11.85	12.60-6.50	14.87-9.32	19.79-12.37
Average Yield %	2.01	2.03	2.29	2.07	1.90	2.02	1.79	1.47

Address: 751 Victoria Square, Montreal
Telephone: 514-286-7425
Web Site: www.powercorporation.com

Officers: Paul Desmarais Jr., OC - Chmn., Co-C.E.O. Andre Desmarais OC - Pres., Co-C.E.O. **Transfer Agents:** Computershare Trust Company of Canada, Toronto, Montreal, and Vancouver

No of Institutions: 4
Shares: 1,317,204 **% Held:** 0.33

POWER FINANCIAL CORP

Exchange	Symbol	Price	52Wk Range	Yield	P/E
TSX	PWF	C$32.36 (5/31/2005)	34.69-26.38	2.69	14.91

***7 Year Price Score 139.19** *NYSE Composite Index=100 ***12 Month Price Score 103.68**

Interim Earnings (Per Share) Can$

Qtr.	Mar	Jun	Sep	Dec
2002	0.33	0.41	0.28	0.33
2003	0.34	0.44	1.58	0.42
2004	0.46	0.59	0.52	0.54
2005	0.52	...	...	...

Interim Dividends (Per Share)

Amt	Decl	Ex	Rec	Pay
0.183Q	7/30/04	9/28/04	9/30/04	11/1/04
0.203Q	11/11/04	12/29/04	12/31/04	2/1/05
0.203Q	3/22/05	4/6/05	4/8/05	4/29/05
0.218Q	5/9/05	6/28/05	6/30/05	8/1/05

Indicated Div: C$0.87

Valuation Analysis

Forecast P/E	13.55 (6/4/05)		
Market Cap	C$22.8 Billion	Book Value	8.8 Billion
Price/Book	2.58	Price/Sales	0.91

Dividend Achiever Status

Rank	12	**5 Year Growth Rate**	19.14%
Total Years of Dividend Growth			12

Business Summary: Insurance (MIC: 8.2 SIC: 311 NAIC: 24113)

Power Financial is a holding company. Through its subsidiaries, Co. is engaged in the following activities: media and entertainment, energy, water, waste services and specialty minerals operations in Europe; providing financial products, benefit plan solutions and services to individuals and corporations in Canada, the U.S. and Europe; savings and investment, retirement income and individual life insurance products and mortgages in Canada, reinsurance products in the U.S. and Europe; the provision of health care, life and disability insurance, annuities, and retirement savings plans and services; and the management and distribution of mutual funds and other managed asset products.

Recent Developments: For the three months ended Mar 31 2005, net earnings climbed 13.1% to C$379.0 million compared with C$335.0 million in the corresponding period of the previous year. Results included pre-tax restructuring charges of C$7.0 million and C$9.0 million in 2005 and 2004, respectively. Revenues advanced 21.9% to C$6.99 billion from C$5.80 billion in the year-earlier period. Premium income jumped 32.7% to C$4.53 billion from C$3.41 billion the year before, while net investment income decreased 4.3% to C$1.33 billion from C$1.39 billion the prior year. Fee income rose 13.0% to C$1.13 billion from C$1.00 billion in 2004.

Prospects: Co. remains on track with restructuring and integrating the operations of Canada Life Financial with its wholly-owned subsidiaries The Great-West Life Assurance Company, London Life Insurance Company and Great-West Life & Annuity Insurance Company. Costs are expected to be incurred as a result and consist primarily of exit and consolidation activities involving operations, facilities, systems and compensation costs. Further, selected administrative functions, facilities and systems are being restructured and integrated with Great-West and London Life. These activities are expected to be completed by the end of 2005.

Financial Data

(Can$ in Thousands)	3 Mos	12/31/2004	12/31/2003	12/31/2002	12/31/2001	12/31/2000	12/31/1999	12/31/1998
Earnings Per Share	2.17	2.11	2.78	1.34	1.21	1.09	1.16	0.94
Cash Flow Per Share	4.94	4.87	3.64	2.53	...	...	...	...
Tang Book Value Per Share	N.M.	N.M.	N.M.	1.05	0.41	6.36	5.64	5.23
Dividends Per Share	0.730	0.730	0.603	0.520	0.440	0.362	0.301	0.250
Dividend Payout %	33.64	34.60	21.67	38.81	36.51	33.26	25.97	26.74
Income Statement								
Total Revenue	6,987,000	23,922,000	15,369,000	18,620,000	17,889,000	16,531,000	14,424,000	14,767,000
Income Before Taxes	812,000	3,304,000	3,569,000	2,198,000	1,953,000	1,756,000	1,704,000	1,449,000
Income Taxes	220,000	832,000	850,000	749,000	642,000	665,000	535,000	483,000
Net Income	379,000	1,558,000	2,023,000	988,000	879,000	786,000	834,000	678,000
Average Shares	707,700	706,300	703,600	703,200	703,400	693,333	693,558	...
Balance Sheet								
Total Assets	105,344,000	104,179,000	105,960,000	68,319,000	67,069,000	59,354,000	56,647,000	58,033,000
Total Liabilities	90,759,000	87,536,000	90,865,000	56,843,000	56,767,000	50,905,000	48,592,000	50,411,000
Stockholders' Equity	8,832,000	8,984,000	8,137,000	6,855,000	5,828,000	4,963,000	4,462,000	4,172,000
Shares Outstanding	704,813	704,813	696,833	693,713	693,403	694,107	693,672	693,160
Statistical Record								
Return on Assets %	1.50	1.48	2.32	1.46	1.39	1.35	1.45	1.20
Return on Equity %	18.51	18.15	26.99	15.58	16.29	16.63	19.32	17.72
Net Margin %	5.42	6.51	13.16	5.31	4.91	4.75	5.78	4.59
Price Range	34.69-26.38	31.99-24.50	25.13-18.15	21.63-15.93	19.30-15.50	17.60-9.55	17.70-10.50	18.45-11.44
P/E Ratio	15.99-12.16	15.16-11.61	9.04-6.53	16.14-11.88	15.95-12.81	16.15-8.76	15.26-9.05	19.63-12.17
Average Yield %	2.47	2.59	2.83	2.76	2.59	2.67	2.21	1.69

Address: 751 Victoria Square, Montreal **Telephone:** 514-286-7425 **Web Site:** www.powerfinancial.com	**Officers:** Paul Desmarais Jr. - Chmn. Andre Desmarais - Dep. Chmn. **Transfer Agents:** Computershare Trust Company of Canada, Toronto, Ontario; Montreal, Quebec; and Winnipeg, Manitoba	**No of Institutions:** 2 **Shares:** 615,375 **% Held:** 0.09

ROTHMANS INC.

Exchange	Symbol	Price	52Wk Range	Yield	P/E
TSX	ROC	C$26.30 (5/31/2005)	26.60-15.65	4.56	19.20

***7 Year Price Score 120.97** *NYSE Composite Index=100 ***12 Month Price Score 121.75**

TRADING VOLUME (thousand shares)

Interim Earnings (Per Share) Can$

Qtr.	Jun	Sep	Dec	Mar
2001-02	0.23	0.36	0.37	0.41
2002-03	0.34	0.35	0.32	0.31
2003-04	0.28	0.42	0.39	0.26
2004-05	0.35	0.39	0.38	0.25

Interim Dividends (Per Share)

Amt	Decl	Ex	Rec	Pay
0.30Q	2/4/2005	3/2/2005	3/4/2005	3/17/2005
100%	2/4/2005	3/2/2005	3/4/2005	3/17/2005
0.30Q	5/20/2005	6/1/2005	6/3/2005	6/17/2005
1.50Sp	5/20/2005	6/1/2005	6/3/2005	6/17/2005

Indicated Div: C$1.20

Valuation Analysis

Forecast P/E	18.70 (6/1/2005)		
Market Cap	C$1.8 Billion	Book Value	196.4 Million
Price/Book	9.04	Price/Sales	2.81

Dividend Achiever Status

Rank	18	**5 Year Growth Rate**	14.14%
Total Years of Dividend Growth			5

Business Summary: Retail - Alcohol & Tobacco (MIC: 5.4 SIC: 194 NAIC: 24940)

Rothmans is a tobacco company. Through its 60.0% owned subsidiary Rothmans, Benson & Hedges Inc. (RBH), Co. is engaged in manufacturing and distribution of tobacco products in Canada. Co.'s products include roll-your-own tobacco products and other tobacco products. Co. produces 140 different cigarette products in different sizes, strengths and package formats. Co.'s brands include Benson & Hedges, Craven A, Rothmans, Belvedere, Number 7, Mark Ten, Viscount, Belmont, Canadian Classics, Dunhill and the Captain Black cigar line.

Recent Developments: For the year ended Mar 31 2005, net earnings rose 3.0% to C$93.0 million compared with C$90.3 million in the previous year. Total revenues increased 2.7% to C$641.0 million from C$623.9 million the year before. Sales, net of excise duty and taxes, grew 2.6% to C$636.8 million from C$620.1 million, primarily due to higher volumes in the cigarette price category, combined with increased prices across all product categories. Investment income increased 10.1% to C$4.2 million from C$3.8 million in 2004. Operating costs excluding amortization rose 1.9% to C$362.6 million from C$355.9 million in the prior year.

Prospects: For fiscal 2006, Co. expects continued volatility in the market as a result of buying patterns, higher taxes and the presence of contraband in the marketplace. Co. will continue to monitor the growth of the contraband market, which it expects to continue to adversely impact legitimate industry stakeholders including Rothmans, Benson & Hedges (RBH). Meanwhile, Co. will continue to seek opportunities for growth through an international tobacco acquisition and continues to assess alternative strategies for utilizing the cash provided by RBH. Furthermore, Co. will reassess its cash reserve position periodically, in the context of its stated acquisition strategy.

Financial Data

(Can$ in Thousands)	9 Mos	6 Mos	3 Mos	03/31/2004	03/31/2003	03/31/2002	03/31/2001	03/31/2000
Earnings Per Share	1.37	1.38	1.41	1.34	1.29	1.37	1.08	0.96
Cash Flow Per Share	2.36	2.38	2.73	3.35	2.06	...	...	...
Tang Book Value Per Share	2.91	2.78	2.63	2.50	1.94	3.82	3.07	2.53
Dividends Per Share	0.969	0.938	0.875	0.813	3.250	0.637	0.550	0.500
Dividend Payout %	70.86	68.14	62.04	60.63	251.94	46.53	50.93	52.08
Income Statement								
Total Revenue	495,561	330,270	162,689	623,943	580,880	579,807	541,875	534,951
EBITDA	224,513	149,412	72,076	268,082	254,569	247,587	205,139	186,677
Depn & Amortn	6,920	4,322	2,127	9,880	7,548	...	...	...
Income Before Taxes	212,959	141,951	68,346	252,683	240,197	245,249	205,484	186,480
Income Taxes	86,248	57,614	27,956	101,585	95,312	100,758	86,650	80,361
Net Income	75,692	50,249	23,842	90,277	86,678	91,484	71,464	63,457
Average Shares	67,924	67,807	67,655	67,377	67,094	66,712	...	...
Balance Sheet								
Current Assets	416,246	428,526	412,056	417,964	353,086	456,596	333,843	310,827
Total Assets	502,652	510,549	494,521	496,757	429,965	526,944	403,239	381,961
Current Liabilities	119,436	139,242	133,275	144,786	110,964	87,494	109,151	143,649
Long-Term Obligations	150,000	150,000	150,000	150,000	150,000	150,000	...	...
Total Liabilities	306,230	322,684	317,141	328,260	299,428	273,670	199,963	214,658
Stockholders' Equity	196,422	187,865	177,380	168,497	130,537	253,274	203,276	167,303
Shares Outstanding	67,544	67,554	67,425	67,351	67,162	66,218	66,128	66,128
Statistical Record								
Return on Assets %	19.32	18.74	21.67	19.43	18.12	19.67	18.20	17.30
Return on Equity %	51.32	54.46	60.37	60.21	45.17	40.08	38.57	41.60
EBITDA Margin %	45.30	45.24	44.30	42.97	43.82	42.70	37.86	34.90
Net Margin %	15.27	15.21	14.65	14.47	14.92	15.78	13.19	11.86
Asset Turnover	1.32	1.28	1.46	1.34	1.21	1.25	1.38	1.46
Current Ratio	3.49	3.08	3.09	2.89	3.18	5.22	3.06	2.16
Debt to Equity	0.76	0.80	0.85	0.89	1.15	0.59	...	...
Price Range	19.95-13.76	17.93-12.23	17.50-12.19	17.41-11.36	17.13-11.61	16.38-11.00	12.28-6.88	17.08-6.80
P/E Ratio	14.56-10.04	12.99-8.86	12.41-8.64	12.99-8.47	13.28-9.00	11.95-8.03	11.37-6.37	17.80-7.08
Average Yield %	5.76	5.96	5.98	5.99	21.50	4.74	5.86	3.91

Address: 1500 Don Mills Road, Toronto
Telephone: 416-449-5525
Web Site: www.rothmansinc.ca

Officers: Joseph J. Heffernan B.Sc. - Chmn. John R. Barnett C.A. - Pres., C.E.O. **Transfer Agents:** CIBC Mellon Trust Company

Investor Contact: 416-442-3483
No of Institutions: 2
Shares: 96,900 **% Held:** 0.14

ROYAL BANK OF CANADA (MONTREAL, QUEBEC)

Exchange	Symbol	Price	52Wk Range	Yield	P/E
TSX	RY	C$75.00 (5/31/2005)	77.00-58.50	3.25	15.50

***7 Year Price Score 115.80** *NYSE Composite Index=100 ***12 Month Price Score 111.06**

Interim Earnings (Per Share) Can$

Qtr.	Jan	Apr	Jul	Oct
2001-02	1.04	1.01	1.02	0.86
2002-03	1.10	0.99	1.14	1.15
2003-04	1.19	1.16	1.15	0.74
2004-05	1.58	1.37	...	...

Interim Dividends (Per Share)

Amt	Decl	Ex	Rec	Pay
0.52Q	8/27/2004	10/22/2004	10/26/2004	11/24/2004
0.55Q	11/30/2004	1/24/2005	1/26/2005	2/24/2005
0.55Q	2/25/2005	4/21/2005	4/25/2005	5/24/2005
0.61Q	5/27/2005	7/22/2005	7/26/2005	8/24/2005

Indicated Div: C$2.44

Valuation Analysis

Forecast P/E	12.93 (6/7/2005)		
Market Cap	C$48.4 Billion	Book Value	19.5 Billion
Price/Book	2.48	Price/Sales	2.12

Dividend Achiever Status

Rank	15	**5 Year Growth Rate**	16.53%
Total Years of Dividend Growth			10

Business Summary: Commercial Banking (MIC: 8.1 SIC: 029 NAIC: 22110)

Royal Bank of Canada is engaged in personal and commercial banking (RBC Banking), wealth management (RBC Investments), insurance (RBC Insurance), corporate and investment banking (RBC Capital Markets) and transaction processing (RBC Global Services). In the U.S., Co. provides personal and commercial banking, mortgage origination, insurance, full-service brokerage and corporate and investment banking services through RBC Centura and its subsidiaries RBC Mortgage and RBC Builder Finance, as well as through RBC Insurance, RBC Dain Rauscher and RBC Capital Markets. As of Oct 31 2004, Co. had total assets of C$447.68 billion, loans of C$175.70 billion and deposits of C$271.58 billion.

Recent Developments: For the second quarter ended Apr 30 2005, net income advanced 19.3% to C$907.0 million compared with C$760.0 million in the equivalent 2004 quarter. Results for 2005 included a business realignment charge of C$4.0 million. Net interest income increased 13.0% to C$1.78 billion from C$1.58 billion a year earlier. Interest income grew 23.2% to C$4.08 billion, while interest expense jumped 32.6% to C$2.30 billion. Provision for credit losses declined 22.1% to C$116.0 million from C$149.0 million in 2004. Non-interest income inched 0.7% higher to C$2.95 billion, while non-interest expense slipped 0.9% to C$2.72 billion.

Prospects: Overall, Co.'s results are benefiting from an expanding North American economy resulting in increasing demand for consumer and business loans and related financial products. However, continuing uncertainty concerning the sustainability of U.S. economic growth alongside rising interest rates and energy prices, widening credit spreads and deterioration in the auto sector is adversely affecting the performance of some of Co.'s capital market businesses. Separately, Co. recently introduced a new Starbucks® Duetto Visa card in Canada and launched two new term life insurance products. Meanwhile, Co.'s Global Private Banking business expanded with a new office in San Francisco.

Financial Data

(Can$ in Thousands)	3 Mos	10/31/2004	10/31/2003	10/31/2002	10/31/2001	10/31/2000	10/31/1999	10/31/1998
Earnings Per Share	4.62	4.23	4.39	3.93	3.55	3.40	2.48	2.65
Cash Flow Per Share	(9.41)	1.15	(11.44)	(4.49)	(9.05)	...	...	...
Tang Book Value Per Share	20.75	19.36	18.87	17.39	15.79	17.26	15.82	15.78
Dividends Per Share	2.110	2.020	1.720	1.520	1.380	1.140	0.940	0.880
Dividend Payout %	45.70	47.75	39.18	38.68	38.87	33.53	37.90	33.21
Income Statement								
Interest Income	3,857,000	13,776,000	14,053,000	14,672,000	17,307,000	16,109,000	14,200,000	14,776,000
Interest Expense	2,086,000	7,083,000	7,411,000	7,514,000	10,810,000	10,830,000	9,083,000	9,712,000
Net Interest Income	1,771,000	6,693,000	6,642,000	7,158,000	6,497,000	5,279,000	5,117,000	5,064,000
Non-Interest Income	2,098,000	8,438,000	7,378,000	5,355,000	5,499,000	4,192,000	3,544,000	3,485,000
Income Before Taxes	1,540,000	4,220,000	4,592,000	4,235,000	3,892,000	3,640,000	2,707,000	3,075,000
Income Taxes	466,000	1,232,000	1,460,000	1,365,000	1,350,000	1,412,000	974,000	1,175,000
Net Income	1,041,000	2,817,000	3,005,000	2,762,000	2,435,000	2,208,000	1,725,000	1,824,000
Average Shares	649,616	655,508	669,016	678,120	647,216	609,865	632,304	633,626
Balance Sheet								
Net Loans & Leases	177,875,000	186,543,000	170,394,000	169,258,000	178,822,000	165,941,000	152,166,000	198,449,000
Total Assets	452,318,000	429,196,000	403,033,000	376,956,000	362,483,000	294,054,000	273,298,000	274,399,000
Total Deposits	280,351,000	270,959,000	259,145,000	243,486,000	235,687,000	206,237,000	187,897,000	180,005,000
Total Liabilities	432,831,000	410,992,000	384,658,000	358,173,000	344,278,000	280,757,000	260,890,000	262,507,000
Stockholders' Equity	19,487,000	18,204,000	18,375,000	18,783,000	18,205,000	13,297,000	12,408,000	11,892,000
Shares Outstanding	644,824	644,747	656,021	665,257	674,020	602,398	617,768	617,581
Statistical Record								
Return on Assets %	0.68	0.68	0.77	0.75	0.74	0.78	0.63	0.70
Return on Equity %	16.23	15.36	16.17	14.93	15.46	17.13	14.20	16.37
Net Interest Margin %	45.92	48.58	47.26	48.79	37.54	32.77	36.04	34.27
Loans to Deposits	0.63	0.69	0.66	0.70	0.76	0.80	0.81	1.10
Price Range	65.59-58.50	65.59-58.50	64.90-53.70	58.70-46.56	53.02-42.75	48.30-27.75	41.88-30.15	45.65-29.10
P/E Ratio	14.20-12.66	15.51-13.83	14.78-12.23	14.94-11.85	14.94-12.04	14.21-8.16	16.89-12.16	17.23-10.98
Average Yield %	3.42	3.28	2.93	2.90	2.85	3.11	2.68	2.23

Address: Royal Bank Plaza, 200 Bay Street, Toronto **Telephone:** 416-974-5151 **Web Site:** www.rbc.com	**Officers:** David P. O'Brien - Chmn. Gordon M. Nixon - Pres., C.E.O. **Transfer Agents:** The Bank of New York, New York, NY	**Investor Contact:** 416-955-7803 **No of Institutions:** 94 **Shares:** 156,160,944 **% Held:** 24.22

SAPUTO INC

Exchange	Symbol	Price	52Wk Range	Yield	P/E
TSX	SAP	C$37.80 (5/31/2005)	38.15-31.14	1.59	17.34

Interim Earnings (Per Share) Can$

Qtr.	Jun	Sep	Dec	Mar
2001-02	0.39	0.40	0.34	0.41
2002-03	0.40	0.40	0.41	0.45
2003-04	0.44	0.56	0.47	0.56
2004-05	0.55	0.53	0.55	...

Interim Dividends (Per Share)

Amt	Decl	Ex	Rec	Pay
0.12Q	6/8/2004	6/21/2004	6/23/2004	7/9/2004
0.15Q	8/4/2004	8/17/2004	8/19/2004	9/3/2004
0.15Q	11/3/2004	11/17/2004	11/19/2004	12/3/2004
0.15Q	2/3/2005	2/16/2005	2/18/2005	3/4/2005

Indicated Div: C$0.60

Valuation Analysis

Forecast P/E	15.54 (6/1/2005)		
Market Cap	C$3.9 Billion	Book Value	1.3 Billion
Price/Book	3.12	Price/Sales	1.01

Dividend Achiever Status

Rank	2	**5 Year Growth Rate**	35.10%
Total Years of Dividend Growth			6

Business Summary: Retail - Food & Beverage (MIC: 5.3 SIC: 143 NAIC: 24430)

Saputo is engaged in the manufacturing and distributing of cheese, and other dairy products such as lactose and whey protein across Canada and the United States. Co.'s business divisions are: the Dairy Products Division in Canada; Dairy Products Division in Argentina; the Cheese Division (USA); and the Bakery Division. In Canada, Co. distributes an assortment of non-dairy products to complement the cheese offerings. Co. also produces by-products such as lactose, whey powder and whey protein, ice cream mixes to clients in Canada, Europe, South America, Asia and Africa.

Recent Developments: For the quarter ended Dec 31 2004, net income advanced 16.5% to C$58.3 million compared with C$50.0 million in the corresponding prior-year period. Revenues grew 5.6% to C$942.2 million from C$892.0 million a year earlier. The improvement in revenues was primarily attributed to increased sales volumes in Co.'s Canadian and Other Dairy Products sector. However, revenues from Co.'s U.S. Dairy Products sector decreased mainly due to the appreciation of the Canadian dollar, which eroded C$22.0 million in revenues compared with the same period last year. Further, revenues from Co.'s Grocery Products sector decreased year over year. Operating income climbed 2.0% to C$80.4 million.

Prospects: Looking ahead, results could benefit from Co.'s recent acquisition activity. On May 16 2005, Co. announced that it has entered into an agreement to acquire Schneider Cheese, Inc., a U.S. manufacturer of string cheese and cheese sticks, for US$23.9 million in cash. Separately, on Apr 18 2005, Co. announced that it has completed the acquisition of the manufacturing, marketing and distribution activities of Fromage Cote S.A. and Distributions Kingsey Inc. for their pressed cheddar and cheddar cheese curd, Swiss-type cheese and other specialty cheeses sold under the brand names Kingsey, Princesse, Sir Laurier d'Arthabaska and Du Village de Warwick. The purchase price was C$52.9 million in cash.

Financial Data

(Can$ in Thousands)	9 Mos	6 Mos	3 Mos	03/31/2004	03/31/2003	03/31/2002	03/31/2001	03/31/2000
Earnings Per Share	2.18	2.10	2.13	2.03	1.66	1.54	1.07	0.94
Cash Flow Per Share	2.60	2.43	2.53	2.77	2.16	...	...	...
Tang Book Value Per Share	7.04	6.67	6.32	5.84	4.50	3.18	1.52	1.50
Dividends Per Share	0.540	0.510	0.480	0.460	0.355	0.210	0.165	0.120
Dividend Payout %	24.73	24.23	22.49	22.66	21.39	13.64	15.42	12.70
Income Statement								
Total Revenue	2,966,244	2,024,009	1,018,900	3,570,190	3,398,112	3,457,412	2,161,671	1,860,878
EBITDA	304,442	207,918	107,018	402,039	354,146	353,223	272,158	233,548
Depn & Amortn	49,870	33,732	17,043	66,038	70,889	68,087	51,763	37,785
Income Before Taxes	231,796	158,019	81,638	301,209	239,585	231,757	179,692	161,579
Income Taxes	59,368	43,861	23,348	88,844	65,857	71,596	55,607	51,386
Net Income	172,428	114,158	58,290	212,365	173,728	160,161	110,241	100,068
Average Shares	105,756	105,663	105,436	104,817	104,454	103,712	103,017	105,873
Balance Sheet								
Current Assets	781,930	776,524	803,945	753,609	687,745	713,515	698,479	397,288
Total Assets	2,063,190	2,074,124	2,124,918	2,069,548	1,970,686	2,046,675	2,012,979	1,373,565
Current Liabilities	370,109	390,463	450,025	456,407	418,419	454,607	455,601	246,726
Long-Term Obligations	301,033	315,941	331,417	327,942	411,135	572,570	700,821	461,353
Total Liabilities	797,716	836,838	912,357	912,719	954,182	1,146,087	1,265,078	744,671
Stockholders' Equity	1,265,474	1,237,286	1,212,561	1,156,829	1,016,504	900,588	747,901	628,894
Shares Outstanding	104,417	104,295	104,200	103,777	103,460	103,184	102,450	102,401
Statistical Record								
Return on Assets %	11.24	10.94	10.96	10.48	8.65	7.83	5.48	8.16
Return on Equity %	19.38	19.17	19.91	19.49	18.12	17.78	14.74	18.50
EBITDA Margin %	10.26	10.27	10.50	11.26	10.42	10.22	12.59	12.55
Net Margin %	5.81	5.64	5.72	5.95	5.11	4.63	5.10	5.38
Asset Turnover	1.91	1.90	1.84	1.76	1.69	1.70	1.28	1.52
Current Ratio	2.11	1.99	1.79	1.65	1.64	1.57	1.53	1.61
Debt to Equity	0.24	0.26	0.27	0.28	0.40	0.64	0.94	0.73
Price Range	36.60-29.50	34.07-25.75	34.07-25.40	33.05-22.00	34.15-21.15	32.20-16.38	20.48-13.50	20.73-13.50
P/E Ratio	16.79-13.53	16.22-12.26	16.00-11.92	16.28-10.84	20.57-12.74	20.91-10.63	19.14-12.62	22.05-14.36
Average Yield %	1.67	1.66	1.63	1.66	1.32	0.92	0.96	0.68

Address: 6869 Metropolitan Blvd. East, Saint-Leonard
Telephone: 514-328-6662
Web Site: www.saputo.com

Officers: Lino Saputo - Chmn. Lino Saputo Jr. - Pres., C.E.O. **Transfer Agents:** National Bank Trust, Montreal, Quebec.

Investor Contact: 514-328-3381
No of Institutions: N/A
Shares: N/A **% Held:** N/A

SICO, INC.

Exchange	Symbol	Price	52Wk Range	Yield	P/E
TSX	SIC	C$16.50 (5/31/2005)	16.65-11.05	1.70	11.87

*7 Year Price Score N/A *NYSE Composite Index=100 *12 Month Price Score 110.40

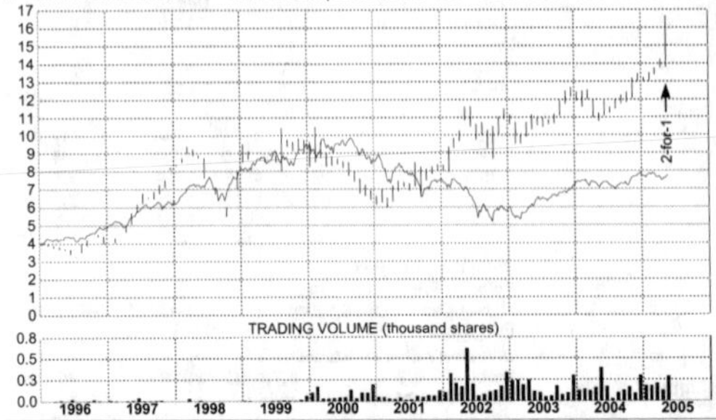

Interim Earnings (Per Share) Can$

Qtr.	Mar	Jun	Sep	Dec
2002	0.14	0.55	0.36	(0.01)
2003	0.16	0.50	0.23	(0.07)
2004	0.17	0.58	0.47	(0.01)
2005	0.39	...	...	...

Interim Dividends (Per Share)

Amt	Decl	Ex	Rec	Pay
0.06Q	10/27/2004	12/1/2004	12/3/2004	12/17/2004
0.07Q	3/3/2005	3/9/2005	3/11/2005	3/25/2005
2-for-1	5/10/2005	5/24/2005	5/26/2005	5/30/2005
0.07Q	5/10/2005	6/1/2005	6/3/2005	6/17/2005

Indicated Div: C$0.28

Valuation Analysis

Forecast P/E 12.39 (6/1/2005)
Market Cap C$112.7 Million Book Value 119.3 Million
Price/Book 0.94 Price/Sales 0.37

Dividend Achiever Status

Rank 27 **5 Year Growth Rate** 8.45%
Total Years of Dividend Growth 5

TRADING VOLUME (thousand shares)

Business Summary: Chemicals (MIC: 11.1 SIC: 851 NAIC: 25510)

Sico is engaged in developing, manufacturing and marketing of architectural paints, metal coatings designed for the transportation industry and related products. Paints, other types of coatings and surface preparation products are mainly sold under the following brand names or trademarks: Sico, Sico Supreme, Cashmere, Chamois, Shantung, Crown Diamond, Chateau, Sico Classic, Sico Expert, Sico Select, Polyprep, Corrostop, Formula, Maxithane, Crystalex, Betonel and Para, in addition to various private labels. Co. operates two significant business units: Architectural and Industrial. Co. operates predominantly in Canada and U.S.

Recent Developments: For the three months ended April 1 2005, net earnings more than doubled to C$2.7 million compared with C$1.2 million in the corresponding quarter of the previous year. The difference in results was attributable to 53 weeks in 2004 compared to 52 in 2005. Sales climbed 8.0% to C$68.0 million from C$63.0 million in the year-earlier period. On a segment basis, Architectural segment sales increased 11.2% to C$59.5 million from C$53.5 million, while Industrial segment sales decreased 9.8% to C$8.5 million from C$9.4 million in the prior-year quarter. Financial expenses dropped 39.4% to C$278,000 from C$458,000 the year before.

Prospects: Co. is confident that it can continue to benefit from favorable conditions in the Canadian architectural paint market, a result of strong renovation spending. Assuming these positive conditions, Co.'s architectural sector will continue to develop its distribution networks across the country. Meanwhile, the industrial sector will seek to capitalize on growing demand in most of its target segments in North America to improve sales and profit margins. Co. remains concerned with rising costs of raw materials, in spite of selling prices increases in some product categories. A strong balance sheet should allow Co. to pursue business acquisitions that should reinforce its market position.

Financial Data

(Can$ in Thousands)	3 Mos	12/31/2004	12/26/2003	12/27/2002	12/28/2001	12/29/2000	12/31/1999	12/25/1998
Earnings Per Share	1.39	1.12	0.83	1.04	0.80	0.68	0.80	0.55
Cash Flow Per Share	2.86	2.52	0.98	1.31	...	...	...	...
Tang Book Value Per Share	5.14	5.01	3.88	5.07	6.13	5.44	4.90	4.21
Dividends Per Share	0.250	0.240	0.220	0.205	0.200	0.190	0.160	0.160
Dividend Payout %	17.96	21.43	26.51	19.71	25.16	28.15	20.00	29.36
Income Statement								
Total Revenue	68,045	303,446	283,644	256,954	224,347	206,934	214,057	206,086
EBITDA	5,636	32,253	32,310	23,286	22,050	19,873	22,655	16,321
Depn & Amortn	1,816	6,787	6,142	5,411	5,020	5,143	5,782	5,321
Income Before Taxes	3,820	23,004	17,051	17,929	15,967	13,398	15,371	9,020
Income Taxes	1,119	7,549	5,890	5,901	6,628	5,661	6,264	3,230
Net Income	2,701	15,455	11,161	12,028	8,609	7,570	9,056	6,156
Average Shares	13,818	13,769	13,444	11,587	10,815	11,518	11,584	10,216
Balance Sheet								
Current Assets	107,461	80,270	91,554	88,051	69,031	64,733	64,255	59,135
Total Assets	197,899	170,733	188,823	155,595	138,500	122,242	104,792	102,844
Current Liabilities	64,494	34,396	45,243	35,453	39,725	30,924	30,784	34,740
Long-Term Obligations	500	5,250	23,993	31,023	20,702	25,196	13,750	15,000
Total Liabilities	78,558	53,341	83,362	78,054	71,962	66,852	54,504	59,751
Stockholders' Equity	119,341	117,392	105,461	77,541	66,538	55,390	50,288	43,093
Shares Outstanding	13,662	13,627	13,509	11,450	10,851	10,180	10,266	10,224
Statistical Record								
Return on Assets %	8.13	8.46	6.50	8.20	6.62	6.69	8.58	6.03
Return on Equity %	14.57	13.65	12.23	16.74	14.16	14.37	19.08	15.18
EBITDA Margin %	8.28	10.63	7.87	9.06	9.83	9.60	10.58	7.92
Net Margin %	3.97	5.09	3.93	4.68	3.84	3.66	4.23	2.99
Asset Turnover	1.49	1.66	1.65	1.75	1.73	1.83	2.03	2.02
Current Ratio	1.67	2.33	2.02	2.48	1.74	2.09	2.09	1.70
Debt to Equity	N.M.	0.04	0.23	0.40	0.31	0.45	0.27	0.35
Price Range	13.75-10.75	13.45-10.75	12.70-9.50	11.63-7.95	8.49-6.00	10.50-6.40	10.45-8.00	9.40-5.50
P/E Ratio	9.89-7.73	12.01-9.60	15.30-11.45	11.18-7.64	10.62-7.50	15.44-9.41	13.06-10.00	17.09-10.00
Average Yield %	2.04	2.01	2.02	2.04	2.76	2.32	1.74	2.01

Address: 3280 Sainte-Anne Boulevard, Quebec City
Telephone: 418-663-9886
Web Site: www.sico.com

Officers: Jean-Paul Lortie - Chmn. Pierre Dufresne CA - Pres., C.E.O. **Transfer Agents:** National Bank Trust Inc., Quebec, Canada

No of Institutions: N/A
Shares: N/A **% Held:** N/A

TERASEN INC

Exchange	Symbol	Price	52Wk Range	Yield	P/E
TSX	TER	C$27.15 (5/31/2005)	29.71-22.05	3.31	21.05

*7 Year Price Score 124.67 *NYSE Composite Index=100 *12 Month Price Score 101.89

TRADING VOLUME (thousand shares)

Interim Earnings (Per Share) Can$

Qtr.	Mar	Jun	Sep	Dec
2002	0.84	0.01	(0.22)	0.64
2003	1.41	0.08	(0.07)	0.56
2004	0.77	0.10	(0.01)	0.57
2005	0.63	...	...	...

Interim Dividends (Per Share)

Amt	Decl	Ex	Rec	Pay
0.21Q	7/29/2004	8/13/2004	8/17/2004	8/31/2004
0.21Q	11/4/2004	11/16/2004	11/18/2004	11/30/2004
0.225Q	2/17/2005	2/23/2005	2/25/2005	2/28/2005
0.225Q	5/4/2005	5/13/2005	5/17/2005	5/31/2005

Indicated Div: C$0.90

Valuation Analysis

Forecast P/E 18.53 (6/4/2005)
Market Cap C$2.9 Billion Book Value 1.4 Billion
Price/Book 2.02 Price/Sales 1.45

Dividend Achiever Status

Rank 28 **5 Year Growth Rate** 7.21%
Total Years of Dividend Growth 8

Business Summary: Oil and Gas (MIC: 14.2 SIC: 623 NAIC: 86910)

Terasen is a provider of energy transportation and utility services. Through Terasen Gas, Co. distributed natural gas in British Columbia (B.C.) to more than 875,000 customers in more than 125 communities at Dec 31 2004. Through Terasen Pipelines, Co. provides petroleum transportation services from Edmonton, Alberta to Vancouver, B.C., Washington state, the U.S. Rocky Mountains region and the U.S. midwest. Terasen Water and Utility Services, subsidiaries of Co., are providers of water and wastewater treatment services as well as product sales related to the water, sewer and irrigation markets, operating over 90 systems in more than 50 communities throughout B.C., Alberta and Alaska.

Recent Developments: For the first quarter ended Mar 31 2005, net earnings decreased 2.4% to C$66.3 million compared with C$67.9 million in the corresponding prior-year quarter. Total revenue increased 2.9% to C$667.3 million from C$648.7 million a year earlier. Natural gas distribution revenues rose 3.4% to C$570.2 million, while water and utility services revenue climbed 24.9% to C$42.7 million. Petroleum transportation revenue fell 17.7% to C$45.9 million, while revenue from other activities grew 18.1% to C$8.5 million. Operating income declined 4.3% to C$134.9 million from C$141.0 million the year before. Comparisons were made with restated results for the prior year.

Prospects: Temporary production outages in the Alberta oilsands have reduced supply from the region which, combined with maintenance turnarounds at refineries connected to the Trans Mountain pipeline, has adversely affected petroleum throughput. However, the pipeline has returned to operating at full capacity and the throughput outlook is strong going forward. In addition, Co. has completed the Express pipeline expansion which provides additional capacity on that system. Meanwhile, Terasen Gas is seeing strong customer growth and improvement in its operating efficiency. With the healthy economic environment in British Columbia, Co. expects customer growth to continue.

Financial Data

(Can$ in Thousands)	3 Mos	12/31/2004	12/31/2003	12/31/2002	12/31/2001	12/31/2000	12/31/1999	12/31/1998
Earnings Per Share	1.29	1.42	1.26	1.22	1.10	1.41	1.06	0.93
Cash Flow Per Share	2.72	3.26	2.60	3.68	...	...	...	...
Tang Book Value Per Share	12.34	13.01	12.75	12.23	10.95	10.56	8.18	7.71
Dividends Per Share	0.855	0.825	0.765	0.705	0.650	0.613	0.583	0.545
Dividend Payout %	66.28	58.10	60.47	58.02	59.36	43.44	54.95	58.92
Income Statement								
Total Revenue	667,300	1,957,000	1,876,600	1,707,200	1,666,300	1,305,600	1,040,600	925,000
EBITDA	175,200	539,300	507,800	452,100	390,300	329,300	339,000	345,100
Depn & Amortn	36,900	147,100	133,400	115,600	95,100	86,200	82,600	84,600
Income Before Taxes	93,000	225,600	198,400	175,700	146,900	125,600	134,800	138,700
Income Taxes	26,700	69,200	59,000	63,200	55,900	8,900	48,900	62,900
Net Income	66,300	156,400	139,400	112,500	91,000	112,700	81,200	71,200
Average Shares	105,300	105,700	104,800	87,200	76,600	76,600	76,600	77,000
Balance Sheet								
Net PPE	3,924,500	3,892,500	3,882,400	3,779,200	3,079,900	2,727,600	2,154,700	2,168,600
Total Assets	5,111,200	4,970,600	4,915,100	4,522,400	3,705,700	3,513,100	2,450,500	2,466,100
Long-Term Obligations	2,147,700	2,166,600	2,301,100	2,123,400	1,928,000	1,561,900	1,001,800	906,700
Total Liabilities	3,692,700	3,474,500	3,485,500	3,156,800	2,865,600	2,703,600	1,824,200	1,876,100
Stockholders' Equity	1,418,500	1,496,100	1,429,600	1,365,600	840,100	809,500	626,300	590,000
Shares Outstanding	105,431	105,171	104,154	103,363	76,687	76,653	76,559	76,532
Statistical Record								
Return on Assets %	2.82	3.16	2.95	2.73	2.52	3.77	3.30	2.93
Return on Equity %	9.64	10.66	9.97	10.20	11.03	15.66	13.35	12.09
EBITDA Margin %	26.26	27.56	27.06	26.48	23.42	25.22	32.58	37.31
Net Margin %	9.94	7.99	7.43	6.59	5.46	8.63	7.80	7.70
PPE Turnover	0.51	0.50	0.49	0.50	0.57	0.53	0.48	0.43
Asset Turnover	0.40	0.39	0.40	0.41	0.46	0.44	0.42	0.38
Debt to Equity	1.51	1.45	1.61	1.55	2.29	1.93	1.60	1.54
Price Range	29.71-22.05	28.40-22.05	24.00-18.18	21.25-16.32	18.20-14.88	16.73-10.75	15.50-10.50	16.98-13.50
P/E Ratio	23.03-17.09	20.00-15.53	19.05-14.42	17.42-13.38	16.55-13.52	11.86-7.62	14.62-9.91	18.25-14.52
Average Yield %	3.35	3.38	3.62	3.68	3.92	4.45	4.16	3.60

Address: 24th Floor, 1111 West Georgia Street, Vancouver
Telephone: 604-443-6500
Web Site: www.terasen.com

Officers: John M. Reid - Pres., C.E.O. Richard T. Ballantyne - Pres., Terasen Pipelines Inc. **Transfer Agents:**CIBC Mellon Trust Company, Vancouver, British Columbia

Investor Contact: 604-443-6566
No of Institutions: 1
Shares: 150,342 **% Held:** 0.14

THOMSON CORP.

Exchange	Symbol	Price	52Wk Range	Yield	P/E
TSX	TOC	C$42.31 (5/31/2005)	47.40-39.36	1.89	26.61

*7 Year Price Score 83.45 *NYSE Composite Index=100 *12 Month Price Score 93.77

Interim Earnings (Per Share)

Qtr.	Mar	Jun	Sep	Dec
2002	(0.05)	0.14	0.39	0.44
2003	0.10	0.17	0.47	0.60
2004	0.05	0.29	0.52	0.67
2005	0.11	...	...	...

Interim Dividends (Per Share)

Amt	Decl	Ex	Rec	Pay
0.19Q	7/28/2004	8/17/2004	8/19/2004	9/15/2004
0.19Q	10/26/2004	11/16/2004	11/18/2004	12/15/2004
0.19Q	2/10/2005	2/17/2005	2/22/2005	3/15/2005
0.20Q	4/26/2005	5/17/2005	5/19/2005	6/15/2005

Indicated Div: $0.80

Valuation Analysis

Forecast P/E	24.34 (6/1/2005)		
Market Cap	$27.7 Billion	Book Value	9.9 Billion
Price/Book	2.81	Price/Sales	3.35

Dividend Achiever Status

Rank	33	5 Year Growth Rate	2.80%
Total Years of Dividend Growth			10

Business Summary: Information Technologies & Communications (MIC: 10 SIC: 375 NAIC: 18210)

Thomson provides value-added information, software tools and applications to users in the fields of law, tax, accounting, financial services, higher education, reference information, corporate training and assessment, scientific research and healthcare. Co. organizes its operations into four market groups that are structured on the basis of the customers they serve: Thomson Legal & Regulatory, Thomson Learning, Thomson Financial and Thomson Scientific & Healthcare.

Recent Developments: For the three months ended Mar 31 2005, income advanced 68.3% to $69.0 million versus income of $41.0 million the year before. Results excluded income of $4.0 million in 2005 and a loss of $4.0 million in 2004 from discontinued operations. Revenues increased 10.0% to $1.85 billion, primarily due to internal growth, acquisitions, and favorable currency translation. Legal and Regulatory segment revenues rose 5.8% to $786.0 million, while Learning segment revenues increased 9.1% to $383.0 million. Financial segment revenues climbed 17.1% to $458.0 million. Operating profit rose 16.5% to $113.0 million from $97.0 million the previous year.

Prospects: Top-line results in 2005 are expected to benefit from revenue growth from existing businesses, as well as contributions from strategic acquisitions. On May 2 2005, Co. announced that it has acquired Macdonald & Associates Ltd., a provider of information about the Canadian venture capital and private equity markets. Separately, on Mar 1 2005, Co. announced that it has acquired Tax Partners®, LLC, a sales and use tax compliance service firm. Terms of these acquisitions were not disclosed. Looking ahead, Co. is projecting full-year 2005 revenue growth to be in line with its long-term target of 7.0% to 9.0%, excluding the effects of currency translation.

Financial Data
(US$ in Thousands)

	3 Mos	12/31/2004	12/31/2003	12/31/2002	12/31/2001	12/31/2000	12/31/1999	12/31/1998
Earnings Per Share	1.59	1.54	1.34	0.93	1.19	1.96	0.86	2.97
Cash Flow Per Share	2.72	2.75	2.53	2.64	...	...	...	...
Dividends Per Share	0.760	0.755	1.153	0.705	0.700	0.685	0.657	0.627
Dividend Payout %	47.80	49.03	86.04	75.81	58.82	34.95	76.45	21.13
Income Statement								
Total Revenue	1,850,000	8,098,000	7,606,000	7,756,000	7,237,000	6,514,000	5,752,000	6,269,000
Depn & Amortn	226,000	906,000	873,000	830,000	920,000	743,000	602,000	644,000
Income Taxes	(8,000)	267,000	156,000	192,000	168,000	(15,000)	105,000	109,000
Net Income	73,000	1,011,000	867,000	615,000	749,000	1,223,000	532,000	1,818,000
Average Shares	656,388	655,927	654,151	641,475	628,239	623,776	618,092	612,000
Balance Sheet								
Current Assets	2,564,000	2,892,000	3,044,000	3,019,000	2,763,000	2,528,000	2,200,000	2,092,000
Total Assets	19,179,000	19,643,000	18,680,000	18,542,000	18,402,000	15,699,000	12,558,000	12,447,000
Current Liabilities	2,806,000	3,083,000	3,145,000	3,202,000	3,830,000	2,965,000	2,477,000	2,073,000
Long-Term Obligations	3,979,000	4,013,000	3,684,000	3,487,000	3,651,000	2,321,000	1,909,000	2,408,000
Total Liabilities	9,328,000	9,681,000	9,480,000	9,588,000	10,182,000	7,881,000	5,562,000	5,702,000
Stockholders' Equity	9,851,000	9,962,000	9,200,000	8,954,000	8,220,000	7,818,000	6,996,000	6,745,000
Shares Outstanding	655,370	655,131	654,579	651,150	630,740	625,764	621,393	616,000
Statistical Record								
Return on Assets %	5.60	5.26	4.66	3.33	4.39	8.63	4.26	14.10
Return on Equity %	11.03	10.52	9.55	7.16	9.34	16.47	7.74	31.10
Net Margin %	3.95	12.48	11.40	7.93	10.35	18.77	9.25	29.00
Asset Turnover	0.44	0.42	0.41	0.42	0.42	0.46	0.46	0.49
Current Ratio	0.91	0.94	0.97	0.94	0.72	0.85	0.89	1.01
Debt to Equity	0.40	0.40	0.40	0.39	0.44	0.30	0.27	0.36
Price Range	47.40-40.10	47.74-40.05	47.08-37.59	56.70-36.25	57.85-42.70	62.40-38.00	51.00-35.75	45.60-29.05
P/E Ratio	29.81-25.22	31.00-26.01	35.13-28.05	60.97-38.98	48.61-35.88	31.84-19.39	59.30-41.57	15.35-9.78
Average Yield %	1.77	1.75	2.76	1.53	1.37	1.31	1.58	1.58

Address: Suite 2706, Toronto Dominion Bank Tower, P.O. Box 24, Toronto-Dominion Centre, Toronto
Telephone: 416-360-8700
Web Site: www.thomson.com

Officers: Richard J. Harrington - Pres., C.E.O. Robert D. Daleo - Exec. V.P., C.F.O. **Transfer Agents:** Computershare Trust Company of Canada, Toronto, Canada

No of Institutions: 67
Shares: 88,205,424 **% Held:** 13.46

TOROMONT INDUSTRIES LTD.

Exchange	Symbol	Price	52Wk Range	Yield	P/E
TSX	TIH	C$21.62 (5/31/2005)	22.90-16.82	1.48	19.65

*7 Year Price Score 150.27 *NYSE Composite Index=100 *12 Month Price Score 104.31

Interim Earnings (Per Share) Can$

Qtr.	Mar	Jun	Sep	Dec
2002	0.04	0.17	0.14	0.30
2003	0.07	0.22	0.26	0.39
2004	0.10	0.29	0.29	0.41
2005	0.11	...	...	...

Interim Dividends (Per Share)

Amt	Decl	Ex	Rec	Pay
0.065Q	4/14/2004	6/14/2004	6/16/2004	7/2/2004
0.065Q	8/16/2004	9/15/2004	9/17/2004	10/1/2004
0.065Q	11/2/2004	12/15/2004	12/17/2004	1/3/2005
0.08Q	2/15/2005	3/16/2005	3/18/2005	4/1/2005

Indicated Div: C$0.32

Valuation Analysis

Forecast P/E	17.31 (6/1/2005)		
Market Cap	C$1.4 Billion	Book Value	420.4 Million
Price/Book	3.25	Price/Sales	0.90

Dividend Achiever Status

Rank	21	5 Year Growth Rate	12.70%
Total Years of Dividend Growth			15

Business Summary: Purpose Machinery (MIC: 11.13 SIC: 353 NAIC: 32412)

Toromont Industries operates in two segments, the Equipment Group and the Compression Group. The Equipment Group sells, rents and services construction equipment and industrial engines through Co.'s Caterpillar dealership and Battlefield operations. The Compression Group is engaged in manufacturing, encompassing the design, installation and servicing of industrial and recreational refrigeration, carbon dioxide compression, process systems, fuel gas compression and natural gas compression. The Compression Group operates through Toromont Process Systems, Toromont Energy Systems Inc., CIMCO Refrigeration, and Aero Tech Manufacturing.

Recent Developments: For the quarter ended Mar 31 2005, net earnings increased 13.6% to C$7.4 million compared with C$6.5 million in the corresponding period of the previous year. Total revenues climbed 12.0% to C$310.0 million from C$276.5 million in the year-earlier quarter Equipment group revenues advanced 17.8% to C$185.8 million, largely due to higher machine sales, rentals and product support activities. Compression group revenues rose 4.4% to C$124.2 million, due to increased product support activity and higher sales of natural gas compression packages. Operating income grew 4.9% to C$13.8 million from C$13.1 million the year before.

Prospects: The economic outlook for North America continues to be relatively positive. The improved balance in Co.'s products and markets, combined with increased after-market activity should allow it to withstand short-term weaknesses in any particular industry. Meanwhile, product supply availability continues to be of some concern, on balance, most customers' equipment needs are covered. Co.'s Compression Group is expected to remain active, given current markets conditions and natural gas prices. Product support in both operating groups should continue to benefit from the large installed base of equipment.

Financial Data

(Can$ in Thousands)	3 Mos	12/31/2004	12/31/2003	12/31/2002	12/31/2001	12/31/2000	12/31/1999	12/31/1998
Earnings Per Share	1.10	1.09	0.94	0.64	0.70	0.54	0.53	0.13
Cash Flow Per Share	0.59	0.95	1.38	1.12	...	...	...	...
Tang Book Value Per Share	6.10	6.04	5.39	5.08	4.69	3.77	3.47	3.12
Dividends Per Share	0.275	0.260	0.210	0.180	0.170	0.160	0.140	0.130
Dividend Payout %	25.00	23.85	22.34	28.13	24.11	29.63	26.67	100.00
Income Statement								
Total Revenue	309,983	1,487,338	1,299,389	1,076,930	911,005	800,464	723,937	683,482
EBITDA	23,867	164,881	144,218	115,711	84,004	66,874	63,910	68,219
Depn & Amortn	9,593	42,756	39,423	36,652	...	...	...	...
Income Before Taxes	11,290	109,765	91,519	67,693	72,042	55,879	55,544	66,309
Income Taxes	3,902	39,247	31,289	26,318	28,342	23,534	23,487	28,121
Net Income	7,388	70,518	60,230	41,375	43,700	32,345	32,057	38,188
Average Shares	64,354	64,655	64,243	64,866	62,107	57,906	78,688	58,860
Balance Sheet								
Current Assets	603,513	587,113	508,477	483,007	444,268	427,985	385,931	336,242
Total Assets	968,636	944,814	856,176	771,902	720,702	613,787	528,050	442,972
Current Liabilities	298,579	348,590	304,900	269,785	226,136	234,579	194,190	190,992
Long-Term Obligations	235,851	166,508	159,694	156,479	171,970	157,187	120,000	60,000
Total Liabilities	548,277	528,959	479,339	436,586	406,454	395,574	324,988	259,376
Stockholders' Equity	420,359	415,855	376,837	335,316	314,248	218,213	203,062	183,596
Shares Outstanding	63,247	63,082	63,563	63,455	64,194	57,951	58,576	58,916
Statistical Record								
Return on Assets %	7.74	7.81	7.40	5.54	6.55	5.65	6.60	8.71
Return on Equity %	17.79	17.74	16.91	12.74	16.41	15.31	16.58	22.50
EBITDA Margin %	7.70	11.09	11.10	10.74	9.22	8.35	8.83	9.98
Net Margin %	2.38	4.74	4.64	3.84	4.80	4.04	4.43	5.59
Asset Turnover	1.65	1.65	1.60	1.44	1.37	1.40	1.49	1.56
Current Ratio	2.02	1.68	1.67	1.79	1.96	1.82	1.99	1.76
Debt to Equity	0.56	0.40	0.42	0.47	0.55	0.72	0.59	0.33
Price Range	22.90-16.82	20.76-16.25	16.62-9.92	13.00-9.32	12.91-7.63	10.38-6.92	9.55-6.88	11.50-7.16
P/E Ratio	20.82-15.29	19.05-14.91	17.68-10.55	20.31-14.57	18.44-10.89	19.21-12.82	18.02-12.97	88.46-55.10
Average Yield %	1.41	1.40	1.67	1.68	1.70	1.87	1.68	1.46

Address: 3131 Highway 7 West, P.O. Box 5511, Concord, 84054 **Telephone:** 416-667-5511 **Web Site:** www.toromont.com	**Officers:** Robert M. Ogilvie - Exec. Chmn. Hugo T. Sorensen - Pres., C.E.O. **Transfer Agents:** CIBC Mellon Trust Company, Toronto, Ontario	**No of Institutions:** 1 **Shares:** 137,400 **% Held:** 0.22

TORONTO DOMINION BANK

Exchange	Symbol	Price	52Wk Range	Yield	P/E
TSX	TD	C$53.59 (5/31/2005)	53.59-42.70	2.99	14.97

Interim Earnings (Per Share) Can$

Qtr.	Jan	Apr	Jul	Oct
2001-02	0.55	0.20	(0.67)	(0.34)
2002-03	0.50	(0.46)	0.73	0.73
2003-04	0.88	0.74	0.86	0.91
2004-05	0.95	0.86	...	...

Interim Dividends (Per Share)

Amt	Decl	Ex	Rec	Pay
0.36Q	8/26/2004	9/14/2004	9/16/2004	10/31/2004
0.36Q	11/24/2004	12/14/2004	12/16/2004	1/31/2005
0.40Q	2/24/2005	3/15/2005	3/17/2005	4/30/2005
0.40Q	5/26/2005	6/14/2005	6/16/2005	7/31/2005

Indicated Div: C$1.60 (Div. Reinv. Plan)

Valuation Analysis

Forecast P/E	12.75 (6/1/2005)		
Market Cap	C$35.3 Billion	Book Value	13.2 Billion
Price/Book	2.67	Price/Sales	2.50

Dividend Achiever Status

Rank	19	5 Year Growth Rate	13.56%
Total Years of Dividend Growth			11

Business Summary: Commercial Banking (MIC: 8.1 SIC: 029 NAIC: 22110)

Toronto Dominion Bank is a bank holding company. Co. is organized into the following operating business segments: Personal and Commercial Banking, Wholesale Banking and Wealth Management. The Personal and Commercial Banking segment provides financial products and services to personal, small business, insurance, and commercial customers. The Wholesale Banking segment provides financial products and services to corporate, government, and institutional customers. The Wealth Management segment provides investment products and services to institutional and retail investors. As of Oct 31 2004, Co.'s total assets were C$311.03 billion and its total deposits were C$206.89 billion.

Recent Developments: For the three months ended Apr 30 2005, net income was C$599.0 million compared with C$490.0 million in the corresponding year-earlier period. Results included a charge of C$22.0 million for 2005 and a credit of C$7.0 million for 2004 related to restructuring initiatives. Net interest income declined 3.3% to C$1.39 billion from C$1.44 billion the previous year, primarily due to Wholesale Banking where there was reduced trading-related net interest income. Co. reported a provision of C$20.0 million in 2005 and a reversal of C$192.0 million from credit losses in 2004. Non-interest income increased 18.1% to C$1.52 billion from C$1.28 billion the year before.

Prospects: Co.'s outlook appears decent. Co. expects its Canadian Personal and Commercial Banking segment to post strong earnings growth for the remainder of 2005 on solid volume growth, lower personal credit losses, positive insurance claims experience and low expense growth. Additionally, Co. expects the U.S. Personal and Commercial Banking segment to report earnings growth within its 8.0% to 10.0% historic range. Co. also expects earnings growth from its advice-based and asset management businesses, which should help offset weakness from Discount Brokerage. Meanwhile, Co.'s Wholesale Banking segment will focus on repositioning the structured products businesses and gaining domestic market share.

Financial Data

(Can$ in Thousands)	3 Mos	10/31/2004	10/31/2003	10/31/2002	10/31/2001	10/31/2000	10/31/1999	10/31/1998
Earnings Per Share	3.45	3.39	1.51	(0.25)	2.07	0.92	4.90	1.81
Cash Flow Per Share	(0.22)	(13.61)	7.93	21.73	(7.71)	(9.49)	(16.37)	(28.24)
Tang Book Value Per Share	13.59	12.65	10.02	7.81	8.43	5.24	17.25	12.94
Dividends Per Share	1.400	1.360	1.160	1.120	1.090	0.920	0.720	0.660
Dividend Payout %	40.56	40.12	76.82	...	52.66	100.00	14.69	36.46
Income Statement								
Interest Income	3,012,000	11,132,000	11,202,000	11,751,000	14,471,000	13,675,000	10,874,000	9,997,000
Interest Expense	1,601,000	5,189,000	5,586,000	6,451,000	10,080,000	10,070,000	7,893,000	7,056,000
Net Interest Income	1,411,000	5,943,000	5,616,000	5,300,000	4,391,000	3,605,000	2,981,000	2,941,000
Provision for Losses	10,000	(386,000)	186,000	2,925,000	920,000	480,000	275,000	450,000
Non-Interest Income	691,000	2,740,000	2,188,000	2,315,000	2,924,000	2,562,000	2,409,000	1,682,000
Income Before Taxes	851,000	3,205,000	1,490,000	(448,000)	1,462,000	1,540,000	4,127,000	1,732,000
Income Taxes	221,000	803,000	322,000	(406,000)	(155,000)	305,000	1,099,000	611,000
Net Income	630,000	2,310,000	1,076,000	(76,000)	1,383,000	1,025,000	2,981,000	1,121,000
Average Shares	661,900	659,400	653,900	646,946	627,047	621,585	599,311	594,040
Balance Sheet								
Net Loans & Leases	125,833,000	123,924,000	118,058,000	122,627,000	119,673,000	120,721,000	87,485,000	84,926,000
Total Assets	333,317,000	311,027,000	273,532,000	278,040,000	287,838,000	264,818,000	214,417,000	181,831,000
Total Deposits	221,962,000	206,893,000	182,880,000	189,190,000	193,914,000	185,808,000	140,386,000	120,677,000
Total Liabilities	320,114,000	297,049,000	260,421,000	264,999,000	274,434,000	252,468,000	202,884,000	173,298,000
Stockholders' Equity	13,203,000	13,978,000	13,111,000	13,041,000	13,404,000	12,350,000	11,533,000	8,533,000
Shares Outstanding	658,349	655,900	656,260	645,399	628,451	622,616	620,343	594,238
Statistical Record								
Return on Assets %	0.72	0.79	0.39	N.M.	0.50	0.43	1.50	0.65
Return on Equity %	17.44	17.01	8.23	N.M.	10.74	8.56	29.71	14.16
Net Interest Margin %	46.85	53.39	50.13	45.10	30.34	26.36	27.41	29.42
Loans to Deposits	0.57	0.60	0.65	0.65	0.62	0.65	0.62	0.70
Price Range	50.00-42.70	49.25-40.92	43.86-28.35	44.94-25.25	45.27-35.49	46.30-33.20	43.50-21.50	36.50-18.93
P/E Ratio	14.49-12.38	14.53-12.07	29.05-18.77	...	21.87-17.14	50.33-36.09	8.88-4.39	20.17-10.46
Average Yield %	3.03	3.04	3.25	2.97	2.70	2.46	2.28	2.34

Address: P.O. Box 1, Toronto-Dominion Centre, King Street West and Bay Street, Toronto **Telephone:** 416-982-8222 **Web Site:** www.td.com	**Officers:** Richard M. Thomson - Chmn. W. Edmund Clark - Pres., C.O.O. **Transfer Agents:** CIBC Mellon Trust Company, Toronto, Canada	**Investor Contact:** 416-944-5743 **No of Institutions:** 94 **Shares:** 202,640,720 **% Held:** 28.81

WEST FRASER TIMBER CO., LTD.

Exchange	Symbol	Price	52Wk Range	Yield	P/E
TSX	WFT	C$46.37 (5/31/2005)	54.95-42.10	1.21	8.27

***7 Year Price Score 129.39** *NYSE Composite Index=100 ***12 Month Price Score 94.09**

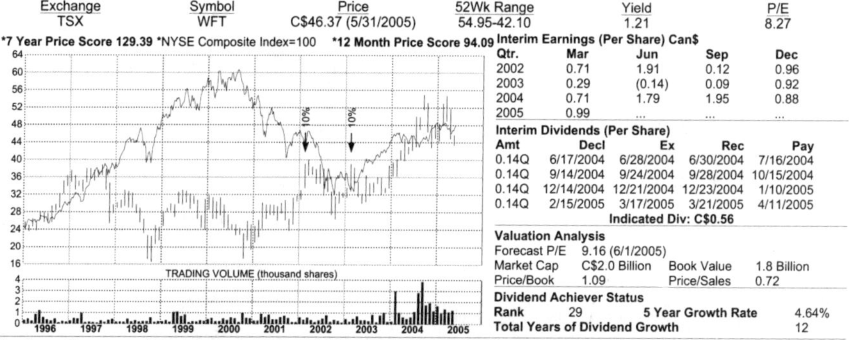

Interim Earnings (Per Share) Can$

Qtr.	Mar	Jun	Sep	Dec
2002	0.71	1.91	0.12	0.96
2003	0.29	(0.14)	0.09	0.92
2004	0.71	1.79	1.95	0.88
2005	0.99	...	...	...

Interim Dividends (Per Share)

Amt	Decl	Ex	Rec	Pay
0.14Q	6/17/2004	6/28/2004	6/30/2004	7/16/2004
0.14Q	9/14/2004	9/24/2004	9/28/2004	10/15/2004
0.14Q	12/14/2004	12/21/2004	12/23/2004	1/10/2005
0.14Q	2/15/2005	3/17/2005	3/21/2005	4/11/2005

Indicated Div: C$0.56

Valuation Analysis

Forecast P/E	9.16 (6/1/2005)		
Market Cap	C$2.0 Billion	Book Value	1.8 Billion
Price/Book	1.09	Price/Sales	0.72

Dividend Achiever Status

Rank	29	**5 Year Growth Rate**	4.64%
Total Years of Dividend Growth			12

Business Summary: Wood Products (MIC: 11.9 SIC: 411 NAIC: 13310)

West Fraser Timber is an integrated forest products company producing lumber, wood chips, LVL, medium density fibreboard, plywood, pulp, linerboard, kraft paper and newsprint. Co. conducts its operations through its subsidiary companies and joint ventures. Most of the forest products manufactured by Co. are sold outside Canada as commodities. Co. operates its facilities in Quesnel and Kitimat in British Columbia; West Monroe in Louisiana; Hinton, Slave Lake and Whitecourt in Alberta.

Recent Developments: For the first quarter ended Mar 31 2005, net earnings were C$42.9 million versus C$26.5 million for the equivalent period a year earlier. Results for 2005 and 2004 included losses of C$3.2 million and C$2.0 million, respectively, on the exchange of long-term debt. Sales jumped 66.8% to C$902.4 million compared with C$541.1 million the year before. The growth in results reflect Co.'s overall productivity and efficiency improvements. Earnings benefited in lumber from sustained higher prices, driven by solid levels of new home construction in the U.S., strong sawmill operations, and the addition of the two Weldwood plywood plants to its panel operations.

Prospects: Co. slated C$105.0 million to build a sawmill in Quesnel, British Columbia to replace its existing facility. The new mill will consists of three-lines and will have an annual capacity of 500.0 million board feet on a two- shift basis. It will be built along side the existing mill. Production is expected to begin in the summer of 2006 when the existing mill will be permanently closed. Separately, Co.'s integration activities are well underway. A detailed systems integration process, which will continue into 2006, is underway to ensure the establishment of common technology platforms that will drive company-wide cost savings and efficiencies. Co. expects that target synergies will be realized.

Financial Data

(Can$ in Thousands)	3 Mos	12/31/2004	12/31/2003	12/31/2002	12/31/2001	12/31/2000	12/31/1999	12/31/1998
Earnings Per Share	5.61	5.36	1.16	3.70	3.35	3.42	3.93	0.04
Cash Flow Per Share	5.06	10.69	4.12	4.61	...	...	...	...
Tang Book Value Per Share	36.07	35.21	35.66	35.07	36.03	30.70	27.96	25.52
Dividends Per Share	0.560	0.560	0.547	0.498	0.463	0.459	0.446	0.438
Dividend Payout %	9.98	10.45	47.16	13.46	13.83	13.42	11.37	N.M.
Income Statement								
Total Revenue	902,400	2,400,007	1,508,147	1,632,239	1,562,306	2,309,440	2,204,115	1,863,399
EBITDA	142,400	466,634	195,422	320,681	266,638	348,928	379,737	216,275
Depn & Amortn	62,700	153,866	142,284	135,434	123,279	136,961	125,142	127,774
Income Before Taxes	67,300	296,724	36,243	185,247	143,359	211,967	254,595	27,278
Income Taxes	23,900	84,754	(6,878)	56,208	34,519	80,509	107,174	21,653
Net Income	42,900	211,970	43,121	137,560	126,488	131,458	147,421	5,625
Average Shares	43,332	39,527	37,102	37,130	33,497	36,707	35,976	35,094
Balance Sheet								
Current Assets	1,063,000	1,209,860	757,317	693,351	759,015	757,665	793,549	634,611
Total Assets	3,761,500	3,927,417	2,087,730	2,115,671	2,352,586	2,453,452	2,264,920	2,108,930
Current Liabilities	593,200	805,978	229,927	212,225	471,224	443,322	449,830	310,067
Long-Term Obligations	742,000	735,536	286,974	337,745	359,589	570,633	589,878	718,449
Total Liabilities	1,943,000	2,145,900	773,584	823,909	1,149,176	1,326,121	1,238,647	1,211,299
Stockholders' Equity	1,818,500	1,781,517	1,314,146	1,291,762	1,203,410	1,127,331	1,026,273	897,631
Shares Outstanding	42,746	42,744	36,856	36,831	33,396	36,716	36,700	35,174
Statistical Record								
Return on Assets %	7.74	7.03	2.05	6.16	5.26	5.56	6.74	0.27
Return on Equity %	14.45	13.66	3.31	11.03	10.85	12.17	15.33	0.63
EBITDA Margin %	15.78	19.44	12.96	19.65	17.07	15.11	17.23	11.61
Net Margin %	4.75	8.83	2.86	8.43	8.10	5.69	6.69	0.30
Asset Turnover	0.94	0.80	0.72	0.73	0.65	0.98	1.01	0.89
Current Ratio	1.79	1.50	3.29	3.27	1.61	1.71	1.76	2.05
Debt to Equity	0.41	0.41	0.22	0.26	0.30	0.51	0.57	0.80
Price Range	54.95-39.75	54.95-36.25	39.05-30.01	40.00-26.36	31.78-21.07	31.82-17.36	33.06-23.97	33.06-16.53
P/E Ratio	9.80-7.09	10.25-6.76	33.66-25.87	10.81-7.13	9.49-6.29	9.30-5.07	8.41-6.10	826.45-413.22
Average Yield %	1.19	1.26	1.58	1.50	1.68	1.87	1.53	1.77

Address: 858 Beatty Street, Suite 500, Vancouver
Telephone: 604-895-2700
Web Site: www.westfraser.com

Officers: Henry H. Ketcham - Chmn., Pres., C.E.O. Gerald J. Miller - Exec. V.P., Pulp & Paper **Transfer Agents:** CIBC Mellon Trust Company, Vancouver, British Columbia; Calgary, Alberta; Regina, Saskatchewan; Winnipeg, Manitoba; Toronto, Ontario; Montreal, Quebec; Halifax, Nova Scotia

Investor Contact: 604-895-2700
No of Institutions: 2
Shares: 143,463 **% Held:** 0.38

WESTON (GEORGE) LIMITED

Exchange	Symbol	Price	52Wk Range	Yield	P/E
TSX	WN	C$110.91 (5/31/2005)	115.00-86.50	1.30	46.21

*7 Year Price Score 105.68 *NYSE Composite Index=100 *12 Month Price Score 106.02

Interim Earnings (Per Share) Can$

Qtr.	Mar	Jun	Sep	Dec
2002	0.79	1.17	1.36	1.70
2003	0.96	1.42	1.54	1.86
2004	0.88	1.04	1.24	(0.60)
2005	0.72	...	...	...

Interim Dividends (Per Share)

Amt	Decl	Ex	Rec	Pay
0.36Q	8/26/2004	9/13/2004	9/15/2004	10/1/2004
0.36Q	11/17/2004	12/13/2004	12/15/2004	1/1/2005
0.36Q	2/11/2005	3/11/2005	3/15/2005	4/1/2005
0.36Q	5/11/2005	6/13/2005	6/15/2005	7/1/2005

Indicated Div: C$1.44

Valuation Analysis

Forecast P/E	17.53 (6/4/2005)		
Market Cap	C$14.3 Billion	Book Value	4.4 Billion
Price/Book	3.22	Price/Sales	N/A

Dividend Achiever Status

Rank	5	5 Year Growth Rate	26.86%
Total Years of Dividend Growth			9

Business Summary: Food (MIC: 4.1 SIC: 051 NAIC: 11812)

George Weston is a holding company. Through its subsidiaries, Co. is engaged in the food processing and distribution industry. Co. has two reportable operating segments: Weston Foods and Food Distribution. The Weston Foods segment is primarily engaged in the baking and dairy industries within North America. Brands include Weston, Arnold, Brownberry, Country Harvest, D'Italiano, Dutch Country, Entenmann's, Freihofer's, Gadoua, Interbake Foods, Maplehurst, Neilson dairy, Ready Bake, Stroehmann, Thomas', and Wonder. The Food Distribution segment, which is operated by Loblaw Companies Limited, concentrates on food retailing while growing its offering of general merchandise products and services.

Recent Developments: For the 12 weeks ended Mar 26 2005, income from continuing operations was C$101.0 million compared with income of C$125.0 million a year earlier. Results for 2005 and 2004 included restructuring and other charges of C$87.0 million and C$4.0 million, respectively. Sales increased 6.4% to C$6.97 billion from C$6.55 billion the previous year. Weston Foods sales fell 1.1%, due primarily to the negative effect of foreign currency translation that reduced Weston Foods reported sales growth by about 5.6%. Sales at Food Distribution, operated by Loblaw, rose 7.9%, with all regions across the country experiencing sales growth over last year. Comparisons were made with restated prior-year figures.

Prospects: On Mar 4 2005, Co. announced a plan to restructure its U.S. biscuit operations operated by Weston Foods. The plan will result in the closure of two biscuit facilities located in Elizabeth, NJ and Richmond, VA over the next 12 to 18 months. The majority of production from the facilities will be moved to a new facility in Virginia and an existing facility in South Dakota. Once completed, Co. anticipates that this initiative will result in lower annual manufacturing costs and strengthen its competitive position within its biscuit operations in the U.S. Co. also continues to evaluate strategic and other cost reduction initiatives, particularly related to the fresh-baked sweet goods category.

Financial Data

(Can$ in Thousands)	3 Mos	12/31/2004	12/31/2003	12/31/2002	12/31/2001	12/31/2000	12/31/1999	12/31/1998
Earnings Per Share	2.40	3.10	5.78	5.02	4.37	3.64	2.67	5.82
Cash Flow Per Share	...	12.19	9.73	10.03	...	...	...	...
Tang Book Value Per Share	7.46	3.38	7.11	2.98	0.45	6.32	5.30	6.08
Dividends Per Share	1.440	1.440	1.200	0.960	0.800	0.700	0.440	0.400
Dividend Payout %	60.00	46.45	20.76	19.12	18.31	19.23	16.48	6.87
Income Statement								
Total Revenue	6,972,000	29,798,000	29,198,000	27,446,000	24,661,000	22,344,000	20,851,000	14,726,000
EBITDA	355,000	2,402,000	2,358,000	2,185,000	1,934,000	1,557,000	1,333,000	1,332,000
Depn & Amortn	150,000	620,000	546,000	507,000	431,000	368,000	357,000	269,000
Income Before Taxes	205,000	1,344,000	1,546,000	1,440,000	1,282,000	1,018,000	840,000	959,000
Income Taxes	49,000	368,000	430,000	469,000	435,000	310,000	301,000	208,000
Net Income	100,000	428,000	792,000	690,000	582,000	481,000	351,000	670,000
Average Shares	129,200	129,200	132,300	132,600	132,800	132,300	131,699	...
Balance Sheet								
Current Assets	4,724,000	4,580,000	4,698,000	4,705,000	5,060,000	3,733,000	3,170,000	2,915,000
Total Assets	18,236,000	17,904,000	17,338,000	16,663,000	16,277,000	11,421,000	10,049,000	9,036,000
Current Liabilities	4,378,000	4,479,000	4,330,000	4,427,000	5,653,000	3,906,000	3,317,000	3,325,000
Long-Term Obligations	6,344,000	6,004,000	5,832,000	5,391,000	4,908,000	2,986,000	2,584,000	1,984,000
Total Liabilities	13,793,000	13,524,000	12,876,000	12,281,000	12,651,000	8,517,000	7,431,000	6,647,000
Stockholders' Equity	4,443,000	4,380,000	4,462,000	4,382,000	3,626,000	2,904,000	2,618,000	2,389,000
Shares Outstanding	129,000	128,913	129,433	132,279	131,467	131,458	131,051	132,000
Statistical Record								
Return on Assets %	2.19	2.42	4.66	4.19	4.20	4.47	3.68	8.98
Return on Equity %	9.00	9.65	17.91	17.23	17.83	17.37	14.02	32.33
EBITDA Margin %	5.09	8.06	8.08	7.96	7.84	6.97	6.39	9.05
Net Margin %	1.43	1.44	2.71	2.51	2.36	2.15	1.68	4.55
Asset Turnover	1.53	1.69	1.72	1.67	1.78	2.08	2.19	1.97
Current Ratio	1.08	1.02	1.08	1.06	0.90	0.96	0.96	0.88
Debt to Equity	1.43	1.37	1.31	1.23	1.35	1.03	0.99	0.83
Price Range	115.00-86.50	111.63-86.50	108.00-89.88	130.65-90.01	105.50-77.00	86.85-45.00	65.50-47.50	59.35-37.67
P/E Ratio	47.92-36.04	36.01-27.90	18.69-15.55	26.03-17.93	24.14-17.62	23.86-12.36	24.53-17.79	10.20-6.47
Average Yield %	1.47	1.50	1.21	0.88	0.86	1.10	0.78	0.84

Address: 22 St. Clair Avenue East, Toronto **Telephone:** 416-922-2500 **Web Site:** www.weston.ca	**Officers:** W. Galen Weston - Chmn., Pres. Richard P. Mavrinac - C.F.O. **Transfer Agents:** Computershare Trust Company of Canada, Toronto	**No of Institutions:** 2 **Shares:** 113,200 **% Held:** 0.09

Take Advantage of Our Multiple Copy Discount!

Copy or detach and send to:

John Wiley & Sons, PT Journals and Periodicals
989 Market Street, San Francisco, CA 94103-1741

For fastest service:

Call or fax toll-free: Phone 888-378-2537; Fax 888-481-2665

Subscriptions Please _ start _ renew my subscription to *Mergent's Dividend Achievers* at the following rate:

U.S.	_ Individual: $180	_ Institutional: $180
Canada/Mexico	_ Individual: $180	_ Institutional: $220
All Others	_ Individual: $204	_ Institutional: $254

Subscribe for multiple copies and save!
Bulk subscription discounts for 10 or more copies will save you 25% on each copy. Save more than 40% on subscription orders for 100 copies or more. To learn more about **bulk subscription discounts**, contact our Special Sales representative Jill Gottlieb at 1-201-748-8839.

Also available in single issues!
For information about ordering single copies of this issue, call 1-888-378-2537. **Multiple copy discounts** also exist for single-issue purchases. Call 1-888-378-2537 for details.

$ ______________ Total subscriptions. (No sales tax for U.S. subscriptions. Canadian residents, add GST for subscription orders.)

_ Payment enclosed (U.S. check or money order only. All payments must be in U.S. dollars.)

_ VISA _ MC _ Amex # ____________________ Exp. Date ____________________

Card Holder Name ____________________ Card Issue # ____________________

Signature ____________________ Day Phone ____________________

_ Bill Me (U.S. institutional orders only. Purchase order required.)

Purchase order # ____

Federal Tax ID13559302 **GST 89102 8052**

Name ____

Address ____

Phone ____________________ E-mail ____________________

_ Yes, I'd like to hear about special discount offers, new products, and more. Place me on the Journals/Periodicals e-mail list.